STREET ATLAS

Birmingham

and West Midlands

...lished in 1998 by

a division of
s Publishing Group Ltd
...n Quays, London E14 4JP

...olour edition 2006
...pression 2006

0   0-540-08837-4 (pocket)
'3   978-0-540-08837-9 (pocket)

's 2006

OS Ordnance Survey®

T   ...uct includes mapping data licensed from
C   ...e Survey® with the permission of the
C   ... of Her Majesty's Stationery Office.
       ...copyright 2006. All rights reserved.
       ...umber 100011710.

       ...' this publication may be reproduced,
       ... retrieval system or transmitted in any
       ... any means, electronic, mechanical,
       ...ving, recording or otherwise, without the
       ...n of the Publishers and the copyright

       ...st of the Publishers' knowledge, the
       ...ion in this atlas was correct at the time of
       ...press. No responsibility can be accepted
       ...rrors or their consequences.

       ...esentation in this atlas of a road, track
       ...s no evidence of the existence of a right

       ...ce Survey and the OS Symbol are
       ...ed trademarks of Ordnance Survey, the
       ...' mapping agency of Great Britain.

       ...ly Toppan, China

Contents

III	**Key to map symbols**
IV	**Key to map pages**
VI	**Route planning**
VIII	**Administrative and Postcode boundaries**
1	**Street maps** at 2⅔ inches to 1 mile
163	**Street maps of centres of Wolverhampton, Birmingham and Coventry** at 5⅓ inches to 1 mile
166	**Index** of towns and villages
169	**Index** of streets, hospitals, industrial estates, railway stations, schools, shopping centres, universities and places of interest

Digital Data

The exceptionally high-quality mapping found in this atlas is available as digital data in TIFF format, which is easily convertible to other bitmapped (raster) image formats.

The index is also available in digital form as a standard database table. It contains all the details found in the printed index together with the National Grid reference for the map square in which each entry is named.

For further information and to discuss your requirements, please contact Philip's on 020 7644 6932 or james.mann@philips-maps.co.uk

Key to map symbols

III

Motorway with junction number	(22a)
Primary route – dual/single carriageway	
A road – dual/single carriageway	
B road – dual/single carriageway	
Minor road – dual/single carriageway	
Other minor road – dual/single carriageway	
Road under construction	
Tunnel, covered road	
Rural track, private road or narrow road in urban area	
Gate or obstruction to traffic (restrictions may not apply at all times or to all vehicles)	
Path, bridleway, byway open to all traffic, road used as a public path	
Pedestrianised area	
DY7 Postcode boundaries	
County and unitary authority boundaries	
Railway, tunnel, railway under construction	
Tramway, tramway under construction	
Miniature railway	
Railway station — Walsall	
Private railway station	
Metro station — South Shields	
Tram stop, tram stop under construction	
Bus, coach station	

◆	Ambulance station
◆	Coastguard station
◆	Fire station
◆	Police station
✚	Accident and Emergency entrance to hospital
H	Hospital
+	Place of worship
i	Information Centre (open all year)
⛟	Shopping Centre
P P&R	Parking, Park and Ride
PO	Post Office
Ⲭ ⛺	Camping site, caravan site
▶ ⊠	Golf course, picnic site
Prim Sch	Important buildings, schools, colleges, universities and hospitals
	Built up area
	Woods
River Medway	Water name
	River, weir, stream
( ) (	Canal, lock, tunnel
	Water
	Tidal water
Church	Non-Roman antiquity
ROMAN FORT	Roman antiquity
87	Adjoining page indicators and overlap bands
237	The colour of the arrow and the band indicates the scale of the adjoining or overlapping page (see scales below)

Abbr	Full	Abbr	Full	Abbr	Full
Acad	Academy	Inst	Institute	Recn Gd	Recreation Ground
Allot Gdns	Allotments	Ct	Law Court		
Cemy	Cemetery	L Ctr	Leisure Centre	Resr	Reservoir
C Ctr	Civic Centre	LC	Level Crossing	Ret Pk	Retail Park
CH	Club House	Liby	Library	Sch	School
Coll	College	Mkt	Market	Sh Ctr	Shopping Centre
Crem	Crematorium	Meml	Memorial	TH	Town Hall/House
Ent	Enterprise	Mon	Monument	Trad Est	Trading Estate
Ex H	Exhibition Hall	Mus	Museum	Univ	University
Ind Est	Industrial Estate	Obsy	Observatory	W Twr	Water Tower
IRB Sta	Inshore Rescue Boat Station	Pal	Royal Palace	Wks	Works
		PH	Public House	YH	Youth Hostel

■ The small numbers around the edges of the maps identify the 1 kilometre National Grid lines
■ The dark grey border on the inside edge of some pages indicates that the mapping does not continue onto the adjacent page

Enlarged mapping only

	Railway or bus station building
	Place of interest
	Parkland

The scale of the maps on the pages numbered in blue is 4.2 cm to 1 km • 2⅔ inches to 1 mile • 1: 23810	0 ¼ ½ ¾ 1 mile — 0 250m 500m 750m 1 kilometre
The scale of the maps on pages numbered in red is 8.4 cm to 1 km • 5⅓ inches to 1 mile • 1: 11900	0 220 yards 440 yards 660 yards ½ mile — 0 125m 250m 375m ½ kilometre

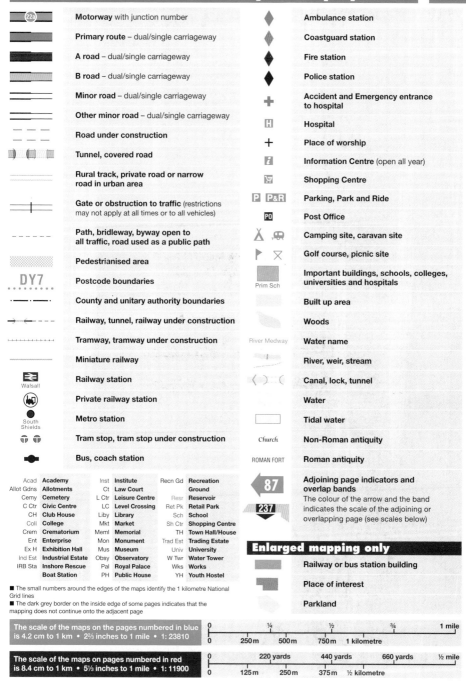

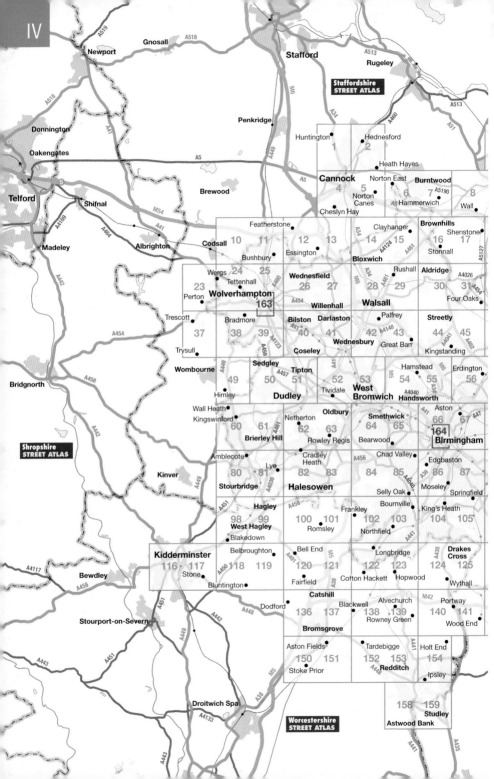

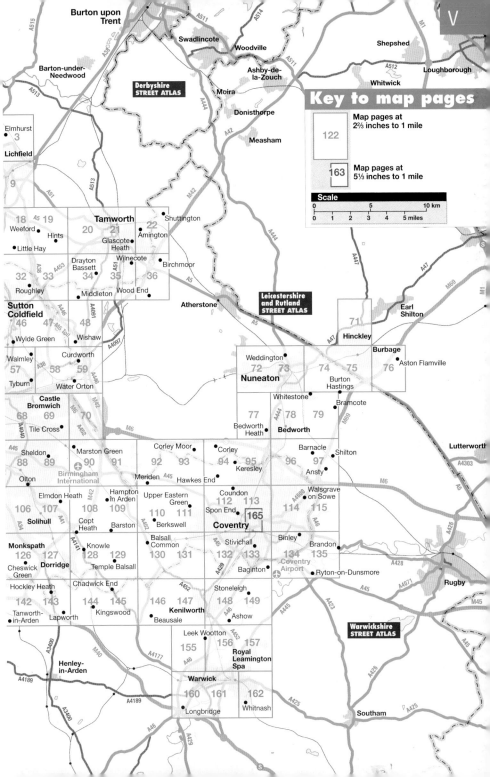

V

Burton upon Trent

Swadlincote

Woodville

Shepshed

Ashby-de-la-Zouch

Whitwick

Loughborough

Barton-under-Needham

Moira

Derbyshire STREET ATLAS

Donisthorpe

Measham

Elmhurst
3

Lichfield

9

Key to map pages

| 122 | Map pages at 2⅔ inches to 1 mile |

| 163 | Map pages at 5⅓ inches to 1 mile |

Scale

0   5   10 km
0   1   2   3   4   5 miles

Shuttington

18 **19**
Weeford

Tamworth

20 **21** **22**
Hints   Amington

Little Hay

Glascote Heath

Wilnecote

Birchmoor

32 **33**
Roughley

Drayton Bassett

34 **35** **36**
Middleton   Wood End

Atherstone

Leicestershire and Rutland STREET ATLAS

Earl Shilton

71

Hinckley

Sutton Coldfield

46 **47** **48**
Wylde Green   Wishaw

Walmley

Curdworth

Burbage

76
Aston Flamville

57 **58** **59**
Tyburn   Water Orton

Weddington

72 **73** **74** **75**

Nuneaton

Burton Hastings

Castle Bromwich

68 **69** **70**
Tile Cross

Whitestone

Bramcote

77 **78** **79**
Bedworth Heath   **Bedworth**

Lutterworth

Sheldon

88 **89** **90** **91**
Olton   Birmingham International

Marston Green

Meriden   Hawkes End

Corley Moor

92 **93** **94** **95** **96** **97**
Corley   Keresley   Ansty

Barnacle

Shilton

Elmdon Heath

106 **107** **108** **109**
Solihull

Hampton in Arden

Copt Heath   Barston

Upper Eastern Green

110 **111**
Berkswell

Coundon

112 **113** **114** **115**
Spon End   **165**   Walsgrave on Sowe

Coventry

Monkspath

126 **127** **128** **129**
Dorridge   Temple Balsall

Cheswick Green

Knowle

Balsall Common

130 **131** **132** **133** **134** **135**
Stivichall   Binley   Brandon

Baginton   Coventry Airport   Ryton-on-Dunsmore

Rugby

Hockley Heath

142 **143** **144** **145** **146** **147** **148** **149**
Tanworth-in-Arden   Lapworth   Kingswood   **Kenilworth**   Ashow

Chadwick End

Stoneleigh

Beausale

Leek Wootton

155 **156** **157**
Royal Leamington Spa

Warwickshire STREET ATLAS

Henley-in-Arden

Warwick

160 **161** **162**
Longbridge   Whitnash

Southam

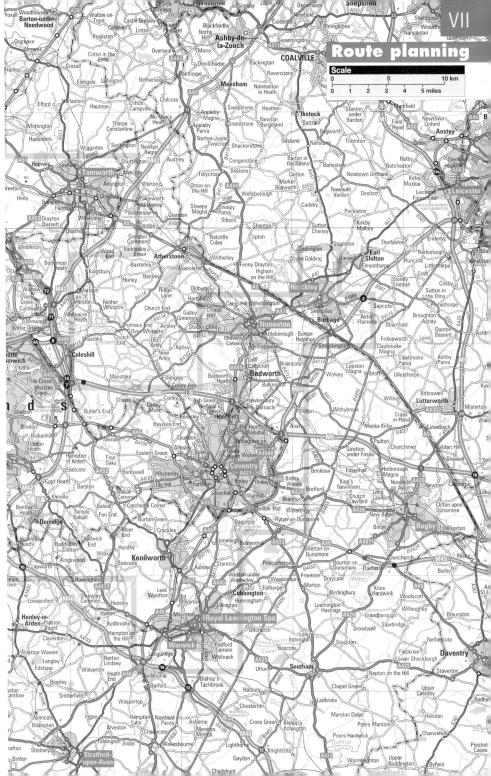

Scale

0   5   10 km

0   1   2   3   4   5 miles

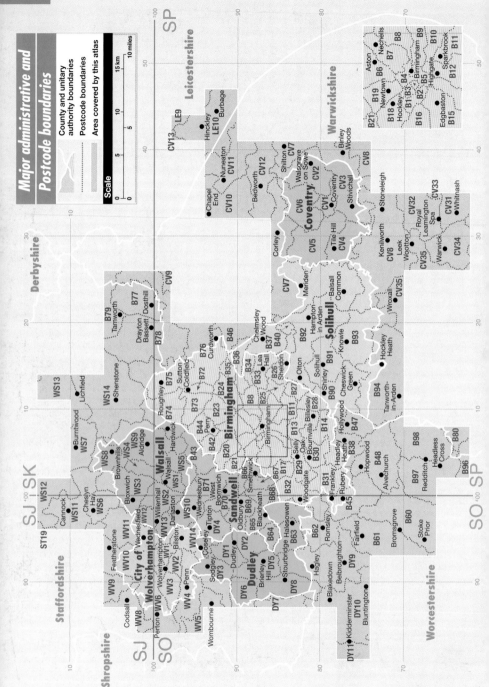

Major administrative and Postcode boundaries

- County and unitary authority boundaries
- Postcode boundaries
- Area covered by this atlas

Scale

0 5 10 15km
0 5 10 miles

Derbyshire

Staffordshire

Shropshire

Leicestershire

Warwickshire

Worcestershire

City of Wolverhampton

Walsall

Sandwell

Dudley

Birmingham

Solihull

Coventry

SP

SK

SJ

SO

ST19

Aston
Nechells
Newtown
Hockley
Edgbaston
Spark brook
Highgate

B21 B19 B6 B7 B8 B9 B10
B18 B1 B3 B4 B5 B11
B16 B2 B12
B15 B13

Codsall
Featherstone
Cheslyn Hay
Cannock
Brownhills
Aldridge
Bloxwich
Willenhall
Wednesfield
Oxley
Perton
Wolverhampton
Bilston
Sedgley
Tipton
Wednesbury
West Bromwich
Oldbury
Smethwick
Woodgate
Brierley Hill
Dudley
Stourbridge
Halesowen
Blackheath
Cradley Heath
Wombourne
Blakedown
Belbroughton
Bluntisdon
Kidderminster
Hagley
Romsley
Fairfield
Bromsgrove
Stoke Prior
Alvechurch
Hopwood
Redditch
Headless Cross

Lichfield
Shenstone
Burntwood
Roughley
Sutton Coldfield
Perry
Selly Oak
Bournville
Billesley
Shirley
Cheswick Green
Knowle
Hockley Heath
Tamworth-in-Arden

Tamworth
Drayton Bassett
Dosthill
Curdworth
Chelmsley Wood
Lea Hall
Sheldon
Olton
Solihull
Hampton-in-Arden
Balsall Common
Meriden
Berkswell

Chapel End
Bedworth
Nuneaton
Hinckley
Burbage
Corley
Shilton
Walsgrave on Sowe
Binley Woods
Coventry
Stivichall
Tile Hill
Kenilworth
Stoneleigh
Leek Wootton
Royal Leamington Spa
Warwick
Whitnash
Wroxall

WV9 WV8 WV10 WV11 WV12 WV1 WV2 WV3 WV4 WV5 WV6 WV13 WV14
WS11 WS12 WS13 WS14 WS1 WS2 WS3 WS4 WS5 WS6 WS7 WS8 WS9 WS10
DY1 DY2 DY3 DY4 DY5 DY6 DY7 DY8 DY9 DY10 DY11
B60 B61 B62 B63 B64 B65 B66 B67 B68 B69 B70 B71 B72 B73 B74 B75 B76 B77 B78 B79 B80 B90 B91 B92 B93 B94 B95 B96 B97 B98
B20 B21 B23 B24 B25 B26 B27 B28 B29 B30 B31 B32 B33 B34 B35 B36 B37 B38 B40 B42 B43 B44 B45 B46 B47 B48
CV1 CV2 CV3 CV4 CV5 CV6 CV7 CV8 CV10 CV11 CV12 CV13 CV31 CV32 CV33 CV34 CV35
LE9 LE10

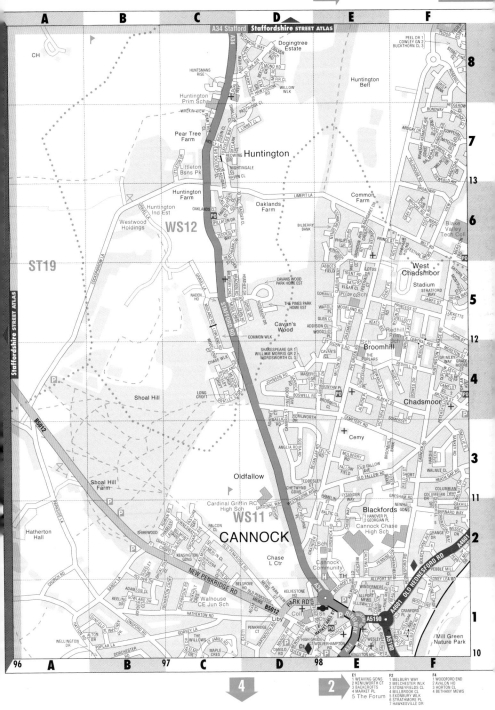

A34 Stafford **Staffordshire** STREET ATLAS

CH

Dogingtree Estate

HUNTSMANS RISE

Huntington Prim Sch

WREKIN VIEW

Pear Tree Farm

Huntington

Littleton Bsns Pk

Huntington Farm

Huntington Ind Est

Westwood Holdings

WS12

ST19

Oaklands Farm

LIMEPIT LA

Common Farm

Huntington Belt

PEEL DR 1
COWLEY GN 2
BUCKTHORN CL 3

BILBERRY BANK

West Chadsmoor

Blake Valley Tech Coll

Stadium

ABBOTS FIELD

Cavans Wood Park Home Est

THE PINES Park Home Est

Cavan's Wood

COMMON WLK

NADEN HO

Broomhill

THE POPLARS

SHAKESPEARE GR 1
WILLIAM MORRIS GR 2
WORDSWORTH CL 3

Shoal Hill

LONG CROFT

Chadsmoor

Cemy

Shoal Hill Farm

Oldfallow

OLD FALLOW AVE
OLD FALLOW RD

Hatherton Hall

Cardinal Griffin RC High Sch

WS11

CANNOK

Blackfords

Cannock Chase High Sch

Chase L Ctr

Cannock Community

Walhouse CE Jun Sch

NEW PENKRIDGE RD

Chase L Ctr

Mill Green Nature Park

WELLINGTON DR

PARK RD

Libr

Coll

A5190

96   A   B   97   C   D   98   E   F

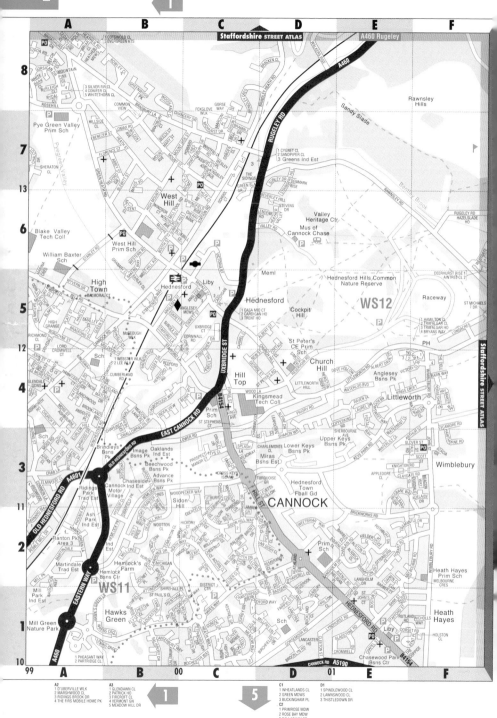

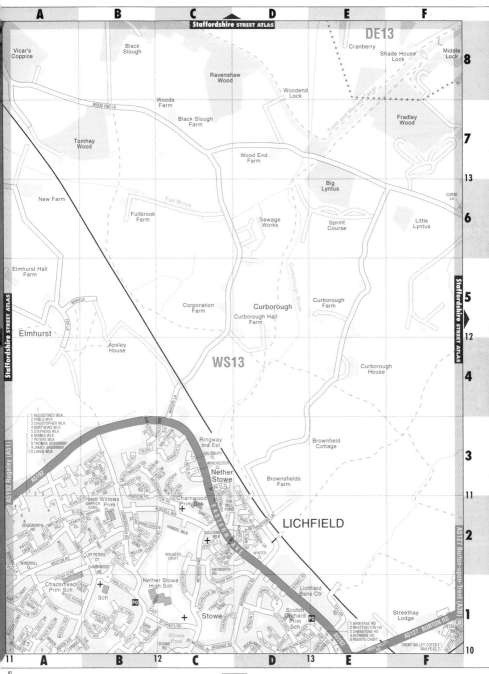

DE13

Cranberry

Shade House
Lock

Middle
Lock

8

Vicar's
Coppice

Black
Slough

Ravenshaw
Wood

Woodend
Lock

Woods
Farm

WOOD END LA

Black Slough
Farm

Fradley
Wood

Trent and Mersey Canal

7

Tomhay
Wood

Wood End
Farm

13

New Farm

Full Brook

GORSE
LA

6

Fullbrook
Farm

Sewage
Works

Sprint
Course

Little
Lyntus

Big
Lyntus

Elmhurst Hall
Farm

Curborough
Farm

Staffordshire STREET ATLAS

5

ASH LA

Corporation
Farm

Curborough

Curborough Brook

Curborough Hall
Farm

12

Elmhurst

Apsley
House

WS13

Curborough
House

4

1 AUGUSTINES WLK
2 PABLS WLK
3 CHRISTOPHER WLK
4 MATTHEWS WLK
5 STEPHENS WLK
6 MARKS WLK
7 PETERS WLK
8 THOMAS GREENWAY
9 JAMES GREENWAY
10 LUKES WLK

Ringway
Ind Est

Brownfield
Cottage

3

A5192 Rugeley (A51)

SALISBURY
CL
WINCHESTER
CL
Nether
Stowe

Brownsfields
Farm

David Willows
Prim Sch

Charnwood
Prim Sch

11

EASTERN AVE

THE
MILL
POND

LICHFIELD

A5127 Burton-upon-Trent (A38)

EDGEWORTH
HO

SULLIVAN
WLK

2

WINDMILL
CL

HAYWORTH

Lichfield
Bsns Ctr

ST PETERS
CT

WALKERS
CROFT

Streethay
Lodge

Chadsmead
Prim Sch

Nether Stowe
High Sch

WINTER
CL

Sch

PO

Nether Stowe
High Sch

Scotch
Orchard
Prim Sch

1 ARMITAGE HO
2 WHITTINGTON HO
3 SHENSTONE HO
4 RIDWARE HO
5 PENNYS CROFT

A5127 BURTON RD

1

Stowe

ST CHAD'S RD

PO

Stowe
Pool

ST MICHAEL RD

WISSAGE RD

TRENT VALLEY COTTS 1
BAILYE CL 2

10

11   12   13

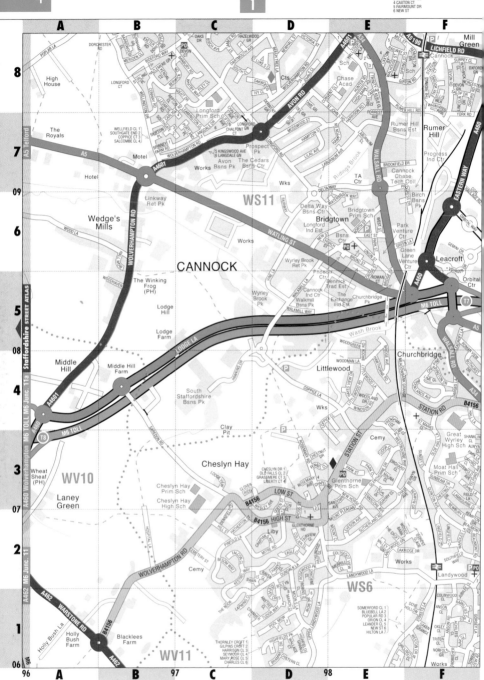

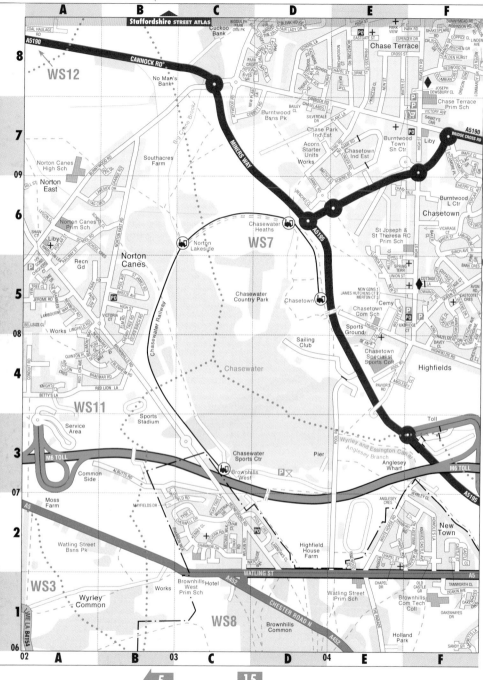

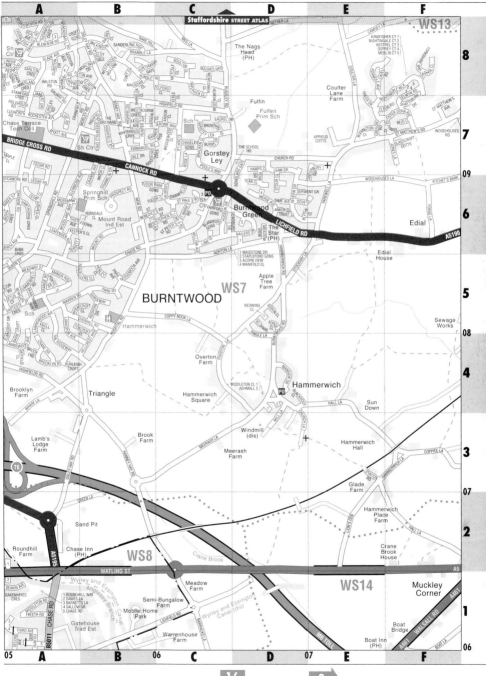

Staffordshire STREET ATLAS

WS13

WS7

BURNTWOOD

WS8

WS14

Muckley Corner

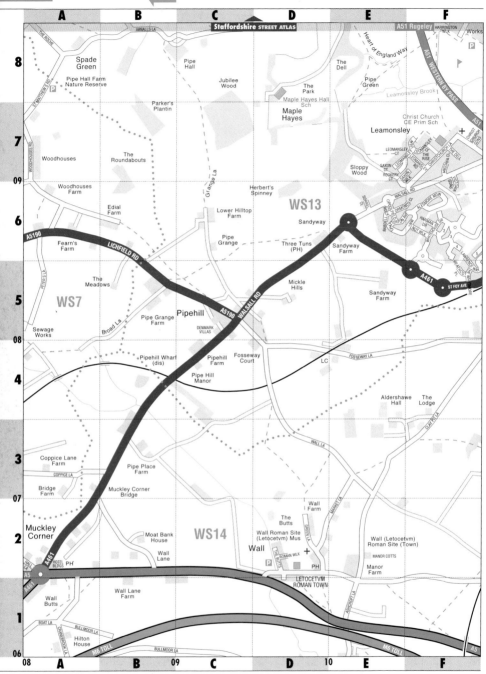

Staffordshire STREET ATLAS

A51 Rugeley

HARRINGTON WK

Works

A51 WESTERN BY PASS

A51

Heart of England Way

Leamonsley Brook

Spade Green

Pipe Hall Farm Nature Reserve

Pipe Hall

Jubilee Wood

The Dell

Pipe Green

Christ Church CE Prim Sch

The Park

Maple Hayes Hall Sch

Parker's Plantin

Maple Hayes

Leamonsley

LEOMANSLEY CT

Woodhouses

The Roundabouts

Sloppy Wood

Grange La

WS13

Woodhouses Farm

Herbert's Spinney

Edial Farm

Lower Hilltop Farm

WALSALL RD

ALESHORE MEW

Sandyway

A5190

Fearn's Farm

LICHFIELD RD

Pipe Grange

Three Tuns (PH)

Sandyway Farm

A461

ST FOY AVE

The Meadows

Mickle Hills

Sandyway Farm

WS7

Broad La

Pipe Grange Farm

Pipehill

WALSALL RD

A5190

DENMARK VILLAS

Sewage Works

PETER'S LA

Pipehill Wharf (dis)

Pipehill Farm

Fosseway Court

LC

FOSSEWAY LA

Pipe Hill Manor

Aldershawe Hall

The Lodge

QUAY LA

WALL LA

Coppice Lane Farm

Pipe Place Farm

COPPICE LA

Muckley Corner Bridge

Wall Farm

Bridge Farm

The Butts

Wall Lane

Muckley Corner

A461

HOTEL BLDGS

Moat Bank House

WS14

Wall

Wall (Letocetvm) Roman Site (Town)

PH

A5

Wall Roman Site (Letocetvm) Mus

LETOCETVM ROMAN WLK

PH

Manor Farm

Wall Butts

Wall Lane Farm

LETOCETVM ROMAN TOWN

BOAT LA

M6 TOLL

Hilton House

BULLMOOR LA

BULLMOOR LA

M6 TOLL

A5

08

A

B

09

C

D

10

E

F

A8	B7	7 HOMELODGE HO	B8	C8		E8	9
1 BEACONFIELDS	1 CITY ARC	8 GREEN CT	1 LOMBARD GDNS	1 HOULBROOKE HO		1 WITLEY DR	
2 LILLINGTON CL	2 SARAH SIDDONS HO	9 FORREST CT	2 ASHWORTH HO	2 WILLIAM LUNN'S HOMES		2 ASPEN CL	
3 SECKHAM RD	3 TUDOR ROW		3 ST CHADS CT	3 THE CHEQUERS		3 MULBERRY DR	
4 JORDAN CL	4 LEVETTS SQ		4 CATHEDRAL CT	4 DRAKE CROFT		4 LAMBOURNE CL	
5 BEACON MEWS	5 BAKER'S LA		5 THE CORN EXCHANGE	5 MALLARD CROFT		5 THE CROSSING	
	6 CASTLE DYKE						

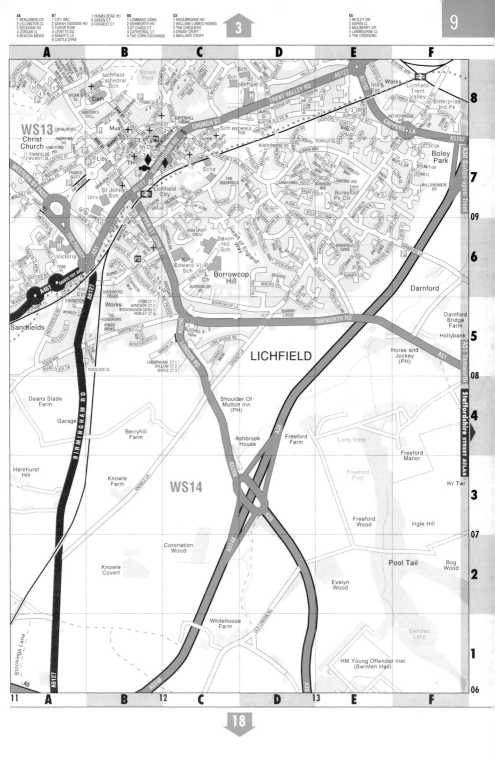

3

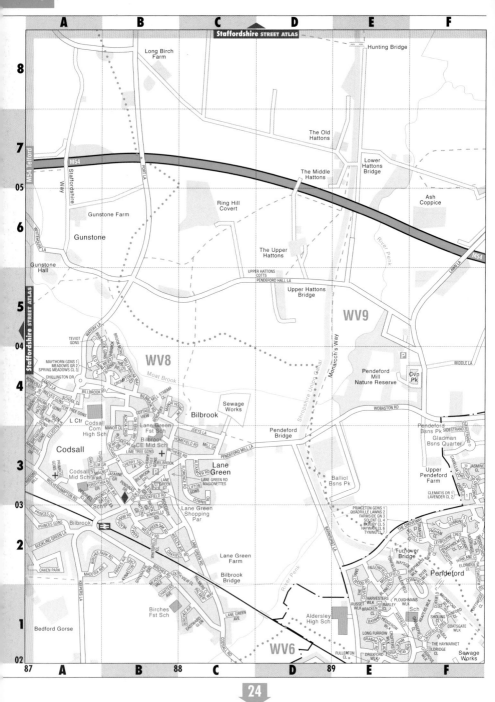

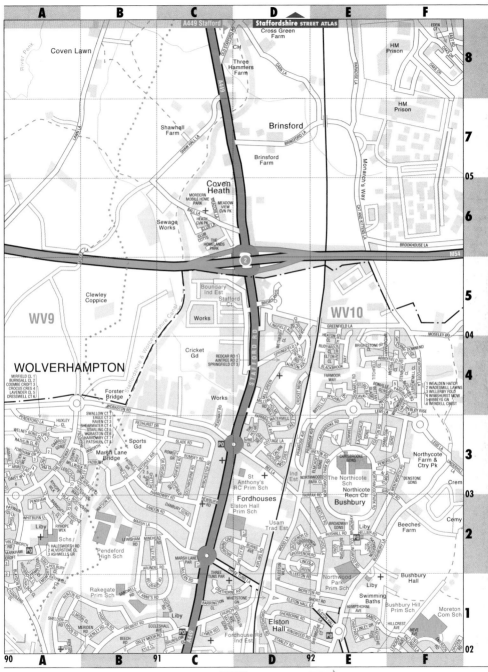

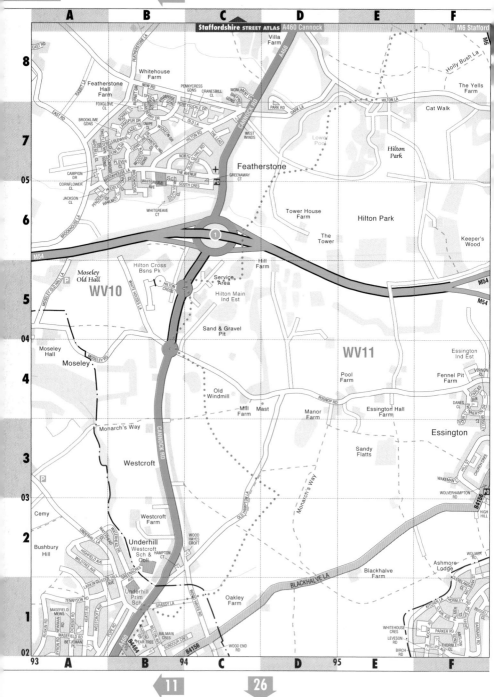

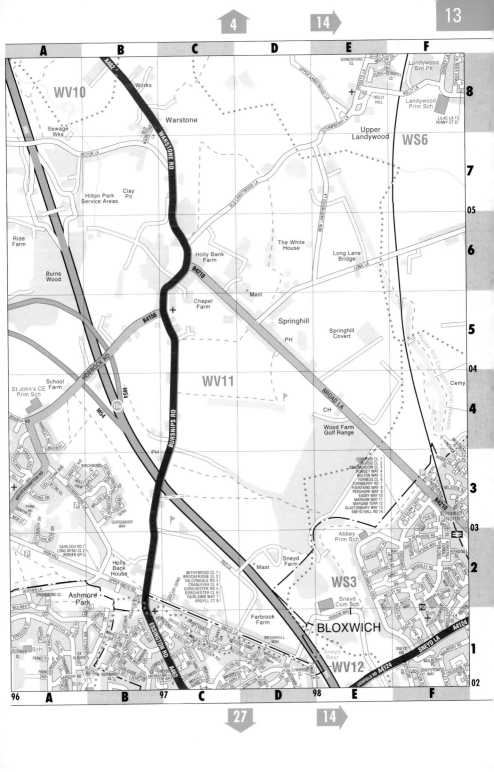

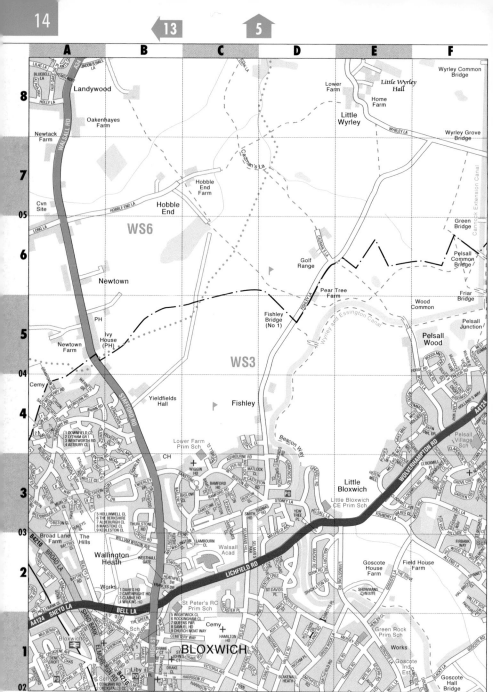

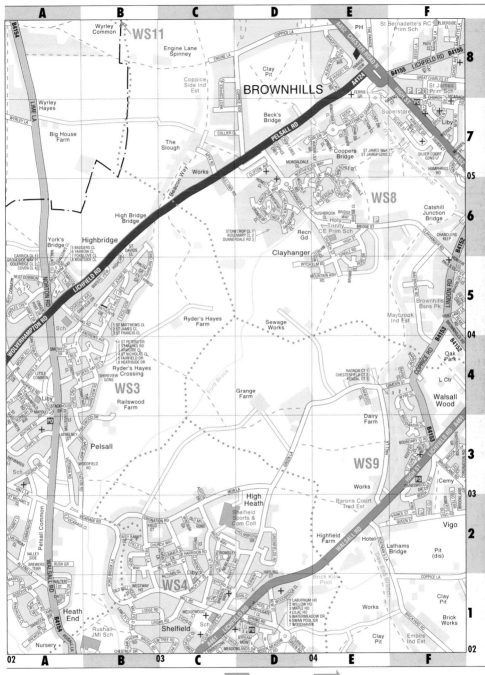

BROWNHILLS

WS11

WS8

WS3

WS9

WS4

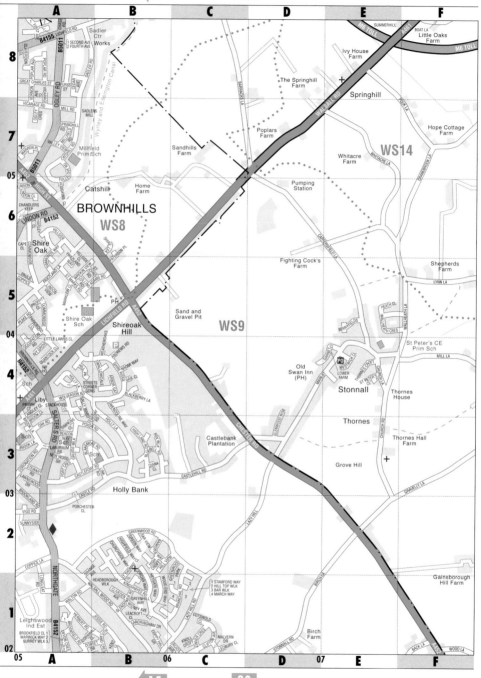

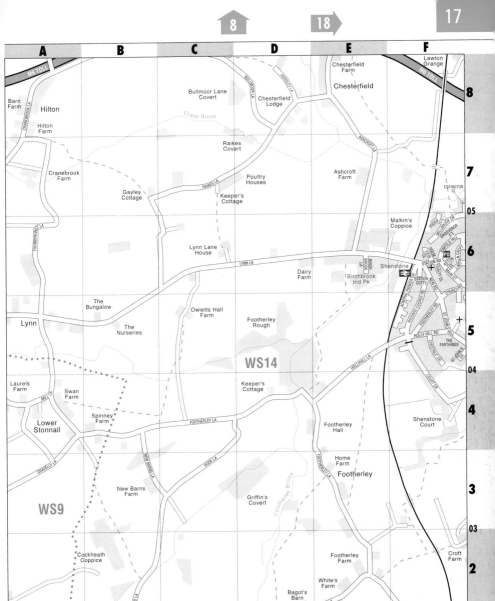

8

18

A **B** **C** **D** **E** **F**

M6 TOLL

Barn Farm

Hilton

Hilton Farm

Cranebrook Farm

THORNYHURST LA

Crane Brook

Bullmoor Lane Covert

Chesterfield Lodge

Chesterfield Farm

Chesterfield

Lawton Grange

M6 TOLL

Raikes Covert

Gayley Cottage

Keeper's Cottage

Poultry Houses

Ashcroft Farm

ESSINGTON CL

Malkin's Coppice

GROSVENOR CT

Lynn Lane House

LYNN LA

Dairy Farm

BIRCH BROOK LA

Birchbrook Ind Pk

Shenstone

SHENSTONE

STATION RD

STATION COTTS

The Bungalow

Lynn

The Nurseries

Owletts Hall Farm

Footherley Rough

WS14

Keeper's Cottage

HOLLY HILL LA

Shenstone Court

HOLLY HILL RD

CHESTNUT DR

THE FARTHINGS

Laurels Farm

MILL LA

Swan Farm

Spinney Farm

Lower Stonnall

GRAVELLY LA

FOOTHERLEY LA

NEW BARNS LA

HOOK LA

Footherley Hall

Home Farm

Footherley

FOOTHERLEY LA

WS9

New Barns Farm

WOOD LA

Griffin's Covert

Footherley Brook

Cockheath Coppice

Footherley Farm

White's Farm

Bagot's Barn

MOOR LA

Footherley Farm

Croft Farm

Biddle's Field Wood

Bosses

BACK LA

FORGE LA

08 **A** **B** 09 **C** **D** 10 **E** **F** 02

8 7 05 6 05 5 04 4 03 3 03 2 1 02

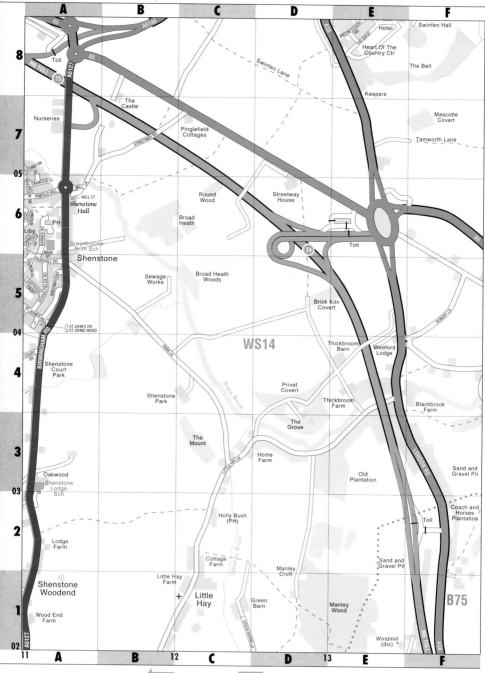

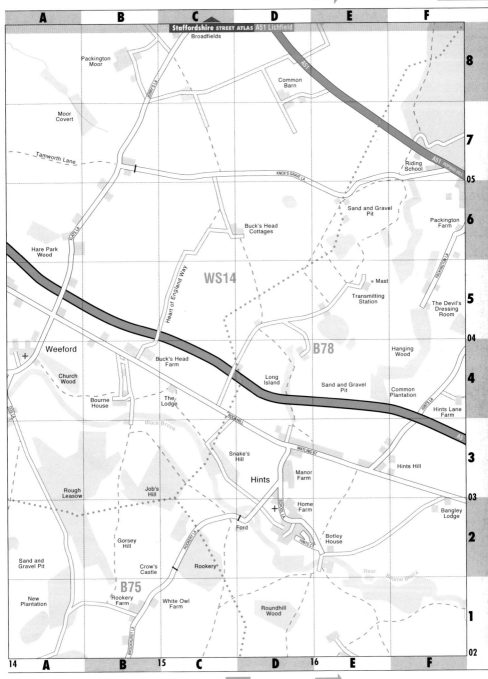

Staffordshire STREET ATLAS A51 Lichfield

Broadfields

Packington Moor

Common Barn

A51

Moor Covert

7

Tamworth Lane

Riding School

A51 HOPWAS HILL

05

KNOX'S GRAVE LA.

Sand and Gravel Pit

Packington Farm

6

Buck's Head Cottages

WS14

Mast

Hare Park Wood

Heart of England Way

Transmitting Station

The Devil's Dressing Room

5

04

Weeford

Buck's Head Farm

B78

Hanging Wood

Church Wood

Bourne House

The Lodge

Long Island

Sand and Gravel Pit

Common Plantation

Hints Lane Farm

4

A5

Black Brook

ROCK HILL

WATLING ST

HINTS LA.

Snake's Hill

Hints Hill

3

03

Rough Leasow

Job's Hill

Hints

Manor Farm

Home Farm

SCHOOL LA.

Bangley Lodge

Gorsey Hill

Ford

Botley House

HINTS CT.

2

Sand and Gravel Pit

Crow's Castle

Rookery

Resr

Bourne Brook

B75

New Plantation

Rookery Farm

White Owl Farm

BROCKHURST LA.

Roundhill Wood

1

02

14

A

B

15

C

D

16

E

F

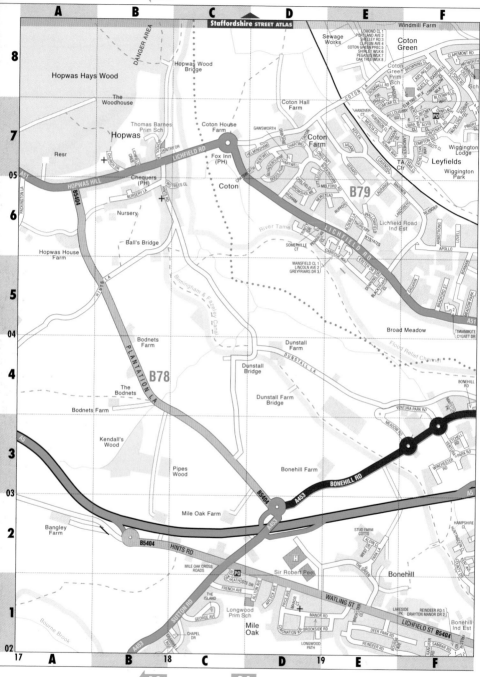

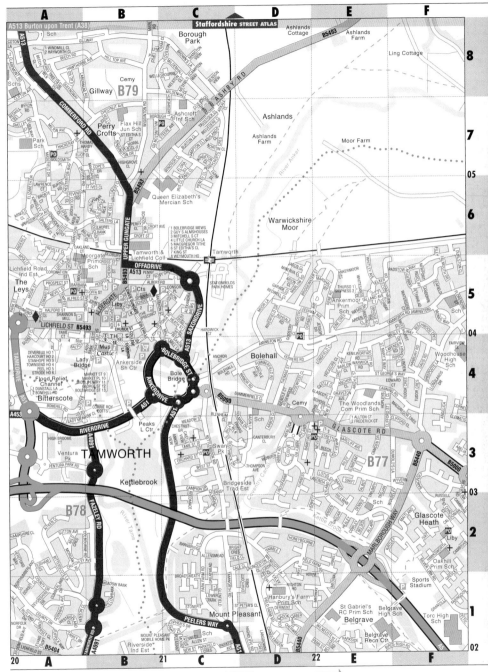

WV7

Simmond's Wood

Wrottesley Hall

The Bradshaws

Wrottesley Park

WV8

Inland Pool

WERGS HALL

The Grange

Salt's Pool

Smith's Rough

Dippons Lane

Cranmoor

Cranmoor Lodge

HEPWORTH CL 1
LOWRY CL 2
MOORE CL 3
THIRLMERE GR 4
WASTWATER CT 5
BUTTERMERE CL 6
CHARTLEY BL 7
KENILWORTH GR 8

SCAMPTON CL 1
HUDSON GR 2
TANGMERE CL 3
LIVINGSTONE AVE 4

Perton

Staffordshire Way / Monarch's Way

THE PADDOCK 1
FALLOWFIELD 2
THE CARTWAY 3
THE WINDROW 4
THE SADDLESTONES 5
MEADOW CROFT 6
WORCESTER GR 7

WV6

Nurton

WOLVERHAMPTON

Nurton Bank

Perton Orchard

Old Perton

Sling Wood

CH

Mast

Boundary Farm

Perton Court

Perton House

South Perton Farm

Middle Wood

Freehold Wood

Wightwick Hall Sch

Wightwick Manor

Wightwick

Cherringham

WV3

A454

23
10

23
38

F3
1 ALBERT RD
2 BROMFORD DALE
3 SLADE HILL
4 ST JUDE'S CT
5 THE CEDARS

F4
1 BRIMFIELD PL
2 BALFOUR CT
3 NEWBRIDGE MEWS
4 GRAFTON CT

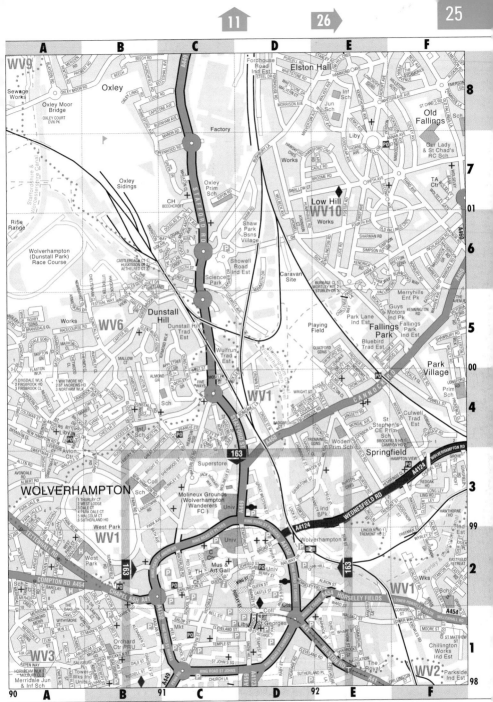

For full street detail of the highlighted area see page 163.

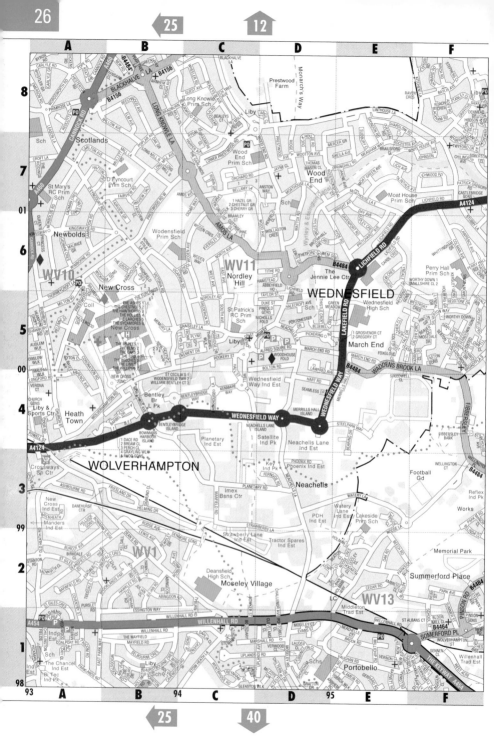

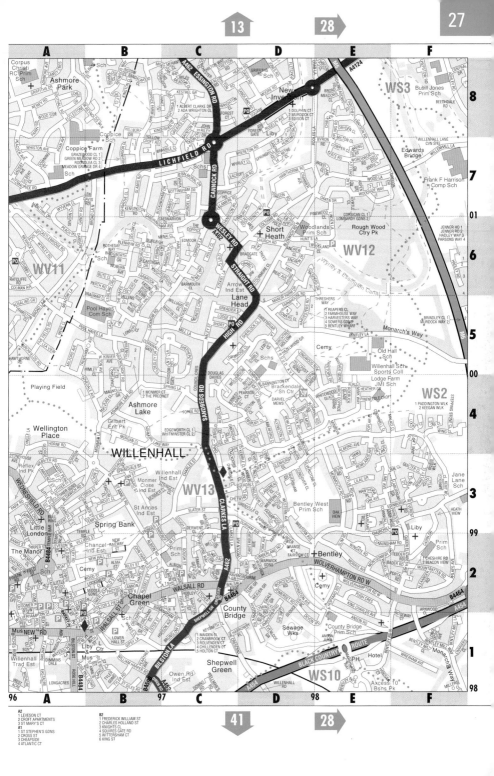

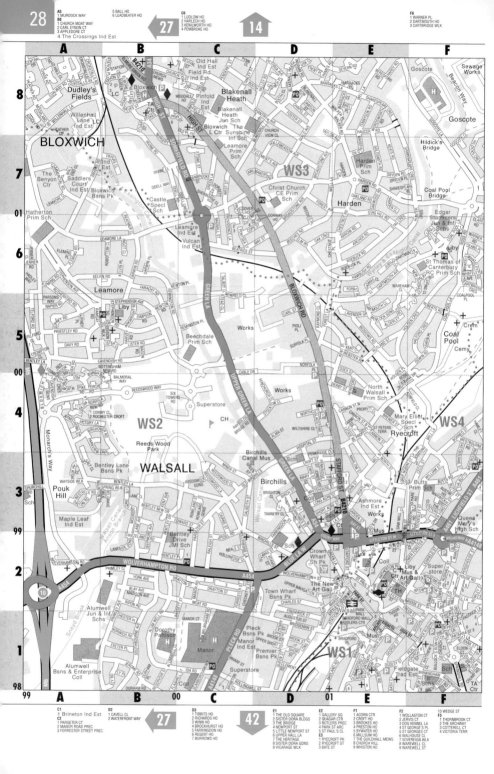

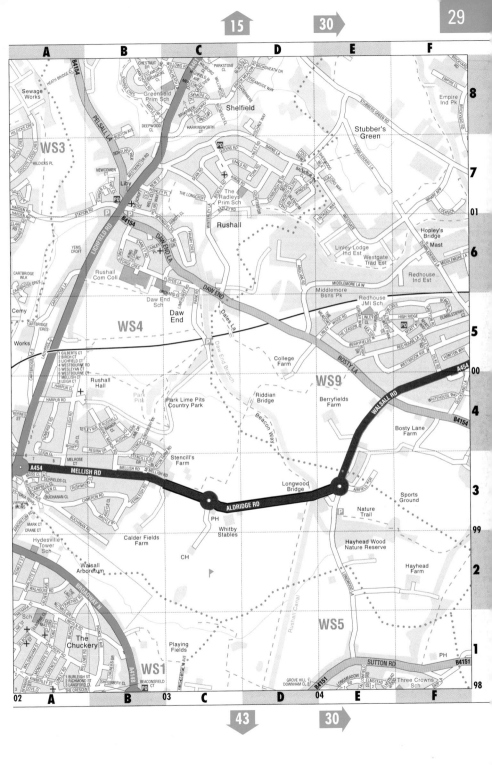

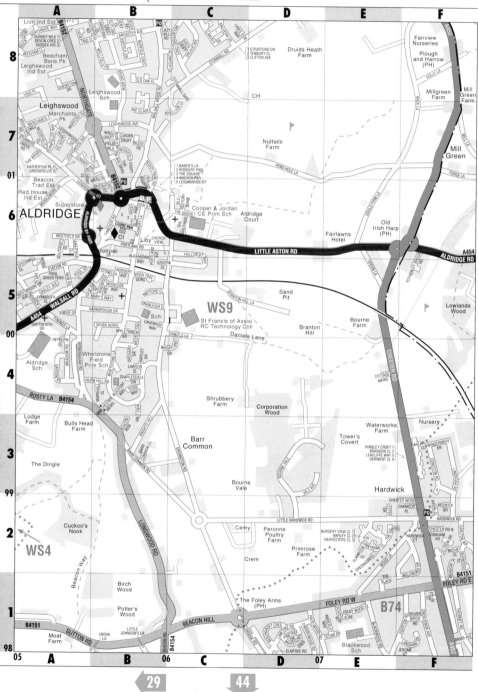

A B C D E F

8

7

6

5

4

3

2

1

01

00

99

98

WOOD LA

French Croft Farm

Forge Farm

Sewage Works

Forge Cottages

Riding Stables

FOOTHERLEY LA

Forge Wood

WS9

FORGE LA

New Wood

WS14

The Belt

BACK LA

CH

A4026

Mill Farm

Home Farm

Aston Prim Sch

Claypit Rough

Cottage Farm

Blake Street

BLAKE ST

Hill Hook

ALDRIDGE RD

A4026

LITTLE ASTON LA

A454

B4138

HILL HOOK HO 1
BICKLEY HO 2

PO

The Spinney

1 BEECH HO
2 OAK HO
3 CEDAR HO
4 BIRCH HO
5 MAPLE HO

ROMANS GRANGE

Hornton Manor

BEECHWOOD CROFT

LITTLE ASTON HALL

Little Aston

KEEPERS RD

Mill Pond

CAMPION 1
CELANDINE 2
BRYONY 3
ASPHODEL 4
GERMANDER 5
MULLEIN 5

Little Aston

CH

Rosemary

Four Oaks Jun & Inf Schs

Wingate

Sch

TANSY 7
VALERIAN 8
GENTIAN 9

A5127

LICHFIELD RD

Roundabout Wood

STONEHOUSE DR

CLAVERDON DR

ROMAN LA

ROSEMARY HILL

WALSALL RD

Four Oaks

THE HEADLANDS

PINEWAYS 1
FOREST LAWNS 2

TALBOT AVE

RUSSELL CT

WATERS RD

HIGHCROFT DR

Streetly

STREETLY LA

HERMES CT

B4151

B74

HARDWICK RD

ROMAN

Sutton Park

SETON HO

B4151

FOLEY RD E

B4138

Streetly Lodge

THORNHILL RD

Sutton Park

Bracebridge Pool

SUTTON COLDFIELD

Gun Slade

Mayor's Arbour

LUTTRELL RD

Sports Ctr
1 THORNEY RD
2 OAKDALE
3 PARKSIDE WAY

CH

Manor Prim Sch

Streetly Lodge

Streetly Belt

Streetly Wood

B4454

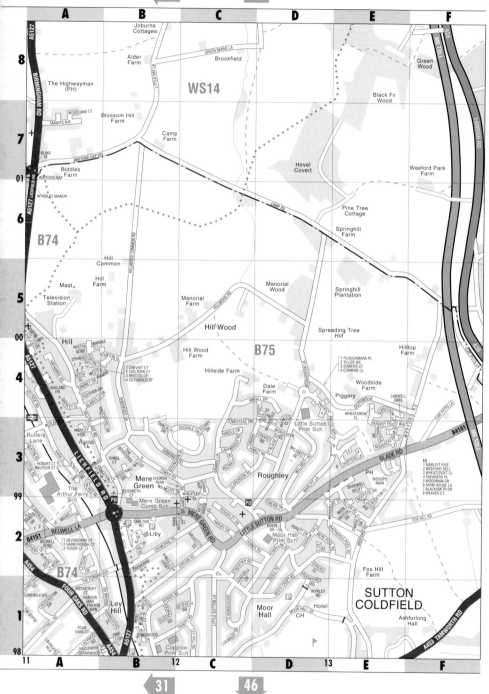

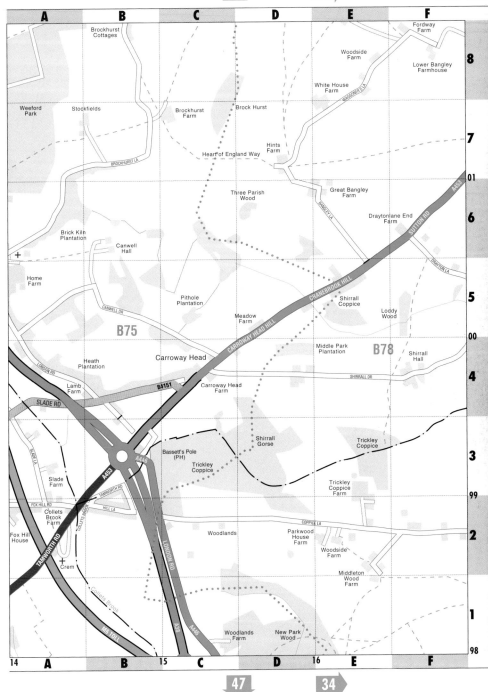

	A	B	C	D	E	F

8

Brockhurst Cottages

Fordway Farm

Woodside Farm

Lower Bangley Farmhouse

White House Farm

WAGGONER'S LA

Weeford Park

Stockfields

Brockhurst Farm

Brock Hurst

7

BROCKHURST LA

Heart of England Way

Hints Farm

A453 01

Three Parish Wood

Great Bangley Farm

BANGLEY LA

Draytonlane End Farm

SUTTON RD

6

Brick Kiln Plantation

Canwell Hall

DRAYTON LA

Home Farm

CRANEBROOK HILL

Shirrall Coppice

Loddy Wood

5

CANWELL DR

Pithole Plantation

Meadow Farm

B75

CARROWAY HEAD HILL

00

Middle Park Plantation

B78

Shirrall Hall

Carroway Head

Heath Plantation

LONDON RD

SHIRRALL DR

4

Lamb Farm

B4151

Carroway Head Farm

SLADE RD

Slade Farm

SLADE LA

Shirrall Gorse

Trickley Coppice

3

Bassett's Pole (PH)

Trickley Coppice

A446

Trickley Coppice Farm

TAMWORTH RD

FOX HILL RD

HILL LA

COLLETS BROOK

Collets Brook Farm

99

Fox Hill House

Crem

COPPICE LA

Woodlands

Parkwood House Farm

2

Woodside Farm

Collets Brook

LONDON RD

A38

Middleton Wood Farm

1

M6 TOLL

A446

Woodlands Farm

New Park Wood

98

14	A	B	15	C	D	16	E	F

33
20

A **B** **C** **D** **E** **F**

New House Farm

BANGLEY LA

SUTTON RD

A453

KIRKLAND AVE
GAINSBOROUGH DR
CASTOR DR

CRANWELL RISE

8

Bourne Bridge

Bourne Brook Cut

Fazeley

YORKSAND RD
REINDEER RD
DAMA RD

MAYAMA RD
DRAYTON MANOR DR

SWISS LODGE DR

Longwood House

Alder Wood

Seventeen Acre

Works

Bourne Brook

Duck Decoy

+

7

A453

01

Hill Farm

Lodge Farm

Drayton Manor Park

CH

DRAYTON MANOR DR

Longwood Stables

COLESHILL RD

6

A4091

Heathley Farm

HEATHLEY LA

Edden's Wood

Bullocks End Farm

5

Oak Farm Craft Ctr

SPIRRAL DR

Stone House

Heart of England Way

DRAYTON LA

Drayton Bassett

CHURCH LA
OLD MANOR CL
VICAR DR
PEEL CL
NEW ROW

EDDENS WOOD CL

PO
+

Manor Prim Sch

Sewage Works

00

Ashdene Farm

B78

RECTORY CL

SALTS LA

Drayton Brick Bridge

Heart of England Way

4

PORTLEYS LA

Brook End Farm

Brook Farm

Birmingham and Fazeley Canal

3

Upper House Farm

99

Gallows Brook

2

COPPICE LA

Quarry

Mill Plantation

Middleton Park

Newhouse Farm

Middleton

CHURCH ROW

INKFORD CL

Highfields Farm

CHURCH LA

Walker's Spinney

Park-gate Farm

Middleton Pool

1

The Green Man (PH)

VICARAGE HILL

CRESSBELT LA

Sewage Works

A4091

Middleton Hall

98

Langley Brook

17 **A** **B** 18 **C** **D** 19 **E** **F**

33
48

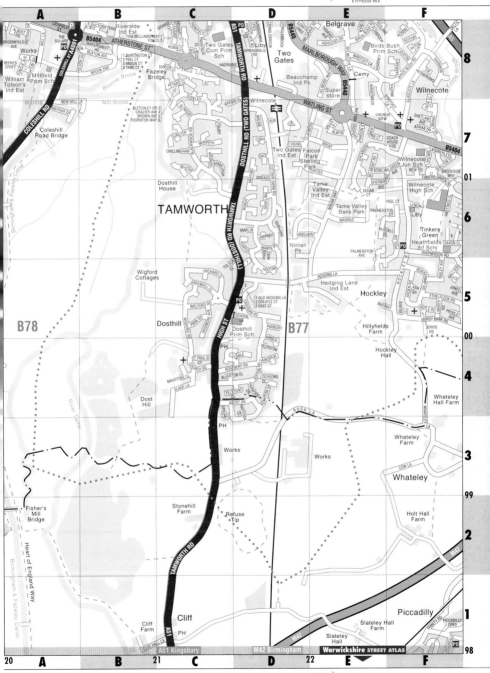

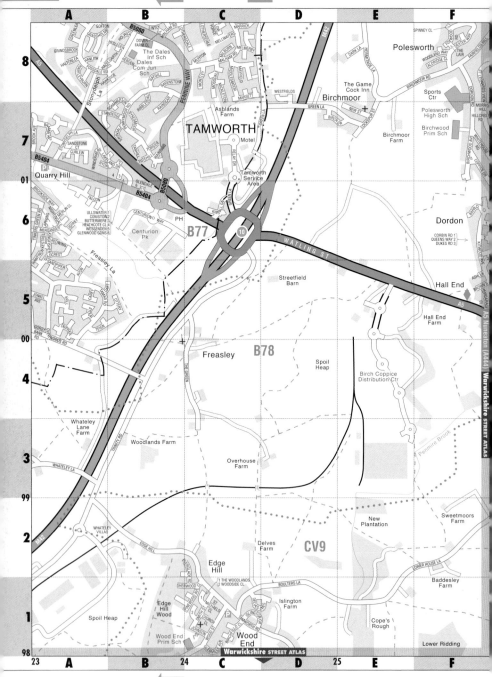

TAMWORTH

Polesworth

Birchmoor

Dordon

Hall End

Quarry Hill

B77

WATLING ST

B78

Freasley

CV9

Edge
Hill

Wood
End

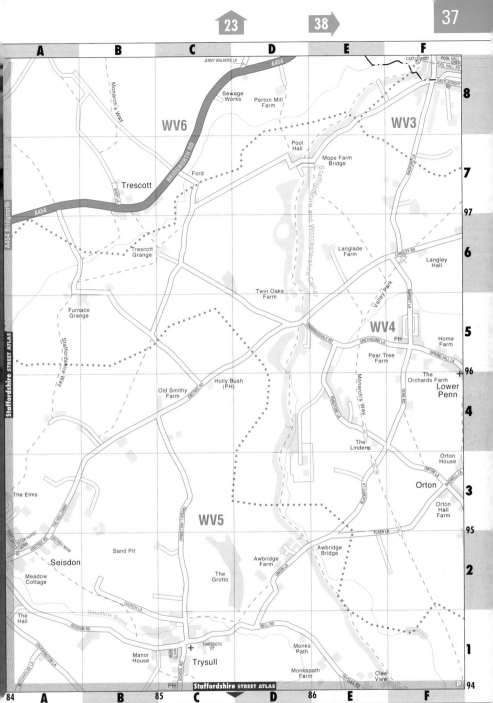

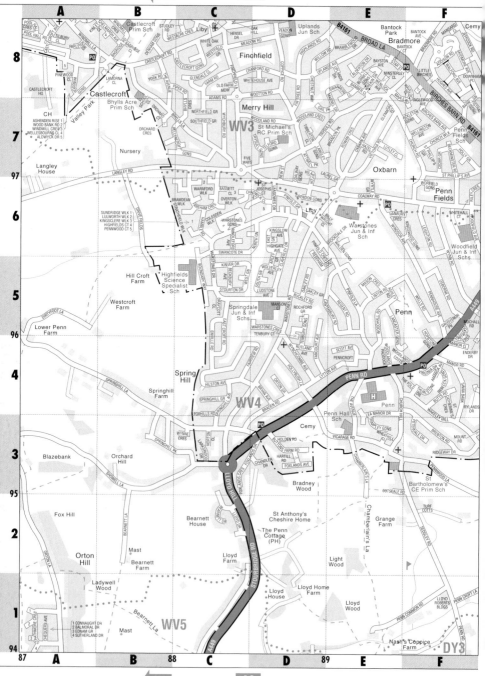

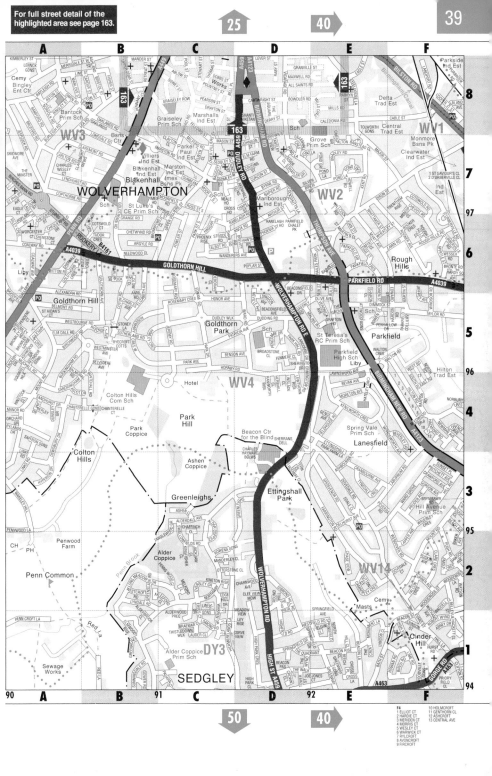

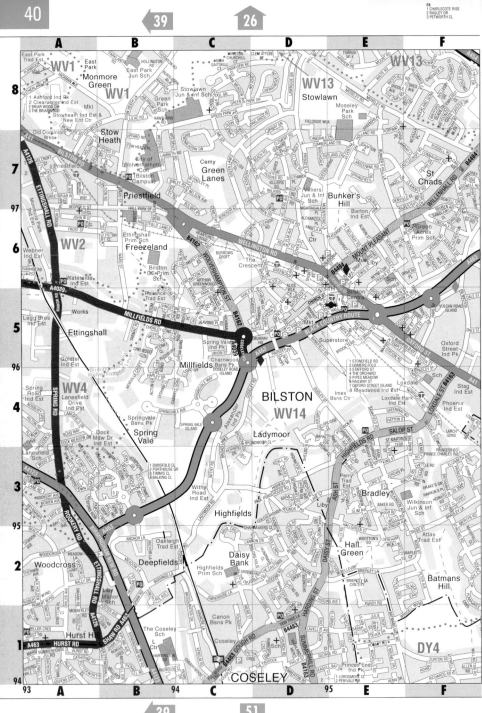

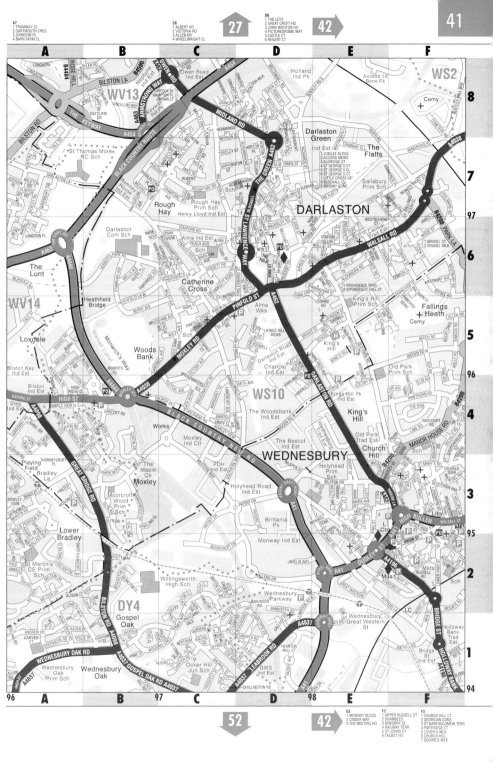

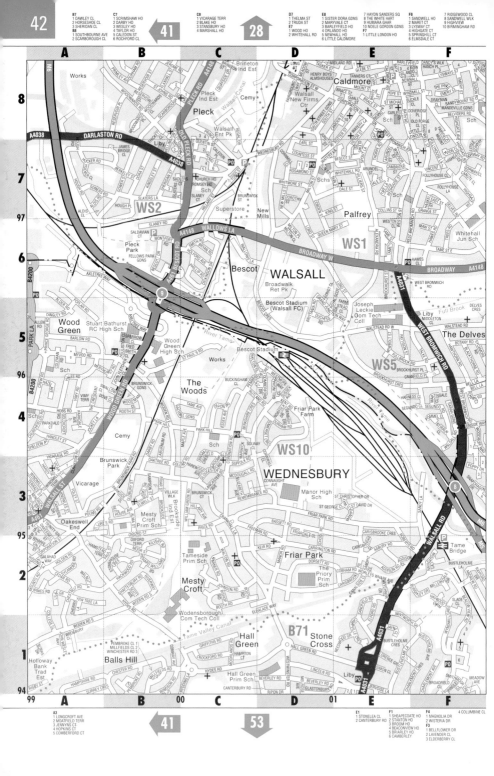

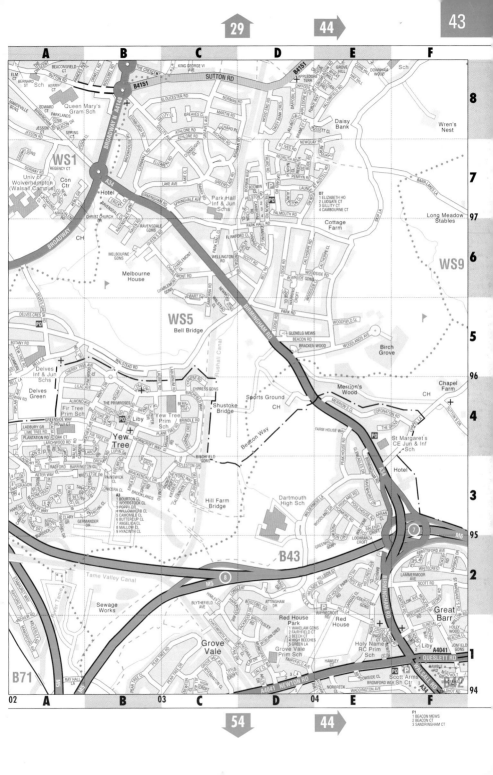

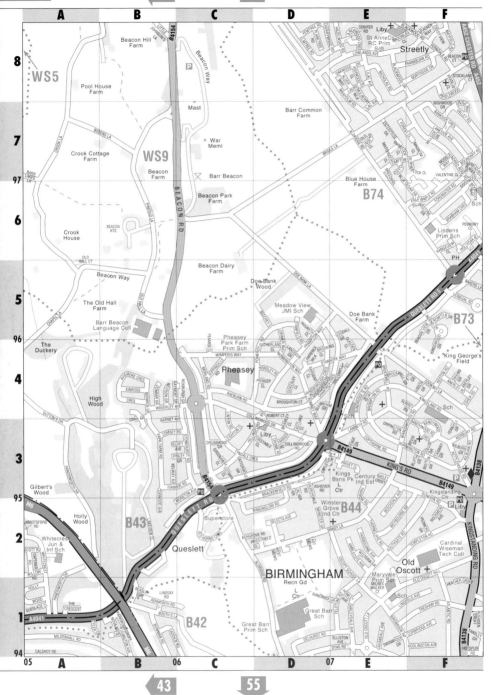

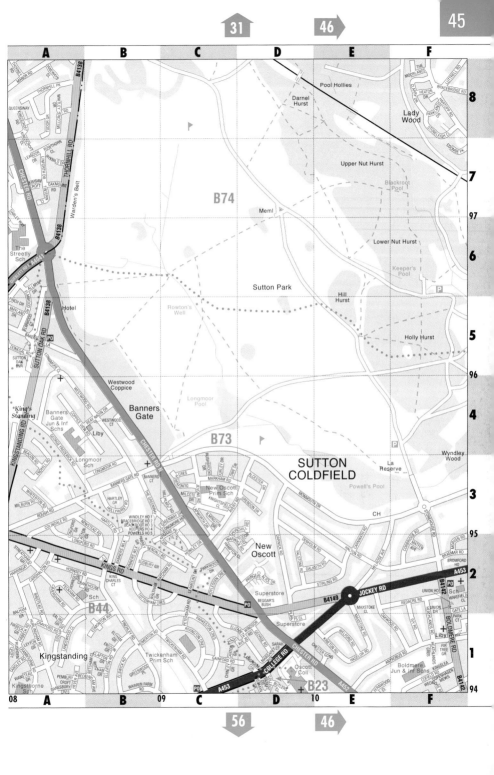

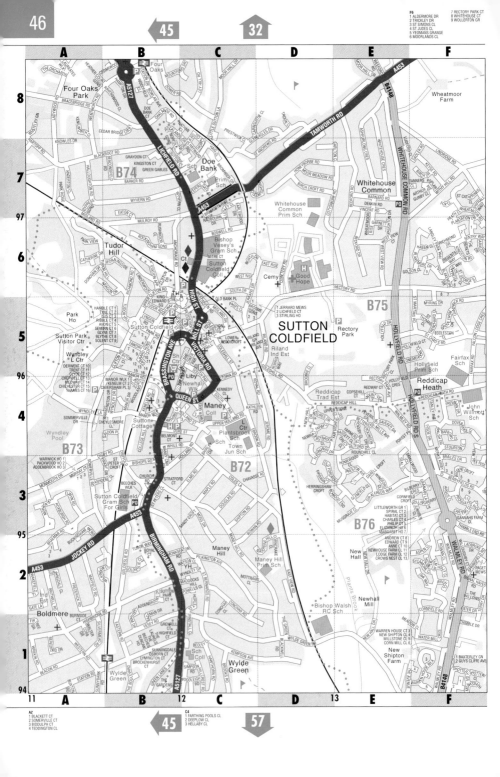

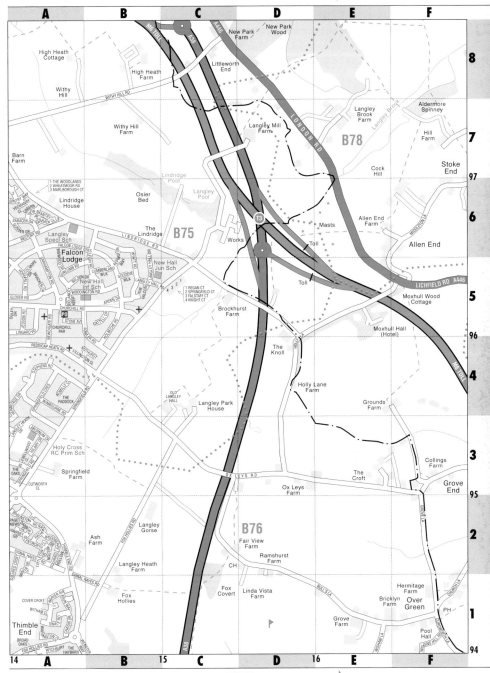

33 **48**

58 **48**

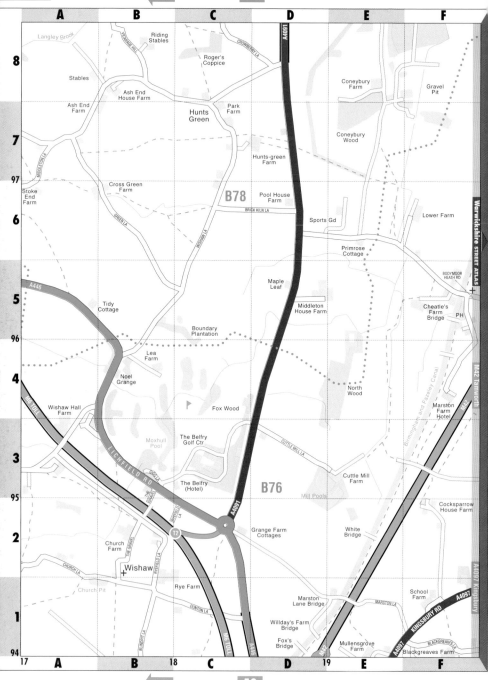

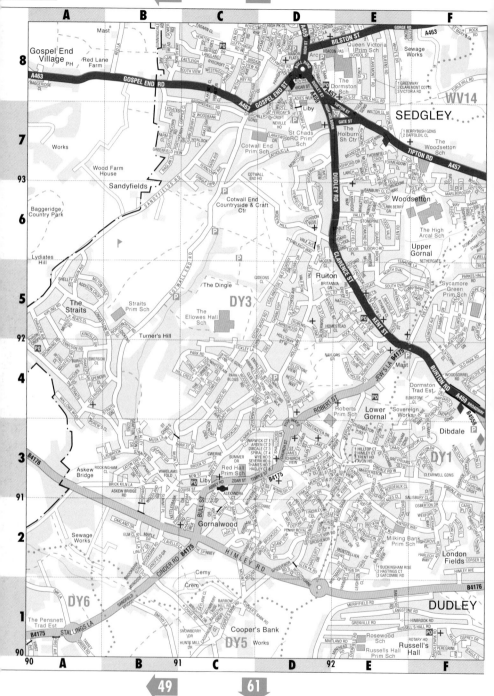

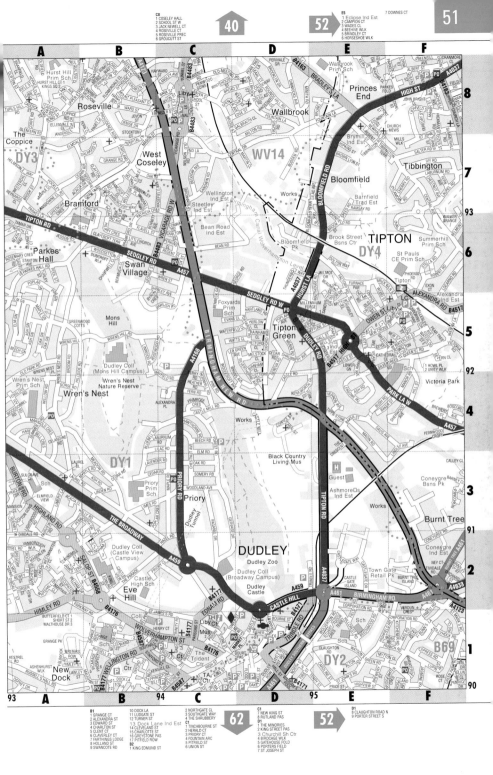

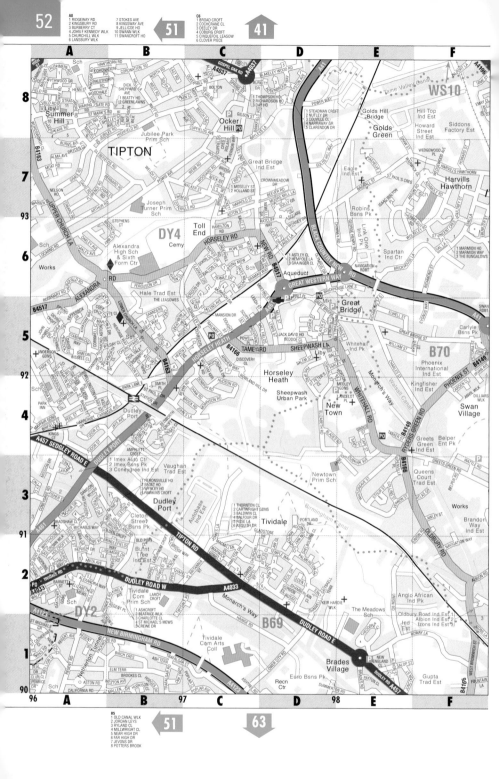

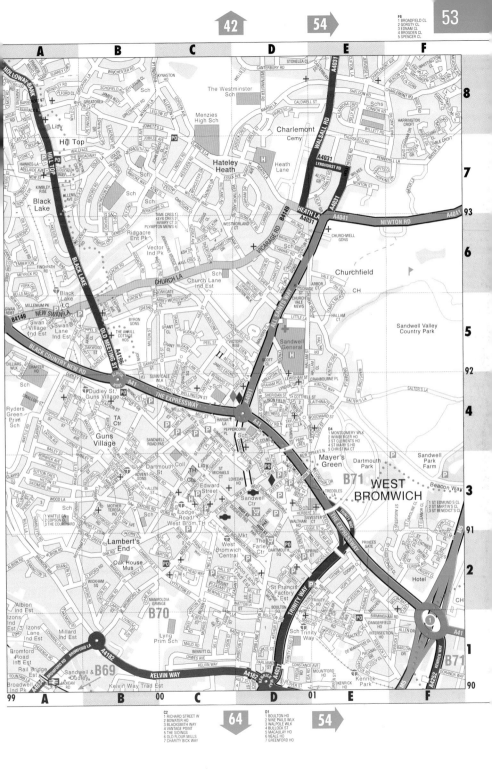

53
43

D8
1 BURRELTON WAY
2 GLENDENE DR
3 FAIRDENE WAY
4 GARSTON WAY

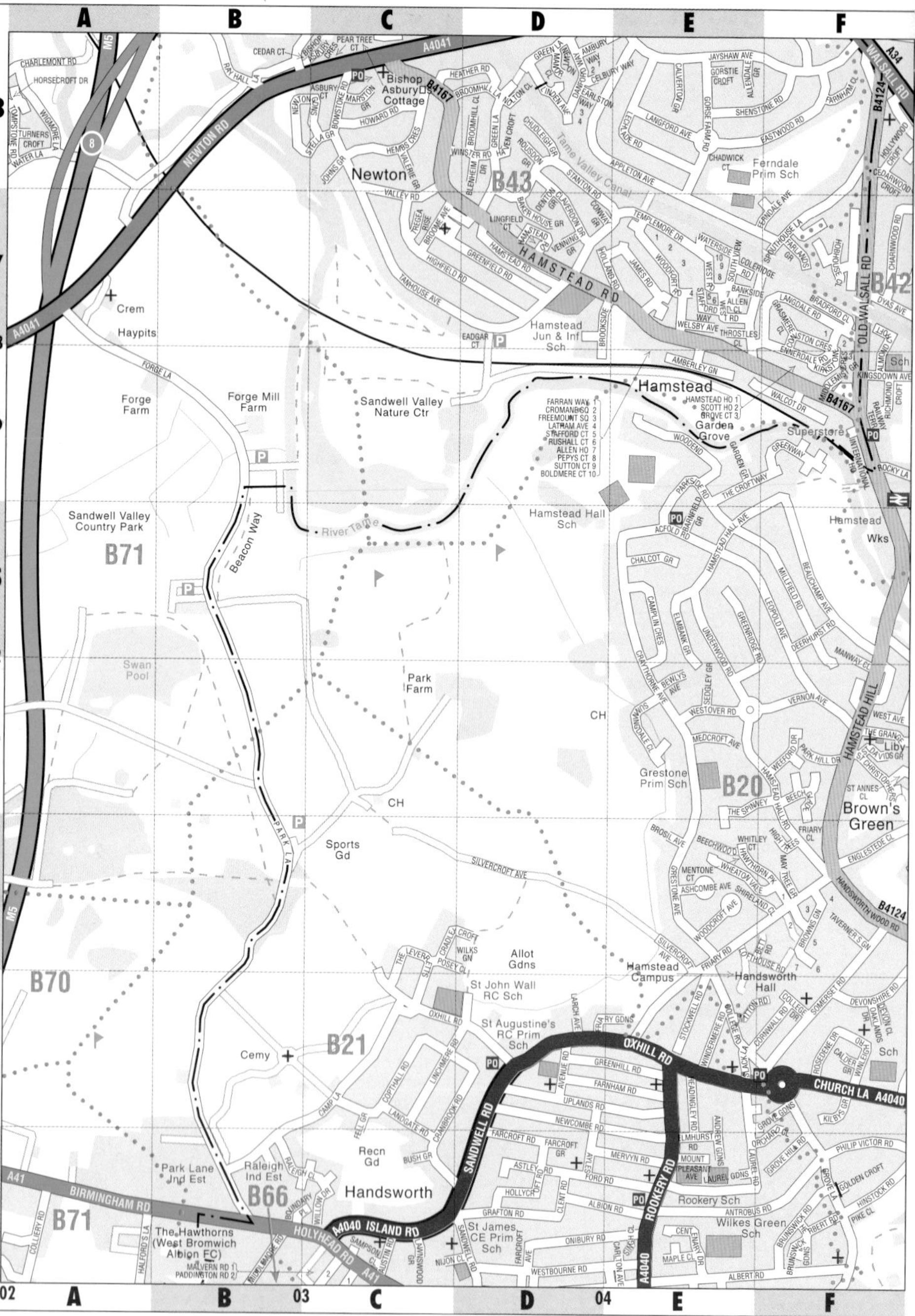

A B C D E F

8

Newton

B43

7

93

Crem
Haypits

Forge Farm
Forge Mill Farm

Hamstead

Hamstead Jun & Inf Sch

FARRAN WAY
CROMANBO 2
FREEMOUNT SQ 3
LATMAN AVE 4
STAFFORD CT 5
RUSHALL CT 6
ALLEN HO 7
PEPYS CT 8
SUTTON CT 9
BOLDMERE CT 10

HAMSTEAD HO 1
SCOTT HO 2
BROVE CT 3

Garden Grove

Superstore

Hamstead Wks

6

Sandwell Valley Country Park

B71

Forge La

Beacon Way

River Tame

Sandwell Valley Nature Ctr

Hamstead Hall Sch

B42

B4167

5

Swan Pool

Park Farm

CH

92

Grestone Prim Sch

B20

Brown's Green

4

M5

Sports Gd

CH

Silvercroft Ave

3

B70

B71

91

Cemy

B21

Allot Gdns

St John Wall RC Sch

St Augustine's RC Prim Sch

Hamstead Campus

Handsworth Hall

OXHILL RD

CHURCH LA A4040

B4124

2

A41 BIRMINGHAM RD

B66

Park Lane Ind Est

Raleigh Ind Est

Recn Gd

Handsworth

SANDWELL RD

GREENHILL RD

FARNHAM RD

ROOKERY RD

Rookery Sch

Wilkes Green Sch

1

B71

The Hawthorns (West Bromwich Albion FC)

HOLYHEAD RD

A4040 ISLAND RD

St James CE Prim Sch

A4040

MALVERN RD 1
PADDINGTON RD 2

WESTBOURNE RD

ALBERT RD

90

02 A B 03 C D 04 E F

53
65

F3
1 HAWTHORN PARK DR
2 CASSOWARY RD
3 QUORN HO
4 ALBRIGHTON HO
5 MEYNELL HO
6 PYTCHLEY HO
7 COTTESMORE HO

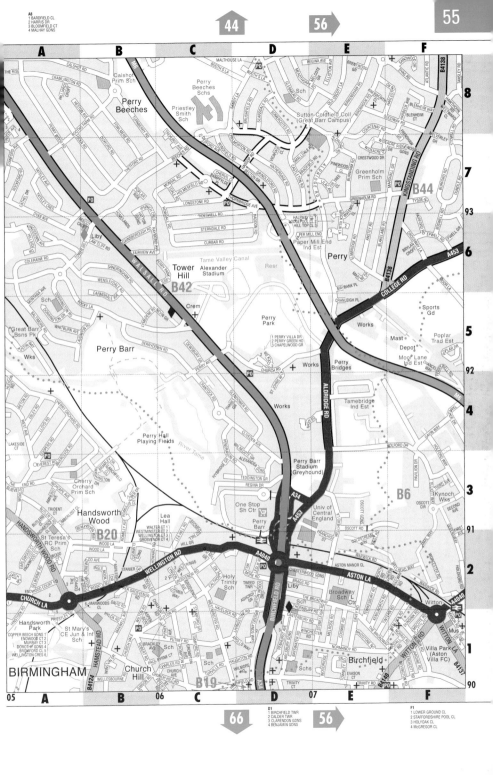

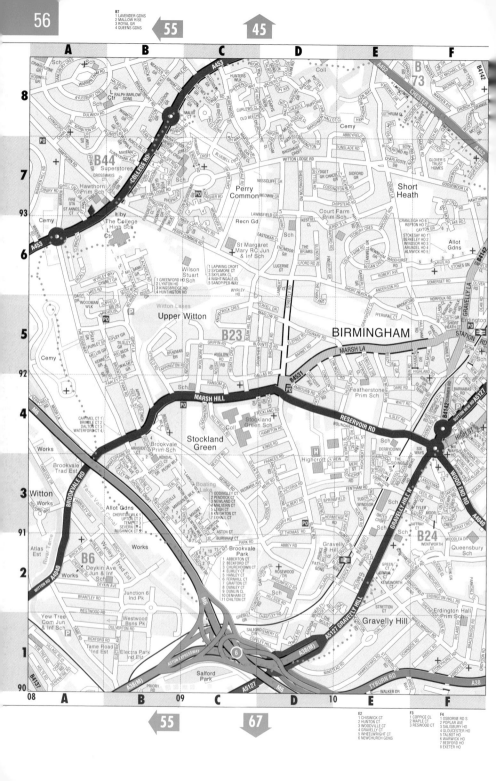

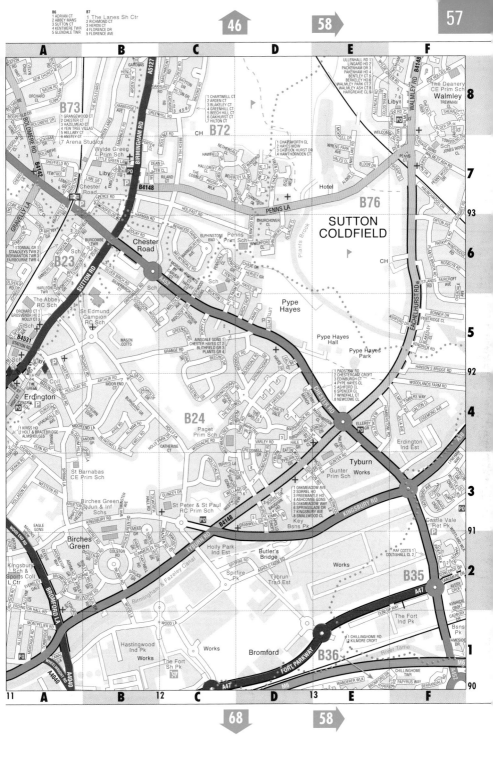

B6
1 ADRIAN CT
2 ABBEY MANS
3 SUTTON CT
4 KENTMERE TWR
5 GLENDALE TWR

B7
1 The Lanes Sh Ctr
2 RICHMOND CT
3 HERON CT
4 FLORENCE DR
5 FLORENCE AVE

46
58
68
58

B73
1 GRANGEWOOD CT
2 CHESTER CT
3 HAZELMEAD CT
4 YEW TREE VILLAS
5 HELLABY CT
6 ANSTEY CT
7 Arena Studios

B23

B72
1 CHARTWELL CT
2 ARDEN CT
3 BLAKELEY CT
4 GREENHILL CT
5 BEECH HILL CT
6 OAKHURST CT
7 HILTON CT

1 CHATSWORTH CL
2 HAYES MDW
3 CATTOCK HURST DR
4 HAWTHORNDEN CT

Walmley

The Deanery
CE Prim Sch

SUTTON
COLDFIELD

B76

Chester Road

Chester
Road

Pype
Hayes

Pype Hayes
Hall

Pype Hayes
Park

The Abbey
RC Sch

St Edmund
Campion
RC Sch

1 PADSTOW RD
2 CHESTERGATE CROFT
3 EDINBURGH CT
4 PYPE HAYES CL
5 ASHFORD CL
6 SPENCER CL
7 WINDFALL CT
8 NEWCOME CL

Erdington

B24

Paget
Prim Sch

Erdington
Ind Est

St Barnabas
CE Prim Sch

Tyburn

Gunter
Prim Sch

Tyburn
Works

Birches Green
Jun & Inf
Schs

St Peter & St Paul
RC Prim Sch

1 OAKMEADOW AVE
2 SORREL HO
3 FREEMANTLE HO
4 ASHCOMBE GDNS
5 OAKMEADOW WAY
6 SPRINGSLADE DR
7 KINGSBURY AVE
8 SMALLWOOD CL

Key
Bsns Pk

Castle Vale
Ret Pk

Birches
Green

Kingsbury
Sch &
Sports Coll
L Ctr

Holly Park
Ind Est

Butler's
Bridge

1 RAF COTTS 1
COLTISHALL CL 2

Works

B35

Spitfire
Pk

Tyburn
Trad Est

The Fort
Ind Pk

Bsns
Pk

Hastingwood
Ind Pk

Works

Works

Bromford

B36

The Fort
Sh Pk

1 CHILLINGHOME RD
2 KILMORE CROFT

Birmingham & Fazeley Canal

FORT PARKWAY

River Tame

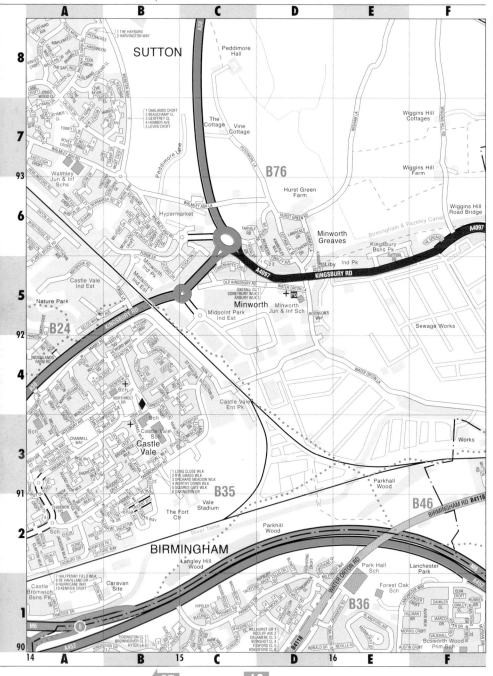

SUTTON

1 THE HAYBARN
2 HARVINGTON WAY

Peddimore
Hall

The
Cottage

Vine
Cottage

1 OAKLANDS CROFT
2 BEAUCHAMP CL
3 GEOFFREY CL
4 HUMBER AVE
5 LEVEN CROFT

B76

Wiggins Hill
Cottages

Wiggins Hill
Farm

Wiggins Hill
Road Bridge

Hurst Green
Farm

Walmley
Jun & Inf
Schs

Hypermarket

Minworth
Greaves

Birmingham & Fazeley Canal

A4097

Kingsbury
Bsns Pk

SUTTON
SQ

Castle Vale
Ind Est

Nature Park

KINGSBURY RD

A4097

KINGSBURY RD

Liby Ind Pk

KINGSBURY RD

OLD KINGSBURY RD

OXSTALL CL 1
CONEYBURY WLK 2
ARBURY WLK 3

WATER ORTON LA

Minworth

Midpoint Park
Ind Est

Minworth
Jun & Inf Sch

ROBINSON'S
WAY

Sewage Works

B24

Metalloys
Ind Est

WATER ORTON LA

Works

Sch

NORTHHOLT
DR

Castle Vale
Ent Pk

Parkhall
Wood

B46

BIRMINGHAM RD B4118

Castle Vale
Sch

Castle
Vale

1 LONG CLOSE WLK
2 RYE GRASS WLK
3 ORCHARD MEADOW WLK
4 WORTHY DOWN WLK
5 SQUIRES GATE WLK
6 OAKINGTON DR

B35

Vale
Stadium

The Fort
Ctr

River Tame

Parkhill
Wood

M6

A452

BIRMINGHAM

Langley Hill
Wood

WATER ORTON RD

Park Hall
Sch

Lanchester
Park

7 HALFPENNY FIELD WLK
8 DE HAVILLAND DR
9 HURRICANE WAY
10 KENRICK CROFT

Caravan
Site

Forest Oak
Sch

B36

Castle
Bromwich
Bsns Pk

M6

A452

1 TIDDINGTON CL 1
BROWNSOVER CL 2
KYTER LA 3

HILLHURST GR 1
REDLIFF AVE 2
DELAMERE CL 3
BOWSHOT CL 4
FOXFORD CL 5
KINGSFORD CL 6

B4118

Bosworth Wood
Prim Sch

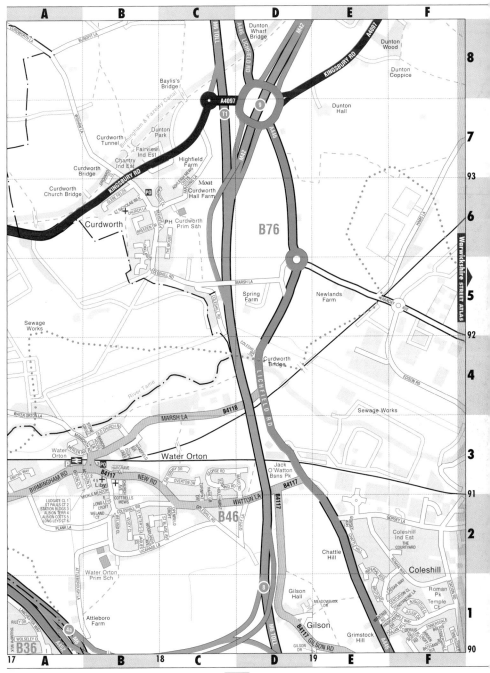

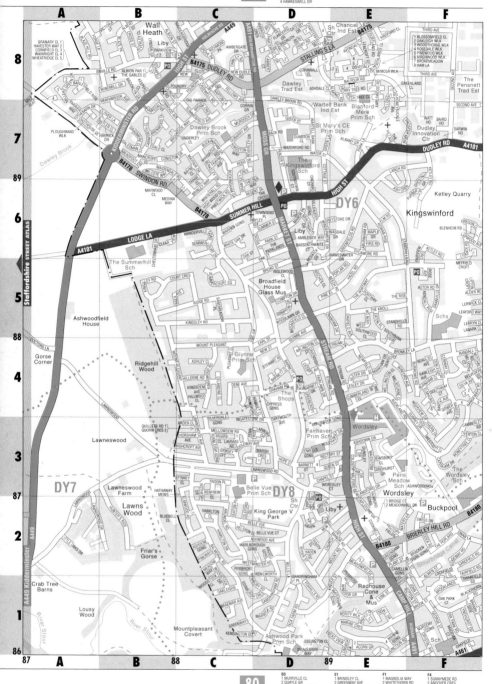

D3
1 MUIRVILLE CL
2 QUAYLE GR
3 ROSE COTTAGE DR
4 CROSS ST

E1
1 BRINDLEY CL
2 GREENWAY AVE
3 DIAMOND PARK DR
4 SWEETBRIER DR
5 GILBEYS CL

F1
1 MAGNOLIA WAY
2 WHITETHORN RD
3 DEWBERRY RD

F4
1 SUNNYMEDE RD
2 ANDOVER CRES
3 FREELAND GR
4 GRANGE LA
5 MADELEY RD

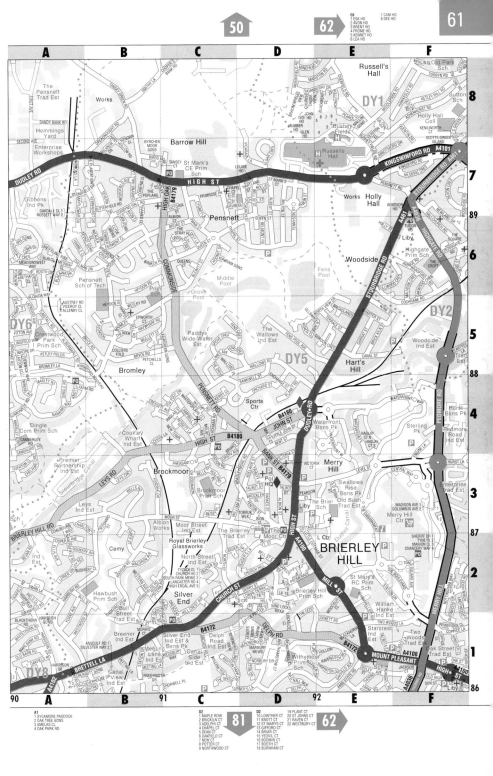

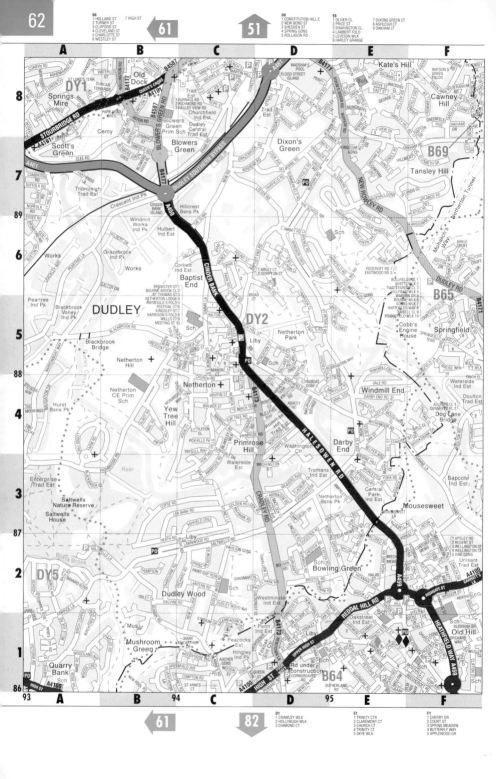

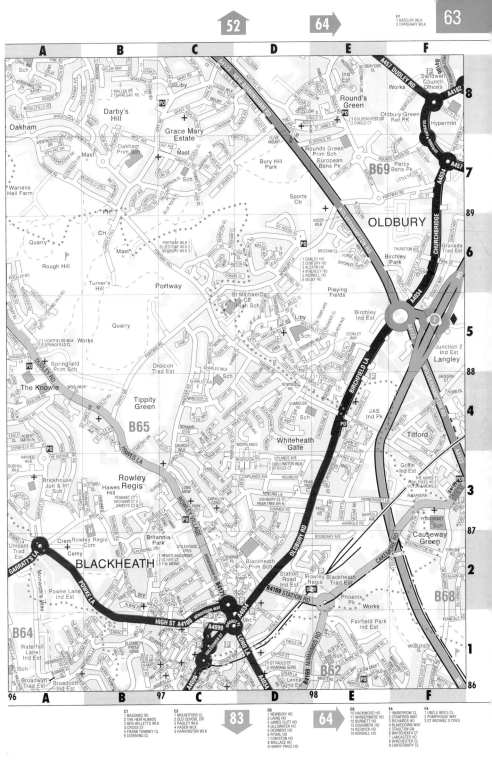

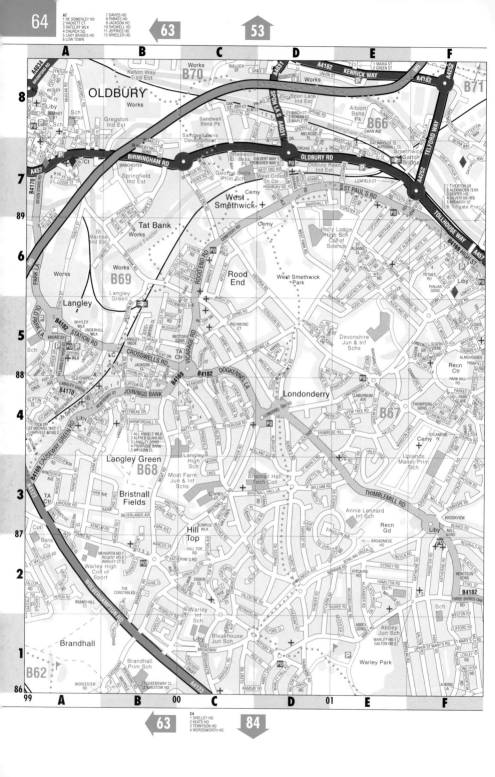

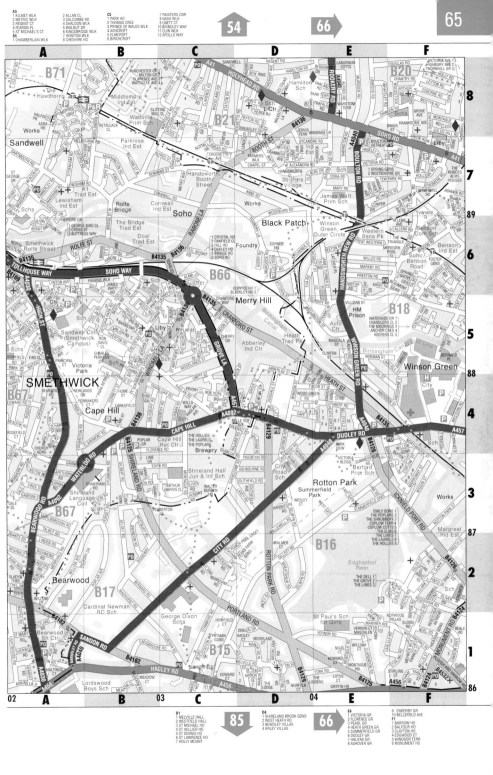

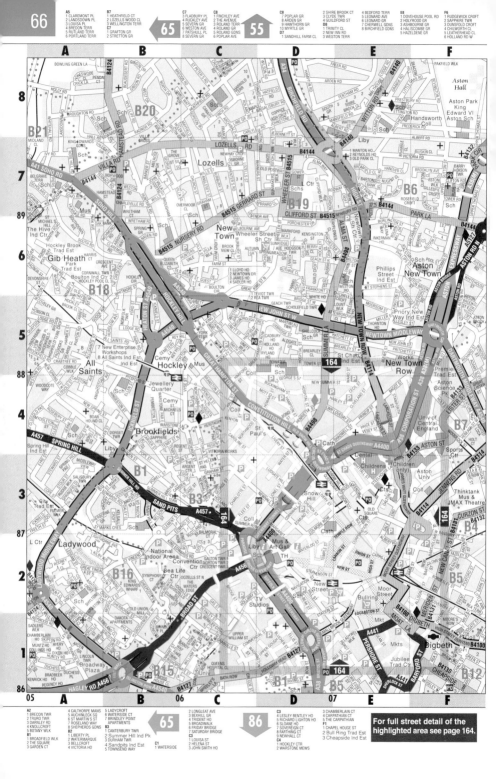

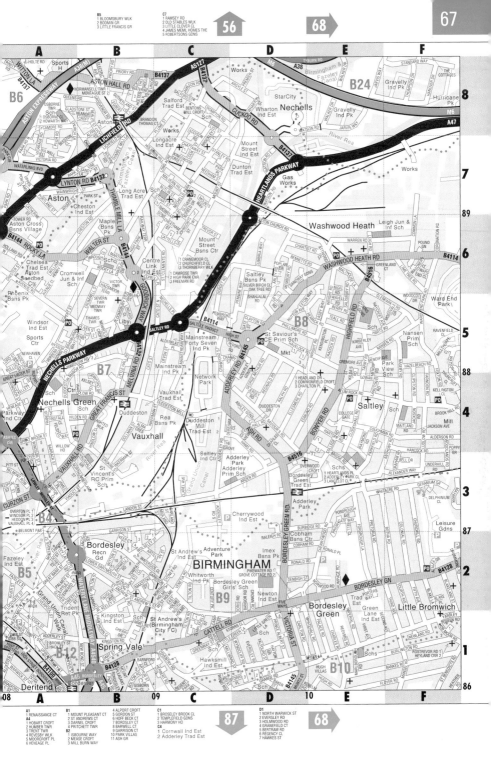

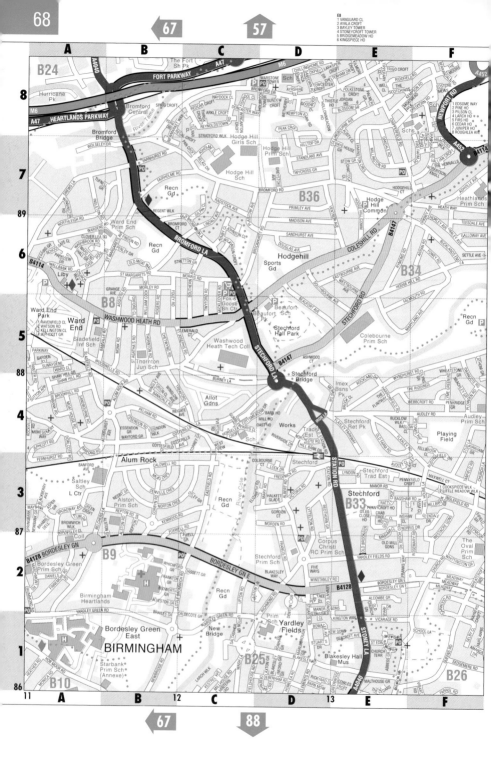

A **B** **C** **D** **E** **F**

M42

Green La

The Belt

B4117 GILSON RD

High Meadow Inf Sch

Cole End

LICHFIELD RD

A446

8

RED WING WLK
GOLDCREST
PHEASANT
NIGHTINGALE AVE
FIELDFARE
CROFT
SWALLOW
JACKDAW
DEE WLK
ISIS GR
FISHER DR
SWAN
WORCESTER

B4117

PRIESTHILLS RD

OLD MILL RD
ORCHARD

HIGH BANK

HIGH ST

OLD RD

7

Kingfisher
Prim Sch

The Catmore

F7
1 RIVERSIDE CT
2 SERVITE HO
3 BRIDGE VIEW
4 WINDMILL AVE
5 ST PAUL'S CRES
6 BRAMBLE CL
7 BLYTHE RD
8 ANGEL MEWS
9 FAIRVIEW MEWS
10 CHAMBERLAIN WLK
11 PARKFIELD CT
12 DUNCOMBE GN

B4114

89

B36

Smiths Wood
Sch

WESTFIELD
HO

SOUTH DR

M42

P
PARK RD
L Ctr

6

B4114

Kingshurst
Jun & Inf Schs

Kingshurst

CHESTER RD

BEDFORD
HO

BIRBECK
HO

SHERWOOD

The Decoy

Cemy

B46

BIRMINGHAM RD

Ct
SUMNER RD

Coleshill

WHEATLEY
GRANGE

Prim
Sch

5

PARADE
MARSTON
DR
Liby

B4114

Waterloo
Ind Est

Coleshill Hall
Bridge

Hall Wlk

BIRMINGHAM

Coleshill Hall
Farm

STONEBRIDGE RD

88

St Antony's
RC Prim Sch

Fordbridge
Inf Sch

NEWHAM HO

TOWER CROFT

River Cole

Coleshill Hall
Farm

4

The City
Tech Coll

Chelmsley
Wood
Ind Est

Bacon's
End

KEELE HO

WESTHAM
HO

WEDGEWOOD
GR

B37

Solihull Coll
(Chelmsley
Campus)

C3
1 BRACKEN CROFT
2 RICHMOND WAY
3 SWANSMOOR GR

Green La

Wheeley
Moor
Farm

M6 TOLL

Warwickshire Street Atlas

Sch

Sports
Ctr

Fordbridge

CONWAY RD

Bacon's End
Bridge

CHESTER RD

Bishop
Wilson
CE Prim Sch

Griffin
Bsns
Pk

1 SOMERVILLE HO
2 SELWYN HO
3 WADHAM HO
4 MANSFIELD HO

3

WOODLODGE
RD

ORIEL
ACRES

B2
1 BEAUCHAMP CL
2 CHESTNUT WLK
3 CRESHAWN HO
4 MAPLE WLK
5 GREENWOOD
6 CEDAR WLK
7 COPPEY WAY
8 DILLINGTON HO
9 WOODBROOK HO

Pol
HQ
Liby

Chelmsley
Wood

P

TRAVELLERS
WAY

7a

87

Prim
Sch

PO

IPSWICH

PINE SQ

VERA
WLK

Croft
Ind Est

Prim
Sch

2

HOLLY LODGE
WLK
CHESTER
WELL CROFT
ARDERNE

MOAT CROFT
KEBLE HO

TRURO
WLK

Chelmsley
Wood

D2
1 HAREBELL WLK
2 MULLINERS CL
3 HIKER GR
4 CHESTER CT
5 WARWICK CT
6 PICTON CROFT

P

Recn Gd

Brickfield
Farm

A452

M42

4

Pool
Wood

7

Coleshill
Pool

1

Alcott Wood

Alcott Hall
Prim Sch

WORCESTER
SHIRLAND RD

HOLBROOK
GR

PINBURY
CROFT

NEVADA WAY

WHEATON

Birmingham
Bsns Pk

A452

86

A 17 **B** 18 **C** 19 **D** **E** **F**

C1
1 TREVELYAN HO
2 RICHMOND HO
3 DARWIN HO

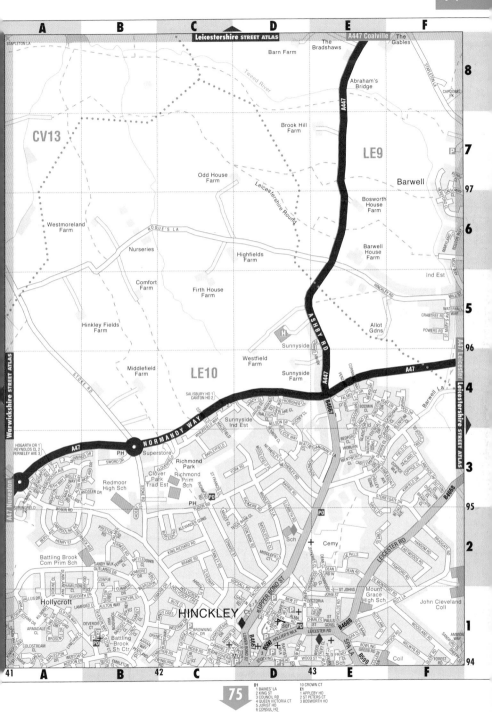

Leicestershire STREET ATLAS

A B C D E F

CV13

LE9

Barwell

Westmoreland Farm

Nurseries

Comfort Farm

Hinkley Fields Farm

Middlefield Farm

LE10

Barn Farm

The Bradshaws

A447 Coalville

The Gables

Abraham's Bridge

Brook Hill Farm

Odd House Farm

Leicestershire Round

Highfields Farm

Firth House Farm

Bosworth House Farm

Barwell House Farm

Ind Est

Sunnyside

Westfield Farm

Sunnyside Farm

Allot Gdns

Salisbury Ho 1
Canton Ho 2

Sunnyside Ind Est

NORMANDY WAY

Superstore

Richmond Park

Clover Park Trad Est

Redmoor High Sch

Richmond Prim Sch

PH

PH

Battling Brook Com Prim Sch

Alexander Gdns

King Richard Rd

Brame Rd

Hollycroft

Battling Brook Sh Ctr

HINCKLEY

ASHBY RD

A447

A447

A47

A47 Nuneaton

Warwickshire STREET ATLAS

Leicestershire STREET ATLAS

A47 Leicester

B4668

B4667

B4668

B4667

B590

B590

Leicester Rd

Mount Grace High Sch

John Cleveland Coll

Cemy

Sch

Sch

PO

PO

Barwell La

Ind Est

Waterfall Way

Crabtree Rd

Powers Rd

Mill St

8

7

97

6

5

96

4

3

95

2

1

94

75

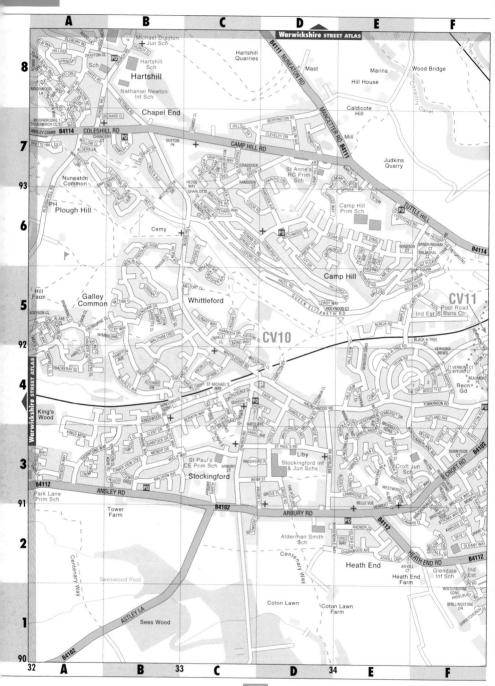

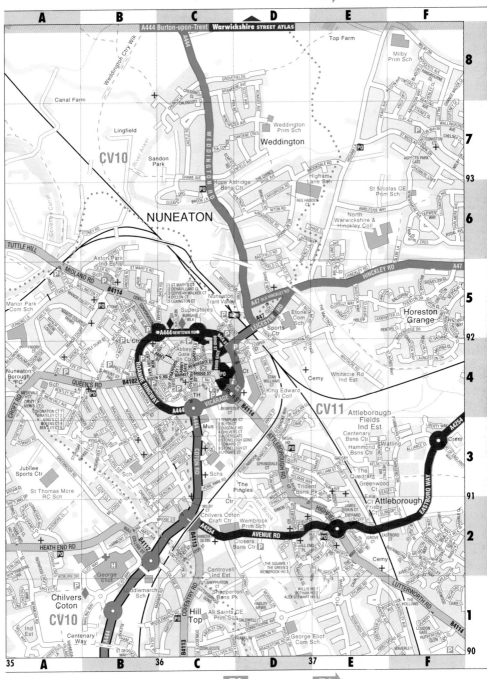

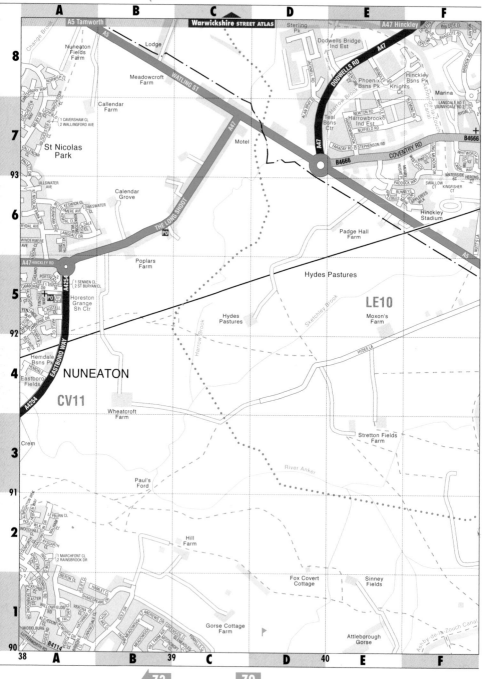

Warwickshire STREET ATLAS

A **B** **C** **D** **E** **F**

A5 Tamworth

A47 Hinckley

Sterling Pk

Dodwells Bridge Ind Est

DODWELLS RD

A47

Hinckley Bsns Pk

Knights Ct

Marina

Nuneaton Fields Farm

Lodge

Meadowcroft Farm

WATLING ST

Phoenix Bsns Pk

Newton Rd

Harrowbrooke Ind Est

Nuffield Rd

LANGDALE RD 1

1 CAVERSHAM CL
2 WALLINGFORD AVE

Callendar Farm

Motel

A47

Teal Bsns Ctr

FARADAY RD

STEPHENSON RD

COVENTRY RD

B4666

St Nicolas Park

Calendar Grove

B4666

WATERSIDE Ct

SWALLOW CT

KINGFISHER CT

ILLSWATER AVE

THE LONGSHOOT

PO

Padge Hall Farm

Hinckley Stadium

A5

Poplars Farm

A47 Hinckley Rd

A4254

1 SENNEN CL
2 ST BURYAN CL

Horeston Grange Sh Ctr

Hydes Pastures

Hyde's Pastures

LE10

Moxon's Farm

HYDES LA

Sketchley Brook

Hemdale Bsns Pk

Eastboro Fields

EASTBORO WAY

NUNEATON

CV11

Wheatcroft Farm

Harrow Brook

Stretton Fields Farm

Crem

River Anker

Paul's Ford

1 MARCHFONT CL
2 RAINSBROOK DR

Hill Farm

Fox Covert Cottage

Sinney Fields

Gorse Cottage Farm

Attleborough Gorse

Ashby-de-la-Zouch Canal

B4114

A **B** **C** **D** **E** **F**

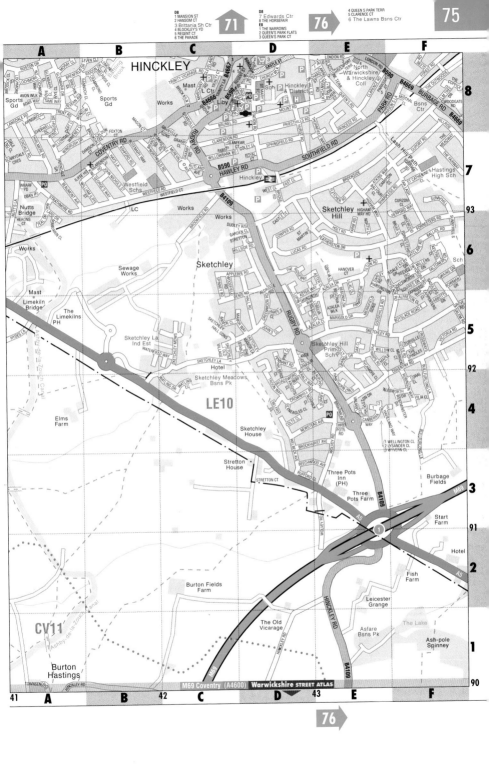

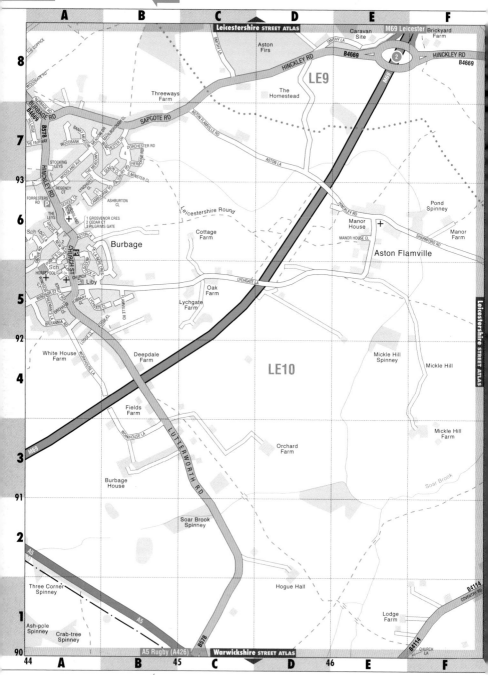

Warwickshire STREET ATLAS

A **B** **C** **D** **E** **F**

ASTLEY LA
B4102

Temple House

Park Farm

Mill

Spring Kidden Wood

The Lawns

Centenary Way
HAREFIELD LA

Dennis Farm

Tea House

8

Old Park

Covents Pool

Garners Pool

Arbury Park

Arbury Hall Park & Gardens

Arbury

7

High Park Pool

Works

GRIFF LA

89

New Park Wood

CV10

Coventry Wood

GRIFF LA

6

Fir Tree Grove

South Farm

Arbury Mill Farm

5

Cowley Wood

Rabbit Lane Wood

Keeper's Close

88

Soar End

Holmes Wood

Sole End Farm

BEDWORTH LA

Woodlands House Farm

Bedworth Woodlands

Norwood Farm

4

Cow Lees

Colliery Wood

DOVE CL

3

CV12

Woodlands Farm

PH

CASTLE LATON RD

87

Taffs Farm

Swain's Wood

Coventry Way

Astley Hall Farm

Market End Farm

MEWTOWN RD
NEWTOWN RD

BROOKLEA

PO

2

JUNIPER CL

THE FIRS

THE FERN

THE WILLOWS

THE LAURELS

HEATHER DR

SWAN LA

CROFT RD

DELAMERE RD

CARLTON RD

1 BLYTH CL
2 HAMILTON CL

DAISY RD

BUTTERCUP RD

CLOVER WAY

THE LIMES

THE ALDER

THE MAPLES

THE CHESTNUTS

THE BEECHES

SMORRALL LA

PH

Market End

Bedworth Heath

CV7

Highfield House Farm

Newdigate Prim Sch

KEEPERS WLK 1
OAKLEY CT 2

ARTHUR ALFORD HO

LAVENDER CL 1
BRYONY RD 2

KATHLEEN AVE

AV444

Church Farm

Mast

POTTERS RD

TOPPS HAMMERS RD

Liby

1

86

D2
1 WILDEY RD
2 HIMLEY RD
3 CAMPION WAY
4 DAFFODIL DRIVE
5 LARKSPUR GR
6 SPEEDWELL CL

F2
1 SYDNEY CT
2 CANBERRA CT
3 MELBOURNE CT
4 QUEENSLAND GDNS

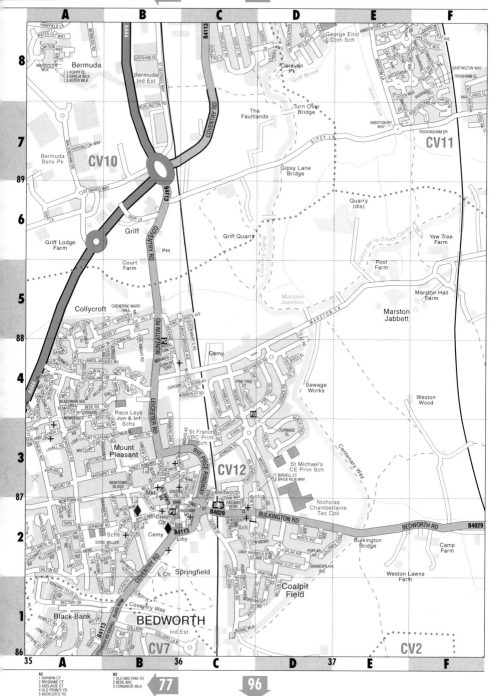

A2
1 DARWIN CT
2 BRISBANE CT
3 ADELAIDE CT
4 OLD PENN'S YD
5 BUCKLER'S YD

B3
1 OLD MEETING YD
2 BEDE ARC
3 CONGREVE WLK

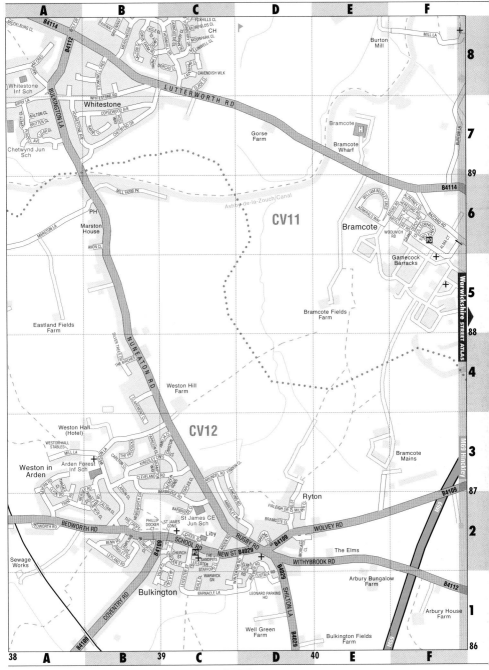

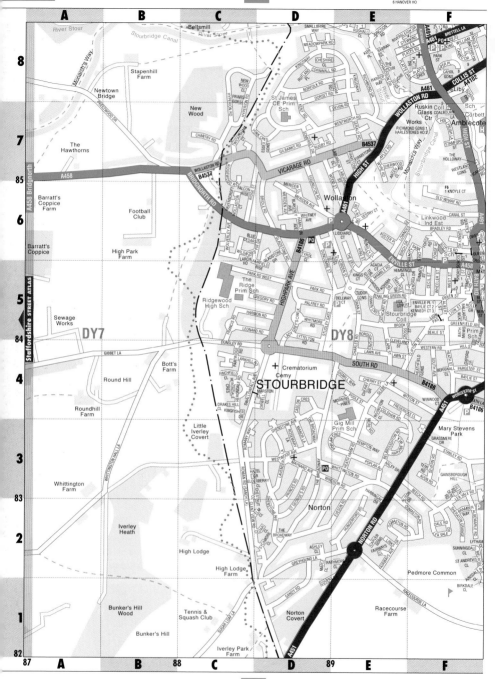

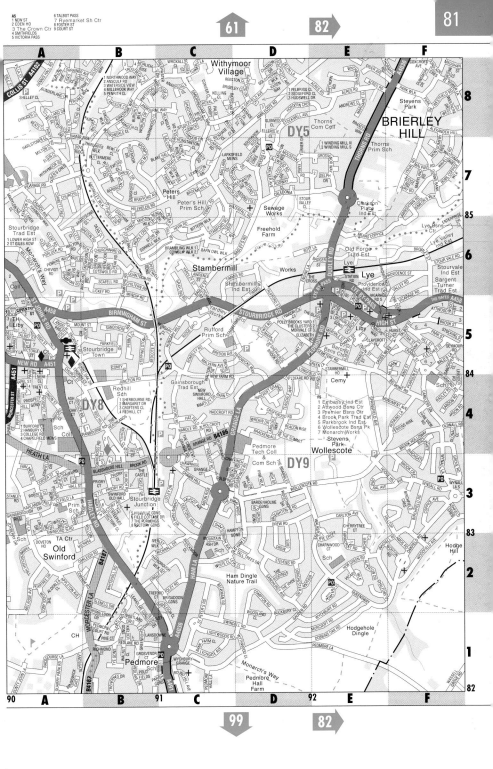

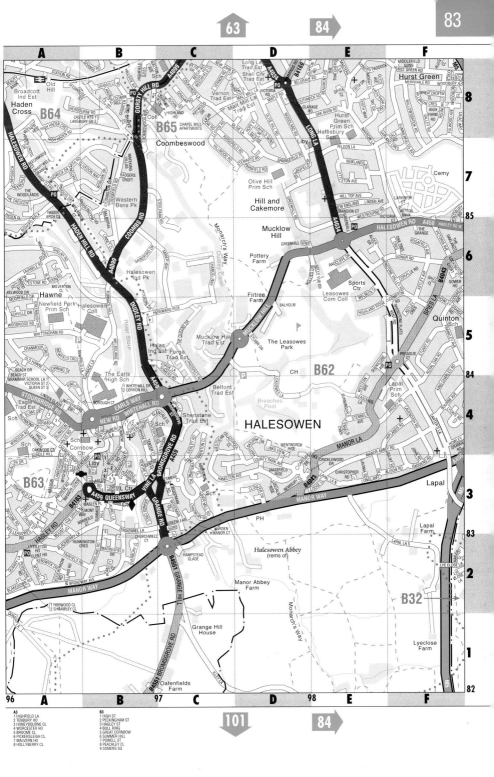

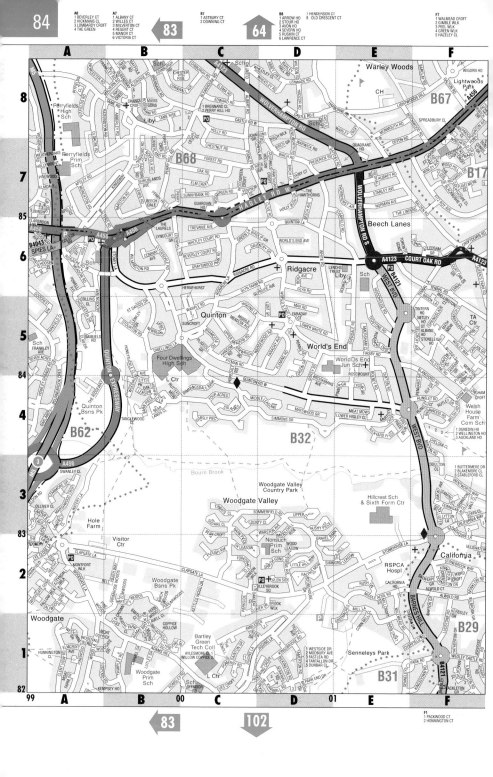

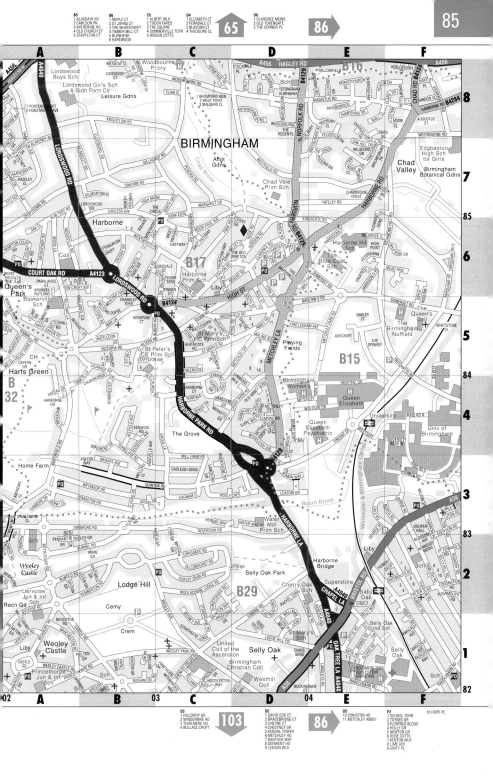

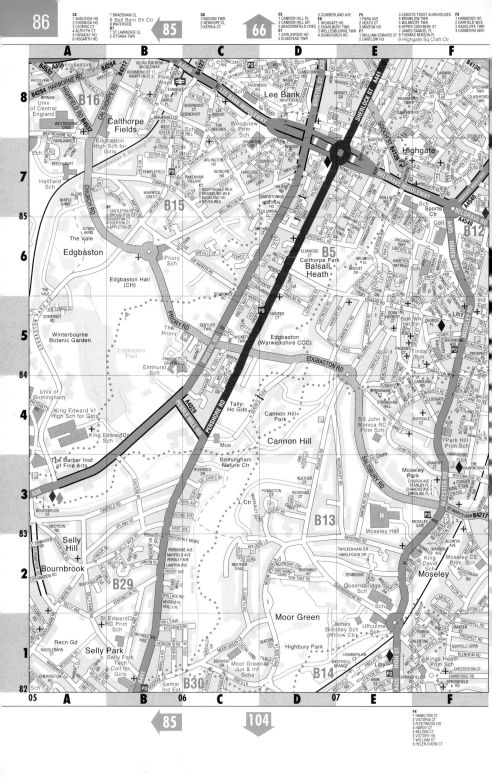

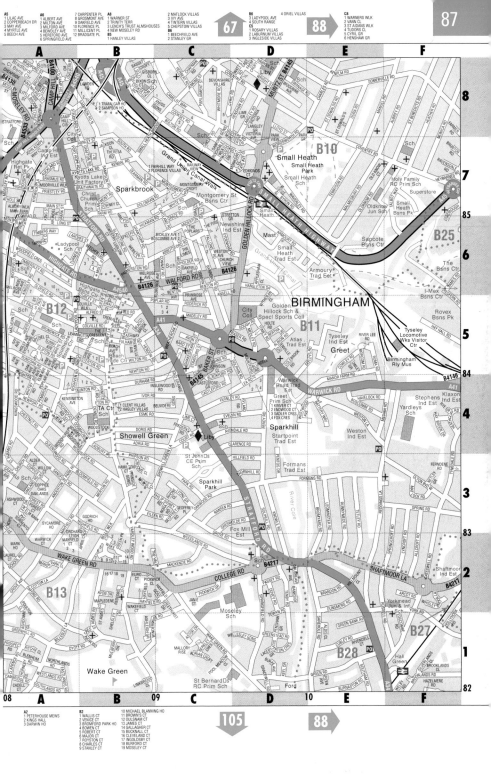

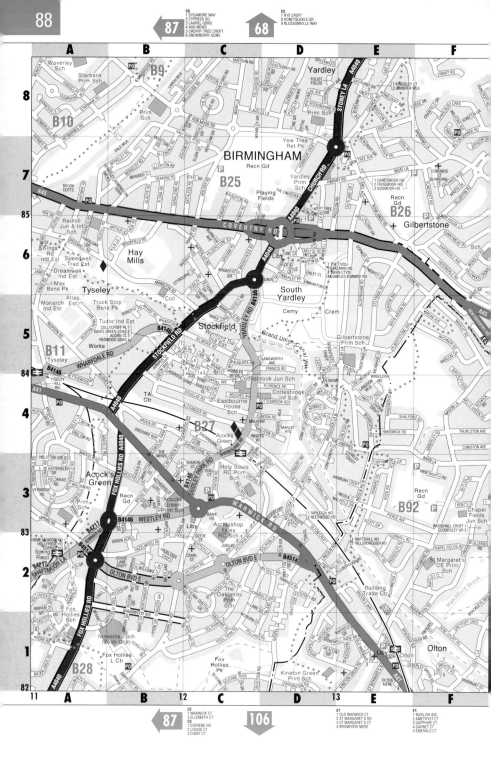

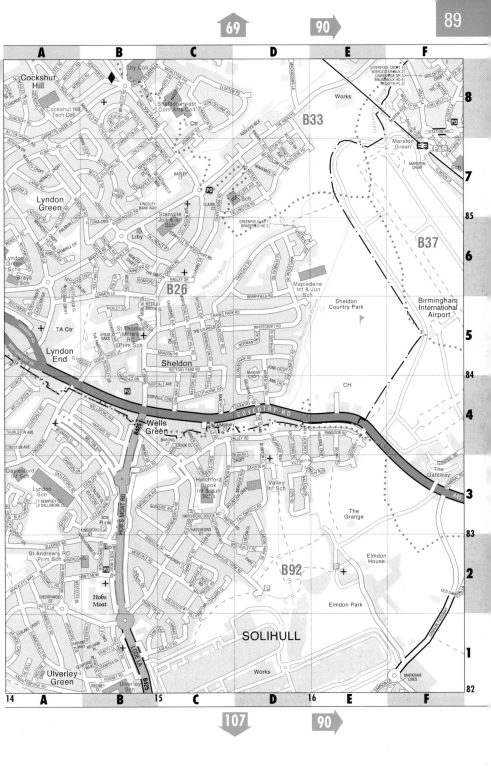

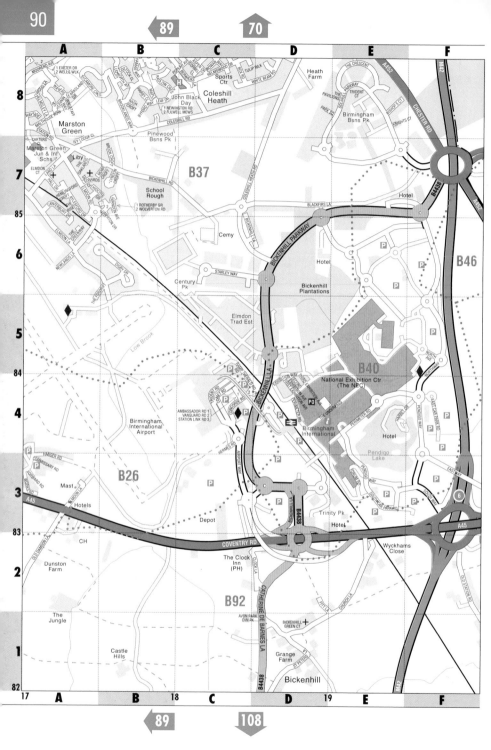

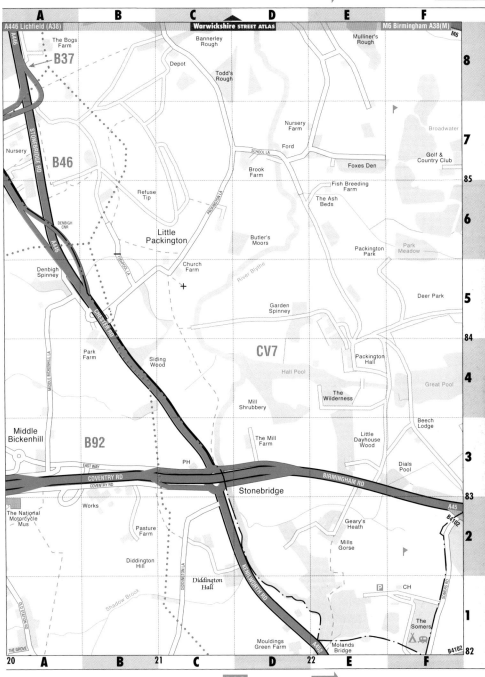

Warwickshire STREET ATLAS

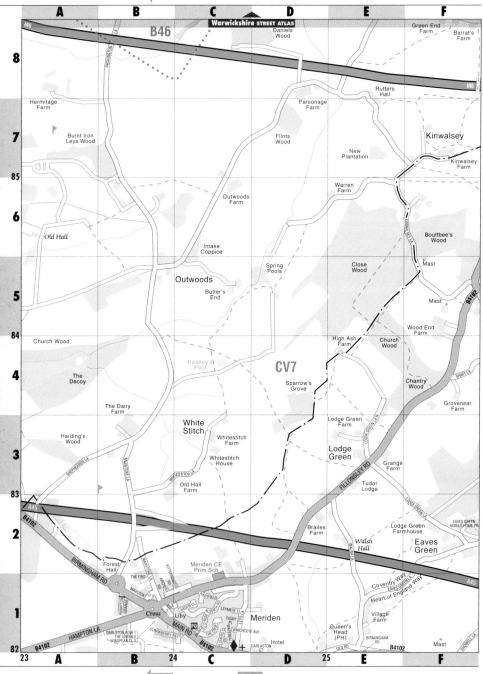

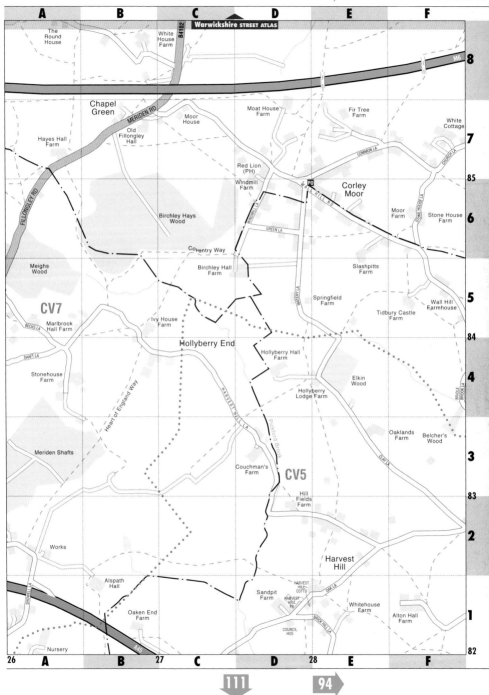

Warwickshire STREET ATLAS

8

7

85

6

5

84

4

3

83

2

1

82

The Round House

White House Farm

Chapel Green

Moor House

Moat House Farm

Fir Tree Farm

White Cottage

MERIDEN RD

Old Fillongley Hall

Hayes Hall Farm

COMMON LA

FILLONGLEY RD

Red Lion (PH)

Windmill Farm

Corley Moor

Moor Farm

Stone House Farm

Birchley Hays Wood

WINDMILL LA

WALL HILL RD

GREEN LA

Coventry Way

Meighs Wood

Birchley Hall Farm

Slashpitts Farm

Wall Hill Farmhouse

CV7

WAVERLY LA

Springfield Farm

Tidbury Castle Farm

BECKS LA

Marlbrook Hall Farm

Ivy House Farm

Hollyberry End

Hollyberry Hall Farm

SHAFT LA

Stonehouse Farm

Elkin Wood

Oaklands Farm

Belcher's Wood

BRIDLE BROOK LA

Hollyberry Lodge Farm

Heart of England Way

Meriden Shafts

HARVEST HILL LA

Pickford Brook

Couchman's Farm

CV5

OAK LA

Works

Hill Fields Farm

SHOWELL LA

Harvest Hill

Alspath Hall

Oaken End Farm

Sandpit Farm

HARVEST HILL COTTS

HARVEST HILL RD

Whitehouse Farm

Alton Hall Farm

BRICK HILL LA

A45

COUNCIL HOS

Nursery

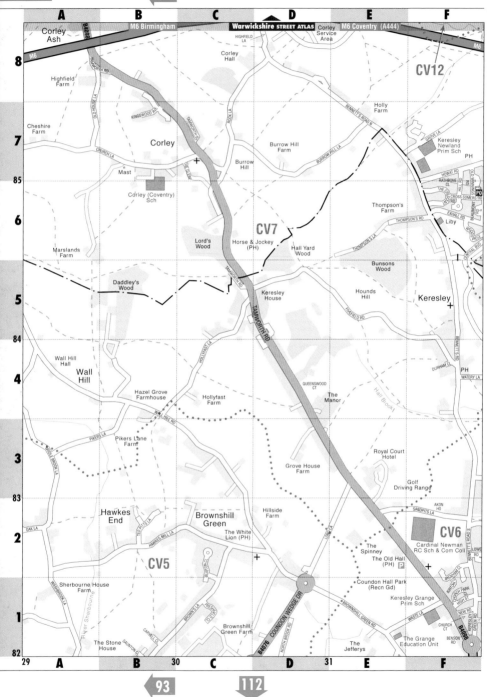

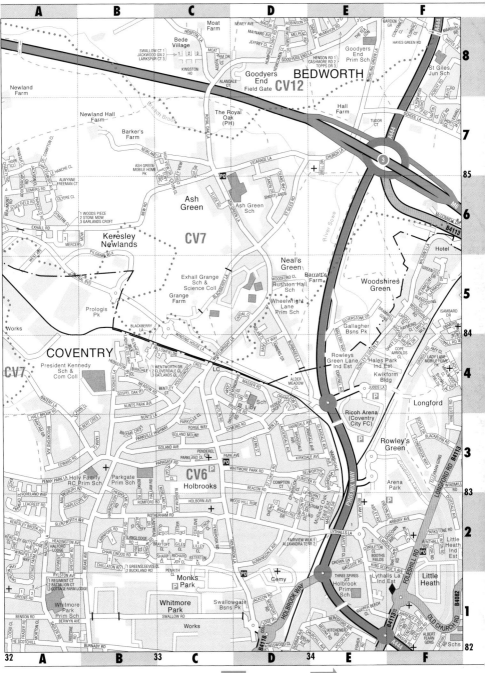

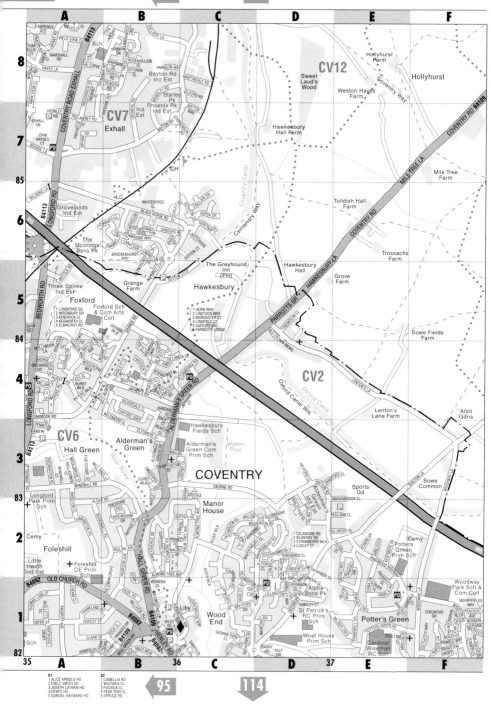

B1
1 ALICE ARNOLD HO
2 EMILY SMITH HO
3 JOSEPH LATHAM HO
4 DEWIS HO
5 SAMUEL HAYWARD HO

B2
1 CAMELLIA RD
2 WISTARIA CL
3 FUCHSIA CL
4 PEAR TREE CL
5 SPRUCE RD

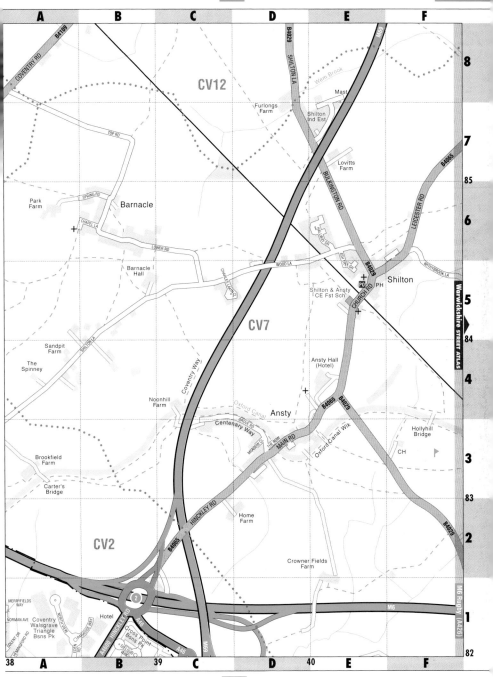

80

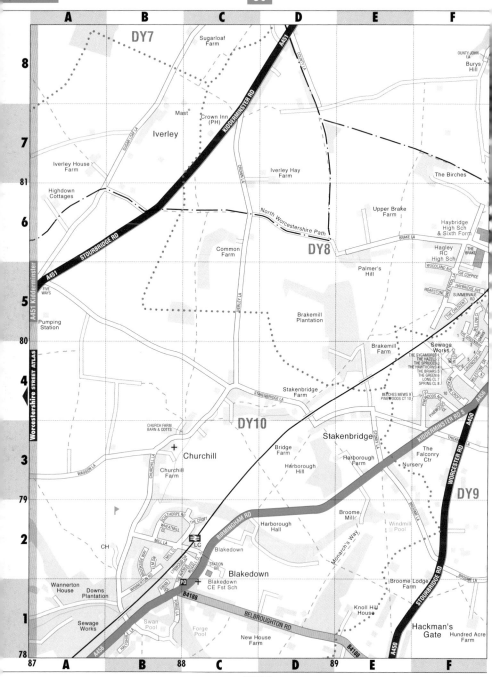

118

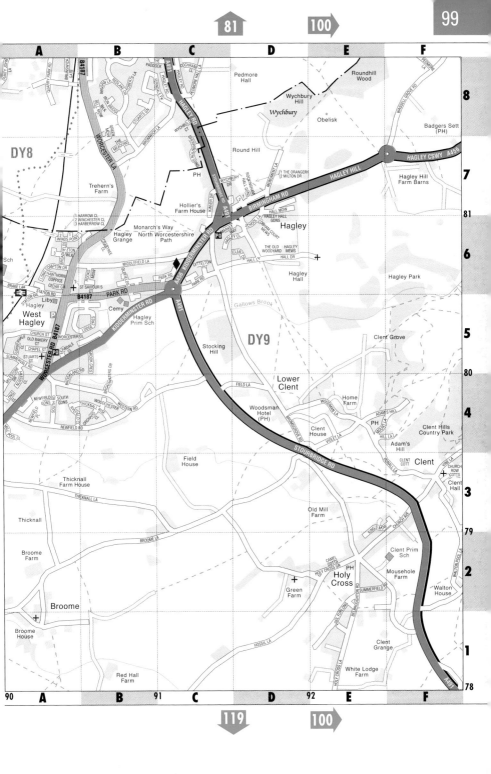

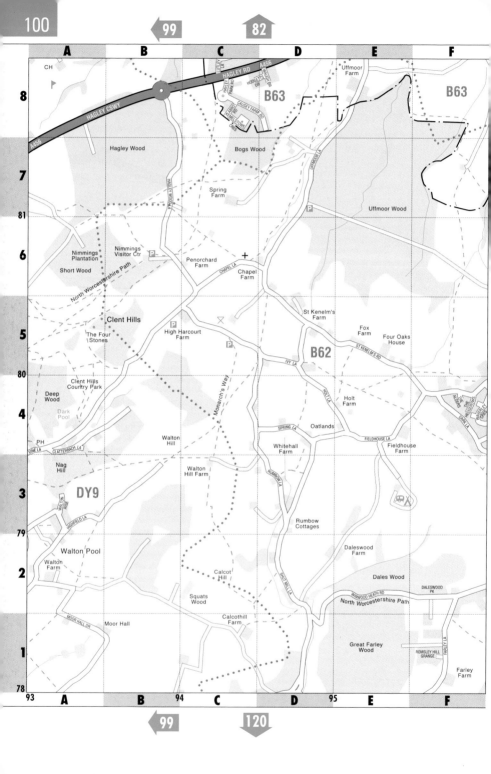

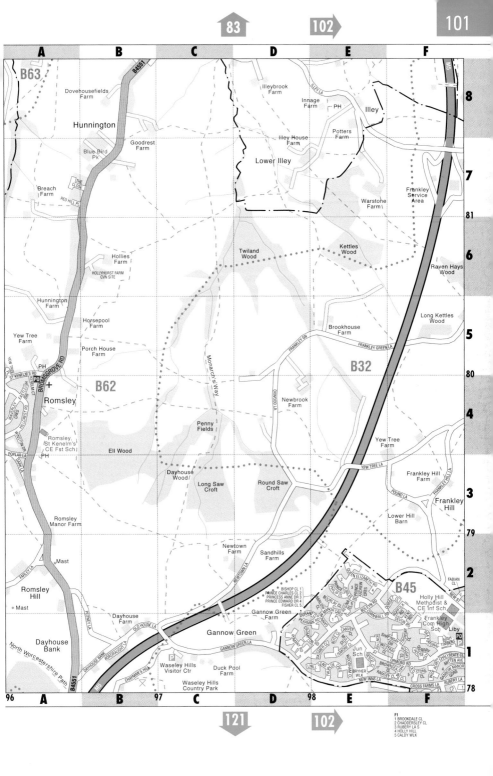

B63

Dovehousefields
Farm

Hunnington

Goodrest
Farm

Blue Bird
Pk

THE CLOSE

Breach
Farm

RED HILL PL

Illeybrook
Farm

Innage
Farm

PH

Illey

Potters
Farm

Illey House
Farm

Lower Illey

Warstone
Farm

Frankley
Service
Area

8

7

81

Hollies
Farm

HOLLYHURST FARM
CVN SITE

Hunnington
Farm

Horsepool
Farm

Yew Tree
Farm

Porch House
Farm

PH

BROMSGROVE RD

ST KENELM'S RD

Romsley

B62

Twiland
Wood

Kettles
Wood

Raven Hays
Wood

Brookhouse
Farm

FRANKLEY GN

FRANKLEY GREEN LA

B32

Long Kettles
Wood

6

5

80

Monarch's Way

Penny
Fields

Ell Wood

Newbrook
Farm

OLDWOOD LA

Yew Tree
Farm

YEW TREE LA

Frankley Hill
Farm

FRANKLEY HILL LA

4

Romsley
St Kenelm's
CE Fst Sch

PH

POPLAR CL

BAKER'S
CRES

PH

EXELBY DR

HELELM CT

WHISTON GR

Dayhouse
Wood

Long Saw
Croft

Round Saw
Croft

ROUND LA

Frankley
Hill

3

79

Romsley
Manor Farm

EARLS LA

Mast

Romsley
Hill

Mast

Newtown
Farm

NEWTOWN LA

Sandhills
Farm

BISHOP CL 1
PRINCE CHARLES CL 2
PRINCESS ANNE DR 3
PRINCE EDWARD DR 4
FISHER CL 5

QUEEN ELIZABETH RD

B45

FABIAN
CL

NEW LN

Holly Hill
Methodist &
CE Inf Sch

2

Dayhouse
Bank

North Worcestershire Path

Dayhouse
Farm

OLD HOUSE LA

DAYHOUSE BANK

MORDAUGHT LA

PUTNEY LA

B4551

A38

CHAPMAN'S HILL

Gannow Green
Farm

Gannow Green

GANNOW GREEN LA

Duck Pool
Farm

Waseley Hills
Visitor Ctr

P

Waseley Hills
Country Park

Frankley
Com High
Sch

Jun
Sch

BRYHER
WLK

NEW INNS LA

CROSS FARMS LA

RUBERY LA

Liby

P

PO

1

78

F1
1 BROOKDALE CL
2 CHADDERSLEY CL
3 RUBERY LA 5
4 HOLLY HILL
5 CALDY WLK

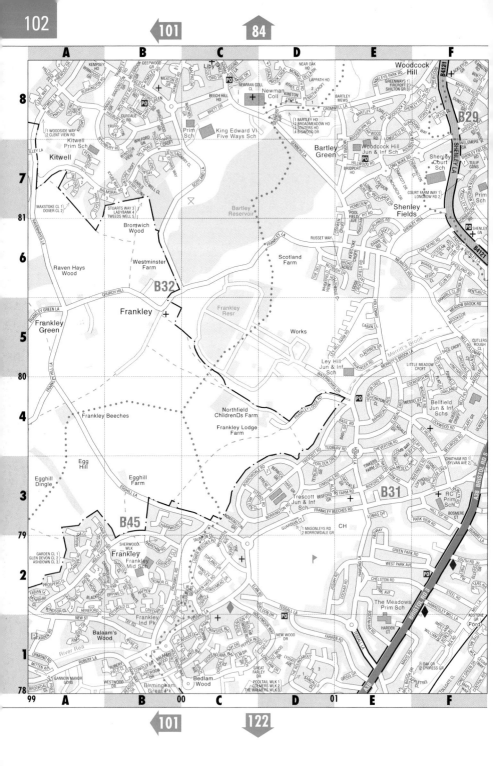

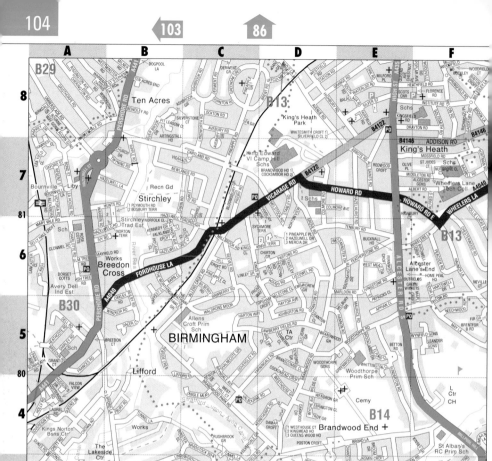

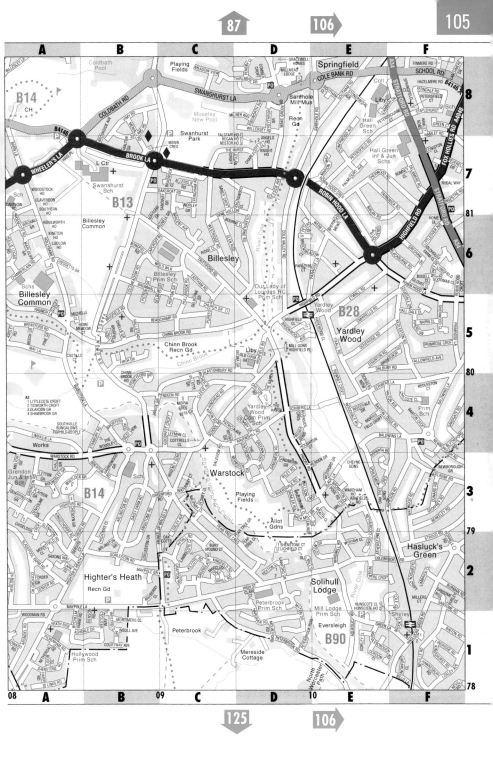

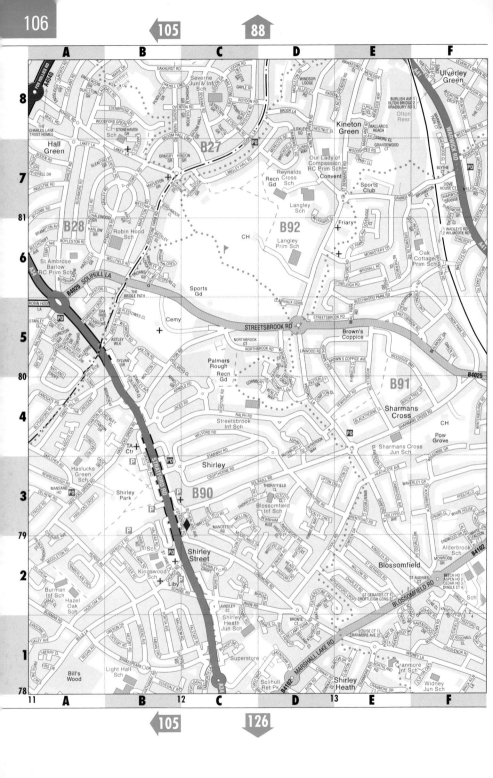

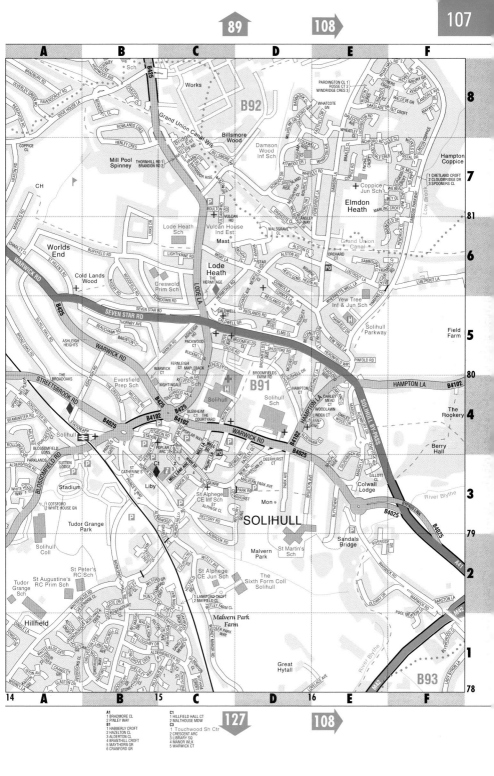

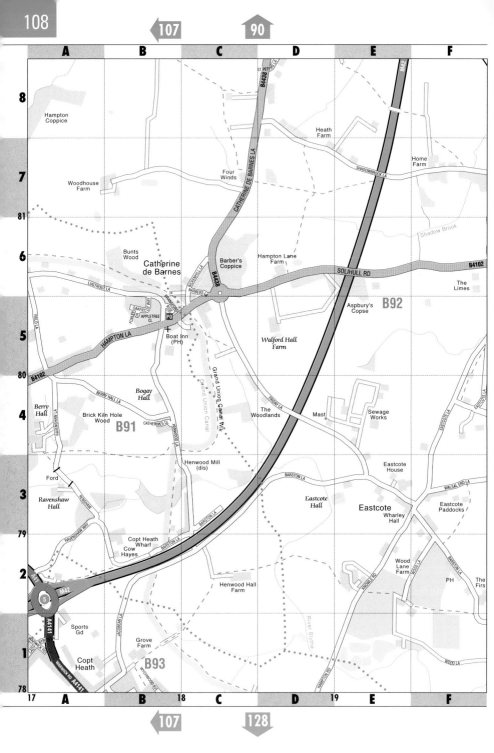

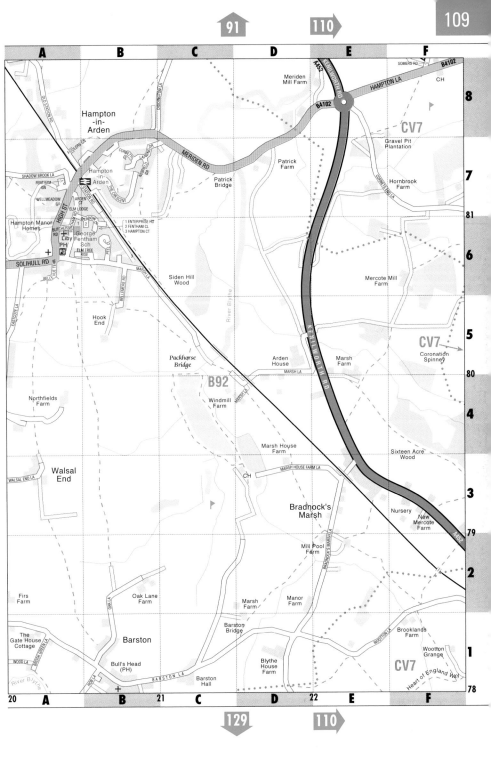

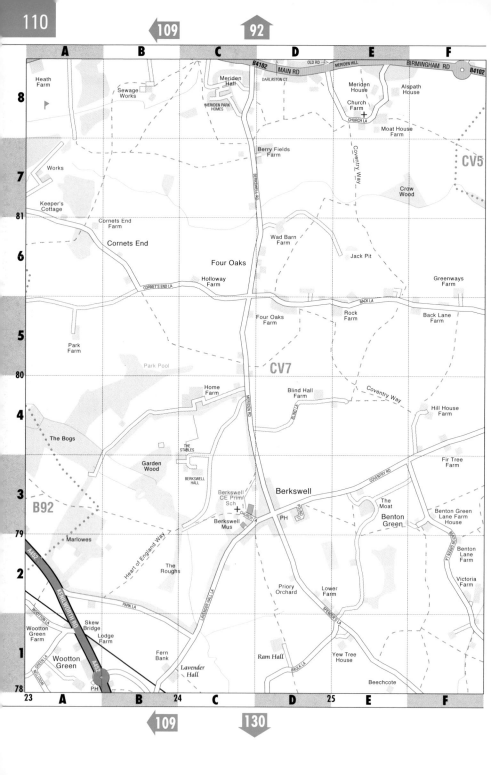

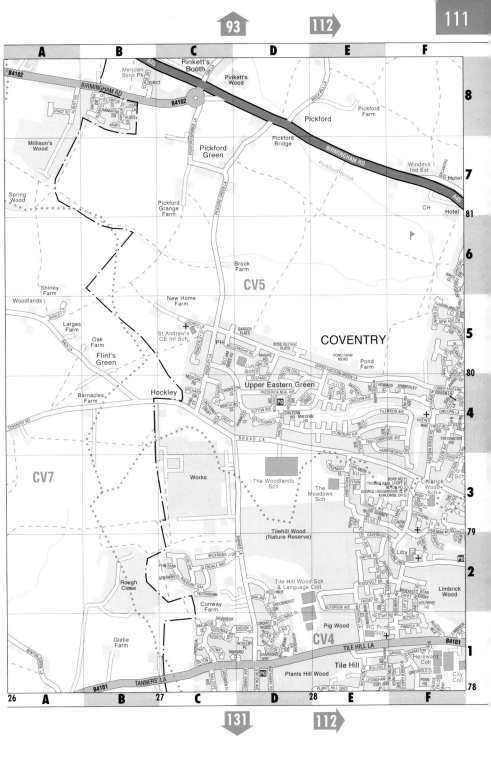

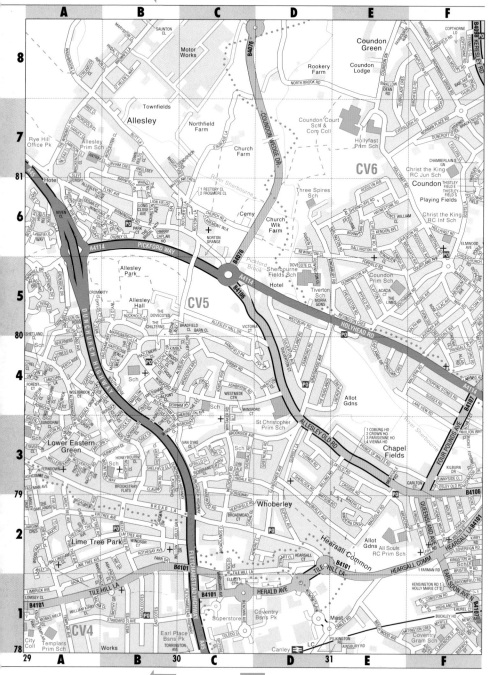

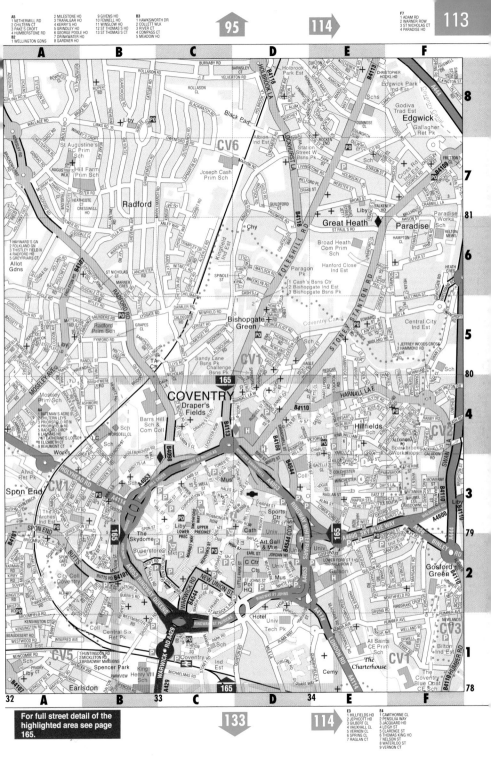

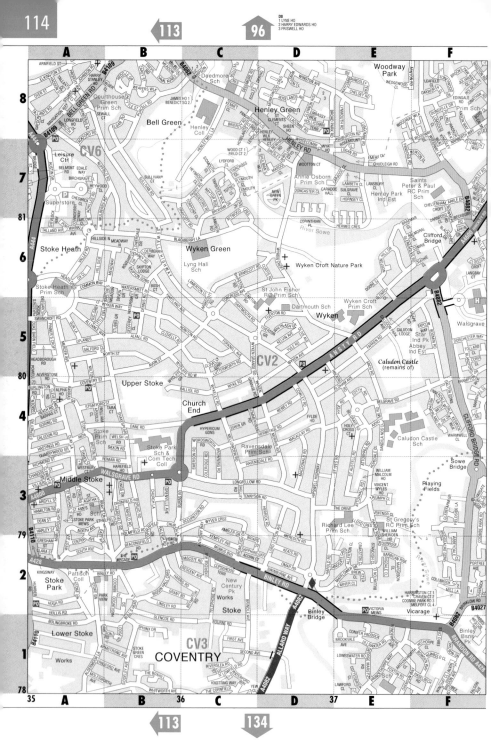

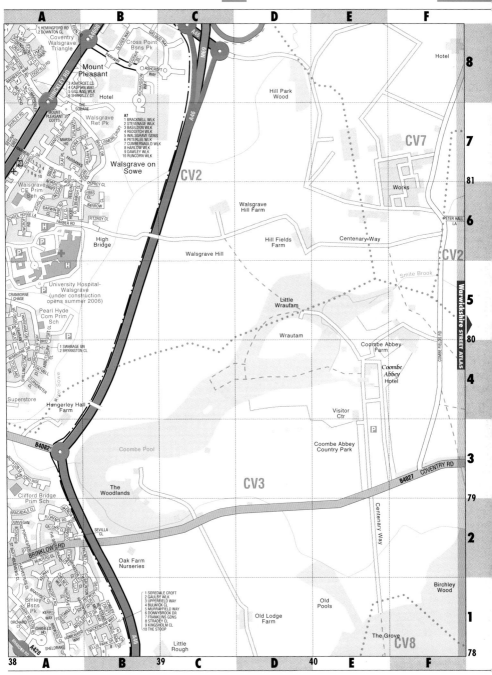

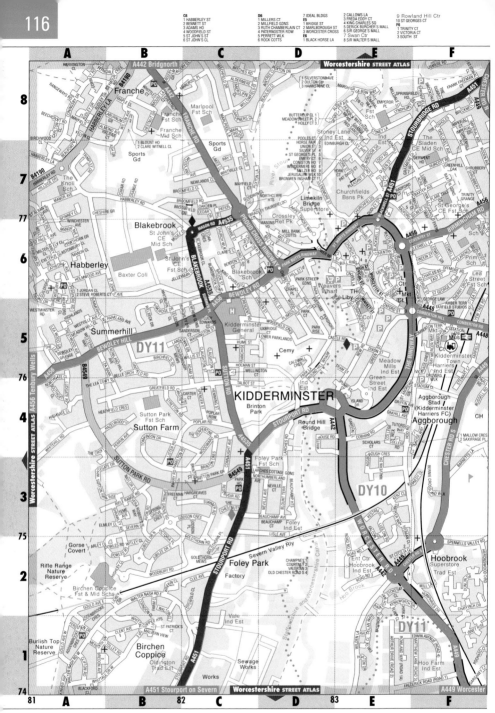

C8
1 HABBERLEY ST
2 BENNETT ST
3 ADAMS HO
4 WOODFIELD ST
5 ST JOHN'S ST
6 ST JOHN'S CL

D6
1 MILLERS CT
2 MILLFIELD GDNS
3 RUTH CHAMBERLAIN CT
4 PATERNOSTER ROW
5 PERRETT WLK
6 ROCK COTTS

7 IDEAL BLDGS
E5
1 BRIDGE ST
2 MARLBOROUGH ST
3 WORCESTER CROSS
E6
1 BLACK HORSE LA

2 CALLOWS LA
3 FREDA EDDY CT
4 KING CHARLES SQ
5 DERICK BURCHER'S MALL
6 SIR GEORGE'S MALL
7 SWAN CTR
8 SIR WALTER'S MALL

9 ROWLAND HILL CTR
10 ST GEORGES CT
F6
1 TRINITY CT
2 VICTORIA CT
3 SOUTH ST

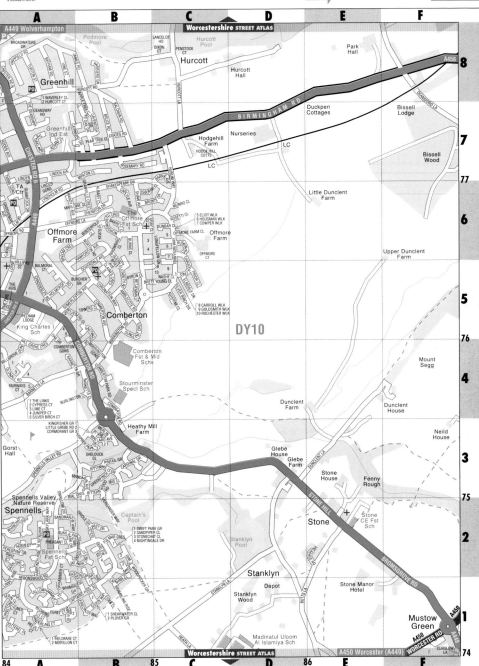

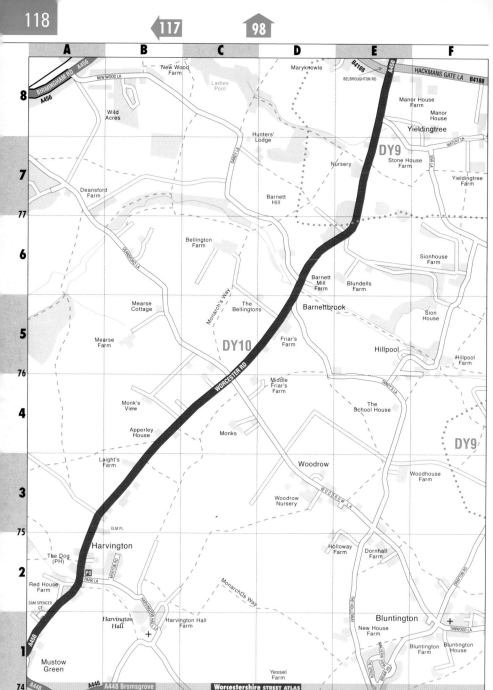

A   B   C   D   E   F

8

7

77

6

5

76

4

3

75

2

1

74

BIRMINGHAM RD A456

NEW WOOD LA

A456

New Wood
Farm

Wild
Acres

Ladies
Pool

Maryknowle

Hunters'
Lodge

Nursery

Barnett
Hill

Deansford
Farm

DEANSFORD LA

Bellington
Farm

SANDY LA

B4188

BELBROUGHTON RD

A450

HACKMANS GATE LA   B4188

Manor House
Farm

Manor
House

Yieldingtree

DY9

Stone House
Farm

WATERY LA

EGG LA

Yieldingtree
Farm

Sionhouse
Farm

Barnett
Mill
Farm

Blundells
Farm

Barnettbrook

Sion
House

Mearse
Cottage

Monarch's Way

The
Bellingtons

Friar's
Farm

Hillpool

Hillpool
Farm

Mearse
Farm

DY10

WORCESTER RD

Middle
Friar's
Farm

TANDY LA

The
School House

DY9

Monk's
View

Monks

Apperley
House

Woodrow

Woodhouse
Farm

WOODROW LA

Laight's
Farm

Woodrow
Nursery

ELM PL

Harvington

The Dog
(PH)

PO

MILTON RD

PARK LA

Red House
Farm

SAM SPENCER
CT

Harvington
Hall

HARVINGTON HALL LA

Harvington Hall
Farm

Monarch's Way

Holloway
Farm

Dornhall
Farm

THE HOLLOWAY

SPRITON RD

Bluntington

New House
Farm

TANWOOD LA

A450

Mustow
Green

A448

A448

A448 Bromsgrove

Worcestershire STREET ATLAS

Yessel
Farm

WALTON POOL HILL

HE GREEN

Bluntington
Farm

Bluntington
House

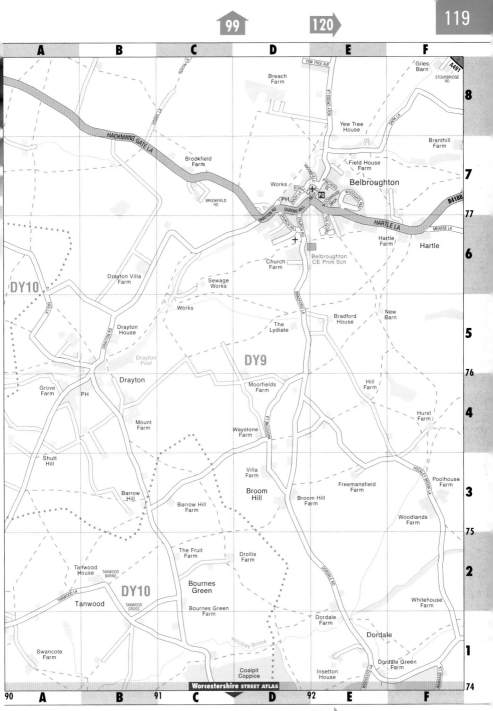

A B C D E F

8

7

77

6

5

76

4

3

75

2

1

74

Yew Tree Ave

Giles Barn

A491
STOURBRIDGE RD

Breach Farm

HODGE LA

HOLY CROSS LA

Yew Tree House

DARK LA

Branthill Farm

HACKMANS GATE LA

Brookfield Farm

Field House Farm

Belbroughton

B4188

Works

WORCESTER RD
PRIESTFIELDS LA
FORGE LA
QUEENS HILL
PH
PO
WOODHOUSE DRIVE
WOODGATE WAY
THE RUE

Brookfield Ho

DRAYTON RD

CHURCH HILL

CHURCH RD

HARTLE LA

MEARSE LA

Hartle Farm

Hartle

DY10

Drayton Villa Farm

Church Farm

Belbroughton CE Prim Sch

Sewage Works

DRAYTON RD

Works

BRADWELL LA

Bradford House

New Barn

Drayton House

The Lydiate

DY9

Drayton Pool

Drayton

Moorfields Farm

WAYSTONE LA

Hill Farm

Hurst Farm

Grove Farm

PH

Mount Farm

Waystone Farm

Villa Farm

Freemansfield Farm

HOCKLEY BROOK LA

Poolhouse Farm

Shutt Hill

Barrow Hill

Barrow Hill Farm

Broom Hill

Broom Hill Farm

Woodlands Farm

The Fruit Farm

Drollis Farm

DORDALE RD

TANWOOD LA

Tanwood House

TANWOOD BARNS

DY10

Bournes Green

Whitehouse Farm

Tanwood

TANWOOD CROSS

Bournes Green Farm

Dordale Farm

Dordale

Swancote Farm

Hockley Brook

Coalpit Coppice

Insetton House

WOODCOTE LA

Dordale Green Farm

PARBAGE LA

90 A B 91 C D 92 E F

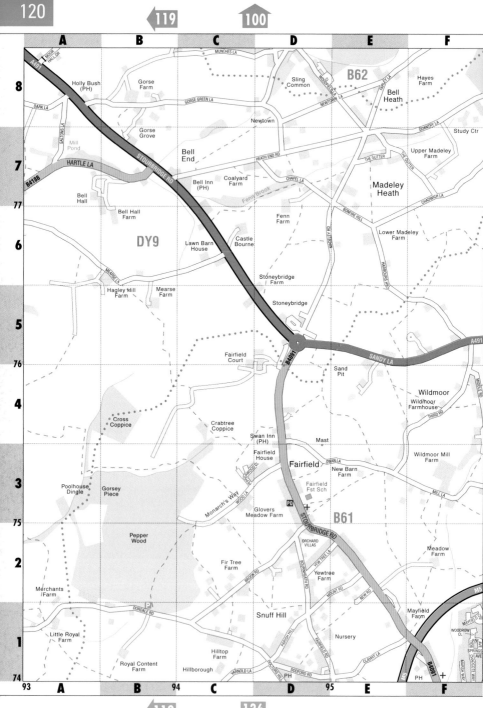

B62

Hayes Farm

Sling Common

Bell Heath

Study Ctr

Holly Bush (PH)

Gorse Farm

Newtown

Upper Madeley Farm

Dark La

Gorse Grove

Bell End

Madeley Heath

Mill Pond

Hartle La

Coalyard Farm

Bell Inn (PH)

Bell Hall

Fenny Brook

Bell Hall Farm

DY9

Fenn Farm

Lower Madeley Farm

Lawn Barn House

Castle Bourne

Stoneybridge Farm

Hagley Hill Farm

Mearse Farm

Stoneybridge

Wildmoor

Fairfield Court

Sand Pit

Wildmoor Farmhouse

Cross Coppice

Crabtree Coppice

Swan Inn (PH)

Mast

Wildmoor Mill Farm

Fairfield House

Fairfield

Swan La

Poolhouse Dingle

Gorsey Piece

Monarch's Way

New Barn Farm

Mill La

Fairfield Fst Sch

B61

Pepper Wood

Glovers Meadow Farm

Stourbridge Rd

Orchard Villas

Meadow Farm

Merchants Farm

Fir Tree Farm

Yewtree Farm

Mayfield Farm

Little Royal Farm

Royal Content Farm

Hilltop Farm

Hillborough

Snuff Hill

Nursery

Woodrow Cl

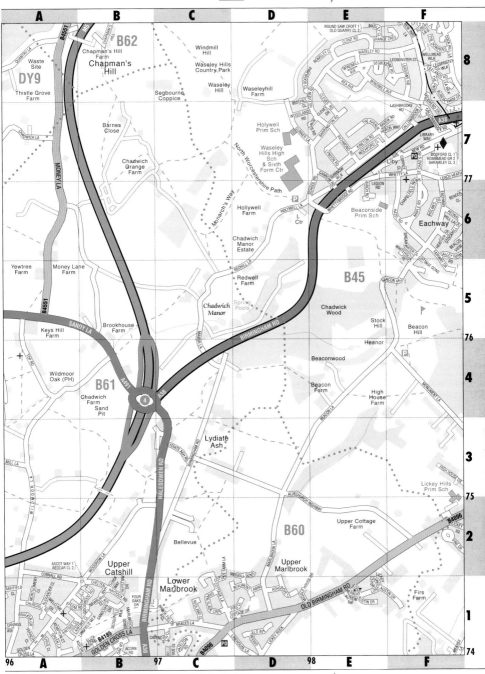

A B C D E F

8

7

77

6

5

76

4

75

3

2

1

74

Birmingham Great Pk

PARK WAY

Callow Brook

Schs

The Leys

1 HOBACRE CL
2 LANCASTER AVE
3 BEGLEY GR

Superstore

Ctr

LC

LYLLBROOK GR

BRISTOL RD S

PO

BEECH CT

ACORN CT

St Columba's RC Prim Sch

COFTON CT

B31

Longbridge

Albert Bradbeer Schs

AUSTIN RISE

DEARMONT RD

HEWELL CL

GRAVEWOOD

SANDSTONE

A38

NEW RD

BRISTOL RD S

STONECROFT AVE

BEECHES CT

CHEWAY CT

KENDAL RD

ROLAND AVE

FOX LN

ROCK AVE

KOVNAR RD

Rubery

KENDAL RD

Sch

LEACH HEATH LA

EACHWAY FARM

LICKEY PARK

SAVILE

BECKLEY GR

Rednal Hill Jun & Inf Sch

SMOOTH WAY

KERSWELL DR

ALFORD CL

Works

Longbridge

WATERHAYNES

RAYBOLD CROFT

THE LANES

WHIMS PL CT

RIDGEACRE

Rednal Hill

STACEY GRANGE GDNS

LICKEY RD

KENDAL RD

JERONGHAM RD

Rednal

Nursery

LONGHILL LA

HARTLAND RD

CANNACOMBE RD

HOPWOOD GR

BAYFORD AVE

B4096

RICHARDS RD

Coft Common

VALLEY RD

BEACON VIEW

PERKMAN

LACHIN

FOREST

Hillside

PINWALL CT

COFTON PARK

Cofton Park

P

WESSMOOR LA

Works

The Grove

Lickey Hills Country Park

Beacon Hill

Hotel P

CH

ROSE HILL

Lickey Hills

P

B4096

Liby

B45

LINDON

COPPICE

TEN ASHES LA

ASHMEAD DR

CRETHAL RD

PICTURE WAY

MIDDLE DR

OAKFIELD DR

THE CHINE

ASHMEAD

Cofton Richards Farm

Bilberry Hill

ASHMEAD

RESEVOIR RD

COFTON LAKE RD

North Worcestershire Path

Tower House

Upper Bittell Resr

MONUMENT LA

Lickey

WARREN LA

Visitor Ctr

Lickey Hills Country Pk

P

Cofton Hill

BARNT GREEN RD

Cofton Hackett

COFTON CHURCH LA

Cofton Hall Farm

Cofton Hall

Mill Shrub

River Arrow

Mast

Mon

OLD BIRMINGHAM RD

PO

HIGH HOUSE DR

LIVINGSTONE

CLAYTON

MALVERN RD

CLEVELAND DR

Lickey Warren

Cofton Plantation

LICKEY RD

BROOKLEY DR

PINE GR

THE BADGERS

BROOKLAND

GREENWOOD DR

EDGEWOOD RD

KENDAL END RD

KENDAL DR

Kendal End

MARGESSON

Bittell Farm House

BITTELL FARM RD

MEGRAVE LA

INGEVA DR

HOLLYWOOD DR

DURNAL

PLYMOUTH DR

Pinfields Wood

CHERRY HILL RD

PH

B4120

B4120

BITTELL RD

Lower Bittell Resr

99 A 00 B C 01 D E F

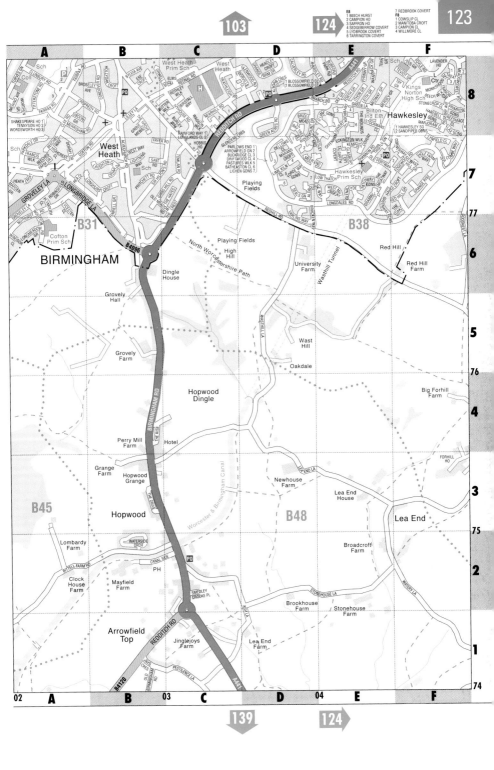

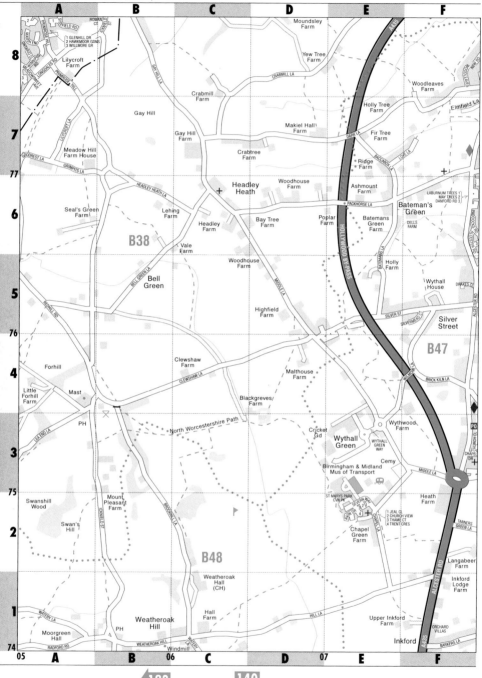

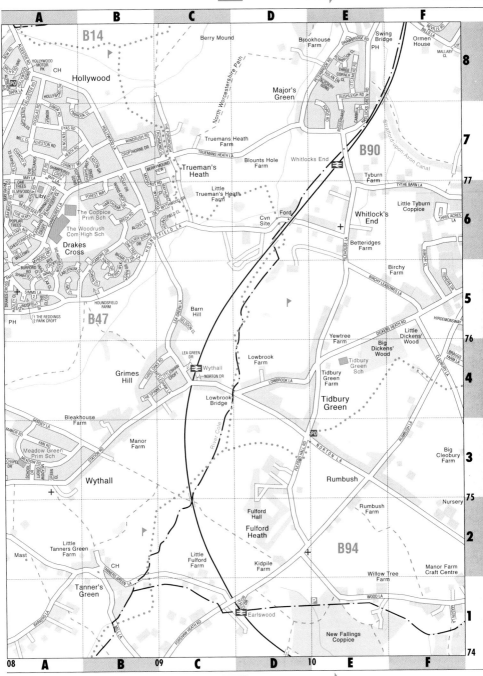

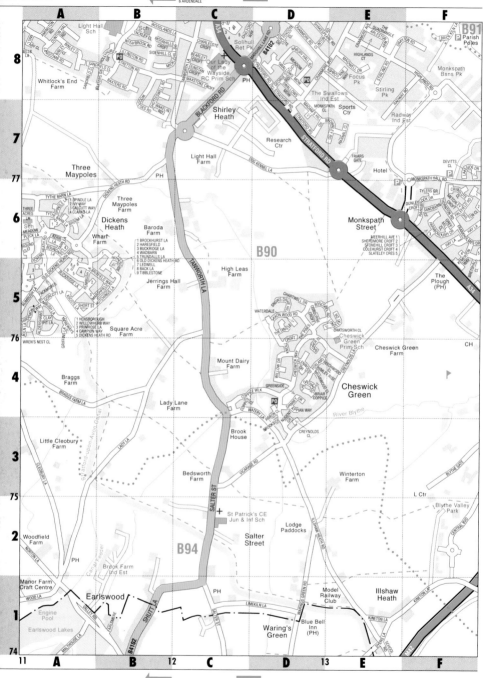

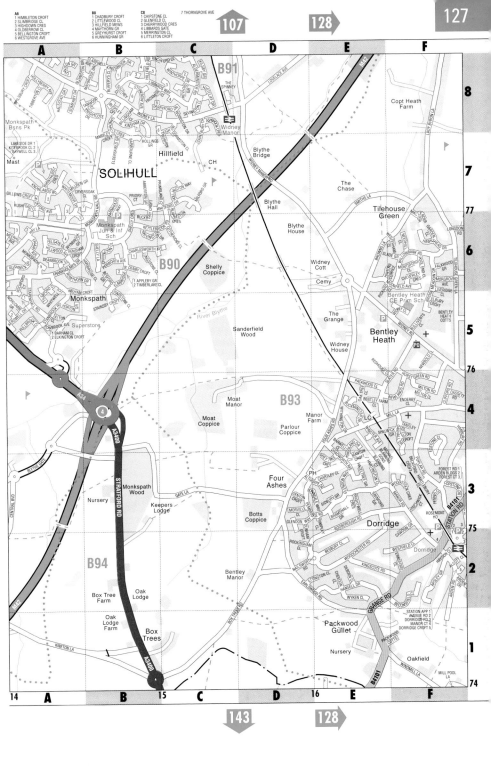

A6
1 HIMBLETON CROFT
2 SLIMBRIDGE CL
3 HIGHDOWN CRES
4 OLDBERROW CL
5 BELLINGTON CROFT
6 WESTGROVE AVE

B8
1 CHADBURY CROFT
2 LITTLEWOOD CL
3 HILLFIELD MEWS
4 MAYTHORN GR
5 GREYHURST CROFT
6 HUNNINGHAM GR

C8
1 CHIPSTONE CL
2 GLENFIELD CL
3 CHERRYWOOD CRES
4 LIBBARDS GATE
5 MERRINGTON CL
6 LITTLETON CROFT

7 THORNGROVE AVE

107   128

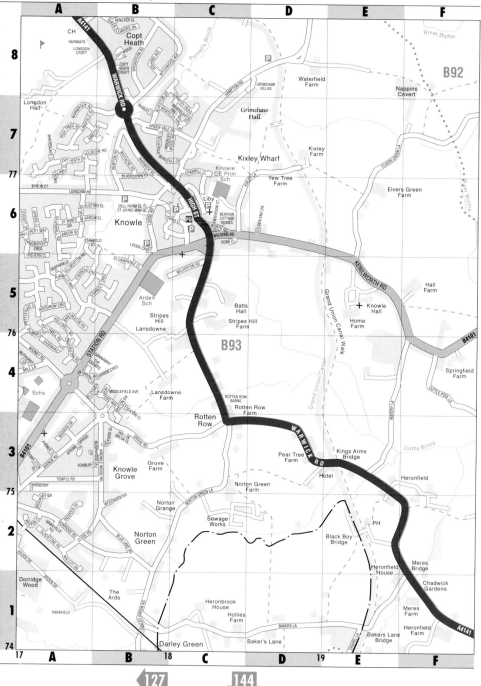

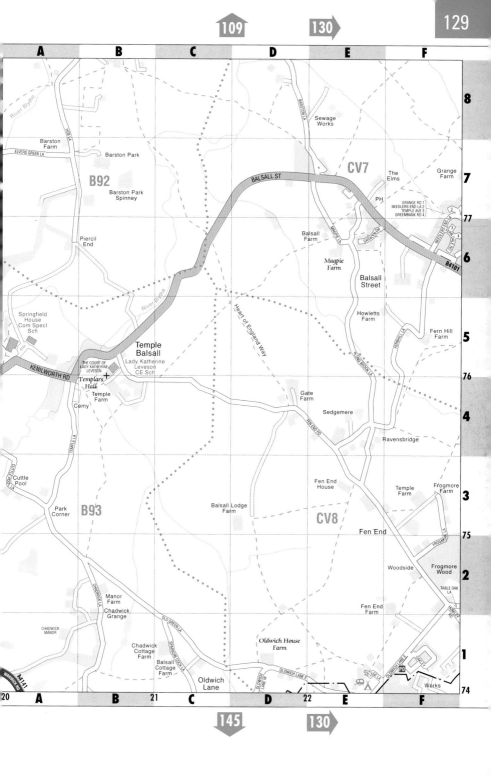

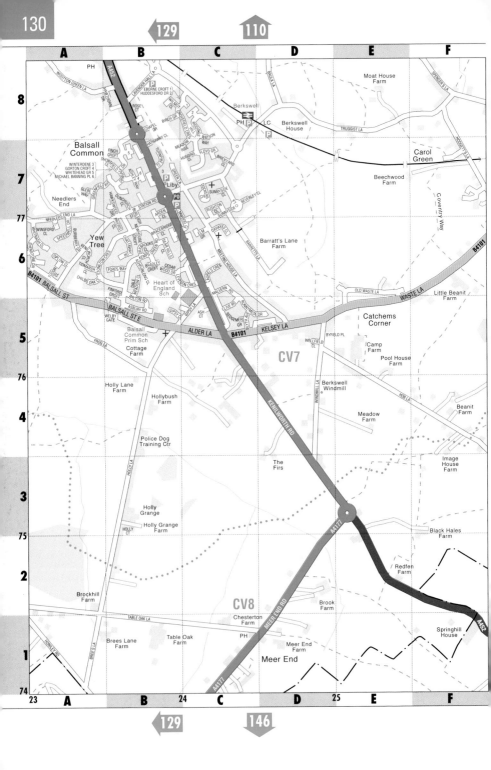

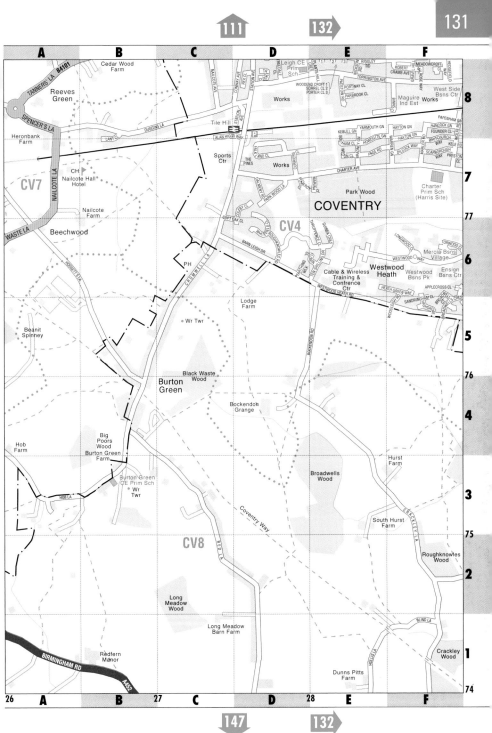

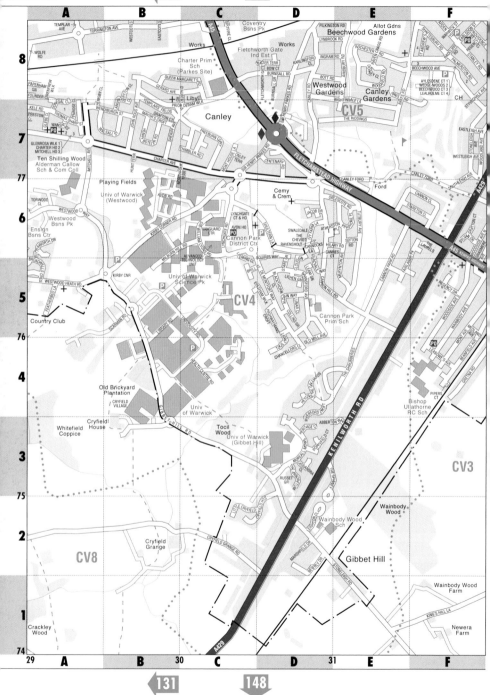

134

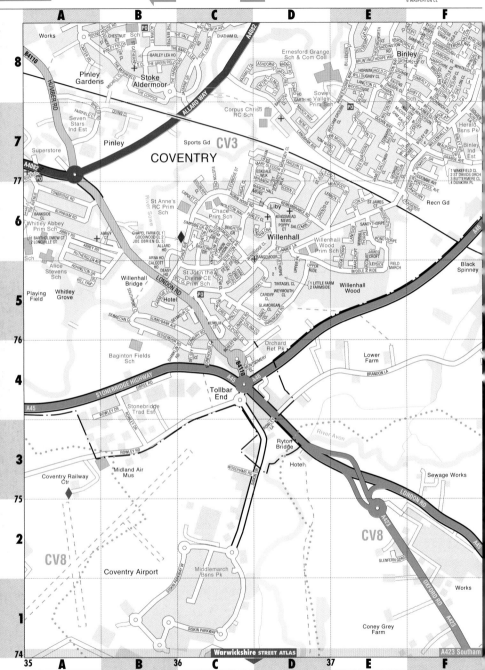

133 114

F8
1 CARDALE CROFT
2 KESTREL CROFT
3 RUTLAND CROFT
4 JIM FORREST CL
5 WILLOWHERB CL
6 WASPERTON CL
7 JOE WILLIAMS CL
8 DEERDALE TERR

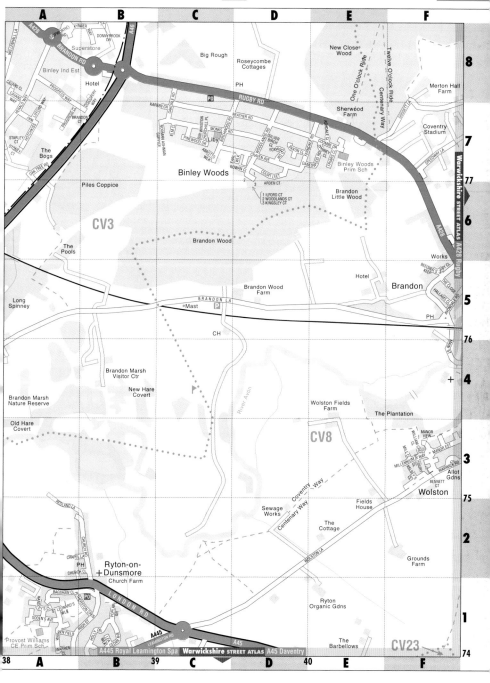

A B C D E F

8
7
77
6
5
76
4
3
75
2
1
74

New Close Wood
Twelve O'Clock Ride
One O'Clock Ride
Centenary Way
Merton Hall Farm
Coventry Stadium
Sherwood Farm
Big Rough
Roseycombe Cottages
PH
RUGBY RD
PO
KAREEN GR
HEATHER RD
MONKS
Binley Woods
Binley Woods Prim Sch
Brandon Little Wood
Piles Coppice
ARDEN CT
1 ILFORD CT
2 WOODLANDS CT
3 KINGSLEY CT
Works
CV3
The Pools
Brandon Wood
Long Spinney
Brandon Wood Farm
Hotel
Brandon
BEECHES KEEP
PH
BRANDON LA
Mast
P
CH
Brandon Marsh Visitor Ctr
New Hare Covert
Brandon Marsh Nature Reserve
Old Hare Covert
River Avon
Wolston Fields Farm
The Plantation
CV8
MANOR VIEW
WILLIAM CL
MANOR EST
WARWICK RD
Allot Gdns
Wolston
Coventry Way
Sewage Works
Centenary Way
Fields House
The Cottage
Grounds Farm
75
Redland La
CHURCH LA
CHAPEL LA
PH
CHURCH END
PO
Ryton-on-Dunsmore
Church Farm
LONDON RD
WOLSTON LA
Ryton Organic Gdns
Provost Williams CE Prim Sch
SODEN'S AVE
WARREN FIELD
A445 Royal Leamington Spa
A45
A445 Daventry
The Barbellows
CV23

BRANDON RD
Superstore
Binley Ind Est
Hotel
The Bogs
A428
A428 Rugby
Warwickshire STREET ATLAS
Warwickshire STREET ATLAS

38 39 40

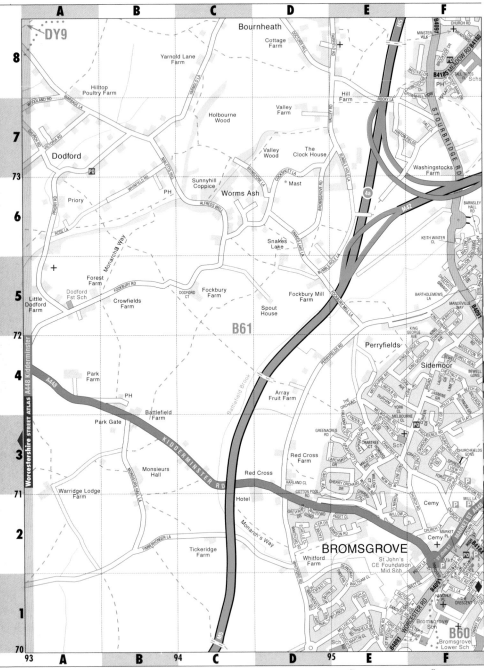

120

DY9

Bournheath

Cottage
Farm

Yarnold Lane
Farm

8

Hilltop
Poultry Farm

Hill
Farm

Holbourne
Wood

Valley
Farm

7

Dodford

Valley
Wood

The
Clock House

73

Sunnyhill
Coppice

Worms Ash

Mast

Priory

PH

6

Snakes
Lake

Forest
Farm

Little
Dodford
Farm

Dodford
Fst Sch

Crowfields
Farm

Dodford
CT

Fockbury
Farm

Fockbury Mill
Farm

5

Spout
House

72

B61

Perryfields

Sidemoor

Park
Farm

4

PH

Array
Fruit Farm

Battlefield
Farm

Park Gate

Red Cross
Farm

Monsieurs
Hall

Red Cross

3

Warridge Lodge
Farm

Hotel

71

BROMSGROVE

Tickeridge
Farm

Whitford
Farm

St John's
CE Foundation
Mid Sch

2

Cemy

Cemy

1

B60

Bromsgrove
Lower Sch

70

93   94   95

150

Worcestershire street atlas

E1
1 Sanders Ind Est
2 WESTBOURNE TERR
3 WESTBOURNE CL

F2
1 GEORGE ST
2 ELGAR MEWS
3 NAILERS CT
4 GUILD CT

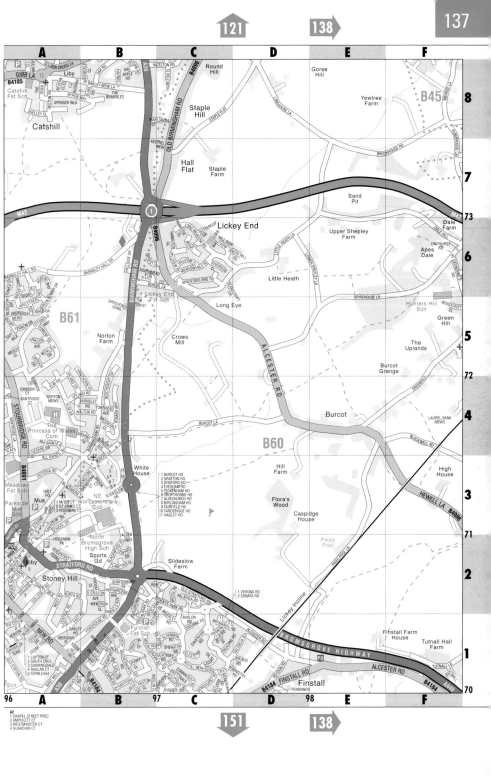

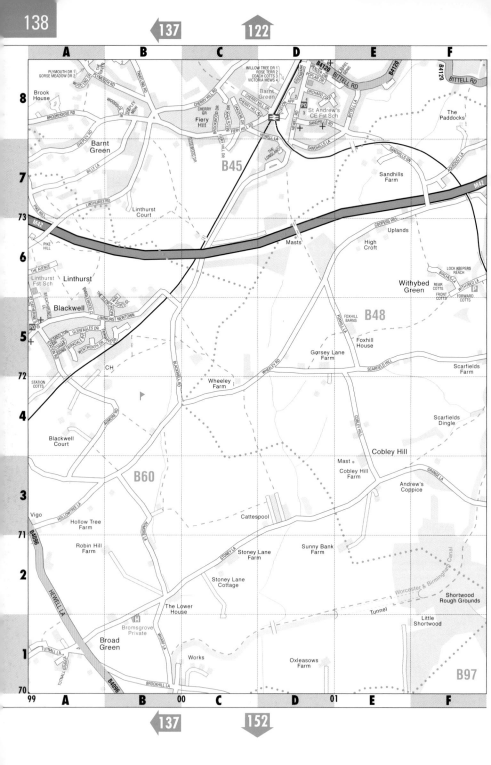

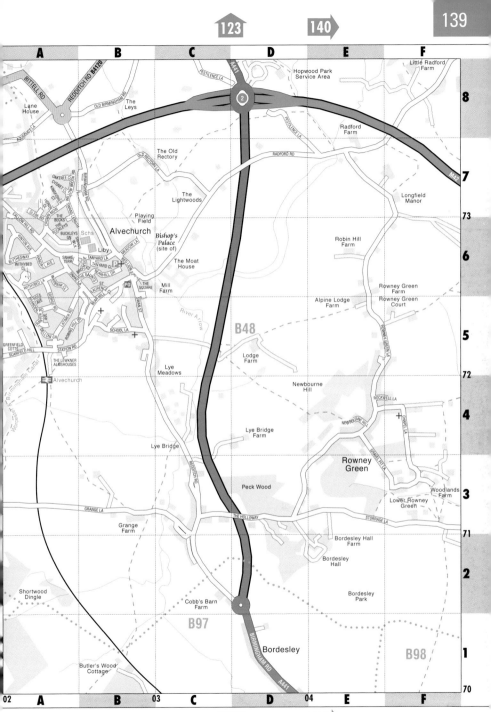

139
124

A B C D E F

8

Newhouse Farm

Lanehouse Farm

Lower Inkford Farm

Brook Priory Farm

ASH CRES 1
THE LAURELS 2
THE LAWNS 3
THE OAKS 4
THE WILLOWS 5

PH

B47

WATERY LA

Birch Acre Farm

DUMBLE PIT LA

HILLCREST

7

Alcott Farm

Birch Acre

HILLCREST PK

Blackoak Wood

M42

Moorfield Coppice

ALCESTER RD

73

M42

3

Seechem Lodge

Moorfield Farm

PH

6

Seechem Farm

BILLESLEY LA

Billesley Farm

Brookside

ICKNIELD ST

Hob Hill Farm

Newlands

HOLLY LA

5

Old House Farm

Hob Hill

Lilley Green Hall Farm

LILLEY GREEN RD

B48

Woodlands Farm

Rose Cottage Farm

72

SEAFIELD LA

WHITEPITS LA

4

Storrage Wood

Barton Farm

Hill Farm

OLD LA

Brockhill Farm

3

Storrage House

Dump House Farm

DUMPHOUSE LA

Old Farm

Chapel Farm

Heath Green Poultry Farm

Heath Green Farm

STORRAGE LA

71

Heath Green

2

Lower Park Farm

ICKNIELD ST

B98

BROCKHILL LA

Carpenters Hill Wood

Poplars Farm

Carpenters Hill Farm

Newlands Rough

1

Hall Farm

Brook Farm

BEOLEY HALL

Carpenter's Hill

70

05 A B 06 C D 07 E F

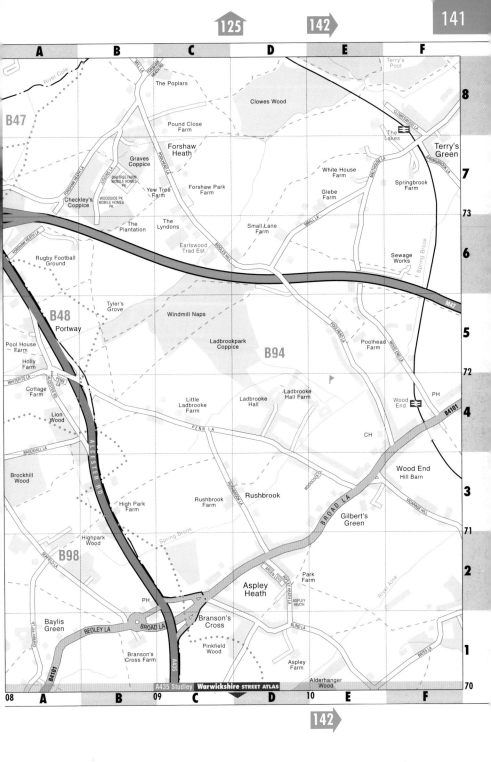

B47

B48

B94

B98

A B C D E F

8

7

73

6

5

72

4

3

71

2

1

70

Terry's
Pool

Clowes Wood

The Poplars

Pound Close
Farm

Forshaw
Heath

Graves
Coppice

OAK TREE FARM
MOBILE HOMES
PK

Yew Tree
Farm

Checkley's
Coppice

WOODSIDE PK
MOBILE HOMES
PK

Forshaw Park
Farm

The
Plantation

The
Lyndons

Earlswood
Trad Est

Rugby Football
Ground

Portway

Tyler's
Grove

Windmill Naps

Ladbrookpark
Coppice

Pool House
Farm

Holly
Farm

Cottage
Farm

Lion
Wood

BROCKHILL LA

Brockhill
Wood

Highpark
Wood

Baylis
Green

Branson's
Cross Farm

The Lakes

Terry's
Green

White House
Farm

Glebe
Farm

Springbrook
Farm

Small Lane
Farm

Sewage
Works

Spring Brook

M42

Poolhead
Farm

Wood
End

PH

Little
Ladbrooke
Farm

Ladbrooke
Hall

Ladbrooke
Hall Farm

PENN LA

CH

B4101

Wood End

Hill Barn

Gilbert's
Green

VICARAGE HILL

High Park
Farm

Rushbrook
Farm

Rushbrook

BROAD LA

Spring Brook

PH

Aspley
Heath

Branson's
Cross

Pinkfield
Wood

Park
Farm

Aspley
Farm

Alderhanger
Wood

BLIND LA

River Alne

BEOLEY LA

BROAD LA

A435

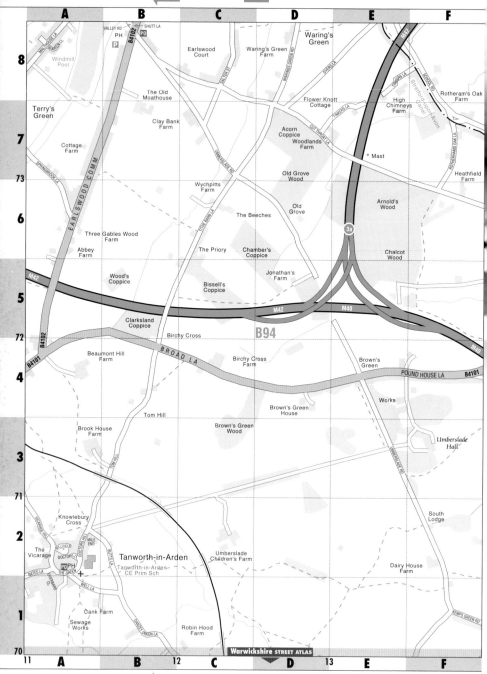

A   **B**   **C**   **D**   **E**   **F**

8

Windmill
Pool

VALLEY RD
PH
SHUTT LA
PO

Earlswood
Court

Waring's Green
Farm

Waring's
Green

Rotheram's Oak
Farm

The Old
Moathouse

Flower Knott
Cottage

High
Chimneys
Farm

Terry's
Green

Clay Bank
Farm

Acorn
Coppice
Woodlands
Farm

7

Cottage
Farm

EARLSWOOD COMM

SPRINGBROOK LA

Old Grove
Wood

Mast

Heathfield
Farm

73

Wychpitts
Farm

TITHE BARN LA

The Beeches

Old
Grove

Arnold's
Wood

6

Three Gables Wood
Farm

Abbey
Farm

The Priory

Chamber's
Coppice

Chalcot
Wood

3a

Wood's
Coppice

Bissell's
Coppice

Jonathan's
Farm

5

M42

B4102

M42

M40

Clarksland
Coppice

Birchy Cross

B94

72

B4101

Beaumont Hill
Farm

BROAD LA

Birchy Cross
Farm

Brown's
Green

POUND HOUSE LA

B4101

4

Tom Hill

Brown's Green
House

Works

Brook House
Farm

Brown's Green
Wood

Umberslade
Hall

3

71

Knowlebury
Cross

South
Lodge

2

The
Vicarage

BELL FIELD
DOCTORS
MILE
END

Tanworth-in-Arden

Umberslade
Children's Farm

Dairy House
Farm

PO PH
THE GREEN

Tanworth-in-Arden
CE Prim Sch

WELL LA

1

BATES LA

Cank Farm

DANZEY GREEN LA

Robin Hood
Farm

KEMPS GREEN RD

Sewage
Works

70

11   **A**   **B**   **12**   **C**   **D**   **13**   **E**   **F**

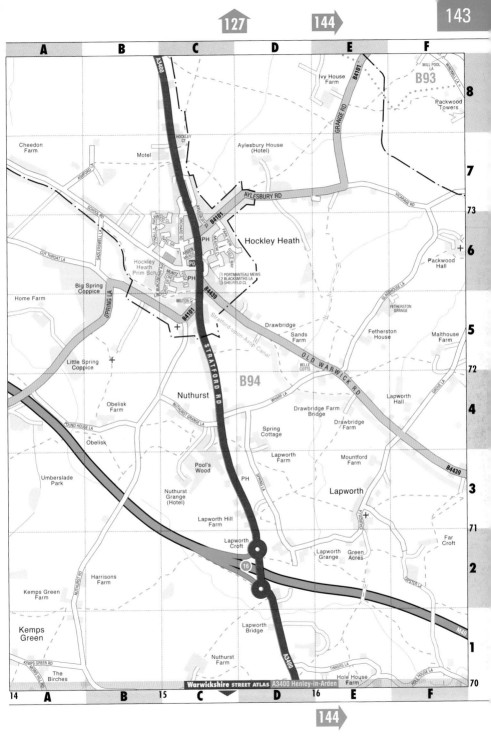

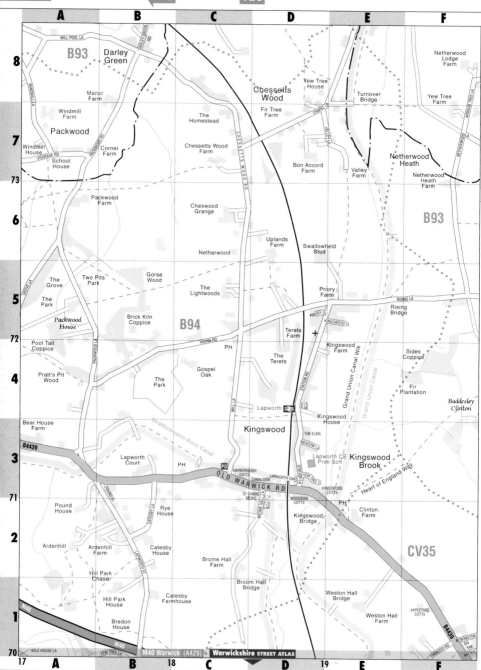

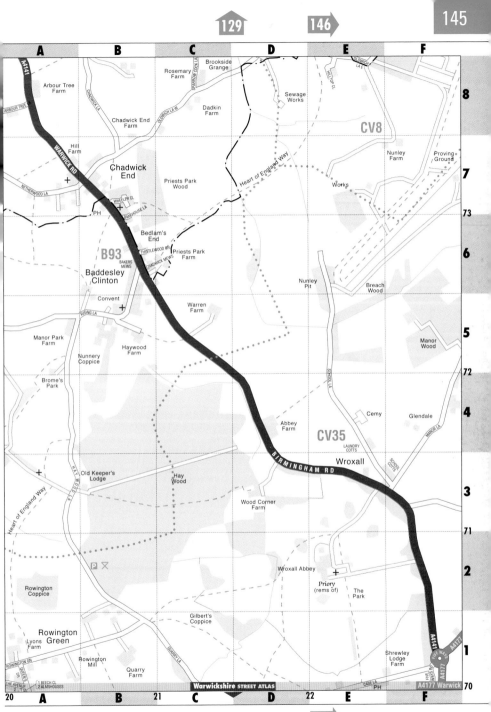

A B C D E F

8

CV8

7

73

6

B93

5

72

4

CV35

3

71

2

1

70

Arbour Tree Farm

Rosemary Farm

Brookside Grange

Sewage Works

Hill Top Cl

OLDWICH LA E

Nunley Farm

Proving Ground

Chadwick End Farm

Dadkin Farm

OLDWICH LA W

SPRING

NETHERWOOD LA

Hill Farm

WARWICK RD

Chadwick End

Priests Park Wood

Heart of England Way

Works

PH

WHEELER CL

BAKEHOUSE LA

Bedlam's End

THISTLEWOOD RD

Priests Park Farm

Nunley Pit

Breach Wood

Baddesley Clinton

BAKERS MEWS

CHADWICK MEWS

Convent

RISING LA

Warren Farm

Manor Park Farm

Haywood Farm

Nunnery Coppice

Manor Wood

Brome's Park

SCHOOL LA

Cemy

Glendale

Abbey Farm

MANOR LA

Heart of England Way

HAY WOOD LA

Old Keeper's Lodge

Hay Wood

BIRMINGHAM RD

Wroxall

LAUNDRY COTTS

SCHOOL COTTS

Wood Corner Farm

Rowington Coppice

P

Wroxall Abbey

Priory (rems of)

The Park

Lyons Farm

Rowington Green

Rowington Mill

Gilbert's Coppice

Quarry Farm

QUARRY LA

Shrewley Lodge Farm

A4141

A4177

FIVE WAYS RD

ROWINGTON GN

THE AVENUE

1 BEECH CL
2 ALMSHOUSES

CASE LA

PH

A4177 Warwick

A B C D E F

8

7

73

6

72

5

4

3

71

2

1

70

Proving Ground

HONLEY RD

Pear Tree Farm

MEER END RD

A4177

Blenheim Farm

Croft Farm

Runway Farm

Black Hill Wood

Poors Wood

Rudfyn Manor

Holly Farm Bsns Pk

Wattcote Farm

HONILEY RD

Warriors Lodge Farm

CHASE LA

CV8

Chase Wood

Honiley Boot (PH)

Yew Tree Cottage

Church Farm

Honiley

Honiley Hall

Featherstons Grove

MANOR LA

Thorny Coppice

Grove Farm

Clattyland Wood

Grove Cottage

Wakefield Wood

PO

Haseley Knob

CV35

Hill Farm Cottage

Cheyneys Farm

SCHOOL CROFT

Hill Farm

Fernwood Farm

ROUNOIL LA

HEATH TERR

The Glade

BUTLERS END

BARRACKS LA

Haseleygreen Farm

Beausale

Lyon Farm

Elmwood Farm

BEAUSALE LA

KITES NEST LA

Holly Farm

Camphill Farm

A4177

Warwickshire STREET ATLAS

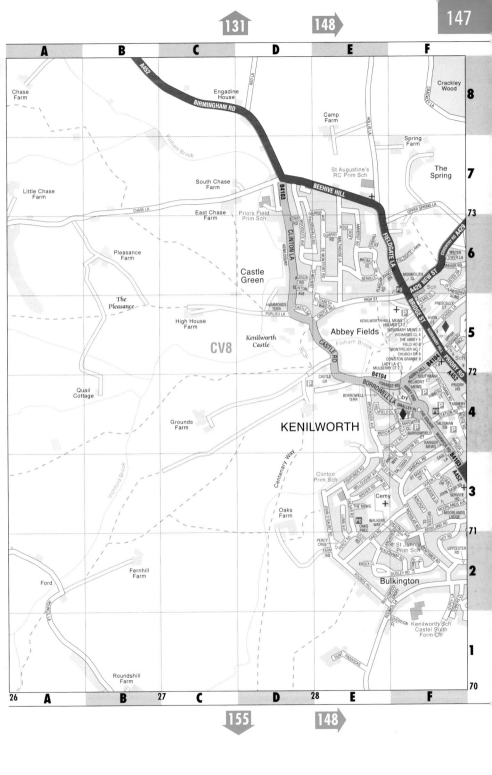

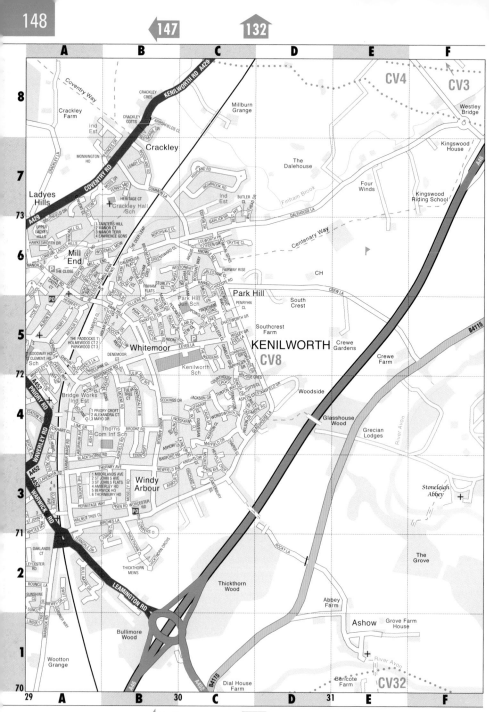

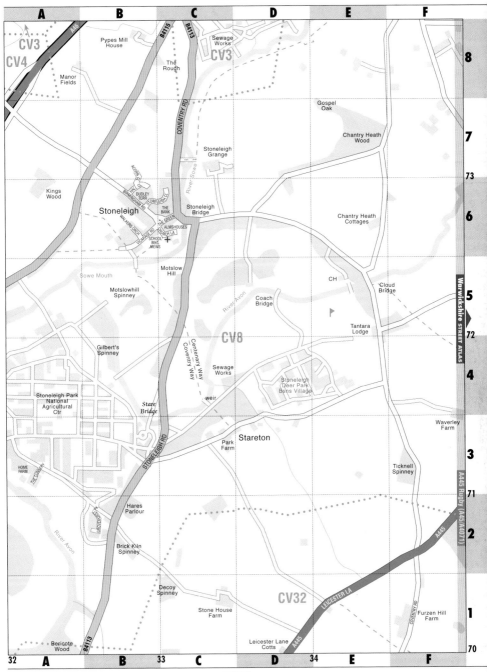

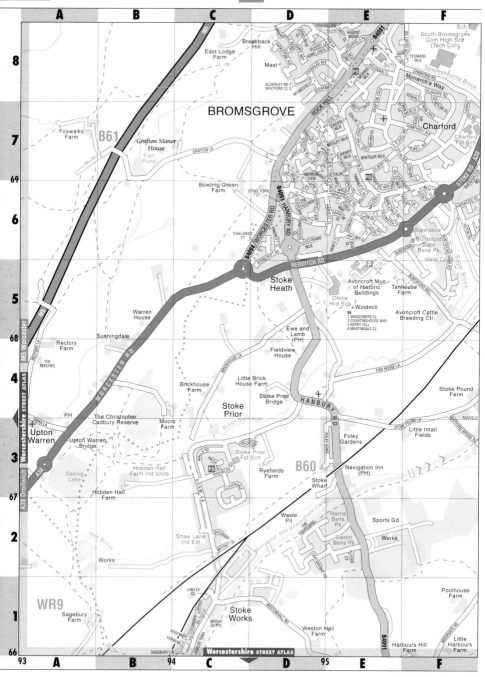

A B C D E F

8

7

69

6

5

68

4

67

3

2

66

1

BROMSGROVE

Charford

Foxwalks Farm

B61

Grafton Manor House

Fish Pond

GRAFTON LA

East Lodge Farm

Breakback Hill

Mast

ALDERLEY RD 1
WHITFORD CL 2

Bowling Green Farm

STOKE TURN CT

OAKLANDS CT

B4091 HANBURY RD

B4091 WORCESTER RD

REDDITCH RD

Stoke Heath

Warren House

Sunningdale

Rectory Farm

THE BEECHES

PH

Upton Warren

Upton Warren Bridge

The Christopher Cadbury Reserve

Moors Farm

Sailing Lake

Hobden Hall Farm Ind Units

Hobden Hall Farm

Brickhouse Farm

Little Brick House Farm

Stoke Prior Bridge

Stoke Prior

River Salwarpe

WORCESTER RD

BROCKHOUSE LA

HANBURY RD

Ewe and Lamb (PH)

Fieldview House

Stoke Pound Farm

FISH HOUSE LA

STOKE POUND LA

FARFIELD

WHITFORD BRIDGE RD

Stoke Pound Farm

Little Intall Fields

Avoncroft Mus of Historic Buildings

Ottilie Hild Sch

Windmill

E6
1 WAGGONERS CL
2 COUNTINGHOUSE WAY
3 KERRY HILL
4 MARTINGALE CL

Tanhouse Farm

Avoncroft Cattle Breeding Ctr

Superstore

Buntsford Gate Bsns Pk

West Cl

Sugar Brook

Foley Gardens

Navigation Inn (PH)

Stoke Wharf

B60

Ryefields Farm

Stoke Prior Fst Sch

WALL'S RD

RYEFIELDS

CLOVERDA

Waste Pit

Worcester and Birmingham Canal

Harris Bsns Pk

Saxon Bsns Pk

Sports Gd

Works

Shaw Lane Ind Est

Hen Brook

Works

WR9

Sagebury Farm

JUBILEE CL

WYCHE COTTS

ROSEMARY DR

VERBENA CL

SAGEBURY DR

Stoke Works

Weston Hall Farm

Harbours Hill Farm

B4091

Poolhouse Farm

Little Harbours Farm

South Bromsgrove Com High Sch (Tech Coll)

Sch

Spadesbourne Brook

YEOMANS WLK

Monarch's Way

Charford Fst Sch

ROCK HILL

STOKE RD

A38

M5

M5 Worcester

A38 Droitwich

Worcestershire STREET ATLAS

Worcestershire STREET ATLAS

93 A B 94 C D 95 E F

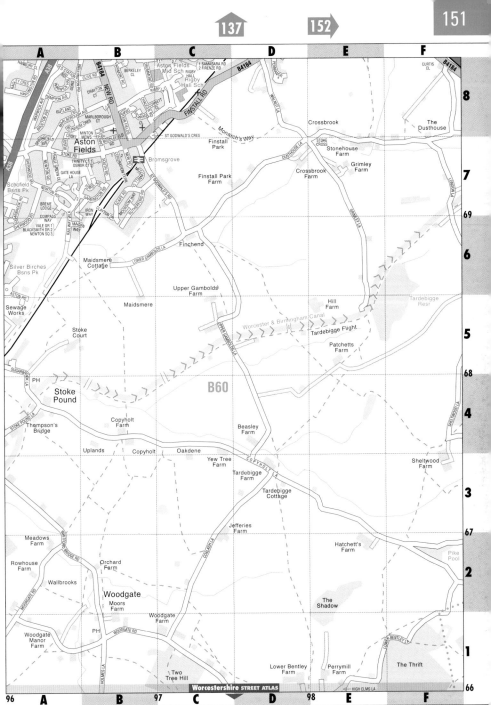

8

7

69

6

5

68

4

3

67

2

1

66

A B C D E F

Hanbury Cl
Berkeley Cl
Aston Fields Mid Sch
1 SAMASARA RD
2 FIRENZE RD
RIGBY HALL
Rigby Hall Sch
CURTIS CL
B4184

Crossbrook
The Dusthouse

Aston Fields
Bromsgrove
ST GODWALD'S CRES
Finstall Park
Monarch's Way
STOKE CROSS
Stonehouse Farm
Grimley Farm

Schofield Bsns Pk
Finstall Park Farm
Crossbrook Farm

Breme Lodge
COMPASS WAY
IRON WAY
VALE GR
BLACKSMITH DR
NEWTON SQ
MAIDEN WAY

Silver Birches Bsns Pk
Maidsmere Cottage
Finchend
Upper Gambolds Farm
Hill Farm
Tardebigge Resr

Sewage Works
Maidsmere
Worcester & Birmingham Canal
Tardebigge Flight
Patchetts Farm

Stoke Court
Stoke Pound
B60

PH
Thompson's Bridge
Copyholt Farm
Beasley Farm

Uplands
Copyholt
Oakdene
Yew Tree Farm
Tardebigge Farm
Sheltwood Farm

Tardebigge Cottage

Meadows Farm
Jefferies Farm
Hatchett's Farm
Pike Pool

Rowhouse Farm
Orchard Farm
Wallbrooks
Woodgate
Moors Farm

Woodgate Manor Farm
PH
Woodgate Farm
The Shadow

Two Tree Hill
Lower Bentley Farm
Perrymill Farm
The Thrift

HIGH ELMS LA
LOWER BENTLEY

96 A B 97 C D 98 E F

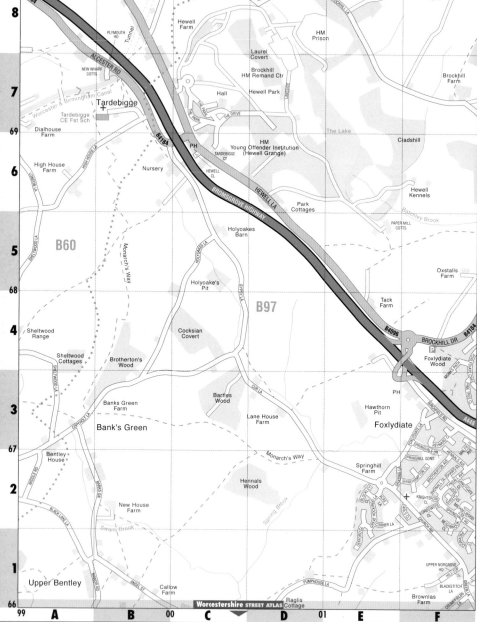

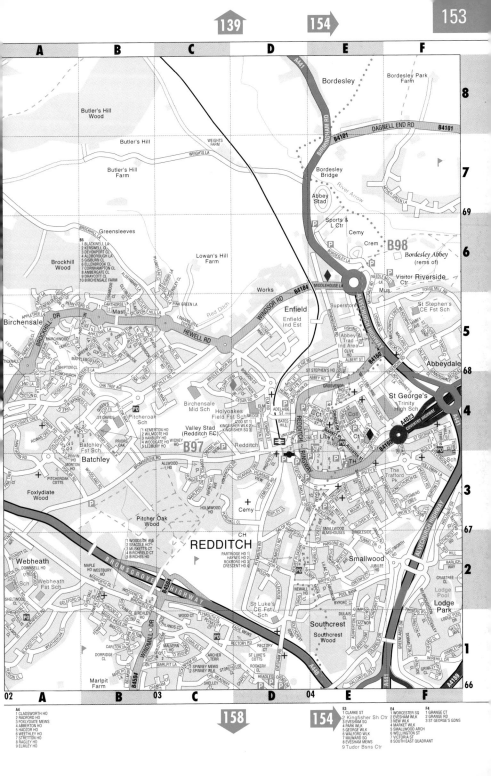

A B C D E F

8 7 69 6 5 68 4 3 67 2 1 66

Bordesley

Bordesley Park Farm

Butler's Hill Wood

Butler's Hill

WEIGHTS FARM

WEIGHTS LA

Butler's Hill Farm

DAGNELL END RD

B4101

BIRMINGHAM RD

B4101

Bordesley Bridge

River Arrow

Abbey Stad

Greensleeves

BROCKHILL LA

1 BLACKWELL LA
2 KERSWELL CL
3 DEVONPORT CL
4 ALDBOROUGH LA
5 GISBURN CL
6 ELLENBROOK CL
7 CORNHAMPTON CL
8 AMBERGATE CL
9 DRAYCOTT CL
10 BIRCHENSALE FARM

Brockhill Wood

Lowan's Hill Farm

Sports & L Ctr

Cemy

Crem

B98

Bordesley Abbey (rems of)

Visitor Ctr

Riverside Ctr

Mus

NEEDLE MILL LA

Works

WINDSOR RD

B4184

Birchensale

BROCKHILL DR

Mast

Red Ditch

PINK GREEN LA

HEWELL RD

Enfield

Enfield Ind Est

Superstore

Abbey Trad Ind Area

CLIVE HO

ALBERT ST

FISHING LA

FORGE MILL RD

ALCESTER RD

St Stephen's CE Fst Sch

Abbeydale

OAK TREE AVE

Birchensale Mid Sch

Holyoakes Field Fst Sch

ELM HO

BRIDGE ST

ADELAIDE ST

ST STEPHEN'S HO

ABBEY RD

GROSVENA

St George's

Trinity High Sch

Col

A4023 COVENTRY HIGHWAY

A441

Pitcheroak Sch

ST DAVIDS

PRIORS OAK

1 KEMERTON HO
2 WILMCOTE HO
3 HANBURY HO
4 WOODGATE HO
5 LEDBURY HO

Valley Stad (Reddich FC)

WIDNEY

KINGFISHER WLK
KINGFISHER SQ

B97

Reddich

REDDITCH RINGWAY

Lib

7TH

The Trafford Pk

ALCESTER RD

Sch

Batchley

MORTON

PINVIN

Batchley Fst Sch

BROMSGROVE RD

ALLOWAY HO

CHURCH RD

SMALLWOOD ALMSHOUSES

DINGLESIDE

Smallwood

HILL

BARLICH WAY

Foxlydiate Wood

Pitcher Oak Wood

Holmwood HO

Cemy

BENTLEY CL

PARSONS RD

MOUNT ST

JUBILEE

CRABTREE CL

Lodge Pool

Lodge Park

WOODSIDE AVE
SEACOLE HO
MUSKETTS CT
BIRCHFIELD CT
BIRCHES HO

REDDITCH

CH

PARTRIDGE HO
HAYNES HO
ROXBORO HO
CRESCENT HO

SLOP LA

LUDLOW

BROAD GROUND RD

POOL BANK

MOSELEY

Webheath

DOWNSELL HO

Webheath Fst Sch

MAPLE HO

WESTBURY HO

BROMSGROVE HIGHWAY

B4504

WINDMILL DR

St Luke's CE Fst Sch

NEWALL HO

BYFORD

SOUTHCREST

COMPTON

Southcrest

Southcrest Wood

St Luke's COTTS

RECTORY CL

RECTORY TERR

ROOKERY

DULAIS CL

EASTNOR

TWINERS

A441

GREEN ARGES DR

SHELTWOOD

PO

COLEFORD CL

MALVERN DR

PLYMOUTH CL

WOOD CT

ARCHER TERR

SPINNEY MEWS

STONEHOUSE

SHELLEY

HEADLESS CROSS

A448

Marlpit Farm

DORRIDGE CL

MARLPIT LA

CRABHAM

B4504

A4189

02 A   B 03 C   D 04 E   F

A4
1 CLADSWORTH HO
2 RADFORD HO
3 FOXLYDIATE MEWS
4 ABBERTON HO
5 HADZOR HO
6 WEETHLEY HO
7 STRETTON HO
8 RAGLEY HO
9 ELMLEY HO

E3
1 CLARKE ST
2 KINGFISHER Sh Ctr
3 EVESHAM SQ
4 PARK WLK
5 GEORGE WLK
6 WALFORD WLK
7 MILLWARD SQ
8 EVESHAM MEWS
9 Tudor Bsns Ctr

E4
1 WORCESTER SQ
2 EVESHAM WLK
3 NEW WLK
4 MARKET WLK
5 SMALLWOOD ARCH
6 WELLINGTON ST
7 VICTORIA ST
8 SOUTH EAST QUADRANT

F4
1 GRANGE CT
2 GRANGE RD
3 ST GEORGE'S GDNS

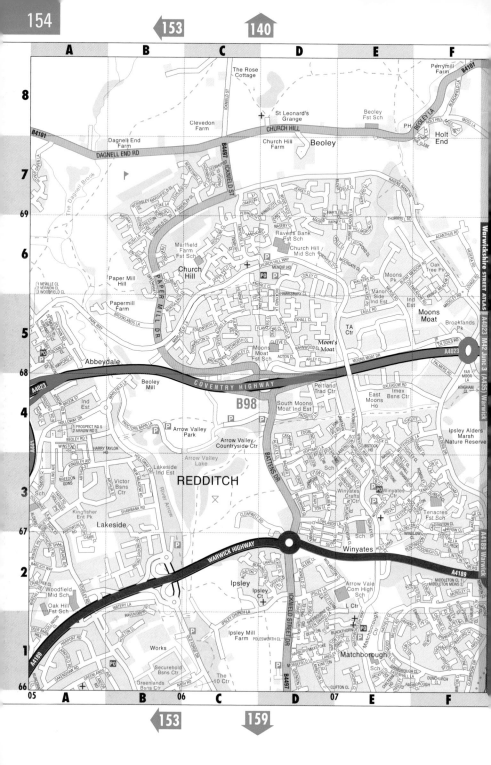

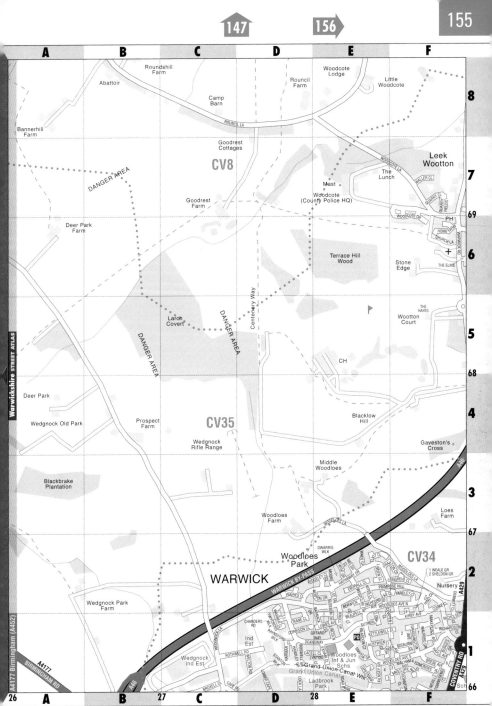

Roundshill Farm

Abattoir

Camp Barn

Rouncil Farm

Woodcote Lodge

Little Woodcote

8

Bannerhill Farm

ROUNCIL LA

Goodrest Cottages

CV8

DANGER AREA

Goodrest Farm

Mast

Woodcote (County Police HQ)

Leek Wootton

The Lunch

WALER CL

WOODCOTE LA

7

69

Deer Park Farm

PH

HOME FARM

CHURCH LA

WARWICK RD

+

Terrace Hill Wood

Stone Edge

THE ELMS

6

DANGER AREA

Larch Covert

DANGER AREA

Centenary Way

THE HAYES

Wootton Court

5

68

CH

Deer Park

Prospect Farm

CV35

Blacklow Hill

4

Wedgnock Old Park

Wedgnock Rifle Range

Gaveston's Cross

A46

Blackbrake Plantation

Middle Woodloes

Loes Farm

3

67

Woodloes Farm

WOODLOES LA

CV34

Woodloes Park

1 WEALE GR
2 SHELDON GR

Nursery

A429

2

WARWICK

WARWICK BY-PASS

DWARRIS WLK

Wedgnock Park Farm

Wedgnock Ind Est

Ind Est

Grand Union Canal

Grand Union Canal

Woodloes Inf & Jun Schs

Ladbrook Park

PO

COVENTRY RD

A429

Sch

1

66

Warwickshire STREET ATLAS

A4177 Birmingham (A452)

A4177 BIRMINGHAM RD

A46

E1
1 NEWSHOLME CL
2 ADDINGHAM CL
3 WATSON CL
4 RYLSTONE WAY
5 KILDWICK WAY

F1
1 HETTON CL
2 BUCKDEN CL
3 LEYBURN CL
4 ARNCLIFFE WAY
5 HUDDISDON CL
6 PHILLIPPES RD

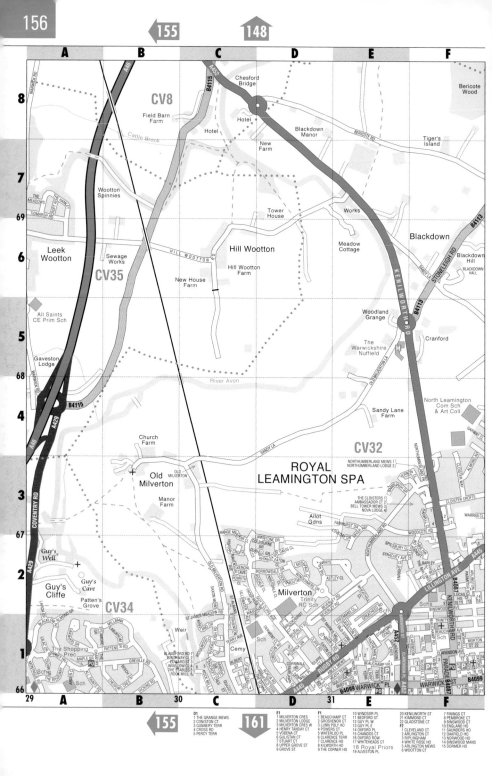

CV8

Chesford Bridge

Field Barn Farm

Hotel

Hotel

New Farm

Blackdown Manor

BERICOTE RD

Tiger's Island

Bericote Wood

Cattle Brook

Wootton Spinnies

THE MEADOWS

TIDMARSH RD

Works

Blackdown

HILL WOOTTON RD

Tower House

Meadow Cottage

Blackdown Hill

Leek Wootton

Sewage Works

Hill Wootton

Hill Wootton Farm

BLACKDOWN HALL

CV35

New House Farm

STONELEIGH RD

All Saints CE Prim Sch

Woodland Grange

Cranford

Gaveston Lodge

The Warwickshire Nuffield

River Avon

KENILWORTH RD

B4113

B4115

A429

A46

Sandy Lane Farm

North Leamington Com Sch & Art Coll

Church Farm

SANDY LA

CV32

Old Milverton

Manor Farm

ROYAL LEAMINGTON SPA

NORTHUMBERLAND MEWS 1
NORTHUMBERLAND LODGE 2

COVENTRY RD

Allot Gdns

THE CLOISTERS 1
AMBASSADOR CT 2
BELL TOWER MEWS 3
NOVA LODGE 4

CLOISTER CROFTS

WARREN CL

Guy's Well

CV34

Guy's Cave

Patten's Grove

Milverton

Trinity RC Sch

Guy's Cliffe

LILLINGTON AVE

KENILWORTH RD

A452

A445

A429

Weir

Cemy

Sch

Sch

WARWICK PL

B4099

WARWICK ST

B4099

A452

PARADE ST

B4087

The Shopping Prec

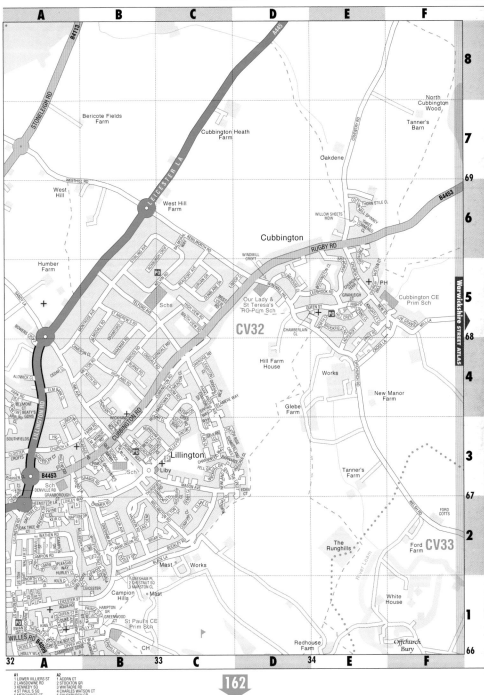

A1
1 LOWER VILLIERS ST
2 LANSDOWNE RD
3 KENNEDY SG
4 ST PAUL S SQ
5 MERCHANTS CT
6 LANSDOWNE CRES
7 WILLIAM THOMAS HO
8 HANOVER GDNS
9 WHITTLE CT

A2
1 ACORN CT
2 STOCKTON GR
3 WHITACRE RD
4 CHARLES WATSON CT
5 SHUCKBURGH GR
6 HELLIDON CL
7 BROWNLOW ST

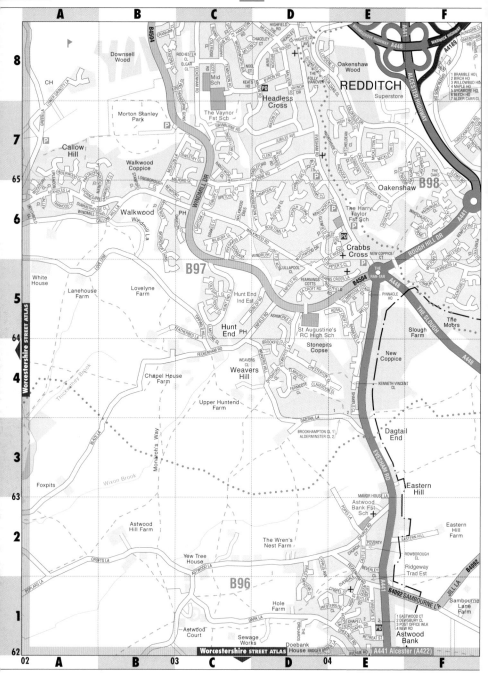

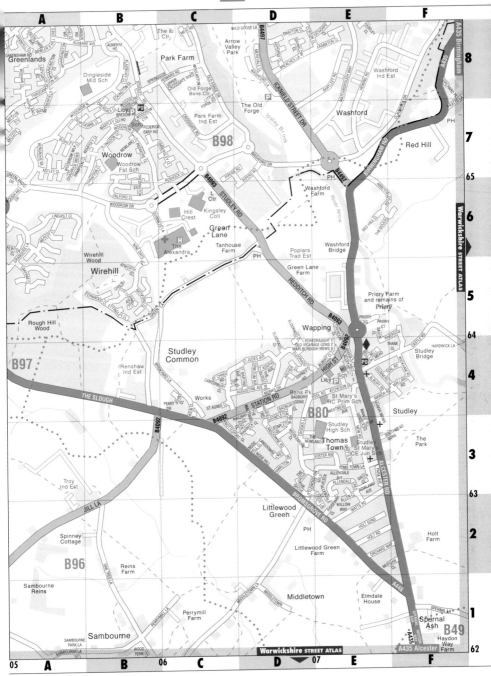

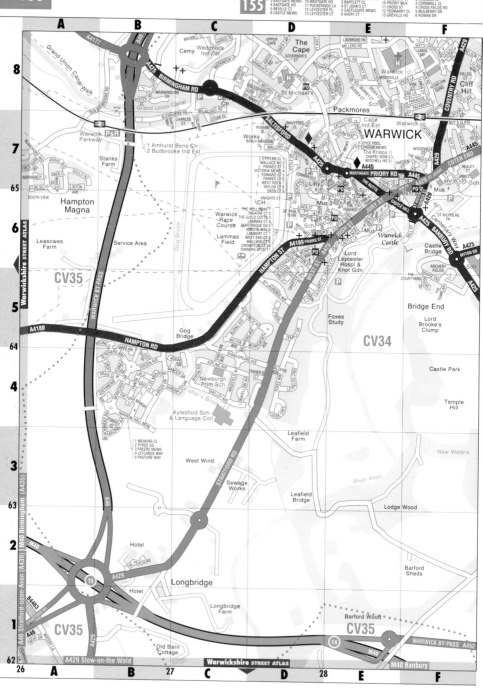

E6	7 MARKS MEWS	F7	7 FAIRFAX CT	F8	7 GAVESTON CL
1 GERRARD ST	8 TIBBITS CT	1 ALEXANDER CT	8 BROOKE MEWS	1 PEMBROKE CL	
2 ALMSHOUSES	9 THE WOOLPACK	2 COACH HOUSE MEWS	9 GOODWAY CT	2 ARUNDEL CL	
3 EASTGATE MEWS	10 WESTGATE HO	3 BARTLETT CL	10 PRIORY WLK	3 CORNWALL CL	
4 EASTGATE HO	11 PUCKERINGS LA	4 ST JOHN'S CT	11 CROSS ST	4 CROSS FIELDS RD	
5 NEVILLE CT	12 LEYCESTER PL	5 CASTLEGATE MEWS	12 YEOMANRY CL	5 MULBERRY DR	
6 CASTLE MEWS	13 LEYCESTER CT	6 AVERY CT	13 GREVILLE HO	6 ROWAN DR	

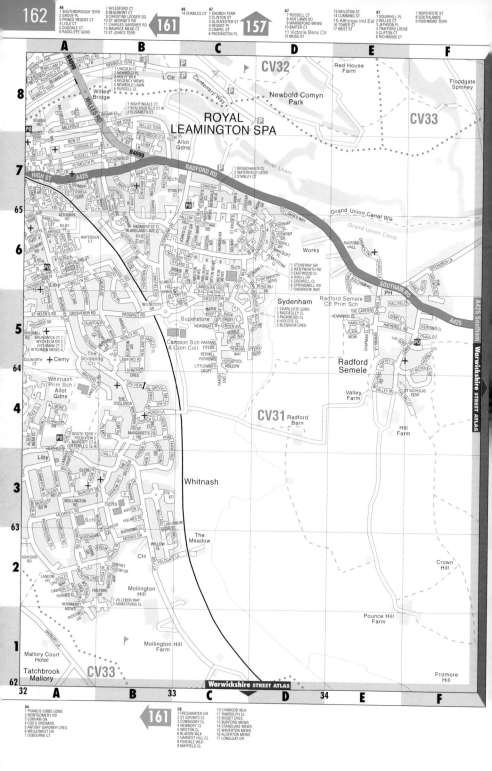

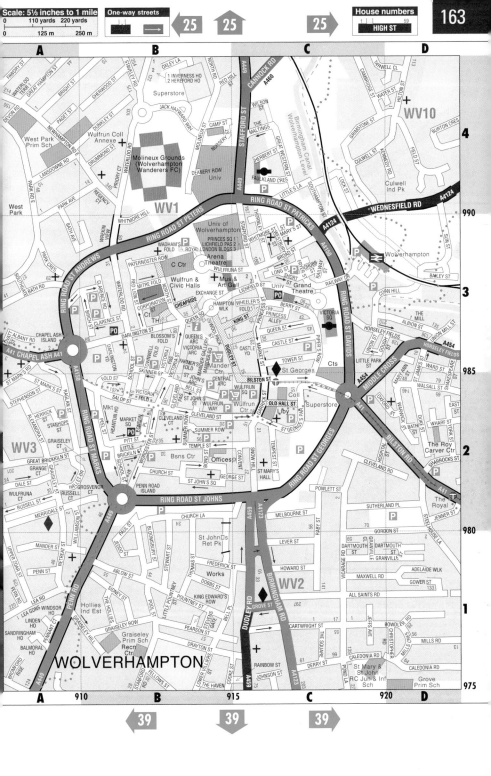

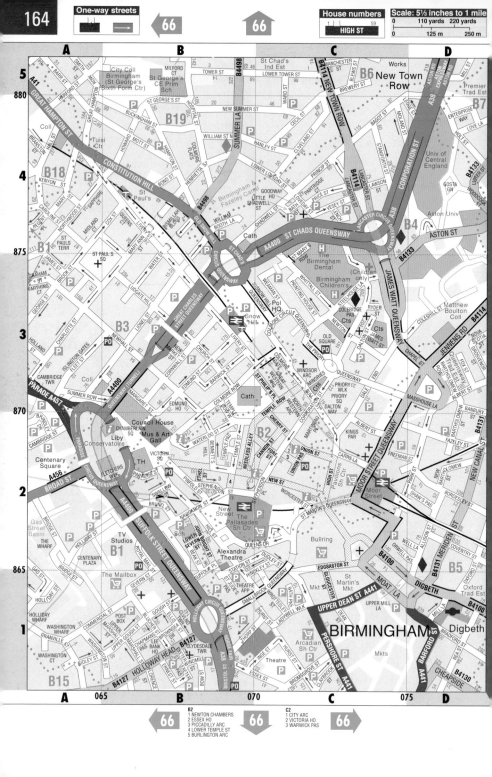

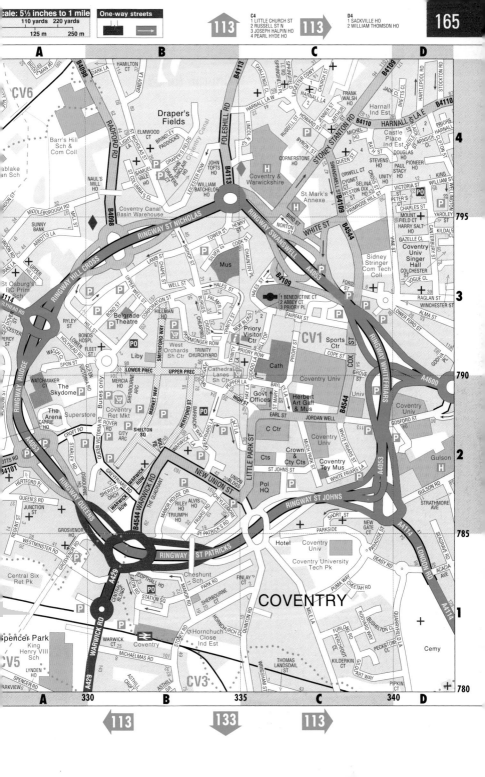

Index

Place name May be abbreviated on the map

Location number Present when a number indicates the place's position in a crowded area of mapping

Locality, town or village Shown when more than one place has the same name

Postcode district District for the indexed place

Page and grid square Page number and grid reference for the standard mapping

Church Rd 6 Beckenham BR2.........**53** C6

Public and commercial buildings are highlighted in magenta   Places of interest are highlighted in blue with a star *

Abbreviations used in the index

Acad	Academy	Comm	Common	Gd	Ground	L	Leisure	Prom	Promenade
App	Approach	Cott	Cottage	Gdn	Garden	La	Lane	Rd	Road
Arc	Arcade	Cres	Crescent	Gn	Green	Liby	Library	Recn	Recreation
Ave	Avenue	Cswy	Causeway	Gr	Grove	Mdw	Meadow	Ret	Retail
Bglw	Bungalow	Ct	Court	H	Hall	Meml	Memorial	Sh	Shopping
Bldg	Building	Ctr	Centre	Ho	House	Mkt	Market	Sq	Square
Bsns, Bus	Business	Ctry	Country	Hospl	Hospital	Mus	Museum	St	Street
Bvd	Boulevard	Cty	County	HQ	Headquarters	Orch	Orchard	Sta	Station
Cath	Cathedral	Dr	Drive	Hts	Heights	Pal	Palace	Terr	Terrace
Cir	Circus	Dro	Drove	Ind	Industrial	Par	Parade	TH	Town Hall
Cl	Close	Ed	Education	Inst	Institute	Pas	Passage	Univ	University
Cnr	Corner	Emb	Embankment	Int	International	Pk	Park	Wk, Wlk	Walk
Coll	College	Est	Estate	Intc	Interchange	Pl	Place	Wr	Water
Com	Community	Ex	Exhibition	Junc	Junction	Prec	Precinct	Yd	Yard

Index of localities, towns and villages

A

Abbeydale.............153 F5
Abbey Fields.........147 E5
Acock's Green.........88 B3
Aggborough.........116 F4
Alderman's Green.....96 B3
Aldersley.............24 F7
Aldridge.............30 A6
Allen End.............47 F6
Allesley.............111 B7
All Saints.............66 A5
Alum Rock.............68 B3
Alvechurch.........139 B6
Alvecote.............22 D6
Amblecote.............80 F7
Amington.............22 B4
Ansty.............97 D4
Arrowfield Top.......123 B1
Ash Green.............95 C6
Ashmore Lake.........27 B4
Ashmore Park.........27 A8
Ashow.............148 E1
Aspley Heath.........141 D2
Aston.............67 A7
Aston Fields.........151 B7
Aston Flamville.......76 E6
Aston New Town.......66 F6
Astwood Bank.........158 F1
Attleborough.........73 F2

B

Bacon's End.............70 B4
Baddesley Clinton....145 B6
Baginton.............133 F2
Balls Hill.............42 B1
Balsall Common.......130 A7
Balsall Heath.........86 C6
Balsall Street.......129 E6
Bank's Green.........152 A3
Banners Gate.........45 B4
Baptist End.............62 C6
Barnacle.............97 B6
Barnt Green.........138 A7
Barr Common.........30 C3
Barrow Hill.............61 C7
Barston.............109 B1
Bartley Green.........102 D7
Barwell.............71 F7
Batchley.............153 B3
Bateman's Green......124 F6
Batmans Hill.........40 F2

Baylis Green.........141 A1
Bearwood.............65 A2
Beausale.............146 C2
Bedworth.............78 B1
Bedworth Heath.......77 E1
Beech Lanes.........84 E6
Beechwood.........131 A6
Beechwood Gardens...132 E8
Belbroughton.......119 E7
Belgrave.............21 E1
Bell End.............120 C7
Belle Vale.............82 E5
Bell Green
  Coventry.............114 B8
  Hollywood.........124 B5
Bell Heath.........120 E8
Bentley.............27 E2
Bentley Heath.......127 E5
Benton Green.........110 E3
Beoley.............154 D7
Berkswell.............110 D3
Bermuda.............78 A8
Bescot.............42 C6
Bickenhill.............90 D1
Bilbrook.............10 C4
Billesley.............105 C6
Billesley Common....105 A5
Bilston.............40 D4
Binley.............134 E8
Binley Woods.........135 C7
Birch Acre.............140 D7
Birchen Coppice.....116 B1
Birchensale.........153 A5
Birches Green.........57 A2
Birchfield.............55 E1
Birchills.............28 D3
Birchmoor.............36 E8
Birmingham.........164 C1
Bishopgate Green....113 D5
Bitterscote.............21 A4
Black Bank.............78 A1
Blackdown.............156 F6
Blackfords.............4 B6
Blackheath.............63 B2
Black Lake.............53 A4
Black Patch.............65 D6
Blackwell.............138 A5
Blakebrook.........116 B6
Blakedown.............98 C2
Blakeley Green.........24 F8
Blakenall Heath.......28 C8
Blakenhall.............39 B7
Bloomfield.............51 E7
Blossomfield.........106 E2
Blowers Green.........62 C7
Bluntington.........118 E1

Boldmere.............46 A1
Bolehall.............21 D4
Boley Park.............9 F7
Bonehill.............20 E2
Bordesley
  Birmingham.........67 B2
  Redditch.............139 D1
Bordesley Green.......67 E2
Bordesley Green East..68 B1
Borough Park.........21 C8
Borrowcop Hill.........9 C6
Bournbrook.............86 A2
Bournes Green.......119 C2
Bournheath.........136 D8
Bournville.............103 E7
Bowling Green.........62 E2
Box Trees.............127 B1
Bradmore.............38 E8
Bradnock's Marsh....109 D3
Bramcote.............79 E6
Bramford.............51 A7
Brandon.............135 F5
Brandwood End.......104 E4
Branson's Cross.....141 C2
Breeden Cross.......104 B6
Bridge End.........160 F5
Brightown.............4 E6
Brierley Hill.........61 E2
Brinsford.............11 D7
Bristnall Fields.......64 B3
Broad Green.........138 B1
Brockmoor.............61 C3
Bromford.............57 D1
Bromley.............61 B5
Bromsgrove.........136 E2
Brookfields.............66 B4
Broome.............99 A2
Broomhill.............1 A4
Broom Hill.........119 D3
Broomhills.............16 B6
Brown's Green.........54 F4
Brownshill Green......94 C2
Brownshill End.........69 A7
Buckpool.............60 F2
Bulkington.............79 B1
Bunker's Hill.........40 E7
Burbage.............76 B6
Burcot.............137 E4
Burnt Tree.............51 F3
Burntwood.............7 C5
Burntwood Green.......7 D6
Burton Green.........131 C4
Burton Hastings......75 A1
Bushbury.............11 E2

C

Caldmore.............42 E8
California.............84 F2
Callow Hill.........158 A7
  Redditch.............139 B1
Camp Hill.............72 E5
Canley.............132 C7
Canley Gardens......132 E8
Cannock.............1 D2
Cannon Hill.........86 D4
Cape Hill.............65 B4
Carol Green.........130 F7
Carpenter's Hill....140 F1
Carroway Head.........33 C4
Castle Bromwich......69 D8
Castlecroft.............38 B8
Castle Green.........147 D6
Castle Vale.............58 B3
Catchems Corner.....130 E5
Catherine Cross.......41 C6
Catherine de Barnes..108 B6
Catshill
  Bromsgrove.........137 A8
  Brownhills.............16 A6
Causeway Green.........63 F2
Cawney Hill.............62 F8
Chadsmoor.............1 F4
Chad Valley.............85 F7
Chadwick End.........145 B7
Chapel End.............72 B7
Chapel Fields.......112 E3
Chapel Green
  Coventry.............93 B7
  Willenhall.............27 B2
Chapman's Hill.......121 B8
Charford.............150 F7
Charlemont.............53 D8
Chase Terrace.........6 E8
Chasetown.............6 F6
Chelmsley Wood.......70 C2
Cheslyn Hay.............4 C3
Chessetts Wood......144 D8
Chesterfield.........17 E8
Chester Road.........57 B6
Cheswick Green......126 E4
Cheylesmore.........133 E7
Chilvers Coton.......73 A1
Christ Church.........9 A8
Churchbridge.........4 F4
Church End.........114 C4
Churchfield.........53 E6
Church Hill
  Birmingham.........55 B1
  Redditch.............154 C6

Wednesbury.............41 E4
Churchill.............98 C3
Cinder Hill.............39 F1
Claregate.............24 E6
Clayhanger.............15 D6
Clent.............99 F3
Cliff.............35 C1
Cliff Hill.........160 F8
Coalpit Field.........78 D1
Coal Pool.............28 F5
Cobley Hill.........138 E4
Cockshut Hill.........89 A8
Codsall.............10 A3
Coft Common.........122 F6
Cole End.............70 E8
Colehall.............69 B5
Coleshill.............70 F6
Coleshill Heath.......90 C8
Collycroft.............78 A5
Colton Hills.........39 B3
Comberton.........117 B5
Compton.............24 D2
Coombeswood.........83 C7
Cooper's Bank.........50 C1
Copt Heath.........108 A1
Corley.............94 B7
Corley Ash.............94 A8
Corley Moor.........93 E6
Cornets End.........110 B6
Coseley.............40 C1
Coton.............20 C6
Coton Green.........20 B5
Cotteridge.........103 E5
Coundon.............112 F6
Coundon Green.......112 E8
County Bridge.........27 C2
Coven Heath.........11 C6
Coven Lawn.............11 A8
Coventry.............165 C1
Crabbs Cross.........158 E6
Crackley.............148 B7
Cradley.............82 D6
Cradley Heath.........82 D8
Cubbington.........157 D6
Curborough.............3 D5
Curdworth.............59 B6

D

Dagtail End.........158 E3
Daisy Bank.............40 C2
Darby End.............62 E4
Darby's Hill.........63 B8
Darlaston.............42 E8
Darlaston Green.......41 E8

Darley Green 144 B8	Great Heath 113 E6	Horseley Heath 52 D5	**M**	Packwood Gullet.....127 E1
Darnford 9 F6	Great Wyrley.....5 B3	Hunnington 101 B8		Palfrey 42 E7
Daw End 29 C5	Greenhill 117 A8	Hunt End 158 C5	Madeley Heath.....120 E7	Palmers Cross 24 D8
Dayhouse Bank 101 A1	Green Lane	Huntington 1 D7	Major's Green 125 D8	Paradise.....113 F6
Deepfields.....40 B2	Coventry 133 B5	Hunts Green 48 C7	Maney.....46 C4	Parkes Hall 51 A6
Deritend.....67 A1	Redditch.....159 C6	Hurcott 117 C8	Manor House 96 C2	Park Farm 159 C8
Dibdale.....50 F3	Green Lanes 40 C7	Hurst Green 83 F8	March End.....26 E5	Parkfield 39 E5
Dickens Heath 126 B6	Greenleighs 39 C3	Hurst Hill.....40 A1	Market End 77 D2	Park Hill 148 C6
Digbeth 164 D1	Greet.....87 E5		Marston Green 90 A8	Park Village.....25 F5
Dixon's Green 62 D7	Griff 78 B6	**I**	Marston Jabbett 78 E5	Pedmore 81 B1
Dodford 136 A7	Griffin's Hill 103 D8		Matchborough 154 E1	Pelsall 15 B3
Doe Bank.....46 C7	Grimes Hill 125 B4	Illey 101 E8	Mayer's Green 53 E3	Pelsall Wood 14 F5
Dordale 119 E1	Grove End 47 F3	Illshaw Heath 126 E1	Meer End 130 D1	Pendeford 10 F2
Dordon 36 F6	Grove Vale 43 C1	Inkford 124 F1	Mere Green 32 B3	Penn 38 E5
Dorridge 127 E3	Gunstone 10 A6	Ipsley 154 C2	Meriden 92 D1	Penn Fields 38 F6
Dosthill.....35 C5	Guns Village 53 B4	Iverley.....98 B7	Merridale 24 E2	Pensett 61 C6
Drakes Cross 125 A6	Guy's Cliffe 156 A2		Merry Hill	Pensnett 61 C6
Draper's Fields 165 B4		**K**	Brierley Hill 61 E3	Perry 55 E6
Drayton 119 B4	**H**		Smethwick 65 D5	Perry Barr 55 B5
Drayton Bassett.....34 D5		Kate's Hill 62 E8	Wolverhampton 38 D7	Perry Beeches 55 B8
Dudley 51 D2	Habberley 116 A6	Kemps Green 143 A1	Mesty Croft.....42 C2	Perry Common 56 C7
Dudley Port.....52 B3	Hackman's Gate 98 F1	Kenilworth 148 D5	Middle 4 A4	Perry Crofts 21 B7
Dudley's Fields 28 A8	Haden Cross 83 A8	Keresley 94 F5	Middle Bickenhill 91 A3	Perryfields 136 E4
Dudley Wood 62 C2	Hagley 99 D6	Keresley Newlands 95 B6	Middle Stoke 114 A3	Perton 23 C4
Dunstall Hill 25 C5	Halesowen 83 D4	Kettlebrook 21 B3	Middleton 34 A1	Pheasey 44 C4
	Hall End 36 F5	Kidderminster 116 D4	Middleton 159 D1	Piccadilly 35 F1
E	Hall Flat 137 C7	Kineton Green 106 E8	Mile Oak 20 D1	Pickford 111 E8
	Hall Green	King's Heath 104 F7	Mill End 148 A6	Pickford Green 111 C7
Eachway.....121 F6	Bilston 40 E2	King's Hill 41 E4	Millfields 40 C5	Pinkett's Booth 111 C8
Earlsdon 113 A1	Birmingham 106 A7	Kingshurst 70 A5	Mill Green	Pinley 134 B7
Earlswood 126 B1	Coventry 96 A3	King's Norton 103 E2	Aldridge 30 F7	Pinley Gdns 134 A8
Eastcote 108 E3	Wednesbury.....42 C1	Kingstanding 45 A1	Cannock 4 F8	Pipehill 8 C5
Eastern Hill.....158 F3	Hammerwich 7 D4	Kingswinford 60 F6	Milverton 156 D2	Pleck 42 C8
Eaves Green 92 F2	Hampton-in-Arden 109 B8	Kingswood 144 D3	Minworth 58 C5	Plough Hill 72 A6
Edgbaston.....86 A6	Hampton Magna 160 A6	King's Wood 104 D1	Minworth Greaves 58 D6	Plowsworth 36 F8
Edge Hill 36 C2	Hamstead 54 E6	Kingswood Brook 144 E3	Monks Park 95 C1	Portobello 26 E1
Edgwick 113 F8	Handsworth 54 C1	Kinwalsey 92 F7	Monkspath 127 B5	Portway
Edial 7 F6	Handsworth Wood 55 B3	Kitt's Green 69 C3	Monkspath Street 126 E6	Olbury 63 C6
Elmdon Heath 107 E7	Harborne 85 B6	Kitwell 102 A7	Monmore Green 40 A8	Redditch 141 A5
Elmhurst 3 A5	Harden 28 E7	Kixley Wharf 128 C7	Moons Moat 154 F5	Potter's Green 96 E1
Elston Hall 25 D8	Hardwick 30 E3	Knowle 128 B6	Moor Green 86 D1	Pouk Hill 28 A3
Emscote 161 B8	Hartle 119 F6	Knowle Grove 128 B3	Moor Hall 32 D1	Priestfield 40 B7
Enfield 153 D5	Harts Green 85 A5		Moseley 86 F2	Primrose Hill 62 C4
Erdington 57 A4	Hartshill 72 B8	**L**	Moseley Village 26 C2	Princes End 51 E8
Essington.....12 F3	Hart's Hill 61 E5		Mount Pleasant	Priory 51 C3
Ettingshall 40 A5	Harvest Hill 93 E2	Ladyes Hills 148 A7	Bedworth 78 B3	Pype Hayes 57 D5
Ettingshall Park.....39 D3	Harvills Hawthorn 52 F7	Ladymoor 40 D4	Coventry 115 B8	
Eve Hill.....51 B2	Harvington 118 B2	Ladywood 66 A2	Tamworth 21 C1	**Q**
Exhall 96 B7	Hasbury 82 E3	Lady Wood 45 F8	Mousesweet 62 F3	
	Haseley Knob 146 A3	Lakeside.....154 B3	Moxley 41 B3	Quarry Bank 82 A8
F	Hasluck's Green 105 F2	Lambert's End 53 B2	Muckley Corner.....8 A2	Quarry Hill 36 A7
	Hateley Heath 53 E7	Landywood 14 A8	Mucklow Hill 83 D6	Queslett 44 C2
Fairfield 120 D3	Hawkesbury 96 C5	Lane Green 10 C3	Mushroom Green 62 B1	Quinton 84 C5
Falcon Lodge 47 A6	Hawkes End 94 B2	Lane Head 27 D5	Mustow Green 117 F1	
Fallings Heath 41 F5	Hawkesley 123 F8	Lanesfield 39 E4		**R**
Fallings Park 25 E5	Hawks Green 2 B1	Laney Green 4 A3	**N**	
Fazeley.....34 E8	Hawne 83 A6	Langley 64 A5		Radford 113 B7
Fen End 129 E3	Hayley Green 82 C1	Langley Green 64 A5	Neachells 26 D3	Radford Semele 162 E5
Finchfield 38 D8	Hay Mills 88 B6	Lapal 83 F3	Neal's Green 95 D5	Reddicap Heath 46 F8
Finham 133 C3	Headless Cross 158 D8	Lapworth 143 E3	Nechells 67 D8	Redditch 153 C2
Finstall 137 D1	Headley Heath 124 C6	Lawns Wood 60 B2	Nechells Green 67 A4	Rednal 122 C6
Fishley 14 C4	Heathcote 161 D3	Lea Hall 69 A2	Nether Stowe 3 C3	Reeves Green 131 A8
Flint's Green 111 B5	Heath End	Leamonsley 18 B5	Netherton 62 C4	Ridgacre 84 D6
Foleshill 96 A2	Bloxwich 15 A1	Leamore 28 B6	Newbolds 26 A6	Riverside 153 F6
Foley Park 116 C2	Nuneaton 72 E2	Lee Bank 86 D8	Newbridge 24 E3	Romsley 101 A4
Footherley.....17 E3	Heath Green 140 F3	Leek Wootton 155 F7	New Cross 26 B6	Romsley Hill 101 A2
Fordbridge.....70 A3	Heath Hayes 2 F1	Leighswood 30 A7	New Dock 51 A1	Rood End 64 C6
Fordhouses 11 D2	Heath Town 26 A4	Leyfields 20 F7	New Invention 27 D8	Roseville 51 B8
Forshaw Heath 141 C7	Hednesford 2 C4	Ley Hill 32 B1	New Oscott 45 D2	Rotten Row 128 C3
Four Ashes 127 D3	Henley Green 114 D8	Lichfield 9 D5	Newton 54 C8	Rotton Park 65 E3
Four Oaks	Highbridge 15 B6	Lickey End 137 C6	Newtown 14 B6	Rough Hay 41 C7
Meriden 110 C6	Highfields	Lifford 104 B5	New Town	Rough Hills 39 F6
Sutton Coldfield 31 F3	Burntwood 6 F4	Lillington 157 C3	Birmingham 66 C6	Roughley 32 D3
Four Oaks Park 46 A8	Coseley 40 C3	Lime Tree Park 112 A2	Brownhills 6 F2	Round's Green 63 E8
Foxford 96 A5	Highgate 86 F7	Linthurst 138 A6	Tipton 52 D4	Rowington Green 145 A1
Foxydale 152 F3	High Heath 15 D2	Little Aston 31 B4	New Town Row 164 C5	Rowley Regis 63 B3
Franche 116 B8	Highter's Heath 124 F6	Little Bloxwich 14 E3	Nordley Hill 26 C6	Rowley's Green 95 B3
Frankley	High Town 2 A5	Little Bromwich 67 F2	Nordfield 103 B4	Rowney Green 139 E3
Birmingham 102 B2	Hill.....32 A4	Little Hay 18 C1	Norton 80 D2	Royal Leamington Spa 156 D3
Frankley Green 102 B5	Hill and Cakemore 83 D7	Little Heath 95 F1	Norton Canes 5 F6	Rubery 122 B7
Frankley Green 102 A5	Hillfield 107 A1	Little London 27 A3	Norton East.....6 A6	Ruiton 50 D5
Frankley Hill 101 F3	Hillfields 113 E4	Little Packington 91 C6	Norton Green 128 B2	Rumbush 125 E3
Freasley.....36 C4	Hill Hook 31 E6	Littlewood 4 E4	Nuneaton 73 C6	Rumer Hill 4 F7
Freezeland 40 B6	Hillpool 118 E5	Littlewood Green 159 D2	Nurton 23 A3	Rushall 29 C6
Friar Park 42 D2	Hill Top	Littleworth 2 E4	Nuthurst 143 C4	Rushbrook 141 D3
Fulford Heath 125 D2	Cannock 2 C4	Little Wyrley 14 E8		Russell's Hall 61 E8
	Nuneaton 73 C1	Lode Heath 107 C6	**O**	Ryecroft 28 E4
G	Dudley 64 C3	Lodge Green 92 E3		Ryton 79 D2
	West Bromwich 53 A7	Lodge Hill 85 B2	Oakenshaw 158 E6	Ryton-on-Dunsmore 135 B2
Galley Common.....72 A5	Hill Wood 32 C5	Lodge Park 153 F2	Oakham 63 A8	
Gannow Green 101 C1	Hill Wooton 156 C6	Londonderry 64 D4	Ocker Hill 52 C8	**S**
Garrett's Green 69 B1	Hilton.....17 A8	London Fields 5 A3	Offmore Farm 117 A6	
Gibbet Hill 132 E2	Himley 49 B3	Longbridge 160 C2	Oldbury 64 A8	St Chads 40 F7
Gib Heath 66 A6	Hinckley.....75 B8	Longford 95 F4	Old Dock 62 B8	St George's 153 F4
Gilbert's Green 141 E3	Hints 19 D3	Lower Bradley 41 A2	Old Fallings 25 F8	St Nicolas Park 74 A7
Gilbertstone 88 F6	Hobble End 14 B7	Lower Clent 99 D4	Oldfallow 1 D3	Salter Street 126 D2
Gillway 21 B8	Hockley	Lower Eastern Green 112 A3	Old Hill 62 F1	Saltley.....67 E4
Gilson 59 D1	Birmingham 66 B5	Lower Gornal 50 E4	Old Milverton 156 B3	Sambourne 159 B1
Glascote Heath 21 F2	Coventry 111 C4	Lower Illey 101 D7	Old Oscott 44 F2	Sandfields 9 A5
Glebe Farm 69 A4	Tamworth.....35 E5	Lower Marlbrook 121 C1	Old Perton 23 B2	Sandhills 65 A7
Golds Green 52 E8	Hockley Heath 143 D6	Lower Penn 37 F4	Oldwich Lane 129 C1	Sandwell 65 A7
Goldthorn Hill 39 A5	Hodgehill.....68 D6	Lower Stoke 114 A1	Olton 88 F1	Scotlands 26 A7
Goldthorn Park 39 C5	Holbrooks 95 C3	Lower Stonnall 17 A4	Orton 37 F3	Scott's Green 62 A7
Goodyers End 95 D8	Holly Bank.....76 F5	Low Hill 37 F3	Outwoods 92 C5	Sedgley 50 F7
Gornalwood 50 C2	Hollyberry End 93 C4	Loxdale.....41 A5	Overend 82 E6	Seisdon 37 A2
Gorstey Ley 7 C7	Hollycroft 71 A1	Lozells 66 D8	Over Green 47 F1	Selly Hill 86 A2
Goscote 28 F8	Holly Hall 61 E7	Lutley 82 C3	Oxbarn 38 E7	Selly Oak 85 D3
Gosford Green 113 F2	Hollyhurst 96 F8	Lydiate Ash 121 C3	Oxley 25 B8	Selly Park 86 A1
Gospel End Village 50 A8	Hollywood 125 B8	Lye 81 E6		Shard End 69 D6
Gospel Oak 41 B1	Holt End 154 F8	Lyndon End 89 A5	**P**	Sharmans Cross 106 E4
Grace Mary Estate 63 C8	Holy Cross 99 E2	Lyndon Green 89 A7		Sheldon 89 C5
Gravelly Hill 56 E1	Homer Hill 82 B6		Packmores 160 E8	Shelfield 15 C1
Great Barr 43 F2	Homily 146 D5		Packwood 144 A8	Shenley Fields 102 E7
Great Bridge.....52 E6	Hoobrook 116 F2			Shenstone 18 A5
	Hopwas 20 B7			Shenstone Woodend 18 A1
	Hopwood 123 B3			
	Horeston Grange 73 F5			

Index of streets, hospitals, industrial estates, railway stations, schools, shopping centres, universities and places of interest

10 Ctr The B98 .... 154 C1
3b Bsns Village B21...... 65 D7

A

A1 Trad Est B66..........65 A7
Aaron Ct B24..........56 F3
Abberley Cl
  Halesowen B63........82 F2
  Redditch B98..........154 C5
Abberley Ind Est B66 ....65 D5
Abberley Rd
  Birmingham B68........84 B8
  Dudley DY3..........50 D4
Abberley St
  Dudley DY2..........62 C8
  Smethwick B66........65 D5
Abberley Rd B77..........22 C2
Abberton Cl B63..........83 C3
Abberton Ct B33..........56 C2
Abberton Gr B90..........127 B7
Abberton Ho 4 B97 ....153 A4
Abberton Way CV4....132 E3
Abbess Gr B25..........68 E1
Abbey CE Inf Sch CV11...73 B5
Abbey Cl
  Bromsgrove B60........137 C2
  West Bromwich B71....53 C5
Abbey Cres
  Halesowen B63........82 D4
  Oldbury B68..........64 D1
Abbey Ct
  Coventry CV1..........165 C3
  Coventry,Pinley CV3...134 B6
Abbeydale Cl CV3..........114 F2
Abbeydale Rd B31......103 A2
Abbey Dr WS3..........15 A5
Abbey End CV8..........147 F4
Abbeyfield Ho WV11....26 D5
Abbeyfield Rd
  Birmingham B23........56 E8
  Wolverhampton WV10....11 F4
Abbeyfields Dr B94......159 E6
Abbey Gate CV11..........73 C4
Abbey Gate S Ctr CV11..73 C4
Abbey Gdns B67..........65 A8
Abbey Gn CV11..........73 B5
Abbey Hill CV8..........147 F5
Abbey Ind Est CV2......114 F5
Abbey Inf Sch B67........64 E2
Abbey Jun Sch B67......64 E1
Abbey Mans 2 B24......57 B6
Abbey Prim Sch WS3 ...13 E2
Abbey RC Jun & Inf Sch The
  B23..........57 A5
Abbey Rd
  Birmingham B17........85 D5
  Birmingham,Gravelly Hill
    B23..........56 D2
  Coventry CV3..........134 A6
  Dudley,Gornalwood DY3 ...50 D3
  Dudley,Netherton DY2...62 D6
  Halesowen B63........82 C4
  Kidderminster DY11 ....116 A6
  Redditch B97..........153 E4
  Smethwick B67..........64 E1
  Tamworth B77..........21 D3
Abbey St N B18..........66 A5
Abbey Sq WS3..........13 E2
Abbey St
  Birmingham B18........66 A5
  Cannock WS12..........2 B7
  Dudley DY3..........50 C3
  Nuneaton CV11..........73 B5
Abbey The CV8..........147 F5
Abbey Trad Ind Area
  B97..........153 E5
Abbey Way CV3..........133 F6
Abbot Rd B63..........100 C8
Abbotsbury Cl CV2......115 A4
Abbotsbury Way CV11...78 E7
Abbots Cl
  Dorridge B93..........128 A7
  Walsall WS4..........29 C6
Abbots Field WS11......1 E5
Abbotsford Ave B43......43 F2
Abbotsford Dr DY1......61 E7
Abbotsford Rd
  Birmingham B11........87 C6
  Lichfield WS14..........9 E7
  Nuneaton CV11..........73 E1
Abbotsford Sch CV8 ....147 F6
Abbots Mews DY5......61 D1
Abbots Rd B14..........104 E7
Abbots Way
  Birmingham B18........66 B6
  Warwick CV34..........160 D6
  Wolverhampton WV3....24 A1
Abbotts Gn LE10..........75 F5
Abbotts La CV1..........165 A3
Abbotts Pl WS3..........14 D1
Abbotts Rd B24..........56 F1
Abbotts St
  4 Royal Leamington Spa
    CV31..........161 F2
  Walsall WS3..........14 D2
Abbotts Wlk CV33......135 C7
Abdon Ave B29..........103 C7
Abelia B77..........21 F3
Abercorn Rd CV5......112 E2
Aberdeen Cl CV5 ....112 A5

Aberdeen Rd CV11.......73 E1
Aberford Cl B18..........65 E4
Aberford Cl WV12......27 D4
Abergavenny Wlk CV3 ..134 F6
Abigails Cl B26..........89 B7
Abingdon Cl WV1......26 B2
Abingdon Rd
  Birmingham B23........56 B7
  Dudley DY2..........62 D3
  Walsall WS3..........13 F2
  Wolverhampton WV1....26 B2
Abingdon Way
  Birmingham B35........58 A3
  Nuneaton CV11..........73 F7
  Walsall WS3..........13 F2
Ablewell St WS1..........28 F1
Ablow St WV2..........163 B1
Abnalls La WS13..........8 B8
Abney Dr WV14..........39 F1
Abney Gr B44..........45 B2
Abourne Ct B65..........86 D6
A B Row B4..........66 F3
Acacia Ave
  Birmingham B37........69 F6
  Coventry CV1..........113 E1
  Walsall WS5..........43 A4
Acacia Cl
  Birmingham B37........69 F6
  Dudley DY1..........51 A3
  Tipton B69..........52 B2
Acacia Cres WV8..........10 B4
Acacia Ct
  Coventry CV1..........112 E5
  Stourbridge DY8......80 E6
Acacia Dr WV14..........51 B7
Acacia Gr WS12..........2 F3
Acacia Rd
  Birmingham B30........103 E8
  Nuneaton CV10..........72 E5
  Royal Leamington Spa
    CV32..........156 D1
Acanthus Rd B98......154 F6
Accord Mews WS10......41 D7
Ace Bsns Pk B33..........69 D2
Acfold Rd B20..........54 E5
Achal Cl CV6..........95 F2
Acheson Rd B28,B90 ...105 F3
Achilles Cl WS6..........4 F3
Achilles Cl CV34......161 F2
Achilles Rd CV6..........114 A7
Ackleton Gdns WV3......38 F7
Ackleton Gr B29..........84 F1
Acocks Green Prim Sch
  B27..........88 B3
Acocks Green Sta B27 ...88 C4
Acorn Cl
  Birmingham,Bournville
    B30..........103 E8
  Birmingham,Stockfield B27 ..88 B5
  Cannock WS11..........2 C2
  Great Wyrley WS6......5 A1
  Stoneleigh CV8..........149 B7
  West Bromwich B70 ....53 B2
Acorn Ct
  1 Royal Leamington Spa
    CV32..........157 A2
  Birmingham B45..........122 D7
  Coventry CV2..........114 C2
Acorn Ctr 1 WS1..........28 F1
Acorn Gdns B30..........104 A7
Acorn Gr
  Birmingham B1..........66 B3
  Stourbridge DY8......60 E1
Acorn Rd
  Catshill B61..........137 B8
  Halesowen B62........83 C8
  Wolverhampton WV11...12 A3
Acorn Starter Units WS7...6 D7
Acorn St CV3..........134 B8
Acorns The B61..........137 B8
Acorn St WV13..........27 C2
Acorn View WS7..........7 C6
Acre Cl CV31..........162 A4
Acre La B97..........152 E2
Acre Rise WV12..........27 B5
Acres Rd DY5..........81 E8
Acres The WV3..........24 C1
Acton Cl B98..........154 D5
Acton Dr DY3..........50 B3
Acton Gr
  Bilston WV14..........40 B4
  Birmingham B44..........45 A2
Acton Ho CV4..........111 F3
Adam Ct
  Cannock WS11..........1 D1
  Halesowen B63........82 F4
Adam Rd 1 CV6..........113 F7
Adams Brook Dr B32......84 B1
Adams Cl
  Smethwick B66........64 D7
  Tipton DY4..........40 F1
Adams Ct DY10......117 A7
Adams Hill B32..........84 B1
Adam's Hill DY9......99 E4
Adams Ho 3 DY11......116 C6
Adams Rd
  Brownhills WS8..........16 B5
  Wolverhampton WV3....38 C8
Adams St
  Birmingham B7..........66 F5

Adams St continued
  Walsall WS2..........28 D2
  West Bromwich B70 ....53 B3
Adam St DY11..........116 C5
Ada Rd
  Birmingham B25........88 B6
  Smethwick B66........65 B3
Adare Dr CV3..........133 C8
Ada Wrighton Cl WV12...27 C7
Adcock Dr CV8..........148 B5
Addenbrooke Dr B73...46 B2
Addenbrooke Pl WS10 ..41 D7
Addenbrooke Rd
  Keresley CV7..........95 A6
  Smethwick B67..........64 F3
Addenbrooke St
  Darlaston WS10..........41 D7
  Walsall WS3..........28 C7
Addenbrook Ho
  8 Cradley Heath B64 ...82 F8
  Sutton Coldfield B73 ...46 A3
Addenbrook Way DY4 ...52 D8
Adderley Gdns B8......67 D5
Adderley Park Cl B8......67 E4
Adderley Park Sta B8......67 D3
Adderley Prim Sch B8 ...67 D4
Adderley Rd B8..........67 C4
Adderley Rd S B8..........67 C3
Adderley St
  Birmingham B9..........67 A1
  Coventry CV1..........113 E4
Adderley Trad Est B8.....67 A1
Addingham Cl 2 CV34 ...155 E1
Addington Way B69......52 D3
Addison Cl
  Cannock WS11..........1 E5
  Nuneaton CV10..........72 A5
  Wednesbury WS10......42 E2
Addison Croft DY3......50 A5
Addison Gr WV11..........12 B1
Addison Pl
  Bilston WV14..........41 A7
  Water Orton B46......59 B3
Addison Rd
  Birmingham,King's Heath
    B14..........104 F7
  Birmingham,Nechells B7...67 C8
  Brierley Hill DY5......61 A2
  Coventry CV6..........113 A8
  Wednesbury WS10......42 E2
  Wolverhampton WV3....38 F8
Addison St WS10..........41 F2
Addison Terr WS10......41 F2
Adelaide Ave B70......53 B3
Adelaide Ct 3 CV12 ....78 A2
Adelaide Dr WS12......2 E3
Adelaide St
  Birmingham B12........86 F8
  Brierley Hill DY5......61 D3
  Coventry CV1..........165 D4
  Redditch B97..........153 D4
Adelaide Wlk WV2......163 D1
Adelphi Ct 3 DY5......61 D2
Adey Rd WV11..........26 F8
Adkins La B67..........65 A1
Admington Rd B33......89 C8
Admiral Gdns CV8......148 C6
Admiral Parker Dr WS14 .17 F5
Admiral Pl B13..........86 F4
Admirals Way
  Bramcote CV11..........79 E6
  Rowley Regis B65......63 B2
Admiral Wlk DY10......116 E8
Adonis Cl B79..........21 C7
Adrian Croft B13......87 C1
Adrian Ct 1 B24..........57 B6
Adria Rd B11..........87 B4
Adshead Rd DY2..........62 C7
Adstone Gr B31..........103 A1
Advance Bsns Pk WS11 ...2 B3
Advanced Tech Unit
  CV4..........132 C6
Advent Gdns B70......53 B3
Adwalton Rd WV6......23 F3
Aethelred Ct WV10......75 C6
Affleck Ave B78..........20 D1
Agenoria Dr DY8......80 F5
Aggborough Cres DY10 ...116 E3
Aggborough Stadium
  (Kidderminster Harriers
  FC) DY10..........116 F4
Agincourt Rd CV3......133 E7
Agmore La B60..........138 D3
Agmore Rd B60..........138 B4
Aiden Ct WS13..........9 C7
Aimsbury Ct B26........89 C4
Ainsbury Rd CV5......132 E8
Ainsdale Cl
  Coventry CV6..........96 B4
  Stourbridge DY8......80 F2
Ainsdale Gdns
  Birmingham B24........84 B1
  Halesowen B63........82 D2
Ainsworth Rd
  6 Birmingham B31....103 D2
  Wolverhampton WV11...11 E4
Aintree Cl
  Bedworth CV12..........78 B4
  Cannock WS12..........2 F6

Aintree Cl continued
  Coventry CV6..........113 E5
  Kidderminster DY11 ....116 D8
  Upper Catshill B61......121 A1
Aintree Dr CV32......157 C3
Aintree Gr B34..........69 D6
Aintree Rd WV10..........11 D4
Aintree Way DY1......50 F2
Aire Croft B31..........103 B1
Airfield Dr WS4,WS9....29 E3
Airport Way B26..........90 C3
Aitken Cl B78..........21 A2
Aitken Wing B15..........86 A6
Ajax Cl WV4..........4 F1
Akon Ho CV6..........94 F2
Akrill Cl B70..........53 B5
Akrill Cottage Hos The
  B70..........53 B5
Alamein Rd WV13......26 E1
Alandale Ave CV5......111 E4
Alandale Ct CV12......95 C8
Alan Bray Cl LE10......74 D7
Alan Higgs Way CV4 ...131 C8
Alasdair Ho 1 B17 ....85 B5
Albany Cl DY10......117 B6
Albany Cres WV14......40 C6
Albany Ct
  1 Birmingham B62....84 A7
  Coventry CV1..........113 A2
Albany Dr WS12..........2 E3
Albany Gdns B91......107 E4
Albany Gr
  Kingswinford DY6......60 E7
  Willenhall WV13..........13 C1
Albany Ho B34..........69 D5
Albany Mews WS10......41 E6
Albany Rd
  Birmingham B17........85 C6
  Coventry CV5..........113 A1
  Wolverhampton WV1....163 A3
Albany Terr CV32......156 E1
Albemarle Rd DY8......80 F2
Albermarle Rd DY6......61 A5
Albert Ave 1 B12........87 A6
Albert Bean Cl CV31 ...162 A4
Albert Bradbeer Inf Sch
  B31..........122 F7
Albert Bradbeer Jun Sch
  B31..........122 C7
Albert Clarke Dr WV12 ...27 C7
Albert Cl B80..........159 E4
Albert Cres CV6..........95 B3
Albert Davie Dr WS12 ...2 F4
Albert Dr B63..........82 F2
Albert Fearn Gdns CV6..95 F1
Albert Ho 1 WS10......41 C6
Albert Pritchard Inf Sch
  WS10..........42 A5
Albert Rd
  Allesley CV5..........111 A8
  Birmingham,Aston B6 ...66 F8
  Birmingham,Brandhall B68 ..84 C8
  Birmingham,Gravelly Hill
    B23..........56 D3
  Birmingham,Handsworth
    B21..........54 E1
  Birmingham,Harborne B17 ..85 B5
  Birmingham,King's Heath
    B14..........104 F7
  Birmingham,Stechford B33 ..68 D3
  Bromsgrove B61..........150 E8
  Fazeley B78..........35 A8
  Hinckley LE10..........71 D1
  Kidderminster DY10....116 F6
  Tamworth B79..........21 B5
  Wolverhampton WV6....25 A3
Albert St E B69..........64 A1
Albert Smith Pl B65......63 A4
Albert St
  Birmingham B5..........164 D3
  Brierley Hill DY5......61 D7
  Cannock,Broomhill WS11...1 E4
  Cannock WS12..........2 D5
  Coventry CV1..........113 E4
  Kingswinford DY6......60 B8
  Nuneaton CV10..........72 E3
  Oldbury B69..........64 A8
  Redditch B97..........153 D4
  Royal Leamington Spa
    CV32..........156 C1
  Stourbridge DY8......80 F5
  Stourbridge,Lye DY9 ...81 E5
  Tipton DY4..........51 F5
  Walsall WS1..........28 E2
  Warwick CV34..........160 E6
  Wednesbury WS10......41 F2
Albion Ave WV13..........27 C2
Albion Bsns Pk B66......64 E8
Albion Cotts B46......59 B3
Albion Ct
  Brierley Hill DY5......61 C6
  Nuneaton CV11..........73 C4
Albion Field Dr B71......53 D4
Albion Ind Est
  Coventry CV6..........113 F7
  West Bromwich B70 ....52 F2
Albion Jun Sch B66......65 A8
Albion Par DY6..........60 B8
Albion Pl WS11..........1 E4

Albion Rd
  Birmingham,Handsworth
    B21..........54 E1
  Birmingham,Sparkhill B11...87 D5
  Brownhills WS8..........15 E8
Albion Rdbt B70..........53 B4
Albion Rd
  West Bromwich B70 ....53 A2
  West Bromwich,Sandwell
    B71..........65 B8
  Willenhall WV13..........27 B2
Albion St
  Bilston WV14..........40 E6
  Birmingham B1..........66 C3
  Brierley Hill DY5......61 D3
  Kenilworth CV8..........148 A5
  Kingswinford DY6......60 B8
  Tipton DY4..........51 F5
  Willenhall WV13..........27 C2
  Wolverhampton WV1....163 B3
Albion Terr B46..........59 B3
Albion Works DY5......61 B3
Alborn Cres B38......123 D8
Albrighton Ho 4 B20...54 F3
Albrighton Rd B63......82 F3
Albrighton Wlk CV11...74 A2
Albright Rd B68..........64 D4
Albury Rd B80..........159 E4
Albury Wlk B11..........87 A4
Albutts Rd WS11..........6 B3
Alcester Dr
  Sutton Coldfield B73 ...45 D3
  Willenhall WV13..........26 D1
Alcester Gdns B14......104 F7
Alcester Highway B98 ..158 F8
Alcester Rd
  Birmingham B13........86 F3
  Finstall B60..........137 F1
  Hollywood B47..........124 F5
  Lickey End B60..........137 D5
  Portway B47,B48......140 F7
Alcester Rd S
  Birmingham,Billesley Common
    B14..........104 E6
  Birmingham,Higher's Heath
    B14..........104 F2
Alcester St
  Birmingham B12........86 F8
  Redditch B98..........153 E4
Alcombe Gr B33..........68 E2
Alcott Cl B93..........127 F2
Alcott Gr B33..........69 E3
Alcott Hall Prim Sch B37..70 B1
Alcott La B37..........89 F8
Alcove The WV14........14 D2
Aldborough La 4 B97 ...53 B5
Aldbourne Rd CV1......113 C5
Aldbury Rd B14..........105 A3
Aldbury Rise CV5......112 C4
Aldeburgh Cl WS3......14 A3
Aldeford Dr DY5......81 D8
Alden Hurst WS7 ......6 F8
Alder Ave DY10......116 E8
Alderbrook Cl
  Redditch B97..........153 B5
  Sedgley DY3..........39 B1
Alderbrook Dr CV11....74 A1
Alderbrook Rd B91......106 F3
Alderbrook Rd B91......106 F2
Alder Carr Cl B98......158 F8
Alder Cl
  Hollywood B47..........125 B6
  Lichfield WS14..........9 F7
  Sutton Coldfield B76 ...57 E7
Alder Coppice Prim Sch
  DY3..........39 C1
Alder Coppice DY3......39 C2
Alder Cres WS5..........43 B4
Alder Ct B13..........87 A3
Alderdale Ave DY3......39 C3
Alderdale Cres B92......107 E2
Alder Dale WV3..........24 E2
Alder Dr B37..........70 B1
Alderflat Pl B7..........67 C5
Alderford Cl WV8 ......24 F8
Aldergate B79..........21 B5
Alder Gr B62..........83 E6
Alderham Cl B91......107 D4
Alderhithe Gr B74......31 B3
Alder Ho 12 CV34......161 D8
Alder La
  Balsall Common CV7 ...130 C5
  Birmingham B30..........103 C6
Alderlea Cl DY8......81 A2
Alderley Cres WS3......28 E5
Alderley Rd B61......150 D8
Alderman Callow Sch & Com
  Coll CV4..........132 A6
Alderman Gee Hall CV12..78 A4
Alderman's Green Com Prim
  Sch CV2..........96 C3
Alderman's Green Ind Est
  CV2..........96 D2

Alderman's Green Rd CV2 96 B3
Aldermans La B97.........153 B6
Alderman Smith Sch
CV10 ....72 D2
Alder Meadow Cl CV6....95 D4
Aldermere Rd DY11....116 C8
Alderminster Cl B97....158 E4
Alderminster Rd
Coventry CV5...........112 A4
Solihull B91............107 C1
Aldermoor Farm Prim Sch
CV3 ....134 B8
Aldermoor La CV3......114 A1
Aldermore Dr 1 B75....46 F6
Alderney Cl
Bramcote CV11.........79 F6
Coventry CV6...........95 B2
Alderney Gdns B38.....103 D1
Alder Park Rd B91.....106 F2
Alderpits Rd B34........69 D6
Alder Rd
Birmingham B12........87 A4
Coventry CV6...........96 A2
Kingswinford DY6.......60 F5
Wednesbury WS10......42 A3
Alders Cl B93..........154 A3
Alders Dr B98.........154 F4
Aldersea Dr B6..........66 F7
Aldersgate CV11........73 C3
Alders Gr CV34........160 D4
Aldershaw Rd B26.......88 E6
Aldershaws B90........126 A5
Alders La
Nuneaton CV10..........72 A7
Tamworth B79...........20 E6
Aldersley Ave WV6......24 E7
Aldersley Cl WV6.......24 F7
Aldersley High Sch WV8 .10 E1
Aldersley Rd WV6.......24 F6
Aldersley Stad WV6.....24 F6
Alders The
Bedworth CV12.........77 E2
Romsley B62...........100 F4
Alderton Cl 1 B91....107 B1
Alderton Dr WV3........38 E8
Alderton Mews 16 CV31. 162 C6
Alder Way
Bromsgrove B60.......137 B2
Sutton Coldfield B74....44 E8
Alderwood Pl B91.....107 C3
Alderwood Prec DY3....39 C1
Alderwood Rise DY3....50 D5
Aldgate Dr DY5.........81 C7
Aldgate Gr B19.........66 D5
Aldin Cl B78............20 E2
Aldington Cl B98......153 F1
Aldin Way LE10.........71 A3
Aldis Cl
Birmingham B28........87 E1
Walsall WS2............42 A7
Aldis Rd WS2...........42 A7
Aldrich Ave CV4.......111 E2
Aldridge By-Pass WS9...30 A6
Aldridge Cl
2 Stourbridge DY8....80 E8
Oldbury B68............64 C4
Polesworth B78.........36 F8
Aldridge Rd
Birmingham,Brandhall
B68 ....84 B8
Birmingham,Perry Barr B42 .55 E4
Hinckley LE10..........75 D6
Sutton Coldfield B74....30 D1
Sutton Coldfield,Little Aston B74,
WS9 ....31 B6
Sutton Coldfield,Streetly
B74..................44 E7
Walsall WS4............29 C3
Aldridge Sch & Science Coll
WS9..................30 A4
Aldridge St WS10.......41 D7
Aldrin Way CV4........132 D5
Aldwick Cl CV32.......157 A4
Aldwick Cl B31.........30 B8
Aldwych Dr WV3........38 A8
Aldwyn Ave B13........86 F2
Alesmore Mdw WS13.....8 F6
Alesworth Dr LE10.....75 F4
Alexander Cl B61.......121 A1
Alexander Ct 1 CV34..160 F7
Alexander Gdns
Birmingham B42........55 D3
Hinckley LE10..........71 C2
Alexander Hill DY5......81 F8
Alexander Ind Pk WV14...40 C4
Alexander Rd
Bedworth CV12.........78 C3
Birmingham B27........88 C4
Codsall WV8............10 C3
Smethwick B67.........64 E2
Willenhall WS2.........27 E5
Alexander Stad B42....55 C6
Alexander Terr B67.....64 F6
Alexandra Ave DY9.....67 F3
Alexandra Ave B21......65 D7
Alexandra Cres B71.....53 E8
Alexandra Ct
Dudley DY3............50 C3
Kenilworth CV8.......148 A4
Oldbury B68............63 E3
Alexandra High Sch & Sixth
Form Ctr DY4..........52 B6

Alexandra Hospl The
B98...................159 C6
Alexandra Ind Est CV4...51 F5
Alexandra Mews B79.....21 C5
Alexandra Pl
Bilston WV14...........40 D6
Dudley DY1............51 C4
Alexandra Rd
Birmingham,Handsworth
B21..................65 D7
Birmingham,Highgate B5...86 E7
Birmingham,Stirchley B30 104 A7
Coventry CV1..........113 F4
Darlaston WS10.........41 E6
Halesowen B63.........82 F4
Royal Leamington Spa
CV31................162 B6
Tipton DY4............52 A6
Wolverhampton WV4....39 A6
Alexandra St
Dudley DY1............51 B1
Wolverhampton WV3...163 A2
Alexandra Terr CV6.....95 E2
Alexandra Theatre B5 .164 B2
Alexandra Way
Aldridge WS9..........30 B5
Tipton B69............52 A2
Alex Grierson Cl CV3...134 E7
Alex Stewart Ho CV11...73 E1
Alfall Rd CV2..........114 B5
Alford Cl B45..........122 C7
Alfreda Ave B47.......125 A8
Alfred Ct B60..........150 E2
Alfred Gunn Ho B68.....64 B4
Alfred Rd
Birmingham,Handsworth
B21..................65 B8
Birmingham,Sparkhill B11...87 B5
Coventry CV1..........113 F4
Alfred Squire Rd WV11...26 D5
Alfred St
Birmingham,Aston B6....67 B8
Birmingham,King's Heath
B14.................104 F7
Birmingham,Sparkbrook
B12..................87 B5
Darlaston WS10.........41 C5
Smethwick B66.........65 C7
Tamworth B79...........21 A5
Walsall WS3............14 B1
West Bromwich B70.....53 D3
Alfreds Well B61.......136 C6
Alfreton Cl LE10........75 F5
Alfriston Rd CV3......133 C4
Alfwyth Ct 4 B15......86 C8
Algate Cl CV6..........95 C3
Algernon Rd B16........65 D4
Alhambra Rd B60......137 C1
Al Hira Sch B12.........87 A6
Alice Arnold Ho 1 CV2 .96 B1
Alice Cl CV12...........77 F1
Alice St WV14..........40 D6
Alice Stevens Sch CV3 .134 A6
Alice Wlk WV14.........40 D6
Alison Cl DY4...........41 A2
Alison Dr DY8...........80 E3
Alison Rd B62...........83 F3
Alison Sq CV6..........96 B4
Allan Cl
5 Smethwick B66.....65 B5
7 Stourbridge DY8....80 F8
All Angels Wlk B68.....64 B4
Allan Rd CV6..........112 F4
Allard Ho CV3.........134 B6
Allard B77.............21 A2
Allard Way CV3........134 C7
Allbut St B64...........62 D1
Allcock St
Birmingham B9..........67 A1
Tipton DY4............52 C8
Allcroft Rd B11.........87 F2
Allenby Cl DY6..........61 A5
Allen Cl
Birmingham B43........54 E7
Studley B80...........159 E3
Allendale Ave B80.....159 E3
Allendale Cres B80....159 E3
Allendale Ct B80......159 E3
Allendale Gr B80.......54 E8
Allendale Rd
Birmingham B25........88 B7
Sutton Coldfield B76....57 E8
Allen Dr
3 Darlaston WS10....41 C6
West Bromwich B70....53 F1
Allen Ho B43..........54 E7
Allen Rd
Tipton DY4............40 F1
Wednesbury WS10......41 F5
Wolverhampton WV6....25 A3
Allens Ave
Birmingham B18........65 F6
West Bromwich B71.....53 A7
Allens Cl WV12.........27 B5
Allens Croft Prim Sch
B14..................104 C5
Allens Croft Rd B14...104 C6
Allens Farm Rd B31...102 E3
Allens La WS3..........14 F2
Allensmead B77........21 C2
Allensmore Cl B98....154 F2
Allens Rd B18..........65 F6
Allen St
Tamworth B77..........21 C1
West Bromwich B70....53 B3
Allerdale Rd WS8.......15 E6

Allerton Cl CV2.......114 E2
Allerton La B71.........53 C8
Allerton Rd B25........88 B7
Allesley Cl B74.........46 C7
Allesley Croft CV5.....112 A6
Allesley Ct CV5........112 A6
Allesley Hall Dr CV5...112 C5
Allesley Hall Prim Sch
CV5..................112 B4
Allesley Old Rd CV5...112 D3
Allesley Prim Sch CV5 .112 A7
Allesley Rd B92........106 D8
Allesley St B6..........66 E5
Alleston Rd WV10.......11 D1
Alleston Wlk WV10.....11 D2
Alleyne Gr B24.........57 A3
Alleyne Rd B24.........57 A1
Alley The DY3...........50 B3
Alliance Cl CV11........73 F3
Alliance Way CV2......114 A5
Allibone Cl CV31......162 A6
Allied Cl CV6...........95 D2
Allingham St B43.......44 D4
Allington Ave 5 WS13...8 F6
Allington Cl WS5........43 D8
Allison St B5..........164 D2
Allitt Gr CV8..........148 B5
Allman Rd B24.........57 B4
Allmyn Dr B74..........45 A6
Allport Mews WS11......1 E1
Allport Rd WS11........1 E1
All Saints CE Inf Sch
CV12.................78 C2
All Saints' CE Jun Sch
CV34.................156 A1
All Saints CE Prim Sch
Coventry CV1..........113 E1
Leek Wootton CV35....156 A5
Nuneaton CV10..........73 C1
West Bromwich B71.....53 C6
All Saints Dr B74.......32 A2
All Saints La CV1.......113 F3
All Saints Pl B61......137 A4
All Saints Rd CV12......77 F1
All Saints' Rd B18......66 B5
All Saints' Rd B14....104 E7
All Saints' Rd
Bromsgrove B61.......137 A3
Darlaston WS10.........41 E6
All Saints Rd
Warwick CV34........161 B8
Wolverhampton WV2...163 C1
All Saints Sq CV12......78 B3
All Saints' St B18......66 A5
All Saints Way B71.....53 C6
Allsops Cl B65.........62 F4
All Souls RC Prim Sch
CV5..................112 A2
Allton Ave B78.........20 D1
Allton Ct B77...........21 E3
Allwell Dr B14.........104 F2
Allwood Gdns B32.......84 A2
Allwood Ho B97........153 C3
Alma Ave DY4...........52 A7
Alma Cres B7..........67 B4
Alma Ct CV11..........79 F6
Alma Ind Est WS10......41 C6
Alma Pl DY2............51 C1
Alma Rd LE10............71 D1
Alma St
Birmingham B19.........66 D6
Coventry CV1..........165 D3
Darlaston WS10.........41 C6
Halesowen B63.........82 C5
Smethwick B66.........65 C6
Walsall WS2............28 D4
Wednesbury WS10......42 B3
Willenhall WV13........27 B2
Wolverhampton WV10...25 F2
Alma Way B19...........66 D7
Alma Wks WS10.........41 D5
Almond Ave
Kidderminster DY11...116 B8
Nuneaton CV10..........72 C6
Royal Leamington Spa
CV32................156 F3
Walsall,Yew Tree WS5...43 A4
Willenhall WS2.........28 E4
Almond Cl
Birmingham B29........103 A6
Cannock WS11...........2 C2
Walsall WS3............14 F2
Almond Croft B42......54 F7
Almond Gr
Warwick CV34.........156 A1
Wolverhampton WV6....25 C4
Almond Rd
Huntington WS12........1 D8
Kingswinford DY6.......60 E8
Almond Tree Ave CV2....96 C2
Almshouses
2 Warwick CV34.....160 E6
Rowington Green CV35..145 A1
Smethwick B67..........65 C7
Stoneleigh CV8........149 C6
Alnwick Cl WS12.........2 C2
Alnwick Ho B23.........56 F4
Alnwick Rd WS3.........14 A4
Alperton Dr DY9........81 C2
Alpha Bsns Pk CV2......96 D1
Alpha Cl B12...........86 E6
Alpha Ho CV2..........114 A4
Alpha Way WS6..........5 A4
Alpine Cl CV10..........72 A5
Alpine Ct CV8.........148 A6
Alpine Dr
Cannock WS12...........2 D4

Alpine Dr *continued*
Dudley DY2............62 B4
Alpine Rise CV3.......133 A5
Alpine Way WV3.........24 C2
Alport Croft 4 B9.....67 B2
Alspath La CV5.........111 F4
Alspath Rd CV7..........92 C1
Alston Cl
Cannock WS12...........2 E2
Solihull B91...........107 D6
Sutton Coldfield B74....32 A2
Alston Gr B9...........68 A3
Alston Ho B69...........63 D6
Alston Prim Sch B9.....68 B3
Alston Rd
Birmingham B9..........68 B3
Oldbury B69............63 F7
Solihull B91...........107 D6
Alston St B16...........66 A2
Althorpe Dr B93.......127 E3
Althorpe Ho CV31......162 A6
Althorpe Ind Est 8
CV31................162 A7
Althorpe St CV31......162 A7
Alton Cl
Coventry CV2...........96 D2
Redditch B97..........153 B1
Wolverhampton WV10....11 E3
Alton Gr
Cannock WS11...........1 B1
Dudley DY2............51 E1
West Bromwich B71.....53 E7
Alton Rd B29...........85 F3
Alum Cl CV6...........113 D8
Alum Dr B9............68 A3
Alumhurst Ave B8......68 B4
Alum Rock Rd B8.......68 B4
Alumwell Bsns & Enterprise
Coll WS2..............28 A1
Alumwell Cl WS2........28 B1
Alumwell Jun & Inf Schs
WS2..................28 B1
Alum Well Rd WS2......28 B1
Alvechurch CE Mid Sch
B48..................139 B6
Alvechurch Crown Meadow
Fst Sch B48...........139 B6
Alvechurch Highway
Lower Marlbrook B60...121 D2
Redditch B98,B97......153 F3
Alvechurch Ho B60.....137 B3
Alvechurch Rd
Birmingham B31........123 B7
Halesowen B63.........82 F2
Alvechurch Sta B48....139 A4
Alvecote Cotts B79.....22 C6
Alvecote La B79........22 C6
Alvecote Pools Nature
Reserve* B79..........22 E6
Aveley Cl B38.........154 D4
Aveley Rd CV6.........113 C6
Alverstoke Cl WV9......11 A2
Alverstone Rd CV2.....114 A4
Alverton Cl B77........35 C4
Alveston Cl B98.......154 C2
Alveston Gr
Birmingham B9..........68 B2
Knowle B93............128 B7
Alveston Pl 15 CV32..156 F1
Alveston Rd B47........125 A7
Alvin Cl
Coventry CV3..........114 F1
Halesowen B62.........83 F8
Alvington Cl WV12......27 D4
Alvis Cl B79............20 F7
Alvis Ho CV1...........165 B2
Alvis Ret Pk CV5......113 A3
Alvis Wlk B36..........69 C8
Alwen St B65...........63 B2
Alwin Rd B65...........63 B2
Alwold Rd B29..........85 A2
Alwynne Freeman Ct CV7 .95 A6
Alwynn Wlk B23........56 C3
Amal Way B6...........55 F2
Amanda Ave WV4........38 F4
Amanda Dr B26.........68 F1
Ambassador Cl CV32..156 F3
Ambassador Rd B26....90 C4
Ambell Cl B65.........63 A4
Amber Bsns Village B77..22 B3
Amber Cl WS11..........2 E2
Amber Ct B77...........22 B3
Amber Dr B69...........63 A6
Ambergate Cl
8 Redditch B97......153 B5
Walsall WS3............14 C3
Ambergate Dr DY6.......60 C8
Amber Gn WS11..........2 E2
Amber Gr WS11..........2 C2
Amberley Ct B44........54 E6
Amberley Gr B6........56 A3
Amberley Ho CV8......148 A3
Amberley Rd B92........88 F4
Amberley Way B74.......31 A6
Amber Terr DY10......116 F5
Amber Way B62.........83 C6
Amberwood Cl WS2......27 D3
Ambion Way LE10........71 F1
Amblecote Ave B44.....44 F2
Amblecote Prim Sch DY8 .80 F8

Amblecote Rd
Brierley Hill DY5.......81 D8
Kidderminster DY10...117 B5
Ambler Gr CV2........114 C3
Ambleside B32..........84 C1
Ambleside Cl WV14......40 E3
Ambleside Dr DY5.......81 C8
Ambleside Gr WV11.....13 B1
Ambleside Rd CV10......78 A2
Ambleside Way
Bromsgrove B60.......137 B1
Kingswinford DY6.......60 D6
Nuneaton CV11..........73 E6
Ambrose Cl WV13.......26 E2
Ambrose Cres DY6......60 D8
Ambury Way B43........54 D8
Amelas Cl 3 DY5......61 A1
Amelia Cl CV12.........79 C3
Amersham Cl
Birmingham B32........84 E5
Amesbury Rd B13.......86 E3
Ames Rd WS10..........41 C7
Amethyst Ct 2 B92....88 F1
Amherst Ave B20........55 A3
Amherst Rd CV8.......147 E6
Amherst Bsns Ctr CV34 .160 B7
Amicombe B77..........22 C1
Amington Cl B75........32 D3
Amington Hall B79.....22 C8
Amington Heath Com Sch
B77..................22 A4
Amington Ind Est B77...22 B3
Amington Pk B77........22 A6
Amington Rd
Birmingham B25........88 B6
Solihull B90..........126 A8
Tamworth B77..........21 D4
Amiss Gdns B10........87 C8
Amity Cl B66...........65 B5
Amos Ave
Nuneaton CV10.........73 B2
Wolverhampton WV11....26 C2
Amos Jacques Rd CV12...78 A4
Amos La WV11...........26 C6
Amos Rd DY9...........81 F2
Amphlett Croft DY4.....52 B4
Amphlett Ct 2 B60...137 A2
Amphletts Cl DY2.......62 E3
Ampton Rd B15.........86 B7
Amroth Cl B45.........122 B7
Amroth Mews CV31.....162 C6
Amwell Gr B14........104 F3
Amy Cl CV6.............95 F4
Anchorage Rd
Birmingham B23........56 D3
Sutton Coldfield B74....46 B6
Anchor Cl
Birmingham B16........65 E1
Tamworth B77..........21 E4
Anchor Cres B18.......65 F5
Anchor Dr B47..........30 F4
Anchor Dr DY4..........52 A3
Anchorfields DY10....116 F6
Anchor Hill DY5........61 C1
Anchor La
Solihull B91..........107 D6
Wolverhampton WV14....40 B2
Anchor Par WS9.........30 B6
Anchor Rd
Aldridge WS9..........30 B6
Bilston WV14...........40 C2
Anchorway Rd CV3.....133 B4
Andersleigh Dr WV14....51 A8
Anderson Cres B43......43 E2
Anderson Dr CV31.....162 A2
Anderson Gdns DY4......52 A4
Anderson Rd
Birmingham B23........56 E6
Smethwick B66.........65 A1
Tipton DY4............52 A4
Anders Sq WV6.........23 E4
Anders B79............21 A6
Anderton Cl B74........46 A7
Anderton Park Prim Sch
B12..................87 B4
Anderton Park Rd B13...87 A3
Anderton Rd
Bedworth CV12.........77 C1
Birmingham B11........87 C6
Coventry CV6..........96 B4
Anderton St B16........66 B3
Andover Cres 2 DY6...60 F4
Andover Pl WS11.........2 B2
Andover St B5..........66 F2
Andressy Mews B61....137 E5
Andrew Cl WV12........27 D6
Andrew Ct B76..........46 F3
Andrew Dr WV12........27 D6
Andrew Gdns B21.......54 E1
Andrew Rd
Halesowen B63.........83 A3
Wednesbury DY4........41 A1
West Bromwich B71.....42 F2
Andrews Cl
Baginton CV8.........133 F2
Brierley Hill DY5......81 E8
Andrews Ho 1 WS13....9 A7
Andrews Rd WS9........16 B4
Anerley Gr B44........44 F4
Anerley Rd B44........44 F4
Angela Ave
Coventry CV2..........96 E1
Rowley Regis B65......63 D4
Angela Pl WV14.........40 D6
Angelica Cl 7 WS5....43 A3
Angelica B77..........21 F4

Angelina St B12 . . . . .86 F7
Angel Mews 8 B46 . . . . . . 70 F7
Angelo Ho B13 . . . . 105 D7
Angel Pas DY8 . . . . .81 A5
Angel St
  Dudley DY1 . . . . .62 B8
  Upper Bentley B97 . . . . . .152 B1
Anglesey Ave B36 . . . . . . .70 B6
Anglesey Bsns Pk WS12 . .2 E4
Anglesey Cl
  Allesley CV5 . . . . .112 B7
  Burntwood WS7 . . . . .6 F4
Anglesey Cres
  Brownhills WS8 . . . . .6 F2
  Cannock WS12 . . . . .2 C5
Anglesey Mews WS12 . . . .2 C5
Anglesey Prim Sch B19 . .66 C7
Anglesey Rd
  Brownhills WS8 . . . . .6 F2
  Lichfield WS13 . . . . .3 B2
Anglesey St
  Birmingham B19 . . . . .66 C7
  Cannock WS12 . . . . .2 B5
Angless Way CV8 . . . . . .147 F3
Anglian Rd WS9 . . . . .29 D6
Anglia Rd WS11 . . . . .1 D3
Anglo African Ind Pk B69 .52 E2
Angorfa Cl WS13 . . . . .8 F7
Angus Cl
  Coventry CV5 . . . . .112 A4
  Kenilworth CV8 . . . . 148 C6
  West Bromwich B71 . . . . .53 C6
Anita Ave DY4 . . . . .52 A2
Anita Croft B23 . . . . .84 E5
Ankadine Rd DY8 . . . . . . .81 B6
Anker Cl WS7 . . . . .7 D6
Ankerdine Ct B63 . . . . . . .83 A3
Ankerdrive B79 . . . . .21 B4
Ankermoor Ct B34 . . . . . . .69 B6
Ankermoor Ct B77 . . . . . . 21 C5
Ankermoor Prim Sch B77 .21 C5
Ankerside Sh Ctr B79 . . . .21 B4
Anker St WS11 . . . . .73 D3
Anker View B77 . . . . .21 C3
Anley Way CV6 . . . . .113 C6
Annan Ave WV10 . . . . .25 F7
Annandale B77 . . . . .22 B1
Ann Cres WS11 . . . . .1 C6
Ann Croft B26 . . . . .89 D4
Anne Cl B70 . . . . .52 E3
Anne Cres CV3 . . . . 134 C5
Anne Ct B76 . . . . .46 F3
Anne Gr DY4 . . . . .41 B1
Anne Rd
  Birmingham B66 . . . . .65 D7
  Brierley Hill DY5 . . . . .62 A1
  Wolverhampton WV4 . . . . 39 B6
Annie Lennard Inf Sch
  B67 . . . . .64 E3
Annie Osborn Prim Sch
  CV2 . . . . 114 D7
Ann Rd B47 . . . . .125 A3
Annscroft B38 . . . . .103 D2
Ann St WV13 . . . . .27 B3
Ansbro Cl B18 . . . . .65 F5
Anscuff Rd DY5 . . . . .61 B1
Ansell Dr CV6 . . . . .96 A5
Ansell Rd
  Birmingham,Gravelly Hill
   B24 . . . . .56 F1
  Birmingham,Sparkbrook
   B11 . . . . .87 C6
Ansell Way CV34 . . . . . . .160 D7
Ansley Cl B98 . . . . 154 F1
Ansley Comm CV10 . . . . .72 A7
Ansley Rd CV10 . . . . .72 B3
Ansley Way WV2 . . . . . . 107 D7
Anslow Gdns WV11 . . . . .12 F1
Anslow Rd B23 . . . . .56 C5
Anson Ave WS13 . . . . .3 A1
Anson Cl
  Burntwood WS7 . . . . .7 C7
  Great Wyrley WS6 . . . . . . .4 F1
  Perton WV6 . . . . .23 E5
Anson Ct B78 . . . . .35 B8
Anson Gr B27 . . . . .88 D2
Anson Junc WS2 . . . . . . .27 E1
Anson Rd
  Great Wyrley WS6 . . . . . . .4 F1
  West Bromwich B70 . . . . .52 E7
Anson Way CV2 . . . . 114 F8
Anstey Croft B37 . . . . . . .70 A4
Anstey Ct B73 . . . . 57 A7
Anstey Gr B27 . . . . .88 B1
Anstey Rd B44 . . . . .55 E6
Anston Way WV11 . . . . . .26 D7
Anstree Cl WS6 . . . . .4 D1
Anstruther Rd B15 . . . . . .85 E8
Ansty Dr WS12 . . . . .2 D1
Ansty Rd CV2 . . . . 114 E5
Antelope Gdns CV34 . . . 160 C8
Anthony Rd B8 . . . . .67 F4
Anthony Way CV2 . . . . . .114 A4
Anton Dr B76 . . . . .58 A6
Antony Gardner Cres 5
  CV31 . . . . .162 A4
Antony Rd B90 . . . . 106 B1
Antrim Cl CV5 . . . . 112 B7
Antringham Gdns B15 . . .85 D8
Antrobus Rd
  Birmingham B21 . . . . .54 E1
  Sutton Coldfield B73 . . . . .45 F1
Anvil Cres WV14 . . . . .40 C5
Anvil Dr B69 . . . . .63 E6
Anvil Wlk B70 . . . . .52 F4
Apex Bsns Pk WS11 . . . . .5 F4
Apex Rd WS8 . . . . .15 C7

Apley Rd DY8 . . . . .80 E7
Apollo Cl WS11 . . . . .2 A5
Apollo Croft B24 . . . . .57 D3
Apollo Rd
  Oldbury B68 . . . . .64 C6
  Stourbridge DY9 . . . . .82 A5
Apollo B79 . . . . .20 F6
Apollo Way
  12 Smethwick B66 . . . . . .65 C5
  Birmingham B20 . . . . .55 D1
  Royal Leamington Spa
   CV34 . . . . .161 D5
Apperley Way B63 . . . . . . .82 B7
Appian Cl
  Birmingham B14 . . . . 104 E5
  Tamworth B77 . . . . 35 D7
Appian Way B90 . . . . 126 C4
Applebee Rd LE10 . . . . . . .75 D6
Applebees Mdw LE10 . . . .74 E6
Applebees Wlk LE10 . . . . .74 F6
Appleby Cl B14 . . . . 104 C6
Appleby Gdns WV11 . . . . .13 C2
Appleby Gr B90 . . . . 127 B6
Appleby Ho 1 LE10 . . . . .71 E1
Applecross Cl CV4 . . . . . .131 F6
Applecross B74 . . . . .31 F1
Appledore Cl
  Cannock WS12 . . . . .2 E3
  Great Wyrley WS6 . . . . . . .5 A3
Appledore Ct 8 WS3 . . . .28 B8
Appledore Dr CV5 . . . . . . 111 F5
Appledore Rd WS5 . . . . . .43 D8
Appledore Terr WS5 . . . . .43 D8
Appledorne Gdns B34 . . . .69 B6
Applesham Cl B11 . . . . . . .87 D6
Appleton Ave
  Birmingham B43 . . . . .54 E8
  Stourbridge DY8 . . . . .81 A2
Appleton Cl B30 . . . . .103 E8
Appleton Cres WV4 . . . . . .39 A5
Appleton Ct 5 B15 . . . . . .86 B7
Apple Tree Cl B23 . . . . . . .56 B4
Appletree Cl
  Catherine de B B91 . . . . .108 B5
Apple Tree Cl DY10 . . . . . 117 B7
Appletree Cotts CV35 . . . 144 F1
Appletree Gr
  Aldridge WS9 . . . . .30 B5
  Wolverhampton WV6 . . . . .25 C5
Appletree La B97 . . . . 153 B5
Appletrees Cres B61 . . . . 137 A5
Apple Wlk WS11 . . . . .2 C2
Applewood Gr 5 B64 . . . .62 F1
Appleyard Cl CV12 . . . . . .78 B2
Approach The CV31 . . . . . 161 F6
April Croft B13 . . . . .87 B3
Apsley Cl B68 . . . . .84 A7
Apsley Croft B38 . . . . . . .104 B2
Apsley Gr
  Birmingham B24 . . . . .57 A2
  Dorridge B93 . . . . .127 F2
Apsley Ho B64 . . . . .62 F2
Apsley Rd B68 . . . . .84 A7
Aqua Ho CV32 . . . . 157 A1
Aqueduct La B48 . . . . 138 F7
Aqueduct Rd B90 . . . . . . .105 E1
Aragon Dr
  Royal Leamington Spa
   CV34 . . . . .161 D5
  Sutton Coldfield B73 . . . . .46 B6
Aragon Ho CV3 . . . . 133 C8
Arbor Ct B7 . . . . .21 D3
Arbor Ct B71 . . . . .53 E6
Arboretum Rd WS1 . . . . . .29 A3
Arboretum The CV4 . . . . .132 D3
Arborfields Cl CV8 . . . . . .148 B8
Arbor Gate WS9 . . . . .16 B4
Arbor Way B37 . . . . .70 C1
Arbour Cl CV8 . . . . 148 B3
Arbour Mews WS11 . . . . . .5 F6
Arbourtree Ct WV5 . . . . . .49 B7
Arbour Tree La B93 . . . . .144 F7
Arbury Dr
  Bedworth CV12 . . . . .78 A3
  Coventry CV6 . . . . .95 F2
Arbury Cl CV32 . . . . 157 A4
Arbury Ct CV10 . . . . .72 C3
Arbury Dr DY8 . . . . .60 D3
Arbury Garth CV10 . . . . . .72 C3
Arbury Hall Park & Gdns *
  CV10 . . . . .77 D7
Arbury Hall Rd B90 . . . . . 126 D8
Arbury Rd CV10 . . . . .72 D2
Arbury Wlk B76 . . . . .58 D5
Arcade The
  Coventry CV3 . . . . 114 B2
  Dudley DY3 . . . . .50 E5
Arcadian WS1 . . . . .28 E1
Arcadian Sh Ctr B5 . . . . . 164 C1
Arcal St DY3 . . . . .50 E7
Archbishop Grimshaw RC
  Sch The B37 . . . . .69 F3
Archbishop Ilsley RC Sch
  B27 . . . . .88 C3
Archer Cl
  Oldbury B68 . . . . .64 B4
  Studley B80 . . . . 159 D4
  Wednesbury WS10 . . . . . .41 E3
Archer Ct CV31 . . . . .81 E2
Archer Gdns B64 . . . . .62 C1
Archer Rd
  Birmingham B14 . . . . 105 C4
  Kenilworth CV8 . . . . .147 E3
  Redditch B98 . . . . .153 E4
  Walsall WS3 . . . . .28 E6
Archers Cl B23 . . . . .56 B5
Archer Terr B97 . . . . 153 C1

Archery Fields CV34 . . . . 160 F6
Archery Rd
  Meriden CV7 . . . . .92 B1
  Royal Leamington Spa
   CV31 . . . . .161 E8
Arches Ind Est The CV5 . 113 A3
Arch Hill St DY2 . . . . .62 C5
Archibald Rd B19 . . . . . . .66 C8
Archway The 2 WS4 . . . . .28 F3
Arcot Rd B28 . . . . .87 F2
Ardath Rd B38 . . . . .104 A2
Ardav Rd B70 . . . . .52 F8
Arden Bldgs B93 . . . . 127 F3
Arden Cl
  Balsall Common CV7 . . . . 130 B7
  Meriden CV7 . . . . .92 C1
  Stourbridge DY8 . . . . .80 E7
  Stourbridge,Wordsley DY8 .60 C3
  Tamworth B77 . . . . 21 E5
  Warwick CV34 . . . . .156 A1
  Whitnash CV31 . . . . 162 B5
Ardencote Rd B13 . . . . . . 105 A6
Arden Croft
  Coleshill B46 . . . . 59 F1
  Solihull B92 . . . . .89 C4
Arden Ct
  Binley Woods CV3 . . . . . . 135 D6
  Dudley DY3 . . . . .50 D3
  Hampton-in-A B92 . . . . . .109 A7
  Sutton Coldfield B72 . . . . .57 C8
Ardendale 6 B90 . . . . . . 126 C8
Arden Dr
  Birmingham B26 . . . . .88 F7
  Dorridge B93 . . . . .128 A1
  Sutton Coldfield,Falcon Lodge
   B75 . . . . .47 B5
  Sutton Coldfield,Wylde Green
   B73 . . . . .57 B8
Arden Forest Inf Sch
  CV12 . . . . .79 B3
Arden Gr
  8 Birmingham,Lozells
   B19 . . . . .66 C8
  Birmingham,Ladywood B16 .66 A1
  Oldbury B69 . . . . .64 A5
Arden Jun & Inf Sch The
  B11 . . . . .87 C5
Ardenleigh Way B24 . . . . .57 A2
Arden Leys B94 . . . . 141 D2
Arden Meads B94 . . . . . . 143 C6
Arden Oak Rd B26 . . . . . . .89 D4
Arden Pl WV14 . . . . .41 B4
Arden Rd
  Birmingham,Acock's Green
   B27 . . . . .88 B4
  Birmingham,Aston B6 . . . .66 D8
  Birmingham,Rubery B45 . .102 A1
  Birmingham,Saltley B8 . . . 67 D3
  Bulkington CV12 . . . . .79 C2
  Dorridge B93 . . . . .127 F2
  Hollywood B47 . . . . 125 A6
  Kenilworth CV8 . . . . .148 B5
  Nuneaton CV11 . . . . 74 A1
  Smethwick B67 . . . . .65 A5
  Tamworth B77 . . . . 35 F5
Arden Sch B93 . . . . 128 B5
Arden St CV5 . . . . 132 F8
Arden Vale Rd B93 . . . . . 128 B7
Arderne Dr B37 . . . . .70 A1
Ardgay Dr WS12 . . . . .1 F7
Ardingley Wlk DY5 . . . . . .62 D8
Ardley Cl DY2 . . . . .62 D8
Ardley Rd B14 . . . . 105 A5
Arena Pk CV6 . . . . .95 F3
Arena Studios B7 . . . . . . .57 A7
Aretha Ct DY6 . . . . .61 A6
Argent Ctr The B1 . . . . . .66 C3
Argingle Pl LE10 . . . . .26 D8
Argus Cl B76 . . . . .46 F3
Argyle Ave B77 . . . . .21 D4
Argyle Cl
  Stourbridge DY8 . . . . .60 E1
  Walsall WS4 . . . . .29 B3
Argyle Rd
  Walsall WS4 . . . . .29 B3
  Wolverhampton WV2 . . . . 39 B6
Argyle St
  Birmingham B7 . . . . .67 D8
  Tamworth B77 . . . . 21 E4
Argyll Ct WV12 . . . . .13 C1
Argyll Ho 5 WV3 . . . . 25 C4
Argyll St CV2 . . . . 114 A3
Ariane B79 . . . . .20 E7
Arion Cl B77 . . . . 21 D5
Arkall Cl B77 . . . . 21 C7
Arkle Croft
  Birmingham B36 . . . . .68 C8
  Rowley Regis B65 . . . . . . .62 F6
Arkle Dr CV2 . . . . 114 F7
Arkle B77 . . . . .35 D4
Arklet Cl CV10 . . . . 72 C5
Arkley Gr B28 . . . . 106 B7
Arkley Rd B28 . . . . 106 B7
Arkwright Rd
  Birmingham B32 . . . . .84 C5
  Walsall WS2 . . . . .28 B5
Arlen Dr B43 . . . . .43 D1
Arlescote Cl B75 . . . . .32 C2
Arlescote Rd B92 . . . . . . .89 C2
Arless Way B17 . . . . .85 B3
Arleston Way B90 . . . . . . 126 E8
Arley Cl
  Kidderminster DY11 . . . . . 116 A2
  Oldbury B69 . . . . .63 D5

Arley Cl continued
  Redditch B98 . . . . .154 D5
Arley Ct DY2 . . . . .62 C6
Arley Dr DY8 . . . . .80 E3
Arley Gr WV4 . . . . 38 D5
Arley Mews CV32 . . . . . . 156 E1
Arley Rd
  Birmingham B29 . . . . .85 F3
  Birmingham,Saltley B8 . . . 67 D6
  Solihull B91 . . . . 107 A4
Arley Villas 4 B18 . . . . . .65 D4
Arlidge Cl WV14 . . . . .40 D4
Arlidge Cres CV8 . . . . 148 C5
Arlington Ave CV32 . . . . . 156 F2
Arlington Cl DY6 . . . . .60 D4
Arlington Ct
  2 Royal Leamington Spa
   CV32 . . . . .156 F2
  Stourbridge DY8 . . . . .81 B4
Arlington Gr B14 . . . . 105 B2
Arlington Ho B15 . . . . 86 C7
Arlington Mews 5 CV32 . 156 F2
Arlington Rd
  Birmingham B14 . . . . 105 B3
  West Bromwich B71 . . . . .53 D6
Arlington Way CV11 . . . . .73 F2
Arlon Ave CV10 . . . . 72 D7
Armada Cl B23 . . . . .56 D1
Armadale Cl LE10 . . . . . . .71 A1
Armarna Dr CV5 . . . . 111 B8
Armfield St CV6 . . . . 114 A8
Armitage Ho WS13 . . . . . .3 E1
Armorial Rd CV3 . . . . 133 B7
Armour Cl LE10 . . . . .75 D5
Armoury Rd B11 . . . . .87 D6
Armoury Trad Est B11 . . . .87 E6
Armscott Rd CV2 . . . . 114 C6
Armside Cl WS3 . . . . 13 B4
Armson Rd CV7 . . . . .78 A1
Armstead Rd WV9 . . . . . . .11 A3
Armstrong Ave CV3 . . . . . 114 B1
Armstrong Cl
  Stourbridge DY8 . . . . .81 B6
  Whitnash CV31 . . . . 162 A2
Armstrong Dr
  Birmingham B36 . . . . .58 F1
  Walsall WS2 . . . . .28 A4
  Wolverhampton WV6 . . . . .25 A5
Armstrong Way WV13 . . . .41 B8
Arna Ho CV2 . . . . 134 B6
Arncliffe Cl CV11 . . . . .74 A2
Arncliffe Way 4 CV34 . . . 155 F1
Arne Rd CV2 . . . . 115 A6
Arnhem Cl WV11 . . . . 26 B8
Arnhem Cnr CV3 . . . . 134 D6
Arnhem Rd WV13 . . . . . . .40 E8
Arnhem Way 8 DY4 . . . . . 52 C5
Arnold Ave CV3 . . . . 133 C5
Arnold Cl
  Tamworth B79 . . . . 21 A6
  Willenhall WS2 . . . . .27 F3
Arnold Gr
  Birmingham B30 . . . . 103 D4
  Solihull B90 . . . . 106 B4
Arnold Lodge Sch CV32 . 156 F2
Arnold Rd B90 . . . . 106 C4
Arnotdale Dr WS12 . . . . . .1 F7
Arnside Cl CV1 . . . . 165 C4
Arnside Ct B23 . . . . .56 B4
Arnwood Cl WS2 . . . . 27 F2
Arosa Dr B17 . . . . 85 B3
Arran Cl
  Birmingham B43 . . . . .43 E3
  Cannock WS11 . . . . .2 A3
  Nuneaton CV10 . . . . 73 A3
Arran Dr B77 . . . . .35 F7
Arran Rd B34 . . . . .68 F6
Arran Way
  Birmingham B36 . . . . .70 B7
  Hinckley LE10 . . . . 71 B1
Arras Bvd CV35 . . . . 160 A7
Arras Rd DY2 . . . . .51 E2
Arrow Cl B93 . . . . 127 F6
Arrowdale Rd B98 . . . . . . 154 A3
Arrowfield Gn B38 . . . . . . 123 D7
Arrow Ho 1 B68 . . . . .84 B8
Arrow Ind Est WV12 . . . . . 27 D6
Arrow Rd N B98 . . . . 154 A4
Arrow Rd S B98 . . . . 154 A3
Arrow Rd WS3 . . . . .28 E6
Arrow Vale Com High Sch
  B98 . . . . 154 E2
Arrow Valley Pk * B98 . . . 154 E2
Arrow Wlk B38 . . . . .104 B1
Arsenal St B9 . . . . 67 C1
Artemis Dr CV34 . . . . 161 E5
Arthingworth Cl CV3 . . . . 114 E1
Arthur Alford Ho CV12 . . .77 D1
Arthur Dr (Road 2) DY11 .116 E1
Arthur Greenwood Ct
  WV14 . . . . 40 C6
Arthur Gunby Cl B75 . . . . .46 F7
Arthur Harris Cl B66 . . . . .65 C3
Arthur Pl B1 . . . . 66 B3
Arthur Rd
  Bilston WV14 . . . . 40 D6
  Birmingham B10 . . . . .67 B1
  Birmingham,Edgbaston
   B15 . . . . .86 B7
  Birmingham,Handsworth B21 .54 E7
  Birmingham,Hay Mills B25 .88 B6
  Tipton DY4 . . . . .52 A7
Arthur St
  Bilston WV14 . . . . 40 D6
  Birmingham B10 . . . . .67 B1
  Cannock,Chadsmoor WS11 . .1 F4
  Cannock WS12 . . . . .2 F3

Arthur St continued
  Coventry CV1 . . . . 165 C4
  Kenilworth CV8 . . . . .148 A5
  Redditch B98 . . . . .154 B3
  West Bromwich B70 . . . . .53 D5
  Wolverhampton WV2 . . . . 39 D7
Arthur Terry Sch The B74. .32 A3
Artillery Rd CV11 . . . . . . .79 F6
Artillery St B10 . . . . .67 C2
Artingstall Ho B30 . . . . . .104 B8
Arton Croft B24 . . . . .57 A2
Arundel Ave WS10 . . . . . . 41 F3
Arundel B17 . . . . .85 A6
Arundel Cres B92 . . . . 89 A1
Arundel Dr 13 B69 . . . . . . 103 C7
Arundel Dr B69 . . . . .62 F8
Arundel Gr WV6 . . . . 23 F3
Arundel Ho B23 . . . . 56 F6
Arundel Pl B11 . . . . 87 A6
Arundel Rd
  Birmingham B14 . . . . 105 A1
  Bromsgrove B60 . . . . 137 B1
  Bulkington CV12 . . . . .79 C3
  Coventry CV3 . . . . 133 D6
  Stourbridge DY8 . . . . .60 C2
  Wolverhampton WV12 . . . .27 C7
Arundel St WS1 . . . . .42 E7
Arundel B77 . . . . 35 C7
Arun Way B76 . . . . .47 A1
Asbury Ct B43 . . . . .54 C8
Asbury Rd
  Balsall Common CV7 . . . . 130 B5
  Wednesbury WS10 . . . . . .42 E2
Ascot Cl
  Bedworth CV12 . . . . .78 B4
  Birmingham B16 . . . . .65 D2
  Coventry CV3 . . . . 134 C6
  Lichfield WS14 . . . . .9 D7
  Oldbury B69 . . . . .63 E6
Ascot Ct 11 B29 . . . . 103 C7
Ascot Dr
  Cannock WS11 . . . . .4 C8
  Dudley DY1 . . . . .50 F2
  Tamworth B77 . . . . 35 D4
  Wolverhampton WV4 . . . . .39 A4
Ascote La B90 . . . . 126 A5
Ascot Gdns DY8 . . . . .60 D2
Ascot Rd B13 . . . . .86 F2
Ascot Ride CV32 . . . . 157 C3
Ascot Way B61 . . . . 121 B1
Ascot Wlk B69 . . . . 63 E6
Asfare Bsns Pk LE10 . . . . 75 E1
Ash Ave B12 . . . . 87 A5
Ashborough Dr B91 . . . . . 127 C8
Ashbourne Cl WS11 . . . . . 2 A4
Ashbourne Gr 3 B6 . . . . . 66 E8
Ashbourne Rd
  Birmingham B16 . . . . .65 D3
  Walsall WS3 . . . . .14 C3
  Wolverhampton,Heath Town
   WV1 . . . . 26 A3
  Wolverhampton,Lanesfield
   WV4 . . . . 39 E3
Ashbourne Ridge B63 . . . .82 E5
Ashbourne Way B90 . . . . 126 E8
Ash Bridge Ct B45 . . . . . . 122 B6
Ashbridge Rd CV5 . . . . . . 112 A3
Ashbrook Cres B91 . . . . . 127 C8
Ashbrook Dr B45 . . . . 122 B8
Ashbrook Gr B30 . . . . 104 C8
Ashbrook Rd B30 . . . . 104 C8
Ashburn Gr WV13 . . . . 27 C2
Ashburton Cl LE10 . . . . . . 76 A2
Ashburton Rd B14 . . . . . . 104 D5
Ashbury Covert 3 B30 . . .104 C3
Ashby Cl
  Birmingham B8 . . . . .68 C6
  Coventry CV3 . . . . 134 F8
Ashby Ct
  Nuneaton CV11 . . . . 73 D3
  Solihull B91 . . . . 107 C1
Ashby Grange LE10 . . . . . .71 E5
Ash Cres
  Birmingham B37 . . . . .69 F6
  Kingswinford DY6 . . . . . . .60 F8
  Portway B47 . . . . 140 F8
Ashcroft
  12 Wolverhampton WV4 . . .39 F4
  4 Smethwick B66 . . . . . . .65 C5
  Birmingham B15 . . . . .85 E5
Ashcroft Cl CV2 . . . . 114 A8
Ashcroft Gr B20 . . . . 55 D2
Ashcroft Inf Sch B79 . . . . 21 C7
Ashcroft La
  Lichfield WS14 . . . . .8 E1
  Shenstone WS14 . . . . 17 E7
Ashcroft DY4 . . . . .52 A2
Ashcroft Way CV2 . . . . . . 115 B8
Ash Ct
  Balsall Common CV7 . . . . 130 C5
  Oldbury B66 . . . . .64 C8
  Stourbridge DY8 . . . . .81 A4

Ashdale Cl
Binley Woods CV3 . . . . .135 E7
Huntington WS12. . . . . .1 C7
Kingswinford DV6 . . . . .60 D8
Ashdale Dr B14. . . . . .105 A1
Ashdale Gr B26. . . . . .89 A8
Ashdale Rd B77 . . . . .21 D5
Ashdene Cl
Kidderminster DY10 . . . . . . .117 C5
Sutton Coldfield B73 . . . . . . .46 A3
Ashdene Gdns
Kenilworth CV8 . . . . .148 B4
Stourbridge DY8 . . . . .60 C2
Ashdown Cl
Birmingham,Frankley
B45. . . . . .102 A2
Birmingham,Highgate B13. . .87 A1
Coventry CV3. . . . . .134 D8
Ashdown Dr
Nuneaton CV10 . . . . .72 F2
Stourbridge DY8 . . . . .60 E3
Ash Dr
Birmingham B31 . . . . .102 C1
Hartshill CV10 . . . . .72 A8
Kenilworth CV8 . . . . .148 A4
Lower Marlbrook B61 . . . . . .121 B1
West Bromwich B71 . . . . . . .53 C6
Ashen Cl DY3. . . . . .39 C3
Ashenden Rise WV3. . . . . . . .38 A8
Ash End House Farm*
B78 . . . . .48 B8
Ashenhurst Rd DY1 . . . . .61 F8
Ashenhurst Wlk DY1 . . . . . . .51 A1
Ashe Rd CV10 . . . . .72 B3
Ashes Rd B69 . . . . .63 F3
Ashes The
Oldbury B69. . . . . .63 F3
Wolverhampton WV11. . . . . .26 B6
Ashfern Dr B76. . . . . .57 F7
Ashfield Ave
Birmingham B14 . . . . .86 F1
Coventry CV4 . . . . .111 D1
Ashfield Cl WS3 . . . . .28 F4
Ashfield Cres
Dudley DY2 . . . . .62 C3
Stourbridge DY9 . . . . .82 A3
Ashfield Ct B38. . . . . .103 E4
Ashfield Gdns B14. . . . . .86 F1
Ashfield Gr
Halesowen B63 . . . . .82 E2
Wolverhampton WV10. . . . . .11 C3
Ashfield Ho B28 . . . . .105 E3
Ashfield Rd
Bilston WV14 . . . . .41 A2
Birmingham B14 . . . . .86 F1
Kenilworth CV8 . . . . .148 B4
Wolverhampton,Fordhouses
WV10 . . . . .11 C3
Wolverhampton WV3 . . . . . .24 D2
Ashford Cl B24 . . . . .57 D4
Ashford Dr
Bedworth CV12 . . . . .78 A3
Sedgley WV3. . . . . .50 E7
Sutton Coldfield B76 . . . . . . .57 F5
Ashford Gdns CV31 . . . . . . .161 F3
Ashford Ind Pk WV2 . . . . . . .40 A7
Ashford La B94 . . . . .143 B7
Ashford Rd
Hinckley LE10 . . . . .75 B7
Whitnash CV31 . . . . .161 F2
Ashford Twr B12. . . . . .66 F8
Ashfurlong Cl CV7 . . . . .130 B6
Ashfurlong Cres B75. . . . . . .46 E7
Ash Gn DY1 . . . . .51 A5
Ash Gr
11 Birmingham,Bordesley
B9 . . . . .67 B2
Ash Green CV7 . . . . .95 C7
Birmingham,Balsall Heath
B12. . . . . .87 A5
Cannock WS11. . . . . .1 F4
Dudley DY3 . . . . .50 C2
Ash Green La CV7 . . . . .95 D6
Ash Green Mobile Home Pk
CV7 . . . . .95 C7
Ash Green Sch CV7 . . . . .95 D6
Ash Gr
Kidderminster DY11 . . . . . . .116 B7
Lichfield WS14. . . . . .9 E8
Ashgrove WS7 . . . . .7 D4
Ashgrove Ct B60. . . . . .121 D1
Ashgrove Rd B44 . . . . .44 C2
Ash Gr
Stourbridge DY9 . . . . .81 D3
Tamworth B77 . . . . .35 F5
Ash Hill WV3 . . . . .24 D2
Ashill Rd B45. . . . . .122 B7
Ashington Gr CV3. . . . . .134 A5
Ashington Rd CV12 . . . . .77 C1
Ash La
Alvechurch B48 . . . . .123 D2
Great Wyrley WS6 . . . . .5 A3
Ashlands Cl B79 . . . . .21 C7
Ashland St
Wolverhampton WV3. . . . . . .25 B1
Wolverhampton WV3 . . . . . . .39 B8
Ashlawn Cres B91. . . . . .106 D5
Ash Lawn Ho 6 CV31. . . . . .162 A7
Ashlea B78 . . . . .36 F5
Ashleigh Ct 8 DY2 . . . . .62 E8
Ashleigh Dr
Birmingham B20 . . . . .55 B2
Nuneaton CV11. . . . . .73 F1
Tamworth B77 . . . . .35 E8
Ashleigh Gr B13. . . . . .87 B1

Ashleigh Ho B91. . . . . .107 C5
Ashleigh Hts B91. . . . . .107 A5
Ashleigh Mews Cotts B76 . .59 C6
Ashleigh Rd
Oldbury B69. . . . . .63 C8
Solihull B91 . . . . .107 B4
Ashley Cl
Birmingham B15 . . . . .86 C7
Kingswinford DV6 . . . . .60 C4
Stourbridge DY8 . . . . .80 D2
Ashley Cres CV34 . . . . .161 B6
Ashley Ct B45 . . . . .122 A1
Ashley Gdns B8. . . . . .67 D4
Ashley Ho DY2. . . . . .62 D4
Ashley Mount WV6. . . . . .24 D5
Ashley Rd
Birmingham B23. . . . . .56 E3
Walsall WS3 . . . . .13 F1
Willenhall WS3 . . . . .27 F8
Wolverhampton WV4. . . . . . .38 E5
Ashley St WV14. . . . . .40 E6
Ashley Way CV7 . . . . .130 B7
Ashmall WS7 . . . . .7 D4
Ashmead Dr B45. . . . . .122 C4
Ashmead Gr B24. . . . . .57 A2
Ashmead Rd WS7. . . . . .7 A8
Ashmead Rise B45. . . . . .122 C4
Ash Mews 4 B27. . . . . .88 C5
Ashmole Ave WS7 . . . . .7 E8
Ashmole Cl WS14. . . . . .9 E6
Ashmole Rd B70. . . . . .52 F7
Ashmore Ave WV11. . . . . . . .13 A1
Ashmore Ind Est WS2 . . . . . .28 E3
Ashmore Lake Rd WV12. . . .27 B4
Ashmore Lake Way WV12. . .27 B4
Ashmore Rd
Birmingham B30 . . . . .103 F5
Coventry CV6 . . . . .113 B4
Ashmore's Ind Est WV1. . . . .51 E3
Ashold Farm Rd B24 . . . . . . .57 D2
Asholme Cl B36 . . . . .68 C7
Ashorne Cl
Birmingham B28 . . . . .106 B7
Coventry CV2. . . . . .96 C2
Redditch B98 . . . . .159 D8
Ashover Gr 8 B18. . . . . .65 E4
Ashover Rd B44 . . . . .44 D3
Ashow Cl CV8 . . . . .148 B4
Ash Park Ind Est WS11. . . . . .2 B3
Ashperton Cl B98. . . . . .153 E1
Ash Priors Cl CV4. . . . . .112 B1
Ash Rd
Birmingham B8 . . . . .67 D4
Dudley DY1 . . . . .51 B3
Tipton DY4 . . . . .51 E4
Wednesbury WS10 . . . . .41 F5
Ashridge Cl CV11 . . . . .78 F8
Ash St
Bilston WV14 . . . . .40 E3
Cradley Heath B64 . . . . .62 F2
Ashstead Cl B76. . . . . .58 B6
Ash St
Walsall WS3 . . . . .14 D1
Wolverhampton WV3. . . . . . .25 A1
Ashted Cir B7 . . . . .67 A4
Ashted Lock B7. . . . . .66 F4
Ashted Wlk B7 . . . . .67 B4
Ash Terr B69. . . . . .52 B1
Ashton Cl B97 . . . . .153 B1
Ashton Croft
Birmingham B16 . . . . .66 A2
Solihull B91 . . . . .107 A1
Ashton Dr WS4 . . . . .15 C2
Ashton Park Dr DY5 . . . . .61 C1
Ashton Rd B25 . . . . .88 F7
Ash Tree Ave CV4 . . . . .112 A2
Ashtree Cl DY5 . . . . .61 B1
Ashtree Ct WS11. . . . . .1 D4
Ash Tree Dr B26 . . . . .88 D7
Ashtree Gr WV14 . . . . .41 B3
Ash Tree Gr CV7 . . . . .97 E5
Ash Tree Rd B30 . . . . .104 A6
Ashtree Rd
Cradley Heath B64 . . . . .62 F2
Oldbury B69. . . . . .63 D8
Ash Tree Rd B97 . . . . .153 B5
Ashtree Rd WS3 . . . . .15 A3
Ashurst Cl CV6 . . . . .96 B5
Ashurst Rd B76. . . . . .57 F7
Ash View WS12 . . . . .1 D8
Ashville Ave B34. . . . . .68 F7
Ashville Dr B63. . . . . .83 A5
Ashwater Dr B14 . . . . .104 D2
Ashway B11 . . . . .87 B5
Ash Way B23 . . . . .56 C7
Ashwell Dr B90. . . . . .106 D4
Ashwells Gr WV9 . . . . .11 A2
Ashwin Rd B21. . . . . .66 A7
Ash Wlk B76 . . . . .46 F2
Ashwood Ave
Coventry CV6. . . . . .112 F5
Stourbridge DY8 . . . . .60 D2
Ashwood Cl
Oldbury B69. . . . . .63 F4
Sutton Coldfield B74 . . . . . . .44 E8
Ashwood Ct
Birmingham B13 . . . . .87 A3
Birmingham,Stechford B34. . .68 D5
Ashwood Dr B37 . . . . .70 D3
Ashwood Gr WV4 . . . . .39 A5
Ashwoodhay DY8 . . . . .60 F3
Ashwood Park Prim Sch
DY8. . . . . .60 D1
Ashwood Rd CV10 . . . . .72 E5
Ashworth Ho
2 Lichfield WS13. . . . . .9 B8
Cannock WS11. . . . . .2 A4

Ashworth Rd B42 . . . . .44 B1
Askew Bridge Rd DY3. . . . . . .50 B3
Askew Cl DY3. . . . . .50 E5
Aspbury Croft B36 . . . . .58 D1
Aspects Park Gate CV11. . . . .73 F7
Aspen Cl
2 Lichfield WS13 . . . . .9 E8
Birmingham B27 . . . . .88 B2
Coventry CV4 . . . . .111 D1
Sutton Coldfield B76 . . . . . . .46 F2
Aspen Dr
Bedworth CV12 . . . . .96 C6
Birmingham B37 . . . . .90 C8
Aspen Gdns B20 . . . . .55 B1
Aspen Gr
Birmingham B9 . . . . .68 A3
Burntwood WS7 . . . . .6 F8
Hollywood B47. . . . . .125 B5
Willenhall WV12 . . . . .27 E7
Aspen Ho B91. . . . . .106 F2
Aspen Way WV3 . . . . .25 A1
Asphodel B74 . . . . .31 F5
Aspen Cl CV8 . . . . .148 C4
Aspley Heath La B94 . . . . . . .141 D2
Aspley Heath B94. . . . . .141 D2
Asquith Dr
Cannock WS11. . . . . .2 C2
Oldbury B69. . . . . .52 D2
Asquith Rd B8 . . . . .68 B5
Assheton Cl B60 . . . . .137 A1
Astbury Ave B67 . . . . .64 F3
Astbury Cl
Walsall WS3 . . . . .14 A4
Wolverhampton WV1. . . . . . .26 A1
Astbury Ct 1 B68 . . . . .84 B7
Aster Cl
Hinckley LE10 . . . . .75 E6
Nuneaton CV11. . . . . .74 A1
Aster Way
Hinckley LE10 . . . . .75 D6
Walsall WS5 . . . . .43 A3
Aster Wlk
Bedworth CV10 . . . . .78 A8
Wolverhampton WV9. . . . . . .11 A3
Asthill Croft CV3. . . . . .133 C8
Asthill Gr CV3. . . . . .133 C8
Astley Ave
Coventry CV6. . . . . .95 E2
Halesowen B62 . . . . .83 F6
Astley Cl
Redditch B98 . . . . .159 A7
Royal Leamington Spa
CV32. . . . . .156 D2
Tipton DY4 . . . . .52 D6
Astley Cres B62. . . . . .83 F5
Astley La
Bedworth CV12 . . . . .77 C4
Nuneaton CV10 . . . . .72 B1
Astley Rd
Birmingham B21 . . . . .54 D1
Bromsgrove B60 . . . . .137 C1
Astley Wlk B90 . . . . .106 B5
Aston Brook Gn B6. . . . . .66 F5
Aston Brook St E B6. . . . . . . .66 F5
Aston Brook St B6. . . . . .66 F5
Aston Bury B15. . . . . .85 D7
Aston Church Rd B7,B8 . . . . .67 D6
Aston Cl
Darlaston WV14. . . . . .41 A4
Shenstone WS14 . . . . .17 F6
Aston Cross Bsns Village
B6. . . . . .67 A6
Aston Ct B23 . . . . .56 C3
Aston Expressway B6 . . . . . . .66 F6
Aston Expressway (Elevated
Rd) B6. . . . . .67 A4
Aston Fields Mid Sch
B60. . . . . .151 C8
Aston Fields Trad Est 2
B60. . . . . .150 F6
Aston Flamville Rd LE10 . . . .76 C7
Aston Hall Rd B6 . . . . .66 F8
Aston La
Aston Flamville LE10 . . . . . . .76 D7
Birmingham B20 . . . . .55 E2
Hinckley LE10 . . . . .76 A6
Aston Manor Rd B20 . . . . . . .55 E2
Aston Manor Sch B6. . . . . . . .66 F6
Aston Manor Transport
Mus* B6. . . . . .55 F1
Aston Pk Ind Est CV11 . . . . . .73 B5
Aston Prim Sch B74 . . . . .31 C6
Aston Rd
Birmingham B6 . . . . .66 F6
Bromsgrove B60 . . . . .150 F6
Coventry CV5. . . . . .112 F1
Dudley DY2 . . . . .62 B8
Aston Rd N B6 . . . . .66 F6
Aston Rd
Nuneaton CV11. . . . . .73 B2
Oldbury B69. . . . . .52 A1
Willenhall WV13 . . . . .26 C1
Aston Science Pk B7 . . . . . . .66 F4
Aston Seedbed Ctr B7 . . . . . .67 A6
Astons Fold DY5. . . . . .81 D7
Aston St
Birmingham B4 . . . . .164 D4
Tipton DY4 . . . . .52 C7
Wolverhampton WV3. . . . . . .39 A8
Aston Tower Com Prim Sch
B6. . . . . .66 F8
Aston Univ B5 . . . . .164 D4

Astor Dr B13 . . . . .87 C1
Astoria Cl WV12 . . . . .13 D1
Astoria Gdns WV12 . . . . .13 D1
Astor Rd
Kingswinford DV6 . . . . .60 F5
Sutton Coldfield B74 . . . . . . .31 A1
Astwell Prep Sch B20 . . . . . .66 B8
Astwood Bank Fst Sch
B96. . . . . .158 E2
Astwood La B96 . . . . .158 C2
Atcham Cl B98 . . . . .154 F3
Atcheson Cl B80. . . . . .159 E4
Athelney Ct WS3. . . . . .15 A3
Athelstan Gr WV6. . . . . .23 F5
Athelstan Way B79. . . . . .20 F7
Athena Dr CV34. . . . . .161 E5
Athena Gdns CV6 . . . . .96 A1
Atherstone Cl
Redditch B98 . . . . .154 F1
Solihull B90 . . . . .105 E2
Atherstone Rd WV1. . . . . .26 B2
Atherstone St B77,B78. . . . . .38 C6
Atherstone Pl CV4 . . . . .132 D6
Athlone Rd WS5 . . . . .43 C8
Athol Cl B32. . . . . .102 D8
Atholl Cres CV10. . . . . .72 E2
Athol Rd CV2 . . . . .115 A6
Atkinson Ct WV10. . . . . .25 D6
Atkins Way LE10 . . . . .75 E7
Atlantic Cl 4 WV13. . . . . .27 A1
Atlantic Rd B44. . . . . .44 F1
Atlantic Way WS10. . . . . .41 E1
Atlas Croft WV10. . . . . .25 C6
Atlas Est
Birmingham,Tyseley B11. . . .88 A5
Birmingham,Witton B6 . . . . .56 A2
Atlas Gr B70 . . . . .52 F3
Atlas Trad Est
Birmingham B11 . . . . .87 D5
Coseley WV14 . . . . .40 F2
Attenborough Cl B19 . . . . . . .66 E5
Attingham Dr
Birmingham B43 . . . . .43 D2
Cannock WS11. . . . . .2 B2
Attleborough Fields Ind Est
CV11. . . . . .73 E3
Attleborough La B46. . . . . . . .59 A1
Attleborough Rd CV11 . . . . . .73 D3
Attlee Cl B69 . . . . .52 D2
Attlee Cres WV14 . . . . .40 E2
Attlee Gr WS11 . . . . .2 C2
Attlee Rd WS2 . . . . .27 E3
Attoxhall Rd CV2. . . . . .114 E4
Attwell Pk WV3 . . . . .38 D7
Attwell Rd DY4 . . . . .40 F1
Attwood Bsns Ctr 2 DY9. . . .81 F1
Attwood Cl B8. . . . . .67 E6
Attwood Cres CV2 . . . . .114 C2
Attwood Gdns WV4 . . . . .39 E5
Attwood Rd WS7. . . . . .6 C7
Attwood St
Halesowen B63 . . . . .82 F5
Stourbridge DY9 . . . . .81 F5
Atworth Cl B98 . . . . .159 B5
Aubrey Rd
Birmingham B32 . . . . .84 E7
Birmingham,Small Heath
B10. . . . . .87 F8
Auchinleck Dr WS13 . . . . .3 C1
Auchinleck Sq 5 B15. . . . . . .66 B1
Auckland Dr B36. . . . . .70 B7
Auckland Ho B32 . . . . .84 F4
Auckland Rd
Birmingham B11 . . . . .87 A7
Kingswinford DY6 . . . . .60 E4
Smethwick B67 . . . . .64 E5
Auden Ct WV6. . . . . .23 F4
Audleigh Ho 8 B15. . . . . .86 C8
Audlem Wlk WV10 . . . . .26 A5
Audley Dr DY11. . . . . .116 A8
Audley Prim Sch B33 . . . . . . .68 F4
Audley Rd B33. . . . . .68 F4
Audnam DY8 . . . . .60 F1
Augusta Pl CV32 . . . . .161 F8
Augusta Rd
Birmingham,Acock's Green
B27 . . . . .88 C5
Birmingham,Moseley B13 . . .86 E4
Augusta Rd E B13 . . . . .86 F4
Augusta St B18. . . . . .66 C4
Augustine Ave B80. . . . . .159 D4
Augustine Gr
Birmingham B18 . . . . .65 F6
Sutton Coldfield B74 . . . . . . .31 F5
Augustines Wlk WS13. . . . . . .3 A3
Augustus Cl B46. . . . . .59 F1
Augustus Ct B15. . . . . .85 F8
Augustus Rd
Birmingham B15 . . . . .85 E8
Coventry CV1. . . . . .113 F4
Augustus St WS2 . . . . .28 D1
Aulton Cres LE10 . . . . .71 B1
Aulton Rd B75. . . . . .32 E2
Aulton Way LE10 . . . . .71 B1
Ault St B70. . . . . .53 D1
Austcliff Cl B97 . . . . .158 D6
Austcliff Dr B91. . . . . .127 C8
Austen Cl CV32. . . . . .157 E5
Austen Pl B15 . . . . .86 B8
Austen Wlk B71 . . . . .53 D6
Austin Cl
Birmingham B27 . . . . .88 D4
Dudley DY1 . . . . .50 F2
Austin Cote La WS14. . . . . . . .9 F7
Austin Croft B36. . . . . .58 E1

Austin Ct 4 B74. . . . . .31 E3
Austin Dr CV6 . . . . .114 A7
Austin Edwards Dr CV34 .161 B8
Austin Rd
Birmingham B21 . . . . .54 C1
Bromsgrove B60 . . . . .150 E7
Austin Rise B31 . . . . .122 F7
Austin St WV6. . . . . .25 A4
Austin Way B42. . . . . .55 A5
Austrey Cl B93. . . . . .128 A6
Austrey Gr B29 . . . . .103 A8
Austrey Rd DY6. . . . . .61 A5
Austwick Cl CV34 . . . . .155 E1
Austy Cl B36 . . . . .68 E8
Autobase Ind Est B69 . . . . . . .52 C3
Auto Ctr B18 . . . . .65 E5
Autumn Berry Gr DY3. . . . . . .50 E6
Autumn Cl WS4. . . . . .15 C1
Autumn Dr
Dudley DY3 . . . . .50 D4
Lichfield WS13. . . . . .3 D2
Walsall WS4 . . . . .15 C2
Autumn Gr B19. . . . . .66 C6
Auxerre Ave B98. . . . . .159 B8
Auxerre Ho B98 . . . . .159 B8
Avalon Cl B24. . . . . .57 A4
Avalon Ho 2 WS11 . . . . .1 F4
Avalon Rd B60. . . . . .137 C2
Avebury Cl CV11 . . . . .73 F2
Avebury Gr B30. . . . . .104 C7
Avebury Rd B30. . . . . .104 C8
Ave Maria Cl B64 . . . . .62 E1
Avenbury Cl B98 . . . . .154 F1
Avenbury Dr B91. . . . . .107 E4
Avenue Cl
Birmingham B7 . . . . .67 A6
Dorridge B93. . . . . .128 A3
Avenue Rd
Astwood Bank B96 . . . . .158 E1
Birmingham,Aston B7,B6. . . .67 A6
Birmingham,Erdington B23 . .56 F4
Birmingham,Handsworth
B21. . . . . .54 D2
Birmingham,King's Heath
B14. . . . . .104 D8
Cannock WS12. . . . . .2 E2
Darlaston WS10. . . . . .41 D6
Dorridge B93. . . . . .128 A3
Dudley,Woodside DY1,DY2. . .61 F6
Kenilworth CV8 . . . . .147 D6
Nuneaton CV11. . . . . .73 D2
Rowley Regis B65 . . . . .63 D1
Royal Leamington Spa
CV31. . . . . .161 F7
Tipton WV14 . . . . .51 C8
Wolverhampton WV3. . . . . . .24 E2
Avenue The
2 Birmingham,Lozells
B19 . . . . .66 C8
Birmingham,Acock's Green
B27. . . . . .88 D3
Birmingham B45 . . . . .121 E7
Blackwell B60 . . . . .138 A6
Blakedown DY10 . . . . .98 B2
Coventry CV3. . . . . .134 A6
Featherstone WV10. . . . . . . .12 C7
Rowington Green CV35 . . . . .145 A1
Rowley Regis B65 . . . . .63 A3
Sutton Coldfield B76 . . . . . . .46 F1
Wolverhampton,Castlecroft
WV3 . . . . .38 B8
Wolverhampton,Park Village
WV10 . . . . .25 F6
Wolverhampton,Penn WV4 . .38 E4
Averill Rd B26 . . . . .69 A1
Avern Cl DY4 . . . . .52 B6
Aversley Rd B38 . . . . .123 E8
Avery Croft B35. . . . . .57 F2
Avery Ct 6 CV34 . . . . .160 F7
Avery Dell Ind Est B30 . . . . .104 A6
Avery Dr B27 . . . . .88 C4
Avery Ho B16. . . . . .66 A3
Avery Myers Cl B68. . . . . .64 B5
Avery Rd
Smethwick B66 . . . . .65 C6
Sutton Coldfield B73 . . . . . . .46 B5
Aviary Ct B21. . . . . .53 C6
Aviemore Cl CV10. . . . . .73 A2
Aviemore Cres B43 . . . . .44 B4
Avill B77 . . . . .36 A5
Avill Gr DY11 . . . . .116 C7
Avington Cl DY3 . . . . .50 D7
Avion Cl WS1 . . . . .42 F7
Avion Ctr WV6 . . . . .25 A4
Avocet Cl
Birmingham B33 . . . . .68 E3
Coventry CV2. . . . . .96 B3
Avocet Dr DY10 . . . . .117 A2
Avonbank Cl B97 . . . . .158 C6
Avon Bsns Pk WS11. . . . . .4 C7
Avon Cl
Brierley Hill DY5 . . . . .61 B7
Bromsgrove B60 . . . . .150 F6
Bulkington CV12 . . . . .79 B6
Perton WV6 . . . . .23 E5
Walsall WS3 . . . . .15 A1
Avoncroft 8 WV4 . . . . .39 F4
Avoncroft Ho B37. . . . . .70 A2
Avoncroft Mus of Historic
Bldgs* B60. . . . . .150 C5
Avon Ct
Kenilworth CV8 . . . . .147 F5
Sutton Coldfield B73 . . . . . . .46 B5
Avondale Cl DY6. . . . . .60 E8
Avondale Rd
Birmingham B11 . . . . .87 D4

Avondale Rd *continued*
Brandon CV8 . . . . .135 F5
Coventry CV5 . . . . .133 A8
Royal Leamington Spa
  CV32 . . . . .157 C4
Wolverhampton WV6 . . . . . .24 F3
Avon Dr
Birmingham,Castle Bromwich
  B36 . . . . .69 F7
Birmingham,Moseley B13 . .87 B2
Willenhall WV13 . . . . .27 C2
Wythall B47 . . . . .124 E2
Avon Ho
2 Dudley,Russell's Hall
  DY1 . . . . .61 E8
3 Birmingham,Brandhall
  B68 . . . . .84 B8
Birmingham,Lee Bank B15 .86 D8
Coventry CV4 . . . . .132 C6
Dudley,Dibdale DY3 . . . . . .50 E3
Avonlea Rise CV32 . . . . .156 D2
Avon Lodge CV11 . . . . . . .73 A5
Avon Park Cvn Pk B92 . . .90 D1
Avon Rd
Burntwood WS7 . . . . .6 F5
Cannock WS11 . . . . .4 D8
Coventry CV4 . . . . .132 B6
Halesowen B63 . . . . .82 B5
Kenilworth CV8 . . . . .147 E3
Kidderminster DY11 . . . . .116 B3
Solihull B90 . . . . .106 D1
Stourbridge DY8 . . . . .80 F3
Walsall WS3 . . . . .14 E1
Whitnash CV31 . . . . .162 A3
Avon St
Birmingham B11 . . . . .87 C5
Coventry CV2 . . . . .114 B5
Warwick CV34 . . . . .161 A7
Avon Wlk LE10 . . . . .75 A8
Avro Way B35 . . . . .58 B2
Awbridge Rd DY2 . . . . . . .62 C3
Awefields Cres B67 . . . . . .64 E4
Awlmakers Gr WS3 . . . . . .28 D7
Awson St CV6 . . . . .113 F6
Axcess 10 Bsns Pk WS10 .41 E8
Axholme Rd CV2 . . . . . . .114 E4
Axletree Way WS10 . . . . . .42 B5
Axminster Cl CV11 . . . . . . .73 F5
Ayala Croft 8 B36 . . . . . . .68 E8
Aylesbury Cl B94 . . . . . . .143 C6
Aylesbury Cres B44 . . . . . .56 A8
Aylesbury Rd B94 . . . . . .143 D7
Aylesdene Ct CV5 . . . . . .132 F8
Aylesford Cl DY3 . . . . .39 C2
Aylesford Ct 7 CV31 . . . .162 A6
Aylesford Dr
Birmingham B37 . . . . .90 A7
Sutton Coldfield B74 . . . . . .31 E5
Aylesford Rd B21 . . . . .54 D1
Aylesford Sch & Language
  Coll CV34 . . . . .160 C4
Aylesford St
Coventry CV1 . . . . .113 E4
Royal Leamington Spa
  CV31 . . . . .162 A6
Aylesmore Cl
Birmingham B32 . . . . .84 C1
Solihull B92 . . . . .106 E8
Aynho Cl CV5 . . . . .112 A3
Aynsley Ct B90 . . . . .106 C2
Ayre Rd B24 . . . . .57 B4
Ayrshire Cl B36 . . . . .68 D8
Ayrton Cl WV6 . . . . .24 A4
Aysgarth Cl CV11 . . . . .74 A2
Azalea Cl
Codsall WV8 . . . . .10 B3
Hinckley LE10 . . . . .75 E5
Azalea Dr LE10 . . . . .75 E5
Azalea Gr B9 . . . . .67 F2
Azalea Wlk LE10 . . . . .75 E5
Aziz Isaac Cl B68 . . . . .64 C6

B

Babbacombe Rd CV3 . . . .133 D5
Babington Rd B21 . . . . . . .65 E7
Bablake Cl CV6 . . . . .112 F8
Bablake Croft B92 . . . . . . .89 A1
Bablake Jun Sch CV1 . . .165 A4
Bablake Sch CV1 . . . . . . .113 B4
Babors Field WV14 . . . . . .40 A3
Babworth Cl WV9 . . . . . . .11 A2
Baccabox La B47 . . . . . . .124 E7
Bacchus Rd B18 . . . . .65 F6
Bache St B70 . . . . .53 D1
Backcester La WS13 . . . . . .9 B8
Backcrofts 5 WS11 . . . . . . .1 E1
Backhouse La WV11 . . . . .26 C4
Back La
Aldridge WS9 . . . . .30 F8
Meriden CV7 . . . . .110 E5
Shenstone WS14 . . . . .17 E1
Solihull B90 . . . . .126 A5
Warwick CV34 . . . . .160 E6
Back Rd
Birmingham B38 . . . . .103 D4
Kingswinford DY6 . . . . .60 D7
Back St CV11 . . . . .73 C5
Badbury Cl B80 . . . . .159 D4
Badbury Gdns B80 . . . . . .159 D4
Baddesley Clinton* B93 .144 F4
Baddesley Cl CV31 . . . . . .162 C5
Baddesley Rd B92 . . . . . . .88 E2

Bader Rd
Perton WV6 . . . . .23 E3
Willenhall WS2 . . . . .27 F2
Bader Wlk B35 . . . . .57 F2
Badger Brook La B96 . . . .158 D1
Badger Cl
Cheswick Green B90 . . . . .126 D4
Huntington WS12 . . . . .1 D6
Redditch B98 . . . . .154 D3
Badger Ct WV10 . . . . .25 D4
Badger Dr WV10 . . . . .25 D4
Badger Rd CV3 . . . . .134 D8
Badgers Bank Rd B74 . . . .31 F5
Badgers Cl WS3 . . . . .15 A5
Badgers Croft B62 . . . . . . .83 B7
Badgers Dr DY3 . . . . .50 E5
Badgers The B45 . . . . . . .122 A2
Badger St DY9 . . . . .81 E6
Badgers Way
Birmingham B34 . . . . .69 A5
Cannock WS12 . . . . .2 D1
Badminton Cl DY1 . . . . . . .50 F3
Badon Covert B14 . . . . . .104 D2
Badsey Cl B31 . . . . .103 C4
Badsey Rd B69 . . . . .63 D5
Baggeridge Ctry Pk DY3 49 E6*
Baggeridge Ctry Pk Visitor
  Ctr* DY3 . . . . .49 F7
Baggott St WV2 . . . . .39 C7
Baginton Cl B91 . . . . .107 B5
Baginton Fields Sch CV3 134 B4
Baginton Rd
Birmingham B35 . . . . .58 B4
Coventry CV3 . . . . .133 C5
Bagley's Rd DY5 . . . . .81 D6
Bagley St DY9 . . . . .81 C6
Bagnall Cl B25 . . . . .88 D6
Bagnall Rd WV14 . . . . . . .40 C5
Bagnall St
Walsall WS3 . . . . .28 C6
Wednesbury DY4 . . . . .41 C1
West Bromwich B70 . . . . . .53 E2
West Bromwich,Harvills
  Hawthorn B70 . . . . .52 E7
Bagnall Wlk DY5 . . . . .61 D1
Bagnall Rd B13 . . . . .104 F7
Bagot Cl B8 . . . . .164 C4
Bagot Way CV34 . . . . . . .161 E3
Bagridge Cl WV3 . . . . .38 B8
Bagridge Rd WV3 . . . . . . .38 B8
Bagshawe Croft B23 . . . . .56 D7
Bagshaw Rd B33 . . . . .68 E3
Bailey Ave B77 . . . . .35 F5
Bailey Cl
Burntwood WS7 . . . . .6 D8
Bailey Ho DY6 . . . . .60 F7
Bailey Rd WV14 . . . . .40 B7
Baileys Ct B65 . . . . .63 B3
Bailey St
West Bromwich B70 . . . . . .53 A4
Wolverhampton WV10 . . . .163 D3
Bailye Cl WS13 . . . . .3 F1
Baines' La 1 LE10 . . . . . . .71 D1
Bains Cl WS13 . . . . .3 A6
Baird Ho DY6 . . . . .60 F7
Bakehouse La B93 . . . . . .145 B6
Bakeman Ho B26 . . . . . . .88 D6
Baker Ave
Royal Leamington Spa
  CV31 . . . . .161 F6
Wolverhampton WV14 . . . .39 F2
Baker Cl WS13 . . . . .3 F1
Baker House Gr B43 . . . . .54 D7
Baker Rd WV14 . . . . .40 E3
Baker's La
  1 Lichfield WS13 . . . . . . .9 B7
Aldridge WS9 . . . . .30 B6
Bakers La
Coventry CV5 . . . . .112 C2
Dorridge B93 . . . . .128 D1
Sutton Coldfield B73,B74 . .45 A5
Bakers Mews B93 . . . . . .145 B6
Baker St
Bedworth CV6 . . . . .96 B6
Birmingham,Handsworth
  B21 . . . . .65 F8
Birmingham,Small Heath
  B10 . . . . .87 C8
Birmingham,Sparkhill B11 . .87 C5
Burntwood WS7 . . . . .6 F6
Tipton DY4 . . . . .51 E4
West Bromwich B70 . . . . . .53 B3
Bakers Way WS12 . . . . . . .2 B5
Bakers Wlk 1 B77 . . . . . . .35 F6
Bakewell Cl
Coventry CV3 . . . . .134 F8
Walsall WS3 . . . . .14 A3
Balaams Wood Dr B31 . . .102 B1
Balaclava Rd B14 . . . . . . .104 E8
Balcaskie Cl B15 . . . . .85 F7
Balden Rd B32 . . . . .84 F7
Baldmoor Lake Rd B23 . . .56 F6
Bald's La DY9 . . . . .81 F5
Baldwin Cl B69 . . . . .52 D2
Baldwin Croft CV6 . . . . . . .96 B1
Baldwin Ho 1 WS11 . . . . . .2 C2
Baldwin Ho B19 . . . . .66 E6
Baldwin Rd
Birmingham B30 . . . . .104 A3
Kidderminster DY10 . . . . . .117 B7
Baldwins La B28 . . . . .105 F4
Baldwin St
Bilston WV14 . . . . .40 F4
Smethwick B66 . . . . .65 B6
Balfour Cl LE10 . . . . .75 E7

Balfour Cres WV6 . . . . . . .24 F4
Balfour Ct
2 Wolverhampton WV6 . . .24 F4
Sutton Coldfield B74 . . . . . .32 A3
Balfour Dr B69 . . . . .52 D2
Balfour Ho 2 B16 . . . . . . .65 F1
Balfour Rd DY6 . . . . .60 E8
Balfour St B12 . . . . .86 E6
Balfour 2 B79 . . . . .21 A4
Balham Gr B44 . . . . .45 A2
Balholm B62 . . . . .83 D5
Balking Cl WV14 . . . . .40 B3
Ballantine Cl CV6 . . . . . . .113 A6
Ballarat Wlk DY8 . . . . .80 F5
Ballard Cres DY2 . . . . .62 D5
Ballard Rd DY2 . . . . .62 D5
Ballard Wlk B37 . . . . .70 A6
Ball Fields B1 . . . . .52 D5
Ball Ho 6 WS3 . . . . .28 B8
Ballingham Cl CV4 . . . . . .112 A2
Balliol Bsns Pk WV9 . . . . .10 E3
Balliol Ho B37 . . . . .69 F2
Balliol Rd
Coventry CV2 . . . . .114 C4
Hinckley LE10 . . . . .75 F6
Ball La WV10 . . . . .11 C6
Ballot St B66 . . . . .65 B5
Balls Hill WS1 . . . . .28 F2
Balls St WS1 . . . . .28 F2
Balmain Cres WV11 . . . . . .12 B1
Balmoral Cl
Coventry CV2 . . . . .114 E6
Halesowen B62 . . . . .83 B7
Lichfield WS14 . . . . .9 D6
Tamworth B79 . . . . .21 B7
Walsall WS4 . . . . .29 D7
Balmoral Ct
Birmingham B31 . . . . .66 C3
Cannock WS11 . . . . .2 A3
Kidderminster DY10 . . . . . .117 A5
Nuneaton CV10 . . . . .72 E5
Balmoral Dr
Cannock WS12 . . . . .1 F7
Willenhall WV12 . . . . .27 C7
Wombourne WV5 . . . . .38 A1
Balmoral Ho WS3 . . . . . . .163 A1
Balmoral Rd
Birmingham B36 . . . . .70 A7
Birmingham,Erdington B23 .56 F5
Birmingham,Kitwell B32 . . .102 B7
Stourbridge DY8 . . . . .60 C2
Sutton Coldfield B74 . . . . . .31 F5
Wolverhampton WV3 . . . . .39 A5
Balmoral View DY1 . . . . . .50 E2
Balmoral Way
Rowley Regis B65 . . . . .63 D4
Royal Leamington Spa
  CV32 . . . . .157 C6
Balsall Common Prim Sch
  CV7 . . . . .130 B5
Balsall Heath Rd B12 . . . . .86 E7
Balsall St E CV7 . . . . .130 B5
Balsall St DY3,CV7 . . . . . .129 D7
Balthazar Cl CV34 . . . . . .161 E4
Baltic Cl WS11 . . . . .1 E2
Baltimore Rd B42 . . . . . . .55 A5
Balvenie Way DY1 . . . . . . .50 F3
Bamber Cl WV3 . . . . .38 E8
Bamburgh Gr CV32 . . . . .156 E3
Bamburgh B77 . . . . .35 C7
Bamford Cl WS3 . . . . .14 C3
Bamford Ho WS3 . . . . .14 C3
Bamford Rd
Walsall WS3 . . . . .14 C3
Wolverhampton WV3 . . . . .39 A8
Bampfylde Pl B42 . . . . . . .55 C2
Bampton Ave 4 WS7 . . . . .7 A8
Bamville Rd B8 . . . . .68 A5
Banbrook Cl B92 . . . . .107 D8
Banbury Cl DY3 . . . . .50 E6
Banbury Croft B37 . . . . . . .69 F2
Banbury Ho B33 . . . . .69 E2
Banbury Rd
Cannock WS11 . . . . .4 C8
Warwick CV34 . . . . .161 A3
Banbury St B5 . . . . .66 F2
Bancroft WV14 . . . . .51 B7
Bancroft B77 . . . . .21 F3
Bandywood Cres B44 . . . . .44 F3
Bandywood Rd B44 . . . . . .44 F3
Banfield Ave WS10 . . . . . . .41 C7
Banfield Rd WS10 . . . . . . .41 C4
Banford Ave B8 . . . . .68 A4
Banford Rd B8 . . . . .68 A4
Bangham Pit Rd B31 . . . . .102 E6
Bangley La
Drayton Bassett B78 . . . . . .33 E6
Mile Oak B78 . . . . .34 A8
Bangor Ho B37 . . . . .70 A6
Bangor Rd B9 . . . . .67 D2
Bank Cres WS7 . . . . .6 F5
Bank Croft CV31 . . . . .162 C5
Bankdale Rd B8 . . . . .68 B4
Bankes Rd B10 . . . . .67 F1
Bankfield Dr CV32 . . . . . .156 C1
Bankfield Rd
Bilston WV14 . . . . .40 D5
Tipton DY4 . . . . .52 C8
Bank Ho B37 . . . . .88 C3
Banklands Rd DY2 . . . . . . .62 E5
Bank Rd
Dudley,Gornalwood DY3 . . .50 C2
Dudley,Netherton DY2 . . . .62 D6
Banks Gn B97 . . . . .152 B2

Bankside
Birmingham,Great Barr
  B43 . . . . .54 E7
Birmingham,Moseley B13 . .87 D2
Bankside Cl CV3 . . . . .134 A6
Bankside Cres B74 . . . . . . .44 F7
Bankside Way WS9 . . . . . .16 B2
Banks Rd CV6 . . . . .113 A5
Banks St WV13 . . . . .27 A2
Bank St
Bilston WV14 . . . . .40 E3
Birmingham B14 . . . . .86 E1
Brierley Hill DY5 . . . . .61 D3
Cannock WS12 . . . . .2 E1
Cradley Heath B64 . . . . . . .62 C1
Stourbridge DY8 . . . . .81 F5
Tipton WV14 . . . . .51 C8
Walsall WS1 . . . . .28 F1
West Bromwich B71 . . . . . .53 D3
Wolverhampton WV10 . . . .25 E5
Bank The CV8 . . . . .149 C6
Bankwell St DY5 . . . . .61 D4
Banky Mdw LE10 . . . . .76 A7
Banner La CV4 . . . . .111 D2
Bannerlea Rd B37 . . . . . . .69 F5
Bannerley Rd B33 . . . . . . .69 C1
Banners Ct B73 . . . . .45 B3
Banners Gate Inf Sch B73 45 A4
Banners Gate Jun Sch
  B73 . . . . .45 B3
Banners Gate Rd B73 . . . .45 A3
Banners St B63 . . . . .82 D6
Banners Wlk B44 . . . . .45 B2
Bannington Ct WV12 . . . . .27 D4
Bannister Rd WS10 . . . . . .41 D2
Bannister St B64 . . . . .62 D2
Banquo App CV34 . . . . . .161 F3
Banstead Cl WV2 . . . . .39 E7
Bantam Gr CV6 . . . . .95 A3
Bantams Cl B33 . . . . .69 C2
Bant Mill Rd B60 . . . . .137 A1
Bantock Ave WV3 . . . . . . .38 F8
Bantock Ct WV3 . . . . .38 E8
Bantock Gdns WV3 . . . . . .24 E1
Bantock House Mus*
  WV3 . . . . .24 F1
Bantock Prim Sch WV3 . . .39 A8
Bantock Rd CV4 . . . . .111 E2
Bantocks The B70 . . . . . . .53 A6
Bantock Way 7 B17 . . . . . .85 D5
Banton Cl B23 . . . . .56 D8
Bantry Cl B26 . . . . .89 C4
Baptist End Rd DY2 . . . . . .62 C6
Baptist Wlk LE10 . . . . .71 D1
Barbara Rd B28 . . . . .105 E4
Barbara St B77 . . . . .21 A5
Barbel Dr WV10 . . . . .26 B4
Barber Inst of Fine Arts The*
  B15 . . . . .86 A3
Barberry Ho B38 . . . . .103 F1
Barbers La B91 . . . . .108 C6
Barbican Rise CV2 . . . . . .114 E2
Barbourne Cl B91 . . . . . . .127 B7
Barbridge Cl CV12 . . . . . . .79 C2
Barbridge Rd CV12 . . . . . .79 C3
Barbrook Dr DY5 . . . . .81 B7
Barcheston Rd
Birmingham B29 . . . . .85 A1
Dorridge B93 . . . . .128 A4
Barclay Ct WV3 . . . . .25 A2
Barclay Rd B67 . . . . .64 E1
Barcliff Ave B7 . . . . .67 A4
Barcroft Prim Sch WV13 . .27 C2
Barcroft WV13 . . . . .27 C2
Bardell Cl WS11 . . . . .3 E6
Bardenholme Gdns DY9 . . .81 D3
Bardfield Cl 1 B42 . . . . . . .55 A8
Bardley Dr B92 . . . . .113 C6
Bardon Dr B90 . . . . .106 D2
Bardsey Cl LE10 . . . . .71 B1
Barford Cl
Birmingham B16 . . . . .65 F3
Kenilworth CV8 . . . . .148 B3
Solihull B90 . . . . .106 D2
Barford St B5 . . . . .86 E8
Bargate Dr WV6 . . . . .25 A4
Bargery Rd WV11 . . . . .13 A3
Barham Cl B90 . . . . .127 A5
Barker Rd B74 . . . . .46 A7
Barker St
Birmingham B19 . . . . .66 B7
Oldbury B68 . . . . .64 C6
Bark Piece B32 . . . . .84 C3
Barlands Croft B34 . . . . . .69 D6
Barle Gr B36 . . . . .70 A7
Barleston Dr LE10 . . . . . . .75 A7
Barley Cl
Cannock WS12 . . . . .2 B5
Dudley DY3 . . . . .50 F7

Barley Cl *continued*
Sutton Coldfield WS9 . . . . .30 E2
Wolverhampton WV8 . . . . .10 E1
Barley Croft
Perton WV6 . . . . .23 D3
Stoke Heath B60 . . . . .150 E6
Barley Ct CV32 . . . . .156 F2
Barleyfield LE10 . . . . .71 C3
Barleyfield Ho 3 WS1 . . . .42 E8
Barleyfield Rise DY6 . . . . . .60 A8
Barleyfield Row WS1 . . . . .42 E8
Barley Lea Ho CV3 . . . . . .134 B8
Barley Lea The CV3 . . . . .134 C8
Barley Mow La B61 . . . . . .137 B8
Barlich Way B98 . . . . .154 A2
Barling Way CV10 . . . . . . .73 B1
Barlow Cl
Birmingham B45 . . . . .101 C2
Oldbury B68 . . . . .64 A3
Tamworth B77 . . . . .21 E4
Barlow Dr B70 . . . . .53 F1
Barlow Rd
Coventry CV2 . . . . .96 D2
Wednesbury WS10 . . . . . . .42 A5
Barlow's Rd B15 . . . . .85 E5
Barmouth Cl WV12 . . . . . .27 C6
Barnabas Rd B23 . . . . .56 F4
Barnaby Sq WV10 . . . . . . .11 F4
Barnack Ave CV3 . . . . . . .133 B5
Barnack Dr CV34 . . . . . . .155 E1
Barnacle La CV12 . . . . . . .79 C1
Barnard Cl
Birmingham B37 . . . . .70 D1
Royal Leamington Spa
  CV32 . . . . .157 C3
Barnard Pl WV2 . . . . .39 E6
Barnard Rd
Sutton Coldfield B75 . . . . . .46 E7
Wolverhampton WV11 . . . .12 F1
Barnard Way WS11 . . . . . .1 F1
Barn Ave DY3 . . . . .50 C7
Barnbridge B77 . . . . .21 C2
Barnbrook Rd B93 . . . . . .128 A7
Barn Cl
Birmingham B30 . . . . .104 B6
Coventry CV5 . . . . .112 C5
Cradley Heath B64 . . . . . . .82 E6
Dordon B78 . . . . .36 F6
Halesowen B63 . . . . .82 E2
Lichfield WS13 . . . . .3 B3
Stoke Heath B60 . . . . .150 E6
Stourbridge DY9 . . . . .81 C4
Whitnash CV31 . . . . .162 B3
Barn Croft
Birmingham B32 . . . . .84 E1
Great Wyrley WS6 . . . . .5 A3
Barncroft Rd B69 . . . . .63 B8
Barncroft St B70 . . . . .53 A8
Barne Cl CV11 . . . . .79 B7
Barnes Cl B37 . . . . .69 E2
Barnes Hill B29 . . . . .84 F2
Barnes Meadow WV14 . . . .51 B8
Barnesville Cl B10 . . . . . . .88 A8
Barnet Rd B23 . . . . .56 D5
Barnett Cl
Bilston WV14 . . . . .40 D4
Kingswinford DY6 . . . . .60 D4
Barnett Gn DY6 . . . . .60 D4
Barnett La DY6,DY8 . . . . . .60 D4
Barnett Rd WV13 . . . . .26 E1
Barnetts Cl DY10 . . . . . . .117 B6
Barnetts Gr DY10 . . . . . . .117 A6
Barnetts La
Brownhills WS8 . . . . .6 F1
Kidderminster DY10 . . . . . .117 A4
Barnett St
Stourbridge DY8 . . . . .60 D3
Tipton B69 . . . . .52 A2
Tipton DY4 . . . . .52 A4
Barney Cl DY4 . . . . .51 F3
Barn Farm Cl 4 WV14 . . . .41 A7
Barnfield Ave CV5 . . . . . . .112 B6
Barnfield Dr B92 . . . . .107 F6
Barnfield Gr B20 . . . . .54 E5
Barnfield Rd
Bromsgrove B61 . . . . .136 E1
Halesowen B62 . . . . .83 D7
Tipton DY4 . . . . .51 E6
Wolverhampton WV11 . . . .26 A2
Barnfield Trad Est DY4 . . .51 E7
Barnford Cl B10 . . . . .67 C1
Barnford Cres B68 . . . . . . .64 B3
Barnfordhill Cl B68 . . . . . .64 B4
Barn Gn WV3 . . . . .38 F7
Barn Ho B8 . . . . .68 D4
Barnhurst La WV8 . . . . . . .10 E2
Barn La
Birmingham,Handsworth
  B21 . . . . .65 E8
Birmingham,King's Heath
  B13 . . . . .105 A7
Solihull B92 . . . . .88 F3
Barn Leigh Dr CV4 . . . . . .131 D6
Barnmoor Rise B91 . . . . . .107 C7
Barn Owl Dr WS3 . . . . .14 F4
Barn Owl Pl DY10 . . . . . . .117 A2
Barnpark Covert 9 B14 .104 C2
Barn Piece B32 . . . . .84 B4
Barnsbury Ave B72 . . . . . .57 C6
Barns Cl WS9 . . . . .15 F4

Barns Croft B74 . . . . 31 B4
Barnsdale Cres B31 . . . . 102 E4
Barns La WS4 . . . . 29 D7
Barnsley Ct CV6 . . . . 113 D8
Barnsley Hall Dr B60 . . . . . 137 B6
Barnsley Hall Rd B61 . . . 137 A6
Barnsley Rd
 Birmingham B17 . . . . 65 A1
 Bromsgrove B61 . . . . 137 B4
Barnstaple Cl CV5 . . . . 111 F5
Barnstaple Rd B66 . . . . 65 B5
Barn St B5 . . . . 66 F2
Barnswood Cl
 Cannock WS11 . . . . 4 B8
 Halesowen B63 . . . . 82 C5
Barnt Green Junc B45 . . 138 D8
Barnt Green Rd B45 . . . . 122 C3
Barn Way WS12 . . . . 2 F4
Barnwood Ct B98 . . . . 154 D5
Barnwood Rd
 Birmingham B32 . . . . 84 F4
 Wolverhampton WV8 . . . . 10 E1
Baron Bsns Ctr DY9 . . . . 81 E5
Barons Cl B17 . . . . 85 B6
Barons Court Trad Est
 WS9 . . . . 15 E2
Baron's Croft CV3 . . . . 133 E7
Barons Croft CV10 . . . . 72 C4
Barons Ct B92 . . . . 89 C4
Baron's Field Rd CV3 . . . 133 E8
Barpool Rd CV10 . . . . 72 F4
Barrack Cl B75 . . . . 47 A6
Barrack La B63 . . . . 82 B6
Barracks Cl WS3 . . . . 28 E8
Barracks La
 Beausale CV35 . . . . 146 C2
 Brownhills WS9,WS14 . . . . . . 16 C8
 Walsall WS3 . . . . 28 E8
Barrack Pl WS3 . . . . 28 E8
Barrack St
 Birmingham B7 . . . . 67 A3
 Warwick CV34 . . . . 160 E7
 West Bromwich B70 . . . . 53 A8
Barracks Way CV1 . . . . 165 B2
Barra Croft B35 . . . . 58 B4
Barrar Cl DY8 . . . . 80 E8
Barras Ct CV2 . . . . 114 A4
Barras Gn CV2 . . . . 114 A4
Barras La CV1 . . . . 113 B3
Barratts Croft DY5 . . . . 50 C1
Barratts Rd B14 . . . . 104 E2
Barratts Rd B38 . . . . 104 A1
Barr Beacon Language Coll
 WS9 . . . . 44 B5
Barr Common Cl WS9 . . . . . 30 B3
Barr Common Rd WS9 . . . . 30 B3
Bar Rd CV3 . . . . 133 E8
Barrett Cl DY10 . . . . 117 B6
Barretts La CV7 . . . . 130 C6
Barrhill Cl B43 . . . . 43 E2
Barrie Ave DY10 . . . . 117 C7
Barrie Rd LE10 . . . . 71 D3
Barrington Cl
 Walsall WS5 . . . . 43 A3
 Wolverhampton WV10 . . . . . . 11 C1
Barrington Rd
 Birmingham B45 . . . . 121 E7
 Solihull B92 . . . . 88 F2
Barr Lakes La
 Birmingham WS9 . . . . 44 A7
 Walsall WS5,WS9 . . . . 43 F7
Barron Rd B31 . . . . 103 B3
Barrow Cl
 Brownhills WS9 . . . . 15 F4
 Coventry CV2 . . . . 115 B6
 Redditch B98 . . . . 154 F3
Barrowfield La CV8 . . . . 147 F4
Barrow Hill Rd DY5 . . . . 50 C1
Barrow Rd CV8 . . . . 147 F4
Barrows La B26 . . . . 89 A6
Barrows Rd B11 . . . . 87 C6
Barrow Wlk B5 . . . . 86 E7
Barrs Cres B64 . . . . 82 F8
Barr's Hill Sch & Com Coll
 CV1 . . . . 165 A4
Barrs Rd B64 . . . . 82 E8
Barrs St B68 . . . . 64 A4
Barr St
 Birmingham B19 . . . . 66 C5
 Dudley DY3 . . . . 50 C3
Barry Ho CV2 . . . . 96 D1
Barry Jackson Twr B6 . . . . . 66 F7
Barry Rd WS5 . . . . 43 C7
Barsham Cl B5 . . . . 86 C6
Barsham Dr DY5 . . . . 81 C8
Barston Cl CV6 . . . . 96 A2
Barston La
 Balsall Common CV7 . . . . . . 129 D8
 Barston B92 . . . . 109 C1
 Catherine de B B91 . . . . 108 B2
 Eastcote B92 . . . . 108 E4
 Solihull B91 . . . . 107 F2
Barston Rd B68 . . . . 84 B7
Bartestree Cl B98 . . . . 154 F1
Bartholomews La B61 . . . 136 F5
Bartholomew Ct CV3 . . . . 134 A6
Bartholomew Row B5 . . . 164 D3
Bartholomew St B5 . . . . . . 164 D2
Bartic Ave DY6 . . . . 60 F4
Bartleet Rd
 Redditch B98 . . . . 159 E8
 Smethwick B67 . . . . 64 D5

Bartlett Cl
 ⓑ Warwick CV34 . . . . 160 F7
 Coventry CV6 . . . . 95 E2
 Wednesbury DY4 . . . . 41 B1
Bartley Cl B92 . . . . 88 F2
Bartley Dr B31 . . . . 102 E8
Bartley Green Tech & Sports
 Coll B32 . . . . 84 C1
Bartley Ho B32 . . . . 102 D8
Bartley Mews B31 . . . . 102 E8
Bartley Woods B32 . . . . 84 B2
Barton Cres LE10 . . . . 162 C6
Barton Croft B28 . . . . 105 F4
Barton Dr B93 . . . . 128 A4
Barton Ind Est WV14 . . . . . . 40 E6
Barton La DY6 . . . . 60 C8
Barton Lodge Rd B28 . . . . 105 E4
Barton Rd
 Bedworth CV12 . . . . 78 A4
 Coventry CV6 . . . . 95 F2
 Nuneaton CV10 . . . . 73 C1
 Wolverhampton WV4 . . . . 39 F4
Bartons Bank B6 . . . . 66 F7
Barton's Mdw CV2 . . . . 114 B6
Barton St B70 . . . . 53 C2
Barwell Cl
 Dorridge B93 . . . . 127 E4
 Royal Leamington Spa
  CV32 . . . . 156 F3
Barwell Ct ❽ B9 . . . . 67 B2
Barwell La LE10 . . . . 71 E3
Barwell Rd B9 . . . . 67 B2
Barwick St B3 . . . . 164 B3
Bar Wlk WS9 . . . . 16 C1
Basalt Cl WS2 . . . . 28 A3
Basant Cl CV34 . . . . 161 A7
Bascote Cl B97 . . . . 153 B1
Baseley Way CV6 . . . . 95 D4
Basford Brook Dr CV6 . . . . . 95 F4
Basildon Wlk ❸ CV2 . . . . . 115 A7
Basil Gr B31 . . . . 102 E4
Basil Rd B31 . . . . 102 E4
Basin La B77 . . . . 21 D3
Baskerville Sch B17 . . . . 85 A5
Baskeyfield Cl WS14 . . . . 9 D7
Baslow Cl
 Birmingham B33 . . . . 68 A4
 Walsall WS3 . . . . 14 C3
Baslow Rd WS3 . . . . 14 B3
Basons La B68 . . . . 64 D5
Bassano Rd ❶ B65 . . . . 63 C1
Bassenthwaite Ct DY6 . . . . . 60 D6
Bassett Cl
 Sutton Coldfield B76 . . . . 46 E4
 Willenhall WV12 . . . . 27 D4
 Wolverhampton WV4 . . . . 38 C6
Bassett Croft B10 . . . . 87 B8
Bassett Rd
 Coventry CV6 . . . . 113 A5
 Stourbridge B63 . . . . 82 A6
 Wednesbury WS10 . . . . 42 D3
Bassetts Gr B37 . . . . 69 E5
Bassett St WS2 . . . . 28 C2
Bassnage Rd B63 . . . . 82 E2
Batchcroft
 Bilston WV14 . . . . 40 D5
 Darlaston WS10 . . . . 41 D8
Batchelor Cl B80 . . . . 80 F8
Batchley Fst Sch B97 . . . . . 153 B4
Batchley Rd B97 . . . . 153 C4
Bateman Dr B73 . . . . 46 B1
Bateman Rd B46 . . . . 59 F1
Bateman's Acre S ❶
 CV6 . . . . 113 A4
Batemans La B47 . . . . 124 E5
Bates Cl B76 . . . . 58 B8
Bates Gr WS10 . . . . 26 A4
Bates Hill B97 . . . . 153 D4
Bates La B94 . . . . 141 F1
Bates Rd CV5 . . . . 132 E8
Bate St
 ❸ Walsall WS2 . . . . 28 E3
 Wolverhampton WV4 . . . . 40 A3
Batham Rd DY10 . . . . 117 A8
Bath Ave WV1 . . . . 163 A4
Bath Ct ❹ B29 . . . . 103 B7
Batheaston Cl B38 . . . . 123 D7
Bath Mdw B63 . . . . 82 E5
Bath Mews DY8 . . . . 80 F5
Bath Pas B5 . . . . 164 C1
Bath Pl ❽ CV31 . . . . 161 F7
Bath Rd
 Brierley Hill DY5 . . . . 62 A2
 Cannock WS11 . . . . 1 E5
 Nuneaton CV11 . . . . 73 B4
 Stourbridge DY8 . . . . 80 F5
 Tipton DY4 . . . . 52 A5
 Walsall WS1 . . . . 42 E8
 Wolverhampton WV1 . . . . . . 163 A3
Bath Row
 Birmingham B15 . . . . 66 C1
 Oldbury B69 . . . . 63 D8
Bath St
 Bilston WV14 . . . . 40 D4
 Birmingham B4 . . . . 164 C4
 Coventry CV1 . . . . 165 C4
 Dudley DY2 . . . . 62 C8
 Royal Leamington Spa
  CV31 . . . . 161 F7
 Sedgley DY3 . . . . 39 E1
 Walsall WS1 . . . . 42 E8
 Willenhall WV13 . . . . 27 B1
 Wolverhampton WV1 . . . . . . 163 D2
Bathurst Rd CV6 . . . . 113 A6
Bathway Rd CV3 . . . . 133 A4
Bath Wlk B12 . . . . 86 E5
Bath Wlk Ind Est B12 . . . . . . 86 E5

Batmans Hill Rd WV14,
 DY4 . . . . 40 E1
Batsford Cl B98 . . . . 159 B5
Batsford Rd CV6 . . . . 112 F4
Batson Rise DY5 . . . . 81 A8
Battalion Ct CV6 . . . . 95 A1
Battenhall Rd B17 . . . . 85 A5
Battens Cl B98 . . . . 153 F3
Battens Dr B98 . . . . 154 D3
Battery Way B11 . . . . 87 E4
Battledown Cl LE10 . . . . 71 B2
Battlefield Hill WV5 . . . . 49 B7
Battlefield La WV5 . . . . 49 B6
Battlefield Terr WV5 . . . . 49 B6
Battling Brook Com Prim Sch
 LE10 . . . . 71 B3
Battling Brook Sh Ctr
 LE10 . . . . 71 B1
Baughan Ho B24 . . . . 57 D3
Baulk La CV7 . . . . 110 D1
Bavaro Gdns DY5 . . . . 62 A2
Baverstock Foundation Sch
 & Specialist Sports Coll
 B14 . . . . 104 E2
Baverstock Rd B14 . . . . 104 E2
Baxter Ave DY10 . . . . 116 F7
Baxter Cl CV4 . . . . 112 A2
Baxter Coll DY11 . . . . 116 B6
Baxter Ct
 ❿ Royal Leamington Spa
  CV31 . . . . 162 A7
 Birmingham B13 . . . . 86 F2
Baxter Gdns DY10 . . . . 116 F7
Baxterley Gn
 Solihull B91 . . . . 106 D4
 Sutton Coldfield B76 . . . . 46 F1
Baxters Gn B90 . . . . 126 B8
Baxters Rd B90 . . . . 126 C8
Bay Ave WV14 . . . . 40 F4
Bayer St WV14 . . . . 51 C8
Bayford Ave
 Birmingham,Coft Common
  B31 . . . . 122 E6
 Birmingham,Sheldon B26 . . . 89 C4
Bayley Cres WS10 . . . . 41 C8
Bayley La CV1 . . . . 165 C2
Bayleys La DY4 . . . . 52 C8
Bayley Twr ❸ B36 . . . . 68 E8
Baylie Ct DY8 . . . . 80 F5
Baylie St DY8 . . . . 80 F4
Baylis Ave WV11 . . . . 26 F8
Bayliss Ave
 Coventry CV6 . . . . 96 A4
 Wolverhampton WV4 . . . . 40 A3
Bayliss Cl
 Bilston WV14 . . . . 40 C7
 Birmingham B31 . . . . 103 B5
Bayliss Ct WV3 . . . . 24 E2
Baynton Rd WV12 . . . . 27 D8
Bayston Ave WV3 . . . . 38 E8
Bayston Rd B14 . . . . 104 E3
Bayswater Rd
 Birmingham B20 . . . . 55 D1
 Dudley DY3 . . . . 50 D2
Bayton Rd CV7 . . . . 96 B8
Bayton Road Ind Est CV7 . . 96 B8
Bayton Way CV7 . . . . 96 C7
Bay Tree Cl
 Birmingham B38 . . . . 123 D8
 Coventry CV2 . . . . 96 D1
Baytree Cl WS3 . . . . 14 A2
Baytree Rd WS3 . . . . 14 A2
Baywell Cl B90 . . . . 127 A7
Bazzard Rd CV11 . . . . 79 F6

Beach Ave
 Birmingham B12 . . . . 87 B5
 Wolverhampton WV4,WV14 . . 40 A2
Beach Brook Cl B11 . . . . 87 B5
Beachburn Way B20 . . . . 55 B3
Beach Cl B31 . . . . 103 C1
Beachcroft Rd DY6 . . . . 49 C1
Beach Dr B63 . . . . 83 A5
Beach Rd
 Bilston WV14 . . . . 40 D7
 Birmingham B11 . . . . 87 B5
Beach St B63 . . . . 83 A5
Beach Trad Ctr B12 . . . . 87 B5
Beachwood Ave DY6 . . . . 49 C1
Beacon Cl
 Birmingham,Great Barr
  B43 . . . . 43 F1
 Birmingham,Rubery B45 . . . 122 A6
 Smethwick B66 . . . . 65 A7
Beacon Ct ❷ B43 . . . . 43 F1
Beacon Ctr for the Blind
 WV4 . . . . 39 D4
Beacon Ct B74 . . . . 44 F8
Beacon Dr WS1 . . . . 43 A8
Beaconfields ❶ WS13 . . . . . . 9 A8
Beacon Gdns WS13 . . . . 3 A1
Beacon Hill
 Birmingham,Aston B6 . . . . . . 66 E8
 Birmingham B45 . . . . 121 F5
 Beacon Hts WS9 . . . . 44 B6
Beacon La
 Birmingham B60,B45 . . . . . . 121 E4
 Sedgley DY3 . . . . 39 E1
Beacon Mews
 ❶ Birmingham B43 . . . . 43 F1
 ❺ Lichfield WS13 . . . . 9 A8
Beacon Pas DY3 . . . . 50 D2
Beacon Prim Sch WV12 . . . . 27 D8
Beacon Rd
 Aldridge WS9 . . . . 30 B1
 Birmingham,Pheasey WS9,
  B43 . . . . 44 C6

Beacon Rd continued
 ❹ Coventry CV6 . . . . 95 D3
 Sutton Coldfield,Banners Gate
  B44 . . . . 45 A3
 Sutton Coldfield,Boldmere
  B73 . . . . 46 A1
 Walsall WS5 . . . . 43 D5
 Willenhall WV12 . . . . 27 C8
Beacon Rise
 Aldridge WS9 . . . . 30 B3
 Sedgley DY3 . . . . 39 E1
 Stourbridge DY9 . . . . 81 D4
Beaconsfield Ave WV4 . . . . . 39 D5
Beaconsfield Cres ❸ B12 . 86 E5
Beaconsfield Ct
 Nuneaton CV11 . . . . 73 D5
 Walsall WS1 . . . . 43 B8
Beaconsfield Dr WV4 . . . . . . 39 D6
Beaconsfield Rd
 Birmingham B12 . . . . 86 E5
 Coventry CV2 . . . . 114 B2
 Sutton Coldfield B74 . . . . 46 B7
Beaconsfield St
 Royal Leamington Spa
  CV31 . . . . 162 B7
 West Bromwich B71 . . . . 53 C5
Beaconside Prim Sch
 B45 . . . . 121 E6
Beacon St
 Lichfield WS13 . . . . 9 A8
 Walsall WS1 . . . . 29 A1
 Wolverhampton WV14 . . . . . . 39 F1
Beacon Trad Est WS9 . . . . . . 30 A6
Beacon View B45 . . . . 122 A6
Beacon View Dr B74 . . . . 44 F5
Beaconview Ho ❹ B71 . . . . . 42 F1
Beacon View Rd B71 . . . . 42 F2
Beacon View WS2 . . . . 27 F2
Beacon Way
 Brownhills WS9 . . . . 16 A3
 Cannock WS12 . . . . 2 F3
Beake Ave CV6 . . . . 113 B7
Beakes Rd B67 . . . . 64 F3
Beaks Farm Gdns B16 . . . . . 65 D2
Beaks Hill Rd B38 . . . . 103 E2
Beak St B1 . . . . 164 B2
Beale Cl B35 . . . . 58 A2
Beale Ho B16 . . . . 65 F1
Beales St B6 . . . . 67 B8
Beale St DY8 . . . . 80 F5
Bealeys Ave WV11 . . . . 26 C8
Bealeys Cl WS3 . . . . 14 A3
Bealeys Ct WV11 . . . . 26 C8
Bealeys La WS3 . . . . 14 A2
Beamans Cl B92 . . . . 89 A4
Beaminster Rd B91 . . . . 107 A4
Beamish Cl CV2 . . . . 115 A6
Bean Croft B32 . . . . 84 C2
Beanfield Ave CV3 . . . . 132 F4
Bean Rd
 Dudley,Dixon's Green DY2 . . . 62 D8
 Dudley,Swan Village DY4 . . . 51 C6
Bean Road Ind Est DY4 . . . . 51 C6
Beardmore Rd B72 . . . . 57 C8
Bear Hill B48 . . . . 139 B5
Bear Hill Dr B48 . . . . 139 B6
Bearing Dr WV11 . . . . 26 E4
Bearley Croft B90 . . . . 126 C8
Bearmore Rd B64 . . . . 62 E1
Bearnett Dr WV4 . . . . 38 B2
Bearnett La WV4 . . . . 38 B2
Bearsdon Cres LE10 . . . . 71 B2
Bearwood Ho B66 . . . . 65 A4
Bearwood Prim Sch B66 . . . 65 A3
Bearwood Rd B66 . . . . 65 A1
Beasley Gr B43 . . . . 44 B1
Beaton Cl WV13 . . . . 26 E2
Beaton Rd B74 . . . . 31 F6
Beatrice St WS3 . . . . 28 C6
Beatrice Wlk B69 . . . . 52 A2
Beattie Cl LE10 . . . . 71 D3
Beatty Ho DY4 . . . . 52 B8
Beaty's Gdns CV32 . . . . 157 A4
Beauchamp Ave
 Birmingham B20 . . . . 54 F5
 Kidderminster DY11 . . . . 116 D3
 Royal Leamington Spa
  CV32 . . . . 156 F1
Beauchamp Cl
 ❶ Birmingham B37 . . . . 70 B2
 Sutton Coldfield B76 . . . . 58 B7
Beauchamp Ct
 ❶ Royal Leamington Spa
  CV32 . . . . 156 F1
 Birmingham B13 . . . . 116 D3
Beauchamp Gdns CV34 . . . 161 B6
Beauchamp Hill CV32 . . . . 156 E1
Beauchamp Ind Pk B77 . . . 35 D8
Beauchamp Rd
 Birmingham B13 . . . . 105 C5
 Kenilworth CV8 . . . . 147 F2
 Royal Leamington Spa
  CV32 . . . . 156 F1
 Solihull B91 . . . . 107 B5
 Tamworth B77 . . . . 35 F5
 Warwick CV34 . . . . 161 B8
Beau Ct WS11 . . . . 1 A6
Beaudesert Cl B47 . . . . 125 A6
Beaudesert Rd
 Birmingham B20 . . . . 66 B8
 Coventry CV5 . . . . 113 A1
 Hollywood B47 . . . . 125 A6
Beaufell Cl CV34 . . . . 155 E1

Beaufort Ave
 Birmingham B34 . . . . 68 D5
 Kidderminster DY11 . . . . 116 A7
 Royal Leamington Spa
  CV32 . . . . 157 C5
Beaufort Cl LE10 . . . . 75 E4
Beaufort Dr CV3 . . . . 134 F7
Beaufort Pk B8 . . . . 68 C5
Beaufort Rd
 Birmingham B17 . . . . 85 B4
 Birmingham B23 . . . . 56 E2
 Birmingham,Lanywood B16 . 66 A1
Beaufort Sch B34 . . . . 68 D5
Beaufort St B98 . . . . 153 E3
Beaufort Way WS9 . . . . 30 B4
Beaulieu Ave DY6 . . . . 60 F4
Beaulieu Cl DY11 . . . . 116 A7
Beaulieu Pk CV31 . . . . 162 D6
Beaumaris Cl
 Coventry CV5 . . . . 111 F5
 Dudley DY1 . . . . 50 F4
Beaumont Ave LE10 . . . . 75 A7
Beaumont Cl
 Great Wyrley WS6 . . . . 4 F2
 Tipton DY4 . . . . 52 A8
Beaumont Cres CV6 . . . . . . 113 A4
Beaumont Dr
 ❸ Royal Leamington Spa
  CV31 . . . . 162 A6
 ❾ Coventry CV6 . . . . 113 A4
Beaumont Dr
 Birmingham B17 . . . . 85 B4
 Brierley Hill DY5 . . . . 81 B7
Beaumont Gdns B18 . . . . 65 F6
Beaumont Gn B91 . . . . 106 C5
Beaumont Lawns B60 . . . . . 121 D1
Beaumont Pk B30 . . . . 103 F4
Beaumont Pl CV11 . . . . 73 A4
Beaumont Rd
 Birmingham B30 . . . . 103 F6
 Great Wyrley WS6 . . . . 4 F2
 Halesowen B62 . . . . 83 E8
 Keresley CV7 . . . . 95 A6
 Nuneaton CV11 . . . . 73 A4
 Wednesbury WS10 . . . . 41 F4
 Beaumont Way WS14 . . . . . . 6 E4
Beaurevoir Way CV34 . . . . 161 A8
Beausale Croft CV5 . . . . . . 112 A3
Beausale Dr B93 . . . . 128 C2
Beauty Bank B64 . . . . 83 A8
Beauty Bank Cres DY8 . . . . . 80 F6
Beauty Bank Prim Sch
 DY8 . . . . 80 F6
Beaver Cl WV11 . . . . 26 F5
Beaver Pk B63 . . . . 82 F6
Bebington Cl WV8 . . . . 24 F8
Beccles Dr WV13 . . . . 40 F8
Beche Way CV5 . . . . 112 B5
Beckbury Ave WV4 . . . . 38 C5
Beckbury Rd
 Birmingham B29 . . . . 85 A1
 Coventry CV2 . . . . 114 F6
Beck Cl B66 . . . . 65 A4
Beckenham Ave B44 . . . . 45 B1
Beckensall Cl DY1 . . . . 51 B1
Becket Cl B74 . . . . 31 F6
Beckett St B98 . . . . 153 F5
Beckett St WV14 . . . . 40 F6
Beckfield Cl
 Birmingham B14 . . . . 104 E2
 Walsall WS4 . . . . 29 C8
Beckfoot Dr CV2 . . . . 96 F1
Beckford Croft B93 . . . . 127 F3
Beckford Ct B23 . . . . 56 C2
Beckman Rd DY9 . . . . 81 C2
Beckminster Rd WV3 . . . . . . 38 F7
Becks The B48 . . . . 139 A7
Beconsfield Ct B93 . . . . 127 F2
Becton Gr B42 . . . . 55 D7
Bedale Ave LE10 . . . . 71 F2
Bedcote Pl DY8 . . . . 81 B5
Beddoe Cl DY4 . . . . 52 D5
Beddow Ave WV14 . . . . 51 C7
Beddows Rd WS3 . . . . 28 E5
Bede Arc ❷ CV12 . . . . 78 B3
Bede Rd
 Bedworth CV12 . . . . 78 A4
 Coventry CV6 . . . . 113 B6
 Nuneaton CV10 . . . . 72 D3
Bedford Cl LE10 . . . . 71 E3
Bedford Dr B75 . . . . 46 F5
Bedford Ho
 ❻ Wolverhampton WV3 . . . . 25 C4
 ❼ Birmingham,Erdington
  B24 . . . . 56 F4
Bedford Ho B36 . . . . 70 B6
Bedford Pl
 ❺ Royal Leamington Spa
  CV32 . . . . 161 F8
 Cannock WS12 . . . . 2 A4
Bedford Rd
 Birmingham B12 . . . . 87 A4
 Sutton Coldfield B75 . . . . 46 E7
 West Bromwich B71 . . . . 53 A7
Bedford St
 Coventry CV1 . . . . 113 A2
 Royal Leamington Spa
  CV32 . . . . 161 F8
 Tipton DY4 . . . . 52 B5
 Wolverhampton WV1 . . . . . . 163 D4
Bedford Terr ❹ B19 . . . . 66 D8
Bedlam La CV6 . . . . 95 E2
Bedlam Wood Rd B31 . . . . 102 C1
Bedworth Cl CV12 . . . . 79 B2
Bedworth Croft DY4 . . . . 52 B4
Bedworth Gr B9 . . . . 68 C3
Bedworth La CV12 . . . . 77 D4

Bedworth Rd
Bedworth CV12 78 F2
Bulkington CV12 79 A2
Coventry CV6,CV7 96 A5
Bedworth Sta CV12 78 C2
Beebee Rd WS10 41 F6
Beecham Bsns Pk WS9 30 A8
Beecham Cl WS9 30 A8
Beech Ave
5 Birmingham,Showell Green B12 87 A5
Birmingham B32 84 D7
Birmingham,Chelmsley Wood B37 70 B1
Halesowen B62 83 C8
Tamworth B77 21 E3
Beech Cl CV10 72 A8
Beech Cliffe CV34 160 F8
Beech Cl
Rowington Green CV35 145 A1
Sedgley DY3 39 E1
Sutton Coldfield B75 32 A4
Tamworth B79 21 A8
Wolverhampton WV10 25 B8
Beech Cres
Burntwood WS7 6 F6
Tipton DY4 52 C8
Wednesbury WS10 41 F5
Beechcroft Ave B28 106 A6
Beechcroft
Bedworth CV12 77 F1
Birmingham B15 86 A7
Beechcroft Cres B74 30 D1
Beechcroft Ct B74 32 A1
Beechcroft Dr B61 137 B4
Beechcroft Est B63 82 C6
Beechcroft Pl WV10 25 C6
Beechcroft Rd
Birmingham B36 69 B8
Cradley Heath B64 62 F1
Kidderminster DY11 116 A8
Beech Ct
Birmingham,Bournville B30 103 E4
Birmingham,Great Barr B43 43 D1
Birmingham,Longbridge B45 122 D7
Birmingham,Short Heath B73 56 F8
Cannock WS12 2 B7
Great Wyrley WS6 5 A4
Oldbury B66 64 C8
Royal Leamington Spa CV34 161 E2
Beechdale Ave B44 44 E2
Beechdale B68 84 B7
Beechdale Prim Sch WS2 28 C5
Beechdale Rd WS3 27 F8
Beech Dene Gr B23 56 E5
Beech Dr CV8 148 B5
Beechen Gr WS7 6 F8
Beecher Pl B63 82 D5
Beecher Rd E B63 82 D5
Beecher Rd B63 82 D5
Beecher's Keep CV8 135 F5
Beecher St B63 82 C5
Beeches Ave B27 88 C4
Beeches Cl
Birmingham B45 121 D8
Kingswinford DY6 60 D5
Beeches Ct B45 122 B7
Beeches Dr B24 57 C5
Beeches Farm Dr B31 123 A7
Beeches Mews DY9 98 F4
Beeches Pl WS3 28 D6
Beeches Rd
Birmingham B42 55 C7
Kidderminster DY11 116 C8
Oldbury B68 64 C3
Rowley Regis B65 63 C1
Walsall WS3 28 D6
West Bromwich B70 53 E3
Beeches The
Bedworth CV12 77 E2
Birmingham B15 86 C8
Sutton Coldfield B74 31 D4
Sutton Coldfield,Wylde Green B73 46 B1
Upton Warren B61 150 A4
West Bromwich B70 53 E2
Wolverhampton,Newbridge WV1 25 A3
Wolverhampton WV11 26 B5
Beeches View Ave B63 82 C4
Beeches Way B31 123 A7
Beeches Wlk B73 46 B3
Beechey Cl B43 44 D5
Beech Farm Croft B31 103 A3
Beechfield Ave 1 B11 87 B6
Beechfield Cl B62 83 C8
Beechfield Dr DY11 116 C8
Beechfield Gr WV14 51 B7
Beechfield Rd
Birmingham B11 87 B6
Smethwick B67 64 F4
Beechfield Rise WS14 9 D8
Beech Gate B74 31 C5
Beech Gdns WS14 9 C6
Beechglade B20 54 F4
Beech Gn DY1 51 A5
Beech Gr
Birmingham B14 105 A5
Huntington WS12 1 D8
Warwick CV34 156 B1
Beech Hill Ct B72 57 C8
Beech Hill Ho B32 102 C8
Beech Hill Rd B72 57 C8
Beech Ho
6 Warwick CV34 161 D8
Redditch B98 158 F8
Solihull B91 106 F2
Sutton Coldfield B74 31 B5
Beechhouse La WV5 37 A1
Beech Hurst 1 B38 123 E8
Beech Hurst Gdns WV5 37 A2
Beech Mews B64 62 E2
Beechmore Rd B26 89 A5
Beechmount Dr B23 57 A6
Beechnut Cl
Coventry CV4 111 D2
Solihull B91 107 D5
Beechnut La B91 107 E4
Beech Park Dr B45 138 C8
Beech Pine Cl WS12 2 A8
Beech Rd
Birmingham,Bournville B30 103 E6
Birmingham,Erdington B23 56 F8
Bromsgrove B61 136 F4
Coventry CV6 113 B5
Dudley DY1 51 C4
Hollywood B47 125 B6
Kingswinford DY6 60 E5
Oldbury B69 63 A8
Stourbridge DY8 80 F3
Tamworth B79 21 A8
Wednesbury WS10 41 F5
Willenhall WV13 26 E2
Wolverhampton WV10 25 B8
Beech Tree Ave
Coventry CV4 112 B2
Wolverhampton WV11 26 C8
Beech Tree Cl
Kingswinford DY6 60 E8
Redditch B97 153 B4
Beech Tree La WS11 4 D8
Beech Tree Rd WS9 15 F3
Beech Way B66 65 B5
Beech Wlk B38 123 F8
Beechwood Ave
Coventry CV5 132 F8
Hinckley LE10 75 D3
Wolverhampton WV11 26 B8
Beechwood B20 54 E3
Beechwood Bsns Pk WS11 2 B3
Beechwood Cl
Cheswick Green B90 126 D4
Walsall WS3 14 B3
Beechwood Cres B77 21 F5
Beechwood Croft
Kenilworth CV8 147 F2
Sutton Coldfield B74 31 D5
Beechwood Ct
1 Birmingham B30 104 C3
Coventry CV5 132 F8
Cradley Heath B64 83 A7
Wolverhampton WV6 24 C3
Beechwood Dr WV6 24 A2
Beechwood Ho 10 WV3 25 A2
Beechwood Park Rd B91 106 E5
Beechwood Rd
Bedworth CV12 78 D4
Birmingham B67 84 F8
Birmingham,Great Barr B43 43 F2
Birmingham,King's Heath B14 104 F5
Dudley DY2 51 E1
Nuneaton CV10 72 D6
West Bromwich B70 53 B3
Beecroft Ave WS13 3 B1
Beecroft Ct WS11 1 E2
Beecroft Hill Sch WS11 1 E2
Beecroft Rd WS11 1 E1
Beehive Cl B61 121 A1
Beehive Hill CV8 147 E7
Beehive La B76 59 C6
Beehive Wlk 4 DY4 51 E5
Beekes Croft B78 35 A8
Bee La WV10 11 D3
Beeston Cl
Birmingham B6 67 A7
Brierley Hill DY5 81 D8
Coventry CV3 134 F8
Beeton Rd B18 65 E6
Beet St B65 63 C1
Beever Rd DY4 52 D7
Beggars Bush La WV5 49 B5
Beggars Bush B73 45 D2
Begonia Cl LE10 75 E5
Begonia Dr LE10 75 E5
Beighton Cl B74 31 F6
Beilby Rd B30 104 B5
Belbroughton CE Prim Sch DY9 119 E6
Belbroughton Cl B98 153 F2
Belbroughton Rd
Blakedown DY10 98 D1
Halesowen B63 82 F2
Holy Cross DY9 99 E2
Stourbridge DY8 80 E3
Belchers La B8,B9 68 A3
Beldray Rd WV14 40 E6
Belfont Trad Est B62 83 C4
Belfry Cl
Hinckley LE10 75 D4
Walsall WS3 14 A3
Belfry Dr DY8 80 E6
Belfry The WV6 23 D4
Belgrade Rd WV10 11 B1
Belgrade Theatre CV1 165 B3
Belgrave Ct DY6 60 F4
Belgrave High Sch B77 21 E1
Belgrave Middleway B5, B12 86 E7
Belgrave Rd
Birmingham B12 86 F6
Coventry CV2 114 E4
Halesowen B62 83 D8
Tamworth B77 35 E8
Belgrave Sq CV2 114 E4
Belgrave Terr B21 66 A7
Belgrave Wlk WS2 28 B3
Belgravia Cl B5 86 E7
Belgravia Ct B37 70 A5
Belgrove Cl B15 85 E6
Belgrove Ho WS11 1 D1
Belinda Cl WV13 26 F3
Bellairs Ave CV12 77 E1
Bellamy Cl B90 106 D1
Bellamy Farm Rd B90 106 D1
Bellamy La WV11 26 C7
Bell Barn Rd B15 86 C8
Bell Barn Sh Ctr 8 B15 86 C8
Bellbrooke Cl CV6 96 B1
Bell Cl
Birmingham B36 70 B6
Birmingham,Bordesley Green B9 67 E3
Darlaston WS10 41 D7
Bellcroft 3 B16 66 B2
Bell Ct CV32 156 F2
Bell Dr
Ash Green CV7 95 E7
Birmingham B9 67 E3
Cannock WS12 2 C7
Walsall WS5 43 A5
Belle Cotts B94 143 D5
Bellefield Ave 10 B18 65 E4
Bellefield Rd B18 65 E4
Belle Isle DY5 61 C3
Bellemere Rd B92 109 B6
Bellencroft Gdns WV3 38 C7
Bell End B65 63 C3
Belle Orch DY11 116 B5
Belle Vale B63 82 E5
Belle Vue Ave B16 65 D4
Bellevue B5 86 D7
Belle Vue Cl B61 121 C1
Belle Vue Ct DY8 60 D2
Belle Vue Dr B62 83 E6
Bellevue WV14 40 E2
Belle Vue Gdns B65 63 C3
Belle Vue CV10 72 E3
Belle Vue Prim Sch DY8 60 C3
Bellevue Rd
Bilston WV14 41 A2
Birmingham B26 89 B7
Belle Vue Rd DY5 62 A1
Belle Vue DY8 60 D2
Bellevue St WV14 39 F2
Belle Vue Terr B92 109 A6
Belle Wlk B13 87 B3
Bellfield B31 102 F4
Bellfield Ho B14 104 D1
Bellfield Jun & Inf Schs B31 102 F4
Bellfield B94 142 A2
Bellflower Cl WV10 12 A7
Bellflower Dr 1 WS5 42 F3
Bell Fold B68 64 C6
Bell Green La B38 124 B5
Bell Green Rd CV6 114 A8
Bell Heather Rd WS8 15 D6
Bell Heath Way B32 84 B2
Bell Hill
3 Birmingham B31 103 A4
Birmingham B31 103 A5
Bell Holloway B31 102 F5
Bellingham B77 22 D1
Bellington Croft 5 B90 127 A6
Bellis St B16 65 F1
Bell La
Birmingham,Kitt's Green B33 69 E1
Birmingham,Northfield B31 103 A4
Studley B80 159 E4
Walsall,Wallington Heath WS3 14 B1
Walsall,Yew Tree WS5 43 A5
Bellman Cl WS10 41 D7
Bell Mdw DY9 99 B8
Bell Meadow Way B14 104 E1
Bell Mead B80 159 E4
Bell Pl WV2 163 B1
Bell Rd
Dudley DY2 62 C5
Trysull WV5 37 D1
Walsall WS5 43 D6
Bell St S DY5 61 D2
Bells Farm Cl B14 104 C2
Bells Farm Jun & Inf Sch B14 104 C2
Bell Sh Ctr The B31 103 A4
Bellsize Cl WS11 5 F5
Bells La
Birmingham B14 104 D2
Stourbridge DY8 60 D2
Bells Moor Rd B70 53 A6
Bell St
Bilston WV14 40 C6
Brierley Hill,Barrow Hill DY5 61 D7
Brierley Hill,Silver End DY5 61 D2
Darlaston WS10 41 D7
Dudley WV14 40 C2
Stourbridge DY8 81 A5
Tipton DY4 51 E5
West Bromwich B70 53 D2
Wolverhampton WV1 163 B2
Bell Tower Mews CV32 156 F3
Bellview Way CV6 96 B1
Bell Vue Rd B65 63 C2
Bellwood Rd B31 102 F4
Belmont Ave WS11 1 C2
Belmont Cl
Aldridge WS9 30 A7
Great Wyrley WS11 5 A4
Redditch B97 153 B1
Tipton DY4 51 F6
Belmont Covert B31 103 B6
Belmont Cres B31 103 B6
Belmont Ct
Royal Leamington Spa CV32 157 A4
Sutton Coldfield B72 46 B4
Belmont Dr CV32 157 A4
Belmont Gdns WV14 41 A4
Belmont Mews CV8 147 F4
Belmont Pas B4 67 A3
Belmont Rd
Birmingham,Handsworth B21 65 C8
Birmingham,Rubery B45 122 A6
Brierley Hill DY5 61 D6
Coventry CV6 114 A7
Belmont Rd E B21 65 C8
Belmont Rd
Smethwick B66 65 A2
Stourbridge DY9 81 F4
Tamworth B77 35 E7
Wolverhampton WV4 39 A5
Belmont Row B4 67 A3
Belmont St WV14 41 A4
Belper DY1 51 B1
Belper Ent Pk B70 52 F4
Belper Rd
Walsall WS3 14 C3
West Bromwich B70 52 F3
Belper Row DY2 62 E4
Belsize B77 21 E2
Belstone Cl B14 104 D6
Belton Ave WV11 12 B1
Belton Cl B94 143 C5
Belton Gr B45 122 C8
Belt Rd WS12,WS11 2 A5
Belvedere Ave WV4 39 B5
Belvedere Cl
Burntwood WS7 6 F5
Kidderminster DY10 117 A5
Kingswinford DY6 60 F4
Tamworth B79 21 C7
Belvedere Dr B61 137 A4
Belvedere Gdns WV6 24 E7
Belvedere Rd
Birmingham B24 57 B2
Coventry CV5 133 A8
Belvide Gr B29 103 B8
Belvidere Gdns B11 87 C4
Belvidere Rd WS1 42 F8
Belvoir Cl DY1 50 E2
Belvoir Rd B60 137 C1
Belvoir B77 35 C7
Belwell Dr B74 32 A2
Belwell Gdns B74 32 A2
Belwell La B74 32 A2
Bembridge Cl WV12 27 B8
Bembridge Rd B33 69 A3
Benacre Dr B5 66 F2
Benbeck Gr DY4 51 C6
Benbow Cl LE10 71 D4
Benches Cl WS7 6 D6
Bencroft WV8 10 B4
Bendall Rd B44 45 B2
Benedictine Ct CV1 165 C3
Benedictine Rd CV3 133 C8
Benedict Sq CV2 114 C8
Benedon Rd B26 89 B7
Bengrove Cl B98 159 A7
Benion Rd WS11 1 F5
Benjamin Gdns 4 B20 55 D1
Benmore Ave B5 86 D7
Bennett Ave DY1 51 B6
Bennett Ct CV8 135 F3
Bennett Dr CV34 161 C7
Bennett Rd B74 31 D3
Bennett's Hill
Birmingham B2 164 B2
Dudley DY2 62 E8
Bennetts Rd B8 67 D6
Bennett's Rd CV7 94 F4
Bennett's Road N CV7 94 E7
Bennett's Road S CV6 94 F2
Bennett St
2 Kidderminster DY11 116 C6
Birmingham B19 66 D8
Bennetts Well Jun & Inf Sch B37 69 F3
Ben Nevis Way DY8 81 A6
Bennick Trad Est WS11 4 E6
Bennitt Cl B70 53 C1
Benn Rd CV12 79 B2
Benson Ave WV4 39 D5
Benson Cl
Lichfield WS13 3 D1
Perton WV6 23 E5
Benson Com Sch B18 65 F6
Benson Ind Est B18 65 F6
Benson Rd
Birmingham,Highter's Heath B14 105 B1
Birmingham,Hockley B18 65 F6
Coventry CV6 95 A1
Benson View B79 21 C8
Bent Ave B32 84 D6
Benthall Rd CV6 95 F2
Bentham Ct B31 102 F5
Bentleybridge Island WV11 26 B4
Bentleybridge Way WV11 26 C4
Bentley Br L Pk WV11 26 B4
Bentley Cl
Redditch B97 153 D3
Royal Leamington Spa CV32 157 B3
Bentley Ct
Coventry CV6 95 C4
Nuneaton CV11 73 A4
Sutton Coldfield B76 57 F8
Bentley Drive JMI Sch WS2 28 B2
Bentley Dr WS2 28 B3
Bentley Farm Cl B93 127 E4
Bentley Gr B29 102 F8
Bentley Heath CE Prim Sch B93 127 F5
Bentley Heath Cotts B93 127 F5
Bentley Lane Bsns Pk WS2 28 B3
Bentley La
Walsall,Birchills WS2 28 B3
Walsall,Leamore WS2 28 A5
Willenhall WV12 27 E5
Bentley Mill Cl WS2 27 F1
Bentley Mill La WS2 27 F1
Bentley Mill Way WS2 27 F1
Bentley New Dr WS2 28 B3
Bentley Pl WS2 28 B2
Bentley Rd
Bedworth CV7 78 A1
Birmingham B36 69 D7
Nuneaton CV11 73 A4
Bentley Rd N WS2 27 E1
Bentley Rd S
Darlaston WS10 41 E8
Walsall WS10 27 E1
Bentley Rd WV10 11 E2
Bentley Way B79 20 F7
Bentley West Prim Sch WS2 27 E3
Bentley Wharf WV12 27 D5
Bentmead Gr B38 104 A1
Benton Ave B11 87 C6
Benton Cl WV12 27 D4
Benton Cres WS3 14 D2
Benton Green La CV7 110 F2
Benton Rd B11 87 C6
Benton's Ct DY11 116 C6
Benton's La WS6 5 A1
Bentons Mill Croft B7 67 C8
Bentree The CV3 134 B8
Bent St DY5 61 D4
Ben Willetts Wlk 3 B65 63 C1
Benyon Ctr The WS2 28 A7
Beoley Cl B72 46 C1
Beoley Fst Sch B98 154 E8
Beoley Gr B45 122 A7
Beoley Hall B98 140 C1
Beoley La
Beoley B98 154 F8
Portway B98 141 B1
Beoley Rd E B98 154 A4
Beoley Rd W B98 153 F4
Berberry Cl B30 103 D6
Berenska Dr CV32 157 A2
Beresford Ave CV6 95 E1
Beresford Cres B70 53 B3
Beresford Dr B73 46 A1
Beresford Rd
Oldbury B69 64 C7
Walsall WS3 28 E8
Berets The B75 46 F6
Bericote Croft B27 88 D3
Bericote Rd CV32 156 E8
Berkeley Cl
Bromsgrove B60 151 B8
Nuneaton CV11 73 B3
Perton WV6 23 F3
Willenhall WS2 27 F3
Berkeley Dr DY6 60 C7
Berkeley Ho
Birmingham B23 56 F6
Sutton Coldfield B76 57 F8
Berkeley Mews B25 88 B7
Berkeley Prec B14 104 F2
Berkeley Rd B25 88 B7
Berkeley Rd E B25 88 B7
Berkeley Rd CV8 147 E6
Berkeley Rd N CV5 113 A1
Berkeley Rd S CV5 133 A8
Berkeley Rd B90 105 F3
Berkeley St WS2 42 B7
Berkeswell Cl B98 154 C7
Berkett Rd CV6 95 B2
Berkley Cres B13 87 C1
Berkley Ct B1 66 C1
Berkley St B1 66 C1
Berkshire Cl
Nuneaton CV10 72 E3
West Bromwich B71 53 B7
Berkshire Cres WS10 42 C4
Berkshire The WS3 14 A3
Berkswell CE Prim Sch CV7 110 C3
Berkswell Cl
Dudley DY1 50 E3
Solihull B91 107 B8
Sutton Coldfield B74 31 E4
Berkswell Hall CV7 110 C3
Berkswell Mus* CV7 110 C3
Berkswell Rd
Birmingham B24 57 B4
Coventry CV6 96 B2
Meriden CV7 110 C7
Berkswell Sta CV7 130 C8

Berkswell Windmill* CV7 130 D4
Bermuda Bsns Pk CV10 78 A7
Bermuda Cl DY1 51 B6
Bermuda Ind Est CV10 78 B8
Bermuda Rd CV10 73 A1
Bernard Pl B18 65 F5
Bernard Rd
  Birmingham B17 65 B2
  Oldbury B68 64 C2
  Tipton DY4 52 B7
Bernard St
  Walsall WS1 29 A1
  West Bromwich B71 53 C4
Berners Cl CV4 111 E2
Berners St B19 66 D7
Bernhard Dr B21 65 E8
Bernie Crossland Wlk DY10 116 F3
Bernwall Cl DY8 80 F4
Berrandale Rd B36 57 F1
Berrington Cl B98 154 D2
Berrington Dr WV14 51 B8
Berrington Rd
  Nuneaton CV10 72 D7
  Royal Leamington Spa CV31 162 B6
Berrington Wlk B5 86 E7
Berrow Cottage Homes B93 128 C6
Berrow Dr B15 85 E7
Berrowside Rd B34 69 E6
Berrow View B61 150 D7
Berry Ave WS10 41 B5
Berrybush Gdns DY3 50 E7
Berry Cl B19 66 D6
Berry Cres WS5 43 C4
Berry Dr
  Aldridge WS9 29 E5
  Barnt Green B45 122 A1
  Smethwick B66 65 A6
Berryfield Rd B26 89 D6
Berryfields WS9 29 E5
Berryfields Rd B76 46 F3
Berryfields WS9 16 E5
Berry Hall La B91 108 B4
Berry Hill WS12 2 C4
Berrymound View B47 125 C7
Berry Rd
  Birmingham B8 67 E5
  Dudley DY1 51 C5
Berry St
  Birmingham B18 65 F6
  Coventry CV1 113 E4
  Wolverhampton WV1 163 C3
Bertha Rd B11 87 D5
Bertie Rd CV8 148 A4
Bertie Terr CV32 156 E1
Bertram Cl DY4 41 C1
Bertram Rd
  [5] Birmingham B10 67 D1
  Smethwick B67 64 E6
Berwick Cl
  Coventry CV5 112 B4
  Warwick CV34 155 E2
Berwick Dr WS11 4 B8
Berwick Gr
  Birmingham,Frankley B31 102 D3
  Birmingham,Pheasey B43 44 B4
Berwick Ho CV8 148 A3
Berwicks La B37 70 B1
Berwood Farm Rd B72 57 C6
Berwood Gdns B24 57 C6
Berwood Gr B92 89 B1
Berwood La B24 57 E3
Berwood Pk B35 58 A2
Berwood Rd B72 57 D6
Berwyn Ave CV6 95 A1
Berwyn Gr WS6 4 F3
Berwyn Way CV10 72 C4
Beryl Ave LE10 71 A2
Besant Gr B27 88 A1
Besbury Cl B93 127 E2
Bescot Cres WS1 42 D5
Bescot Croft B42 55 B6
Bescot Dr WS2 42 B6
Bescot Ind Est The WS10 41 D4
Bescot Rd WS2 42 B6
Bescot Stadium Sta WS1 42 D5
Bescot St WS1 42 E7
Besford Gr
  Birmingham B31 102 D3
  Solihull B90 127 B6
Besom Way WS6 4 C2
Bessborough Rd B25 88 D8
Best Ave CV8 148 C7
Best Rd WV14 40 D7
Best St B64 62 F2
Beswick Gr B33 69 A4
Beta Gr B14 105 C4
Bethany Mews [4] WS11 1 F4
Betjeman Ct DY10 117 B5
Betjeman Pl WV10 12 A1
Betley Gr B33 69 A5
Betony Cl WS5 43 A3
Betsham Cl B44 45 B1
Bettany Glade WV10 11 E4
Betteridge Dr B76 46 E4
Bettina Cl CV10 72 B5
Bettman Cl CV3 133 E6
Betton Rd B14 104 E5
Bett Rd B20 54 F3
Betty's La WS11 6 A4
Bevan Ave WV4 39 E4
Bevan Cl
  Bilston WV14 40 F6
  Walsall WS4 15 C1
Bevan Ct CV3 133 D7
Bevan Lee Rd WS11 1 D3
Bevan Rd
  Brierley Hill DY5 61 A2
  Tipton DY4 52 B4
Bevan Way B66 64 F7
Beverley Ave CV10 72 B4
Beverley Cl
  Astwood Bank B96 158 E2
  Balsall Common CV7 130 C7
  Sutton Coldfield B72 57 D7
Beverley Court Rd B32 84 C6
Beverley Cres WV4 39 F4
Beverley Croft B23 56 D2
Beverley Ct [1] B62 84 A6
Beverley Dr DY6 60 C7
Beverley Gr B26 89 B5
Beverley Hill WS12 2 D6
Beverley Rd
  Birmingham B45 122 A7
  Royal Leamington Spa CV32 156 D1
  West Bromwich B71 42 D1
Beverly Dr CV4 132 D2
Beverston Rd
  Perton WV6 24 A4
  Wednesbury DY4 41 B2
Bevington Cres CV6 112 E5
Bevington Rd B6 66 F8
Bevin Rd WS2 27 E3
Bevis Gr B44 44 F3
Bewdley Ave [4] B12 87 A6
Bewdley Dr WV1 26 B2
Bewdley Grange DY11 116 A5
Bewdley Hill DY11 116 B5
Bewdley Rd
  Birmingham B30 104 B8
  Kidderminster DY11 116 C6
Bewdley Villas [3] B18 65 D4
Bewell Ct B61 136 F4
Bewell Gdns B61 136 F4
Bewell Head B61 136 F4
Bewick Ct WV6 24 C2
Bewlay Cl DY5 81 B7
Bewley Rd WV12 27 D4
Bewlys Ave B20 54 E4
Bexfield Cl CV5 112 A6
Bexhill Gr [3] B15 66 C1
Bexley Gr B71 53 E7
Bexley Rd B44 56 B8
Bexmore Dr WS13 3 F1
Beyer Cl B77 22 A2
Bhylls Acre Prim Sch WV3 38 B7
Bhylls Cres WV3 38 C7
Bhylls La WV3 38 C7
Bibbey's Gn WV10 11 F4
Bibsworth Ave B13 105 D8
Bibury Rd B28 105 E7
Bicester Sq B35 58 B4
Bickenhill Green Ct B92 90 D1
Bickenhill La
  Birmingham B37 90 C6
  Birmingham B40 90 D4
  Catherine de B B92 108 C6
Bickenhill Park Rd B92 88 E1
Bickenhill Parkway B37 90 D6
Bickenhill Rd B37 90 B7
Bickford Rd
  Birmingham B6 56 A1
  Wolverhampton WV10 25 F5
Bickington Rd B32 84 D1
Bickley Ave
  Birmingham B11 87 C6
  Sutton Coldfield B74 31 E5
Bickley Gr B26 89 B5
Bickley Ho B74 31 E5
Bickley Rd
  Bilston WV14 41 A7
  Walsall WS4 29 C7
Bicknell Croft B14 104 E2
Bickton Cl B24 57 C5
Biddings La WV14 40 B2
Biddles Hill B94 141 C6
Biddlestone Pl WS10 41 B7
Biddleston Gr WS5 43 C3
Biddulph Ct [3] B73 46 A2
Bideford Dr B29 85 C1
Bideford Rd
  Coventry CV2 114 C7
  Smethwick B66 65 B5
Bideford Way WS11 4 B8
Bidford Cl B90 106 D2
Bidford Rd B31 102 E3
Bierton Rd B25 88 C8
Bigbury Cl CV3 133 E5
Biggin Cl
  Birmingham B35 58 A3
  Perton WV6 23 E5
Biggin Hall Cres CV3 114 B2
Bigwood Dr
  Birmingham B32 84 D1
  Sutton Coldfield B75 47 A5
Bilberry Bank WS11 1 E6
Bilberry Cres
  Huntington WS12 1 C5
  Sutton Coldfield B76 46 F3
Bilberry Dr B45 122 A6
Bilberry Rd
  Birmingham B14 104 C6
  Coventry CV2 96 D2
Bilboe Rd WV14 41 A3
Bilbrook CE Mid Sch WV8 10 B3
Bilbrook Ct WV8 10 B3
Bilbrook Gr
  Birmingham B29 84 F2
  Codsall WV8 10 B3
Bilbrook Rd WV8 10 B4
Bilbrook Sta WV8 10 A2
Bilbury Cl B97 158 C6
Bilhay La B70 53 A5
Bilhay St B70 53 B5
Billau Rd WV14 40 D2
Billesden Cl CV3 134 E8
Billesley La
  Birmingham B13 87 A1
  Portway B48 140 E6
Billesley Prim Sch B13 105 C6
Billingham Cl B91 127 B8
Billing Rd CV5 112 D3
Billingsley Rd B26 89 A8
Billinton Cl CV2 114 E2
Bills La B90 106 A1
Billsmore Gn B92 107 C7
Bills St WS10 41 E6
Billy Buns La WV5 49 B8
Billy La B45,B60 138 A7
Billy Wright Cl WV4 38 D6
Bilport La WS10 52 F8
Bilston Central Sta WV14 40 E5
Bilston CE Prim Sch WV14 40 B6
Bilston Ind Est WV14 41 A4
Bilston Key Ind Est WV14 41 A5
Bilston La WV13 41 B8
Bilston Mus & Art Gall WV14 40 E6
Bilston Rd
  Darlaston WV13 41 A8
  Wednesbury,Church Hill WS10 41 E3
  Wednesbury,Gospel Oak DY4 41 B2
  Wolverhampton WV2 39 F8
Bilston St
  Darlaston WS10 41 D6
  Sedgley DY3 50 E8
  Willenhall WV13 27 A1
  Wolverhampton WV1 163 C2
Bilton Grange Rd B26 88 F8
Bilton Ind Est
  Birmingham B38 123 E8
  Coventry CV3 113 F1
Binbrook Rd WV12 27 D4
Bincomb Ave B26 89 B6
Binfield St DY4 52 A4
Bingley Ave B8 68 B4
Bingley Ent Ctr WV3 39 A8
Bingley St WV3 39 A8
Binley Ave CV3 134 F7
Binley Bsns Pk CV3 115 A1
Binley Cl
  Birmingham B26 88 D6
  Solihull B90 126 A8
Binley Gr CV3 134 F7
Binley Ind Est CV3 135 A8
Binley Rd CV2,CV3 114 D1
Binley Woods Prim Sch CV3 135 E7
Binns Cl CV4 131 F8
Binstead Rd B44 45 A2
Binswood Ave CV32 156 F2
Binswood Cl CV2 96 D2
Binswood Ct [9] CV32 156 F2
Binswood Mans [14] CV32 156 F2
Binswood Rd B62 84 A7
Binswood St CV32 156 E1
Binton Cl B98 154 F1
Binton Croft B13 104 F8
Binton Rd
  Coventry CV2 96 D2
  Solihull B90 105 F1
Birbeck Ho B36 70 B6
Birbeck Pl DY5 61 B6
Birchall St B12 66 F1
Birch Ave
  Birmingham B31 102 C1
  Brierley Hill DY5 62 A2
  Brownhills WS8 15 E8
  Burntwood WS7 6 F6
  Cannock WS11 4 C8
Birchbrook Ind Pk WS14 17 E6
Birch Brook La WS14 17 E6
Birch Bsns Pk WS11 4 F6
Birch Cl
  Bedworth CV12 78 D4
  Birmingham B30 103 E6
  Coventry CV5 111 F6
  Sutton Coldfield B76 46 F2
Birch Coppice DY5 62 A1
Birch Coppice Distribution Ctr B78 36 E4
Birch Coppice Gdns WV12 27 E4
Birch Cres B69 52 B1
Birchcroft [6] B66 65 C5
Birch Croft
  Aldridge WS9 30 C8
  Birmingham B37 70 C1
Birch Croft Rd B75 46 D7
Birch Croft B24 57 D5
Birch Ct
  [11] Wolverhampton WV3 25 C4
  Birmingham B30 103 E4
  Oldbury B66 64 D8
  Royal Leamington Spa CV34 161 E2
  Walsall WS4 29 A4
Birchdale Ave B23 56 E3
Birchdale WV14 40 D7
Birchdale Rd B23 56 D5
Birch Dr
  Halesowen B62 63 E1
  Stourbridge DY8 80 E6
  Sutton Coldfield,Little Aston B74 31 D5
  Sutton Coldfield,Whitehouse Common B75 46 F7
Birchen Coppice Fst Sch DY11 116 B2
Birchen Coppice Mid Sch DY11 116 B2
Birch End CV34 161 B8
Birchensale Farm [10] B97 153 B5
Birchensale Mid Sch B97 153 C4
Birchensale Rd B97 153 C5
Birches Ave WV8 10 C1
Birches Barn Ave WV3 38 F7
Birches Barn Rd WV3 38 F7
Birches Cl B13 86 F1
Birches Fst Sch WV8 10 B1
Birches Green Inf Sch B24 57 B2
Birches Green Jun Sch B24 57 B3
Birches Green Rd B24 57 B2
Birches Ho B97 153 B2
Birches La
  Alvechurch B48 138 F6
  Kenilworth CV8 148 B3
Birches Park Rd WV8 10 A2
Birches Rd WV8 10 B2
Birches Rise WV13 26 F1
Birches The CV12 79 B4
Birchfield Ave WV6 24 B6
Birchfield Cl
  Halesowen B63 82 E2
  Wood End CV9 36 C1
Birchfield Com Sch B20 55 D1
Birchfield Cres DY9 81 F3
Birchfield Ct B97 153 B2
Birchfield Gdns
  [8] Birmingham B6 66 D8
  Walsall WS5 43 C4
Birchfield La
  Oldbury,Round's Green B69 63 F6
  Oldbury,Whiteheath Gate B69 63 E4
Birchfield Rd
  Birmingham B20 55 D2
  Coventry CV6 112 F8
  Kidderminster DY11 116 B5
  Redditch B97 153 B2
  Stourbridge DY9 81 F3
Birchfields Dr WS12 2 D1
Birchfields Rd WV12 27 A5
Birchfield Twr [1] B20 55 D1
Birchfield Way WS5 43 C4
Birchgate DY9 81 F4
Birchglade WV3 24 D1
Birchgrave Cl CV6 114 A7
Birch Gr
  Balsall Common CV7 130 B8
  Birchmoor B78 36 D7
  Birmingham B68 84 D7
  Lichfield WS14 9 D8
Birch Hollow B15 85 F6
Birch Ho
  Redditch B98 158 F8
  Sutton Coldfield B74 31 B5
Birchills Canal Mus* WS2 28 C3
Birchills CE Prim Com Sch WS2 28 D2
Birchills St WS2 28 D2
Birch La
  Aldridge WS9 16 D1
  Birmingham B68 84 D7
  Walsall WS4 15 C1
Birchley Ho
  Oldbury B69 63 D6
  Redditch B97 153 B1
Birchley Ind Est B69 63 E5
Birchley Park Ave B69 63 E6
Birchley Rise B92 88 F4
Birch Meadow Cl CV34 160 D7
Birchmoor Cl B28 106 B7
Birchmoor Rd B78 36 F8
Birchover Rd WS2 28 A4
Birch Rd
  Birmingham,Rubery B45 121 E6
  Birmingham,Warley Woods B68 84 D7
  Birmingham,Witton B6 56 A2
Birch Rd E B6 56 B2
Birch Rd
  Sedgley DY3 39 F1
  Wednesfield WV11 26 F8
  Wolverhampton WV11 12 F1
Birch St
  Oldbury B68 64 C5
  Tipton DY4 51 F5
  Walsall WS2 28 D3
  Wolverhampton WV1 163 B3
Birch Terr DY2 62 C4
Birch Tree Gdns WS9 30 B5
Birchtree Gdns DY5 62 A1
Birch Tree Gr B91 106 F4
Birchtree Hollow WV12 27 D5
Birchtree Rd CV10 72 C6
Birchtrees Croft B26 88 D5
Birchtrees Dr B33 69 D2
Birchtrees B24 57 D4
Birchway Cl CV32 156 C1
Birch Wlk B68 84 D8
Birchwood Ave B78 36 F7
Birchwood Cl
  Essington WV11 13 A3
  Kidderminster DY11 116 A7
Birchwood Cres B12 87 B4
Birchwood Prim Sch B78 36 F7
Birchwood Rd
  Binley Woods CV3 135 C7
  Birmingham B12 87 A4
  Lichfield WS14 9 F7
  Wolverhampton WV4 39 A5
Birchwoods B32 84 B2
Birchwood Wlk DY6 60 E8
Birchy Cl B90 125 F6
Birchy Leasowes La B90 125 E5
Birdbrook Rd B44 55 E8
Birdcage Wlk [4] DY2 51 D1
Bird Cage Wlk B38 103 F2
Bird End B71 53 F8
Bird Grove Ct CV1 113 D5
Birdhope B77 22 C1
Birdie Cl B38 103 D1
Birdlip Gr B32 84 C6
Bird Rd CV34 161 D4
Birds Bush Prim Sch B77 35 E8
Birds Bush Rd B77 35 F8
Birds Mdw DY5 61 B7
Bird St
  Coventry CV1 165 C3
  Dudley DY3 50 C3
  Lichfield WS13 9 B7
Birdwell Croft B13 104 F6
Birkdale Ave
  Birmingham B29 85 F1
  Blackwell B60 138 A5
Birkdale Cl
  Coventry CV6 95 B4
  Nuneaton CV11 74 A1
  Stourbridge DY8 80 F2
  Wolverhampton WV1 26 A2
Birkdale Dr B69 63 A7
Birkdale Gr B29 104 A8
Birkdale Rd WS3 14 A3
Birkenshaw Rd B44 55 E8
Birley Gr B63 82 C1
Birlingham Ho B60 137 B3
Birmingham Botanical Gdns* B15 85 F7
Birmingham Bsns Pk B37 90 E8
Birmingham Children's Hospl B4 164 C3
Birmingham Christian Coll B29 85 C1
Birmingham Coll of Food, Tourism & Creative Studies B3 164 A3
Birmingham Conservatoire B1 164 B2
Birmingham Dental Hospl The B4 164 C4
Birmingham Great Pk B45 122 B8
Birmingham Heartlands Hospl B9 68 B2
Birmingham Hippodrome Theatre* B5 164 C1
Birmingham Int Airport B40 90 B4
Birmingham Int Convention Ctr* B1 66 C2
Birmingham Int Sta B40 90 D4
Birmingham & Midland Mus of Transport* B47 124 E3
Birmingham Mus & Art Gal* B3 164 B2
Birmingham Nature Ctr* B5 86 C3
Birmingham New Rd
  Dudley DY1,DY4,WV14 51 C4
  Wolverhampton WV4 39 E4
Birmingham Nuffield Hospl The B15 85 F5
Birmingham Rd
  Aldridge WS9 30 A4
  Allesley CV5 111 E7
  Alvechurch B48 139 B7
  Birmingham,Buckland End B36 69 A8
  Birmingham,Rubery B45, B61 121 D5
  Blakedown DY10 98 C2
  Burton Green CV8 131 A1
  Coleshill B46 70 E5
  Dudley DY1 51 E2
  Hagley DY9 99 D7
  Halesowen B63 83 B4
  Hopwood B31,B48 123 B4
  Kenilworth CV8 147 C8
  Kidderminster DY10 117 D7
  Lichfield WS14 9 A4
  Lickey End B60,B61 137 B6
  Little Packington CV7 91 E3
  Lower Marlbrook B61 121 B1
  Oldbury B69 64 B7
  Redditch B97,B98 153 E8
  Rowley Regis B65 63 C2
  Shenstone WS14 18 A4
  Stoneleigh CV8 149 B6
  Studley B80,B98 159 E7
  Sutton Coldfield B72,B73 46 B2
  Walsall B43,WS1,WS5 43 D5
  Warwick CV34 160 B8
  Water Orton B46 59 A3
  West Bromwich B71 54 A1
  Wolverhampton WV2 39 D7
  Wroxall B93,CV35 145 D3
Birmingham Rly Mus* B11 87 F5

Birmingham Sch of Acting B1 164 B2
Birmingham Sch of Speech & Drama B15 86 A7
Birmingham St
Darlaston WS10 41 E6
Dudley DY2 51 D1
Halesowen B63 83 B3
Oldbury B69 64 A7
Stourbridge DY8 81 B5
Walsall WS1 28 F1
Willenhall WV13 27 C2
Birmingham Women's Hospl B15 85 D4
Birnam B15 86 A8
Birnham Cl DY4 51 D5
Birstall Way B38 123 C8
Birvell Ct CV12 78 D3
Bisell Way DY5 81 C6
Biset Ave DY10 117 B5
Bishbury Cl B15 85 E8
Bishop Asbury Cres B43 54 C8
Bishop Asbury's Cottage* B43 54 C8
Bishop Challoner RC Sch B14 104 F8
Bishop Cl
Birmingham B45 101 E1
Cannock WS11 1 D2
Dudley DY2 62 E8
Bishopgate Bsns Pk CV1 113 D5
Bishopgate Ind Est CV1 113 D5
Bishop Hall Cres B60 150 E7
Bishop Milner RC Sch DY1 51 A3
Bishop Rd WS10 42 C2
Bishops Cl B66 65 C4
Bishop's Ct
Birmingham,Coleshill Heath B37 90 E8
Birmingham,Northfield B31 103 B3
Bishops Gate B31 103 A2
Bishopsgate St B15 66 B1
Bishops Mdw B75 32 E3
Bishops Rd B73 46 B3
Bishop St
Birmingham B5 86 E8
Coventry CV1 165 B3
Bishopstone Cl B98 154 F2
Bishops Way B74 31 F6
Bishops Wlk
Coventry CV5 133 B8
Halesowen B64 83 A6
Bishopton Cl
Coventry CV5 112 B3
Solihull B90 106 C1
Bishopton Rd B67 64 F1
Bishop Ullathorne RC Sch CV3 132 F4
Bishop Vesey's Gram Sch B74 46 C6
Bishop Walsh RC Sch B72 46 D1
Bishop Wilson CE Prim Sch B37 70 C3
Bishton Gr DY2 62 D4
Bisley Gr B24 57 B2
Bismillah Bldgs B19 164 B4
Bissell Cl B28 105 F6
Bissell Dr WS10 42 B3
Bissell St
Birmingham B32 84 A6
Birmingham,Highgate B5 86 E8
Bissel St WV14 40 F5
Bisset Cres 12 CV31 162 C6
Bi Tec Ind Pk WV1 26 A1
Biton Cl B17 85 B5
Bittell Cl
Birmingham B31 122 F7
Wolverhampton WV10 11 E4
Bittell Ct B31 122 F7
Bittell Farm Rd B48 123 A2
Bittell La B45 138 E8
Bittell Rd
Alvechurch B48 139 A8
Barnt Green B45 138 E8
Bitterne Dr WV6 25 A4
Bittern Wlk DY5 81 C6
Bittern Wood Rd DY10 117 B3
Bitterscote La B78 21 A2
Blackacre Rd DY2 62 D8
Black-a-Tree Ct CV10 72 F5
Black-A-Tree Rd CV10 72 E4
Blackbades Bvd CV34 160 B4
Black Bank CV7 78 B1
Blackberry Ave
Birmingham B9 68 A3
Hockley Heath B94 143 C6
Blackberry Cl DY1 61 E8
Blackberry La
Brownhills WS9 16 B4
Coventry,Neal's Green CV7 95 C5
Coventry,Wyken Green CV2 114 C6
Halesowen B63 83 A2
Rowley Regis B65 62 F5
Sutton Coldfield B74 31 E4
Blackbird Croft B36 70 A7
Blackbrook Cl DY2 62 A3
Blackbrook Rd DY2 62 B5
Blackbrook Valley Ind Pk DY2 62 A5
Blackbrook Way WV10 11 E4
Blackburn Ave WV6 24 F7
Blackburne Rd B28 105 F6
Blackburn Rd CV6 95 F3
Blackbushe Cl B17 84 F7
Blackcat Cl B37 70 A3
Black Country Living Mus* DY1 51 D3
Black Country New Rd
Darlaston WS10 41 C4
Tipton B70,DY4 52 D6
Black Country Route
Bilston WV14 40 E5
Darlaston WV13,WS10 41 B7
Walsall WS2,WS10 27 E1
Blackdown Cl B45 102 A2
Blackdown Hall CV32 156 F6
Blackdown Rd B93 128 B6
Blackdown B77 22 C1
Blackett Ct 1 B73 46 A2
Blackfirs La B37,B46 90 D7
Blackford Cl
Halesowen B63 82 D2
Kidderminster DY11 116 A1
Blackford Rd
Birmingham B11 87 C4
Solihull B90 126 C8
Blackford St B18 65 E5
Blackfriars Cl B79 20 E5
Blackgreaves La B76 48 F1
Blackhalve La WV11 12 D1
Blackham Dr B73 57 A7
Blackham Rd WV11 26 F8
Black Haynes Rd B29 103 A6
Blackheath Mkt B65 63 C1
Blackheath Prim Sch B65 63 D2
Blackheath Trad Est B65 63 E2
Black Horse La 1 DY10 116 E6
Blackhorse La DY5 61 E1
Black Horse Rd CV6,CV7 96 B6
Black Lake La B60,B97 152 A2
Black Lake Sta B70 53 A6
Black Lake B70 53 A6
Black La CV32 157 C2
Blackley Ho B66 65 D6
Blacklow Rd CV34 156 A1
Blackmoor Croft B33 69 D2
Blackmore La B60 137 A3
Blackpit La WV4 37 E3
Black Prince Ave CV3 133 E6
Blackrock Rd B23 56 B6
Blackroot Cl WS7 7 D4
Blackroot Ho B73 45 C2
Blackroot Rd B74 46 B7
Blackshaw Dr CV2 114 F6
Blacksmith Dr
7 Sutton Coldfield B75 32 E3
Bromsgrove B60 151 A7
Blacksmiths La B94 143 C6
Blacksmith Way 3 B70 53 C2
Black Soils Rd B98 154 F5
Blackstitch La B97 153 A1
Blackthorn Ave WS7 6 F4
Blackthorn Cl
Birmingham B30 103 C6
Coventry CV4 132 D5
Blackthorn Ct B98 154 E1
Blackthorne Cl
Dudley DY1 50 F4
Solihull B91 106 E4
Blackthorne Rd
Dudley DY1 50 F5
Kenilworth CV8 148 A3
Lichfield WS14 9 D7
Smethwick B67 64 D4
Walsall WS5 42 F5
Blackthorn Gr CV11 73 F2
Blackthorn Rd
Birmingham,Bournville B30 103 D6
Birmingham,Castle Bromwich B36 69 C8
Stourbridge DY8 61 A1
Blackwatch Rd CV6 113 C8
Blackwater Cl DY5 61 A6
Blackwell La 1 B97 153 B5
Blackwell Rd
Barnt Green B45,B60 138 B5
Coventry CV6 113 E8
Sutton Coldfield B72 46 D1
Blackwell St DY10 116 E6
Blackwood Ave WV11 26 C8
Blackwood Dr B74 44 E8
Blackwood Rd
Bromsgrove B60 137 B2
Sutton Coldfield B74 30 E1
Tamworth B77 35 C7
Blackwood Sch B74 30 E1
Blades Rd B70 52 D4
Bladon Cl CV11 73 F8
Bladon Wlk 6 CV31 162 C6
Blaenwern Dr B63 82 B7
Blagdon Rd B63 83 A6
Blair Dr CV12 77 D1
Blair Gr B37 70 D1
Blakebrook Cl DY11 116 C6
Blakebrook Gdns DY11 116 C6
Blakebrook DY11 116 C6
Blakebrook Sch DY11 116 C6
Blake Cl
Cannock WS11 2 A5
Hinckley LE10 71 D4
Nuneaton CV10 72 A5
Blakedon Rd WS10 41 E3
Blakedown CE Fst Sch DY10 98 C1
Blakedown Rd B63 82 F1
Blakedown Sta DY10 98 C2
Blakedown Way 4 B69 63 E4
Blake Hall Cl DY5 81 C7
Blake Ho 2 WS2 42 C8
Blake La B9 67 F2
Blakeland Rd B44 55 E6
Blakelands Ave CV31 162 B6
Blakeland St B9 67 F2
Blakeley Ave WV6 24 F7
Blakeley Ct B72 57 C8
Blakeley Hall Gdns B69 64 B7
Blakeley Hall Rd B69 64 B7
Blakeley Heath Dr WV5 49 A5
Blakeley Heath Prim Sch WV5 49 A5
Blakeley Rise WV6 24 F7
Blakeley Wood Rd DY4 52 D8
Blakemere Ave B25 88 E8
Blakemere Cl B98 154 F3
Blakemore Cl B32 84 F3
Blakemore Dr B75 46 F6
Blakemore Rd
Brownhills WS9 16 A3
West Bromwich B70 53 A1
Blakenall Heath Jun Sch WS3 28 C8
Blakenall Heath WS3 28 D8
Blakenall La WS3 28 D8
Blakenall Row WS3 28 D8
Blakeney Ave
Birmingham B17 85 A7
Stourbridge DY8 80 D6
Blakeney Cl DY3 50 C8
Blakenhale Jun & Inf Schs B33 69 B1
Blakenhale Rd B33 69 B1
Blakenhall Gdns WV2 39 D7
Blakenhall Ind Est WV2 39 B7
Blake Pl B9 67 F2
Blake Rd B61 137 B8
Blakes Field Dr B45 122 A1
Blakesley Cl B76 57 F5
Blakesley Gr B25 68 D1
Blakesley Hall Mus* B25 68 E1
Blakesley Hall Prim Sch B25 68 D1
Blakesley Mews B25 88 D8
Blakesley Rd B25 68 D1
Blakesley Way B33 68 D2
Blake Street Sta B74 31 F6
Blake St B74 31 E6
Blake Valley Tech Coll WS12 1 F6
Blakewood Cl B34 69 C5
Blandford Ave B36 58 E1
Blandford Dr
Coventry CV2 114 F5
Stourbridge DY8 60 E3
Blandford Gdns WS7 7 C6
Blandford Rd
Birmingham B32 84 F5
Royal Leamington Spa CV32 156 C1
Blandford Way CV35 160 A7
Blanefield WV8 10 E2
Blanford Mere Prim Sch DY6 60 E8
Blanning Ct B93 127 E3
Blay Ave WS2 28 B2
Blaydon Ave B75 32 E2
Blaydon Ct 3 B17 85 D4
Blaydon Rd WV9,WV10 11 A1
Blaythorn Ave B92 89 A3
Blaze Hill Rd DY6 60 A8
Blaze La B96,B97 158 A3
Blaze Pk DY6 60 B8
Bleachfield La B98 154 F8
Bleak Hill Rd B23 56 C5
Bleak House Dr WS7 6 D8
Bleakhouse Jun Sch B68 64 C1
Bleakhouse Rd B68 64 C1
Bleak St B67 64 F6
Blenheim 5 B17 85 B6
Blenheim Ave CV6 95 C2
Blenheim Cl
Hinckley LE10 71 F4
Nuneaton CV11 73 F2
Tamworth B77 21 C4
Walsall WS4 29 D7
Blenheim Cres
Bromsgrove B60 151 A8
Royal Leamington Spa CV31 162 C5
Blenheim Ct
Birmingham B44 55 F8
Solihull B91 107 C4
Blenheim Dr
Birmingham B43 54 D8
Darlaston WS10 41 E5
Blenheim Rd
Birmingham B13 86 F1
Burntwood WS7 7 A8
Kingswinford DY6 61 A6
Norton Canes WS11 6 B4
Solihull B90 106 D2
Willenhall WV12 27 B6
Blenheim Way
Birmingham,Castle Vale B35 58 B2
Birmingham,Old Oscott B44 55 F8
Dudley DY1 50 E2
Blenheim Wlk CV6 95 B4
Bletchley Dr
Coventry CV5 112 B4
Tamworth B77 35 C8
Bletchley Rd B24 57 E4
Blewitt Cl B36 58 D2
Blewitt St
Brierley Hill DY5 61 C6
Cannock WS12 2 B7
Blews St B6 66 E5
Blick Rd CV34 161 C4
Blind La
Berkswell CV7 110 D4
Blind La continued
Kenilworth CV8 131 F1
Tanworth-In-A B94 141 D1
Blindpit La B76 59 B8
Bliss Cl CV4 111 E3
Blithe Cl DY8 81 A8
Blithfield Dr DY5 81 B7
Blithfield Gr B24 57 C5
Blithfield Pl WS11 2 B1
Blithfield Rd WS8 6 C2
Blockall Cl WS10 41 D7
Blockall WS10 41 D7
Blockley Cl B97 152 E2
Blockley Rd CV12 78 C4
Blockley's Yd 4 LE10 75 D8
Blondvil St CV3 133 D7
Bloomfield Cres WS13 3 B2
Bloomfield Ct 3 B42 55 A8
Bloomfield Dr WV12 13 D1
Bloomfield Pk DY4 51 D6
Bloomfield Rd
Birmingham B13 87 B3
Tipton DY4 51 E7
Bloomfield St N B63 82 F5
Bloomfield St W B63 82 F4
Bloomfield Terr DY4 51 E7
Bloomfield Way B79 20 F8
Bloomsbury Gr B14 104 C7
Bloomsbury St
Birmingham B7 67 B5
Wolverhampton WV2 163 B1
Bloomsbury Way WS14 9 E7
Bloomsbury Wlk 1 B7 67 B5
Bloor Mill Cl WV13 26 F1
Blossom Ave B29 85 F2
Blossom Dr B61 137 A5
Blossomfield Cl
Birmingham B38 123 D8
Kingswinford DY6 60 E8
Blossomfield Ct B38 123 D8
Blossomfield Gdns B91 107 A4
Blossomfield Inf Sch B90 106 D3
Blossomfield Rd B91 106 F2
Blossom Gr
Birmingham B36 68 E8
Cradley Heath B64 62 F1
Blossom Hill B24 57 A4
Blossom Rd B24 57 C4
Blossom's Fold WV1 163 B3
Blossomville Way 9 B27 88 C5
Blount Ho DY11 116 B8
Blounts Rd B23 56 D5
Blount Terr DY11 116 D3
Blowers Green Cres DY2 62 B7
Blowers Green Pl DY2 62 B7
Blowers Green Prim Sch DY2 62 B8
Blower's Green Rd DY2 62 B8
Bloxcidge St B68 64 B4
Bloxwich Bsns Pk WS2 28 A7
Bloxwich CE Prim Sch WS3 14 B1
Bloxwich Hospl WS3 28 B8
Bloxwich La WS2 28 A4
Bloxwich L Ctr WS3 28 C8
Bloxwich North Sta WS3 13 F2
Bloxwich Rd N WV12 27 D6
Bloxwich Rd S WV13 27 A3
Bloxwich Rd WS2,WS3 28 D5
Bloxwich Sta WS3 14 A1
Blucher St B1 164 B1
Blue Ball La B63 82 C7
Bluebell Cl
Cannock WS12 2 B6
Stourbridge DY8 60 C2
Bluebell Cres WV11 26 D5
Bluebell Croft
Birmingham,Northfield B31 102 F4
Birmingham,Perry Common B23 56 C7
Bluebell Dr
Bedworth CV12 77 E2
Birmingham B37 70 E2
Bluebell La WS6 5 A1
Bluebell Rd
Brownhills WS9 16 B3
Cradley Heath B64 62 E3
Dudley DY1 51 B4
Bluebell Wlk CV4 111 F1
Bluebellwood Cl B76 47 A3
Bluebird Cl WS14 9 D8
Blue Bird Pk B62 101 B7
Bluebird Trad Est WV10 25 E5
Blue Cedar Dr B74 44 F6
Blue Cedars DY8 80 C6
Blue Coat CE Comp Sch WS1 28 F1
Blue Coat CE Inf Sch WS1 28 F1
Blue Coat CE Jun Sch WS1 28 F1
Blue Coat Sch The B17 85 E6
Blue La E WS2 28 E3
Blue Lake Rd B93 128 B2
Blue La W WS2 28 D2
Blue Rock Pl B69 63 C7
Bluestone Wlk B65 63 C6
Blundell Rd B11 87 D5
Blundells The CV8 148 A5
Blyth Ave CV7 130 C5
Blyth Cl CV12 77 C1
Blyth Ct CV11 73 C3
Blythe Cl
Burntwood WS7 7 D6
Redditch B97 158 D7
Blythe Ct
Solihull B91 106 F7
Blythe Ct continued
Sutton Coldfield B73 46 B5
Blythefield Ave B43 43 C2
Blythe Gate B90 126 F3
Blythe Gr B44 44 F3
Blythe Rd
7 Coleshill B46 70 F7
Coventry CV1 113 E4
Blythe St B77 21 C4
Blythesway B48 139 A6
Blythe Valley Pk B90 126 F2
Blytheway B91 107 E3
Blythewood Cl B91 107 F1
Blythsford Rd B28 106 A4
Blythswood Rd B11 88 A4
Blyton Cl B16 65 F3
Boar Croft CV4 111 F2
Board School Gdns DY3 50 E6
Boar Hound Cl B18 66 A4
Boat La WS14 7 F1
Boatman's La WS9 15 E2
Bobbington Way DY2 62 E5
Bobs Coppice Wlk DY5 81 F7
Bockendon Rd CV4 131 E5
Boddington Cl CV32 157 E5
Bodenham Cl B98 154 D3
Bodenham Rd
Birmingham,Brandhall B68 84 B8
Birmingham,Frankley B31 102 E1
Boden Rd B28 106 A7
Bodens La WS9 44 B7
Bodiam Ct WV6 24 A3
Bodicote Gr B75 32 E3
Bodington Cl WS7 7 E7
Bodington Rd B75 32 B3
Bodmin Cl
Hinckley LE10 71 E4
Walsall WS5 43 D7
Bodmin Ct 16 DY5 61 D2
Bodmin Gr 2 B7 67 B5
Bodmin Rd
Coventry CV2 114 F5
Dudley DY2 62 D2
Bodmin Rise WS5 43 D7
Bodnant Way CV8 148 C6
Bodymoor Heath Rd B76 48 F5
Bognop Rd WV11 12 D4
Bohun St CV4 111 F1
Boldmere Cl B73 57 A7
Boldmere Ct B43 54 E7
Boldmere Dr B73 57 A8
Boldmere Gdns B73 57 A8
Boldmere Inf Sch B73 45 F1
Boldmere Jun Sch B73 45 F1
Boldmere Rd B73 57 A8
Bolebridge Mews B79 21 B5
Bolebridge St B79 21 C4
Bolehall Ho B77 21 C4
Boley Cl WS14 9 D7
Boley Cottage La WS14 9 E7
Boley La WS14 9 D7
Boleyn Cl
Cheslyn Hay WS6 4 D2
Warwick CV34 161 C6
Boleyn Rd B45 101 E2
Boley Park Ctr WS14 9 E7
Bolingbroke Dr CV34 161 E3
Bolingbroke Rd CV3 114 A1
Bolney Rd B32 84 E4
Bolton Cl CV3 133 E5
Bolton Ct DY4 52 C8
Bolton Rd
Birmingham B10 87 C8
Wednesfield WV11 26 D5
Bolton St B9 67 B2
Bolton Way WS3 13 F3
Bolyfant Cres CV31 162 A2
Bomers Field B45 122 C7
Bond Dr B35 58 A3
Bondfield Rd B13 105 B6
Bond Gate CV11 73 C4
Bonds Hospl CV1 165 A3
Bond Sq B18 66 A4
Bond St
Birmingham,Ladywood B19 164 B4
Birmingham,Stirchley B30 104 A7
Coventry CV1 165 B3
Dudley WV14 51 A8
Nuneaton CV11 73 C5
Rowley Regis B65 63 E3
West Bromwich B70 53 C2
Wolverhampton WV2 163 B2
Bondway WS12 1 F7
Bonehill Ind Est B78 20 F1
Bonehill Rd B78 20 E3
Bone Mill La WV1 25 D4
Boney Hay Rd WS7 7 B7
Bonfire Hill DY9 120 E6
Bonham Gr B25 68 D1
Boningale Way B93 127 E3
Bonington Dr CV12 78 A4
Bonner Dr B76 57 F5
Bonner Gr WS9 29 F5
Bonneville Cl CV5 111 B8
Bonniksen Cl 7 CV31 161 F5
Bonnington Way B43 44 D4
Bonny Stile La WV11 26 B6
Bonsall Rd B23 57 A6
Bonville Gdns WV10 11 E4
Booth Cl
Kingswinford DY6 61 A6
Lichfield WS13 3 A2
Walsall WS3 28 D8

Booth Ct 17 DY5 .....61 D2
Booth Ho WS4 .....28 F3
Booth Rd WS10 .....42 C2
Booths Farm Rd B42 .....55 B8
Booths Fields CV6 .....95 E2
Booth's La B42 .....44 B1
Booth St
  Birmingham B21 .....65 D7
  Cannock WS12 .....2 B6
  Darlaston WS10 .....41 D8
  Walsall WS3 .....28 C8
Boot Piece La B97 .....153 B5
Bordeaux Cl WV1 .....50 E3
Borden Cl WV8 .....24 F8
Bordesley Abbey* B98 .....153 F6
Bordesley Abbey Visitor Ctr* B98 .....153 F6
Bordesley Cir B10 .....67 B1
Bordesley Cl B9 .....68 A2
Bordesley Ct CV32 .....157 A3
Bordesley Gn B9 .....67 E2
Bordesley Gn E B9,B33 .....68 C2
Bordesley Green Girls' Sch B9 .....67 D2
Bordesley Green Prim Sch B9 .....68 A2
Bordesley Green Rd B8 .....67 D2
Bordesley Green Trad Est B9 .....67 D3
Bordesley La B98 .....153 E6
Bordesley Middleway B12 .....87 A8
Bordesley Park Rd B10 .....67 B1
Bordesley Sta B10 .....67 A1
Bordesley St B5 .....164 D2
Bordsley Ct 7 B9 .....67 B2
Bore St WS13 .....9 B7
Borman B79 .....20 F5
Borneo St WS4 .....28 F4
Borough Cres
  Oldbury B65 .....63 E4
  Stourbridge DY8 .....80 E5
Borough Ct B63 .....83 B4
Borough Rd B79 .....21 C7
Borough The LE10 .....75 D8
Borrington Gdns DY10 .....117 B4
Borrington Rd DY10 .....117 B5
Borrowcop Ho WS14 .....9 C6
Borrowcop La WS14 .....9 C5
Borrowdale Cl
  Brierley Hill DY5 .....81 B8
  Coventry CV6 .....113 A8
Borrowdale Dr CV32 .....156 D2
Borrowdale Gr B31 .....102 D3
Borrowdale Rd B31 .....102 C3
Borrowell La CV8 .....147 E4
Borrowell Terr CV8 .....147 E4
Borrow St WV13 .....27 A3
Borwick Ave B70 .....53 A3
Bosbury Terr B30 .....104 B7
Boscobel Cl DY1 .....50 F3
Boscobel Cres WV1 .....25 C4
Boscobel Rd
  Birmingham B43 .....43 D2
  Cheswick Green B90 .....126 D5
  Walsall WS3 .....43 B8
Boscombe Ave B11 .....87 C6
Boscombe Rd B11 .....87 E4
Bosmere Ct B31 .....102 F3
Boss Dr DY2 .....62 C7
Boss Gate Cl WV5 .....49 A5
Boston Cl WS12 .....2 E1
Boston Gr B44 .....56 B8
Boston Pl CV6 .....113 D8
Boston Way LE9 .....71 F6
Bosty La WS9 .....29 E5
Boswell Cl
  Darlaston WS9 .....41 D5
  Wednesbury WS10 .....41 C1
Boswell Dr CV2 .....115 A7
Boswell Gr CV34 .....155 D1
Boswell Rd
  Bilston WV14 .....40 F7
  Birmingham B44 .....55 F6
  Cannock WS11 .....1 D4
  Sutton Coldfield B74 .....46 C6
Bosworth Cl
  Baginton CV8 .....133 E2
  Dudley DY3 .....51 A6
  Hinckley LE10 .....71 A1
  Sedgley DY3 .....50 F7
Bosworth Dr B37 .....70 A2
Bosworth Ho 3 B10 .....71 E1
Bosworth Rd B26 .....88 E4
Bosworth Wood Prim Sch
  Birmingham B36 .....58 F1
  Birmingham B36 .....59 D8
Botany Dr DY3 .....50 D6
Botany Rd WS5 .....43 A5
Botany Wlk 3 B16 .....66 A2
Botham Ho CV1 .....73 E1
Botha Rd B9 .....67 F2
Botoner Rd CV1 .....113 F2
Botteley Rd B70 .....53 A6
Bottetourt Rd B29 .....85 A2
Botteville Rd B27 .....88 C3
Bott La
  Stourbridge DY9 .....81 E6
  Walsall WS1 .....28 F1
Bottle Cotts 817 .....85 D4
Bott Rd CV5 .....132 D8
Bottrill St CV11 .....73 B5
Boughton Rd B25 .....88 C7
Boulevard The
  Brierley Hill DY5 .....61 F2

Boulevard The continued
  Sutton Coldfield B73 .....57 B8
Boultbee Rd B72 .....57 C7
Boulters La CV9 .....36 D1
Boulton Cir B19 .....66 C6
Boulton Cl WS7 .....7 C8
Boulton Ho 1 B70 .....53 D1
Boulton Ind Ctr B18 .....66 B5
Boulton Rd
  Birmingham B21 .....65 E7
  Smethwick B66 .....65 D6
  Solihull B91 .....107 C7
  West Bromwich B70 .....53 D1
Boulton Retreat B21 .....65 E7
Boultons La B97 .....158 D6
Boulton Sq B70 .....53 D1
Boulton Wlk B23 .....56 B4
Boundary Ave B65 .....63 E2
Boundary Cl WV13 .....26 C1
Boundary Cres DY3 .....50 C3
Boundary Ct B37 .....69 E2
Boundary Dr B13 .....86 D2
Boundary Farm WV6 .....23 F2
Boundary Hill DY3 .....50 C4
Boundary Ho B15 .....86 D8
Boundary Ind Est WV10 .....11 C5
Boundary La B90 .....126 A6
Boundary Pl B21 .....54 B1
Boundary Rd
  Birmingham B23 .....56 E4
  Brownhills WS9 .....15 F3
  Sutton Coldfield B74 .....44 F7
Boundary Way
  Wolverhampton,Penn WV4 .....38 C5
  Wolverhampton,Tettenhall Wood WV6 .....23 F2
Bourlay Cl B45 .....101 E2
Bournbrook Ct B5 .....86 A3
Bournbrook Rd B29 .....86 A2
Bourne Ave
  Fairfield B61 .....120 F1
  Fazeley B78 .....20 E1
  Halesowen B62 .....83 F4
  Tipton DY4 .....52 C7
Bournebrook Cl DY2 .....62 C5
Bournebrook Cres B62 .....84 A4
Bourne Cl
  Birmingham B13 .....105 D6
  Cannock WS12 .....2 E2
  Solihull B91 .....107 E6
Bourne Gn B32 .....84 E6
Bourne Hill Cl DY2 .....62 E3
Bourne Rd
  Birmingham B6 .....67 B7
  Coventry CV3 .....114 C1
Bournes Cl B63 .....82 F3
Bournes Cres B63 .....82 E4
Bournes Hill B63 .....82 E4
Bourne St
  Dudley,Bramford DY3, WV14 .....51 A7
  Dudley DY2,DY3 .....51 D1
Bourne Vale WS9 .....30 D3
Bourne Way Gdns B29 .....104 A8
Bourne Wlk B65 .....62 F5
Bourn Mill Dr B6 .....66 E6
Bournville Coll of F Ed
  Birmingham B30 .....103 E7
  Birmingham B31 .....103 C7
Bournville Inf Sch B30 .....103 E6
Bournville Jun Sch B30 .....103 E7
Bournville La B30 .....103 E6
Bournville Mews B30 .....103 E5
Bournville Sch of Art B30 .....103 E7
Bournville Sch & Sixth Form Ctr B30 .....103 C6
Bournville Sta B30 .....104 A7
Bourton Cl 1 WS5 .....43 A3
Bourton Croft B92 .....106 F8
Bourton Dr CV31 .....162 B5
Bourton Rd B92 .....106 F8
Bovey Croft B76 .....58 A7
Bowater Ave B33 .....68 D1
Bowater Ho
  2 West Bromwich B70 .....53 C2
  Birmingham B19 .....66 D5
Bowater St B70 .....53 C2
Bowbrook Ave B90 .....127 A5
Bowcroft Gr B24 .....57 C6
Bow Ct CV5 .....132 D8
Bowden Rd B67 .....64 E6
Bowden Way CV3 .....114 F1
Bowdler Rd WV2 .....163 D1
Bowen Ave WV4 .....40 A3
Bowen-Cooke Ave WV6 .....23 E6
Bowen Ct 4 B13 .....87 B2
Bowen St WV4 .....39 E5
Bower Cl WS13 .....3 D2
Bowercourt Cl B91 .....107 B2
Bower La DY5 .....82 A8
Bowers Croft CV32 .....157 A5
Bowes Dr WS11 .....1 F4
Bowes Rd B45 .....121 E7
Bowfell Cl CV5 .....112 B4
Bowker St WV13 .....26 C1
Bowlas Ave B74 .....46 B8
Bowling Green Ave B77 .....35 F7
Bowling Green Cl
  Birmingham B23 .....56 E7
  Darlaston WS10 .....41 D7
Bowling Green Dr B67 .....64 E2
Bowling Green La
  Bedworth CV7,CV12 .....95 E8
  Birmingham B20 .....66 A8

Bowling Green Rd
  Dudley DY2 .....62 E2
  Hinckley LE10 .....71 E1
  Stourbridge DY8 .....80 E5
Bowling Green St CV34 .....160 D6
Bowls Ct CV5 .....112 F3
Bowman Gn LE10 .....75 F6
Bowman Rd B42 .....44 B1
Bowmans Harbour Island WV10 .....26 A8
Bowman's Rise WV1 .....26 B3
Bowmore Rd B60 .....137 B1
Bowness Cl CV6 .....113 A8
Bowness Gr WV11 .....13 B1
Bowness Ho B65 .....63 D4
Bowood Cres B31 .....103 B2
Bowood Dr WV6 .....27 D8
Bowood End B76 .....46 E3
Bowshot Cl B36 .....58 D1
Bow St
  Bilston WV14 .....40 E6
  Birmingham B1 .....164 B1
Bowstoke Rd B43 .....54 C8
Bowyer Rd B8 .....67 E4
Bowyer St B10 .....67 A1
Box Cl CV31 .....162 B3
Boxhill Cl B6 .....66 F6
Boxhill The CV3 .....114 B1
Boxnott Cl B97 .....153 A2
Box Rd B37 .....90 C8
Box St WS1 .....28 F1
Box Trees Rd B93,B94 .....127 C1
Boyd Cl CV2 .....115 A8
Boyden Cl WS11 .....1 B1
Boyd Gr B27 .....88 B2
Boydon Cl WV2 .....40 A6
Boyleston Rd B28 .....106 A6
Boyne Rd B26 .....89 B7
Boyslade Rd LE10 .....75 F5
Boyslade Road E LE10 .....75 F5
Boyton Gr B44 .....44 F3
Brabazon Gr B35 .....57 F3
Brabham Cres B74 .....44 F6
Bracadale Ave B44 .....57 A4
Bracadale Cl CV3 .....115 A2
Bracebridge Cl CV7 .....130 B6
Bracebridge Rd
  Birmingham B24 .....56 F1
  Sutton Coldfield B73 .....46 A8
Bracebridge St
  Birmingham B6 .....66 E6
  Nuneaton CV11 .....73 B3
Braceby Ave B13 .....105 C6
Braces La B60 .....121 C1
Brace St WS1 .....42 E8
Brackenbury Rd B44 .....56 B8
Bracken Cl
  Burntwood WS7 .....7 C7
  Cannock WS12 .....2 D8
  Lichfield WS14 .....9 D8
  Wolverhampton WV8 .....10 E1
Bracken Croft 1 B37 .....70 C2
Brackendale Dr
  Nuneaton CV10 .....72 F3
  Walsall WS5 .....43 A3
Brackendale Sh Ctr WV12 .....27 D4
Brackendale Way DY9 .....81 D4
Bracken Dr B75 .....47 A5
Brackenfield Rd
  Birmingham B44 .....44 D3
  Halesowen B63 .....82 E3
Brackenfield View DY1 .....61 D8
Bracken Ho B8 .....68 A3
Brackley Ave B20 .....55 C1
Brackley Cl CV6 .....112 F7
Brackleys Way B92 .....89 A2
Bracknell Wlk 1 CV2 .....115 A7
Bradbeer Ho B16 .....66 A1
Bradburne Way B7 .....67 A5
Bradburn Rd WV11 .....26 B8
Bradbury Cl WS8 .....15 F5
Bradbury La WS12 .....2 B8
Bradbury Rd B92 .....107 A8
Braddock Cl CV3 .....115 A1
Brade Dr CV2 .....115 B7
Braden Rd WV4 .....38 D4
Brades Cl B63 .....82 B7
Brades Rise B69 .....63 D8
Bradestone Rd CV11 .....73 D1
Bradewell Rd B36 .....58 D1
Bradfield Cl CV5 .....112 C5
Bradfield Ho B36 .....89 D6
Bradfield Rd B42 .....55 D7
Bradford Cl B43 .....54 F7
Bradford Court Bsns Ctr B12 .....87 A8

Bradford La
  Belbroughton DY9 .....119 D5
  Walsall WS3 .....28 E1
Bradford Mall WS1 .....28 E1
Bradford Pl WS1 .....28 E1
Bradford Rd
  Birmingham B36 .....69 B7
  Brownhills WS8 .....15 E8
  Dudley DY2 .....61 F6
Bradford St
  Birmingham B12,B5 .....66 F1
  Cannock WS11 .....2 A5
  Tamworth B79 .....20 F5
  Walsall WS1 .....28 E1
Bradgate Cl WV12 .....27 C6
Bradgate Dr B74 .....31 E5
Bradgate Pl 12 B12 .....87 A6
Bradgate Rd LE10 .....71 F2
Brading Rd CV10 .....73 D6
Bradley Croft CV7 .....130 B6
Bradley Ho 5 WS4 .....41 A3
Bradley La Sta WV14 .....41 A3
B:adleymore Rd DY5 .....61 D3
Bradley Rd
  Birmingham B34 .....69 D6
  Stourbridge DY8 .....80 F6
  Wolverhampton WV2 .....39 E7
Bradleys Cl B64 .....82 E7
Bradley's La DY4,WV14 .....51 E8
Bradley St
  Bilston WV14 .....40 F4
  Brierley Hill DY5 .....61 C7
  Tipton DY4 .....51 F2
Bradmore Cl 1 B91 .....107 A1
Bradmore Gr B29 .....103 A8
Bradmore Rd WV3 .....38 F8
Bradney Gn CV4 .....131 E7
Bradnick Pl CV4 .....111 F1
Bradnock Cl B13 .....105 C7
Bradnock's Marsh La B92 .....109 E2
Bradshaw Ave
  Birmingham B38 .....103 D1
  Darlaston WS10 .....41 C5
Bradshaw Cl
  7 Birmingham B15 .....86 C8
  Tipton DY4 .....52 A3
Bradshawe Cl B28 .....105 D3
Bradstock Rd B30 .....104 C4
Bradwell Croft B75 .....32 E3
Braeburn Cl WS13 .....3 D1
Braemar Ave CV4 .....60 C1
Braemar Cl
  Coventry CV2 .....114 E6
  Sedgley DY3 .....39 C1
  Willenhall WV12 .....27 B5
Braemar Dr B23 .....56 B5
Braemar Gdns WS12 .....1 F7
Braemar Rd
  Norton Canes WS11 .....6 B4
  Royal Leamington Spa CV32 .....157 B4
  Solihull B92 .....88 E1
  Sutton Coldfield B73 .....46 A2
Braemar Way CV10 .....73 A2
Braeside Croft B37 .....70 D2
Braeside Way WS3 .....14 F3
Bragg Rd B20 .....55 D2
Braggs Farm La B90 .....126 A4
Braham B79 .....20 D6
Braid Cl B38 .....103 D1
Brailes Cl B92 .....107 E7
Brailes Dr B76 .....46 F3
Brailes Gr B9 .....68 B1
Brailsford Cl WV11 .....26 E8
Brailsford Dr B66 .....65 A5
Brain St B77 .....22 A2
Braithwaite Dr DY6 .....60 D6
Braithwaite Rd B11 .....87 B7
Brake La DY8 .....98 E6
Brakesmead CV31 .....161 F5
Brake The DY8 .....98 F6
Bramah Way DY4 .....52 C6
Bramber Dr WV5 .....49 A6
Bramber Rd B77 .....21 D1
Bramber Way DY8 .....80 F2
Bramble Cl
  6 Coleshill B46 .....70 F7
  Birmingham,Aston B6 .....66 E7
  Birmingham,Shenley Fields B31 .....102 F6
  Brownhills WS8 .....15 E5
  Cradley Heath B64 .....62 F4
  Nuneaton CV11 .....73 F2
  Willenhall WV12 .....27 C7
Bramble Dell B8 .....68 A3
Bramble Dr
  Birmingham B26 .....89 A6
  Cannock WS12 .....2 C7
Bramble Gn DY1 .....50 F5
Bramble Ho B98 .....158 F8
Brambles The WS14 .....7 B8
Brambleside DY8 .....60 F1
Bramble St CV1 .....113 F2
Brambles The
  Catshill B61 .....137 A8
  Lichfield WS14 .....9 D6
  Norton Canes WS11 .....6 A5
  Stourbridge DY9 .....81 D3
  Sutton Coldfield B76 .....58 A8
Bramblewood DY3 .....50 B8
Bramblewoods B34 .....69 C5
Bramblewood WV5 .....49 A7
Brambling B77 .....36 A7
Brambling Rise D10 .....117 B1
Brambling Wlk

Brambling Wlk
  2 Birmingham B15 .....86 C7
  Brierley Hill DY5 .....81 C6
Bramcote Cl
  Bulkington CV12 .....79 D2
  Hinckley LE10 .....71 F3
Bramcote Dr B91 .....107 C7
Bramcote Hospl CV11 .....79 E7
Bramcote Rd B32 .....84 C5
Bramcote Rise B75 .....46 C7
Bramdean Wlk WV4 .....38 C6
Bramdene Ave CV10 .....73 D8
Brame Rd LE10 .....71 C2
Bramerton Cl WV11 .....26 A6
Bramford Dr DY1 .....51 B6
Bramford Prim Sch DY1 .....51 B6
Bramley Cl
  Birmingham B43 .....44 D3
  Walsall WS5 .....43 D8
Bramley Croft B90 .....106 C2
Bramley Ct WV11 .....26 C6
Bramley Dr
  Birmingham B20 .....55 B3
  Hollywood B47 .....125 B6
Bramley Mews Ct B27 .....88 C4
Bramley Rd
  Birmingham B27 .....88 C5
  Walsall WS5 .....43 B4
Brampton Ave B28 .....106 A6
Brampton Cres B90 .....106 B6
Brampton Dr WS12 .....2 E2
Brampton Way CV12 .....79 B3
Bramshall Dr B93 .....127 E3
Bramshaw Cl B14 .....104 F2
Bramshill Ct B15 .....86 B8
Bramstead Ave WV6 .....24 B2
Bramston Cres CV4 .....111 F1
Bramwell Dr WS6 .....4 D1
Bramwell Gdns CV6 .....95 F5
Brancaster Cl B77 .....22 A5
Branchal Rd WS9 .....16 C1
Branch Rd B38 .....123 E8
Branden Rd B48 .....139 A5
Brandfield Rd CV6 .....112 F8
Brandhall Ct B68 .....64 A2
Brandhall La B68 .....64 B1
Brandhall Prim Sch B68 .....64 B1
Brandhall Rd B68 .....64 B2
Brandon Cl
  Sedgley DY3 .....50 E7
  Sutton Coldfield WS9 .....30 F3
  West Bromwich B70 .....53 A2
Brandon Ct
  Birmingham B31 .....103 B1
  Coventry CV3 .....135 A7
Brandon Gr B31 .....122 F7
Brandon La CV3,CV8 .....135 C5
Brandon Marsh Nature Reserve* CV3 .....135 A4
Brandon Marsh Visitor Ctr* CV3 .....135 B4
Brandon Par CV32 .....162 A8
Brandon Pk WV3 .....38 E7
Brandon Pl B34 .....69 D7
Brandon Rd
  Birmingham B28 .....87 E2
  Coventry CV3 .....135 A8
  Halesowen B62 .....63 E1
  Hinckley LE10 .....75 B7
  Solihull B91 .....107 C2
Brandon Thomas Ct B6 .....67 B8
Brandon Way B70 .....81 E8
Brandon Way Ind Est B70 .....52 F3
Brandon Way B70 .....53 A2
Brandon Wood Farm* CV8 .....135 D5
Brandwood Cres B30 .....104 D3
Brandwood Gr B14 .....104 D3
Brandwood Ho B14 .....104 D3
Brandwood Park Rd B14 .....104 C4
Brandwood Rd B14 .....104 D5
Branfield Cl WV14 .....51 A8
Branksome Ave B21 .....65 F8
Branksome Rd CV6 .....112 E6
Branscombe Cl B14 .....104 D5
Bransdale Ave CV6 .....95 D3
Bransdale Cl WV6 .....25 A5
Bransdale Rd WS8 .....15 F6
Bransford Ave CV4 .....132 D5
Bransford Rise B91 .....108 B5
Branston St B18 .....66 C4
Branstree Dr CV6 .....95 D2
Brantford Rd B25 .....88 C8
Branthill Croft 4 B91 .....107 B1
Branthwaite Rd CV6 .....113 A8
Brantley Ave WV3 .....24 C1
Brantley Rd B6 .....56 B6
Branton Hill La WS9 .....30 C5
Brantwood Ave WS7 .....7 A5
Brascote Rd LE10 .....74 F8
Brasshouse Inf Sch B66 .....65 A7
Brasshouse La B66 .....65 A7
Brassie Cl B38 .....103 D1
Bratch Cl DY2 .....62 C3
Bratch Hollow WV5 .....49 A8
Brathay Cl CV3 .....133 D6
Bratt St B70 .....53 C4
Braunston Cl B76 .....47 A2
Brawnes Hurst B26 .....89 A8
Brayford Ave
  Brierley Hill DY5 .....81 B7
  Coventry CV3 .....133 C6
Braymoor Rd B33 .....69 E1
Bray's La CV2 .....114 A3
Brays Rd B26 .....89 B6
Brays Sch B26 .....89 A6

Bray St WV13. . . . . .27 B2
Braytoft Cl CV6 . . . . .95 C2
Brazil St CV4 . . . . .111 E2
Breaches La B98. . . . . .159 D8
Breadmarket St WS13. . . . . . .9 B8
Breakback Rd B61. . . . . . . .150 D8
Bream Cl
 Birmingham B37 . . . . .70 C2
 Wolverhampton WV10. . . . . .26 B4
Breamore Cres DY1 . . . . .50 F3
Bream B77. . . . . .35 D7
Brean Ave B92. . . . . .88 F5
Brearley Cl B19. . . . . .66 E5
Brearley St
 Birmingham,Handsworth
 B21. . . . . .65 D8
 Birmingham,Hockley B19. . . . .66 E5
Brechin Cl I.E10. . . . . .75 A8
Brecknell Rise DY10. . . . . . .116 F8
Brecknock Rd B71. . . . . . . .53 A6
Brecon Ave B61 . . . . .137 A5
Brecon Dr DY8 . . . . .81 B6
Brecon Rd B20. . . . . .66 B8
Brecon Twr I B16. . . . . . . .66 A2
Bredon Ave
 Coventry CV3. . . . . .134 F8
 Kidderminster DY11 . . . . . .116 A1
 Stourbridge DY9 . . . . .81 C5
Bredon Ct
 Halesowen B63 . . . . .83 A3
 Sutton Coldfield B75 . . . . . .32 A4
Bredon Ho B98 . . . . .159 B7
Bredon Rd
 Bromsgrove B61. . . . . . . .150 D7
 Oldbury B69. . . . . .63 D5
 Stourbridge DY8 . . . . .81 B6
Bredon Terr I B18. . . . . . . .66 A5
Bredon View B97 . . . . .158 D8
Breech Cl B74. . . . . .44 F7
Bree Cl CV5 . . . . .112 A7
Breeden Dr B76. . . . . .59 B6
Breedon Cl B30. . . . . .104 A5
Breedon Gdns B98. . . . . . . .154 A3
Breedon Rd B30. . . . . .104 A5
Breedon Way WS4. . . . . . . .15 C1
Breener Ind Est DY5. . . . . . .61 B1
Breen Rydding Dr WV14. .51 B8
Bree's La CV8 . . . . .130 A1
Breeze Ave WS11 . . . . .6 B5
Brelades Cl DY1 . . . . .50 E3
Breme Lodge B60. . . . . . . .151 A7
Brendon B77. . . . . .22 B1
Brendon Way CV10 . . . . . . .72 A3
Brenfield Dr LE10. . . . . . . .75 A8
Brennand Cl B68. . . . . .84 C8
Brennand Rd B68. . . . . . . .84 B8
Brentford Rd
 Birmingham B14 . . . . .105 A5
 Solihull B91. . . . . .106 E3
Brent Ho I B31 . . . . .61 E8
Brentmill Cl WV10 . . . . . . .11 F4
Brentnall Dr B75. . . . . .32 B3
Brenton Rd WV4. . . . . .38 F3
Brent Rd B30. . . . . .104 D8
Brent B77. . . . . .35 E7
Brentwood Ave CV3 . . . . . .133 C3
Brentwood Cl B91. . . . . . . .106 E3
Brentwood Gdns B91. . . . . .106 E3
Brentwood Gr B44. . . . . . . .55 E8
Brenwood Cl DY6. . . . . . . .60 B7
Brereton Cl DY2 . . . . .62 E8
Brereton Rd WV12 . . . . . . .27 D7
Brese Ave CV34. . . . . .155 F1
Bretby Gr B23 . . . . .57 A6
Bretford Rd CV2. . . . . .96 C1
Bretshall Cl B90. . . . . .126 F5
Brett Dr B32. . . . . .102 C8
Brettell Ct
 Brierley Hill DY5,DY8. . . . . .61 B1
 Stourbridge DY8 . . . . .80 F8
Brettell St I DY1. . . . . .62 B8
Bretton Gdns WV10 . . . . . .25 F6
Bretton Rd B27. . . . . .88 D2
Bretts Cl CV1 . . . . .165 D4
Bretts Hall Est CV10. . . . . . .72 A7
Brett St B71. . . . . .53 B5
Brett Young Cl DY10 . . . . . .117 B5
Brevitt Rd WV2 . . . . .39 D6
Brewer Rd CV12 . . . . .79 D2
Brewers Cl CV3 . . . . .115 A1
Brewers Dr WS3. . . . . .15 A1
Brewers Terr WS3. . . . . . . .15 A2
Brewer St WS2 . . . . .28 E4
Brewery St
 Birmingham,Handsworth
 B21. . . . . .65 D8
 Birmingham,New Town Row
 B6. . . . . .164 C5
 Dudley DY2. . . . . .51 E1
 Smethwick B67 . . . . .64 F6
 Tipton DY4. . . . . .51 F4
Brewins Way DY5. . . . . . . .62 A4
Brewster Cl
 Coventry CV2. . . . . .114 E2
 Fazeley B78. . . . . .20 E1
Brewster St I DY2. . . . . . . .62 C5
Breydon Gr WV13 . . . . . . .40 F8
Brian Rd B67. . . . . .64 E5
BrianswAY CV6. . . . . .95 E3
Briar Ave B74. . . . . .31 A1
Briarbeck WS4 . . . . .29 C8
Briar Cl
 Birmingham B24. . . . . .57 A4
 Cannock WS12. . . . . .2 A8
 Hinckley LE10. . . . . .75 F6
 Lickey End B60. . . . . .137 C6

Briar Cl continued
 Royal Leamington Spa
 CV32. . . . . .157 B2
Briar Coppice B90. . . . . . . .126 D4
Briar Ct
 I Brierley Hill DY5. . . . . . .61 D2
 Dudley DY2. . . . . .62 C6
Briardene Ave CV12. . . . . . .78 B2
Briarfield Rd B11. . . . . .88 A3
Briar Hill DY10. . . . . .118 E1
Briar Hill Inf Sch CV31. . .162 B3
Briarley Ho I B71. . . . . . . .42 F1
Briarmead LE10. . . . . .75 E4
Briars Cl
 Brierley Hill DY5. . . . . . . .61 C4
 Coventry CV2. . . . . .114 C2
 Nuneaton CV11 . . . . .73 E5
Briars The
 Aldridge WS9. . . . . .30 A7
 Birmingham B23. . . . . .56 D6
 West Hagley DY9. . . . . . . .98 F4
Briar B77. . . . . .22 A3
Briarwood Cl B90. . . . . . . .126 D4
Briar Wood Cl WV2 . . . . . . .40 A7
Briarwood The WV2. . . . . . .40 A7
Brickfield Rd B25. . . . . .88 B6
Brickheath Rd WV1. . . . . . .26 A3
Brickhill Dr B37. . . . . .70 A2
Brick Hill La CV5 . . . . .111 E8
Brickhouse Jun & Inf Sch
 B65. . . . . .63 A3
Brickhouse Lane S DY4. . .52 E6
Brickhouse La
 Stoke Prior B60. . . . . .150 C4
 West Bromwich B70 . . . . . .52 E6
Brickhouse Rd B65. . . . . . . .63 A4
Brickiln Ct I DY5. . . . . .61 D2
Brickiln St WS8. . . . . .15 F7
Brick Kiln La
 Birmingham B44. . . . . .55 E6
 Dudley DY3. . . . . .50 B3
 Middleton B78. . . . . .48 D6
 Solihull B47. . . . . .126 F8
 Wythall B47. . . . . .124 F4
Brick Kiln St
 Brierley Hill,Hart's Hill
 DY5. . . . . .61 E5
 Brierley Hill,Quarry Bank
 DY5. . . . . .82 A8
 Hinckley LE10. . . . . .75 C8
 Tipton DY4. . . . . .51 F6
Brickkiln St WV13. . . . . . . .26 F1
Brick Kiln Way CV12. . . . . . .78 D3
Brick St DY3. . . . . .50 D8
Brickworks Rd WS12. . . . . . .2 E2
Brickyard Cl CV7 . . . . .130 C7
Brickyard La B80. . . . . .159 C4
Brickyard Rd
 Aldridge,Leighswood WS9. . .30 A7
 Aldridge,Leighswood WS9. . .30 A8
 Aldridge,Vigo WS9. . . . . . .15 F1
Bridal Path The CV5. . . . . . .112 B6
Briddsland Rd B33. . . . . . . .69 E2
Bridgeacre Gdns CV3 . . . . .114 F2
Bridge Ave
 Cheslyn Hay WS6. . . . . . . .4 E4
 Tipton DY4. . . . . .52 C7
Bridgeburn Rd B31. . . . . . .102 E8
Bridge Cl
 Birmingham B11. . . . . .87 B3
 Brownhills WS8 . . . . .15 E6
Bridgecote CV3. . . . . .134 E6
Bridge Croft B12 . . . . .86 E6
Bridge Cross Rd WS7. . . . . . .7 A7
Bridge Ct DY8 . . . . .60 E2
Bridge End CV34. . . . . .160 F5
Bridgefield Wlk B65 . . . . . . .62 F5
Bridgefoot Wlk WV8 . . . . . .10 F1
Bridgeford Rd B34. . . . . . . .69 B6
Bridge Ho
 Royal Leamington Spa
 CV31. . . . . .162 A8
 Smethwick B66 . . . . .65 C6
Bridge Ind Est B91. . . . . . .107 C7
Bridgelands Way B20. . . . . . .55 D1
Bridgeman Croft B36 . . . . . .58 E1
Bridgeman Rd CV6. . . . . . .113 B4
Bridgeman St WS2. . . . . . . .28 D1
Bridgemary Cl WV10 . . . . . .11 E3
Bridge Meadow Dr B93. . .127 F6
Bridgemeadow Ho B36 B8 E8
Bridgend Croft DY5. . . . . . .61 B6
Bridgenorth Ho B33 . . . . . . .69 B2
Bridge Piece B31. . . . . .103 B2
Bridge Rd
 Birmingham B8 . . . . .67 E3
 Hinckley LE10. . . . . .75 D7
 Tipton DY4. . . . . .52 C7
 Walsall WS4 . . . . .15 B1
Bridge St Ind Est WS10 . .41 C1
Bridge St N B66. . . . . .65 B7
Bridge St S B66. . . . . .65 B6
Bridge St W B19. . . . . .66 D5
Bridge Sch The B23. . . . . . .56 E4
Bridges Cres WS11 . . . . .5 F5
Bridgeside Trad Est B77. . .21 C3
Bridges Rd WS11 . . . . .5 F5
Bridge St
 I Kidderminster DY10. . .116 C5
 Bilston WV14. . . . . .40 E6
 Birmingham B1. . . . . .164 A2
 Brownhills WS8 . . . . .15 E6
 Cannock WS11. . . . . .4 E5
 Coventry CV6. . . . . .114 A7
 Halesowen B63. . . . . .82 C7
 Kenilworth CV8. . . . . .147 F5
 Nuneaton,Chilvers Coton
 CV11. . . . . .73 C2

Bridge St continued
 Nuneaton CV11 . . . . .73 C4
 Oldbury B69. . . . . .64 A8
 Redditch B97. . . . . .153 D4
 Stourbridge DY8 . . . . .60 E1
 Tamworth B77. . . . . .21 E5
 Tipton WV14 . . . . .51 C8
 Walsall WS1 . . . . .28 F2
 Warwick CV34 . . . . .161 C8
 Wednesbury WS10 . . . . . . .41 F1
 West Bromwich B70 . . . . . .53 B4
 Willenhall WV13 . . . . .26 F1
 Wolverhampton WV10. . . . .25 E5
Bridge The I WS1. . . . . . . .28 E1
Bridge Trad Ctr The B64. .82 D8
Bridge Trad Est The B66. . .65 B6
Bridge View
 I Coleshill B46. . . . . .70 F7
 Baginton CV8. . . . . .133 B3
Bridgewater Ave B69. . . . . . .64 A4
Bridgewater Cres DY2 . . . . . .51 F4
Bridgewater Dr WV14. . . . . .40 C2
Bridgewater St B77. . . . . . . .21 D5
Bridge Way WS8. . . . . .15 E6
Bridgnorth Gr WV12 . . . . . .27 B6
Bridgnorth Rd
 Himley B63 . . . . .49 B3
 Stourbridge DY7,DY8. . . . . .80 C6
 Trescott WV6. . . . . .37 C7
 Wolverhampton WV6. . . . . .24 B2
Bridgtown Bsns Ctr WS11 .4 E6
Bridgtown Prim Sch WS11 .4 E6
Bridgwater Cl WS9. . . . . . . .15 F3
Bridle Brook La CV5,CV7. .94 A3
Bridle Gr B71. . . . . .53 F7
Bridle La B74,WS9 . . . . .44 E7
Bridle Mead B31. . . . . .103 B2
Bridle Path The B90. . . . . . .106 B6
Bridle Rd DY8 . . . . .80 D6
Bridlewood B74. . . . . .44 F8
Bridley Moor Rd B97. . . . . .153 C5
Bridport Cl CV2. . . . . .115 A4
Bridport Ho B31. . . . . .102 E7
Brierley Hill Prim Sch
 DY5. . . . . .61 D2
Brierley Hill Rd DY8. . . . . . .60 F2
Brierley La WV14 . . . . .40 E2
Brierley La Cvn Site WV14 .40 E2
Brierley Rd
 Bromsgrove B60. . . . . . . .137 C1
 Coventry CV2. . . . . .114 C8
Brierley Trad Est The DY5 .61 C3
Brier Mill Rd B63. . . . . .83 C3
Brier Sch The DY6 . . . . .60 F5
Brier Specl Sch The DY5. .61 E2
Briery Cl B64. . . . . .82 F7
Briery Rd B63. . . . . .82 E3
Brigadoon Gdns DY9 . . . . . .81 C2
Brigfield Cres B13 . . . . .105 B5
Brigfield Rd B13 . . . . .105 B5
Bright Cres B77 . . . . .21 C2
Brightmere Rd CV6 . . . . . . .113 B4
Brighton Cl WS2. . . . . .28 D3
Brighton Mews I WV3 . . . . .25 A2
Brighton Rd B27 . . . . .87 A5
Brighton St CV2 . . . . .114 B3
Bright Rd B68. . . . . .64 B5
Bright St
 Coventry CV6. . . . . .113 C4
 Darlaston WS10. . . . . .41 D5
Brightstone Cl WV10 . . . . . .11 E4
Brightstone Rd B45. . . . . . .102 B2
Bright St
 Stourbridge DY8 . . . . .80 D6
 Wolverhampton WV1. . . . . .163 A4
Brightwalton Rd CV3. . . . . .133 D7
Brightwell Cres B93 . . . . . .127 E3
Brill Cl CV4 . . . . .132 C5
Brimfield Pl I WV6 . . . . . . .24 F4
Brimstone La B61. . . . . .136 D7
Brindle Ave CV3 . . . . .114 C2
Brindle Cl B26. . . . . .88 E5
Brindle Ct B23. . . . . .56 B3
Brindlefields Way DY4 . . . . . .52 B2
Brindle Rd WS5. . . . . .43 C4
Brindley Ave WV11 . . . . . . .13 A1
Brindley Cl
 I Stourbridge DY8. . . . . . .60 E1
 Willenhall WS2 . . . . .27 F5
Brindley Cres WS12. . . . . . . .2 C8
Brindley Ct I B70. . . . . . . .53 A1
Brindley Dr B1. . . . . .164 A2
Brindley Heath Rd WS12 . .2 D8
Brindley Paddocks CV1 . .165 B4
Brindley Pl B1. . . . . .66 B2
Brindley Point Apartments I
 B16. . . . . .66 B2
Brindley Rd
 Bedworth CV7 . . . . .96 B8
 Hinckley LE10. . . . . .75 F4
 West Bromwich B71 . . . . . .53 A8
Brindley Bsns Pk WS11 . . .2 B3
Brindley Way I B66. . . . . . .65 C5
Brineton Gr B29. . . . . .85 A1
Brineton Ind Est I WS2. .28 C1
Brineton St WS2. . . . . .28 C1
Bringewood Gr B32. . . . . . .102 B8
Brinklow Cl B98 . . . . .159 D8
Brinklow Croft B34 . . . . . . .69 D7
Brinklow Rd
 Birmingham B29. . . . . .84 F2
 Coventry CV3 . . . . .115 A2
Brinklow Twr I B12. . . . . . .86 F7
Brinley Way DY6. . . . . .60 C6
Brinsford La WV10 . . . . . . .11 D7
Brinsford Rd WV10. . . . . . .11 C3
Brinsley Cl B91. . . . . .107 B2
Brinsley Rd B26. . . . . .89 B8

Brinton Cl DY11. . . . . .116 C3
Brinton Cres DY11 . . . . . . .116 C3
Brisbane Cl CV3 . . . . .133 E6
Brisbane Ct I CV12. . . . . . .78 A2
Brisbane Rd B67. . . . . .64 E5
Brisbane Way WS12. . . . . . . .2 E3
Briscoe Rd CV6. . . . . .95 D4
Brisely Cl DY5. . . . . .81 D8
Bristam Cl B69. . . . . .63 E6
Bristnall Hall Cres B68. . . .64 A3
Bristnall Hall La B68. . . . . . .64 C3
Bristnall Hall Rd B68. . . . . . .64 C3
Bristnall Hall Tech Coll
 B68. . . . . .64 D3
Bristol Cl WS11. . . . . .2 B1
Bristol Ct I B29. . . . . .103 C7
Bristol Rd
 Birmingham,Balsall Heath
 B5. . . . . .86 C5
 Birmingham,Gravelly Hill
 B23. . . . . .56 E3
 Dudley DY2. . . . . .62 D2
Bristol Rd S
 Birmingham B31. . . . . . . .102 F2
 Birmingham,Bournville B29,B30,
 B31. . . . . .103 C7
 Birmingham,Longbridge B31,
 B45. . . . . .122 C8
Bristol St
 Birmingham B15 . . . . .86 D8
 Wolverhampton WV3. . . . . .39 B8
Briston Cl DY5. . . . . .81 C8
Britannia Cl B98. . . . . .153 F3
Britannia Gdns B65. . . . . . . .63 C3
Britannia Rd DY3 . . . . .50 E5
Britannia Rd
 Bilston WV14. . . . . .40 F3
 Hinckley LE10. . . . . .76 A5
 Rowley Regis B65. . . . . . . .63 C2
Britannia St
 Coventry CV2. . . . . .113 F3
 Oldbury B69. . . . . .52 C2
Britannia Way WS13 . . . . . . .9 F8
Britannic Gdns B13. . . . . . . .86 D2
Britannic Ho B13. . . . . .86 D2
Britford Cl B14 . . . . .104 F3
Briton Rd CV2 . . . . .114 A4
Brittan Cl B34 . . . . .69 E6
Brittania Pk WS10. . . . . . . .41 D3
Brittania Rd WS1. . . . . .42 E8
Brittania Sh Ctr I LE10. . .75 D8
Britten Cl CV11. . . . . .79 A7
Britten St B97. . . . . .153 D4
Britton Dr B72. . . . . .57 C8
Britwell Rd B73. . . . . .46 A2
Brixfield Way B90. . . . . . . .126 E5
Brixham Cl CV11. . . . . .73 F5
Brixham Dr CV2 . . . . .114 C7
Brixham Rd B16. . . . . .65 D2
Brixworth Cl CV3 . . . . .134 E8
Broad Acres B31. . . . . .102 E6
Broadbent Cl I WS13. . . . . .8 F6
Broadcott Ind Est B64. . . .83 A8
Broad Croft I DY4 . . . . . . .52 C6
Broadfern Rd B93 . . . . .128 B8
Broadfield Cl
 Kingswinford DY6 . . . . . . .60 D5
 West Bromwich B71 . . . . . .42 F1
Broadfield House Glass
 Mus* DY6 . . . . .60 D5
Broadfields DY9 . . . . .99 A6
Broadfield Wlk I B16. . . . . .66 B1
Broad Ground Rd B98. . . .154 E2
Broadhaven Cl CV31 . . . . . .162 C7
Broad Heath Cl B97. . . . . .153 B5
Broad Heath Com Prim Sch
 CV6. . . . . .113 C6
Broadheath Dr WS4. . . . . . .29 D8
Broadhidley Dr B32. . . . . . . .84 B1
Broadhurst Grn WS12. . . . . .2 A8
Broad La
 Birmingham B14. . . . . . . .104 E4
 Burntwood WS7. . . . . .8 B5
 Coventry CV5. . . . . .111 D4
 Lichfield WS14. . . . . .9 C6
Broad Mdw WV5. . . . . .30 B8
Broadmeadow Cl CV5. . . . .112 C2
Broadmeadow Cl B30. . . . .104 B3
Broadmeadow Ho B32 . . . .102 D8
Broadmeadow Inf Sch
 B30. . . . . .104 B2
Broadmeadow Jun Sch
 B30. . . . . .104 B2
Broadmeadow WV4. . . . . . . .60 E8
Broad Meadow La
 Birmingham B30 . . . . .104 B3
 Great Wyrley WS6. . . . . . . .5 A4
Broadmeadows Cl WV12. . .27 E8
Broadmeadows Rd WV12. . .27 E8
Broadmede Ho B67. . . . . . .64 E2

 Bra – Bro 179

Broadmere Rise CV5. . . . . .112 A2
Broadmoor Ave B68. . . . . . .64 D2
Broadmoor Cl WV14. . . . . . .40 C4
Broadmoor Rd WV14. . . . . . .40 C4
Broadoaks Cl WS11 . . . . .5 F6
Broad Oaks Rd B91 . . . . . . .107 A5
Broad Oaks B76 . . . . .47 A1
Broadoaks The B91 . . . . . . .107 A4
Broad Park Rd CV2 . . . . . . .114 D8
Broad Rd B27 . . . . .88 B3
Broadsmeath B77. . . . . .21 C1
Broad St
 Bilston WV14. . . . . .40 D6
 Birmingham B15,B1. . . . . . .66 C2
 Brierley Hill DY5 . . . . .61 C6
 Bromsgrove B61 . . . . .136 F4
 Cannock WS11 . . . . .4 E6
 Coventry CV6. . . . . .113 E7
 Kidderminster DY10 . . . . . .116 E7
 Kingswinford DY6. . . . . . . .60 D5
 Oldbury B69. . . . . .64 A5
Broadstone Ave
 Halesowen B63 . . . . .82 B4
 Walsall WS3 . . . . .28 D7
Broadstone Cl WV4 . . . . . . .39 D5
Broadstone Rd B26. . . . . . . .69 A1
Broad Street Jetty CV6. . .113 E7
Broad St
 Tipton WV14 . . . . .51 C8
 Warwick CV34 . . . . .160 F7
 Wolverhampton WV1. . . . . .163 C3
Broadsword Way LE10. . . . . .75 D4
Broadwalk I B1 . . . . .66 C1
Broadwalk Ret Pk WS1. . . . .42 D6
Broadwas B38 . . . . .154 C5
Broadwater CV5. . . . . .133 A8
Broadwaters Ave WS10. . . . .41 C4
Broadwaters Dr
 Kidderminster DY10 . . . . . .117 A8
 West Hagley DY9. . . . . . . .99 B4
Broadwaters Rd WS10 . . . . .41 C4
Broadway Ave
 Birmingham B9 . . . . .68 A3
 Halesowen B63 . . . . .83 A2
Broadway
 Cannock WS12. . . . . .1 F6
 Coventry CV5. . . . . .113 A1
Broadway Croft
 Birmingham B26 . . . . .89 A6
 Oldbury B68. . . . . .64 C1
Broadway CV32. . . . . .157 D3
Broadway Gdns WV10 . . . . .11 E2
Broadway Mans CV5 . . . . . .113 A1
Broadway N WS1. . . . . .29 B2
Broadway Plaza B16. . . . . . .66 A1
Broadway B20. . . . . .55 E2
Broadway Sch The (Aston
 Campus) B6 . . . . .66 E8
Broadway B90. . . . . .106 B4
Broadway The
 Birmingham B20 . . . . .55 E2
 Dudley DY1. . . . . .51 B3
 Stourbridge DY8 . . . . .80 D3
 West Bromwich B71 . . . . . .53 B7
 Wombourne WV5. . . . . . . .49 A5
Broad Way WS4 . . . . .15 C2
Broadway
 Walsall WS5 . . . . .43 A6
 Wolverhampton,Bushbury
 WV10. . . . . .11 E2
 Wolverhampton WV10. . . . .24 C2
Broadway W WS1. . . . . .42 D6
Broadwell Cl CV4 . . . . .131 F6
Broadwell Ind Pk B69. . . . . .53 A1
Broadwell Rd
 Oldbury B69. . . . . .64 A8
 Solihull B92 . . . . .89 A2
Broadwells Cres CV4. . . . . .132 A5
Broadyates Gr B25. . . . . . . .88 C6
Broadyates Rd B25. . . . . . . .88 C6
Brobury Croft B91. . . . . . . .106 D4
Brockencote Ct B73. . . . . . . .46 B1
Brockenhurst Way CV6. . . . . .96 B6
Brockeridge Cl WV12 . . . . . .13 C1
Brockfield Ho WV10 . . . . . . .25 F4
Brockhall Gr B37. . . . . .69 F5
Brockhill Rd B97 . . . . .153 A5
Brockhill La
 Alvechurch B48. . . . . .124 B2
 Beoley B98. . . . . .140 F2
 Tardebigge B97. . . . . .152 B2
Brockhurst Ave LE10. . . . . . .75 D4
Brockhurst Cres WS5. . . . . .42 E4
Brockhurst Dr
 Birmingham B28 . . . . .106 A5
 Coventry CV4 . . . . .111 D2
 Wolverhampton WV1. . . . . .25 A4
Brockhurst Ho I WS2 . . . . .28 D3
Brockhurst La
 Solihull B90. . . . . .126 B5
 Weeford B75. . . . . .33 B7
Brockhurst Pl WS5. . . . . . . .42 F5
Brockhurst Rd
 Birmingham B36 . . . . .68 D6
 Sutton Coldfield B75 . . . . . .32 D1
Brockhurst St WS1. . . . . . . .42 E6
Brockley Cl DY5. . . . . .61 D3
Brockley Gr B13 . . . . .86 C6
Brockley Pl B7 . . . . .67 C7
Brockmoor Cl DY9 . . . . .81 B3
Brockmoor Prim Sch DY5 .61 C3
Brock Rd DY4 . . . . .52 C5
Brockton Rd B29. . . . . .85 A1
Brockwell Gr B44. . . . . .44 E4

Brockwell Rd B44 . . . . .44 E4
Brockworth Rd B14 . . . . . .104 C2
Brocton CI WV14 . . . . .40 A3
Brodick CI LE10 . . . . .75 A8
Brodick Rd LE10 . . . . .74 F8
Brodick Way CV10 . . . . .72 F3
Brogden CI 4 B71 . . . . .53 F8
Brome Hall La B94 . . . . . . .144 D2
Bromfield CI B6 . . . . .66 E7
Bromfield Cres WS10 . . . . . .42 C4
Bromfield Ct WV6 . . . . .24 E3
Bromfield Rd B97 . . . . .153 D2
Bromford Central B8 . . . . . .68 B8
Bromford CI
  Birmingham,Erdington
  B23 . . . . .56 E5
  Birmingham,Handsworth
  B20 . . . . .55 A2
Bromford Cres B24 . . . . . . .57 A2
Bromford Ct B8 . . . . .68 B6
Bromford Dale 2 WV6 . . . . .24 E3
Bromford Dell B31 . . . . .103 C4
Bromford Dr B36 . . . . .68 D8
Bromford Gdns B15 . . . . . . .85 C8
Bromford Hill B20 . . . . .55 C3
Bromford Ho B73 . . . . .45 F2
Bromford La
  Birmingham B8,B36 . . . . . . .68 C6
  West Bromwich B70 . . . . . . .53 B2
Bromford Mere 4 B92 . . . . .88 E1
Bromford Park Ho 3 B13 .87 B2
Bromford Rd
  Birmingham B36 . . . . .68 D7
  Dudley DY2 . . . . .62 A6
  West Bromwich B69,B70 . . . .53 A1
Bromford Rise WV3 . . . . . .163 A1
Bromford Road Ind Est
  B70 . . . . .53 A1
Bromford Wlk B43 . . . . .43 F1
Bromhurst Way CV34 . . . . .160 B4
Bromleigh Dr CV2 . . . . .114 C2
Bromleigh Villas CV8 . . . . .133 F2
Bromley DY5 . . . . .61 B5
Bromley CI
  Cannock WS12 . . . . .2 C7
  Kenilworth CV8 . . . . .147 E6
Bromley Gdns WV8 . . . . .10 A4
Bromley Hills Prim Sch
  DY6 . . . . .60 F5
Bromley Ho WV4 . . . . .39 A5
Bromley La DY6 . . . . .60 E4
Bromley Lodge WV4 . . . . . . .39 A5
Bromley-Pennsett Prim Sch
  The DY5 . . . . .61 B5
Bromley PI WV4 . . . . .39 A5
Bromley St
  Birmingham B9 . . . . .67 A1
  Stourbridge DY9 . . . . .81 F6
  Wolverhampton WV2 . . . . . . .39 C7
Brompton Dr DY5 . . . . .81 B7
Brompton Lawns WV6 . . . . .24 A3
Brompton Pool Rd B28 . . .105 E3
Brompton Rd B44 . . . . .44 E4
Bromsgrove Highway
  Bromsgrove B60 . . . . .137 D1
  Redditch B97 . . . . .153 B2
  Tardebigge B60,B97 . . . . . .152 C6
Bromsgrove Lower Sch
  B60 . . . . .136 F1
Bromsgrove Mus * B61. .137 A3
Bromsgrove Private Hospl
  B60 . . . . .138 B1
Bromsgrove Rd
  Clent DY9 . . . . .99 D4
  Dodford B61 . . . . .136 D6
  Halesowen B63 . . . . .83 C4
  Mustow Green DY10 . . . . . . .117 F2
  Redditch B97 . . . . .153 B3
  Romsley B62 . . . . .101 A5
  Studley B80 . . . . .159 D2
Bromsgrove Sch B61 . . . . .136 F1
Bromsgrove Sta B60 . . . . . .151 B7
Bromsgrove St
  Birmingham B5 . . . . .164 C1
  Halesowen B63 . . . . .83 C4
  Kidderminster DY10 . . . . . . .116 E6
Bromwall Rd B13 . . . . .105 B6
Bromwich CI CV3 . . . . .134 F8
Bromwich Dr B75 . . . . .46 C7
Bromwich La DY9 . . . . .99 B8
Bromwich Wlk B9 . . . . .68 A3
Bromwynd CI WV2 . . . . .39 B6
Bromyard Ave B76 . . . . .58 A8
Bromyard Rd B11 . . . . .87 E3
Bronte Ct B90 . . . . .106 D1
Bronte Dr
  Cannock WS11 . . . . .2 C2
  Kidderminster DY10 . . . . . . .117 C6
Bronte Farm Rd B90 . . . . . .106 D1
Bronte Rd WV2 . . . . .39 F6
Bronwen Ingham Ct
  DY10 .116 E7
Bronwen Rd WV14 . . . . .51 C7
Bronze CI CV11 . . . . .78 E8
Brook Ave B77 . . . . .36 A7
Brookbank Ave B34 . . . . .69 D6
Brookbank Gdns DY3 . . . . . .50 B2
Brookbank Rd DY3 . . . . .50 B2
Brook CI
  Birmingham B33 . . . . .68 E4
  Brownhills WS9 . . . . .16 A3
  Coventry CV1 . . . . .113 E4

Brook CI continued
  Lichfield WS13 . . . . .3 A1
  Solihull B90 . . . . .105 F1
Brook Cotts B25 . . . . .88 A7
Brook Cres
  Kingswinford DY6 . . . . .60 C7
  Stourbridge DY9 . . . . .81 F3
  West Hagley DY9 . . . . .99 B5
Brook Croft
  Birmingham,Lyndon Green
  B26 . . . . .89 B7
  Birmingham,Marston Green
  B37 . . . . .90 B7
Brook Ct B60 . . . . .137 B3
Brookdale CI B45 . . . . .102 A1
Brookdale Dr WV4 . . . . .38 E6
Brookdale
  Dudley DY3 . . . . .50 C3
  Hinckley LE10 . . . . .75 B7
  Kidderminster DY10 . . . . . . .116 F8
Brookdale Rd CV10 . . . . .73 E7
Brook Dr B32 . . . . .84 D1
Brooke CI CV34 . . . . .160 B8
Brooke Mews 4 CV34 . . . .160 F7
Brook End WS7 . . . . .7 A4
Brookend Dr B45 . . . . .121 F7
Brook End B78 . . . . .35 B8
Brooke Rd
  Cannock WS12 . . . . .1 F6
  Kenilworth CV8 . . . . .148 B4
Brookes CI B69 . . . . .52 B1
Brookes Ho 6 WS1 . . . . .28 E1
Brooke St DY2 . . . . .51 D1
Brook Farm Ind Est B94 . .126 B2
Brook Farm Wlk B37 . . . . . .70 D2
Brookfield CI
  Aldridge WS9 . . . . .16 A1
  Redditch B97 . . . . .158 D4
Brookfield Dr WS11 . . . . .4 E7
Brookfield Ho DY9 . . . . .119 C7
Brookfield Rd
  Aldridge WS9 . . . . .16 A1
  Birmingham B18 . . . . .66 A5
  Birmingham,Brandwood End
  B30 . . . . .104 D3
  Codsall WV8 . . . . .10 B3
  Cubbington CV32 . . . . .157 E5
  Hinckley LE10 . . . . .75 C6
Brook Fields CI B60 . . . . . .121 C1
Brookfields Prim Sch B18 .66 A4
Brookfields Rd B68 . . . . .64 C4
Brookfield Terr B18 . . . . . . .66 A5
Brookfield Way
  Solihull B92 . . . . .106 D7
  Tipton DY4 . . . . .52 B6
Brookford Ave CV6 . . . . .95 A3
Brook Green La B92 . . . . . .109 A1
Brookhampton Ct B97 . . . .158 E4
Brookhill CI WV12 . . . . .13 D1
Brookhill Rd B8 . . . . .68 A4
Brookhill Way WV12 . . . . . . .13 D1
Brook Holloway DY9 . . . . . . .81 F4
Brookhouse CI WV10 . . . . . . .12 B6
Brookhouse La
  Featherstone WV10 . . . . .12 B7
  Wolverhampton WV10 . . . . . .11 F6
Brookhouse Rd
  Blackwell B45 . . . . .137 F7
  Walsall WS5 . . . . .43 B7
Brookhurst Ct CV32 . . . . . .156 D1
Brookhurst Prim Sch
  CV32 .156 C1
Brookhus Farm Rd B76 . . . .58 A8
Brooking CI B43 . . . . .44 D4
Brook La
  Birmingham B32 . . . . .84 F5
  Birmingham,Billesley B13 . .105 B7
  Brownhills WS9 . . . . .15 F3
  Cradley Heath B64 . . . . .62 E2
  Great Wyrley WS6 . . . . .5 A3
Brookland Gr WS9 . . . . .15 F3
Brookland Rd
  Brownhills WS9 . . . . .15 F3
  West Hagley DY9 . . . . .99 A4
Brooklands Ave WS6 . . . . . . .4 F4
Brooklands CI B28 . . . . .87 F1
Brooklands Dr B14 . . . . .104 E5
Brooklands Ho 8 CV34 . . .161 D8
Brooklands La B98 . . . . .154 B5
Brooklands Par WV1 . . . . . . .26 B2
Brooklands Pk B98 . . . . .154 F5
Brooklands Rd
  Birmingham B28 . . . . .87 F1
  Cannock WS11 . . . . .2 A4
Brooklands
  Stourbridge DY8 . . . . .60 F1
  Walsall WS5 . . . . .43 B3
Brooklands Way B37 . . . . . . .90 A8
Brook La
  Nuneaton CV10 . . . . .73 C6
  Solihull B92 . . . . .106 D8
Brooklea CV12 . . . . .77 F2
Brooklea Gr B38 . . . . .104 A1
Brookline Gdns WV10 . . . . .12 B7
Brooklyn Ave B6 . . . . .66 F7
Brooklyn Gr
  Dudley WV14 . . . . .51 D8
  Kingswinford DY6 . . . . .60 B8
Brooklyn Rd
  Burntwood WS7 . . . . .7 A4
  Cannock WS12 . . . . .2 D1
  Coventry CV1 . . . . .113 D6
Brookmans Ave B32 . . . . . . .84 D4
Brook Mdws WV8 . . . . .10 B4
Brookmeadow Ct B28 . . . .105 D6
Brook Meadow Rd
  Birmingham B34 . . . . .69 B6

Brook Meadow Rd continued
  Walsall WS4 . . . . .29 D8
Brook Park Trad Est 4
  DY9 . . . . .81 F5
Brookpiece Ho B14 . . . . . . .104 C2
Brook Piece Wlk B35 . . . . . .58 B3
Brook Prim Sch DY6 . . . . . . .60 F1
Brook Rd
  Birmingham,Chad Valley
  B15 . . . . .85 E7
  Birmingham,Rubery B45 . . .121 E7
  Bromsgrove B61 . . . . .136 E1
  Cheslyn Hay WS6 . . . . .4 E4
  Fairfield B61 . . . . .120 C2
  Oldbury B68 . . . . .64 A2
  Stourbridge DY8 . . . . .81 B3
  Wollaston WV13 . . . . .26 E1
Brooksbank Dr B64 . . . . .62 F4
Brooksby Gr B93 . . . . .128 A2
Brooks Croft B35 . . . . .58 A2
Brookshaw Way CV2 . . . . . .114 F8
Brookside Ave
  Birmingham B13 . . . . .105 B7
  Coventry CV5 . . . . .112 C3
  Kenilworth CV8 . . . . .147 E4
Brookside
  Birmingham,Great Barr
  B43 . . . . .54 D7
  Birmingham,Northfield
  B31 . . . . .102 F5
  Cheswick Green B90 . . . . . . .126 D3
Brookside CI
  Alvechurch B48 . . . . .139 B6
  Birmingham B23 . . . . .56 C7
  Halesowen B63 . . . . .82 D3
Brookside Dr B61 . . . . .136 F8
Brookside
  Dudley DY3 . . . . .50 D2
  Hinckley LE10 . . . . .75 E7
Brookside Ind Est WS10 . . .42 B3
Brookside Rd B78 . . . . .20 D1
Brookside Way
  Blakedown DY10 . . . . .98 B2
  Kingswinford DY6 . . . . .60 C7
  Tamworth B77 . . . . .36 A6
Brooks Rd B72 . . . . .57 C8
Brook St
  Bedworth CV12 . . . . .78 B5
  Bilston WV14 . . . . .40 E5
  Birmingham B3 . . . . .164 A3
  Brierley Hill DY5 . . . . .82 A8
  Dudley DY3 . . . . .51 A7
  Dudley,Gornalwood DY3 . . . .50 C3
  Kingswinford DY6 . . . . .49 B1
Brookstray Flats CV5 . . . . .112 B3
Brook St B98 . . . . .154 A4
Brook Street Bsns Ctr
  DY4 . . . . .51 E6
Brook St
  Smethwick B66 . . . . .65 B6
  Stourbridge,Amblecote DY8 .60 F1
  Stourbridge DY8 . . . . .80 E5
  Stourbridge,Lye DY9 . . . . . . .81 F5
  Tipton DY4 . . . . .51 E6
  Walsall WS2 . . . . .28 D1
  Warwick CV34 . . . . .160 E6
  West Bromwich B70 . . . . . . .53 B3
Brook Terr WV14 . . . . .40 E5
Brookthorpe Dr WV12 . . . . .27 C4
Brookvale Ave CV3 . . . . .114 C1
Brook Vale WS11 . . . . .4 F8
Brookvale CI B61 . . . . .137 B4
Brookvale Gr B92 . . . . .88 D1
Brookvale Mews B29 . . . . . . .86 B2
Brookvale Park Rd B23 . . . .56 B4
Brookvale Prim Sch B23 . . .56 B3
Brookvale Rd
  Birmingham B23,B6 . . . . .56 A3
  Solihull B92 . . . . .88 D1
Brookvale Trad Est B6 . . . . .56 A3
Brook View CI B19 . . . . .66 C6
Brookview B67 . . . . .64 F3
Brookweed B77 . . . . .22 A3
Brookwillow Rd B63 . . . . .82 E1
Brook Wlk B32 . . . . .84 D2
Brookwood Ave B28 . . . . . . .105 D5
Brookwood Dr B45 . . . . .138 C8
Broom CI B60 . . . . .137 B2
Broom Covert Rd WS14 . . . .18 E8
Broom Cres DY10 . . . . .117 A6
Broomcroft Rd B37 . . . . .69 F5
Bromedene Ave B34 . . . . . . .69 A7
Broom Dr B14 . . . . .104 E4
Broome Ave B43 . . . . .54 C7
Broome CI 5 B63 . . . . .83 A3
Broome Croft CV6 . . . . .95 B3
Broome Ct B36 . . . . .69 C8
Broome Gdns B75 . . . . .46 F6
Broomehill CI DY5 . . . . .81 C7
Broome Rd WV10 . . . . .25 C7
Broomfield Ave B78 . . . . .35 A8
Broomfield CI DY11 . . . . . . .116 C7
Broomfield Gn DY11 . . . . . . .116 C7
Broomfield PI CV5 . . . . .120 B2
Broomfield Rd
  Birmingham B23 . . . . .56 D3
  Coventry CV5 . . . . .113 A1
  Kidderminster DY11 . . . . . . .116 C7
  Wednesbury WS10 . . . . .42 C3
Broomfield Rise CV10 . . . . . .72 F2
Broomfields Ave B91 . . . . . .107 D5
Broomfields CI B91 . . . . . . .107 D5
Broomfields Farm Rd
  B91 . . . . .107 D5
Broomfield B67 . . . . .64 F5

Broomhall Ave WV11 . . . . . . .26 D6
Broom Hall Cres B27 . . . . . .106 B8
Broom Hall Gr B27 . . . . .106 C8
Broomhill Bank WS11 . . . . . . .1 E3
Broomhill CI
  Birmingham B43 . . . . .54 D8
  Cannock WS11 . . . . .1 E4
Broomhill La B43 . . . . .54 D8
Broomhill Rd B23 . . . . .56 B7
Broom Ho 3 B71 . . . . .42 F1
Broomhurst B15 . . . . .85 E8
Broomie CI B75 . . . . .46 D4
Broomlea La B90 . . . . .126 A6
Broomlea CI B74 . . . . .44 E8
Broom Rd
  Dudley DY1 . . . . .51 A5
  Walsall WS5 . . . . .43 B3
Broom St B12 . . . . .87 A8
Broomybank CV8 . . . . .148 B6
Broomy CI B34 . . . . .69 A5
Brosdale Dr LE10 . . . . .71 A1
Broseley Ave B31 . . . . .123 B8
Broseley Brook CI 1 B9 . . . .67 C1
Brosil Ave B20 . . . . .54 E3
Brotherton Ave B97 . . . . . . .152 F2
Brougham St B19 . . . . .66 B7
Brough CI
  Birmingham B7 . . . . .67 B6
  Wolverhampton WV4,WV14 . .39 F3
Broughton Ct B15 . . . . .86 B7
Broughton Cres B31 . . . . . . .122 D8
Broughton Ct
  2 Birmingham,Edgbaston
  B15 . . . . .86 B7
  Birmingham,Pheasey B43 . . .44 D4
  Perton WV6 . . . . .24 A3
Broughton Rd
  Birmingham B20 . . . . .66 A8
  Stourbridge DY9 . . . . .81 D3
  Wolverhampton WV3 . . . . . . .24 C1
Browett Rd CV6 . . . . .113 A5
Brown Ave B77 . . . . .35 C8
Brownfield Rd B34 . . . . .69 C7
Brownhills Com Tech Coll
  WS8 . . . . .16 A4
Brownhills Rd
  Brownhills WS8 . . . . .16 A4
  Norton Canes WS11 . . . . .6 B4
Brownhills West Prim Sch
  WS8 . . . . .6 C2
Brownhills West Sta * WS7 .6 C3
Brownhills Way CV34 . . . . .160 C5
Browning CI
  Kidderminster DY10 . . . . . . .117 B6
  Nuneaton CV10 . . . . .72 A5
  Tamworth B79 . . . . .20 B8
  Willenhall WV12 . . . . .27 C7
Browning Cres WV10 . . . . . . .11 C2
Browning Dr LE10 . . . . .71 C1
Browning Gr WV6 . . . . .23 E4
Browning Rd
  Burntwood WS7 . . . . .7 C2
  Coventry CV2 . . . . .114 C3
  Dudley DY3 . . . . .50 A4
Browning St B16 . . . . .66 B2
Brown Lion St DY4 . . . . .51 E7
Browning St 7 B16 . . . . . . .157 A2
Brownmead Jun & Inf Sch
  B34 . . . . .69 A6
Brown Rd WS10 . . . . .41 C7
Brown's Coppice Ave
  B91 . . . . .106 C5
Brown's Ct B13 . . . . .87 B2
Browns Dr B73 . . . . .56 F8
Brownsea CI B45 . . . . .101 F1
Brownsea Dr B1 . . . . .164 B1
Brownsfield Rd WS13 . . . . . . .3 D1
Browns Gn B20 . . . . .54 E3
Brownshill Bsns Pk WS8 . . .15 F5
Brownshill Green CI CV6 . . .94 E1
Brownshore La WV11 . . . . . . .13 A8
Brown's La
  Brownshill Green CV5 . . . . . .94 C1
  Dordon B78 . . . . .36 F5
Browns La B93 . . . . .127 E6
Brown's La CV7 . . . . .21 C8
Brownsover CI B36 . . . . .58 B1
Brown St WV2 . . . . .39 D7
Brownswall Rd DY3 . . . . .50 C7
Broxell CI CV34 . . . . .155 C1
Broxwood Pk WV6 . . . . .24 B3
Bruce Rd
  Bedworth CV7 . . . . .95 F7
  Coventry CV6 . . . . .113 B8
  Kidderminster DY10 . . . . . . .117 B7
Brueton Ave
  Bromsgrove B60 . . . . .151 A8
  Solihull B91 . . . . .107 D3
Brueton Dr
  Birmingham B24 . . . . .57 A3
  Redditch B98 . . . . .154 A3
Brueton Rd WV14 . . . . .41 A7
Bruford Rd WV3 . . . . .39 A8
Brunel CI
  Birmingham B12 . . . . .87 A5
  Burntwood WS7 . . . . .7 B8
  Coventry CV2 . . . . .113 F3
  Whitnash CV31 . . . . .162 B2

Brunel Rd
  Hinckley LE10 . . . . .75 C1
  Oldbury B69 . . . . .63 D6
Brunel St B1 . . . . .164 B2
Brunel Way WV2 . . . . .40 A2
Brunel Wlk WS10 . . . . .41 F6
Brunslow CI
  Willenhall WV13 . . . . .27 C1
  Wolverhampton WV10 . . . . . .11 C2
Brunswick Arc B1 . . . . .66 B2
Brunswick Ct
  Wednesbury WS10 . . . . .42 C3
  Whitnash CV31 . . . . .162 A5
Brunswick Gate DY8 . . . . . . .81 A4
Brunswick Gdns
  Birmingham B21 . . . . .54 F7
  Wednesbury WS10 . . . . .42 B6
Brunswick Ho
  Birmingham,Buckland End
  B34 . . . . .69 A7
  Birmingham,Marston Green
  B37 . . . . .89 F8
Brunswick Park Rd WS10 .42 B3
Brunswick Rd
  Birmingham,Handsworth
  B21 . . . . .54 F7
  Birmingham,Sparkbrook
  B12 . . . . .87 A5
  Cannock WS11 . . . . .1 E2
  Coventry CV1 . . . . .113 B2
Brunswick St
  Birmingham B1 . . . . .66 B2
  Royal Leamington Spa
  CV32 .162 A5
  Walsall WS2 . . . . .42 C7
Brunswick Terr WS10 . . . . . . .41 F3
Bruntingthorpe Way
  CV3 . . . . .134 E8
Brunton CI CV3 . . . . .115 B1
Brunton Rd B10 . . . . .87 F7
Brushfield Rd B42 . . . . .55 D8
Brutus Dr B46 . . . . .59 E1
Bryan Ave WV4 . . . . .38 D4
Bryan Rd WS2 . . . . .42 C4
Bryanston Ct CV2 . . . . .115 A4
Bryanston Rd B91 . . . . .106 F1
Bryanston Rd B91 . . . . .106 F6
Bryans Way WS12 . . . . .2 F4
Bryant Rd CV7 . . . . .96 A7
Bryant St B18 . . . . .65 E5
Bryce Rd DY5 . . . . .61 B5
Bryher Wlk B45 . . . . .101 E1
Brylan Croft B44 . . . . .56 A7
Brymill Ind Est DY4 . . . . .51 E7
Brympton Rd CV3 . . . . .114 C2
Bryn Arden Rd B26 . . . . .88 E5
Bryndale Ave B14 . . . . .104 C4
Bryn Jones CI CV3 . . . . .134 F7
Brynmawr Rd WV4,WV14 . . .40 A3
Bryn Rd B70 . . . . .113 F7
Brynside CI B14 . . . . .104 D2
Bryony CI CV12 . . . . .77 E1
Bryony Croft B23 . . . . .56 B7
Bryony Gdns WS10 . . . . .41 D7
Bryony Rd B29 . . . . .103 B7
Bryony R4 . . . . .31 F5
Bsns Ctr The B11 . . . . .87 F6
Bubbenhall Rd CV8 . . . . .133 F1
Buchanan Ave WS4 . . . . .29 A3
Buchanan CI WS4 . . . . .29 A3
Buchanan Rd WS4 . . . . .29 A3
Buckbury CI DY9 . . . . .81 D2
Buckbury Croft B90 . . . . . . .127 B6
Buckden CI 2 CV34 . . . . . . .155 F1
Buckden B77 . . . . .22 C1
Buckfast CI
  Bromsgrove B61 . . . . .136 D1
  Coventry CV3 . . . . .133 E5
Buckhold Dr CV5 . . . . .112 B5
Buckingham CI
  Hinckley LE10 . . . . .71 F4
  Nuneaton CV10 . . . . .73 B1
  Wednesbury WS10 . . . . .42 D4
Buckingham Ct
  Birmingham B29 . . . . .85 D1
  Birmingham,Griffin's Hill
  B29 . . . . .103 D8
Buckingham Dr WV12 . . . . . .27 B7
Buckingham Gdns WS14 . . . .9 B6
Buckingham Gr DY6 . . . . .60 C7
Buckingham Mews B73 . . . .46 A3
Buckingham PI 3 WS12 . . . . .2 E1
Buckingham Rd
  Birmingham B36 . . . . .69 F7
  Rowley Regis B65 . . . . .63 D4
  Tamworth B79 . . . . .20 E7
  Wolverhampton WV4 . . . . . . .39 A5
Buckingham Rise
  Coventry CV5 . . . . .112 B4
  Dudley DY1 . . . . .50 E2
Buckingham St B19 . . . . . . .164 B4
Buckland CI WS12 . . . . .2 D1
Buckland End B34 . . . . .69 A6
Buckland Ho 8 B15 . . . . .86 C7
Buckland Rd CV6 . . . . .95 B2
Bucklands End La B34 . . . . . .68 F6
Buckle CI WS1 . . . . .42 E8
Buckler's Yd 5 CV12 . . . . . . .78 A2
Buckley Ct B14 . . . . .104 F8
Buckley Ho CV5 . . . . .112 F1
Buckley Rd
  Royal Leamington Spa
  CV32 .157 C2
  Wolverhampton WV4 . . . . . . .38 D5
Buckleys Gn B48 . . . . .139 A6
Buckleys The B48 . . . . .139 A6
Bucklow Wlk B33 . . . . .68 E4
Buckminster Dr B93 . . . . . . .127 E4

ucknall Cres B32 . . . . 102 A8
ucknall Ct **15** B13 . . . . 87 B2
ucknall Ho B14 . . . . 104 E6
ucknell Rd WV11 . . . . 13 B1
ucknell Cl B91 . . . . 107 C5
uckridge Cl B38 . . . . 123 D7
uckridge La B90 . . . . 126 A5
ucks Hill CV10 . . . . 72 C6
uckthorn Cl WS12 . . . . 1 F8
uckton Cl B75 . . . . 32 E2
udbrooke Cl CV7 . . . . 96 D2
udbrooke Ind Est CV34 . 160 B7
udbrooke Rd CV34 . . . . 160 B7
udbrook Gr B34 . . . . 69 E6
udden Rd WV14 . . . . 51 D7
ude Rd WS5 . . . . 43 D7
uffery Rd DY2 . . . . 62 D7
ufferys Cl B11 . . . . 96 D2
uilding Trade Ctr B92 . . . . 88 E2
uildwas Cl WS3 . . . . 13 F2
ulford Cl B14 . . . . 104 F2
ulger Rd WV14 . . . . 40 C7
ulkington La CV11 . . . . 79 A7
ulkington Rd
  Bedworth CV12 . . . . 78 D2
  Shilton CV7 . . . . 97 E6
ullace Croft **4** B15 . . . . . . 85 D3
ulldog La WS13 . . . . 3 B1
uller St WV4 . . . . 39 E6
ullfield Ave CV4 . . . . 111 E1
ullfields Cl B60 . . . . 151 C7
ullfinch Cl DY1 . . . . 61 E8
ullfurlong La LE10 . . . . 75 F4
ullimore Gr CV8 . . . . 148 A2
ullivents Cl B93 . . . . 127 F5
ull La
  Darlaston WV14,WS10 . . . . 41 B3
  West Bromwich B70 . . . . . . 53 A3
  Wombourne WV5 . . . . 49 B7
ullmeadow La WV5 . . . . 49 A8
ullmoor La
  Muckley Corner WS14 . . . . . 8 A1
  Muckley Corner WS11 . . . . . 8 B1
ullock's Row WS1 . . . . 28 F1
ullock St
  4 West Bromwich B70 . . 53 D1
  Birmingham B7 . . . . 67 A5
ullows Rd WS8 . . . . 15 C6
ull Ring **4** B63 . . . . 83 B3
ullring B5 . . . . 164 C2
ull Ring
  Kidderminster DY10 . . . . . 116 C6
  Nuneaton CV10 . . . . 73 B2
  Sedgley DY3 . . . . 50 D8
ull Ring Trad Est **2** B12 . 66 F1
ull Ring WV13 . . . . 27 A3
ull's Head La CV3 . . . . 114 B2
ull's La B76 . . . . 47 E1
ull St
  Birmingham B17 . . . . 85 D5
  Birmingham,Brookfields
    B4 . . . . 164 C3
  Brierley Hill DY5 . . . . 61 B1
  Darlaston WS10 . . . . 41 E6
  Dudley,Gornalwood DY3 . . 50 D2
  Dudley,Springs Mire DY1 . . 62 A8
  Nuneaton CV11 . . . . 73 D2
ull Street Trad Est DY5 . . 61 B2
ull St B70 . . . . 53 D3
ull Yd CV1 . . . . 165 B2
ulwell Cl B6 . . . . 67 A7
ulwer Rd CV6 . . . . 113 A6
ulwick Cl CV3 . . . . 115 B1
umble Hole La B61 . . . . . . 136 E7
unbury Gdns B30 . . . . 103 D4
unbury Rd B30,B31 . . . . . . 103 C4
undle Hill B63 . . . . 83 A4
ungalows The B70 . . . . 52 F6
unker's Hill La WV14 . . . . . 40 E7
unns Mdw LE10 . . . . 74 E6
unn's La DY2 . . . . 51 F1
untsford Dr B60 . . . . 150 E6
untsford Gate Bsns Pk
  B60 . . . . 150 F6
untsford Hill B60 . . . . 150 F6
untsford Park Rd B60 . . 150 F6
unyan Pl WS11 . . . . 1 E4
urbage CE Inf Sch LE10 . 76 A5
urbage Cl WV10 . . . . 25 E6
urbage Jun Sch LE10 . . . . 75 F6
urbage Rd LE10 . . . . 76 A7
urbages La CV6 . . . . 95 D4
urberry Ct **3** DY4 . . . . . . 52 A8
urberry Gr CV7 . . . . 130 A6
urbidge Rd B9 . . . . 67 E3
urbury Cl
  Bedworth CV12 . . . . 78 C4
  Royal Leamington Spa
    CV32 . . . . 157 C2
urbury Ct CV34 . . . . 161 B8
urbury St B19 . . . . 66 C6
urbury St B19 . . . . 66 C7
urcher Gn DY10 . . . . 117 B5
urcombe Twr B23 . . . . 57 B6
urcot Ave
  Bromsgrove B60 . . . . 137 B4
  Wolverhampton WV1 . . . . . 26 A2
urcot Ct **1** B74 . . . . 31 F2
urcote Rd B24 . . . . 57 D3
urcot Ho B60 . . . . 137 B3
urcot La
  Bromsgrove,Burcot B60 . . 137 B3
  Bromsgrove,Stoney Hill
    B60 . . . . 137 C1
urdock Cl
  Cannock WS11 . . . . 2 B3
  Walsall WS5 . . . . 43 A3

Burdock Ho B38 . . . . 103 F1
Burdock Rd B29 . . . . 103 A6
Burdons Cl B34 . . . . 69 A5
Burfield Rd WV13 . . . . 27 C1
Burford Rd B63 . . . . 82 C6
Burford Cl
  Solihull B92 . . . . 89 A3
  Walsall WS5 . . . . 43 A4
Burford Ct
  18 Birmingham B13 . . . . 87 B2
  Stourbridge DY8 . . . . 81 A4
Burford Mews **13** CV31 . 162 C6
Burford Park Rd B38 . . . . 123 E8
Burford Rd
  Birmingham B44 . . . . 55 F7
  Hollywood B47 . . . . 125 A6
Burgage Pl CV11 . . . . 73 C4
Burgage Wlk CV11 . . . . 73 C4
Burges CV1 . . . . 165 B3
Burges Gr CV34 . . . . 155 F1
Burgess Croft B92 . . . . . . 107 F7
Burghley Cl CV11 . . . . 73 F2
Burghley Dr
  Kidderminster DY11 . . . . . 116 C5
  West Bromwich B71 . . . . . . 42 F2
Burghley Wlk B31 . . . . 81 B8
Burgh Way CV34 . . . . 28 A4
Burgoyne St WS11 . . . . 2 A5
Burhill Way B37 . . . . 70 B5
Burke Ave B13 . . . . 87 E2
Burkitt Dr DY4 . . . . 52 C8
Burland Ave WV6 . . . . 24 E6
Burleigh Cl
  Balsall Common CV7 . . . . 130 B7
  Cannock WS12 . . . . 2 A8
  Willenhall WV12 . . . . 27 B6
Burleigh Croft WS7 . . . . 7 A4
Burleigh Rd
  Hinckley LE10 . . . . 71 C2
  Wolverhampton WV3 . . . . . 39 A8
Burleigh St WS1 . . . . 29 A1
Burleton Rd B33 . . . . 69 E2
Burley Cl B90 . . . . 105 F2
Burley Way B38 . . . . 123 C8
Burlington Arc **2** B42 . . 164 B2
Burlington Ave B70 . . . . . . 53 E1
Burlington Ct DY10 . . . . . 117 B4
Burlington Pas DY10 . . . . . 35 B8
Burlington Rd
  Birmingham B10 . . . . 67 F1
  Coventry CV2 . . . . 113 F4
  Nuneaton CV10 . . . . 78 B7
  West Bromwich B70 . . . . . . 53 E1
Burlington St B6 . . . . 66 E6
Burlish Ave **1** B92 . . . . . . 88 F1
Burman Cl B90 . . . . 106 A2
Burman Dr B46 . . . . 70 F5
Burman Inf Sch B90 . . . . . 106 A1
Burman Rd B90 . . . . 106 A1
Burmarsh Wlk WV8 . . . . 24 F8
Burmese Way B65 . . . . 62 F6
Burnaby Cl CV10 . . . . 72 B5
Burnaby Rd CV6 . . . . 95 B1
Burnaston Cres B90 . . . . . 127 C6
Burnaston Rd B28 . . . . 87 F1
Burnbank Gr B24 . . . . 57 B4
Burn Cl B66 . . . . 65 A4
Burncross Way WV10 . . . . . 25 F6
Burnell Gdns WV3 . . . . 38 E8
Burnel Rd B29 . . . . 85 B2
Burnett Ho **12** B69 . . . . . 63 D5
Burnett Rd B74 . . . . 31 E2
Burney La B8 . . . . 68 C4
Burnfields Way WS9 . . . . . . 30 A7
Burnham Ave
  Birmingham B25 . . . . 88 C6
  Wolverhampton WV10 . . . . 25 C8
Burnham Cl DY6 . . . . 60 F4
Burnham Ct
  18 Brierley Hill DY5 . . . . 61 D2
  Birmingham B23 . . . . 56 C2
Burnham Gn WS11 . . . . 4 B8
Burnham Mdw B28 . . . . . . 106 A6
Burnham Rd
  Birmingham B44 . . . . 55 F7
  Coventry CV3 . . . . 134 A6
Burnham Rise CV11 . . . . . . 74 A6
Burnhill Gr B29 . . . . 103 A8
Burnlea Gr B31 . . . . 103 C1
Burnsall Cl
  Birmingham B37 . . . . 69 F2
  Wolverhampton WV9 . . . . . 11 A3
Burnsall Gr CV5 . . . . 132 D8
Burnsall Rd CV5 . . . . 132 D8
Burns Ave
  Tipton DY4 . . . . 52 A7
  Warwick CV34 . . . . 160 C5
  Wolverhampton WV10 . . . . 11 D2
Burns Cl
  Kidderminster DY10 . . . . . 117 B6
  Lichfield WS13 . . . . 9 B6
  Redditch B97 . . . . 158 C8
  Stourbridge DY8 . . . . 81 A8
Burns Dr WS7 . . . . 7 C7
Burns Gr DY3 . . . . 50 A4
Burnside CV3 . . . . 134 E8
Burnside Ct B73 . . . . 46 A1
Burnside Gdns WS5 . . . . . . 43 D6
Burnside Way B31 . . . . 122 F7
Burns Pl WS10 . . . . 41 A5
Burns Rd
  Coventry CV2 . . . . 114 B3
  Darlaston WS10 . . . . 41 B5
  Royal Leamington Spa
    CV32 . . . . 157 B4
  Burns St WS11 . . . . 2 A3

Bursnway LE10 . . . . 71 C1
Burns Wlk CV12 . . . . 78 C2
Burnthurst Cres B90 . . . . 127 A7
Burnt Meadow Rd B98 . 154 F4
Burnt Oak Dr DY8 . . . . 81 B5
Burnt Tree Ind Est B69 . . . 52 B2
Burnt Tree Island DY1,DY4 . 51 F2
Burnt Tree Jun & Inf Sch
  B69 . . . . 52 A2
Burnt Tree DY4 . . . . 51 F2
Burntwood Bsns Pk WS7 . . 6 D7
Burntwood Rd
  Hammerwich WS7 . . . . 7 D4
  Norton Canes WS11 . . . . . . 6 A7
Burntwood Town Sh Ctr
  WS7 . . . . 6 F6
Burrelton Way B43 . . . . 54 D8
Burrington Rd B32 . . . . . . 102 A8
Burrowes St WS2 . . . . 28 D3
Burrow Hill Cl B36 . . . . 69 C8
Burrow Hill La CV7 . . . . 94 D7
Burrows Cl CV31 . . . . 162 B3
Burrows Croft WV14 . . . . . . 40 C6
Burrows Ho **7** WS2 . . . . . 28 D3
Burrows Rd DY6 . . . . 60 F4
Burrs Dr WS10 . . . . 42 A1
Burslem Wlk WV1 . . . . 40 B8
Burslem Cl WS3 . . . . 14 A3
Burnips Ave WV1 . . . . 13 C4
Burnan Ave WS4 . . . . 29 B8
Burton Cl
  Brownshill Green CV5 . . . . 94 C2
  Tamworth B79 . . . . 21 C7
Burton Cres WV10 . . . . 163 D4
Burton Farm Rd WS4 . . . . . 29 B3
Burton Gr B64 . . . . 82 E8
Burton Green CE Prim Sch
  CV8 . . . . 131 B3
Burton La
  Bramcote CV11 . . . . 79 F7
  Redditch B98 . . . . 153 F3
Burton Old Rd E WS14 . . . . 9 E8
Burton Old Rd
  Lichfield WS13 . . . . 3 F1
  Lichfield WS14 . . . . 9 F8
Burton Old Rd W WS14 . . . . 9 D8
Burton Rd
  Dudley DY1 . . . . 50 F4
  Lichfield WS13 . . . . 3 F1
  Wolverhampton WV10 . . . . 25 E3
Burton Wood Dr B20 . . . . . 55 D2
Burwaye CV13 . . . . 9 A6
Buryfield B91 . . . . 107 B6
Bury Hill Rd B69 . . . . 63 D8
Bury Ho CV4 . . . . 111 F3
Bury Mound Ct B90 . . . . . 105 C2
Bury Rd CV31 . . . . 161 F7
Busby Cl CV3 . . . . 134 F7
Bush Ave B66 . . . . 65 C5
Bushbery Ave CV4 . . . . . . 111 F2
Bushbury Croft B37 . . . . . . 70 C3
Bushbury Hill Prim Sch
  WV10 . . . . 11 F1
Bushbury La
  Wolverhampton,Bushbury
    WV10 . . . . 11 E2
  Wolverhampton,Elston Hall
    WV10 . . . . 25 D7
Bushbury Rd
  Birmingham B33 . . . . 69 C3
  Wolverhampton WV10 . . . . 26 A5
Bushbury St WV10 . . . . 25 D7
Bush Cl CV4 . . . . 111 F3
Bush Ct CV2 . . . . 114 B8
Bushell Dr B91 . . . . 107 D4
Bushelton Cl CV1 . . . . 165 C1
Bushey Cl B74 . . . . 30 F2
Bushey Fields Hospl DY5 . 61 E8
Bushey Fields Rd DY1 . . . . 61 E7
Bushfield Gr WV14 . . . . 40 F5
Bush Gr
  Birmingham B21 . . . . 54 C1
  Walsall WS3 . . . . 15 A2
Bushley Cl B98 . . . . 159 A7
Bushley Croft B91 . . . . 127 B8
Bushman Way B34 . . . . 69 E5
Bushmore Rd B28 . . . . 106 A4
Bush Rd
  Dudley DY2 . . . . 62 C2
  Tipton DY4 . . . . 51 E4
Bush St WS10 . . . . 41 D7
Bushway Cl DY5 . . . . 61 B2
Bushwood Cl B15 . . . . 86 C8
Bushwood Dr B93 . . . . 128 B3
Bushwood Rd B29 . . . . 85 B1
Bushy End CV34 . . . . 161 E4
Busill Jones Prim Sch
  WS3 . . . . 27 F8
Bustleholme Ave B71 . . . . . 42 F1
Bustleholme Cres B71 . . . . 42 E1
Bustleholme La B71 . . . . . . 42 E1
Butcher's La CV5 . . . . 112 C6
Butchers La B63 . . . . 82 C7
Butchers Rd B92 . . . . 109 A6
Butcroft Gdns WS10 . . . . . . 41 E6
Bute Cl
  Birmingham B45 . . . . 101 E1
  Hinckley LE10 . . . . 71 C1
  Willenhall WV12 . . . . 27 B6
Butler Cl CV8 . . . . 148 C2
Butler Rd B92 . . . . 88 F3
Butlers Cl
  Birmingham,Handsworth
    B20 . . . . 55 A3
  Birmingham,Perry Common
    B23 . . . . 56 E5
Butlers Cres CV7 . . . . 78 A1
Butlers End CV35 . . . . 146 C2
Butler's Hill La B97 . . . . . 153 B5

Butlers Lane Sta B74 . . . . . 32 A3
Butlers La B74 . . . . 32 A3
Butlers Prec **3** WS1 . . . . 28 E2
Butler's Rd B20 . . . . 55 A3
Butler St
  Astwood Bank B96 . . . . . 158 E1
  West Bromwich B70 . . . . . . 53 A4
Butlin Rd CV6 . . . . 95 C4
Butlin St B7 . . . . 67 C7
Buttercup Cl
  6 Walsall WS5 . . . . 43 A3
  Kidderminster DY10 . . . . . 116 E8
Buttercup Dr B60 . . . . 137 C6
Buttercup Way CV12 . . . . . 77 D2
Butterfield Cl WV6 . . . . 23 D3
Butterfield Ct DY1 . . . . 51 A2
Butterfield Rd DY5 . . . . 61 B7
Butterfly Way **4** B64 . . . . 62 F1
Buttermere Ave CV11 . . . . . 74 A6
Buttermere Cl
  Brierley Hill DY5 . . . . 81 B7
  Cannock WS11 . . . . 2 B3
  Coventry CV3 . . . . 134 F7
  Wolverhampton WV6 . . . . . 24 D8
Buttermere Dr
  Birmingham B32 . . . . 84 F3
  Essington WV11 . . . . 13 A2
Buttermere Rd WV11 . . . . . 13 B1
Buttermere **7** B77 . . . . . . 36 B7
Butter Wlk B38 . . . . 123 C8
Butterworth Cl WV14 . . . . . 40 A1
Butterworth Dr CV4 . . . . . . 132 A6
Buttery Rd B67 . . . . 64 E6
Butt La
  Allesley CV5 . . . . 112 B7
  Hinckley LE10 . . . . 71 E1
Butt Lane Cl LE10 . . . . 71 E1
Buttons Farm Rd WV4 . . . . 38 D3
Buttress Way B66 . . . . 65 A6
Butts Cl WS11 . . . . 5 E4
Butts La CV13 . . . . 113 A2
Butts The
  Lichfield WS14 . . . . 8 D2
  Walsall WS4 . . . . 29 A4
  Warwick CV34 . . . . 160 E7
Butts Way WS11 . . . . 5 E4
Buxton Ave B79 . . . . 35 B8
Buxton Cl WS3 . . . . 14 C3
Buxton Rd
  Birmingham B23 . . . . 56 B7
  Dudley DY2 . . . . 62 A6
  Sutton Coldfield B73 . . . . . 57 A8
  Walsall WS3 . . . . 14 C3
Byfield Cl B33 . . . . 69 E1
Byfield Pl CV7 . . . . 130 D5
Byfield Rd CV6 . . . . 112 E5
Byfleet Cl WV14 . . . . 40 A3
Byford Cl B98 . . . . 153 E2
Byford Ct CV10 . . . . 72 F4
Byford St CV10 . . . . 73 A4
Byford Way B37 . . . . 90 B8
Bylands Cl B61 . . . . 136 E1
Byland B77 . . . . 21 D3
Byland Way WS3 . . . . 13 F2
Bypass Link B91 . . . . 107 F3
By Pass Rd B77 . . . . 22 A6
Byrchen Moor Gdns DY5 . 61 B7
Byrne Rd WV2 . . . . 39 D7
Byron Ave
  Birmingham CV12 . . . . 78 D2
  Birmingham B23 . . . . 56 B3
  Lichfield WS14 . . . . 9 B5
  Warwick CV34 . . . . 160 C4
Byron Cl
  Birmingham B10 . . . . 87 D7
  Kidderminster DY10 . . . . . 117 B5
Byron Cres DY1 . . . . 51 B6
Byron Croft
  Dudley DY3 . . . . 50 A5
  Sutton Coldfield B74 . . . . . 31 F6
Byron Ct
  Dorridge B93 . . . . 128 A6
  Sutton Coldfield B74 . . . . . 32 A5
Byron Gdns B71 . . . . 53 B5
Byron Pl WS11 . . . . 1 F5
Byron Rd
  Birmingham B10 . . . . 87 D7
  Redditch B97 . . . . 158 D8
  Tamworth B79 . . . . 21 A7
  Willenhall WV12 . . . . 27 E7
  Wolverhampton WV10 . . . . 12 A1
Byron St
  Brierley Hill DY5 . . . . 61 D6
  Coventry CV1 . . . . 165 C4
Byron Way B61 . . . . 137 A8
Bywater Cl CV3 . . . . 133 B5
Bywater Ho **5** WS1 . . . . . 28 E1
Byways WS3 . . . . 14 C3

C

Caban Cl B31 . . . . 102 E5
Cable Dr WS2 . . . . 28 C5
Cable St WV2 . . . . 39 F8
Cabot Gr WV6 . . . . 23 E4

Cadbury Dr B35 . . . . 58 A2
Cadbury Ho B19 . . . . 66 D5
Cadbury Rd B13 . . . . 87 B4
Cadbury Sixth Form Coll
  B38 . . . . 103 F1
Cadbury Way B17 . . . . 85 B5
Cadbury World* B30 . . . . 103 F7
Cadden Dr CV4 . . . . 132 B2
Caddick Cres B71 . . . . 53 D7
Caddick Rd B42 . . . . 44 B1
Caddick St WV14 . . . . 51 A8
Cadeby Cl LE10 . . . . 71 B3
Cadell Ct B13 . . . . 87 A1
Cadet Dr B90 . . . . 106 A3
Cadgwith Gdns WV14 . . . . 41 A2
Cadine Gdns B13 . . . . 86 C1
Cadleigh Gdns B17 . . . . . . 85 C1
Cadle Rd WV10 . . . . 25 E7
Cadman Cl CV12 . . . . 78 C3
Cadman Cres WV10 . . . . . . 26 A7
Cadman's La WS6,WS3 . . . 14 D6
Cadnam Cl
  Birmingham B17 . . . . 85 C3
  Darlaston WV13 . . . . 41 B8
Cadogan Rd B77 . . . . 35 D5
Caen Cl CV35 . . . . 160 A7
Caernarfon Dr CV11 . . . . . . 73 D3
Caernarvon Cl WV12 . . . . . 27 C7
Caernarvon Way DY1 . . . . . 50 E2
Caesar Rd CV8 . . . . 147 E3
Caesar Way B46 . . . . 59 E1
Cairndhu Dr DY10 . . . . 117 B7
Cairn Dr WS2 . . . . 28 C3
Cairns St WS2 . . . . 28 C3
Caister Dr WV13 . . . . 40 F8
Caister B77 . . . . 22 A6
Caistor Cl B78 . . . . 34 B8
Caithness Cl CV5 . . . . 112 A4
Cakemore Rd B65 . . . . 63 E2
Cala Dr B15 . . . . 86 B7
Calcot Dr WV6 . . . . 24 E7
Calcot Cl CV4 . . . . 134 B5
Calcutt Way B90 . . . . 126 A6
Caldecote Cl CV10 . . . . 73 C8
Caldecote Gr B9 . . . . 68 C1
Caldecott Cl CV6 . . . . 113 C5
Caldeford Ave B90 . . . . . . 127 A7
Calder Ave WS1 . . . . 29 A2
Calder Cl
  Bulkington CV12 . . . . 79 B2
  Coventry CV3 . . . . 133 E7
Calder Dr B76 . . . . 58 A7
Calderfields Cl WS4 . . . . . . 29 A3
Calder Gr B20 . . . . 54 F2
Calder Rise DY3 . . . . 50 F6
Calder B77 . . . . 22 B2
Calder Twr **2** B20 . . . . . . 55 D1
Calder Wlk CV31 . . . . 162 C6
Caldmore Com Prim Sch
  WS1 . . . . 42 E8
Caldmore Gn WS1 . . . . 42 E8
Caldmore Rd WS1 . . . . 42 E8
Caldon Cl LE10 . . . . 75 B8
Caldwall Cres DY11 . . . . . 116 D5
Caldwell Ct
  Nuneaton CV11 . . . . 73 B5
  Solihull B91 . . . . 107 C5
Caldwell Rd
  Birmingham B9 . . . . 68 B3
  Nuneaton CV11 . . . . 73 D1
Caldwell St B71 . . . . 53 D8
Caldy Wlk **6** B45 . . . . . . 101 F1
Cale Cl B77 . . . . 21 C2
Caledonia DY5 . . . . 81 D7
Caledonian CV11 . . . . 43 C3
Caledonia Rd WV2 . . . . . . 163 D1
Caledon Pl WS2 . . . . 40 E6
Caledon St WV2 . . . . 42 C7
Caledon St **5** WS2 . . . . . 42 C7
Calewood Rd DY5 . . . . 81 D7
Calgary Cl CV3 . . . . 115 A2
Caliban Mews CV34 . . . . . 161 E3
California Ho B32 . . . . 84 E2
California Gr WS7 . . . . 6 B8
California Rd B69 . . . . 63 B8
California Way B32 . . . . 84 F3
Callaghan Gr **3** WS11 . . . 2 C2
Callcott Dr DY5 . . . . 81 D7
Callear Rd WS10 . . . . 41 D1
Callendar Cl CV11 . . . . 74 A7
Calley Cl DY4 . . . . 52 A3
Callis Wlk **2** B77 . . . . 35 F6
Callowbridge Rd B45 . . . . 121 F7
Callowbrook La B45 . . . . . 121 F7
Callow Hill Rd B48 . . . . . . 139 A6
Callows La **2** DY10 . . . . 116 E6
Calmere Cl CV2 . . . . 114 F8
Calpurnia Ave CV34 . . . . . 161 E2
Calshot Prim Sch B42 . . . . 55 B8
Calshot Rd B42 . . . . 55 A8
Calstock Rd WV12 . . . . 27 D4
Calthorpe Cl WS5 . . . . 43 E6
Calthorpe Mans **4** B15 . 66 B1
Calthorpe Rd
  Birmingham,Edgbaston
    B15 . . . . 86 B8
  Birmingham,Handsworth Wood
    B20 . . . . 55 C2
  Walsall WS5 . . . . 43 D6
Calthorpe Sch Sports Coll
  B12 . . . . 87 A8
Caludon Castle Sch CV2 . 114 E4

Caludon Lodge CV2 . . . . .114 E5
Caludon Park Ave CV2 . . .114 E5
Caludon Rd CV2 . . . . 114 A4
Calver Cres WV11 . . . . .26 F5
Calverley Rd B38 . . . . 123 D8
Calvert Cl CV3 . . . . .133 D6
Calverton Gr B43 . . . . .54 E8
Calves Croft WV13 . . . . .27 A3
Calvin Cl WV10 . . . . .11 D3
Calving Hill WS11 . . . . .1 E2
Camberley **6** B71 . . . . .42 F1
Camberley Cres WV4 . . . . . .39 E2
Camberley Dr WV4 . . . . .39 A4
Camberley Gr B23 . . . . .56 E6
Camberley Rd DY6 . . . . .61 A4
Camberwell Terr CV31 . . . . .162 A7
Camborne Cl B6 . . . . .66 E7
Camborne Dr CV11 . . . . .73 F5
Camborne Rd WS5 . . . . .43 D7
Cambourne Rd
   Hinckley LE10 . . . . .76 A6
   Rowley Regis B65 . . . . .63 C3
Cambrai Dr B28 . . . . 105 F8
Cambria Cl B90 . . . . 125 E7
Cambrian B77 . . . . .22 A2
Cambria St WS11 . . . . .1 D4
Cambridge Ave
   Solihull B91 . . . . 106 E3
   Sutton Coldfield B73 . . . . . . .57 B8
Cambridge Cl WS9 . . . . .30 B8
Cambridge Cres B15 . . . . . . .86 D7
Cambridge Dr
   Birmingham B37 . . . . .69 F1
   Nuneaton CV10 . . . . .72 E3
Cambridge Gdns CV32 . . . .157 A1
Cambridge Rd
   Birmingham B13 . . . . .86 F1
   Dudley DY2 . . . . .62 A7
   Smethwick B66 . . . . .65 A4
Cambridge St
   Birmingham B1 . . . . 164 A2
   Coventry CV1 . . . . 113 E5
   Walsall WS1 . . . . .42 E7
   West Bromwich B70 . . . . . . .53 B2
   Wolverhampton WV10 . . . . .163 C4
Cambridge Twr B1 . . . . 164 A2
Cambridge Way B27 . . . . . . .88 D4
Camden Cl
   Birmingham B36 . . . . .69 A8
   Walsall WS5 . . . . .43 A4
Camden Dr
   Birmingham B1 . . . . .66 C3
   Tamworth B77 . . . . .21 E3
Camden St
   Birmingham B18,B1 . . . . . . .66 B4
   Brownhills WS9 . . . . .15 F4
   Coventry CV2 . . . . 114 A4
   Walsall WS1 . . . . .42 E8
Camden Way DY6 . . . . .49 D1
Camel Cotts DY9 . . . . .99 E2
Camellia Gdns
   Stourbridge DY8 . . . . .60 E2
   Wolverhampton WV9 . . . . . . .10 F3
Camellia Rd CV2 . . . . .96 B2
Camelot Cl WS11 . . . . .1 F4
Camelot Gr CV8 . . . . 148 C5
Camelot Way B10 . . . . .87 C8
Cameo Dr DY8 . . . . .80 F8
Cameron Cl
   Allesley CV5 . . . . 112 A7
   Royal Leamington Spa
   CV32 . . . . 157 A4
Cameron Rd WS4 . . . . .29 B3
Camford Gr B14 . . . . 104 F3
Cam Gdns DY5 . . . . .61 B6
Cam Ho B7 DY1 . . . . .61 E8
Camhouses B77 . . . . .22 B1
Camino Rd B32 . . . . .84 F3
Camomile Cl **5** WS5 . . . . . .43 A3
Campbell Cl
   Nuneaton CV10 . . . . .72 A4
   Tamworth B79 . . . . .20 F8
   Walsall WS4 . . . . .29 A3
Campbells Gn B26 . . . . .89 B4
Campbell St DY5 . . . . .61 C4
Campden Gn B92 . . . . .89 A3
Camp Hill B12 . . . . .87 A8
Camp Hill Cir B12 . . . . .87 A8
Camp Hill Ind Est B12 . . . . . .87 A7
Camphill La WV13 . . . . .41 F2
Camp Hill Middleway B12 . .87 A7
Camp Hill Prim Sch CV10 . . .72 E6
Camp Hill Rd CV10 . . . . .72 C7
Camp Hill DY8 . . . . .60 E1
Campian's Ave WS6 . . . . .4 D2
Campion Cl
   3 Birmingham B38 . . . . . .123 F8
   Coventry CV3 . . . . 133 D6
   Walsall WS5 . . . . .43 A3
Campion Ct **2** DY4 . . . . . . .51 E5
Campion Dr
   Featherstone WV10 . . . . .12 A7
   Tamworth B77 . . . . .21 C3
Campion Gr CV32 . . . . 157 A2
Campion Gr B63 . . . . .82 D3
Campion Ho
   2 Birmingham B38 . . . . . .123 E8
   Wolverhampton WV10 . . . . . . .25 F4
Campion Rd CV32 . . . . 157 A2
Campion Sch & Com Coll
   CV31 . . . . 162 C5

Campion B74 . . . . .31 F5
Campion Terr CV32 . . . . 157 A1
Campion Way
   3 Bedworth CV12 . . . . . .77 D2
   Solihull B90 . . . . 126 A5
Camp La
   Birmingham,Handsworth
   B21 . . . . .54 C2
   Birmingham,King's Norton
   B38 . . . . .103 F3
Camplea Croft B37 . . . . .70 A2
Camplin Cres B20 . . . . .54 F5
Campling Cl CV12 . . . . .79 B2
Camp Rd B75 . . . . .32 D6
Campriano Dr CV34 . . . . 161 A8
Camp St
   Birmingham B9 . . . . .67 C1
   Wednesbury WS10 . . . . .41 F2
   Wolverhampton WV1 . . . . . . 163 B4
Campton Cl LE10 . . . . .75 E7
Campville Cres B71 . . . . .42 E1
Campville Gr B37 . . . . .69 F5
Camp Wood Cl B30 . . . . 103 F8
Camrose Croft
   Birmingham,Balsall Heath
   B12 . . . . .86 F5
   Birmingham,Castle Bromwich
   B34 . . . . .69 B6
Camrose Gdns WV9 . . . . .11 A3
Camrose Twr B7 . . . . .67 B6
Camsey La WS7 . . . . .7 E8
Camville CV3 . . . . .115 A2
Canal La B24 . . . . .57 A1
Canal Rd CV6 . . . . .113 F8
Canalside CV6 . . . . .96 B6
Canalside Cl
   Walsall WS3 . . . . .14 F1
   Wednesbury WS10 . . . . .42 E2
Canal Side
   Dudley DY2 . . . . .62 E4
   Hopwood B48 . . . . 123 B2
Canal Side Ind Est DY5 . . . . .61 C1
Canalside B94 . . . . 144 D3
Canal St
   Brierley Hill DY5 . . . . .61 E5
   Dudley DY1 . . . . .51 D4
   Oldbury B69 . . . . .64 D2
   Stourbridge DY8 . . . . .80 F6
   Tipton DY4 . . . . .51 C8
Canal View Ind Est DY5 . . . . .61 B1
Canal Way LE10 . . . . .74 F7
Canary Gr B19 . . . . .66 C8
Canberra Ct **2** CV12 . . . . . .77 F2
Canberra Ho B34 . . . . .69 E6
Canberra Rd
   Coventry CV2 . . . . .96 C4
   Walsall WS5 . . . . .43 C6
Canberra Way
   4 Birmingham B12 . . . . . .86 F8
   Hinckley LE10 . . . . .75 E4
Canford Cl
   Birmingham B12 . . . . .86 F7
   Coventry CV3 . . . . 133 C3
Canley Ford CV4,CV5 . . . . . . 132 B7
Canley Rd CV5 . . . . 132 D8
Canley Sta CV5 . . . . 112 D1
Cannel Rd WS7 . . . . .6 D6
Cannes Ct CV4 . . . . 132 D6
Canning Cl WS5 . . . . .43 D6
Canning Gdns B18 . . . . .65 E4
Canning Rd
   Tamworth B77 . . . . .21 F4
   Walsall WS5 . . . . .43 D6
Canning St LE10 . . . . .71 C1
Cannock Chase High Sch
   WS11 . . . . .1 E2
Cannock Chase Tech Coll
   Cannock,Blackfords WS11 . . .1 D1
   Cannock,Bridgtown WS11 . . .4 E7
   Cannock Com Hospl WS11 . .1 E2
   Cannock Ind Ctr WS11 . . . . .4 D5
   Cannock Motor Village
   WS11 . . . . .2 B3
Cannock Rd
   Burntwood,Chase Terrace
   WS7 . . . . .6 D7
   Burntwood,Gorstey Ley WS7. .7 B7
   Cannock,Heath Hayes WS12. .5 C8
   Cannock WS12,WS11 . . . . . .2 A5
   Featherstone WV10 . . . . .12 C7
   Willenhall WV12 . . . . .27 C7
   Cannock Sh Ctr WS11 . . . . . .1 E1
Cannocks La CV4 . . . . 132 D6
Cannock Sta WS11 . . . . .4 F8
Cannon Cl CV4 . . . . 132 F6
Cannon Dr WV14 . . . . .40 D2
Cannon Hill Gr **2** B12 . . . . .86 E5
Cannon Hill Pl **1** B12 . . . . .86 E5
Cannon Hill Rd
   Birmingham B12 . . . . .86 E5
   Coventry CV4 . . . . 132 D5
Cannon Park District Ctr
   CV4 . . . . 132 C6
Cannon Park Prim Sch
   CV4 . . . . 132 D5
Cannon Park Rd CV4 . . . . . . 132 E5
Cannon Rd WV5 . . . . .49 A7
Cannon St N WS2 . . . . .28 E4
Cannon St
   Birmingham B2 . . . . 164 C2
   Walsall WS2 . . . . .28 E4
   Willenhall WV13 . . . . .27 B2
Canon Bsns Pk WV14 . . . . . . .40 C1
Canon Dr CV7 . . . . .95 D6
Canon Evans CE Inf Sch
   CV12 . . . . .78 A2
Canon Hudson Cl CV3. . . . . . 134 C6

Canon Maggs CE Jun Sch
   CV12 . . . . .78 B2
Canon Young Rd CV31. . . . . .162 B3
Canterbury Ave WV13 . . . . . . .27 D2
Canterbury Cl
   9 Rowley Regis B65 . . . . .63 E4
   Birmingham B23 . . . . .56 D2
   Kenilworth CV8 . . . . 148 C3
   Lichfield WS13 . . . . .3 C3
   Studley B80 . . . . .159 C4
   Tamworth B77 . . . . .21 D6
   Walsall WS3 . . . . .15 A4
   West Bromwich B71 . . . . . . .53 E8
Canterbury Cross Prim Sch
   B20. . . . . .55 D1
Canterbury Dr
   Birmingham B37 . . . . .90 A7
   Burntwood WV7 . . . . .7 E7
   Perton WV6 . . . . .23 E4
Canterbury Rd
   Birmingham B20 . . . . .55 D1
   Kidderminster DY11 . . . . . . 116 A6
   West Bromwich B71 . . . . . . .53 D8
   Wolverhampton WV4 . . . . . . .38 E5
Canterbury St CV1 . . . . 165 D3
Canterbury Twr **1** B1 . . . . .66 B3
Canterbury Way
   Cannock WS12 . . . . .2 B1
   Nuneaton CV11 . . . . .74 A8
Cantlow Cl CV5 . . . . 112 A3
Cantlow Ho **2** B12 . . . . .86 F7
Cantlow Rd B13 . . . . 105 A6
Canton Ho LE10 . . . . .71 C4
Canute Cl WS1 . . . . .42 F7
Canvey Cl B45 . . . . 101 E1
Canwell Ave B37 . . . . .69 F5
Canwell Dr B75 . . . . .33 B5
Canwell Gate B75 . . . . .32 E4
Canwell Gdns WV14 . . . . .40 C4
Capcroft Rd B13 . . . . 105 B6
Cape Cl WS8 . . . . .16 A6
Cape Hill Ret Ctr B66 . . . . . . .65 C4
Cape Hill B66 . . . . .65 C4
Cape Ind Est CV34 . . . . 160 E7
Capener Rd B43 . . . . .44 A2
Cape Prim Sch B66 . . . . .65 C4
Cape Rd CV34 . . . . 160 D8
Capern Gr B32 . . . . .84 F5
Cape St
   Birmingham B18 . . . . .65 D4
   West Bromwich B70 . . . . . . .52 E4
Capethorn Rd B66 . . . . .65 A3
Capilano Rd B23 . . . . .56 C7
Capmartin Rd CV6 . . . . 113 C7
Cappers La WS13,WS14 . . . . . .9 F8
Capponfield Cl WV14 . . . . . . .40 B3
Capstone Ave
   Birmingham B18 . . . . .66 A4
   Wolverhampton WV10. . . . . .25 C8
Captain's Cl WV3 . . . . .24 D2
Captains Pool Rd DY10 . . . . .117 A1
Captain's Pool Rd DY10 . . . .117 A1
Capulet Cl CV3 . . . . 134 C6
Capulet Dr CV34 . . . . 161 E6
Caradoc Cl CV2 . . . . 114 D7
Caradoc Hall CV2 . . . . 114 D7
Caradoc B77 . . . . .22 A2
Carcroft Rd B25 . . . . .88 D8
Cardale Croft **1** CV3. . . . . .134 F8
Cardale St B65 . . . . .63 D1
Carden Cl B70 . . . . .52 F4
Carder Cres WV14 . . . . .40 D4
Carder Dr DY5 . . . . .61 C2
Cardiff Cl CV3 . . . . 134 D5
Cardiff St WV3 . . . . .39 B8
Cardigan Cl B71 . . . . .53 C7
Cardigan Dr WV12 . . . . .27 B6
Cardigan Ho WS12 . . . . .2 C5
Cardigan Pl WS12 . . . . .2 C5
Cardigan Rd CV12 . . . . .77 C1
Cardigan St B4 . . . . 164 D3
Cardinal Cres B61 . . . . 136 D1
Cardinal Dr DY10 . . . . .117 B3
Cardinal Griffin RC High Sch
   WS11 . . . . .1 D2
Cardinal Newman RC Sch
   B17. . . . . .65 A2
Cardinal Newman RC Sch &
   Com Coll CV6 . . . . .94 F2
Cardinal Way WS11 . . . . .1 D2
Cardinal Wiseman RC Sch
   CV2. . . . . .96 E1
Cardinal Wiseman Tech Coll
   B44. . . . . .44 F2
Carding Cl CV5 . . . . .111 F4
Cardington Ave B42. . . . . .44 A1
Cardington Cl B98 . . . . .154 F3
Cardoness Pl DY1 . . . . .50 F2
Cardy Cl B97 . . . . 153 B4
Careless Gn DY9 . . . . .81 F4
Carey St CV6 . . . . 114 B8
Carey B77 . . . . .36 A5
Carfax B77 . . . . .4 E8
Cargill Cl CV6 . . . . .95 F5
Carhampton Rd B75 . . . . .47 A5
Carillon Gdns B65 . . . . .63 D3
Carisbroke Ave B37. . . . . .70 C2
Carisbrook Cl WS10 . . . . .42 E3
Carisbrooke B77 . . . . .22 C1
Carisbrooke Ave B37. . . . . . . .70 C2
Carisbrooke Cl WS10 . . . . .42 E3
Carisbrooke Cres B62 . . . . . .83 D3
Carisbrooke Dr B62 . . . . .83 D3
Carisbrooke Gdns WV10 . . . .11 E3
Carisbrooke Rd
   Birmingham B17 . . . . .65 B5
   Perton WV6 . . . . .24 A3
   Wednesbury WS10 . . . . .42 E3
   Wolverhampton WV6 . . . . . . .24 B3
Carisbrooke Rd CV10. . . . . . . .73 D6

Carlcroft B77 . . . . .22 B2
Carless Ave B17 . . . . .85 B7
Carless St WS1 . . . . .42 E8
Carl Eynon Cl **2** WS3. . . . . .28 B8
Carl Ho WS11 . . . . .4 B7
Carlisle St B18 . . . . .65 F5
Carlson Pk **2** B17 . . . . .85 B5
Carl St WS2 . . . . .28 D5
Carlton Ave
   Bilston WV14 . . . . .40 F7
   Birmingham B21 . . . . .54 E1
   Stourbridge DY9 . . . . .81 E3
   Wolverhampton WV11 . . . . . .26 A7
Carlton Cl
   Bulkington CV12 . . . . .79 B3
   Cannock WS12 . . . . .2 D1
   Dudley DY1 . . . . .51 C6
   Kidderminster DY11 . . . . . . 116 A8
   Redditch B97 . . . . 153 B1
   Sutton Coldfield B75 . . . . . . .46 E7
Carlton Cres
   Burntwood WS7. . . . . .7 A8
   Tamworth B79 . . . . .20 F8
Carlton Croft B74. . . . . .31 A2
Carlton Ct CV5 . . . . 112 F2
Carlton Gdns CV5 . . . . 133 A8
Carlton Ho
   8 Royal Leamington Spa
   CV32. . . . . .161 F8
   Sutton Coldfield B75 . . . . . . .32 B2
Carlton Mews B36 . . . . .69 D7
Carlton Mews Flats B36. . . . .69 D7
Carlton Rd
   Birmingham B9 . . . . .67 D1
   Coventry CV6 . . . . .95 F1
   Smethwick B66 . . . . .65 B8
   Wolverhampton WV3 . . . . . . .39 A7
Carlyle Ave DY10 . . . . 117 B6
Carlyle Bsns Pk B70 . . . . .52 F5
Carlyle Gr WV10 . . . . .26 A8
Carlyle Rd
   Birmingham,Edgbaston
   B16. . . . . .65 C1
   Birmingham,Lozells B19 . . . .66 C8
   Bromsgrove B60 . . . . 151 B8
   Rowley Regis B65 . . . . .63 C2
   Wolverhampton WV10 . . . . . .26 A8
Carmel Cl WS12 . . . . .2 C5
Carmel Gr B32 . . . . .84 B1
Carmelite Rd CV1 . . . . 113 E2
Carmichael Cl WS14 . . . . .9 D7
Carmodale Ave B42 . . . . .55 B5
Carnation Way CV10 . . . . .78 A8
Carnbroe Ave CV3 . . . . 134 F7
Carnegie Ave CV3 . . . . .54 B4
Carnegie Cl CV3 . . . . 134 B8
Carnegie Dr WS10 . . . . .42 A3
Carnegie Rd B65 . . . . .63 B2
Carnford Rd B26. . . . . .89 B6
Carnforth Cl DY6 . . . . .60 B7
Carnforth Rd B60 . . . . .137 B1
Carnoustie Cl
   Bromsgrove B61 . . . . 150 D8
   Nuneaton CV11 . . . . .79 C8
   Sutton Coldfield B75 . . . . . . .46 C8
   Walsall WS3 . . . . .14 A3
Carnoustie B77 . . . . .22 C5
Carnwath Rd B73 . . . . .45 E2
Carol Ave B61 . . . . 136 D3
Carol Cres
   Halesowen B63 . . . . .82 F5
   Wednesfield WV11 . . . . .26 E6
Carol Gdns DY8 . . . . .80 F8
Caroline Cl CV11 . . . . .78 F7
Caroline Pl B13 . . . . .86 F3
Caroline Rd B13 . . . . .86 F4
Caroline St
   Birmingham B3 . . . . 164 A4
   Dudley DY2 . . . . .51 E1
   West Bromwich B70 . . . . . . .53 B1
Carousel Pk LE9 . . . . .71 F8
Carpathian Ct **4** B18 . . . . . .66 C4
Carpathian The **8** B18. . . . .66 C4
Carpenter Glade B63 . . . . . . .82 D5
Carpenter Pl **7** B12 . . . . . . .87 A6
Carpenter Rd B15 . . . . .86 B7
Carpenters Cl LE10 . . . . .75 F5
Carpenters Ct B12 . . . . .86 F8
Carpenter's Rd B19 . . . . .66 C7
Carpet Trades Way
   WS11 . . . . 116 D7
Carrick Cl WS3 . . . . .15 A5
Carrie Ho CV1 . . . . 165 A2
Carriers Cl WS2 . . . . .27 F1
Carriers Fold WV5 . . . . .49 B7
Carrington Rd WS10 . . . . .42 D2
Carroll Wlk DY10 . . . . 117 C5
Carraway Head Hill B78. . . . .33 D4
Carrs La B4 . . . . 164 C2
Carsal Cl CV7 . . . . .95 D6
Carshalton Gr WV2 . . . . .39 E7
Carshalton Rd B44. . . . . .45 A2
Cartbridge Cres WS3. . . . . . . .28 F6
Cartbridge La S WS4 . . . . .29 A5
Cartbridge La WS4 . . . . .29 A6
Cartbridge Wlk WS3 . . . . .29 A6
Carter Ave
   Codsall WV8 . . . . .10 B3
   Kidderminster DY11 . . . . . . 116 B4
   Carter Ct DY11 . . . . 116 C4
Carter Rd
   Birmingham B43 . . . . .43 F2
   Coventry CV3. . . . . 134 A8
   Wolverhampton WV6. . . . . . .25 B3
Carters Cl
   Birmingham B77 . . . . .90 A7
   Bromsgrove B61 . . . . 150 D7

Carters Cl *continued*
   Sutton Coldfield B76 . . . . . . .46 F2
Cartersfield La WS9. . . . . .16 E4
Carter's Gn B70 . . . . .53 B4
Carters Hurst B33 . . . . .69 B1
Carter's La
   Birmingham B62 . . . . .84 A3
   Halesowen B62 . . . . .83 F4
Carthorse La B97 . . . . 153 B5
Carthusian Rd CV3. . . . . 133 C2
Cartland Rd
   Birmingham,Sparkbrook
   B11. . . . . .87 C6
   Birmingham,Stirchley B14,
   B30. . . . . 104 C2
Cartmel Cl CV5 . . . . 112 A4
Cartmel Ct B23 . . . . .56 B6
Cartway The WV6 . . . . .23 D4
Cartwright Gdns B69. . . . . . . .52 C2
Cartwright Ho WS3 . . . . .14 B3
Cartwright Rd
   Stoke Prior B60 . . . . 150 D2
   Sutton Coldfield B75 . . . . . . .32 C3
Cartwright St WV2 . . . . 163 C3
Carvell Cl CV5 . . . . .94 B1
Carver Cl CV2 . . . . 114 E2
Carver Ct
   Sutton Coldfield B24 . . . . . . .57 C6
   Wednesbury DY4 . . . . .41 A1
Carver Gdns DY8 . . . . .80 E2
Carver St B1 . . . . .66 B4
Casa Mia Ct WS12 . . . . .2 C5
Cascade Cl CV3 . . . . 133 E6
Case La CV35. . . . . .145 E1
Casern View B75. . . . . .47 A6
Casewell Rd DY6 . . . . .60 C8
Casey Ave B23. . . . . .56 D8
Cash Joynson Ave WS10. . . .41 C8
Cashmore Ave CV31. . . . . . . .161 F5
Cashmore Rd
   Bedworth CV12 . . . . .77 E1
   Kenilworth CV8 . . . . 148 C4
Cash's Bsns Ctr CV1 . . . . 113 D5
Cash's La CV1 . . . . 113 D6
Casita Gr CV8 . . . . 148 C4
Caslon Cres DY8. . . . . .80 D4
Caslon Flats B63 . . . . .82 C4
Caslon Prim Sch B63 . . . . . . .82 C4
Caslon Rd B63 . . . . .82 C6
Caspian Way CV2 . . . . 115 A8
Cassandra Cl
   Coventry CV4 . . . . 132 D3
   Dudley DY5 . . . . .50 C1
Cassandra Gr CV34 . . . . 161 D4
Cassowary Rd B20 . . . . .54 F3
Castello Dr B36 . . . . .58 D1
Castillo Cl B14 . . . . 105 A5
Castings The WV14 . . . . .40 D2
Castlebridge Gdns WV11 . . . .26 F7
Castlebridge Rd WV11 . . . . . .27 A6
Castle Bromwich Bsns Pk
   B35. . . . . .58 A1
Castle Bromwich Hall Gdns*
   B36. . . . . .69 E8
Castle Bromwich Inf Sch
   B36. . . . . .69 E8
Castle Bromwich Jun Sch
   B36. . . . . .69 E7
Castle Cl
   Brownhills WS8 . . . . .6 F2
   Coventry CV3. . . . . 133 D4
   Cradley Heath B64 . . . . .63 B1
   Solihull B92 . . . . .89 B1
   Tamworth B77 . . . . .21 E4
   Warwick CV34 . . . . 160 E6
Castle Cres B36 . . . . .69 C8
Castlecroft Ave WV3 . . . . .38 A8
Castle Croft B68 . . . . .84 D8
Castlecroft Gdns WV3 . . . . . .38 C8
Castlecroft Ho WV3 . . . . .38 A8
Castlecroft La WV6 . . . . .23 F1
Castlecroft WS11 . . . . .5 E5
Castlecroft Prim Sch
   WV3. . . . . .38 B8
Castlecroft Rd
   Bilston WV14 . . . . .40 F7
   Wolverhampton WV3 . . . . . . .38 B8
Castle Ct
   5 Darlaston WS10 . . . . . .41 D6
   Hinckley LE10 . . . . .75 D6
   Kenilworth CV8 . . . . 148 A6
Castleditch La B98. . . . . 158 E7
Castle Dr
   Coleshill B46 . . . . .70 F5
   Willenhall WV12 . . . . .27 B5
Castleford Gr B11. . . . . .87 C4
Castleford Rd B11 . . . . .87 C4
Castlefort Jun Mix & Inf Sch
   WS9. . . . . .16 B3
Castlefort Rd WS9 . . . . .16 B3
Castlegate Dr DY1 . . . . .51 E2
Castle Gate Island DY1 . . . . .51 E2
Castlegate Mews **5**
   CV34. . . . . .160 F7
Castlegate Way DY1 . . . . .51 E2
Castle Gn CV8 . . . . 147 D5
Castle Gr
   Kenilworth CV8 . . . . 147 E4
   Stourbridge DY8 . . . . .81 B3
Castlehall **7** B77 . . . . .22 A2
Castle High Sch DY1 . . . . . . .51 A4
Castle Hill
   Dudley DY1 . . . . .51 D2
   Kenilworth CV8 . . . . 147 E5
Castlehill Rd WS9. . . . . .16 C3
Castlehills Dr B36 . . . . .69 A8
Castle Hill CV34 . . . . 160 E6

Castle Ho B33 . . . . .69 B2
Castle Hts B64. . . . . .83 B8
Castle La
Solihull B92 . . . . .89 A2
Warwick CV34 . . . . .160 E6
Castlemaine Dr LE10 . . . .71 E3
Castle Mews 6 CV34 . . . .160 E6
Castle Mill D91 . . . . .51 D4
Castle Mill Rd B60 . . . . .51 C4
Castle Place Ind Est CV1 165 D4
Castle Rd
Birmingham B29 . . . . .85 B1
Birmingham,Kings Norton
B30 . . . . .103 F4
Brownhills WS9 . . . . .16 A2
Castle Rd E B68 . . . . .84 D8
Castle Rd
Kenilworth CV8 . . . . .147 E5
Kidderminster DY11 . . . . . .116 E5
Nuneaton CV10 . . . . .73 C7
Studley B80 . . . . .159 F4
Tamworth B77 . . . . .35 F5
Tipton DY4 . . . . .51 D4
Castle Rd W B68 . . . . .84 C8
Castlereagh Cl WV10 . . . . .25 C6
Castle Specl Sch WS3 . . . .28 B7
Castle Sq B29 . . . . .85 A1
Castle St
Astwood Bank B96 . . . . . . .158 E2
Brownhills WS8 . . . . .6 F2
Coventry CV1 . . . . .165 D4
Darlaston WS10 . . . . .41 D8
Dudley DY1 . . . . .51 D1
Hinckley LE10 . . . . .75 D8
Sedgley DY3 . . . . .50 E5
Tipton DY4 . . . . .51 E5
Warwick CV34 . . . . .160 E6
West Bromwich B70 . . . . . . .53 A8
Wolverhampton WV1 . . . . .163 C3
Castle The DY8 . . . . .81 B3
Castleton St 1 B15 . . . . . . .86 B7
Castleton Rd
Birmingham B42 . . . . .55 D7
Walsall WS3 . . . . .14 C2
Castleton St DY2 . . . . .62 C4
Castle Vale Ent Pk B76 . . .58 A5
Castle Vale Ind Est B76 . . .58 A5
Castle Vale Ret Pk B35 . . .57 F3
Castle Vale Sch B35 . . . . . .58 B3
Castle View Cl WS10 . . . . .41 A4
Castle View Rd WV14,
WS10 .41 B4
Castle Yd WV1 . . . . .163 C3
Caswell Rd
Royal Leamington Spa
CV31 . . . . .162 B6
Sedgley DY3 . . . . .50 C8
Caterbank Way 2 WS13 . .8 F6
Cater Dr B76 . . . . .46 F2
Caterham Dr DY6 . . . . .60 F8
Catesby Dr DY6 . . . . .60 D8
Catesby Ho B37 . . . . .69 F4
Catesby La B94 . . . . .144 B2
Catesby Pk
Birmingham B38 . . . . .103 E3
Birmingham B38 . . . . .103 E3
Catesby Rd
Coventry CV6 . . . . .113 B8
Solihull B90 . . . . .106 B1
Cateswell Rd B11,B28 . . . .87 F2
Cathcart Rd DY8 . . . . .80 E5
Cathedral Ave DY11 . . . . .116 A6
Cathedral Cl DY11 . . . . .9 B8
Cathedral Ct 4 WS13 . . . . . .9 B8
Catherines Cl B91 . . . . . . .108 B4
Catherine St
Birmingham B6 . . . . .67 A7
Coventry CV2 . . . . .114 A3
Catherine Ward Hall CV12 78 B5
Catherton Cl DY4 . . . . .41 C1
Catholic La DY3 . . . . .50 D7
Catisfield Cres WV8 . . . . . . .11 B4
Cat & Kittens La WV10 . . .11 E6
Cat La B34 . . . . .69 B7
Caton Gr B28 . . . . .106 A7
Cato St N B7 . . . . .67 C5
Cato St N B7 . . . . .67 C5
Catshill Fst Sch B61 . . . . .137 A8
Catshill Mid Sch B61 . . . .136 F8
Catshill Rd WS8 . . . . .16 A7
Cattell Dr B75 . . . . .47 B5
Cattell Rd
Birmingham B9 . . . . .67 C1
Warwick CV34 . . . . .160 E7
Cattells Gr B7 . . . . .67 C6
Cattermole Gr B43 . . . . .44 C3
Cattock Hurst Dr B72 . . . . .57 D7
Causeway Green Prim Sch
B68 . . . . .63 F3
Causeway Gn B68 . . . . .64 A4
Causeway Rd WV14 . . . . . . .51 D8
Causeway B65 . . . . .63 C2
Causeway The B25 . . . . .88 D7
Causey Farm Rd B63 . . . . .100 C8
Cavalier Cir WV10 . . . . .11 E4

Cavalier Cl CV11 . . . . .73 E2
Cavalier Dr B63 . . . . .83 A3
Cavandale Ave B44 . . . . .44 E1
Cavan's Cl WS11 . . . . .1 E4
Cavans Cl CV3 . . . . .135 A8
Cavans Way CV3 . . . . .135 A8
Cavans Wood Park Home Est
WS12 .1 D5
Cavell Cl 1 WS2 . . . . .28 D2
Cavell Rd
Burntwood WS7 . . . . .7 E8
Dudley DY2 . . . . .51 F1
Cavendish Cl
Birmingham B38 . . . . .104 B1
Kingswinford DY6 . . . . .60 D4
Lower Marlbrook B60 . . . . .121 C1
Cavendish Ct
Birmingham B17 . . . . .85 B8
Dorridge B93 . . . . .128 A3
Cavendish Dr
Kidderminster DY10 . . . . . .117 B7
West Hagley DY9 . . . . .98 F4
Cavendish Gdns
Walsall WS2 . . . . .28 A4
Wolverhampton WV1 . . . . . .26 C1
Cavendish Rd
Birmingham B16 . . . . .65 D4
Coventry CV4 . . . . .111 E2
Halesowen B62 . . . . .83 F4
Walsall WS2 . . . . .28 B5
Wolverhampton WV1 . . . . . .26 B1
Cavendish Way WS9 . . . . . .30 B5
Cavendish Wlk CV11 . . . . . .79 C8
Caversham Cl CV11 . . . . . . .74 A2
Caversham Pl B73 . . . . .46 B4
Caversham Rd B44. . . . . . . .45 A2
Cawdon Gr B93 . . . . .127 F3
Cawdor Cres B16 . . . . .65 F1
Cawnpore Rd CV6 . . . . .95 B2
Cawthorne Cl 1 CV1 . . . . .113 E4
Caxton Ct 4 WS11 . . . . .4 E8
Caxton Gr B44 . . . . .45 C1
Caxton St WS11 . . . . .4 E8
Caynham Cl B98 . . . . .154 D4
Caynham Rd B32 . . . . .102 B8
Cayton Gr B23 . . . . .56 F6
Cearl Ct B27 . . . . .88 C2
Cecil Ave B27 . . . . .162 A8
Cecil Dr B69. . . . . .52 D2
Cecil Leonard Knox Cres
CV11 .79 F6
Cecil Rd
Birmingham,Gravelly Hill
B24 .56 F3
Birmingham,Selly Park B13. .86 C1
Cecil St
Birmingham B19 . . . . .164 C4
Cannock WS11 . . . . .1 F4
Stourbridge DY8 . . . . .80 F5
Walsall WS4 . . . . .28 F3
Cecily Rd CV3 . . . . .133 E7
Cedar Ave
Birmingham B36 . . . . .69 C8
Brownhills WS8 . . . . .16 A8
Dudley WV14 . . . . .51 B7
Ryton-on-D CV8. . . . . .135 B1
Cedar Bridge Croft B74 . .46 B8
Cedar Cl
Birmingham,Bournville
B30 . . . . .103 C8
Birmingham,Brandhall B68 . .84 C8
Cannock WS12 . . . . .2 A8
Lichfield WS14. . . . . .9 F7
Royal Leamington Spa
CV32 . . . . .157 A4
Stourbridge DY8 . . . . .80 D2
Walsall WS5 . . . . .43 B4
Cedar Cres DY11 . . . . .116 C6
Cedar Ct
Allesley CV5. . . . . .112 A6
Birmingham B43 . . . . .54 B8
Hinckley LE10 . . . . .76 A6
Tamworth B77 . . . . .35 E6
Cedar Dr
Bilston WV14 . . . . .40 F7
Cobsall WV8 . . . . .10 B3
Great Wyrley WS6 . . . . .5 B4
Warwick CV34 . . . . .156 A1
West Hagley DY9 . . . . .99 A6
Wolverhampton WV3 . . . . . .38 C7
Cedarhill Dr WS11 . . . . .1 F3
Cedar Ho
7 Royal Leamington Spa
CV32 . . . . .161 E8
Birmingham B36 . . . . .68 F8
Solihull B91 . . . . .106 F1
Sutton Coldfield B74 . . . . . .31 B5
Cedar Park Rd
Redditch B97 . . . . .153 D4
Willenhall WV12 . . . . .13 C1
Cedar Rd
Birmingham B30 . . . . .103 E6
Burntwood WS7 . . . . .7 A3
Dudley DY1 . . . . .51 B3

Cedar Rd continued
Nuneaton CV10 . . . . .72 D6
Redditch B97 . . . . .153 D4
Tipton DY4 . . . . .51 D5
Wednesbury WS10 . . . . .42 A2
Willenhall WV13 . . . . .26 E2
Cedars Ave
Birmingham B27 . . . . .88 C4
Coventry CV6 . . . . .112 F5
Kingswinford DY6 . . . . .60 D4
Wombourne WV5 . . . . .49 A5
Cedars Bsns Ctr The WS11 .4 C7
Cedars Hort Unit The
WV3 . . . . .24 A1
Cedars Mews The 3
CV32 . . . . .161 D8
Cedars Rd CV7 . . . . .78 B1
Cedars The
5 Wolverhampton,Newbridge
WV6 .24 F3
Birmingham B25 . . . . .68 E1
Dorridge B93 . . . . .128 A4
Wolverhampton,Tettenhall
WV6 .24 D5
Cedar Terr B60 . . . . .137 A1
Cedar View B97 . . . . .153 C4
Cedar Way
Birmingham B31 . . . . .102 F1
Wolverhampton WV11. . . . . .26 C7
Cedar Wlk 6 B37 . . . . .70 B2
Cedarwood Croft B42. . . . . .54 F8
Cedar Wood Dr CV7 . . . . .130 B6
Cedar Wood Rd DY3 . . . . . .50 D5
Celandine CV10 . . . . .60 C4
Celandine Rd
Coventry CV2. . . . . .96 D2
Dudley DY1 . . . . .51 A4
Celandine
Sutton Coldfield B74 . . . . . .31 F5
Tamworth B77 . . . . .21 C3
Celbury Way B43 . . . . .54 D8
Celeste Rd B60 . . . . .137 C1
Celtic Rd WS11 . . . . .1 E3
Celts Cl B65 . . . . .66 B5
Cemetery La B18 . . . . .66 B5
Cemetery Rd
Cannock WS11 . . . . .1 E4
Darlaston WS10 . . . . .41 F8
Oldbury B68. . . . . .64 C6
Redditch B97 . . . . .153 D3
Smethwick B67 . . . . .64 F4
Stourbridge DY9 . . . . .81 E5
Sutton Coldfield B75 . . . . . .46 D6
Willenhall WV13 . . . . .27 A2
Cemetery St
Bilston WV14 . . . . .40 C6
Cheslyn Hay WS6. . . . . .4 C2
Cemetery Way WS10 . . . . . .41 E6
Centaur Rd CV5 . . . . .112 F2
Centenary Bsns Ctr CV1 . .73 E3
Centenary Cl 1 B31 . . . . .103 A1
Centenary Dr B21. . . . . .54 E1
Centenary Plaza B1. . . . . . .164 A2
Centenary Rd CV4 . . . . .132 D7
Centenary Sq B1. . . . . .164 A2
Central Ave
13 Wolverhampton WV4 . . . .39 F4
Bilston WV14 . . . . .40 E7
Birmingham B31 . . . . .122 F8
Cannock WS11 . . . . .1 F5
Coventry CV2 . . . . .114 A2
Cradley Heath B64 . . . . .82 D7
Nuneaton CV11 . . . . .73 B5
Rowley Regis B65 . . . . .63 C2
Royal Leamington Spa
CV31 . . . . .161 F6
Stourbridge DY9 . . . . .81 E3
Tipton DY4 . . . . .51 D5
Central Bldgs CV3 . . . . . . .165 B1
Central Bsns Pk B33 . . . . .69 F1
Central City Ind Est CV6. .113 F5
Central Cl WS3 . . . . .14 A1
Central Dr
Dudley,Gornalwood DY3 . . . .50 D2
Dudley,West Coseley WV14. .51 D7
Walsall WS3 . . . . .14 A1
Central Gr B27 . . . . .88 C2
Central Park Dr B18 . . . . . .65 F5
Central Park Ind Est DY2. .62 E3
Central Rd B60 . . . . .137 A2
Central Six Ret Pk CV1. . .165 A1
Central Sq B23 . . . . .57 A4
Central Trad Est
Darlaston WS10 . . . . .41 E6
Wolverhampton WV2. . . . . . .39 F8
Central Way DY5. . . . . .61 F3
Centre City B63 . . . . .83 B3
Centre La B63 . . . . .83 B3
Centre Link Ind Est B7 . . .67 B6
Centreway The B14 . . . . . .105 D4
Centrovell Ind Est CV11 . . .73 C2
Centurion Cl B46 . . . . .59 F1
Centurion Pk B77. . . . . .36 B6
Centurion Way B77 . . . . . . .36 B6
Century Ho B7. . . . . .66 E5
Century Ind Est B44 . . . . . .44 E3
Century Mews B64. . . . . . . .62 F2
Century Pk
Birmingham,Bordesley Green
B9 . . . . .67 C2

Century Pk continued
Birmingham,Marston Green
B26 .90 C6
Century Rd B69. . . . . .64 A8
Century Ter B5. . . . . .86 C5
Ceolmund Cres B37. . . . . . .70 B2
CE Prim Sch of St Edmund &
St John The DY2 . . . . .51 E1
Chace Ave CV3 . . . . .134 C6
Chaceley Cl CV2 . . . . .115 A8
Chaceley Ct B97 . . . . .158 D8
Chaceley Gr B23. . . . . .56 E7
Chace Prim Sch CV3. . . . . .134 C6
Chadbrook Crest B15 . . . . .85 F7
Chadbury Croft 1 B91. . . .127 B8
Chadbury Rd B63. . . . . .83 C3
Chadcote Way B61. . . . . . . .120 F1
Chaddersley Cl 2 B45 . . .101 F1
Chaddesley Cl
Oldbury B69. . . . . .63 D5
Redditch B98 . . . . .153 F1
Chaddesley Dr DY9 . . . . . . .81 B1
Chaddesley Gdns 2
DY10. . . . . .117 A5
Chaddesley Rd
Birmingham B31 . . . . .103 D2
Halesowen B63 . . . . .82 F2
Kidderminster DY10 . . . . . .117 A5
Chadley Cl B91 . . . . .107 A6
Chad Rd
Birmingham B15 . . . . .85 F8
Dudley WV14 . . . . .51 B7
Chadsgrove Sch B61. . . . . .136 F8
Chadshunt Cl B36 . . . . .58 D2
Chadsmead Prim Sch
WS13 .3 A1
Chadsmoor CE Jun Sch
WS11. .2 A3
Chadsmoor Inf Sch WS11 . .2 A4
Chadsmoor Terr B77 . . . . . .67 B6
Chad Sq B15. . . . . .85 E8
Chadstone Dr B90 . . . . . . .127 B6
Chadswell Heights WS13. . . .3 B2
Chad Vale Prim Sch B15 . .85 D7
Chad Valley Cl B17. . . . . . . .85 D6
Chadwell Dr B90 . . . . .106 B6
Chadwick La CV7. . . . . .130 F2
Chadwick Ave B45 . . . . . . .122 B6
Chadwick Cl
Coventry CV5. . . . . .112 B3
Wolverhampton WV4 . . . . . .38 D6
Chadwick Ct B42 . . . . .54 E8
Chadwick La
Chadwick End B93 . . . . . . .145 B8
Temple Balsall B93 . . . . . . .129 B2
Chadwick Manor B93. . . . .129 A1
Chadwick Mews
Chadwick End B93 . . . . . . .145 B8
Redditch B98 . . . . .159 A7
Chadwick Rd B75. . . . . .46 F5
Chadworth Ave B93 . . . . . .127 E3
Chaffcombe Rd B26 . . . . . .89 C7
Chaffinch Cl
Cannock WS12. . . . . .2 B4
Sedgley DY3 . . . . .39 C3
Chaffinch Dr
Birmingham B36 . . . . .70 B7
Kidderminster DY10 . . . . . .116 F2
Chaffinch Rd DY9 . . . . .81 D3
Chainmakers Cl WV14. . . . .40 D2
Chainshop Mus* DY2. . . . .62 B3
Chain Wlk B19 . . . . .66 D7
Chalcot Dr WS12. . . . . .2 A7
Chalcot Gr B20 . . . . .54 E5
Chaldon Cl WV9 . . . . .11 A1
Chale Gr B14 . . . . .105 A3
Chalfield Cl B79. . . . . .20 C6
Chalfont Ave WS11. . . . . .4 C7
Chalfont Cl
Bedworth CV12 . . . . .78 A4
Coventry CV5. . . . . .112 B4
Chalfont Ct WS11. . . . . .4 C7
Chalfont PI DY9. . . . . .81 E2
Chalfont Rd B20 . . . . .55 C1
Chalford Rd B23. . . . . .56 C8
Chalgrove Ave B38. . . . . . .103 E1
Chalgrove Cres B91. . . . . .107 B1
Challenge Bsns Pk CV1 . .113 D5
Challenge Cl CV1 . . . . .165 C4
Challenge Way WV10 . . . . .25 E5
Challenor Ave WV13 . . . . . .26 D1
Chalybeate Cl B45 . . . . . . .101 F1
Chamberlain Cl
Cubbington CV32 . . . . .157 E5
Oldbury B69. . . . . .63 E4
Chamberlain Cres B90 . .106 A2
Chamberlain Ct
3 Birmingham,Hockley
B18. .66 C4
Birmingham,King's Heath
B14. .86 E1
Chamberlaine St CV12 . . .78 B3
Chamberlain Ho B16. . . . . .66 A1
Chamberlain Rd B13 . . . . . .87 A1
Chamberlain's Gn CV6 . . .112 F7
Chamberlain's La WV4 . . . .38 E3
Chamberlain Sq B3. . . . . . .164 B2
Chamberlain Wlk
10 Coleshill B46 . . . . .70 F7
Chambley Gr B37 . . . . .70 B1
Champney Dr DY10 . . . . . .116 E2
Chance Croft B68 . . . . .84 B8
Chance Fields CV31 . . . . .162 F6
Chancel Ct B91 . . . . .107 C2
Chancel Ind Est
Darlaston WS10 . . . . .41 D5
Kingswinford DY6 . . . . .49 E1

Chancel Ind Est The WV1..26 A1
Chancel Ind Est WV13. . . . .27 B2
Chancellor's Cl B15. . . . . . .85 E8
Chancellors Cl CV4 . . . . . .132 D4
Chancel Way
Birmingham B6 . . . . .55 F5
Halesowen B62 . . . . .83 C6
Chancery Ct CV10. . . . . .72 A7
Chancery Dr WS12 . . . . .2 C7
Chancery La CV10 . . . . .72 B7
Chancery Way DY5. . . . . . . .61 F2
Chanders Rd CV34 . . . . . . .155 D1
Chandler Dr WV4 . . . . .38 D3
Chandler Ho B65 . . . . .63 D4
Chandlers Cl
Birmingham B18 . . . . .65 F5
Redditch B97 . . . . .158 D7
Wolverhampton WV9 . . . . . .11 A1
Chandlers Dr B77. . . . . .22 B5
Chandlers Keep WS8. . . . . .16 A6
Chandlers Rd CV31. . . . . . .162 A2
Chandlers CV31. . . . . .161 D7
Chandos Ave B13 . . . . .86 F3
Chandos Ct 15 CV32 . . . . .156 F1
Chandos Prim Sch B12. . . .86 E8
Chandos St
Coventry CV2 . . . . .114 A3
Nuneaton CV11 . . . . .73 A4
Royal Leamington Spa
CV32. . . . . .156 F1
Change Brook Cl CV11. . . . .73 F8
Channel Way CV6. . . . . .96 B6
Channon Dr DY5. . . . . .81 D8
Chanston Ave B14 . . . . . . .104 E4
Chanterelle Ct WV4 . . . . . . .39 B4
Chanterelle Gdns WV4 . . . .39 B4
Chantrey Cres
Bilston WV14 . . . . .40 F7
Birmingham B43 . . . . .44 D4
Chantries The CV1 . . . . . . .113 E5
Chantry Ave WS3 . . . . .28 D8
Chantry Cl B47 . . . . .125 A7
Chantry Ct B13 . . . . .86 F3
Chantry Dr B62. . . . . .84 A6
Chantry Heath Cres B93. .128 C7
Chantry Ind Est B7. . . . . . . .59 B7
Chantry Rd
Birmingham,Handsworth
B21. .65 F8
Birmingham,Moseley B13 . .86 F4
Stourbridge DY7 . . . . .80 C7
Chantry The CV34 . . . . .156 A3
Chapel Ash WV3 . . . . .25 B2
Chapel Ave WS8 . . . . .6 E2
Chapel Ct B64 . . . . .83 B8
Chapel Dr
2 Royal Leamington Spa
CV32. . . . . .161 F8
4 Brierley Hill,Silver End
DY5. . . . . .61 D2
Astwood Bank B96 . . . . . . .158 E1
Brierley Hill,Barrow Hill
DY5. . . . . .61 C7
Chapel Dr
Balsall Common CV7 . . . . . .130 B8
Brownhills WS8 . . . . .6 E2
Mile Oak B78. . . . . .20 C1
Wythall B47 . . . . .124 F3
Chapel Farm Cl CV3 . . . . .134 C6
Chapelfield Mews
Birmingham B45 . . . . .121 F6
Stourbridge DY8 . . . . .81 A4
Chapelfield Rd B45 . . . . . .122 A7
Chapel Fields Jun Sch
B92. .88 F3
Chapel Fields Rd B92. . . . . .88 F2
Chapel Gn WV13 . . . . .27 B2
Chapel House La B63 . . . . .82 C6
Chapelhouse Rd B37. . . . . .69 F1
Chapel House St 1 B12. .66 F1
Chapel La
Barnacle CV7 . . . . .97 B6
Beoley B98. . . . . .154 F8
Birmingham B29 . . . . .85 E2
Birmingham,Great Barr B43,
WS9 . . . . .44 A5
Kingswood B94 . . . . .144 D7
Lichfield WS14. . . . . .9 B6
Madeley Heath DY9 . . . . . .120 D7
Romsley B62 . . . . .100 C6
Rowney Green B48 . . . . . . .139 F4
Ryton-on-D CV8 . . . . .135 B2
Walsall B43 . . . . .43 F4
Wythall B47 . . . . .124 E2
Chapel Mews B77 . . . . .22 A5
Chapel Mill Apartments
B62. .83 C8
Chaplon B72 . . . . .22 A2
Chapel PI DY11 . . . . .116 D6
Chapel Rd B96 . . . . .158 E1
Chapel Row CV34 . . . . .160 E7
Chapel Sq WS6 . . . . .4 D3
Chapel St
5 Royal Leamington Spa
CV31. . . . . .162 A7
Astwood Bank B96 . . . . . . .158 E1
Bedworth CV12 . . . . .78 C3
Bilston WV14 . . . . .40 F4
Birmingham B4 . . . . .164 D3
Birmingham,Handsworth
B21. .65 D7
Brierley Hill,Barrow Hill
DY5. . . . . .61 C6

Chapel St continued
Brierley Hill,Quarry Bank
DY5 . . . . .61 F1
Brierley Hill,Silver End DY5 . .61 D2
Bromsgrove B60 . . . . .137 A2
Brownhills WS8 . . . . .6 E2
Burntwood WS7 . . . . .7 D7
Cannock WS12 . . . . .2 E1
Coventry CV1 . . . . .165 B3
Dudley DY2 . . . . .62 D4
Halesowen B63 . . . . .83 A3
Kidderminster DY11 . . . . . .116 D6
Kingswinford DY6 . . . . .60 B8
Norton Canes WS11 . . . . .5 F5
Nuneaton CV11 . . . . .73 C4
Redditch B97 . . . . .153 D1
Chapel Street Prec ◪
B60 . . . . .137 A2
Chapel St
Stourbridge,Lye DY9 . . . . . . .81 E5
Stourbridge,Wollaston DY8 . .81 A4
Stourbridge,Wordsley DY8 . . .60 D3
Tipton DY4 . . . . .51 E5
Walsall,Blakenall Heath
WS3 . . . . .28 D8
Walsall WS3 . . . . .15 A3
Warwick CV34 . . . . .160 E7
Wednesbury WS10 . . . . .41 E3
West Bromwich B70 . . . . . . .53 B5
West Hagley WV9 . . . . .99 A5
Wolverhampton WV2 . . . . . .39 D7
Chapel View B67 . . . . .64 F4
Chapel Wlk
Birmingham B30 . . . . .104 A2
Bromsgrove B60 . . . . .137 A2
Dudley DY3 . . . . .50 C2
Chapelwood Gr B42 . . . . . . .55 D5
Chaplain Rd WS12 . . . . .2 E2
Chapman Cl CV31 . . . . .162 E5
Chapman Ct CV34 . . . . .161 C8
Chapman Rd B10 . . . . .87 C8
Chapman's Hill B62 . . . . . . .101 B1
Chapmans Pas B1 . . . . .164 B1
Chapman St B70 . . . . .53 B3
Chapter Ho B70 . . . . .53 A5
Chard Rd CV3 . . . . .134 D8
Charfield Cl B30 . . . . .103 D7
Charford Fst Sch B60 . . . . . .150 F7
Charford Rd B60 . . . . .150 F8
Charingworth Rd B92 . . . . . .89 C3
Charity Bick Way B77 . . . . . .53 C2
Charity Rd CV7 . . . . .95 A7
Charlbury Ave B37 . . . . .69 F2
Charlbury Cres B26 . . . . . . .88 F8
Charlbury Mews CV31 . . . . . .162 C6
Charlbury Twr ◪ B5 . . . . . . .86 E8
Charlecote Cl B98 . . . . .154 D2
Charlecote Croft B90 . . . . . .126 C8
Charlecote Dr
Birmingham B23 . . . . .56 E7
Dudley DY1 . . . . .50 E3
Charlecote Gdns
Royal Leamington Spa
CV31 . . . . .162 D5
Sutton Coldfield B73 . . . . . .57 A8
Charlecote Rd CV6 . . . . .9 A2
Charlecote Rise ◪ WV13 . . . . .40 F8
Charlecote Wlk CV11 . . . . . . .78 F8
Charlcott Cl B13 . . . . .105 D7
Charlemont Ave B71 . . . . . . .53 E8
Charlemont Cres B71 . . . . . . .42 E1
Charlemont Cl WS12 . . . . .2 D3
Charlemont Gdns WS5 . . . . . . .43 C6
Charlemont Jun & Inf Sch
B71 . . . . .53 E8
Charlemont Rd
Walsall WS5 . . . . .43 C6
West Bromwich B71 . . . . . . .53 F8
Charles Ave
Essington WV11 . . . . .12 F4
Rowley Regis B65 . . . . .63 C4
Wolverhampton WV4 . . . . . . .39 B5
Charles Burns Sch B13 . . . . .86 E1
Charles Cl
Birmingham B8 . . . . .67 D4
Cheslyn Hay WS6 . . . . .4 D1
Charles Cres WS3 . . . . .15 A5
Charles Ct ◪
Royal Leamington Spa
CV31 . . . . .162 A6
◪ Warwick,Emscote
CV34 . . . . .161 B8
◪ Birmingham B37 . . . . .87 B2
Sutton Coldfield B76 . . . . . .46 F3
Warwick CV34 . . . . .160 C7
Charlesdale Dr WS9 . . . . .30 B4
Charles Dr B7 . . . . .67 B6
Charles Eaton Rd CV12 . . . . . .77 F3
Charles Edward Rd B26 . . . . . .88 D6
Charles Foster St WS10 . . . . . .41 C6
Charles Gardner Rd ◪
CV31 . . . . .161 F6
Charles Hayward Bglws
WV4 . . . . .39 D3
Charles Henry St B12 . . . . . .86 F8
Charles Holland St ◪
WV13 . . . . .27 B2
Charles Lakin Cl CV7 . . . . . . .97 C5
Charles Lane Trust Homes
The B28 . . . . .106 A8
Charles Pearson Ct B66 . . . . .65 B5
Charles Rd
Birmingham,Aston B6 . . . . . .56 A1

Charles Rd continued
Birmingham,Bordesley Green B9,
B10 . . . . .67 E1
Birmingham,Handsworth
B20 . . . . .55 C1
Brierley Hill DY5 . . . . .62 B1
Halesowen B63 . . . . .82 F4
Solihull B91 . . . . .106 E2
Stourbridge DY8 . . . . .80 E4
Tipton DY4 . . . . .52 A7
Charles St
Coventry CV1 . . . . .165 D4
Hinckley LE10 . . . . .71 E1
Kidderminster DY10 . . . . . .116 F6
Nuneaton CV11 . . . . .73 A5
Redditch B97 . . . . .153 C1
Smethwick B66 . . . . .65 C7
Walsall WS2 . . . . .28 D2
Warwick CV34 . . . . .161 A8
West Bromwich B70 . . . . . . .52 E5
Willenhall WV13 . . . . .27 C3
Charles Watson Ct ◪
CV32 . . . . .157 A2
Charles Wesley Ct WV3 . . . . . .39 A7
Charles Wlk B65 . . . . .63 C5
Charlesworth Ave B90 . . . . . .127 B6
Charleville Rd B19 . . . . .66 B7
Charlewood Rd CV6 . . . . .95 B2
Charlock Gr WS11 . . . . .2 C3
Charlotte Cl
Nuneaton CV10 . . . . .72 C6
Tipton B69 . . . . .52 A2
Charlotte Rd
Birmingham,Edgbaston
B15 . . . . .86 C7
Birmingham,Stirchley B30 . .104 A6
Wednesbury WS10 . . . . .41 C2
Charlotte St
◪ Dudley DY1 . . . . .51 B1
Birmingham B3 . . . . .164 A3
Royal Leamington Spa
CV31 . . . . .161 F6
Walsall WS1 . . . . .29 A2
Charlton Dr B64 . . . . .82 D7
Charlton Pl B8 . . . . .67 D5
Charlton Rd B44 . . . . .56 A8
Charlton St
◪ Dudley DY1 . . . . .51 B1
Brierley Hill DY5 . . . . .61 A3
Charminster Ave B25 . . . . . . .88 D8
Charminster Dr CV3 . . . . . . .133 D4
Charnley Dr B75 . . . . .32 E2
Charnwood Ave
Nuneaton CV10 . . . . .72 E2
Sedgley DY3 . . . . .39 D2
Charnwood Bsns Pk
WV14 . . . . .40 C5
Charnwood Cl
Birmingham B45 . . . . .102 B3
Brierley Hill DY5 . . . . .81 B8
Cannock WS12 . . . . .2 C2
Darlaston WV14 . . . . .41 B3
Hinckley LE10 . . . . .71 E2
Lichfield WS13 . . . . .3 C1
Charnwood Ct DY9 . . . . .81 E2
Charnwood Ho WS13 . . . . .3 B2
Charnwood Prim Sch
WS13 . . . . .3 C2
Charnwood Rd
Birmingham B42 . . . . .54 F7
Hinckley LE10 . . . . .71 D2
Walsall WS5 . . . . .43 A4
Charnwood Way CV32 . . . . . .157 C3
Charter App CV34 . . . . .160 D5
Charter Ave CV4 . . . . .132 B7
Charter Cl WS11 . . . . .5 E4
Charter Cres B64 . . . . .83 B8
Charterfield Dr
Cannock WS12 . . . . .2 C1
Kingswinford DY6 . . . . .60 D8
Charter Ho CV4 . . . . .132 A7
Charterhouse Dr B91 . . . . . .107 C1
Charterhouse Rd CV1 . . . . . .113 E2
Charter Prim Sch (Harris
Site) CV4 . . . . .131 F7
Charter Prim Sch (Parkes
Site) CV4 . . . . .132 C8
Charter Rd DY4 . . . . .41 C1
Charters Ave WV8 . . . . .10 B1
Charter St DY5 . . . . .61 E5
Charters The WS13 . . . . .3 B1
Chartist Rd B8 . . . . .67 D6
Chartley Cl
Dorridge B93 . . . . .127 E3
Perton WV6 . . . . .23 F4
Chartley Rd
Birmingham B23 . . . . .56 F3
West Bromwich B71 . . . . . . .53 D6
Chartway The WS3 . . . . .15 B4
Chartwell Cl
Dudley DY1 . . . . .51 B6
Nuneaton CV11 . . . . .73 F1
Chartwell Dr
Cheswick Green B90 . . . . . .126 D5
Sutton Coldfield B74 . . . . . .31 D4
Wolverhampton WV10 . . . . .11 E1
Chartwell Grange B64 . . . . . .83 A7
Chartwell Rd B79 . . . . .20 D7
Chase Acad WS11 . . . . .4 E8
Chase Ave WS6 . . . . .4 E3
Chase Cl CV11 . . . . .73 E6
Chase Gr B24 . . . . .57 E6
Chase La CV4 . . . . .147 B7
Chaselands WS11 . . . . .6 D7
Chase L Ctr WS11 . . . . .1 D2
Chaseley Ave WS11 . . . . .1 C2

Chaseley Croft WS11 . . . . .1 C2
Chaseley Gdns WS7 . . . . .7 C7
Chase Park Ind Est WS7 . . . . . .6 D7
Chase Rd
Brownhills WS8 . . . . .7 A1
Burntwood WS7 . . . . .7 B6
Dudley DY3,DY5 . . . . .50 C1
Walsall WS3 . . . . .28 A8
Chaseside Dr WV11 . . . . .2 B3
Chaseside Ind Est WS11 . . . . . .2 B3
Chase Terrace Prim Sch
WS7 . . . . .6 F7
Chase Terrace Tech Coll
WS7 . . . . .6 F6
Chase The
Sutton Coldfield B76 . . . . . .57 D7
Wolverhampton WV6 . . . . . .25 B6
Chasetown Com Sch WS7 . . . . .6 E7
Chasetown Ind Est WS7 . . . . . .6 E7
Chasetown Specialist Sports
Coll WS7 . . . . .6 E6
Chasetown Sta* WS7 . . . . . . .6 D5
Chase Vale WV7 . . . . .6 C4
Chase View WV4 . . . . .39 E2
Chasewater* WV7 . . . . .6 C4
Chasewater Country Pk*
WS7 . . . . .6 D5
Chasewater Heaths Sta*
WS7 . . . . .6 D6
Chasewater Rly* WS11 . . . . . . .6 B5
Chasewater Way WS11 . . . . . . .5 F5
Chase Wlk WS11 . . . . .1 C4
Chasewood Park Bsns Ctr
WS12 . . . . .1 F1
Chater Dr B76 . . . . .47 A1
Chaters Cl DY4 . . . . .51 E5
Chatham Cl CV3 . . . . .134 C8
Chatham Rd B31 . . . . .103 A3
Chatillon Cl CV34 . . . . .161 E3
Chatsworth Ave B43 . . . . . . .43 C1
Chatsworth Cl
Cheswick Green B90 . . . . . .126 E5
Hinckley LE10 . . . . .75 F6
Sutton Coldfield B72 . . . . . .57 D7
Willenhall WV12 . . . . .27 B5
Chatsworth Cres WS4 . . . . . . .29 D7
Chatsworth Dr
Cannock WS11 . . . . .2 A4
Nuneaton CV11 . . . . .73 F2
Chatsworth Gdns
Royal Leamington Spa
CV31 . . . . .162 D6
Wolverhampton WV6 . . . . . .24 A7
Chatsworth Gr CV8 . . . . . . .148 C5
Chatsworth Rd B62 . . . . .83 A7
Chatsworth Rise CV3 . . . . . .133 E6
Chatsworth Tower B15 . . . . . .86 C8
Chattaway Dr CV7 . . . . .130 B6
Chattaway St B7 . . . . .67 C2
Chatterton Ave B13 . . . . .86 E6
Chatterton Wlk ◪ DY10 . . . . .117 B6
Chattle Hill B46 . . . . .59 E2
Chattock Ave B91 . . . . .107 E3
Chattock Cl B36 . . . . .68 E7
Chatwell Gr B29 . . . . .85 B2
Chatwin Pl WV14 . . . . .40 E3
Chatwin St B66 . . . . .64 F7
Chatwins Wharf DY4 . . . . . . .51 F5
Chaucer Ave
Dudley DY3 . . . . .50 A5
Tipton DY4 . . . . .52 B8
Willenhall WV12 . . . . .27 E8
Chaucer Cl
Birmingham B23 . . . . .56 B3
Dudley WV14 . . . . .51 D8
Lichfield WS14 . . . . .9 B6
Chaucer Cres DY10 . . . . . . .117 C5
Chaucer Dr CV11 . . . . .72 A4
Chaucer Gr B27 . . . . .88 B2
Chaucer Ho B63 . . . . .82 B5
Chaucer Rd
Bromsgrove B60 . . . . .151 B8
Walsall WS3 . . . . .28 C8
Chauntry Pl CV1 . . . . .165 C3
Chauson Gr B91 . . . . .127 A8
Chavasse Rd B72 . . . . .46 D3
Chawnhill Cl DY9 . . . . .81 C3
Chawn Hill DY9 . . . . .81 C3
Chawn Park Dr DY9 . . . . .81 C3
Chaynes Gr B33 . . . . .69 D2
Chaytor Dr CV10 . . . . .72 B6
Cheadle Cl CV2 . . . . .96 A4
Cheadle Dr B23 . . . . .56 D8
Cheam Cl CV6 . . . . .96 A1
Cheam Gdns WV6 . . . . .24 E8
Cheapside
◪ Willenhall WV13 . . . . . . .27 A1
Birmingham B5,B12 . . . . . . .66 F1
Cheapside Ind Est ◪ B12 . .66 F1
Cheapside WV1 . . . . .163 B3
Cheatham St B7 . . . . .67 C6
Cheatle Ct B97 . . . . .35 D5
Checketts St WS2 . . . . .28 C2
Checkley Cl B90 . . . . .106 B4
Checkley Croft B76 . . . . .57 F8
Cheddar Rd B12 . . . . .86 E6
Chedworth Cl
Birmingham B29 . . . . .103 B6
Redditch B98 . . . . .154 C5
Cheedon Cl B93 . . . . .127 E2
Chelford Cl CV10 . . . . .72 B5
Chelford Cres DY6 . . . . .61 A3
Chells Gr B13 . . . . .105 B5
Chelmar Cl B36 . . . . .69 E8
Chelmar Dr DY5 . . . . .61 A6
Chelmarsh Ave WV3 . . . . .38 B8

Chelmarsh Cl B98 . . . . .154 C7
Chelmarsh CV6 . . . . .113 C6
Chelmorton Rd B42 . . . . .55 D7
Chelmscote Rd B92 . . . . .88 F1
Chelmsley Ave B46 . . . . .70 F6
Chelmsley Circ B37 . . . . .70 B2
Chelmsley Gr B33 . . . . .69 E3
Chelmsley La B37 . . . . .90 A8
Chelmsley Rd B37 . . . . .70 B3
Chelmsley Wood Ind Est
B37 . . . . .70 D4
Chelney Wlk CV3 . . . . .115 A1
Chelsea B37 . . . . .69 F5
Chelsea Cl
Birmingham B32 . . . . .84 F4
Nuneaton CV11 . . . . .73 F7
Chelsea Ct ◪ B29 . . . . .103 B7
Chelsea Dr B74 . . . . .31 F4
Chelsea Trad Est B7 . . . . . . .67 A6
Chelsea Way DY6 . . . . .60 C6
Chelsey Rd CV2 . . . . .114 E8
Chelston Dr WV6 . . . . .24 C4
Chelston Rd B31 . . . . .102 E2
Cheltenham Ave B61 . . . . . .121 B1
Cheltenham Cl
Bedworth CV12 . . . . .78 B4
Wolverhampton WV6 . . . . . .25 B5
Cheltenham Croft CV2 . . . . .114 F7
Cheltenham Dr
Birmingham B36 . . . . .68 D8
Kingswinford DY6 . . . . .60 B6
Chelthorn Way B91 . . . . . . .107 C2
Cheltondale ◪ B90 . . . . . . .126 C8
Cheltondale Rd B91 . . . . . . .106 F6
Chelveston Cres B91 . . . . . .107 B1
Chelveston Rd CV6 . . . . .112 E5
Chelwood Gdns WV14 . . . . . .40 B5
Chelwood Gr CV2 . . . . .96 F1
Chelworth Rd B38 . . . . .104 B2
Chem Rd WV14 . . . . .40 C5
Chenet Way WS11 . . . . .1 E2
Chenies Cl CV5 . . . . .112 B3
Cheniston Rd WV12 . . . . .27 C7
Chepstow Cl
Coventry CV3 . . . . .134 C5
Perton WV6 . . . . .23 F4
Chepstow Dr B61 . . . . .121 B1
Chepstow Gr B45 . . . . .122 B6
Chepstow Rd
Walsall WS3 . . . . .13 F1
Wolverhampton WV10 . . . . .11 D5
Chepstow Villas ◪ B12 . . . .87 B5
Chepstow Way WS3 . . . . .13 F1
Chequerfield Dr WV4 . . . . . . .39 A4
Chequers Ave WV5 . . . . .38 A1
Chequers Ct WS12 . . . . .2 A5
Chequer St CV12 . . . . .79 C2
Chequers The ◪ WS13 . . . . . . .9 C8
Cherhill Covert ◪ B14 . . . . .104 C2
Cherington Cl B98 . . . . .154 F1
Cherington Rd B29 . . . . . . .104 A8
Cherington Way WS9 . . . . . . .16 C1
Cheriton Gr WV6 . . . . .23 E3
Cheriton Wlk B23 . . . . .56 B3
Cherrington Cl B31 . . . . . . .102 F7
Cherrington Dr WS6 . . . . .4 F4
Cherrington Gdns
Stourbridge DY9 . . . . .99 C2
Wolverhampton WV6 . . . . . .24 B2
Cherrington Way B91 . . . . . .107 B1
Cherry Bank WS12 . . . . .2 C6
Cherry Blossom Gr CV31 . . . .162 B2
Cherrybrook Way CV2 . . . . . . .96 C1
Cherry Cl
Burntwood WS7 . . . . .6 F6
Coventry CV6 . . . . .95 D2
Cherry Cres B24 . . . . .56 F3
Bromsgrove B61 . . . . .136 E2
Cherrydale Ct DY1 . . . . .50 F2
Cherry Dr
Birmingham B9 . . . . .67 B1
Cherry Gn DY1 . . . . .50 F4
Cherry La
Himley DY3 . . . . .49 C3
Sutton Coldfield B73 . . . . . .57 A7
Wednesbury WS10 . . . . .42 A2
Cherry Lea B34 . . . . .69 B6
Cherryl Ho B3 B64 . . . . .31 E3
Cherry Oak Sch B29 . . . . . . .85 D2
Cherry Orchard Ave B63 . . . .82 F6
Cherry Orchard Cres B63 . . .82 F6
Cherry Orchard Prim Sch
B20 . . . . .55 A3
Cherry Orchard Rd B20 . . . . .55 A4
Cherry Orch
Cradley Heath B64 . . . . .62 F1
Kenilworth CV8 . . . . .148 A5
Kidderminster DY10 . . . . . .116 F6
Lichfield WS14 . . . . .9 C7
Cherry Pit La B98 . . . . .141 A1
Cherry Rd DY4 . . . . .51 F7
Cherry St
Birmingham B2 . . . . .164 C2
Halesowen B63 . . . . .82 F5
Stourbridge DY8 . . . . .80 E4

Cherry St continued
Tamworth B79 . . . . .21 B5
Warwick CV34 . . . . .160 F7
Wolverhampton WV3 . . . . . .25 B1
Cherry Tree Ave
Nuneaton CV10 . . . . .72 E6
Walsall WS5 . . . . .43 A5
Cherry Tree Croft ◪ B27 . . .88 C5
Cherrytree Ct DY9 . . . . .81 E3
Cherry Tree Gdns WV8 . . . . .10 B3
Cherry Tree La
Codsall WV8 . . . . .10 B3
Halesowen B63 . . . . .82 D1
Cherry Tree Rd
Huntington WS12 . . . . .1 D8
Kingswinford DY6 . . . . .60 E8
Norton Canes WS11 . . . . .6 B5
Cherry Tree Wlk
Redditch B97 . . . . .153 B4
Tamworth B79 . . . . .21 A8
Cherry Way CV8 . . . . .148 A5
Cherry Wlk B47 . . . . .125 B5
Cherrywood Cl WV14 . . . . . . .40 C1
Cherrywood Cres ◪
B91 . . . . .127 C8
Cherrywood Ct B92 . . . . .89 A2
Cherrywood Gn WV14 . . . . . .40 D8
Cherrywood Gr CV5 . . . . . . .111 F5
Cherrywood Ind Est B9 . . . . .67 D3
Cherrywood Rd
Birmingham B9 . . . . .67 E2
Sutton Coldfield B74 . . . . . .30 D1
Sutton Coldfield B74 . . . . . .44 D8
Cherrywood Way WV4 . . . . . .31 D4
Chervil Cl B42 . . . . .55 C7
Chervil Rise WV10 . . . . .25 F3
Cherwell Cl LE10 . . . . .75 A8
Cherwell Ct B73 . . . . .46 B5
Cherwell Dr
Birmingham B36 . . . . .69 F8
Brownhills WS8 . . . . .6 C2
Cherwell Gdns ◪ B6 . . . . . .66 D8
Cherwell B77 . . . . .21 D1
Chesford Cres
Coventry CV6 . . . . .96 B2
Warwick CV34 . . . . .156 B1
Chesham St CV31 . . . . .162 B7
Cheshire Ave B90 . . . . .106 A2
Cheshire Cl
Burntwood WS7 . . . . .7 F8
Stourbridge DY8 . . . . .80 D8
Cheshire Gr
Kidderminster DY11 . . . . . .116 A7
Perton WV6 . . . . .23 E4
Cheshire Ho ◪ B66 . . . . .65 B5
Cheshire Rd
Birmingham B6 . . . . .56 A2
Smethwick B67 . . . . .65 A4
Walsall WS2 . . . . .27 F2
Cheslyn Dr WS6 . . . . .4 C3
Cheslyn Gr B14 . . . . .105 A3
Cheslyn Hay High Sch WS6 . . .4 C3
Cheslyn Hay Prim Sch
WS6 . . . . .4 C2
Chessetts Gr B13 . . . . .105 A6
Chessetts Wood Rd B94 . . . .144 C7
Chessher St LE10 . . . . .71 C1
Chester Ave WV6 . . . . .24 F7
Chester Cl
Birmingham B37 . . . . .70 A2
Cannock WS11 . . . . .2 B1
Lichfield WS13 . . . . .3 C3
Willenhall WV13 . . . . .27 D2
Chester Ct
◪ Birmingham,Chelmsley
Wood B37 . . . . .70 D2
◪ Birmingham,Weoley Castle
B29 . . . . .103 B7
Birmingham,Chester Road
B73 . . . . .57 A7
Chesterfield Cl B31 . . . . . .103 B2
Chesterfield Ct
Birmingham B38 . . . . .103 E4
Brownhills WS9 . . . . .15 F4
Chesterfield Rd WS14 . . . . . .43 A5
Chestergate Croft B24 . . . . .57 D4
Chester Gdns B73 . . . . .45 C1
Chester Hayes Ct B24 . . . . . .57 C5
Chester Pl WS2 . . . . .28 B1
Chester Rd
Aldridge B74 . . . . .30 C4
Birmingham,Castle Bromwich
B36 . . . . .69 E7
Birmingham,Chelmsley Wood
B37 . . . . .90 F8
Cradley Heath B64 . . . . .82 C8
Dudley DY2 . . . . .62 D2
Hampton-in-Arden B46,B92,CV7 . .91 B5
Chester Rd N
Kidderminster DY10 . . . . . .117 A7
Sutton Coldfield B73 . . . . . .45 B4
Sutton Coldfield B74 . . . . . .30 F2
Chester Rd S DY10 . . . . . . .116 F4
Chester Rd
Stonnall WS9 . . . . .16 D3
Sutton Coldfield B23,B24,B35,
B73 . . . . .57 A7
West Bromwich B71 . . . . . . .42 B1
Chester Rise B68 . . . . .84 B8
Chester Road Sta B73 . . . . . .57 A7
Chester St
Birmingham B6 . . . . .67 A6
Coventry CV1 . . . . .113 A3

Chester St continued
Wolverhampton WV6 . . . . .25 B4
Chesterton Ave B12 . . . . .87 B5
Chesterton Cl
Redditch B97 . . . . .158 D4
Solihull B91 . . . . .106 E5
Chesterton Ct B13 . . . . .86 F1
Chesterton Dr
Nuneaton CV10 . . . . .72 A5
Royal Leamington Spa
CV31 . . . . .162 C5
Chesterton Rd
Birmingham B12 . . . . .87 B5
Coventry CV6 . . . . .113 A7
Wolverhampton WV10 . . . . . .26 A8
Chesterton Way B71 . . . . .53 C6
Chesterwood Gdns B20 . . .55 D2
Chesterwood B47 . . . . .125 A6
Chesterwood Rd B13 . . . . . .104 F6
Chester Wood WS9 . . . . .30 F2
Chestnut Ave
Dudley DY1 . . . . .51 C3
Kenilworth CV8 . . . . .147 F3
Tamworth B79 . . . . .21 B7
Tipton DY4 . . . . .51 F7
Chestnut Cl
Birmingham B27 . . . . .88 C4
Cannock WS11 . . . . .2 C2
Solihull B92 . . . . .106 D8
Stourbridge DY8 . . . . .80 D3
Sutton Coldfield B74 . . . . . . .31 A3
Chestnut Cres CV10 . . . . . . .72 E6
Chestnut Ct
Birmingham B36 . . . . .69 E7
Burntwood WS7 . . . . .6 F4
Coventry CV3 . . . . .134 B8
Kidderminster DY11 . . . . . . .116 B8
Royal Leamington Spa
CV34 . . . . .161 D2
Chestnut Dr
Birmingham,Buckland End
B36 .69 B7
Birmingham,Erdington B24 . .57 C4
Cheslyn Hay WS6 . . . . .4 F3
Great Wyrley WS6 . . . . .4 E3
Nuneaton CV11 . . . . .73 E3
Shenstone WS14 . . . . .17 F5
Walsall WS4 . . . . .29 B8
West Hagley DY9 . . . . .98 F4
Wombourne WV5 . . . . .49 A5
Chestnut Gr
4 Birmingham B17 . . . . .85 D5
Coventry CV4 . . . . .112 A2
Kidderminster DY11 . . . . . . .116 B8
Kingswinford DY6 . . . . .60 F6
Tamworth B77 . . . . .21 C3
Wolverhampton WV11 . . . . . .26 C7
Chestnut Pl
Birmingham B14 . . . . .104 E8
Walsall WS3 . . . . .28 D6
Chestnut Rd
Astwood Bank B96 . . . . .158 E1
Bedworth CV12 . . . . .78 D4
Birmingham,Brandhall B68 . .84 C7
Birmingham,Showell Green
B13 .87 A4
Bromsgrove B61 . . . . .136 F4
Walsall WS3 . . . . .28 E6
Wednesbury WS10 . . . . .42 A2
Chestnuts Ave B26 . . . . .89 B7
Chestnuts Sq CV32 . . . . . . .157 B2
Chestnuts The
Bedworth CV12 . . . . .77 E2
Kidderminster DY11 . . . . . . .116 C3
Wolverhampton WV11 . . . . . .26 B6
Chestnut Tree Ave CV4 . .112 A2
Chestnut Wlk 2 B37 . . . . . .70 B2
Cheston Rd WV14 . . . . .40 B5
Cheston Ind Est 67 A7
Cheston Rd B7 . . . . .67 A7
Cheswell Cl WV6 . . . . .24 B2
Cheswick Cl
Coventry CV6 . . . . .114 A7
Willenhall WV13 . . . . .27 B5
Cheswick Green Prim Sch
B90 . . . . .126 C4
Cheswick Way B90 . . . . . . .126 C4
Cheswood Dr B76 . . . . .58 B6
Chesworth Rd B60 . . . . .137 B1
Chetland Croft B92 . . . . . . .107 F7
Chettle Rd WV14 . . . . .40 F3
Chetton Ave CV6 . . . . .113 C6
Chetton Gn WV10 . . . . .11 B3
Chetwode Cl CV5 . . . . .112 B4
Chetwood Cl WV6 . . . . .25 A5
Chetwynd Cl WS2 . . . . .27 D3
Chetwynd Dr CV11 . . . . .79 F2
Chetwynd Jun Sch CV11 . .79 A7
Chetwynd Rd
Birmingham B8 . . . . .68 B5
Wolverhampton WV2 . . . . . . .39 B6
Cheveley Ave B45 . . . . .122 B7
Chevening Cl DY3 . . . . .50 C7
Cheveral Ave CV6 . . . . .113 B6
Cheveral Rd CV12 . . . . .78 A3
Cheverel Pl CV11 . . . . .73 B2
Cheverel St CV11 . . . . .73 B3
Cheveridge CV31 . . . . .107 A2
Cheverton Rd B31 . . . . .102 E4
Cheviot Cl CV10 . . . . .72 B3
Cheviot Ct B75 . . . . .32 A4
Cheviot Rd
Stourbridge DY8 . . . . .81 A6
Wolverhampton WV2 . . . . . . .39 F7

Cheviot Rise
Cannock WS12 . . . . .2 C5
Royal Leamington Spa
CV32 . . . . .157 C3
Cheviot B77 . . . . .22 C1
Cheviot The CV4 . . . . .132 D6
Cheviot Way B63 . . . . .82 D2
Cheylesmore Cl B73 . . . . . . .46 B4
Cheylesmore CV1 . . . . .165 B2
Cheyne Ct 3 B17 . . . . .85 D5
Cheyne Gdns B28 . . . . .105 E3
Cheyne Pl B17 . . . . .85 D5
Cheyne Wlk DY5 . . . . .81 C7
Cheyney Cl WV6 . . . . .25 A5
Chichester Ave DY2 . . . . .62 D5
Chichester Ct CV11 . . . . .74 A7
Chichester Ct B73 . . . . .46 B5
Chichester Dr
Birmingham B32 . . . . .84 A5
Cannock WS12 . . . . .2 C1
Chichester Gr B37 . . . . .70 B1
Chideock Hill CV3 . . . . .133 A6
Chiel Cl CV5 . . . . .111 F4
Chigwell Cl B35 . . . . .58 A3
Chilcote Cl B28 . . . . .105 F4
Chilcote Prim Sch B28 . . . .105 F4
Childs Ave WV14 . . . . .40 A2
Childs Oak Cl CV7 . . . . .130 A6
Chilgrove Gdns WV6 . . . . .24 C5
Chilham Dr B37 . . . . .70 C2
Chillaton Rd CV6 . . . . .95 B2
Chillenden Ct WV13 . . . . .27 C2
Chillinden B77 . . . . .35 C7
Chillinghome Rd B36 . . . . . . .68 D8
Chillinghome Twr B36 . . . . . .57 F1
Chillington Cl WS6 . . . . .4 F1
Chillington Dr
Codsall WV8 . . . . .10 A4
Dudley DY1 . . . . .50 F3
Chillington Fields WV1 . . . .26 A1
Chillington Pl WV14 . . . . .40 C5
Chillington Rd DY4 . . . . .41 C1
Chillington St WV1 . . . . .25 F1
Chillington Wlk B65 . . . . .63 D3
Chillington Works Ind Est
WV1 .25 F1
Chiltern Cl
Cheslyn Hay WS6 . . . . .4 D1
Dudley DY3 . . . . .50 D3
Halesowen B63 . . . . .82 D1
Chiltern Ct
2 Coventry CV4 . . . . .113 A5
Sutton Coldfield B75 . . . . . . .32 A4
Chiltern Dr WV13 . . . . .26 D1
Chiltern Ho
Coventry CV5 . . . . .111 D4
Redditch B98 . . . . .154 E1
Chiltern Leys 2 CV6 . . . . . .113 A4
Chiltern Rd
Stourbridge DY8 . . . . .81 B6
Tamworth B77 . . . . .22 C1
Chilterns The
Coventry CV5 . . . . .112 B4
Oldbury B69 . . . . .63 E5
Chilton Cl B23 . . . . .56 C2
Chilton Rd B14 . . . . .105 D4
Chilvers Coton Com Inf Sch
CV11 .73 B3
Chilvers Coton Craft Ctr
CV11 .73 C2
Chilvers Ct CV11 . . . . .73 C3
Chilvers Gr B37 . . . . .69 F5
Chilwell Cl B91 . . . . .107 B1
Chilwell Croft B19 . . . . .66 E6
Chilworth Ave WV11 . . . . .26 F7
Chilworth Cl
4 Birmingham B6 . . . . .66 F6
Nuneaton CV11 . . . . .78 E8
Chimes Cl B33 . . . . .69 E1
Chimney Rd DY4 . . . . .52 D6
Chines The CV10 . . . . .73 D7
Chingford Cl DY8 . . . . .60 C4
Chingford Rd
Birmingham B44 . . . . .56 A8
Coventry CV6 . . . . .96 A4
Chinley Gr B44 . . . . .45 C1
Chinn Brook Ho B14 . . . . . .105 B4
Chinn Brook Rd B13 . . . . . .105 C5
Chip Cl B38 . . . . .103 D2
Chipperfield Rd B36 . . . . . . .68 E8
Chipstead Rd B23 . . . . .56 E7
Chipstone Cl B91 . . . . .107 C1
Chirbury Gr B31 . . . . .103 B1
Chirk Cl DY10 . . . . .116 E2
Chirton Gr B14 . . . . .104 D6
Chiseldon Croft B14 . . . . . . .105 A4
Chisholm Gr B27 . . . . .106 C8
Chiswell Rd B18 . . . . .65 E4
Chiswick Ct 1 B23 . . . . .56 E2
Chiswick Ho 2 B15 . . . . .86 C8
Chiswick Wlk B37 . . . . .70 E2
Chivenor Ho B35 . . . . .58 A2
Chivenor Jun & Inf Sch
B35 .58 A2
Chivington Cl B90 . . . . .127 B6
Chorley Ave B34 . . . . .68 F6
Chorley Gdns WV14 . . . . .40 B5
Chorley Way CV6 . . . . .113 C6
Christ Church CE Inf Sch
Wolverhampton,Dunstall Hill
WV6 .25 B4
Wolverhampton WV6 . . . . . . .25 B4
Christ Church CE Jun Sch
WV6 .24 C4
Christ Church CE Prim Sch
Birmingham B11 . . . . .87 B7
Dudley WV14 . . . . .40 D1

Christ Church CE Prim Sch
continued
Lichfield WS13 . . . . .8 F7
Oldbury B69 . . . . .64 A8
Walsall WS3 . . . . .28 D7
Christchurch Cl
Birmingham B15 . . . . .85 E8
Nuneaton CV10 . . . . .72 F1
Christ Church Gdns WS13 . .8 F7
Christ Church Gr WS1 . . . . .43 A7
Christchurch La WS13 . . . . . . .8 F7
Christchurch Rd CV6 . . . . . .113 A5
Christina Ct 5 B71 . . . . .53 D4
Christine Cl DY4 . . . . .41 C2
Christine Ledger Sq 9
CV31 . . . . .162 A6
Christopher Cadbury Reserve
The ★ B61 . . . . .153 C3
Christopher Hooke Ho
CV6 .113 E8
Christopher Rd
Birmingham B29 . . . . .85 C2
Halesowen B62 . . . . .83 E3
Wolverhampton WV2 . . . . . .163 D1
Christopher Wlk WS13 . . . . . .8 F7
Christ the King RC Inf Sch
CV6 .112 F6
Christ the King RC Jun Sch
CV6 .112 F7
Christ The King RC Prim Sch
B44 . . . . .56 A8
Chubb St WV1 . . . . .163 C3
Chub B77 . . . . .35 D7
Chuckery Prim Sch WS1 . .29 A1
Chuckery Rd WS1 . . . . .29 A1
Chudleigh Gr B43 . . . . .54 D8
Chudleigh Rd
Birmingham B23 . . . . .56 E4
Coventry CV2 . . . . .114 E7
Churchacre B23 . . . . .56 C8
Church Ave
Birmingham,Handsworth
B20 .55 C1
Birmingham,Moseley B13 . . .86 F3
Clent DY9 . . . . .99 F3
Stourbridge DY8 . . . . .81 A7
Water Orton B46 . . . . .59 B3
Churchbridge B69 . . . . .63 F6
Churchbridge Pk WS11 . . . . .4 E5
Church Cl
Birmingham B37 . . . . .70 A6
Drayton Bassett B78 . . . . .34 E5
Hartshill CV10 . . . . .72 B8
Hinckley LE10 . . . . .76 A5
Ryton-on-D CV8 . . . . .135 B2
Shenstone WS14 . . . . .18 A5
Whitnash CV31 . . . . .162 B4
Wood End CV9 . . . . .36 C1
Wythall B47 . . . . .124 F3
Church Cres WV11 . . . . .12 F3
Church Croft
Birmingham B17 . . . . .85 B4
Halesowen B63 . . . . .83 A4
Church Cross View DY1 . .61 D8
Church Ct
3 Cradley Heath B64 . . . . . . .62 E1
Astwood Bank B96 . . . . .158 E2
Coventry CV6 . . . . .94 F1
Stourbridge DY8 . . . . .81 A5
Churchdale Cl CV10 . . . . .72 C4
Churchdale Rd B44 . . . . .44 D3
Church Down Ct B23 . . . . . .158 D6
Churchdown Ct B23 . . . . .56 C2
Church Dr
Birmingham B30 . . . . .104 B7
Hopwas B78 . . . . .20 D7
Kenilworth CV8 . . . . .147 F5
Church End CV31 . . . . .162 E6
Church Farm Barn & Cotts
DY10 .98 B3
Churchfield Ave DY4 . . . . . . .51 F8
Churchfield Cl B7 . . . . .67 C6
Churchfield Ind Est DY2 . . .62 C8
Churchfield Rd B10 . . . . .25 B8
Churchfields
Birmingham B43 . . . . .44 D4
Bromsgrove B61 . . . . .136 F3
Churchfields Bsns Pk
DY10 . . . . .116 E7
Churchfields Cl B61 . . . . . . .136 F3
Churchfields Gdns B61 . . . .136 F3
Churchfields DY10 . . . . .116 E7
Churchfields Rd
Bromsgrove B61 . . . . .136 F3
Wednesbury WS10 . . . . .42 A4
Churchfield St DY2 . . . . .62 C8
Church Gdns
Smethwick B67 . . . . .65 A4
Wolverhampton WV10 . . . . . .26 A4
Church Gn
Bilston WV14 . . . . .40 D8
Birmingham B20 . . . . .55 A2
Church Gn E B98 . . . . .153 E4
Church Gn W B97 . . . . .153 E4
Church Gr B13 . . . . .105 C5
Church Hill
6 Wednesbury WS10 . . . . . .41 F3
8 Walsall WS1 . . . . .42 F8
Belbroughton DY9 . . . . .119 D6
Beoley B98 . . . . .154 D8
Birmingham,Northfield
B31 . . . . .103 A3
Brierley Hill DY5 . . . . .61 D2
Cannock WS12 . . . . .2 D4

Church Hill Dr WV6 . . . . .24 E5
Church Hill B32 . . . . .102 B6
Church Hill Mid Sch
B98 .154 D6
Church Hill Rd
Birmingham B20 . . . . .55 C1
Solihull B91 . . . . .107 C3
Wolverhampton WV6 . . . . . . .24 D5
Church Hill CV32 . . . . .161 E8
Church Hill St B67 . . . . .64 F6
Church Hill Way B98 . . . . . .154 D6
Church Hill WV4 . . . . .38 E4
Church Ho
Brierley Hill DY5 . . . . .61 C2
Walsall WS2 . . . . .42 C7
Churchill Ave
Coventry CV6 . . . . .113 E8
Kenilworth CV8 . . . . .148 A6
Churchill Ct B69 . . . . .52 C2
Churchill Dr
Rowley Regis B65 . . . . .63 B2
Stourbridge DY8 . . . . .81 A7
Churchill Gdns DY3 . . . . .50 C7
Churchill La DY10 . . . . .98 B3
Churchill Par B75 . . . . .47 A5
Churchill Pl B33 . . . . .69 C3
Churchill Rd
Birmingham B9 . . . . .67 F3
Halesowen B63 . . . . .82 F2
Shenstone WS14 . . . . .18 A5
Sutton Coldfield,Falcon Lodge
B75 .47 A5
Sutton Coldfield,New Oscott
B73 .45 C3
Upper Catshill B61 . . . . .121 A1
Walsall WS2 . . . . .27 E3
Churchill Sh Ctr 3 DY2 . . .51 D1
Churchill Wlk 5 DY4 . . . . . .52 A8
Church La
Ash Green CV7 . . . . .95 E7
Aston Flamville LE10 . . . . . . .76 F1
Berkswell CV7 . . . . .110 C3
Bickenhill B92 . . . . .90 E2
Birmingham,Aston B6 . . . . . . .67 A8
Birmingham,Handsworth
B20 .55 A2
Birmingham,Kitt's Green
B33 .69 A3
Bromsgrove B61 . . . . .136 F2
Corley CV7 . . . . .94 B7
Coventry,Middle Stoke
CV2 . . . . .114 B3
Coventry,Upper Eastern Green
CV5 . . . . .111 C5
Cubbington CV32 . . . . .157 E5
Curdworth B76 . . . . .59 B6
Halesowen B63 . . . . .83 B4
Hammerwich WS7 . . . . .7 D3
Lapworth B94 . . . . .143 E3
Lighthorne CV35 . . . . .155 F6
Meriden CV7 . . . . .110 E8
Middleton B78 . . . . .34 C1
Church Lane Ind Est B71 . .53 C6
Church La
Nuneaton CV10 . . . . .73 C7
Radford Semele CV31 . . . . .162 E6
Royal Leamington Spa
CV32 . . . . .157 A3
Stratton B79 . . . . .22 E7
Stoneleigh CV8 . . . . .149 C6
Stonnall WS9 . . . . .16 E4
Tamworth B79 . . . . .21 B5
Trysull WV5 . . . . .37 B2
West Bromwich B71 . . . . .53 C6
Whitnash CV31 . . . . .162 B4
Wishaw B76 . . . . .48 A2
Wolverhampton WV2 . . . . . .163 B2
Church Mews
Tipton DY4 . . . . .51 E8
Walsall WS3 . . . . .28 E8
Church Moat Way 1 WS3 .28 B8
Church of the Ascension CE
Prim Sch DY6 . . . . .60 C8
Churchover Cl B76 . . . . .57 D6
Church Park CV6 . . . . .94 F1
Church Pl
Birmingham B12 . . . . .86 F5
Walsall WS3 . . . . .28 D8
Church Rd
Astwood Bank B96 . . . . .158 E2
Baginton CV8 . . . . .133 F2
Belbroughton DY9 . . . . .119 D6
Birmingham,Aston B6 . . . . . . .67 B7
Birmingham,Edgbaston B15 .86 A7
Birmingham,Erdington B24 . .57 A4
Birmingham,Moseley B13 . . .87 A3
Birmingham,Northfield
B31 . . . . .103 A4
Birmingham,Perry Barr B42 . .55 D5
Birmingham,Sheldon B26 . . .89 C6
Birmingham,South Yardley
B25 .88 E8
Birmingham,Stechford B33 . .68 F2
Bromsgrove B61 . . . . .136 F4
Brownhills WS8 . . . . .15 F7
Burntwood WS7 . . . . .7 D2
Catshill B61 . . . . .136 F6
Coseley,Daisy Bank WV14 . .40 D1
Dodford DY9 . . . . .136 A2
Dudley,Netherton DY2 . . . . . .62 A8
Halesowen B63 . . . . .82 C7
Huntington WS11 . . . . .1 A2
Norton Canes WS11 . . . . .5 E4
Nuneaton,Stockingford
CV10 . . . . .72 C3
Perton WV6 . . . . .23 E4

Che – Chu 185

Church Rd continued
Redditch,St George's B97 . .153 E4
Redditch,Webheath B97 . . .152 F2
Rowley Regis B65 . . . . .63 C3
Ryton-on-D CV8 . . . . .135 B2
Shenstone WS14 . . . . .17 F5
Shilton CV7 . . . . .97 E5
Smethwick B67 . . . . .65 A4
Solihull B90 . . . . .106 B2
Stonnall WS9 . . . . .16 E3
Stourbridge DY8 . . . . .60 E2
Stourbridge,Lye DY9 . . . . .81 E5
Stourbridge,Old Swinford
DY8 .81 B3
Sutton Coldfield B73 . . . . . . .56 F8
Sutton Coldfield,Maney B72,
B73 .46 B3
Tamworth B77 . . . . .35 C4
Walsall WS3 . . . . .15 A3
Willenhall WV12 . . . . .27 D6
Wolverhampton,Oxbarn
WV3 .38 F7
Wolverhampton,Oxley
WV10 . . . . .11 C1
Wolverhampton,Tettenhall Wood
WV6 .24 B3
Wolverhampton,Tettenhall
WV6 .24 B3
Wombourne WV5 . . . . .49 B7
Church Row Cotts DY9 . . . . .99 F3
Church Row B78 . . . . .34 B1
Churchside Way WS9 . . . . . .16 B2
Church Sq 4 B69 . . . . .64 A7
Church St
Bilston WV14 . . . . .40 D5
Birmingham B3 . . . . .164 B3
Brierley Hill,Quarry Bank
DY5 .61 D7
Brierley Hill,Silver End DY5 . .61 C2
Bromsgrove B61 . . . . .136 F2
Brownhills WS8 . . . . .15 E6
Bulkington CV12 . . . . .79 C2
Burntwood WS7 . . . . .6 E5
Cannock,Bridgtown WS11 . . .2 A4
Cannock,Chadsmoor WS11 . .2 A4
Cannock WS11 . . . . .2 B3
Coventry CV1 . . . . .165 C4
Cradley Heath B64 . . . . .62 E1
Darlaston,Woods Bank
WS10 . . . . .41 C4
Darlaston WS10 . . . . .41 D6
Dudley,Gornalwood DY3 . . . .50 D3
Dudley,Kate's Hill DY2 . . . . . .62 C8
Halesowen B62 . . . . .83 D1
Hinckley LE10 . . . . .76 A5
Kidderminster DY10 . . . . . . .116 E6
Lichfield WS13,WS14 . . . . .9 C8
Nuneaton CV11 . . . . .73 C4
Oldbury B69 . . . . .64 A8
Royal Leamington Spa
CV31 . . . . .162 A7
Stourbridge DY8 . . . . .81 A5
Studley B80 . . . . .159 E3
Tamworth B79 . . . . .21 B5
Tipton DY4 . . . . .52 A2
Walsall,Blakenall Heath
WS3 .28 F1
Walsall WS1 . . . . .28 F1
Warwick CV34 . . . . .160 E6
Wednesfield WV11 . . . . .26 C5
West Bromwich B70 . . . . .53 C4
West Hagley DY9 . . . . .99 A5
Willenhall WV13 . . . . .27 B2
Wolverhampton,Heath Town
WV10 . . . . .26 A4
Wolverhampton WV2 . . . . . .163 B2
Church Terr
1 Royal Leamington Spa
CV31 . . . . .162 A7
Cubbington CV32 . . . . .157 E5
Sutton Coldfield B75 . . . . . . .32 C3
Church Vale B20 . . . . .55 B1
Church Vale Mews B71 . . . .53 F5
Church Vale
Norton Canes WS11 . . . . .5 E4
West Bromwich B71 . . . . .53 D5
Church View
Aldridge WS9 . . . . .30 B6
Birmingham B11 . . . . .87 C6
Brownhills WS9 . . . . .15 F3
Church View Cl WS3 . . . . .28 D8
Church View Dr B64 . . . . . . .62 F1
Church View
Dudley DY3 . . . . .50 D3
Wythall B47 . . . . .35 F7
Churchward Cl DY8 . . . . .81 B6
Churchward Gr WV5 . . . . . . .49 A8
Church Way
Bedworth CV12 . . . . .78 B2
Walsall WS4 . . . . .15 C2
Churchwell Ct
Halesowen B63 . . . . .83 B2
Wombourne WV5 . . . . .49 A6
Churchwell Gdns B71 . . . . .53 E6
Church Wlk
1 Royal Leamington Spa
CV31 . . . . .161 F7
Allesley CV5 . . . . .112 C6
Birmingham B8 . . . . .68 A6

Church Wlk continued
Hinckley LE10 . . . . .75 D8
Kidderminster DY11 . . . . . 116 C6
Rowley Regis B65 . . . . .63 C4
Wolverhampton,Oxbarn
WV3 . . . . .38 F7
Wolverhampton,Tettenhall
WV6 . . . . .24 E5
Churchyard Rd DY4 . . . . . . .52 B5
Churnet Gr WV6 . . . . .23 F4
Churn Hill Rd WS9 . . . . .30 B4
Churns Hill La DY3 . . . . .49 B3
Churston CI WS3 . . . . .14 A3
Chylds Ct CV5 . . . . 112 A5
Cicero App CV34 . . . . 161 E2
Cider Ave DY5 . . . . .81 E8
Cinder Bank DY2 . . . . .62 C6
Cinder Bank Island DY2 . .62 B7
Cinder Rd
Burntwood WS7 . . . . .6 E7
Dudley DY3 . . . . .50 B2
Cinder Way 2 WS10 . . . . . .41 E3
Cinquefoil Leasow 5
DY4 . . . . .52 C6
Circle The
Birmingham B17 . . . . .85 C6
Nuneaton CV10 . . . . .72 F4
Circuit CI WV13 . . . . .27 B3
Circular Rd B27 . . . . .88 C2
Circus Ave B37 . . . . .70 C2
Cirencester CI B60 . . . . . . 137 B2
City Arc
1 Birmingham B2 . . . . 164 C2
1 Lichfield WS13 . . . . .9 B7
Coventry CV1 . . . . 165 B2
City Coll
Birmingham B33 . . . . .89 B8
Birmingham,Sparkbrook
B11 . . . . .87 A7
Birmingham,Sparkhill B11 . .87 D5
City Coll Birmingham (St
George's Sixth Form Ctr)
B19 . . . . 164 B5
City Coll Coventry (Butts Ctr)
CV1 . . . . 113 A2
City Coll Coventry (Maxwell
Ctr) CV1 . . . . 113 A4
City College Coventry (Tile
Hill Ctr) CV4 . . . . 111 F1
City Coll (Handsworth
Campus) B21 . . . . .65 F8
City Est B64 . . . . .82 D8
City Hospl B18 . . . . .65 F4
City of Wolverhampton Coll
(Bilston Campus) WV14 . .40 F7
City of Wolverhampton Coll
(Metro One Campus)
WV1 . . . . 163 C2
City Rd
Birmingham B16 . . . . .65 C2
Oldbury B69 . . . . .63 D8
City Road Prim Sch B16 . . .65 D3
City Tech Coll The B37 . . . . .70 A4
City Trad Est B16 . . . . .66 A3
City View
Birmingham,Saltley B8 . . . .67 D4
Birmingham,Stockland Green
B23 . . . . .56 E6
Civic CI B1 . . . . .66 C2
Civic Hall * WV1 . . . . 163 B3
Cladswell Ho 1 B47 . . . . . 153 A4
Claerwen Gr B31 . . . . 102 E5
Claines Cres DY10 . . . . . . 117 B5
Claines Rd
Birmingham B31 . . . . 103 C4
Halesowen B63 . . . . .82 D5
Claire Ct B26 . . . . .89 C7
Clairvaux Gdns B91 . . . . . 106 D5
Clandon CI B14 . . . . 104 C2
Clanfield Ave WV11 . . . . . . .26 F7
Clapgate Gdns WV14 . . . . .40 A3
Clapgate La B32 . . . . .84 C2
Clapham Sq CV31 . . . . 162 B7
Clapham St CV31 . . . . 162 B6
Clapham Terrace Com Prim
Sch CV31 . . . . 162 B7
Clapham Terr CV31 . . . . . . 162 B7
Clapton Gr B44 . . . . .45 B1
Clarage Ho B62 . . . . .83 D8
Clara St CV2 . . . . 114 A2
Clare Ave WV11 . . . . .12 F1
Clare CI CV32 . . . . 157 C2
Clare Cres WV14 . . . . .39 F2
Clare Ct B90 . . . . 105 D2
Clare Dr B15 . . . . .85 F8
Claregate Prim Sch WV6 . . .24 F7
Clarel Ave B8 . . . . .67 C3
Claremont CI CV12 . . . . .79 B4
Claremont Cotts DY3 . . . . .50 E8
Claremont Ct 2 B64 . . . . . .62 E1
Claremont Mews WV1 . . . .39 A7
Claremont PI 1 B18 . . . . . .66 A5
Claremont Rd
Birmingham,Hockley B18 . .66 B6
Birmingham,Sparkbrook
B11 . . . . .87 B7
Royal Leamington Spa
CV31 . . . . 161 F6
Sedgley DY3 . . . . .50 E8
Smethwick B66 . . . . .65 B4
Tamworth B79 . . . . .21 A8
Wolverhampton WV3 . . . . . .39 B7
Claremont St
Bilston WV14 . . . . .40 C6
Cradley Heath B64 . . . . . . .62 E1

Claremont Way B63 . . . . . . .83 A3
Claremont Wlk CV5 . . . . . 112 C6
Clarence Ave B21 . . . . .65 C8
Clarence Ct
5 Hinckley LE10 . . . . .75 E8
Oldbury B68 . . . . .64 C2
Clarence Gdns B74 . . . . . . .31 F3
Clarence Ho 7 CV32 . . . . 156 F1
Clarence Mews 1 B17 . . . .85 D6
Clarence Rd
Bilston WV14 . . . . .40 F7
Birmingham B17 . . . . .85 D6
Birmingham,Gravelly Hill
B23 . . . . .56 D3
Birmingham,Handsworth
B21 . . . . .65 C8
Birmingham,King's Heath
B13 . . . . .87 A1
Birmingham,Sparkhill B11 . .87 D4
Dudley DY2 . . . . .62 D6
Hinckley LE10 . . . . .75 E8
Sutton Coldfield B74 . . . . . .31 F4
Wolverhampton WV1 . . . . 163 B3
Clarence St
5 Coventry CV1 . . . . 113 E4
Dudley DY3 . . . . .50 E5
Kidderminster DY10 . . . . . 116 F6
Nuneaton CV11 . . . . .73 A4
Royal Leamington Spa
CV31 . . . . 162 A6
Wolverhampton WV1 . . . . 163 B3
Clarence Terr 6 CV32 . . . 156 F1
Clarendon PI B17 . . . . .85 C5
Clarendon Ave CV32 . . . . . 156 F1
Clarendon CI B97 . . . . 153 B5
Clarendon Cres CV32 . . . . 156 E1
Clarendon Dr DY4 . . . . .52 D8
Clarendon Gdns 8 B20 . . .55 D1
Clarendon Ho LE10 . . . . . . .75 B7
Clarendon PI
Birmingham B62 . . . . .84 A6
Royal Leamington Spa
CV32 . . . . 156 E1
Walsall WS3 . . . . .14 F3
Clarendon Rd
Birmingham B16 . . . . .65 E1
Hinckley LE10 . . . . .75 C7
Kenilworth CV8 . . . . 148 A3
Smethwick B67 . . . . .64 F4
Sutton Coldfield B75 . . . . . .32 C3
Walsall WS4 . . . . .15 C2
Clarendon Sq CV32 . . . . . 156 F1
Clarendon St
Coventry CV5 . . . . 112 F1
Royal Leamington Spa
CV32 . . . . 157 A1
Walsall WS3 . . . . .14 B1
Wolverhampton WV3 . . . . . .25 A2
Clare Rd
Walsall WS3 . . . . .29 A6
Wolverhampton WV10 . . . . .25 E7
Clare's Ct DY11 . . . . 116 C6
Clarewell Ave B91 . . . . 127 B8
Clare Witnell CI DY11 . . . . 116 B8
Clarion Way WS11 . . . . .1 E5
Clarke Ho WS3 . . . . .14 B1
Clarke's Ave CV8 . . . . 148 A3
Clarkes Gr DY4 . . . . .52 C6
Clarkes Ind Est B73 . . . . . .46 A2
Clarke's La B71 . . . . .53 C7
Clarkes La WV13 . . . . .27 C3
Clarke St 1 B97 . . . . 153 E3
Clark Rd WV3 . . . . .24 F2
Clarksland Gr B37 . . . . .90 A8
Clarks La B90 . . . . 126 A6
Clarkson Dr CV31 . . . . 162 A4
Clarkson Place Ind Est
DY5 . . . . .81 E7
Clarkson Rd WS10 . . . . .42 A3
Clark St
Birmingham B16 . . . . .65 F2
Coventry CV6 . . . . .96 A1
Stourbridge DY8 . . . . .80 E4
Clarry Dr B74 . . . . .45 F8
Clary Gr WS5 . . . . .43 A3
Clatterbach La DY9 . . . . . . 100 A4
Claughton Ct DY11 . . . . . . 116 C5
Claughton Rd DY2 . . . . .51 D1
Claughton Road N 8 DY2 .51 D1
Claughton St B71 . . . . 116 C5
Clausen CI B43 . . . . .44 E4
Clavedon CI B31 . . . . 102 E7
Claverdon CI
Brownhills WS8 . . . . .16 A8
Redditch B97 . . . . 158 D4
Solihull B91 . . . . 106 E3
Claverdon Dr
Birmingham B43 . . . . .54 D7
Sutton Coldfield B74 . . . . . .31 B4
Claverdon Gdns B27 . . . . . .88 B5
Claverdon Ho
Birmingham B13 . . . . 105 A7
Warwick CV34 . . . . 161 B8
Claverdon Rd CV5 . . . . 112 B3
Claverley Dr 6 DY1 . . . . . . .51 B1
Claverley Dr WV4 . . . . .38 D5
Clay Ave CV11 . . . . .73 F7
Claybrook Dr B98 . . . . 159 F7
Claybrook St B5 . . . . 164 C1
Claycroft PI DY9 . . . . .81 E5
Claycroft Terr 2 DY1 . . . . .51 E1
Claydon Gr 3 B14 . . . . . . 105 A3
Claydon Rd DY6 . . . . .49 C1
Clay Dr B32 . . . . .84 A5
Claygate Rd WS12 . . . . .2 E3
Clayhanger La WS8 . . . . . . .15 D6
Clayhanger Rd WS8 . . . . . . .15 F6

Clay La
Birmingham B26 . . . . .88 E5
Coventry CV2 . . . . 114 A4
Harvest Hill CV5 . . . . .93 E3
Oldbury B69 . . . . .64 A4
Claymore B77 . . . . .35 E7
Claypit CI B70 . . . . .53 A3
Claypit La B61 . . . . 120 E1
Clay Pit La
Lichfield WS14 . . . . .8 F3
Solihull B90 . . . . 126 A5
Claypit La B70 . . . . .53 A4
Clayton CI WV2 . . . . .39 C7
Clayton Dr
Birmingham B36 . . . . .69 C7
Bromsgrove B60 . . . . 151 B7
Clayton Gdns B45 . . . . 122 A2
Clayton Ho 3 B16 . . . . .65 F1
Clayton Rd
Birmingham B8 . . . . .67 D5
Coventry CV6 . . . . 112 E5
Dudley WV14 . . . . .51 B7
Clayton Wlk B35 . . . . .58 A2
Clear View DY6 . . . . .60 B6
Clearwater Ind Est WV2 . . .40 A7
Clearwell Gdns CV32 . . . . . 156 C1
Clearwell Rd B98 . . . . 154 C3
Cleasby B77 . . . . .22 C1
Cleaveland Mews 2 WS13 .3 A1
Cleaver Gdns CV10 . . . . .73 C6
Clee Ave CV31 . . . . 116 C2
Clee Hill Dr WV3 . . . . .24 A1
Clee Hill Rd DY3 . . . . .50 D4
Clee Rd
Birmingham B31 . . . . 123 A8
Dudley DY2 . . . . .62 A7
Oldbury B68 . . . . .64 C4
Stourbridge DY8 . . . . .81 A6
Cleeton St WS12 . . . . .2 D1
Cleeve CI B98 . . . . 154 D5
Cleeve Dr B74 . . . . .31 F6
Cleeve Ho B24 . . . . .57 A2
Cleeve Rd
Birmingham B14 . . . . 105 C4
Walsall WS3 . . . . .13 F3
Cleeves Ave CV34 . . . . 161 D6
Clee CV7 . . . . .21 D3
Cleeve Way WS3 . . . . .13 F3
Clee View Mdw DY3 . . . . . .39 D2
Clegg Rd WS7 . . . . .7 E7
Clematis Dr WV9 . . . . .10 F3
Clematis B77 . . . . .22 A1
Clem Attlee Ct WV13 . . . . . .40 D8
Clemens St CV31 . . . . 162 A7
Clement Ho B24 . . . . 148 A5
Clement PI WV14 . . . . .40 D7
Clement Rd
Bilston WV14 . . . . .40 D7
Halesowen B62 . . . . .63 D1
Clements CI
Kenilworth CV8 . . . . 148 A5
Oldbury B69 . . . . .63 F4
Clements Rd B25 . . . . .88 D8
Clements St CV2 . . . . 114 A3
Clement St
Birmingham B1 . . . . .66 B3
Nuneaton CV11 . . . . .73 B3
Walsall WS2 . . . . .28 D1
Clemson St WV13 . . . . .27 A2
Clennon Rise CV2 . . . . 114 D8
Clensmore St DY10 . . . . . . 116 D7
Clent Ave
Kidderminster DY11 . . . . . 116 B1
Redditch B97 . . . . 158 D7
Clent Cott DY9 . . . . .99 F3
Clent Ct 1 DY1 . . . . .51 B1
Clent Dr
Hagley DY9 . . . . .99 D6
Nuneaton CV10 . . . . .72 B3
Clent Hill Dr B65 . . . . .63 A5
Clent Hills Ctry Pk * DY9 100 A4
Clent Ho B63 . . . . .83 A2
Clent Prim Sch DY9 . . . . . . .99 F2
Clent Rd
Birmingham B45 . . . . 121 E8
Birmingham,Handsworth
B21 . . . . .54 D1
Oldbury B68 . . . . .64 C1
Stourbridge DY8 . . . . .81 A6
Clent View Rd
Birmingham B32 . . . . .84 A1
Halesowen B63 . . . . .82 C5
Stourbridge DY8 . . . . .80 C2
Clent View B66 . . . . .65 B3
Clent Villas B12 . . . . .87 B4
Clent Way B32 . . . . 102 A8
Cleobury CI B97 . . . . 153 B5
Cleobury La B94 . . . . 126 A3
Cleopatra Gr CV34 . . . . . . 155 E1
Cleton Street Bsns Pk
DY4 . . . . .52 B3
Cleton St DY4 . . . . .52 B3
Clevedon Ave B36 . . . . .69 E8
Clevedon Rd B12 . . . . .86 F6
Cleveland CI
Willenhall WV13 . . . . .26 D1
Wolverhampton WV11 . . . . .12 F1
Cleveland Ct
10 Birmingham B13 . . . . . .87 B2
1 Royal Leamington Spa
CV32 . . . . 156 F2
Wolverhampton WV2 . . . . 163 B2
Cleveland Dr
Barnt Green B45 . . . . 122 A4
Cannock WS11 . . . . .2 B4
Cleveland Pas WV1 . . . . . . 163 B2
Cleveland Rd
Bulkington CV12 . . . . .79 B3

Cleveland Rd continued
Coventry CV2 . . . . 114 A4
Hinckley LE10 . . . . .75 C8
Wolverhampton WV2 . . . . 163 C2
Cleveland St
14 Dudley,New Dock DY1 . .51 B1
4 Dudley,Old Dock DY1 . .62 B8
Stourbridge DY8 . . . . .80 E4
Wolverhampton WV1 . . . . 163 B2
Cleveland Twr B1 . . . . 164 B1
Cleveley Dr CV10 . . . . .72 D7
Cleves Cres WS6 . . . . .4 D1
Cleves Dr B45 . . . . 121 E7
Cleves Rd B45 . . . . 121 E8
Clewley Dr WV9 . . . . .11 B3
Clewley Gr B32 . . . . .84 B5
Clews CI WS1 . . . . .42 E7
Clewshaw La B38 . . . . 124 C4
Clews Rd B98 . . . . 158 F7
Cley CI B5 . . . . .86 D6
Clifden Gr CV8 . . . . 148 C6
Cliffe Dr CV32 . . . . 157 D3
Cliffe Dr B33 . . . . .69 C3
Cliffe Rd CV32 . . . . 156 D1
Cliff Hall La B78 . . . . .35 C1
Clifford Bridge Prim Sch
CV3 . . . . 115 A3
Clifford Bridge Rd CV3 . . . 114 F4
Clifford CI B77 . . . . .21 F3
Clifford Rd
Bentley Heath B93 . . . . . . 127 F4
Smethwick B67 . . . . .64 F1
West Bromwich B70 . . . . . .53 B2
Clifford St
3 Dudley DY1 . . . . .62 B8
Birmingham B19 . . . . .66 D7
Tamworth B77 . . . . .21 E3
Wolverhampton WV6 . . . . . .25 A3
Clifford Wlk B19 . . . . .66 D7
Cliff Rock Rd B45 . . . . 122 B7
Clift CI WV12 . . . . .27 C6
Clifton Ave
Aldridge WS9 . . . . .16 C1
Brownhills WS8 . . . . .15 D7
Cannock WS11 . . . . .4 C7
Tamworth B79 . . . . .21 A7
Clifton CI
Birmingham B6 . . . . .66 F7
Oldbury B69 . . . . .64 A4
Redditch B98 . . . . 159 E8
Clifton Cres B91 . . . . 106 F1
Clifton Ct
5 Royal Leamington Spa
CV31 . . . . 162 B7
Hinckley LE10 . . . . .71 B1
Clifton Dr B73 . . . . .46 B5
Clifton Gdns WV8 . . . . .10 C3
Clifton Gn B28 . . . . 106 A5
Clifton La B71 . . . . .53 E8
Clifton Prim Sch B12 . . . . . .87 A5
Clifton Rd
Birmingham,Aston B6 . . . . .66 F7
Birmingham,Balsall Heath
B12 . . . . .87 A5
Birmingham,Castle Bromwich
B36 . . . . .69 E8
Halesowen B63 . . . . .83 E8
Kidderminster DY11 . . . . . 116 A1
Nuneaton CV10 . . . . .72 F4
Smethwick B67 . . . . .64 F4
Sutton Coldfield B73 . . . . . .46 B5
Wolverhampton WV6 . . . . . .24 D5
Clifton Road Ind Est B12 . .86 F5
Clifton St
Coventry CV1 . . . . 165 D4
Cradley Heath B64 . . . . . . .62 F1
Dudley WV14 . . . . .51 A8
Sedgley WV14 . . . . .39 F1
Stourbridge DY8 . . . . .80 F4
Wolverhampton WV3 . . . . . .25 B2
Clifton Terr B23 . . . . .56 F4
Clifton Way LE10 . . . . .71 A1
Clinic Dr
Nuneaton CV11 . . . . .73 C3
Stourbridge DY9 . . . . .81 E5
Clinton Ave
Hampton Magna CV35 . . . 160 A7
Kenilworth CV8 . . . . 147 D6
Clinton Cres WS7 . . . . .7 B8
Clinton Gr B90 . . . . 106 E1
Clinton La CV8 . . . . 147 B6
Clinton Prim Sch CV8 . . . . 147 E3
Clinton Rd
Bilston WV14 . . . . .41 A7
Coleshill B46 . . . . .70 F6
Coventry CV6 . . . . .95 F2
Solihull B90 . . . . 106 E1
Clinton St
2 Royal Leamington Spa
CV31 . . . . 162 A7
Birmingham B18 . . . . .65 E5
Clipper View B16 . . . . .65 E1
Clipstone Rd CV6 . . . . 112 E6
Clipston Rd B8 . . . . .67 F4
Clissold CI B12 . . . . .86 E7
Clissold Pas B18 . . . . .66 A4
Clissold St B18 . . . . .66 A4
Clive CI B75 . . . . .32 D2
Cliveden Ave
Aldridge WS9 . . . . .16 B1
Birmingham B42 . . . . .55 D4
Cliveden Coppice B74 . . . . .31 F1
Cliveden Wlk CV11 . . . . . . .78 E8
Clivedon Way B32 . . . . .83 B7
Cliveland St B19 . . . . 164 C4
Clive Rd
Balsall Common CV7 . . . . . 130 C5

Clive Rd continued
Birmingham B32 . . . . .84 D7
Bromsgrove B60 . . . . 151 B8
Burntwood WS7 . . . . .7 A7
Redditch B97 . . . . 153 D5
Clive St B71 . . . . .53 C5
Clivesway LE10 . . . . .71 C2
Clockfields Dr DY5 . . . . .61 A1
Clock La B92 . . . . .90 D2
Clockmill Ave WS3 . . . . .14 E3
Clockmill PI WS3 . . . . .14 F3
Clockmill Rd WS3 . . . . .14 E3
Clodeshall Rd B8 . . . . .67 E4
Cloister Croft CV2 . . . . 114 F6
Cloister Crofts CV32 . . . . . 156 F3
Cloister Dr B62 . . . . .83 D3
Cloisters The
Royal Leamington Spa
CV32 . . . . 156 F3
Studley B80 . . . . 159 D4
Walsall WS4 . . . . .28 F3
Cloister Way CV32 . . . . 156 F3
Clonmel Rd B30 . . . . 104 A6
Clopton Cres B37 . . . . .70 C4
Clopton Rd B33 . . . . .89 C8
Closers Bsns Ctr DY11 . . . .73 D2
Close The
Birmingham B17 . . . . .84 F7
Birmingham,Griffin's Hill
B29 . . . . 103 D8
Dudley DY3 . . . . .50 C4
Halesowen B63 . . . . .82 D6
Hollywood B47 . . . . 125 A5
Hunnington B62 . . . . 101 A7
Kenilworth CV8 . . . . 148 A6
Lichfield WS13 . . . . .9 B8
Wednesbury WS10 . . . . . . .41 E3
Whitnash CV31 . . . . 162 A5
Clothier Gdns WS13 . . . . . .27 A3
Clothier Street Prim Sch
WV13 . . . . .27 A3
Clothier St WV13 . . . . .27 A3
Cloudbridge Dr B92 . . . . . 107 F7
Cloud Gn CV4 . . . . 132 D5
Cloudsley Gr B92 . . . . .88 F3
Clovelly Gdns CV2 . . . . 114 C5
Clovelly Rd CV2 . . . . 114 B5
Clovelly Way CV11 . . . . .73 E5
Clover Ave B37 . . . . .70 D2
Clover Ct B38 . . . . 103 D2
Cloverdale CI CV6 . . . . .95 B4
Cloverdale
Perton WV6 . . . . .23 D4
Stoke Prior B60 . . . . 150 C3
Clover Dr B32 . . . . .84 D2
Cloverfield LE10 . . . . .71 C3
Clover Hill WS5 . . . . .43 E8
Clover La DY6 . . . . .60 B7
Clover Lea Sq B8 . . . . .68 A6
Clover Ley WV10 . . . . .25 F3
Clover Mdws WS12 . . . . .2 C1
Clover Piece 6 DY4 . . . . . . .52 C6
Clover Pk Trad Est LE10 . . .71 B3
Clover Rd B29 . . . . 103 A6
Clover Ridge WS6 . . . . .4 C3
Clover Way CV12 . . . . .77 D2
Clowes Wood La B94 . . . . . 141 F8
Club Cotts WV10 . . . . .11 C6
Club La WV10 . . . . .11 C6
Club Row DY3 . . . . .50 E5
Club View B38 . . . . 103 D2
Clunbury Croft B34 . . . . . . .69 E5
Clunbury Rd B31 . . . . 123 A8
Clun CI B69 . . . . .52 A1
Clunes Ave CV11 . . . . .73 E6
Clun Rd B31 . . . . 102 F6
Clusters The DY9 . . . . .81 E5
Clyde Ave B62 . . . . .83 E8
Clyde Ct B73 . . . . .46 B5
Clyde Mews DY5 . . . . .61 B6
Clyde Rd
Bulkington CV12 . . . . .79 A2
Dorridge B93 . . . . 128 A2
Clydesdale B26 . . . . .89 B5
Clydesdale Rd
Birmingham B32 . . . . .84 B6
Brownhills WS8 . . . . .15 E6
Clydesdale Twr B1 . . . . 164 B1
Clyde St
Birmingham B12 . . . . .67 A1
Cradley Heath B64 . . . . . . .62 E1
Clyde Twr 3 B19 . . . . .66 D7
Coach Cotts B45 . . . . 138 D8
Coach House Mews 2
CV34 . . . . 160 F2
Coach House Rise B77 . . . .35 F7
Coalash La B60 . . . . 151 C2
Coalbourne Gdns B63 . . . . .82 C5
Coalbourn La DY8 . . . . .80 F7
Coalbourn Way DY5 . . . . . . .61 A3
Coal Haulage Rd WS12 . . . .5 F8
Coalheath La WS4 . . . . .29 C8
Coalmeadow CI WS3 . . . . . .13 F3
Coalpit Fields Rd CV12 . . . .78 C1
Coal Pool La WS3 . . . . .28 F5
Coalpool PI WS3 . . . . .28 F6
Coalport Rd WV1 . . . . .26 A1
Coalway Ave
Birmingham B26 . . . . .89 C4
Wolverhampton WV3 . . . . . .39 A6
Coalway Gdns WV3 . . . . . . .38 D7
Coalway Rd
Walsall WS3 . . . . .28 F6
Wolverhampton WV3 . . . . . .38 E6
Coates Rd DY10 . . . . 117 B7

Coat Of Arms Bridge Rd
CV3 . . . . 133 A6
Coatsgate Wlk WV8 . . . . . . 10 F1
Cobbett Rd WS7 . . . . 6 D7
Cobbles The B72 . . . . 57 C7
Cobble Wlk B18 . . . . 66 A5
Cobbs Rd CV8 . . . . 147 D6
Cobbs Wlk B65 . . . . 62 F5
Cobden Ave CV31 . . . . 162 C5
Cobden Cl
Cannock WS10 . . . . 2 C7
Darlaston WS10 . . . . 41 F6
Tipton DY4 . . . . 51 F8
Cobden Gdns B12 . . . . 86 E6
Cobden St
Coventry CV6 . . . . 113 E5
Darlaston WS10 . . . . 41 F6
Kidderminster DY11 . . . . . . 116 D5
Stourbridge DY9 . . . . 80 E5
Walsall WS1 . . . . 42 D7
Cobham Bsns Ctr B9 . . . . 67 D2
Cobham Cl
Birmingham B35 . . . . 57 F3
Bromsgrove B60 . . . . 150 F7
Cobham Court Mews DY9 . 99 D6
Cobham Rd
Birmingham B9 . . . . 67 D2
Halesowen B63 . . . . 83 B4
Kidderminster DY10 . . . . . . 116 E4
Stourbridge DY9 . . . . 81 B2
Wednesbury WS10 . . . . 42 E2
Cobia B77 . . . . 35 D7
Cob La B30 . . . . 103 C6
Cobley Hill B48 . . . . 138 E4
Cobnall Rd B61 . . . . 121 A2
Cobs Field B30 . . . . 103 C6
Coburg Croft DY4 . . . . 52 C6
Coburg Ho CV5 . . . . 112 E3
Coburn Dr B75 . . . . 32 D2
Cochrane Cl
Tipton DY4 . . . . 52 C6
Stourbridge DY9 . . . . 99 C8
Cochrane Rd DY2 . . . . 61 F5
Cockermouth Cl CV32 . . . 156 D2
Cock Hill La B45 . . . . 121 C8
Cocksheds La B62 . . . . 83 E8
Cockshut Hill B26 . . . . 89 A8
Cockshut Hill Tech Coll
B26 . . . . 89 A8
Cockshutt La B61 . . . . 136 D7
Cockshutts La WV2 . . . . 3 D2
Cocksmead Croft B14 . . . 104 D5
Cocksmoor Ho B14 . . . . . . 104 D5
Cocksparrow La WS12,
WS19 . . . . 1 B5
Cocksparrow St CV34 . . . 160 D7
Cockspur St B78 . . . . 36 E7
Cockthorpe Cl B17 . . . . . . 84 F7
Cocton Cl WV6 . . . . 23 E5
Codsall Com High Sch
WV8 . . . . 10 A4
Codsall Mid Sch WV8 . . . . 10 A4
Codsall Rd
Codsall WV8 . . . . 10 C1
Cradley Heath B64 . . . . 82 E8
Wolverhampton WV6 . . . . . . 24 D7
Cofield Rd B73 . . . . 45 F1
Cofton Church La B45 . . . 122 F3
Cofton Cl B97 . . . . 153 B5
Cofton Ct B45 . . . . 122 D7
Cofton Dr B31 . . . . 122 D8
Cofton Lake Rd B45 . . . . . 122 C3
Cofton Prim Sch B31 . . . . 123 A6
Cofton Rd B31 . . . . 123 B7
Cokeland Pl B64 . . . . 82 D8
Colaton Cl WV10 . . . . 25 E4
Colbourne Ct B33 . . . . 68 D3
Colbourne Gr CV32 . . . . . 156 D2
Colbourne Rd
Tipton DY4 . . . . 21 A2
Tipton DY4 . . . . 52 A4
Colbrand Gr B15 . . . . 86 D8
Colbrook Rd B21 . . . . 21 D1
Coldbath Rd B13 . . . . 105 B8
Coldfield Dr B98 . . . . 158 E7
Coldridge Cl WV8 . . . . 10 F1
Coldstream Cl LE10 . . . . . . 71 A1
Coldstream Dr DY8 . . . . . . 60 E3
Coldstream Rd B76 . . . . . . 57 E8
Cole Bank Rd B28 . . . . . . 105 F8
Colebourne Prim Sch B33 68 E5
Colebourne Rd B13 . . . . . 105 D6
Colebridge Cres B46 . . . . . 70 F8
Colebrook Cl CV3 . . . . . . 114 F1
Colebrook Croft B90 . . . . 105 F2
Colebrook Rd
Birmingham B11 . . . . 87 D5
Solihull B90 . . . . 105 F2
Coleby Cl CV4 . . . . 131 D7
Cole Ct B37 . . . . 70 B2
Coleford Cl
Redditch B97 . . . . 153 A2
Stourbridge DY9 . . . . 60 C2
Coleford Dr B37 . . . . 70 A2
Cole Gn B90 . . . . 105 F2
Cole Hall La B34 . . . . 69 A5
Colehill B79 . . . . 21 B5
Colehurst Croft B90 . . . . . 126 F6
Coleman Rd WS10 . . . . 42 A5
Coleman St
Coventry CV4 . . . . 111 F3
Wolverhampton WV6 . . . . . . 24 F5
Colemeadow Rd
Birmingham B13 . . . . 105 B6
Coleshill B46 . . . . 70 F7
Redditch B98 . . . . 154 F6
Colenso Rd B16 . . . . 65 D4

Coleraine Rd B42 . . . . 55 A6
Coleridge Cl
Redditch B97 . . . . 158 C8
Tamworth B79 . . . . 21 A6
Walsall WS3 . . . . 15 A5
Willenhall WV12 . . . . 27 E7
Coleridge Dr WV6 . . . . 23 E4
Coleridge Pas B4 . . . . 164 C3
Coleridge Rd
Birmingham B43 . . . . 54 E7
Coventry CV2 . . . . 114 C3
Coleridge Rise DY3 . . . . . . 50 A4
Colesbourne Ave B14 . . . . 104 C2
Colesbourne Rd B92 . . . . . 89 B3
Coles Cres B71 . . . . 53 B7
Colesden Wlk WV4 . . . . . . 38 C6
Coleshill CE Prim Sch
B46 . . . . 70 F6
Coleshill Cl B97 . . . . 158 C5
Coleshill Heath Rd
Birmingham B37 . . . . 90 C7
Coleshill B37,B46 . . . . 70 E2
Coleshill Heath Sch B37 . 70 C1
Coleshill Ind Est B46 . . . . 59 F2
Coleshill Rd
Birmingham,Hodgehill B34,
B36 . . . . 68 G6
Birmingham,Marston Green
B37 . . . . 90 B8
Curdworth B76 . . . . 59 C5
Fazeley B78 . . . . 35 A7
Hartshill CV10 . . . . 72 A7
Sutton Coldfield B75 . . . . . . 46 D5
Water Orton B46 . . . . 59 B2
Coleshill St
Birmingham B5 . . . . 164 D3
Fazeley B78 . . . . 35 A8
Sutton Coldfield B72 . . . . . . 46 C5
Coleside Ave B13 . . . . 105 D7
Coles La
Sutton Coldfield B72 . . . . . . 46 C3
West Bromwich B71 . . . . . . 53 B7
Cole St DY2 . . . . 62 E4
Cole Valley Rd B28 . . . . . 105 D6
Coleview Cres B33 . . . . . . 69 E3
Coleville Rd B76 . . . . 58 B6
Coley Cl LE10 . . . . 75 D7
Coleys La B31 . . . . 103 A2
Colgreave Ave B13 . . . . . . 87 D2
Colina Cl CV3 . . . . 134 C5
Colindale Rd B44 . . . . 45 A3
Colinwood Cl WS6 . . . . 4 F1
Colledge Rd CV6 . . . . 95 D1
Colleen Ave B30 . . . . 104 B3
College Ct B24 . . . . 57 B2
College Cl WS10 . . . . 42 A1
College Ct WV6 . . . . 24 D4
College Dr
Birmingham B20 . . . . 54 F2
Royal Leamington Spa
CV32 . . . . 156 F2
College Farm Dr B73 . . . . 45 D1
College Gate B8 . . . . 67 E4
College High Sch The
B44 . . . . 56 B6
College Hill B73 . . . . 46 B4
College La
Balsall Common CV8 . . . . . 129 E1
Hinckley LE10 . . . . 71 E1
Tamworth B79 . . . . 21 B5
College of Law The B8 . . 164 A4
College Rd
Birmingham,Alum Rock B8 . 67 E4
Birmingham B32 . . . . 84 A6
Birmingham,Handsworth
B20 . . . . 54 F2
Birmingham,Moseley B13 . . 87 C2
Birmingham,Perry Common
B44 . . . . 56 B7
Bromsgrove B60 . . . . 137 A2
Kidderminster DY10 . . . . . . 116 E4
Wolverhampton WV6 . . . . . . 24 D4
College St
Birmingham B18 . . . . 66 A4
Nuneaton CV10 . . . . 73 C1
College View WV6 . . . . 24 D3
College Wlk
Birmingham B29 . . . . 103 D8
Bromsgrove B60 . . . . 137 A2
Kidderminster DY10 . . . . . . 116 E4
Collet Rd WV6 . . . . 23 E5
Collets Brook B75 . . . . 33 A2
Collett Cl DY8 . . . . 81 A6
Colletts Gr B37 . . . . 69 F4
Collett St B7 . . . . 22 A1
Collett Wlk CV1 . . . . 113 B3
Colley Ave WV10 . . . . 25 F7
Colley Gate B63 . . . . 82 C6
Colley La B63 . . . . 82 C6
Colley Lane Prim Sch
B63 . . . . 82 C6
Colley Orch B63 . . . . 82 C6
Colley St B70 . . . . 53 D4
Collier Cl
Cheslyn Hay WS6 . . . . 4 D2
Walsall WS8 . . . . 15 C7
Colliers Cl WV12 . . . . 27 B6
Colliers Fold DY5 . . . . 61 B5
Colliery Dr WS3 . . . . 13 F3
Colliery La CV7 . . . . 78 B1
Colliery La N CV7 . . . . 78 B1
Colliery Rd
Smethwick B71 . . . . 65 A8
West Bromwich B71 . . . . . . 54 A1
Collindale Ct DY6 . . . . 49 D1
Collingbourne Ave B36 . . . 68 E8

Collings Ho B16 . . . . 66 A1
Colling Wlk B37 . . . . 70 A5
Collingwood Dr B43 . . . . . . 44 D3
Collingwood Ho B43 . . . . . 44 D3
Collingwood Rd
Birmingham,Brandwood End
B30 . . . . 104 D3
Coventry CV5 . . . . 113 A2
Wolverhampton WV10 . . . . . 11 E2
Collins Cl B32 . . . . 84 A5
Collins Dr B8 WS13 . . . . . . 8 F6
Collins Gr CV4 . . . . 132 D5
Collins Hill WS13 . . . . 3 A2
Collinson Cl B98 . . . . 154 A1
Collins Rd
Brownhills WS8 . . . . 16 A4
Royal Leamington Spa
CV34 . . . . 161 D5
Wednesbury WS10 . . . . 42 C3
Collins St
Walsall WS1 . . . . 42 E7
West Bromwich B70 . . . . . . 52 E3
Collis Cl B60 . . . . 151 A8
Collis St DY8 . . . . 80 F8
Collister Cl B90 . . . . 106 A4
Colly Croft B37 . . . . 69 F5
Collycroft Pl B27 . . . . 88 B5
Colman Ave WV11 . . . . 26 F6
Colman Cres B68 . . . . 64 C2
Colman Hill Ave B63 . . . . 82 D6
Colman Hill B63 . . . . 82 D5
Colmers Farm Inf Sch
B45 . . . . 122 B8
Colmers Farm Jun Sch
B45 . . . . 122 B8
Colmers Sch & Sports Coll
B45 . . . . 122 B8
Colmore Ave B14 . . . . 104 D7
Colmore Circus Queensway
B4 . . . . 164 C3
Colmore Cres B13 . . . . 87 B1
Colmore Dr B75 . . . . 47 A5
Colmore Flats B19 . . . . . . 164 B4
Colmore Gate B2 . . . . 164 C3
Colmore Jun Sch B14 . . . 104 D7
Colmore Rd B14 . . . . 104 D7
Colmore Row B3 . . . . 164 B3
Coln Cl B31 . . . . 102 F6
Colonial Ind Pk B64 . . . . . 82 D7
Colonial Rd B9 . . . . 67 F2
Colshaw Rd DY8 . . . . 80 E4
Colt Cl B74 . . . . 44 E7
Coltham Rd WV12 . . . . 27 D7
Coltishall Cl B35 . . . . 57 F2
Coltman Cl WS14 . . . . 9 D7
Colton Hills Com Sch
WV4 . . . . 39 B4
Colts Cl LE10 . . . . 75 D4
Coltsfoot Cl WV11 . . . . 26 E5
Coltsfoot View WS6 . . . . . . 4 E2
Colts La B98 . . . . 154 D3
Columbia Cl B5 . . . . 86 D7
Columbia Gdns CV12 . . . . 78 E2
Columbian Cres WS7 . . . . . 6 F8
Columbian Dr WS11 . . . . . . 1 F3
Columbian Way WS11 . . . . 1 F3
Columbus Ave DY5 . . . . . . 61 F3
Colville Cl DY4 . . . . 52 D8
Colville Rd B12 . . . . 87 B5
Colville Wlk B12 . . . . 87 B5
Colwall Rd DY3 . . . . 50 D4
Colwall Wlk B27 . . . . 88 D4
Colworth Rd B31 . . . . 102 F4
Colyere Cl CV7 . . . . 95 A6
Colyns Gr B33 . . . . 68 F5
Combe Fields Rd CV3 . . . 115 F4
Comber Croft B13 . . . . . . 105 D8
Comber Dr DY5 . . . . 61 B6
Comberford Ct B WS10 . . 42 A3
Comberford Dr B WS10 . . 42 D4
Comberford Rd B79 . . . . . . 21 A5
Comberton Ave DY10 . . . . 117 B5
Comberton Ct B DY10 . . 117 A5
Comberton Fst Sch
DY10 . . . . 117 B4
Comberton Gdns DY10 . . 117 B5
Comberton Hill DY10 . . . . 116 F5
Comberton Mans B
DY10 . . . . 117 A4
Comberton Mid Sch
DY10 . . . . 117 B4
Comberton Park Rd
DY10 . . . . 117 B4
Comberton Pl DY10 . . . . . 116 F5
Comberton Rd
Birmingham B26 . . . . 89 B8
Kidderminster DY10 . . . . . . 117 B4
Comberton Terr DY10 . . . . 116 F5
Combine Cl B75 . . . . 32 D4
Combrook Gn B34 . . . . 69 D6
Comet Rd B26 . . . . 90 C4
Commainge Cl CV34 . . . . 160 D7
Commercial Rd
Walsall WS2 . . . . 28 A7
Wolverhampton WV1 . . . . . . 25 E1
Commercial St B1 . . . . . . 164 A2
Commissary Rd B26 . . . . . 90 A3
Commonfield Croft B8 . . . 67 D5
Common La
Birmingham,Sheldon B26 . . 89 B6
Birmingham,Washwood Heath
B8 . . . . 67 F6
Cannock WS11 . . . . 2 A3

Common La continued
Corley Moor CV7 . . . . 93 E7
Kenilworth CV8 . . . . 148 B7
Tamworth B79 . . . . 21 B4
Common Rd WV5 . . . . 49 A6
Commonside
Brierley Hill DY5 . . . . 61 C6
Brownhills WS8 . . . . 16 A6
Walsall WS3 . . . . 15 A2
Common View WS12 . . . . . . 2 B7
Common Way CV2 . . . . . . 114 A6
Common Wlk WS12 . . . . 1 C5
Communication Row B15 . 66 C1
Compass Ct 4 CV1 . . . . . 113 B3
Compass Way B60 . . . . . . 151 A7
Compton Cl
Redditch B98 . . . . 153 E2
Royal Leamington Spa
CV32 . . . . 157 C2
Solihull B91 . . . . 106 D4
Compton Croft B37 . . . . . . 70 D1
Compton Ct
1 Sutton Coldfield B74 . . . 31 F3
7 Wolverhampton WV3 . . . 25 A2
Coventry CV6 . . . . 95 D2
Dudley DY2 . . . . 62 C6
Compton Dr
Dudley DY2 . . . . 62 F8
Kingswinford DY6 . . . . 60 D5
Sutton Coldfield B74 . . . . . . 44 E7
Compton Grange B64 . . . . 82 C8
Compton Gr
Halesowen B63 . . . . 82 C4
Kingswinford DY6 . . . . 60 D5
Compton Hill Dr WV3 . . . . 24 D2
Compton Ho B33 . . . . 69 B2
Compton Mews WV6 . . . . . 24 E3
Compton Rd
Birmingham B24 . . . . 56 E1
Coventry CV6 . . . . 95 D2
Cradley Heath B64 . . . . 62 C1
Halesowen B62 . . . . 83 F5
Stourbridge DY9 . . . . 81 D2
Tamworth B79 . . . . 20 F7
Wolverhampton WV3 . . . . . . 24 F2
Compton Rd W WV3 . . . . . 24 D2
Comrie Cl CV2 . . . . 114 F6
Comsey Rd B43 . . . . 44 B3
Comwall Cl WS3 . . . . 28 C7
Comyn St CV32 . . . . 157 B1
Conchar Cl B72 . . . . 46 C2
Conchar Rd B72 . . . . 46 C2
Concorde Dr B35 . . . . 57 F2
Concorde Rd B26 . . . . 90 C4
Condor Gr WS12 . . . . 2 C1
Condover Cl WS2 . . . . 27 D3
Condover Rd B31 . . . . 123 B8
Conduit Rd WS11 . . . . 6 A4
Conduit St WS13 . . . . 9 B8
Coneybury Wlk B76 . . . . . . 58 D5
Coneyford Rd B34 . . . . 69 C6
Coney Gn DY8 . . . . 81 B5
Coneygre Bsns Pk DY4 . . 51 F3
Coneygre Ind Est DY4 . . . 52 A3
Coneygre Rd DY4 . . . . 51 F3
Congleton Cl
Coventry CV6 . . . . 95 E2
Redditch B97 . . . . 153 B5
Congregve Cl CV34 . . . . . 155 F2
Congreve Wlk 3 CV12 . . . 78 B3
Conifer Cl
Bedworth CV12 . . . . 78 C4
Brierley Hill DY5 . . . . 81 C8
Cannock WS12 . . . . 2 A8
Conifer Ct B13 . . . . 86 E2
Conifer Dr
Birmingham,Handsworth
B21 . . . . 65 E7
Birmingham,Northfield
B31 . . . . 103 B3
Conifer Gr
3 Royal Leamington Spa
CV31 . . . . 161 D5
Bromsgrove B61 . . . . 136 F3
Conifer Paddock
Coventry CV3 . . . . 114 E1
Halesowen B62 . . . . 83 E8
Conifer Rd B74 . . . . 44 E8
Conifers The CV8 . . . . 148 A7
Coningsby Cl 3 CV31 . . 162 C6
Coningsby Dr DY11 . . . . . 116 C5
Conington Gr B17 . . . . 85 A5
Coniston Ave B92 . . . . 88 F4
Coniston Cl
Birmingham B28 . . . . 105 F7
Bromsgrove B60 . . . . 137 B1
Bulkington CV12 . . . . 79 C3
Coniston Cres B43 . . . . . . 54 F7
Coniston Ct
2 Royal Leamington Spa
CV32 . . . . 156 D1
Nuneaton CV11 . . . . 73 F7
Coniston Dr
Coventry CV5 . . . . 111 D4
Kingswinford DY6 . . . . 60 B7
Coniston Grange CV8 . . . 147 F5
Coniston Ho
10 Birmingham B17 . . . . . . 85 D5
7 Oldbury B69 . . . . 63 E4
Kidderminster DY10 . . . . . . 116 E7
Coniston Rd
Birmingham B23 . . . . 56 D4
Coventry CV5 . . . . 112 F1
Royal Leamington Spa
CV32 . . . . 156 D1
Sutton Coldfield B74 . . . . . . 30 F3

Coniston Rd continued
Wolverhampton WV6 . . . . . . 24 D8
Coniston B77 . . . . 36 B7
Coniston Way
Cannock WS11 . . . . 1 E1
Nuneaton CV11 . . . . 73 F7
Connaught Ave
Kidderminster DY11 . . . . . . 116 C4
Wednesbury WS10 . . . . 42 C3
Connaught Cl WS5 . . . . 43 C7
Connaught Dr WV5 . . . . . . 38 A1
Connaught Gdns B5 . . . . . 86 E6
Connaught Ho 1 WV3 . . . 25 A2
Connaught Rd
Bilston WV14 . . . . 40 F7
Bromsgrove B60 . . . . 137 C1
Wolverhampton WV1 . . . . . . 25 A2
Connops Way DY9 . . . . 81 E5
Connor Rd B71 . . . . 53 E8
Conolly Dr B45 . . . . 102 B1
Conrad Cl B11 . . . . 87 A7
Conrad Rd CV6 . . . . 113 A7
Consort Cres DY5 . . . . 61 C6
Consort Dr WS10 . . . . 41 C8
Consort Pl B79 . . . . 21 C5
Consort Rd B30 . . . . 104 A3
Constable Cl
Bedworth CV12 . . . . 78 A5
Birmingham B43 . . . . 44 D3
Constables The B68 . . . . . 64 B2
Constance Ave B70 . . . . . . 53 D1
Constance Rd B5 . . . . 86 D5
Constance La B46 . . . . 59 F1
Constantine Way WV14 . . . 41 A2
Constitution Hill
1 Dudley DY2 . . . . 62 D8
Birmingham B19 . . . . 164 B4
Constitution Hill E DY2 . . 62 D8
Consul Ho 6 LE10 . . . . . . 71 D1
Convent Cl
Cannock WS11 . . . . 4 D8
Kenilworth CV8 . . . . 148 A7
Wolverhampton WV1 . . . . . 163 C2
Conway Ave
Birmingham B32 . . . . 84 B6
Coventry CV4 . . . . 131 D8
Oldbury B68 . . . . 64 B2
West Bromwich B71 . . . . . . 42 B1
Conway Cl
Dudley DY1 . . . . 51 C6
Kingswinford DY6 . . . . 60 F4
Solihull B90 . . . . 106 D1
Conway Cres WV12 . . . . . . 27 C7
Conway Gr B43 . . . . 54 D7
Conway Ho WS3 . . . . 28 D6
Conway Prim Sch B11 . . . 87 C6
Conway Rd
Birmingham B37 . . . . 70 B3
Birmingham,Sparkbrook
B11 . . . . 87 C6
Bromsgrove B60 . . . . 136 F1
Cannock WS11 . . . . 4 B8
Perton WV6 . . . . 23 F3
Royal Leamington Spa
CV32 . . . . 161 D8
Solihull B90 . . . . 106 D1
Conwy Cl
Nuneaton CV11 . . . . 73 D3
Walsall WS2 . . . . 28 A4
Conybere St B12 . . . . 86 F7
Conyworth Cl B27 . . . . 88 D4
Cook Ave DY2 . . . . 62 D7
Cook Cl
Knowle B93 . . . . 128 C6
Coventry CV6 . . . . 23 E4
Cooke Cl
Coventry CV6 . . . . 96 A4
Warwick CV34 . . . . 155 F2
Cookes Croft B31 . . . . 103 B3
Cookesley Cl B43 . . . . 44 D4
Cooke St WV2 . . . . 163 B1
Cookley Cl B63 . . . . 82 F2
Cookley Way B69 . . . . 63 E5
Cookley Wharf Ind Est
DY5 . . . . 61 B4
Cooknell Dr DY8 . . . . 60 E2
Cook Rd WS3 . . . . 14 D2
Cooksey La B44 . . . . 44 F3
Cooksey Rd B10 . . . . 87 C8
Cooks La B37 . . . . 70 A4
Cookspiece Wlk B33 . . . . . 68 F3
Cook St
Birmingham B7 . . . . 67 C7
Coventry CV1 . . . . 165 B3
Darlaston WS10 . . . . 41 F6
Coombe Abbey Ctry Pk . . 115 E3
Coombe Abbey Visitor Ctr . 115 E4
Coombe Ave CV3 . . . . 134 F7
Coombe Croft WV9 . . . . . . 11 A3
Coombe Dr CV3 . . . . 115 A2
Coombe Ho
Binley Woods CV3 . . . . 135 E4
Nuneaton CV10 . . . . 72 B4
Coombe Hill B64 . . . . 83 B8
Coombe Park Rd CV3 . . . . 114 F2
Coombe Pk B74 . . . . 45 F7
Coombe Rd
Birmingham B20 . . . . 55 E1
Solihull B90 . . . . 106 C2
Coombes La B31 . . . . 122 F7
Coombes Rd B62 . . . . 83 B7
Coombe St CV3 . . . . 114 B2

Coombs Rd B62 . . . . .83 B7
Coombswood Way B65 . . . .83 B8
Co-Operative St CV2 . . . . . . .96 B3
Cooper Ave DY5 . . . . .61 A2
Cooper Cl
  Bromsgrove B60 . . . . .150 E6
  West Bromwich B70 . . . . . . .53 E2
Cooper & Jordan CE Prim
  Sch WS9 . . . . .30 C6
Coppice View Rd B73 . . . . . .45 A4
Coppice Way ⁊ B37 . . . . . .70 B2
Coppice Wlk
  Cheswick Green B90 . . . . . .126 D4
  Hinckley LE10 . . . . .71 F3
Copplestone Cl B34 . . . . . . .69 B6
Copps Rd CV32 . . . . .161 D8
Coppy Hall Gr WS9 . . . . .16 B1
Coppy Nook La WS7 . . . . . . .7 C5
Copse Cl B31 . . . . .103 A2
Copse Cres WS3 . . . . .15 A4
Copse Dr CV5 . . . . .111 B8
Copsehill Ct B75 . . . . .46 E4
Copse Rd DY2 . . . . .62 B3
Copse The
  Bedworth CV7 . . . . .96 A8
  Sutton Coldfield B74 . . . . . . .31 F1
Copsewood Ave CV11 . . . . .79 B7
Copsewood Terr CV3 . . . . .114 C2
Copson Cl B70 . . . . .53 A3
Copstone Dr B93 . . . . .127 F3
Copston Gr B29 . . . . .103 B8
Copthall Ho CV1 . . . . .165 B1
Copthall Rd B21 . . . . .54 C2
Copt Heath Croft B93 . . . .128 B8
Copt Heath Dr B93 . . . . . . .128 A7
Copthorne Ave WS7 . . . . .6 F4
Copthorne La CV6 . . . . .112 F8
Copthorne Rd
  Birmingham B44 . . . . .44 E3
  Coventry CV6 . . . . .112 F8
  Wolverhampton WV3 . . . . . . .39 A7
Copt Oak Cl CV4 . . . . .131 C6
Copyholt La
  Stoke Prior B60 . . . . .151 D3
  Upper Bentley B60,B97 . . . .152 A3
Coral Cl
  Coventry CV5 . . . . .112 C2
  Hinckley LE10 . . . . .75 F4
Coralin Cl B37 . . . . .70 C2
Corbett Rd CV6 . . . . .113 C7
Corbett Cl B60 . . . . .151 B8
Corbett Cres DY8 . . . . .81 A7
Corbett Ho ⁊ B70 . . . . . . .80 F8
Corbett Hospl DY8 . . . . .80 F7
Corbett Ind Est DY2 . . . . . . .62 C6
Corbett Rd
  Brierley Hill DY5 . . . . .61 E1
  Hollywood B47 . . . . .125 A4
  Kidderminster DY11 . . . . . .116 A8
Corbetts Cl B92 . . . . .109 B7
Corbett St B66 . . . . .65 B4
Corbin Rd B78 . . . . .36 F6
Corbison Cl CV34 . . . . .155 D1
Corbizum Ave B80 . . . . .159 D4
Corbridge Ave B44 . . . . .44 F1
Corbridge Rd B73 . . . . .45 F2
Corbyn Rd
  Birmingham B9 . . . . .68 B3
  Dudley DY1 . . . . .61 F8
Corbyns Cl DY5 . . . . .61 B7
Corbyns Hall La DY5 . . . . . . .61 B7
Corbyns Hall Rd DY5 . . . . . .61 B7
Cordelia Gn CV34 . . . . .161 D4
Cordley St B70 . . . . .53 B4
Corfe Cl
  Birmingham B32 . . . . .84 F5
  Coventry CV2 . . . . .114 F5
  Perton WV6 . . . . .23 F3
Corfe Dr B69 . . . . .63 A8
Corfe Rd WV14 . . . . .51 A8
Corfton Dr WV6 . . . . .24 C3
Coriander Cl
  Birmingham B45 . . . . .102 B2
  Stoke Prior B60 . . . . .150 C1
Corinne Cl B45 . . . . .122 A6
Corinne Croft B37 . . . . .70 A4
Corinthian Pl CV2 . . . . .114 D6
Coriolanus Sq CV34 . . . . . .161 F3
Corisande Rd B29 . . . . .85 C2
Corley Ave B31 . . . . .103 B3
Corley Cl B90 . . . . .105 E1
Corley (Coventry) Sch
  CV7 . . . . .94 B6
Corley View CV7 . . . . .95 C6
Cormorant Gr DY10 . . . . . .117 B3
Cornbow Ctr B63 . . . . .83 B3
Cornbrook Rd B29 . . . . .102 F7
Cornbury Gr B91 . . . . .106 D4
Corncrake Cl B72 . . . . .46 D2
Corncrake Dr B36 . . . . .70 A7
Corncrake Rd DY1,DY3 . . . . .50 E3
Corndon Cl DY11 . . . . .116 A8
Cornel Cl B37 . . . . .90 C8
Cornelius St CV3 . . . . .133 D8
Cornel Rd B77 . . . . .21 F4
Corner Ho B66 . . . . .65 D6
Corner Ho The ⁊ CV32 . . .156 F1
Corner La B97 . . . . .152 E2
Corner Pl The ⁊ B17 . . . . .85 D6
Cornerstone B13 . . . . .86 F3
Cornerstone Ho CV1 . . . . . .165 C4
Cornerway B38 . . . . .123 F7
Cornet's End La CV7 . . . . . .110 B6
Cornets End La CV7 . . . . . . .109 E7

Coppice The
  Birmingham,Frankley
    B31 . . . . .102 C2
  Birmingham,Handsworth Wood
    B20 . . . . .55 A2
  Cannock WS12 . . . . .2 E1
  Coventry CV3 . . . . .134 B8
  Hinckley LE10 . . . . .75 F8
  Nuneaton CV10 . . . . .73 C7
  Wednesbury DY4 . . . . .41 C1
  West Hagley DY8 . . . . .98 F5
  Willenhall WV12 . . . . .27 C6
Coppice View Rd B73 . . . . . .45 A4

Corn Exchange The ⁊
  WS13 . . . . .9 B8
Cornfield Ave B60 . . . . .150 D6
Cornfield Cl DY6 . . . . .60 A8
Cornfield Croft
  Birmingham B37 . . . . .70 D3
  Sutton Coldfield B76 . . . . . . .46 F3
Cornfield Dr WS14 . . . . .9 E7
Cornfield Cl LE10 . . . . .71 C4
Cornfield Pl B65 . . . . .62 F4
Cornfield Rd
  Birmingham B31 . . . . .103 B4
  Rowley Regis B65 . . . . .62 F4
Cornfield Wlk B60 . . . . .10 F2
Cornfield The CV3 . . . . .114 C1
Cornflower Cl WV10 . . . . . . .12 A7
Cornflower Cres DY2 . . . . . .62 F8
Cornflower Rd WS8 . . . . .15 D6
Corngreaves Jun & Inf Sch
  B64 . . . . .62 D1
Corngreaves Rd B64 . . . . . . .82 E7
Corngreaves The B34 . . . . . .69 B6
Corngreaves Trad Est
  B64 . . . . .82 D7
Cornhampton Cl ⁊ B97 . .153 B5
Cornhill WS11 . . . . .1 E5
Cornhill Gr
  Birmingham B30 . . . . .104 C2
  Kenilworth CV8 . . . . .148 C5
Corn Hill
  Walsall WS5 . . . . .43 E8
  Wolverhampton WV10 . . . . .163 D3
Cornish Cres CV10 . . . . .73 A2
Corn Mdws CV12 . . . . .78 C2
Corn Mill Cl
  Birmingham B32 . . . . .84 E1
  Sutton Coldfield B76 . . . . . . .46 F1
Cornmill Cl WS1 . . . . .42 D7
Cornmill Gdns B60 . . . . . . .138 A5
Cornmill Gr WV6 . . . . .23 D5
Cornovian Cl WV6 . . . . .23 E5
Corns Ho WS10 . . . . .41 E6
Cornwall Ave
  Birmingham B68 . . . . .84 B8
  Tamworth B78 . . . . .21 A1
Cornwall Cl
  ⁊ Warwick CV34 . . . . .160 F8
  Aldridge WS9 . . . . .16 A1
  Kingswinford DY6 . . . . .60 D8
  Wednesbury WS10 . . . . .42 D3
Cornwall Gate WV12 . . . . . .27 B5
Cornwall Ho CV12 . . . . .156 D1
Cornwall Ind Est
  Birmingham B8 . . . . .67 C4
  Smethwick B66 . . . . .65 C7
Cornwalls Rd B70 . . . . .53 A1
Cornwall Pl
  Royal Leamington Spa
    CV32 . . . . .156 D1
  Walsall WS2 . . . . .27 E3
Cornwall Rd
  Birmingham,Handsworth
    B20 . . . . .54 F2
  Birmingham,Rubery B45 . . .101 E1
  Cannock WS12 . . . . .2 B5
  Coventry CV1 . . . . .113 E1
  Smethwick B66 . . . . .65 C7
  Stourbridge DY8 . . . . .80 D8
  Walsall WS5 . . . . .43 B7
  Wolverhampton WV6 . . . . . .24 C4
Cornwall St B3 . . . . .164 B3
Cornwall Twr B18 . . . . .66 B5
Cornwall Way LE10 . . . . .71 E4
Cornwell Cl
  Redditch B98 . . . . .159 B5
  Tipton DY4 . . . . .52 A5
Cornyx La B91 . . . . .107 D6
Coronation Ave
  Mile Oak B78 . . . . .20 D1
  Willenhall WV13 . . . . .27 D2
Coronation Cres B79 . . . . . .22 F7
Coronation Ct CV11 . . . . . . .73 B4
Coronation Rd
  Bilston WV14 . . . . .40 C6
  Birmingham B29 . . . . .85 F2
  Birmingham,Great Barr B43 .43 E4
  Birmingham,Washwood Heath
    B8 . . . . .67 F6
  Brownhills WS9 . . . . .16 A3
  Coventry CV1 . . . . .113 F4
  Tipton DY4 . . . . .52 A5
  Walsall WS4 . . . . .15 B2
  Wednesbury WS10 . . . . .42 C4
  Wolverhampton WV10 . . . . .26 A5
Coronation St B79 . . . . .21 A4
Coronation Terr B60 . . . . . .151 B7
Coronation Way DY10 . . . . .117 B5
Coronel Ave CV6 . . . . .95 E4
Corporation Rd DY2 . . . . . . .51 F1
Corporation St W WS1 . . . . .42 D8
Corporation St
  Birmingham B2 . . . . .164 C3
  Coventry CV1 . . . . .165 B3
  Nuneaton CV10 . . . . .116 E5
  Nuneaton CV11 . . . . .73 B5
  Tamworth B79 . . . . .21 B5
  Walsall WS1 . . . . .42 E7
  Wednesbury WS10 . . . . .42 A4
Corpus Christi RC Prim Sch
  Birmingham B33 . . . . .68 D2
  Wednesfield WV11 . . . . .27 A8
Corpus Christi RC Sch
  CV3 . . . . .134 D7

Correen B77 . . . . .22 C1
Corrie Croft
  Birmingham,Bartley Green
    B32 . . . . .102 B7
  Birmingham,Lyndon Green
    B26 . . . . .89 B7
Corrie Roy Cotts B78 . . . . . .21 A4
Corrin Gr DY6 . . . . .60 C8
Corron Hill B63 . . . . .83 B4
Corser St
  Dudley DY1 . . . . .51 A2
  Stourbridge DY8 . . . . .81 A3
  Wolverhampton WV1 . . . . . . .25 F1
Corsican Cl
  Burntwood WS7 . . . . .7 A8
  Willenhall WV12 . . . . .27 E7
Corsican Dr WS12 . . . . .2 A8
Corsican Dr WS12 . . . . .2 A8
Corunna Rd CV34 . . . . .160 C7
Corvedale Rd B29 . . . . .103 A6
Corve Gdns WV6 . . . . .24 E5
Corve View DY3 . . . . .39 C1
Corville Gdns B26 . . . . .89 C4
Corville Rd B62 . . . . .83 F6
Corwen Croft B31 . . . . .102 E6
Cory Croft DY4 . . . . .52 A5
Coseley Hall ⁊ WV14 . . . . . .51 C8
Coseley Rd WV14 . . . . .40 C4
Coseley Road Island
  WV14 . . . . .40 C4
Coseley Sch The WV14 . . . . .40 D4
Coseley Sta WV14 . . . . .40 A3
Cosford Cl
  Redditch B98 . . . . .154 F1
  Royal Leamington Spa
    CV32 . . . . .157 B3
Cosford Cres B35 . . . . .58 A3
Cosford Ct B17 . . . . .23 E5
Cosford Dr DY2 . . . . .62 E5
Cosgrove Wlk WV8 . . . . .10 F1
Cossington Rd B23 . . . . .56 E7
Costard Ave CV34 . . . . .161 E3
Costers La B98 . . . . .154 F2
Costock Cl B37 . . . . .90 B8
Coten End Prim Sch
  CV34 . . . . .160 F7
Cotes Rd LE10 . . . . .75 F5
Cotford Rd B14 . . . . .105 A2
Cotheridge Cl B90 . . . . .127 C6
Cot La DY6,DY8 . . . . .60 C5
Cotleigh Gr B43 . . . . .44 D3
Cotman Cl
  Bedworth CV12 . . . . .78 A4
  Birmingham B43 . . . . .44 C3
Cotman Dr LE10 . . . . .71 A3
Coton Green Prec B79 . . . . .20 F7
Coton Green Prim Sch
  B79 . . . . .20 F8
Coton Gr B90 . . . . .105 E2
Coton La
  Birmingham B23 . . . . .56 F4
  Tamworth B79 . . . . .20 E8
Coton Rd
  Nuneaton CV11 . . . . .73 C3
  Wolverhampton WV4 . . . . . .39 B5
Cotsdale Rd WV4 . . . . .38 E3
Cotsford B91 . . . . .107 A3
Cotswold Cl
  Aldridge WS9 . . . . .16 C1
  Birmingham B45 . . . . .102 B2
  Cannock WS12 . . . . .2 A8
  Kidderminster DY11 . . . . . .116 C7
  Oldbury B69 . . . . .63 E5
Cotswold Cres CV10 . . . . . . .72 B3
Cotswold Croft B63 . . . . .82 C1
Cotswold Dr
  Sutton Coldfield B75 . . . . . . .32 A4
  Wolverhampton WV3 . . . . . .39 B6
Cotswold Dr CV3 . . . . .133 C3
Cotswold Gr WV12 . . . . .13 B1
Cotswold Rd
  Cannock WS12 . . . . .2 A8
  Stourbridge DY8 . . . . .81 B6
  Wolverhampton WV2 . . . . . .39 F7
Cotswold Way B61 . . . . .137 A5
Cottage Cl
  Burntwood WS7 . . . . .6 F5
  Cannock WS12 . . . . .2 D5
  Nuneaton CV11 . . . . .73 D4
  Royal Leamington Spa
    CV31 . . . . .162 C6
  Wolverhampton WV11 . . . . . .26 C6
Cottage Ct WS7 . . . . .6 F5
Cottage Dr B60 . . . . .121 D1
Cottage Farm La B60 . . . . .121 C1
Cottage Farm Lodge CV6 . .95 A1
Cottage Farm Rd
  Coventry CV6 . . . . .95 A2
  Tamworth B77 . . . . .35 D7
Cottage Gdns B45 . . . . .121 F6
Cottage La
  Burntwood WS7 . . . . .6 F5
  Lower Marlbrook B60 . . . . .121 C1
  Minworth B76 . . . . .58 D6
  Wolverhampton WV10 . . . . . .11 D3
Cottage Mews WS9 . . . . .30 E4
Cottage Sq CV31 . . . . .162 C6
Cottage St DY5 . . . . .61 D3
Cottages The
  Birmingham B24 . . . . .67 F8
  Cradley Heath B63 . . . . .82 E6
Cottage St DY5 . . . . .60 D7
Cottage View WV8 . . . . .10 B4
Cottage Wlk
  ⁊ Tamworth B77 . . . . .35 F6

Cottage Wlk continued
  West Bromwich B70 . . . . . . .53 D2
Cotterell Ct ⁊ WS4 . . . . . . .28 F3
Cotteridge Jun & Inf Sch
  B30 . . . . .104 A5
Cotteridge Rd B30 . . . . .104 A4
Cotterills Ave B8 . . . . .68 C4
Cotterills Cl CV31 . . . . .162 B3
Cotterills La B8 . . . . .68 C4
Cotterills Rd DY4 . . . . .52 B7
Cottesbrook Cl CV3 . . . . . .134 D8
Cottesbrook Inf Sch B27 . .88 D4
Cottesbrook Jun Sch B27 .88 C4
Cottesbrook Rd B27 . . . . . . .88 D4
Cottesfield Cl B8 . . . . .68 B4
Cottesmore Cl B71 . . . . .53 F8
Cottesmore Ho ⁊ B20 . . . . .54 F3
Cottle Cl WS2 . . . . .27 F3
Cotton Dr CV8 . . . . .148 C6
Cotton La B13 . . . . .87 A2
Cotton Mill Spinney
  CV32 . . . . .157 E6
Cotton Pool Rd B61 . . . . . . .136 E2
Cottrells Cl B14 . . . . .105 C4
Cottrells Mews B46 . . . . . . .59 B2
Cottrell St B71 . . . . .53 D4
Cottsmeadow Dr B8 . . . . . . .68 C4
Cotwall End Countryside &
  Craft Ctr* DY3 . . . . .50 C6
Cotwall End Ho DY3 . . . . . . .50 C7
Cotwall End Prim Sch
  DY3 . . . . .50 D3
Cotwall End Rd DY3 . . . . . . .50 C5
Cotysmore Rd B75 . . . . .46 D2
Couchman Rd B8 . . . . .67 E4
Coughton Dr CV31 . . . . .162 D5
Coulter Gr WV6 . . . . .23 D4
Coulter La WS7 . . . . .7 E8
Council Cres WV12 . . . . .27 C4
Council Ho* B3 . . . . .164 B2
Council Hos CV5 . . . . .93 D1
Council Rd ⁊ LE10 . . . . .71 D1
Coundon Court Sch & Com
  Coll CV6 . . . . .112 E7
Coundon Gn CV6 . . . . .112 E8
Coundon Prim Sch CV6 . .112 E5
Coundon Rd CV1 . . . . .113 B3
Coundon St CV1 . . . . .165 A4
Coundon Wedge Dr CV5,
  CV6 . . . . .112 D7
Counterfield Dr B65 . . . . . . .62 F5
Countess Dr WS4 . . . . .29 C7
Countess Rd CV11 . . . . .73 A4
Countess's Croft The
  CV3 . . . . .133 D7
Countess St WS1 . . . . .42 D6
Countinghouse Way ⁊
  B60 . . . . .150 E6
County Bridge Prim Sch
  WS2 . . . . .27 E1
County Cl
  Birmingham B32 . . . . .84 D3
  Birmingham,Stirchley B30 . .104 C6
County Dr B78 . . . . .21 A2
County La DY8 . . . . .98 D8
County Park Ave B62 . . . . . .83 D2
Courtaulds Way CV6 . . . . . .113 D6
Court Cres DY6 . . . . .60 C5
Court Dr WS14 . . . . .17 F4
Courtenay Gdns B43 . . . . . .43 E2
Courtenay Rd B44 . . . . .55 E8
Court Farm Prim Sch B23 .56 E6
Court Farm Rd B23 . . . . .56 E6
Court Farm Way B29 . . . . .102 F7
Courthouse Croft CV8 . . . .148 C4
Courthouse Green Prim Sch
  CV6 . . . . .114 A8
Court La B23 . . . . .56 F7
Courtland Ave CV6 . . . . .112 F5
Courtland Rd DY6 . . . . .60 E8
Courtlands Cl B5 . . . . .86 C6
Courtlands The WV6 . . . . . . .24 E4
Court Leet B65 . . . . .63 C3
Court Leet Rd CV3 . . . . .133 E7
Courtney Cl CV11 . . . . .73 F7
Courtney DY10 . . . . .116 E2
Court Oak Gr B17 . . . . .85 A6
Court of Lady Katherine
  Leveson The B93 . . . . . . .129 B5
Court Par WS9 . . . . .30 B6
Court Pas DY1 . . . . .51 C1
Court Rd
  Birmingham,Balsall Heath
    B12 . . . . .86 E6
  Birmingham,Sparkhill B11 . . .87 C4
  Wolverhampton WV6 . . . . . .24 F4
  Woodcross WV4 . . . . .40 A3
Court St
  ⁊ Cradley Heath B64 . . . . . .62 F1
  ⁊ Stourbridge DY8 . . . . .81 A5
  Royal Leamington Spa
    CV31 . . . . .162 A7
Courtway Ave B14 . . . . .105 B1
Court Way WS2 . . . . .28 E2
Courtyard The
  Coleshill B46 . . . . .59 F2
  Solihull B91 . . . . .107 C4
  Stoke Prior B60 . . . . .150 D2
  Warwick CV34 . . . . .160 E5
  West Bromwich B70 . . . . . . .53 A3
Cousins St WV2 . . . . .39 D7
Coveley Gr B18 . . . . .66 A5
Coven Cl WS3 . . . . .15 A5
Coven Gr B29 . . . . .85 B2
Coven St WV10 . . . . .25 D4
Coventry Airport CV8 . . . . .134 B2
Coventry Blue Coat CE Sch
  The CV1 . . . . .113 F1

Coventry Bsns Pk CV5 . . . . 112 D1
Coventry Canal Basin
Warehouse CV1 . . . . .165 B4
Coventry Cath Church of St
Michael* CV1. . . . . .165 C3
Coventry Gram Sch CV5. . .112 F1
Coventry Highway B98 . . . . 154 C4
Coventry Muslim Sch
CV6 . . . . .113 E8
Coventry Prep Sch CV3 . .133 B8
Coventry Railway Ctr
CV8 . . . . 134 A3
Coventry Rd
Aston Flamville LE10. . . . . .76 F1
Baginton CV8. . . . . .133 F2
Barnacle CV7,CV12 . . . . . . .97 A8
Bedworth CV12 . . . . .78 B2
Bedworth,Hawkesbury CV2. .96 E6
Berkswell CV7 . . . . 110 C3
Bickenhill B26,B92. . . . . . . .90 C2
Birmingham B10,B25,B26 . .88 C6
Bulkington CV12 . . . . .79 B1
Coventry CV3. . . . . .115 F3
Cubbington CV32 . . . . .157 E7
Hampton-in-A B92 . . . . .91 B3
Hinckley LE10 . . . . .75 B7
Hinckley,Sketchley Hill LE10 .75 F5
Kenilworth CV8 . . . . .148 A3
Nuneaton CV10 . . . . .78 C7
Stoneleigh CV8,CV3. . . . . .149 C7
Warwick CV34. . . . . 160 F8
Coventry Ret Mkt CV1. . . .165 B2
Coventry Road Exhall CV7 .96 A8
Coventry Sta CV1 . . . . 165 B1
Coventry St
Birmingham B5 . . . . .164 D2
Coventry CV2. . . . . 114 A4
Kidderminster DY10 . . . . . .116 F6
Nuneaton CV11 . . . . .73 C4
Stourbridge DY8 . . . . .81 A5
Wolverhampton WV1. . . . . .26 A2
Coventry Toy Mus* CV1 . .165 C2
Coventry Univ CV1. . . . . . .165 C2
Coventry University Tech Pk
CV1 . . . . .165 C1
Coventry Walsgrave Triangle
Bsns Pk CV2 . . . . .97 A1
Coventry & Warwickshire
Hospl CV1 . . . . .165 C4
Cove Pl CV2 . . . . 114 C7
Cover Croft B76 . . . . .47 A1
Coverdale Rd B92 . . . . .89 A4
Covers The B80. . . . . .159 E6
Covert La DY8 . . . . .80 D2
Covert The WV8. . . . . .10 E1
Covey Cl WS13. . . . . .3 D1
Cowdray Cl CV31 . . . . .162 C7
Cow La B78 . . . . .35 F3
Cowles Croft B25. . . . . .68 E1
Cowley Cl B36. . . . . .58 F1
Cowley Dr
Birmingham B27 . . . . .88 D4
Dudley DY1 . . . . .50 F2
Cowley Gn WS12. . . . . .1 F8
Cowley Gr B11. . . . . .87 E5
Cowley Rd
Birmingham B11 . . . . .87 E5
Coventry CV2. . . . . 114 D4
Cowley B77. . . . . .21 E2
Cowper Cl
Warwick CV34 . . . . .155 C1
Willenhall WV12 . . . . .27 E7
Cowper Rd LE10 . . . . .75 D6
Cowper Wlk DY10. . . . . . . .117 C6
Cowslip Cl
1 Birmingham,Hawkesley
B38. . . . . .123 F8
Birmingham,Selly Oak B29 .103 A7
Cowslip Wlk DY5 . . . . .81 C6
Coxcroft Ave DY5 . . . . .81 F8
Coxmoor Cl WS3. . . . . .13 F3
Cox Rd WV14 . . . . .40 E1
Cox's Cl CV10. . . . . .73 B3
Cox's La B64 . . . . .62 F2
Cox's Orch 4 CV31 . . . . . .162 A4
Cox St
Birmingham B3 . . . . .164 B4
Coventry CV1. . . . . 165 C3
Coxwell Ave WV10 . . . . . . .25 C5
Coxwell Gdns B16 . . . . .65 F2
Coyne Cl DY4. . . . . .51 D5
Coyne Rd B70 . . . . .53 B2
Cozens Cl CV12 . . . . .78 A4
Crabbe St DY9 . . . . .81 F5
Crabbs Cross La B97. . . . .158 E5
Crab La
Cannock WS11. . . . . .2 A3
Willenhall WV12 . . . . .13 D1
Crabmill Cl
Birmingham B38 . . . . .123 E7
Redditch B98 . . . . .128 C7
Crabmill La
Birmingham B38 . . . . .124 D8
Coventry CV6. . . . . .113 F7
Crabourne Rd DY2 . . . . . . .62 B2
Crabtree Cl
Birmingham B31 . . . . .103 C2
Redditch B98 . . . . .154 A2
West Bromwich B71 . . . . . .53 F8
West Hagley DY9 . . . . .99 B6
Crabtree Dr
Bromsgrove B61. . . . . .136 F3
Crabtree Gr CV31 . . . . .162 C6
Crab Tree Ho B33. . . . . .68 E3
Crabtree La B61. . . . . .136 E3

Crabtree Rd
Barwell LE9 . . . . .71 F5
Birmingham B18 . . . . .66 A5
Walsall WS1 . . . . .29 A2
Crackley Cotts CV8 . . . . . .148 B8
Crackley Cres CV8 . . . . . . .148 B8
Crackley Hall Sch CV8 . .148 B7
Crackley La
Coventry CV4. . . . . .131 F3
Kenilworth CV8 . . . . .148 A7
Crackley Way DY2 . . . . .62 A6
Craddock Ct CV10 . . . . .72 C7
Craddock Dr CV10 . . . . .72 C7
Craddock Rd B67. . . . . .64 F8
Craddock St WV6 . . . . .25 B4
Cradley CE Prim Sch B63 .82 C7
Cradley Cl B98 . . . . .154 F2
Cradley Croft B21. . . . . .54 C3
Cradley Fields B63. . . . . . . .82 D5
Cradley Forge DY5. . . . . . . .82 A8
Cradley Heath Factory Ctr
B64. . . . . .82 B8
Cradley Heath Sta B64. . .82 B8
Cradley High Sch B63. . . . .82 D6
Cradley Park Rd DY2. . . . . .62 D2
Cradley Rd
Cradley Heath B64 . . . . . . .82 C8
Dudley DY2 . . . . .62 D3
Cradock Rd B8 . . . . .67 E5
Craigends Ave CV3 . . . . . .134 E6
Crail Gr B43 . . . . .44 B4
Crakston Cl CV2 . . . . .114 E2
Cramlington Rd B42 . . . . . .55 A8
Crammond Cl LE10 . . . . . . .75 B8
Cramore Cl DY4 . . . . .52 A8
Cramp Hill WS10. . . . . .41 D6
Cranborne Chase CV2 . . .115 A5
Cranbourne Ave WV6 . . . . .39 E3
Cranbourne Cl B45 . . . . . .102 B2
Cranbourne Gr B44 . . . . . . .56 A8
Cranbourne Pl B71 . . . . . . .53 D4
Cranbourne Rd
Birmingham B44 . . . . .45 A1
Stourbridge DY8 . . . . .81 B4
Cranbrook Ct WV13 . . . . . . .27 C2
Cranbrook Gr WV6. . . . . . . .23 F3
Cranbrook Rd B21 . . . . .54 C2
Cranby St B8 . . . . .67 C5
Craneberry Rd B37 . . . . . . .69 E3
Cranebrook Hill B78 . . . . . .33 E5
Cranebrook La WS14. . . . . .16 F7
Crane Cl CV34 . . . . .155 D1
Crane Cl WS1 . . . . .29 A3
Crane Dr WS7 . . . . .7 A4
Crane Field WS13. . . . . .3 B1
Cranehouse Rd B44 . . . . . . .45 A2
Cranemoor Cl B7 . . . . .67 C6
Crane Rd WV14 . . . . .40 F3
Craner's Rd CV1 . . . . .113 F4
Cranesbill Cl CV10 . . . . . . .12 C7
Cranesbill Rd B29 . . . . . . .103 A6
Cranes Park Rd B26 . . . . . .89 C5
Crane St DY11 . . . . .116 D6
Crane Terr WV6 . . . . .24 E5
Cranfield Gr B26. . . . . .88 F8
Cranfield Pl WS5 . . . . .42 F5
Cranfield Rd WS7. . . . . .7 A7
Cranford Gr 6 B91 . . . . . .107 B1
Cranford Pl WS11. . . . . .1 F1
Cranford Rd
Coventry CV5. . . . . .112 D4
Wolverhampton WV3. . . . . .38 D8
Cranford St B66. . . . . .65 C5
Cranford Way B66 . . . . .65 C5
Cranham Cl B97 . . . . .153 B1
Cranham Dr DY6. . . . . .60 E5
Cranhill Cl B92 . . . . .89 B1
Crankhall La WS10. . . . . . . .42 C3
Cranleigh Cl
Aldridge WS9 . . . . .30 B5
Willenhall WV12 . . . . .13 C1
Cranleigh Ho B23. . . . . .56 F6
Cranleigh Pl B44 . . . . .55 E5
Cranleigh Way WS14. . . . . . .9 E7
Cranmer Ave WV12 . . . . . . .27 D7
Cranmer Cl WS6. . . . . .4 D1
Cranmere Ave WV6 . . . . . . .24 A6
Cranmere Ct WV6. . . . . .24 A6
Cranmore Ave
Birmingham B21 . . . . .65 D7
Solihull B90 . . . . .126 E8
Cranmore Bvd B90. . . . . . .126 D8
Cranmore Dr B90. . . . . . . .106 E1
Cranmore Inf Sch B91 . .106 C1
Cranmore Rd
Birmingham B36 . . . . .58 E1
Solihull B90 . . . . .126 D8
Wolverhampton WV3. . . . . .24 F3
Cransley Gr B91 . . . . .107 A1
Crantock Cl WV11 . . . . .13 C1
Crantock Rd B42 . . . . .55 C4
Crantock Way CV11 . . . . . . .73 F4
Cranwell Gr B24 . . . . .57 D3
Cranwell Rise B78 . . . . .20 C1
Cranwell Way B35 . . . . .58 B3
Crathie Cl CV2. . . . . .114 F6
Crathorne Ave WV10 . . . . . .11 C1
Craufurd Ct DY8 . . . . .81 A3
Craufurd St DY8 . . . . .81 A3
Craven Ave CV3 . . . . .135 D7

Craven Ct CV3. . . . . .114 F2
Craven St
Coventry CV5. . . . . .112 F2
Wolverhampton WV2. . . . . .39 F6
Craven B77 . . . . .22 B1
Crawford Ave
Darlaston WS10. . . . . .41 C7
Smethwick B67 . . . . .64 F4
Wolverhampton WV4 . . . . . .39 F3
Crawford Cl CV32. . . . . . . .157 B5
Crawford Rd
Sutton Coldfield B76 . . . . . .57 F8
Wolverhampton WV3. . . . . .25 A2
Crawford St B8 . . . . .67 C5
Crawley Wlk 1 B64. . . . . . .62 D1
Crawshaws Rd B36 . . . . . . .58 C1
Crayford Rd B44. . . . . .45 A1
Craythorne Ave B20. . . . . . .54 E4
Crecy Cl B76 . . . . .46 E4
Crecy Rd CV3 . . . . .133 E7
Credenda Rd B70. . . . . .53 A1
Crediton Cl CV11 . . . . .73 F5
Cregoe St B15. . . . . .86 C8
Cremore Ave B8 . . . . .67 E5
Cremorne Rd B75. . . . . .32 B2
Cremorne Wlk B75 . . . . . . .32 B2
Crendon Cl B80. . . . . .159 E5
Crendon Rd B65 . . . . .63 A6
Crescent Arc 2 B91 . . . . .107 C3
Crescent Ave
Birmingham B18 . . . . .66 B6
Brierley Hill DY5 . . . . .61 C1
Coventry CV3. . . . . .114 C2
Crescent Grange Rd The
DY9 . . . . .81 C4
Crescent Ho B97 . . . . .153 D2
Crescent Ind Pk DY2 . . . .62 B7
Crescent Rd
Darlaston WS10. . . . . .41 D6
Dudley DY2 . . . . .62 B5
Kidderminster DY11 . . . . . .116 C5
Willenhall WV13 . . . . .27 C2
Crescent Sta The WV14. . .40 D6
Crescent The
Bilston WV14 . . . . .40 D6
Birmingham,Coleshill Heath
B37. . . . . .90 E8
Birmingham,Great Barr B43 .44 A1
Birmingham,Hockley B18. . .66 B6
Birmingham,Sparkbrook
B12. . . . . .87 B5
Bromsgrove B60. . . . . .136 F1
Cradley Heath B64 . . . . . . .83 A7
Dudley DY1 . . . . .51 E4
Great Wyrley WS6 . . . . .5 A3
Hampton-in-A B92 . . . . . . .109 B7
Kersley CV7 . . . . .96 A6
Rowley Regis B65 . . . . .63 C2
Solihull,Lode Heath B91 . .107 B4
Solihull,Shirley B90 . . . . . .106 A4
Walsall WS1 . . . . .43 A8
Wednesbury WS10 . . . . . . .42 A4
West Hagley DY9. . . . . .98 F5
Willenhall WS10,WV13 . . . .27 C1
Wolverhampton WV6. . . . . .24 B3
Crescent Twr B1. . . . . .66 C2
Cressage Ave B31. . . . . . . .103 A1
Cressage Rd CV2 . . . . .115 A6
Cressett Ave DY5 . . . . .61 C4
Cressett La DY5. . . . . .61 C4
Cressida Cl CV34 . . . . .161 F3
Cressington Dr B74 . . . . . . .32 A1
Cresswell Cl CV10 . . . . .73 C8
Cresswell Cres WS3. . . . . . .13 F2
Cresswell Ct WV10 . . . . . . .11 A3
Cresswell Gr B24 . . . . .57 D4
Cresswell Ho B24 . . . . .113 B7
Crest The
Birmingham B31 . . . . .123 C7
Royal Leamington Spa
CV32. . . . . .157 D3
Crest View
Birmingham B14 . . . . .105 B4
Sutton Coldfield B74 . . . . . .44 F8
Crestwood Ave DY11 . . . . .116 A5
Crestwood Dr B44 . . . . .55 E7
Crestwood Glen WV6 . . . . .24 E7
Crestwood Park Prim Sch
DY6 . . . . .61 A5
Crestwood Sch The DY6. . .60 F5
Crestwood B77 . . . . .22 A5
Creswell Rd B28. . . . . .106 B7
Creswicke Gr B45 . . . . .122 C7
Crewe Dr CV7 . . . . .52 A2
Crew La CV8. . . . . .148 E6
Crew Rd WS10. . . . . .42 A4
Creynolds Cl B90 . . . . .126 D3
Creynolds La B90 . . . . .126 E4
Cricket Cl
Coventry CV5. . . . . .112 F3
Walsall WS5 . . . . .43 B7
Cricketers Mdw B64 . . . . . .82 F7
Cricket La WS14 . . . . .9 C5
Cricket Mdw
Dudley DY3 . . . . .50 E5
Wolverhampton WV10. . . . .11 D4
Crick La B20. . . . . .66 A8
Cricklewood Dr B62 . . . . . . .83 D3
Crigdon B77 . . . . .22 C1
Crimmond Rise B63. . . . . . .82 E5
Crimscote Cl B90 . . . . .126 F6
Cringlebrook B77. . . . . .21 D1
Cripps Rd WS2 . . . . .27 E3
Crockett's Ave B21. . . . . . . .65 D7
Crockett's Lane Prim Sch
B66. . . . . .65 B5
Crockett's La B66. . . . . .65 A6
Crockett's Rd B21 . . . . .65 D7

Crockett St DY1. . . . . .51 A2
Crockford Dr B75. . . . . .32 B3
Crockford Rd B71. . . . . .42 C1
Crockington La WV5 . . . . . .37 A1
Crocus Cres WV9 . . . . .11 A3
Croft Apartments 2
WV13 . . . . .27 A2
Croft Ave CV2 . . . . .21 B6
Croft Cl
Birmingham B25 . . . . .88 E8
Redditch B98 . . . . .154 D3
Warwick CV34 . . . . .161 C7
Croft Cres WS8 . . . . .15 D7
Croft Ct B36. . . . . .69 B8
Croftdown Rd B17 . . . . .85 A7
Croft Down Rd B92 . . . . . . .89 D4
Crofters Cl DY8. . . . . .81 B4
Crofters Ct B15. . . . . .85 E6
Crofters La B75. . . . . .32 E3
Crofters Wlk WV8. . . . . .10 E1
Croft Fields CV12. . . . . .78 B2
Croft Gdns WS7. . . . . .7 A8
Croft Ho 2 WS1. . . . . .28 F1
Croft Ind Est B37 . . . . .70 D2
Croft Jun Sch CV10 . . . . .72 F3
Croft La WV10 . . . . .26 A7
Croftleigh Gdns B91 . . . . .106 C2
Croft Mews CV12. . . . . .73 A4
Croft Par WS9 . . . . .30 B6
Croft Pool CV12 . . . . .77 F2
Croft Rd
Bedworth CV12 . . . . .77 F2
Birmingham B26 . . . . .88 E8
Coventry CV1. . . . . .165 A2
Leek Wootton CV35. . . . . . .156 A7
Nuneaton CV10 . . . . .72 F3
Crofts La B96. . . . . .158 B2
Crofts The B76. . . . . .58 A8
Croft Street JMI Sch WS2 .28 D3
Croft The
Birmingham B31 . . . . .103 B2
Blakedown DY10 . . . . .98 C2
Bulkington CV12 . . . . .79 B2
Cheslyn Hay WS6. . . . . .4 E2
Coventry CV6. . . . . .95 F4
Dudley DY2 . . . . .61 F6
Kidderminster DY11 . . . . . .116 A4
Meriden CV7 . . . . .92 C1
Sedgley DY3. . . . . .39 E1
Walsall WS5 . . . . .43 E8
Croftway The B20. . . . . .54 E6
Croftwood Dr DY9 . . . . .81 D4
Cromane Sq B43. . . . . .54 E7
Cromarty Cl CV5 . . . . .112 A5
Cromdale Cl CV10 . . . . .72 A3
Cromdale Dr B63. . . . . .82 D3
Cromdale B77 . . . . .22 D1
Crome Rd B43. . . . . .44 D3
Cromer Gdns WV6 . . . . .24 F5
Cromer Rd
Birmingham B12 . . . . .86 F5
Royal Leamington Spa
CV32. . . . . .157 B2
Cromes Wood CV4. . . . . . .111 D1
Crompton Ave B20. . . . . . . .55 C1
Crompton Cl WS2. . . . . .28 A5
Crompton Ct
Codsall WV8 . . . . .10 B4
Warwick CV34 . . . . .160 D6
Crompton Rd
Birmingham,Handsworth
B20. . . . . .55 C1
Birmingham,Nechells B7 . .67 C8
Birmingham,Rubery B45 . .101 D1
Tipton DY4 . . . . .51 D5
Crompton St CV34 . . . . . . .160 D6
Cromwell Cl
Rowley Regis B65 . . . . .63 A5
Walsall WS2 . . . . .5 A1
Cromwell Dr DY2 . . . . .62 F8
Cromwell Jun & Inf Sch
B7. . . . . .67 B6
Cromwell La
Birmingham B31 . . . . .102 E8
Coventry CV4,CV8 . . . . . . .131 C6
Cromwell Rd
Cannock WS12. . . . . .2 E1
Tamworth B79 . . . . .20 E8
Wolverhampton WV10. . . . .11 E4
Cromwells Mdw WS14 . . . . .9 C5
Cromwell St
Birmingham B7 . . . . .67 B6
Coventry CV6. . . . . .113 F6
Dudley DY2 . . . . .62 A8
West Bromwich B71 . . . . . .53 C4
Crondal Pl B15. . . . . .86 B7
Crondal Rd CV7 . . . . .96 B7
Cronehills Jun & Inf Sch
B70. . . . . .53 D4
Cronehills Linkway B70 . . .53 D4
Cronehills St B70. . . . . .53 D4
Crookham Cl B17. . . . . .84 F7
Crookhay La B71 . . . . .53 B8
Crook La
Aldridge WS9 . . . . .30 B1
Birmingham WS9 . . . . .30 B1
Crooks La B80. . . . . .159 D3
Croome Cl
Birmingham B11 . . . . .87 B3
Coventry CV6. . . . . .113 F6
Redditch B98 . . . . .154 F1
Cropredy Rd B81 . . . . .123 B8
Cropthorne Cl B98 . . . . . . .159 B7

Cropthorne Dr B47 . . . . . . .125 B7
Cropthorne Ho B60 . . . . . .137 B3
Cropthorne Rd B90 . . . . . .106 C3
Crosbie Rd
Birmingham B17 . . . . .85 B6
Coventry CV5. . . . . .112 E3
Crosby Cl
Birmingham B1 . . . . .66 B3
Wolverhampton WV6 . . . . . .24 F5
Cross Cheaping CV1 . . . . .165 B3
Cross Cl B64 . . . . .62 F2
Cross Farm Rd B17 . . . . . . .85 D4
Cross Farms La B45 . . . . . .101 F1
Crossfell B77 . . . . .22 B1
Crossfield Rd B33. . . . . .69 A3
Crossfield Rd WS13 . . . . . . .9 E8
Cross Fields Rd 4 CV34 .160 F8
Crossgate Rd
Dudley DY2 . . . . .61 F6
Redditch B98 . . . . .159 C7
Cross Ho WV2 . . . . .39 C7
Crossings Ind Est The 4
WS3. . . . . .28 B8
Crossings The 5 WS14. . . .9 E8
Crosskey Cl B33 . . . . .69 E2
Cross Keys Island WS12 . .2 C3
Cross Keys WV11 . . . . .9 B8
Cross La
Birmingham B43 . . . . .43 E1
Cubbington CV32 . . . . .157 E1
Lichfield WS14. . . . . .9 C6
Crossland Cres WV6 . . . . . .24 F7
Crossland Row LE10 . . . . . .76 A6
Cross La DY3 . . . . .39 E1
Crossley Ct CV3 . . . . .113 F7
Crossley Ret Pk DY11 . . .116 D6
Crossley St DY2. . . . . .62 D4
Crossley Wlk B60 . . . . .150 E7
Cross Pl DY3 . . . . .39 E1
Cross Point Bsns Pk CV2 115 B8
Cross Rd
4 Royal Leamington Spa
CV32. . . . . .156 D1
Coventry CV6. . . . . .113 F8
Keresley CV7 . . . . .94 F6
Cross Road Ind Est CV6 .113 F7
Cross St N WV1. . . . . .25 D4
Cross St S WV2. . . . . .39 C7
Cross St
1 Warwick CV34 . . . . .160 F7
2 Willenhall WV13 . . . . . . .27 A1
4 Rowley Regis B65 . . . . . .63 C1
5 Stourbridge,Wordsley
DY6. . . . . .60 D3
Bilston WV14 . . . . .40 F2
Birmingham B21 . . . . .66 C8
Burntwood WS7. . . . . .6 E8
Cannock,Bridgtown WS11 . .4 E5
Cannock WS12. . . . . .2 E1
Cheslyn Hay WS6. . . . . .4 D2
Coventry CV1. . . . . .165 C4
Dudley DY1 . . . . .51 C1
Halesowen B63. . . . . .83 A3
Kingswinford DY6 . . . . .60 D6
Kingswinford,Wall Heath
DY6. . . . . .60 B8
Nuneaton CV10 . . . . .72 D3
Oldbury B68. . . . . .64 A4
Royal Leamington Spa
CV32. . . . . .157 A1
Smethwick B66 . . . . .65 A6
Stourbridge DY8 . . . . .80 E5
Tamworth B79 . . . . .21 B5
Tamworth,Kettlebrook B77 .21 C3
Walsall WS3 . . . . .15 A1
Wednesbury WS10 . . . . . . .41 E3
Wolverhampton WV1. . . . . .25 F1
Cross The
Kingswinford DY6 . . . . .60 D6
Stourbridge DY9 . . . . .81 E6
Crossway La B44. . . . . .55 F6
Crossway Rd CV3 . . . . .133 B4
Crossways Ct B44. . . . . .56 B7
Crossways Gn B44. . . . . . . .56 B7
Crossways WS10 . . . . .41 D6
Crossways Sh Ctr WV10 . . .26 A3
Crossways The B68 . . . . . . .64 B5
Cross Wlk B69 . . . . .63 C8
Cross Wlks DY9. . . . . .81 E5
Crowberry Cl WS8 . . . . .15 D6
Crowberry La B78 . . . . .48 C8
Crowden Rd B71 . . . . .42 A1
Crowesbridge Mews
WV14 . . . . .51 B8
Crowhall Rd CV11. . . . . .74 A1
Crowhurst Rd B31. . . . . . . .122 E7
Crowland Ave WV6. . . . . . . .23 E4
Crowle Dr DY9. . . . . .81 C5
Crowmere Rd CV2 . . . . . . .114 F7
Crown Cl
Bromsgrove B61. . . . . .136 F2
Rowley Regis B65 . . . . .63 C4
Sedgley DY3. . . . . .39 D1
Crown Ct
10 Hinckley LE10. . . . . . . .71 D1
1 Sutton Coldfield B74 . . . .31 C3
Darlaston WS10. . . . . .41 C8
Crown Ctr The 3 DY8. . . . .81 A5
Crown Gn CV6. . . . . .95 C2
Crownhill Mdw B61. . . . . . .136 F3
Crownhill Rd LE10 . . . . .75 D4
Crown Ho
Coventry CV5. . . . . .112 E3

Crown La
Iverley DY8 . . . . .98 C7
Kidderminster DY10 . . . .116 E6
Stourbridge DY8 . . . . .80 F5
Sutton Coldfield B74 . . . . . .31 E3
Crown Mdw B48 . . . . .139 A7
Crownmeadow Dr DY4 . . .52 D7
Crown Rd
Birmingham,Bordesley Green
B9 . . . . .67 D2
Birmingham,King's Norton
B30 . . . . .104 A4
Crown St WV1 . . . . .25 D4
Crown Terr CV31 . . . . .161 F7
Crown Way CV32 . . . . .157 B3
Crown Wharf Sh Pk WS2 . .28 D2
Crown Wlk DY4 . . . . .52 A2
Crows Nest Cl B76 . . . . . . .46 F3
Crowther Gdns B63 . . . . . .82 C7
Crowther Gr WV6 . . . . .24 F4
Crowther Rd
Birmingham B23 . . . . .56 D5
Wolverhampton WV6 . . . . .24 F5
Crowther St
Kidderminster DY11 . . . . .116 C6
Wolverhampton WV10 . . . .25 E4
Croxall Way B66 . . . . .65 B5
Croxdene Ave WS3 . . . . . . .14 A1
Croxhall St CV12 . . . . .78 C3
Croxley Dr WS12 . . . . .2 C3
Croxley Gdns WV13 . . . . . . .40 F8
Croxstalls Ave WS3 . . . . . . .28 A8
Croxstalls Cl WS3 . . . . .14 A1
Croxstalls Pl WS3 . . . . .28 A8
Croxstalls Rd WS3 . . . . .28 A8
Croxton Gr B33 . . . . .69 A4
Croyde Ave B42 . . . . .55 A8
Croydon Cl CV3 . . . . .133 E6
Croydon Ct **20** B29 . . . . .103 C7
Croydon Rd
Birmingham B29 . . . . .85 F3
Birmingham,Erdington B24 . .57 A2
Croy Dr B35 . . . . .58 B4
Crucible The WV14 . . . . . . .40 B6
Crummock Cl CV4 . . . . .95 D3
Crumpfields La B97 . . . . . .152 F1
Crump Ho WS1 . . . . .28 F1
Crusader Cl B69 . . . . .63 E5
Crutchley Ave B78 . . . . .21 A2
Crutchley Way CV31 . . . . .162 A2
Crychan Cl B45 . . . . .102 B2
Cryersoak Cl B90 . . . . .127 B7
Cryfield Grange Rd CV4,
CV8 . . . . .132 C2
Cryfield Hts CV4 . . . . .132 D2
Cryfield Village CV4 . . . . .132 B4
Crystal Ave DY8 . . . . .60 F1
Crystal Dr B66 . . . . .64 C8
Crystal Ho B66 . . . . .65 C6
Cubbington CE Prim Sch
CV32 . . . . .157 F5
Cubbington Rd
Coventry CV6 . . . . .96 A2
Royal Leamington Spa
CV32 . . . . .157 B3
Cubley Rd B28 . . . . .87 E1
Cuckoo Cl WS11 . . . . .2 C2
Cuckoo La CV1 . . . . .165 C3
Cuckoo Rd B7 . . . . .67 D8
Cue La B66 . . . . .65 C5
Culey Gr B33 . . . . .69 D2
Culford Dr B32 . . . . .102 C8
Culham C B27 . . . . .88 D2
Cullwick St WV1 . . . . .40 A8
Culmington Rd B31 . . . . . .122 F8
Culmore Cl WV12 . . . . .27 D4
Culmore Rd B62 . . . . .63 E1
Culpepper Cl CV10 . . . . . . .72 E4
Culverhouse Dr DY5 . . . . . .61 A1
Culverley Cres B93 . . . . . .127 F6
Culvert Way B66 . . . . .64 D7
Culwell Ind Pk WV10 . . . .163 D4
Culwell St WV10 . . . . .163 C4
Culwell Trad Est WV10 . . .25 F4
Culworth Cl CV31 . . . . .161 F5
Culworth Ct
Coventry CV6 . . . . .113 E7
Whitnash CV31 . . . . .162 A5
Culworth Row CV6 . . . . . .113 E8
Cumberford Ave B33 . . . . . .69 E1
Cumberland Ave **3** B5 . . .86 E7
Cumberland Cl DY6 . . . . . . .60 E4
Cumberland Cres
Burntwood WS7 . . . . .7 A8
Royal Leamington Spa
CV32 . . . . .157 C3
Cumberland Dr
Nuneaton CV10 . . . . .72 E3
Tamworth B78 . . . . .21 A1
Cumberland Ho **7** WV3 . .25 C4
Cumberland Rd
Bilston WV14 . . . . .40 D7
Birmingham B68 . . . . .84 B7
Cannock WS11 . . . . .1 C5
West Bromwich B71 . . . . . . .53 D7
Willenhall WV13 . . . . .27 D2
Cumberland St B1 . . . . .66 B2
Cumberland Wlk B75 . . . . .47 B4
Cumbernauld Wlk **7**
CV2 . . . . .115 A7
Cumbrae Dr LE10 . . . . .71 B2
Cumbria Cl CV1 . . . . .113 A3
Cumbrian Croft B63 . . . . . .82 D2

Cumbria Way B8 . . . . .67 D6
Cumming St **14** CV31 . . .162 A7
Cundall Cl CV31 . . . . .162 B6
Cunnery The CV8 . . . . .149 A3
Cunningham Rd
Perton WV6 . . . . .23 E4
Walsall WS2 . . . . .27 E2
Cupfields Ave DY4 . . . . .52 C8
Cupfields Cres DY4 . . . . . . .52 C7
Curbar Rd B42 . . . . .55 C6
Curborough Rd WS13 . . . . . .3 B2
Curdale Rd B32 . . . . .102 B8
Curdworth La B76 . . . . .59 A8
Curdworth Prim Sch B76 . .59 C6
Cur La B97 . . . . .152 D3
Curlew Cl
Kidderminster DY10 . . . . .117 B2
Lichfield WS14 . . . . .9 E7
Curlew Dr WS8 . . . . .15 E7
Curlew Hill WS11 . . . . .2 A3
Curlews Cl B23 . . . . .56 C8
Curlew B77 . . . . .36 A7
Curlieu Cl CV35 . . . . .160 A7
Curral Rd B65 . . . . .63 C3
Curran Cl CV31 . . . . .162 B6
Curriers Cl CV4 . . . . .131 D7
Curslow La DY10 . . . . .117 F1
Curtin Dr WS10 . . . . .41 B4
Curtis Cl
Finstall B60 . . . . .151 F8
Smethwick B66 . . . . .65 C4
Curtis Rd CV2 . . . . .114 D6
Curzon Ave CV6 . . . . .113 E8
Curzon Cl LE10 . . . . .75 F7
Curzon Gr CV31 . . . . .162 C6
Curzon St
Birmingham B4 . . . . .67 A3
Wolverhampton WV2 . . . . . .39 D7
Cuthbert Rd B18 . . . . .65 E4
Cutlers Rough Cl B31 . . . .102 F5
Cutler St B66 . . . . .65 B6
Cutsdean Cl B31 . . . . .102 F6
Cutshill Cl B36 . . . . .69 C8
Cut Throat La B94 . . . . . . .142 D7
Cutting The WS4 . . . . .28 F4
Cuttle Mill La B76 . . . . .48 D3
Cuttle Pool La B93 . . . . . .128 F4
Cutworth Cl B76 . . . . .47 A3
Cwerne Ct DY3 . . . . .50 E6
Cygnet Cl
Alvechurch B48 . . . . .139 A7
Cannock WS12 . . . . .2 C7
Wolverhampton WV6 . . . . . .24 C2
Cygnet Ct
Coventry CV1 . . . . .165 C4
Kidderminster DY10 . . . . .117 A1
Cygnet Dr
Brownhills WS8 . . . . .15 E7
Tamworth B79 . . . . .20 F5
Cygnet Gr B23 . . . . .56 B6
Cygnet La DY5 . . . . .61 C7
Cygnet Rd B70 . . . . .53 A5
Cygnus Way B70 . . . . .52 F5
Cymbeline Way CV34 . . . .161 E4
Cypress Ave DY3 . . . . .50 D5
Cypress Croft CV3 . . . . . . .134 F8
Cypress Ct DY10 . . . . .117 A4
Cypress Gdns
Kingswinford DY6 . . . . .60 C8
Sutton Coldfield B74 . . . . . .46 A7
Walsall WS5 . . . . .43 C4
Cypress Gr B31 . . . . .102 E1
Cypress La CV31 . . . . .162 B3
Cypress Rd
Dudley DY2 . . . . .51 F1
Walsall WS5 . . . . .43 C4
Cypress Sq **2** B27 . . . . . .88 C5
Cypress Way
Birmingham B31 . . . . .122 F8
Nuneaton CV10 . . . . .72 D6
Cyprus Ave B96 . . . . .158 D2
Cyprus Cl B29 . . . . .103 A7
Cyprus St
Oldbury B69 . . . . .64 A8
Wolverhampton WV2 . . . . . .39 C6
Cyril Gr **5** B10 . . . . .87 C8
Cyril Rd B10 . . . . .87 D8

D

Dacer Cl B30 . . . . .104 B5
Dace Rd WV10 . . . . .26 B4
Dace B77 . . . . .35 D7
Dadford View DY5 . . . . .61 B2
Dad's La B13 . . . . .86 C1
Daffern Rd CV7 . . . . .78 A1
Daffodil Cl DY3 . . . . .50 E7
Daffodil Dr **4** CV12 . . . . . .77 D2
Daffodil Pl WS5 . . . . .43 D8
Daffodil Rd WS5 . . . . .43 D8
Daffodil Way B31 . . . . .122 E8
Dagger La B71 . . . . .53 E4
Dagnall Rd B27 . . . . .88 D3
Dagnell End Rd B98 . . . . .154 B7
Dagtail La B97 . . . . .158 D3
Dahlia Cl
Hinckley LE10 . . . . .75 E6
Wolverhampton WV1 . . . . . .26 C1
Dahlia Wlk CV10 . . . . .78 A8
Daimler Cl B36 . . . . .58 F1
Daimler Rd
Birmingham B14 . . . . .105 D3
Coventry CV6 . . . . .113 C5
Dainton Gr B32 . . . . .84 C1
Daintree Croft CV3 . . . . . .133 C7
Daintry Dr B78 . . . . .20 B7
Dairy Cl DY4 . . . . .52 B5

Dairy Ct B68 . . . . .84 D7
Dairy La B97 . . . . .153 A5
Daisy Bank WS12 . . . . .1 F8
Daisy Bank Cl WS3 . . . . . . .15 B2
Daisy Bank Cres WS5 . . . . .43 D8
Daisy Croft CV12 . . . . .77 D2
Daisy Dr B23 . . . . .56 A5
Daisy Farm Rd B14 . . . . . .105 B3
Daisy Mdw DY4 . . . . .52 C6
Daisy Rd B16 . . . . .65 F2
Daisy St
Dudley WV14 . . . . .40 D2
Wolverhampton WV6 . . . . . .25 A4
Daisy Walk WV9 . . . . .11 A3
Dakota Apartments B16 . .66 B1
Dalbeg Cl WV8 . . . . .24 E8
Dalbury Rd B28 . . . . .105 E5
Dalby Cl CV3 . . . . .134 E8
Dalby Rd WS3 . . . . .28 F6
Dale Cl
Birmingham B43 . . . . .43 D1
Catshill B61 . . . . .136 F7
Smethwick B66 . . . . .65 A4
Tipton DY4 . . . . .52 D5
Warwick CV34 . . . . .161 A8
Dalecote Ave B92 . . . . .107 E8
Dale Ct WV1 . . . . .25 A3
Dale Dr WS7 . . . . .7 B7
Dale End B4 . . . . .164 C3
Dale End Cl LE10 . . . . .75 A7
Dale End
Darlaston WS10 . . . . .41 D6
Nuneaton CV10 . . . . .72 E5
Dale Hill B60 . . . . .137 D4
Dalehouse Flats CV8 . . . .148 B6
Dalehouse La CV8 . . . . . . .148 D7
Dale Meadow Cl CV7 . . . .130 B6
Dale Rd
Birmingham B29 . . . . .85 E3
Halesowen B62 . . . . .83 F8
Redditch B98 . . . . .153 F5
Stourbridge DY8 . . . . .80 F2
Dales Cl WV6 . . . . .25 A5
Dales Com Jun Sch B77 . . .36 B8
Dales Inf Sch The B77 . . . .36 B8
Dalesman Cl DY6 . . . . .60 B7
Dale St
Bilston WV14 . . . . .41 A5
Royal Leamington Spa
CV32 . . . . .161 E8
Smethwick B66 . . . . .65 A3
Walsall WS1 . . . . .42 E7
Wednesbury WS10 . . . . . . .41 E3
Wolverhampton WV3 . . . . . .163 A3
Daleswood Pk B62 . . . . . .100 F2
Dale Terr B69 . . . . .63 C8
Daleview Rd B14 . . . . .105 C4
Daleway Rd CV3 . . . . .133 B4
Dale Wlk B25 . . . . .88 B7
Dalewood Croft B26 . . . . . .89 A5
Dalewood Rd B37 . . . . .69 F5
Daley Cl B1 . . . . .66 B3
Daley Rd WV14 . . . . .40 F2
Dalkeith Rd B73 . . . . .45 E2
Dalkeith St WS2 . . . . .28 C3
Dallas Rd B23 . . . . .56 D5
Dallimore Cl B92 . . . . .89 A3
Dallington Rd CV6 . . . . . . .112 E6
Dalloway Cl B5 . . . . .86 D6
Dalmahoy Cl CV11 . . . . .79 C8
Dalmeny Rd CV4 . . . . .131 D7
Dalston Cl DY2 . . . . .62 D6
Dalston Rd B27 . . . . .88 C4
Dalton Ct B23 . . . . .56 B3
Dalton Gdns CV2 . . . . .114 F4
Dalton Rd
Bedworth CV12 . . . . .78 A2
Coventry CV5 . . . . .113 A1
Walsall WS2 . . . . .28 A3
Dalton St
Birmingham B4 . . . . .164 C3
Wolverhampton WV3 . . . . . .39 B8
Dalton Way B4 . . . . .164 C3
Dalvine Rd DY2 . . . . .62 B2
Dalwood Cl WV14 . . . . .51 B7
Dalwood Way CV6 . . . . .96 B4
Damar Croft B14 . . . . .104 D4
Dama Rd B78 . . . . .34 F8
Dame Agnes Gr CV6 . . . . .114 B8
Dame Elizabeth Cadbury
Tech Coll B30 . . . . .103 D7
Dame Ellen Pinsent Sch
B13 . . . . .105 D8
Damien Cl B67 . . . . .64 F5
Damson Cl
Redditch B97 . . . . .158 C6
Wednesfield WV12 . . . . . . .27 A6
Damson Ct LE10 . . . . .75 B7
Damson La B91,B92 . . . . .107 C7
Damson Parkway B91,
B92 . . . . .107 C7
Damson Wharf DY4 . . . . . . .52 A3
Damson Wood Inf Sch
B92 . . . . .107 D7
Dam St WS13 . . . . .9 B8
Danbury Cl B76 . . . . .47 A2
Danbury Gdns CV10 . . . . . .11 C2
Danbury Rd B90 . . . . .106 B2
Danby Gr B24 . . . . .57 B2
Dando Rd DY2 . . . . .62 D8
Dandy Bank Rd DY6 . . . . . .61 A8
Dandy's Wlk WS1 . . . . .42 F8
Dane Gr B13 . . . . .104 E7
Danehill Wlk WV8 . . . . .24 F8
Danehurst Ctr WV1 . . . . . . .26 A3
Danelagh Cl B79 . . . . .20 F7
Dane Rd CV2 . . . . .114 B4

Danesbury Cres
Birmingham B44 . . . . .56 A8
Royal Leamington Spa
CV31 . . . . .162 D6
Danes Cl WV11 . . . . .12 F4
Danescourt Rd WV6 . . . . . .24 C6
Danesmoor Ho B26 . . . . . .88 E7
Danesmore Park Jun & Inf
Sch WV11 . . . . .13 A1
Daneswood Dr WS9 . . . . . .15 F3
Daneswood Rd CV3 . . . . . .135 E7
Dane Terr B65 . . . . .63 C5
Daneways Ct B74 . . . . .45 A8
Danford Cl DY8 . . . . .81 A4
Danford Gdns B10 . . . . .87 C8
Danford La B91 . . . . .106 E3
Danford Rd B47 . . . . .124 F6
Danford Way B43 . . . . .54 D8
Dangerfield Ho B70 . . . . . . .53 E1
Dangerfield La WS10 . . . . . .41 C4
Daniel Ave CV10 . . . . .72 C3
Daniels La WS9 . . . . .30 C5
Daniels Rd B9 . . . . .68 A2
Danilo Rd WS11 . . . . .1 D1
Danks St DY4 . . . . .52 A2
Danzey Cl B98 . . . . .159 B5
Danzey Gr B14 . . . . .104 C2
Danzey Green La B94 . . . .142 B1
Danzey Green Rd B36 . . . . .58 B1
Daphne Cl CV2 . . . . .96 C3
Darby Cl WV14 . . . . .40 B2
Darby End Rd DY2 . . . . .62 E4
Darby Ho **2** WS2 . . . . .42 C7
Darby Rd
Oldbury B68 . . . . .64 C5
Wednesbury WS10 . . . . . . .42 B4
Darbys Hill Rd B69 . . . . . . .63 B7
Darby St B65 . . . . .63 C1
Darbys Way DY4 . . . . .52 B5
Darcel Croft B76 . . . . .46 E3
Daren Cl B36 . . . . .69 F8
Dare Rd B23 . . . . .56 E4
Dare's Wlk LE10 . . . . .71 D1
Darfield Wlk **2** B12 . . . . . .86 F8
Darges La WS6 . . . . .4 F4
Darkhouse La WV14 . . . . . .40 C2
Dark La
Astwood Bank B96 . . . . . .158 D1
Bedworth CV12 . . . . .77 D1
Belbroughton DY9 . . . . . . .119 F8
Birchmoor B78 . . . . .36 E8
Brinsford WV10 . . . . .11 D8
Coventry CV1 . . . . .165 B4
Featherstone WV10 . . . . . . .12 D7
Great Wyrley WS6 . . . . .5 C1
Heywood B38,B47 . . . . . .124 E7
Romsley B62 . . . . .100 F4
Stoke Heath B60 . . . . .150 D6
Darlaston Com Science Coll
WS10 . . . . .41 B6
Darlaston Ct CV7 . . . . .92 D1
Darlaston La WV14 . . . . . . .41 A7
Darlaston Rd
Walsall WS2 . . . . .42 A8
Wednesbury WS10 . . . . . . .41 C6
Darlaston Road Ind Est
WS10 . . . . .41 D5
Darley Ave B34 . . . . .68 F6
Darleydale Ave B44 . . . . . . .44 E1
Darley Dr WV6 . . . . .25 B5
Darley Green Rd B93 . . . .128 B1
Darley Ho B69 . . . . .63 D6
Darley Mead Ct B91 . . . . .107 E4
Darley Rd LE10 . . . . .75 E6
Darley Way B74 . . . . .45 A7
Darlington St
Darlaston WS10 . . . . .41 D5
Wolverhampton WV1 . . . . .163 B3
Darlington Yd WV1 . . . . . .163 B3
Darlston Row CV7 . . . . .92 B1
Darnbrook B77 . . . . .22 C1
Darnel Croft **3** B10 . . . . . .67 B1
Darnel Hurst Rd B75 . . . . . .32 D3
Darnford Cl
Birmingham B28 . . . . .106 A5
Coventry CV2 . . . . .114 F7
Sutton Coldfield B72 . . . . . .57 D7
Darnford La WS14 . . . . .9 F6
Darnford Moors WS14 . . . . .9 E6
Darnford View WS13 . . . . . .3 E1
Darnick Rd B73 . . . . .45 D2
Darnley Rd **3** B16 . . . . . . .66 A2
Darrach Cl CV2 . . . . .96 E1
Darris Rd B29 . . . . .104 A8
Dart Cl LE10 . . . . .75 A8
Dartford Rd WS3 . . . . .13 F1
Dartington Way CV11 . . . . .78 F8
Dartmoor Cl B45 . . . . .102 A2
Dartmouth Ave
Cannock WS11 . . . . .4 C8
Stourbridge DY8 . . . . .60 D3
Walsall WS3 . . . . .28 E6
Willenhall WV13 . . . . .27 A2
Dartmouth Cir B6 . . . . .66 F5
Dartmouth Cl WS3 . . . . .28 E5
Dartmouth Cres **2** WV14 .41 A7
Dartmouth Dr WS9 . . . . .30 A5
Dartmouth High Sch B43 . .43 D3
Dartmouth Ho WS13 . . . . . . .3 B1
Dartmouth Middleway B7 .66 F4
Dartmouth Pl WS3 . . . . .28 F6
Dartmouth Rd
Birmingham B29 . . . . .85 F2
Cannock WS11 . . . . .1 D1
Coventry CV2 . . . . .114 C5
Smethwick B66 . . . . .64 F8
Dartmouth Sch CV2 . . . . .114 D5
Dartmouth Sq B70 . . . . .53 D2

Dartmouth Street Sta B70 .53 B3
Dartmouth St
West Bromwich B70 . . . . . . .53 B3
Wolverhampton WV2 . . . . .163 C1
Wolverhampton WV2 . . . . .163 D1
Dart St B9 . . . . .67 B1
Dart B77 . . . . .36 A5
Darvel Mews WV12 . . . . . . .27 C4
Darvel Rd WV12 . . . . .27 D4
Darwall St WS1 . . . . .28 E2
Darwell Pk B77 . . . . .22 B2
Darwin Cl
Burntwood WS7 . . . . .7 B7
Cannock WS12 . . . . .2 E2
Coventry CV2 . . . . .115 A6
Hinckley LE10 . . . . .71 E3
Lichfield WS13 . . . . .9 A8
Darwin Ct
1 Bedworth CV12 . . . . . .78 A2
Perton WV6 . . . . .23 E4
Darwin Ho
3 Birmingham,Chelmsley
Wood B37 . . . . .70 C1
3 Birmingham,Showell Green
B13 .87 A2
Kingswinford DY6 . . . . .60 F7
Darwin Pl WS2 . . . . .28 B6
Darwin Rd WS2 . . . . .28 B6
Darwin St B12 . . . . .86 F8
Dassett Gr B9 . . . . .68 A2
Dassett Rd B93 . . . . .127 F4
Datchet Cl CV5 . . . . .112 C4
Datteln Rd WS11 . . . . .2 A4
D'aubeny Rd CV4 . . . . .132 C8
Dauntsey Covert B14 . . . .104 D2
Davena Dr B29 . . . . .84 E2
Davena Gr WV14 . . . . .40 D3
Davenham Rd B60 . . . . . . .137 C1
Davenport Dr
Birmingham B35 . . . . .58 C3
Bromsgrove B60 . . . . .137 B1
Davenport Lodge Sch
CV5 . . . . .133 B8
Davenport Rd
Coventry CV5 . . . . .133 B8
Wednesfield WV11 . . . . . . .26 E6
Daventry Gr B32 . . . . .84 D5
Daventry Rd CV3 . . . . .133 D7
Davey Rd
Birmingham B20 . . . . .55 E1
West Bromwich B70 . . . . . . .53 A5
David Cox Ct **1** B17 . . . . .85 D5
David Harman Dr B71 . . . . .53 F7
David Peacock Cl CV4 . . . .52 A5
David Rd
Bedworth CV12 . . . . .95 F8
Birmingham B20 . . . . .55 B2
Coventry CV1 . . . . .113 F2
Tipton DY4 . . . . .52 A7
Davidson Ave CV31 . . . . . .162 A7
Davidson Rd WS14 . . . . .9 B7
Davids The B31 . . . . .103 C5
Davies Ave WV14 . . . . .40 D3
Davies Ho
7 Oldbury B69 . . . . .64 A7
Walsall WS3 . . . . .14 B1
Davies Rd CV7 . . . . .95 F7
Davis Ave DY4 . . . . .51 E4
Davis Cl CV32 . . . . .156 D2
Davis Gr B25 . . . . .88 D6
Davison Rd B67 . . . . .64 F3
Davis Rd
Tamworth B77 . . . . .21 F4
Willenhall WV12 . . . . .27 D8
Davy Rd WS2 . . . . .28 A5
Dawberry Cl B14 . . . . .104 D5
Dawberry Fields Rd B14 . .104 D5
Dawberry Rd B14 . . . . .104 C6
Daw End La WS4 . . . . .29 C6
Daw End WS4,WS9 . . . . . . .29 C6
Dawes Ave B70 . . . . .53 C1
Dawes Cl CV2 . . . . .114 A3
Dawes La WS8 . . . . .7 A1
Dawlish Cl CV11 . . . . .73 E5
Dawlish Cl CV3 . . . . .133 D5
Dawlish Rd
Birmingham B29 . . . . .85 F2
Dudley DY1 . . . . .51 C5
Smethwick B66 . . . . .65 B5
Dawn Dr DY4 . . . . .41 C2
Dawney Dr B75 . . . . .32 A4
Dawn Rd B31 . . . . .102 E6
Dawson Ave WV14 . . . . .39 F2
Dawson Cl CV31 . . . . .162 A2
Dawson Cl B24 . . . . .56 F4
Dawson Rd
Birmingham B21 . . . . .65 F8
Bromsgrove B61 . . . . .136 E2
Coventry CV3 . . . . .114 A1
Dawson Sq WV14 . . . . .40 C5
Dawson St
Smethwick B66 . . . . .65 A3
Walsall WS3 . . . . .28 D8
Day Ave WV11 . . . . .26 E7
Daybrook Cl B97 . . . . .153 B5

Day Ho DY4 . . . . .52 C8
Dayhouse Bank B62. . . . .101 B1
Daylesford Inf Sch B92. . . .89 A3
Daylesford Rd B92. . . . . . .89 A3
Days Cl CV1 . . . . .113 E3
Day's La CV1 . . . . .113 F3
Day St WS2. . . . . .28 E3
Daytona Dr CV5 . . . . . . .111 B8
Deacon St CV11 . . . . .73 C3
Deakin Rd
  Birmingham B24 . . . . . .57 A3
  Sutton Coldfield B75 . . . .46 E7
Deakins Rd B25 . . . . .88 B7
Deal Ave WS7 . . . . .7 A8
Deal Dr B69 . . . . .52 A1
Deal Gr B31 . . . . .103 A3
Deanbrook Cl B90. . . . . .127 A6
Dean Cl
  Brierley Hill WS5 . . . . . .61 D2
  Perton WV6. . . . . .23 E6
Deanery CE Prim Sch The
  B76. . . . . .57 F8
Deanery Row WV1. . . . . .163 B4
Dean Rd
  Birmingham B23 . . . . . .56 F5
  Hinckley LE10 . . . . .71 E2
  Walsall WS4 . . . . .29 C7
Dean Rd W LE10 . . . . . . .71 E2
Deans Cl B98. . . . . .154 D5
Deanscroft Dr B60 . . . . .137 C6
Deans Croft WS14 . . . . . . .9 C8
Deansfield High Sch WV1. .26 C2
Deansfield Rd WV1. . . . . .26 A2
Dansford La DY10. . . . . .118 B6
Deans Pl WS3 . . . . .28 F6
Dean's Rd WV1 . . . . .26 B2
Deans Slade Dr WS14 . . . .9 A5
Dean St
  Birmingham B5 . . . . . . .164 C1
  Coventry CV2 . . . . .114 A3
Deanston Croft CV2. . . . . .96 F1
Dean St DY3. . . . . .50 D8
Deansway B61. . . . . . . .136 E2
Deans Way CV7. . . . . . . .95 D6
Deansway Ho DY10 . . . .117 A7
Deansway The DY10. . . .117 A7
Deansway CV34. . . . . . .155 E1
Dearman Rd B11. . . . . . .87 B7
Dearmont Rd B31. . . . . .122 E7
Dearne Ct DY3. . . . . .51 A6
Deasy Ho CV3 . . . . .134 B5
Deasy Rd CV1 . . . . .165 C1
Deavall Way WS11 . . . . . . .2 B2
Debden Cl B93. . . . . . . .127 E2
Debenham Cres B25 . . . .68 D1
Debenham Rd B25. . . . . .68 D1
Deblen Dr B16 . . . . .65 D1
Deborah Cl WV14 . . . . . .51 A7
De-Compton Cl CV7 . . . .95 A7
Deedmore Rd CV2 . . . . . .96 D1
Deedmore Sch CV2 . . . .114 C8
Deegan Cl CV2 . . . . . . .114 A5
Dee Gr
  Birmingham B38 . . . . . .123 E8
  Cannock WS11. . . . . .4 D8
De Ho DY1 . . . . .61 E8
Deelands Rd B45. . . . . . .121 F8
Deeley Cl
  Birmingham B15. . . . . . .86 C7
  Cradley Heath B64. . . . . .82 E7
Deeley Dr DY4 . . . . . . .52 C6
Deeley Pl WS3 . . . . .28 B8
Deeley St
  Brierley Hill DY5 . . . . . .61 E1
  Walsall WS3 . . . . .28 B8
Deeley B77 . . . . .22 A3
Deepdale Ave B26. . . . . .89 A4
Deepdale La DY3 . . . . . .50 E3
Deepdale B77. . . . . .22 D2
Deeplow Cl DY4 . . . . . .46 C4
Deepmoor Rd B33. . . . . .68 F3
Deepmore Ave WS2. . . . .28 B2
Deepwood Cl WS4 . . . . .29 D8
Deepwood Gr B32 . . . . .102 B8
Deer Barn Hill B98. . . . .154 A1
Deer Cl
  Huntington WS12. . . . . . .1 C6
  Norton Canes WS11 . . . . .6 B7
  Walsall WS3 . . . . .14 C3
Deerdale Terr CV3 . . . .134 F8
Deerdale Way CV3 . . . . .134 F8
Dee Rd WS3 . . . . .14 E1
Deerfold Cres WS7. . . . . . .7 B7
Deerham Cl B23 . . . . . . .56 C6
Deerhill B77. . . . . .22 C1
Deerhurst Cl B98 . . . . . .154 C7
Deerhurst Ct B91. . . . . .107 D4
Deerhurst Rd
  Birmingham B20 . . . . . .54 F5
  Coventry CV6. . . . . .95 B2
Deerhurst Rise WS12 . . . . .2 F6
Deer Leap The CV8 . . . .148 B6
Deerpark Dr CV34. . . . . .160 E8
Deer Park Rd B78 . . . . . .20 E1
Deer Park Way B91 . . . .107 C1
Deer Wlk WV8. . . . . .10 F3
Deer Wlk
  Birmingham B36 . . . . . .70 A7
  Birmingham B36 . . . . . .70 A8
Defford Ave WS4 . . . . . .15 D1
Defford Cl B97 . . . . . . .152 E1
Defford Dr B68. . . . . . . .64 B4

Dehavilland Cl CV11 . . . .73 B5
De Havilland Dr B35 . . . .58 A2
De Havilland Way LE10. .75 E4
Deighton Gr CV3. . . . . . .134 C6
Deighton Rd WS5. . . . . . .43 B4
De-La-Bere Cres LE10 . . .76 A6
Delage Cl CV6. . . . . .96 B4
Delamere Cl B36 . . . . . .58 D1
Delamere St WS5. . . . . . .43 C3
Delamere Rd
  Bedworth CV12 . . . . . . .77 F2
  Birmingham B28 . . . . . .105 F7
  Willenhall WV12 . . . . . . .27 C7
Delamere Way CV32 . . . .157 C4
Delancey Keep B75. . . . . .47 A5
Delaware Rd CV3 . . . . . .133 C5
Delf Ho CV2 . . . . .96 D1
Delhi Ave CV6 . . . . .95 D1
Delhurst Ave WV4 . . . . . .39 E3
Delhurst Rd B44 . . . . . . .44 D1
Delingpole Wlk B44. . . .82 E8
Delius St CV4. . . . . .111 E3
Della Dr B32 . . . . .102 D8
Dell Cl CV3. . . . . .134 C5
Dell Farm Cl B93 . . . . . .128 B6
Dellow Gr B48. . . . . .139 A5
Dellows Cl B38 . . . . . . .123 D7
Dell Rd
  Birmingham B30 . . . . . .104 A5
  Brierley Hill DY5 . . . . . .61 B5
Dells Farm B47 . . . . . . .124 F6
Dell The
  Birmingham,Edgbaston
  B5. . . . . .65 F2
  Birmingham,Shenley Fields
  B31. . . . . .102 D6
  Cannock WS12. . . . . .2 D4
  Lichfield WS13. . . . . .8 F7
  Solihull B92. . . . . .89 A1
  Stourbridge DY8 . . . . . . .80 E6
  Tamworth B79 . . . . .21 B6
Dellway The DY8. . . . . . .80 E5
Delmore Way B76 . . . . . .58 B6
Delph Dr DY5. . . . . .81 E7
Delphinium Cl B9. . . . . . .67 F3
Delph La DY5 . . . . .61 D6
Delphi Cl CV34 . . . . . . .161 E4
Delph Rd DY5 . . . . .61 D1
Delph Road Ind Est DY5. .61 C1
Delrene Rd B90. . . . . . . .105 F3
Delta Trad Est WV2 . . . . .39 F8
Delta Way WS11 . . . . .4 D7
Deltic B77. . . . . .35 F8
Deltic B77. . . . . .22 A1
Delves Cres
  Walsall WS5 . . . . .43 A5
  Wood End CV9. . . . . . . .36 C1
Delves Green Rd WS5. . . .43 A5
Delves Inf Sch WS5 . . . . .43 A5
Delves Jun Sch WS5. . . . .43 A5
Delves Rd WS1 . . . . .42 F7
Delville Cl WS10 . . . . . . .41 F4
Delville Rd WS10 . . . . . . .41 F4
Delville Terr WS10 . . . . . .41 F3
De Marnham Ct B70 . . . .53 E1
De Montfort Ho B37. . . . .69 F5
De Montfort Rd
  Hinckley LE10 . . . . .71 E1
  Kenilworth CV8 . . . . . . .147 E6
De Montfort Way CV4. . .132 D5
De Moram Gr B92. . . . . .107 F2
Dempster Ct CV11 . . . . . .73 C4
Dempster Rd CV12. . . . . .78 A4
Demuth Way B69. . . . . . .63 F6
Denaby Gr B14 . . . . . . .105 D4
Denbigh Cl DY1. . . . . . . .50 F2
Denbigh Cnr B46. . . . . . .91 A6
Denbigh Cres B71. . . . . . .53 B6
Denbigh Ct B29. . . . . . .103 C7
Denbigh Dr
  Wednesbury WS10 . . . . .42 D4
  West Bromwich B71. . . . .53 B6
Denbigh Rd
  Coventry CV6. . . . . .112 E5
  Tipton DY4. . . . . .52 C4
Denbigh St B9. . . . . .67 D2
Denbury CV34 . . . . .2 D1
Denby Bldgs CV32 . . . .161 F8
Denby Cl
  Birmingham B7. . . . . . . .67 B5
  Royal Leamington Spa
  CV32. . . . . .157 C3
Denby Croft B90. . . . . . .127 B6
Dencer Cl B45 . . . . .122 A8
Dencer Dr CV8 . . . . . . .148 C4
Dencil Cl B63. . . . . .82 D5
Dene Ave DY6 . . . . .60 C4
Dene Court Rd B92 . . . . .88 F1
Dene Croft WS3 . . . . . . .14 A1
Denegate Cl B76. . . . . . .58 B6
Dene Hollow B13 . . . . . .105 C7
Denehurst Cl B45. . . . . .122 A1
Denehurst Way CV10. . . .72 F3
Denemoor Ct CV8 . . . . .148 B5
Dene Rd
  Dexter Penn WV4 . . . . . .37 F4
  Stourbridge DY8 . . . . . . .80 F3
Denewood Ave B20 . . . . .55 B2
Denewood Way CV8. . . . .148 C6
Denford Gr B14. . . . . . . .104 D5
Dengate Dr CV7 . . . . . . .130 B7
Denham Ave CV5 . . . . . .112 C4
Denham Ct B23. . . . . . . .56 C2
Denham Gdns WV3 . . . . .38 A8
Denham Rd B27 . . . . . . .88 C5
Denholme Gr B14 . . . . . .105 A3
Denholm Rd B73. . . . . . .45 D2

Denise Dr
  Birmingham B17 . . . . . .85 C4
  Birmingham,Kingshurst B37 .69 F4
  Dudley WV14 . . . . .51 B8
Denis Rd LE10 . . . . .75 D5
Denleigh Rd DY6 . . . . . .60 F4
Denmark Cl WV6 . . . . . .25 A4
Denmark Rise WS12 . . . . .2 D7
Denmark Villas WS13. . . .8 C5
Denmead Dr WV11. . . . . .26 F8
Dennis Gdns WV1 . . . . . .26 C2
Dennett Cl CV34. . . . . . .155 F2
Dennfield Dr WS6. . . . . . .4 C2
Dennis Hall DY8 . . . . . .80 F8
Dennis Hall Rd DY8 . . . . .81 A8
Dennis Rd
  Birmingham B12. . . . . . .87 B4
  Coventry CV2. . . . . .114 B6
Dennis St DY8 . . . . .80 F8
Dennis B77. . . . . .21 E2
Denshaw Croft CV2. . . . .115 A8
Denshaw Rd B14 . . . . . .104 D6
Denston Ct B64 . . . . . .31 F2
Denstone Gdns WV10 . . .11 F3
Denton Cl CV8. . . . . . . .147 D6
Denton Croft B93. . . . . .127 D3
Denton Gr
  Birmingham,Great Barr
  B43. . . . . .54 D7
  Birmingham,Stechford B33 .68 D2
Denton Rd DY9. . . . . . . .82 A4
Dent St B79 . . . . .21 C5
Denver Rd B14 . . . . . . .105 A2
Denville Cl WV14 . . . . . .40 E7
Denville Cres B9. . . . . . .68 B3
Denville Rd CV32 . . . . . .157 A3
Derby Ave WV6 . . . . . . .24 F7
Derby Dr B37. . . . . .70 B2
Derby Rd LE10. . . . . . . .71 D1
Derby St
  Birmingham B9 . . . . . . .67 A2
  Walsall WS2 . . . . .28 E4
Dereham Cl B8. . . . . . . .67 C4
Dereham Ct CV32. . . . . .157 A2
Dereham Wlk WV14. . . . .40 E2
Derek Ave DY5 . . . . .61 E8
Derick Burcher's Mall
  DY10. . . . . .116 E6
Dering Cl CV2 . . . . .114 D8
Deronda Cl CV12 . . . . . .78 A3
Derron Ave B26. . . . . . . .88 E5
Derry Cl B17 . . . . .85 A3
Derrydown Cl B23. . . . . .56 E3
Derrydown Rd B42. . . . . .55 B5
Derry St
  Brierley Hill DY5 . . . . . .61 D2
  Wolverhampton WV2. . . .163 C1
Dersingham Dr CV6. . . . .96 B2
Derwent Cl
  Brierley Hill DY5 . . . . . .61 B6
  Coventry CV5. . . . . .111 E4
  Royal Leamington Spa
  CV32. . . . . .156 D1
  Sutton Coldfield WS9. . . .30 F3
  Willenhall WV13 . . . . . . .27 C2
Derwent Ct B73 . . . . . . .46 B5
Derwent Gr
  Birmingham B13 . . . . . .86 C1
  Burntwood WS7. . . . . . . .7 D6
  Cannock WS11. . . . . .4 C6
Derwent Ho
  Oldbury B69 . . . . .63 D5
  Birmingham B17. . . . . .85 D5
  Kidderminster DY10 . . . .116 F7
Derwent Rd
  Bedworth CV12 . . . . . . .78 A2
  Birmingham B30 . . . . . .104 C8
  Coventry CV6. . . . . .95 A2
  Wolverhampton WV6. . . .24 E8
Derwent B77 . . . . .21 D1
Derwent Way
  Bromsgrove B60 . . . . . .137 B1
  Nuneaton CV34 . . . . . .161 E4
Desdemona Ave CV34. . .161 E4
Desford Ave B42. . . . . . .55 C7
De Somerley Ho B69. . .64 A1
Despard Rd CV5. . . . . . .111 D4
Dettonford Rd B32. . . . .102 B8
Devereux Cl
  Birmingham B36 . . . . . .69 C8
  Coventry CV4. . . . . .111 C1
Devereux Rd
  Sutton Coldfield B75. . . .32 C1
  West Bromwich B70 . . . .53 E1
Deveron Ct LE10. . . . . . .71 B1
Deveron Way LE10 . . . . .71 B1
Devey Dr DY4. . . . . .52 D6
Devine Croft DY4 . . . . . .52 A5
Devitts Cl B90 . . . . .126 F7
Devon Cl
  Birmingham B20 . . . . . .54 F2
  Nuneaton CV10 . . . . . . .72 F3
Devon Cres
  Aldridge WS9. . . . . .16 A1
  Dudley DY2 . . . . .61 F7
  Wolverhampton B71 . . . .53 C6
Devon Ct
  Birmingham B29. . . . .103 B7
  Cannock WS11. . . . . .4 C8
Devon Gn WS11. . . . . . . .4 C8
Devon Ho DY4 . . . . . . .80 F8
Devonport Cl B97. . . . .153 B5
Devon Rd

Devon Rd continued
  Stourbridge DY8 . . . . . . .80 E7
  Wednesbury WS10 . . . . .42 C4
  Willenhall WV13 . . . . . . .27 D1
  Wolverhampton WV1. . . .163 A4
Devonshire Ave B18 . . . .65 F6
Devonshire Ct B74. . . . . .32 A2
Devonshire Dr
  Tamworth B78 . . . . .21 A1
  West Bromwich B71. . . . .53 E3
Devonshire Inf Sch B67. . .64 E5
Devonshire Jun Sch B67. .64 E5
Devonshire Rd
  Birmingham B20 . . . . . .54 F2
  Smethwick B67 . . . . . . .64 E6
Devonshire St B18. . . . . .66 A6
Devonshire Villas B10. . . .87 D8
Devon St B7. . . . . .67 C5
Devoran Cl
  Bedworth CV7 . . . . .96 B8
  Wolverhampton WV6. . . .25 B4
Dewberry Dr WS5. . . . . . .43 A3
Dewberry Rd DY8 . . . . .60 F1
Dewhurst Croft B33. . . . .69 B3
Dewis Ho CV2 . . . . .96 B1
Dewsbury Ave CV3 . . . . .133 B5
Dewsbury Cl
  Astwood Bank B96 . . . .158 E1
  Stourbridge DY8 . . . . . . .60 E3
Dewsbury Dr
  Burntwood WS7. . . . . . . .7 C6
  Wolverhampton WV4 . . . .39 A4
Dewsbury Gr B42. . . . . . .55 C5
Dexter B67. . . . . .64 F6
Dexter Way B78 . . . . . . .36 F8
Dey Croft CV34 . . . . . . .160 B4
Deykin Ave B6. . . . . .56 B2
Deykin Avenue Jun & Inf Sch
  B6. . . . . .56 B2
Deykin Rd WS13 . . . . . . .9 A6
D'Eyncourt Prim Sch
  WV11. . . . . .26 B7
D'Eyncourt Rd WV10. . . .26 A7
Dial Cl B14 . . . . .104 E2
Dial House La CV5 . . . . .111 F4
Dial La
  Stourbridge DY8 . . . . . . .80 E8
  West Bromwich B70 . . . .53 C2
Diamond Ct B64 . . . . . .62 D1
Diamond Gr WS11 . . . . . .2 C3
Diamond Park Dr DY8. .60 E1
Diana Cl WS9 . . . . .16 B3
Diana Dr CV2. . . . . .96 E1
Diane Cl DY4 . . . . .41 B8
Dibble Cl WV12 . . . . . . .27 D5
Dibble Rd B67. . . . . .64 F6
Dibdale Ct DY1 . . . . .50 F3
Dibdale Rd DY1 . . . . . . .50 F3
Dibdale Rd W DY1 . . . . .50 F3
Dibdale St DY1 . . . . .51 A2
Dice Pleck B31. . . . . . . .103 C2
Dickens Cl
  Dudley DY3 . . . . .50 B5
  Nuneaton CV10 . . . . . . .72 A4
Dickens Heath Prim Sch
  B90. . . . . .126 A6
Dickens Heath Rd
  Solihull B90. . . . . .126 A6
  Solihull B90. . . . . .126 A6
  Solihull B90. . . . . .126 B8
Dickens Rd
  Coventry CV6. . . . . .113 A8
  Dudley WV14 . . . . .40 D2
  Wolverhampton WV10. . . .12 A1
Dickinson Av WV10 . . . . .25 F8
Dickinson Dr
  Sutton Coldfield B76. . . .46 E4
  Walsall WS2 . . . . .42 C6
Dickinson Rd WV5. . . . . .49 A4
Dickins Rd CV34 . . . . . .156 B1
Dick Sheppard Ave DY4 . .52 B8
Didcot Cl B97 . . . . .158 C5
Diddington Ave B28. . . . .106 A5
Diddington La B92,CV7 . .91 C5
Didgley Gr B37 . . . . .70 A5
Didsbury Rd CV7. . . . . . .95 A3
Digbeth
  Birmingham B5 . . . . . . .164 D1
  Walsall WS1 . . . . .28 E2
Digbey Cl CV5. . . . . .112 B6
Digby Cres B46 . . . . . . .59 B3
Digby Ct B27 . . . . .88 C3
Digby Dr B37. . . . . .90 A6
Digby Ho B37. . . . . .69 F4
Digby Pl CV7 . . . . .92 C1
Digby Rd
  Coleshill B46 . . . . .70 F6
  Kingswinford DY6 . . . . . .60 D8
  Sutton Coldfield B73. . . .46 B4
Dilcock Way CV4 . . . . . .131 F7
Dilke Rd WS9. . . . . .29 F5
Dillam Cl CV6. . . . . .96 A4
Dilliars Wlk B70 . . . . . . .53 A5
Dillington Ho B37. . . . .70 D2
Dillon Ct CV11. . . . . . . .73 B5
Dillotford Ave CV3 . . . . .133 D6
Dilloways La WV13 . . . . .40 F8
Dilwyn Cl B98 . . . . .154 F1
Dimbles La WS13 . . . . . .3 B1
Dimbles La WS13 . . . . . .3 A2
Dimmingsdale Bank B32. .84 C4
Dimmingsdale Rd WV4. . .37 E5
Dimminsdale WV13 . . . . .27 A1
Dimmocks Ave WV14. . . .51 D8
Dimsdale Gr B31 . . . . . .102 E3
Dimsdale Rd B31 . . . . . .102 D3
Dinedor Cl B98 . . . . . . .154 D3

Dingle Ave B64 . . . . .82 E8
Dingle Cl
  Birmingham B30 . . . . . .103 D7
  Coventry CV6. . . . . .113 A6
  Dudley DY2 . . . . .62 E7
Dingle Com Prim Sch
  DY6 . . . . .61 A4
Dingle Dr DY8 . . . . .106 F1
Dingle Hollow B69. . . . . .63 D8
Dingle La
  Solihull B91. . . . . .106 F2
  Willenhall WV13 . . . . . . .27 A4
Dingle Mead B14 . . . . . .104 C4
Dingle Rd
  Brownhills WS8 . . . . . . .15 E6
  Dudley DY2 . . . . .62 E7
  Kingswinford DY6 . . . . . .61 A3
  Stourbridge DY9 . . . . . . .81 E3
Dingleside Mid Sch B98..159 B8
Dingleside B98 . . . . .153 E2
Dingle St B69 . . . . .63 E8
Dingle The
  Birmingham B29 . . . . . .85 E2
  Cheswick Green B90. . . .126 D5
  Nuneaton CV10 . . . . . . .72 E6
  Oldbury B69. . . . . .63 D8
  Wolverhampton WV3 . . . .24 D1
Dingle View DY3 . . . . . . .50 C7
Dingley Rd
  Bulkington CV12 . . . . . . .79 B2
  Wednesbury WS10 . . . . .42 A5
Dinham Gdns DY1 . . . . . .50 E3
Dinmore Ave B31. . . . . .103 B4
Dinmore Cl B98 . . . . . . .154 D3
Dinsdale Wlk WV6. . . . . .25 A5
Dippons Dr WV6. . . . . . .24 A3
Dippons Ho WV6. . . . . . .24 A3
Dippons Mill Cl WV6. . . .24 A3
Dirtyfoot La WV4 . . . . . .38 A5
Discovery Cl DY4 . . . . . .52 C5
Discovery Way CV3 . . . .135 B7
District Ctr WS12 . . . . . . .2 C2
Ditchford Cl B97. . . . . . .158 D4
Ditch The WS1. . . . . .28 F1
Ditton Gr B31 . . . . .122 F6
Dixon Cl
  Birmingham B35 . . . . . .58 A2
  Tipton DY4. . . . . .52 C6
Dixon Ct DY10 . . . . . . .117 C8
Dixon Ho B16. . . . . .66 A1
Dixon Rd B10 . . . . .87 B8
Dixons Green Ct DY2. . .62 E8
Dixon's Green Rd DY2. . .62 E8
Dixon St
  Kidderminster DY10 . . . .116 E5
  Wolverhampton WV2. . . .39 E7
Doal Trad Est B66. . . . . .65 B6
Dobbins Oak Rd DY9. . . .81 E1
Dobbs Mill Cl B29 . . . . .86 B2
Dobbs St WV2 . . . . .163 B1
Dobson La CV31 . . . . . .162 A4
Dockar Rd B31 . . . . . . .102 E2
Dockers Cl CV7 . . . . . . .130 C7
Dock La DY1 . . . . .51 B1
Dock Lane Ind Est DY1 . .51 B1
Dock Mdw Dr Ind Est
  WV4. . . . . .40 B4
Dock Meadow Dr WV4 . . .40 A4
Dock Rd DY8 . . . . .60 F2
Dock The
  Catshill B61. . . . . .137 A8
  Stourbridge DY9 . . . . . . .81 F5
Doctors Cl B94 . . . . . . .142 A2
Doctors Hill
  Bournheath B61. . . . . . .136 E6
  Stourbridge DY9 . . . . . . .81 C3
Doctor's Piece
  Tamworth-In-A B94 . . . .142 A2
Doctors La
  Kingswinford DY6 . . . . . .60 A4
  Shenstone WS14 . . . . . .18 A6
Doctor's Piece CV13. . . . .27 B2
Dodd Ave CV34 . . . . . . .161 C2
Doddington Gr B32 . . . .102 B8
Dodford Cl B45. . . . . . . .121 F7
Dodford Ct B61 . . . . . . .136 C6
Dodford Fst Sch B61. . . .136 A3
Dodford Rd B61 . . . . . . .137 B3
Dodgson Cl CV6 . . . . . . .96 A4
Dodwells Bridge Ind Est
  LE10. . . . . .74 E8
Dodwells Rd LE10. . . . . .74 E8
Doe Bank Ct B74 . . . . . .46 B8
Doe Bank La
  Birmingham B43,WS9 . . .44 D5
  Coventry CV1. . . . . .113 A3
Doe Bank Rd DY4. . . . . .41 C1
Dogberry Cl CV3. . . . . . .134 C6
Dogberry Way CV34. . . . .161 C2
Dogge Lane Croft B27 . . .88 B2
Dog Kennel La WS1. . .28 F2
Dogkennel La
  Halesowen B63. . . . . . . .83 B3
  Oldbury B68. . . . . .64 C5
Doglands The CV31 . . . .162 B4
Dog La
  Tamworth B77 . . . . .22 B6
  Weeford WS14 . . . . .19 A4
Dogpool La B30 . . . . . . .86 B1
Doidge Rd B23 . . . . .56 D3
Dollery Dr B5 . . . . .86 C5
Dollis Gr B44. . . . . .44 F3
Dollman St B7. . . . . .67 B4

Dolman Rd B6 . . . . .66 E8
Dolobran Rd B11 . . . . .87 B7
Dolomite Ave CV4 . . . .112 D1
Dolphin Cl WS3 . . . . .14 F1
Dolphin Ct WV12 . . . . .27 D8
Dolphin La B27 . . . . .88 C1
Dolphin Rd
  Birmingham B11 . . . . .87 D5
  Redditch B98 . . . . .154 A5
Dolton Way DY4 . . . . .51 E6
Domar Rd DY11 . . . . .116 B7
Dominic Dr B30 . . . . .103 D4
Donalbain Cl CV34 . . . . . .161 F3
Doncaster Cl CV2 . . . . .114 D7
Doncaster Way B36 . . . . . .68 C8
Don Cl B15 . . . . .85 D8
Donegal Cl CV4 . . . . .132 A7
Donegal Rd B74 . . . . .44 F5
Dongan Rd CV34 . . . . .160 E7
Don Gr WS11 . . . . .4 D7
Donibristle Croft B35 . . .58 A4
Donnington Ave CV6 . . . .112 E5
Donnington Cl B98 . . . . . .154 C5
Donnington Ho B33 . . . . . .69 B2
Donnithorne Ave CV10,
  CV11 .73 D1
Donovan Dr B73 . . . . .46 A6
Dooley Cl WV13 . . . . .26 E2
Doone Cl CV2 . . . . .114 E6
Dorado B77 . . . . .35 D7
Dora Herbert Ct B12 . . . .86 E5
Doran Cl B63 . . . . .82 D1
Doranda Way B71 . . . . .53 F1
Dora Rd
  Birmingham B10 . . . . .87 E8
  Birmingham,Handsworth
  B21 . . . . .65 E7
  West Bromwich B70 . . . . . .53 C1
Dora St WS2 . . . . .42 B7
Dorcas Cl CV11 . . . . .79 C8
Dorchester Cl WV12 . . . . .27 C8
Dorchester Dr B17 . . . . . . .85 B4
Dorchester Rd
  Cannock WS11 . . . . .1 B1
  Hinckley LE10 . . . . .76 B7
  Solihull B91 . . . . .107 A4
  Stourbridge DY9 . . . . .81 D2
  Willenhall WV12 . . . . .13 C1
Dorchester Way
  Coventry CV2 . . . . .115 A4
  Nuneaton CV11 . . . . .74 A7
Dordale Cl B31 . . . . .102 C1
Dordale Rd DY9 . . . . .119 E2
Dordon Cl B90 . . . . .105 E1
Dordon Rd B78 . . . . .36 F8
Doreen Gr B24 . . . . .57 B2
Doris Rd
  Birmingham B11 . . . . .87 B4
  Birmingham,Bordesley Green
  B9 . . . . .67 E2
  Coleshill B46 . . . . .70 F8
Dorlecote Rd B8 . . . . .68 A4
Dorlecote Ct CV10 . . . . . . .73 C1
Dorlecote Pl CV10 . . . . . . .78 C8
Dorlecote Rd CV10 . . . . . . .78 C8
Dormer Ave B77 . . . . .21 D5
Dormer Ho B6 CV32 . . . . .156 F2
Dormer Pl CV32 . . . . .161 E8
Dormie Cl B38 . . . . .103 D1
Dormington Rd B44 . . . . . .44 F3
Dormston Cl
  Redditch B98 . . . . .153 F1
  Solihull B91 . . . . .127 C8
Dormston Dr
  Birmingham B29 . . . . .84 F2
  Sedgley DY3 . . . . .50 E8
Dormston Sch The DY3 . .50 E8
Dormston Trad Est DY1 . .50 F4
Dormy Dr B31 . . . . .123 A7
Dorncliffe Ave B33 . . . . . . .89 D7
Dorney Cl CV5 . . . . .132 E8
Dornie Dr B38 . . . . .103 F1
Dornton Rd B30 . . . . .104 B8
Dorothy Adams Cl B3 B64 .82 E8
Dorothy Gdns B20 . . . . . . .55 A2
Dorothy Goodman Spec1 Sch
  LE10 .71 D2
Dorothy Pattison Hospl
  WS2 . . . . .28 B1
Dorothy Powell Way CV2 .96 F1
Dorothy Rd
  Birmingham B11 . . . . .88 B5
  Smethwick B67 . . . . .65 A4
Dorridge Cl B97 . . . . .153 A4
Dorridge Ct B93 . . . . .153 B1
Dorridge Croft B93 . . . . .127 F2
Dorridge Jun & Inf Schs
  B93 .128 A4
Dorridge Rd B93 . . . . .128 A2
Dorridge Sta B93 . . . . . . .127 F2
Dorrington Gn B42 . . . . . . .55 A5
Dorrington Prim Sch B42 .55 A5
Dorrington Rd B42 . . . . . . .55 A5
Dorset Cl
  Birmingham B45 . . . . .101 F2
  Nuneaton CV10 . . . . .72 F3
  Tamworth B78 . . . . .21 A1
Dorset Cotts B30 . . . . . . .104 A6
Dorset Ct B2 B29 . . . . . . .103 B7
Dorset Dr WS9 . . . . .16 B1
Dorset Pl WS3 . . . . .28 C7
Dorset Rd
  Birmingham B8 . . . . .67 C6

Dorset Rd *continued*
  Cannock WS12 . . . . .2 E1
  Coventry CV1 . . . . .113 C5
  Smethwick B17 . . . . .65 B3
  Stourbridge DY8 . . . . .80 D8
Dorsett Rd
  Darlaston WS10 . . . . .41 C6
  Wednesbury WS10 . . . . .42 D2
Dorsett Road Terr WS10 .41 C6
Dorset Twr B18 . . . . .66 B4
Dorsheath Gdns B23 . . . . .56 F4
Dorsington Rd B27 . . . . . . .88 D1
Dorstone Covert B14 . . .104 C2
Dorville C23 B8 . . . . .123 D8
Dosthill Prim Sch B77 . . .35 D5
Dosthill Rd (Two Gates)
  B77 . . . . .35 D7
Dotterel Pl DY10 . . . . .117 A1
Douay Rd B24 . . . . .57 B6
Double Row DY2 . . . . .62 E4
Doughty St DY4 . . . . .52 C5
Douglas Ave
  Birmingham B36 . . . . .68 D6
  Oldbury B68 . . . . .64 D5
Douglas Davies Cl WV12 .27 C4
Douglas Ho CV1 . . . . .165 D4
Douglas Pl WV10 . . . . .25 C6
Douglas Rd
  Birmingham B27 . . . . .88 C4
  Birmingham,Handsworth
  B21 . . . . .65 F8
  Dudley WV14 . . . . .51 D8
  Halesowen B62 . . . . .63 E1
  Hollywood B47 . . . . .125 A7
  Oldbury B68 . . . . .64 D4
  Sutton Coldfield B72 . . . . . .46 C3
Douglass Rd DY2 . . . . .62 D8
Doulton Cl
  Birmingham B32 . . . . .84 F3
  Coventry CV2 . . . . .96 E1
Doulton Dr B66 . . . . .65 A6
Doulton Rd B64,B65 . . . . . .62 F4
Doulton Trad Est B65 . . . .62 F4
Douper Hall B29 . . . . .85 F3
Dovebridge Cl B76 . . . . . . .46 F4
Dove Cl
  Bedworth CV12 . . . . .77 E3
  Birmingham B25 . . . . .88 E8
  Burntwood WS7 . . . . .7 C6
  Hinckley LE10 . . . . .75 A8
  Kidderminster DY10 . . . . .117 B2
  Walsall WS1 . . . . .29 A1
  Wednesbury WS10 . . . . .42 B4
Dovecote Cl
  Coventry CV6 . . . . .112 D5
  Solihull B91 . . . . .107 B8
  Tipton DY4 . . . . .52 C5
  Wolverhampton WV6 . . . . .24 C4
Dovecote Rd B61 . . . . .136 E1
Dovecotes Prim Sch WV8 .10 F1
Dovecotes The
  Coventry CV5 . . . . .112 B5
  Sutton Coldfield B75 . . . . . .32 B3
Dovedale Ave
  Coventry CV6 . . . . .95 F2
  Solihull B90 . . . . .106 B1
  Walsall WS3 . . . . .15 B5
  Willenhall WV12 . . . . .27 B4
Dovedale Cl WS11 . . . . .2 A5
Dovedale Ct
  B5 Birmingham B29 . . . . .103 C7
  Wolverhampton WV4 . . . . .39 F2
Dovedale Dr B28 . . . . .105 F5
Dovedale Rd
  Birmingham B23 . . . . .56 C2
  Kingswinford DY6 . . . . .60 E8
  Wolverhampton WV4 . . . . .39 E3
Dove Dr DY8 . . . . .81 A8
Dove Gdns B38 . . . . .104 B2
Dove Hollow
  Cannock WS12 . . . . .2 E4
  Great Wyrley WS6 . . . . .4 F1
Dove House Ct B91 . . . . .106 F7
Dovehouse Fields WS14 . . .9 B6
Dove House La B91 . . . . . .106 F7
Dove House La B91 . . . . . .107 A8
Dovehouse Pool Rd B6 B6 .66 E8
Dover Cl B32 . . . . .102 A7
Dovercourt Rd B26 . . . . . . .89 C5
Doverdale Ave DY10 . . . . .117 B5
Doverdale Cl
  Halesowen B63 . . . . .82 E5
  Redditch B98 . . . . .159 B7
Dover Farm Cl B77 . . . . . . .36 B8
Dover Ho WS3 . . . . .28 C7
Doveridge Cl B91 . . . . . . .106 E6
Doveridge Pl WS1 . . . . .42 F8
Doveridge Rd B28 . . . . . . .105 E5
Dove Ridge DY8 . . . . .81 A7
Doversley Rd B14 . . . . . . .104 C5
Dover St
  Bilston WV14 . . . . .40 D6
  Birmingham B18 . . . . .66 A6
  Coventry CV1 . . . . .165 A3
Dovestone B77 . . . . .22 D1
Doveton Ho DY8 . . . . .81 A3
Dove Way B36 . . . . .69 F8
Dove Dr B76 . . . . .58 A7
Dovey Rd
  Birmingham B13 . . . . .87 D2
  Oldbury B69 . . . . .63 D8
Dowar Rd B45 . . . . .122 C7
Dowells Cl B13 . . . . .86 F2
Dowells Gdns DY8 . . . . . . .60 D3
Doweries The B45 . . . . . . .121 F8
Dower Rd B75 . . . . .32 B1
Dowler's Hill Cres B98 . .159 A8
Dowles Cl B29 . . . . .103 B6

Dowles Rd DY11 . . . . .116 B2
Dowley Croft CV3 . . . . . . .115 B1
Downcroft Ave B38 . . . . . .103 E2
Downderry Way CV6 . . . .114 A6
Downend Cl WV10 . . . . .11 F4
Downes Ct B7 Dy4 . . . . .51 E5
Downesway WS11 . . . . .1 C2
Downey Cl B11 . . . . .87 B7
Downfield Cl WS3 . . . . .14 A4
Downfield Dr DY3 . . . . .50 E6
Downham Cl WS5 . . . . .29 E1
Downham Pl WV3 . . . . .38 F8
Downham Wood WS5 . . . . .43 E8
Downie Rd WV8 . . . . .10 C3
Downing Cl
  B6 Rowley Regis B65 . . . . .63 C1
  Dorridge B93 . . . . .128 A4
  Wednesfield WV11 . . . . .27 A7
Downing Cres CV12 . . . . . .78 C4
Downing Ct B2 B68 . . . . . . .84 B7
Downing Dr B79 . . . . .20 E5
Downing Ho B37 . . . . .70 B1
Downing St
  Halesowen B63 . . . . .83 A5
  Smethwick B66 . . . . .65 B4
Downland Cl B38 . . . . .103 F1
Downsell Ho B97 . . . . .153 A2
Downsell Rd B97 . . . . .153 A2
Downsfield Rd B26 . . . . . . .89 B7
Downside Rd B24 . . . . .56 E1
Downs Rd WV13 . . . . .41 C8
Downs The
  Sutton Coldfield WS9 . . . . .30 E2
  Wolverhampton WV10 . . . .25 C6
Downton Cl CV2 . . . . .115 A8
Downton Cres B33 . . . . . . .69 E3
Dowty Ave CV12 . . . . .77 D1
Dowty Way WV9 . . . . .11 A3
Doyle Dr CV6 . . . . .95 F3
Dragoon Fields B60 . . . . .151 B8
Drake Cl WS3 . . . . .14 B1
Drake Cres DY11 . . . . .116 A7
Drake Croft B4 WS13 . . . . . .9 C8
Drake Ct WS13 . . . . .14 B1
Drake Rd
  Birmingham B23 . . . . .56 C3
  Smethwick B66 . . . . .64 E7
  Walsall WS3 . . . . .14 C1
Drakes Cl
  Redditch B97 . . . . .158 C6
  Wythall B47 . . . . .124 F4
Drakes Cross Par B47 . . .125 A5
Drake's Gn WV14 . . . . .40 F3
Drakes Hill Cl DY8 . . . . . . .80 C4
Drake St
  Coventry CV6 . . . . .113 D7
  West Bromwich B71 . . . . . . .53 C5
Drake Way LE10 . . . . .71 D4
Drancy Ave WV12 . . . . .27 D6
Draper Cl CV8 . . . . .148 C4
Drapers Ct CV11 . . . . .165 B4
Draper's Fields CV1 . . . . .165 B4
Drawbridge Rd B90 . . . . .125 E8
Draycote Cl B92 . . . . .107 D6
Draycot Ave B23 . . . . .56 D4
Draycott Cl
  B9 Redditch B97 . . . . .153 B5
  Wolverhampton WV4 . . . . .38 C5
Draycott Cres B77 . . . . . . .21 D1
Draycott Dr B31 . . . . .102 E7
Draycott Rd
  Coventry CV2 . . . . .114 C7
  Smethwick B66 . . . . .64 E7
Drayman Cl WS1 . . . . .42 F8
Drayton Cl
  Hartshill CV10 . . . . .72 A8
  Redditch B98 . . . . .159 D8
  Sutton Coldfield B75 . . . . . .32 B3
Drayton Cres CV5 . . . . . . .111 D5
Drayton Ct
  Bromsgrove B60 . . . . .151 B8
  Warwick CV34 . . . . .155 E2
Drayton La B78 . . . . .34 C5
Drayton Manor Dr
  Drayton Bassett B78 . . . . . .34 F7
  Fazeley B78 . . . . .34 E7
Drayton Manor Pk* B78 .34 E7
Drayton Rd
  Bedworth CV12 . . . . .78 D2
  Belbroughton DY9 . . . . . . .119 B5
  Birmingham B14 . . . . .104 F8
  Smethwick B66 . . . . .65 A1
  Solihull B90 . . . . .126 C8
Drayton St
  Walsall WS2 . . . . .28 C2
  Wolverhampton WV2 . . . . .163 B1
Drayton Way CV10 . . . . . . .72 C7
Dreadnought Rd DY5 . . . . .61 B8
Dreamwell Ind Est B11 . . .88 A6
Dreel The B15 . . . . .85 E7
Dreghorn Rd B36 . . . . .68 F8
Drem Croft B35 . . . . .58 A2
Dresden Cl WV1 . . . . .40 A4
Drew Cres
  Kenilworth CV8 . . . . .148 A4
  Stourbridge DY9 . . . . .81 D2
Drew Rd DY9 . . . . .81 D3
Drews Holloway B63 . . . . .82 D5
Drews Holloway S B63 . . .82 D5
Drews La B8 . . . . .68 A7
Drews Meadow Cl B1
  B14 .104 C2
Driffield Cl B98 . . . . .154 D2
Driffold B73 . . . . .46 B4
Driftwood Cl B38 . . . . .123 D7
Drinkwater Ho B7 CV1 . . .113 B2
Drive Fields WV4 . . . . .38 B6

Drive Sch (Tettenhall Coll)
  The WV6 . . . . .24 D4
Drive The
  Birmingham,Gravelly Hill
  B23 . . . . .56 E2
  Birmingham,Handsworth
  B20 . . . . .55 B2
  Brierley Hill DY5 . . . . .61 C5
  Coventry CV2 . . . . .114 E8
  Halesowen,Cradley B63 . . .82 D5
  Halesowen,Hasbury B63 . . .83 A3
  Hopwood B48 . . . . .123 B3
  Redditch B97 . . . . .152 C7
  Shenstone WS14 . . . . .18 E8
  Walsall,Pelsall WS3 . . . . . . .14 E2
  Walsall WS4 . . . . .15 C1
  Wolverhampton WV6 . . . . .24 C5
Droicon Trad Est B65 . . . .63 C5
Dronfield Rd CV2 . . . . .114 B3
Drovers Way B60 . . . . .150 E6
Drovers Wlk DY10 . . . . . . .116 A8
Droveway The WV9 . . . . . . .10 F2
Droxford Wlk WV8 . . . . . . .10 F1
Droylsdon Park Rd CV3 .133 B3
Dr Phillip Sh Ctr The
  CV2 . . . . .96 D1
Druid Park Rd WV12 . . . . .13 C1
Druid Rd CV2 . . . . .114 B3
Druids Ave
  Aldridge WS9 . . . . .30 C8
  Rowley Regis B65 . . . . .63 D4
Druids La B14 . . . . .104 D1
Druid St LE10 . . . . .71 D1
Druids Wlk WS9 . . . . .16 A3
Drummond Cl
  Coventry CV6 . . . . .112 F7
  Wolverhampton WV11 . . . .13 A2
Drummond Gr B43 . . . . .44 C3
Drummond Rd
  Birmingham B9 . . . . .68 A2
  Bromsgrove B60 . . . . .151 B8
  Stourbridge DY9 . . . . .81 F4
Drummond St WV1 . . . . . .163 B4
Drummond Way B37 . . . . . .70 C2
Drury La
  Solihull B91 . . . . .107 C3
  Stourbridge DY8 . . . . .81 A5
Drybrook Cl B38 . . . . .123 E8
Drybrooks Cl CV7 . . . . . . .130 B6
Dryden Cl
  Kenilworth CV8 . . . . .147 F3
  Tipton DY4 . . . . .52 A7
  Willenhall WV12 . . . . .27 E8
Dryden Gr B27 . . . . .88 B2
Dryden Pl WS3 . . . . .28 E7
Dryden Rd
  Tamworth B79 . . . . .21 A6
  Walsall WS3 . . . . .28 E7
  Wolverhampton WV10 . . . .11 F1
Drylea Gr B36 . . . . .68 F8
Dual Way WS12 . . . . .1 D8
Dubarry Ave DY6 . . . . .60 C7
Duchess Cl B16 . . . . .66 A1
Duchess Rd
  Birmingham B16 . . . . .66 A1
  Walsall WS1 . . . . .42 D5
Duckhouse Rd WV11 . . . . .26 D7
Duck La WV8 . . . . .10 B3
Duddeston Dr B8 . . . . .67 D4
Duddeston Manor Rd B7 .67 A4
Duddeston Mill Rd B7,B8 .67 C4
Duddeston Mill Trad Est
  B7 . . . . .67 B4
Duddeston Sta B7 . . . . .67 B4
Dudding Rd WV4 . . . . .39 D5
Dudhill Rd B65 . . . . .63 A3
Dudhill Wlk B65 . . . . .63 A3
Dudley Castle* DY1 . . . . . .51 D2
Dudley Central Trad Est
  DY2 . . . . .62 C8
Dudley Cl B65 . . . . .63 A5
Dudley Coll (Castle View
  Campus) DY1 . . . . .51 B2
Dudley Coll (International
  Glass Ctr) DY5 . . . . .61 D3
Dudley Coll of Tech
  (Broadway Campus)
  DY1 . . . . .51 C2
Dudley Coll of Tech (Mons
  Hill Campus) DY1 . . . . . . .51 B5
Dudley Coll of Tech
  (Wolverhampton St**
  Campus) DY1 . . . . .51 B1
Dudley Cres WV11 . . . . .26 E6
Dudley Gn CV32 . . . . .157 B2
Dudley Gr B6 B18 . . . . .65 E4
Dudley Innovation Ctr
  DY6 . . . . .60 F7
Dudley L Ctr DY1 . . . . .51 B1
Dudley Mus & Art Gall*
  DY1 . . . . .51 C1
Dudley Park Rd B27 . . . . . .88 C3
Dudley Port Sta DY4 . . . . .52 B4
Dudley Port DY4 . . . . .52 A3
Dudley Rd
  Birmingham B18 . . . . .65 F4
  Brierley Hill DY5,DY6 . . . . . .61 D4
  Dudley DY3 . . . . .50 E6
  Halesowen B63 . . . . .83 B5
  Himley DY3 . . . . .49 D3
  Kenilworth CV8 . . . . .147 F2
  Kingswinford DY6 . . . . .60 F7
  Kingswinford,Wall Heath
  DY6 . . . . .60 C8
  Oldbury B69 . . . . .63 E8
  Rowley Regis B65 . . . . .63 A5
  Stourbridge DY9 . . . . .81 E5
  Tipton DY4 . . . . .51 E5

Dudley Rd *continued*
  Wolverhampton WV2 . . . . .39 C7
Dudley Rise LE10 . . . . .75 D6
Dudley Road E B69 . . . . . . .52 D1
Dudley Road W B69 . . . . . . .52 B2
Dudley Row DY2 . . . . .51 E6
Dudley Southern Bypass
  DY2 . . . . .62 C7
Dudley St
  Bilston WV14 . . . . .40 D4
  Birmingham B5 . . . . .164 C2
  Coventry CV6 . . . . .96 A1
  Kidderminster DY10 . . . . .116 E6
  Sedgley DY3 . . . . .50 D8
  Walsall WS1 . . . . .28 E1
  Wednesbury WS10 . . . . .41 E2
  West Bromwich B70 . . . . . . .53 A5
  Wolverhampton WV1 . . . .163 B3
Dudley Walker Dr WV14 . .40 C6
Dudley Wlk WV4 . . . . .39 C5
Dudley Wood Ave DY2 . . . .62 C2
Dudley Wood Prim Sch
  DY2 . . . . .62 C2
Dudley Wood Rd DY2 . . . . .62 C2
Dudley Zoo* DY1 . . . . .51 D2
Dudmaston Way DY1 . . . . .50 E3
Dudnill Gr B32 . . . . .102 A8
Duffield Cl WV8 . . . . .10 F1
Dufton Rd B32 . . . . .84 E4
Dugdale Cl WS12 . . . . .2 F3
Dugdale Cres B75 . . . . .32 C3
Dugdale Ho CV11 . . . . .73 C3
Dugdale Rd CV6 . . . . .113 B6
Dugdale St
  Nuneaton CV11 . . . . .73 C4
  Smethwick B18 . . . . .65 C4
Duggins La CV4,CV7 . . . . .131 B8
Duke Barn Field CV2 . . . .114 A5
Dukes Rd
  Birmingham B30 . . . . .104 A3
  Dordon B78 . . . . .36 F6
Duke St
  Coventry CV5 . . . . .112 F2
  Dudley DY3 . . . . .50 C5
  Nuneaton CV11 . . . . .73 B4
  Rowley Regis B65 . . . . .63 B2
  Royal Leamington Spa
  CV32 . . . . .157 A1
  Stourbridge DY8 . . . . .81 A6
  Sutton Coldfield B72 . . . . . .46 B4
  Wednesfield WV11 . . . . .26 D5
  West Bromwich B70 . . . . . . .53 B4
  Wolverhampton,Springfield
  WV1 .163 D2
  Wolverhampton WV3 . . . . .39 A7
Dulais Cl B98 . . . . .153 E1
Dulvern Gr B14 . . . . .104 D5
Dulverton Ave CV5 . . . . . .112 C4
Dulverton Ct CV5 . . . . .112 D4
Dulverton Rd B6 . . . . .56 B1
Dulwich Gr B44 . . . . .56 B8
Dulwich Rd B44 . . . . .56 A8
Dumblederry Ave CV9 . . . .50 C7
Dumblederry Cl WS9 . . . . . .29 F5
Dumblederry La
  Aldridge WS9 . . . . .29 F6
  Walsall WS9 . . . . .29 E5
Dumble Pit La B47,B48 . . .140 F7
Dumolo's La B77 . . . . .21 F3
Dumphouse La B48 . . . . . .140 C3
Dunard Rd B90 . . . . .105 F3
Dunbar Cl
  Birmingham B32 . . . . .84 D1
  Kidderminster DY10 . . . . .117 C6
Dunbar Gr B43 . . . . .44 B4
Dunblane Dr CV32 . . . . . . .157 C5
Dunblane Way LE10 . . . . . . .71 A2
Duncalfe Dr B75 . . . . .32 B3
Duncan Edwards Cl DY1 . .62 A8
Duncan Ho B13 . . . . .46 B1
Duncan St WV2 . . . . .39 C7
Dunchurch Cl
  Balsall Common CV7 . . . . .130 B7
  Redditch B98 . . . . .154 F1
Dunchurch Cres B73 . . . . . .45 C3
Dunchurch Dr B31 . . . . . . .102 E7
Dunchurch Highway
  CV5 .112 A4
Dunchurch Ho B4 B65 . . . . .86 C8
Dunclent Cres DY10 . . . . .117 B5
Dunclent La DY10 . . . . .117 C3
Duncombe Dr CV32 . . . . . .157 C5
Duncombe Gr B17 . . . . .85 A7
Duncombe St DY8 . . . . .80 D5
Duncroft Ave CV6 . . . . .112 F7
Duncroft Rd B26 . . . . .89 A8
Duncroft Wlk DY1 . . . . .51 B6
Duncumb Rd B75 . . . . .47 A5
Dundalk La WS6 . . . . .4 D2
Dundas Ave DY2 . . . . .62 F8
Dunedin Dr B45 . . . . .122 B1
Dunedin Ho B32 . . . . .84 F4
Dunedin Rd B44 . . . . .44 F3
Dunedin B77 . . . . .22 A2
Dunham Croft B93 . . . . . .127 D3
Dunhill Ave CV4 . . . . .111 E3
Dunkirk Ave B70 . . . . .52 E3
Dunkirk Pl CV3 . . . . .134 F7
Dunkley St WV1 . . . . .163 B4
Dunley Croft B90 . . . . .126 F6
Dunley Ct B23 . . . . .56 C2
Dunlin Cl
  Birmingham B23 . . . . .56 C2
  Kingswinford DY6 . . . . .61 A6

Dunlin Dr
Featherstone WV10 12 B7
Kidderminster DY10 116 F2
Dunlop Rd B97 158 D5
Dunlop Way B35 57 F2
Dunnerdale Rd WS8 15 D6
Dunnigan Rd B32 84 F3
Dunnose Cl CV6 113 E8
Dunns Bank DY5 81 F7
Dunrose Cl CV2 114 E2
Dunsfold Cl WV14 40 A3
Dunsfold Croft 3 B6 66 F6
Dunsford Cl DY5 81 B7
Dunsford Rd B66 65 A2
Dunsink Rd B6 55 F1
Dunslade Cres DY5 81 F8
Dunslade Rd B23 56 E7
Dunsley Dr DY8 60 E3
Dunsley Gr WV4 39 A4
Dunsley Rd DY8 80 C4
Dunsmore Ave CV3 134 C6
Dunsmore Dr DY5 81 F8
Dunsmore Gr B91 106 F7
Dunsmore Rd B28 87 E2
Dunstall Ave WV6 25 C4
Dunstall Cl B97 153 B2
Dunstall Gr B29 102 F8
Dunstall Hill Jun & Inf Sch WV6 25 C4
Dunstall Hill Trad Est WV6 25 C5
Dunstall Hill WV6 25 C5
Dunstall La
Hopwas B78 20 D4
Wolverhampton WV6 25 B5
Dunstall Rd
Halesowen B63 82 D3
Wolverhampton WV6 25 B4
Dunstan Croft B90 126 C8
Dunstan Ct 3 B15 86 B7
Dunster Cl B30 104 C4
Dunster Gr WV6 23 F3
Dunster Pl CV6 95 D3
Dunster Rd B37 70 D2
Dunster B77 35 C7
Dunston Cl
Great Wyrley WS6 13 E8
Kingswinford DY6 60 D7
Dunston Dr WS7 7 A8
Dunsville Dr CV2 114 F8
Dunton Cl B75 32 A4
Dunton Hall Rd B90 126 A8
Dunton La B76 48 C1
Dunton Pk B76 59 C7
Dunton Rd B37 69 F5
Dunton Trad Est B7 67 D7
Dunvegan Cl
Coventry CV3 115 A2
Kenilworth CV8 148 C4
Dunvegan Rd B24 57 A4
Duport Rd LE10 75 F7
Durant Cl B45 101 D1
Durban Rd B66 65 C4
Durbar Ave CV6 113 D8
D'Urberville Cl WV2 39 F6
D'Urberville Rd WV2 39 F6
D'Urberville Wlk 1 WS11 2 A2
Durham Ave WV13 27 D3
Durham Cl
Bromsgrove B61 136 E4
Keresley CV7 94 F4
Tamworth B78 21 A2
Durham Cres CV5 112 B7
Durham Croft B37 70 B2
Durham Dr B71 53 D7
Durham Ho 1 WV3 25 C4
Durham Pl WS2 28 B1
Durham Rd
Birmingham B11 87 B4
Dudley DY2 62 D2
Rowley Regis B65 63 E4
Stourbridge DY8 80 D8
Walsall WS2 42 B8
Wednesbury WS10 42 D4
Durham Twr 3 B1 66 B3
Durley Dean Rd B29 85 C2
Durley Dr B73 45 C3
Durley Rd B25 88 C6
Durlston Cl B77 21 F5
Durlston Gr B28 106 A8
Durnford Croft B14 104 E1
Dursley Cl
Solihull B92 107 B8
Willenhall WV12 27 D4
Dursley Dr WS11 1 B2
Dursley Rd WS7 7 A7
Dusthouse La B60 151 D7
Dutton Rd CV2 96 D3
Dutton's La B75 32 E4
Duxford Cl B97 158 B8
Duxford Rd B42 55 B7
Dwarris Wlk CV34 155 E2
Dwellings La B32 84 B5
Dyas Ave B42 55 A7
Dyas Rd
Birmingham B44 44 E1
Hollywood B47 125 A7
Dyce Cl B35 58 A4
Dyers La B94 142 D8
Dyers Rd CV11 79 F6
Dymoke St B12 86 F8
Dymond Rd CV6 95 D3
Dynes Wlk B67 65 A5
Dyott Rd B13 87 A1
Dysart Cl CV1 113 E4
Dyson Cl WS2 27 F3
Dysons Gdns B8 67 E5
Dyson St CV4 111 E3

E

Eachelhurst Rd B24,B76 57 F5
Eachus Rd WV14 51 D8
Eachway B45 121 F6
Eachway Farm Cl B45 122 A6
Eachway La B45 122 A6
Eacott Cl CV6 95 A3
Eadgar Ct B43 54 D7
Eadie Mews B97 153 D1
Eadie St CV10 72 D4
Eagle Cl
Cheslyn Hay WS6 4 D2
Dudley DY1 50 F1
Nuneaton CV11 79 B8
Rowley Regis B65 63 A4
Eagle Croft B14 104 E2
Eagle Ct
Wolverhampton,Pendeford WV10 11 B3
Wolverhampton WV3 39 A7
Eagle Dr B77 22 C4
Eagle Gdns B24 57 A2
Eagle Gr
Birmingham B36 70 A8
Cannock WS12 2 C1
Eagle Ho CV1 113 D5
Eagle Ind Est DY4 52 E7
Eagle La
Kenilworth CV8 147 F3
Tipton DY4 52 D6
Eagle Rd B98 154 E5
Eagle St E CV1 113 D5
Eagle St
Coventry CV1 113 D5
Royal Leamington Spa CV31 162 A6
Tipton DY4 52 C6
Wolverhampton,Penn Fields WV3 39 A7
Wolverhampton WV2 39 E8
Eagle Trad Est B63 83 A4
Eales Yd 9 LE10 71 D1
Ealing Gr B44 45 A1
Ealingham B77 22 B1
Eanwulf Ct B15 86 C8
Eardisley Cl B98 154 F1
Earl Place Bsns Pk CV4 112 B1
Earlsbury Gdns B20 55 D1
Earls Cl B97 152 F2
Earls Court Rd B17 85 A6
Earl's Croft The CV3 133 D7
Earlsdon Ave CV5 133 A8
Earlsdon Ave N CV5 112 F1
Earlsdon Ave S CV5 133 A8
Earlsdon Ho CV5 133 A8
Earlsdon Prim Sch CV5 113 A1
Earlsdon St CV5 132 F8
Earls Ferry Gdns B32 102 B7
Earls High Sch The B63 83 B4
Earlsmead Rd B21 65 C7
Earlsmere B94 126 B1
Earls Rd
Nuneaton CV11 73 A5
Walsall WS4 29 D7
Earls Rivers Ave CV34 161 D3
Earl St
Bedworth CV12 78 C2
Bilston WV14 40 D5
Coventry CV1 165 C2
Dudley WV14 51 D8
Kingswinford DY6 60 D4
Earlston Way B43 54 D8
Earl St
Royal Leamington Spa CV32 157 A1
Walsall WS1 42 D7
West Bromwich B70 53 B4
Earls Way B63 83 B4
Earl's Wlk CV3 135 D7
Earlswood Comm B94 142 A6
Earlswood Cres WV9 11 A3
Earlswood Ct B20 55 A2
Earlswood Dr B74 46 C7
Earlswood Ho 1 B5 86 E7
Earlswood Rd
Birmingham,Brandwood End B30 104 D3
Dorridge B93 127 D2
Kingswinford DY6 60 E8
Earlswood Sta B94 125 D1
Earlswood Trad Est B94 141 C6
Easby Way
Birmingham B8 67 E5
Walsall WS3 13 F2
Easedale Cl
Coventry CV3 133 B6
Nuneaton CV11 74 A6
Easemore Rd B98 153 F5
Easenhall Cl B93 128 A4
Easenhall La B98 154 E1
Easmore Cl B14 104 D2
Eastacre WV13 27 A1
East Ave
Bedworth CV12 78 D2
Coventry CV2 114 A2
Oldbury B69 63 C7
Wolverhampton WV11 26 C6
East Birmingham Coll Bordesley Green Campus B9 68 A2
Eastboro Ct CV11 73 E2
Eastboro Fields CV11 74 A4
Eastboro Way CV11 73 F2
Eastbourne Ave B34 68 E6
Eastbourne Cl CV6 112 E6
Eastbourne House Sch B27 88 C4
Eastbourne St WS4 28 F3
Eastbrook Cl B76 46 D4
Eastbury Dr B92 89 A3
East Cannock Rd WS12 2 C4
East Car Park Rd B40 90 F4
East Cl LE10 75 D7
Eastcote Cl B90 106 D3
Eastcote Cres WS7 7 A5
Eastcote La B92 108 F4
Eastcote Rd
Birmingham B27 88 A1
Wolverhampton WV10 25 F5
Eastcotes CV4 112 B1
East Croft Rd WV4 38 C5
Eastdean Cl B23 56 D6
East Dene CV32 157 B2
East Dr B5 86 C4
Eastern Ave
Brierley Hill DY5 61 B2
Lichfield WS13 3 C2
Eastern Green Jun Sch CV5 111 D5
Eastern Green Rd CV5 111 F4
Eastern Hill B96 158 F2
Eastern Rd
Birmingham B29 86 B3
Sutton Coldfield B73 46 B1
Eastern Way WS11 2 A2
Easterton Croft B14 104 E2
East Farm Croft B10 87 D8
Eastfield Cl WS9 30 A6
Eastfield Dr B92 107 E8
Eastfield Gr WV1 25 F2
Eastfield Jun & Inf Sch WV1 25 F2
Eastfield Rd
Birmingham B9 68 C3
Nuneaton CV10 73 D6
Royal Leamington Spa CV32 162 A8
Tipton DY4 52 A8
Wolverhampton WV1 25 F2
Eastfield Retreat WV1 25 F2
East Gate B16 65 E3
Eastgate Ct WS14 9 C6
Eastgate Ho 4 CV34 160 E6
Eastgate Mews 3 CV34 160 E6
Eastgate St WS7 6 E8
East Gn WV4 38 D6
East Gr CV31 162 A6
Eastham Rd B13 105 C6
East Holme B9 67 C2
Easthope Rd B33 69 A4
Eastlake Cl B43 44 D3
Eastlands Gr CV5 112 E4
Eastlands Rd B13 87 A1
Eastleigh Ave CV5 132 F7
Eastleigh Croft B76 58 A7
Eastleigh Dr B62 101 A4
Eastleigh Gr B25 88 D8
Eastleigh DY3 50 C8
Eastley Cres CV34 160 B8
East Meadway B33 69 E3
East Mews B44 44 D2
East Moons Ho B98 154 E4
Eastmoor Cl B74 31 B2
Eastney Cres WV8 24 F8
Eastnor Cl
Kidderminster DY10 116 E2
Redditch B98 153 E1
Eastnor Gr CV31 162 B7
Easton Gdns WV11 26 F5
Easton Gr
Birmingham B27 88 C1
Hollywood B47 125 B7
East Park Inf Sch WV1 26 B1
East Park Jun Sch WV1 40 B8
East Park Trad Est WV1 40 A8
East Park Way WV1 26 A1
East Pathway B17 85 C6
East Rd
Bromsgrove B60 137 A1
Featherstone WV10 12 A7
Tipton DY4 52 B8
Wolverhampton WV4 39 F4
Eastridge Croft WS14 18 A5
East Rise B75 46 D6
East St
Brierley Hill DY5 82 A8
Cannock WS11 4 E6
Coventry CV1 113 E3
Dudley,Gornalwood DY3 50 D3
Dudley,Kate's Hill DY2 62 E8
Kidderminster DY10 116 F6
Tamworth B77 35 D5
Wolverhampton WV1 163 D2
East View Rd B72 46 D2
East View
Shuttington B79 22 F7
Tamworth B77 21 E3
Eastville B31 103 B3
Eastward Glen WV8 10 C1
Eastway B17 85 C6
East Way B92 91 B3
Eastway B40 90 F3
Eastwood Ave WS7 7 A8
Eastwood Cl CV31 162 D6
Eastwood Ct B96 158 E1
Eastwood Dr DY10 117 B5
Eastwood Rd
Birmingham,Balsall Heath B12 86 D5
Birmingham,Great Barr B43 54 F8
Dudley DY2 62 E6
Eastwoods Rd LE10 71 F2
Eatesbrook Rd B33 69 C3
Eathorpe Cl
Birmingham B34 69 D6
Coventry CV2 96 C1
Redditch B98 154 E1
Eaton Ave B70 53 A4
Eaton Cl CV32 156 D2
Eaton Cres DY3 50 B3
Eaton Ct
Royal Leamington Spa CV32 156 D1
Sutton Coldfield B74 46 B7
Eaton Pl DY6 60 E5
Eaton Rd CV1 165 B1
Eaton Rise WV12 27 B6
Eaton Wood Dr B26 88 D5
Eaton Wood B24 57 D4
Eaves Court Dr DY3 39 C1
Eaves Green Gdns B27 88 B5
Eaves Green La CV7 92 E1
Eaves Green Mobile Home Pk CV7 92 F2
Ebbw Vale Terr CV3 133 D7
Ebenezer St
Cannock WS12 2 A7
Tipton WV14 51 C8
West Bromwich B70 52 F6
Ebley Rd B20 55 A4
Ebmore Dr B14 104 D2
Eboral Cl CV34 155 E2
Eborne Croft CV7 130 C8
Ebourne Cl CV8 148 A4
Ebrington Ave B92 89 B3
Ebrington Cl B14 104 D4
Ebrington Rd B71 53 D6
Ebro Cres CV3 114 F1
Ebrook Rd B72 46 C4
Ebstree Mdw WV5 37 A2
Ebstree Rd
Seisdon WV5 37 A2
Seisdon WV5 37 C4
Eburne Rd CV2 96 C3
Ebury Rd B30 104 B4
Eccles Cl CV2 114 C8
Eccleshall Ave WV10 25 C8
Eccleston Cl B75 46 F5
Ecclestone Rd WV11 27 A8
Eccleston Sch B17 85 B5
Echells Cl B61 136 D2
Echo Way WV4 40 A4
Eckersall Rd B38 103 E3
Eckington Cl B98 159 B8
Eckington Wlk B38 123 E7
Eclipse Ind Est 1 DY4 51 E5
Edale Cl
Kingswinford DY6 60 B7
Wolverhampton WV4 39 E3
Edale Gn LE10 75 F6
Edale Rd B42 55 C7
Edale B77 22 B1
Edale Way CV6 114 A7
Eddens Wood Cl B78 34 E5
Eddie Miller Ct CV12 78 B2
Eddish Rd B33 69 B3
Eddy Rd DY10 116 E7
Edelweiss Cl WS5 43 B3
Edenbridge Rd B28 106 B8
Edenbridge View DY1 50 E3
Eden Cl
Birmingham B31 122 E8
Cannock WS12 2 E2
Oldbury B69 52 D2
Studley B80 159 D3
Edencroft B15 86 C8
Eden Croft CV8 148 B3
Eden Ct
Featherstone WV10 11 F8
Nuneaton CV10 72 C7
Royal Leamington Spa CV32 157 D3
Edendale Dr LE10 71 E4
Edendale Rd B26 89 B6
Edenfield Cl B97 153 A5
Edenfield Pl B77 22 B1
Eden Gdns
Rowley Regis B65 63 B2
Sedgley DY3 50 E8
Eden Gr
Birmingham B37 70 D1
West Bromwich B71 53 D5
Edenhall Rd B32 84 B6
Eden Ho 2 DY8 81 A5
Edenhurst Rd B31 122 F7
Eden Rd
Coventry CV2 115 A8
Solihull B92 89 D3
Edensor Cl WV10 25 E4
Eden St CV6 113 F7
Edgar Cl B79 20 F7
Edgar Stammers Jun & Inf Schs WS3 28 F6
Edgbaston High Sch for Girls
Birmingham B15 85 F7
Birmingham,Calthorpe Fields B15 86 B8
Edgbaston Park Rd B15 86 A5
Edgbaston Rd B12 86 D5
Edgbaston Rd E B12 86 F5
Edgbaston Rd B66 65 A4
Edgbaston Sh Ctr B16 86 A8
Edgbaston St B5 164 C2
Edgbaston (Warwickshire Cty Cricket Club) B5 86 D5
Edgcombe Rd B28 87 F1
Edgefield Rd CV2 115 A8
Edge Hill Ave WV10 12 B1
Edge Hill Dr
Perton WV6 23 E3
Sedgley DY3 39 C2
Edgehill Pl CV4 111 C1
Edgehill Rd B31 103 B1
Edge Hill Rd B74 31 E4
Edge Hill CV9 36 B2
Edgemond Ave B24 57 F4
Edgemoor Mdw WS12 2 C1
Edge St WV14 51 D8
Edgewick Com Prim Sch CV6 113 E8
Edgewood Cl 2 B64 82 F8
Edgewood Dr B45 122 B1
Edgewood Rd
Birmingham,King's Norton B38 123 F7
Birmingham,Rednal B45 122 B6
Edgeworth Cl
Redditch B98 154 C5
Willenhall WV12 27 C4
Edgeworth Ho WS13 3 A2
Edgmond Cl B98 154 D4
Edgware Rd B23 56 D5
Edgwick Park Ind Est CV6 113 F8
Edgwick Rd CV6 113 F7
Edgwood Ct 4 B16 65 F1
Edinburgh Ave WS2 27 F3
Edinburgh Cl DY10 116 E8
Edinburgh Cres
Royal Leamington Spa CV31 161 F6
Stourbridge DY8 60 C1
Edinburgh Ct B24 57 D4
Edinburgh Dr
Walsall WS4 29 D7
Willenhall WV12 27 B6
Edinburgh La WS2 28 A4
Edinburgh Rd
Bilston WV14 40 F3
Birmingham B68 84 B8
Dudley DY2 62 D6
Nuneaton CV10 72 D6
Walsall WS5 43 B8
Edinburgh Villas CV8 133 F2
Edingale Rd CV2 114 F8
Edison Cl WS12 2 C7
Edison Ct WV12 27 D7
Edison Gr B32 84 D5
Edison Rd
Curdworth B46,B76 59 F4
Walsall WS2 28 B5
Edison Wlk WS2 28 B5
Edith Rd B66 65 C3
Edith St B70 53 B3
Edmondes Cl CV34 155 F1
Edmonds Cl B33 69 B2
Edmondscote Rd CV32 161 D8
Edmonds Ct
Birmingham,Gilbertstone B26 88 F7
Birmingham,Small Heath B10 87 D7
Edmonds Rd B68 64 C2
Edmonton Ave B44 45 B1
Edmonton Cl WS11 2 B2
Edmonton Ho B5 86 D7
Edmoor Cl WV12 27 C6
Edmund Ho B3 164 B3
Edmund Rd
Birmingham B8 67 D4
Coventry CV1 113 D5
Dudley DY3 50 E6
Edmund St B3 164 B3
Ednall La B60 136 F1
Ednam Cl 3 B71 53 F8
Ednam Gr WV5 38 A1
Ednam Rd
Dudley DY1 51 C2
Wolverhampton WV4 39 C5
Edsome Way B36 68 F8
Edstone Cl B93 127 F4
Edstone Mews B36 68 F8
Education Ctr The DY5 61 D7
Edward Ave WS9 30 A7
Edward Bailey Cl CV3 134 E7
Edward Cl WV14 40 E3
Edward Ct
Birmingham B16 65 C1
Nuneaton CV11 73 C3
Sutton Coldfield B76 46 F3
Tamworth B77 21 F4
Walsall WS1 43 A8
Edward Fisher Dr DY4 52 A5
Edward Mews CV34 160 E7
Edward Rd
Bedworth CV12 78 C3
Birmingham B68 84 C8
Birmingham,Balsall Heath B12 86 E5
Birmingham,Highter's Heath B14 105 A1
Coventry CV6 95 A3
Halesowen B63 82 F4
Perton WV6 23 E5
Smethwick B67 65 A4
Tipton DY4 52 A7
Water Orton B46 59 C3
Edwards Ctr 7 LE10 75 D8
Edwards Gr CV8 148 C5
Edwards Rd
Birmingham B24 57 A4
Burntwood WS7 6 F5
Dudley DY2 62 C4
Sutton Coldfield B75 32 D3
Edward St
3 Dudley DY1 51 B1

Edward St continued
Birmingham B1 . . . . .66 C3
Cannock WS11 . . . . .1 E4
Coventry CV6 . . . . .113 E5
Darlaston WS10 . . . . .41 E6
Hinckley LE10 . . . . .71 C2
Nuneaton CV11 . . . . .73 C3
Oldbury B68 . . . . .64 A4
Redditch B97 . . . . .153 E4
Edward Street Hospl B70 .53 C3
Edward St
Royal Leamington Spa
CV32 . . . . .156 C1
Tamworth B79 . . . . .21 A5
Walsall WS2 . . . . .28 C3
Warwick CV34 . . . . .160 D7
Wolverhampton WV4 . . . . . . .39 F5
Edward Tyler Rd CV7 . . .78 A1
Edwin Ave (Road 4)
DY10 . . . . .116 F1
Edwin Ave B60 . . . . .150 F7
Edwin Ct
Bromsgrove B60 . . . . .150 F7
Bromsgrove B60 . . . . .150 F7
Edwin Phillips Dr B71 . . .53 B8
Edwin Rd B30 . . . . .104 B7
Edyth Rd CV2 . . . . .114 E4
Edyvean Walker Ct CV11 .73 B5
Eel St B69 . . . . .63 F7
Effingham Rd B13 . . . . . .105 C7
Egbert Cl B6 . . . . .67 B8
Egelwin Cl WV6 . . . . .23 E5
Egerton Ct 4 B15 . . . . . . .86 B7
Egerton Rd
Birmingham B24 . . . . .57 E3
Sutton Coldfield B74 . . . . . . .30 F1
Wolverhampton WV10 . . . . . .11 E3
Egghill La B31,B45 . . . . . .102 B3
Eggington Rd DY8 . . . . . . .80 D6
Egginton Rd B28 . . . . .105 E5
Egg La DY9,DY10 . . . . .119 A5
Eglamour Way CV34 . . . .161 F3
Egmont Gdns WV11 . . . . .26 F5
Egret Ct DY10 . . . . .117 A1
Egret Wlk CV2 . . . . .96 B3
Eider Cl DY10 . . . . .117 B1
Eights Croft WS7 . . . . .6 D8
Eileen Gdns B37 . . . . .69 F4
Eileen Rd B11 . . . . .87 C3
Elan Cl
Dudley DY3 . . . . .50 D3
Royal Leamington Spa
CV32 . . . . .157 C3
Elan Rd
Birmingham B31 . . . . .102 C2
Sedgley DY3 . . . . .50 C8
Elbow St B64 . . . . .62 F2
Elbury Croft B93 . . . . .127 F5
Elcock Dr B42 . . . . .55 D5
Eldalade Way WS10 . . . . . .42 D2
Elderberry Cl
3 Walsall WS5 . . . . .42 F3
Stourbridge DY8 . . . . .80 C3
Elderberry Way CV2 . . . .114 B6
Elder Cl WS11 . . . . .2 C2
Elderfield Rd B30 . . . . . . .104 B3
Elder La WS7 . . . . .7 C7
Eldersfield Cl B98 . . . . . .154 E7
Eldersfield Gr B91 . . . . . .127 B7
Elderside Cl WS8 . . . . .15 F8
Elder Way B23 . . . . .56 E2
Eldon Ct WS1 . . . . .28 F1
Eldon Dr B76 . . . . .57 E7
Eldon Rd
Birmingham B32 . . . . .84 A3
Birmingham,Edgbaston B16 .65 F2
Halesowen B62 . . . . .83 F3
Eldon St
Darlaston WS10 . . . . .41 D7
Walsall WS1 . . . . .28 F1
Eldorado Cl B80 . . . . .159 D4
Eld Rd CV6 . . . . .113 E7
Eldridge Cl WV9 . . . . .10 F2
Eleanor Rd WV14 . . . . .40 D6
Electra Park Ind Pk B6 . .56 B1
Electric Ave B6 . . . . .56 B1
Elford Cl
Birmingham B14 . . . . .104 E5
Sutton Coldfield B74 . . . . . . .31 A2
Elford Gr
Bilston WV14 . . . . .40 C4
Birmingham B37 . . . . .70 B1
Elford Rd
Birmingham B17,B29 . . . . . . .85 B3
West Bromwich B71 . . . . .42 E2
Elgar Cl
Cannock WS11 . . . . .1 E5
Lichfield WS13 . . . . .3 B2
Nuneaton CV11 . . . . .79 A7
Redditch B97 . . . . .158 C8
Elgar Cres DY5 . . . . .61 D7
Elgar Ct B15 . . . . .86 A7
Elgar Mews 2 B60 . . . . .136 F2
Elgar Rd CV6 . . . . .114 B8
Elgin Cl
Sedgley DY3 . . . . .39 E1
Stourbridge DY8 . . . . .81 A7
Elgin Ct WV6 . . . . .23 E4
Elgin Gr B25 . . . . .88 C7
Elgin Rd WS3 . . . . .14 A4
Elias Cl WS14 . . . . .9 E6
Eliot Cl
Tamworth B79 . . . . .21 A7
Warwick CV34 . . . . .155 E2

Eliot Croft WV14 . . . . .40 D2
Eliot St B7 . . . . .67 C8
Eliot Way CV10 . . . . .73 B2
Eliot Wlk DY10 . . . . .117 C6
Elisabeth Ct
Royal Leamington Spa
CV31 . . . . .162 B8
Sutton Coldfield B74 . . . . . . .32 B3
Elizabeth Ave
Bilston WV14 . . . . .40 F3
Wednesbury WS10 . . . . .42 C3
Wolverhampton WV4 . . . . . . .39 B5
Elizabeth Cres B68 . . . . . .64 D2
Elizabeth Ct
1 Birmingham B17 . . . . .85 D4
2 Birmingham,Acock's Green
B27 .88 C2
6 Coventry CV6 . . . . .113 A4
Warwick CV34 . . . . .161 B6
Elizabeth Dr B79 . . . . .21 A6
Elizabeth Gr
Dudley DY2 . . . . .62 F7
Solihull B90 . . . . .106 C2
Elizabeth Ho
1 Walsall WS5 . . . . .43 D7
Stourbridge DY9 . . . . .81 E5
Elizabeth Mews B69 . . . . .52 A2
Elizabeth Prout Gdns B65 63 B1
Elizabeth Rd
Birmingham,Moseley B13 . . .86 C2
Birmingham,New Oscott
B73 .45 D1
Birmingham,Stechford B33 . .68 D3
Cannock WS11 . . . . .1 E6
Halesowen B63 . . . . .82 F3
Hinckley LE10 . . . . .71 D2
Royal Leamington Spa
CV31 . . . . .161 F6
Walsall WS5 . . . . .43 C7
West Bromwich B70 . . . . .52 D4
Elizabeth Way
Coventry CV2 . . . . .114 F7
Kenilworth CV8 . . . . .147 E5
Redditch B97 . . . . .153 D5
Elizabeth Wlk DY4 . . . . . . .41 A2
Eliza Gdns B61 . . . . .121 B1
Elkington Croft B90 . . . .127 A5
Elkington St
Birmingham B6 . . . . .66 E5
Coventry CV6 . . . . .113 F8
Elkstone Cl B92 . . . . .89 B3
Elkstone Covert B14 . . . .104 C2
Ellacombe Rd CV2 . . . . . .114 D8
Elland Gr B27 . . . . .88 D2
Ellards Dr WV11 . . . . .26 F5
Ellenbrook Cl 6 B97 . . . .153 B5
Ellen St B18 . . . . .66 A4
Ellenvale Cl WV14 . . . . . . .51 A8
Ellerbeck B77 . . . . .22 B1
Ellerby Gr B24 . . . . .57 E4
Ellerdene Cl B98 . . . . .158 D8
Ellerman Gdns CV6 . . . . . .95 F3
Ellerside Gr B31 . . . . .102 F2
Ellerslie Cl DY5 . . . . .81 D8
Ellerslie Rd B13 . . . . .105 C7
Ellerton Rd B44 . . . . .45 D1
Ellerton Wlk WV10 . . . . . . .25 F5
Ellesboro' Rd B17 . . . . .85 B7
Ellesmere Rd
Bedworth CV12 . . . . .78 A2
Birmingham B8 . . . . .67 D4
Perton WV6 . . . . .23 F3
Ellice Dr B36 . . . . .70 B7
Elliot Ct 1 WV14 . . . . .39 F4
Elliot Gdns B45 . . . . .122 B5
Elliott Cl WS11 . . . . .1 F5
Elliott Ct CV5 . . . . .112 C1
Elliott Rd B29 . . . . .85 E1
Elliotts La WV8 . . . . .10 B3
Elliott's Rd DY4 . . . . .51 E5
Elliott Way B6 . . . . .55 F3
Ellis Ave DY5 . . . . .61 A2
Ellison St B70 . . . . .53 C1
Ellis Park Dr CV3 . . . . .115 B1
Ellis St B1 . . . . .164 B1
Elliston Ave B44 . . . . .55 E8
Elliston Gr CV31 . . . . .162 C6
Ellis Wlk WS11 . . . . .4 F8
Ellowes Hall Sch The DY3 .50 C5
Ellowes Rd DY3 . . . . .50 C4
Ellsmore Mdw WS13 . . . . . .9 A6
Ellys Rd CV1 . . . . .113 C5
Elm Ave
Bilston WV14 . . . . .40 D6
Birmingham B12 . . . . .87 A5
Wednesbury WS10 . . . . .41 F4
Wolverhampton WV11 . . . . . .26 B8
Elmay Rd B26 . . . . .89 A7
Elm Bank B13 . . . . .87 A3
Elm Bank Cl CV32 . . . . . . .157 A4
Elmbank Gr B20 . . . . .54 E5
Elmbank Rd
Kenilworth CV8 . . . . .147 E6
Walsall WS5 . . . . .43 C4
Elmbridge Cl B63 . . . . .82 D5
Elmbridge Dr B90 . . . . . . .126 F6
Elmbridge Rd B44 . . . . .55 E6
Elmbridge Way
1 Birmingham B31 . . . . .103 D2
Sedgley DY3 . . . . .50 C8
Elm Cl
Binley Woods CV3 . . . . .135 C7
Dudley DY3 . . . . .50 E2
Stourbridge DY8 . . . . .80 D2
Elmcroft 6 B66 . . . . .65 C5
Elmcroft Ave B32 . . . . .84 A1
Elm Croft B68 . . . . .84 C4

Elmcroft Gdns WV10 . . . . .11 E3
Elmcroft Rd B26 . . . . .88 F7
Elm Ct
Allesley CV5 . . . . .111 B8
Birmingham B13 . . . . .86 F4
Oldbury B66 . . . . .64 C8
Redditch B97 . . . . .153 D4
Walsall WS1 . . . . .43 A8
Elmdale B62 . . . . .84 A7
Elmdale Cres B31 . . . . . . .102 E4
Elmdale Dr
Aldridge WS9 . . . . .30 C8
Kidderminster DY10 . . . . . . .117 C5
Elmdale Rd
Birmingham B62 . . . . .102 E4
Wolverhampton WV14 . . . . . .51 A7
Elm Dale Rd WV4 . . . . .39 A5
Elmdene Rd CV8 . . . . .148 B4
Elmdon Cl
Solihull B92 . . . . .89 D2
Wolverhampton WV10 . . . . . .11 A1
Elmdon Coppice B92 . . . .107 F7
Elmdon Ct B37 . . . . .90 A7
Elmdon La
Birmingham B37 . . . . .90 A6
Solihull B26 . . . . .90 A6
Elmdon Park Rd B92 . . . . .89 D2
Elmdon Rd
Birmingham,Acock's Green
B27 .88 D4
Birmingham,Marston Green
B37 .90 A7
Birmingham,Selly Park B29 . .86 A2
Wolverhampton WV10 . . . . . .11 A1
Elmdon Trad Est B37 . . . . .90 C5
Elm Dr
Birmingham,Frankley
B31 . . . . .102 E7
Birmingham,Grove Vale B43 .43 D1
Blakedown DY10 . . . . .98 B2
Halesowen B62 . . . . .63 E1
Elm Farm Ave B37 . . . . . . .89 F7
Elm Farm Rd WV2 . . . . . . .39 D7
Elmfield Ave B24 . . . . .57 E2
Elmfield Cres B13 . . . . .86 F2
Elmfield Rd
Birmingham B36 . . . . .69 F7
Nuneaton CV10 . . . . .73 C7
Elmfield Rudolf Steiner Sch
Ltd DY8 . . . . .81 A3
Elmfield View DY1 . . . . . . .51 A3
Elm Gdns WS14 . . . . .9 C7
Elm Gn DY1 . . . . .51 A5
Elm Gr
Balsall Common CV7 . . . . . .130 C6
Birmingham B37 . . . . .69 F6
Bromsgrove B61 . . . . .137 A4
Codsall WV8 . . . . .10 A3
Huntington WS12 . . . . .1 D8
Elmhurst Ave B65 . . . . . . .63 C3
Elmhurst B15 . . . . .85 D8
Elmhurst Cl B97 . . . . .158 D4
Elmhurst Dr
Burntwood WS7 . . . . .7 A4
Kingswinford DY6 . . . . .60 F4
Elmhurst Rd
Birmingham B21 . . . . .54 E1
Coventry CV6 . . . . .96 A4
Hinckley Tech Sch B5 . . . . . .86 B5
Elmley Cl
Dudley WV14 . . . . .51 B7
Kidderminster DY11 . . . . . . .116 B3
Elmley Ct B33 . . . . .56 C2
Elmley Gr
Birmingham B30 . . . . .104 B2
Perton WV6 . . . . .23 F3
Elmley Ho 8 B97 . . . . .153 A4
Elm Lodge B92 . . . . .109 A7
Elmore Cl
Birmingham B37 . . . . .70 A4
Coventry CV3 . . . . .134 B8
Elmore Green Cl WS3 . . . .28 B8
Elmore Green Prim Sch
WS3 .14 B1
Elmore Green Rd WS3 . . .14 B1
Elmore Rd B33 . . . . .69 A3
Elmore Row WS3 . . . . .14 B1
Elm Pl DY10 . . . . .118 B3
Elm Rd
Birmingham B15 . . . . .85 F5
Birmingham,Bournville
B30 . . . . .103 F8
Dudley DY1 . . . . .51 C4
Kidderminster DY10 . . . . . . .117 A6
Kingswinford DY6 . . . . .60 E6
Norton Canes WS11 . . . . .6 A1
Redditch B97 . . . . .153 D4
Royal Leamington Spa
CV32 . . . . .157 B3
Sutton Coldfield B76 . . . . . . .46 F2
Walsall WS3 . . . . .28 C8
Elms Cl
Birmingham B38 . . . . .123 C8
Solihull B91 . . . . .107 D5
Elmsdale Ave CV6 . . . . .95 F2
Elmsdale Ct 6 WS1 . . . . . .42 F8
Elmsdale Gr B31 . . . . .123 B7
Elms Farm Prim Sch B33 .89 D7
Elms Rd B72 . . . . .46 C3
Elmstead Ave B33 . . . . . . .89 D7
Elmstead Cl WS5 . . . . .29 E1
Elmstead Twr 2 B5 . . . . . .86 E7
Elmstead Wood WS5 . . . . .29 E1
Elms The
Bedworth CV12 . . . . .77 E2
Birmingham B16 . . . . .65 F3
Kingswood B94 . . . . .144 D3
Leek Wootton CV35 . . . . . . .155 F6

Elms The continued
Wolverhampton WV11 . . . . . .26 B5
Elmstone Cl
Dudley DY3 . . . . .50 F4
Redditch B97 . . . . .158 C5
Elm St
Willenhall WV13 . . . . .27 C2
Wolverhampton WV3 . . . . . . .25 A1
Elm Terr B69 . . . . .52 B1
Elm Tree Ave CV4 . . . . . . .112 B2
Elm Tree Dr LE10 . . . . .75 F8
Elm Tree Gr B63 . . . . .82 D6
Elm Tree Rd
Birmingham B17 . . . . .85 A7
Birmingham,Stirchley B30 . .104 A6
Bulkington CV12 . . . . .79 D2
Elmtree Rd
Sutton Coldfield B74 . . . . . . .30 D1
Sutton Coldfield B74 . . . . . . .44 D8
Elm Tree Rise B92 . . . . . .109 B6
Elm Tree Way B64 . . . . .62 F1
Elm Tree Wlk B79 . . . . .20 F8
Elm Way CV10 . . . . .72 A8
Elmwood Ave
Coventry CV6 . . . . .112 F5
Essington WV11 . . . . .13 A3
Elmwood Cl
Balsall Common CV7 . . . . . .130 C7
Cannock WS11 . . . . .2 A2
Elmwood Ct
Birmingham B5 . . . . .86 D6
Coventry CV1 . . . . .165 B4
Sutton Coldfield B74 . . . . . . .45 A5
Elmwood Gdns B20 . . . . . .55 B2
Elmwood Gr B47 . . . . .125 A6
Elmwood Rd
Birmingham B24 . . . . .57 C2
Stourbridge DY8 . . . . .60 C2
Sutton Coldfield B74 . . . . . . .45 A5
Elmwood Rise DY3 . . . . . . .39 E1
Elmwoods B32 . . . . .84 B2
Elphin Cl CV6 . . . . .95 A4
Elphinstone End B24 . . . . .57 C6
Elsma Rd B68 . . . . .84 C8
Elston Hall La WV10 . . . . . .11 C1
Elston Hall Prim Sch
WV10 . . . . .11 D2
Elstree Rd B23 . . . . .56 D5
Elswick Gr B44 . . . . .56 B8
Elswick Rd B44 . . . . .45 B1
Elsworth Gr B25 . . . . .88 C6
Elsworth Rd B31 . . . . .103 D2
Eltham Gr B44 . . . . .45 B1
Eltham Rd CV3 . . . . .133 E7
Elton Cl
Royal Leamington Spa
CV32 . . . . .157 C2
Wolverhampton WV10 . . . . . .11 E4
Elton Croft B93 . . . . .127 F4
Elton Gr B27 . . . . .88 A2
Eltonia Croft B26 . . . . .89 B6
Elunda Gr WS7 . . . . .6 E8
Elva Croft B36 . . . . .58 F1
Elvers Green La B92,B93 .128 E7
Elvetham Rd B15 . . . . .86 C8
Elviron Dr WV6 . . . . .24 B5
Elwell Cres DY1 . . . . .50 F6
Elwells Cl WV14 . . . . .40 A3
Elwell St
Wednesbury WS10 . . . . .42 B3
West Bromwich B70 . . . . .52 E5
Elwy Circ CV7 . . . . .95 C6
Elwyn Rd B73 . . . . .46 A3
Ely Cl
Birmingham B37 . . . . .70 B2
Cannock WS11 . . . . .2 B1
Coventry CV2 . . . . .115 A6
Kidderminster DY11 . . . . . . .116 A6
Rowley Regis B65 . . . . .63 D3
Ely Cres B71 . . . . .53 B7
Ely Gr B32 . . . . .84 F4
Ely Pl WS2 . . . . .28 B1
Ely Rd WS2 . . . . .28 B1
Emay Cl B70 . . . . .52 F8
Embankment The DY5 . . . .61 E3
Embassy Dr
Birmingham B15 . . . . .86 B8
Oldbury B69 . . . . .63 E8
Embassy Ind Est 1 DY9 . .81 F5
Embassy Rd B69 . . . . .63 E8
Embassy Wlk CV2 . . . . . . .114 D8
Emberton Way B77 . . . . . . .21 F5
Embleton Cl LE10 . . . . .71 B1
Embleton Gr B34 . . . . .69 A6
Emerald Ct
3 Solihull B92 . . . . .88 F1
Birmingham B8 . . . . .68 C5
Emerald Way CV31 . . . . . .161 F5
Emerson Cl DY3 . . . . .50 A4
Emerson Gr WV10 . . . . .25 F8
Emerson Rd
Birmingham B17 . . . . .85 C6
Coventry CV2 . . . . .114 C3
Wolverhampton WV10 . . . . . .25 E8
Emery Cl
Birmingham B23 . . . . .56 D1
Coventry CV2 . . . . .114 F2
Walsall WS1 . . . . .42 F8
Emery Ct DY10 . . . . .116 F2
Emery St DY10 . . . . .116 F2
Emily Gdns B16 . . . . .65 F3
Emily Rd B26 . . . . .88 D6
Emily Smith Ho 2 CV2 . . .96 B1
Emily St
Birmingham B12 . . . . .86 F7
West Bromwich B70 . . . . .53 B2
Emmanuel Rd
Burntwood WS7 . . . . .7 B7

Emmanuel Rd continued
Sutton Coldfield B73 . . . . . . .57 B8
Emmeline St B9 . . . . .67 B2
Emmott Dr CV31 . . . . .162 B5
Emperor Pl DY10 . . . . .116 E8
Empire Cl WS9 . . . . .29 F8
Empire Ind Est WS9 . . . . . .15 F1
Empire Ind Pk WS9 . . . . . .29 F8
Empire Rd CV4 . . . . .111 E2
Empress Way WS10 . . . . . .41 D8
Emscote Dr B73 . . . . .57 B2
Emscote Gn B91 . . . . .106 C2
Emscote Inf Sch CV34 . . .161 B8
Emscote Rd
Birmingham B6 . . . . .55 F1
Coventry CV3 . . . . .114 C2
Warwick CV34 . . . . .161 B8
Emsworth Cres WV9 . . . . . .11 A2
Emsworth Gr B14 . . . . .104 D6
Ena Rd CV1 . . . . .113 D5
Endemere Rd CV6 . . . . . . .113 D7
Enderby Cl B93 . . . . .127 F4
Enderby Dr WV4 . . . . .39 A5
Enderby Gr 9 B18 . . . . .65 E4
Enderby Rd B23 . . . . .56 C7
Enderley Cl WS3 . . . . .14 B3
Enderley Dr WS3 . . . . .14 B3
End Hall Rd WV6 . . . . .24 A3
Endhill Rd B44 . . . . .45 A3
Endicott Rd B6 . . . . .55 F1
Endmoor Gr B23 . . . . .56 C6
Endsleigh Gdns CV31 . . . .162 B6
Endsleigh Gr B28 . . . . .106 A8
Endwood Court Rd B20 . . .55 A2
Endwood Ct
Birmingham B11 . . . . .87 D4
Birmingham,Handsworth Wood
B20 .55 A2
Endwood Dr
Solihull B91 . . . . .106 F2
Sutton Coldfield B74 . . . . . . .31 C4
Enfield Cl B23 . . . . .56 F6
Enfield Ind Est B97 . . . . . .153 D5
Enfield Rd
Birmingham B15 . . . . .86 B8
Coventry CV2 . . . . .114 B3
Redditch B97 . . . . .158 D5
Rowley Regis B65 . . . . .63 D3
Enford Cl B34 . . . . .69 D6
Engadine Rd B60 . . . . .137 C1
Engine La
Brierley Hill DY5 . . . . .61 F4
Darlaston WS10 . . . . .41 A4
Stourbridge DY9 . . . . .81 D6
Tamworth B77 . . . . .22 A2
Walsall WS8 . . . . .15 C8
Engine St
Oldbury B69 . . . . .64 B6
Smethwick B66 . . . . .65 B6
England Cres CV31 . . . . . .161 E2
England Ho 10 CV32 . . . . .156 F2
Englestede Cl B20 . . . . .54 F3
Engleton Rd CV6 . . . . .113 A6
Englewood Dr B28 . . . . . . .106 A6
English Martyrs CE Prim Sch
B11 .87 C4
Ennerdale Cl
Brownhills WS8 . . . . .15 E7
Royal Leamington Spa
CV32 . . . . .156 D2
Ennerdale Cres CV11 . . . . .73 E3
Ennerdale Dr
Halesowen B63 . . . . .82 D2
Perton WV6 . . . . .23 F4
Ennerdale La CV2 . . . . . . .114 F4
Ennerdale Rd
Birmingham B43 . . . . .54 F6
Wolverhampton WV6 . . . . . . .24 D8
Ennersdale Bglws B46 . . .59 F1
Ennersdale Cl B46 . . . . .59 F1
Ennersdale Rd B46 . . . . . . .59 F1
Enright Cl CV32 . . . . .156 E2
Ensall Dr DY8 . . . . .60 E1
Ensbury Cl WV12 . . . . .27 D4
Ensdale Row WV13 . . . . . . .27 A1
Ensdon Gr B44 . . . . .45 B1
Ensford Cl B74 . . . . .31 E5
Ensign Cl CV4 . . . . .111 D1
Ensor Cl CV11 . . . . .74 A6
Ensor Dr B78 . . . . .22 F1
Enstone Rd
Birmingham B23 . . . . .57 A7
Dudley DY1 . . . . .61 F8
Enterprise Dr
Stourbridge DY9 . . . . .81 F6
Sutton Coldfield B74 . . . . . . .44 E7
Enterprise Gr WS3 . . . . . . .13 B5
Enterprise Ho B92 . . . . . .109 A6
Enterprise Ind Pk WS13 . . .9 F8
Enterprise Trad Est DY5 . .61 F3
Enterprise Way B7 . . . . . .164 D4
Enterprise Workshops
DY6 .61 A7
Enville Cl
Birmingham B37 . . . . .70 B1
Walsall WS3 . . . . .14 A3
Enville Gr B11 . . . . .87 D5
Enville Pl DY8 . . . . .80 E5
Enville Rd
Dudley DY3 . . . . .50 D8
Kingswinford DY6 . . . . .60 D8
Wolverhampton WV4 . . . . . . .38 C4
Enville St DY8 . . . . .80 F5
Epperston Ct CV31 . . . . . .161 F7
Epping Cl
Birmingham B45 . . . . .102 B2
Walsall WS3 . . . . .28 C6

Epping Gr B44......56 A7
Epping Way CV32......157 C4
Epsom Cl
  Bedworth CV12......78 B4
  Lichfield WS14......9 D7
  Perton WV6......23 F4
  Redditch B97......158 C8
  Tamworth B77......35 C4
Epsom Ct 16 B29......103 C7
Epsom Dr CV3......134 C6
Epsom Rd B44......56 B8
Epsom Rd
  Royal Leamington Spa
  CV32......157 C4
  Upper Catshill B61......121 A1
Epwell Gr B44......55 F6
Epwell Rd B44......55 F6
Epworth Ct DY5......61 B5
Erasmus Rd B11......87 A7
Erasmus Way WS13......9 A8
Ercall Cl B23......56 A6
Erdington Hall Prim Sch
  B24......114 A1
Erdington Hall Rd B24......56 F2
Erdington Ind Pk B24......57 F4
Erdington Rd WS9......30 C3
Erdington Sta B23......56 F5
Erica Cl CV4......77 F2
Erica Dr B29......103 A8
Erica Dr CV31......162 B2
Erica Rd WS5......43 B3
Eric Grey Cl CV2......114 A5
Eringden B77......22 B1
Erithway Rd CV3......133 B4
Ermington Cres B36......68 F7
Ermington Rd WV4......39 D4
Ernesford Grange Prim Sch
  CV3......114 E1
Ernesford Grange Sch & Com
  Coll CV3......134 D8
Ernest Clarke Cl WV12......27 C4
Ernest Ct B38......104 A1
Ernest Rd
  Birmingham B12......87 B4
  Dudley DY2......51 F1
  Smethwick B67......64 E6
Ernest Richards Rd CV12......78 B4
Ernest St B1......164 B1
Ernsford Ave CV3......114 B1
Ernsford Cl B93......127 F2
Erskine Cl LE10......71 A2
Erskine St B7......67 B3
Erwood Cl B97......153 B2
Esher Rd
  Birmingham B44......44 F4
  West Bromwich B71......53 D6
Eskdale Cl WV1......26 A2
Eskdale Rd LE10......75 A7
Eskdale Wlk
  Brierley Hill DY5......81 B8
  Coventry CV3......134 D7
Esk Ho 1 B11......61 E8
Eskrett St WS2......2 C5
Esme Rd B11......87 B4
Esmond Cl B30......103 D5
Essendon Gr B8......68 B4
Essendon Rd B8......68 B4
Essendon Wlk B8......68 B4
Essex Ave
  Kingswinford DY6......60 B5
  Wednesbury WS10......42 C4
  West Bromwich B71......53 D7
Essex Cl
  Coventry CV5......112 B3
  Kenilworth CV8......147 E2
Essex Ct
  5 Birmingham B29......103 C2
  Warwick CV34......160 E8
Essex Gdns DY8......80 D7
Essex Ho
  2 Birmingham B2......164 B4
  2 Wolverhampton WV3......25 C4
Essex Rd
  Dudley DY2......62 A6
  Sutton Coldfield B75......32 D2
Essex St
  Birmingham B5......164 C1
  Walsall WS2......28 E5
Essington Cl
  Lichfield WS14......9 A5
  Shenstone WS14......18 A7
  Stourbridge DY8......60 E1
Essington Ind Est WV11......12 F4
Essington Rd WV12......13 B5
Essington St B16......66 B1
Essington Way WV1......26 B6
Este Rd B26......69 A1
Esterton Cl CV6......95 C2
Estone Wlk B6......67 A4
Estria Rd B15......86 B7
Estridge La WS6......5 A2
Etchell Rd B78......20 F3
Ethelfield Rd CV2......114 B3
Ethelfleda Rd B77......35 F5
Ethelfleda Terr WS10......41 F3
Ethel Rd B17......85 D5
Ethelred Cl B74......32 A3
Ethel St
  Birmingham B2......164 B2
  Oldbury B68......64 A4
  Smethwick B67......64 F2
Etheridge Rd WV14......40 D7
Eton Cl
  1 Sutton Coldfield B74......31 F2
  Lichfield WS14......9 B6

Eton Dr DY8......81 A3
Etone Com Sch CV11......73 D5
Eton Cl......73 B5
Eton Rd B12......87 B4
Eton Wlk DY9......99 A6
Etruria Way WV14......40 E7
Etta Gr B44......44 F4
Ettingley Cl B98......159 B5
Ettingshall Park Farm La
  WV4......39 E4
Ettingshall Prim Sch
  WV14......40 B6
Ettingshall Rd
  Bilston WV14......40 A2
  Wolverhampton WV2......40 A7
Ettington Cl B93......127 D2
Ettington Rd
  Birmingham B6......66 E8
  Coventry CV5......112 A3
Ettymore Cl DY3......50 D8
Ettymore Rd DY3......50 D8
Ettymore Rd W DY3......50 C8
Etwall Rd B28......105 E6
Euan Cl B17......85 C8
Eunal Ct B97......158 E5
Euro Bsns Pk B69......52 D1
Euro Cl B73......87 B2
Europa Ave B70......53 F2
Europa Way
  Lichfield WS13......9 F8
  Royal Leamington Spa
  CV34......161 D5
European Bsns Pk B69......63 E7
Eustace Rd CV12......79 D1
Euston Cres CV3......134 C6
Euston Pl CV32......161 F8
Euston Sq 1 CV32......161 F8
Evans Cl
  Willenhall WS11......26 D1
  Dudley DY4......51 C5
Evans Croft B78......21 A1
Evans Gdns B29......85 D1
Evans Gr CV31......162 A2
Evans Pl WV14......40 E7
Evans St
  Willenhall WS11......26 D1
  Wolverhampton,Dunstall Hill
  WV6......25 A4
  Wolverhampton WV4,WV4......39 F1
Eva Rd
  Birmingham B18......65 D6
  Oldbury B68......64 D3
Evason Ct B6......55 E1
Eve La DY1......50 F5
Evelyn Ave CV6......95 F2
Evelyn Croft B73......57 A8
Evelyn Rd B11......87 D4
Evenlode Cl
  Redditch B98......153 F1
  Solihull B92......115 A8
Evenlode Cres CV6......112 F5
Evenlode Gr WV13......27 D1
Evenlode Rd B92......89 B3
Everard Ct CV11......73 E2
Everdon Rd CV6......95 B2
Everene Ho 1 B27......88 C3
Everest Cl B66......64 F8
Everest Rd
  Birmingham B20......55 A3
  Willenhall WS2......27 F3
Everglade Rd CV9......36 C2
Evergreen Cl WV14......51 B8
Evergreen Hts WS1......2 A8
Evergreens The CV10......72 F6
Everitt Dr B93......128 A6
Eversfield Prep Sch B91......107 B4
Eversleigh Rd CV6......112 E7
Eversley Dale B24......57 A2
Eversley Gr
  Sedgley DY3......39 C2
  Wolverhampton WV11......26 C6
Eversley Rd 2 B9......67 D1
Evers St DY5......82 A8
Everton Rd B8......68 C4
Eves Croft B32......84 C1
Evesham Cres WS3......13 F3
Evesham Ct DY11......116 D5
Evesham Ho B62......137 B3
Evesham Mews 3 B97......153 E3
Evesham Rise B96,B97......158 D4
Evesham Rise DY2......62 D3
Evesham Sq 3 B97......153 E3
Evesham St B97......153 E3
Evesham Wlk
  2 Redditch B97......153 E4
  Coventry CV6......132 D5
Eveson Rd DY8......80 E2
Ewart Rd WS2......27 F3
Ewell Rd B24......57 B4
Ewhurst Ave B29......85 F1
Ewhurst Cl WV13......40 F8
Ewloe Cl DY10......116 E1
Exbury Cl WV9......10 F2
Exbury Way CV11......78 E8
Excelsior Gr WS3......15 B5
Exchange Ind Est The
  WS11......4 E5
Exchange St
  Brierley Hill DY5......61 D4
  Kidderminster DY10......116 E6
  Wolverhampton WV1......163 B3
Exchange The WS3......14 B1
Exe Croft B31......123 D8
Exeter Cl
  Coventry CV3......134 D8
  Kidderminster DY11......116 A6
Exeter Dr
  Birmingham B37......89 F8

Exeter Dr continued
  Tamworth B79......20 E5
Exeter Ho 8 B24......56 F4
Exeter Pas B1......164 B1
Exeter Pl WS2......28 B1
Exeter Rd
  Birmingham B29......85 F2
  Cannock WS11......4 C4
  Dudley DY2......62 D2
  Smethwick B66......65 B5
Exeter St B1......164 B1
Exford Cl DY5......81 B7
Exhall Cedars Inf Sch CV7 96 A8
Exhall Cl
  Redditch B98......154 D5
  Solihull B91......106 E2
Exhall Ct B23......56 C2
Exhall Gn CV7......95 F7
Exhall Grange Sch & Science
  Coll CV7......95 C5
Exhall Rd CV7......95 A6
Exham Cl CV34......155 E1
Exhibition Way B40......90 D4
Exis Ct CV11......73 E2
Exley CV31......21 D1
Exminster Rd CV3......133 E5
Exmoor Ct B61......137 A4
Exmoor Dr
  Bromsgrove B61......137 A4
  Royal Leamington Spa
  CV32......157 C4
Exmoor Gn WV11......26 C7
Exmouth Cl CV2......114 C7
Exonbury Wlk 5 WS11......1 F2
Exon Ct DY4......51 F6
Expressway The B70......53 C4
Exton Cl
  Ash Green CV7......95 C6
  Wednesfield WV11......26 F8
Exton Way B8......67 D5
Eyffler Cl CV34......160 D7
Eyland Gr WS1......28 F2
Eymore Cl B29......103 B6
Eynsham Cl CV4......131 F7
Eyre St B18......66 A3
Eyston Ave DY4......52 D8
Eyton Cl B98......154 D3
Eyton Croft B12......86 F7
Ezekiel La WV12......27 C6

F

Fabian Cl
  Birmingham B45......102 A2
  Coventry CV3......134 D7
Fabian Cres B90......106 B1
Fabius Cl LE10......75 C7
Facet Rd B38......104 A2
Factory La B61......136 F1
Factory Rd
  Birmingham B18......66 A6
  Hinckley LE10......71 D1
  Tipton DY4......51 E6
Factory St WS10......41 C6
Fairbanks Cl CV2......115 A7
Fairbourne Ave
  Birmingham B44......44 E2
  Rowley Regis B65......63 E4
Fairbourne Gdns B97......158 C2
Fairbourne Twr B23......57 A6
Fairbourne Way CV6......112 E8
Fairburn Cres WS3......15 B5
Faircroft Ave B76......57 F6
Faircroft CV8......147 F3
Faircroft Rd B36......58 D1
Fairdene Way B43......54 D8
Fairfax Ct 7 B43......160 F7
Fairfax Rd
  Birmingham B31......123 A8
  Sutton Coldfield B75......46 F5
  Wolverhampton WV10......11 E3
Fairfax St CV1......165 C3
Fairfield Cl WS12......2 D1
Fairfield Ct CV3......134 A7
Fairfield Dr
  Halesowen B62......63 E1
  Walsall WS3......15 B4
Fairfield Gr B62......63 E1
Fairfield Ho B60......137 B3
Fairfield Mount WS1......42 F8
Fairfield Park Ind Est B62 63 E1
Fairfield Rd
  Birmingham B14......104 E8
  Dudley DY2......62 D7
  Halesowen B63......83 A2
  Halesowen,Hurst Green B62 63 E1
  Stourbridge DY8......60 F2
Fairfield Rise
  Meriden CV7......92 C1
  Stourbridge DY8......80 D5
Fairfields Hill B78......36 F8
Fairford Cl
  Redditch B98......154 C7
  Solihull B91......106 D5
Fairford Gdns
  Burntwood WS7......7 C6
  Stourbridge DY8......60 E3
Fairford Rd B44......55 F6
Fairgreen Gdns DY5......61 C5
Fairgreen Way
  Birmingham B29......85 F1
  Sutton Coldfield B74......31 A1
Fairground Way WS1......42 D8
Fairhaven Croft B62......63 E1

Fairhaven Prim Sch DY8......60 D3
Fairhills DY3......50 D8
Fairhill Way B11......87 C7
Fairholme Rd B36......68 B7
Fairhurst Dr CV32......156 E3
Fair Isle Dr CV10......72 F2
Fair Lady Dr WS7......6 D8
Fairlands Pk CV4......132 E5
Fairlawn B15......86 A7
Fairlawn Cl
  Royal Leamington Spa
  CV32......156 D1
  Willenhall WV12......13 C1
Fairlawn Dr DY6......60 D4
Fairlawns
  Birmingham B26......69 A1
  Sutton Coldfield B76......58 A8
Fairlawn Way WV12......13 C1
Fairlie Cres B38......103 D1
Fairlight Dr B45......122 A1
Fairmead Rise B38......103 E1
Fairmile Cl CV3......134 D8
Fairmile Rd B63......83 A6
Fairmont Rd B60......151 B8
Fairmount Dr 5 WS11......4 E8
Fairoak Dr
  Bromsgrove B60......150 F6
  Wolverhampton WV6......24 B3
Fair Oaks Dr WS6......14 A8
Fairview Ave B42......55 B6
Fairview Cl
  Cheslyn Hay WS6......4 C2
  Tamworth B77......21 F5
  Wolverhampton WV11......26 B7
Fairview Cres
  Kingswinford DY6......60 F6
  Wolverhampton WV11......26 B7
Fairview Ct WS2......27 D2
Fairview Gr WV11......26 B7
Fairview Ind Est B76......59 B7
Fairview Mews 9 B46......70 F7
Fairview Rd
  Dudley DY1......51 A3
  Wolverhampton,Scotlands
  WV11......26 B7
  Wolverhampton,Spring Hill
  WV4......38 C4
Fairview Wlk CV6......95 E2
Fairway B69......63 A8
Fairway
  Birmingham B31......102 E3
  Cannock WS11......4 D6
Fairway Ct B77......22 B3
Fairway Dr B45......121 F6
Fairway Gn WV14......40 D8
Fairway Rd CV11......79 B8
Fairway Rd B68......63 F2
Fairways Ave B93......128 A8
Fairways Dr B60......138 B5
Fairways The CV32......156 F2
Fairway The......35 F5
Fairway The
  Birmingham B38......103 D2
  Hinckley LE10......75 F7
Fairway WS4......15 D1
Fairyfield Ct B43......43 D1
Fairyfield Ho B43......43 D1
Fakenham Croft B17......84 F7
Falcon Ave CV3......134 F8
Falcon Cl
  Cannock WS11......1 C2
  Cheslyn Hay WS6......4 C2
  Kidderminster DY10......116 C8
  Nuneaton CV11......79 B8
Falcon Cres WV14......39 C7
Falcondale Rd WV12......13 C1
Falconers Gn LE10......75 E6
Falconhurst Rd B29......84 F3
Falcon Lodge Cres B75......47 A6
Falcon Pk B77......35 E7
Falcon Pl B68......63 C7
Falcon Rd B68......80 C6
Falcons The B75......47 B5
Falcon View B30......104 A4
Falcon Way WV14......50 F1
Falfield Cl B65......63 D6
Falfield Gr B31......122 C7
Falkener Ho CV6......113 E7
Falkland Cl CV4......131 D7
Falkland Croft B30......104 B6
Falkland Way B36......70 B6
Falkwood Gr B93......127 F6
Fallindale Rd B26......89 B6
Fallings Heath Cl WV10......41 F7
Fallings Park Ind Est
  WV10......25 F5
Fallings Park Prim Sch
  WV10......26 A8
Fallowfield Ave B28......105 F5
Fallowfield B15......85 E8
Fallow Field
  Cannock WS11......1 E3
  Lichfield WS13......3 C3
Fallowfield WV6......23 D4
Fallowfield Rd
  Halesowen B63......82 D3
  Rowley Regis B65......63 A3
  Solihull B92......89 D3
  Walsall WS5......43 E8

Fallowfields Cl B61......136 E3
Fallow Cl......95 C4
Fallow Field B74......31 B3
Fallowfield WV8......10 E2
Fallow Hill CV31......162 C6
Fallow Rd B78......20 F1
Fallows Ho B19......66 E5
Fallows Rd B11......87 C6
Fallow Wlk B32......84 A2
Falmouth Cl CV11......74 A5
Falmouth Dr
  Hinckley LE10......71 E4
  Tamworth B77......21 F5
Falmouth Rd
  Birmingham B34......68 F6
  Walsall WS5......43 D7
Falna Cres B79......20 F7
Falstaff Av CV4......125 A6
Falstaff Cl
  Nuneaton CV11......74 A1
  Sutton Coldfield B76......58 B7
Falstaff Ct B75......47 C5
Falstaff Gr CV34......161 E3
Falstaff Ho B13......105 F7
Falstaff Rd
  Coventry CV4......111 E1
  Solihull B90......106 C1
Falstone Rd B73......45 D2
Fanad Ho B23......56 E3
Fancott Dr CV8......147 F6
Fancott Rd B31......103 A5
Fancourt Ave WV4......38 D4
Fane Rd WV11......13 B2
Fanshawe Rd B27......88 C1
Faraday Ave
  Birmingham B32......84 D5
  Curdworth B46,B76......59 F5
Faraday Cr B32......84 D5
Faraday Ho 6 B15......86 C8
Faraday Rd
  Hinckley LE10......74 E7
  Walsall WS2......28 B1
Farber Rd CV2......115 A6
Farbrook Way WV12......27 B6
Farclose Ho B15......86 C7
Farcroft Ave
  Birmingham B21......65 D8
  Coventry CV6......111 D4
Farcroft Gr B21......54 D1
Farcroft Rd B21......54 D1
Fardon Way B23......56 B8
Fareham Cres WV4......38 C6
Farewell La WS7......7 E6
Farfield
  Kidderminster DY10......116 F5
  Stoke Prior B60......150 F4
Far Gosford St CV1......113 E2
Far High Dr B74......52 B5
Far Highfield B76......46 E4
Far Hill Cl B17......53 F8
Farington B77......21 F1
Farlands Dr DY8......81 A3
Farlands Gr B43......54 F7
Farlands Rd DY8......81 A3
Far Lash LE10......75 F7
Farleigh Dr WV3......38 A8
Farleigh Rd WV6......24 A3
Farley Ctr The B70......53 D2
Farley La B62......100 F1
Farley Rd B23......56 B4
Farley St
  Royal Leamington Spa
  CV31......162 B7
  Tipton DY4......52 D5
Farlow Cl
  Coventry CV6......114 A4
  Redditch B98......154 D3
Farlow Croft B37......89 F8
Farlow Rd B31......103 C3
Farmacre B9......67 C2
Farman Rd CV5......113 A2
Farm Ave B68......64 A3
Farmbridge Cl WS2......27 C3
Farmbridge Rd WS2......27 C3
Farmbridge Way WS2......27 D3
Farmbrook Ave WV10......11 F2
Farm Cl
  Birmingham B33......68 F3
  Cannock WS12......2 C3
  Codsall WV8......10 B2
  Coventry CV6......96 B4
  Kidderminster DY11......116 B2
  Sedgley DY3......50 B7
  Solihull B92......21 C7
  Tamworth B79......21 C7
Farmcote Cl B97......158 D4
Farmcote Lodge CV2......96 B4
Farmcote Rd
  Birmingham B33......69 A4
  Coventry CV2......96 B4
Farmcroft Rd DY9......81 E2
Farmdale Gr B45......122 A6
Farm End B20......88 A7
Farmers Cl B76......46 E4
Farmers Ct B63......82 F4
Farmer's Fold WV1......163 B3
Farmers Rd B60......150 E7
Farmers Wlk B21......54 F7
Farmer Ward Rd CV8......148 A3
Farmer Way DY4......41 C1
Farm House La B75......32 E3
Farmhouse Rd WV12......27 D5

Farm House Way B43 . . . . . **43** E4
Farmhouse Way
Solihull B90 . . . . **127** B7
Willenhall WV12 . . . . **27** D5
Farmoor Gr B34 . . . . **69** E6
Far Moor La B98. . . . . **154** F5
Farmoor Way WV10 . . . . . **11** E4
Farm Rd
Birmingham B11 . . . . **87** B7
Brierley Hill DY5 . . . . **61** E1
Dudley DY2 . . . . **62** A4
Hinckley LE10 . . . . **75** E6
Kenilworth CV8 . . . . **147** E2
Oldbury B68. . . . . **64** A3
Redditch B98. . . . . **154** A3
Rowley Regis B65 . . . . **63** A4
Royal Leamington Spa
CV32. . . . . **157** B3
Smethwick B67 . . . . **64** E3
Tipton DY4. . . . . **52** B7
Wolverhampton WV3 . . . . . . **38** C8
Farmside Cl DY9. . . . . **81** A2
Farmside CV3 . . . . **134** D5
Farmside Gn WV9. . . . . . . **10** F2
Farm St B19 . . . . **66** C6
Farmstead Cl WS1 . . . . . . **42** E5
Farmstead Rd B92 . . . . . . **89** C2
Farmstead The CV3 . . . . . **134** B8
Farm St
Walsall WS2 . . . . **28** E4
West Bromwich B70 . . . . **53** C1
Farnborough Cl B98 . . . . . **154** F1
Farnborough Ct B75 . . . . . **32** C2
Farnborough Dr B90. . . . . **126** F6
Farnborough Rd B35. . . . . **58** B3
Farnbury Croft B38 . . . . . **104** B2
Farncote Dr B74. . . . . **31** F3
Farndale Ave
Coventry CV6 . . . . **95** D3
Wolverhampton WV6. . . . . . **24** F5
Farndale Cl DY5 . . . . **81** B6
Farndon Ave B37 . . . . **90** B7
Farndon Cl CV12. . . . . **79** B3
Farndon Rd B8. . . . . **67** F4
Farneway LE10 . . . . **71** B1
Farnham Cl B43 . . . . **54** F8
Farnham Rd B21. . . . . **54** F2
Farnhurst Rd B8. . . . . **68** B7
Farnol Rd B26 . . . . **68** F1
Farnworth Gr B36 . . . . **58** E1
Farquhar Rd
Birmingham B15 . . . . **85** F6
Birmingham, Moseley B13 . . . **86** F3
Farquhar Rd E B15 . . . . . . **85** F6
Farran Way B43 . . . . **54** E7
Farr Dr CV4 . . . . **112** B2
Farren Rd
Birmingham B31 . . . . **102** D1
Coventry CV2 . . . . **114** E5
Farrier Cl
Bromsgrove B60 . . . . **150** E6
Sutton Coldfield B76 . . . . **57** F8
Farrier Rd B43 . . . . **44** D3
Farriers Mill WS3 . . . . **14** E4
Farriers The B26. . . . . **89** B5
Farriers Way
Hinckley LE10 . . . . **75** F6
Nuneaton CV11 . . . . **73** F2
Farrier Way DY6. . . . . **60** A7
Farringdon Ho WS2 . . . . . **28** D3
Farringdon St WS2 . . . . . . **28** D3
Farrington Rd
Birmingham B23 . . . . **56** B5
Wolverhampton WV4. . . . . . **39** E3
Farrow Rd B44 . . . . **44** E3
Farthing Ct B18 . . . . **66** C3
Farthing La
Curdworth B76 . . . . **59** C6
Redditch B97 . . . . **153** B5
Sutton Coldfield B72 . . . . **46** B4
Farthing Pools Cl B72. . **46** C4
Farthings La DY2 . . . . **62** A7
Farthings Lodge DY1. . . **51** B1
Farthings The
Birmingham B17 . . . . **85** D6
Shenstone WS14 . . . . **17** F5
Farthing Wlk CV4. . . . . . . **131** D6
Farvale Rd B76 . . . . **58** C6
Far View WS9 . . . . **16** B2
Far Wood Rd B31 . . . . **102** E8
Farzens Ave CV34 . . . . **160** B3
Faseman Ave CV4. . . . . . . **111** F3
Fashoda Rd B29 . . . . **86** B1
Fasson Cl B77 . . . . **35** C8
Fastlea Rd B32 . . . . **84** D1
Fastmoor Oval B33 . . . . . . **69** E1
Fast Pits Rd B25. . . . . **88** C7
Fatherless Barn Cres B63 . **82** D5
Faulconbridge Ave CV5 . . **111** E4
Faulconbridge Way
CV34 . . . . **161** E3
Faulkland Cres WV1 . . . . . **163** C4
Faulkner Cl DY8 . . . . **80** F4
Faulkner Rd B92. . . . . **89** B1
Faulkners Farm Dr B23 . . . **56** B6
Faulknor Dr DY5 . . . . **61** B7
Faultlands Cl CV11. . . . . . **78** F8
Faversham Cl
Willenhall WS2 . . . . **27** D3
Wolverhampton WV8. . . . . . **24** E8
Fawdry Cl B73 . . . . **46** B5
Fawdry St
Birmingham B9 . . . . **67** A2
Smethwick B66 . . . . **65** C5
Wolverhampton WV1. . . . . . **163** A4

Fawley Cl
Coventry CV3. . . . . **134** C6
Willenhall WV13 . . . . **26** F1
Fawley Gr B14. . . . . **104** B5
Fawn Cl WS12 . . . . **1** C6
Faygate Cl CV3 . . . . **114** F3
Fazeley Cl B91. . . . . **107** D4
Fazeley Ind Est B5. . . . . . **67** A2
Fazeley Rd
Tamworth B78 . . . . **21** A4
Tamworth, Fazeley B78 . . . . . **21** B2
Fazeley St B5. . . . . **66** F2
Fearnings Cotts B97 . . . . . **158** D5
Fearon Pl 4 B66 . . . . **65** A5
Featherbed La
Coventry CV4. . . . . **132** A5
Redditch B97 . . . . **158** C5
Featherston Dr LE10 . . . . . **75** E6
Featherstone Cl
Nuneaton CV10 . . . . **73** C2
Solihull B90 . . . . **106** D2
Featherstone Cres B90. . . **106** D2
Featherstone La WV10 . . . **12** B8
Featherstone Prim Sch
B23. . . . . **56** E4
Featherstone Rd B14. . . . . **104** E6
Featherston Rd B74. . . . . . **31** A2
Feckenham Ho B60 . . . . . **137** B3
Feckenham Rd
Astwood Bank B96 . . . . **158** E2
Redditch, Headless Cross
B97. . . . . **158** C4
Feckenham Way WS13 . . . . **3** C1
Felding Cl CV2 . . . . **115** A6
Feilding Way CV10. . . . . . . **72** A5
Fein Bank CV4 . . . . **111** C2
Felbrigg Cl DY5. . . . . **81** D8
Feldings The B24 . . . . **57** C4
Feldon La B62. . . . . **83** E7
Felgate Cl B90. . . . . **127** A6
Fellbrook Cl B33. . . . . **68** F4
Fell Gr
Birmingham B21 . . . . **54** C2
Royal Leamington Spa
CV32. . . . . **157** C3
Fellmeadow Rd B33 . . . . . **69** A2
Fellmeadow Way DY3 . . . . **50** E2
Fellmore Gr CV31. . . . . **162** D7
Fellows Ave DY6. . . . . **60** C8
Fellows La B17. . . . . **85** A5
Fellows Park Gdns WS2 . . . **42** B6
Fellows Rd WV14 . . . . **40** D7
Fellows St WV2. . . . . **163** B1
Felspar Rd B77 . . . . **22** B3
Felstead Cl B77. . . . . **35** C4
Felsted Way B7. . . . . **67** A4
Felstone Rd B44. . . . . **44** E1
Feltham Cl B33 . . . . **69** E1
Felton Cl
Coventry CV2. . . . . **96** E1
Redditch B98 . . . . **154** E1
Felton Croft B33. . . . . **69** A3
Felton Gr B91 . . . . **107** C1
Fenbourne Cl WS4. . . . . . . **29** C8
Fenchurch Cl WS2 . . . . **28** D4
Fen Cl DY10 . . . . **116** E8
Fencote Ave B37. . . . . **70** A4
Fen End Rd CV8 . . . . **129** E4
Fenmere Cl WV4. . . . . **39** D5
Fennel Cl WS6. . . . . **4** D3
Fennel Croft B34 . . . . **69** B7
Fennell Ho 10 CV1 . . . . . . **113** B2
Fennel Rd DY5. . . . . **81** C7
Fennis Cl B93 . . . . **127** F3
Fenn Rise
Stourbridge DY8 . . . . **60** D3
Willenhall WV12 . . . . **27** B5
Fenn St B77. . . . . **21** E1
Fennyland La CV8 . . . . **148** B7
Fens Cres DY5. . . . . **61** C5
Fenside Ave CV3. . . . . **133** D4
Fens Pool Ave DY5. . . . . . . **61** D5
Fenswood Ave B34 . . . . . . **69** A5
Fensway The B34 . . . . **69** A5
Fenter Cl B13 . . . . **86** F5
Fentham Cl B92 . . . . **109** B6
Fentham Gn B92. . . . . **109** A7
Fentham Rd
Birmingham, Aston B6 . . . . . **66** E8
Birmingham, Gravelly Hill
B23. . . . . **56** E3
Hampton-in-A B92 . . . . **109** A6
Fenton Rd
Birmingham B27 . . . . **88** B5
Hollywood B47. . . . . **125** A7
Fenton St
Brierley Hill DY5 . . . . **61** D3
Smethwick B66 . . . . **64** D7
Fenton Way B27 . . . . **88** B5
Fenwick Cl B97. . . . . **153** B1
Fereday's Croft DY3. . . . . . **50** D7
Fereday St DY1 . . . . **51** F4
Ferguson Dr
Kidderminster DY11 . . . . **116** A1
Tipton DY4 . . . . **52** B6
Ferguson Rd B68. . . . . **64** B3
Ferguson St WV11. . . . . . . **13** A1
Fern Ave DY4 . . . . **51** F7
Fern Bank Cl B63. . . . . **82** C2
Fernbank Cres WS5. . . . . . **43** C4
Fernbank Rd B8 . . . . **68** C4
Fern Cl
Coventry CV2 . . . . **96** C2
Dudley WV14 . . . . **51** B8
Ferncliffe Rd B17. . . . . **85** B4
Fern Cl WS4. . . . . **15** D1

Ferndale Ave B43. . . . . . . **54** F7
Ferndale Cl
Burntwood WS7. . . . . **7** B6
Nuneaton CV11 . . . . **73** E5
Upper Catshill B61. . . . . **121** A1
West Hagley DY9. . . . . **99** A5
Ferndale Cres
Birmingham B12 . . . . **87** A8
Kidderminster DY11 . . . . **116** B8
Ferndale Ct 8 B17 . . . . . . **85** D4
Ferndale Dr CV8 . . . . **148** A2
Ferndale Gr LE10 . . . . **75** A7
Ferndale Pk DY9. . . . . **99** C8
Ferndale Prim Sch B43 . . . **54** E8
Fern Dale Rd CV7. . . . . **129** F6
Ferndale Rd
Binley Woods CV3 . . . . **135** D7
Birmingham B28 . . . . **105** F8
Essington WV11. . . . . **13** B3
Oldbury B68. . . . . **64** A2
Sutton Coldfield B74 . . . . **44** F8
Fern Dell Cl WS11 . . . . **1** C2
Ferndene Rd B11. . . . . **88** A3
Ferndown Ave DY3. . . . . . . **50** C7
Ferndown Cl
Birmingham B26 . . . . **69** A1
Coventry CV4. . . . . **112** A3
Walsall WS3 . . . . **14** B4
Ferndown Gdns WV11. . . . **26** F5
Ferndown Rd B91. . . . . **107** C5
Fern Dr WS6 . . . . **5** A4
Ferneley Ave LE10 . . . . **71** A3
Ferness Cl LE10 . . . . **71** B2
Ferness Rd LE10. . . . . **71** B2
Ferney Hill Ave B97. . . . . . **153** C3
Fern Gr CV12 . . . . **77** E2
Fernhill Cl CV8 . . . . **147** E6
Fernhill Ct B23 . . . . **56** C2
Fernhill Dr CV32. . . . . **157** B1
Fernhill Gr B44 . . . . **44** F3
Fernhill La CV7, CV8 . . . . . **129** F5
Fernhill Rd B92. . . . . **88** E2
Fernhurst Dr DY5 . . . . **61** B7
Fernhurst Rd B8. . . . . **68** A3
Fernleigh Ave WS7. . . . . . . **7** A8
Fernleigh Cl B91. . . . . **107** C5
Fernleigh Gdns DY8. . . . . . **60** C3
Fernleigh Rd WS4 . . . . **29** B3
Fernley Ave B29 . . . . **86** B2
Fernley Rd B11. . . . . **87** C4
Fern Leys WV3. . . . . **24** D1
Fern Rd
Birmingham B24. . . . . **57** A4
Dudley DY1 . . . . **51** C4
Huntington WS12. . . . . **1** D5
Wolverhampton WV3. . . . . . **163** A1
Fernside Gdns B13 . . . . . . **87** B3
Fernside Rd WV13 . . . . **26** D3
Fern St
Redditch B98 . . . . **159** B5
Sutton Coldfield B73 . . . . **45** E1
Fernwood Croft
Birmingham B14 . . . . **104** E6
Tipton DY4. . . . . **51** F4
Fernwood Rd B73 . . . . **45** E1
Fernwoods B32 . . . . **84** B2
Ferrers Cl
Coventry CV4. . . . . **111** F2
Sutton Coldfield B75 . . . . **32** D2
Ferrers Rd B77. . . . . **21** D4
Ferrie Gr WS8. . . . . **15** E8
Ferris Gr B27 . . . . **88** A1
Festival Ave WS10 . . . . . . **41** C4
Festival Ct
Cannock WS11 . . . . **1** E5
Dudley DY2 . . . . **62** C5
Lichfield WS13 . . . . **9** A7
Festival Mews WS10 . . . . . **41** C4
Festival Way WV6. . . . . **25** B6
Fetherston Cres CV8. . . . . **135** B1
Fetherston Ct 4 CV31 . . . **161** F6
Fetherston Grange B94 . . . **143** F5
Ffernfail Ct B23 . . . . **56** E3
Fibbersley Bank WV13 . . . . **26** F1
Fibbersley WV13, WV11. . . **26** F4
Fiddlers Gn B92 . . . . **109** A7
Field Ave B31 . . . . **102** F5
Field Barn Rd CV35. . . . . . **160** A2
Field Cl
Birmingham B26 . . . . **89** A6
Bromsgrove B60 . . . . **150** E6
Hinckley LE10 . . . . **71** F3
Kenilworth CV8 . . . . **148** B5
Stourbridge DY8 . . . . **61** A2
Tamworth B77 . . . . **21** C2
Walsall, Blakenall Heath
WS3 . . . . **14** C1
Walsall WS4 . . . . **15** B2
Warwick CV34 . . . . **161** B7
Field Cottage Dr DY8 . . . . . **81** B3
Field Ct
Coventry CV2. . . . . **114** D7
Walsall WS4 . . . . **15** C1
Fieldfare B64 . . . . **83** A8
Fieldfare Croft B36 . . . . . . **70** A8
Fieldfare Cl DY10 . . . . **117** A1
Fieldfare WS7 . . . . **7** D5
Fieldfare Rd DY9. . . . . **81** D4
Field Farm La B98. . . . . . . **154** D2
Field Farm Rd B77. . . . . . . **21** D6
Fieldgate La
Kenilworth CV8 . . . . **147** F6
Whitnash CV31 . . . . **162** B2
Fieldgate Lawn CV8. . . . . . **147** F6
Fieldgate Trad Est WS1. . . . **28** F1
Field Head La CV34 . . . . . . **161** B6
Field Head Pl WV6. . . . . . . **24** B4

Fieldhead Rd B11. . . . . . . **88** A3
Field Ho CV8 . . . . **147** F5
Fieldhouse La B62 . . . . . . **100** E4
Fieldhouse Rd
Birmingham B25 . . . . **88** C8
Burntwood WS7 . . . . **7** A7
Cannock WS12 . . . . **1** F7
Wolverhampton WV4. . . . . . **39** E4
Field La
9 Birmingham B32 . . . . . . **102** B8
Catherine de B B91 . . . . **108** A5
Clent DY9 . . . . **99** D4
Great Wyrley WS6 . . . . **4** F3
Stourbridge DY8 . . . . **81** A3
Walsall WS4 . . . . **15** B2
Field Maple Rd B74. . . . . . **44** F6
Field March CV3. . . . . **134** E5
Field Mews DY2 . . . . **62** E2
Fieldon Cl B90. . . . . **106** C2
Field Rd DY2 . . . . **51** E2
Field Rd Ind Est WS3 . . . . **28** C8
Field Rd
Lichfield WS13. . . . . **3** B3
Tipton DY4. . . . . **52** A8
Walsall WS3 . . . . **14** C1
Fields Ct CV34 . . . . **160** F8
Fieldside La CV3. . . . . **114** F3
Fieldside Wlk WV14. . . . . . **40** D8
Field St
Bilston WV14. . . . . **40** E3
Cannock WS11 . . . . **1** F3
Fields The WV8 . . . . **10** B4
Fieldstone View DY3. . . . . . **50** D4
Field St
Willenhall WV13 . . . . **27** A2
Wolverhampton WV10. . . . . **163** D4
Field View Cl CV7. . . . . **96** A8
Fieldview Cl WV14 . . . . **40** E2
Field View Dr B65. . . . . **63** F3
Field View CV31. . . . . **162** B3
Field Way B94 . . . . **143** C6
Fieldways Cl B47 . . . . **125** A7
Field Wlk WS9 . . . . **30** B7
Fiery Hill Dr B45. . . . . **138** C8
Fiery Hill Rd B45 . . . . **138** C8
Fife Rd CV5 . . . . **112** F2
Fife St CV11 . . . . **73** A4
Fifield Cl CV11. . . . . **73** D2
Fifield Gr B33 . . . . **68** F3
Fifth Ave
Birmingham B9 . . . . **67** F2
Wolverhampton WV10 . . . . . **25** E7
Fifty Cl WS11. . . . . **4** C8
Filey Cl WS12 . . . . **2** D1
Filey B77 . . . . **21** F6
Fillingham Cl B37 . . . . **70** D1
Fillongley Rd CV7. . . . . **92** E3
Filton Ave WS7 . . . . **7** A8
Filton Croft B35 . . . . **58** A4
Fimbrell Cl DY5. . . . . **81** A8
Finbury Cl B92 . . . . **88** F1
Finchall Croft B92 . . . . **107** F2
Fincham Cl WV9 . . . . **11** A3
Finch Cl
Coventry CV6. . . . . **95** C2
Rowley Regis B65 . . . . **62** F4
Finch Croft CV7 . . . . **130** B7
Finchdene Gr WV3 . . . . **24** D1
Finch Dr B74 . . . . **45** A5
Finches End B34. . . . . **69** C5
Finchfield Cl DY8 . . . . **60** C3
Finchfield Gdns WV3 . . . . . **24** E1
Finchfield Hill WV3 . . . . . . **24** C1
Finchfield La WV3 . . . . **38** C8
Finchfield Rd W WV3 . . . . . **24** D1
Finchley Ave 1 B19 . . . . . . **66** C8
Finchley Cl DY3. . . . . **50** D2
Finchley Rd B44. . . . . **45** B1
Finchmead Rd B33 . . . . . . **69** E2
Finchpath Rd B70 . . . . **53** A4
Finch Rd B19 . . . . **66** C8
Findlay Rd B14 . . . . **86** E1
Findon Cl
Bulkington CV12 . . . . **79** C3
Redditch B97 . . . . **153** A5
Findon Rd B8 . . . . **68** B6
Findon St DY10 . . . . **116** F6
Finford Croft CV7 . . . . **130** B6
Fingal Cl CV3 . . . . **134** C6
Finger Post Dr WS3 . . . . . . **15** A5
Finham Cl CV5. . . . . **112** B4
Finham Cres CV8 . . . . **148** B6
Finham Flats CV8 . . . . **148** B6
Finham Gr CV3. . . . . **133** C3
Finham Green Rd CV3 . . . . **133** B3
Finham Park Sch CV3. . . . . **133** B4
Finham Prim Sch CV3. . . . **133** B3
Finham Rd CV8. . . . . **148** B6
Finings Ct 7 CV32. . . . . . . **156** F2
Finlarigg Dr B15. . . . . **85** F6
Finlay Ct CV1 . . . . **165** C1
Finmere Rd B28 . . . . **105** F8
Finmere Way B90. . . . . **106** D3
Finnemore Rd CV3. . . . . . . **133** B5
Finney Well Cl WV14 . . . . . **40** B3
Finsbury Dr DY5. . . . . **81** C7
Finsbury Gr B23 . . . . **56** D6
Finstall Cl
Birmingham B7 . . . . **67** A4
Sutton Coldfield B72 . . . . **46** C1
Finstall Fst Sch B60 . . . . . **137** B1
Finstall Rd
Bromsgrove B60 . . . . **151** C8
Finstall B60 . . . . **137** D1
Finwood Cl B92 . . . . **107** E8
Finwood Rd CV35. . . . . **144** F1

Fir Ave B12. . . . . **87** A5
Firbank Cl B30 . . . . **103** E1
Firbank Way WS3. . . . . **14** F2
Firbarn Cl B76. . . . . **46** D2
Firbeck Gr B44 . . . . **45** A3
Firbeck Rd B44. . . . . **45** A3
Fircroft 9 Wolverhampton WV4 . . . **39** F4
Birmingham B31 . . . . **102** F8
Fir Croft DY5 . . . . **81** C8
Fircroft Cl
3 Cannock WS11 . . . . **2** A3
Stoke Heath B60 . . . . **150** D6
Fircroft Coll B29. . . . . **103** D8
Fircroft WV14. . . . . **41** A3
Fircroft Ho B37. . . . . **70** A2
Fircroft B91 . . . . **106** F1
Firecrest Cl
Birmingham B23 . . . . **56** B7
Cannock WS11 . . . . **2** C2
Firecrest Way DY10 . . . . . . **117** B1
Firedrake Croft CV1. . . . . . **113** F2
Firenze B60 . . . . **137** C1
Fire Sta B44 . . . . **56** A7
Fire Station Flats B30. . . . **103** F4
Firethorn Cres CV31 . . . . . **162** A2
Fir Gr
Birmingham B14 . . . . **104** F5
Coventry CV4. . . . . **112** A2
Stourbridge DY8 . . . . **80** D6
Wolverhampton WV3. . . . . . **25** A1
Firhill Croft B14. . . . . **104** D2
Firleigh Dr CV12. . . . . **79** D2
Firmstone Ct DY8. . . . . **80** E7
Firmstone St DY8. . . . . **80** E7
Firsbrook Ho WV6 . . . . **25** A5
Firsbrook Rd WV6 . . . . **25** A5
Firsby Rd B32 . . . . **84** E5
Firs Cl
Lower Marlbrook B60 . . . . . . **121** D1
Smethwick B67 . . . . **65** A5
Firs Cl The DY10 . . . . **117** A5
Firs Dr B90 . . . . **106** A1
Firs Farm Dr B36. . . . . **68** F7
Firs Ho B36 . . . . **68** F7
Firsholm Cl B73 . . . . **57** A7
Firs La B67 . . . . **65** A5
Firs Mobile Home Pk The 4 WS11 . . . . **2** A2
Firs Prim Sch B36 . . . . **68** F8
Firs Rd DY6 . . . . **60** E6
Firs St DY2. . . . . **51** D1
First Ave
Birmingham, Bordesley Green
B9 . . . . **67** E1
Birmingham, Selly Oak B29 . . **86** B3
Birmingham, Tyburn B35 . . . . **58** A5
Birmingham, Witton B6 . . . . . **55** F2
Brownhills WS8 . . . . **16** A8
Coventry CV3. . . . . **114** C1
Kingswinford DY6 . . . . **50** A1
Wolverhampton WV10. . . . . **25** D6
First Exhibition Ave B40. . . **90** D4
Fir St DY3 . . . . **49** F7
Firs The
Bedworth CV12 . . . . **77** E2
Birmingham B11 . . . . **87** C6
Coventry CV5. . . . . **133** B8
Kidderminster DY10 . . . . **117** A5
Meriden CV7 . . . . **92** B1
First Meadow Piece B32 . . **84** E4
Firsvale Rd WV11. . . . . **26** F5
Firsway WV6 . . . . **24** A2
Firswood Rd B33 . . . . **69** C1
Firth Dr
Birmingham B14 . . . . **105** B5
Halesowen B62 . . . . **83** E8
Firth Park Cres B62. . . . . . **83** E8
Fir Tree Ave CV4 . . . . **112** B2
Fir Tree Cl
Birmingham B44. . . . . **55** F2
Redditch B97 . . . . **153** D4
Tamworth B79. . . . . **20** E7
Fir Tree Dr
Dudley DY2 . . . . **50** E7
Walsall WS5 . . . . **43** B4
Fir Tree Gr
Nuneaton CV11 . . . . **78** D8
Sutton Coldfield B73 . . . . **45** F1
Fir Tree Prim Sch WS5. . . . **43** A4
Firtree Rd B24. . . . . **57** B2
Fir Tree Rd WV3 . . . . **38** C8
Fisher Cl B45. . . . . **101** E2
Fisher Rd
Coventry CV6. . . . . **113** C8
Oldbury B65 . . . . **64** C7
Walsall WS3 . . . . **13** F2
Fisher's Ct CV34 . . . . **160** D4
Fishers Dr B90 . . . . **125** F5
Fisher St
Brierley Hill DY5 . . . . **61** B2
Cannock WS12. . . . . **1** F8
Dudley DY2 . . . . **51** D1
Tipton, Burnt Tree DY4. . . . . **52** A3
Tipton, Great Bridge DY4 . . . **52** D5
Willenhall WV13 . . . . **27** C2
Wolverhampton WV3. . . . . . **38** F8
Fish Hill B97 . . . . **153** E4
Fish House La B60 . . . . **150** E4
Fishing Line Rd B97. . . . . . **153** E5
Fishley Cl WS3. . . . . **14** C4
Fishley La WS3. . . . . **14** D5
Fishponds Rd CV8 . . . . **147** E3
Fishpool Cl B36. . . . . **68** D8
Fishpool La CV7. . . . . **91** B5
Fistral Gdns WV3 . . . . **38** C7

itchet's Bank WS7 . . . . 7 F6
ithern Cl DY3. . . . . 50 E5
itters Mill Cl B5 . . . . 56 A6
itton Ave DY6. . . . . 61 A5
itton St CV11 . . . . 73 B3
itzgerald Pl DY5 . . . . 81 B6
itzguy Cl B70. . . . . 53 E1
itzmaurice Rd WV11 . . . . . 27 A7
itz Roy Ave B17. . . . . 84 F7
itzroy Cl CV2 . . . . 115 B6
itzroy Rd B31 . . . . 102 D3
ivefield Rd CV7 . . . . 94 E5
Five Fields Rd WV12 . . . . . 27 A5
Five Oaks Rd WV13 . . . . . . 40 E8
Fives Gr WS7 . . . . 6 C8
Five Ways
 Birmingham B33 . . . . 68 D2
 Birmingham,Bordesley Green
 B9 . . . . 67 D2
 Birmingham,Ladywood B16. 66 B1
 Churchill DY10. . . . . 98 A5
 Cradley Heath B64 . . . . . . 82 C8
 Dudley DY3 . . . . 50 D3
Five Ways Prim Sch WS12 . . 2 D2
Five Ways Rd WS9 . . . . . . 145 F1
Five Ways Sta B15 . . . . 86 B8
Five Ways
 Wolverhampton,Dunstall Hill
 WV3 . . . . 25 C4
 Wolverhampton WV3. . . . . 38 C7
 Wroxall CV35. . . . . 145 F1
Flackwell Rd B23 . . . . 56 E7
Fladbury Cl
 Dudley DY2 . . . . 62 D3
 Redditch B98 . . . . 159 B8
Fladbury Cres B29 . . . . 85 D1
Fladbury Gdns B20 . . . . 66 C8
Fladbury Pl 1 B19 . . . . 66 C7
Flamboro' Cl CV3 . . . . 134 F8
Flamborough Cl B34. . . . . . 69 A7
Flamborough Way WV14 . . 51 B7
Flamville Rd LE10. . . . . 76 B5
Flanders Cl B98 . . . . 154 D5
Flanders Dr DY6 . . . . 60 D8
Flash La WV4 . . . . 37 E2
Flash Rd B69. . . . . 63 E7
Flatlea B31. . . . . 102 F4
Flats La WS14 . . . . 19 A6
Flats The B61. . . . . 136 F3
Flatts The WS10 . . . . 41 E7
Flaunden Cl CV5. . . . . 112 B4
Flavel Cres CV31. . . . . 161 F7
Flavell Ave WV14 . . . . 40 D1
Flavell Cl B32 . . . . 84 B1
Flavells La
 Birmingham B25 . . . . 88 C8
 Dudley DY3 . . . . 50 B2
Flavell St DY1 . . . . 51 B6
Flavel Rd B60 . . . . 150 E7
Flax Cl B47. . . . . 125 A5
Flax Gdns B38. . . . . 123 F8
Flaxhall St WS2. . . . . 42 B8
Flax Hill Jun Sch B73. . . . . 21 B7
Flaxley Cl B33 . . . . 68 F3
Flaxley Parkway B33. . . . . . 68 E4
Flaxley Rd B33 . . . . 68 E4
Flaxton Gr B33 . . . . 69 A4
Flaxton Wlk WV6 . . . . 25 A5
Flecknoe Cl B36. . . . . 58 C1
Flecknose St CV3 . . . . 134 C6
Fledburgh Dr B76. . . . . 46 D4
Fleet St
 Birmingham B3 . . . . 164 A3
 Coventry CV1. . . . . 165 B3
Fleetwood Gdns B37. . . . . . 70 D1
Fleetwood Ho 3 B13 . . . . . 86 F4
Fleming Pl WS2 . . . . 28 A6
Fleming Rd
 Birmingham B32 . . . . 84 D5
 Hinckley LE10 . . . . 74 F7
 Walsall WS2 . . . . 28 A6
Fletchamstead Highway
 CV5 . . . . 132 D7
Fletcher Gr B93 . . . . 128 B4
Fletcher Rd
 Hinckley LE10 . . . . 75 E7
 Walsall WV12 . . . . 13 D1
 Willenhall WV12 . . . . 27 D8
Fletcher's La WV13 . . . . . . 27 C2
Fletcher St DY9. . . . . 81 F5
Fletchers Wlk B3 . . . . 164 B2
Fletchworth Gate CV5 . . . . 132 D8
Fletchworth Gate Ind Est
 CV4 . . . . 132 D8
Fletton Gr B14. . . . . 105 A3
Fleur de-lys Ct CV34 . . . . . 161 B8
Flinkford Cl WS5. . . . . 43 D6
Flinn Cl WV14 . . . . 9 D7
Flint Cl DY10 . . . . 116 E2
Flint Green Rd B27 . . . . . . 88 B3
Flintham Cl B92 . . . . 88 E3
Flint Ho 3 WV3 . . . . 25 C4
Flintway The B33 . . . . 68 E4
Floodgate St B5 . . . . 66 F1
Flood St DY2 . . . . 51 D1
Flood Street Island DY2. . . 62 D8
Flora Cl DY9 . . . . 21 C7
Flora Rd B25 . . . . 88 D7
Florence Ave
 5 Sutton Coldfield B73 . . 57 B7
 Birmingham B11 . . . . 87 C5
 Wolverhampton WV4. . . . . 40 A4
Florence Bldgs 3 B29 . . . . 85 F2
Florence Cl CV12 . . . . 95 F8
Florence Dr 4 B73 . . . . . . 57 B7
Florence Gr
 5 Sutton Coldfield B18. . . 65 E4
 West Bromwich B71 . . . . . 42 E1

Florence Pl 10 B12 . . . . 87 A6
Florence Rd
 Birmingham,Acock's Green
 B27 . . . . 88 D4
 Birmingham,Handsworth
 B21. . . . . 65 D8
 Birmingham,King's Heath
 B14. . . . . 104 F8
 Codsall WV8 . . . . 10 C3
 Coventry CV3. . . . . 115 A2
 Oldbury B69. . . . . 63 F4
 Smethwick B66 . . . . 65 B4
 Sutton Coldfield B73 . . . . 57 B7
 Tipton DY4. . . . . 52 A7
 West Bromwich B70 . . . . . 53 E1
Florence St
 Birmingham B1 . . . . 164 B1
 Cannock WS12 . . . . 2 B1
 Walsall WS1 . . . . 29 A1
Florence Villas B17 . . . . . . 87 C7
Florendine Com Prim Sch
 B77. . . . . 21 F5
Florence St B77 . . . . 21 F5
Florian Gr WS10 . . . . 41 E7
Florian Way LE10 . . . . 71 A1
Florida Way DY6 . . . . 61 A6
Florin Cl CV4 . . . . 131 E6
Flowerdale Cl WV14 . . . . . . 51 A8
Flowerdale Dr CV2. . . . . . . 114 B6
Floyd Gr CV7 . . . . 130 C7
Floyds La WS4 . . . . 29 C6
Floyer Rd B10 . . . . 67 F1
Flude Rd CV7. . . . . 95 C6
Flyford Cl B98 . . . . 153 F1
Flyford Croft B29 . . . . 84 F2
Flynt Ave CV5 . . . . 112 B6
Fockbury Mill La B61 . . . . 136 E5
Fockbury Rd B61 . . . . 136 B5
Focus Pk B90. . . . . 126 E8
Foden Cl WS14 . . . . 17 F6
Foden Rd B42 . . . . 55 A7
Foinavon Cl B65. . . . . 62 F6
Fold St WV1 . . . . 163 B2
Fold The
 Birmingham B38 . . . . . . 104 A1
 Darlaston WS10. . . . . 41 D6
 Wolverhampton WV4 . . . . . 38 F4
Foldyard Cl B76 . . . . 58 A8
Foleshill CE Prim Sch
 CV6 . . . . 96 A2
Foleshill Rd CV1,CV6 . . . . . 113 D6
Foley Ave WV6. . . . . 24 C3
Foley Church Cl B74. . . . . . 31 A2
Foley Ct B74 . . . . 46 A6
Foley Dr WV6. . . . . 24 C3
Foley Gdns B60. . . . . 150 E3
Foley Ind Est DY11. . . . . . 116 D3
Foley Park Fst Sch DY11 . . 116 D3
Foley Rd B8 . . . . 68 B5
Foley Rd E B74 . . . . 31 A2
Foley Rd DY9 . . . . 81 C2
Foley Rd W B74 . . . . 30 E1
Foley St WS10 . . . . 42 A4
Foley Wood Cl B74 . . . . 30 E1
Foliot Fields B25 . . . . 88 D8
Folkes Rd DY9 . . . . 82 A6
Folkestone Croft B36 . . . . . 68 E8
Folkland Gn CV6. . . . . 113 A7
Folliott Rd B33 . . . . 69 B3
Follyhouse Cl WS1 . . . . 42 F7
Follyhouse La WS1. . . . . . . 42 F7
Folly The B97 . . . . 158 D8
Fontenaye Rd B79 . . . . 20 F7
Fontley Cl B26. . . . . 69 A2
Fontmell Cl CV2 . . . . 115 A4
Fontwell Rd WV10 . . . . 11 D4
Footherley La WS14. . . . . . 17 C4
Footherley Rd WS14 . . . . . . 17 F5
Fordbridge Cl B97 . . . . 153 C1
Fordbridge Inf Sch B37 . . . 70 A5
Fordbridge Rd B37. . . . . . . 70 A5
Ford Brook La WS3 . . . . . . 15 B2
Ford Cotts CV33 . . . . 157 F2
Forder Gr B14 . . . . 105 A2
Forde Way Gdns B38. . . . . 123 D7
Fordfield Rd B33 . . . . 69 C4
Fordham Gr WV9 . . . . 11 A3
Fordhouse La B30 . . . . 104 B6
Fordhouse Rd B60. . . . . . . 137 B1
Fordhouse Rd Ind Est
 WV10. . . . . 11 D1
Fordhouse Rd WV10 . . . . . . 11 D1
Fordhouse Road Ind Est
 WV10. . . . . 25 D8
Fordraught La B62. . . . . . . 101 B1
Ford Rd B61. . . . . 136 E1
Fordrift The B37 . . . . 90 A8
Fordrough Ave B9 . . . . 67 E3
Fordrough B25 . . . . 87 F7
Fordrough La B9 . . . . 67 E2
Fordrough The
 Birmingham B31 . . . . . . 103 C1
 Hollywood B90. . . . . 125 C7
 Sutton Coldfield B75 . . . . 32 A1
Fords Rd B90. . . . . 125 E7
Ford St
 Birmingham B18 . . . . 66 B5
 Coventry CV1. . . . . 165 C3
 Nuneaton CV10 . . . . 72 E4
 Smethwick B67 . . . . 64 F6
 Walsall WS2 . . . . 42 C7
Fordwater Rd B74 . . . . 44 F6
Fordwell Cl CV5 . . . . 112 F3
Foredraft Cl B32 . . . . 84 C3
Foredraft St B63 . . . . 82 D5
Foredraught B80 . . . . 159 E4
Foredrift Cl B98 . . . . 153 E2
Foredrove La B92 . . . . 107 F7

Foregate St B96 . . . . 158 E1
Forelands Gr B61 . . . . 150 D8
Foreland Way CV6. . . . . 95 A3
Forest Ave WS3. . . . . 28 D7
Fore St B2 . . . . 164 C2
Forest Cl
 Lickey End B60 . . . . 137 B6
 Smethwick B66 . . . . 64 E7
 Sutton Coldfield B74 . . . . 44 E7
Forest Ct
 Birmingham B13 . . . . 87 A3
 Coventry CV5. . . . . 112 A4
 Dorridge B93 . . . . 127 F3
 Willenhall WV12 . . . . 27 C8
Forest Dale B45 . . . . 122 B6
Forest Dr
 Birmingham B17 . . . . 85 D6
 Cradley Heath B64 . . . . . . 62 F3
Forester's Rd CV3 . . . . . . 133 E6
Forester Way B14. . . . . . . 116 E3
Forest Gate WV12. . . . . 27 D8
Forest Glade WS6. . . . . 4 F2
Forest Hill Rd B26 . . . . 89 C5
Forest La WS2 . . . . 28 D5
Forest Lawns B74. . . . . 31 C3
Forest Oak Sch B36. . . . . . 58 E1
Forest Pk B76 . . . . 46 F4
Forest Pl WS3 . . . . 28 E6
Forest Rd
 Birmingham B68 . . . . 84 C7
 Birmingham,Moseley B13 . . 87 A3
 Birmingham,South Yardley
 B25. . . . . 88 C6
 Dorridge B93. . . . . 127 F3
 Dudley DY1 . . . . 51 C4
 Hinckley LE10 . . . . 75 F8
Forest View B97 . . . . 158 E6
Forest Way
 Great Wyrley WS6 . . . . . . 5 A1
 Hollywood B47. . . . . 125 B6
 Nuneaton CV10 . . . . 72 E2
Forfar Wlk B38 . . . . 103 D2
Forfield Pl CV31 . . . . 162 A7
Forfield Rd CV6. . . . . 112 E5
Forge Ave WS9 . . . . 16 B7
Forge Cl
 Hammerwich WS7 . . . . 7 D5
 Wolverhampton WV8 . . . . . 10 C1
Forge Croft B76 . . . . 58 B6
Forge Dr B61. . . . . 136 F3
Forge La
 Aldridge,Leighswood WS9. . 30 A5
 Aldridge,Mill Green WS9 . . 30 F7
 Belbroughton DY9 . . . . . 119 D7
 Blakedown DY10. . . . . 98 B1
 Burntwood WS7 . . . . 7 F6
 Cradley Heath B64 . . . . . . 82 B8
 Halesowen B62 . . . . 83 C5
 Kingswinford DY6 . . . . . . 60 A8
 Lichfield WS13. . . . . 3 A1
 Shenstone B74,WS14 . . . . 31 C7
 Sutton Coldfield B76 . . . . 58 B5
 West Bromwich B71 . . . . . 54 A6
Forge Mill Farm* B71 . . . . 54 B6
Forge Mill Needle Mus*
 B98 . . . . 153 F6
Forge Mill Rd B98 . . . . 153 F6
Forge Rd
 Darlaston WS10. . . . . 41 C6
 Kenilworth CV8 . . . . 148 A6
 Stourbridge DY8 . . . . 80 F6
 Walsall WS3 . . . . 14 F5
 Willenhall WV12 . . . . 27 C4
Forge St
 Cannock WS12 . . . . 2 C4
 Wednesbury WS10 . . . . . . 41 E4
Forge The B63 . . . . 82 B8
Forge Trad Est B62. . . . . . . 83 C5
Forge Way
 Coventry CV6. . . . . 95 C3
 Oldbury B69. . . . . 63 E6
Forhill Ho B38. . . . . 123 F3
Forknell Ave CV2 . . . . 114 C5
Formans Rd B11. . . . . 87 E3
Formans Trad Est B11. . . . . 87 D3
Formby Ave WV6 . . . . 23 D4
Formby Way WS3 . . . . 14 A3
Forrell Gr B31. . . . . 123 B7
Forrest Ave
 Cannock WS11. . . . . 4 B8
 Essington WV11. . . . . 13 A4
Forrest Ct 9 WS13 . . . . 9 B7
Forresters Cl LE10 . . . . 75 F6
Forresters Rd LE10 . . . . . . 75 F6
Forrester Street Prec 3
 WS2 . . . . 28 C2
Forrester St WS2 . . . . 28 C2
Forrest Rd CV8 . . . . 147 E4
Forryan Rd LE10 . . . . 75 F7
Forshaw Heath La B94. . . . 141 A7
Forshaw Heath Rd B94. . . . 125 C1
Forster St
 Birmingham B7 . . . . 67 A3
 Birmingham B7 . . . . 64 E7
Forsythia Cl B31 . . . . 102 F8
Forsythia Gr WV8. . . . . 10 A3
Fort Cres WS9 . . . . 16 A3
Forth Dr B37 . . . . 70 B4
Forth Gr B38 . . . . 123 E8
Forth Way B62 . . . . 83 E8
Forties 1 B77 . . . . 35 E7
Fort Ind Pk The B35 . . . . . 57 F1
Fortnum Cl B33 . . . . 69 D2
Forton Cl WV6. . . . . 24 B2
Fort Parkway B24,B35,B36 . . 57 D1
Fort Sh Pk The B24 . . . . . . 57 C1
Forum Rd B40 . . . . 90 E3
Forum The 5 WS11 . . . . 1 E1

Foxfield Dr DY8. . . . . 81 A3
Foxfields Way WS12. . . . . . 1 C7
Fox Foot Dr DY5 . . . . 61 C4
Foxford Cl
 Birmingham B36 . . . . 58 D1
 Sutton Coldfield B72 . . . . 57 D7
Foxford Cres CV2 . . . . 96 B4
Foxford Sch & Com Arts Coll
 CV6 . . . . 96 A5
Foxglove Cl
 Bedworth CV12 . . . . 77 E1
 Birmingham B27 . . . . 88 B1
 Coventry CV6 . . . . 95 C2
 Featherstone WV10. . . . . . 12 B7
 Lichfield WS14 . . . . 3 A1
 Walsall WS3 . . . . 15 A5
 Wednesfield WV11 . . . . . . 26 E5
Foxglove Cres B37. . . . . . . 69 E3
Foxglove Rd DY1 . . . . 51 A4
Foxglove B77 . . . . 22 A4
Foxglove Way B21 . . . . 65 D2
Fox Glove Way B23 . . . . . . 56 B7
Foxglove Way B60 . . . . . . 137 C6
Foxglove Wlk WV12 . . . . . . 27 C2
Fox & Goose Sh Ctr B8 . . . 68 C5
Fox Gr B27 . . . . 88 A2
Fox Green Cres B27. . . . . . 88 A2
Foxhill Barns B48. . . . . . . 138 E5
Fox Hill B29 . . . . 103 C8
Fox Hill Cl B29 . . . . 103 C8
Foxhill Cl WS12. . . . . 2 D7
Foxhill La B48 . . . . 138 E5
Fox Hill Rd B75 . . . . 32 F2
Foxhill's Cl WS7 . . . . 7 A5
Foxhills Cl CV11 . . . . 74 C1
Foxhills Pk DY2 . . . . 62 C4
Foxhills Rd
 Stourbridge DY8 . . . . 60 D1
 Wolverhampton WV4 . . . . . 38 C4
Foxholes La B97. . . . . 158 B6
Foxholes The DY10. . . . . . 116 F8
Foxhollies L Ctr B63. . . . . . 82 E4
Fox Hollies L Ctr B27. . . . . 88 B1
Fox Hollies Rd
 Birmingham,Acock's Green
 B27 . . . . 88 A1
 Birmingham,Moseley B13 . . 86 E2
Foxhollow B61. . . . . 150 D8
Fox Hollow Cl B45 . . . . . . 122 C7
Fox Hollow WV6. . . . . 24 C2
Foxhope Cl B38. . . . . 104 B2
Foxhunt Rd B63 . . . . 82 E2
Fox La
 Bromsgrove B61 . . . . 150 E8
 Great Wyrley WS6 . . . . . . 3 A5
Foxland Ave
 Birmingham B45 . . . . . . 122 C7
 Great Wyrley WS6 . . . . . . 5 A3
Foxland Cl
 Birmingham B37 . . . . 70 D2
 Cheswick Green B90. . . . . 126 D4
Foxlands Ave WV4 . . . . 38 D3
Foxlands Cres WV4 . . . . . . 38 C3
Foxlands Dr
 Dudley DY3 . . . . 50 D5
 Gospel End Village WV4 . . 38 C3
 Sutton Coldfield B72 . . . . 57 D7
Foxlea Rd B63 . . . . 82 D1
Foxley Dr B91 . . . . 108 B5
Foxmeadow Cl DY3 . . . . . . 50 E7
Fox Mill Est B11 . . . . 87 D3
Foxoak Ent Ctr B64 . . . . . . 62 D1
Foxoak St B64 . . . . 62 C1
Fox's La WV6 . . . . 25 C4
Fox St
 Birmingham B5 . . . . 164 D3
 Dudley DY1 . . . . 62 E4
Foxtail Way WS12. . . . . 2 E4
Foxton Cl CV10 . . . . 75 B7
Foxton Man B74 . . . . 32 A1
Foxton Rd
 Birmingham B8 . . . . 67 F4
 Coventry CV3. . . . . 114 E1
Foxwalks Ave B61 . . . . 150 D8
Foxwell Gr B9 . . . . 68 C3
Foxwell Rd B9 . . . . 68 C3
Fox Wlk WS9 . . . . 16 B3
Foxwood Ave B43 . . . . 44 B2
Foxwood Dr CV3 . . . . 135 D7
Foxwood Gr B37 . . . . 69 E5
Foxwood Rd B78. . . . . 36 F8
Foxyards Cl DY4 . . . . 51 D5
Foxyards Prim Sch DY4 . . . 51 C5
Foyle Rd B38. . . . . 103 F1
Fozdar Cres WV14 . . . . 40 B1
Fradley Cl B30. . . . . 103 D4
Framefield Dr B91 . . . . . . 107 F6
Framlingham Gr
 Kenilworth CV8 . . . . 148 C6
 Perton WV6 . . . . 24 A1
Frampton Cl
 Birmingham,Bournville
 B30. . . . . 103 D7
 Birmingham,Chelmsley Wood
 B37. . . . . 70 D3
Frampton Way B43 . . . . . . 44 D5
Frampton Wlk CV2. . . . . . . 114 F4
Frances Ave CV34. . . . . . . 161 A7

Frances Cres CV12 ....78 A3
Frances Dr WS3 ....14 B2
Frances Havergal Cl **2**
CV31 ....161 F6
Frances Rd
  Baginton CV8 ....133 F3
  Birmingham,King's Norton
  B30 ....104 A5
  Birmingham,Lozells B19 ....66 C8
  Birmingham,Stockland Green
  B23 ....56 D3
Franche Fst Sch DY11....116 B8
Franche Mid Sch DY11...116 B8
Franche Rd DY11 ....116 C8
Franchise Gdns WS10 ....41 F6
Franchise St
  Birmingham B42 ....55 E2
  Darlaston WS10 ....41 F6
  Kidderminster DY11 ....116 C5
Franciscan Rd CV3 ......133 D8
Francis Cl
  1 Kingswinford DY6.....60 D8
  Sutton Coldfield B74 ....44 F8
Francis Gibbs Gdns **1**
WV13 ....162 A4
Francis Rd
  Birmingham,Acock's Green
  B27 ....88 C5
  Birmingham,Edgbaston B16 ..66 A1
  Birmingham,South Yardley
  B25 ....88 A6
  Bromsgrove B60 ....150 F7
  Lichfield WS13 ....3 A2
  Smethwick B67 ....64 D4
  Stourbridge DY8 ....80 C5
Francis St
  Birmingham B7 ....67 A4
  Coventry CV6 ....113 E7
  West Bromwich B70 .....53 D1
  Wolverhampton WV1 .....25 C4
Francis Ward Cl B71 .....53 A8
Francis Wlk B31 ....123 A7
Frankburn Rd B74 ....44 F8
Frank F Harrison Comp Sch
WS2 ....27 F7
Frank Fisher Way B70 ....53 C2
Frankfort St B19 ....66 D6
Frank Freeman Ct DY10..116 F8
Frankholmes Dr B90 ....127 A6
Frankland Ave CV4 ......96 A1
Frankley Ave B62 ....83 F5
Frankley Beeches Rd
B31 ....102 D3
Frankley Com High Sch
B45 ....101 F1
Frankley Gn B32 ....101 D5
Frankley Green La B32...101 E5
Frankley Hill La B32 ....102 A4
Frankley Ind Pk B45 ....102 B1
Frankley La B31,B32 ....100 D6
Frankley Lodge Rd B31 .102 D4
Frankley Mid Sch B45...102 B2
Frankley Rd B68 ....84 B8
Frankley Terr B17 ....85 B5
Franklin Cl CV11 ....73 D1
Franklin Dr WS7 ....7 B7
Franklin Gr CV4 ....111 E1
Franklin Rd
  Birmingham B30 ....103 F5
  Nuneaton CV11 ....73 D1
  Whitnash CV31 ....162 A3
Franklins Gdns CV3 ....115 B1
Franklin St B18 ....65 E5
Franklin Way B30 ......103 F6
Franklyn Cl WV6 ....23 E5
Frankpledge Rd CV3 ....133 E7
Frank Rd B67 ....64 E6
Frank St
  Birmingham B12 ....86 F7
  Nuneaton CV11 ....73 B3
Franks Way B33 ....68 E2
Frank Tommey Cl **5** B65 .63 C1
Frankton Ave CV3 ......133 C5
Frankton Cl
  Redditch B98 ....159 E8
  Solihull B92 ....89 B2
Frankton Gr B9 ....68 B2
Frank Walsh Ho CV1 ....165 C4
Frankwell Dr CV2 ....96 E1
Fraser Cl CV10 ....72 B6
Fraser Rd
  Birmingham B11 ....87 D5
  Coventry CV6 ....95 A1
Fraser St WV14 ....40 E6
Frayne Ave DY6 ....60 C7
Freasley Cl B90 ....106 D3
Freasley Rd B34 ....69 E6
Freda Eddy Ct **3** DY10 ..116 E6
Freda Rd B70 ....53 D1
Freda Rise B69 ....63 D8
Fredas Gr B17 ....85 A4
Frederick Ave L10 ......117 B2
Frederick Bird Prim Sch
CV2 ....113 F5
Frederick Ct B77 ....21 E3
Frederick Eary Ho B98 .159 B7
Frederick Neal Ave CV5 .111 D4
Frederick Rd
  Birmingham,Aston B6 ....66 F8
  Birmingham,Beech Lanes
  B68 ....84 D7
  Birmingham,Erdington B15 .86 B8
  Birmingham,Gravelly Hill
  B23 ....56 E2

Frederick Rd continued
  Birmingham,Selly Oak B29 .85 D2
  Birmingham,Sparkhill B11 ..87 C4
  Birmingham,Stechford B33 ..68 D3
Frederick Rd (Road 1)
DY10 ....116 F1
Frederick St
  Sutton Coldfield B73 ....46 A2
  Wolverhampton WV1 .....26 C5
Fredericks Cl DY8 ......80 E4
Frederick St
  Birmingham B1 ....66 C4
  Walsall WS2 ....28 D1
  West Bromwich B70 .....53 C4
  Wolverhampton WV2 ....163 B1
Frederick William St **1**
WV13 ....27 B2
Fred Lee Gr CV3 ....133 D4
Fred Smith Cl WS10 .....42 B5
Freeburn Cswy CV4 ....132 C7
Freeford Gdns WS14 .....9 E6
Freehold St CV1 ....113 F4
Freeland Gr **3** DY6 .....60 F4
Freeman Cl CV10 ....72 D4
Freeman Ct DY11 ....116 B3
Freeman Dr B76 ....46 F4
Freeman Pl WV14 ....40 E8
Freeman Rd
  Birmingham B7 ....67 B6
  Wednesbury WS10 ....42 D3
Freemans Cl CV32 ......156 E2
Freeman's La L10 ....76 A5
Freeman St
  Birmingham B5 ....164 C2
  Coventry CV6 ....113 F6
  Wolverhampton WV10 ....25 F2
Freemantle Ct B37 ......69 F5
Freemantle Ho B34 .....57 D3
Freemount Sq B43 ....54 E7
Freer Dr WS7 ....7 E7
Freer Rd B6 ....66 E8
Freers Mews CV34 ......160 B4
Freer St
  Nuneaton CV11 ....73 E2
  Walsall WS1 ....28 F2
Freesland Rise CV10 .....72 B6
Freeth Rd WS8 ....7 A1
Freeth St
  Birmingham B16 ....65 F2
  Oldbury B69 ....63 F8
Freezeland St WV14 .....40 B6
Fremantle Dr WS12 ......2 F2
Fremantle Ho B34 ......69 E6
Fremont Dr DY1 ....50 E3
French Ave B78 ....20 C1
French Rd DY2 ....51 F1
Frensham Cl
  Birmingham B37 ....70 C2
  Cheslyn Hay WS6 ....4 E4
Frensham Dr CV10 ......72 B5
Frensham Way B17 ......85 C6
Frenshaw Gr B44 ....55 F7
Freshfield Cl CV5 ....94 C1
Freshwater Dr B13 ......81 B8
Freshwater Gr **1** CV31 .162 C6
Fretton Cl CV6 ....113 F7
Freville Cl B79 ....21 A5
Frevill Rd CV6 ....114 B8
Friardale Cl WS10 ......42 D3
Friar Park Rd WS10 .....42 D3
Friar's Alley WS13 ....9 B7
Friars Cl
  Binley Woods CV3 ......135 E7
  Stourbridge DY8 ....60 C3
Friars Gate B90 ....126 E7
Friars Gorse DY7 ....80 C8
Friars' Rd CV1 ....94 C1
Friars' St CV34 ....160 D6
Friar St WS10 ....42 B3
Friars Wlk
  Birmingham B37 ....70 D2
  Tamworth B77 ....21 C3
Friary Ave
  Lichfield WS13 ....9 A6
  Solihull B90 ....127 A6
Friary Cl
  Birmingham B20 ....54 F3
  Hinckley LE10 ....71 E1
Friary Cres WS4 ....29 C6
Friary Dr B74 ....31 F3
Friary Gdns
  Birmingham B21 ....54 D2
  Lichfield WS13 ....9 A7
Friary Rd
  Birmingham B20 ....54 E3
  Lichfield WS13 ....9 A7
Friary The WS13 ....73 B5
Friday Ave B92 ....108 D4
Friday Bridge **6** B11 ...66 C1
Friday La B92 ....108 D4
Friesland Dr WV1 ....26 B3
Friezeland Rd WS2 ......28 B2
Friezland La WS8 ....16 A5
Friezland Way WS8 .....16 A5
Frilsham Way CV5 ......112 B4
Fringe Green Cl B60 ....151 A7
Fringe Meadow Rd B98 .154 F6
Frinton Gr B21 ....65 C2
Frisby Ct CV11 ....73 E2
Frisby Rd CV4 ....111 E2
Friston Ave B16 ....66 B1
Friswell Dr CV6 ....114 A8
Friswell Ho **3** CV2 ....114 D8
Frith Way LE10 ....71 A3
Frobisher Cl
  Great Wyrley WS6 ....4 F1
  Hinckley LE10 ....71 D4

Frobisher Rd CV3 ....133 C5
Frobisher Way B66 ......64 D7
Frodesley Rd B26 ....89 B8
Froggatt Rd WV14 ....40 D7
Froggatts Ride B76 ......46 F3
Frog La
  Balsall Common CV7 ....130 A5
  Lichfield WS13 ....9 B7
Frogmere Cl CV5 ....112 C6
Frogmill Rd B45 ....102 B2
Frogmoor Ho B26 ....88 E7
Frogmore La CV8 ....129 F2
Frome Cl DY3 ....50 D2
Frome Dr WV11 ....26 C5
Frome Ho **4** DY1 ....61 E8
Frome Way B14 ....104 D6
Front Cotts B48 ....138 F6
Frost St WV2 ....40 A6
Froxmere Cl B91 ....127 C8
Froyle Cl WV6 ....24 C5
Froysell St WV13 ....27 B2
Fryer Ave CV32 ....156 E3
Fryer Rd B31 ....123 B7
Fryers Cl WS3 ....28 B7
Fryers Rd WS2,WS3 ......28 A7
Fryer St WV1 ....163 C3
Frythe Cl CV8 ....148 C6
Fuchsia Cl **3** CV2 ......96 B2
Fuchsia Dr WV9 ....10 F3
Fugelmere Cl B17 ....84 F7
Fulbrook Cl B98 ....154 C5
Fulbrook Gr B29 ....102 F8
Fulbrook Rd
  Coventry CV2 ....96 C2
  Dudley DY1 ....51 A1
Fulford Dr B76 ....58 B5
Fulford Gr B26 ....89 C6
Fulford Hall Rd B90,B94 .125 D3
Fulham Rd B11 ....87 B5
Fullbrook Cl B90 ......127 A4
Fullbrook Rd WS5 ....42 E5
Fullelove Rd WS8 ....16 A7
Fullers Cl CV6 ....112 F7
Fullerton Cl WV8 ....10 E1
Fullwood Cl CV2 ....96 E2
Fullwood Cres DY1,DY2 ..61 F6
Fullwoods End WV14 .....40 C1
Fulmar Cres DY10 ......117 B2
Fulmer Wlk B18 ....66 A3
Fulton Cl B60 ....137 B1
Fulwell Gr B44 ....56 A8
Fulwell Mews B37 ....90 B8
Fulwood Ave B62 ....83 F8
Fulwood Pl DY6 ....60 F6
Furlong Cl B63 ....82 C6
Furlong La B63 ....82 C6
Furlong Mdw B31 ......103 C2
Furlong Rd CV1 ....165 C1
Furlongs Rd DY3 ....50 D6
Furlongs The
  Stourbridge DY8 ....81 B3
  Wolverhampton WV11 ....26 B5
Furlong The WS10 ....41 E5
Furlong Wlk DY3 ....50 D4
Furnace Cl CV12 ....78 D3
Furnace Hill B63 ....83 B5
Furnace La B63 ....83 A5
Furnace Par DY4 ....51 E6
Furnace Rd
  Bedworth CV12 ....78 D4
  Dudley DY2 ....62 C8
Furness Cl WS3 ....13 F3
Furness B77 ....21 D3
Furnivall Cres WS13 .....3 D1
Furr Marsh The CV34 ...160 B4
Furrows The B60 ....150 D6
Furst St WS8 ....16 A8
Furzebank Way WV12 ....27 F4
Furze Way WS5 ....43 E8
Fylde Ho CV2 ....114 D4
Fynford Rd CV6 ....113 B5

G

Gable Croft WS14 ....9 F6
Gables The
  Kingswinford DY6 ....60 B8
  Sutton Coldfield B24 ....57 D4
Gaddesby Rd B14 ......104 F8
Gadds Dr B65 ....63 D4
Gadsby Ave WV11 ....27 A7
Gadsby St CV11 ....73 E3
Gads Gn DY2 ....62 E5
Gads Green Cres DY2 ....62 E6
Gadshill CV34 ....161 E4
Gads La
  Dudley DY1 ....51 C1
  West Bromwich B70 .....53 A3
Gadwall Croft B23 ......56 B3
Gaelic Rd WS11 ....1 D4
Gagarin B79 ....20 F5
Gaiafields Rd WS13 ......3 B1
Gaia La WS13 ....9 B8
Gaialands Cres WS13 .....3 B1
Gaia Stowe WS13 ....3 B1
Gail Cl WS9 ....16 B4
Gailey Croft B44 ....44 E3
Gail Pk WV3 ....38 D7
Gainford Cl DY8 ....60 F1
Gainford Rd B44 ....45 A1
Gainford Rise CV3 .....115 A3
Gainsborough Ave LE10 ..71 A3
Gainsborough Cres
  Birmingham B43 ....44 D4
  Dorridge B93 ....128 A6

Gainsborough Dr
  Bedworth CV12 ....78 A4
  Mile Oak B78 ....34 B8
  Perton WV6 ....23 E5
  Royal Leamington Spa
  CV31 ....162 D6
Gainsborough Hill DY8 ...81 A3
Gainsborough Mews
DY11 ....116 B5
Gainsborough Pl DY1 ....50 E2
Gainsborough Rd B42 ....55 B6
Gainsborough Trad Est
DY9 ....81 C4
Gainsbrook Cres WS11 ....5 F5
Gainsford Dr B62 ....83 B6
Gains La WS3,WS11 ....5 D2
Gairloch Rd WV11 ....13 B1
Gaitskell Terr B69 ......52 D2
Gaitskell Way B66 ......64 F7
Galahad Way WS10 ......42 A2
Galbraith Cl WV14 .....151 D8
Galena Cl B77 ....22 B2
Galena Way B6 ....66 E6
Gale Wlk B65 ....62 F5
Galey's Rd CV3 ....133 D8
Gallagher Bsns Pk CV6 ...95 E5
Gallagher Ct **14** B13 ....87 B2
Gallagher Rd CV12 ......78 A2
Gallagher Ret Pk CV6 ...113 F8
Gallery Sq **1** WS1 .....28 E2
Gallery The WV4 ....39 A6
Galliards The CV4 .....132 D4
Galliers Cl B77 ....35 F5
Galloway Ave B34 ....68 F6
Galloway Cl LE9 ....71 F7
Gallows Hill CV34 .....161 B4
Gallus Dr LE10 ....71 A1
Galmington Dr CV3 ....133 B6
Galton Cl
  Sutton Coldfield B24 ....57 F4
  Tipton DY4 ....52 C6
Galton Dr DY2 ....62 B6
Galton Ho B67 ....64 F2
Galton Rd B67 ....64 F1
Galtons La DY9 ....120 A7
Galton Twr B1 ....66 C2
Galway Rd WS7 ....24 F1
Gamesfield Gn WV3 ......24 E1
Gammage St DY2 ....62 B8
Gamson Cl DY10 ....116 E4
Ganborough Cl B98 ....154 E1
Gandy Rd WV12 ....27 A7
Gannahs Farm Cl B76 ....46 F3
Gannaway B93 ....128 A6
Gannow Green La B45 ..101 D1
Gannow Manor Cres
B45 ....101 E2
Gannow Manor Gdns
B45 ....101 F1
Gannow Rd B45 ....121 E7
Gannow Wlk B45 ......121 E7
Ganton Rd WS3 ....14 A3
Ganton Wlk WV8 ....24 F8
Garage Cl B77 ....21 D5
Garden Cl
  Birmingham,Frankley
  B45 ....102 A2
  Birmingham,Ward End B8 ..68 A5
  Hinckley LE10 ....75 D6
  Knowle B93 ....127 F6
Garden Cres WS3 ....14 F3
Garden Croft WS9 ....30 B7
Garden Gr
  8 Birmingham B16.....66 B1
  Warwick,Emscote CV34...161 C8
  Warwick,Packmores CV34.160 E7
Gardeners Cl DY11 .....116 C8
Garden Flats CV5 ......111 D5
Garden Gr
  Bedworth CV12 ....95 F8
  Birmingham B20 ....54 E6
  Birmingham B6 ....112 B6
Garden Rd LE10 ....71 D1
Gardens The
  Birmingham,Chester Road
  B73 ....57 B8
  Birmingham,Stockland Green
  B23 ....56 E3
  Kenilworth CV8 ....148 A3
  Royal Leamington Spa
  CV32 ....156 F4
  Sutton Coldfield B76 ....46 B1
Garden St WS2 ....28 E3
Garden Wlk
  Bilston WV14 ....40 F6
  Dudley DY3 ....50 C2
Gardner Ho **8** CV1 ....113 B2
Gardner Way CV8 ....148 A2
Garfield Rd B26 ....89 B8
Garganey Ct DY10 ......116 F1
Garibaldi Terr B60 .....137 A1
Garland Cres B62 ....83 E8
Garlands Croft CV7 .....95 A6
Garland St B9 ....67 C3
Garlands Way WV11 .....26 C7
Garland Way B31 ......103 C4
Garlick Dr CV8 ....148 C6
Garman Cl B43 ....43 E2
Garner Cl WV14 ....40 D6
Garnet Ave B43 ....44 B3
Garnet Cl WS9 ....16 E4
Garnet Ct **4** B92 ......88 F1
Garnette Cl CV10 ....72 B5
Garnet Cl CV10 ....72 B5
Garrard Gdns B73 ......46 B5
Garratt Cl B31 ....123 B8
Garratt St B77 ....63 B5
Garratt St B71 ....53 B5

Garratts Wlk B14 ......104 E1
Garret Cl DY6 ....60 D8
Garretts Green La B26,
  B33 ....89 C5
Garrett St CV11 ....73 E2
Garrick Cl
  Coventry CV5 ....111 C4
  Dudley DY1 ....50 F3
Garrick Rd
  Bromsgrove B60 ....137 C1
  Cannock WS11 ....1 D4
Garrick Rise WS7 ....7 B7
Garrick St WV1 ....163 C2
Garrigill B77 ....22 B1
Garrington Rd B60 .....151 B7
Garrington St WS10 .....41 C7
Garrison Ct **9** B9 .....67 B2
Garrison La B9 ....67 C2
Garrison St B9 ....67 B3
Garston Way **4** B43 ....54 D8
Garth Cres CV3 ....134 D8
Garth Ho CV3 ....134 D8
Garth The
Birmingham B14 ....105 D4
Lichfield WS13 ....3 B2
Garway Cl
  Redditch B98 ....154 E1
  Royal Leamington Spa
  CV32 ....156 F4
Garway Gr B25 ....88 C6
Garwood Rd B26 ....88 F7
Gas Sq B61 ....136 F1
Gas St B1 ....66 C2
Gas Street Basin* B1 ..164 A2
Gatacre St DY3 ....50 D3
Gatcombe Cl WV10 ......11 F4
Gatcombe Rd DY1 ....50 E2
Gatehouse Fold **4** DY2 ..51 D1
Gatehouse La CV12 ......78 A2
Gate House La B60 .....151 A7
Gatehouse CV31 ....161 D2
Gatehouse Trad Est WS8 ..7 B1
Gate La
  Dorridge B93,B94 .....127 C3
  Sutton Coldfield B73 ....45 F2
Gateside Rd CV6 ....95 E2
Gate St
  Birmingham B8 ....67 D5
  Sedgley DY3 ....50 E7
  Tipton DY4 ....52 A2
Gateway The B26 ....89 F3
Gatis St WV6 ....25 A5
Gatwick Rd B35 ....58 B4
Gauden Rd DY9 ....81 D2
Gaulby Wlk CV3 ....115 A1
Gaunts The B48 ....139 B6
Gaveston Cl **7** CV34 ..160 F8
Gaveston Rd
  Coventry CV6 ....112 F6
  Royal Leamington Spa
  CV32 ....156 E2
Gavin Way B6 ....55 F4
Gawne La B64 ....62 F3
Gawsworth B79 ....20 D7
Gaydon Cl
  Coventry CV6 ....114 A8
  Perton WV6 ....23 E5
  Redditch B98 ....153 F1
Gaydon Gr B29 ....85 A2
Gaydon Pl B73 ....46 B4
Gaydon Rd
  Aldridge WS9 ....30 A4
  Solihull B92 ....89 D3
Gayer St CV6 ....96 A1
Gayfield Ave DY5 ....61 E1
Gay Hill La B38 ....124 B8
Gayhurst Cl CV3 ......134 E8
Gayhurst Dr B25 ....88 E8
Gayle B77 ....20 C8
Gayle Gr B27 ....106 C8
Gaylon B21 ....42 A1
Gayton Rd B71 ....53 D6
Gaywood Croft B15 .....86 C8
Gaza Cl CV4 ....112 A1
Gazelle Cl CV1 ....165 D3
Geach St B19 ....66 D6
Geach Twr B19 ....66 D5
Gedney Cl B90 ....105 C3
Geeson Cl B35 ....58 B4
Gee St B19 ....66 D6
Gemini Dr WS11 ....4 F6
Gendle Ct B77 ....21 D4
Geneva Rd DY4 ....51 D5
Genge Ave WV4 ....39 E4
Genners App B31 ......102 D8
Genners La B31 ....102 D7
Genthorn Cl **11** WV4 ...39 F4
Gentian B74 ....31 F4
Gentian Cl B31 ....102 F6
Geoffrey Cl
  Coventry CV2 ....114 B5
  Sutton Coldfield B76 ....58 B7
Geoffrey Pl B11 ....87 C3
Geoffrey Rd
  Birmingham B11 ....87 C3
  Solihull B90 ....105 F3
George Arthur Rd B8 ....67 D5
George Ave
  Mile Oak B78 ....20 C1
  Rowley Regis B65 ......63 D2
George Betts Prim Sch
B66 ....64 C7
George Bird Cl B66 .....65 A6
George Cl DY2 ....62 E8
George Dance Cl **2**
DY10 ....117 B6

George Dixon Int Sch & Sixth Form Ctr B17 65 C2
George Dixon Jun & Inf Sch B17 65 C2
George Eliot Ave CV12 78 D2
George Eliot Com Sch
Nuneaton CV11 73 D1
Nuneaton CV11 78 D8
George Eliot Hospl CV10 73 B2
George Eliot Rd CV1 113 D5
George Eliot St CV11 73 C2
George Fentham Endowed Sch B92 109 B6
George Frederick Rd B73 45 A4
George Henry Rd DY4 52 E6
George Hodgkinson Cl CV4 111 F3
George La WS13 9 C8
George Law Ct DY10 116 F5
George Marston Rd CV3 114 E1
George Park Cl CV2 96 C1
George Poole Ho 6 CV1 113 B2
George Rd
Alvechurch B48 139 A5
Birmingham B29 85 E3
Birmingham,Edgbaston B15 86 B8
Birmingham,Great Barr B43 43 F2
Birmingham,South Yardley B25 88 A6
Birmingham,Stockland Green B23 56 C3
Coseley,Daisy Bank WV14 40 D1
Dudley,Tipton Green DY4 51 D6
Halesowen B63 82 F4
Oldbury B68 64 C2
Solihull B91 107 D3
Sutton Coldfield B73 45 D1
Warwick CV34 161 A8
Water Orton B46 59 C3
George Robertson Cl CV3 134 E7
George Rose Gdns WS10 41 C6
George St W B18 66 A4
George Salter High Sch B70 53 A4
George St
1 Bromsgrove B61 136 F2
Birmingham,Balsall Heath B12 86 F5
Birmingham,Brookfields B3 164 A3
Birmingham,Handsworth B21 65 C8
Birmingham,Lozells B19 66 B7
Cannock WS12 2 C4
Coventry CV1 113 E5
Dudley DY1 51 B6
Hinckley LE10 75 D8
Kidderminster DY10 116 F6
Nuneaton CV11 73 E2
George Street Ringway CV12 78 B3
George St
Royal Leamington Spa CV31 162 A7
Stourbridge DY8 60 F1
Stow Heath WV2 40 A7
Tamworth B79 21 B4
Walsall WS1 28 E1
West Bromwich B70 53 D2
Willenhall WV13 27 A4
Wolverhampton WV2 163 C2
George Wlk 5 B97 153 E3
Georgian Gdns 2 WS10 41 F3
Georgian Pl WS11 1 E2
Georgina Ave WV14 40 D3
Geraghty Ct DY4 41 A2
Geraldine Rd B25 88 B7
Gerald Rd DY8 80 E7
Geranium Gr B9 67 F3
Geranium Rd DY2 62 F8
Gerard Ave CV4 132 B8
Gerardsfield Rd B33 69 E2
Gerard B79 20 E7
Germander Dr WS5 43 A3
Germander B74 31 F5
Gerrard Cl B19 66 D7
Gerrard Rd WV13 26 E1
Gerrard St
1 Warwick CV34 160 E6
Birmingham B19 66 C7
Gertrude Pl B18 66 A5
Gervase Dr DY1 51 C3
Geston Rd DY1 61 F8
Gettings Cl WS7 7 F7
Gheluvelt Ave DY10 116 F7
Gibbet Hill Rd CV4 132 B3
Gibbet La DY7 80 B4
Gibbins Rd B29 85 D2
Gibb La B61 137 A8
Gibbons Cl CV4 111 F2
Gibbons Gr WV6 24 F4
Gibbons Hill Rd DY3 39 D2
Gibbons Ind Pk DY6 61 A7
Gibbons La DY5 61 A7
Gibbons Rd
Sutton Coldfield B75 32 B3
Wolverhampton WV6 24 F4
Gibbs Cl CV2 115 B6
Gibbs Hill Rd B31 123 C7
Gibb Sq B12 67 A1
Gibbs Rd
Redditch B98 154 A5
Stourbridge DY9 82 A5
Gibbs St WV6 25 A4
Gibb St B9 66 F1
Gibson Cres CV12 78 A1
Gibson Dr
Birmingham B20 66 B8
Smethwick B66 65 A6
Gibson Rd
Birmingham B20 66 B8
Perton WV6 23 E3
Gideon Cl B25 88 D6
Gideons Cl DY3 50 D5
Gielgud Way CV2 115 B8
Giffard RC Prim Sch The WV6 24 F5
Giffard Rd
Bilston WV1 40 B7
Wolverhampton WV10 11 F3
Giffard Way CV34 155 E1
Gifford Ct 13 DY5 61 D2
Giffords Croft WS13 3 A1
Gigg La B76 48 B3
Gig Mill Prim Sch DY8 80 E4
Gigmill Way DY8 80 E4
Gilbanks Rd DY8 80 D7
Gilberry Cl B93 128 A4
Gilbert Ave B69 63 B7
Gilbert Cl
3 Coventry CV1 113 E3
Bedworth CV12 78 B2
Wednesfield WV11 27 A7
Gilbert Ent Pk WV12 27 B4
Gilbert La WV5 49 B7
Gilbert Rd
Bromsgrove B60 150 E7
Lichfield WS13 3 C2
Smethwick B66 65 B3
Gilbert Scott Way DY10 116 F7
Gilberts Ct WS4 29 A4
Gilbertstone Ave B26 88 E5
Gilbertstone Cl B98 153 E1
Gilbertstone Prim Sch B26 88 E5
Gilbert St DY4 52 A2
Gilbert Wlk WS13 3 C2
Gilbeys Cl 5 DY8 60 E1
Gilby Rd B16 66 A1
Gilchrist Dr B15 85 E8
Gildas Ave B38 104 A1
Giles Cl
Birmingham B33 68 E3
Coventry CV6 95 C2
Giles Close Ho B33 68 E3
Giles Cl B92 107 F7
Giles Rd
Lichfield WS13 3 A3
Oldbury B68 64 B5
Gilfil Rd CV10 73 B1
Gilldown Pl B15 86 B7
Gillespie Croft B6 66 F7
Gillet Cl CV11 73 B3
Gillhurst Rd B17 85 C7
Gillians Wlk CV2 115 A8
Gilling Gr B34 69 A6
Gillingham Cl WS10 42 D4
Gillity Ave WS5 43 C8
Gillity Cl WS5 43 C8
Gillity Ct 3 WS5 43 D7
Gilliver Rd B90 106 B2
Gillman Cl B26 89 D4
Gillott Cl B91 107 E3
Gillott Rd B16 65 D2
Gillows Croft B90 127 A7
Gillscroft Rd B33 69 A3
Gill St
Dudley DY2 62 E4
West Bromwich B70 53 C1
Gillway B79 21 B8
Gilmorton Cl
Birmingham B17 85 B7
Solihull B91 107 C1
Gilpin Cl B8 68 C7
Gilpin Cres WS3 15 A4
Gilpins Croft WS6 4 D1
Gilquart Way CV1 165 C1
Gilson Dr B46 70 D8
Gilson Rd B46 70 E8
Gilson St DY4 52 C8
Gilson Way B37 70 A5
Gilwell Rd B34 69 E6
Gimble Wlk 2 B17 84 F7
Ginkgo Wlk 2 CV31 161 F5
Gipsy Cl CV7 130 B5
Gipsy La
Balsall Common CV7 130 C5
Birmingham B23 56 B5
Nuneaton CV10,CV11 78 D7
Willenhall WV13 27 B1
Girdlers Cl CV3 133 B5
Girtin Cl CV12 78 A4
Girton Ho B36 69 F8
Girton Rd WS11 4 F8
Girvan Gr CV32 157 C5
Gisborn Cl B10 87 B8
Gisburn Cl
5 Redditch B97 153 B5
Warwick CV34 155 F1
Givens Ho 9 CV1 113 B2
GK Davies Trad Est DY9 82 A6
Gladeside Cl WS4 29 D8
Glades The WS9 30 B7
Glade The
Birmingham B26 89 D4
Cannock WS11 1 C2
Coventry CV5 111 F3
Stourbridge DY9 81 E5
Sutton Coldfield B74 30 E1
Wolverhampton WV8 10 E1
Gladman Bsns Quarter WV9 10 F3
Gladstone Cl LE10 71 E4
Gladstone Ct 22 CV32 156 F1
Gladstone Dr
Oldbury B69 52 D3
Stourbridge DY8 80 D6
Gladstone Gr 3 DY6 60 D8
Gladstone Rd
Birmingham,Gravelly Hill B23 56 D3
Birmingham,South Yardley B26 88 D6
Birmingham,Sparkbrook B11 87 B6
Cannock WS12 2 E1
Dorridge B93 128 A2
Stourbridge DY8 80 D6
Gladstone St
Birmingham B6 67 B8
Darlaston WS10 41 E6
Walsall WS2 28 D4
West Bromwich B71 53 C5
Gladstone Terr LE10 75 E8
Gladys Rd
Birmingham B25 88 B7
Smethwick B67 64 F2
Gladys Terr B67 65 A2
Glaisdale Ave CV6 95 E3
Glaisdale Gdns WV6 25 A5
Glaisdale Rd B28 106 B8
Glaisedale Gr WV13 27 C2
Glaisher Dr WV10 25 C6
Glamis Rd WV12 27 B7
Glamorgan Cl CV3 134 D5
Glanville Dr B75 32 A4
Glasbury Croft B38 123 E7
Glascote Cl B90 106 A4
Glascote Ct B77 21 E4
Glascote Gr B34 69 C6
Glascote Heath Prim Sch B77 22 A2
Glascote La B77 35 F8
Glascote Rd
Tamworth B77 22 B2
Tamworth,Glascote Heath B77 21 E3
Glasscroft Cotts WS7 7 F7
Glassford Dr WV6 24 E6
Glasshouse Coll DY8 80 F7
Glasshouse Hill DY8 81 B3
Glasshouse La
Hockley Heath B94 143 F6
Kenilworth CV8 148 D4
Glastonbury Cl DY11 116 A6
Glastonbury Cres WS3 13 E2
Glastonbury Rd
Birmingham B14 105 C5
West Bromwich B71 42 D1
Glastonbury Way WS3 13 E1
Glaston Dr B91 107 A1
Gleads Croft B62 84 A3
Gleaston Wlk WV1 26 C1
Gleave Rd
Birmingham B29 85 E1
Whitnash CV31 162 A3
Glebe Ave CV12 77 E1
Glebe Cl
Coventry CV4 132 A7
Redditch B98 154 D2
Glebe Cres CV8 148 A3
Glebe Ct CV31 162 A3
Glebe Dr B73 56 F8
Glebefarm Gr CV3 114 F3
Glebe Farm Rd B33 69 A5
Glebe Fields B76 59 B6
Glebefields Prim Sch DY4 52 A8
Glebefields Rd DY4 52 A7
Glebeland Cl B16 66 B1
Glebe La
Nuneaton CV11 73 F6
Stourbridge DY8 80 E4
Glebe Pl
Darlaston WS10 41 B6
Royal Leamington Spa CV31 162 B7
Glebe Rd
Alvechurch B48 139 A7
Hinckley LE10 71 F1
Nuneaton CV11 73 D4
Solihull B91 107 D5
Willenhall WV13 40 F8
Glebe St WS1 42 E8
Glebe The
Belbroughton DY9 119 E6
Beoley B98 154 F7
Corley CV7 94 C7
Glebe Way CV7 130 A7
Gledhill Pk WS14 9 C5
Gleeson Dr CV34 155 E1
Glenavon Rd B14 105 A3
Glen Bank LE10 71 E1
Glenbarr Cl LE10 75 A8
Glenbarr Dr LE10 75 A8
Glen Cl
Cannock WS11 1 E5
Walsall WS4 29 A3
Glencoe Dr WS11 2 A4
Glencoe Rd
Birmingham B16 65 C4
Coventry CV3 114 B1
Glencroft Rd B92 89 D4
Glen Ct
Codsall WV8 10 A4
Wolverhampton WV6 24 E2
Glendale Ave CV8 148 A6
Glendale Cl
Halesowen B63 83 B4
Wolverhampton WV3 38 C8
Glendale Ct B77 36 B6
Glendale Dr
Birmingham B33 68 F3
Glendale Dr *continued*
Wombourne WV5 49 A6
Glendale Gdns WS11 2 A4
Glendale Inf Sch CV10 72 F2
Glendale Twr 5 B23 57 B6
Glendale Way CV4 111 C2
Glendawn Cl 1 WS11 2 A3
Glendene Cres B38 123 C7
Glendene Dr 2 B43 54 D8
Glendene Rd WS12 2 D6
Glen Devon Cl B45 102 A2
Glendon Gdns CV12 79 C3
Glendon Rd B23 56 D6
Glendon Way B93 127 E3
Glendower App CV34 161 E3
Glendower Ave CV5 112 D3
Glendower Rd
Aldridge WS9 16 B1
Birmingham B42 55 D4
Gleneagles Cl
Hinckley LE10 75 D4
Nuneaton CV11 74 C1
Gleneagles Dr
Birmingham B43 43 E3
Blackwell B60 138 A5
Oldbury B69 63 A7
Sutton Coldfield B75 46 D8
Gleneagles Rd
Birmingham B26 89 A8
Coventry CV2 114 E6
Perton WV6 23 D5
Walsall WS3 13 F3
Gleneagles B77 22 B5
Glenelg Dr DY8 81 B2
Glenelg Mews WS5 43 D5
Glenfern Gdns CV8 134 E2
Glenfern Rd WV14 51 A8
Glenfield Ave CV10 73 D7
Glenfield Cl
2 Solihull B91 127 C8
Redditch B97 158 D6
Sutton Coldfield B76 46 E3
Glenfield Gr B29 86 A1
Glenfield
Tamworth B77 21 C1
Wolverhampton WV8 10 E2
Glengarry Cl B32 102 B7
Glengarry Gdns WV3 24 F1
Glenhill Dr B38 124 A8
Glen Ho DY1 61 D8
Glenhurst Cl WS2 27 D3
Glenmead Prim Sch B44 55 D8
Glenmead Rd B44 55 D8
Glenmore Ave WS7 7 A6
Glenmore Cl WV3 38 E7
Glenmore Dr
Birmingham B38 103 D2
Coventry CV6 95 F5
Glenmount Ave CV6 95 F5
Glenn St CV6 95 D3
Glenpark Rd B8 67 F5
Glen Park Rd DY3 50 D2
Glen Rd
Dudley DY3 50 E6
Stourbridge DY8 80 F3
Glenridding Cl CV6 95 F5
Glen Rise B13 105 C6
Glenrosa Wlk CV4 132 A7
Glenroy Cl CV2 114 E6
Glenroyde B38 123 E7
Glenside Ave B92 89 C3
Glen Side B32 84 D2
Glen The B60 138 A5
Glenthorne Dr WS6 4 E3
Glenthorne Ho WS6 4 D2
Glenthorne Prim Sch WS6 4 E3
Glenthorne Rd B24 57 A2
Glentworth Ave CV6 95 A2
Glentworth Gdns WV6 25 B5
Glentworth B76 47 A2
Glenville Ave CV9 36 C1
Glenville Dr B23 56 E5
Glenwood Cl DY5 81 D8
Glenwood Dr B90 126 D4
Glenwood Gdns
Bedworth CV12 78 A5
Tamworth B77 36 B6
Glenwood Rd B38 123 D8
Glenwood Rise WS9 16 D3
Globe St WS10 41 F1
Gloster Dr CV8 147 F6
Gloucester Cl
Lichfield WS13 3 B3
Nuneaton CV11 74 A7
Gloucester Ho
4 Birmingham B24 56 F4
4 Wolverhampton WV3 25 C4
Gloucester Pl WV13 27 D2
Gloucester Rd
Dudley DY2 62 D2
Walsall WS5 43 C8
Wednesbury WS10 42 C3
Gloucester St
3 Royal Leamington Spa CV31 162 A7
Birmingham B5 164 C1
Coventry CV1 113 B3
Wolverhampton WV6 25 B4
Gloucester Way
Birmingham B37 70 A1
Cannock WS11 2 B1
Glover Cl
Birmingham B28 105 F6
Warwick CV34 160 B4
Glover Rd B75 47 A5
Glovers Cl CV7 92 C1
Glovers Croft B37 69 F3
Glovers Field Dr B7 67 C7
Glovers Rd B10 87 D8
Glover St
Birmingham B9 67 A2
Cannock WS12 2 F3
Coventry CV3 133 D8
Redditch B98 153 E3
Glover's Trust Homes B73 56 F7
Glover St B70 53 D1
Glyde Ct B27 88 B2
Glyme Dr WV6 24 E5
Glyn Ave WV14 41 B3
Glyndebourne B79 20 D7
Glyn Dr WV14 41 B3
Glyne Ct B73 46 B5
Glyn Farm Rd B32 84 C6
Glynn Cres B63 82 B7
Glynne Ave DY6 60 D5
Glynne Prim Sch DY6 60 C4
Glyn Rd B32 84 D6
Glynside Ave B32 84 D6
Godfrey Cl CV31 162 E5
Godiva Pl CV1 165 D3
Godiva Trad Est CV6 113 F8
Godolphin B79 20 D7
Godrich Ho B13 87 B3
Godson Cres DY11 116 C3
Godson Pl DY11 116 C3
Goffs Cl B32 84 F3
Gofton B77 36 A8
Goldacre Cl CV31 161 F4
Goldborough Cl WV14 40 D3
Goldby Dr WS10 41 E4
Gold Cl CV11 78 E8
Goldcrest Cl DY2 62 D2
Goldcrest Croft B36 70 A8
Goldcrest Dr DY10 117 B2
Goldcrest B77 36 A6
Golden Acres La CV3 134 F7
Goldencrest Dr B69 63 E8
Golden Croft B20 54 F1
Golden Cross La B61 121 B1
Goldencross Way DY5 61 B1
Golden End Dr B93 128 D6
Golden Hillock Rd
Birmingham B11 87 D6
Dudley DY2 62 C3
Golden Hillock Sch & Specialist Sports Coll B11 87 D5
Goldfinch Cl B30 103 D8
Goldfinch Rd DY9 81 C3
Goldicroft Rd WS10 42 A4
Goldieslie Cl B73 46 B2
Goldieslie Rd B73 46 B2
Goldsborough B77 22 A1
Golds Hill Gdns B21 65 F7
Golds Hill Rd B21 65 F8
Golds Hill Way DY4 52 D7
Goldsmith Ave CV34 160 C5
Goldsmith Pl B79 21 A7
Goldsmith Rd
Birmingham B14 104 F8
Walsall WS3 28 E7
Goldsmith Wlk DY10 117 C5
Goldstar Way B33 69 C2
Goldtel Ind Est WV4 40 A5
Goldthorn Ave WV4 39 B6
Goldthorn Cl CV5 111 D4
Goldthorn Cres WV4 39 A6
Goldthorne Ave
Birmingham B26 89 C4
Cannock WS11 1 F2
Goldthorne Cl B97 153 C1
Goldthorne Wlk DY5 81 D8
Goldthorn Hill WV2,WV4 39 C6
Goldthorn Mews DY11 116 C2
Goldthorn Park Prim Sch WV4 39 D5
Goldthorn Pl DY11 116 C2
Goldthorn Rd
Kidderminster DY11 116 C2
Wolverhampton WV2,WV3 39 B6
Golf Dr CV11 74 B1
Golf La
Bilston WV14 40 D7
Whitnash CV31 162 B2
Golson Cl B75 46 F6
Gomeldon Ave B14 104 F3
Gomer St W WV13 27 A2
Gomer St WV13 27 A2
Gonville Ho B36 69 F8
Gooch Cl DY8 81 B6
Gooch St N B5 86 E8
Gooch St B5 86 E8
Goodall Gr B43 44 E5
Goodall St WS1 28 F1
Goodby Rd B13 86 D3
Goode Ave B18 66 A5
Goode Cl
Oldbury B68 64 C4
Warwick CV34 160 C7
Goode Croft CV4 111 F2
Goodeve Wlk B75 47 B5
Goodfellow St CV32 156 C1
Good Hope Hospl B75 46 D6
Goodison Gdns B24 57 B5
Goodleigh Ave B45 122 E6
Goodman Cl B28 105 F6
Goodman St B1 66 B3
Goodman Way CV4 111 C1
Goodrest Ave B62 84 A5
Goodrest Croft B14 105 C4
Goodrest La B38 123 F6
Goodrich Ave WV6 24 A3
Goodrich Cl B98 154 F2

Goodrich Covert 🔟 B14 . 104 C2
Goodrick Way B7 . . . . .67 B6
Good Shepherd RC Sch
  CV6 . . . . .95 F1
Goodway Ct 🟨 CV34 . . . .160 F7
Goodway Ho
  🟨 Royal Leamington Spa
  CV32 . . . . .161 D8
  Birmingham B4 . . . . .164 C4
  Kenilworth CV8 . . . . .148 A5
Goodway Rd
  Birmingham B44 . . . . .55 F8
  Solihull B92 . . . . .89 E4
Goodwin Cl DY11 . . . . . . .116 C7
Goodwood Cl
  Birmingham B36 . . . . .68 D8
  Coventry CV3 . . . . .134 C6
  Lichfield WS14 . . . . .9 D7
Goodwood Dr B74 . . . . . . .44 F7
Goodwood Rd B61 . . . . . .121 B1
Goodwyn Ave B68 . . . . . . .84 C7
Goodyear Ave WS10 . . . . .41 C5
Goodyear Rd B67 . . . . .64 E2
Goodyers End La CV12 . . . .95 D8
Goodyers End Prim Sch
  CV12 . . . . .95 E8
Goosehill Cl B98 . . . . .154 E1
Gooseshills Rd LE10 . . . . . .75 E5
Goosemoor La B23 . . . . . . .56 F7
Goostry Cl B77 . . . . .21 D5
Goostry Rd B77 . . . . .21 D5
Gopsall Rd LE10 . . . . .71 D2
Gopsal St B4 . . . . .67 A3
Gorcott La B90 . . . . .126 A5
Gordon Ave
  Birmingham B19 . . . . .66 D7
  West Bromwich B71 . . . . . .53 C8
  Wolverhampton WV4 . . . . .39 F3
Gordon Cl
  Bedworth CV12 . . . . .78 C4
  Oldbury B69 . . . . .52 D2
Gordon Cres DY5 . . . . .61 E5
Gordon Ct B33 . . . . .68 D3
Gordon Dr DY4 . . . . .52 C6
Gordon Pl WV14 . . . . .40 C5
Gordon Rd
  Birmingham B17 . . . . .85 D6
  Birmingham,Lozells B19 . . .66 C8
Gordon St
  🟨 Birmingham B9 . . . . . . .67 B2
  Coventry CV1 . . . . .113 B2
  Darlaston WS10 . . . . .41 E6
  Royal Leamington Spa
  CV31 . . . . .162 A7
  Wolverhampton WV2 . . . .163 C2
Gorey Cl WV12 . . . . .27 B8
Gorge Rd
  Sedgley DY3 . . . . .50 E8
  Wolverhampton WV14,DY3 . .39 F1
Goring Rd CV2 . . . . .114 A4
Gorleston Gr B14 . . . . . . .105 B2
Gorleston Rd B14 . . . . . . .105 B2
Gorsebrook Rd WV6 . . . . . .25 B5
Gorse Cl
  Birmingham,Fordbridge
  B37 . . . . .70 B3
  Birmingham,Selly Oak B29 103 A8
Gorse Dr WS12 . . . . .1 D5
Gorse Farm Rd
  Birmingham B43 . . . . .54 E8
  Nuneaton CV11 . . . . .79 B8
Gorsefield Rd B34 . . . . . . .69 C5
Gorse Green La DY9 . . . . .120 C8
Gorse La WS14 . . . . .1 C4
Gorse Meadow Dr B45 . . .138 B8
Gorsemoor Prim Sch
  WS12 . . . . .2 D1
Gorsemoor Rd WS12 . . . . . .2 D1
Gorsemoor Way WV11 . . . .13 B3
Gorse Rd
  Dudley DY1 . . . . .51 A4
  Wednesfield WV11 . . . . . . .27 A8
Gorseway WS7 . . . . .7 B5
Gorse Way WS12 . . . . .2 C8
Gorseway CV5 . . . . .112 C3
Gorsey La
  Cannock WS11 . . . . .1 C1
  Coleshill B46 . . . . .59 F2
  Great Wyrley WS6 . . . . .4 F1
  Norton Canes WS3 . . . . .5 E1
  Wythall B47 . . . . .125 A3
Gorsey Way
  Aldridge WS9 . . . . .29 E5
  Coleshill B46 . . . . .59 E2
Gorsly Piece B32 . . . . .84 C4
Gorstey Lea WS7 . . . . .7 C7
Gorstie Croft B43 . . . . .54 E8
Gorsty Ave DY5 . . . . .61 C3
Gorsty Bank WS14 . . . . .9 E8
Gorsty Cl 🟨 B71 . . . . .53 F8
Gorsty Hill Rd B65 . . . . . . .83 B8
Gorsty Bank Rd B77 . . . . . .35 F5
Gorsymead Gr B31 . . . . . .102 C2
Gorsy Rd B32 . . . . .84 D5
Gorsy Way CV10 . . . . .72 D5
Gorton Croft CV7 . . . . . . .130 B7
Gorway Cl WS1 . . . . .42 F7
Gorway Gdns WS1 . . . . . . .43 A7
Gorway Rd WS1 . . . . .43 A7
Goscote Cl
  Redditch B97 . . . . .153 A5
  Walsall WS3 . . . . .28 F7
Goscote Hospl WS3 . . . . . .28 F8
Goscote Ind Est WS3 . . . . .14 E1
Goscote La WS3 . . . . .28 F8

Goscote Lodge Cres WS3 .29 A7
Goscote Pl WS3 . . . . .29 A7
Goscote Rd WS3 . . . . .15 A1
Gosford Dr LE10 . . . . .71 A1
Gosford Ind Est CV1 . . . . .113 F2
Gosford Park Prim Sch
  CV1 . . . . .113 F2
Gosford St
  Birmingham B12 . . . . .86 F6
  Coventry CV1 . . . . .165 D2
Gosford Wlk B92 . . . . .89 B1
Gosmoor Ho B26 . . . . .88 E7
Gospel End Dr DY3 . . . . . . .50 B8
Gospel End St DY3 . . . . . . .50 D8
Gospel Farm Rd B27 . . . .106 B8
Gospel La B27 . . . . .106 C8
Gospel Oak Rd
  Coventry CV6 . . . . .95 A4
  Wednesbury DY4 . . . . .41 B1
Gosport Cl WV1 . . . . .40 B7
Gosport Rd CV6 . . . . .113 E8
Goss Croft B29 . . . . .85 D1
Gossett La CV8 . . . . .135 F7
Gossey La B33 . . . . .69 C2
Gossey Lane Jun & Inf Sch
  B33 . . . . .69 C2
Goss The DY5 . . . . .61 D1
Gosta Gn B4 . . . . .164 D4
Gotham Rd B26 . . . . .88 E6
Goths Cl B65 . . . . .63 C4
Gough Ave WV11 . . . . .26 B8
Gough Rd
  Birmingham,Edgbaston
  B15 . . . . .86 C7
  Birmingham,Sparkhill B11 . .87 D5
  Dudley WV14 . . . . .40 C1
Gough St
  Birmingham B1 . . . . .164 B1
  Willenhall WV13 . . . . .27 C2
  Wolverhampton WV1 . . . .163 C3
Gould Ave E DY11 . . . . . .116 A2
Gould Ave W DY11 . . . . . .116 A1
Gould Firm La WS9 . . . . . . .30 E6
Gould Rd CV35 . . . . .160 A7
Governor's Ct CV34 . . . . .160 D8
Gowan Rd B8 . . . . .67 E4
Gower Ave DY6 . . . . .60 F4
Gower Ho B62 . . . . .83 F6
Gower St
  Birmingham B19 . . . . .66 D7
  Walsall WS2 . . . . .42 B7
  Willenhall WV13 . . . . .27 A2
  Wolverhampton WV2 . . . .163 D1
Gowland Dr WS11 . . . . .1 B1
Gowrie Cl LE10 . . . . .71 B2
Goya Cl WS11 . . . . .2 C2
Gozzard St WV14 . . . . .40 E5
Gracechurch Sh Ctr B72 . .46 B5
Grace Mary Prim Sch B69 .63 C7
Gracemere Cres B28 . . . .105 E3
Grace Moore Ct WS11 . . . . .1 F4
Grace Rd
  Allesley CV5 . . . . .111 A8
  Birmingham B11 . . . . .87 C7
  Oldbury B69 . . . . .63 C8
  Tipton DY4 . . . . .52 A7
Gracewell Homes B13 . . .105 D6
Gracewell Rd B13 . . . . .87 D1
Grafton Cl B98 . . . . .159 B7
Grafton Cres B60 . . . . . . .150 E8
Grafton Ct
  🟨 Wolverhampton WV6 . . .24 F4
  Birmingham B23 . . . . .56 C2
  Coventry CV4 . . . . .132 B7
Grafton Dr WV13 . . . . .26 D1
Grafton Gdns DY3 . . . . .50 B3
Grafton Gr 🟨 B19 . . . . .66 C7
Grafton Ho
  Bromsgrove B60 . . . . .137 B3
  Wolverhampton WV4 . . . . .39 E5
Grafton La B61 . . . . .150 C7
Grafton Pl WV14 . . . . .40 E7
Grafton Rd
  Birmingham,Handsworth
  B21 . . . . .54 D1
  Birmingham,Sparkbrook
  B11 . . . . .87 B7
  Oldbury B68 . . . . .63 F2
  Solihull B90 . . . . .105 C2
  West Bromwich B71 . . . . . .53 D4
Grafton St CV1 . . . . .113 F2
Graham Cl
  Coventry CV6 . . . . .96 B1
  Wednesbury DY4 . . . . .41 B1
Graham Cres B45 . . . . . . .122 A7
Graham Ho B74 . . . . .30 F2
Graham Rd
  Birmingham,Saltley B9 . . . .67 F2
  Birmingham,South Yardley
  B25 . . . . .88 C6
  Halesowen B62 . . . . .83 C8
  Kingswinford DY6,DY8 . . . .60 D4
  West Bromwich B71 . . . . . .53 D4
Graham St
  Birmingham,Hockley B1 . . .66 C3
  Birmingham,Lozells B19 . . .66 C7
  Nuneaton CV11 . . . . .73 C5
Grainger Cl DY4 . . . . .52 D6
Grainger Ct WS11 . . . . .1 D2
Grainger La B64 . . . . .82 D8
Grainger St DY2 . . . . .62 D7
Graiseley Ct WV3 . . . . . . .163 B2
Graiseley Hill WV2 . . . . . .163 B1
Graiseley La WV11 . . . . . . .26 C5
Graiseley Prim Sch WV2 .163 B1

Graiseley Row WV2 . . . . . .163 B1
Graiseley St WV3 . . . . . . .163 A2
Graith Cl B28 . . . . .105 E2
Grammar School La B63 . .83 A4
Grampian Rd DY8 . . . . .81 A6
Granada Trad Est B69 . . . . .63 F6
Granary Cl
  Cannock WS12 . . . . .2 B5
  Kingswinford DY6 . . . . .60 A8
Granary La B76 . . . . .46 F3
Granary Rd
  Stoke Heath B60 . . . . .150 E6
  Wolverhampton WV8 . . . . .10 E1
Granary The WS9 . . . . .30 B6
Granborough Cl CV3 . . . . .134 F8
Granborough Ct CV32 . . . .157 A3
Granbourne Rd WS2 . . . . . .27 D4
Granby Ave B33 . . . . .69 C1
Granby Bsns Pk B33 . . . . . .69 D1
Granby Cl
  Hinckley LE10 . . . . .75 C7
  Redditch B98 . . . . .154 F4
  Solihull B92 . . . . .106 E7
Granby Rd
  Hinckley LE10 . . . . .75 C7
  Nuneaton CV10 . . . . .72 F3
Grandborough Dr B91 . . . .107 A1
Grand Cl B66 . . . . .65 B3
Grand Depot Rd CV11 . . . .79 F6
Grand Junction Way WS1 .42 D5
Grand Theatre* WV1 . . . .163 C3
Grandys Croft B37 . . . . . . .69 F2
Granefield Ct 🟨 B9 . . . . . . .67 D1
Grange Ave
  Aldridge WS9 . . . . .16 A1
  Birmingham B8 . . . . .68 B6
  Burntwood WS7 . . . . .7 B7
  Coventry,Binley CV3 . . . . .134 F7
  Coventry,Finham CV3 . . . .133 C3
  Kenilworth CV8 . . . . .147 E4
  Sutton Coldfield B75 . . . . . .32 C3
Grange Cl
  Nuneaton CV10 . . . . .72 C7
  Tamworth B77 . . . . .35 C8
  Warwick CV34 . . . . .161 C8
Grange Cres
  Birmingham B45 . . . . .121 F8
  Halesowen B63 . . . . .83 B3
  Walsall WS4 . . . . .29 B8
Grange Ct
  🟨 Dudley DY1 . . . . .51 B1
  🟨 Redditch B98 . . . . .153 F4
  Stourbridge DY9 . . . . .81 C3
  Willenhall WS2 . . . . .27 D2
  Wolverhampton WV3 . . . .163 A2
Grange Dr
  Cannock WS11 . . . . .1 C4
  Hinckley LE10 . . . . .75 E5
Grange Education Unit The
  CV6 . . . . .94 E1
Grange Farm Dr B38 . . . . .123 D8
Grange Farm Prim Sch
  CV3 . . . . .133 B5
Grangefield Cl WV8 . . . . . . .10 F1
Grange Hill B62 . . . . .83 C2
Grange Hill Rd B38 . . . . . .103 E1
Grangehurst Prim Sch
  CV6 . . . . .96 B4
Grange La
  Kingswinford DY6 . . . . .60 F4
  Alvechurch B48 . . . . .139 B3
  Stourbridge DY9 . . . . .81 D4
  Sutton Coldfield B75 . . . . . .32 C3
Grange Mews The 🟨
  CV32 . . . . .156 D1
Grangemouth Rd CV6 . . . .113 B7
Grange Pk DY1 . . . . .51 A1
Grange Rd
  🟨 Birmingham B98 . . . . . .153 F4
  Balsall Common CV7 . . . . .129 F7
  Birmingham,Aston B6 . . . . .66 E8
  Birmingham B29 . . . . .85 F3
  Birmingham,Bordesley Green
  B10 . . . . .67 D1
  Birmingham,Erdington B24 . .57 C5
  Birmingham,King's Heath
  B14 . . . . .104 E8
  Burntwood WS7 . . . . .7 A5
  Coventry CV6 . . . . .96 B5
  Cradley Heath B64 . . . . . . .83 B8
  Dorridge B93 . . . . .127 C2
  Dudley,New Dock DY1 . . . .51 B1
  Dudley,Roseville WV14 . . . .51 B7
  Halesowen B63 . . . . .83 C3
  Hockley Heath B94 . . . . . .143 E8
  Kidderminster DY11 . . . . . .116 B7
  Norton Canes WS11 . . . . . . .6 B6
  Royal Leamington Spa
  CV32 . . . . .157 B3
  Smethwick B66 . . . . .65 A3
  Solihull B91 . . . . .106 C4
  Stourbridge DY9 . . . . .81 C4
  West Bromwich B71 . . . . . .53 B3
  Wolverhampton,Blakenall
  WV2 . . . . .39 B6
  Wolverhampton,Tettenhall Wood
  WV6 . . . . .24 C4
Grange Rise B38 . . . . .123 F7
Grangers La B98 . . . . .158 F5
Grange St
  Dudley DY1 . . . . .51 B1
  Walsall WS1 . . . . .42 F7
Grange The
  Birmingham B24 . . . . .57 C3
  Cubbington CV32 . . . . . . .157 F5
  Halesowen B63 . . . . .83 F6
  Royal Leamington Spa
  CV32 . . . . .157 D3

Grange The continued
  Warwick CV34 . . . . .161 C7
  Wombourne WV5 . . . . .49 A7
Grange Wlk CV6 . . . . .96 B5
Grangewood Ct
  Solihull B92 . . . . .106 F2
  Sutton Coldfield B73 . . . . . .57 A7
Granhill Cl B98 . . . . .159 A8
Granleigh Ct CV32 . . . . . .157 E5
Granoe Cl CV3 . . . . .134 E8
Gransden Ave B14 . . . . . . .105 A2
Grant Cl
  Kingswinford DY6 . . . . .60 D8
  West Bromwich B71 . . . . . .53 C5
Grant Ct B30 . . . . .104 A5
Grantham Rd
  Birmingham B11 . . . . .87 B6
  Smethwick B66 . . . . .65 B3
Grantley Cres DY6 . . . . . . .60 C7
Grantley Dr B37 . . . . .70 B3
Granton Cl B14 . . . . .104 D5
Granton Rd B14 . . . . .104 D5
Grantown Gr WS3 . . . . .14 A4
Grant Rd
  Bedworth CV7 . . . . .78 A1
  Coventry CV3 . . . . .114 B2
Granville Cl
  Bromsgrove B60 . . . . .137 B1
  Wolverhampton WV2 . . . .163 D3
Granville Crest B10 . . . . . .117 B6
Granville Dr DY6 . . . . .60 F5
Granville Gdns LE10 . . . . . .75 C8
Granville Rd
  Cradley Heath B64 . . . . . . .83 B8
  Dorridge B93 . . . . .128 A2
  Hinckley LE10 . . . . .75 C8
Granville Sq 🟨 B1 . . . . .66 B1
Granville St
  Birmingham B1 . . . . .164 A1
  Royal Leamington Spa
  CV32 . . . . .157 A2
  Willenhall WV13 . . . . .27 A3
  Wolverhampton WV2 . . . .163 C1
Grapes Cl CV6 . . . . .113 B5
Grasdene Gr B17 . . . . .85 C4
Grasmere Ave
  Coventry CV3 . . . . .132 F6
  Perton WV6 . . . . .23 F4
  Sutton Coldfield B74 . . . . . .31 A2
Grasmere Cl
  Birmingham B43 . . . . .54 F7
  Kidderminster DY10 . . . . .116 E7
  Kingswinford DY6 . . . . .60 B7
  Wolverhampton,Palmers Cross
  WV6 . . . . .24 E8
  Wolverhampton WV11 . . . .26 C7
Grasmere Ct CV11 . . . . . . .73 F7
Grasmere Ho 🟨 B69 . . . . . .63 D5
Grasmere Pl WS11 . . . . .1 E5
Grasmere Rd
  Bedworth CV12 . . . . .78 B2
  Birmingham B21 . . . . .65 F7
Grasscroft Dr CV3 . . . . . . .133 C6
Grassholme B77 . . . . .36 A8
Grassington Ave CV34 . . . .155 F1
Grassington Dr
  Birmingham B37 . . . . .69 F1
  Nuneaton CV11 . . . . .74 A2
Grassmere Ct WS6 . . . . .4 D3
Grassmere Dr DY8 . . . . . . .80 F3
Grassmoor Rd B38 . . . . . .103 E2
Grassy La WV10,WV11 . . . .12 B1
Graston Cl B16 . . . . .66 A2
Gratham Cl B77 . . . . .35 C8
Gratley Croft WS12 . . . . . . .1 C4
Gratidge Rd B27 . . . . .88 D2
Gratton Ct CV3 . . . . .132 F6
Gravel Bank B32 . . . . .84 D2
Gravel Hill
  Coventry CV4 . . . . .111 F1
  Wolverhampton WV5 . . . . .49 B6
Gravel La WS12 . . . . .1 C5
Gravelly Ct 🟨 B23 . . . . .56 E2
Gravelly Hill B23 . . . . .56 E3
Gravelly Hill N B23 . . . . . . .56 E3
Gravelly Hill Sta B23 . . . . . .56 E2
Gravelly Ind Pk B24 . . . . . .67 F8
Gravelly La
  Birmingham B23 . . . . .56 F5
  Stonnall WS9 . . . . .16 F3
Gravel Pit La B48 . . . . . . .139 E3
Gravel The B76 . . . . .48 B2
Gray Cl DY10 . . . . .116 F2
Graydon Ct B74 . . . . .46 B7
Grayfield Ave B13 . . . . .87 A3
Grayland Cl B27 . . . . .88 B2
Graylands The CV3 . . . . . .133 C4
Grayling Cl WS10 . . . . .41 B3
Grayling Rd DY9 . . . . .81 C6
Grayling Wlk B37 . . . . .70 D6
Gray Rd WS12 . . . . .1 F6
Grayshott Cl
  Birmingham B23 . . . . .56 E5
  Bromsgrove B61 . . . . .136 E3
Grays Rd B17 . . . . .85 D6
Grayson Ave B7 . . . . .21 E4
Grayswood Ave CV5 . . . . .111 E4
Grayswood Park Rd B32 . .84 C6
Grayswood Rd B31 . . . . . .122 F7

Grazebrook Croft B32 . . . .102 C6
Grazebrook Ind Pk DY2 . . .62 B6
Grazebrook Rd DY2 . . . . . .62 C7
Grazewood Cl WV12 . . . . .27 B6
Grazier Ave B77 . . . . .35 C8
Grazing La B97 . . . . .152 F2
Greadier St WV12 . . . . .27 C5
Great Arthur St B66 . . . . . .64 F7
Great Barn La B97 . . . . . . .153 B1
Great Barr Bsna Pk B42 . . .55 A5
Great Barr Prim Sch B44 . .44 D1
Great Barr Sch B44 . . . . . . .44 D1
Great Barr St B9 . . . . .67 A2
Great Brickkiln St WV3 . . .25 B1
Great Bridge Ind Est DY4 . .52 C7
Great Bridge Prim Sch
  DY4 . . . . .52 C6
Great Bridge Rd WV14 . . . .41 B3
Great Bridge St B70 . . . . . .52 E5
Great Bridge W DY4 . . . . . .52 D5
Great Brook St B7 . . . . .67 A4
Great Charles St WS8 . . . . .15 F8
Great Charles Street
  Queensway B3 . . . . .164 B3
Great Colmore St B15 . . . .164 B1
Great Cornbow 🟨 B63 . . . .83 B3
Great Croft Ho 🟨 WS10 . . .41 D6
Great Farley Dr B31 . . . . . .102 C1
Greatfield Rd DY11 . . . . . .116 B4
Great Francis St B7 . . . . . . .67 B4
Great Hampton Row
  B19 . . . . .164 A4
Great Hampton St
  Birmingham B18 . . . . .164 A4
  Wolverhampton WV1 . . . . .25 B4
Greatheed Rd CV32 . . . . . .156 E2
Great Hockings La B97 . . .152 E2
Great King St N B19 . . . . . .66 C5
Great King St B19 . . . . .66 C5
Great Lister St B7 . . . . .67 A4
Great Mdw DY4 . . . . .52 B5
Greatmead B77 . . . . .21 C1
Great Moor Rd WV6 . . . . . .23 A3
Great Oaks B26 . . . . .89 B5
Greatorex Ct B71 . . . . .53 B8
Great Stone Rd B31 . . . . . .103 A1
Great Tindal St B16 . . . . . . .66 A2
Great Western Arc B2 . . . .164 C3
Great Western Ct B18 . . . . .65 E6
Great Western Ct B64 . . . . .63 A1
Great Western St
  Wednesbury WS10 . . . . . . .41 E2
  Wolverhampton WV1 . . . .163 C4
Great Western Way CV4 . . .52 D6
Great Wood Rd B10 . . . . . . .87 E8
Great Wyrley High Sch
  WS6 . . . . .4 F3
Greaves Ave WS5 . . . . .43 C8
Greaves Cl
  Walsall WS5 . . . . .43 C8
  Warwick CV34 . . . . .161 C1
Greaves Cres WV12 . . . . . .27 C8
Greaves Rd DY2 . . . . .62 D4
Greaves Sq B38 . . . . .104 B1
Grebe Cl B23 . . . . .56 B3
Greenacre Cl B77 . . . . .22 B5
Greenacre Dr WV8 . . . . . . .10 B2
Greenacre Rd DY4 . . . . .41 A1
Greenacres Ave WV10 . . . .12 B2
Green Acres B27 . . . . .88 B3
Greenacres B26 . . . . .84 E2
Greenacres Cl WS9 . . . . . . .30 E2
Green Acres Prim Sch
  WV14 . . . . .40 F6
Greenacres Prim Sch B77 .22 B5
Green Acres Rd B38 . . . . .123 D8
Greenacres Rd B61 . . . . . .136 E3
Greenacres
  Sedgley DY3 . . . . .39 B1
  Sutton Coldfield B76 . . . . . .58 A8
  Wolverhampton WV6 . . . . .24 B5
Greenaleigh Rd B14 . . . . . .105 D3
Green Ave B28 . . . . .87 E1
Greenaway Cl B43 . . . . .44 C3
Greenaway Ct WV10 . . . . . .12 C7
Green Bank Ave B28 . . . . . .87 E1
Greenbank B45 . . . . .138 D8
Greenbank Gdns DY8 . . . . .60 E2
Greenbank Rd CV7 . . . . . .129 F6
Green Barns La WS14 . . . . .32 C8
Green Bower Dr B61 . . . . .137 A5
Greenbush Dr B63 . . . . .83 A5
Green Cl
  Studley B80 . . . . .159 E3
  Whitnash CV31 . . . . .162 B4
  Wythall B47 . . . . .125 A3
Greencroft WV14 . . . . .40 D6
Green Croft B9 . . . . .68 A3
Greencroft
  Kingswinford DY6 . . . . .60 D4
  Lichfield WS13 . . . . .3 A2
Green Ct
  🟨 Lichfield WS13 . . . . .9 B7
  Birmingham,Gravelly Hill
  B23 . . . . .56 E2
  Birmingham,Hall Green
  B28 . . . . .105 F8
Green Dr
  Birmingham B32 . . . . .84 C1
  Wolverhampton WV10 . . . .25 C7
Greenend Rd B13 . . . . .86 F2
Greenfield Ave
  Balsall Common CV7 . . . . .130 A7

Greenfield Ave continued
Cradley Heath B64 . . . . .62 B1
Lower Marlbrook B60 . . . . . 121 D1
Stourbridge DY8 . . . . .80 F5
Greenfield Bldgs WV5 . . . . .29 A7
Greenfield Cotts B48. . . . 139 A5
Greenfield Cres B15 . . . . . .86 A8
Greenfield Croft WV14 . . .40 D2
Greenfield Ho B26 . . . . . . .89 D6
Greenfield La WV10 . . . . . .11 E5
Greenfield Prim Sch
Stourbridge DY8 . . . . .80 F5
Walsall WS4 . . . . .29 C8
Greenfield Rd
Birmingham B17 . . . . .85 D5
Birmingham,Newton B43. . .54 D7
Smethwick B67 . . . . .64 E4
Greenfields
Aldridge WS9 . . . . .30 B7
Cannock WS11 . . . . .1 E2
Greenfields
Kingswinford DY6 . . . . .60 E6
Walsall WS4 . . . . .15 D2
Wombourne WV5 . . . . .49 A7
Green Field The CV3 . . . .134 B8
Greenfield View DY3 . . . . .50 B7
Greenfinch Cl
Birmingham B36 . . . . .70 A7
Kidderminster DY10 . . . . . .117 B3
Greenfinch Rd
Birmingham B36 . . . . .70 A7
Stourbridge DY9 . . . . .81 D3
Greenford Cl B97 . . . . . . .153 B5
Greenford Ho
7 West Bromwich B70. . . . .53 D1
Birmingham B23 . . . . .56 B6
Greenford Rd B14 . . . . . .105 C3
Green Gables
Hollywood B47. . . . . .125 A4
Sutton Coldfield B74 . . . . . .46 B7
Greenheart B77. . . . . .22 A4
Greenhill Ave DY10 . . . . .116 F7
Greenhill B60 . . . . .137 F4
Green Hill Cl B60 . . . . . . .137 D6
Greenhill Cl
Tamworth B77 . . . . .35 C5
Willenhall WV12 . . . . .27 B5
Greenhill Ct
Halesowen B62 . . . . .83 E7
Sutton Coldfield B72 . . . . . .57 C8
Wombourne WV5 . . . . .49 B5
Greenhill Dr B29 . . . . .85 C1
Greenhill Gdns
Birmingham B43 . . . . .43 E2
Halesowen B62 . . . . .83 D6
Wombourne WV5 . . . . .49 B5
Greenhill Ind Est DY10 . .117 A7
Greenhill WS13 . . . . .9 C8
Greenhill Mews WS13 . . . . .9 C8
Greenhill Oak DY10 . . . . .116 F7
Greenhill Rd
Birmingham,Handsworth
B21 . . . . .54 E2
Birmingham,Moseley B13 . .87 A1
Dudley DY3 . . . . .50 E5
Halesowen B62 . . . . .83 E7
Sutton Coldfield B72 . . . . . .57 C8
Whitnash CV31 . . . . .162 B4
Greenhill Way WS9 . . . . . .16 B1
Green Hill Way B90 . . . . .106 B5
Greenhill WV5 . . . . .49 B6
Greenholm Prim Sch B44 .55 E7
Greenholm Rd B44 . . . . . . .55 E7
Greenhough Rd WS13 . . . . .9 A8
Greenhurst Dr B45. . . . . .122 A1
Greening Dr B15. . . . . .86 B7
Green La
Aldridge WS9 . . . . .30 E5
Balsall Common CV7 . . . . .130 B7
Birchmoor B77,B78 . . . . . . .36 D7
Birmingham B32 . . . . .84 C6
Birmingham,Bordesley Green
B9 . . . . .67 E1
Birmingham,Castle Bromwich
B36 . . . . .69 E8
Birmingham,Great Barr B43 .43 D1
Birmingham,Handsworth
B21 . . . . .65 C8
Birmingham,Hawkesley
B38 . . . . .123 E8
Birmingham,Newton B43. . .54 D8
Brownhills WS8 . . . . .7 B2
Cannock WS11 . . . . .4 E6
Coleshill B46 . . . . .70 F5
Corley Moor CV7 . . . . .93 D6
Coventry CV3 . . . . .133 B4
Dudley DY3 . . . . .50 F5
Halesowen B62 . . . . .63 D1
Kingswinford DY6 . . . . .60 D7
Lichfield WS14 . . . . .48 B6
Middleton B78 . . . . .48 B6

Green Lanes Prim Sch
B36. . . . . .69 F8
Green Lanes B73 . . . . .57 B8
Green Lane Venture Ctr
WS11 . . . . .4 E6
Green La
Nuneaton CV10 . . . . .72 C7
Redditch B97 . . . . .158 A7
Solihull B90 . . . . .105 E1
Stourbridge DY8 . . . . .81 E5
Studley B80 . . . . .159 B5
Tamworth B77 . . . . .36 C6
Upper Catshill B61. . . . . . .121 A1
Walsall,Birchills WS2,WS3 .28 C5
Walsall,High Heath WS4,
WS9 . . . . .15 D3
Walsall,Pelsall WS3. . . . . . .15 A4
Warwick CV34 . . . . .160 F8
Greenlawns DY4 . . . . .52 B8
Green La WV6 . . . . .24 F7
Greenleaf Cl CV5 . . . . . . .112 A3
Greenleas Gdns B63 . . . . .83 C3
Greenlea B77. . . . . .36 A8
Green Leigh B23. . . . . .56 F8
Greenleighs DY3 . . . . .39 D3
Greenly Rd WV4 . . . . .39 D5
Green Mdws **2** WS12 . . . . .2 C1
Green Mdw
Stourbridge DY9 . . . . .99 B7
Wednesfield WV11 . . . . .26 E5
Green Meadow Prim Sch
B29. . . . . .102 F7
Green Meadow Rd
Birmingham B29 . . . . .103 A7
Willenhall WV12 . . . . .27 B7
Greenmoor Rd
Hinckley LE10 . . . . .75 D5
Nuneaton CV10 . . . . .73 A3
Greenoak Cres
Birmingham B30 . . . . .104 C8
Dudley WV14. . . . . .51 A7
Green Oak Rd WV8 . . . . . .10 B2
Greenodd Dr CV6 . . . . .95 F5
Green Park Ave WV14 . . . .40 C8
Green Park Dr WV14 . . . . .40 C8
Green Park Rd
Birmingham B31 . . . . .102 E2
Bromsgrove B60 . . . . .137 B2
Dudley DY2 . . . . .62 F8
Green Park WV14. . . . . . . .40 B8
Green Rd
Birmingham B28 . . . . .87 E1
Dudley DY2 . . . . .62 D7
Greenridge Rd B20 . . . . . . .54 E5
Green Rock La WS3. . . . . . .14 D1
Green Rock Prim Sch
WS3 . . . . .14 E1
Greenroyde DY9 . . . . .81 B1
Greensand Dr WV14. . . . . .40 D2
Greenside
Birmingham B17 . . . . .85 C5
Cheswick Green B90 . . . . .126 D4
Greenside Cl CV11 . . . . . . .74 C1
Greenside Rd B24 . . . . .57 C5
Greenside B60. . . . . .150 C2
Greensill Ave WS5 . . . . . . .43 A4
Greensill Av DY4. . . . . .51 F8
Greens Ind Est WV10 . . . .11 B2
Green Slade Cres B60. . . .121 C1
Greenslade Croft B31 . . .103 A2
Green Slade Gr WS12 . . . . .2 C7
Greenslade Rd
Sedgley DY3. . . . . .39 B2
Solihull B90 . . . . .105 C2
Walsall WS5 . . . . .43 C7
Greensleeves Cl CV6 . . . . .95 B2
Greensleeves B74. . . . . .31 F1
Greens Rd CV6 . . . . .95 A1
Green St B12 . . . . .66 F1
Greens Rd B13 . . . . .87 D1
Greens The WV6 . . . . .23 E3
Green St
Kidderminster DY10 . . . . . .116 E5
Oldbury B69. . . . . .64 A7
Green Street Ind Est
DY10. . . . . .116 E4
Green St
Smethwick B67 . . . . .64 F5
Stourbridge DY8 . . . . .80 F5
Tipton WV14 . . . . .51 C8
Walsall WS2 . . . . .28 C3
West Bromwich B70 . . . . . .64 E8
Greensward Cl CV8 . . . . . .148 B6
Green Sward La B98 . . . . .154 D1
Greensward The CV3 . . . .115 A2
Greensway WV11 . . . . .26 B8
Greens Yd CV12. . . . . .78 C3
Green The
4 Birmingham,Quinton
B32. . . . . .84 A6
Aldridge WS9. . . . . .30 C6
Birmingham,Castle Bromwich
B36. . . . . .69 B7
Birmingham,Erdington B23 .57 A4
Birmingham,Frankley B31 .102 C2
Birmingham,King's Norton
B38. . . . . .103 F2
Bluntington DY10. . . . . . . .118 E1
Darlaston WS10. . . . . .41 D7
Fazeley B78. . . . . .35 B7
Freasley B78. . . . . .36 C4
Meriden CV7 . . . . .92 B1
Nuneaton CV11 . . . . .73 E2
Oldbury B68. . . . . .64 B1
Solihull B91 . . . . .107 D5
Stoneleigh CV8 . . . . .149 C6
Stourbridge DY8 . . . . .60 D2
Sutton Coldfield B72 . . . . . .46 D1

Green The continued
Tamworth B77 . . . . .22 B5
Tanworth-in-A B94 . . . . . .142 A2
Walsall WS3 . . . . .14 B1
West Hagley DY9. . . . . .98 F4
Greenvale Ave B26. . . . . . . .89 D6
Greenvale B31. . . . . .102 F5
Green Way WS9. . . . . .16 B2
Greenway Ave **2** DY8 . . . .60 E1
Greenway B20. . . . . .54 F6
Greenway Dr B73. . . . . .45 C3
Greenway Gdns
Birmingham B38 . . . . .123 E7
Sedgley DY3. . . . . .39 E1
Greenway CV11. . . . . .79 B8
Greenway Rd WV14 . . . . . .40 E4
Greenways
Birmingham B31 . . . . .102 F8
Coventry CV4 . . . . .111 C2
Dudley DY3 . . . . .39 E1
Greenways
Halesowen B63 . . . . .82 C6
Stourbridge DY8 . . . . .60 C1
Greenway St B9 . . . . .67 C1
Greenways The CV32 . . . .157 B3
Greenway The
Birmingham,Marston Green
B37. . . . . .90 A6
Sutton Coldfield,New Oscott
B73. . . . . .45 A2
West Hagley DY9. . . . . .98 F5
Greenway Wlk B33 . . . . . . .69 E1
Green Wickets B13 . . . . . .104 E6
Green Wlk 4 B17 . . . . .84 F7
Greenwood Ave
Birmingham B27 . . . . .88 B1
Oldbury B68. . . . . .64 C5
Rowley Regis B65 . . . . .63 D3
Greenwood B25 . . . . .88 D8
Greenwood Cl B14. . . . . . .104 E5
Greenwood Cotts DY1 . . . .51 A5
Greenwood Ct
Nuneaton CV11 . . . . .73 E3
Royal Leamington Spa
CV32 . . . . .157 B1
Greenwood Dr WS14 . . . . . .9 B6
Greenwood Pk
Aldridge WS9 . . . . .16 C2
Cannock WS12. . . . . .2 B8
Greenwood Pl B44. . . . . . . .45 B1
Greenwood Rd
Aldridge WS9 . . . . .16 B2
West Bromwich B71 . . . . . .53 B8
Wolverhampton WV10 . . . . .25 C7
Greenwood Sq 5 B37 . . . . .70 B2
Greenwoods The DY8 . . . . .80 E5
Greenwood Way B37 . . . . . .70 B2
Greethurst Dr B13 . . . . . . .87 C2
Greet Prim Sch B11. . . . . . .87 D4
Greets Green Ind Est B70 .52 F4
Greets Green Rd B70 . . . . .52 F3
Greetville Cl B34 . . . . .69 A5
Gregory Ave
Birmingham B29 . . . . .103 A8
Coventry CV3. . . . . .133 A6
Gregory Cl 3 WS10. . . . . . .41 F2
Gregory Ct WV11 . . . . .26 E5
Gregory Dr DY1. . . . . .51 A2
Gregory Hood Rd CV3. . . .133 E4
Gregory Rd
Burntwood WS7 . . . . .7 E7
Stourbridge DY8 . . . . .80 D5
Gregston Ind Est B69 . . . . .64 B8
Greig Ct WS11 . . . . .2 C2
Grendon Cl
Coventry CV4 . . . . .111 C1
Redditch B98. . . . . .154 D1
Grendon Dr B73. . . . . .45 D3
Grendon Gdns WV3 . . . . . . .38 D6
Grendon Jun & Inf Sch
B14. . . . . .105 A3
Grendon Rd
Birmingham B14 . . . . .105 A3
Solihull B92 . . . . .106 E8
Grenfell Cl CV31. . . . . .162 D6
Grenfell Ct B73. . . . . .46 B1
Grenfell Dr B15. . . . . .85 F8
Grenfell Rd WS3 . . . . .14 D3
Grenville Ave CV2. . . . . . .114 B3
Grenville Cl WS2. . . . . .27 D3
Grenville Dr
Birmingham B23 . . . . .56 B3
Smethwick B66 . . . . .64 D8
Grenville Pl B70 . . . . .52 E3
Grenville Rd
Dudley DY1. . . . . .50 E1
Solihull B90 . . . . .106 B2
Gresham Ave CV32. . . . . . .157 B2
Gresham Pl CV32 . . . . .157 B2
Gresham Rd
Birmingham B28 . . . . .105 F6
Cannock WS11. . . . . .1 F3
Nuneaton CV10 . . . . .78 B8
Oldbury B68. . . . . .64 C6
Gresham St CV2 . . . . .114 A2
Gresham Twr B12 . . . . .86 F8
Gresley Cl B74 . . . . .32 A4
Gresley Gr B23 . . . . .56 C1
Gresley Rd CV2. . . . . .114 D8
Gresley Row WS13 . . . . .9 C8
Gresley B77 . . . . .21 F1
Gressel La B33 . . . . .69 D3
Grestone Ave B20. . . . . . . .54 E3
Grestone Prim Sch B20 . . .54 E4
Greswold Cl CV4 . . . . .111 F1
Greswolde Dr B24 . . . . .57 B4
Greswolde Park Rd B27. . .88 B4

Greswolde Rd
Birmingham B11 . . . . .87 D3
Solihull B91 . . . . .106 E6
Greswoldes The CV31 . . . .162 F6
Greswold Gdns B34 . . . . . .69 A5
Greswold Prim Sch B91. . .107 C6
Greswold St B71 . . . . .53 B5
Gretna Rd CV3 . . . . .132 F4
Gretton Cres WS9. . . . . . . .29 E5
Gretton Rd
Aldridge WS9 . . . . .29 F5
Birmingham B23 . . . . .56 D7
Greville Dr B15. . . . . .86 C6
Greville Ho **13** CV34. . . . .160 F7
Greville Rd
Kenilworth CV8 . . . . .147 F4
Warwick CV34 . . . . .160 E8
Greville Smith Ave CV31 .162 B4
Grevis Cl B13. . . . . .86 F4
Grevis Rd B25 . . . . .68 E1
Greycoat Rd CV6 . . . . .95 A2
Greyfort Cres B92. . . . . . . .88 F1
Greyfriars Cl
Dudley DY1 . . . . .50 E3
Solihull B92 . . . . .106 D6
Greyfriars La CV1. . . . . . . .165 B2
Greyfriars Rd CV1 . . . . . . .165 B2
Greyfriars Dr
Bromsgrove B61 . . . . .136 D2
Tamworth B79 . . . . .20 E6
Greyfriars La CV1. . . . . . . .165 B2
Greyfriars Rd CV1 . . . . . . .165 B2
Greyhound La
Lower Penn WV4 . . . . .37 E5
Stourbridge DY8 . . . . .80 D2
Greyhurst Croft 5 B91. . .127 B8
Grey Mill La B90 . . . . .126 F6
Greysbrooke Prim Sch
WS14 . . . . .18 A6
Greysbrooke WS14. . . . . . .18 A5
Grey's Rd B60. . . . . .159 E3
Greystoke Ave B36. . . . . . . .68 F7
Greystoke Dr DY6 . . . . .60 D6
Greystone Cl B98 . . . . .154 C5
Greystone Pas **10** DY1. . . .51 B1
Grey Tree Cres B93 . . . . . .127 E3
Grice St B70. . . . . .64 D8
Griffin Ave DY10 . . . . .116 E4
Griffin Bsns Pk B37 . . . . . .70 C3
Griffin Cl
Birmingham B31 . . . . .103 B6
Burntwood WS7 . . . . .6 E8
Griffin Ct B5 . . . . .86 C5
Griffin Gdns B17. . . . . .85 D4
Griffin Ho B16 . . . . .65 E1
Griffin Ind Est B65. . . . . . .63 F3
Griffin Rd
Birmingham B23 . . . . .56 C5
Warwick CV34 . . . . .161 C7
Griffins Brook Cl B30 . . . .103 D7
Griffins Brook La B30 . . . .103 D6
Griffins La B90 . . . . .126 A5
Griffin St
Dudley DY2 . . . . .62 C4
West Bromwich B70 . . . . . .53 D3
Wolverhampton WV1 . . . . . .25 F1
Griffiths Dr
Wolverhampton WV11 . . . . .13 A1
Wombourne WV5 . . . . .49 A5
Griffiths Rd
Dudley DY1 . . . . .51 A6
West Bromwich B71 . . . . . .42 C1
Willenhall WV12 . . . . .27 D8
Griffiths St WV14 . . . . .51 E5
Griff La
Nuneaton CV10 . . . . .78 A6
Nuneaton CV10 . . . . .78 B6
Grigg Gr B31 . . . . .102 E1
Grimley La B60 . . . . .151 E6
Grimley Rd 2 B31. . . . . . .103 D2
Grimley WS11 . . . . .1 F4
Grimpits La B38 . . . . .124 A7
Grimshaw Rd B27 . . . . .88 A1
Grimshaw Villas B93 . . . . .128 D8
Grimston Cl CV3. . . . . .115 A2
Grimstone St WV10 . . . . . .163 C4
Grindleford Rd B42 . . . . . . .55 D7
Grindle Rd CV6 . . . . .95 F4
Grindley Ho 5 CV1. . . . . . .113 B2
Grindsbrook B77. . . . . .36 A8
Gristhorpe Rd B29 . . . . . . .104 A8
Grizebeck Dr CV5. . . . . . . .112 A5
Grizedale Cl B45. . . . . .102 B2
Grocott Rd WV10 . . . . .41 B4
Grosmont Ave 8 B12. . . . . .87 A6
Grosvenor Ave
Birmingham B20 . . . . .55 C2
Kidderminster DY10 . . . . . .117 A8
Sutton Coldfield B74 . . . . . .30 F1
Grosvenor Cl
Lichfield WS14. . . . . .9 D6
Sutton Coldfield B75 . . . . . .32 C1
Wolverhampton WV10 . . . . .11 D2
Grosvenor Cres
Hinckley LE10 . . . . .75 E6
Wolverhampton WV10 . . . . .11 D2
Grosvenor Ct
2 Royal Leamington Spa
CV32 . . . . .156 F1
Birmingham,Handsworth
B20 . . . . .55 C2
Dudley DY3 . . . . .50 C8
Shenstone WS14 . . . . .17 F6
Stourbridge DY9 . . . . .81 F3
Wednesfield WV11 . . . . .26 E5
WV6 . . . . .24 A3
Wolverhampton WV3 . . . . .163 B2

Grosvenor Gdns B61. . . . .137 B5
Grosvenor Ho
Birmingham,Erdington
B23. . . . . .57 A5
Coventry CV1. . . . . .165 A2
Redditch B97 . . . . .153 E4
Grosvenor Pk WV4. . . . . . .38 F5
Grosvenor Rd
Birmingham,Aston B6 . . . . .67 B8
Birmingham,Aston B6 . . . . .85 A6
Birmingham,Handsworth
B20 . . . . .55 C2
Coventry CV1 . . . . .165 A1
Dudley DY3 . . . . .50 D2
Oldbury B68. . . . . .64 A3
Solihull B91 . . . . .106 F1
Whitnash CV31 . . . . .162 A5
Wolverhampton,Bushbury
WV10 . . . . .11 D2
Wolverhampton WV4 . . . . . .39 E3
Grosvenor Road S DY3 . . . .50 D2
Grosvenor St W B16 . . . . . .66 B1
Grosvenor Sh Ctr B31. . . .103 A4
Grosvenor Sq B28 . . . . . . .105 F5
Grosvenor St
Birmingham B5 . . . . .164 D3
Wolverhampton WV10 . . . . .25 F3
Wolverhampton WV4 . . . . . .39 E7
Grotto La WV6 . . . . .24 E5
Groucutt St 6 WV14 . . . . . .51 C8
Grounds Dr B74 . . . . .31 F3
Grounds Rd B74 . . . . .31 F3
Grout St B70 . . . . .52 E4
Grove Ave
Birmingham B27 . . . . .88 B3
Birmingham,Handsworth
B21 . . . . .65 D8
Birmingham,Moseley B13 . .87 A2
Halesowen B63 . . . . .82 F3
Solihull B91 . . . . .107 C5
Grove Cl WS11. . . . . .1 E3
Grove Cottage Rd B9 . . . . .67 D2
Grove Cres
Brierley Hill DY5 . . . . .61 C5
Walsall WS3 . . . . .14 F3
Grove Ct
Birmingham B43 . . . . .54 F6
Coventry CV5. . . . . .133 B8
Nuneaton CV11. . . . . .73 E2
Grove Farm Dr B75. . . . . . .46 F5
Grovefield Cres CV7 . . . . .130 C8
Grove Fields CV10 . . . . .73 D8
Grove Gdns
Birmingham B20 . . . . .54 F2
Bromsgrove B61 . . . . .137 A6
Grove Hill Rd B21. . . . . .54 F1
Grove Hill WS5 . . . . .29 E1
Grovehurst Pk CV8. . . . . . .149 B2
Grove La
Birmingham B17 . . . . .85 C4
Birmingham,Handsworth
B20 . . . . .54 F1
Keresley CV7 . . . . .94 F7
Lapworth B94 . . . . .143 F4
Groveland Rd DY4 . . . . .52 B3
Grovelands Cres WV10 . . . .11 D6
Grovelands Ind Est CV7 . . .96 A6
Grove La
Norton Canes WS3 . . . . .5 E1
Smethwick B66 . . . . .65 C5
Shaw B76 . . . . .47 F2
Wolverhampton WV6 . . . . . .24 B2
Groveley La B31,B45. . . . .122 E5
Grove Mews B31. . . . . .123 B8
Grove Pk
Hinckley LE10 . . . . .76 A6
Kingswinford DY6 . . . . .60 C8
Grove Pl
2 Royal Leamington Spa
CV31 . . . . .162 A6
Nuneaton CV10 . . . . .72 D3
Grove Prim Sch WV2 . . . . .163 D1
Grove Rd
Ansty CV7 . . . . .97 D3
Birmingham,King's Heath
B14. . . . . .104 D6
Birmingham,Sparkhill B11. .87 C2
Birmingham B93 . . . . .128 B3
Hinckley LE10 . . . . .76 A6
Nuneaton CV10 . . . . .72 D3
Oldbury B68. . . . . .64 D1
Solihull B91 . . . . .107 C5
Stourbridge DY9 . . . . .81 F3
Grove Sch B21. . . . . .65 F8
Groveside Way WS3 . . . . . .15 A5
Grove St
Coventry CV1 . . . . .165 C3
Dudley DY2 . . . . .62 E8
Redditch B98 . . . . .153 E4
Royal Leamington Spa
CV32 . . . . .161 E8
Smethwick B66 . . . . .65 D4
Wolverhampton,Springfield
WV10 . . . . .25 D4
Grove Terr WS1 . . . . .28 F1
Grove The
Bedworth CV12 . . . . .78 C3
Birmingham,Edgbaston B16 .65 F1
Birmingham,Great Barr B43 .43 E4
Birmingham,Lozells B19 . . .66 B7
Birmingham,Rednal B45 . .122 D4
Birmingham,Saltley B8 . . . .67 C4
Birmingham,West Heath
B31. . . . . .123 B8

Grove The *continued*
Brierley Hill DY5 61 C1
Burntwood WS7 6 D8
Coleshill B46 70 F4
Hampton-in-A B92 91 A1
Hinckley LE10 75 C8
Rowley Regis B65 63 C2
Studley B80 159 D3
Sutton Coldfield B74 31 D6
Walsall WS5 43 B3
Wolverhampton,New Cross WV11 26 B6
Wolverhampton,Parkfield WV4 39 E5
Grove Vale Ave B43 43 C1
Grove Vale Prim Sch B43 43 D1
Grove Villas B64 82 D7
Grove Way B74 44 F7
Grovewood Dr 2 B38 103 E1
Guardhouse Rd CV6 113 B8
Guardian Angels RC Prim Sch B34 69 E6
Guardian Ct
4 Bromsgrove B60 137 A2
Birmingham,Frankley B31 102 D3
Birmingham,Gilbertstone B26 88 F7
Solihull B91 107 D3
Guardian Ho B68 84 C7
Guardians Way B31 102 E8
Guernsey Dr B36 70 B6
Guest Ave WV11 26 C8
Guest Gr B19 66 C6
Guest Hospl DY1 51 E3
Guild Ave WS3 28 D8
Guild Cl B16 66 A2
Guild Cotts The CV34 160 D6
Guild Croft B19 66 D6
Guild Ct 4 B60 136 F2
Guildford Cl DY11 116 A6
Guildford Croft B37 89 F8
Guildford Ct
12 Birmingham B29 103 C7
Coventry CV6 113 D7
Guildford Dr B19 66 D6
Guildford St 4 B19 66 D7
Guildhall Mews The 7 WS1 28 F1
Guild Rd
Bromsgrove B60 136 F1
Coventry CV6 113 D7
Guillemard Ct B37 70 B1
Guilsborough Rd CV3 134 E8
Guinea Cres CV4 131 E6
Guinness Cl B98 158 D8
Guiting Cl B97 153 B1
Guiting Rd B29 103 A7
Gulistan Ct 6 CV32 156 E1
Gulistan Rd CV32 156 E1
Gullane Cl B38 103 D1
Gullet The B78 22 F1
Gullick Way WS7 6 D8
Gulliman's Way CV31 162 D7
Gullswood Cl B14 104 D2
Gulson Hospl CV1 165 D2
Gulson Rd CV1 113 E2
Gumbleberrys Cl B8 68 C4
Gun Barrel Ind Ctr B63 82 F6
Gundry Cl CV31 162 A7
Gun La CV2 114 A5
Gunmakers Wlk B19 66 D7
Gunner Gr B75 47 A6
Gunner La B45 121 D7
Gunners La B80 159 E4
Gunnery Terr 3 CV32 156 D1
Gunns Way B92 106 D7
Guns La B70 53 B4
Gunstock Cl B74 44 E7
Guns Village Prim Sch B70 53 A3
Gunter Prim Sch B24 57 E3
Gunter Rd B24 57 E3
Gunton Ave CV3 134 C6
Guphill Ave CV5 112 D2
Guphill La CV5 112 D3
Gupta Trad Est B69 52 F1
Gurnard Cl WV12 13 B1
Gurnard B77 35 D6
Gurney Cl CV4 111 E3
Gurney Pl WS2 28 A5
Gurney Rd WS2 28 A5
Guthrie Cl B19 66 D6
Guthrum Cl
Birmingham B23 56 E8
Perton WV6 23 F5
Gutteridge Ave CV6 95 A2
Gutter The DY9 120 E7
Guy Ave WV10 25 E6
Guy Pl E 13 CV32 156 F1
Guy Pl W 12 CV32 156 F1
Guy Rd CV8 147 F2
Guy's Almshouses B79 21 B5
Guy's Cliffe Ave CV32 156 D2
Guys Cliffe Ave B76 46 F1
Guy's Cliffe Rd CV32 161 E8
Guy's Cliffe Terr CV34 160 F7
Guys Cl B79 20 F7
Guy's Cl CV34 161 A8
Guy's Cross Park Rd CV34 160 F8
Guy's La DY3 50 B2
Guys Motors Ind Pk WV10 25 F5
Guy St
Royal Leamington Spa CV32 156 F1
Guy St *continued*
Warwick CV34 160 F7
Guy's Wlk B61 137 A5
Gwalia Gr B23 56 F4
Gwendoline Ave LE10 71 A2
Gwendoline Way WS9 16 B4
GWS Ind Est WS10 41 D1
Gypsy La
Kenilworth CV8 147 F2
Redditch B97 152 C5
Water Orton B46 59 D2

H

Habberley La DY11 116 A8
Habberley Rd
Kidderminster DY11 116 B7
Rowley Regis B65 63 D2
Habberley St 1 DY11 116 C6
Habberly Croft 1 B91 107 B1
Habitat Ct B76 46 F3
Hackett Cl WV14 39 F1
Hackett Ct 2 B69 64 A7
Hackett Dr B66 64 D7
Hackett Rd B65 63 E3
Hackett St DY4 52 C7
Hackford Rd WV4 39 F4
Hackmans Gate La DY9 119 B7
Hack St B9 67 A1
Hackwood Ho 10 B69 63 D5
Hackwood Rd WS10 42 B2
Hadcroft Grange DY9 81 D4
Hadcroft Rd DY9 81 C4
Haddock Rd WV14 40 C7
Haddon Cres WV12 27 C7
Haddon Croft B63 82 C1
Haddon End CV3 133 E6
Haddon Rd
Birmingham B42 55 D6
Royal Leamington Spa CV32 157 B2
Haddon St CV6 114 A8
Haddon Twr 1 B15 86 D8
Haden Arch Ct B64 83 A7
Haden Cl
Cradley Heath B64 83 A7
Stourbridge DY8 60 D2
Haden Cres WV11 26 F6
Haden Cross Dr B64 83 A7
Haden Ct 5 WV3 25 A2
Hadendale B64 83 A7
Haden Hill Rd B63 83 B6
Haden Hill WV3 25 A2
Haden Park Rd B64 82 F7
Haden Rd
Cradley Heath B64 62 E2
Wednesbury DY4 41 A1
Haden St B12 86 F6
Haden Way B12 86 F6
Haden Wlk 4 B65 63 C3
Hadfield Cl B24 57 E3
Hadfield Croft B19 66 C5
Hadfield Way B37 70 A4
Hadland Rd B33 69 B1
Hadleigh Croft B76 58 A6
Hadleigh Rd CV3 133 C4
Hadley Cl
Dudley DY2 62 E4
Hollywood B47 125 A5
Hadley Croft B66 65 A7
Hadley Ct B16 65 D1
Hadley Mews CV11 73 D1
Hadley Pl WV14 40 C7
Hadley Rd
Bilston WV14 40 C7
Willenhall WS2 27 F6
Hadley St B68 64 A4
Hadley Way WS2 28 A6
Hadlow Croft B33 89 D7
Hadrian Cl CV32 157 B4
Hadrian Dr B46 59 F1
Hadrians Cl B77 35 D8
Hadyn Gr B26 89 B6
Hadzor Ho 5 B97 153 A4
Hadzor Rd B68 84 D8
Hafren Cl B45 102 B2
Hafton Gr B9 67 D1
Haggar St WV2 39 C6
Haglay Ct N DY5 61 E4
Haglay Ct S DY5 61 E4
Hagley Cl DY9 99 C6
Hagley Cswy DY9 100 B8
Hagley Ct DY3 50 D3
Hagley Hall Gdns DY9 99 D6
Hagley Hall* DY9 99 D6
Hagley Hill DY9 99 E7
Hagley Ho B60 137 B3
Hagley Mews DY9 99 D6
Hagley Park Dr B45 122 A6
Hagley Prim Sch DY9 99 B5
Hagley RC High Sch DY8 98 F6
Hagley Rd
Birmingham B16 65 C1
Halesowen B63 82 E2
Stourbridge DY8 81 B3
Hagley Rd W B32,B68 84 D7
Hagley St 3 B63 83 B3
Hagley Sta DY9 99 A6
Hagley View Rd DY2 62 C8
Hagley Villas B12 87 B4
Hagley Wood La DY9,B62 100 B7
Haig Cl
Cannock WS11 2 A5
Sutton Coldfield B75 46 C7
Haig Pl B13 105 A7
Haig Rd DY2 51 F1
Haig St B71 53 C5
Hailes Park Cl WV2 39 E6
Hailsham Rd B23 56 F5
Hailstone Cl B65 63 A5
Haines Cl DY4 52 B4
Haines St B70 53 D2
Hainfield Dr B91 107 E5
Hainge Rd B69 52 C1
Hainult Cl DY8 60 D4
Halas Ct B64 62 E2
Halas Ind Est B62 83 C5
Halberd Cl LE10 75 D5
Halberton St B66 65 D4
Haldane Ct B33 69 B2
Haldon Gr B31 122 E7
Halecroft Ave WV11 26 D5
Hale Gr B24 57 D4
Halesbury Ct B63 82 F2
Halesbury Sch B62 83 E7
Hales Cres B67 64 E4
Halescroft Sq B31 102 E6
Hales Gdns B23 56 C8
Hales La B67 64 E4
Halesmere Way B63 83 C3
Halesowen CE Prim Sch B63 83 B4
Halesowen Coll (E-Business Ctr) B62 83 C8
Halesowen Coll (Whittingham main campus) B63 83 B5
Halesowen Ind Pk B62 83 B6
Halesowen Rd
Dudley BY2,B64 62 D4
Halesowen B62 83 F6
Lower Marlbrook B61 121 C3
Halesowen St
Oldbury B69 63 F7
Rowley Regis B65 63 C1
Hales Park Ind Est CV6 95 E4
Hales Rd
Halesowen B63 83 A4
Wednesbury WS10 42 A5
Hales St CV1 165 C3
Hales Way B69 63 F7
Halesworth Rd WV9 10 F2
Hale Trad Est DY4 52 B6
Halewood Gr B28 106 A7
Haley St WV12 27 C5
Halfcot Ave DY9 81 C3
Halford Cres WS3 28 F5
Halford Gr B24 57 E4
Halford La CV6 95 A2
Halford Lodge CV6 95 A2
Halford Rd B91 106 E6
Halford's La B66 65 A8
Halfords Pk B66 65 A8
Halford St B79 21 A5
Halfpenny Field Wlk B35 58 A3
Halfshire La DY10 98 B1
Halfway Cl B44 55 E6
Halifax Cl CV5 112 A7
Halifax Ct DY11 116 B8
Halifax Gr 7 B18 65 E4
Halifax Ho B5 86 D7
Halifax Rd B90 106 B2
Haliscombe Gr 4 B6 66 E8
Halkett Glade B33 68 D3
Halladale B38 103 F1
Hallam Cl B71 53 E5
Hallam Cres WV10 25 E6
Hallam Ct B71 53 E5
Hallam Dr B71 53 E5
Hallam Rd CV6 95 B2
Hallams Cl CV8 135 F5
Hallam St
Birmingham B12 86 E5
West Bromwich B71 53 D5
Hallbridge Cl WS3 14 F2
Hallbridge Way B69 52 B2
Hall Brook Rd CV6 95 A4
Hallchurch Rd DY2 61 F6
Hall Cl CV8 149 B6
Hallcourt Cl 3 WS11 4 E8
Hallcourt Cres 2 WS11 4 E8
Hallcourt La WS11 4 E8
Hall Cres B71 53 C6
Hallcroft Cl B72 57 C7
Hallcroft Way
Aldridge WS9 30 C5
Dorridge B93 128 A6
Hall Dale Cl B28 105 F5
Hall Dr
Baginton CV8 133 E3
Birmingham B37 90 A7
Hagley DY9 99 D6
Hall End CV11 73 D2
Hall End Pl CV11 73 D2
Hall End WS10 41 F3
Hallens Dr WS10 41 D2
Hallet Dr WV3 163 A2
Hallewell Rd B16 65 D3
Hallfield Sch B15 86 A7
Hallfields CV31 162 E5
Hall Green Inf Sch B28 105 F7
Hall Green Jun Sch B28 105 F7
Hall Green Prim Sch B71 42 D1
Hall Green Rd
Coventry CV2,CV6 96 B2
West Bromwich B71 42 D1
Hall Green Sch B28 105 E8
Hall Green Sta B28 87 F1
Hallgreen St WV14 40 E2
Hall Gr WV14 51 C8
Hall Hays Rd B34 69 E7
Hall La
Brownhills WS9 15 E3
Coventry CV2 114 F6
Dudley DY2 62 C6
Hall La *continued*
Great Wyrley WS6 5 A3
Hagley DY9 99 D6
Hammerwich WS7 7 E4
Muckley Corner WS7,WS14 7 F2
Tipton DY4 52 B8
Walsall WS3 14 F3
Wolverhampton WV14 39 F1
Hall Mdw
Hagley DY9 99 D7
Wedges Mills WS11 4 B6
Hallmoor Rd B33 69 B3
Hallmoor Sch B33 69 B3
Hallot Cl B23 56 D8
Halloughton Rd B74 46 A7
Hallow Cl 3 B31 103 D2
Hallowfields Cl B98 153 E1
Hall Park St WV14 40 B7
Hall Rd
Birmingham,Castle Bromwich B36 69 A8
Birmingham,Handsworth B20 66 A8
Birmingham,Saltley B8 67 D4
Hinckley LE10 75 D5
Royal Leamington Spa CV32 156 F1
Smethwick B67 64 E4
Hall St E WS10 41 C7
Hall St S B70 64 D8
Hall's Cl CV31 162 B3
Hall St
Bilston WV14 40 E5
Birmingham B18 164 A4
Cradley Heath B64 62 F2
Darlaston WS10 41 B7
Dudley DY2 51 D1
Hallstead Rd B13 105 B5
Hall St
Oldbury B68 64 B5
Sedgley DY3 50 D8
Stourbridge DY8 81 A3
Tipton DY4 51 E5
Walsall WS2 28 D3
West Bromwich B70 53 C2
Willenhall WV13 27 B1
Wolverhampton WV11 26 C5
Hallswelle Gr B43 44 E4
Hallway Dr CV7 97 E6
Hall Wlk B46 70 F4
Halsbury Gr B44 56 B8
Halstead Gr B91 127 A8
Halston Rd WS7 7 B8
Haltonlea B77 36 A8
Halton Rd B73 45 E2
Halton St DY2 62 C5
Hamar Way B37 70 B1
Hamberley Ct B18 65 D5
Hamble Cl DY5 61 A6
Hamble Ct B73 46 B5
Hambledon Cl WV9 11 A2
Hamble Gr WV6 23 E4
Hamble Rd
Birmingham B42 43 F1
Wolverhampton WV4 38 C6
Hamble B77 21 D2
Hambleton Rd B63 82 D2
Hambletts Rd B70 53 A3
Hambrook Cl WV6 25 A5
Hambury Dr B14 104 D7
Ham Dingle Prim Sch DY9 81 C2
Hamelin St WS11 1 E3
Hamilton Ave
Birmingham B17 85 A7
Halesowen B62 83 C3
Stourbridge DY8 80 D6
Hamilton Cl
Bedworth CV12 77 C1
Cannock WS12 2 F4
Hinckley LE10 71 A2
Lickey End B60 137 C6
Sedgley DY3 50 C8
Stourbridge DY8 60 C2
Hamilton Ct
1 Birmingham,Moseley B13 86 F4
Birmingham,Showell Green B13 87 B3
Coventry CV1 165 B4
Nuneaton CV10 72 D4
Hamilton Dr
Birmingham B29 103 D8
Oldbury B69 52 C2
Stourbridge DY8 60 C2
Studley B80 159 D3
Hamilton Gdns WV10 11 F3
Hamilton Ho WS3 14 C1
Hamilton Lea WS11 6 A6
Hamilton Rd
Birmingham B21 65 D8
Coventry CV2 114 A3
Kidderminster DY11 116 B3
Radford Semele CV31 162 E5
Redditch B97 158 C8
Smethwick B67 64 E2
Tipton DY4 52 C6
Hamilton Sch B21 65 D8
Hamilton St WS3 14 D1
Hamilton Terr CV32 161 F8
Ham La
Kingswinford DY6 49 E1
Stourbridge DY9 81 C2
Hamlet Cl CV11 74 B1
Hamlet Gdns B28 105 F8
Hamlet Rd B28 105 F8
Hamlet The
Leek Wootton CV35 156 A7
Hamlet The *continued*
Norton Canes WS11 5 E5
Hammer Bank DY5 82 A8
Hammersley Cl B63 82 C7
Hammersley St CV12 77 E1
Hammerwich Hospl WS7 7 B5
Hammerwich La WS7 7 F3
Hammerwich Rd WS7 7 D5
Hammond Ave WV10 25 E8
Hammond Bsns Ctr CV11 73 E3
Hammond Cl CV11 73 E3
Hammond Dr B23 56 F5
Hammond Rd CV2 113 F4
Hammonds Terr CV8 147 D5
Hammond Way DY8 81 A7
Hampden Cl 3 DY5 82 A8
Hampden Retreat B12 86 E6
Hamps Cl WS7 7 D7
Hampshire Cl
Coventry CV3 134 F8
Tamworth B78 20 F2
Hampshire Ct 1 B29 103 B7
Hampshire Dr B15 85 E8
Hampshire Rd B71 42 A1
Hampson Cl B11 87 B6
Hampstead Glade B63 83 C2
Hampton Ave
Bromsgrove B60 151 A8
Nuneaton CV10 72 B4
Hampton Cl
Coventry CV6 113 F6
Redditch B98 159 B7
Sutton Coldfield B73 45 C2
Tamworth B79 21 C7
Hampton Court Rd B17 85 A6
Hampton Ct
Birmingham B15 86 B8
Hampton-in-A B92 109 B6
Solihull B91 107 D4
Wednesbury B71 42 C1
Wolverhampton WV10 12 B2
Hampton Dr B74 46 B8
Hampton Gdns DY9 81 D3
Hampton Gn WS11 4 E7
Hampton Grange CV7 92 B1
Hampton Gr
Royal Leamington Spa CV32 157 B1
Walsall WS3 15 A4
Hampton-in-Arden Sta B92 109 B7
Hampton La
Catherine de B B91 108 B5
Meriden CV7 109 E8
Hampton Pl WS10 41 C8
Hampton Rd
Birmingham,Aston B6 66 D8
Birmingham,Stockland Green B23 56 D4
Coventry CV6 113 F6
Knowle B93 128 C8
Warwick CV34 160 B5
Wolverhampton WV10 11 B1
Hampton St
Birmingham B19 164 B4
Cannock WS11 4 D7
Dudley,Netherton DY2 62 C5
Dudley WV14 51 B8
Warwick CV34 160 D6
Hampton View WV10 25 F3
Hampton Wlk WV1 163 B3
Hams La B76 59 F6
Hams Rd B8 67 D4
Hamstead Cl WV11 26 D6
Hamstead Ct B19 66 B7
Hamstead Hall Ave B20 54 E5
Hamstead Hall Rd B20 54 F4
Hamstead Hall Sch B20 54 E6
Hamstead Hill B20 54 F4
Hamstead Ho B43 54 F7
Hamstead Jun & Inf Sch B43 54 D7
Hamstead Rd
Birmingham,Hamstead B43 54 D7
Birmingham,Lozells B19,B20 66 B7
Hamstead Sta B42 54 F6
Hamstead Terr WS10 42 A2
Hanam Cl B75 46 F6
Hanbury Cl
Bromsgrove B60 151 A8
Halesowen B63 82 F2
Hanbury Cres WV4 38 E6
Hanbury Croft B27 88 E3
Hanbury Ct DY8 81 A4
Hanbury Hill DY8 81 A4
Hanbury Ho B97 153 B4
Hanbury Rd
Bedworth CV12 78 C4
Brownhills WS8 6 F2
Dorridge B93 127 F4
Norton Canes WS11 5 F5
Stoke Heath B60 150 D4
Tamworth B77 21 F4
West Bromwich B70 53 A3
Hanbury's Farm Com Prim Sch B77 21 D1
Hanch Pl WS1 42 F8
Hancock Gn CV4 131 F8
Hancock Rd B8 67 F4
Hancox St B68 64 B2
Handcross Gr CV3 133 A5
Handel Ct WS11 2 C2
Handel Wlk WS13 3 C2
Handley Gr
Birmingham B31 102 C2
Warwick CV34 155 D1
Handley's Cl CV8 135 A1

Handley St WS10 . . . . .42 A4
Handsworth, Booth Street
  Sta B21 . . . . .65 C7
Handsworth Cl B21 . . . . .65 D7
Handsworth Coll B6 . . . . .66 E8
Handsworth Cres CV5. . . . .111 E4
Handsworth Dr B43 . . . . .44 A3
Handsworth Gram Sch
  B21. . . . . .65 F8
Handsworth New Rd B18. . .65 E6
Handsworth Wood Girls' Sch
  B20. . . . . .54 F2
Handsworth Wood Rd
  B20. . . . . .55 A2
Hanford Cl CV6. . . . . .113 E6
Hanford Close Ind Est
  CV6 . . . . .113 E6
Hanger Rd B26 . . . . .90 A3
Hanging La B31 . . . . .102 E2
Hangleton Dr B11 . . . . .87 D6
Hangman's La LE10 . . . . .71 E3
Hanley Cl B63 . . . . .82 E4
Hanley Ct B23 . . . . .56 C2
Hanley St B19 . . . . .164 C4
Hanley Villas ■ B12 . . . . . . .87 B5
Hanlith B77 . . . . .36 A8
Hannaford Way WS11 . . . . . . .1 F2
Hannaford Rd B16 . . . . .65 D8
Hannah Rd WV14 . . . . .41 A3
Hanney Hay Rd WS7,WS8 . . .7 B3
Hannon Rd B14. . . . . .104 E5
Hanover Cl B6. . . . . .66 E7
Hanover Ct
  Hinckley LE10 . . . . .75 E6
  Redditch B97. . . . . .158 D8
  Tamworth B79 . . . . .20 E7
  Walsall WS2 . . . . .27 E1
  Wolverhampton WV6. . . . . .24 C4
Hanover Dr B24 . . . . .67 F8
Hanover Gdns ⑧ CV32. . .157 A1
Hanover Glebe CV11. . . . . . .73 C2
Hanover Ho ⑥ DY8 . . . . .80 F8
Hanover Pl
  Bromsgrove B60 . . . . .136 F1
  Cannock WS11. . . . . .1 E2
Hanover Rd B65 . . . . .63 C4
Hanover St B61. . . . . .136 F1
Hans Cl CV2 . . . . .113 F4
Hansell Dr B93 . . . . .127 E2
Hansom Ct ② LE10 . . . . . . .75 D8
Hansom Rd
  Birmingham B32 . . . . .84 C5
  Hinckley LE10 . . . . .71 F2
Hanson Ct B92 . . . . .88 F5
Hanson Man B74 . . . . .32 A1
Hanson's Bridge Rd B24 . .57 F5
Hanson Way CV6 . . . . .96 A4
Hanwell Cl B76. . . . . .58 B7
Hanwood Cl
  Birmingham B12 . . . . .86 F8
  Coventry CV5 . . . . .111 D4
Hanwood Ho ■ B12 . . . . . .86 F8
Hanworth Cl CV32. . . . . . . .157 C2
Hanworth Rd CV34. . . . . . . .160 D8
Harald Cl WV6. . . . . .23 E5
Harbeck Ave B44 . . . . .55 F8
Harberrow Cl DY9 . . . . .99 A6
Harbet Dr B40. . . . . .90 E4
Harbinger Rd B38 . . . . .104 B2
Harborne Ct B17. . . . . .85 C4
Harborne Hill Sch B15. . . . .85 A6
Harborne Ho B17. . . . . .85 A4
Harborne La B17 . . . . .85 D3
Harborne Park Rd B17. . . . .85 C6
Harborne Prim Sch B17. . . .85 C6
Harborne Rd
  Birmingham,Chad Valley
    B15. . . . . .85 E7
  Birmingham,Warley Woods
    B68. . . . . .84 E8
Harborough Cotts B94 . .144 D3
Harborough Ct B74 . . . . .32 A2
Harborough Dr
  Aldridge WS9. . . . . .30 B5
  Birmingham B36 . . . . .58 D1
Harborough Rd CV6. . . . . . .95 B2
Harborough Wlk DY9 . . . . . .81 E2
Harbourne Cl CV8 . . . . .148 A5
Harbours Cl B61. . . . . .150 D7
Harbours Hill DY9 . . . . .120 E6
Harbury Cl
  Redditch B98 . . . . .154 D1
  Sutton Coldfield B76 . . . . . .58 B6
Harbury La CV33,CV34 . . .161 E2
Harbury Rd B12 . . . . .86 D5
Harbury St B17. . . . . .90 B8
Harcourt CV3 . . . . .134 E5
Harcourt Dr
  Dudley DY3 . . . . .50 D2
  Sutton Coldfield B74 . . . . . .31 F4
Harcourt Gdns CV11 . . . . . . .73 C3
Harcourt Ho B79 . . . . .21 A4
Harcourt Rd
  Birmingham B23 . . . . .56 E6
  Cradley Heath B64 . . . . . . .82 E8
  Wednesbury WS10 . . . . . . .41 F4
Harden Cl WS3 . . . . .28 E7
Harden Ct B31. . . . . .102 E1
Harden Gr WS3 . . . . .28 E7
Harden Keep B66. . . . . .65 A4
Harden Manor Ct B63. . . . . .82 F2
Harden Prim Sch WS3 . . . . .28 E7
Harden Rd WS3. . . . . .28 E7
Harden Vale B63 . . . . .82 F3
Hardie Ct ② WV4. . . . . .39 F4
Hardie Gn WS11 . . . . .1 F3
Harding St WV14. . . . . .40 D2
Hardon Rd WV4. . . . . .39 F5

Hardware St B70 . . . . .53 D4
Hardwick Cl CV5. . . . . .112 A4
Hardwick Ct
  Stourbridge DY9 . . . . .81 D5
  Sutton Coldfield B74 . . . . . .30 F2
  Tamworth B79 . . . . .21 C5
Hardwick Dr B62 . . . . .83 A7
Hardwicke Way DY9. . . . . . . .81 D5
Hardwick La B80 . . . . .159 F4
Hardwick Rd
  Solihull B92 . . . . .88 E4
  Sutton Coldfield B74 . . . . . .31 A2
Hardwick Wlk B14 . . . . .104 D2
Hardwyn Cl CV3 . . . . .115 A1
Hardy Ave DY10. . . . . .117 A6
Hardy Cl
  Hinckley LE10 . . . . .71 D4
  Nuneaton CV10 . . . . .72 A4
Hardy Ct ❹ B13 . . . . .86 F4
Hardy Rd
  Coventry CV6. . . . . .113 A8
  Walsall WS3 . . . . .28 E8
  Wednesbury WS10 . . . . . . .42 A3
Hardy Sq WV2 . . . . .39 F6
Harebell Cl
  Cannock WS12. . . . . .2 D2
  Featherstone WV10. . . . . . .12 A7
  Walsall WS5 . . . . .43 A3
Harebell Cres DY1 . . . . .51 A4
Harebell Gdns B38. . . . . . . .123 F8
Harebell B77 . . . . .22 A4
Harebell Wlk ■ B37 . . . . . . .70 D2
Harefield Ho CV2 . . . . .114 B3
Harefield La CV12. . . . . .77 F8
Harefield Rd
  Coventry CV2. . . . . .114 B3
  Nuneaton CV11 . . . . .73 C4
Hare Gr B31. . . . . .102 D3
Hare & Hounds La CV10. . .73 A2
Haresfield Cl B97. . . . . .153 D3
Haresfield B90. . . . . .126 A5
Hare St WV14. . . . . .40 F5
Harewell Dr B75. . . . . .32 C1
Harewood ⑥ B17. . . . . .85 B6
Harewood Ave
  Birmingham B43 . . . . .43 C2
  Wednesbury WS10 . . . . . . .42 C3
Harewood Rd CV5 . . . . .112 C2
Harford St B18,B19. . . . . . .164 A5
Hargate La B71. . . . . .53 D4
Hargate Prim Sch B71 . . . . .53 C4
Harger Ct CV8. . . . . .147 F4
Harger Mews CV8 . . . . .147 F4
Hargrave Cl
  Coventry CV3 . . . . .115 A1
  Water Orton B46. . . . . .59 B3
Hargrave Rd B90 . . . . .105 D1
Hargreave Cl B76 . . . . .57 F8
Hargreaves Ct DY11. . . . . . . .16 C2
Hargreaves St WV1 . . . . .40 A7
Harington Rd CV6. . . . . .113 A5
Harland Cl B61. . . . . .136 D3
Harland Rd B74. . . . . .32 A3
Harlech Cl
  Birmingham B32 . . . . .102 A7
  Kenilworth CV8 . . . . .148 C5
  Oldbury B69. . . . . .52 A1
Harlech Ho ② WS3 . . . . . . .28 C6
Harlech Rd WV12 . . . . .27 C6
Harlech Twr B23. . . . . .57 A6
Harlech Way
  Dudley DY1 . . . . .50 F2
  Kidderminster DY10 . . . . . .116 E2
Harlequin Dr B13. . . . . .86 E2
Harlestones Ho DY8 . . . . . . .80 F7
Harleston Rd B44. . . . . .55 F8
Harley Cl WS8 . . . . .16 A6
Harley Dr WV14. . . . . .40 E4
Harley Grange ⑥ DY2. . . . .62 E8
Harley St CV2 . . . . .114 A3
Harlow Gr B28. . . . . .106 A6
Harlow Wlk ⑧ CV2 . . . . . .115 A7
Harlstones Cl DY8 . . . . .81 A8
Harlyn Cl WV14 . . . . .41 A2
Harman Dr WS13 . . . . .3 F6
Harman Rd B72. . . . . .57 B6
Harmar Cl CV34 . . . . .155 D1
Harmer Cl CV2 . . . . .115 A7
Harmer St B18 . . . . .66 A5
Harmon Rd DY8 . . . . .80 C5
Harmony Ct CV10. . . . . .73 B2
Harmony Ho ❸ B12 . . . . . . .67 C1
Harnall Cl B90. . . . . .126 E7
Harnall Ind Est CV1 . . . . . . .165 C4
Harnall La E CV1 . . . . .165 C4
Harnall La W CV1. . . . . .165 C4
Harnall Row
  Coventry CV1. . . . . .113 E2
  Coventry CV1. . . . . .113 E3
Harness Cl WS5 . . . . .43 D8
Harold Evers Way DY10 . .116 F7
Harold Rd
  Birmingham B16 . . . . .65 F1
  Coventry CV2. . . . . .114 D2
  Smethwick B67 . . . . .64 E3
Harold St CV11 . . . . .73 C3
Harpenden Dr CV5. . . . . . . .112 A5
Harper Ave WV11. . . . . .26 C7
Harper Bell Sch The B12 . .87 A8
Harper Rd
  Bilston WV14. . . . . .40 D6
  Coventry CV1. . . . . .113 E2
Harpers Rd
  Birmingham,Higher's Heath
    B14. . . . . .105 A1

Harpers Rd continued
  Birmingham,Northfield
    B31. . . . . .103 A2
Harper St WV13. . . . . .27 A2
Harport Rd B98. . . . . .154 A1
Harpur Cl WS4 . . . . .29 A4
Harpur Rd WS4 . . . . .29 A4
Harrier Rd B27 . . . . .88 D2
Harriers Gn DY10 . . . . .117 B8
Harriers Ind Est DY10 . . . .116 F5
Harriet Cl DY5 . . . . .61 B5
Harringay Dr DY8. . . . . .80 E3
Harringay Rd B44. . . . . .45 A2
Harrington Croft B71 . . . . . .53 F7
Harrington Ct CV3 . . . . .114 F2
Harrington Way CV10 . . . . . .78 A7
Harrington Wlk WS13 . . . . . .8 F8
Harringworth CV34 . . . . .29 C8
Harriott Dr CV34. . . . . .161 D4
Harris Bsns Pk B60. . . . . . .150 E2
Harris Cl B98 . . . . .158 F8
Harris Ct B18. . . . . .66 A6
Harris Dr
  ② Birmingham B42. . . . . . .55 A8
  Smethwick B66 . . . . .65 B3
Harrison Cl
  Cheslyn Hay WS6. . . . . .4 D1
  Walsall WS3 . . . . .14 C1
Harrison Cres CV12. . . . . . . .78 A2
Harrison Ct DY8 . . . . .61 A1
Harrison Ho B14. . . . . .104 F3
Harrison Rd
  Birmingham B24 . . . . .56 F4
  Cannock WS11. . . . . .4 E7
  Redditch B97 . . . . .158 C8
  Stourbridge DY8 . . . . .61 A1
  Sutton Coldfield B74 . . . . . .31 E5
  Walsall WS4 . . . . .15 C2
Harrison's Fold DY2 . . . . . . .62 C5
Harrisons Gn B15. . . . . .85 E6
Harrisons Pleck B13 . . . . . .86 F3
Harrison's Rd B15 . . . . .85 E6
Harrison St WS3. . . . . .14 C1
Harrison Way CV31 . . . . . . .161 F5
Harris Rd
  Coventry CV3. . . . . .114 B2
  Warwick CV34 . . . . .160 C8
Harrold Ave B65. . . . . .63 E3
Harrold Rd B65 . . . . .63 E3
Harrold St DY4 . . . . .52 C7
Harrold Terr B19. . . . . .66 C8
Harrop Way DY9 . . . . .80 E8
Harrowbrook Ind Est
  LE10. . . . . .74 E7
Harrowbrook Rd LE10. . . . . .74 E7
Harrowby Ct WV10. . . . . .11 B3
Harrowby Dr DY4 . . . . .52 A4
Harrowby Pl WV13 . . . . .27 D1
Harrowby Rd
  Darlaston WV14. . . . . .41 A4
  Wolverhampton WV10. . . . .11 C2
Harrow Cl
  Coventry CV6. . . . . .96 A4
  Stoke Heath B60 . . . . .150 E6
  West Hagley DY9. . . . . .99 A6
Harrow Ct ❺ DY4. . . . . .31 F2
Harrowfield Rd B33. . . . . . . .68 E4
Harrow Rd
  Birmingham B29 . . . . .85 F3
  Kingswinford DY6 . . . . .49 D1
  Whitnash CV31. . . . . .162 B3
Harrow St WV1 . . . . .25 B4
Harry Caplan Ho CV5 . . . . .112 B6
Harry Edwards Ho ②
  CV2 . . . . .114 D8
Harry Perks St WV13. . . . . . .27 A3
Harry Price Ho B68 . . . . .84 A8
Harry Rose Rd CV2 . . . . . . .114 E3
Harry Salt Ho CV1 . . . . .165 D3
Harry Stanley Ho CV6. . . . . .96 C2
Harry Taylor Fst Sch The
  B97. . . . . .158 E6
Harry Taylor Ho B98 . . . . . .154 A4
Harry Truslove Cl CV6 . . . .113 A7
Harry Weston Rd CV3 . . . . .115 A1
Hart Dr B73. . . . . .57 A6
Hartfield Cres B27 . . . . .88 B2
Hartfields Way B65 . . . . .62 F5
Hartford Cl B17. . . . . .85 A7
Hartill Rd WV4. . . . . .38 D3
Hartill St WV13 . . . . .41 B8
Hartington Cl B93 . . . . .127 E3
Hartington Cres CV5. . . . . .112 F1
Hartington Gn LE10 . . . . . . .75 E6
Hartington Rd B19. . . . . .66 D7
Hartland Ave
  Coventry CV2. . . . . .114 B5
  Dudley WV14. . . . . .51 A8
Hartland Rd
  Birmingham B31 . . . . .122 E6
  Tipton DY4. . . . . .51 D5
  West Bromwich B71. . . . . . .53 F8
Hartland St DY5. . . . . .61 D7
Hartlebury Cl
  Cannock WS11. . . . . .2 C1
  Dorridge B93. . . . . .127 F3
  Redditch B98 . . . . .154 E1
Hartlebury Rd
  Halesowen B63 . . . . .82 F2
  Oldbury B69. . . . . .63 F5
Hartledon Rd B17. . . . . .85 B5
Hartle La B63 . . . . .119 F6
Hartlepool Rd CV1 . . . . . . .165 D4
Hartleyburn B77. . . . . .36 A8
Hartley Dr WS9 . . . . .30 B4
Hartley Gr B44 . . . . .45 B3
Hartley Pl B15. . . . . .85 F8

Hartley Rd B44 . . . . .45 B3
Hartley St WV3 . . . . .25 A2
Harton Way B14 . . . . .104 C5
Hartopp Rd
  Birmingham B8 . . . . .67 E4
  Sutton Coldfield B74 . . . . . .45 F8
Hart Rd
  Birmingham B24 . . . . .57 A5
  Willenhall WV11 . . . . .26 D4
Hartridge Wlk CV4. . . . . . . .112 B4
Hartsbourne Dr B62 . . . . . . .83 D4
Harts Cl B17. . . . . .85 D6
Harts Green Rd B17. . . . . . . .85 A5
Hartshill Cl B34. . . . . .69 A6
Hartshill Ho B27. . . . . .88 E2
Hartshill Rd
  Birmingham B34 . . . . .69 A6
  Solihull B27 . . . . .88 D2
Hartshill Sch CV10 . . . . .72 B8
Hartshorn St WV14. . . . . .40 D5
Hartside Cl B63. . . . . .82 D2
Hartslade WS14. . . . . .9 E6
Harts Rd B8 . . . . .67 E5
Hart St WS1 . . . . .42 E8
Hartswell Dr B13 . . . . .104 F6
Hartwell Cl B91. . . . . .107 B1
Hartwell La WS6. . . . . .5 A3
Hartwell Rd B24. . . . . .56 E4
Hartwood Cres WV3 . . . . . . .38 F5
Harvard Cl DY1 . . . . .50 F4
Harvard Rd B92 . . . . .89 B4
Harvest Cl
  Birmingham B30 . . . . .104 B6
  Dudley DY3 . . . . .50 C3
  Stoke Heath B60 . . . . .150 E6
Harvesters Cl
  Coventry CV3. . . . . .115 A2
  Sutton Coldfield WS9 . . . . . .30 E2
Harvesters Rd WV12 . . . . . . .27 D5
Harvesters Way WV12. . . . . .27 D5
Harvesters Wlk WV8 . . . . . . .10 E1
Harvester Way B43 . . . . .60 A8
Harvest Fields Way
  Sutton Coldfield B75. . . . . . .32 D4
  Sutton Coldfield B75. . . . . . .32 E3
Harvest Gdns B68. . . . . .64 A4
Harvest Hill Cl ❼ CV31. .162 C6
Harvest Hill Cotts CV5 . . . .93 D1
Harvest Hill La CV5,CV7 . . .93 C4
Harvest Hill Pk CV5. . . . . . . .93 D1
Harvest Rd
  Rowley Regis B65 . . . . .63 A3
  Smethwick B67 . . . . .64 D3
Harvest Wlk B65. . . . . .63 A3
Harvey Cl CV5 . . . . .112 A7
Harvey Ct B33 . . . . .69 D3
Harvey Dr B75. . . . . .32 C2
Harvey Mews B30. . . . . .103 D7
Harvey Rd
  Birmingham B26 . . . . .88 D7
  Walsall WS2 . . . . .28 B5
Harveys Terr CV2 . . . . .114 F8
Harvey Works Ind Est B63 .82 F6
Harvills Hawthorn Prim Sch
  B70. . . . . .52 F7
Harvills Hawthorn B70 . . . .52 F7
Harvine Wlk DY8 . . . . .80 E3
Harvington Cl
  Kidderminster DY11 . . . . . .116 A8
  Redditch B97 . . . . .153 B5
Harvington Dr B90. . . . . . . .127 B6
Harvington Hall* DY10 . .118 B1
Harvington Hall La DY10 .118 B3
Harvington Rd
  Birmingham,Brandhall
    B68. . . . . .84 A8
  Birmingham,Weoley Castle
    B29 . . . . .103 A8
  Bromsgrove B60 . . . . .151 A8
  Dudley WV14. . . . . .51 A8
  Halesowen B63 . . . . .82 F2
Harvington Way ❺ B65 . . .63 C3
Harwell Cl B79 . . . . .21 C7
Harwin Cl WV6 . . . . .24 F7
Harwood Dr
  Hinckley LE10 . . . . .71 F4
  Tamworth B77 . . . . .35 D4
Harwood Gr ■ B90 . . . . . .126 C8
Harwood Rd WS13 . . . . .3 B3
Harwood St B70 . . . . .53 B2
Hasbury CE Prim Sch B63 .82 F2
Hasbury Cl B63. . . . . .82 E2
Hasbury Rd B32 . . . . .102 B8
Haselbech Rd CV3. . . . . . . .114 F1
Haselbury Cnr CV10. . . . . . .72 F1
Haseley Cl
  Redditch B98 . . . . .154 C1
  Whitnash CV31. . . . . .162 B5
Haseley Rd
  Birmingham B21 . . . . .65 E7
  Coventry CV2. . . . . .96 C1
  Solihull B91. . . . . .106 C6
Haselor Cl B63 . . . . .45 E1
Haselour Rd B37 . . . . .69 E8
Haselwell Dr B30 . . . . .104 D3
Hasilwood Sq CV3 . . . . .114 A2
Haskell St WS1 . . . . .42 F7
Haslucks Croft B90 . . . . . . .106 A3
Haslucks Green Rd
  Solihull,Major's Green
    B90. . . . . .105 F6
  Solihull,Shirley B90 . . . . . .106 A4
Haslucks Green Sch B90 .106 A3
Hassop Rd B42 . . . . .55 D7
Hastang Fields CV31 . . . . .162 C5
Hastings Cl B77 . . . . .35 F6
Hastings Ct DY1 . . . . .50 E2

Hastings High Sch LE10. . .75 F7
Hastings Rd
  Birmingham B23 . . . . .56 B7
  Bromsgrove B60 . . . . .150 E7
  Coventry CV2. . . . . .114 A4
Hastingwood Ind Pk B24 . .57 B1
Haswell Rd B63. . . . . .82 D4
Hatcham Rd B44. . . . . .45 C2
Hatchford Ave B92. . . . . .89 C3
Hatchford Brook Inf Sch
  B92. . . . . .89 C3
Hatchford Brook Jun Sch
  B92. . . . . .89 C3
Hatchford Brook Rd B92 . .89 C3
Hatchford Com Prim Sch
  B37. . . . . .69 F2
Hatchford Ct B92 . . . . .89 C3
Hatchford Wlk B37 . . . . .70 B1
Hateley Dr WV4 . . . . .39 E4
Hateley Heath Prim Sch
  B71. . . . . .53 B7
Hatfield Cl
  Birmingham B23 . . . . .56 D8
  Redditch B98 . . . . .154 E1
Hatfield Rd
  Birmingham B19 . . . . .66 D8
  Stourbridge DY9 . . . . .81 C4
Hathaway Cl
  Balsall Common CV7 . . . . .130 B7
  Willenhall WV13 . . . . .40 F8
Hathaway Dr
  Nuneaton CV11 . . . . .74 A1
  Warwick CV34 . . . . .155 C2
Hathaway Mews DY8. . . . . . .60 C3
Hathaway Rd
  Coventry CV4. . . . . .111 D1
  Solihull B90 . . . . .106 B1
  Sutton Coldfield B75 . . . . . .32 A4
Hatherden Dr B76 . . . . .47 C4
Hatherell Rd CV31. . . . . . . .162 E5
Hathersage Rd B42 . . . . .55 D7
Hatherton Croft WS11. . . . . .1 C1
Hatherton Gdns WV10. . . . .11 E2
Hatherton Gr B29 . . . . .84 F1
Hatherton Pl WS9. . . . . .30 A7
Hatherton Prim Sch WS2 . .28 A6
Hatherton Rd
  Bilston WV14. . . . . .40 F6
  Cannock WS11. . . . . .1 C1
  Walsall WS1 . . . . .28 E2
Hatherton St
  Cheslyn Hay WS6. . . . . .4 C1
  Walsall WS1,WS4 . . . . .28 E2
Hatters Ct CV12. . . . . .78 D2
Hattersley Gr B11. . . . . .88 A3
Hatton Gdns B42 . . . . .55 B7
Hatton Rd
  Cannock WS11. . . . . .1 A1
  Wolverhampton WV6. . . . . .24 F3
Hattons Gr WV8 . . . . .10 B2
Hatton St WV14 . . . . .40 E4
Haughton Rd B20. . . . . .55 D1
Haunch La B13 . . . . .105 A5
Haunchwood Rd CV10. . . . . .72 D4
Havacre La WV14 . . . . .40 C1
Havefield Ave WS14 . . . . .9 E7
Havelock Cl WV3 . . . . .38 F8
Havelock Rd
  Birmingham,Handsworth
    B20. . . . . .55 C1
  Birmingham,Saltley B8 . . . .67 D5
  Birmingham,Sparkhill B11. .87 E4
Haven Croft B43. . . . . .54 D8
Havendale Cl CV6. . . . . .113 B5
Haven Dr B27 . . . . .88 B3
Haven The
  Barnt Green B45 . . . . .138 A8
  Birmingham B14 . . . . .105 D4
  Stourbridge DY9 . . . . .60 D2
  Wolverhampton WV2. . . . .163 B1
Haverford Dr B45 . . . . .122 B6
Havergal Wlk B63 . . . . .82 B4
Haverhill Cl WS3. . . . . .14 A3
Hawbridge Cl B90 . . . . .127 B6
Hawbush Gdns DY5. . . . . . . .61 A1
Hawbush Prim Sch DY5. . . .61 A2
Hawbush Rd
  Brierley Hill DY5. . . . . .61 A2
  Walsall WS3 . . . . .28 E6
Hawcroft Gr B34. . . . . .69 C6
Hawes Cl WS1. . . . . .42 F6
Hawes La B65 . . . . .63 B3
Hawes Rd WS1 . . . . .42 F6
Haweswater Dr DY6. . . . . . . .60 D6
Hawfield Cl B69 . . . . .63 F3
Hawfield Gr B72. . . . . .57 C7
Hawfield Rd B69. . . . . .63 F3
Hawfinch Rise DY10. . . . . . .117 B2
Hawfinch B77 . . . . .36 A6
Hawk Cl CV11 . . . . .79 B8
Hawker Dr B35. . . . . .57 F2
Hawkesbury Fields Sch
  CV6. . . . . .96 C3
Hawkesbury La CV2. . . . . . . .96 D5
Hawkesbury Rd B90 . . . . . .105 F1
Hawkes Cl B30 . . . . .104 A7
Hawkes Dr CV34 . . . . .161 D4
Hawkes La B70 . . . . .53 A7

Hawkesley CE & Methodist
Prim Sch B38 ....123 E7
Hawkesley Cres B31 ... 103 A1
Hawkesley Dr B31 ......122 F8
Hawkesley End B38 .....123 E7
Hawkesley Mill La B31 ..102 F2
Hawkesley Rd DY1 ......61 F8
Hawkesley Sq B38 ......123 E7
Hawkes Mill La CV5 .....94 B2
Hawkesmoor Dr WS14 .....9 D8
Hawkes St B10 ....87 D8
Hawkestone Cres B70 ....53 A6
Hawkestone Rd B29 .....103 A7
Hawkesville Dr ▉ WS11... 1 F2
Hawkeswell Cl B92 .....106 E8
Hawkeswell Dr B36 .....60 D8
Hawkesworth Dr CV8 ...148 A6
Hawkesyard Rd B24 .....56 E1
Hawkhurst Rd B14 ......104 F2
Hawkinge Dr B35 ....58 A4
Hawkins Cl
  Birmingham B5 ....86 E6
  Hinckley LE10 ....71 D4
  Lichfield WS13 ....3 B2
Hawkins Croft CV4 .....52 A3
Hawkins Dr WS11 ....4 C4
Hawkin's Pl WV14 ......40 F3
Hawkins Rd CV5 ....113 A2
Hawkins St B70 ....53 A8
Hawkley Cl WV1 ....26 B2
Hawkley Rd WV1 ....26 B2
Hawkmoor Gdns B38 ...124 A8
Hawksbury Cl B98 .....154 D5
Hawks Cl WS6 ....4 D2
Hawksford Cres WV10 ...25 E7
Hawks Green La WS11 ....2 A1
Hawkshead Dr B93 .....127 F6
Hawkside ▉ B77 ....36 B8
Hawksmill Ind Est B9 ...67 C1
Hawksmoor Dr WV6 .....23 D3
Hawkstone Cl DY11 ....116 D8
Hawkstone Ct CV6 ......23 D5
Hawkswell Ave WV5 ....49 A5
Hawkswell Dr WV13 ....40 F8
Hawkswood Dr
  Balsall Common CV7 ...130 B7
  Darlaston WS10 ....41 B3
Hawkswood Gr B14 ....105 B3
Hawksworth Cres B37 ...70 D3
Hawksworth Dr ▉ CV1 ..113 B3
Hawksworth B77 ....21 F2
Hawkyard Ct WS11 ....2 A4
Hawley Cl WS4 ....28 F4
Hawley Ct B43 ....43 E1
Hawley Rd LE10 ....75 D7
Hawnby Gr B76 ....47 A2
Hawne Cl B63 ....82 E6
Hawne La B63 ....82 E6
Hawnelands The B63 ....82 F5
Hawskford Cres WV10 ...25 D7
Hawthorn Ave WS6 ......5 A1
Hawthorn Brook Way B23 56 E8
Hawthorn Cl
  Birmingham,Erdington
   B23 ....56 F7
  Birmingham,Spring Vale B9 ..67 B1
  Lichfield WS14 ....9 D8
Hawthorn Coppice DY9 ..99 A6
Hawthorn Cres LE10 ....75 E4
Hawthorn Croft B68 ....84 D7
Hawthorn Ct CV4 ......111 E1
Hawthornden Ct B76 ....57 D7
Hawthorn Dr
  Balsall Common CV7 ...130 B8
  Birmingham B29 ....85 C1
Hawthorne Ave B79 ....21 B8
Hawthorne Cres WS7 ....7 A6
Hawthorne Croft B30 ..103 D5
Hawthorne Dr B47 .....125 B6
Hawthorne Gr DY3 ......50 D2
Hawthorne Ho WV10 .....25 F3
Hawthorne Rd
  Birmingham B15 ....85 E7
  Birmingham,Castle Bromwich
   B36 ....69 F7
  Birmingham,King's Norton
   B30 ....103 D5
  Cannock WS12 ....2 F3
  Cheslyn Hay WS6 ....4 E4
  Dudley DY1 ....51 C4
  Essington WV11 ....13 A3
  Halesowen B63 ....82 E2
  Huntington WS12 ......14 C1
  Wednesfield WV11 .....27 A5
  Willenhall WV12 ......27 D7
  Wolverhampton WV2 ....39 D6
Hawthorne Terr CV10 ...72 F5
Hawthorn Gr
  ▉ Birmingham B19 ....66 C8
  Kidderminster DY11 ...116 A6
Hawthorn La CV4 ....111 E1
Hawthorn Park Dr ▉ B20 58 F3
Hawthorn Pk B20 ....54 E3
Hawthorn Pl WS2 ....27 E3
Hawthorn Prim Sch B44 .56 A7
Hawthorn Rd
  Bilston WV1 ....40 B8
  Birmingham B44 ....56 A7
  Brierley Hill DY5 .....81 E8
  Bromsgrove B61 ....137 B4
  Redditch B97 ....153 A4
  Royal Leamington Spa
   CV31 ....161 F6
  Sutton Coldfield,Streetly
   B74 ....31 A1

Hawthorn Rd continued
  Sutton Coldfield,Wylde Green
   B72 ....46 C1
  Tipton DY4 ....52 B8
  Walsall,Bescot WS5 ....42 F5
  Walsall,Shelfield WS4 ..29 B8
  Walsall WS4 ....15 B1
  Wednesbury WS10 ......41 F4
Hawthorns Sta The B71 ..65 A8
Hawthorns The
  ▉ Kidderminster DY10... 117 A5
  Birmingham,Showell Green
   B13 ....86 F3
  Birmingham,Warley Woods
   B68 ....84 D7
Hawthorns The (West
  Bromwich Albion FC)
   B21 ....54 B1
Hawthorns The
  West Hagley DY9 ....98 F4
  Wolverhampton WV11 ...26 B6
Hawthorn Terr WS10 ....41 F4
Hawthorn Way CV10 .....72 A8
Haxby Ave B34 ....69 A6
Haybarn The B76 ....58 A8
Haybridge Ave DY8 .....98 F5
Haybridge High Sch & Sixth
  Form DY8 ....98 F6
Hay Brook Dr B11 ......87 F4
Hay Cl DY11 ....116 C7
Haycock Pl WS10 ....41 C8
Haycroft Ave B8 ....67 E5
Haycroft Dr B74 ....32 A4
Haydn Sanders Sq ▉
   ....42 E8
Haydock Cl
  Birmingham B36 ....68 C8
  Coventry CV6 ....96 B4
  Tamworth B77 ....35 D4
  Wolverhampton WV6 ....25 B5
Haydock Rd B61 ....121 B1
Haydon Cl B93 ....127 F2
Haydon Croft B33 ......69 A3
Haydon Way B49 ....159 F1
Haye House Gr B36 .....68 E7
Hayes Cres B68 ....64 D5
Hayes Croft B38 ......123 F7
Hayes Dr B24 ....57 D5
Hayes Green Rd CV12 ...95 F8
Hayes Gr B24 ....57 D6
Hayes La
  Bedworth CV7 ....96 A8
  Stourbridge DY9 ......82 A6
Hayes Mdw B72 ....52 D7
Hayes Rd
  Hartshill CV10 ....72 A8
  Oldbury B68 ....64 D5
Hayes St B70 ....53 A4
Hayes The
  Birmingham B31 ......123 C7
  Leek Wootton CV35 ....155 F5
  Stourbridge DY9 ......82 A5
  Willenhall WV12 ......27 B6
Hayes Trad Est DY9 ....82 A6
Hayes View Dr WS6 ......4 E4
Hayes Way WS12 ....2 C1
Hayfield Ct B13 ....87 B2
Hayfield Gdns B13 .....87 C2
Hayfield Rd B13 ....87 B2
Hayford Cl B98 ....154 A5
Hay Gn DY9 ....81 D5
Hay Gr WS8 ....15 F8
Hay Green Cl B30 .....103 D6
Hay Green La B30 .....103 D6
Hay Hall Rd B11 ....87 C5
Hayhead Wood Nature
  Reserve* WS4 ....29 E2
Hay Hill WS5 ....43 E8
Hay La CV1 ....165 C2
Hayland Rd B23 ....56 E6
Hay La B90 ....127 A6
Hayle Ave CV34 ....155 F1
Hayle Cl
  Birmingham B38 ......104 B2
  Nuneaton CV11 ....74 A5
Hayle Rd B77 ....21 D2
Hayley Ct
  Kingswinford DY6 .....60 D6
  Sutton Coldfield B24 ..57 C6
Hayley Green Rd B32 ..102 B8
Hayley Park Rd B63 ...100 C8
Hayling Cl B45 ....101 F1
Hayling Ct WS4 ....29 B8
Hayling Gr WV2 ....39 B6
Hayloft Cl B60 ....150 E6
Haylofts The B63 ......82 C1
Haymaker Way WS12 .....2 F4
Haymarket The WV8 ....10 E1
Haymoor WS14 ....9 E7
Haynes Cl B61 ....137 B8
Haynes Ho B97 ....153 D2
Haynes La WS5 ....43 B4
Haynestone Rd CV6 ...112 E6
Haypits Cl B71 ....53 E7
Hay Pk B5 ....86 D6
Hay Rd B25 ....88 A7
Hayrick Dr DY6 ....60 B7
Hayseech B64 ....83 A7
Hayseech Rd B64 ....82 F6
Hays Kent's Moat The
   B26 ....88 F6
Hays La LE10 ....75 B7
Hayton Gn CV4 ....131 F8
Haytor Ave B14 ....104 D5
Haytor Rise CV2 ......114 C7
Haywain Cl WV9 ....10 F2
Hayward Rd B75 ....46 F2

Haywards Cl
  Birmingham B23 ....56 E5
  Walsall WS3 ....14 F3
Hayward's Gn CV6 .....113 A7
Hayward St WV14 ....51 B8
Haywharf Rd DY5 ....61 B5
Haywood Dr
  Halesowen B62 ....83 C8
  Wolverhampton WV6 ....24 C8
Hay Wood La B93,CV35 .145 A3
Haywood Rd B33 ....69 F2
Haywood's Farm B71 ...42 F2
Hayworth Cl B79 ....20 F8
Hayworth Rd WS13 ......3 C2
Hazel Ave
  Birmingham B73 ....45 C1
  Wednesbury WS10 ......42 A1
Hazelbeach Rd B8 ......67 F5
Hazelbeech Rd B70 ....53 B3
Hazel Cl
  Hartshill CV10 ....72 A8
  Royal Leamington Spa
   CV32 ....157 A2
Hazel Croft
  Birmingham,Chelmsley Wood
   B37 ....70 B1
  Birmingham,Northfield
   B31 ....103 A3
Hazeldene Gr ▉ B6 ....66 E8
Hazeldene Rd
  Birmingham B33 ....89 D7
  Halesowen B63 ....82 E2
Hazel Dr B47 ....125 B5
Hazeley Cl B17 ....85 A7
Hazelgarth B77 ....36 B8
Hazel Gdns
  Birmingham B27 ....88 C5
  Codsall WV8 ....10 A4
Hazel Gr
  Bedworth CV12 ....78 D3
  Bilston WV14 ....40 E7
  Hockley Heath B94 ...143 C6
  Lichfield WS14 ....9 C7
  West Bromwich B70 ....53 C1
  Wolverhampton WV11 ...26 C7
  Wombourne WV5 ....49 A7
Hazelhurst Rd
  Birmingham,Castle Bromwich
   B36 ....69 E7
  Birmingham,King's Heath
   B14 ....104 E2
Hazell Way WV10 ....73 A1
Hazelmead Ct B73 .....57 A7
Hazelmere Dr
  Burntwood WS7 ....6 F4
  Wolverhampton WV3 ....24 A1
Hazelmere Rd B28 ....105 F8
Hazeloak Rd B90 .....106 A2
Hazel Oak Sch B90 ...106 A2
Hazel Rd
  Birmingham B45 ......121 F6
  Coventry CV6 ....96 B1
  Dudley DY1 ....51 C2
  Kingswinford DY6 .....60 E5
  Nuneaton CV10 ....72 D5
  Redditch B97 ....153 C5
  Wednesbury DY4 ....41 D1
  Wolverhampton WV3 ....38 E7
Hazelslade Ho WS12 ....2 F6
Hazels The DY9 ....98 F5
Hazelton Cl
  ▉ Solihull B91 ......107 B1
  Catshill B61 ....137 C8
Hazelton Rd B61 ......121 C1
Hazeltree Croft B27 ...88 B2
Hazelville Gr B28 ....106 A6
Hazelville Rd B28 ....106 A7
Hazelwell Cres B30 ...104 D6
Hazelwell Dr B14 .....104 D6
Hazelwell Fordrough
   B30 ....104 B6
Hazelwell La B30 .....104 A6
Hazelwell Rd B30 .....104 A6
Hazelwell St B30 .....104 A7
Hazelwood Cl
  Cheslyn Hay WS6 ....4 D2
  Kidderminster DY11 ..116 B4
Hazelwood Dr WV11 ....26 A5
Hazelwood Gr
  Cannock WS11 ....4 C8
  Willenhall WV12 ......27 D5
Hazelwood Rd
  Birmingham B27 ....88 B2
  Dudley DY1 ....50 F5
  Sutton Coldfield B74 ..30 D1
Hazlemere Cl CV5 .....112 B4
Hazlemere Dr B74 ......32 B1
Hazlemere Gr WS11 .....4 B8
Hazlitt Gr B30 ....103 D4
Headborough Rd CV2 ..114 A5
Headborough Wlk WS9 ..16 B1
Headingley Rd A21 ....54 E2
Headington Ave CV6 ...95 A2
Headland Dr B8 ....67 D5
Headland Rd WV3 ......24 A1
Headlands The
  Coventry CV5 ....112 D4
  Sutton Coldfield B74 ..31 C3
Headless Cross Dr B97 153 D1
Headley Croft B38 ...123 D8
Headley Dr B97 ....153 D1
Headley Heath La B38 .124 B6
Headley Rise B90 ....106 D2
Headway Rd WV10 ......11 C3

Heale Cl B63 ....82 A7
Healey Ct CV34 ....160 F7
Healey B77 ....21 D2
Health Centre Rd CV4 .132 C4
Heanor Croft B6 ....67 B8
Heantun Croft WV10 ....26 A5
Heantun Ct WV3 ....163 B2
Heantun Ho WV3 ....163 B2
Heantun Lodge WV14 ...40 C6
Heantun Mill Ct WS10 ..51 B1
Heantun Rise WV3 .....25 C4
Heantun Row WV11 .....13 B2
Hearsall Comm CV5 ...112 F2
Hearsall Com Prim Sch
   CV5 ....112 F2
Hearsall Ct CV4 ......112 D2
Hearsall La CV5 ......112 F2
Heartland Mews B65 ....63 B2
Heartlands High Sch B7 .67 B4
Heartlands Parkway B7 ..67 D7
Heartlands Pl B8 ......67 E4
Heart of England Sch
   CV7 ....130 C6
Heart of England Way
   CV11 ....130 F3
Heart Of The Country Ctr*
   WS14 ....18 E8
Heath Acres WS10 ......41 C4
Heath Ave CV12 ....77 E1
Heathbank Dr WV12 .....1 C6
Heath Bridge Cl WS4 ...29 A8
Heathbrook Ave DY6 ....60 B7
Heath Cl
  Birmingham B30 ......103 D5
  Bromsgrove B60 ......150 E6
Heathcliff Rd
  Birmingham B11 ....87 F4
  Dudley DY2 ....62 F7
Heath Cl
  Stonnall WS14 ....16 E5
  Sutton Coldfield B75 ..46 F7
  Tipton DY4 ....52 B5
Heathcote Ave B91 ...106 E3
Heathcote Cl B77 ......36 B7
Heathcote Ct CV6 .....113 A7
Heathcote Dr B78 .....20 D6
Heathcote Ho B17 ......85 C5
Heathcote Ind Est CV34 161 D4
Heathcote La
  Royal Leamington Spa
   CV34 ....161 D4
  Warwick CV34 ....161 A5
Heathcote Rd
  Birmingham B30 ......104 A5
  Whitnash CV31 ....162 A4
Heathcote St CV6 .....113 A7
Heathcote Way CV34 ..161 D4
Heath Cres CV2 ....114 A6
Heath Croft B75 ......123 A7
Heath Ct B75 ....32 D1
Heath Cvn Pk WV10 .....11 C6
Heath End Rd
  Madeley Heath DY9 ...120 D7
  Nuneaton CV10 ....72 F2
Heather Ave WS5 ....43 B4
Heather Cl
  Birmingham B36 ....70 A8
  Lichfield WS13 ....3 D1
  Walsall WS3 ....28 A8
  Wednesfield WV11 .....26 B5
Heather Court Gdns B74 .46 A8
Heather Croft B44 .....44 F1
Heather Ct B13 ....86 D3
Heather Dale B13 ......86 C2
Heather Dr
  Bedworth CV12 ....77 E2
  Birmingham B45 ......121 F6
  Huntington WS12 ......1 D5
Heather Gr
  Solihull B91 ....107 E6
  Willenhall WV12 ......27 E4
Heather Ho B38 ......103 F1
Heatherleigh Rd B36 ..69 F8
Heather Mews WS12 .....2 B8
Heather Rd
  Binley Woods CV3 ....135 D7
  Birmingham,Great Barr B43 .54 D8
  Birmingham,Small Heath
   B10 ....87 F8
  Cannock WS12 ....2 A8
  Coventry CV2 ....96 C2
  Dudley DY1 ....51 C4
  Smethwick B67 ....64 E6
  Walsall WS3 ....28 A8
Heather Valley WS12 ....2 D6
Heath Farm Rd
  Codsall WV8 ....10 B2
  Stourbridge DY8 ......80 E3
Heathfield Cl
  Cradley Heath B64 .....62 F2
  Dorridge B93 ....128 A5
Heathfield Cres DY11 ..116 B4
Heathfield Ct ▉ B19 ...66 B7
Heathfield Dr WS3 .....14 B2
Heathfield Foundation
  Technology Coll The
   B64 ....62 F1
Heathfield Gdns DY8 ...80 F4
Heathfield La W WS10 ..41 C6
Heathfield La W WS10 ..41 B6
Heathfield Prim Sch B19 ..66 C8
Heathfield Rd
  Birmingham,King's Heath
   B14 ....104 F8

Heathfield Rd continued
  Birmingham,Lozells B19 ..66 C8
  Coventry CV5 ....112 C2
  Halesowen B63 ....82 E3
  Redditch B97 ....153 A1
  Sutton Coldfield B74 ..31 F3
Heathfields WV8 ....23 E8
Heathfields Inf Sch B77 .35 F6
Heathfield Way B64 ....62 F1
Heath Gap Rd WS11 .....1 F3
Heath Gdns B91 ......107 D6
Heath Gn DY1 ....50 F5
Heath Gr WV8 ....10 B3
Heathgreen Cl B37 ....70 D3
Heath Green Gr ▉ B18 .65 E4
Heath Green Rd B18 ...65 E4
Heath Green Way CV4 .131 F6
Heath Hayes Prim Sch
   WS12 ....2 F2
Heath Hill Rd WV6 .....23 C1
Heath Ho B14 ....104 F2
Heath House La WV8 ...23 E8
Heath La DY10 ....117 C1
Heathland Ave B34 ....69 A7
Heathland Cl WS12 .....2 D2
Heathlands Cl DY6 .....60 E8
Heathlands Cres B73 ...45 F1
Heathlands Gr B31 ...103 A1
Heathlands Prim Sch B34 .68 F7
Heathlands Rd B73 ....45 F1
Heathlands The
  ▉ Rowley Regis B65 ...63 C1
  Stourbridge DY8 ......81 B4
Heath Lane Hospl B71 ..53 D7
Heath La
  Stourbridge DY8 ......81 A4
  West Bromwich B71 ....53 D7
Heathleigh Rd B38 ....123 C8
Heathley La B78 ....34 E5
Heathmere Ave B25 ....88 D8
Heathmere Dr B37 .....69 F2
Heath Mill La B9 ......67 A1
Heath Mount Prim Sch
   B12 ....86 F6
Heath Park Bsns & Ent Coll
   WV11 ....26 A5
Heath Rd
  Bedworth CV12 ....77 F1
  Birmingham B30 ......103 D5
  Coventry CV2 ....114 A4
  Darlaston WS10 ....41 E8
  Dudley DY2 ....62 C2
  Hollywood B47 ....125 A7
  Solihull B91 ....107 D6
Heath Rd S B31 ....103 B4
Heath Rd
  Solihull B91 ....107 D6
  Willenhall WV12 ......13 D1
Heath Rise B14 ....105 A1
Heath St S B18 ....65 F4
Heathside Dr
  Birmingham B38 ......104 B2
  Cannock WS12 ....2 B7
  Rowley Regis B65 .....63 C1
  Tamworth B79 ....21 C5
Heath Terr
  Beausale CV35 ....146 C2
  Royal Leamington Spa
   CV32 ....156 E1
Heath Trad Pk B66 .....65 D5
Heath View
  Cannock WS12 ....5 E8
  Willenhall WS2 ....27 F3
Heath Way
  Birmingham B34 ....69 B6
  Cannock WS11 ....2 B2
Heathway Cl B34 ....69 A7
Heathy Farm Cl B32 ...84 B1
Heathy Rise B32 ......84 A2
Heaton Cl WV10 ....11 E5
Heaton Dr
  Birmingham B15 ....85 E8
  Sutton Coldfield B73 ..45 F8
Heaton Rd B91 ....107 A7
Heaton St B18 ....66 B5
Hebden Ave CV34 .....155 F1
Hebden Gr
  Birmingham B28 .....105 E3
  Willenhall WV11 ......13 B1
Hebden B77 ....36 B8
Hebden Way CV11 ......74 A2
Heckley Rd CV7 ....96 A7
Heddle Gr CV6 ....114 B8
Heddon Pl B7 ....67 A3
Hedera Cl B8 ....67 E5
Hedera Rd B98 ....154 F6
Hedgefield Gr B63 ....82 C4
Hedgefield Way CV4 ..131 F8
Hedgerow Cl WS12 .....1 F7
Hedgerow Dr B76 ......49 D1
Hedgerows The
  Lichfield WS14 ....9 B5
  Nuneaton CV10 ....72 F6
  Romsley B62 ....100 F4
  Tamworth B77 ....35 F8
Hedgerow Wlk
  Coventry CV5 ....95 B4
  Wolverhampton WV8 ...10 E1
Hedges Way B60 ......137 B1
Hedgetree Croft B37 ...70 C2
Hedge Way CV10 ....72 C7
Hedging Lane Ind Est B77 35 E5
Hedging La B77 ....35 E5
Hedgings The B34 .....69 B6
Hedgley Gr B33 ....69 A4
Hedingham Gr B37 .....70 D2

Hedley Croft B35 58 B4
Hednesford Hills Common
  Nature Reserve* WS12 2 E5
Hednesford Rd
  Brownhills WS8 6 C2
  Cannock,Blackfords WS11 1 F2
  Cannock WS12 2 E1
  Norton Canes WS11 5 F6
Hednesford Sta WS12 2 B5
Hednesford St WS11 1 A1
Heeley Rd B29 85 F1
Heemstede La CV32 157 A2
Heera Cl CV6 113 D8
Hefford Dr B26 65 A6
Helena Cl CV10 72 F3
Helena St 2 B1 66 C3
Helen Dixon Ct 8 B13 86 F4
Helenny Cl WV11 26 A5
Helen St CV6 113 F6
Hele Rd CV3 133 D6
Helford Cl DY4 51 D4
Heligan Pl WS12 2 E2
Hellaby Cl 3 B22 46 C4
Hellaby Cl B73 57 A7
Hellaby Ho B74 31 F3
Hellidon Cl 6 CV32 157 A2
Hellier Ave DY4 52 B4
Hellier Rd WV10 11 E2
Hellier St DY2 62 C8
Helming Dr WV1 26 B3
Helmingham B79 20 D7
Helmsdale Rd CV32 157 B5
Helmsdale Way B79 51 A7
Helmsley Cl DY5 81 C8
Helmsley Rd WV11 26 C8
Helmswood Dr B37 90 C8
Helston Cl
  Nuneaton CV11 74 A5
  Stourbridge DY8 60 C2
  Tamworth B79 21 C8
  Walsall WS5 43 D7
Helstone Gr B11 88 A3
Helston Rd WS5 43 D7
Hembs Cres B43 54 C8
Hemdale Bsns Pk CV11 74 A4
Hemdale CV11 74 A4
Hemingford Rd CV2 115 A8
Heming Rd B98 159 E8
Hemlingford Croft B37 90 A7
Hemlingford Rd
  Birmingham B37 69 F6
  Sutton Coldfield B76 58 A6
Hemlock Bsns Ctr WS11 2 B2
Hemlock Pk WS11 2 B2
Hemlock Way WS11 2 B3
Hemmings Cl
  Radford Semele CV31 162 E5
  Stourbridge DY8 80 F5
  Wolverhampton WV10 25 E3
Hemmings St WS10 41 C8
Hemming St DY11 116 C4
Hemmings Yd DY6 61 A8
Hemplands Rd DY8 80 F5
Hempole La DY4 52 D6
Hemsby Cl CV4 132 A7
Hemsworth Dr CV12 79 B2
Hemyock Rd B29 103 B8
Henbury Rd B27 88 D3
Henderson Cl
  Allesley CV5 112 C7
  Lichfield WS14 9 D7
Henderson Ct 7 B68 84 B8
Henderson Way B65 63 C1
Henderson Wlk DY4 52 B8
Hendon Cl
  Dudley DY3 50 D2
  Wolverhampton WV10 25 E7
Hendon Rd B11 87 B5
Hendre Cl CV5 112 D2
Heneage Pl 8 B7 67 A4
Heneage St W 2 66 F4
Heneage St B7 67 A4
Henfield Cl WV11 26 D7
Hengham Rd B26 69 A1
Hen La CV6 95 D3
Henley Cl
  Burntwood WS7 7 B5
  Nuneaton CV11 73 F8
  Sutton Coldfield B73 57 B8
  Tamworth B79 21 C6
  Tipton DY4 52 D5
  Walsall WS3 14 E1
Henley Coll CV2 114 C8
Henley Cres B91 107 B7
Henley Ct
  Coventry CV2 114 D7
  Lichfield WS14 9 B6
Henleydale 8 B90 126 C8
Henley Dr B74 32 A3
Henley Mill La CV2 114 C7
Henley Park Ind Est CV2 114 E7
Henley Rd
  Coventry CV2 114 D7
  Whitnash CV31 162 B5
  Wolverhampton WV10 11 B1
Henley St B11 87 B7
Henley Wlk CV2 114 D8
Henlow Cl DY4 51 D5
Henlow Rd B14 105 A2
Hennalls The B36 68 F7
Hennals Ave B97 152 F2
Henn Dr DY4 40 E1
Henne Dr WV14 40 C1
Henn St DY4 52 A8
Henrietta St
  Birmingham B19 164 B4
  Coventry CV6 113 E5
Henry Boteler Rd CV4 132 B7

Henry Boys' Almshouses
  WS1 42 D8
Henry Cl WS7 51 B1
Henry Lloyd Ind Est WS10 41 C7
Henry Rd B25 88 C7
Henry St
  Coventry CV1 165 B3
  Hinckley LE10 71 A2
  Kenilworth CV8 148 A5
  Nuneaton CV11 73 C2
  Walsall WS2 28 D1
Henry Tanday Ct 4
  CV32 156 E1
Henry Wlk B60 150 E7
Hensborough B90 126 A5
Hensel Dr WV3 38 C8
Henshaw Gr
  6 Birmingham,Small Heath
  B10 87 C8
  Birmingham,Yardley B25 88 C7
Henshaw Rd B10 87 D8
Henson Rd CV12 77 E1
Henstead St B5 86 D8
Hentland Cl B98 154 D4
Henwood Cl WV6 24 C3
Henwood La B91 108 B4
Henwood Rd WV6 24 C3
Hepburn Cl WS9 30 A5
Hepburn Edge B24 57 B4
Hepworth Cl WV6 23 F4
Hepworth Rd CV3 115 B1
Herald Ave CV5 112 D1
Herald Ct 2 DY1 51 C1
Herald Rd B26 90 C4
Heralds Ct 6 CV34 161 B8
Herald Way
  Coventry CV3 135 A7
  Hinckley LE10 75 D4
Herbert Art Gall & Mus*
  CV1 165 C2
Herbert Austin Dr B60 121 E1
Herbert Rd
  Aldridge WS9 16 A1
  Birmingham,Handsworth
  B21 54 F1
  Birmingham,Small Heath
  B10 87 C8
  Smethwick B67 65 A1
  Solihull B91 107 B4
Herbert's La CV8 148 A5
Herberts Park Rd WS10 41 B6
Herbert St
  Bilston WV14 40 B6
  Nuneaton CV10 72 E3
  Redditch B98 153 E4
  West Bromwich B70 53 D3
  Wolverhampton WV1 163 C4
Herbhill Cl WV4 39 D4
Hereford Ave 5 B12 87 A6
Hereford Cl
  Aldridge WS9 30 A8
  Barwell LE9 71 F6
  Birmingham B45 102 A2
  Kidderminster DY11 116 A5
  Nuneaton CV10 72 E4
Hereford Ho WV1 163 B4
Hereford Pl B71 53 B7
Hereford Rd
  Birmingham B68 84 B7
  Bramcote CV11 79 F6
  Cannock WS12 2 B4
  Dudley DY2 62 E3
Hereford Sq B8 67 C5
Hereford St WS2 28 E4
Hereford Way B78 21 A2
Hereford Wlk B37 69 F1
Hereward Rise B62 83 C5
Hereward Way LE10 75 F6
Heritage Cl B68 64 C4
Heritage Ct
  Birmingham B18 66 C4
  Coventry CV4 132 D3
  Kenilworth CV8 148 B7
  Lichfield WS14 9 D6
Heritage Dr CV6 96 C6
Heritage The 7 WS1 28 E1
Heritage Way
  Birmingham B33 69 D3
  Tipton DY4 52 B5
Hermes Cl CV34 161 E5
Hermes Cres CV2 114 E6
Hermes Ct
  Royal Leamington Spa
  CV34 161 E5
  Sutton Coldfield B74 31 F3
Hermes Rd
  Birmingham B26 90 C4
  Lichfield WS13 3 D1
Hermione Cl CV34 161 F3
Hermitage Cl B78 22 F1
Hermitage Dr B76 47 A4
Hermitage Rd
  Birmingham B15 85 C8
  Birmingham,Gravelly Hill
  B23 56 D3
  Coventry CV2 114 D4
  Solihull B91 107 C6
Hermitage The B91 107 C6
Hermitage Way CV8 148 A3
Hermit's Croft CV3 133 D8
Hermit's Wlk DY3 50 D5
Hernall Croft B26 89 A7
Herne Cl B18 66 A4
Hernefield Rd B34 69 A7
Hernehurst B32 84 C6
Hern Rd DY5 81 C6

Heronbank CV4 111 C2
Heron Cl
  Alvechurch B48 139 A7
  Brownhills WS8 15 E7
  Cheswick Green B90 126 D4
Heron Ct 8 B73 57 B7
Herondale WS12 2 A4
Herondale Cres DY8 80 C4
Herondale Rd
  Birmingham B26 88 F6
  Stourbridge DY8 80 C4
Heronfield Cl B98 154 C5
Heronfield Dr B31 122 F6
Heronfield Way B91 107 E5
Heron Ho CV3 114 B2
Heron Mill WS3 14 E3
Heron Rd B68 64 A2
Heronry The WV6 23 F2
Herons Ct LE10 75 A7
Heronsville Ho CV4 52 B3
Herons Way B29 85 C3
Heronswood Dr DY5 61 D1
Heronswood Rd
  Birmingham B45 122 B6
  Kidderminster DY10 117 A2
Heronville Dr B70 53 A7
Heronville Rd B70 53 A6
Heron Way B45 121 F7
Herrick Rd
  Birmingham B8 67 E5
  Coventry CV2 114 D3
Herrick St WV3 163 A2
Herringshaw Croft B76 46 E3
Hertford Pl CV1 165 A2
Hertford St
  Birmingham B12 87 A5
  Coventry CV1 165 B2
Hertford Way B91 128 B4
Hervey Gr B24 57 D6
Hesket Ave B68 64 C1
Hesketh Cres B23 56 C5
Hesketh Pl B37 89 F8
Hesleden B77 36 B8
Heslop Cl CV3 134 F8
Hessian Cl WV14 40 B2
Hestia Dr B29 103 E8
Heston Ave B42 55 B8
Hetton Cl 1 CV34 155 F1
Hever Ave B44 45 A1
Hever Cl DY1 50 E2
Hewell Ave B60 150 F7
Hewell Cl
  Birmingham B31 122 F7
  Kingswinford DY6 49 D1
  Redditch B97 152 C6
Hewell La
  Barnt Green B45 138 D8
  Redditch B60,B97 152 D6
Hewell Rd
  Barnt Green B45 138 D8
  Redditch B97 153 D4
Hewitson Gdns B67 64 F2
Hewitt Ave CV6 113 B4
Hewitt Cl WS13 3 A2
Hewitt St WS10 41 C5
Hewston Croft WS12 2 D4
Hexby Cl CV2 115 A6
Hexham Way DY1 50 F2
Hexton Cl B90 105 D2
Hexworthy Ave CV3 133 B5
Heybarnes Cir B10 87 F7
Heybarnes Rd B10 88 A8
Heybrook Cl CV2 114 C7
Heycott Gr B38 104 C2
Heycroft CV4 132 D4
Heydon Rd
  Brierley Hill DY5 61 B6
  Finstall B60 137 D1
Heyford Cl CV2 96 D3
Heyford Gr B91 127 C8
Heyford Way B35 58 B5
Heygate Way WS9 16 B1
Heyland Cnr B10 67 F1
Heynesfield Rd B33 69 C3
Heythrop Gr B13 105 D8
Heyville Croft CV8 148 C3
Heywood Cl CV6 114 A7
Hibberd Ct CV8 147 F4
Hickman Ave WV1,WV2 40 A8
Hickman Gdns B16 65 F1
Hickman Rd
  Bilston WV14 40 C5
  Birmingham B11 87 B6
  Brierley Hill DY5 61 C4
  Tipton DY4 51 F8
Hickman's Ave B64 62 E2
Hickmans Cl 1 B62 84 A6
Hickman St DY9 81 C6
Hickmerelands La DY3 39 C1
Hickory Cl WS11 2 C2
Hickory Dr B17 65 A2
Hicks Cl CV34 155 E2
Hidcote Ave B76 58 A8
Hidcote Cl
  Nuneaton CV11 78 F8
  Royal Leamington Spa
  CV31 162 C5
Hidcote Gr
  Birmingham,Garret's Green
  B33 89 C8
  Birmingham,Marston Green
  B37 90 A7
Hidcote Rd CV8 148 C6
Hidson Rd B23 56 C5
Higgins Ave WV14 40 D2
Higgins La B32 84 C5
Higgins Wlk B66 65 B6
Higgs Field Cres B64 63 B1

Higgs Rd WV11 13 A1
Higham Lane Sch CV10 73 D6
Higham La CV11 73 E7
Higham's Cl B65 63 B3
Higham Way B10 75 E7
Higham Way Ho LE10 75 E7
Higham Way WV10 25 E6
High Arcal Dr DY3 50 F7
High Arcal Rd DY3 49 F4
High Arcal Sch The DY3 50 F6
High Ash Cl CV7 95 F7
High Ave B64 82 F8
High Bank WS11 4 E8
High Beech CV5 112 A6
High Beeches B43 43 D1
Highbridge Rd
  Dudley DY2 62 B3
  Sutton Coldfield B73 46 A1
High Brink Rd B46 70 F7
Highbrook Cl WV9 11 A2
High Broome Ct B78 21 A3
High Brow B17 85 B7
High Bullen WS10 41 F3
Highbury Ave
  Birmingham B21 65 F8
  Rowley Regis B65 63 D3
Highbury Cl B65 63 D3
Highbury Ct B13 104 E7
Highbury Gn CV10 72 C7
Highbury Rd
  Birmingham B14 104 D8
  Oldbury B68 64 B5
  Smethwick B66 64 D7
  Sutton Coldfield B74 31 C3
Highclare Sch B23 57 A5
Highclare Sch St Paul's
  B74 46 C7
Highclare Woodfield Sch
  B72 46 C1
High Clere B64 83 A7
Highcliffe Rd B77 35 D8
Highcrest Cl B31 123 A7
High Croft WS9 16 B2
Highcroft Ave DY8 60 C3
High Croft B43 43 C1
Highcroft Cl CV11 74 A3
Highcroft Cres CV32 156 C1
Highcroft Dr B74 31 E3
Highcroft Hospl B23 56 E3
Highcroft Rd B23 56 E3
Highcroft WS11 15 B6
Highdown Cres 8 B90 127 A6
Highdown Rd CV31 162 B6
High Elms La B60 151 E1
High Ercal Ave CV3 61 C2
High Farm Rd
  Halesowen,Hasbury B63 82 F3
  Halesowen,Hurst Green B62 83 F8
Highfield Ave
  Bilston WV14 40 E4
  Burntwood WS7 7 B7
  Redditch B97 158 D8
  Tamworth B77 22 A5
  Walsall WS4 29 C8
  Wolverhampton WV10 12 A2
Highfield Cl
  Birmingham B28 105 D5
  Burntwood WS7 7 B7
  Kenilworth CV8 147 E4
Highfield Cres
  Halesowen B63 82 D6
  Rowley Regis B65 63 B3
  Wolverhampton WV11 26 B6
Highfield Ct
  Cannock WS11 2 B5
  Sutton Coldfield B73 46 B1
Highfield Dr B73 56 F7
Highfield Gdns WS14 9 C8
Highfield Inf & Jun Sch
  B8 67 E5
Highfield La
  1 Halesowen B63 83 A3
  Birmingham B32 84 B4
  Clent DY9 100 A3
  Corley CV7 94 D8
Highfield Mews B63 82 C1
Highfield Pl B14 105 D5
Highfield Rd
  Birmingham,Edgbaston
  B15 86 A8
  Birmingham,Moseley B13 87 B3
  Birmingham,Newton B43 54 C7
  Birmingham,Saltley B8 67 E5
  Birmingham,Yardley Wood B14
  B28 105 D5
  Bromsgrove B60 150 E8
  Burntwood WS7 7 C7
  Cannock WS12 2 E1
  Coventry CV2 113 F4
  Dudley DY2 62 C5
  Halesowen B63 82 D5
  Kidderminster DY10 117 A8
  Nuneaton CV11 73 E2
  Redditch B97 158 D8
  Rowley Regis B65 63 B3
  Sedgley DY3 39 D1
  Smethwick B67 64 F3
  Stourbridge DY8 61 A2
  Studley B80 159 D4
  Tipton DY4 52 B8
  Walsall WS3 15 A4
Highfields
  Bromsgrove B61 136 C1
  Burntwood WS7 7 B7

Highfields Ct WV4 38 D6
Highfields Dr
  Dudley DY14 40 D3
  Wombourne WV5 49 A5
Highfields Grange WS6 4 D1
Highfields Pk
  Burntwood WS7 7 C7
  Cradley Heath B65 83 C8
  Dudley WV14 40 C2
Highfields Rd
  Burntwood WS7 6 F4
  Dudley WV14 40 D3
  Hinckley LE10 71 E1
Highfields Science Specialist
  Sch WV4 38 C5
Highfields The WV6 24 A3
Highfield Terr
  Birmingham B18 66 A5
  Royal Leamington Spa
  CV32 156 D1
Highfield Way WS9 16 B2
Highgate Ave
  Walsall WS1 42 F8
  Wolverhampton WV4 38 D6
Highgate Bsns Ctr B12 87 B6
Highgate Cl
  Birmingham B12 86 F7
  Kidderminster DY11 116 A4
  Walsall WS1 42 F7
Highgate Ct 4 WS1 42 F8
Highgate Dr WV4 42 F7
Highgate Ho B15 56 E8
Highgate Middleway B12 86 F7
Highgate Pl B12 87 A7
Highgate Prim Sch DY2 61 F6
Highgate Rd
  Birmingham B12 87 A6
  Dudley DY1,DY2 61 F6
  Walsall WS1 42 F7
  Highgate Ret Pk B12 87 A7
  Highgate Sq B12 86 F7
Highgate Sq Craft Ctr 9
  B12 86 F7
Highgate St
  Birmingham B12 86 F7
  Cradley Heath B64 62 F2
Highgate St 4 B64 31 A1
High Gn WS11 1 D1
High Grange WS11 2 A5
High Gr CV8 WS11 1 D1
Highgrove Cl
  Tamworth B79 21 B7
  Willenhall WV12 27 B7
Highgrove CV4 131 F5
Highgrove Pl DY1 50 F2
Highgrove WV6 24 C3
High Haden Cres B64 83 A8
High Haden Rd B64 83 A8
High Heath Cl B30 103 D5
High Hill WV11 13 C4
High Holborn DY3 50 D7
High House Dr B45 121 F3
High House La B60 152 A6
Highland Ho B62 83 C8
Highland Mews WV14 40 D1
Highland Rd
  Birmingham,Erdington
  B23 56 F5
  Birmingham,Great Barr B43 43 E3
High Land Rd WS9 16 B3
Highland Rd
  Cannock WS11 1 C4
  Coventry CV5 112 F1
  Cradley Heath B64 62 E2
  Dudley DY1 51 A3
  Kenilworth CV8 148 C7
  Royal Leamington Spa
  CV32 157 B4
Highland Ridge B62 83 E5
Highlands Cl
  Kidderminster DY11 116 A5
  Warwick CV34 161 A8
Highlands Ct B90 126 E8
Highlands Rd
  Solihull B90 126 F8
  Wolverhampton WV3 38 D8
Highlands Way WV8 159 A7
High Leasowes B63 83 A4
Highley Cl
  Kidderminster DY11 116 B2
  Redditch B98 154 E4
High Mdws
  Bromsgrove B60 150 D7
  Wolverhampton WV6 24 C3
  Wombourne WV5 49 B6
High Meadow Inf Sch B46 70 F8
High Meadow Rd B38 104 A2
Highmoor Cl
  Dudley WV14 40 D3
  Willenhall WV12 27 B7
Highmoor Rd B65 63 B3
Highmore Dr B32 102 C8
High Mount St WS12 2 B6
High Oak DY5 61 C7
Highover Dr B75 32 A4
Highpark Ave DY8 80 D5
High Park Cl
  Coventry CV5 111 F3
  Sedgley DY3 50 D8
  Smethwick B66 65 B5
High Park Cres DY3 39 D1
High Park Rd B63 82 C5

High Park St B7 . . . .**67** B6
High Point B15 . . . .**85** E6
High Rd WV12 . . . .**27** C5
High Ridge WS9 . . . .**29** F5
High Ridge Cl
  Aldridge WS9 . . . .**29** E5
  Darlaston WS10 . . . .**41** A4
High St Duchess Par B70 .**53** D3
High St Princess Par B70 .**53** D3
High St
  1 Halesowen B63 . . . .**83** B3
  7 Dudley,Old Dock DY1 . . .**62** B8
  Aldridge WS9 . . . .**30** B6
  Astwood Bank B96 . . . .**158** C1
  Bedworth CV12 . . . .**78** B2
  Belbroughton DY9 . . . .**119** E2
  Bilston WV14 . . . .**40** D5
  Birmingham,Aston B6,B19 . .**66** E7
  Birmingham B4 . . . .**164** C2
  Birmingham,Castle Vale B35 **58** B4
  Birmingham,Erdington B23 . .**56** F4
  Birmingham,Harborne B17 . .**85** A6
  Birmingham,King's Heath
    B14 . . . .**104** E8
  Birmingham,Quinton B32 . .**84** A6
  Birmingham,Saltley B8 . . . .**67** D5
  Brierley Hill,Barrow Hill
    DY5 . . . .**61** C7
  Brierley Hill,Brockmoor DY5 .**61** C4
  Brierley Hill,Quarry Bank
    DY5 . . . .**82** A8
  Bromsgrove B61 . . . .**137** A2
  Brownhills,Clayhanger WS8 .**15** E6
  Brownhills,Vigo WS9 . . . . . .**15** F3
  Brownhills WS8 . . . .**15** F8
  Burntwood,Chasetown WS7 . .**6** F6
  Cheslyn Hay WS6 . . . .**4** D2
  Coleshill B46 . . . .**70** F7
  Coventry CV1 . . . .**165** C2
  Coventry,Keresley CV6 . . . . .**94** F1
  Cradley Heath B64 . . . .**62** D1
  Cubbington CV32 . . . .**157** E5
  Darlaston WS10 . . . .**41** A4
  Dudley DY1 . . . .**51** C1
  Hampton-in-A B92 . . . .**109** A2
  Kenilworth CV8 . . . .**147** E5
  Kidderminster DY10 . . . . . .**116** E6
  Kingswinford DY6 . . . .**60** E6
  Kingswinford,Wall Heath
    DY6 . . . .**60** C8
  Knowle B93 . . . .**128** C6
  Norton Canes WS11 . . . .**6** B5
  Nuneaton CV11 . . . .**73** B4
High Street Bordesley
  B12. . . . .**67** A1
High Street Deritend B12 .**66** F1
High St
  Rowley Regis B65 . . . .**63** C1
  Royal Leamington Spa
    CV31 . . . .**162** A7
  Ryton-on-D CV8 . . . .**135** B1
  Sedgley DY3. . . . .**50** D8
  Smethwick B66 . . . .**65** A5
  Solihull B91 . . . .**107** C3
  Solihull,Shirley B90 . . . .**105** D2
  Stourbridge,Amblecote DY8 .**80** F7
  Stourbridge DY8 . . . .**81** A5
  Stourbridge,Lye DY9 . . . .**81** F5
  Stourbridge,Wollaston DY8 .**80** E7
  Stourbridge,Wordsley DY8 . .**60** E2
  Studley B80. . . . .**159** E4
  Sutton Coldfield B72 . . . .**46** C5
  Tamworth B77 . . . .**35** C5
  Tipton,Princes End DY4 . . . . .**51** F8
  Tipton,Tipton Green DY4 . . . .**51** E5
  Walsall,Pelsall WS3. . . . .**15** A4
  Walsall,Wallington Heath
    WS3 . . . .**14** B1
  Walsall WS1 . . . .**28** E1
  Warwick CV34 . . . .**160** E6
  Wednesfield WV11 . . . .**26** D5
  West Bromwich B70 . . . .**53** C3
  Wolverhampton WV6 . . . .**24** D4
  Wombourne WV5 . . . .**49** B7
Highters Cl B14 . . . .**105** B2
Highter's Heath La B14 .**105** A2
Highters Heath Prim Sch
  B14. . . . .**105** B3
Highters Rd B14 . . . .**105** A3
High Timbers B45. . . . .**101** F1
Hightown B63 . . . .**82** C6
Hightree Cl B32 . . . .**84** B1
High Trees B20 . . . .**54** F3
High Trees Cl B98 . . . .**158** E7
High Trees Ho B69 . . . .**63** F3
High Trees Rd B93 . . . .**128** A7
Highview **9** WS1 . . . .**42** F8
High View Dr CV7 . . . .**95** C7
Highview Dr DY6 . . . .**60** F4
High View Rd CV32 . . . . . .**157** C5
Highview St DY2 . . . .**51** E1
High View WV14 . . . .**39** F1
Highwaymans Croft CV4 .**132** D5
Highwood Ave DY2 . . . .**89** A1
High Wood Cl DY6 . . . .**60** C6
Highwood Croft B38 . . . . . .**103** D1
Hiker Gr **3** B37 . . . .**70** D2
Hilary Cres DY1. . . . .**51** B6
Hilary Dr
  Aldridge WS9. . . . .**30** A5
  Sutton Coldfield B76 . . . .**47** A3
  Wolverhampton WV3 . . . .**38** D7
Hilary Gr B31. . . . .**102** F4
Hilary Rd
  Coventry CV4. . . . .**132** E6

Hilary Rd continued
  Nuneaton CV10 . . . .**72** F5
Hilden Rd B7 . . . .**67** B4
Hideric Cres DY1. . . . .**61** F7
Hilderstone Rd B25 . . . .**88** C6
Hildicks Cres WS3 . . . .**28** F7
Hildicks Pl WS3. . . . .**29** A7
Hilditch Way CV11. . . . .**73** E2
Hillaire Cl B38 . . . .**104** C2
Hillaries Rd B23 . . . .**56** D2
Hillary Ave WS10 . . . .**42** C3
Hillary Crest DY3 . . . .**50** E5
Hillary Prim Sch WS2 . . . . . .**42** C7
Hillary St WS2 . . . .**42** C7
Hill Avenue Prim Sch
  WV4 . . . .**39** F3
Hill Ave WV4 . . . .**39** F3
Hill Bank Dr B33. . . . .**68** D4
Hillbank B69 . . . .**63** D8
Hill Bank Rd
  Birmingham B38 . . . .**104** A2
  Halesowen B63 . . . .**82** D6
Hill Bank DY9 . . . .**81** F5
Hillborough Rd B27. . . . .**88** D2
Hillbrook Gr B33 . . . .**68** F3
Hillbrow Cres B62 . . . .**83** F8
Hillbury Dr WV12 . . . .**27** B8
Hill Cl
  Birmingham B31 . . . .**103** C1
  Royal Leamington Spa
    CV32. . . . .**157** A3
  Sedgley DY3. . . . .**39** E1
Hillcrest Ave B43 . . . .**43** E2
Hill Crest Ave DY5 . . . .**61** C2
Hillcrest Ave
  Halesowen B63 . . . .**82** B7
  Wolverhampton WV10 . . . . . .**11** E1
Hillcrest Bsns Pk DY2 . . . . . .**62** C7
Hillcrest Cl
  Dudley DY2 . . . .**62** C5
  Tamworth B79 . . . .**21** B6
Hill Crest CV32 . . . .**157** F5
Hill Crest Dr WS13 . . . .**3** A1
Hill Crest DY3 . . . .**50** C4
Hillcrest Gdns WV12 . . . .**27** D5
Hill Crest Gr B44 . . . .**56** A7
Hill Crest Hospl B98 . . . . . .**159** C6
Hillcrest Ind Est B64. . . . . . .**82** D8
Hillcrest Pk B47 . . . .**140** F8
Hill Crest Rd B13 . . . .**86** E2
Hillcrest Rd
  Birmingham B43 . . . .**43** E2
  Dudley DY2 . . . .**51** E1
  Nuneaton CV10 . . . .**72** E5
  Polesworth B78 . . . .**36** F7
  Romsley B62 . . . .**101** A4
  Sutton Coldfield B72 . . . .**46** C1
Hillcrest Rise WS7 . . . .**7** B4
Hillcrest Sch & Com Coll The
  DY2 . . . .**62** C5
Hillcrest Sch & Sixth Form
  Ctr B32. . . . .**84** E3
Hillcroft Ho B14 . . . .**104** F2
Hill Croft Rd B14 . . . .**104** C6
Hillcroft Rd DY6 . . . .**60** E7
Hillcross Wlk B36. . . . .**68** F8
Hilldene Rd DY6 . . . .**60** C4
Hilldrop Gr **1** B17 . . . .**85** D3
Hilleys Croft B37 . . . .**69** F2
Hill Farm Ave CV11 . . . .**74** B1
Hill Farm Prim Sch CV6 .**113** B7
Hillfield Hall Ct **1** B91. . . . .**107** C1
Hillfield Mews **3** B91. . . . .**127** B8
Hillfield Rd
  Birmingham B11 . . . .**87** D3
  Solihull B91 . . . .**107** C2
  Solihull,Hillfield B91 . . . .**107** B1
Hillfields Ho **1** CV1. . . . . . .**113** E3
Hillfields Rd DY5 . . . .**81** B7
Hillfields B67. . . . .**64** D3
Hillfield Wlk B65 . . . .**62** F5
Hill Fray Dr CV3 . . . .**134** A5
Hill Gr B20 . . . .**55** C2
Hill Grove Cres DY10 . . . . . .**117** A4
Hillgrove Gdns DY10 . . . . . .**117** A4
Hillhampton Cl B92 . . . .**89** C1
Hill Hook Rd B74 . . . .**31** E5
Hill Hook Rd B74 . . . .**31** F5
Hill Ho B66. . . . .**65** C6
Hill House La B33 . . . .**68** F3
Hillhurst Gr B36. . . . .**58** D1
Hillhurst Rd B73. . . . .**45** C3
Hilliard Cl CV12. . . . .**78** B4
Hilliards Croft B42. . . . .**55** A8
Hillingford Ave B43 . . . .**44** D3
Hill La
  Alvechurch B47,B48. . . . . . .**124** C1
  Birmingham B43 . . . .**43** E2
  Bromsgrove B60 . . . .**136** F1
  Clent DY9 . . . .**99** E4
  Middleton B75 . . . .**33** B2
Hillman Dr DY2 . . . .**62** E7
Hillman Gr B36. . . . .**58** F1
Hillman Ho CV1 . . . .**165** B3
Hillman B77. . . . .**21** E2
Hillmeads Dr DY2 . . . .**62** E7
Hillmeads Rd B38. . . . .**104** A1
Hillmorton CV8 . . . .**154** E6
Hillmorton Rd
  Coventry CV2. . . . .**96** C1
  Dorridge B93 . . . .**128** A5
  Sutton Coldfield B74 . . . .**31** F4
Hillmorton B78 . . . .**31** F3
Hillmount Cl B28 . . . .**87** E2
Hill Pas B64 . . . .**62** E2
Hill Pk WS9 . . . .**16** A4
Hill Pl WV11 . . . .**13** A1

Hill Rd
  Keresley CV7 . . . .**94** F6
  Tipton B69. . . . .**52** A2
  Willenhall WV13 . . . .**26** E1
Hillrise LE10 . . . .**75** F8
Hill Rise View B60 . . . .**137** C6
Hillsborough Ho B27. . . . . . .**88** E2
Hillside Ave
  Brierley Hill DY5 . . . .**82** A8
  Cradley Heath B65 . . . .**83** B8
  Halesowen B63 . . . .**82** D6
Hillside WS8 . . . .**16** A6
Hillside Cl
  Birmingham B32 . . . .**102** A8
  Brownhills WS8 . . . .**16** A6
  Burntwood WS7. . . . .**6** E5
  Cannock WS12 . . . .**2** A7
  Kidderminster DY11 . . . . . .**116** A7
Hillside Cres WS3. . . . .**14** F3
Hillside Croft B92. . . . .**89** E4
Hillside Ct B43 . . . .**43** E2
Hillside Dr
  Birmingham B37 . . . .**69** F4
  Wolverhampton WV1. . . . . . .**26** A3
Hillside
  Hartshill CV10 . . . .**72** A8
  Lichfield WS14. . . . .**9** D6
Hillside N CV2 . . . .**114** A6
Hillside Rd
  Birmingham,Gravelly Hill
    B23. . . . .**56** F4
  Birmingham,Great Barr B43 .**43** D2
  Dudley DY1 . . . .**51** A5
  Hinckley LE10 . . . .**75** D6
  Sutton Coldfield B74 . . . .**32** A4
Hillside B98 . . . .**153** D2
Hill St
  Bedworth CV12 . . . .**78** B5
  Bilston WV14. . . . .**40** E3
  Birmingham B5 . . . .**164** B2
  Brierley Hill,Quarry Bank
    DY5 . . . .**82** A8
  Brierley Hill,Silver End DY5 .**61** D2
  Burntwood WS7. . . . .**6** E5
  Cannock WS12 . . . .**2** C7
  Cheslyn Hay WS6. . . . .**4** C2
  Coventry CV1. . . . .**165** B3
  Darlaston WS10. . . . .**41** E6
  Dudley,Netherton DY2 . . . . . .**62** C4
  Dudley,Upper Gornal DY3 . . .**50** D5
  Essington WV11 . . . .**12** F3
  Halesowen B63 . . . .**83** A3
  Hinckley LE10 . . . .**75** E8
  Kidderminster DY11 . . . . . .**116** D6
  Norton Canes WS11 . . . .**5** F6
  Nuneaton CV10 . . . .**72** D4
Hillstone Gdns WV10. . . . . . .**25** F8
Hillstone Prim Sch B34 . . . . .**69** D5
Hillstone Rd B34. . . . .**69** D5
Hill St
  Royal Leamington Spa
    CV32. . . . .**157** A1
  Smethwick B66 . . . .**65** A6
  Stourbridge,Amblecote DY8 .**80** F8
  Stourbridge DY8 . . . .**80** F4
  Stourbridge,Lye DY9 . . . .**81** F5
  Tipton DY4 . . . .**51** F4
  Walsall WS1 . . . .**28** F1
  Warwick CV34 . . . .**161** B8
Hill The B32 . . . .**84** E2
Hill Top Ave
  Halesowen B62 . . . .**83** E7
  Tamworth B79 . . . .**21** B8
Hill Top Cl B44. . . . .**55** E6
Hilltop Cl CV8 . . . .**145** E8
Hill Top CV1 . . . .**165** C3
Hilltop Ct CV3 . . . .**50** E3
Hill Top Dr B36 . . . .**68** D7
Hill Top Ind Est B70. . . . .**52** F8
Hill Top Rd B31 . . . .**102** F3
Hilltop Rd DY2 . . . .**62** F1
Hill Top B68 . . . .**64** C2
Hill Top B97 . . . .**152** F1
Hilltop DY3 . . . .**81** F3
Hill Top Rd B70 . . . .**53** A7
Hill Top Wlk WS9 . . . .**16** C1
Hillview Cl
  Halesowen B63 . . . .**82** E6
  Lickey End B60 . . . .**137** C6
Hillview Rd
  Birmingham B45 . . . .**121** E8
  Lickey End B60 . . . .**137** C6
Hill Village Rd B75 . . . .**32** A4
Hillville Gdns DY8 . . . .**81** B3
Hillwood Ave Prim Sch B74 . .**31** F4
Hillwood Ave B90 . . . .**127** A6
Hillwood Cl CV6 . . . .**95** C2
Hillwood Common Rd
  B75. . . . .**32** B6
Hillwood Rd
  Birmingham B31 . . . .**102** F7
  Halesowen B62 . . . .**83** C7
  Sutton Coldfield B75 . . . .**32** C5
Hill Wood WS3 . . . .**14** F2
Hill Wootton Rd CV32,
  CV35 . . . .**156** C6
Hillyfields Rd B23. . . . .**56** C4

Hilly Rd WV14 . . . .**40** E2
Hilmore Way B77 . . . .**35** E8
Hilsea Cl WV8 . . . .**10** F1
Hilston Ave
  Halesowen B63 . . . .**82** F4
  Wolverhampton WV4 . . . .**38** C4
Hilton Ave
  Birmingham B28 . . . .**105** F4
  Nuneaton CV10 . . . .**72** B6
Hilton Cl WS3 . . . .**14** A2
Hilton Cross Bsns Pk
  WV10 . . . .**12** B5
Hilton Cross WV10. . . . .**12** B5
Hilton Ct
  Coventry CV5. . . . .**112** F2
  Sutton Coldfield B72 . . . .**57** C8
Hilton Dr B72. . . . .**57** C8
Hilton La
  Featherstone WV10,WV11 . .**12** E8
  Great Wyrley,Warstone
    WV11 . . . .**12** B7
  Great Wyrley WS6 . . . .**5** A2
Hilton Main Ind Est WV11 .**12** C5
Hilton Pl WV14 . . . .**40** F5
Hilton Rd
  Burntwood WS7. . . . .**6** C8
  Featherstone WV10 . . . .**12** C7
  Oldbury B69 . . . .**63** B6
  Willenhall WV12 . . . .**13** C1
  Wolverhampton WV4 . . . .**39** F4
Hilton St
  West Bromwich B70 . . . .**53** A3
  Wolverhampton WV10 . . . . .**163** D4
Hilton Trad Est WV4. . . . .**39** F4
Hilton Way WV12 . . . .**27** C8
Himbleton Cl B98. . . . .**159** B7
Himbleton Croft **1** B90 .**127** A6
Himley Ave DY1. . . . .**50** F2
Himley Cl
  Birmingham B43 . . . .**43** C2
  Willenhall WV12 . . . .**27** B5
Himley Cres WV4 . . . .**39** B5
Himley Ct DY3 . . . .**50** E3
Himley Gardens DY3 . . . .**49** F4
Himley Gr B45. . . . .**122** B6
Himley Hall* DY3. . . . .**49** D4
Himley Rd
  2 Bedworth CV12 . . . .**77** D2
  Dudley DY1,DY3 . . . .**50** C2
Himley Rise B90 . . . .**126** E4
Himley St DY1 . . . .**51** A1
Hinbrook Rd DY1 . . . .**50** E1
Hinchliffe Ave WV14 . . . .**40** B2
Hinchwick Ct B93. . . . .**127** F3
Hinckes Rd WV6 . . . .**24** A3
Hinckley Bsns Pk LE10. . . . .**74** F8
Hinckley Coll LE10 . . . .**71** F1
Hinckley & District Hospl
  LE10. . . . .**75** D8
Hinckley & District Mus*
  LE10. . . . .**71** D1
Hinckley Rd
  Ansty CV2,CV7 . . . .**97** C2
  Aston Flamville LE10. . . . . . .**76** E6
  Barwell LE9 . . . .**71** E5
  Burbage LE9 . . . .**76** D8
  Burton Hastings CV11 . . . . . .**75** A1
  Burton Hastings CV11,LE10 . .**75** D1
  Coventry CV2 . . . .**115** A8
  Hinckley LE10 . . . .**71** A5
  Nuneaton CV11 . . . .**73** E5
Hinckley Sta LE10. . . . .**75** D7
Hinckley St B5 . . . .**164** C2
Hincks St WV2 . . . .**40** A7
Hind Cl CV34 . . . .**155** F2
Hindhead Rd B14 . . . .**105** C4
Hindlip Cl B63. . . . .**82** F2
Hindlow Cl B7 . . . .**67** A4
Hindon Gr B27 . . . .**106** C7
Hindon Sq **6** B15 . . . .**85** F8
Hindon Wlk B32 . . . .**84** C2
Hingeston St B18. . . . .**66** B4
Hingley Croft WS9 . . . .**30** F3
Hingley Ind Pk B64 . . . .**62** C1
Hingley Rd B64 . . . .**82** A6
Hingley St B64 . . . .**62** D1
Hinksford Cl DY6 . . . .**60** E8
Hinksford La DY6,DY7 . . . . . .**60** C8
Hinstock Cl WV4 . . . .**39** A4
Hinstock Rd B20. . . . .**54** F1
Hintlesham Ave B15 . . . .**85** D5
Hinton Gr WV11 . . . .**26** F5
Hintons Coppice B93 . . . . .**127** E6
Hinton Cl B78. . . . .**19** D2
Hints La
  Hopwas B78 . . . .**20** B5
  Weeford B78 . . . .**19** F4
Hints Rd
  Hopwas B78 . . . .**20** B6
  Mile Oak B78. . . . .**20** C2
Hipkins St DY4 . . . .**51** E7
Hiplands Rd B62. . . . .**83** F4
Hipsley Cl B36 . . . .**58** C1
Hipsmoor Cl B37 . . . .**69** F2
Hipswell Highway CV2 . . . .**114** D3
Hirdemonsway B90 . . . .**126** A5
Hiron Croft CV3 . . . .**133** C8
Hiron The CV3 . . . .**133** C8
Hiron Way CV34 . . . .**160** B7
Histons Hill WV8 . . . .**10** A3
Histons Dr WV8 . . . .**10** A3
Hitches La B15 . . . .**86** D7
Hitchman Cl CV31. . . . .**162** A5
Hitchman Rd CV31 . . . .**162** A5

Hither Green La B98. . . . . .**153** F7
Hitherside B90 . . . .**126** B5
Hive Ind Ctr The B18. . . . . . .**66** A6
HM Young Offender Inst
  (Swinfen Hall) WS14. . . . .**9** E1
Hoarestone Ave CV11 . . . . . .**79** A7
Hoarstone DY9 . . . .**98** F5
Hobacre Cl B45. . . . .**122** A8
Hobart Croft **1** B7 . . . .**67** A4
Hobart Ct B74 . . . .**32** A3
Hobart Dr WS5 . . . .**43** C6
Hobart Rd
  Cannock WS12. . . . .**2** E2
  Tipton DY4. . . . .**40** E1
Hobbis Ho B38 . . . .**123** C7
Hobble End La WS6. . . . .**14** B7
Hobden Hall Farm Ind Units
  B60. . . . .**150** B3
Hobgate Cl WV10 . . . .**25** F4
Hobgate Rd WV10 . . . .**25** F4
Hob Green Prim Sch DY9 .**81** E2
Hob Green Rd DY9 . . . .**81** E2
Hobhouse Cl B43 . . . .**54** F7
Hob La
  Balsall Common CV7 . . . . . .**130** C4
  Burton Green CV8 . . . .**131** A3
  Temple Balsall B92 . . . .**129** A8
Hobley St WV13. . . . .**27** C2
Hobmoor Prim Sch B25. . . . .**88** D8
Hob Moor Rd B10,B25 . . . . . .**88** C8
Hobnock Rd WV11 . . . .**13** B5
Hobs Rd WS10 . . . .**42** A4
Hockett St CV3 . . . .**133** D8
Hocking Rd CV2 . . . .**114** E4
Hockley Brook Cl B18. . . . . . .**66** A5
Hockley Brook La DY9 . . . . .**119** F3
Hockley Brook Trad Est
  B18. . . . .**66** A6
Hockley Ctr B18 . . . .**66** B6
Hockley Cl B19 . . . .**66** D6
Hockley Cr B94 . . . .**143** C7
Hockley Heath Prim Sch
  B94. . . . .**143** C6
Hockley Hill B18. . . . .**66** B5
Hockley La
  Coventry CV5. . . . .**111** C5
  Dudley DY2 . . . .**62** C4
Hockley Pool Cl B18 . . . .**66** B5
Hockley Rd
  Birmingham B23 . . . .**56** D4
  Dudley WV14. . . . .**51** A7
  Tamworth B77 . . . .**35** F5
Hockley St B19 . . . .**66** C5
Hodder Gr B71 . . . .**53** F7
Hodge Hill Ave DY9 . . . .**81** F3
Hodge Hill Comm B36 . . . . . .**68** E7
Hodge Hill Cotts DY10 . . . .**117** C7
Hodgehill Ct B36 . . . .**68** E7
Hodge Hill Girls Sch B36. .**68** C7
Hodge Hill Prim Sch B36. .**68** E6
Hodge Hill Rd B34 . . . .**68** E6
Hodge Hill Sch B36 . . . .**68** C7
Hodge La B77 . . . .**22** B6
Hodges Dr B69 . . . .**63** B8
Hodgetts Cl B67 . . . .**64** D3
Hodgetts Dr B63 . . . .**100** C8
Hodgett's La
  Balsall Common CV7 . . . . . .**130** F7
  Coventry CV7,CV8 . . . .**131** A6
Hodgkins Cl WS8 . . . .**16** A6
Hodgkiss Cl WS10 . . . .**41** E4
Hodgson Twr B19. . . . .**66** D6
Hodnell Cl B36 . . . .**58** C1
Hodnet Cl
  Bilston WV14. . . . .**40** B5
  Kenilworth CV8 . . . .**148** B5
Hodnet Dr DY5 . . . .**61** C6
Hodnet Gr B5 . . . .**86** E8
Hodnet Pl WS11 . . . .**2** B2
Hodson Ave WV13 . . . .**27** C1
Hodson Cl WV11 . . . .**26** F8
Hodson Way WS11 . . . .**2** B2
Hoff Beck Ct **8** B9 . . . .**67** B2
Hogarth Cl
  Bedworth CV12 . . . .**78** A4
  Birmingham B43 . . . .**44** D5
  Hinckley LE10 . . . .**71** A3
  Willenhall WV13 . . . .**26** E2
Hogarth Dr LE10 . . . .**71** A3
Hogarth Ho **6** B15 . . . .**86** C8
Hoggs La B31 . . . .**102** E4
Holbeache La DY6 . . . .**49** D1
Holbeache Rd DY6. . . . .**60** D1
Holbeach Rd B33. . . . .**69** B2
Holbeche Rd
  Dorridge B93 . . . .**128** A7
  Sutton Coldfield B75 . . . .**47** B5
Holbein Cl CV12 . . . .**78** A4
Holberg Gr WV11 . . . .**26** E5
Holborn Ave CV6 . . . .**95** C2
Holborn Hill B6,B7 . . . .**67** C7
Holborn Sh Ctr The DY3 . .**50** D7
Holbrook Gr B37. . . . .**70** A1
Holbrook La CV6. . . . .**95** D2
Holbrook Park Est CV6. . . .**113** D8
Holbrook Prim Sch CV6 . . . . .**95** E1
Holbrook Twr B36. . . . .**68** D8
Holbrook Way CV6 . . . .**95** D1
Holbury Cl WV9 . . . .**11** A2
Holcombe Rd B11 . . . .**88** A3

Holcroft Rd
Halesowen B63 . . . . .82 C5
Kingswinford DY6 . . . . .49 C1
Stourbridge DY9 . . . . .81 C4
Holcroft St
Tipton DY4 . . . . .52 A2
Wolverhampton WV2 . . . . .40 A7
Holden Cl B23 . . . . .56 E2
Holden Cres WS3 . . . . .28 F5
Holden Croft DY4 . . . . .52 A3
Holden Pl WS3 . . . . .28 E5
Holden Rd
Wednesbury WS10 . . . . . . .42 A2
Wolverhampton WV4 . . . . .38 D3
Holdens The B28 . . . . .105 E6
Holder Dr WS11 . . . . .1 B2
Holder Rd
Birmingham,South Yardley
B25 . . . . .88 C7
Birmingham,Sparkbrook
B11 . . . . .88 C7
Holders Gdns B13 . . . . .86 C2
Holders La B13 . . . . .86 C2
Holdford Rd B6 . . . . .55 F2
Holdgate Rd B29 . . . . .103 C7
Hole Farm Rd B31 . . . . . . .103 C5
Hole Farm Way B38 . . . . . .123 F2
Hole House La B94 . . . . . . .143 F1
Hole La B31 . . . . .103 C5
Holford Ave WS2 . . . . .42 C6
Holford Dr B42,B6 . . . . . . .55 F4
Holford Way B6 . . . . .55 F3
Holifast Rd B72 . . . . .57 C7
Holioak Dr CV34 . . . . .161 B6
Holland Ave
Knowle B93 . . . . .128 B8
Oldbury B68 . . . . .64 D4
Holland Ho B19 . . . . .66 D5
Holland House Inf Sch
B72 . . . . .46 C4
Holland Ind Pk WS10 . . . . .41 D8
Holland Rd
Bilston WV14 . . . . .40 E7
Birmingham B43 . . . . .54 D7
Coventry CV6 . . . . .113 A6
Sutton Coldfield B72 . . . . .46 C4
Holland Rd W B6 . . . . .66 F6
Hollands Pl WS3 . . . . .14 D1
Hollands Rd WS3 . . . . .14 D1
Holland St
1 Dudley DY1 . . . . .62 B8
Birmingham B3 . . . . .164 A3
Sutton Coldfield B72 . . . . .46 C4
Tipton DY4 . . . . .52 C2
Hollands Way WS3 . . . . . . .14 F4
Hollemeadow Ave WS3 . . .28 D7
Holliars Gr B37 . . . . .69 F5
Hollicombe Terr CV2 . . . . .114 D8
Holliday Rd
Birmingham,Erdington
B24 . . . . .57 A4
Birmingham,Handsworth
B21 . . . . .65 F7
Holliday St
Birmingham B1 . . . . .164 A2
Birmingham B1 . . . . .66 C1
Holliday Wharf B1 . . . . . . .164 A1
Hollie Lucas Rd B13 . . . . . .104 F7
Holliers Walk Prim Sch
LE10 . . . . .71 D1
Hollier's Wlk LE10 . . . . .71 D1
Hollies Ave WS11 . . . . .1 F1
Hollies Croft B5 . . . . .86 C5
Hollies Ct WS11 . . . . .1 F1
Hollies Dr
Halesowen B62 . . . . .83 E6
Wednesbury WS10 . . . . . .41 F3
Hollies Ind Est WV2 . . . . . .163 B1
Hollies La WV6 . . . . .23 A4
Hollies Park Rd WS11 . . . . .1 F1
Hollies Rd B69 . . . . .63 B8
Hollies Rise B64 . . . . .82 F8
Hollies St DY5 . . . . .61 D7
Hollies The
Barnt Green B45 . . . . .122 A1
Birmingham,Aston B6 . . . .67 B8
Birmingham,Winson Green
B16 . . . . .65 F3
Smethwick B66 . . . . .65 C4
Wolverhampton,New Cross
WV11 . . . . .26 B5
Wolverhampton WV3 . . . . .38 F7
Hollin Brow Cl B93 . . . . . . .128 B3
Hollingberry La B76 . . . . . .46 F3
Hollings Gr B91 . . . . .127 B8
Hollington Cres B33 . . . . . .69 A4
Hollington Rd WV1 . . . . . . .26 B1
Hollington Way B90 . . . . . .127 C7
Hollinwell Cl
Nuneaton CV11 . . . . .79 C8
Walsall WS3 . . . . .14 A3
Hollis La CV8 . . . . .147 E8
Hollis Rd CV3 . . . . .114 A2
Hollister Dr B32 . . . . .84 F3
Holloway Bank Trad Est
WS10 . . . . .41 F1
Holloway Bank
Wednesbury WS10 . . . . . .41 F1
West Bromwich B70,B71 . .53 A8
Holloway B31 . . . . .102 E5
Holloway Circus Queensway
B1 .164 B1
Holloway Dr B98 . . . . .154 B3
Holloway Field CV6 . . . . . .113 A6
Holloway Head B1 . . . . . . .164 B1
Holloway La B98 . . . . .153 F3
Holloway Pk B98 . . . . .154 A3

Holloway St W DY3 . . . . . .50 D4
Holloway St
Dudley DY3 . . . . .50 D4
Wolverhampton WV1 . . . . .40 A7
Holloway B79 . . . . .21 B4
Holloway The
Alvechurch B48 . . . . .139 D3
Bluntington DY10 . . . . . . .118 E2
Seisdon WV5 . . . . .37 A3
Stourbridge DY8 . . . . .80 F7
Warwick CV34 . . . . .160 C6
Wolverhampton WV6 . . . . .24 C2
Hollow Cres CV6 . . . . .113 B5
Hollow Croft B31 . . . . .103 B3
Hollow Croft Rd WV12 . . . .27 B7
Hollowmeadow Ho B36 . . .68 D8
Hollows The CV11 . . . . .73 F1
Hollow The B13 . . . . .86 E4
Hollowtree La B60 . . . . . . .138 A3
Holly Ave
Birmingham,Balsall Heath
B12 . . . . .87 A5
Birmingham,Selly Oak B29 .86 B1
Hollybank Ave WV11 . . . . .13 A3
Hollybank Cl WS3 . . . . .14 A2
Hollybank B13 . . . . .82 D1
Hollybank Rd B13 . . . . . . .105 A6
Hollyberry Ave B91 . . . . . .127 A8
Hollyberry Cl 8 B63 . . . . . .83 A3
Hollyberry Croft B34 . . . . . .69 C6
Hollybrow B29 . . . . .103 B7
Holly Bush Gr B32 . . . . .84 D7
Hollybush La
Coventry CV6 . . . . .96 A4
Stourbridge DY8 . . . . .80 F7
Wolverhampton WV4 . . . . .38 D4
Hollybush Wlk 2 B64 . . . . .62 D1
Holly Cl
Hinckley LE10 . . . . .75 E5
Sutton Coldfield B76 . . . . .46 F2
Tamworth B79 . . . . .21 B7
Willenhall WV12 . . . . .27 C6
Hollycot Gdns B12 . . . . . . .86 F6
Hollycroft Cres LE10 . . . . . .71 C1
Hollycroft Gdns WV6 . . . . .24 B6
Hollycroft LE10 . . . . .71 C1
Hollycroft Rd B21 . . . . .54 D1
Holly Ct
Balsall Common CV7 . . . . .130 B3
Birmingham B23 . . . . .57 A5
Kidderminster DY10 . . . . .116 D8
Walsall WS5 . . . . .43 A4
Hollydale Rd
Birmingham B24 . . . . .57 C3
Rowley Regis B65 . . . . . . .63 D2
Holly Dr
Birmingham B27 . . . . .88 B2
Hollywood B47 . . . . .125 B7
Ryton-on-D CV8 . . . . .135 B1
Holly Farm Bsns Pk CV8 . .146 B7
Hollyfaste Rd B33 . . . . .69 B1
Hollyfast La CV7 . . . . .94 C4
Hollyfast Prim Sch CV6 . . .112 E7
Hollyfast Rd CV6 . . . . .112 E6
Hollyfield Ave B91 . . . . . . .106 E3
Hollyfield Cres B75 . . . . . . .46 E4
Hollyfield Ct B75 . . . . .46 E5
Hollyfield Dr
Barnt Green B45 . . . . .122 A1
Sutton Coldfield B75 . . . . .46 E5
Hollyfield Prim Sch B75 . .46 F5
Hollyfield Rd S B76 . . . . . . .46 F4
Hollyfield Rd B75 . . . . .46 E5
Holly Gr 4 B29 . . . . .85 F2
Holly Grange B64 . . . . .64 D7
Holly Gr
Birmingham,Bournville
B30 . . . . .103 F8
Birmingham,Lozells B19 . .66 B8
Bromsgrove B61 . . . . .136 F3
Coventry CV4 . . . . .112 B2
Stourbridge DY8 . . . . .80 F5
Wolverhampton WV3 . . . . .38 F7
Holly Hall Maths &
Computing Coll DY1 . . . .61 F8
Holly Hall Rd DY2 . . . . .62 A7
Hollyhedge Cl
Birmingham B31 . . . . .102 D6
Walsall WS2 . . . . .28 C2
Hollyhedge La WS2 . . . . . . .28 C2
Hollyhedge Prim Sch B71 .53 E8
Hollyhedge Rd B71 . . . . . . .53 E7
Holly Hill
4 Birmingham B45 . . . . .101 F1
Great Wyrley WS6 . . . . . . .13 E8
Hollyhill La WS14 . . . . .17 C5
Holly Hill Meth & CE Inf Sch
B45 . . . . .101 F2
Holly Hill Rd
Birmingham B45 . . . . .102 A2
Shenstone WS14 . . . . .17 F5
Hollyhock Rd
Birmingham B27 . . . . .88 A2
Dudley DY2 . . . . .51 F1
Hollyhurst CV12 . . . . .77 F1
Hollyhurst Dr DY6 . . . . .60 E3
Hollyhurst Farm Cvn Site
B62 . . . . .101 B6
Hollyhurst Gr
Birmingham B26 . . . . .88 E6
Solihull B90 . . . . .126 B8
Hollyhurst Rd B73 . . . . .45 B3
Hollyhurst B46 . . . . .59 C2
Holly La
Aldridge WS9 . . . . .30 F8
Balsall Common CV7 . . . .130 B3

Holly La continued
Birmingham,Erdington B24 . .57 C4
Birmingham,Marston Green
B37 . . . . .89 F8
Brownhills WS9 . . . . .16 A4
Great Wyrley WS6 . . . . . . .13 F8
Huntington WS12 . . . . .1 C7
Portway B48 . . . . .140 F5
Smethwick B66 . . . . .64 E6
Sutton Coldfield B74 . . . . .32 A3
Wishaw B76 . . . . .47 D4
Holly Lodge High Sch Coll of
Science B67 . . . . .64 D6
Holly Lodge Wlk B37 . . . . . .69 F2
Holly Marie Ct CV5 . . . . . .112 F1
Hollymoor Way
Birmingham B31 . . . . .102 B1
Birmingham B31 . . . . .102 D1
Holly Mount 7 B15 . . . . . . .65 D1
Hollymount B62 . . . . .84 A7
Hollyoak Croft B31 . . . . . . .123 B8
Hollyoake Cl B68 . . . . .64 A2
Hollyoak Gr B91 . . . . .107 A1
Hollyoak Rd B74 . . . . .44 F6
Hollyoak St B71 . . . . .53 D4
Hollyoak Way WS11 . . . . . .1 F1
Holly Park Dr B24 . . . . .57 C2
Holly Park Ind Est B24 . . . .57 C2
Hollypiece Ho B27 . . . . .88 A2
Holly Pl B29 . . . . .86 B2
Holly Rd
Birmingham B68 . . . . .84 D4
Birmingham,Edgbaston B16 .65 D1
Birmingham,Handsworth
B20 . . . . .66 A8
Birmingham,King's Norton
B30 . . . . .104 A4
Dorridge B93 . . . . .127 D3
Dudley DY1 . . . . .51 A3
Rowley Regis B65 . . . . . . .63 B1
Wednesbury WS10 . . . . . .41 F5
West Bromwich B71 . . . . . .53 E8
Holly St
Cannock WS12 . . . . .1 F6
Dudley DY1 . . . . .61 E6
Hollystitches Rd CV10 . . . .72 E6
Holly St
Royal Leamington Spa
CV32 . . . . .157 B1
Smethwick B67 . . . . .64 F5
Holly View WV11 . . . . .13 A3
Hollywell Rd
Birmingham B26 . . . . .89 B6
Dorridge B93 . . . . .128 A5
Hollywell St WV14 . . . . . . .40 A1
Holly Wlk
Baginton CV8 . . . . .133 E2
Nuneaton CV11 . . . . .73 F2
Royal Leamington Spa
CV32 . . . . .157 A1
Holly Wood B43 . . . . .44 A1
Hollywood By-Pass
Birmingham B47 . . . . .104 F1
Hollywood B38,B47 . . . . .124 E6
Hollywood Croft B42 . . . . . .54 F8
Hollywood Gdns B47 . . . . .125 A8
Hollywood La B47 . . . . . . .125 B7
Hollywood Motor Pk
B47 . . . . .125 A8
Hollywood Prim Sch
B14 . . . . .105 A1
Hollywood Rd B14 . . . . . . .125 A8
Holman Cl WV13 . . . . .26 E2
Holman Rd WV13 . . . . .26 E2
Holman St DY11 . . . . .116 C5
Holman Way
Nuneaton CV11 . . . . .73 D3
Willenhall WV13 . . . . .26 E2
Holmbridge Gr WS4 . . . . . .15 D2
Holmcroft CV2 . . . . .114 F8
Holme Mill WV10 . . . . .11 D4
Holmes Ct CV8 . . . . .147 F5
Holmes Dr
Birmingham B45 . . . . .121 F6
Coventry CV5 . . . . .111 D5
Holmesfield Rd B42 . . . . . . .55 C7
Holmes La B60 . . . . .151 B1
Holmes Rd
Whitnash CV31 . . . . .162 B3
Willenhall WV13 . . . . .27 D6
Holmes The WV10 . . . . . . .11 D3
Holme Way WS4 . . . . .29 B7
Holmewood Cl CV8 . . . . . .148 B5
Holmewood Ct CV8 . . . . . .148 B5
Holmfield Rd CV2 . . . . .114 B3
Holmsdale Rd CV6 . . . . . . .113 E7
Holm View Cl WS14 . . . . . .17 F6
Holmwood Ave DY11 . . . . .116 A6
Holmwood Dr B97 . . . . . . .153 C3
Holmwood Ho B97 . . . . . . .153 C3
Holmwood Rd B10 . . . . . . .67 D1
Holroyd Ho CV4 . . . . .111 F2
Holston Cl WS12 . . . . .2 E3
Holsworth Cl B77 . . . . .21 D1
Holsworthy Cl CV11 . . . . . .73 E5
Holt & Bracebridge
Almshouses B24 . . . . . . .57 A4
Holt Cres WS11 . . . . .2 B2
Holt Ct B7 . . . . .66 F4
Holte Dr B75 . . . . .32 D2
Holte Rd
Birmingham,Aston B6 . . . .56 A1
Birmingham,Sparkhill B11 . .87 D5
Holte Sch B19 . . . . .66 D7
Holtes Wlk B6 . . . . .67 B8

Holt Farm Prim Sch B62 . .63 E1
Holt Gdns B80 . . . . .159 E2
Holt Hill B98 . . . . .154 F8
Holt Ho B61 . . . . .137 A3
Holt La B62 . . . . .100 D4
Holton Ct WV13 . . . . .27 C2
Holt Rd
Halesowen B62 . . . . .63 E1
Hinckley LE10 . . . . .75 E6
Studley B80 . . . . .159 E2
Holtshill La WS1 . . . . .28 F2
Holt St B7 . . . . .164 D4
Holt The CV32 . . . . .157 B3
Holwick B77 . . . . .36 B8
Holy Cross Ct CV2 . . . . . . .114 E4
Holy Cross Gn DY9 . . . . . . .99 E2
Holy Cross La DY9 . . . . . . .119 E8
Holy Cross RC Prim Sch
B76 . . . . .47 A3
Holy Family RC Prim Sch
Birmingham B10 . . . . .87 F7
Coventry CV6 . . . . .95 B3
Holyhead L Ctr B21 . . . . . . .65 D8
Holyhead Prim Sch WS10 .41 E3
Holyhead Rd
Birmingham B21 . . . . .65 D8
Codsall WV8 . . . . .23 E7
Coventry CV5 . . . . .112 E5
Darlaston WS10 . . . . .41 C4
Wednesbury WS10 . . . . . .41 E3
Holyhead Road Ind Est
WS10 . . . . .41 B4
Holyhead Sch B21 . . . . .65 D8
Holyhead Way B21 . . . . . . .65 D8
Holy Name RC Prim Sch
B43 . . . . .43 E1
Holyoak Cl
3 Birmingham B6 . . . . . .55 F1
Bedworth CV12 . . . . .77 F1
Holyoakes Field Fst Sch
B97 . . . . .153 D4
Holy Oaks Cl B98 . . . . .154 E2
Holyoke Gr CV31 . . . . .162 B2
Holyrood Ct CV10 . . . . .72 D5
Holyrood Gr B6 . . . . .66 E8
Holy Rosary RC Prim Sch
WV1 . . . . .26 A1
Holy Souls RC Prim Sch
B27 . . . . .88 C3
Holy Trinity CE Prim Sch
Birmingham B20 . . . . .55 C2
Brownhills WS8 . . . . .15 E6
West Bromwich B70 . . . . . .53 C1
Holy Trinity RC Prim Sch
WV14 . . . . .40 E6
Holy Trinity RC Sch B37 . . .87 C8
Holy Trinity Sch DY10 . . . .116 F6
Holy Well Cl B16 . . . . .66 A1
Holywell Cl CV4 . . . . .111 D1
Holywell La B45 . . . . .121 D7
Holywell Rise WS14 . . . . . . .9 D6
Home Cl B28 . . . . .105 F6
Homecroft Rd B26 . . . . .88 E8
Homedene Rd B31 . . . . . . .102 E5
Home Farm Cres CV31 . . . .162 B4
Home Farm
Leek Wootton CV35 . . . . .155 F6
Stoneleigh CV8 . . . . .149 A3
Homefield Rd WV8 . . . . . . .10 C3
Homelands B42 . . . . .55 B7
Homelands Park The
WV10 . . . . .11 C6
Homelea Rd B25 . . . . .88 D8
Homelodge Ho 7 WS13 . . .9 B7
Homemead Gr B45 . . . . . .121 F7
Home Meadow Ct B13 . . . .105 A5
Home Meadow Ho B27 . . . .88 A2
Home Meadow La B98 . . . .154 E6
Home Park Rd CV11 . . . . . .73 C3
Home Peal Ho B14 . . . . . . .104 E6
Homer Cl CV34 . . . . .161 E5
Homer Hill Rd B63 . . . . .82 C7
Homer Rd
Solihull B91 . . . . .107 B3
Sutton Coldfield B75 . . . . .32 D2
Homers Fold WV14 . . . . . . .40 D5
Homer St B12 . . . . .86 F5
Homerton Rd B44 . . . . .45 B1
Homestead Cl DY3 . . . . . . .50 E3
Homestead Dr B75 . . . . . . .32 C3
Homestead Rd B33 . . . . . . .69 B1
Homeward Way CV3 . . . . .115 A1
Homewood Cl B76 . . . . .46 F4
Homings Cl WS8 . . . . .15 D6
Honesome Rd B26 . . . . .68 A8
Honeyborne Rd B75 . . . . . .46 D7
Honeybourne Cl
3 Halesowen B63 . . . . . .83 A3
Coventry CV5 . . . . .112 B3
Honeybourne Rd
Birmingham B33 . . . . .89 C8
Halesowen B63 . . . . .83 C3
Honeybourne Way
Birmingham B26 . . . . .105 H8
Willenhall WV13 . . . . .26 D1
Honeychurch Cl B98 . . . . .153 F3
Honeycomb Way B98 . . . .153 D5
Honeyfield Rd CV1 . . . . . . .113 D5
Honeysuckle Ave DY6 . . . . .60 E7
Honeysuckle Cl B32 . . . . . .84 B5
Honeysuckle Dr
Coventry CV2 . . . . .96 B2
Featherstone WV10 . . . . . .12 C7
Walsall WS5 . . . . .43 A3
Honeysuckle Gr 8 B27 . . . .88 C5
Honeysuckle Way WS6 . . . .5 B4

Honeytree Cl DY6 . . . . .60 F3
Honiley Ct CV2 . . . . .96 D1
Honiley Dr B73 . . . . .45 C2
Honiley Rd
Birmingham B33 . . . . .69 A2
Honiley CV8 . . . . .146 B6
Meer End CV8 . . . . .130 A1
Honiley Way CV2 . . . . .96 D1
Honister Cl DY5 . . . . .61 F1
Honiton Cl B31 . . . . .102 E4
Honiton Cres B31 . . . . .102 E4
Honiton Rd CV2 . . . . .114 C5
Honiton Wlk 7 B66 . . . . . . .65 B5
Honington Cl 2 B29 . . . . . . .84 F1
Honor Ave WV4 . . . . .39 C5
Hoobrook Ent Ctr DY10 . . .116 E2
Hoobrook Ind Est DY10 . . .116 E2
Hood Gr B30 . . . . .103 D4
Hood St CV1 . . . . .113 E3
Hoo Farm Ind Est DY10 . .116 F1
Hook Dr B74 . . . . .31 F4
Hook La WS14 . . . . .17 C2
Hoopers La B96 . . . . .158 E1
Hooper St B18 . . . . .65 F4
Hoo Rd DY10 . . . . .116 E4
Hoosen Cl B62 . . . . .84 A6
Hope Aldridge Bsns Ctr
CV10 . . . . .73 C6
Hope Cl CV7 . . . . .95 A7
Hopedale Cl CV2 . . . . .114 E3
Hopedale Rd B32 . . . . .84 C5
Hope Pl 11 B29 . . . . .85 F2
Hope Rd DY4 . . . . .52 C6
Hope St
Birmingham B5 . . . . .86 E8
Coventry CV1 . . . . .113 E2
Dudley DY2 . . . . .62 C8
Halesowen B62 . . . . .83 D8
Stourbridge DY8 . . . . .81 A5
Walsall WS1 . . . . .42 E8
West Bromwich B70 . . . . . .53 E2
Hope Terr DY2 . . . . .62 C5
Hopgardens Ave B60 . . . . .137 B2
Hopkins Ct 4 WS13 . . . . . . .42 A3
Hopkins Dr B71 . . . . .53 E7
Hopkins Rd CV6 . . . . .113 A4
Hopkins St DY4 . . . . .52 A2
Hopleys Cl B77 . . . . .21 E4
Hopstone Gdns WV4 . . . . . .38 F4
Hopstone Rd B29 . . . . .85 A1
Hopton Cl
Coventry CV4 . . . . .112 A4
Perton WV6 . . . . .23 F3
Wednesbury DY4 . . . . .41 C2
Hopton Cres WV11 . . . . . . .26 E6
Hopton Crofts CV32 . . . . . .156 C2
Hopton Dr DY10 . . . . .116 E1
Hopton Gdns DY1 . . . . .51 A3
Hopton Gr B13 . . . . .105 C5
Hopton Mdw WS12 . . . . . . .2 C1
Hopwas Gr B37 . . . . .69 F5
Hopwas Hill B78 . . . . .20 A6
Hopwood Cl B63 . . . . .83 A2
Hopwood Gr B31 . . . . .122 E6
Hopyard Cl DY3 . . . . .50 B3
Hopyard Gdns WV14 . . . . . .40 B3
Hopyard La
Dudley DY3 . . . . .50 B3
Redditch B98 . . . . .154 D4
Hopyard Rd WS2 . . . . .27 C2
Horace Partridge Rd
WS10 . . . . .41 A5
Horace St WV14 . . . . .51 A8
Horatio Dr B13 . . . . .86 F4
Hordern Cl WV6 . . . . .24 F5
Hordern Cres DY5 . . . . .81 D8
Hordern Gr WV6 . . . . .24 F5
Hordern Rd WV6 . . . . .24 F5
Horeston Grange Sh Ctr
CV11 . . . . .74 A5
Hornbeam Cl B29 . . . . .103 B7
Hornbeam Dr CV4 . . . . . . .111 D1
Hornbeam Gr CV31 . . . . . .162 C5
Hornbeam B77 . . . . .22 A4
Hornbeam Wlk WV3 . . . . . .25 A1
Hornbrook Gr B92 . . . . . . .106 C7
Hornby Gr B14 . . . . .105 A3
Hornby Rd WV4 . . . . .39 C5
Hornchurch Close Ind Est
CV1 . . . . .165 B1
Horndean Cl CV6 . . . . .165 B1
Horndean Cl CV6 . . . . .113 E8
Horner Way B62 . . . . .63 C1
Horne Way B34 . . . . .69 E5
Horning Dr WV14 . . . . .40 C3
Horninghold Cl CV3 . . . . . .134 E8
Hornsey Cl CV2 . . . . .114 E7
Hornsey Gr B44 . . . . .45 A2
Hornsey Rd B44 . . . . .45 A2
Hornton Cl B74 . . . . .31 D5
Horrell Rd
Birmingham B26 . . . . .89 B7
Solihull B90 . . . . .105 F2
Horsecroft Dr B71 . . . . .54 A8
Horse Fair
Birmingham B1 . . . . .164 B1
Kidderminster DY10 . . . . .116 E6
Horsecroft B77 . . . .
Horse The 3 LE10 . . . . .75 D8
Horsehills Dr WV3 . . . . .24 E2
Horselea Croft B8 . . . . .68 C4
Horseley Fields WV1 . . . . . .163 D3
Horseley Heath DY4 . . . . . .52 C5
Horseley Rd
Tipton DY4 . . . . .52 C5

Horseley Rd *continued*
Tipton DY4 . . . . .52 C6
Horsepool LE10 . . . . .76 A5
Horsepool Hollow CV31 . 162 C5
Horseshoe CI **2** WS2 . . . .42 B7
Horseshoe Dr WS12 . . . . .2 F4
Horse Shoe Rd CV4 . . . . . . .96 A4
Horse Shoes La B26 . . . . . .89 B5
Horseshoe The B68 . . . . . . .64 C2
Horseshoe Wlk **6** DY4 . .51 E5
Horsfall Rd B75 . . . . .47 A5
Horsford Rd CV3 . . . . .133 C6
Horsham Ave DY8 . . . . .60 C3
Horsley La WS14 . . . . .17 D8
Horsley Rd
Birmingham B43 . . . . .44 D4
Sutton Coldfield B74 . . . . . .31 B2
Horton CI
3 Cannock WS11 . . . . .1 F4
Bedworth CV7 . . . . .95 F7
Darlaston WS10 . . . . .41 D7
Sedgley DY3 . . . . .50 C8
Horton Gr B90 . . . . .127 A5
Horton Pl WV10 . . . . .41 D7
Horton Sq B12 . . . . .86 E7
Horton St
Darlaston WS10 . . . . .41 D7
Tipton DY4 . . . . .52 D5
West Bromwich B70 . . . . . .53 C2
Hosiery St CV12 . . . . .78 C2
Hospital Dr B15 . . . . .85 E4
Hospital La
Bedworth CV12 . . . . .77 B1
Cheslyn Hay WS6 . . . . .4 B2
Dudley WV14 . . . . .51 B7
Hospital Rd WS7 . . . . .7 B8
Hospital St
Birmingham B19 . . . . .164 B4
Birmingham,Newtown B19 . .66 D6
Birmingham,Stockland Green
B23 . . . . .56 E4
Tamworth B79 . . . . .21 B5
Walsall WS2 . . . . .28 D4
Wolverhampton WV2 . . . . .163 C2
Hossil La
Belbroughton DY9 . . . . . . .119 C8
Clent DY9 . . . . .99 D1
Hotchkiss Way CV3 . . . . . .135 A4
Hotel Bldgs WS14 . . . . .8 A2
Hothersall Dr B73 . . . . .56 F8
Hothorpe CI CV3 . . . . .114 F1
Hotspur Rd B44 . . . . .44 F1
Hough Pl WS2 . . . . .42 B7
Hough Rd
Birmingham B14 . . . . .104 D6
Walsall WS2 . . . . .42 A7
Houghton Ct B28 . . . . .105 D4
Houghton St
Oldbury B69 . . . . .63 F6
West Bromwich B70 . . . . . .64 D8
Houlbrooke Ho **1** WS14 . . .9 C8
Houldey Rd B31 . . . . .103 B1
Houldsworth Cres CV6 . . .95 C4
Houliston CI WS10 . . . . .42 B5
Houndsfield CI B47 . . . . . .125 C6
Houndsfield Farm B47 . . .125 B5
Houndsfield Gr B47 . . . . . .125 B5
Houndsfield La B47 . . . . . .125 C6
Housman Rd
Housman CI B60 . . . . .150 E8
Housman Pk B60 . . . . .137 A3
Housman Wlk DY10 . . . . . .117 C6
Houting B77 . . . . .35 D5
Houx The DY9 . . . . .80 E8
Hove Ave CV5 . . . . .111 E4
Hovelands CI CV2 . . . . . . .114 C8
Hove Rd B27 . . . . .88 C1
Hoveton CI B98 . . . . .154 B2
Howard Ave B61 . . . . .136 E3
Howard CI CV5 . . . . .111 E4
Howard Cres WS12 . . . . .2 C7
Howard Ct B16 . . . . .65 E1
Howard Rd
Bilston WV14 . . . . .40 F3
Birmingham,Handsworth
B20 . . . . .55 B2
Birmingham,King's Heath
B14 . . . . .104 E7
Birmingham,Newtown B43 . .54 C8
Birmingham,South Yardley
B25 . . . . .88 C2
Howard Rd E B13 . . . . . . .104 F7
Howard St
Nuneaton CV10 . . . . .73 A3
Redditch B98 . . . . .159 C8
Solihull B92 . . . . .88 E3
Wednesfield WV11 . . . . .26 F8
Howard St
Birmingham B19 . . . . .164 B4
Coventry CV1 . . . . .165 C4
Howard Street Ind Est
B70 . . . . .52 F8
Howard St
Tipton DY4 . . . . .52 B5
West Bromwich B70 . . . . . .52 F7
Wolverhampton WV2 . . . . .163 C1
Howarth Way B6 . . . . .67 A7
Howat Rd CV7 . . . . .94 F7
Howcotte Gn CV4 . . . . .131 E8
Howden Pl B33 . . . . .69 C5
Howdle's La WS8 . . . . .6 F2
Howe Cres WV12 . . . . .27 C6
Howell Rd WV2 . . . . .39 E7
Howells CI CV12 . . . . .77 D1

Howes Com Prim Sch
CV3 . . . . .133 E5
Howes Croft B35 . . . . .58 A2
Howes La CV3 . . . . .133 D3
Howe St B4 . . . . .66 F3
Howfield Ct B16 . . . . .65 C1
Howford Gr B7 . . . . .67 B4
Howland CI WV9 . . . . .10 F2
Howlette Rd CV4 . . . . .111 E2
Howley Ave B44 . . . . .44 E1
Howley Grange Prim Sch
B62 . . . . .83 F5
Howley Grange Rd B62 . .84 A4
Howl Pl DY4 . . . . .51 F5
Hoylake CI
Nuneaton CV11 . . . . .74 B1
Walsall WS3 . . . . .14 B4
Hoylake Dr B69 . . . . .63 A7
Hoylake Rd WV6 . . . . .23 D5
Hoyland Way B30 . . . . . . .103 E8
HRS Bsns Pk B33 . . . . .69 C1
Huband CI B98 . . . . .154 A5
Hubert Croft B29 . . . . .85 F2
Hubert Rd B29 . . . . .85 F2
Hubert St B6 . . . . .66 F5
Hucker CI WS2 . . . . .42 A7
Hucker Rd WS2 . . . . .42 A7
Huddesford Dr CV7 . . . . . .130 C8
Huddisdon CI **5** CV34 . . .155 F1
Huddlestone CI WV10 . . . . .12 B6
Huddleston Way B29 . . . . . .85 C1
Huddocks View WS3 . . . . . .14 F5
Hudson Ave B46 . . . . .70 F6
Hudson CI WS11 . . . . .2 B2
Hudson Dr WS7 . . . . .7 C6
Hudson Gr WV6 . . . . .23 E5
Hudson Rd
Birmingham B20 . . . . .55 A4
Tipton DY4 . . . . .52 C4
Hudson's Dr B30 . . . . .104 A4
Hudswell Dr DY5 . . . . .81 D8
Huggins CI CV7 . . . . .130 C7
Hughes Ave WV3 . . . . .38 F8
Hughes CI
Warwick CV34 . . . . .155 D2
Whitnash CV31 . . . . .162 A2
Hughes Pl WV14 . . . . .40 D7
Hughes Rd
Bilston WV14 . . . . .40 D7
Darlaston WS10 . . . . .41 A5
Hughes The CV34 . . . . .160 E6
Hugh Gaitskill Ct WV14 . .40 C8
Hugh Porter Way WV6 . . .24 F6
Hugh Rd
Birmingham B10 . . . . .67 E1
Coventry CV3 . . . . .114 A2
Smethwick B67 . . . . .64 E5
Hugh Villas B10 . . . . .67 E1
Huins CI B98 . . . . .154 A4
Hulbert Dr DY2 . . . . .62 B6
Hulbert Ind Est DY2 . . . . . .62 B6
Hulland Pl DY5 . . . . .61 C3
Hullbrook Rd B13 . . . . . . .105 C6
Hulme CI CV3 . . . . .115 B1
Humara Ghar **9** WS1 . . . .42 E8
Humber Ave
Coventry CV1 . . . . .113 F1
Sutton Coldfield B76 . . . . . .58 A7
Humber Gdns B63 . . . . .82 C5
Humber Gr B36 . . . . .58 F1
Humber Ho DY1 . . . . .61 D8
Humber Rd
Coventry CV3 . . . . .134 A8
Wolverhampton WV3 . . . . . .25 A1
Humberstone Rd
4 Coventry CV6 . . . . .113 A5
Sutton Coldfield B24 . . . . . .57 E4
Humber Twr **2** B7 . . . . . .67 A4
Hume St
Kidderminster DY11 . . . . .116 C5
Smethwick B66 . . . . .65 B4
Humpage Rd B9 . . . . .67 E2
Humphrey Ave B60 . . . . . .150 F7
Humphrey Burton's Rd
CV3 . . . . .133 C8
Humphrey-Davy Rd CV12 . .95 D8
Humphrey Middlemore Dr
B17 . . . . .85 D4
Humphrey St DY3 . . . . .50 D3
Humphries Cres WV14 . . . .40 F2
Humphries Dr DY10 . . . . . .116 F2
Humphries Ho WS8 . . . . . . .15 F7
Humphries Rd WV10 . . . . . .25 D6
Humphris St CV34 . . . . . . .161 B8
Hundred Acre Rd B74 . . . .44 F7
Hungary CI DY9 . . . . .81 C5
Hungary Hill DY9 . . . . .81 C5
Hungerfield Rd B36 . . . . . . .58 C1
Hungerford Rd DY8 . . . . . . .80 E2
Hungry La WS14 . . . . .18 F5
Hunningham Gr **6** B91 .127 B8
Hunnington CI B32 . . . . . . .84 A1
Hunnington Cres B63 . . . . .83 B2
Hunscote CI B90 . . . . .105 F1
Hunscote Ho B90 . . . . .105 F1
Hunslet CI B32 . . . . .84 F4
Hunslet Rd
Birmingham B32 . . . . .84 F4
Burntwood WS7 . . . . .7 B8
Hunstanton Ave B17 . . . . . .84 F6
Hunstanton CI DY5 . . . . .81 C7
Hunt End Cl B97 . . . . .158 C5
Hunt End La B97 . . . . .158 C5
Hunter Ave WS7 . . . . .7 B7
Hunter CI WS14 . . . . .9 D6
Hunter Cres WS3 . . . . .28 F7
Hunter Ct B5 . . . . .86 D5

Hunter Rd WS11 . . . . .4 E8
Hunters CI
Bilston WV14 . . . . .41 A7
Coventry CV3 . . . . .115 A2
Hunters Hill Sch B60 . . . .137 F6
Hunters Rd B19 . . . . .66 B7
Hunter's Ride DY7 . . . . .60 B2
Hunters Rise B63 . . . . .82 D1
Hunter St WV6 . . . . .25 A4
Hunters Vale B19 . . . . .66 C6
Hunters Wlk B23 . . . . .56 E8
Hunter Terr CV5 . . . . .132 D8
Huntington CI
Redditch B98 . . . . .154 F2
Tamworth B78 . . . . .20 F2
Huntington Rd
Coventry CV5 . . . . .133 A8
West Bromwich B71 . . . . . .53 B7
Huntington Way CV10 . . . .72 E3
Huntingtree Rd B63 . . . . . .56 B6
Huntington Ind Est WS12 . .1 B6
Huntington Prim Sch
WS12 . . . . .1 C8
Huntington Rd WV12 . . . . .27 D8
Huntington Terrace Rd
WS11 . . . . .1 F4
Huntingtree Prim Sch
B63 . . . . .82 E3
Huntingtree Rd B63 . . . . . .82 E3
Huntlands Rd B63 . . . . .82 F2
Huntley Dr B91 . . . . .107 B2
Huntly Rd B16 . . . . .66 A1
Hunton CI **2** B23 . . . . . . .56 E2
Hunton Hill B23 . . . . .56 E3
Hunton Rd B23 . . . . .56 E3
Hunt Paddocks CV8 . . . . .147 E1
Hunt's La WV12 . . . . .27 D6
Huntsman CI WV14 . . . . . . .40 D2
Huntsmans Gate WS7 . . . . .7 B8
Huntsmans Rise WS12 . . . . .1 C8
Hunts Mill Dr DY5 . . . . .50 C1
Hunts Rd B30 . . . . .104 B7
Hunt Terr CV4 . . . . .132 B7
Hurcott CI DY10 . . . . .117 A8
Hurcott La DY10 . . . . .117 C8
Hurcott Rd DY10 . . . . .117 B8
Hurdis Rd B90 . . . . .106 A2
Hurdlow Ave B18 . . . . .66 A5
Hurlbutt Rd CV34 . . . . .161 C4
Hurley CI
Royal Leamington Spa
CV32 . . . . .157 A2
Sutton Coldfield B72 . . . . . .46 C2
Walsall WS5 . . . . .43 D6
Hurley Gr B37 . . . . .69 F5
Hurleys Fold DY2 . . . . .62 C5
Hurlingham Rd B44 . . . . . . .45 A1
Hurn Way CV6 . . . . .96 B4
Huron CI WS11 . . . . .2 B2
Hurricane Pk B24 . . . . .68 A8
Hurricane Way B35 . . . . . . .58 A2
Hursey Dr B77 . . . . .52 A6
Hurstbourne Cres WV1 . . .26 B1
Hurst Bsns Pk DY6 . . . . . . .62 A4
Hurst CI B36 . . . . .69 E7
Hurstcroft Rd B33 . . . . .69 B3
Hurst Ct DY9 . . . . .81 F5
Hurst Green Prim Sch
B62 . . . . .83 E8
Hurst Green Rd
Bentley Heath B93 . . . . . .127 F4
Halesowen B62 . . . . .83 F8
Minworth B76 . . . . .58 D6
Hurst Hill CI WV14 . . . . . . .51 A8
Hurst Hill Prim Sch WV14 .51 A8
Hurst La
Birmingham B34 . . . . .69 E6
Brierley Hill DY5 . . . . .61 F3
Hurst La N B36 . . . . .69 F7
Hurst La DY4 . . . . .51 D6
Hurst Rd
Bedworth CV12 . . . . .78 B3
Coventry CV6 . . . . .96 A4
Dudley WV14 . . . . .40 A1
Hinckley LE10 . . . . .75 D8
Sedgley WV14 . . . . .39 F1
Smethwick B67 . . . . .64 D2
Hurst St B5 . . . . .164 C1
Hurst The
Birmingham B13 . . . . .105 D7
Hollywood B47 . . . . .125 A6
Hurstway The B23 . . . . .56 C8
Hurst Wlk CV6 . . . . .96 A4
Hurstwood Rd B23 . . . . .56 C8
Huskison CI B69 . . . . .52 B1
Huskisson St CV10 . . . . .25 C6
Hussey Rd
Brownhills WS8 . . . . .15 E8
Norton Canes WS11 . . . . . . .5 F7
Husum Way DY10 . . . . .117 C2
Hutchings La B90 . . . . .126 B5
Hut Hill La WS6 . . . . .5 A4
Hutton Ave B8 . . . . .67 D5
Hutton Rd
Birmingham,Handsworth
B20 . . . . .55 C1
Birmingham,Saltley B8 . . . .67 D5
Huxbey Dr B92 . . . . .107 F8
Huxley CI WV9 . . . . .11 A3
Hyacinth CI **9** WS5 . . . . .43 A3
Hyacinth Way LE10 . . . . . . .75 D5
Hyatt Sq DY5 . . . . .81 C7
Hyatts Wlk B65 . . . . .62 F5
Hyde CI B60 . . . . .137 B2
Hyde Pl CV32 . . . . .161 E8
Hyde Rd
Coventry CV2 . . . . .114 E4
Kenilworth CV8 . . . . .148 A5

Hyde Rd *continued*
Wednesfield WV11 . . . . . . .26 E6
Hydes La LE10 . . . . .74 E4
Hydes Rd
Wednesbury WS10 . . . . . . .42 B2
West Bromwich B71 . . . . . .42 C1
Hydesville Tower Sch
WS1 . . . . .29 A2
Hyde The DY9 . . . . .81 D2
Hyett Way WV14 . . . . .41 B2
Hylda Rd B20 . . . . .55 B1
Hylstone Cres WV11 . . . . . .26 D6
Hylton St B18 . . . . .66 C5
Hypericum Gdns CV2 . . . .114 C6
Hyperion Dr WV4 . . . . .39 A3
Hyperion Rd
Stourbridge DY7 . . . . .80 C7
Sutton Coldfield B36 . . . . . .57 F1
Hyron Hall Rd B27 . . . . .88 C2
Hyssop CI
Birmingham B7 . . . . .67 A5
Cannock WS11 . . . . .2 B3
Hytall Rd B90 . . . . .105 C2
Hythe Gr B25 . . . . .88 D8

I

Ibberton Rd B14 . . . . .105 B3
Ibex CI CV3 . . . . .114 F1
Ibis CI DY10 . . . . .117 B3
Ibis Gdns DY6 . . . . .61 A6
Ibstock CI B98 . . . . .154 E4
Ibstock Dr DY8 . . . . .81 A4
Ibstock Ho B98 . . . . .154 E4
Ibstock Rd CV6 . . . . .96 A5
Icknield CI B74 . . . . .31 A1
Icknield Fst Sch B98 . . . . .154 D1
Icknield Port Rd B16 . . . . .65 F3
Icknield Sq B16 . . . . .66 A3
Icknield St
Alvechurch B38 . . . . .124 B2
Beoley B48,B98 . . . . .140 C2
Birmingham B18 . . . . .66 B4
Redditch,Church Hill B98 . .154 C2
Redditch,Ipsley B98 . . . . . .154 D2
Icknield Street Dr B98 . . .159 D7
Icknield St B48 . . . . .140 B6
Ida Rd
Walsall WS2 . . . . .28 C1
West Bromwich B70 . . . . . .53 D1
Idbury Rd B44 . . . . .56 A7
Ideal Bldgs **7** DY11 . . . .116 D6
Ideal Wks DY9 . . . . .82 A6
Iden Rd CV1 . . . . .113 E4
Idmiston Croft B14 . . . . . .104 F2
Idonia Rd WV6 . . . . .23 F5
Ilam Pk CV8 . . . . .148 C5
Ilex CI CV34 . . . . .161 A7
Ilford CI CV12 . . . . .78 A3
Ilford Ct CV3 . . . . .135 D7
Ilford Dr CV3 . . . . .133 B5
Ilford Rd B23 . . . . .56 D6
Ilfracombe Gr CV3 . . . . . . .133 A5
Iliffe Ho LE10 . . . . .75 B7
Iliffe Way B17 . . . . .85 D4
Ilkley Gr B37 . . . . .69 F2
Illeybrook Sq B32 . . . . .84 D2
Illey CI B31 . . . . .102 C1
Illey La
Birmingham B32 . . . . .102 A7
Halesowen B62 . . . . .101 E8
Illshaw Heath Rd B90,
B94 . . . . .126 D2
Illshaw WV1 . . . . .11 A3
Ilmington CI
Coventry CV3 . . . . .133 B5
Redditch B98 . . . . .154 D1
Ilmington Dr B73 . . . . .45 C3
Ilmington Rd B29 . . . . .84 F1
Ilminster CI LE10 . . . . .76 B7
Ilsham Gr B31 . . . . .122 F6
Ilsley Rd B23 . . . . .56 E4
Image Bsns Pk WS11 . . . . . .2 B3
I-Max Bsns Pk B11 . . . . . . .88 A6
Imber Rd DY10 . . . . .117 A1
Imex Auto Ctr DY4 . . . . . . .52 A3
Imex Bsns Ctr
Bilston WV14 . . . . .40 E4
Redditch B98 . . . . .154 E4
Wolverhampton WV13 . . . .26 C3
Imex Bsns Pk
Birmingham,Bordesley Green
B9 .67 D2
Birmingham,Stechford B33 . .68 E4
Tipton DY4 . . . . .52 A4
Wolverhampton WV2 . . . . . .39 C7
Imex Ho WV2 . . . . .39 E7
Imogen Gdns CV34 . . . . . .161 E3
Imperial Ave DY10 . . . . . . .116 F8
Imperial Ct DY10 . . . . .116 F8
Imperial Gr DY10 . . . . .116 F8
Imperial Rd B9 . . . . .67 E1
Imperial Rise B46 . . . . .59 E2
Impey Rd B31 . . . . .102 F1
Impsley CI B36 . . . . .69 F8
Impsley CI B36 . . . . .69 F8
Inca CI CV3 . . . . .134 F8
Ince Rd WS10 . . . . .41 C7
Incestre Dr B43 . . . . .43 D1
Inchbrook Rd CV8 . . . . . . .148 C7
Inchcape Ave B20 . . . . .55 A3
Inchford Ave CV34 . . . . . . .155 E2
Inchford CI CV11 . . . . .73 F1
Inchford Rd B92 . . . . .107 F2
Inchlaggan Rd WV10 . . . . .25 F6
Infantry Pl B75 . . . . .47 A6
Ingatestone Dr DY8 . . . . . . .60 C3

Inge St B5 . . . . .164 C1
Ingestre CI
Cannock WS11 . . . . .2 B1
Walsall WS3 . . . . .13 F3
Ingestre Dr B43 . . . . .43 C1
Ingestre Ho WV6 . . . . .24 E5
Ingestre Rd
Birmingham B28 . . . . .106 A7
Wolverhampton WV10 . . . .11 C1
Ingeva Dr B45 . . . . .122 A1
Ingham Way B17 . . . . .85 A8
Ingleby Gdns WV6 . . . . .24 E5
Ingle Ct CV31 . . . . .161 E7
Ingledew CI WS2 . . . . .27 D3
Inglefield Rd B33 . . . . .68 F3
Inglemere Gr B29 . . . . . . .102 F7
Inglenook Dr B20 . . . . .55 B2
Ingleside Villas **3** B11 . . .87 C5
Ingleton CI CV11 . . . . .74 A2
Ingleton Rd B8 . . . . .68 A7
Inglewood Ave WV3 . . . . . .38 F8
Inglewood CI
Kingswinford DY6 . . . . .60 D5
Royal Leamington Spa
CV32 . . . . .157 A3
Inglewood Gr B74 . . . . .30 F2
Inglewood Rd B11 . . . . .87 C5
Ingoldsby Rd **17** B13 . . . . .87 B2
Ingoldsby Rd B31 . . . . .103 C3
Ingram Gr B27 . . . . .88 A2
Ingram Pit La B77 . . . . .22 A5
Ingram Pl WS3 . . . . .14 D1
Ingram Rd
Coventry CV5 . . . . .132 D8
Walsall WS3 . . . . .14 D1
Inhedge St DY3 . . . . .50 E5
Inhedge The DY1 . . . . .51 C1
Inkberrow CI **4** B63 . . . . .82 F2
Inkberrow Rd B63 . . . . .82 F2
Inkerman Gr WV10 . . . . . . .25 F2
Inkerman Ho B19 . . . . .66 E6
Inkerman St
Birmingham B7 . . . . .67 B4
Wolverhampton WV10 . . . .25 F3
Inland Rd B24 . . . . .57 B2
Innage Cl CV31 . . . . .162 B8
Innage Rd B31 . . . . .103 B4
Innage The B47 . . . . .125 A5
Innis Rd CV5 . . . . .132 E8
Innsworth Dr B35 . . . . .58 A4
Insetton CI B98 . . . . .154 D4
Inshaw CI B33 . . . . .68 E3
Institute Rd B14 . . . . .104 F8
Instone Rd
Coventry CV6 . . . . .95 A1
Halesowen B63 . . . . .83 A3
Instow CI WV12 . . . . .27 B8
Insull Ave B14 . . . . .105 B1
Intended St B63 . . . . .82 C7
International Ho B43 . . . . . .54 F6
Intersection Ho B70 . . . . . .53 F1
Intown Row WV1 . . . . .28 F2
Intown WS1 . . . . .28 F2
Int Sch & Com Coll The
B33 . . . . .69 D3
Inveraray CI CV8 . . . . .148 C4
Inverclyde Rd B20 . . . . .55 A3
Inverness CI CV5 . . . . .112 A4
Inverness Ho WV1 . . . . .163 B4
Inverness Rd B31 . . . . .102 F3
Invicta Rd CV3 . . . . .134 F8
Inworth WV9 . . . . .11 B3
Io Ctr The B98 . . . . .159 C8
Ipsley Alders Marsh Nature
Reserve* B98 . . . . .154 F4
Ipsley CE Mid Sch B98 . . .154 E3
Ipsley Church La B98 . . . .154 C1
Ipsley Gr B23 . . . . .56 A5
Ipsley La B98 . . . . .154 D2
Ipsley St B98 . . . . .153 E3
Ipstones Ave B33 . . . . .68 F4
Ipswich Cres B42 . . . . .55 B7
Ipswich Wlk B37 . . . . .70 B2
Ireland Green Rd B70 . . . . .53 B2
Ireton CI CV4 . . . . .111 C1
Ireton Rd
Birmingham B20 . . . . .55 A4
Wolverhampton WV10 . . . .11 E3
Iris CI
Birmingham B29 . . . . .103 B8
Dudley DY2 . . . . .51 F1
Hinckley LE10 . . . . .75 E5
Tamworth B79 . . . . .21 C6
Iris Dr B14 . . . . .104 D3
Irnham Rd B74 . . . . .32 B1
Ironbridge Way CV6 . . . . . .96 B6
Iron Bridge Wlk DY9 . . . . . .99 B8
Ironmonger Row CV1 . . . .165 B3
Ironstone Rd WS7 . . . . .6 E8
Iron Way B60 . . . . .151 B7
Irvan Ave B70 . . . . .52 F5
Irvine CI WS3 . . . . .28 B7
Irvine Rd WS3 . . . . .28 B7
Irving CI DY3 . . . . .50 A4
Irving Rd
Coventry CV1 . . . . .113 E2
Solihull B92 . . . . .89 E3
Wednesbury DY4 . . . . .41 A1
Irving St B1 . . . . .66 D1
Irwell B77 . . . . .21 E2
Irwin Ave B45 . . . . .122 C7
Isaac Walton Pl B70 . . . . . .52 E7
Isambard Dr CV6 . . . . .95 F5
Isbourne Way **1** B9 . . . . .67 B2
Isis CI B73 . . . . .46 B5

Isis Gr
  Birmingham B36 . . . . .69 F8
  Willenhall WV13 . . . . .27 C2
Isis Ho DY1 . . . . .61 D8
Island Cl LE10 . . . . .71 E2
Island Dr DY10 . . . . .116 E4
Island The B78 . . . . .20 C1
Islington Cres CV9 . . . . .36 C1
Islington Gates B3 . . . . .164 A3
Islington B63 . . . . .83 A4
Islington Row B15 . . . . .66 B1
Islington Row Middleway
  B15 .86 C8
Ismere Rd B24 . . . . .57 B2
Itchen Gr WV6 . . . . .23 E4
Ithon Gr B38 . . . . .123 E8
Ivanhoe Ave CV11 . . . . .73 E1
Ivanhoe Rd
  Birmingham B43 . . . . .44 C3
  Lichfield WS14 . . . . .9 B6
  Wolverhampton WV2 . . . . . .40 A6
Ivanhoe St DY2 . . . . .62 A7
Ivatt Cl WS4 . . . . .29 B7
Ivatt B77 . . . . .21 F2
Iverley La DY10,DY8 . . . . .98 C5
Iverley Rd B63 . . . . .83 C4
Iverley Wlk DY9 . . . . .81 C2
Ivor Rd
  Birmingham B11 . . . . .87 B4
  Coventry CV6 . . . . .95 F2
  Redditch B97 . . . . .153 D2
Ivy Ave
  3 Birmingham B12 . . . . .87 A5
  Birmingham B12 . . . . .87 A5
Ivybridge Gr B42 . . . . .55 C3
Ivybridge Rd CV3 . . . . .133 D6
Ivy Cl WS11 . . . . .4 D8
Ivy Croft WV9 . . . . .10 F3
Ivydale Ave B26 . . . . .89 C5
Ivy Farm La CV4 . . . . .132 D6
Ivyfield Rd B23 . . . . .56 B5
Ivy Gdns WS11 . . . . .6 A5
Ivy Gr
  Brownhills WS8 . . . . .16 A4
  Nuneaton CV10 . . . . .72 D6
Ivy Ho WS9 . . . . .16 A4
Ivyhouse La WV14 . . . . .51 B8
Ivyhouse Rd B38 . . . . .123 C8
Ivy House Rd B69 . . . . .63 D6
Ivyhouse Wlk 6 B77 . . . . .35 F6
Ivy La
  Birmingham B9 . . . . .67 A2
  Romsley B62 . . . . .100 D5
Ivy Lodge Cl B37 . . . . .90 A7
Ivy Rd
  Birmingham,Handsworth
    B21 . . . . .66 A7
  Birmingham,Stirchley B30 . .104 A6
  Dudley DY1 . . . . .51 A4
  Sutton Coldfield B73 . . . . . .45 F1
  Tipton DY4 . . . . .51 F7
Ivy Way B90 . . . . .126 A6
Izod St B97 . . . . .153 D4
Izons La Ind Est B70 . . . . .53 A1
Izons Lane Ind Est B70 . . . . . .53 A1
Izons La B70 . . . . .53 A1
Izons Rd B70 . . . . .53 C3

J

Jacey Rd
  Birmingham B16 . . . . .65 D2
  Solihull B90 . . . . .106 B4
Jack Cade Way CV34 . . . . . . .161 E4
Jack David Ho DY4 . . . . .52 D5
Jackdaw Cl DY3 . . . . .39 C2
Jackdaw Dr B36 . . . . .70 A8
Jacker's Rd CV2 . . . . .96 B4
Jackfield Cl B98 . . . . .154 E1
Jack Hayward Way WV14 . . .163 B4
Jacklin Dr CV3 . . . . .133 C4
Jacknell Rd LE10 . . . . .74 D8
Jack Newell Ct 3 WV14 . . . .51 C8
Jack O'Watton Bsns Pk
  B46 . . . . .59 D3
Jackson Ave B8 . . . . .67 F4
Jackson Cl
  Birmingham B11 . . . . .87 B7
  Featherstone WV10 . . . . . . .12 A6
  Keresley CV7 . . . . .95 A7
  Norton Canes WS11 . . . . .5 E4
  Oldbury B68 . . . . .64 B5
  Wednesbury DY4 . . . . .41 B1
Jackson Ct
  Brierley Hill DY5 . . . . .61 F1
  Oldbury B69 . . . . .63 F4
Jackson Dr B67 . . . . .64 D5
Jackson Gr CV8 . . . . .148 C4
Jackson Ho 9 B69 . . . . .64 A7
Jackson Rd
  Birmingham B8 . . . . .67 F4
  Coventry CV6 . . . . .95 D1
  Lichfield WS13 . . . . .3 B7
Jackson St
  Oldbury B68 . . . . .64 B4
  Stourbridge DY9 . . . . .81 E6
  Wolverhampton WV6 . . . . . .25 A4
Jackson Way B32 . . . . .84 A5
Jackwood Gn CV12 . . . . .95 C8
Jacmar Cres B67 . . . . .64 E6
Jacob Dr CV4 . . . . .132 D6
Jacobean La B93 . . . . .108 B1
Jacob's Hall La WS6 . . . . .5 B1
Jacoby Pl B5 . . . . .86 C5

Jacox Cres CV8 . . . . .148 C5
Jacquard Cl CV3 . . . . .133 D4
Jacquard Ho 3 CV1 . . . . . . .113 E4
Jade Cl CV1 . . . . .165 D4
Jade Gr WS11 . . . . .2 C2
Jaffray Cres B24 . . . . .56 F3
Jaffray Ct B23 . . . . .56 E3
Jaffray Rd B24 . . . . .56 F3
Jaguar B77 . . . . .21 E2
Jakeman Cl B98 . . . . .154 E4
Jakeman Rd B12 . . . . .86 E5
James Beattie Ho WV6 . . . . . .24 C4
James Bridge Cl WS2 . . . . . . .42 B7
James Brindley Sch
  (Parkway Ctr) B15 . . . . .86 C8
James Brindley Sch (Willow
  Ctr) B13 . . . . .86 E1
James Cl WS10 . . . . .41 F7
James Clift Ho 3 B69 . . . . . .63 D5
James Cl B63 . . . . .65 A5
Jamescroft CV3 . . . . .134 E6
James Ct
  13 Birmingham,Moseley
    B13 . . . . .87 B2
  Birmingham,King's Norton
    B38 . . . . .103 F2
  Warwick CV34 . . . . .160 F7
James Dawson Dr CV5 . . . . .111 B8
James Dee Cl DY5 . . . . .62 A1
James Diskin Ct CV11 . . . . . . .73 E2
James Eaton Cl B71 . . . . .53 C5
James Galloway Cl CV3 . . . . .134 E7
James Green Rd CV4 . . . . . . .111 F2
James Greenway WS13 . . . . . . .3 A2
James Ho
  Birmingham B19 . . . . .66 C6
  Coventry CV2 . . . . .114 C8
James Hutchens Ct WS7 . . . . .6 F5
James Lloyd Trust Flats
  B30 . . . . .103 C5
James Meml Homes The 4
  B7 .67 C7
Jameson Rd B6 . . . . .67 C8
Jameson St WV6 . . . . .25 B4
James Rd
  Birmingham,Great Barr
    B43 . . . . .54 E7
  Birmingham,Tyseley B11 . . . .87 F6
  Coleshill B46 . . . . .70 F8
  Kidderminster DY10 . . . . . .117 A8
James Samuel Pl 2 B12 . .86 F7
James Scott Rd B63 . . . . .82 A6
James St
  Bilston WV14 . . . . .40 E6
  Birmingham B3 . . . . .164 A3
  Cannock WS11 . . . . .1 F5
  Nuneaton CV11 . . . . .73 A5
  Willenhall WV13 . . . . .27 A3
James Turner St B18 . . . . . . .65 E6
James Watt Dr B19 . . . . .66 C8
James Watt Prim Sch
  B21 . . . . .65 E7
James Watt Queensway
  B4 . . . . .164 C3
James Watt St
  Birmingham B4 . . . . .164 C3
  West Bromwich B71 . . . . . . .53 B8
Jane Lane Cl WS2 . . . . .27 F3
Jane Lane Sch WS2 . . . . .27 F3
Janice Gr B14 . . . . .105 B4
Janice Ct B13 . . . . .87 C2
Janine Ave WV11 . . . . .26 E7
Jaques Cl B46 . . . . .59 B2
Jardine Cres CV4 . . . . .111 F2
Jardine Rd B6 . . . . .55 F1
Jarvis Cl LE10 . . . . .71 D4
Jarvis Cres B69 . . . . .64 A6
Jarvis Rd B23 . . . . .56 F6
Jarvis Way B24 . . . . .67 E8
JAS Ind Pk B65 . . . . .63 E4
Jasmin Croft B14 . . . . .104 E3
Jasmine Gr WV8 . . . . .11 A3
Jasmine Rd
  Bromsgrove B61 . . . . .136 F4
  Codsall WV8 . . . . .10 B3
  Coventry CV8 . . . . .134 C8
  Royal Leamington Spa
    CV32 . . . . .157 A2
Jasmine Rd
  Dudley DY2 . . . . .51 F1
  Tamworth B77 . . . . .22 A4
Jasmine Way WS10 . . . . .41 D7
Jason Cl B77 . . . . .21 D5
Jason Rd DY9 . . . . .81 F4
Javelin Ave B35 . . . . .58 B2
Javelin Way WS10 . . . . .41 D2
Jayne Cl
  Wednesfield WV11 . . . . .26 D7
  West Bromwich B71 . . . . . . .42 E1
Jay Park Cres DY10 . . . . .117 B2
Jay Rd DY6 . . . . .60 D8
Jays Ave DY4 . . . . .52 D5
Jays Cres B48 . . . . .123 B1
Jayshaw Ave B43 . . . . .54 E8
Jeal Cl B47 . . . . .124 E2
Jean Dr DY4 . . . . .52 D6
Jeavons Pl WV14 . . . . .40 C5
Jedburgh Ave WV6 . . . . .23 E4
Jedburgh Gr CV3 . . . . .133 A4
Jeddo St WV2 . . . . .163 B1
Jeffcock Rd WV3 . . . . .39 B7
Jefferies Cl LE10 . . . . .71 E2
Jefferson Cl B71 . . . . .53 B8
Jeffrey Ave WV4 . . . . .39 F5
Jeffrey Cl CV12 . . . . .79 C3
Jeffrey Rd B65 . . . . .63 E3

Jeffrey Woods Cross
  CV1 . . . . .113 F4
Jeffries Ho 11 B69 . . . . .64 A7
Jeffs Ave WV13 . . . . .163 C1
Jeliff St CV4 . . . . .111 F2
Jelleyman Cl DY11 . . . . .116 C6
Jellicoe Ho 9 DY4 . . . . .52 A8
Jellicoe Way LE10 . . . . .71 D3
Jenkins Ave CV5 . . . . .111 F4
Jenkins Cl WV14 . . . . .40 C5
Jenkinson Rd WS10 . . . . .41 D1
Jenkins St B10 . . . . .87 C8
Jenks Ave WV10 . . . . .25 E8
Jennens Rd B4 . . . . .66 F3
Jenner Cl WS2 . . . . .28 A6
Jenner Ho WS2 . . . . .27 F6
Jenner Rd WS2 . . . . .28 A6
Jenner St
  Coventry CV1 . . . . .165 C4
  Wolverhampton WV2 . . . . .163 D2
Jennifer Wlk B25 . . . . .88 E8
Jennings St B64 . . . . .62 F2
Jenny Cl WV14 . . . . .40 E1
Jennyns Ct 3 WS10 . . . . .42 A3
Jenny Walkers La WV6 . . . . . .23 D1
Jensen B77 . . . . .21 E2
Jenton Rd CV31 . . . . .162 B6
Jephcott Gr B8 . . . . .68 A4
Jephcott Ho 2 CV1 . . . . .113 E3
Jephcott Rd B8 . . . . .68 A4
Jephson Cl CV2 . . . . .96 C4
Jephson Dr B26 . . . . .88 F7
Jephson Pl 3 CV31 . . . . .162 B7
Jeremy Gr B92 . . . . .89 B3
Jeremy Rd WV4 . . . . .39 C5
Jerome Ct B74 . . . . .30 F1
Jerome Dr WS11 . . . . .6 A5
Jerome K Jerome Mus*
  WS1 . . . . .28 E1
Jerome Prim Sch WS11 . . . . . . .5 F5
Jerome Rd
  Norton Canes WS11 . . . . .6 A5
  Sutton Coldfield B72 . . . . . .46 D4
  Walsall WS2 . . . . .28 B1
Jerome Way WS7 . . . . .7 C7
Jerrard Dr B75 . . . . .46 C4
Jerrard Mews B75 . . . . .46 C5
Jerry's La
  Birmingham B23 . . . . .56 E6
  Weeford WS14 . . . . .19 B8
Jersey Cl B98 . . . . .154 E1
Jersey Croft B36 . . . . .70 B6
Jersey Rd B8 . . . . .67 D4
Jerusalem Wlk DY10 . . . . . . .116 E7
Jervis Cl DY5 . . . . .61 C7
Jervis Cres B74 . . . . .31 D3
Jervis Ct 3 WS1 . . . . .28 F2
Jervis Pk B74 . . . . .31 C4
Jervis Rd B77 . . . . .35 F5
Jervis Terr B21 . . . . .65 D8
Jervoise Dr B31 . . . . .103 B5
Jervoise Jun & Inf Sch
  B29 . . . . .85 A1
Jervoise La B71 . . . . .42 E1
Jervoise Rd B29 . . . . .85 A2
Jervoise St B70 . . . . .53 A4
Jesmond Gr B24 . . . . .57 E4
Jesmond Rd CV1 . . . . .113 F4
Jessel Rd WS2 . . . . .28 B2
Jessie Rd WS9 . . . . .16 B1
Jesson Cl WS1 . . . . .43 A7
Jesson Ct WS1 . . . . .43 A8
Jesson Rd
  Dudley DY3 . . . . .51 A6
  Sutton Coldfield B75 . . . . . . .47 A5
  Walsall WS1 . . . . .43 A8
Jesson's CE Prim Sch
  DY1 . . . . .51 B1
Jesson St B70 . . . . .53 E2
Jessop Dr B77 . . . . .21 E5
Jevons Dr 7 DY4 . . . . .52 B5
Jevons Rd B73 . . . . .45 C3
Jevon St WV14 . . . . .51 B8
Jewellery Quarter Sta
  B18 . . . . .66 B4
Jew's La CV1 . . . . .50 E4
Jiggins La B32 . . . . .84 D1
Jill Ave B43 . . . . .43 C1
Jillcot Rd B92 . . . . .89 B3
Jill La B96 . . . . .159 B2
Jim Forrest Cl 4 CV3 . . . . . .134 F8
Jinnah Cl B12 . . . . .86 F8
Jinnah Rd B98 . . . . .153 E2
Joanna Dr CV3 . . . . .133 C5
Joan of Arc Ho CV3 . . . . .133 E6
Joan's Cl CV31 . . . . .162 C6
Joan St WV2 . . . . .39 E6
Joan Ward St CV3 . . . . .133 D8
Job's La CV4 . . . . .112 A2
Jockey Field DY3 . . . . .50 E6
Jockey La WS10 . . . . .42 A4
Jodrell St CV11 . . . . .73 A3
Joe Jones Ct DY3 . . . . .39 D1
Joe O'Brien Cl CV3 . . . . .134 C6
Joe Williams Cl 7 CV3 . . . . .134 F8
Joeys La WV8 . . . . .10 C3
John Black Day Hospl
  B37 . . . . .90 C8
John Bosco Cl B71 . . . . .53 B7
John Bright Cl B19 . . . . .66 B7
John Bright St 1 B1,B2 . . . .164 B2
John Cleveland Coll LE10 . . . .71 F1
Johndory 2 B77 . . . . .35 D6
John F Kennedy Wlk 4
  DY4 . . . . .52 A8
John Fletcher Cl WS10 . . . . . .42 B4
John Grace St CV3 . . . . .133 D8

John Gulson Prim Sch
  CV1 . . . . .113 D5
John Harper St WV13 . . . . . . .27 B2
John Haynes Ct CV7 . . . . .96 A7
John Ho DY1 . . . . .61 D8
John Howell Dr DY4 . . . . .52 A5
John Kempe Way B12 . . . . . . .87 A7
John Knight Rd CV12 . . . . .78 B5
John McGuire Cres CV3 . . . . .134 E7
John Nash Sq CV8 . . . . .147 F3
John Nichols St LE10 . . . . .75 B7
John of Gaunt Ho CV3 . . . . . .133 E6
John O'Gaunt Rd CV8 . . . . . .147 E3
John Rd B62 . . . . .83 F3
John Riley Dr WV12 . . . . .27 C8
John Rous Ave CV4 . . . . .132 B7
John's Cl LE10 . . . . .75 D5
John's Cl B80 . . . . .159 C4
Johns Gr B43 . . . . .54 C8
John Shelton Com Prim Sch
  CV6 . . . . .95 D4
John Shelton Dr CV6 . . . . .95 D4
John Sinclair Ho CV1 . . . . . . .165 B4
Johns La WS10 . . . . .21 A2
John's La
  Oldbury B69 . . . . .52 C3
  Tipton DY4 . . . . .52 B4
John Smith Ho 3 B1 . . . . .66 C3
Johnson Ave WV11 . . . . .26 F7
Johnson Cl
  Birmingham,Sparkhill B11 . . .87 C5
  Birmingham,Ward End B8 . . .68 C6
  Darlaston WS10 . . . . .41 D5
  Darlaston WS10 . . . . .3 C1
  Redditch B98 . . . . .154 A5
Johnson Dr B35 . . . . .57 F3
Johnson Pl 3 WV14 . . . . .41 A7
Johnson Rd
  Bedworth CV12 . . . . .78 C3
  Birmingham B23 . . . . .57 A6
  Burntwood WS7 . . . . .6 F8
  Cannock WS11 . . . . .1 D4
  Coventry CV6 . . . . .114 A8
  Darlaston WS10 . . . . .41 D5
  Wednesbury WS10 . . . . .42 C2
  Willenhall WV12 . . . . .27 D7
Johnsons Bridge Rd B71 . . . . .53 C6
Johnsons Gr B68 . . . . .84 D8
Johnson St
  Birmingham B7 . . . . .67 C6
  Wolverhampton,Cinder Hill
    WV14 . . . . .39 F1
  Wolverhampton WV2 . . . . . .39 D7
  Wood End CV9 . . . . .36 C1
John St
  Bedworth CV12 . . . . .78 A2
  Birmingham B19 . . . . .66 D7
  Brierley Hill DY5 . . . . .61 D4
  Cannock,Chadsmoor WS11 . . .2 A4
  Cannock,Wimblebury WS12 . .2 F3
  Hinckley LE10 . . . . .71 E1
  Nuneaton,Coton CV11 . . . . .73 C2
  Nuneaton,Stockingford
    CV10 . . . . .72 E3
  Oldbury B69 . . . . .64 A7
  Royal Leamington Spa
    CV32 . . . . .161 F8
  Stourbridge DY8 . . . . .60 F2
  Tamworth B77 . . . . .21 E4
  Walsall WS2 . . . . .28 E4
  West Bromwich,Great Bridge
    B70 . . . . .52 F5
  West Bromwich,Guns Village
    B70 . . . . .53 B4
  Willenhall WV13 . . . . .27 A1
  Wolverhampton WV2 . . . . . .40 A6
John Tofts Ho CV1 . . . . .165 B4
John Wesley Way WS10 . . . . .42 A1
John Whitworth Sch B76 . . . . .46 F4
John Wooton Ho 3
  WS10 . . . . .41 D6
Joiners Croft B92 . . . . .107 E8
Joinings Bank B68 . . . . .64 B4
Jonathan Rd CV2 . . . . .114 F8
Jon Baker Ct LE10 . . . . .75 E8
Jonesfield Cres WV1 . . . . .26 D3
Jones Ho WS2 . . . . .28 D3
Jones La
  Burntwood WS7 . . . . .7 F7
  Great Wyrley WS6 . . . . .5 B1
Jones Rd
  Bedworth CV7 . . . . .78 A1
  Walsall WV12 . . . . .13 D1
  Willenhall WV12 . . . . .27 D8
  Wolverhampton WV2 . . . . . .25 C6
Jones Wood Cl B76 . . . . .58 A7
Jonfield Gdns B43 . . . . .43 F3
Jonkel Ave B77 . . . . .36 A5
Jonquil Cl B31 . . . . .122 E6
Jordan Cl
  4 Lichfield WS13 . . . . .9 A8
  Kenilworth CV8 . . . . .148 B2
  Kidderminster DY11 . . . . . .116 A6
  Sutton Coldfield B75 . . . . . . .32 B1
Jordan Leys 3 DY4 . . . . .52 B5
Jordan Pl WV14 . . . . .40 E3
Jordan Rd B75 . . . . .32 B1
Jordans Cl B97 . . . . .158 D6
Jordans The CV5 . . . . .112 C4
Jordan Way WS9 . . . . .16 B1
Jordan Well CV1 . . . . .165 C2

Joseph Cash Prim Sch
  CV6 . . . . .113 C7
Joseph Chamberlain Coll
  B12 . . . . .86 F6
Joseph Creighton Cl
  CV3 . . . . .134 E7
Joseph Dewsbury Cl WS7 . . .6 F8
Joseph Halpin Ho 3
  CV1 . . . . .165 C4
Joseph Leckie Com Tech
  Coll WS5 . . . . .42 E5
Joseph Luckman Rd CV12 .78 B4
Joseph St B63 . . . . .63 F6
Joseph Turner Prim Sch
  DY4 . . . . .52 B7
Josiah Mason Coll B23 . . . .56 C4
Josiah Rd B31 . . . . .102 D2
Jourdain Pk CV34 . . . . .161 E3
Jovian Dr LE10 . . . . .71 A1
Jowett's La B71 . . . . .53 B8
Jowett B77 . . . . .21 E2
Joyberry Dr DY8 . . . . .81 A3
Joyce Pool CV34 . . . . .160 E7
Joynson St WS10 . . . . .41 E5
Jubilee Ave
  Redditch B97 . . . . .158 D7
  West Bromwich B71 . . . . . . .53 B7
Jubilee Bldgs WS10 . . . . .41 D7
Jubilee Bsns Pk DY9 . . . . .82 A5
Jubilee Cl
  Great Wyrley WS6 . . . . .4 F2
  Stoke Prior B60 . . . . .150 C1
  Walsall WS3 . . . . .28 E6
Jubilee Cres CV6 . . . . .113 B7
Jubilee Ct
  Birmingham,Acock's Green
    B27 . . . . .88 C2
  Birmingham,Turves Green
    B31 . . . . .103 B1
Jubilee Dr N DY11 . . . . .116 B2
Jubilee Dr S DY11 . . . . .116 B2
Jubilee Gdns B23 . . . . .56 B7
Jubilee Ho B98 . . . . .153 E2
Jubilee Park Prim Sch
  DY4 . . . . .52 B8
Jubilee Rd
  Birmingham B45 . . . . .101 E2
  Darlaston WV14 . . . . .41 A4
  Tipton DY4 . . . . .52 B8
Jubilee St B71 . . . . .53 D8
Jubilee Terr
  Bedworth CV12 . . . . .78 B4
  Stoke Prior B60 . . . . .150 C1
Jubilee Trad Ctr B5 . . . . .66 E1
Judd Cl CV12 . . . . .77 F3
Judds La CV6 . . . . .95 E4
Judge Cl B69 . . . . .64 A7
Judge Rd DY5 . . . . .81 F7
Juggins La B94 . . . . .141 B7
Julia Ave B24 . . . . .57 F4
Julia Gdns B71 . . . . .53 F8
Julian Cl
  Catshill B61 . . . . .137 A8
  Coventry CV2 . . . . .114 F8
  Great Wyrley WS6 . . . . .5 A3
  Wolverhampton WV1 . . . . . .26 B2
Julian Rd WV1 . . . . .26 B2
Julie Croft WV14 . . . . .40 E1
Juliet Cl CV11 . . . . .74 A1
Juliet Dr CV34 . . . . .161 F3
Juliet Rd B62 . . . . .83 F3
Julius Dr B46 . . . . .59 F1
Junction 2 Ind Est B69 . . . . . .63 F5
Junction 6 Ind Pk B6 . . . . .56 B2
Junction Rd
  Birmingham B21 . . . . .65 C8
  Bromsgrove B61 . . . . .136 E3
  Stourbridge,Amblecote DY8 .60 E1
  Stourbridge DY8 . . . . .81 B4
  Wolverhampton WV2 . . . . . .40 B7
Junction St S B69 . . . . .64 A5
Junction St
  Coventry CV1 . . . . .165 A2
  Dudley DY2 . . . . .62 B8
  Oldbury B69 . . . . .52 E1
  Walsall WS1 . . . . .28 E2
Junction The 1 DY8 . . . . .80 E8
June Cres B77 . . . . .21 E5
June Croft B26 . . . . .89 D5
Juniper Cl
  Bedworth CV12 . . . . .77 E2
  Birmingham B27 . . . . .88 B5
  Burntwood WS7 . . . . .7 A6
  Sutton Coldfield B76 . . . . . . .46 F3
Juniper Ct DY10 . . . . .117 A4
Juniper Dr
  Coventry CV5 . . . . .111 F5
  Sutton Coldfield B76 . . . . . . .58 A7
  Walsall WS5 . . . . .43 B4
Juniper Ho B20 . . . . .55 B7
Juniper Rise B63 . . . . .82 C5
Juniper B77 . . . . .22 A4
Juno Dr CV31 . . . . .161 F5
Jurist Ho 5 LE10 . . . . .71 D1
Jury Rd DY5 . . . . .81 F7
Jury St CV34 . . . . .160 E6
Justice Cl CV31 . . . . .162 A5
Jutland Rd B13 . . . . .105 B8

K

Kanzan Rd CV2 . . . . .96 B4

Kareen Gr CV3. . . . . 135 C2
Karen Cl CV10 . . . . 72 E7
Karen Way DY5 . . . . 81 D8
Karlingford Cl CV5 . . . . 132 D8
Kate's Hill Prim Sch DY2. . 62 E8
Katherine Ho **8** B17. . . . . . 85 B5
Katherine Rd B67. . . . . 64 F2
Kathleen Ave CV12. . . . . 77 E1
Kathleen Rd
Birmingham B25 . . . . 88 C7
Sutton Coldfield B72 . . . . . . 46 C4
Katie Rd B29 . . . . 85 E1
Katmandu Rd B60 . . . . 137 C1
Katrine Ct CV10. . . . . 72 C5
Kayne Cl DY6 . . . . 60 C7
Keanscott Dr B68 . . . . 64 C4
Keasden Gr WV13. . . . . 27 C3
Keating Gdns B75. . . . . 32 A4
Keatley Ave B33 . . . . 69 E2
Keats Ave
Birmingham B10 . . . . 87 D7
Cannock WS11. . . . . 1 E5
Keats Cl
Dudley DY3 . . . . 50 A5
Nuneaton CV10 . . . . 72 A4
Stourbridge DY8 . . . . 81 A8
Sutton Coldfield B74 . . . . . . 31 F6
Tamworth B79 . . . . 20 F8
Keats Gr
Birmingham B27 . . . . 88 B1
Wolverhampton WV10. . . . . . 26 A8
Keats Ho
2 Oldbury B68. . . . . 64 C4
Redditch B97. . . . . 158 C8
Keats Pl DY10 . . . . 117 B6
Keats Rd
Coventry CV2. . . . . 114 D2
Walsall WS3 . . . . 28 E2
Willenhall WV12 . . . . 27 E7
Wolverhampton WV10. . . . . . 12 A1
Keble Cl
Burntwood WS7 . . . . 7 C7
Cannock WS11. . . . . 4 E8
Keble Gr
Birmingham B26 . . . . 89 B6
Walsall WS1 . . . . 43 A7
Keble Ho B33 . . . . 70 A2
Keble Wlk B79 . . . . 21 A6
Kebull Gn CV4 . . . . 131 E8
Kedleston Cl WS3. . . . . 14 A3
Kedleston Ct B28. . . . . 105 F4
Kedleston Rd B28. . . . . 105 F5
Keegan Wlk WS2 . . . . 27 F4
Keel Dr B13 . . . . 87 D1
Keele Cl B98 . . . . 154 E6
Keele Ho B37 . . . . 70 B4
Keeley St B9 . . . . 67 B2
Keeling Dr WS11. . . . . 1 B1
Keelinge St DY4 . . . . 52 B5
Keeling Rd CV8. . . . . 148 B5
Keenan Dr CV12 . . . . 77 D1
Keen St B66 . . . . 65 D5
Keepers Cl
Birmingham B18 . . . . 65 F5
Brownhills WS9 . . . . 15 F3
Keeper's Cl WS7 . . . . 7 A6
Keepers Cl
Kingswinford DY6 . . . . 60 B8
Lichfield WS14 . . . . 9 E7
Keepers Gate Cl B74. . . . . . 46 C7
Keepers Ho B73 . . . . 45 C2
Keepers La WV6,WV8. . . . . . 10 A1
Keepers Rd B74 . . . . 31 C5
Keepers Wlk CV12 . . . . 77 D1
Keer Ct B9 . . . . 67 B2
Kegworth Cl CV6 . . . . 96 A4
Kegworth Rd B23. . . . . 56 C2
Keir Cl CV32. . . . . 157 A2
Keir Hardie Wlk B69 . . . . . . 52 D2
Keir Rd WS10. . . . . 42 D2
Keith Rd CV32 . . . . 157 B4
Keith Winter Cl B61. . . . . . 136 F6
Kelby Cl B31 . . . . 102 E4
Kelby Rd B31. . . . . 102 F4
Keldy Cl WV6 . . . . 24 F5
Kele Rd CV4 . . . . 132 A7
Kelfield Ave B17. . . . . 85 B4
Kelham Pl B92. . . . . 89 B1
Kelia Dr B67. . . . . 64 F6
Kellett Rd B7 . . . . 67 A4
Kelling Cl DY5 . . . . 81 C8
Kellington Cl B8. . . . . 67 F4
Kelmarsh Dr B91. . . . . 107 B1
Kelmscote Rd CV6 . . . . 112 F8
Kelmscott Rd B17. . . . . 85 B7
Kelsall Cl WV1 . . . . 26 B2
Kelsall Croft B1 . . . . 66 B3
Kelsey Cl
Birmingham B7 . . . . 67 B4
Nuneaton CV11 . . . . 73 E3
Kelsey La CV7 . . . . 130 D5
Kelsey's Cl CV8 . . . . 135 F3
Kelso Gdns WV6 . . . . 23 D4
Kelsull Croft B37. . . . . 70 A2
Kelton Ct B15 . . . . 86 A7
Kelverdale Gr B14 . . . . 104 C4
Kelverley Gr B71. . . . . 43 A1
Kelvestone Ho WS11. . . . . . . 1 D1
Kelvin Ave CV2 . . . . 114 D5
Kelvin Cl DY11. . . . . 116 A8
Kelvin Dr WS11. . . . . 2 A3
Kelvin Pl WS2 . . . . 28 B6

Kelvin Rd
Birmingham B31 . . . . 103 B1
Royal Leamington Spa
CV32. . . . . 157 C5
Walsall WS2 . . . . 28 B6
Kelvin Way Trad Est B70. . . 53 B1
Kelvin Way B70. . . . . 53 C1
Kelway Ave B43 . . . . 44 B3
Kelway CV3. . . . . 115 A2
Kelwood Dr B63 . . . . 83 A5
Kelynmead Rd B33. . . . . 69 A2
Kemberton Cl WV3. . . . . 24 C1
Kemberton Rd
Birmingham B29 . . . . 85 B2
Wolverhampton WV3 . . . . . . 24 C1
Kemble Cl WV12 . . . . 27 D3
Kemble Croft B5. . . . . 86 E7
Kemble Dr B35. . . . . 58 A3
Kemelstowe Cres B63. . . . 100 C8
Kemerton Ho B97. . . . . 153 B4
Kemerton Way B90 . . . . . . 126 F6
Kemp Cl CV34. . . . . 161 A2
Kempe Rd B33. . . . . 69 A4
Kempley Ave CV2 . . . . 114 C2
Kempsey Cl
Halesowen B63 . . . . 82 E4
Oldbury B69 . . . . 63 E4
Redditch B98. . . . . 159 B7
Solihull B92 . . . . 89 A3
Kempsey Covert B38. . . . . 123 E7
Kempsey Ho B32 . . . . 102 A8
Kempsford Cl B98 . . . . 158 F6
Kemps Green Rd
Balsall Common CV7,
CV8. . . . . 130 B6
Kemps Green B94 . . . . 143 A1
Kempson Ave
Sutton Coldfield B72 . . . . . . 46 C1
West Bromwich B71 . . . . . . 53 B5
Kempson Rd B36 . . . . 68 F8
Kempsons Gr WV14 . . . . 40 B3
Kempthorne Ave
Wolverhampton WV10. . . . . . 11 E1
Wolverhampton WV10. . . . . . 25 E8
Kempthorne Gdns WS3 . . . 14 A2
Kempthorne Rd WV14. . . . . 40 F6
Kempton Cres CV32. . . . . . 157 C4
Kempton Ct B61. . . . . 121 A1
Kempton Dr
Great Wyrley WS6 . . . . 4 F2
Tamworth B77. . . . . 35 D4
Kempton Park Rd B36 . . . . . 68 D8
Kempton Way DY8 . . . . 60 F3
Kemsey Dr WV14. . . . . 40 F3
Kemshead Ave B31 . . . . . . 122 E8
Kemsley Rd B14 . . . . 104 F2
Ken St CV11. . . . . 73 E2
Kenchester Cl B98. . . . . . . 154 F2
Kendal Ave
Birmingham B45 . . . . 122 B7
Coleshill B46 . . . . 70 F7
Royal Leamington Spa
CV32. . . . . 156 C2
Kendal Cl
Bromsgrove B60 . . . . 137 B1
Nuneaton CV11 . . . . 74 A6
Wolverhampton WV6 . . . . . . 24 F6
Kendal Ct
14 Birmingham,Selly Oak
B29. . . . . 103 C7
Birmingham,Stockland Green
B23. . . . . 56 B3
Brownhills WS9 . . . . 15 F4
Cannock WS11. . . . . 4 B8
Kendal Dr B45. . . . . 122 D1
Kendal End Rd B45 . . . . . . 122 D1
Kendal Gr B92 . . . . 107 F8
Kendall Ho **15** B69 . . . . 63 D5
Kendal Rise DY6 . . . . 60 F5
Kendal Rise Rd B45. . . . . . 122 B7
Kendal Rd B11 . . . . 87 B7
Kendal Rise
Coventry CV5. . . . . 112 C4
Oldbury B68. . . . . 64 B3
Kendal Rise Rd B45. . . . . . 122 B7
Kendal Rise Wv6 . . . . 24 F6
Kendal Twr **5** B17 . . . . 85 D5
Kenderdine Montessori Sch
CV5 . . . . 133 A8
Kendon Ave CV6 . . . . 112 C6
Kendrick Ave B34. . . . . 69 E5
Kendrick Cl
Coventry CV6. . . . . 96 A4
Solihull B92 . . . . 107 F6
Kendrick Pl WV14. . . . . 41 A4
Kendrick Rd
Darlaston WV14. . . . . 41 A4
Sutton Coldfield B76 . . . . . . 57 F5
Wolverhampton WV10. . . . . . 25 E6
Kendricks Rd WS10 . . . . . . 41 F7
Kendrick St WS10 . . . . 42 A3
Kenelm Ct
Coventry CV3 . . . . 134 C5
Romsley B62 . . . . 101 A4
Sutton Coldfield B73 . . . . . . 46 B4
Kenelm Rd
Birmingham B10 . . . . 87 D8
Dudley WV14 . . . . 40 C1
Oldbury B68. . . . . 64 A3
Sutton Coldfield B73 . . . . . . 46 B4
Kenilcourt CV8. . . . . 147 D5
Kenilworth Castle * CV8. . 147 D5
Kenilworth Cl
Balsall Common CV7. . . . . 130 A8
Redditch B97 . . . . 158 D6
Stourbridge DY8 . . . . 60 D2
Sutton Coldfield B74 . . . . . . 46 A8
Tipton DY4 . . . . 51 D4
Kenilworth Cres
Walsall WS2 . . . . 28 A4

Kenilworth Cres continued
Wolverhampton WV4. . . . . . . 39 E4
Kenilworth Ct
2 Cannock WS11. . . . . 1 E1
Birmingham B15 . . . . 85 F8
Birmingham,Gravelly Hill
B24. . . . . 56 E2
Coventry CV3. . . . . 133 C8
Dudley DY1. . . . . 61 F8
Kenilworth Dr
Cannock WS11. . . . . 1 D4
Kidderminster DY10 . . . . . . 116 E2
Nuneaton CV11 . . . . 73 B3
Kenilworth Hall Mews
CV8 . . . . 147 F5
Kenilworth Ho
3 Walsall WS3 . . . . 28 C6
Birmingham B13 . . . . 105 A6
Kenilworth Rd
Balsall Common CV7,
CV8. . . . . 130 D4
Birmingham,Birchfield B20. . 55 E2
Birmingham,Warley Woods
B68. . . . . 84 D7
Blackdown CV32 . . . . 156 E5
Bradnock's Marsh B92 . . . . 109 E5
Coventry CV4 . . . . 132 E3
Kenilworth CV8 . . . . 148 C8
Knowle B93 . . . . 128 E5
Lichfield WS14. . . . . 9 B6
Meriden CV7 . . . . 91 D1
Perton WV6 . . . . 23 F4
Royal Leamington Spa
CV32. . . . . 157 C6
Tamworth B77 . . . . 21 E4
Kenilworth Sch Castle Hall
Sixth Form CV8. . . . . 147 F2
Kenilworth Sch CV8. . . . . . 148 C5
Kenilworth St **20** CV32. . 156 F1
Kenley Gr B30 . . . . 104 B3
Kenley Way B91. . . . . 106 D4
Kenmare Way WV11. . . . . . . 26 D4
Kenmore Ave WS12 . . . . 1 F7
Kenmore Dr B LE10 . . . . . . 71 B2
Kenmure Rd B33 . . . . 89 C8
Kennan Ave CV31 . . . . 161 F6
Kennedy Cl
Kidderminster DY10 . . . . . . 116 F3
Sutton Coldfield B74 . . . . . . 46 C4
Tamworth B77 . . . . 21 C1
Kennedy Cres
Darlaston WS10. . . . . 41 C7
Dudley DY3 . . . . 50 D4
Kennedy Croft B26. . . . . . . 89 A7
Kennedy Ct B98 . . . . 159 A3
Kennedy Gr B30 . . . . 104 B6
Kennedy Rd WV10 . . . . 11 C1
Kennedy Sq **3** CV32. . . . 157 A1
Kenneggy Mews B29. . . . . . 85 F2
Kennerley Rd B25. . . . . 88 D6
Kennet Cl
Brownhills WS8. . . . . 6 C2
Coventry CV2 . . . . 114 C8
Kennet Gr B36. . . . . 69 F8
Kenneth Gr B23 . . . . 56 B5
Kennet Ho **5** DY1 . . . . 61 F8
Kenneth Vincent Cl B97. . 158 E4
Kennet B77. . . . . 21 D1
Kennford Cl B65. . . . . 63 C6
Kennington Rd WV10. . . . . . 25 F5
Kenpas Highway CV3 . . . . 133 A5
Kenrick Croft B35 . . . . 57 F2
Kenrick Ho
Birmingham B16 . . . . 66 A1
West Bromwich B70 . . . . . . 53 E1
Kenrick Park Sta B70. . . . . 53 E1
Kenrick Way B70 . . . . 64 E8
Kensington Ave B12 . . . . . . 87 A4
Kensington Ct
Coventry CV5. . . . . 113 A1
Nuneaton CV10 . . . . 72 C6
Kensington Dr
Sutton Coldfield B74 . . . . . . 31 F5
Tamworth B79 . . . . 21 B7
Kensington Gdns
Cannock WS11. . . . . 1 C2
Stourbridge DY8 . . . . 60 C1
Kensington Pl
Birmingham B8 . . . . 67 D5
Cannock WS12. . . . . 5 C1
Kensington Rd
Birmingham B29 . . . . 86 B2
Coventry CV5. . . . . 113 A1
Willenhall WV12 . . . . 27 B7
Kensington St B19 . . . . 66 D6
Kenswick Dr B63 . . . . 83 A2
Kent Ave
Fazeley B78. . . . . 20 F2
Walsall WS2 . . . . 28 B3
Kent Cl
Aldridge WS9. . . . . 16 B1
Coventry CV3. . . . . 133 E6
Kidderminster DY10 . . . . . . 116 E3
Kent Close Jun & Inf Sch
B71 . . . . 53 B7
Kent Ct
Walsall WS2 . . . . 28 C5
West Bromwich B71 . . . . . . 53 C7
Kent Dr B LE10 . . . . 71 F4
Kenthurst Cl CV5 . . . . 111 C4
Kentish Rd B21 . . . . 65 C8
Kentmere CV2 . . . . 96 E2
Kentmere Rd B60 . . . . 137 C1
Kentmere Twr **8** B23. . . . . 57 B6
Kenton Ave WV6. . . . . 24 F4
Kenton Wlk **7** B29 . . . . . . 85 F2
Kent Pl
Cannock WS12. . . . . 2 F1

Kent Pl continued
Dudley DY2 . . . . 62 A6
Kent Rd
Birmingham B45 . . . . 101 F1
Halesowen B62 . . . . 83 F5
Stourbridge DY8 . . . . 80 D7
Wednesbury WS10 . . . . 42 D4
Willenhall WS2 . . . . 27 F3
Wolverhampton WV2. . . . . . . 39 E7
Kent St N B18 . . . . 65 F5
Kent's Cl B92. . . . . 88 F3
Kents Ho B33. . . . . 69 B2
Kent St
Birmingham B5 . . . . 66 E1
Dudley DY3 . . . . 50 E5
Walsall WS2 . . . . 28 B3
Kentwell B79. . . . . 20 D7
Kenward Croft B17 . . . . 84 F7
Kenward Rd B47 . . . . 125 A7
Kenwick Rd B17. . . . . 85 B4
Kenwood Rd B9 . . . . 68 B3
Kenwyn Gn CV7. . . . . 96 B8
Kenyon Cl
Bromsgrove B60 . . . . 137 A1
Stourbridge DY8 . . . . 81 A7
Kenyon St B18. . . . . 164 A4
Kepler B77 . . . . 22 B1
Kepler Dr 20 E7
Keppel St CV1. . . . . 113 E5
Kerby Rd B23. . . . . 56 C5
Kererwin Cl B64. . . . . 63 A1
Keresley Brook Rd CV6. . . . 95 A2
Keresley Cl
Coventry CV6. . . . . 95 A2
Solihull B91 . . . . 107 C5
Keresley Grange Prim Sch
CV6 . . . . 94 F1
Keresley Gr B29 . . . . 84 F2
Keresley Green Rd CV6 . . . . 94 F1
Keresley Newland Prim Sch
CV7 . . . . 94 F7
Keresley Rd CV6 . . . . 113 A8
Kernthorpe Rd B14 . . . . . . 104 D4
Kerr Dr DY4 . . . . 51 E8
Kerria Ct **3** B15. . . . . 86 D8
Kerria Cir B77. . . . . 22 A4
Kerria Rd B77 . . . . 22 B4
Kerridge Cl WV9. . . . . 11 A2
Kerris Way CV3 . . . . 115 A1
Kerr La B90 . . . . 126 A6
Kerry Cl
Barwell LE9 . . . . 71 F7
Birmingham B31 . . . . 102 F6
Brierley Hill DY5 . . . . 61 C4
Kerry Croft CV6. . . . . 158 E5
Kerry Ct WS1. . . . . 43 A7
Kerry Hill **1** B60 . . . . 150 E6
Kerry's Ho CV1 . . . . 113 B2
Kersley Gdns WV11. . . . . . . 26 F5
Kerswell Cl B97 . . . . 153 B5
Kerswell Dr B90. . . . . 127 A5
Kesterton Rd B74. . . . . 31 E5
Kesteven Cl B15. . . . . 86 B6
Kesteven Rd B71 . . . . 53 C7
Keston Rd B44. . . . . 44 C8
Kestrel Ave B25. . . . . 88 C8
Kestrel Cl
Birmingham,Castle Vale
B35. . . . . 58 B3
Birmingham,Short Heath
B23. . . . . 56 D6
Hinckley LE10 . . . . 75 F6
Kidderminster DY10 . . . . . . 116 E3
Kestrel Croft **2** CV3 . . . . 134 F8
Kestrel Ct WS7 . . . . 7 F8
Kestrel Dr B74 . . . . 31 F5
Kestrel Gr
Birmingham B30 . . . . 103 D8
Cannock WS12. . . . . 2 C1
Willenhall WV12 . . . . 27 C8
Kestrel Ho
Dudley DY1. . . . . 51 A1
Halesowen B63 . . . . 82 B7
Oldbury B68. . . . . 63 F2
Kestrel Rise WV6 . . . . 24 F7
Kestrel B77. . . . . 36 A6
Kestrel View B60. . . . . 137 C7
Kestrel Way WS6 . . . . 4 C2
Keswick Cl CV11. . . . . 74 A6
Keswick Dr DY6 . . . . 60 F8
Keswick Gn CV32 . . . . 156 D1
Keswick Ho B74 . . . . 30 F2
Keswick Ho **14** B69 . . . . . 63 D5
Keswick Rd B92 . . . . 89 A4
Keswick Wlk CV2 . . . . 114 F4
Ketley Croft B12 . . . . 86 F7
Ketley Fields DY6 . . . . 61 A5
Ketley Hill Rd DY1 . . . . 61 F8
Ketley Rd
Kingswinford DY6 . . . . 60 F6
Oldbury B69 . . . . 64 A7
Kettlebrook Rd
Solihull B90 . . . . 127 C6
Tamworth B77 . . . . 21 C3
Kettlehouse Rd B44. . . . . . . 44 F3
Kettlesbank Rd DY3. . . . . . 50 B2
Kettles Wood Dr B32. . . . . . 84 C2
Kettlewell Cl CV34 . . . . 155 E1
Kettlewell Way B37. . . . . . . 69 F1
Ketton Gr B33 . . . . 89 D7
Kevilliok St CV3 . . . . 133 D6
Kew Cl
Birmingham B37. . . . . 69 F3
Kenilworth CV8 . . . . 148 C5
Kew Dr DY1 . . . . 51 A2
Kew Gdns B33 . . . . 68 E2
Kew Ho CV4 . . . . 111 F3
Kewstoke Cl WV12 . . . . 13 B1
Kewstoke Croft B31. . . . . . 102 E6

Kewstoke Rd WV12 . . . . 13 C1
Key Bsns Pk B24. . . . . 57 D3
Keyes Dr DY6. . . . . 49 D1
Key Hill B18 . . . . 66 B5
Key Hill Dr B18. . . . . 66 B5
Key Ind Pk WS13. . . . . 26 D3
Keynell Covert B30 . . . . . . 104 C2
Keynes Dr WV14 . . . . 40 E6
Keys Cl WS12 . . . . 2 C3
Keys Cres B71. . . . . 53 C6
Keyse Rd B75. . . . . 46 F7
Keysmith Cl WV13 . . . . 27 C1
Keys Park Rd WS12 . . . . 2 E3
Keyte Cl CV37 . . . . 52 A5
Keyway Jct WV13 . . . . 41 B8
Keyway Ret Pk WV13. . . . . . 41 B8
Keyway The WV13 . . . . 41 A8
Keyworth Cl DY4. . . . . 52 B5
Khyber Cl WS10 . . . . 41 C8
Kidd Croft DY4 . . . . 41 C2
Kidderminster Coll DY10 . 116 F5
Kidderminster General Hospl
DY11. . . . . 116 F5
Kidderminster Railway Mus*
DY10 . . . . 116 F5
Kidderminster Rd
Bromsgrove B61 . . . . 136 C3
Iverley DY8 . . . . 98 C7
Kingswinford DY6 . . . . 60 B7
Kidderminster Rd S DY9 . . 99 F3
Kidderminster Rd WV6 . . . . 99 B5
Kidderminster Sta DY10 . . 116 F5
Kidderminster Town Sta*
DY10 . . . . 116 F5
Kidson Eventide Homes
WV6 . . . . 24 F5
Kielder Cl
Cannock WS12. . . . . 2 E2
Walsall WS5 . . . . 43 C3
Kielder Dr CV10 . . . . 72 E2
Kielder Gdns DY9. . . . . 81 B1
Kier's Bridge Cl DY4 . . . . . 52 B3
Kilberry Cl LE10 . . . . 71 A1
Kilburn Dr
Coventry CV5. . . . . 112 F3
Kingswinford DY6 . . . . 49 E1
Kilburn Gr B44 . . . . 44 F3
Kilburn Pl DY2. . . . . 62 D6
Kilburn Rd B44. . . . . 44 F3
Kilby Ave B16. . . . . 66 A2
Kilby Gr CV31. . . . . 162 A6
Kilbye Cl B77. . . . . 35 F5
Kilby Gn LE10. . . . . 75 F6
Kilbys Gr B20. . . . . 54 F2
Kilcote Rd B90 . . . . 105 C2
Kildale Cl CV1 . . . . 165 D3
Kilderkin Ct CV1 . . . . 165 C1
Kildwick Way **5** CV34. . . 155 E1
Kilmarie Cl LE10. . . . . 71 A1
Kilmet Wlk **1** B67. . . . . . . 65 A5
Kilmore Croft B36. . . . . 68 E8
Kilmorie Rd
Birmingham B27 . . . . 88 C5
Cannock WS11. . . . . 1 C2
Kiln Cl
Nuneaton CV10 . . . . 72 E3
Royal Leamington Spa
CV32. . . . . 157 A1
Studley B80 . . . . 159 C4
Kiln Croft B65 . . . . 63 A4
Kiln La
Birmingham B11 . . . . 88 B6
Solihull B90 . . . . 126 A5
Kilnsey Gr CV34. . . . . 155 E1
Kiln Way B78 . . . . 22 F1
Kilpeck Cl B98. . . . . 154 F2
Kilsall Ct **15** WV3 . . . . . . 25 C4
Kilsby Gr B91. . . . . 127 C8
Kilvert Rd WS10 . . . . 42 B2
Kilworth Ave **8** B11 . . . . . 87 B5
Kilworth Ho **4** CV32. . . . 156 F1
Kimberley Cl
Coventry CV5. . . . . 111 F4
Redditch B98. . . . . 154 B7
Sutton Coldfield B74 . . . . . . 31 A2
Kimberley Pl WV14 . . . . 51 B7
Kimberley Rd
Baginton CV8. . . . . 133 F2
Bedworth CV12 . . . . 78 C4
Smethwick B66 . . . . 65 A7
Solihull B92 . . . . 89 A1
Kimberley St WV3 . . . . 25 A1
Kimberley B77. . . . . 35 F7
Kimberley Wlk B76 . . . . 58 C6
Kimble Cl CV5 . . . . 112 B4
Kimble Gr B24 . . . . 57 D3
Kimbley Rise B20. . . . . 54 F2
Kimbolton Dr B60 . . . . 138 A5
Kimmond Ct **21** CV32. . . 156 F1
Kimpton Cl B14. . . . . 104 E2
Kimsan Croft B74. . . . . 45 A7
Kinchford Cl B91 . . . . 127 B8
Kineton Cl B98 . . . . 154 D3
Kineton Croft B32 . . . . 102 D8
Kineton Green Prim Sch
B92. . . . . 88 D1
Kineton Green Rd B92. . . . 106 D8
Kineton Ho B13. . . . . 105 A6
Kineton La B90,B94. . . . . . 127 A1
Kineton Rd
Birmingham B45 . . . . 121 E7
Coventry CV2. . . . . 114 C6
Kenilworth CV8 . . . . 148 C4
Sutton Coldfield B73 . . . . . . 45 E1
Kineton Rise DY3 . . . . 39 C2
Kinfare Dr WV6. . . . . 24 B4
Kinfare Rise DY3. . . . . 50 E4

King Charles Ave WS2 . . . . . .27 E2
Kingsclere Wlk WV4 . . . . .38 C6
Kingsoak Gdns DY2 . . . . .62 E7
Kington Cl WV12 . . . . .27 B8
King Charles Cl DY11 . . . . .116 C6
Kingscliff Rd B10 . . . . .88 A8
Kings Par B4 . . . . .164 C2
Kington Gdns B37 . . . . .69 F2
King Charles Ct B44 . . . . . . .45 B2
Kingscote Cl B98 . . . . .154 D7
Kings Park Dr CV3 . . . . .115 B1
Kington Way B33 . . . . .68 E1
King Charles I Sch DY10 117 A5
Kingscote Gr CV3 . . . . .133 A4
Kingspiece Ho 8 B36 . . . . . .68 E8
King William St
WS2 . . . . .27 E2
Kingscote Rd
King's Rd B44 . . . . .44 E3
Coventry CV1 . . . . .113 E4
King Charles Prim Sch
Birmingham B15 . . . . .85 E6
Kiniths Cres B71 . . . . .53 E5
Stourbridge DY8 . . . . .80 F8
WS2 . . . . .27 E2
Dorridge B93 . . . . .127 E2
Kings Rd
Kiniths Way
King Charles Rd B62 . . . . . . .83 F4
Kings Croft
Birmingham,Stirchley
Halesowen B62 . . . . .63 E1
King Charles Sq 4 DY10 116 C6
Birmingham,Castle Bromwich
B14 . . . . .104 C6
West Bromwich B71 . . . . . . .53 E4
King David Jun & Inf Sch
B36 . . . . .69 F7
Birmingham,Stockland Green
Kinlet Cl
B13 .86 F2
Birmingham,Sheldon B26 . .89 A5
B23 . . . . .56 D4
Redditch B98 . . . . .154 E3
King Edmund St 1 B61 . . . .136 F5
Cannock WS12 . . . . .2 E4
Birmingham,Tyseley B11 . . .88 A6
Wolverhampton WV3 . . . . . .38 A8
King Edward Rd
Kingscroft Cl B74 . . . . .45 A8
King's Rd DY11 . . . . .116 C6
Kinlet Gn B37 . . . . .70 C1
Birmingham B13 . . . . .86 F3
Kingscroft Rd B74 . . . . .45 A8
Kings Rd
Kinloch Dr DY1 . . . . .50 F3
Bromsgrove B61 . . . . .136 F5
King's Ct CV11 . . . . .73 B4
Sedgley DY3 . . . . .50 E8
Kinnerley St WS1 . . . . .29 A1
Coventry CV1 . . . . .113 F4
Kings Ct
Sutton Coldfield B44,B73 . . .45 B2
Kinnersley Cl B98 . . . . .154 E3
Nuneaton CV11 . . . . .73 D4
Kings Ct
Sutton Coldfield B44,B73 . . .45 B2
Walsall WS4 . . . . .29 C7
Kinnersley Gn B98 . . . . .63 D5
King Edwards Cl B20 . . . . . . .66 B8
Stourbridge DY8 . . . . .80 E5
King's Rise Com Prim Sch
Kinnerton Cres B29 . . . . . . .84 F2
King Edwards Gdns B20 . . . .66 B7
Sutton Coldfield B75 . . . . . . .32 B3
B44 . . . . .45 A2
Kinross Ave WS12 . . . . .1 F7
King Edward's Rd B1 . . . . . . .66 B7
Tipton DY4 . . . . .52 A4
Kings Road Ind Est B25 . . . .88 A6
Kinross Cl CV10 . . . . .72 F2
King Edward's Row WV2 .163 B1
Kingsdene Ave B30 . . . . .60 C4
Kings Sq WV14 . . . . .51 A8
Kinross Cres B43 . . . . .44 B4
King Edward's Sch B15 . . . .86 A4
Kingsdown Ave B42 . . . . .55 A6
King St
Kinross Rd CV32 . . . . .157 B4
King Edward St WS10 . . . . . .41 D6
Kingsdown Rd B31 . . . . .84 F1
2 Hinckley LE10 . . . . .71 D1
Kinross Way LE10 . . . . .71 A1
King Edward Wharf B16 . . . .66 B2
Kingsfield Rd B14 . . . . .104 E8
6 Willenhall WV13 . . . . . . .27 B2
Kinsall Gn B77 . . . . .36 C6
King Edward VI Aston Sch
Kingsford Cl B36 . . . . .58 D1
Kingstanding Ctr B44 . . . . . .44 F3
Kinsey Gr B14 . . . . .104 F4
B6 . . . . .66 F8
Kingsford Ct B92 . . . . .89 B3
Kingstanding Rd B44 . . . . . .44 F5
Kinsham Dr B91 . . . . .127 B8
King Edward VI Camp Hill
Kingsford Nouveau DY6 . .61 A5
Kingstanding Sch B44 . . . . .44 E1
Kintore Croft B32 . . . . .102 B7
Sch For Boys B14 . . . . . . .104 D7
Kingsford Rd CV6 . . . . .113 C7
King St
Kintyre Cl
King Edward VI Camp Hill
Kingsgate Ho B37 . . . . .70 A2
Bedworth CV12 . . . . .78 C2
Birmingham B45 . . . . .101 E1
Sch For Girls B14 . . . . . . .104 D7
Kings Gdn B30 . . . . .103 E4
Bilston WV14 . . . . .40 E3
Hinckley LE10 . . . . .71 B1
King Edward VI Coll
Kings Gdns CV12 . . . . .78 C2
Birmingham B11 . . . . .87 A7
Kintyre The CV2 . . . . .115 B7
Nuneaton CV11 . . . . .73 D4
Kings Gr CV2 . . . . .114 B3
Brierley Hill DY5 . . . . .82 A8
Kinver Ave
Stourbridge DY8 . . . . .81 A6
Kings Green Ave B38 . . . . . .103 F2
Brownhills WS9 . . . . .15 F2
Birmingham DY11 . . . . . . .116 A1
King Edward VI Five Ways
Kings Hall 2 B13 . . . . .87 A2
Burntwood WS7 . . . . .6 F5
Willenhall WV12 . . . . .27 B5
Sch B32 . . . . .102 C8
Kingshayes Rd WS9 . . . . . . .16 B1
Cradley Heath B64 . . . . .62 F1
Kinver Cl CV2 . . . . .96 E1
King Edward VI Handsworth
Kings Heath Boys
Darlaston WS10 . . . . .41 D6
Kinver Cres WS9 . . . . .16 C1
Sch B21 . . . . .86 A4
Mathematics & Computing
Dudley DY2 . . . . .51 C1
Kinver Croft
King Edward VI High Sch for
Coll B13 . . . . .105 A6
Dudley,The Coppice WV14 . .51 A8
Birmingham B12 . . . . .86 E7
Girls B15 . . . . .86 A4
Kings Heath Jun Sch B14 .86 F1
Kings Terr B14 . . . . .104 D6
Sutton Coldfield B76 . . . . . . .58 A8
King Edward VI Sch WS14 . . .9 C6
King's High Sch for Girls The
King St B63 . . . . .83 A4
Kinver Ct B11 . . . . .87 D4
Kingfield Ind Est CV1 . . . . .113 C6
CV34 . . . . .160 E7
Kingsthorne Prim Sch
Kinver Dr
Kingfield Rd
King's Hill Day Hospl
B44 .45 A1
Hagley WV9 . . . . .99 C7
Coventry CV1,CV6 . . . . .113 D7
WS10 . . . . .41 E5
Kingston Arc WS11 . . . . .1 E1
Wolverhampton WV4 . . . . . .38 C5
Solihull B90 . . . . .105 C2
Kingshill Dr B38 . . . . .103 F2
Kingston Cl B79 . . . . .21 C7
Kinver Rd B31 . . . . .103 D2
Kingfisher Ave CV10 . . . . . . .72 C5
King's Hill Inf Sch WS10 . . .41 E5
Kingston Ct 8 B29 . . . . .103 C7
Kinver St DY8 . . . . .60 E1
Kingfisher Cl
King's Hill La CV3 . . . . .133 B2
Kingston Ctr PRU WV6 . . . .24 F5
Kinwalsey La CV7 . . . . .92 F6
Birmingham B26 . . . . .89 A6
King's Hill Mews WS10 . . . .41 D5
Kingston Dr LE10 . . . . .71 A4
Kinwarton Cl B26 . . . . .88 D6
Brownhills WS8 . . . . .15 F7
King's Hill Pk Ind Est
Kingston Ho CV12 . . . . .95 C8
Kinwarton Croft
Sedgley DY3 . . . . .39 C2
WS10 . . . . .41 E5
Kingston Ind Est B9 . . . . . . .67 B1
Birmingham B12 . . . . .86 E7
Kingfisher Ct
King's Hill Prim Sch
Kingston Mews CV31 . . . . . .162 C6
Sutton Coldfield B76 . . . . . . .58 A8
Alvechurch B48 . . . . .139 A7
WS10 . . . . .41 E5
Kingston Rd
Kinver Terr DY7 . . . . .60 A7
Burntwood WS7 . . . . .7 F8
King's Hill Rd WS14 . . . . .9 C6
Birmingham B9 . . . . .67 B1
Kipling Ave
Hinckley LE10 . . . . .74 F6
Kings Ho B24 . . . . .57 A4
Coventry CV5 . . . . .112 F2
Dudley DY4 . . . . .40 B1
Kingfisher Dr
Kingsholm Cl CV3 . . . . .115 B1
Sutton Coldfield B75 . . . . . . .46 F6
Warwick CV34 . . . . .160 C4
Birmingham B36 . . . . .70 A8
Kingshurst Inf Sch B37 . . . .70 A6
Kingston Row B1 . . . . .66 C2
Kipling Cl
Cannock WS12 . . . . .2 C5
Kingshurst Jun Sch B37 . . .70 A6
Kingston Way DY6 . . . . .60 C7
Nuneaton CV10 . . . . .72 A5
Stourbridge DY8 . . . . .80 C4
Kingshurst Rd
King Street Pas
Tipton DY4 . . . . .52 A8
Kingfisher Ent Pk B98 . . . .154 A3
Birmingham B31 . . . . .103 A3
2 Dudley DY2 . . . . .51 D1
Kipling Rd
Kingfisher Gr
Solihull B90 . . . . .105 F1
Brierley Hill DY5 . . . . .82 A8
Birmingham B30 . . . . .103 C4
Kidderminster DY10 . . . . . .117 B3
Kingshurst Way B37 . . . . . . .69 F5
King St
Coventry DY3 . . . . .113 A8
Willenhall WV12 . . . . .27 C8
Kingsland Ave CV5 . . . . .112 F2
Royal Leamington Spa
Dudley DY3 . . . . .50 A5
Kingfisher Ind Est B70 . . . . .52 F4
Kingsland Dr B93 . . . . .127 E4
B32 . . . . .157 A1
Wednesfield WV10 . . . . .27 E8
Kingfisher Prim Sch B36 . . .70 A8
Kingsland Prim Sch B44 . . .44 F4
Smethwick B66 . . . . .65 C5
Wolverhampton WV10 . . . . .26 A6
Kingfisher Rd B23 . . . . .56 C7
Kingsland Rd
Stourbridge DY8 . . . . .80 E6
Kipling Rise B79 . . . . .20 F8
Kingfisher Sh Ctr 2 B97 153 E3
Birmingham B44 . . . . .44 F4
Stourbridge,The Lye DY9 . . .81 F5
Kipling Wlk 3 DY10 . . . . . .117 B6
Kingfisher B77 . . . . .36 A6
Wolverhampton WV1 . . . . . .25 B3
Tamworth B79 . . . . .21 B5
Kirby Ave CV34 . . . . .155 F1
Kingfisher View B34 . . . . . . .69 A5
Kingslea Rd B91 . . . . .127 B8
Walsall WS1 . . . . .42 D7
Kirby Cl
Kingfisher Way B30 . . . . . . .103 D8
Kingslea Rd B91 . . . . .45 F1
Wednesbury WS10 . . . . .41 E3
Bilston WV14 . . . . .40 E3
Kingfisher Wlk B97 . . . . . . .153 E4
Kingsleigh Croft B75 . . . . . . .32 B2
Wolverhampton WV1 . . . . .163 C3
Brandon CV8 . . . . .135 F5
King George Ave B61 . . . . .136 F4
Kingsleigh Dr B20 . . . . .69 A8
Kingsway B63 . . . . .82 A8
Coventry CV1 . . . . .113 D6
King George Cres WS4 . . . .29 B6
Kingsleigh Rd B20 . . . . .55 B2
Kingsway 8 DY4 . . . . .52 A8
Kirby Corner Rd CV4 . . . . . .132 B6
King George Pl WS4 . . . . . .29 B6
Kingsley Ave
Kingsway
Kirby Dr DY1 . . . . .50 E3
King George's Ave
Cannock WS12 . . . . .2 C7
Birmingham B68 . . . . .84 B7
Kirby Rd
Bedworth CV12 . . . . .78 B5
Kingsley Bank Way B26 . . . .89 B7
Cannock WS11 . . . . .2 A4
Birmingham B18 . . . . .65 E6
Coventry CV6 . . . . .95 F2
Kingsley Cl B79 . . . . .21 A6
Kingsway Com Prim Sch
Coventry CV5 . . . . .112 F2
King George's Way WS11 5 B7
Kingsley Coll B98 . . . . .159 C6
CV31 . . . . .161 F6
Kirfield Dr LE10 . . . . .71 F3
King George VI Ave WS5 . .29 C1
Kingsley Cres CV12 . . . . .79 B3
Kingsway CV2 . . . . .114 A3
Kirkby Bri B73 . . . . .46 B3
King George V Prim Sch
Kingsley Ct
Kingsway Dr B38 . . . . .103 F2
Kirkdale Ave CV6 . . . . .95 D3
B70 .53 D3
Binley Woods CV3 . . . . .135 D6
Kingsway WV11 . . . . .13 A4
Kirkham Gdns DY5 . . . . .61 C6
Kingham Cl
Birmingham B25 . . . . .88 E8
Kingsway Ho CV12 . . . . .78 C2
Kirkham Gr B33 . . . . .68 F3
Dudley DY3 . . . . .50 C2
Kingsley Gr DY3 . . . . .50 A5
Kingsway CV11 . . . . .73 B4
Kirkham Way DY4 . . . . .52 A5
Redditch B98 . . . . .154 F4
Kingsley Prep Sch B93 . . . .128 A4
Kingsway Rd WV10 . . . . .26 A6
Kirkland Way B78 . . . . .34 B8
Kingham Covert B14 . . . . . .104 D2
Kingsley Rd
Kingsway
Kirkside Gr WS8 . . . . .15 F7
King Henry VIII Sch CV3 . .165 A1
Birmingham,Balsall Heath
Royal Leamington Spa
Kirkstall Cl WS3 . . . . .13 F2
Kingland Dr CV32 . . . . .156 C1
B12 . . . . .87 A6
CV31 . . . . .161 F6
Kirkstall Cres WS3 . . . . .13 F2
Kingmead Ho B14 . . . . .104 D4
Birmingham,King's Norton
Stourbridge DY8 . . . . .80 E8
Kirkstone Cres
King Richard Rd LE10 . . . . . .71 C2
B30 . . . . .103 D4
Wolverhampton WV10 . . . . .26 A6
Birmingham B43 . . . . .54 F6
King Richard St CV2 . . . . . .113 F3
Kingswinford DY6 . . . . .60 C5
Kingswear Ave WV6 . . . . . . .23 F3
Wombourne WV5 . . . . .49 A6
Kings Ave WS12 . . . . .2 C4
Kingsley Sch The CV32 . . .156 F1
Kingswinford Rd DY1 . . . . . .61 F7
Kirkstone Ct DY5 . . . . .81 B8
King's Ave DY3 . . . . .50 E2
Kingsley St
Kingswinford Sch The
Kirkstone Way DY5 . . . . .81 B8
Kingsbridge Ho B23 . . . . . . .56 B6
Dudley DY2 . . . . .62 C5
DY6 . . . . .60 D7
Kirkstone Wlk CV11 . . . . . . .74 A6
Kingsbridge Rd
Walsall WS2 . . . . .42 B7
Kingswood Ave
Kirkwall Rd B32 . . . . .84 D1
Birmingham B32 . . . . .84 D1
Kingsley Terr CV2 . . . . .114 E8
Cannock WS11 . . . . .4 C7
Kirkwood Ave B23 . . . . .56 F7
Nuneaton CV10 . . . . .73 D6
Kingsley Wlk CV2 . . . . .114 F7
Corley CV7 . . . . .94 B8
Kirmond Wlk WV6 . . . . .25 C5
Kingsbridge Wlk 6 B66 . . .65 B5
Kingslow Ave WV4 . . . . .38 D6
Kingswood Cl
Kirstead Gdns WV6 . . . . .24 B3
Kingsbrook Dr B91 . . . . .127 B8
King's Mdw DY9 . . . . .99 E3
Coventry CV6 . . . . .95 D1
Kirtley B77 . . . . .21 E2
Kings Bsns Pk B44 . . . . .44 E3
Kings Mdw CV10 . . . . .72 A3
Whitnash CV31 . . . . .162 B3
Kirton Cl
Kingsbury Ave B24 . . . . .57 D3
Kingsmead Mews CV3 . . . .134 D6
Kingswood Ctr The
Coventry CV6 . . . . .94 F1
Kingsbury Bsns Pk B76 . . .58 B6
Kingsmead Tech Coll
WS6 . . . . .95 D1
Whitnash CV31 . . . . .162 B3
Kingsbury Cl
WS12 . . . . .2 C4
Kingswood Colliery Cvn Site
Kirton Gr
Minworth B76 . . . . .58 C6
Kingsmere Cl B24 . . . . .56 F2
WS6 . . . . .95 D1
Birmingham B33 . . . . .69 C2
Walsall WS4 . . . . .29 B4
Kings Mews WS14 . . . . .9 B5
Kingswood Cotts B94 . . . . .144 D3
Solihull B91 . . . . .107 A1
Kingsbury Rd
King's Norton Boys Sch
Kingswood Croft B7 . . . . . . .67 C4
Wolverhampton WV10 . . . . .26 A6
2 Tipton DY4 . . . . .52 A8
B30 . . . . .103 E4
Kingswood Dr
Kitchener Rd
Birmingham B35,B76 . . . . . .58 B5
Kings Norton Bsns Ctr
Birmingham B30 . . . . .104 C3
Birmingham B29 . . . . .86 B1
Birmingham,Birches Green
B30 . . . . .104 A4
Great Wyrley WS6 . . . . .5 A4
Coventry CV6 . . . . .113 E8
B24 .57 B3
King's Norton Girls Sch
Norton Canes WS11 . . . . . . .5 F5
Dudley DY2 . . . . .51 F1
Birmingham,Tyburn B24,B35 57 E3
B30 . . . . .103 F5
Sutton Coldfield B74 . . . . . . .44 F5
Kitchener St B66 . . . . .65 D7
Curdworth B76 . . . . .59 B6
Kings Norton High Sch
Kingswood Gdns
Kitchen La
Minworth B76 . . . . .58 D5
B38 . . . . .123 F8
Nuneaton CV10 . . . . .72 B4
Wednesfield WV11 . . . . .26 F8
Kingsbury Sch & Sports Coll
King's Norton Prim Sch
Wolverhampton WV4 . . . . . .38 F6
Wolverhampton WV11 . . . . .12 F1
B24 .57 E3
B30 . . . . .104 A2
Kingswood Ho B14 . . . . . . .104 E2
Kitebrook Cl
King's CE Sch The WV6 . . . .24 B5
King's Norton Sta B30 . . . .103 F4
Kingswood Sch B90 . . . . . .106 B2
Redditch B98 . . . . .154 E4
Kings Cl B14 . . . . .104 C6
Solihull B90 . . . . .127 A7
Kite La B97 . . . . .153 A5
Kites Cl CV34 . . . . .155 C2
Kites Nest La CV35 . . . . . . .146 C1
Kitsland Rd B34 . . . . .69 E6
Kitswell Gdns B32 . . . . .102 A8

Kittermaster Rd CV7 . . . . . . .92 C1
Kittiwake Dr
Brierley Hill DY5 . . . . .81 D7
Kidderminster DY10 . . . . . .117 B3
Kittoe Rd B74 . . . . .32 A3
Kitt's Green Rd B33 . . . . .69 B3
Kitwell La B32 . . . . .102 A8
Kitwell Prim Sch B32 . . . . .102 A7
Kitwood Ave B78 . . . . .36 F6
Kitwood Dr B92 . . . . .107 D7
Kixley La B93 . . . . .128 C6
Klaxon Ind Est B11 . . . . .87 F4
Klevedon Cl CV11 . . . . .74 A1
Knapton Cl LE10 . . . . .71 A3
Knaresdale Cl DY5 . . . . .81 C8
Knaves Castle Ave WS8 . . . .6 F2
Knebley Cres CV10 . . . . .73 C1
Knebworth Cl B44 . . . . .55 E8
Knibbs The CV34 . . . . .160 E7
Knight Ave CV1 . . . . .113 E1
Knightcote Dr
Royal Leamington Spa
CV32 . . . . .161 E8
Solihull B91 . . . . .127 B8
Knight Ct B75 . . . . .47 C5
Knight Ho B13 . . . . .105 D7
Knightley Cl CV32 . . . . .157 E5
Knightley Rd B91 . . . . .106 F2
Knightlow Ave CV3 . . . . .134 C6
Knightlow Cl CV8 . . . . .148 C3
Knightlow Rd B17 . . . . .85 B8
Knighton Cl B74 . . . . .31 F3
Knighton Ct B74 . . . . .31 F3
Knighton Ct B74 . . . . .31 F3
Knighton Dr B74 . . . . .31 F3
Knighton Rd
Birmingham B31 . . . . .103 C4
Cannock WS12 . . . . .2 E3
Dudley DY2 . . . . .62 D4
Sutton Coldfield B74 . . . . . . .31 D5
Knights Ave B20 . . . . .24 E6
Knightsbridge Ave CV12 . . .78 C4
Knightsbridge Cl B74 . . . . . .31 F4
Knightsbridge Ct B837 . . . . .69 F5
Knightsbridge La CV12 . . . . .27 C5
Knightsbridge Rd B92 . . . . . .89 A1
Knights Cl
3 Willenhall WV13 . . . . . . .27 B2
Birmingham B23 . . . . .56 E2
Hinckley LE10 . . . . .75 D4
Knights Cres WV6 . . . . .24 E7
Knights Ct
Birmingham B37 . . . . .90 E8
Hinckley LE10 . . . . .74 D4
Norton Canes WS11 . . . . . . .6 A4
Warwick CV34 . . . . .160 D6
Knightsfield Cl B73 . . . . .45 C3
Knightsford Cl B97 . . . . . . .152 F2
Knights Hill WS9 . . . . .30 B3
Knights Rd B11 . . . . .88 A4
Knights Templar Way
CV4 . . . . .112 A1
Knightstone Ave B18 . . . . . . .66 A4
Knights Wood Cl B75 . . . . . .46 D7
Knightwick Cres B23 . . . . . . .56 C5
Knipersley Rd B73 . . . . .57 A7
Knoll Cl WS7 . . . . .7 B5
Knollcroft 4 B16 . . . . .66 A2
Knoll Croft
Aldridge WS9 . . . . .16 C1
Cheswick Green B90 . . . . . .126 D4
Coventry CV3 . . . . .133 C6
Knoll Dr
Coventry CV3 . . . . .133 C6
Warwick CV34 . . . . .155 E1
Knoll Sch The DY11 . . . . . .116 A7
Knoll The
Birmingham B32 . . . . .84 C1
Kingswinford DY6 . . . . .60 E5
Knott Ct 11 DY5 . . . . .61 D2
Knottesford Cl B80 . . . . . . .159 C3
Knotting Way CV3 . . . . .114 C1
Knottsall La B68 . . . . .64 B3
Knotts Farm Rd DY6 . . . . . . .61 A4
Knowesley Cl B60 . . . . .137 B2
Knowlands Rd B90 . . . . .127 A7
Knowle CE Prim Sch
B93 . . . . .128 C6
Knowle Cl
Birmingham B45 . . . . .122 D7
Redditch B98 . . . . .154 C6
Knowle Hill CV8 . . . . .148 C6
Knowle Hill Rd DY2 . . . . .62 B4
Knowle La WS14 . . . . .9 B3
Knowle Rd
Birmingham B11 . . . . .87 D3
Eastcote B92 . . . . .108 E2
Rowley Regis B65 . . . . .63 A4
Knowles Ave CV10 . . . . .72 C4
Knowles Dr CV34 . . . . .46 B8
Knowles Rd WV1 . . . . .25 F1
Knowles St WS10 . . . . .42 A3
Knowle Wood Rd B93 . . . . .128 B3
Knox Cres CV11 . . . . .73 F8
Knox Rd WV2 . . . . .39 D6
Knox's Grave La WS14,B78 19 D7
Knoyle Ct 1 DY8 . . . . .80 F6
Knutswood Cl B13 . . . . .105 D7
Kohima Dr DY8 . . . . .80 D5
Kossuth Rd WV14 . . . . .40 A1
Kurtus B77 . . . . .35 D6
Kwikform Bldg CV6 . . . . .95 E4
Kyle Cl WV10 . . . . .11 B1
Kyles Way B32 . . . . .102 B7
Kynaston Cres WV8 . . . . .10 B3
Kynaston Ho B71 . . . . .53 C8

Kyngsford Rd B33 . . . . .69 D3
Kynner Way CV3 . . . . . . .135 B8
Kynoch Wks B6. . . . . .55 F3
Kyotts Lake Rd B11 . . . . . . .87 B7
Kyotts Lake Unit Factory
  B11. . . . . .87 B7
Kyrwicks La B11 . . . . .87 A7
Kyter La B36 . . . . .69 B8

L

Laburnham Ct WS14 . . . . .9 C5
Laburnham Rd DY6 . . . . . . .60 E6
Laburnum Ave
  Birmingham B37 . . . . .69 F6
  Cannock WS11 . . . . .4 E7
  Coventry CV6. . . . . .112 F5
  Kenilworth CV8 . . . . .148 A4
  Smethwick B67 . . . . .64 E4
  Tamworth B79 . . . . .21 B8
Laburnum Cl
  Bedworth CV12 . . . . .77 E2
  Birmingham B37 . . . . .69 F6
  Cannock WS11. . . . . .4 E7
  Hollywood B47. . . . . .125 A5
  Redditch B98 . . . . .153 E2
  Stourbridge DY8 . . . . .80 E7
  Walsall WS3 . . . . .9 A5
Laburnum Cotts B21 . . . . . .65 E8
Laburnum Croft B69 . . . . . .52 B2
Laburnum Dr
  Sutton Coldfield B76 . . . . . .47 A3
  Whitnash CV31 . . . . .162 B3
Laburnum Gr
  Birmingham B13 . . . . .86 F3
  Bromsgrove B61 . . . . .136 F4
  Burntwood WS7. . . . . .6 F6
  Kidderminster DY11 . . . . .116 B8
  Nuneaton CV10 . . . . .72 D6
  Warwick CV34 . . . . .156 B1
  Willenhall WS2 . . . . .27 F3
Laburnum Ho WS4. . . . . . . .15 D1
Laburnum Rd
  Bilston WV1. . . . . .40 B8
  Birmingham B30 . . . . . . .103 F8
  Brownhills WS9 . . . . .16 A3
  Dudley DY1 . . . . .51 F4
  Tipton DY4. . . . . .51 F7
  Walsall WS5 . . . . .43 C4
  Wednesbury WS10 . . . . . .42 B4
  Wolverhampton WV4 . . . . .39 F3
Laburnum St
  Stourbridge DY8 . . . . .80 E7
  Wolverhampton WV3 . . . . .25 B1
Laburnum Trees B47 . . . . .124 F7
Laburnum Villas 2 B11 . . .87 C5
Laburnum Way B31 . . . . . .103 A1
Laceby Gr B13. . . . . .87 D1
Lacell Cl CV34 . . . . .155 E1
Ladbroke Dr B76 . . . . .46 F2
Ladbroke Gr B27. . . . . . . .106 C8
Ladbroke Pk CV34 . . . . . . .155 E1
Ladbrook Cl B98. . . . . .158 E7
Ladbrook Gr DY3 . . . . .50 B3
Ladbrook Rd
  Coventry CV5. . . . . .112 A4
  Solihull B91 . . . . .107 C2
Ladbury Gr WS5 . . . . .43 A4
Ladbury Rd WS5 . . . . .43 A3
Ladeler Gr B33 . . . . .69 E2
Ladies Wlk DY3 . . . . .50 D8
Lady Bank
  Birmingham B32 . . . . . . .102 B7
  Tamworth B79 . . . . .21 B4
Lady Bracknell Mews
  B31. . . . . .103 C4
Lady Brades Ho 5 B69 . . .64 A7
Lady Byron La B93. . . . . . .127 F8
Ladycroft
  5 Birmingham B16. . . . . . .66 B2
  Cubbington CV32 . . . . . . .157 E5
Ladyfields Way CV6. . . . . . .95 B4
Lady Grey Ave CV34 . . . . .161 E3
Lady Grey's Wlk DY8 . . . . .80 D5
Ladygrove Cl B98 . . . . . . .159 A8
Lady Harriet's La B98. . . . .153 F4
Lady Katherine Leveson CE
  Sch B93 . . . . .129 B5
Lady La
  Coventry CV6. . . . . .95 F4
  Earlswood B90,B94 . . . . . .126 B3
  Kenilworth CV8 . . . . .147 F4
Lady Lane Mobile Home Pk
  CV6 . . . . .95 F4
Ladymead Dr CV6. . . . . . . .95 B2
Lady Meadow Cl B78 . . . . .21 A3
Ladymoor Rd WV14 . . . . . .40 C3
Ladypool Ave 3 B11. . . . . .87 B6
Ladypool Cl
  Halesowen B62 . . . . .83 C4
  Walsall WS4 . . . . .29 A5
Ladypool Rd B11,B12. . . . .87 A5
Ladypool Sch B11 . . . . . . .87 B6
Ladysmith Rd B63 . . . . . . .82 C6
Lady Warwick Ave CV12. . .78 D2
Ladywell Cl WV5. . . . . .49 A8
Ladywell Wlk B5. . . . . . . .164 C1
Ladywood Cl DY5. . . . . . . .61 F2
Ladywood Middleway
  B16. . . . . .66 A2
Ladywood Rd
  Birmingham B16. . . . . .66 A1
  Sutton Coldfield B74 . . . . . .46 A8
Laertes Gr CV34 . . . . .161 F2

Laggan Cl CV10 . . . . .72 C5
Lagonda B77 . . . . .21 E3
Lagrange B79 . . . . .20 E6
Laing Ho 2 B69. . . . . .63 D5
Lair The B78. . . . . .36 F8
Lake Ave WS5 . . . . .43 C7
Lake Cl WS5. . . . . .43 C7
Lakedown Cl B14. . . . . . . .104 E1
Lakefield B31. . . . . .102 D4
Lakefield Cl B28. . . . . .106 B7
Lakefield Rd WV11. . . . . . . .26 E5
Lakehouse Ct B23 . . . . .56 E8
Lakehouse Gr B38 . . . . . . .103 D3
Lakehouse Rd B73 . . . . . . .56 F8
Lakeland Dr B37 . . . . .36 B7
Lakeland Ho CV34 . . . . . . .161 A7
Lakenheath B79 . . . . .21 C7
Laker Cl DY8 . . . . .81 A7
Lakes Cl DY11 . . . . .116 C7
Lakeside CV12 . . . . .78 A2
Lakeside CV WV13. . . . . . . .26 E3
Lakeside Ct
  Birmingham B20 . . . . .55 A4
  Brierley Hill DY5 . . . . .81 B8
Lakeside Dr
  Birmingham B23 . . . . .56 B6
  Norton Canes WS11 . . . . . . .6 B6
  Solihull B90 . . . . .126 F7
Lakeside Ind Est B98. . . . .154 B3
Lakeside Pk B78. . . . . .20 F1
Lakeside Prim Sch
  Tamworth B77 . . . . .21 E2
  Willenhall WV13. . . . . .26 E3
Lakeside Rd B70. . . . . .53 A6
Lakeside
  Redditch B97 . . . . .152 D7
  Sutton Coldfield B74 . . . . . .31 B5
Lakeside Wlk B23. . . . . . . .56 C3
Lakes Rd B23 . . . . .56 A6
Lake St DY3 . . . . .50 D3
Lakes The B94 . . . . .141 F8
Lakeview Cl B43 . . . . .44 B2
Lake View Rd CV5. . . . . . .112 F4
Lakewood Dr B45. . . . . . . .102 B1
Lakey La B28 . . . . .106 B7
Lakey Lane Jun & Inf Sch
  B28. . . . . .106 B7
Lakin Cl CV34 . . . . .160 F4
Lakin Ho CV34 . . . . .160 F4
Lakin Rd CV34 . . . . .160 F4
Lambah Cl WV14. . . . . .40 F7
Lamb Cl B34 . . . . .69 E5
Lambert Cl B23. . . . . .56 D6
Lambert Ct
  Kingswinford DY6 . . . . .60 D8
  Warwick CV34 . . . . .160 D6
Lambert End B70. . . . . .53 B3
Lambert Fold 4 DY2. . . . . .62 E8
Lambert Rd WV10. . . . . . . .25 F6
Lambert St B70. . . . . .53 B3
Lambeth Cl
  Birmingham B37 . . . . .70 B4
  Coventry CV2. . . . . .114 E7
Lambeth Rd
  Bilston WV14. . . . . .40 B7
  Birmingham B44. . . . . .44 E3
Lamburn Cl WS3 . . . . .14 C2
Lambourn Cres CV31. . . . .162 C6
Lambourne Cl
  4 Lichfield WS14. . . . . .9 E8
  Coventry CV5. . . . . .112 A4
  Great Wyrley WS6 . . . . .4 F3
Lambourne Gr B37 . . . . . . .69 E2
Lambourne Way
  Brierley Hill DY5 . . . . .81 B8
  Norton Canes WS11 . . . . . . .6 A5
Lambourn Rd
  Birmingham B23 . . . . .56 D4
  Willenhall WV13. . . . . .27 D1
Lambscote Cl B90 . . . . . . .105 C2
Lamb St CV1 . . . . .165 B3
Lamerton Cl CV2 . . . . .114 C6
Lamford Cl LE10 . . . . .71 B1
Lamintone Dr CV32 . . . . . .156 D2
Lammas Cl B92. . . . . .89 C1
Lammas Croft CV31. . . . . .162 A3
Lammas Ct CV34. . . . . . . .160 D6
Lammas Ho 6 CV6 . . . . . .113 A4
Lammas Rd
  Coventry CV6. . . . . .112 F4
  Stourbridge DY8 . . . . .60 C3
Lammas Wlk CV34 . . . . . . .160 D7
Lammermoor Ave B43 . . . .43 F2
Lamont Ave B32 . . . . .84 F3
Lamorna Cl
  Nuneaton CV11 . . . . .73 F4
  Wolverhampton WV3 . . . . .38 B8
Lamprey B77 . . . . .35 D6
Lanark Cl DY6 . . . . .60 F5
Lanark Croft B35 . . . . .57 F3
Lancaster Ave
  Aldridge WS9. . . . . .30 B8
  Birmingham B45 . . . . .122 A8
  Wednesbury WS10 . . . . . . .42 C3
Lancaster Circus Queensway
  B4. . . . . .164 C4
Lancaster Cl B30 . . . . .104 A6
Lancaster Dr B35. . . . . .58 B2
Lancaster Gdns WV4 . . . . .38 E5
Lancaster Ho
  5 Stourbridge DY8 . . . . . .80 F8
  7 Rowley Regis B65 . . . . . .63 E4
  Cannock WS12. . . . . .2 D1
Lancaster Pl
  Kenilworth CV8 . . . . .147 E2
  Walsall WS3 . . . . .14 E2

Lancaster Rd
  Brierley Hill DY5 . . . . .61 C2
  Hinckley LE10 . . . . .75 D8
Lancaster St B4 . . . . .164 C4
Lance Cl LE10 . . . . .75 D5
Lancelot Cl B8 . . . . .67 E3
Lancelot Ho DY10 . . . . . . .117 C8
Lancelot Pl B70 . . . . .52 E4
Lanchester Cl B79 . . . . . . .20 E7
Lanchester Rd
  Birmingham B38 . . . . .104 A1
  Coventry CV6. . . . . .113 B6
Lanchester Way B36 . . . . . .58 F1
Lancia Cl CV6 . . . . .96 B4
Lancing Rd CV12. . . . . .79 C2
Lander Cl B45 . . . . .122 A6
Landgate Rd B21 . . . . .54 C2
Land La B32 . . . . .90 A7
Land Oak Dr DY10 . . . . . . .117 B7
Landor Ho CV31 . . . . .162 A4
Landor Rd
  Dorridge B93. . . . . .128 A6
  Redditch B98 . . . . .154 A1
  Warwick CV34 . . . . .160 D8
  Whitnash CV31 . . . . .162 A3
Landor St B8 . . . . .67 B3
Landport Rd WV2 . . . . .39 B8
Landrail Wlk B36. . . . . .70 A8
Landrake Rd DY6 . . . . .61 A5
Landsberg B79 . . . . .20 F6
Landsdown Pl 2 B18. . . . .66 A5
Landseer Dr LE10 . . . . .71 B3
Landseer Gr B43. . . . . .44 D4
Landsgate DY8 . . . . .81 A1
Landswood Cl B44 . . . . . . .45 A1
Landswood Rd B68 . . . . . .64 C4
Landywood Ent Pk WS6. . .13 F8
Landywood Gn WS6. . . . . . .4 E2
Landywood La WS6 . . . . . . .4 E2
Landywood Prim Sch
  WS6 . . . . .13 F8
Landywood Sta WS6 . . . . . .4 E2
Lane Ave WS2 . . . . .28 B3
Lane Cl WS2 . . . . .28 B3
Lane Croft B76 . . . . .58 A8
Lane Ct 8 WV3. . . . . .25 C4
Lane Green Ave WV8. . . . . .10 C1
Lane Green Ct WV8 . . . . . .10 B3
Lane Green Fst Sch WV8 .10 B4
Lane Green Rd WV8 . . . . . .10 B3
Lane Green Rd Masionettes
  WV8. . . . . .10 B3
Lane Green S Par WV8. . . .10 B3
Lane Rd WV4 . . . . .40 A4
Lanesfield Drive Ind Est
  WV4 . . . . .40 A4
Lanesfield Dr WV4 . . . . . . .40 A4
Lanesfield Jun & Inf Sch
  WV4. . . . . .40 A4
Laneside B74. . . . . .44 F7
Laneside CV3. . . . . .134 E6
Laneside Dr LE10 . . . . .71 F3
Laneside Gdns WS2. . . . . . .28 B2
Lanes Sh Ctr The 1 B73 . .57 B7
Lane St WV14 . . . . .40 D3
Lanfear Ct LE10. . . . . .75 C7
Langbank Ave CV3 . . . . . .134 D7
Langbay Ct CV2 . . . . .114 F6
Langcliffe Ave CV34. . . . . .155 F1
Langcomb Rd B90 . . . . . . .126 A8
Langdale Ave CV6 . . . . .95 D3
Langdale Cl
  Brownhills WS8 . . . . .15 E6
  Royal Leamington Spa
  CV32 . . . . .157 D3
Langdale Croft B21 . . . . . .65 E7
Langdale Ct B77. . . . . .22 A6
Langdale Dr
  Bilston WV14 . . . . .40 D7
  Cannock WS11. . . . . .4 C7
  Nuneaton CV11 . . . . .74 A6
Langdale Gn WS11. . . . . . . .4 C7
Langdale Rd
  Birmingham B43 . . . . .44 F2
  Hinckley LE10 . . . . .75 A8
Langdale Way DY9 . . . . . . .81 D4
Langdon St B9 . . . . .67 B2
Langdon Wlk B27 . . . . .88 E4
Langfield Rd B93 . . . . .128 A7
Langford Ave B43. . . . . . . .54 E8
Langford Cl WS1. . . . . .29 A1
Langford Croft B91 . . . . . .107 C2
Langford Gr B17 . . . . .85 C3
Langham Cl B26. . . . . .89 A7
Langham Gr B17 . . . . .85 B5
Langholm Dr
  Birmingham B44. . . . . .45 D1
  Cannock WS12. . . . . .2 E2
Langland Dr DY3 . . . . .50 C8
Langley Ave WV14 . . . . . . .51 C8
Langley Cl
  Brownhills WS9 . . . . .16 A3
  Redditch B98 . . . . .154 D1
Langley Cres B68 . . . . .64 B4
Langley Croft CV4 . . . . . . .112 A2
Langley Dr B35. . . . . .58 A1
Langley Gdns
  Oldbury B68. . . . . .64 B4
  Wolverhampton WV3 . . . . .38 D7
Langley Gr B10 . . . . .87 D8
Langley Green Rd B69. . . .64 A4
Langley Green Sta B68. . . .64 B5
Langley Hall Dr B75 . . . . . .47 B5
Langley Hall Rd
  Solihull B92 . . . . .106 C7
  Sutton Coldfield B75 . . . . . .47 B5
Langley Heath Dr B76. . . . .47 A3
Langley High Sch B68. . . . .64 C4

Langley High St B69 . . . . . .64 A5
Langley Mede B68. . . . . . . .64 B5
Langley Park Way B75 . . . .46 F6
Langley Prim Sch
  Oldbury B69. . . . . .64 A5
  Solihull B92 . . . . .106 D6
Langley Rd
  Birmingham B10 . . . . .87 D8
  Oldbury B68. . . . . .64 B4
  Whitnash CV31. . . . . .162 A4
  Wolverhampton WV3,WV4. .38 B7
Langley Rise B92 . . . . .89 D3
Langley Sch B92. . . . . . . .106 D7
Langley Specl Sch B75. . . .47 A6
Langleys Rd B29 . . . . .85 E1
Langley Wlk B37. . . . . .70 D2
Langlodge Rd CV6. . . . . . . .95 B2
Langmead Cl WS2 . . . . . . .27 D3
Langnor Rd CV2 . . . . .114 C6
Langsett Rd WV10 . . . . . . .25 C4
Langstone Rd
  Birmingham B14 . . . . .105 B3
  Dudley DY1 . . . . .50 F1
Langton Cl
  Birmingham B36 . . . . .70 B6
  Coventry CV3. . . . . .134 E8
Langton Fld 1 WS13 . . . . . .3 A1
Langton Pl WV14 . . . . .41 A4
Langton Rd B8 . . . . .67 E4
Langtree Ave B91 . . . . . . .107 B1
Langtree Cl WS12. . . . . .2 D1
Langwood Cl CV4 . . . . . . .132 B7
Langwood Ct B36. . . . . . . .69 B8
Langworth Ave B27 . . . . . .88 C5
Lannacombe Rd B31. . . . . .122 E6
Lansbury Ave WS10 . . . . . .41 C4
Lansbury Cl CV2 . . . . .114 E7
Lansbury Dr WS11 . . . . .1 E4
Lansbury Gn B64 . . . . .83 B8
Lansbury Rd B64 . . . . .83 B8
Lansbury Wlk 6 DY4 . . . . .52 A8
Lansdale Ave B92. . . . . . . .107 F8
Lansdowne Cir CV32 . . . . .157 A1
Lansdowne Cl
  Bedworth CV12 . . . . .78 A3
  Dudley,West Coseley WV14. .51 A7
  Rowley Regis CV2 . . . . . . .62 F6
Lansdowne Cres
  6 Royal Leamington Spa
  CV32 . . . . .157 A1
  Studley B80 . . . . .159 D3
  Tamworth B77 . . . . .35 D8
Lansdowne Ct CV9 . . . . . . .81 C1
Lansdowne Rd
  2 Royal Leamington Spa
  CV32 . . . . .157 A1
  Birmingham,Erdington B24 . .56 F3
  Birmingham,Handsworth
  B21. . . . . .66 A8
  Halesowen,Hasbury B63 . . .82 D2
  Halesowen,Hurst Green B62 .63 F1
  Studley B80 . . . . .159 D3
  Wolverhampton WV1 . . . . .163 A4
Lansdowne St
  Birmingham B18 . . . . .65 F4
  Coventry CV2. . . . . .113 F3
  Royal Leamington Spa
  CV32 . . . . .157 A1
Lansdown Cl
  Lansdown Gn DY11 . . . . . .116 C5
  Lansdown Ho B15 . . . . .86 D8
  Lant Cl CV7. . . . . .131 B7
  Lantern Rd DY2 . . . . .62 C2
  Lanthorn Cl WS13. . . . . .9 A7
  Lapal La B62 . . . . .82 A2
  Lapal La N B62 . . . . .83 B3
  Lapal La S B32,B62 . . . . . .83 F2
  Lapal Prim Sch B62 . . . . . .83 F4
  Lapley Cl WV1 . . . . .26 B2
  Lappath Ho B32 . . . . .102 D8
  Lapper Ave WV4 . . . . .39 F2
  Lapwing Cl
  Brownhills WS8 . . . . .15 C1
  Cheslyn Hay WS6. . . . . .4 E3
  Kidderminster DY10 . . . . .117 B1
Lapwing Croft B23. . . . . . . .56 C7
Lapwing Dr B92 . . . . .109 B7
Lapwing Rd DY9 . . . . .81 A1
Lapwood Ave DY6. . . . . . . .61 A5
Lapworth CE Prim Sch
  B94. . . . . .144 D3
Lapworth Cl B98. . . . . . . .158 F7
Lapworth Dr B73 . . . . .45 C3
Lapworth Gr B12. . . . . .86 F6
Lapworth Oaks B94 . . . . . .144 D3
Lapworth Rd CV2 . . . . .96 C1
Lapworth Sta B94 . . . . . . .144 D4
Lapworth St B94. . . . . . . .144 B2
Lara Cl B17. . . . . .85 B8
Lara Gr DY4 . . . . .52 A2
Larch Ave B21 . . . . .54 D2
Larch Cl WS14 . . . . .9 E7
Larch Croft
  Birmingham B37 . . . . .70 B2
  Tividale B69. . . . . .52 B2
Larch Dr B31 . . . . .102 C1
Larches Cottage Gdns
  DY11. . . . . .116 C3
Larches La WV3 . . . . .25 A2
Larches Rd DY11. . . . . . . .116 D4
Larches St B11 . . . . .87 B6
Larches The
  Bedworth CV7. . . . . .96 B8
  Wolverhampton WV11 . . . .26 B5
Larchfield Cl B20 . . . . .55 A3
Larch Gdns WV14 . . . . . . .40 F4
Larch Gr
  Sedgley DY3. . . . . .50 E7

Larch Gr continued
  Warwick CV34 . . . . .156 A1
Larch Ho
  Birmingham B36 . . . . .68 F8
  Stourbridge DY8 . . . . .80 C6
Larchmere Dr
  Birmingham B28 . . . . .105 F8
  Bromsgrove B61 . . . . .136 E5
  Essington WV11. . . . . .13 B1
Larch Rd DY6. . . . . .60 E4
Larch Tree Ave CV4 . . . . . .112 A2
Larch Wlk B25. . . . . .88 B8
Larchwood Cres B74 . . . . . .44 E8
Larchwood Dr WS11 . . . . . . .2 A4
Larchwood Gn WS5 . . . . . .43 B4
Larchwood Rd
  Bedworth CV7 . . . . .78 B3
  Walsall WS5 . . . . .43 A4
Larcombe Dr WV4 . . . . . . .39 D5
Large Ave WS10 . . . . .41 C4
Lark Cl B14. . . . . .105 A2
Larkfield Ave B36. . . . . .69 B8
Larkfield Rd B98 . . . . .154 A3
Larkfield Way CV5 . . . . . . .112 A4
Lark Hall Com Inf Sch
  B79. . . . . .21 A1
Larkhill DY10 . . . . .116 E2
Larkhill Rd DY8 . . . . .80 C4
Larkhill Wlk B14. . . . . . . .104 D1
Larkin Cl
  Bulkington CV12 . . . . .79 B3
  Wolverhampton WV10. . . . .12 A1
Larkin Gr CV2 . . . . .114 F6
Lark Meadow Dr B37 . . . . .69 F3
Larkspur B77 . . . . .35 C7
Larkspur Ave WS7 . . . . .7 A5
Larkspur Croft B36 . . . . . . .68 D8
Larkspur Ct
  Bedworth CV12 . . . . .95 C8
  Halesowen B62 . . . . .83 F7
Larkspur Dr WV10 . . . . . . .12 B7
Larkspur Gr 5 CV12 . . . . . .77 D2
Larkspur Rd DY2. . . . . .62 F8
Larkspur Way WS8. . . . . . .15 D6
Larkswood Dr
  Sedgley DY3. . . . . .50 D7
  Wolverhampton WV4 . . . . .38 C3
Larne Rd B26. . . . . .89 A7
Lashbrooke Ho B45. . . . . .121 F7
Lassington Cl B98 . . . . . . .154 E4
Latches Cl WS10. . . . . .41 E6
Latchford Cl B98. . . . . . . .154 E6
Latelow Rd B33 . . . . .69 A2
Latham Ave B43 . . . . .54 E7
Latham Cres DY4 . . . . .52 A3
Latham Rd CV5 . . . . .113 A2
Lath La B66 . . . . .64 D8
Lathom Gr B33 . . . . .68 F5
Latimer Cl CV8. . . . . .147 F2
Latimer Gdns B15 . . . . .86 D7
Latimer Pl B18 . . . . .65 E6
Latimer Rd B48 . . . . .139 A5
Latimer St WV13. . . . . .27 B3
Latymer Cl B76. . . . . .58 A7
Lauder Cl
  Sedgley DY3. . . . . .39 C1
  Willenhall WV13 . . . . .26 D1
Lauderdale Ave CV6 . . . . . .95 D3
Lauderdale Cl
  Lanterham B13 . . . . .87 A2
  Coventry CV5. . . . . .112 F1
Lauderdale Gdns WV10. . .11 E3
Laughton Cl B31 . . . . .123 B7
Launce Gr CV34 . . . . .161 F2
Launceston Cl
  Tamworth B77 . . . . .21 D2
  Walsall WS5 . . . . .43 D7
Launceston Dr CV11 . . . . . .73 F4
Launceston Rd WS5 . . . . . .43 D7
Launde The B28 . . . . .105 E3
Laundry Cotts CV35 . . . . .145 E4
Laundry Rd B66 . . . . .65 C3
Laureates Wlk B74. . . . . . .46 A8
Laurel Bank Mews B60. . .137 F4
Laurel Bank B77 . . . . .21 B6
Laurel Cl
  Coventry CV2. . . . . .96 E2
  Dudley DY1 . . . . .51 A3
  Lichfield WS14. . . . . .9 D8
  Redditch B98 . . . . .153 E2
Laurel Ct
  Birmingham B13 . . . . .87 A2
  Coventry CV5. . . . . .112 F1
Laurel Dr
  Burntwood WS7. . . . . .7 C7
  Cannock WS12. . . . . .2 E4
  Hartshill CV10 . . . . .72 A7
  Smethwick B66 . . . . .65 A8
  Sutton Coldfield B74 . . . . . .44 E8
Laurel Gdns
  3 Birmingham,Stockfield
  B27. . . . . .88 C5
  Barnt Green B45 . . . . .138 E8
  Birmingham B21 . . . . .54 E1
Laurel Gr
  Birmingham B30 . . . . .103 E6
  Bromsgrove B61 . . . . .136 F4
  Darlaston WV14. . . . . .41 A4
  Wolverhampton WV4 . . . . .38 E6
Laurel La B63 . . . . .83 B3
Laurel Rd
  Birmingham,Handsworth
  B21. . . . . .54 F1
  Birmingham,King's Norton
  B30. . . . . .104 A4
  Dudley DY1 . . . . .51 A3

x

x

Laurel Rd continued
Tipton DY4 . . . . 51 F7
Walsall WS5 . . . . 43 B4
Laurels Cres CV7 . . . . . 130 C6
Laurels The
Bedworth CV12 . . . . 77 E2
Birmingham B68 . . . . 84 B6
Birmingham,Ladywood B16 . 65 F5
Birmingham,Sheldon B26 . . 89 C5
Coventry CV4 . . . . 132 F6
Portway B47 . . . . 140 F8
Smethwick B66 . . . . 65 C4
Sutton Coldfield B73 . . . . 46 B1
Laurence Ct B31 . . . . . 103 B5
Laurence Gr WV6 . . . . . 24 E7
Lauriston Cl CV1 . . . . . . 50 F3
Lavender Ave CV6 . . . . 112 F5
Lavender Cl
[2] Walsall WS5 . . . . 42 F3
Bedworth CV12 . . . . 77 E1
Wolverhampton WV9 . . . . . 10 F3
Lavender Gdns [1] B23 . . 56 B7
Lavender Gr
Bilston WV14 . . . . 40 F6
Walsall WS3 . . . . 28 E5
Lavender Hall La CV7 . . 110 C2
Lavender Ho B38 . . . . . 123 F8
Lavender La DY8 . . . . . . 80 D3
Lavender Rd
Dudley DY1 . . . . 51 B3
Tamworth B77 . . . . 21 F4
Lavendon Rd B42 . . . . . 55 B5
Lavenham Cl CV11 . . . . . 79 C8
Lavinia Rd B42 . . . . 55 B6
Law Cliff Rd B42 . . . . . . 55 B6
Law Cl B69 . . . . 52 D2
Lawden Rd B10 . . . . 87 B8
Lawford Ave WS14 . . . . . . 9 E7
Lawford Cl
Birmingham B7 . . . . 67 A3
Coventry CV3 . . . . 114 E1
Lawford Gr
Birmingham B5 . . . . 86 E8
Solihull B90 . . . . 105 D2
Lawford Rd CV31 . . . . . 162 B5
Lawfred Ave WV11 . . . . . 26 D5
Lawley Cl
Coventry CV4 . . . . 112 A2
Walsall WS4 . . . . 15 B1
Lawley Middleway B4 . . . 67 A3
Lawley Rd WV14 . . . . 40 B6
Lawley St
Dudley DY1 . . . . 51 A1
West Bromwich B70 . . . . . 52 F3
Lawley The B63 . . . . 82 D1
Lawn Ave DY8 . . . . 80 E4
Lawn La WV9 . . . . 11 A7
Lawnoaks Cl WS8 . . . . 6 D2
Lawn Rd WV2 . . . . 40 A6
Lawns Bsns Ctr The LE10 . 75 E8
Lawns Cl WS9 . . . . 9 C8
Lawnsdown Rd WV5 . . . . 81 F6
Lawnsfield Gr B23 . . . . . 56 D7
Lawnside Gn WV14 . . . . . 40 D8
Lawns The
Bedworth CV12 . . . . 77 C2
Hinckley LE10 . . . . 75 E8
Portway B47 . . . . 140 F7
Lawn St DY8 . . . . 80 E4
Lawnswood Ave
Burntwood WS7 . . . . 6 F5
Solihull B90 . . . . 106 D3
Stourbridge DY8 . . . . 60 C3
Wolverhampton,Parkfield
WV4 . . . . 39 E4
Wolverhampton WV6 . . . . . 24 E8
Lawnswood Cl [2] WS12 . . . 2 D2
Lawnswood Dr
Brownhills WS9 . . . . 16 A3
Stourbridge DY7 . . . . 60 D3
Lawnswood Gr B21 . . . . . 54 C1
Lawnswood Rd
Dudley DY3 . . . . 50 D5
Stourbridge DY8 . . . . 60 D3
Lawnswood Rise WV6 . . . 24 F8
Lawnwood
Stourbridge DY8 . . . . 60 A2
Sutton Coldfield B76 . . . . 58 A8
Lawnwood Rd DY2 . . . . . 62 C2
Lawrence Ave
Wednesfield WV11 . . . . . . 26 F6
Wolverhampton WV10 . . . . 26 A4
Lawrence Ct
[6] Birmingham B68 . . . . . 84 B8
Tamworth B79 . . . . 21 A6
Lawrence Dr B76 . . . . . . 58 D6
Lawrence Gdns CV8 . . . 148 A6
Lawrence La B64 . . . . . . 62 E1
Lawrence Rd CV7 . . . . . . 96 B8
Lawrence Saunders Rd
CV6 . . . . 113 B5
Lawrence St
Stourbridge DY9 . . . . 81 C6
Willenhall WV13 . . . . 27 A3
Lawrence Way WS13 . . . . . 8 F5
Lawrence Wlk B43 . . . . . 44 D4
Lawson Cl WS9 . . . . 30 B4
Lawson St B4 . . . . 164 C4
Law St B71 . . . . 53 C5
Lawton Ave B29 . . . . 86 B7
Lawton Cl
Hinckley LE10 . . . . 74 F8
Rowley Regis B65 . . . . . . 63 D6
Laxton Cl CV3 . . . . 25 B1
Laxey Rd B16 . . . . 65 D3
Laxford Cl B12 . . . . 86 E6
Laxton Cl DY6 . . . . 61 A5

Laxton Gr
Birmingham B25 . . . . 68 D1
Solihull B91 . . . . 107 C7
Lay Gdns CV31 . . . . 162 E5
Lazy Hill B38 . . . . 104 B2
Lazy Hill WS9 . . . . 16 C1
Lazy Hill Rd WS9 . . . . . . 16 C2
Lea Ave WS10 . . . . 41 D1
Lea Bank Ave DY11 . . . . 116 B5
Lea Bank Rd DY2 . . . . . . 62 C3
Leabon Gr B17 . . . . 85 C4
Leabrook B26 . . . . 88 F8
Leabrook Rd N WS10 . . . . 41 D2
Leabrook Rd WS10 . . . . . 41 D1
Leach Green La B45 . . . . 122 B6
Leach Heath La B45 . . . . 122 A7
Leacliffe Way WV9 . . . . . . 30 F3
Leacote Dr WV6 . . . . 24 C4
Leacrest Rd CV6 . . . . 95 A2
Leacroft Ave WV10 . . . . . 25 E8
Leacroft Cl WS9 . . . . 16 B1
Leacroft Gr B71 . . . . 53 B7
Leacroft La WS11 . . . . 4 F5
Leacroft Rd DY6 . . . . 60 E8
Lea Croft Rd B97 . . . . . 158 D5
Leacroft CV7 . . . . 27 C2
Lea Cswy The DY11 . . . . 116 A4
Leadbeater Ho [6] B63 . . . 83 A8
Leadbetter Dr B61 . . . . . 136 D2
Lea Dr B26 . . . . 89 A6
Lea End La B48 . . . . . . 123 D3
Leaf Ct CV3 . . . . 133 D4
Leafdown Cl WS12 . . . . . . 2 D3
Leafenden Ave WS7 . . . . . 7 A6
Leafield Cl CV2 . . . . 114 F8
Leafield Cres B33 . . . . . . 69 A5
Leafield Gdns B62 . . . . . 83 D8
Leafield Rd B92 . . . . 89 C1
Leafield CV3 . . . . 133 E5
Lea Ford Rd B33 . . . . . . 69 C4
Leaford Way DY6 . . . . . . 61 A5
Leafy Glade B74 . . . . 31 A3
Leafy Rise DY3 . . . . 50 D4
Lea Gdns WV3 . . . . 163 A1
Leagh Cl CV8 . . . . 148 B2
Lea Green Ave DY4 . . . . . 51 D5
Lea Green Dr B47 . . . . . 125 C4
Lea Green La B47 . . . . . 125 C5
Lea Hall Rd B33 . . . . 69 A2
Lea Hall Sta B33 . . . . 69 A2
Leahill Croft B37 . . . . . . 69 F2
Lea Hill Rd B20 . . . . 55 C2
Lea Ho [6] B15 . . . . 61 E8
Leaholme Gdns DY9 . . . . 81 B2
Leahouse Gdns B68 . . . . 64 A3
Lea House Rd B30 . . . . . 104 A7
Leahurst Cres B17 . . . . . . 85 B4
Leahurst Cres B17 . . . . . . 64 A3
Lea La WS6 . . . . 5 A3
Leaholme Ct CV5 . . . . . 132 F8
Lea Manor Dr WV4 . . . . . 38 E4
Leam Cl CV11 . . . . 73 F1
Leam Cres B92 . . . . 89 B1
Leam Dr WS7 . . . . 7 D7
Leam Gn CV4 . . . . 132 D5
Leamington Cl WS11 . . . . 4 C7
Leamington Rd
Birmingham B12 . . . . 87 B5
Coventry CV3 . . . . 133 C6
Kenilworth CV8 . . . . 148 B2
Ryton-on-D CV8 . . . . . . 135 B1
**Leamington Spa Art Gallery
& Mus*** CV32 . . . . 161 F8
Leamington Spa Sta
CV31 . . . . 161 F7
Leamore Cl WS2 . . . . 28 A7
Leamore Ind Est WS2 . . . 28 C6
Leamore La WS3 . . . . 28 C7
Leamore Prim Sch WS3 . . 28 C7
Leamount Dr B44 . . . . . . 45 C2
Leam Rd CV31 . . . . 161 D7
Leam Side Ho [9] CV34 . . 161 D8
Leam St CV31 . . . . 162 B7
Leam Terr CV31 . . . . . . 162 B8
Leander Cl WS6 . . . . 4 F2
Leander Gdns B14 . . . . . 104 F5
Leander Rd DY9 . . . . 81 F4
Leander Dr B74 . . . . 45 A7
Lea Park Rise B61 . . . . . 136 F5
Lea Rd
Birmingham B11 . . . . 87 D4
Wolverhampton WV3 . . . . . 39 B8
Lear Gr CV34 . . . . 161 E4
Lear Rd WV5 . . . . 49 B8
Leas Cl CV12 . . . . 78 A3
Leason La WV10 . . . . 26 A7
Leasow Dr B15 . . . . 85 D3
Leasowe Rd
Birmingham B45 . . . . . . 121 F8
Tipton DY4 . . . . 51 E4
Leasowe's Ave CV3 . . . . 132 F4
Leasowes Com Coll B62 . . 83 F6
Leasowes Ct B63 . . . . . . 82 F3
Leasowes Dr
Perton WV6 . . . . 23 D4
Wolverhampton WV4 . . . . . 38 D6
Leasowes La B62 . . . . . . 83 D4
Leasowes Rd B14 . . . . . . 104 F1
Leasowes The WS13 . . . . . 3 C1
Leasow The WS13 . . . . . . 29 E5
Leas The WV10 . . . . 11 F8
Lea St DY10 . . . . 116 F6
Lea Street Fst Sch DY10 . 116 F6
Lea The
Birmingham B33 . . . . 69 A2
Kidderminster DY11 . . . . 116 A5
Leatherhead Cl [5] B6 . . . 66 F6

Lea Vale Rd DY8 . . . . . . 80 F3
Leavesden Gr B26 . . . . . 89 A5
Lea View
Aldridge WS9 . . . . 29 E5
Wednesfield WV12 . . . . . . 27 A5
Lea Village B33 . . . . 69 B3
Leaward Cl CV10 . . . . 72 E2
Lea Wlk
Birmingham B45 . . . . . . 121 F8
Ryton-on-D CV8 . . . . . . 135 B1
Lea Wood Gr DY11 . . . . . 116 A5
Lea Yield Cl B30 . . . . . . 104 A7
Lebanon Gr WS7 . . . . 6 F8
Lebanon Cl B98 . . . . . . 154 B7
Lechlade Rd B43 . . . . 54 B8
Leckie Rd WS2 . . . . 28 E4
Ledbrook Rd CV32 . . . . . 157 E5
Ledbury Cl
Aldridge WS9 . . . . 16 C1
Birmingham B16 . . . . 66 A2
Redditch B98 . . . . 154 F2
Walsall WV11 . . . . 26 B1
Ledbury Ho
Birmingham B33 . . . . 69 E2
Redditch B97 . . . . 153 B4
Ledbury Rd CV31 . . . . . 162 C6
Ledbury Way B76 . . . . . . 58 A8
Ledsam Gr B32 . . . . 84 F6
Ledsam St B16 . . . . 66 A2
Ledwell B90 . . . . 126 A5
Lee Bank Ho B1 . . . . . . 164 B1
Lee Bank Middleway B15 . 86 C8
Leebank Rd B63 . . . . 82 E2
Leech St DY4 . . . . 52 C5
Lee Cl CV34 . . . . 155 E2
Lee Cres B15 . . . . 86 C8
Lee Ct WS9 . . . . 16 B1
Leeder Cl CV6 . . . . 95 C2
Leedham Ave DY4 . . . . . . 51 F3
Lee Gdns B67 . . . . 64 A6
Lee Meadowe CV34 . . . . 160 B4
Leeming Cl CV4 . . . . . . 132 C6
Lee Mount B15 . . . . 86 C8
Lee Rd
Cradley Heath B64 . . . . . . 82 F8
Hollywood B47 . . . . 125 A7
Royal Leamington Spa
CV31 . . . . 161 E6
Leeson Wlk [8] B17 . . . . . 85 D5
Lees Rd WV14 . . . . 40 F3
Lees St B18 . . . . 65 F6
Lees Terr WV14 . . . . 40 F3
Lee St B70 . . . . 53 A8
Lee The CV5 . . . . 112 C4
Lee Wlk WS11 . . . . 2 B4
Legg Bros Ind Est WV4 . . 40 A5
Legge La
Birmingham B1 . . . . 66 C3
Dudley WV14 . . . . 40 D1
Legge St
Birmingham B4 . . . . 164 D4
West Bromwich B70 . . . . . 53 E3
Wolverhampton WV2 . . . . . 39 E6
Legion Cl WS11 . . . . 4 A6
Legion Rd B45 . . . . 121 E7
Legs La WV10 . . . . 11 F3
Le Hanche Cl CV7 . . . . . . 95 A7
Leicester Cl B67 . . . . 64 E1
Leicester Cswy CV1 . . . . 113 D5
Leicester Ct CV12 . . . . . . 79 C2
Leicester La
Cubbington CV32 . . . . . . 149 E1
Royal Leamington Spa
CV32 . . . . 157 C6
Leicester Pl B71 . . . . 53 C7
Leicester Rd
Bedworth CV12 . . . . 78 B4
Hinckley LE10 . . . . 71 F2
Nuneaton CV11 . . . . 73 D5
Shilton CV7 . . . . 97 F6
Leicester Row CV1 . . . . . 165 B4
Leicester St
Bedworth CV12 . . . . 78 B3
Bulkington CV12 . . . . 79 C2
Royal Leamington Spa
CV32 . . . . 157 A1
Walsall WS1 . . . . 28 E2
Wolverhampton WV6 . . . . . 25 B4
Leigham Dr B17 . . . . 85 A7
Leigh Ave
Burntwood WS7 . . . . 7 B7
Coventry CV3 . . . . 133 C3
Leigh CE Prim Sch CV4 . 131 D8
Leigh Cl WS4 . . . . 29 A4
Leigh Ct
Birmingham B23 . . . . 56 C2
Walsall WS4 . . . . 29 A3
Leigh Jun &Inf Sch B8 . . . 67 E6
Leigh Rd
Birmingham B8 . . . . 67 E6
Sutton Coldfield B75 . . . . 47 B5
Walsall WS4 . . . . 29 A4
Leighs Rd WS4 . . . . 15 C1
Leigh St [4] WS1 . . . . . . 113 E4
Leighswood Ave WS9 . . . . 30 B7
Leighswood Cl WS11 . . . . . 1 C5
Leighswood Ct WS9 . . . . . 30 B6
Leighswood Gr WS9 . . . . . 30 A7
Leighswood Ind Est WS9 . 30 A6
Leighswood Rd WS9 . . . . . 30 B6
Leighton Cl
Birmingham B43 . . . . 44 C3
Coventry CV4 . . . . 132 D2
Dudley DY1 . . . . 50 E2
Royal Leamington Spa
CV32 . . . . 157 C4

Leighton Rd
Birmingham B13 . . . . 86 F2
Darlaston WV14 . . . . 41 A4
Wolverhampton WV6 . . . . . 38 F6
Leisure Wlk [7] B77 . . . . . 35 F6
Leith Gr B38 . . . . 123 E8
Lelant Gr B17 . . . . 85 A5
Lellow St B71 . . . . 53 C8
Le More B74 . . . . 32 A2
Lemox Rd B70 . . . . 53 A8
Lench Cl
Halesowen B62 . . . . 63 C1
Redditch B97 . . . . 153 A5
Lench's Cl B13 . . . . 87 A3
Lenchs Gn B5 . . . . 86 E7
Lench St B4 . . . . 164 C4
Lench's Trust Almshouses
[3] Birmingham,Edgbaston
B12 . . . . 87 A8
[3] Birmingham,Highgate
B12 . . . . 87 A8
Lenchs Trust B32 . . . . . . 84 E6
Len Davis Rd WV12 . . . . . 27 B7
Lennard Cl CV3 . . . . . . 134 E6
Lennox Gdns WV3 . . . . . . 39 A8
Lennox Gr B73 . . . . 57 A7
Lennox St B19 . . . . 66 D6
Lenton Croft B26 . . . . . . 88 E4
Lenton's La CV2 . . . . 96 E4
Lenwade Rd B68 . . . . 84 D8
Leofric Ct [3] B15 . . . . . . 86 C8
Leofric St CV6 . . . . 113 A5
Leomansley Cl WS13 . . . . . 8 F7
Leomansley Rd WS13 . . . . 8 E7
Leomansley View WS13 . . . 8 E7
Leominster Cl WS5 . . . . 121 F8
Leominster Ho B33 . . . . . 69 E2
Leominster Rd B11 . . . . . 87 E3
Leominster Wlk B45 . . . . 121 F8
Leona Ind Est B62 . . . . . . 63 A1
Leonard Ave [5] B19 . . . . 66 D8
Leonard Gr [3] B19 . . . . . 66 D8
Leonard Parkins Ho CV12 . 79 D2
Leonard Rd
Birmingham B19 . . . . 66 D8
Stourbridge DY8 . . . . 80 C5
Leontes Mdws CV34 . . . . 161 E3
Leopold Ave B20 . . . . 54 F5
Leopold Rd CV1 . . . . . . 113 F4
Leopold St B12 . . . . 86 F8
Lepid Gr B29 . . . . 85 C2
Lerryn Cl DY6 . . . . 60 F5
Lesingham Dr CV4 . . . . . 111 E1
Lesley Bentley Ho [4] B66 . 66 C3
Lesley Dr DY6 . . . . 60 E4
Leslie Dr DY4 . . . . 41 B1
Leslie Rd
Birmingham,Edgbaston
B16 . . . . 65 F2
Birmingham,Handsworth
B20 . . . . 55 D2
Sutton Coldfield B74 . . . . 31 B2
Wolverhampton WV10 . . . . 25 F4
Leslie Rise B69 . . . . 63 D5
Lesscroft Cl WV9 . . . . . . 11 A3
Lester Gr WS9 . . . . 30 E2
Lester St WV14 . . . . 40 F5
Leswell Gr DY10 . . . . . . 116 F6
Leswell La DY10 . . . . . . 116 F6
Leswell St DY10 . . . . . . 116 F6
Letchlade Cl CV2 . . . . . . 114 C8
Levante Gdns B33 . . . . . . 68 D2
Leve La WV13 . . . . 27 A2
Level St DY5 . . . . 61 E3
Leven Cl LE10 . . . . 75 B8
Leven Croft B76 . . . . 58 A7
Leven Dr WV14 . . . . 13 B1
Leven Way CV2 . . . . 115 A8
Levenwick Way DY6 . . . . . 61 A5
Leverretts The B21 . . . . . 54 C3
Lever St WV2 . . . . 163 C1
Leverton Rise WV10 . . . . . 25 C6
Leveson Ave WS6 . . . . 4 E2
Leveson Cl DY2 . . . . 62 E7
Leveson Cres CV7 . . . . . 130 B6
Leveson Ct
[1] Willenhall WV13 . . . . . 27 A2
Wolverhampton WV6 . . . . . 25 A4
Leveson Dr DY4 . . . . 51 E6
Leveson Rd
Wednesfield WV11 . . . . . . 12 F1
Leveson St WV13 . . . . 27 A2
Leveson Wlk [5] DY2 . . . . 62 E8
Levett Rd B77 . . . . 22 B5
Levetts Fields WS14 . . . . . 9 C7
Levetts Hollow WS12 . . . . . 2 D3
Levetts Sq [4] WS1 . . . . . . 9 B7
Levington Cl WV6 . . . . . . 23 F5
Leviss Trad Est B33 . . . . . 68 D4
Lewis Ave WV1 . . . . 26 B2
Lewis Cl
Lichfield WS14 . . . . 9 E7
Willenhall WV12 . . . . 27 D5
Lewis Rd
Birmingham B30 . . . . . . 104 B8
Coventry CV1 . . . . 113 D5

Lewis Rd
Radford Semele CV31 . . . 162 F5
Stourbridge DY9 . . . . 81 D5
Lewis St
Bilston WV14 . . . . 40 E6
Tipton DY4 . . . . 52 D5
Walsall WS2 . . . . 28 D3
Lewkner Almshouses The
B48 . . . . 139 A5
Lewthorn Rise WV4 . . . . . 39 D4
Lexington Ct CV11 . . . . . . 73 B5
Lexington Gn DY5 . . . . . . 81 C7
Leybourne Cres WV9 . . . . 10 F2
Leybourne Gr B25 . . . . . . 88 C6
Leybrook Rd B45 . . . . . . 122 B8
Leyburn Cl
[1] Warwick CV34 . . . . . 155 F1
Coventry CV6 . . . . 95 E2
Nuneaton CV11 . . . . 74 A2
Willenhall WS2 . . . . 27 D3
Leyburn Rd B16 . . . . 66 A1
Leycester Cl B31 . . . . . . 123 A7
Leycester Ct [3] CV34 . . . 160 E6
Leycester Pl [2] CV34 . . . 160 E6
Leycester Rd CV8 . . . . . . 148 A2
Leycroft Ave B33 . . . . 69 D3
Leydon Croft B38 . . . . . . 104 B2
Leyes La CV8 . . . . 148 C5
Leyfields Cres CV34 . . . . 160 B6
Leyfields WS13 . . . . 3 B2
Ley Hill Farm Rd B31 . . . 102 C5
Ley Hill Jun & Inf Sch
B31 . . . . 102 E5
Leyland Croft B13 . . . . . 105 D7
Leyland Ave WV3 . . . . 24 F1
Leyland Rd
Bulkington CV12 . . . . 79 B2
Coventry CV5 . . . . 112 D4
Nuneaton CV11 . . . . 73 E1
Tamworth B77 . . . . 21 E3
Leylands Way CV34 . . . . 160 B4
Leyman Cl B14 . . . . 105 C4
Leymere Cl CV7 . . . . 92 C1
Ley Rise DY3 . . . . 39 C1
Leys Cres DY5 . . . . 61 B3
Leys La CV7 . . . . 92 C1
Leysdown Gr B27 . . . . . . 106 C8
Leysdown Rd B27 . . . . . . 106 C8
Leys Hill CV3 . . . . 134 E5
Leys Ind Est DY5 . . . . . . 61 A3
Leys La CV7 . . . . 92 C1
Leys Rd DY5 . . . . 61 B3
Leysters Cl B98 . . . . 154 E3
Leys The
[1] Darlaston WS10 . . . . . 41 D6
Birmingham B31 . . . . . . 103 B5
Hinckley LE10 . . . . 76 A6
Leys Wood Croft B26 . . . . 89 B6
Leyton Cl DY5 . . . . 81 D8
Leyton Gr B44 . . . . 45 A1
Leyton Rd B21 . . . . 65 F8
Libbards Gate [4] B91 . . 127 C8
Libbards Way B91 . . . . . 127 B8
Liberty Cl WS6 . . . . 11 F4
Liberty Ho [1] B16 . . . . . . 66 B2
Liberty Rd B77 . . . . 35 F5
Liberty Way CV11 . . . . . . 73 F3
Libra Cl B79 . . . . 20 F7
Library Cl LE10 . . . . 76 A5
Library Rd CV4 . . . . 132 B5
Library Sq B31 . . . . 107 C3
Library Way B45 . . . . . . 121 F7
Lich Ave WV11 . . . . 26 F7
Lichen Cl WS12 . . . . 1 C6
Lichen Gdns B38 . . . . . . 123 D7
Lichen Gn CV4 . . . . 132 D5
Lichfield Bsns Ctr WS13 . . 3 D1
Lichfield Cathedral Sch
WS13 . . . . 9 B8
Lichfield Cath* WS13 . . . . 9 B8
Lichfield City Sta WS14 . . . 9 C7
Lichfield Cl CV11 . . . . 74 A7
Lichfield Cres B78 . . . . . . 20 E7
Lichfield Ct
Solihull B90 . . . . 105 D2
Sutton Coldfield B75 . . . . 46 C5
Walsall WS4 . . . . 29 A2
Lichfield Pas WV1 . . . . . 163 C3
Lichfield Rd
Birmingham B6 . . . . 67 B8
Brownhills,Shireoak Hill WS8,
WS9 . . . . 16 B5
Brownhills WS8,WS14 . . . . 16 A8
Burntwood WS7 . . . . 7 D6
Cannock WS11 . . . . 1 D4
Coventry CV3 . . . . 133 D8
Sutton Coldfield B74 . . . . 20 E6
Tamworth B78,B79 . . . . . 20 E6
Walsall B75 . . . . 15 B5
Walsall,New Invention WS3,WS4,
WS8,WS9 . . . . 13 E1
Walsall,Rushall WS4 . . . . . 29 A4
Walsall,Shelfield WS4 . . . . 15 C1
Walsall,Wallington Heath
WS3 . . . . 14 C2
Water Orton B46,B76 . . . . 59 F4
Wednesfield WV12 . . . . . . 27 D8
Wishaw B76,B78 . . . . 48 B3
Lichfield Road Ind Est
B79 . . . . 20 E6

Lichfield St
Bilston WV14 . . . . .40 E5
Fazeley B78 . . . . .20 F1
Tamworth B79 . . . . .21 A5
Tipton DY4 . . . . .51 F8
Wolverhampton WV1 . . . . .9 F8
Lichfield Trent Valley Sta
WS13 . . . . .9 F8
Lichwood Rd WV11 . . . . . .26 F7
Lickey Coppice B45 . . . . .122 C4
Lickey End Fst Sch B60 . .137 C6
Lickey Grange Dr B60 . . .121 E1
Lickey Gr DY11 . . . . .116 B2
Lickey Hills Country Pk &
Visitor Ctr* B45 . . . . . . .122 B2
Lickey Hills Prim Sch
B45 . . . . .121 F3
Lickey Rd
Birmingham B45 . . . . . . .122 C6
Stourbridge DY9 . . . . . . .81 B6
Lickey Rock B60 . . . . . . .121 D1
Lickey Sq B45 . . . . .122 A2
Liddiard Ct DY8 . . . . .80 E6
Liddon Dr B27 . . . . .106 C8
Liddon Rd B27 . . . . .106 C8
Lifford Cl B14 . . . . .104 C4
Lifford La B30 . . . . .104 B4
Lifford Way CV3 . . . . . . .135 A7
Lifton Croft DY6 . . . . . . .60 F5
Lightfields Wlk B65 . . . . .63 A5
Light Hall Sch B90 . . . . . .126 B8
Lighthorne Ave B16 . . . . .66 B2
Lighthorne Rd B91 . . . . .107 C6
Light La CV1 . . . . .165 B4
Lightning Way B31 . . . . .123 B7
Lightoak Cl B97 . . . . . . .158 C6
Lightwood Cl B93 . . . . . .128 B8
Lightwood Rd DY1 . . . . . .51 A3
Lightwoods Hill B67 . . . . .84 E8
Lightwoods Jun & Inf Sch
B68 . . . . .84 D8
Lightwoods Rd
Smethwick B67 . . . . .65 A1
Stourbridge DY9 . . . . . . .81 C1
Lilac Ave
1 Birmingham,Balsall Heath
B12 . . . . .87 A5
Birmingham,Perry B44 . . . .55 E7
Cannock WS11 . . . . .4 D7
Coventry CV6 . . . . .113 A5
Sutton Coldfield B74 . . . . .44 E8
Tipton DY4 . . . . .51 E7
Walsall WS5 . . . . .43 A4
Lilac Cl
Hinckley LE10 . . . . .75 E6
Redditch B98 . . . . .153 E2
Lilac Gr
Burntwood WS7 . . . . .6 F7
Walsall WS2 . . . . .27 E3
Warwick CV34 . . . . .156 A1
Wednesbury WS10 . . . . . .42 A2
Lilac Ho WS4 . . . . .15 D1
Lilac La WS6 . . . . .14 A8
Lilac Rd
Bedworth CV12 . . . . .78 D5
Bilston WV1 . . . . .40 B8
Dudley DY1 . . . . .51 C4
Tamworth B79 . . . . .21 A8
Willenhall WV12 . . . . .27 E7
Lilacvale Way CV4 . . . . .132 D5
Lilac Way B62 . . . . .83 F8
Lilian Gr WV14 . . . . .40 E1
Lilleburne Dr CV10 . . . . . .72 B7
Lilleshall Cl B98 . . . . . . .154 E3
Lilleshall Cres WV2 . . . . .39 D7
Lilleshall Rd B26 . . . . . . .89 B7
Lilley Cl CV6 . . . . .95 C2
Lilley Green Rd B48 . . . .140 D5
Lilley La B31 . . . . .123 B8
Lillington Ave CV32 . . . .156 F2
Lillington Cl
2 Lichfield WS13 . . . . .9 A8
Royal Leamington Spa
CV32 . . . . .157 A3
Sutton Coldfield B75 . . . . .47 A4
Lillington Gr B34 . . . . . . .69 D5
Lillington Prim Sch
CV32 . . . . .157 B3
Lillington Rd
Coventry CV2 . . . . .96 D1
Royal Leamington Spa
CV32 . . . . .157 A3
Solihull B90 . . . . .126 B8
Lilycroft La B38 . . . . . . .124 A7
Lily Green La B97 . . . . . .153 A4
Lily Rd B26 . . . . .88 D7
Lily St B71 . . . . .53 C5
Limberlost Cl B20 . . . . . .55 A3
Limbrick Ave CV4 . . . . . .112 A1
Limbrick Cl B90 . . . . . . .105 F2
Limbrick Wood Prim Sch
CV4 . . . . .111 F3
Limbury Gr B92 . . . . .107 F8
Lime Ave
8 Birmingham B29 . . . . . .85 F2
Royal Leamington Spa
CV32 . . . . .157 A4
Walsall WS2 . . . . .27 E3
Lime Cl
Great Wyrley WS6 . . . . . . .4 F4
Hollywood B47 . . . . .125 A5
Tipton DY4 . . . . .51 E5
Walsall WS2 . . . . .27 E3
West Bromwich B70 . . . . .53 A4

Lime Ct
Birmingham B11 . . . . . . .87 C4
Kidderminster DY10 . . . .117 A4
Lime Gr
Bilston WV14 . . . . .40 C7
Birmingham B25,B26 . . . .88 D6
Birmingham,Balsall Heath
B12 . . . . .86 F5
Birmingham,Chemsley Wood
B37 . . . . .70 B1
Birmingham,Lozells B19 . .66 C8
Birmingham,Small Heath
B10 . . . . .87 D8
Bromsgrove B61 . . . . . . .136 F4
Burntwood WS7 . . . . .7 C6
Coventry CV4 . . . . .112 B2
Kenilworth CV8 . . . . .148 A4
Lichfield WS14 . . . . .9 D8
Nuneaton CV10 . . . . .72 E5
Smethwick B66 . . . . .65 B3
Smethwick B66 . . . . .65 B3
Sutton Coldfield B73 . . . . .57 B7
Walsall WS4 . . . . .29 C6
Limehurst Ave WS4 . . . . .24 C1
Limehurst Rd WS4 . . . . . .29 C6
Lime Kiln Cl B38 . . . . . . .123 D7
Limekiln La
Birmingham B14 . . . . . . .105 A4
Earlswood B94 . . . . .126 D1
Lime La
Norton Canes WS3 . . . . . . .6 A1
Walsall WS3 . . . . .15 A7
Limepit La
Dudley DY1 . . . . .51 A3
Huntington WS11,WS12 . . .1 D6
Lime Rd
Huntington WS12 . . . . .1 D8
Sedgley DY3 . . . . .39 F1
Wednesbury WS10 . . . . . .41 F4
Limes Ave
Brierley Hill DY5 . . . . . . .61 C5
Rowley Regis B65 . . . . . .63 C2
Limescroft Cl WS4 . . . . . .29 B7
Limes Ct WV6 . . . . .24 D5
Limes Rd
Dudley DY1 . . . . .51 B3
Wolverhampton WV6 . . . .24 D4
Lime St WV14 . . . . .51 A6
Limes The
Bedworth CV12 . . . . .77 E2
Birmingham,Gravelly Hill
B24 . . . . .56 F3
Birmingham,Ladywood B16 .65 F2
Birmingham,Rotton Park
B16 . . . . .65 F3
Birmingham,Sparkbrook
B11 . . . . .87 C6
Coventry CV6 . . . . .112 E5
Himley DY3 . . . . .49 B3
Walsall WS1 . . . . .29 A2
Wolverhampton WV11 . . . .26 B5
Lime St
Walsall WS1 . . . . .29 A1
Wolverhampton WV3 . . . . .39 B8
Limes View DY3 . . . . .50 D7
Lime Tree Ave
Coventry CV4 . . . . .112 A2
Wolverhampton WV6 . . . .24 A3
Lime Tree Cres B97 . . . .153 B4
Lime Tree Gdns WV8 . . . .10 B3
Lime Tree Gr B31 . . . . . .103 C2
Lime Tree Rd
Birmingham,Acock's Green
B27 . . . . .88 C5
Birmingham,Saltley B8 . . .67 F6
Codsall WV8 . . . . .10 A4
Limetree Rd B74 . . . . . . .30 D1
Lime Tree Rd WS5 . . . . . .43 A4
Linacre Ho B37 . . . . .69 F2
Linaker Rd CV3 . . . . .134 C5
Linchmere Rd B21 . . . . . .54 C2
Lincoln Ave
Nuneaton CV10 . . . . .72 B7
Tamworth B79 . . . . .20 E6
Willenhall WV13 . . . . .27 D2
Lincoln Cl
Birmingham B27 . . . . .88 E3
Lichfield WS13 . . . . .3 C3
Warwick CV34 . . . . .155 E1
Lincoln Croft WS14 . . . . .17 F6
Lincoln Ct
9 Birmingham B29 . . . . .103 C7
Royal Leamington Spa
CV32 . . . . .162 A8
Lincoln Dr WS11 . . . . .4 F8
Lincoln Gn WV10 . . . . . . .11 D2
Lincoln Gr B37 . . . . .70 A1
Lincoln Ho WV10 . . . . . . .11 D2
Lincoln Rd
Birmingham B27 . . . . .88 D2
Bromsgrove B61 . . . . . . .136 E4
Dudley DY2 . . . . .62 D2
Lincoln Rd N B27 . . . . . . .88 E3
Lincoln Rd
Smethwick B67 . . . . .64 E2
Walsall WS1 . . . . .29 A1
West Bromwich B71 . . . . .42 D1
Lincoln St
Birmingham B12 . . . . . . .86 E6
Coventry CV1 . . . . .165 C4
Wolverhampton WV10 . . . .25 E3
Lincoln Tower B16 . . . . . .66 A1
Lincroft Cres CV5 . . . . . .112 A4
Lindale B94 . . . . .68 C6
Lindale Cres DY5 . . . . . . .81 B6
Linden Ave
Birmingham B43 . . . . .54 D8
Burntwood WS7 . . . . .7 A8

Linden Ave continued
Halesowen B62 . . . . .83 E7
Kidderminster DY10 . . . .117 A7
Oldbury B69 . . . . .63 D8
Linden Cl
Tamworth B77 . . . . .21 F4
Warwick CV34 . . . . .155 E2
Willenhall WV12 . . . . .27 D2
Linden Ct B91 . . . . .107 E4
Linden Dr DY8 . . . . .81 A3
Linden Gdns DY10 . . . . .117 A6
Linden Glade B63 . . . . . . .83 A4
Linden Gr DY10 . . . . .117 A7
Linden Ho WV3 . . . . .163 A1
Linden La WV12 . . . . .27 E6
Linden Lea
Bedworth CV12 . . . . .78 B3
Wolverhampton WV3 . . . .24 D1
Linden Rd
Birmingham B30 . . . . . . .103 E7
Dudley DY1 . . . . .51 B3
Hinckley LE10 . . . . .71 C1
Smethwick B66 . . . . .65 A2
Lindens Dr B74 . . . . .44 F5
Lindens Prim Sch B74 . . .44 F6
Lindens The
Birmingham B32 . . . . .84 E7
Birmingham,Edgbaston B16 .65 D1
Wolverhampton WV6 . . . .24 E3
Linden View WS12 . . . . . . .2 B4
Lindenwood B73 . . . . .66 A6
Lindera B77 . . . . .22 A4
Lindfield The CV3 . . . . . .134 C8
Lindford Way B38 . . . . . .104 B2
Lindhurst Dr B94 . . . . . . .143 C6
Lindisfarne Dr CV8 . . . . .148 C4
Lindisfarne B77 . . . . .21 D3
Lindley Ave DY4 . . . . .51 F4
Lindley Rd
Bedworth CV12 . . . . .77 D2
Coventry CV3 . . . . .114 B2
Lindon Cl WS8 . . . . .15 F7
Lindon Dr WS8 . . . . .15 F7
Lindon Rd WS8 . . . . .15 F6
Lindon View WS8 . . . . . . .16 A5
Lindop Cl CV32 . . . . .157 D5
Lindrick Cl WS3 . . . . .13 F3
Lindridge Dr B76 . . . . . . .58 D6
Lindridge Rd
Birmingham B23 . . . . .56 C5
Solihull B90 . . . . .105 F1
Sutton Coldfield B75,B76 . .47 B6
Lindrosa Rd B74 . . . . .30 F3
Lindsay Rd B42 . . . . .44 B1
Lindsey Ave B31 . . . . . . .103 C4
Lindsey Cres CV8 . . . . . .148 A1
Lindsey Pl DY5 . . . . .61 C3
Lindsey Rd B71 . . . . .53 C7
Lindsworth App B30 . . . .104 C3
Lindsworth Ct **2** B30 . . .104 C3
Lindsworth Rd B30 . . . . .104 C3
Lindsworth Sch (North)
B23 . . . . .57 A6
Lindsworth Sch (South)
B30 . . . . .104 C3
Lineholt Cl B98 . . . . .159 A6
Linehouse La
Catshill B60 . . . . .137 D8
Lower Marlbrook B60 . . . .121 D1
Linen St CV34 . . . . .160 D6
Linfield Gdns DV5 . . . . . . .39 C1
Linford Wlk CV2 . . . . .96 F1
Linforth Dr B74 . . . . .45 A7
Lingard Cl B7 . . . . .67 A5
Lingard Ho B76 . . . . .58 F8
Lingard Rd B75 . . . . .47 A5
Lingen Cl B98 . . . . .154 E3
Lingfield Ave
Birmingham B44 . . . . .44 F1
Wolverhampton WV10 . . . .11 D5
Lingfield Cl WS6 . . . . .4 F2
Lingfield Ct
Birmingham B43 . . . . .54 D7
Coventry CV6 . . . . .96 B4
Lingfield Dr WS6 . . . . .4 F2
Lingfield Gdns B34 . . . . . .69 B6
Lingfield Gr WV6 . . . . .23 F4
Lingfield Rd WV11 . . . . . . .6 A5
Lingfield Way DY6 . . . . . .61 A5
Lingfield Wlk B61 . . . . . .121 B1
Lingham Cl B92 . . . . .107 E7
Ling Ho WV10 . . . . .25 F3
Ling Rd WS12 . . . . .1 C5
Lingwood Dr CV10 . . . . . .72 F3
Linhope Dr DY6 . . . . .61 A5
Link One Ind Pk DY4 . . . . .52 E6
Link Rd
Birmingham B16 . . . . .65 E3
Brownhills WS9 . . . . .16 B3
Wombourne WV5 . . . . . . .49 A7
Links Ave WV6 . . . . .24 D7
Links Cres B68 . . . . .84 B8
Links Dr
Birmingham B45 . . . . . . .122 A6
Solihull B91 . . . . .107 B6
Stourbridge DY8 . . . . .80 E2
Links Rd
Birmingham,Brandhall
B68 . . . . .84 B8
Birmingham,Higher's Heath
B14 . . . . .105 A4
Coventry CV6 . . . . .113 B8
Wolverhampton WV4 . . . .39 A3
Links Side Way WS9 . . . . .30 C8
Links The DY10 . . . . .117 A4

Links View
Halesowen B62 . . . . .83 D4
Sutton Coldfield B74 . . . . .31 B1
Linkswood Cl B13 . . . . . . .87 B1
Link The B27 . . . . .88 A1
Linkway Ret Pk WS11 . . . . .4 B6
Linkway CV31 . . . . .161 E6
Linkwood Ind Est DY8 . . . .80 F6
Linley Cl WS9 . . . . .29 E7
Linley Dr WV10 . . . . .11 E1
Linley Gr
Birmingham B14 . . . . . . .104 C6
Dudley DY3 . . . . .50 B2
Linley Lodge Ind Est WS9 .29 E6
Linley Rd WS4 . . . . .29 D7
Linley Wood Rd WS9 . . . .29 E5
Linnet Cl
Birmingham B30 . . . . . . .103 E8
Coventry CV3 . . . . .134 D5
Halesowen B62 . . . . .83 B6
Huntington WS12 . . . . .1 D7
Linnet Gr
Birmingham B23 . . . . .56 B6
Willenhall WV12 . . . . .27 C8
Linnet Rise DY10 . . . . . . .116 F1
Linpole Wlk B14 . . . . . . .104 D2
Linsey Rd B92 . . . . .89 C2
Linslade CV1 . . . . .39 D4
Linstock Way CV6 . . . . . . .96 B4
Linthouse La WV11 . . . . . .26 B6
Linthouse Wlk **3** B77 . . .35 F6
Linthurst Fst Sch B60 . . .138 A6
Linthurst Newtown B60 . .138 B5
Linthurst Rd B45,B60 . . .138 A7
Lintly B77 . . . . .22 A2
Linton Ave B91 . . . . .107 A1
Linton Cl
Halesowen B63 . . . . .82 D5
Redditch B98 . . . . .154 F2
Linton Croft WV14 . . . . . .40 D5
Linton News B98 . . . . . . .154 F2
Linton Rd
Birmingham,Acock's Green
B11 . . . . .88 A4
Cradley Heath B64 . . . . . .62 F3
Wolverhampton WV4 . . . .38 E5
Linton Wlk B23 . . . . .56 C3
Linwood Cl LE10 . . . . .71 B2
Linwood Ct B15 . . . . .86 D7
Linwood Dr
Cannock WS12 . . . . .1 F7
Coventry CV2 . . . . .96 F1
Linwood Rd
Birmingham B21 . . . . .65 E8
Dudley DY1 . . . . .51 B5
Solihull B91 . . . . .106 D5
Lionel St B3 . . . . .164 B3
Lion Fields Ave CV5 . . . .112 B6
Lion Ind Est WS9 . . . . . . .30 A8
Lion Pas DY8 . . . . .80 E8
Lion's Den WS7,WS14 . . . .7 E2
Lion Sq DY10 . . . . .116 E6
Lion St
Kidderminster DY10 . . . .116 E6
Stourbridge DY8 . . . . .80 F5
Liskeard Cl CV11 . . . . .74 A5
Liskeard Rd WS5 . . . . .43 D7
Lisko Cl DY5 . . . . .81 A8
Lisle Ave DY11 . . . . .116 D3
Lisle St **4** CV31 . . . . . . .162 A6
Lismore Cl B45 . . . . .101 E1
Lismore Croft CV2 . . . . .115 B7
Lismore Dr
Birmingham B17 . . . . .85 A3
Hinckley LE10 . . . . .71 C1
Lissimore Dr DY4 . . . . . . .52 B8
Lisson Gr B44 . . . . .44 F4
Listelow Cl B36 . . . . .69 B8
Lister Cl
Tipton DY4 . . . . .52 A4
Walsall WS2 . . . . .28 B5
Lister Rd
Dudley DY2 . . . . .62 D7
Kidderminster DY11 . . . .116 B4
Walsall WS2 . . . . .28 B5
Lister St
Birmingham B7 . . . . .66 F4
Nuneaton CV11 . . . . .73 D3
Willenhall WV13 . . . . .27 B1
Listowel Rd B14 . . . . . . .104 D6
Lisures Dr B76 . . . . .46 D4
Little Acre B97 . . . . .158 D6
Little Albert St WS2 . . . . .28 E2
Little Ann St B5 . . . . .66 F2
Little Aston Hall Dr B74 . .31 B5
Little Aston Hospl B74 . . .31 B5
Little Aston La B74 . . . . . .31 D6
Little Aston Park Rd B74 . .31 A3
Little Aston Rd WS9 . . . . .30 D6
Little Barrow Wlk **3** WS3 .14 A1
Little Barr St B9 . . . . .67 A2
Little Birches
Wolverhampton WV3 . . . .38 F8
Little Bloxwich CE Prim Sch
WS3 . . . . .14 D3
Little Brickiln St **3** B63 . .163 B2
Little Bromwich Rd B9 . . .68 C2
Little Broom St B12 . . . . .87 A8
Little Caldmore B11 . . . . .42 E8
Little Church La B79 . . . . .21 B5
Little Church St B4 CV1 . .165 C4
Little Clothier St WV13 . . .27 A3
Little Clover Cl **3** B7 . . . .67 C7
Little Comm 15 A4
Little Cornbow B63 . . . . . .83 B3
Littlecote Croft **B** B14 . .105 A3
Littlecote Dr B23 . . . . . . .56 F7

Littlecote B79 . . . . .20 D2
Little Cottage St DY5 . . . .61 D2
Little Croft B43 . . . . .43 C1
Little Cross St WS10 . . . . .41 D7
Little Cryfield CV4 . . . . . .132 C2
Little Duke St CV11 . . . . . .73 B4
Little Edward St B9 . . . . . .67 A2
Little Farm CV3 . . . . .134 D5
Little Field CV2 . . . . .114 C3
Little Fields Way B69 . . . .63 F2
Little Forge Rd B98 . . . . .159 C6
Little Francis Gr **3** B7 . . . .67 B5
Little Gorway WS1 . . . . . . .42 F7
Little Grebe Rd DY10 . . . .117 B3
Little Green La B9 . . . . . . .67 C1
Little Green Lanes B73 . . .57 B2
Little Hall Rd B7 . . . . .67 B5
Little Hardwick Rd WS9 . . .30 D2
Little Hay La WS14 . . . . . .18 C3
Little Heath Croft B34 . . . .69 B7
Little Heath Ind Est CV6 . . .96 A1
Little Heath La B60 . . . . .137 D6
Little Heath Prim Sch CV6 .95 F1
Little Hill Gr B38 . . . . . . .104 A1
Little Hill Way B32 . . . . . .84 D2
Little Hill WS10 . . . . .41 F3
Little Johnson's La
WS13 . . . . .27 A2
Aldridge WS9 . . . . .30 B1
Walsall WS9 . . . . .44 B8
Little John St DY5 . . . . . . .61 D4
Little La
West Bromwich B71 . . . . .53 D5
Willenhall WV12 . . . . .27 D7
Little Lawns Cl WS9 . . . . .16 A4
Little London Ho **1** WS1 . .42 F7
Little London JMI Sch
WS1 . . . . .42 F8
Little London WS1 . . . . . . .42 F8
Littlemead Ave B31 . . . .103 C1
Little Meadow Croft B31 .102 F4
Little Meadow Wlk B33 . . .68 F3
Littlemead Rd B90 . . . . .125 E8
Little Moor Hill B67 . . . . . .64 F5
Little Newport St **5** WS1 .28 F2
Little Oaks Dr WS9 . . . . . .60 A2
Little Oaks Rd B6 . . . . . . .66 E8
Littleover Ave B28 . . . . . .105 F6
Little Park St
Coventry CV1 . . . . .165 C2
Wolverhampton WV1 . . . .163 C3
Little Pk B32 . . . . .84 B4
Little Potter St DY5 . . . . . .61 D2
Little Pountney St WV2 . .163 B1
Little Shadwell St B4 . . . .164 C4
Littleshaw Croft B47 . . . .125 C4
Littleshaw La B47 . . . . . .125 C4
Little's La WV1 . . . . .163 C4
Little South St CV1 . . . . .113 E3
Little Station St WS2 . . . . .28 E2
Little St DY2 . . . . .51 D1
Little Sutton La B75 . . . . .46 C8
Little Sutton Prim Sch
B75 . . . . .32 D3
Little Sutton Rd B75 . . . . .32 D2
Littlethorpe CV3 . . . . . . .134 D6
Littleton Bsns Pk WS12 . . .1 C7
Littleton Cl
Kenilworth CV8 . . . . .148 A7
Sutton Coldfield B76 . . . . .47 A2
Littleton Croft **6** B91 . . .127 C8
Littleton Rd WV12 . . . . . .27 D7
Littleton St E WS1 . . . . . . .28 F3
Littleton St W WS1 . . . . . .28 E2
Littlewood Cl **3** B91 . . . .127 B8
Littlewood Gn B80 . . . . . .159 D3
Littlewood La WS6 . . . . . . .4 E4
Littlewood Rd WS6 . . . . . . .4 E4
Little Woods B97 . . . . . . .158 E6
Little Wood St WV13 . . . . .27 A2
Littleworth Ave DY1 . . . . .51 A5
Littleworth Croft CV31 . . .162 C5
Littleworth Gr B76 . . . . . .46 F4
Littleworth Hill WS12 . . . . .2 D4
Littleworth Rd WS12 . . . . .2 D4
Litton B77 . . . . .22 C1
Liveridge Cl B93 . . . . . . .127 F6
Liverpool Croft B37 . . . . .89 F8
Liverpool St B9 . . . . .67 A2
Livery St
Birmingham B3 . . . . .164 B3
Birmingham B3 . . . . .164 B4
Royal Leamington Spa
CV32 . . . . .161 F8
Livingstone Ave WV6 . . . .23 E5
Livingstone Rd
Bilston WV14 . . . . .40 E5
Birmingham,Handsworth
B20 . . . . .55 D1
Birmingham,King's Heath
B14 . . . . .104 E6
Coventry CV6 . . . . .113 E7
Walsall WS3 . . . . .15 A4
Lizafield Ct B66 . . . . .64 E7
Llewellyn Rd CV31 . . . . . .162 A6
Lloyd Cl CV11 . . . . .73 D7
Lloyd Cres CV2 . . . . .114 E3
Lloyd Dr WV4 . . . . .38 C2
Lloyd George Gr WS11 . . . .2 C2
Lloyd Ho B19 . . . . .164 C4
Lloyd Rd
Birmingham B20 . . . . .55 A4
Wolverhampton WV6 . . . .24 E5
Lloyd Roberts Bldgs WV4 .38 F1
Lloyds Rd B62 . . . . .83 C8

Lloyd St
Birmingham B10 . . . . .87 D8
Cannock WS11. . . . . .1 D1
Dudley DY2 . . . . .62 D8
Wednesbury WS10 . . . . . . .41 E3
West Bromwich B71 . . . . . .53 E4
Wolverhampton WV6 . . . . .24 F4
Loach Dr CV2 . . . . .96 B4
Lobelia Cl LE10 . . . . .75 E5
Locarno Rd DY4 . . . . .52 A6
Lochalsh Gr WV11 . . . . . . .13 B1
Lochmore Cl LE10 . . . . . . .75 A8
Lochmore Dr LE10 . . . . . . .75 A8
Lochmore Way LE10 . . . . .75 A8
Lochranza Croft B43 . . . . .43 E2
Lochsong Cl B77 . . . . .35 D4
Loch St CV3 . . . . .114 C1
Lock Cl B97 . . . . .153 A4
Lock Dr B33 . . . . .68 D3
Locke Cl CV6 . . . . .95 A1
Locket Cl WS2 . . . . .27 F4
Locketts Ct WS11 . . . . .1 F5
Lockfield Cl B9 . . . . .60 F2
Lockhart Cl CV8 . . . . .148 A3
Lockhart Dr B75. . . . . .32 C1
Lockheed Cl B13 . . . . .161 F5
Lockhurst La CV6 . . . . . . .113 D7
Locking Croft B35 . . . . . . .58 B3
Lockington Croft B62 . . . .83 F6
Lock Keepers Cl WS11 . . . .5 F4
Lock Keepers Reach
  B48. . . . . .138 F6
Lock La CV34 . . . . .160 D8
Lockley Cl WV10 . . . . .25 F4
Lock Mus The* WV13 . . . . .27 A1
Lockside WS9 . . . . .29 F7
Lockside Cl DY5 . . . . .61 D1
Locksmith Cl WV13 . . . . . .27 B2
Locks The CV31 . . . . .161 D7
Locks View DY8 . . . . .60 E1
Lockton Rd B30 . . . . .104 C6
Lockwood Rd B31 . . . . . . .102 F4
Lode Heath Sch B91 . . . . .107 C6
Lode La B91 . . . . .107 C6
Loder Cl CV4 . . . . .111 F3
Lodge Cl
Halesowen B62 . . . . .83 E3
Hinckley LE10 . . . . .76 A5
Walsall WS5 . . . . .43 D6
Lodge Cres
Dudley DY2 . . . . .62 A4
Warwick CV34 . . . . .160 D4
West Hagley DY9 . . . . .99 B5
Lodge Croft
Birmingham B31 . . . . . . .102 E6
Knowle B93 . . . . .128 B6
Lodge Dr B26 . . . . .88 F8
Lodge Farm Cl B76 . . . . . .46 F5
Lodge Farm JMI Sch
  WV12. . . . . .27 E4
Lodgefield Rd B62 . . . . . . .83 B7
Lodge Forge Trad Est
  B64. . . . . .82 C7
Lodge Gr WS9 . . . . .30 A5
Lodge Green La CV7 . . . . .92 F3
Lodge Green La N CV7 . . .92 F3
Lodge Hill Rd B29 . . . . . . .85 D1
Lodge La
Cheslyn Hay WS11. . . . . . . .4 C5
Kingswinford DY6 . . . . . . .60 B6
Lodgepool Cl B44. . . . . . . .55 E6
Lodge Pool Dr B98 . . . . . .153 F1
Lodge Prim Sch B70 . . . . .53 B3
Lodge Rd
Bilston WV14 . . . . .40 F4
Birmingham B18 . . . . .65 F5
Coventry CV3 . . . . .114 B1
Darlaston WS10 . . . . .41 D5
Knowle B93 . . . . .128 B6
Redditch B98 . . . . .153 E3
Smethwick B67 . . . . .64 F7
Walsall,The Chuckery WS5 . .43 D6
Walsall WS4 . . . . .15 B1
West Bromwich B70 . . . . .53 C3
Lodge Rd/ West Bromwich
  TH Sta B70. . . . . .53 C3
Lodge Rd WV10 . . . . .25 B8
Lodge St
Oldbury B69. . . . . .64 A7
Willenhall WV12 . . . . .27 C5
Lodge The B15 . . . . .65 D1
Lodge View WS6 . . . . .4 C3
Loeless Rd B33 . . . . .69 A3
Lofthouse Cres B31 . . . . .102 F3
Lofthouse Gr B31 . . . . . . .102 F3
Lofthouse Rd B20. . . . . . . .54 F3
Loftus Cl B29 . . . . .102 F8
Loftus Ct WS7 . . . . .7 A5
Logan Cl WV10 . . . . .25 C6
Logan Rd CV2 . . . . .114 F7
Lole Cl CV6 . . . . .96 A4
Lollard Croft CV3 . . . . . . .133 D8
Lomaine Dr B30 . . . . .103 E4
Lomas Dr B31 . . . . .102 E4
Lomas St WV1 . . . . .25 C4
Lomax Cl WS13 . . . . .3 A1
Lomax Rd WS12 . . . . .2 B7
Lombard Ave DY2 . . . . . . .62 D3
Lombard Gdns WS13 . . . . .9 B8
Lombard St W B70 . . . . . . .53 C3
Lombard St
Birmingham B12 . . . . .86 F8
Lichfield WS13. . . . . .9 B8
West Bromwich B70 . . . . .53 C3
Lombardy Croft B62 . . . . .84 A6
Lombardy Gdns WV12 . . . .27 E7
Lombardy Gr WS7 . . . . .6 F8

Lomita Cres B77 . . . . .35 D8
Lomond Cl
Birmingham B34 . . . . .69 E6
Hinckley LE10 . . . . .75 E8
Tamworth B79 . . . . .20 F8
Lomond Rd DY3 . . . . .39 C1
Lomond Way WV10 . . . . . .72 C5
Lomsey Cl CV4 . . . . .112 A1
Londonderry Gr B67 . . . . .64 F5
Londonderry La B67 . . . . .64 E4
Londonderry Rd B68. . . . . .64 D4
London Hts DY1 . . . . .51 A2
London La
Bromsgrove B60 . . . . .151 F7
Tardebigge B60 . . . . .152 A6
London Pl WV2 . . . . .163 B2
London Rd
Birmingham B20 . . . . .55 C2
Coventry,Cheylesmore
  CV3. . . . . .133 E8
Coventry,Willenhall CV3. . .134 B5
Hinckley LE10 . . . . .75 E8
Lichfield WS14. . . . . .9 C2
Middleton B75,B78 . . . . . .47 D7
Ryton-on-D CV8. . . . . .135 B1
Shenstone B75,WS14 . . . . .32 F7
Sutton Coldfield B75 . . . . .33 A4
Weeford WS14 . . . . .18 F3
London St B66. . . . . .65 C5
Lones Rd B71 . . . . .65 B8
Long Acre B7. . . . . .67 C7
Longacre WS10. . . . . .41 A8
Longacre Ind Est B7 . . . . .67 C7
Long Acre CV10 . . . . .116 F7
Longacres
Cannock WS12. . . . . .2 F5
Sutton Coldfield B74 . . . . .31 C4
Long Acre St WS2 . . . . . . .28 D3
Long Acre Trad Est B7 . . . .67 B7
Longbank Rd B69. . . . . . . .63 C8
Longboat La DY8 . . . . .60 F1
Longboat Quay DY2 . . . . . .62 D4
Longborough Cl B97. . . . .158 B6
Longbow Rd B29 . . . . .102 F7
Longbridge La B31 . . . . . .122 E8
Long Bridge Rd WS14 . . . . .9 C5
Longbridge Sta B31. . . . . .122 E8
Long Brook La CV7,CV8. . .129 E5
Long Close Ave CV5 . . . . .112 B6
Long Close Wlk B35 . . . . . .58 A3
Long Cl DY9 . . . . .99 A4
Long Compton Dr DY9 . . . .99 A6
Longcroft Ave WS10. . . . . .42 A3
Long Croft WS12. . . . . .1 C4
Longcroft Cl B35 . . . . .58 A3
Longcroft The
Halesowen B63 . . . . .82 E4
Walsall WS4 . . . . .29 C7
Longdales Rd B38 . . . . . . .123 E7
Longdon Ave WV4 . . . . . . .39 D5
Longdon Cl B98 . . . . .159 B7
Longdon Croft B93 . . . . . .128 A8
Longdon Dr B74 . . . . .31 E4
Longdon Rd B93 . . . . .128 A6
Longfellow Ave CV34. . . . .160 C4
Longfellow Cl B97 . . . . . . .158 C7
Longfellow Gn DY10 . . . . .117 C6
Longfellow Pl WS11. . . . . . .1 C4
Longfellow Rd
Birmingham B30 . . . . .103 D4
Coventry CV2 . . . . .114 C3
Dudley DY3 . . . . .50 B5
Longfellow Wlk B79 . . . . . .20 F8
Longfield Cl
Birmingham B28 . . . . .105 F6
Tamworth B77 . . . . .21 E4
Longfield Dr B74 . . . . .31 D4
Longfield Ho
Coventry CV6 . . . . .114 A8
Wolverhampton WV10. . . . .25 F3
Longfield Rd
Birmingham B31 . . . . .102 E8
Royal Leamington Spa
  CV31. . . . . .162 B6
Stourbridge DY9 . . . . .81 D5
Longford Cl
Birmingham B32 . . . . .102 A7
Dorridge B93. . . . . .128 B3
Longford Ct WS11 . . . . .4 B8
Longford Gn WS11 . . . . . . .4 C7
Longford Gr B44. . . . . .45 A3
Longford Ind Est WS11. . . . .4 D6
Longford Park Prim Sch
  CV6. . . . . .96 A3
Longford Rd
Bedworth CV7 . . . . .96 A6
Birmingham B44 . . . . .45 A2
Cannock WS11. . . . . .4 D7
Coventry CV6 . . . . .96 A4
Wolverhampton WV10. . . . .26 A4
Longford Sq CV6 . . . . .96 A4
Long Furrow WV8 . . . . .10 E1
Longham Croft B32 . . . . . .84 F4
Longhurst Croft B31 . . . . .123 B7
Long Hyde Rd B67 . . . . . . .64 F1
Long Innage B63 . . . . .82 B6
Long Knowle La WV11 . . . .26 B8
Long Knowle Prim Sch
  WV11. . . . . .26 C8
Long La
Brownhills Green CV5,
  CV7. . . . . .94 D2
Great Wyrley WS6 . . . . . . .13 C6
Halesowen B62 . . . . .83 E8
Longlake Ave WV6 . . . . . . .24 B3
Longlands Cl B38 . . . . . . .123 C8
Longlands Dr B77 . . . . . . .21 F4

Longlands Rd B62 . . . . . . .83 E3
Longlands The
Barnt Green B45 . . . . .138 D7
Wombourne WV5. . . . . . . .49 A6
Long La Trad Est B62 . . . . .83 D8
Long Leasow B29. . . . . . . .103 B7
Longleat Ave 2 B15 . . . . . .86 C1
Longleat B43 . . . . .43 C2
Longleat Dr
Cheswick Green B90 . . . . .126 E5
Dudley DY1 . . . . .50 E2
Longleat Gr 17 CV31 . . . . .162 A5
Longleat Rd WS9 . . . . .16 A1
Longleat B79 . . . . .20 D7
Longley Ave B76. . . . . .58 D5
Longley Cres B26. . . . . .88 E4
Long Leys Croft B46 . . . . .59 B2
Long Leys Ct B46 . . . . .59 B2
Long Ley WV10 . . . . .25 F3
Long Mdw B65 . . . . .63 C3
Longmeadow Cl B75. . . . . .46 F5
Long Meadow Dr
Hinckley LE10 . . . . .74 F7
Sedgley DY3. . . . . .39 B3
Longmeadow Gr B31. . . . .123 A6
Long Meadow Rd B60. . . .137 C6
Longmeadow Rd WS5 . . . . .43 E8
Long Mill Ave WV11. . . . . .26 B7
Long Mill N WV11. . . . . . . .26 B7
Long Mill S WV11. . . . . . . .26 B7
Longmoor Cl
Redditch B97 . . . . .153 B5
Wednesfield WV11 . . . . . . .27 A8
Longmoor Ho 13 B74 . . . . .31 F2
Longmoor Rd
Halesowen B63 . . . . .82 E3
Sutton Coldfield B73 . . . . .45 B3
Longmoor Sch B73 . . . . . . .45 A4
Longmore Ave WS2 . . . . . .27 F1
Longmore Cl B73 . . . . .45 A5
Longmore Ho B73 . . . . .45 C3
Longmore Rd B90 . . . . . . .106 D2
Longmore St
Birmingham B12 . . . . .86 E7
Wednesbury WS10 . . . . . . .41 F3
Long Mynd Cl WV11. . . . . .13 B1
Long Mynd B63. . . . . .82 D1
Long Mynd Rd B31. . . . . .102 F6
Long Nuke Rd B31. . . . . . .102 E7
Long Saw Dr B31. . . . . . . .102 F4
Longshaw Gr B34. . . . . . . .69 D6
Long Shoot The CV11 . . . . .74 C6
Long St
Birmingham B11 . . . . .87 A6
Bulkington CV12 . . . . .79 D2
Coventry CV1 CV90. . . . . .127 B6
Longstone Rd B42. . . . . . . .55 C7
Long St
Walsall WS2 . . . . .28 D1
Wolverhampton WV1. . . . .163 C3
Longville Ct CV3. . . . . .134 A6
Longwill Prim Sch For Deaf
Children B31. . . . . .103 A5
Long Wood B30 . . . . .103 E5
Longwood Cl CV4. . . . . . . .131 F6
Longwood La WS4,WS5 . . .29 E2
Longwood Path B78. . . . . .20 D1
Longwood Prim Sch B78. .20 D1
Longwood Rd
Aldridge WS9. . . . . .30 B2
Birmingham B45 . . . . .122 A7
Longwood Rise WV12 . . . . .27 D5
Lonicera Cl WS5 . . . . .43 B3
Lonscale Dr CV3. . . . . .133 B5
Lonsdale Cl
Birmingham B33 . . . . .68 D2
Willenhall WV12 . . . . .27 B5
Lonsdale Ct B17. . . . . .85 C6
Lonsdale Rd
Bilston WV14 . . . . .40 F6
Birmingham B17 . . . . .85 B6
Royal Leamington Spa
  CV32 . . . . .157 B4
Smethwick B66 . . . . .64 D7
Walsall WS5 . . . . .43 B3
Wolverhampton WV3. . . . . .39 B7
Lord Austin Dr B60 . . . . . .121 E1
Lord Cromwell Ct WS11. . . .2 A5
Lord Leycester Hosp & Knot
  Gdn* CV34. . . . . .160 E6
Lord Lytton Ave CV2 . . . . .114 D2
Lord St W WV14 . . . . .40 E3
Lord's Dr WS2. . . . . .28 E3
Lords La B80 . . . . .159 E2
Lordsmore Cl WV14. . . . . . .40 D1
Lord St
Bilston WV14 . . . . .40 E3
Birmingham B7 . . . . .66 F5
Coventry CV5. . . . . .112 F2
Walsall WS1 . . . . .42 E6
Wolverhampton WV1. . . . .163 A1
Lords Wood B17 . . . . .85 A8
Lordswood Boys Sch B17 .65 A1
Lordswood Rd B17. . . . . . . .85 B7
Lordswood Girls Sch & Sixth
Form Ctr B17 . . . . .85 A8
Lordswood Rd B17. . . . . . . .85 A7
Lorenzo Cl CV3 . . . . .134 D6
Lorimer Way B43 . . . . .44 D5
Loriners Gr WV11. . . . . . . .26 C7
Lorne Gr DY10. . . . . .117 A6
Lorne St
Burntwood WS7. . . . . .6 E8
Kidderminster DY10 . . . . .117 A5
Tipton DY4. . . . . .51 F8
Lorrainer Ave DY5 . . . . . . .81 A8

Lorton B79 . . . . .20 D7
Lothersdale B77 . . . . .36 C8
Lothians Rd
Walsall WS3 . . . . .15 A5
Wolverhampton WV6 . . . . .24 E6
Lottie Rd B29. . . . . .103 B8
Lotus Croft B67. . . . . .64 F4
Lotus Ct B16 . . . . .65 E1
Lotus Dr
Cannock WS11. . . . . .1 E5
Cradley Heath B64 . . . . . . .62 F2
Tipton B77 . . . . .21 E3
Lotus Way B65 . . . . .63 A4
Loudon Ave CV6 . . . . .113 A5
Loudon Gate CV11 . . . . . . .73 F1
Loughshaw B77 . . . . .22 C1
Loughton Gr B63 . . . . .82 F4
Louisa Pl 3 B18. . . . . .66 A5
Louisa St 1 B1 . . . . .66 C3
Louis Ct B67 . . . . .64 F5
Louise Croft B14. . . . . . . .104 E2
Louise Ct
  2 Birmingham B27. . . . . . .88 C3
Solihull B91 . . . . .106 E1
Louise Ho DY5. . . . . .61 D7
Louise Lorne Rd B13. . . . . .86 F4
Louise Rd B21. . . . . .65 F7
Louise St DY3 . . . . .50 C3
Lount Wlk B19. . . . . .66 E5
Lovage Rd B98 . . . . .154 F6
Lovatt Cl DY4 . . . . .41 C1
Lovatt Pl WS11 . . . . .1 C5
Lovatt St WV1 . . . . .163 A3
Loveday Dr CV32. . . . . . . .156 E2
Loveday Ho B70 . . . . .53 D3
Loveday St B4 . . . . .164 C4
Love La B7 . . . . .164 D4
Lovelace Ave B91. . . . . . . .127 D8
Love La
Great Wyrley WS6 . . . . .5 B3
Hinckley LE10 . . . . .76 A6
Hollywood B47. . . . . .124 F7
Stourbridge,Lye DY9 . . . . .81 F5
Stourbridge,Old Swinford
  DY8 . . . . .81 A3
Walsall WS1 . . . . .42 E7
Wolverhampton WV6. . . . . .24 D6
Lovell Cl
Bedworth CV7 . . . . .96 A8
Birmingham B29 . . . . .103 B6
Lovell Rd CV12 . . . . .78 A3
Lovell B79. . . . . .20 F6
Love Lyne B97 . . . . .158 B5
Lover's Wlk 5 WS10. . . . . .41 F3
Lovett Ave B69 . . . . .63 D5
Lovetts Cl LE10 . . . . .74 F8
Lowans Hill Cotts B97 . . .153 C5
Lowans Hill View B97 . . . .153 C4
Low Ave B43 . . . . .43 F2
Lowbridge Cl WV12 . . . . . .27 C5
Lowbrook La B90. . . . . . . .125 D4
Lowcroft Gdns WV10. . . . . .25 B5
Lowden Croft B26. . . . . .88 E4
Lowdham B77 . . . . .22 C1
Lowe Ave WS10. . . . . .41 C7
Lowe Dr
Kingswinford DY6 . . . . . . .60 E4
Sutton Coldfield B73 . . . . .45 C3
Lower Ave CV31 . . . . .161 F7
Lower Beeches Rd B31 . . .102 C2
Lower Bentley La B60. . . .151 F1
Lower Bond St LE10 . . . . . .71 D1
Lower Cape CV34 . . . . .160 D8
Lower Chapel St B69 . . . . .52 C2
Lower Church La DY4 . . . . .52 B5
Lower City Rd B69 . . . . .52 D1
Lower Common La B97 . . .153 B2
Lowercroft Way B74 . . . . . .31 E6
Lower Dartmouth St B9. . .67 B2
Lower Darwin St B12 . . . . .86 F8
Lower Rd CV6 . . . . .95 A2
Lower Derry St DY5. . . . . . .61 D7
Lower Eastern Green La
  CV5 . . . . .111 F4
Lower Essex St B5. . . . . . . .66 E1
Lower Farm Prim Sch
  WS3 . . . . .14 C3
Lower Farm WS9 . . . . .16 E4
Lower Ford St CV1. . . . . . .165 D3
Lower Forster St WS1. . . . .28 F2
Lower Gambolds La B60 .151 B6
Lower Gn
Tipton DY4. . . . . .51 E5
Wolverhampton WV6. . . . . .24 E5
Lower Grinsty La B97. . . . .158 A8
Lower Ground Cl 1 B6 . . . .55 F1
Lower Gungate B79. . . . . . .21 B5
Lower Hall La WS1. . . . . . . .28 F1
Lower Hall St WV13. . . . . . .27 B1
Lower High St
Cradley Heath B64 . . . . . . .82 C8
Stourbridge DY8 . . . . .80 F6
Wednesbury WS10 . . . . . . .41 E2
Lower Higley Cl B32 . . . . . .84 E4
Lower Holyhead Rd CV1 . .165 A3
Lower Horseley Fields
  WV1 . . . . .25 F2
Lower House La CV9 . . . . . .36 F2
Lower Keys Bsns Pk WS12. .2 D3
Lower Ladyes Hills CV8 . .148 A6
Lower Leam St CV31. . . . .162 B7
Lower Lichfield St WV13 . .27 A1
Lower Loveday St B19 . . . .164 C4
Lower Mill St DY10 . . . . . .116 E5
Lower Moor B30. . . . . .103 E8
Lower North St WS4 . . . . . .28 F4
Lower Parklands DY11 . . . .116 C5
Lowerpark B77. . . . . .21 C1

Lower Par The B72 . . . . . .46 C5
Lower Prec CV1 . . . . .165 B3
Lower Prestwood Rd
  WV11 . . . . .26 C7
Lower Queen St B72 . . . . . .46 C4
Lower Rd
Barnacle CV7 . . . . .97 C6
Cannock WS12. . . . . .2 C3
Lower Reddicroft B73. . . . .46 C5
Lower Rushall St WS1. . . . .28 F2
Lower Sandford St WS13 . . .9 A7
Lower Severn St B1 . . . . . .164 B2
Lower Shepley La B60 . . . .137 E6
Lowerstack Croft B37. . . . .69 F3
Lower St WV6 . . . . .24 E5
Lower Temple St 4 B2. . . .164 B2
Lower Tower St B19. . . . . .164 C5
Lower Trinity St B9 . . . . . . .67 A1
Lower Valley Rd DY5 . . . . .61 A2
Lower Vauxhall WV1 . . . . .25 A3
Lower Villiers St
  1 Royal Leamington Spa
    CV32 . . . . .157 A1
Wolverhampton WV2. . . . . .39 C7
Lower Walsall St WV1. . . . .25 F1
Lower White Rd B32. . . . . .84 D5
Lowes Ave CV34 . . . . .155 E1
Lowesmoor Rd B26. . . . . . .89 C7
Lowe St
Birmingham B12 . . . . .87 A8
Wolverhampton WV6. . . . . .25 B4
Loweswater Cl CV11 . . . . . .74 A6
Loweswater Rd CV3. . . . . . .50 D3
Loweswater Ho B38 . . . . .104 B1
Loweswater Rd CV3. . . . . .114 E1
Lowfield Cl B62. . . . . .84 A3
Lowfield La B97 . . . . .153 B5
Lowford Cl WS13 . . . . .114 C1
Lowforce B77 . . . . .22 C1
Low Hill Cres WV10 . . . . . .25 B8
Lowhill La B45 . . . . .122 D6
Lowland Cl B64. . . . . .62 F1
Lowland Rd WS12. . . . . .1 C5
Lowlands Ave
Sutton Coldfield B74 . . . . .44 E8
Wolverhampton WV6. . . . . .24 E6
Lowlands Ct WV6 . . . . .24 E6
Lowlands La B98 . . . . .154 D3
Lowndes Rd DY8. . . . . .80 E6
Lowrey Ct B68. . . . . .64 C3
Lowry Cl
Bedworth CV12 . . . . .78 A4
Perton WV6 . . . . .23 F4
Smethwick B67 . . . . .64 F6
Willenhall WV13 . . . . .26 E2
Low Thatch B38 . . . . .123 E7
Lowther Ct 10 DY5. . . . . . .61 D2
Lowther St CV2 . . . . .113 F4
Low Town 6 B69 . . . . .64 A7
Low Wood Rd B23 . . . . .56 E5
Loxdale Park Ind Est
  WV14 . . . . .40 E4
Loxdale Prim Sch WV14. . .40 F4
Loxdale Sidings WV14. . . . .40 F4
Loxdale St WV14. . . . . .40 F4
Loxley Ave
Birmingham B14 . . . . .105 C3
Solihull B90 . . . . .105 F1
Loxley Cl
Birmingham B31 . . . . .102 E8
Coventry CV2 . . . . .96 D2
Redditch B98 . . . . .154 D6
Loxley Ct CV2. . . . . .96 D2
Loxley Rd
Smethwick B67 . . . . .64 F1
Sutton Coldfield B75 . . . . .32 D3
Loxley Sq B92 . . . . .106 D8
Loxley Way CV32. . . . . . . .157 A2
Loxton Cl B74 . . . . .31 C5
Loynells Rd B45 . . . . .122 B7
Loyns Cl B37 . . . . .69 B3
Lozells Inf & Jun Sch B19 .66 C7
Lozells Rd B19. . . . . .66 C7
Lozells St B19 . . . . .66 C7
Lozells Wood Cl 2 B19 . . . .66 C7
Luanne Cl B64. . . . . .63 A1
Lucas Ct CV32 . . . . .161 D8
Lucas Ho CV32 . . . . .156 F2
Lucas Rd LE10 . . . . .75 D6
Luce Cl B35 . . . . .58 B4
Luce Rd WV10 . . . . .25 E6
Lucerne Cl CV2 . . . . .96 C3
Lucerne Ct B23 . . . . .56 D6
Lucian Cl CV2 . . . . .115 B7
Lucknow Rd WV12 . . . . . . .27 B5
Lucy Edwards Ct DY11 . . .116 C5
Luddington Rd B92 . . . . . .107 E8
Ludford Cl B75 . . . . .46 A7
Ludford Rd
Birmingham B32 . . . . .84 A1
Nuneaton CV10 . . . . .72 C6
Ludgate Ave DY11 . . . . . . .116 A4
Ludgate Cl
Oldbury B69. . . . . .63 B8
Water Orton B46 . . . . .59 B3
Ludgate Ct 2 WS5. . . . . . . .43 D7
Ludgate Hill B3. . . . . .164 B3
Ludgate Ho B13 . . . . .86 F4
Ludgate St 1 DY1 . . . . .51 B1
Ludgate B79. . . . . .21 A5
Lud La B79 . . . . .21 A5

Ludlow Cl
Birmingham B37 . . . .**70** C2
Cannock WS11. . . . .**2** C2
Willenhall WV12 . . . .**27** B6
Ludlow Ct B11. . . . .**87** B6
Ludlow Ho
1 Walsall WS3 . . . .**28** C6
Birmingham B13 . . . .**105** A6
Ludlow La WS2 . . . .**28** A4
Ludlow Rd
Birmingham B8 . . . .**67** F4
Coventry CV5. . . . .**113** A2
Kidderminster DY10 . . . . . .**116** E3
Redditch B97. . . . .**153** E3
Ludlow Way DY1. . . . .**50** E2
Ludmer Way B20 . . . .**55** C2
Ludstone Ave WV4 . . . .**38** D5
Ludstone Rd B29 . . . .**84** F1
Ludworth Ave B37 . . . .**90** B8
Luff Cl CV5 . . . .**134** B8
Lugtrout La
Catherine de B B91 . . . . . .**108** A6
Solihull B91 . . . .**107** F6
Lukes The B64 . . . .**62** C1
Lukes Wlk WS13 . . . .**3** A2
Lulworth Cl B63 . . . .**82** C6
Lulworth Pk CV8. . . . .**148** C6
Lulworth Rd
Birmingham B28 . . . .**88** A1
Burntwood WS7. . . . .**7** A7
Lulworth Wlk WV4 . . . .**38** C6
Lumley Gr B37 . . . .**70** D2
Lumley Rd WS1 . . . .**29** A1
Lumsden Cl CV2 . . . .**114** F8
Lunar Cl CV4 . . . .**132** D5
Lundy Cl LE10 . . . .**71** B1
Lundy View B36. . . . .**70** B6
Lunn Ave CV8 . . . .**147** E3
Lunn Poly Ho 3 CV32. . . .**156** F1
Lunns Croft WS13. . . . .**9** C8
Lunt Gr B32 . . . .**84** D5
Lunt Jct The WV14 . . . .**41** A6
Lunt Pl WV14 . . . .**41** A6
Lunt Rd WV14 . . . .**40** F6
Lunt The ★ CV8 . . . .**133** E3
Lupin Cl LE10. . . . .**75** D5
Lupin Gr
Birmingham B9 . . . .**67** F3
Walsall WS5 . . . .**43** B4
Lupin Rd DY2. . . . .**51** F1
Lupton Ave CV3. . . . .**133** C7
Lupton Ct B60 . . . .**137** A1
Lusbridge Cl B63. . . . .**82** B4
Luscombe Rd CV2 . . . .**114** E8
Luther Way CV5. . . . .**111** F4
Lutley Ave B63 . . . .**82** E4
Lutley Cl WV3 . . . .**38** E7
Lutley Dr DY9. . . . .**81** C3
Lutley Gr B32. . . . .**84** B1
Lutley La B63. . . . .**82** C2
Lutley Mill Rd B63 . . . .**82** E4
Lutley Prim Sch B63 . . . . . .**82** D1
Luton Rd B29. . . . .**85** F3
Lutterworth Rd
Coventry CV2. . . . .**114** C5
Hinckley LE10 . . . .**76** C3
Nuneaton CV11 . . . .**79** C8
Luttrell Rd B74 . . . .**32** A1
Luxor La CV5 . . . .**111** B8
Lyall Gdns B45 . . . .**101** E1
Lyall Gr B27 . . . .**88** A2
Lychgate Ave WV3. . . . .**81** C1
Lychgate Cl LE10 . . . .**76** C5
Lychgate La LE10 . . . .**76** C5
Lydate Rd B62. . . . .**83** F4
Lydbrook Covert 6 B38. . .**123** E8
Lydbury Gr B33. . . . .**69** A4
Lyd Cl WV11 . . . .**26** B5
Lydd Croft B35 . . . .**58** B4
Lyddington Dr B62. . . . .**83** B7
Lyde Gn B63. . . . .**82** B7
Lydford Cl CV2 . . . .**114** C7
Lydford Gr B24 . . . .**57** A1
Lydford Rd WS3 . . . .**14** B3
Lydgate Ct
Bedworth CV12 . . . .**78** A4
Nuneaton CV11 . . . .**73** C3
Lydgate Rd
Coventry CV6. . . . .**113** B5
Kingswinford DY6 . . . .**60** F6
Lydget Gr B23 . . . .**56** D7
Lydham Cl
Bilston WV14. . . . .**40** B4
Birmingham B44 . . . .**56** A6
Redditch B98 . . . .**153** E5
Lydia Croft B74. . . . .**31** E6
Lydian Cl WV6 . . . .**25** B4
Lydiate Ash Rd B60 . . . . . .**121** C3
Lydiate Ave B31 . . . .**102** D1
Lydiates Cl DY3. . . . .**50** B7
Lydney Cl
Redditch B98 . . . .**154** D7
Willenhall WV12. . . . .**27** D4
Lydney Gr B31. . . . .**102** F3
Lydstep Gr CV31. . . . .**162** C2
Lye Ave B32 . . . .**84** A2
Lye Bsns Ctr DY9 . . . .**81** F6
Lye By-Pass DY9. . . . .**81** E6
Lye Close La B32 . . . .**84** A2
Lyecroft Ave B37 . . . .**70** D2
Lye Cross Rd B69 . . . .**63** B7
Lye Sta DY9 . . . .**81** E6
Lye Valley Ind Est DY9. . . . .**81** F6
Lygon Cl B98. . . . .**154** A5
Lygon Gr B32. . . . .**84** E4

Lymedene Rd B42 . . . .**55** B5
Lyme Green Rd B33. . . . . . .**68** F4
Lymer Rd WV10. . . . .**11** C1
Lymesy St CV3. . . . .**133** D7
Lymington Cl CV6. . . . .**113** D8
Lymington Ct B73 . . . .**46** B1
Lymington Dr CV6 . . . .**96** B6
Lymington Rd WV13 . . . .**27** D2
Lymore Croft CV2. . . . .**115** A8
Lymsey Croft DY8. . . . .**60** C3
Lynbrook Cl
Dudley DY2 . . . .**62** D5
Hollywood B47. . . . .**125** A7
Lynbrook Rd CV5 . . . .**132** D8
Lynchgate Ct CV4 . . . .**132** C6
Lynchgate Ho CV4 . . . .**132** C6
Lynchgate Rd CV4 . . . .**132** C6
Lynch The
Nuneaton CV11 . . . .**73** D2
Polesworth B78. . . . .**22** F1
Lyncourt Gr B32 . . . .**84** B6
Lyncroft Rd B11. . . . .**87** F2
Lyndale Cl CV5 . . . .**112** C3
Lyndale Dr WV11. . . . .**26** E6
Lyndale Rd
Coventry CV5. . . . .**112** C3
Dudley DY2 . . . .**62** E6
Sedgley DY3. . . . .**39** B2
Lyndale B77. . . . .**35** F6
Lynden Cl B61. . . . .**136** E3
Lynden Ho CV5 . . . .**133** B8
Lyndenwood B97 . . . .**153** A2
Lyndholm Rd B10 . . . .**117** A6
Lyndhurst Cl
Bedworth CV6 . . . .**96** B6
Hinckley LE10 . . . .**76** A7
Lyndhurst Croft CV5 . . . . .**111** C4
Lyndhurst Dr
Kidderminster DY10 . . . . . .**116** E8
Stourbridge DY8 . . . .**60** F1
Lyndhurst Rd
Birmingham B24 . . . .**56** F2
Cannock WS12. . . . .**2** E1
West Bromwich B71 . . . .**53** E7
Wolverhampton WV3. . . . . . .**39** A7
Lyndon Cl
Birmingham,Castle Bromwich
B36. . . . .**69** C8
Birmingham,Handsworth
B20. . . . .**55** C2
Halesowen B63 . . . .**82** F4
Sedgley DY3. . . . .**39** E1
Lyndon Croft B37 . . . .**90** B7
Lyndon Ct CV32. . . . .**161** E8
Lyndon Green Inf Sch
B26. . . . .**89** A6
Lyndon Green Jun Sch
B26. . . . .**89** A6
Lyndon Gr
Kingswinford DY6 . . . .**60** B8
West Bromwich B71 . . . .**53** D4
Lyndon Ho B31. . . . .**103** B3
Lyndon Rd
Birmingham,Rubery B45. . . .**121** E7
Birmingham,Stechford B33. . .**68** E3
Solihull B92 . . . .**88** F2
Sutton Coldfield B73 . . . . . .**46** B5
Sutton Coldfield B92 . . . . . .**89** A3
Lyndon B71 . . . .**53** D5
Lyndworth Rd B30 . . . . . .**104** C8
Lyneham Cl
Hinckley LE10 . . . .**71** A1
Tamworth B79 . . . .**21** C8
Lyneham Gdns B76 . . . .**58** B6
Lyneham Way B35 . . . .**57** F3
Lyne Ho 1 CV2. . . . .**114** D8
Lynfield Cl B38. . . . .**123** F7
Lyng Cl CV5 . . . .**112** A4
Lyng Hall Sch CV2 . . . .**114** C6
Lyng La B70 . . . .**53** C2
Lyng Prim Sch B70 . . . .**53** C1
Lynmouth Cl
Aldridge WS9. . . . .**30** A5
Nuneaton CV11 . . . .**73** E5
Lynmouth Rd CV2. . . . . . .**114** E8
Lynn Gr B29. . . . .**85** C3
Lynn La WS14 . . . .**17** D6
Lynon Field CV34 . . . .**160** B4
Lynton Ave
Smethwick B66 . . . .**65** A6
West Bromwich B71 . . . .**53** C7
Wolverhampton WV6. . . . . . .**24** F6
Lynton Cl CV34 . . . .**155** E1
Lynton Ho B23. . . . .**56** B6
Lynton Rd
Birmingham B6 . . . .**67** B7
Coventry CV6. . . . .**95** F1
Lynval Rd DY5. . . . .**81** F7
Lynwood Ave DY6. . . . .**60** B7
Lynwood Cl
Walsall WV12. . . . .**13** E1
Willenhall WV12 . . . .**27** E8
Lynwood Dr DY10. . . . .**98** C2
Lynwood Way B45 . . . .**122** A3
Lynwood Wlk
10 Royal Leamington Spa
CV31. . . . .**162** C6
Birmingham B17 . . . .**85** D4
Lyon Ct B72 . . . .**46** C5
Lyons Gr B11. . . . .**87** C3
Lysander Cl LE10 . . . .**75** E4
Lysander Rd B45 . . . .**102** A2
Lysander Way
Birmingham B35 . . . .**58** B2
Cannock WS11. . . . .**1** E3
Lyster Cl CV34 . . . .**160** B8
Lysway Ct 3 WS1 . . . .**42** F8
Lysways St WS1 . . . .**42** F8

Lythall Cl CV31 . . . .**162** F5
Lythalls La CV6 . . . .**95** E2
Lythalls Lane Ind Est CV6 .**95** E1
Lytham
Stourbridge DY8 . . . .**80** F2
Sutton Coldfield B76 . . . . . .**58** B6
Lytham Croft B15. . . . .**86** D8
Lytham Gr WS3 . . . .**14** A3
Lytham Rd WV6. . . . .**23** D4
Lytham B77 . . . .**22** C5
Lythwood Dr DY5. . . . .**81** C8
Lyttelton Pl DY9 . . . .**99** C6
Lyttelton Rd
Birmingham,Edgbaston
B16. . . . .**65** D1
Birmingham,Stechford B33 . .**68** D3
Stourbridge DY8 . . . .**80** D5
Warwick CV34. . . . .**160** E8
Lyttleton Ave
Bromsgrove B60 . . . .**150** E7
Halesowen B62 . . . .**83** E7
Lyttleton Cl
Coventry CV3. . . . .**115** A1
Dudley DY2 . . . .**62** C4
Lyttleton Ho B63 . . . .**83** A2
Lyttleton St B70 . . . .**53** C2
Lytton Ave WV4 . . . .**38** E4
Lytton Gr B27 . . . .**88** B1
Lytton La B32 . . . .**84** F3

M

Maas Rd B31. . . . .**103** A4
Mabey Ave B98 . . . .**153** F5
MacAdam Cl WS7. . . . .**7** B8
MacArthur Rd B64. . . . .**82** C8
Macaulay Ho 5 B70 . . . . . .**53** D1
Macaulay Rd CV2. . . . .**114** D4
McBean Rd WV6. . . . .**24** F4
Macbeth App CV34. . . . .**155** A1
McCalla Ho WV3. . . . .**25** B1
McConnell Cl B60 . . . .**151** B7
MacDonald Cl B69 . . . .**52** D2
MacDonald Rd CV2 . . . . . .**114** D3
MacDonald St B5. . . . .**86** E8
McDonnell Dr CV6,CV7 . . . . .**95** F6
McDougall Rd WS10 . . . . . .**42** C3
Macefield Cl CV2 . . . .**96** D2
Mace St B64. . . . .**62** E1
McGeough Wlk WS11 . . . . . .**2** B5
McGhie St WS12. . . . .**2** B6
McGregor Cl 4 B6. . . . .**55** F1
MacGregor Cres B77. . . . . . .**21** F3
MacGregor Tithe B79 . . . . . .**21** B5
Machin Rd B23 . . . .**56** F4
Mackadown La B33. . . . .**69** D2
Mackay Rd WS3 . . . .**14** D2
McKean Rd
Oldbury B69. . . . .**64** A8
West Bromwich B70 . . . .**53** C1
Mcken Ct B70 . . . .**53** C2
Mackenzie Cl CV5 . . . .**112** A7
Mackenzie Rd B11. . . . .**87** C2
Mackmillan Rd B65 . . . .**63** C2
McLean Rd WV10 . . . .**11** C1
McMahon Rd CV12. . . . .**95** E8
Macmillan Cl B69. . . . .**52** A1
Macrome Rd WV6. . . . .**24** E8
Madam's Hill Rd B90 . . . .**126** D7
Maddocke Wlk 4 WS13. . . . .**8** F6
Maddocks Hill B72. . . . .**46** C2
Madehurst Rd B23. . . . .**56** E6
Madeira Ave WV8 . . . .**10** A2
Madeira Croft CV5 . . . .**112** E2
Madeira Ct DY8. . . . .**60** F1
Madeley Rd
Birmingham B11 . . . .**87** C5
Kingswinford DY6 . . . .**61** A4
Madeley Heath DY9. . . . . . .**120** D6
Redditch B98. . . . .**154** F5
Madinatul Uloom Al Islamiya
Sch DY10 . . . .**117** D1
Madin Rd DY4. . . . .**51** E4
Madison Ave
Birmingham B36 . . . .**68** D6
Brierley Hill DY5 . . . .**61** F3
Walsall WS2 . . . .**28** B2
Madley Cl B45. . . . .**121** E8
Madox Cl B79 . . . .**20** E8
Madresfield Dr B63 . . . .**83** B2
Madrona B77 . . . .**22** B4
Maer Cl B65. . . . .**63** C3
Mafeking Rd B66 . . . .**65** A4
Mafeking Villas B62 . . . .**83** B7
Magdala St B18 . . . .**65** E5
Magdalen Cl DY1 . . . .**51** A2
Magdalen B16 . . . .**65** E1
Magdalene Rd WS1 . . . .**43** A7
Magee Cl LE10. . . . .**71** C2
Magna Cl WS6. . . . .**4** E3
Magness Cres WV12 . . . .**27** C5
Magnet Wlk B23. . . . .**56** C5
Magnolia Cl
Birmingham B29 . . . .**103** A4
Coventry CV3. . . . .**133** B5
Magnolia Dr 1 WS5 . . . . . .**42** F4
Magnolia Gr
Codsall WV8 . . . .**10** B3
Willenhall WV12 . . . .**27** B4
Magnolia B27 . . . .**22** A4
Magnolia Way 1 DY8. . . . . .**60** F1
Magnum Cl B74 . . . .**44** F7
Magnus B77. . . . .**35** E6
Magpie Cl DY2. . . . .**62** E3
Magpie Ho CV5 . . . .**111** D5
Magpie La CV7. . . . .**129** E6
Magpie Way DY10. . . . .**117** B2

Maguire Ind Est CV4 . . . .**131** F8
Magyar Cres CV11 . . . .**79** A8
Maidavale Cres CV3. . . . . . .**133** C4
Maiden Cl WV13 . . . .**27** C2
Maidendale Rd DY6. . . . .**60** B7
Maidensbridge Dr DY6. . . . .**60** C8
Maidensbridge Gdns DY6 .**49** B1
Maidensbridge Prim Sch
DY6 . . . .**49** B1
Maidensbridge Rd DY6. . . . .**49** B1
Maiden Way B60. . . . .**151** A6
Maidstone Dr
Burntwood WS7. . . . .**7** D6
Stourbridge DY8 . . . .**60** E3
Maidstone Rd B20. . . . .**55** E1
Maidwell Dr B90. . . . .**126** E8
Mailbox The B1. . . . .**164** B1
Main Rd
Ansty CV7 . . . .**97** D3
Meriden CV7 . . . .**110** D8
Tamworth B79 . . . .**21** B8
Main St
Birmingham B11 . . . .**87** A7
Brandon CV8 . . . .**135** F4
Mainstone Cl B98. . . . .**154** E3
Mainstream Forty Seven Ind
Pk B7. . . . .**67** C5
Main St
Shenstone WS14 . . . .**17** F6
Stonnall WS9 . . . .**16** D4
Main Terr B11 . . . .**87** A7
Mainwaring Dr B75. . . . .**32** E2
Maisemore Cl B98 . . . .**154** D6
Maitland Rd
Birmingham B8 . . . .**67** F4
Dudley DY1 . . . .**50** E1
Maitland B77. . . . .**21** F2
Maizefield LE10 . . . .**71** C4
Majestic Way B65. . . . .**63** D4
Major Ct 6 B13 . . . .**87** B2
Major St WV2. . . . .**39** E7
Majuba Rd B16 . . . .**65** C4
Makepeace Ave CV34 . . . . .**155** F1
Malam Cl CV4 . . . .**112** A1
Malcolm Ave
Birmingham B24 . . . .**57** C5
Bromsgrove B61. . . . .**136** E3
Malcolm Ct WV1. . . . .**25** A3
Malcolm Gr B45. . . . .**122** A7
Malcolm Rd B90. . . . .**106** B1
Malcolmson Cl B15. . . . .**85** F8
Maldale B77. . . . .**22** C1
Malfield Ave B97 . . . .**152** F3
Malfield Dr B27. . . . .**88** E3
Malham Cl CV11 . . . .**74** A2
Malham Rd
Tamworth B77 . . . .**36** C8
Warwick CV34. . . . .**155** F1
Malhay Gdns 4 B42 . . . .**55** A8
Malins Rd
Birmingham B17 . . . .**85** D5
Wolverhampton WV4 . . . . . .**39** E5
Malins The CV34 . . . .**161** B6
Malkit Cl WS2 . . . .**27** F4
Mallaby Cl B90. . . . .**126** A8
Mallard Ave
Kidderminster DY10 . . . . . .**117** B3
Nuneaton CV10 . . . .**72** C6
Mallard Cl
Birmingham B27 . . . .**88** C3
Brierley Hill DY5 . . . .**81** C7
Redditch B98. . . . .**153** F5
Walsall WS3 . . . .**14** A3
Mallard Croft 5 WS13. . . . . .**9** C8
Mallard Dr
Birmingham B23 . . . .**56** B3
Hinckley LE10 . . . .**75** A7
Oldbury B69. . . . .**63** F4
Mallard Rd B80. . . . .**159** F4
Mallards Reach B92 . . . . . .**106** E8
Mallender Dr B93. . . . .**127** F6
Mallen Dr B69 . . . .**52** B1
Mallerin Croft CV10. . . . .**72** B5
Mallicot Cl WS13 . . . .**3** D1
Mallin Gdns DY1 . . . .**61** E8
Mallin St B66. . . . .**64** D7
Mallory Cres WS3. . . . .**14** D2
Mallory Dr
Kidderminster DY11 . . . . . .**116** D8
Warwick CV34. . . . .**160** D7
Mallory Rd WV6 . . . .**23** E3
Mallory Rise B13 . . . .**87** C1
Mallow Cl CV6 . . . .**95** E4
Mallow Cl 1 WS5 . . . .**43** A3
Mallow Cres DY10 . . . .**116** F4
Mallow Croft CV12. . . . .**77** E2
Mallow Rd B61. . . . .**136** F6
Mallow Rise 2 B23. . . . .**56** B7
Malmesbury Pk B15 . . . .**85** E7
Malmesbury Rd
Birmingham B10 . . . .**87** E7
Coventry CV6. . . . .**95** A3
Malpas Dr B32. . . . .**102** C8
Malpass Rd DY5. . . . .**81** F7
Malt Cl B17 . . . .**85** D6
Malthouse Croft B6. . . . .**66** E8
Malthouse Dr DY1 . . . .**51** A2
Malthouse Gdns B19. . . . . . .**66** D8
Malthouse Gr B25 . . . .**68** E1
Malthouse La
Birmingham B8 . . . .**67** E4
Birmingham,Great Barr B42 .**55** D8
Earlswood B94. . . . .**141** E7

Malthouse La continued
Kenilworth CV8 . . . .**147** E6
Wolverhampton WV6. . . . . . .**24** F4
Malthouse Mdw 2 B91. . . .**107** C1
Malthouse Rd DY4. . . . .**51** E5
Malthouse Row B37 . . . .**90** A8
Maltings Ct B17 . . . .**65** A1
Maltings The
Aldridge WS9. . . . .**30** C6
Nuneaton CV11 . . . .**73** E5
Royal Leamington Spa
CV32. . . . .**156** F2
Studley B80 . . . .**159** D4
Wolverhampton WV1. . . . . .**163** C4
Malt Mill La B62. . . . .**83** D8
Malt Mill Lane Trad Est
B62. . . . .**83** D8
Malton Ave B65. . . . .**63** D6
Malton Gr B13. . . . .**105** B7
Malvern Ave
Nuneaton CV10 . . . .**72** B3
Stourbridge DY9 . . . .**81** C5
Malvern Cl
Birmingham B15 . . . .**85** C8
West Bromwich B71 . . . .**53** D5
Willenhall WV12 . . . .**27** B4
Malvern Cres DY2. . . . .**61** F6
Malvern Ct
8 Sutton Coldfield B74 . . . .**31** F2
Birmingham,Stockfield B27. .**88** C4
Birmingham,Stockland Green
B23. . . . .**56** C2
Wolverhampton WV10. . . . . .**25** D8
Malvern Dr
Aldridge WS9. . . . .**30** C8
Kidderminster DY10 . . . . . .**116** E3
Sutton Coldfield B76. . . . . . .**58** A8
Wolverhampton WV11. . . . . .**26** B1
Malvern Hill Rd B7 . . . .**67** C7
Malvern Ho
7 Halesowen B63 . . . .**83** A3
Coventry CV5. . . . .**111** D4
Redditch B97 . . . .**153** C1
Malvern Park Ave WV1 . . . .**107** D3
Malvern Rd
Balsall Common CV7 . . . . . .**130** C6
Barnt Green B45 . . . .**122** A2
Birmingham,Acock's Green
B27. . . . .**88** B4
Birmingham B68 . . . .**84** B8
Birmingham,Handsworth
B21. . . . .**54** C1
Bromsgrove B61. . . . .**150** D7
Coventry CV5. . . . .**112** F4
Redditch B97 . . . .**158** D8
Malvern St B12. . . . .**87** A5
Malvern View
Dudley DY10 . . . .**118** C1
Willenhall WV11. . . . .**116** B1
Malvern View Rd DY3 . . . . . .**50** D4
Mamble Rd DY8 . . . .**80** E5
Mammoth Dr WV10 . . . .**25** D6
Manby Cl WV6. . . . .**25** A4
Manby Rd B35. . . . .**58** A4
Manby St DY4. . . . .**51** F8
Mancetter Rd
Nuneaton CV10 . . . .**72** D7
Solihull B90 . . . .**106** C3
Manchester St
Birmingham B6 . . . .**164** C5
Oldbury B69. . . . .**64** B7
Mancroft Cl DY6. . . . .**60** B7
Mancroft Gdns WV6. . . . . . .**24** C5
Mancroft Rd WV6. . . . .**24** C5
Mandale Rd WV10 . . . .**25** F6
Mandarin Ave DY10 . . . . . .**117** B3
Mandarin Cl LE10. . . . .**75** A6
Mander Ctr WV1 . . . .**163** B3
Mander Gallery WV1 . . . . . .**163** B3
Mander Gr CV34 . . . .**160** C4
Manderley Cl
Coventry CV5. . . . .**111** C5
Sedgley DY3. . . . .**39** C2
Manders Ind Est WV1 . . . . . .**26** A3
Mander Sq WV1 . . . .**163** B3
Manderston Cl DY1 . . . .**50** E3
Mander St WV3. . . . .**163** A1
Mandeville Gdns DY6. . . . . .**60** C6
Mandeville Gdns WS1. . . . . .**42** F8
Mandeville Way B61 . . . . . .**136** F5
Mandrake Cl CV6 . . . .**95** D4
Maney Cnr B72. . . . .**46** B4
Maney Hill Prim Sch B72. .**46** D2
Maney Hill Rd B72. . . . .**46** C2
Manfield Ave CV2. . . . .**115** A7
Manfield Rd WV13 . . . .**26** C3
Manfield Cl WS7. . . . .**7** D6
Manifoldia Grange B70 . . . . .**53** B2
Manifold Way WS10. . . . .**42** E3
Manilla Rd B29. . . . .**86** A1
Manitoba Croft 2 B38. . . . .**123** F8
Manley Cl B70. . . . .**53** A3
Manley Rd WS13. . . . .**3** D1
Manlove St WV3. . . . .**39** A8
Manningford Ct B14 . . . . . .**104** F3
Manningford Rd B14. . . . . .**104** E3
Manor Abbey Rd B62. . . . . . .**83** E4
Manor Ave
Cannock WS11. . . . .**1** D1
Great Wyrley WS6 . . . .**5** A4
Kidderminster DY11 . . . . . .**116** A7
Manor Ave S DY11 . . . .**116** A6
Manor Cl
Birmingham B16 . . . .**65** D1
Codsall WV8 . . . .**10** B4
Hinckley LE10 . . . .**75** C5
Kidderminster DY11 . . . . . .**116** A6
Willenhall WV13 . . . .**26** F3

Manor Cl continued
Wolverhampton WV4 . . . . .38 F4
Manor Cotts WS11 . . . . .8 E2
Manor Court Ave CV11 . . . . . .73 B5
Manor Court Mews CV11 . .73 A5
Manor Court Rd
Bromsgrove B60 . . . . .150 F8
Nuneaton CV11 . . . . .73 A5
Manor Ct
🔢 Birmingham,Hurst Green
B62 . . . . .84 A7
Birmingham,King's Norton
B30 . . . . .104 A2
Dorridge B93 . . . . .127 F2
Dudley DY2 . . . . .62 C5
Kenilworth CV8 . . . . .148 A6
Mile Oak B78 . . . . .20 D1
Royal Leamington Spa
CV31 . . . . .161 F7
Walsall WS2 . . . . .28 C1
Manor Dr
Dudley DY3 . . . . .50 B3
Sutton Coldfield B73 . . . . .46 B4
Manor Est CV8 . . . . .135 F3
Manor Farm Craft Ctr*
B94 .125 F2
Manor Farm Dr WV12 . . . . . .27 D5
Manor Farm Rd B11 . . . . .87 E4
Manor Flats DY3 . . . . .50 D8
Manorford Ave B71 . . . . .43 A1
Manor Gdns
Birmingham B33 . . . . .68 D2
Wednesbury WS10 . . . . .41 F4
Wombourne WV5 . . . . .49 B7
Manor Hall Mews CV3 . .134 D6
Manor High Sch WS10 . . . . . .42 D3
Manor Hill B73 . . . . .46 B4
Manor Hospl WS2 . . . . .28 C1
Manor Ho The CV31 . . . . .161 F7
Manor House Cl
Aston Flamville LE10 . . . . .76 E6
Birmingham B29 . . . . .84 F1
Manor House Dr
Birmingham B29 . . . . .103 B7
Coventry CV1 . . . . .165 B2
Manor House La
Astwood Bank B96 . . . . .158 E3
Birmingham B26 . . . . .88 F6
Water Orton B46 . . . . .59 B3
Manor House Pk WV8 . . . .10 B4
Manor House Rd WS10 . . .41 F4
Manor Ho WV6 . . . . .24 D5
Manorial Rd B75 . . . . .32 E3
Manor Ind Est WS2 . . . . .28 C1
Manor Jun & Inf Sch
WV14 . . . . .40 B2
Manor La
Halesowen B62 . . . . .83 E4
Honiley CV8,CV35 . . . . .146 A5
Lower Marlbrook B61 . . . . . . .121 C4
Stourbridge DY8 . . . . .80 D3
Wroxall CV35 . . . . .145 F4
Manor Mews B80 . . . . .159 E4
Manor Park B13 . . . . .87 A2
Manor Park Com Sch
CV11 . . . . .73 A5
Manor Park Gr B31 . . . . . . .102 C1
Manor Park Prim Sch
Birmingham B6 . . . . .67 A8
Coventry CV3 . . . . .133 D7
Manor Park Rd
Birmingham B36 . . . . .69 D8
Nuneaton CV11 . . . . .73 A5
Manor Pk DY6 . . . . .60 D6
Manor Pl LE10 . . . . .71 D1
Manor Prim Sch
Drayton Bassett B78 . . . . .34 E5
Sutton Coldfield B74 . . . . .31 A1
Manor Rd
Birmingham,Birchfield B6 . . . .55 F1
Birmingham,Edgbaston B16 . .65 D1
Birmingham,Stechford B33 . . .68 E3
Coventry CV1 . . . . .165 B1
Dorridge B93 . . . . .127 F3
Ettingshall WV4 . . . . .40 A5
Kenilworth CV8 . . . . .147 F6
Mile Oak B78 . . . . .20 D1
Manor Rd N B16 . . . . .65 D1
Manor Rd
Royal Leamington Spa
CV32 . . . . .157 B3
Smethwick B67 . . . . .64 E4
Solihull B91 . . . . .107 C5
Stourbridge DY8 . . . . .60 E2
Studley B80 . . . . .159 E4
Sutton Coldfield B74 . . . . .31 A1
Sutton Coldfield,Maney B73 . .46 B4
Sutton Coldfield,Streetly
B74 .45 A8
Tamworth B77 . . . . .21 D4
Tipton DY4 . . . . .51 F4
Upper Bentley B97 . . . . .152 B1
Walsall WS2 . . . . .28 C2
Wednesbury WS10 . . . . .42 D2
Wythall B47 . . . . .125 A3
Manor Rise
Burntwood WS7 . . . . .7 A5
Lichfield WS14 . . . . .9 C7
Manor Road Prec 🔢 WS2 .28 C1
Manor Side Ind Est B98 . .154 E4
Manor Sq B91 . . . . .107 C3
Manor St
Hinckley LE10 . . . . .71 C1
Wolverhampton WV6 . . . . .24 D5
Manor Terr CV8 . . . . .148 A6

Manor View CV8 . . . . .135 F3
Manor Way
Halesowen B62,B63 . . . . .83 D3
Hinckley LE10 . . . . .75 D5
Manor Way Prim Sch B63 .83 C3
Manor Wlk
🔢 Solihull B91 . . . . .107 C3
Sutton Coldfield B73 . . . . .46 B4
Mansard Cl
Wolverhampton,Bradmore
WV3 .38 F8
Wolverhampton,Scotlands
WV10 . . . . .26 B8
Mansard Ho B90 . . . . .106 A3
Manse Cl CV7 . . . . .78 A1
Manse Gdns B80 . . . . .159 E3
Mansell Cl B63 . . . . .82 B7
Mansell Rd
Redditch B97 . . . . .158 D7
Tipton DY4 . . . . .52 A8
Mansel Rd B10 . . . . .87 E8
Mansel St CV6 . . . . .113 E8
Mansfield Cl B79 . . . . .20 E6
Mansfield Green Com Sch
B6 . . . . .66 E8
Mansfield Ho B37 . . . . .70 D3
Mansfield Rd
Birmingham,Aston B6 . . . . . . .66 E8
Birmingham,South Yardley
B25 . . . . .88 C5
Mansion Cl DY1 . . . . .51 A3
Mansion Cres B67 . . . . .64 E4
Mansion Ct B62 . . . . .83 E7
Mansion Dr
Hammerwich WS7 . . . . .7 D4
Tipton DY4 . . . . .52 C5
Manson St 🔢 LE10 . . . . . . .75 D8
Manston Ct WV4 . . . . .38 D5
Manston Dr B64 . . . . .63 A1
Manston Rd B26 . . . . .89 B7
Manston View B79 . . . . .21 C8
Manta Rd B77 . . . . .35 D6
Mantilla Dr CV3 . . . . .133 A8
Manton Croft B93 . . . . .127 E3
Manton Ho B19 . . . . .66 E7
Manway Cl B20 . . . . .54 F4
Manwoods Cl B20 . . . . .55 B2
Maple Ave
Bedworth CV7 . . . . .78 B1
Wednesbury WS10 . . . . .42 C4
Mapleback Cl B91 . . . . .107 C5
Maple Bank B15 . . . . .86 A7
Maplebeck Cl CV5 . . . . .113 A3
Maple Bsns Pk B7 . . . . .67 B6
Maple Cl
🔢 Birmingham,Harborne
B17 .85 B6
🔢 Birmingham,Erdington
B24 .56 F3
Bilston WV14 . . . . .40 F2
Lichfield WS14 . . . . .9 C8
Oldbury B66 . . . . .64 D8
Maple Ctr The WS10 . . . . .41 B3
Mapledene B13 . . . . .87 B2
Mapledene Inf Sch B26 . . . .89 D6
Mapledene Jun Sch B26 . .89 D6
Mapledene Rd B26 . . . . .89 D6
Maple Dr
Birmingham B44 . . . . .56 C8
Dudley DY3 . . . . .50 B2
Huntington WS12 . . . . .1 D8
Walsall,Shelfield WS4 . . . . .29 B8
Walsall,Yew Tree WS5 . . . . . . .43 B4
Maple Gn DY1 . . . . .51 A5
Maple Gr
Bilston WV14 . . . . .40 F4
Birmingham,Aston B19 . . . . . .66 D8
Birmingham,Kingshurst B37 .69 F6
Kingswinford DY6 . . . . .60 E6
Lichfield WS14 . . . . .9 E7
Warwick CV34 . . . . .156 A1
Wolverhampton WV3 . . . . .24 C2
Maple Hayes Hall Sch
WS13 .8 B3
Maple Ho
Redditch,Greenlands
B98 . . . . .158 F8
Redditch,Webheath B97 . . . .153 B2
Sutton Coldfield B74 . . . . .31 B5
Walsall WS4 . . . . .15 D1
Maple Leaf Dr B37 . . . . .90 B8
Maple Leaf Ind Est WS2 . .28 A4
Maple Leaf Rd WS10 . . . . . .41 C1
Maple Rd
Birmingham B45 . . . . .121 F6
Birmingham,Selly Oak B30 .103 E8
Dudley DY1 . . . . .51 C3
Halesowen B62 . . . . .83 D8
Nuneaton CV10 . . . . .72 E5
Maple Rise
Oldbury B68 . . . . .64 C2
Tamworth B77 . . . . .22 A4
Maple Row 🔢 DY5 . . . . .61 D2

Maples The
Bedworth CV12 . . . . .77 E2
Wolverhampton WV11 . . . . . . .26 B5
Maple St WS3 . . . . .14 D2
Mapleton Gr B28 . . . . .106 B7
Mapleton Rd
Birmingham B28 . . . . .106 B7
Coventry CV6 . . . . .112 F8
Maple Tree La B63 . . . . .82 C6
Maple Way B31 . . . . .102 F1
Maple Wlk
🔢 Birmingham B37 . . . . .70 B2
Coventry CV6 . . . . .95 F5
Maplewood B76 . . . . .58 A8
Mapperley Cl CV2 . . . . .115 A8
Mapperley Gdns B13 . . . . .86 C3
Mappleb, Town in B97 .153 B5
Mapleborough Rd B90 .105 C1
Mapps Cl B63 . . . . .82 C6
Marans Croft B38 . . . . .123 D7
Marble Alley B80 . . . . .159 E4
Marbury Cl B38 . . . . .103 D2
Marbury Dr WV14 . . . . .41 A6
Marbury Mews DY5 . . . . . . .61 D1
Marchant Rd
Bilston WV14 . . . . .40 D7
Wolverhampton WV6 . . . . .24 F2
March Cl WS6 . . . . .4 D1
March End Rd WV11 . . . . . . .26 D5
Marchfont Cl CV11 . . . . .74 A1
Marchmont Rd B9 . . . . .68 A2
Marchmount Rd B72 . . . . . .57 C8
March Way
Aldridge WS9 . . . . .16 C1
Coventry CV3 . . . . .134 D7
Marchwood Cl B97 . . . . . . .153 A5
Marcliff Cres B90 . . . . .105 C2
Marconi Pl WS12 . . . . .2 C7
Marcos Dr B36 . . . . .58 F1
Marcot Rd B92 . . . . .88 F5
Marcroft Pl CV31 . . . . .162 D6
Marden Cl WV13 . . . . .26 F1
Marden Rd B31 . . . . .123 A7
Marden Wlk B23 . . . . .56 C3
Mardol Cl CV2 . . . . .114 D7
Mardon Rd B26 . . . . .89 C5
Maree Gr WV11 . . . . .13 B1
Maret Ct 🔢 WS1 . . . . .42 F8
Marfield Cl B76 . . . . .58 A6
Margam Cres WS3 . . . . .13 F2
Margam Terr WS3 . . . . .13 F2
Margam Way WS3 . . . . .13 F2
Margaret Ave
Bedworth CV12 . . . . .78 B3
Halesowen B63 . . . . .82 F4
Margaret Cl DY5 . . . . .81 E8
Margaret Dr
Cannock WS11 . . . . .1 E6
Stourbridge DY8 . . . . .81 B4
Margaret Gdns B67 . . . . . . .64 E5
Margaret Gr B17 . . . . .85 C7
Margaret Rd B76 . . . . .46 F3
Margaret Rd
Birmingham,Harborne
B17 .85 C5
Birmingham,New Oscott
B73 .57 A5
Darlaston WS10 . . . . .41 C4
Wolverhampton WV3 . . . . .38 F8
Margaret St
Birmingham B3 . . . . .164 B3
West Bromwich B70 . . . . .53 B2
Margaret Vale DY4 . . . . .41 C1
Margaret Vine B62 . . . . .63 F1
Margeson Cl CV2 . . . . .114 E2
Margesson Dr B45 . . . . .122 D1
Margetts Cl CV8 . . . . .147 F4
Margreal Ind Est B70 . . . . . .53 A2
Marholm Cl WV9 . . . . .10 F2
Marian Croft B26 . . . . .89 D5
Maria St B70 . . . . .64 E8
Marie Brock Cl CV4 . . . . . .112 B1
Marie Dr B27 . . . . .106 B8
Marigold Cl WS11 . . . . .2 C3
Marigold Cres DY1 . . . . .51 A4
Marigold Dr LE10 . . . . .75 E5
Marigold Wlk CV10 . . . . .78 A8
Marina Cl CV4 . . . . .131 E7
Marina Cres WS12 . . . . .2 A5
Marine Cres DY8 . . . . .60 E1
Marine Dr B44 . . . . .55 E6
Marine Gdns DY8 . . . . .60 E1
Mariner Ave B16 . . . . .65 E1
Mariner B79 . . . . .20 E6
Marion Cl DY5 . . . . .61 F2
Marion Rd
Coventry CV6 . . . . .113 D7
Smethwick B67 . . . . .64 E5
Marion Way B28 . . . . .105 E7
Marita Cl DY2 . . . . .62 E3
Marjoram Cl B38 . . . . .123 F8
Marjorie Ave B30 . . . . .104 B3
Mark Antony Dr CV34 . . . .161 D4
Mark Ave WS10 . . . . .41 E3
Markby Rd B18 . . . . .65 E6
Mark Cl B98 . . . . .153 E2
Mark Ct WS1 . . . . .29 A3
Market Cnr
🔢 Royal Leamington Spa
CV31 . . . . .161 F6
Baginton CV8 . . . . .133 F2
Market End Cl CV12 . . . . . . .77 C2
Market Hall St WS11 . . . . . . .1 E1
Market La
Lichfield WS14 . . . . .8 E2
Lower Penn WV4 . . . . .37 F5

Market Pl
🔢 Cannock WS11 . . . . .1 E1
Bromsgrove B61 . . . . .136 F2
Dudley DY1 . . . . .51 D1
Hinckley LE10 . . . . .75 D8
Nuneaton CV11 . . . . .73 C4
Redditch B98 . . . . .153 E4
Rowley Regis B65 . . . . .63 C1
Tamworth B79 . . . . .21 B4
Tipton DY4 . . . . .52 D5
Walsall WS3 . . . . .14 B1
Warwick CV34 . . . . .160 E6
Wednesbury WS10 . . . . .41 F2
Willenhall WV13 . . . . .27 A1
Market Sq
Cradley Heath B64 . . . . .82 C8
Wolverhampton WV3 . . . . . . .163 B2
Market St
Bromsgrove B61 . . . . .136 F2
Cannock WS12 . . . . .2 C5
Kidderminster DY10 . . . . .116 E5
Kingswinford DY6 . . . . .60 D6
Lichfield WS13 . . . . .9 B8
Oldbury B69 . . . . .64 A8
Stourbridge DY8 . . . . .81 A5
Tamworth B79 . . . . .21 B4
Warwick CV34 . . . . .160 D6
Wolverhampton WV1 . .163 C3
Market Way
Bilston WV14 . . . . .40 D5
Coventry CV1 . . . . .165 B2
Hagley DY9 . . . . .99 C6
Market Wlk 🔢 B97 . . . . . . .153 E4
Markfield Rd B26 . . . . .89 B8
Markford Wlk B19 . . . . .66 D6
Markham Cres B92 . . . . .89 F1
Markham Croft WV9 . . . . . . .11 A2
Markham Dr
Kingswinford DY6 . . . . .60 E4
Whitnash CV31 . . . . .162 B3
Markham Rd B73 . . . . .45 C3
Mark Ho B13 . . . . .87 A2
Marklew Cl WS8 . . . . .16 A5
Marklin Ave WV10 . . . . .11 D1
Mark Rd WS10 . . . . .41 E3
Marksbury Cl WV6 . . . . .25 A5
Marks Mews 🔢 CV34 . . . . .160 E6
Marks Wlk WS13 . . . . .3 A2
Marlbank Rd DY8 . . . . .61 A1
Marlborough Ave B60 . . . .151 A8
Marlborough Cl
Hinckley LE10 . . . . .76 B7
Sutton Coldfield B74 . . . . .31 E6
Marlborough Ct
🔢 Sutton Coldfield B74 . . .31 F2
Bromsgrove B60 . . . . .151 B8
Marlborough Dr
Royal Leamington Spa
CV31 . . . . .162 D5
Stourbridge DY8 . . . . .81 A3
Marlborough Gdns
Stourbridge DY8 . . . . .60 D2
Wolverhampton WV6 . . . . .24 E4
Marlborough Gr B25 . . . . . .68 C1
Marlborough Ind Est
WV2 .39 D7
Marlborough Jun Sch
B10 . . . . .67 E1
Marlborough Mews B80 .159 E4
Marlborough Rd
Birmingham,Castle Bromwich
B36 .69 D8
Birmingham,Small Heath
B10 .67 E1
Coventry CV2 . . . . .114 A3
Dudley DY3 . . . . .50 F6
Nuneaton CV11 . . . . .73 B3
Smethwick B66 . . . . .65 A3
Marlborough St
🔢 Kidderminster DY10 . . .116 E5
Walsall WS3 . . . . .14 B1
Marlborough Way B77 . . . .21 F2
Marlbrook Cl B92 . . . . .89 C4
Marlbrook Dr WV4 . . . . .39 B6
Marlbrook Gdns B61 . . . . . .121 B1
Marlbrook La B60 . . . . .121 D2
Marlcliff Gr B13 . . . . .105 A6
Marlcroft CV3 . . . . .134 E5
Marldon Rd B14 . . . . .104 E6
Marlene Croft B37 . . . . .70 C1
Marler Rd CV4 . . . . .131 F7
Marley Hts B27 . . . . .88 D4
Marley Rd DY6 . . . . .61 A4
Marlfield Farm Fst Sch
B98 .154 C6
Marlfield La
Redditch,Abbeydale B98 . . .154 B4
Redditch,Church Hill B98 . .154 B5
Marlgrove Ct B61 . . . . .137 B8
Marling Croft B92 . . . . .107 F7
Marlin B77 . . . . .35 D6
Marlissa Dr CV6 . . . . .95 E2
Marloes Wlk CV31 . . . . .162 C6
Marlow Cl
Coventry CV5 . . . . .112 B4
Dudley DY2 . . . . .62 E3
Marlowe Cl DY10 . . . . .117 B6
Marlowe Dr WV12 . . . . .27 C4
Marlow Rd
Birmingham B23 . . . . .56 D5
Tamworth B77 . . . . .21 D5
Marlow St
Rowley Regis B65 . . . . .63 B1
Walsall WS2 . . . . .28 E3

Marlpit La
Redditch B97 . . . . .153 C1
Sutton Coldfield B75 . . . . .32 D3
Marlpit Rise 🔢 B75 . . . . . . .32 E3
Marlpool Dr
Redditch B97 . . . . .153 C3
Walsall WS3 . . . . .15 A1
Marlpool Fst Sch DY11 . .116 C8
Marlpool La DY11 . . . . .116 C8
Marlpool Pl DY11 . . . . .116 C8
Marl Rd DY2 . . . . .62 B4
Marlston Wlk CV5 . . . . .112 B4
Marl Top B38 . . . . .103 F2
Marlwood Cl CV6 . . . . .95 F4
Marmion Dr B43 . . . . .43 F2
Marmion Gr DY1 . . . . .62 A8
Marmion Ho B70 . . . . .52 F6
Marmion St B79 . . . . .21 B6
Marmion St B79 . . . . .21 B5
Marmion Way B70 . . . . .52 F6
Marne Cl CV34 . . . . .161 A8
Marnel Dr WV3 . . . . .38 E7
Marner Cres CV6 . . . . .113 B5
Marner Rd
Bedworth CV12 . . . . .78 A3
Nuneaton CV10 . . . . .73 B1
Marnhull Cl CV2 . . . . .114 F4
Marquis Dr B62 . . . . .83 A7
Marrick B77 . . . . .22 C1
Marriners La CV5 . . . . .112 B5
Marriott Rd
Bedworth CV12 . . . . .77 D2
Coventry CV6 . . . . .113 A4
Dudley DY2 . . . . .62 C4
Smethwick B66 . . . . .64 D7
Marroway St B16 . . . . .65 F3
Marrowfat La B21 . . . . .65 F7
Mars Cl WV14 . . . . .40 A1
Marsdale Dr CV10 . . . . .72 E4
Marsden Cl B92 . . . . .88 E1
Marsden Rd B98 . . . . .153 E3
Marsett B77 . . . . .36 C8
Marshall Cl WS9 . . . . .30 B4
Marshall Gr B44 . . . . .55 F7
Marshall Ho 🔢 WS2 . . . . . .42 C8
Marshall Lake Rd B90 . . .106 C1
Marshall Rd
Birmingham B1 . . . . .164 B1
Smethwick B67 . . . . .64 D7
Tamworth B77 . . . . .21 E5
Marsham Cl CV34 . . . . .161 B8
Marsham Court Rd B91 .106 F7
Marsham Rd B14 . . . . .104 F3
Marshbrook Cl
Coventry CV2 . . . . .96 E3
Sutton Coldfield B24 . . . . .57 E4
Marshbrook Rd B24 . . . . . . .57 D4
Marsh Cl WS3 . . . . .56 F5
Marsh Cres DY8 . . . . .60 D3
Marsh End B38 . . . . .124 A8
Marshfield B98 . . . . .154 B7
Marshfield Dr CV4 . . . . .132 D2
Marshfield Gdns B24 . . . . . .56 F2
Marshfield Rd B90 . . . . .126 B5
Marsh Gr DY10 . . . . .116 E8
Marsh Hill B23 . . . . .56 C4
Marsh Hill Jun & Inf Sch
B23 . . . . .56 C4
Marsh Ho CV2 . . . . .115 A7
Marsh House Farm La
B92 .109 D3
Marsh La
Birmingham B23 . . . . .56 E5
Bradnock's Marsh B92 . . . . .109 D5
Curdworth B76 . . . . .59 D5
Hampton-in-A B92 . . . . .109 B6
Lichfield WS14 . . . . .9 C5
Marshland Way WS2 . . . . . .27 E1
Marsh Lane Par WV10 . . .11 C2
Marsh La
Solihull B91 . . . . .107 E3
Walsall WS2 . . . . .28 E2
Water Orton B46 . . . . .59 C3
West Bromwich B71 . . . . .53 D8
Wolverhampton WV10 . . . . . .11 B2
Marshmont Way B23 . . . . . .56 D8
Marsh St WS2 . . . . .28 E2
Marsh The WS10 . . . . .41 E3
Marsh Way B61 . . . . .120 F1
Marshwood Cl 🔢 WS11 . . . .2 A2
Marshwood Croft B62 . . . . .84 A3
Marsland Cl B17 . . . . .65 C1
Marsland Rd B92 . . . . .106 C8
Marston Ave WS10 . . . . .41 C6
Marston Cl
Royal Leamington Spa
CV32 . . . . .157 B2
Stourbridge DY8 . . . . .80 D3
Marston Croft B37 . . . . .89 F7
Marston Dr B37 . . . . .70 A5
Marston Gn B37 . . . . .90 A7
Marston Green Inf Sch
B37 . . . . .90 A7
Marston Green Jun Sch
B37 . . . . .90 A7
Marston Green Sta B37 . .89 F7
Marston Ind Est WV2 . . . . .39 C7

Marston La
Bedworth CV12 . . . . .78 D5
Nuneaton CV11 . . . . .78 E8
Wishaw B76. . . . . .48 E1
Marston Pk B78 . . . . .20 F4
Marston Rd
Birmingham B29 . . . . . . .102 F8
Cannock WS12. . . . . .1 F6
Dudley DY1 . . . . .61 E8
Sutton Coldfield B73 . . . .57 A7
Wolverhampton WV2. . . . .39 C7
Marston St WV13 . . . . . . .27 C2
Marten Cl CV35. . . . . . . .160 A7
Martham Dr WV6 . . . . . . .24 B2
Martin Cl
Birmingham B26 . . . . .88 D6
Bromsgrove B61. . . . . . . .136 E1
Coventry CV5. . . . . .111 E4
Dudley WV14. . . . . .51 D7
Martin Croft WS13 . . . . . . .3 A1
Martindale WS11 . . . . .2 A2
Martindale Rd CV7. . . . . . .96 C8
Martindale Trad Est WS11 . .2 A2
Martindale Wlk DY5 . . . . .81 B6
Martin Dr WV12 . . . . .27 C5
Martineau Pl B2 . . . . . . .164 C2
Martineau Twr B19. . . . . .66 D5
Martingale Cl
[9] Bromsgrove B60 . . . . .150 E6
Walsall WS5 . . . . .42 F4
Martin Hill St DY2 . . . . . .62 C8
Martinique Sq CV34. . . . .160 D6
Martin Rd
Bilston WV14 . . . . .40 F3
Tipton DY4. . . . . .52 A4
Walsall WS5 . . . . .43 C8
Martin Rise B37 . . . . .89 F8
Martins Rd CV12. . . . . . . .77 E1
Martin St WV4 . . . . .39 F5
Martlesham Sq B35. . . . . .58 A4
Martley Cl B98 . . . . .159 B7
Martley Croft
Birmingham B32 . . . . .84 E4
Solihull B91 . . . . .127 B8
Martley Dr DY9 . . . . .81 C4
Martley Rd
Oldbury B69. . . . . .63 D5
Walsall WS4 . . . . .15 C2
Marton Ave WS7 . . . . .7 A8
Marton Cl B7. . . . . .67 B6
Martyrs' Cl The CV3. . . . .133 D8
Marwood Cl CV11. . . . . . .78 E7
Marwood Croft B74. . . . . .31 A2
Mary Ann St
Birmingham B3 . . . . .164 B4
Wolverhampton WV1. . . . .163 D2
Mary Elliot Specl Sch
WS2. . . . . .28 C4
Mary Herbert St CV3. . . .133 D7
Maryland Ave B34 . . . . . .68 F5
Maryland Cl LE9 . . . . . . .71 F6
Maryland Dr B31 . . . . . . .103 B5
Maryland Rd DY5 . . . . . . .81 F7
Marylebone Cl DY8 . . . . . .81 A7
Mary Macarthur Dr B64. . .62 C1
Mary Rd
Birmingham,Handsworth
B21. . . . . .86 E5
Birmingham,Stechford B33. .68 D3
Oldbury B69. . . . . .63 C8
West Bromwich B70 . . . . .53 D1
Mary Rose Cl WS6 . . . . . . .4 D1
Mary Slessor St CV3 . . . .134 D7
Mary St
Birmingham,Balsall Heath
B12. . . . . .86 E5
Birmingham,Brookfields
B3. . . . . .164 A4
Cannock WS12. . . . . .2 B7
Marystow Cl CV5 . . . . . . .112 B8
Mary St WS3 . . . . .28 D3
Maryvale Ct
[2] Walsall WS1. . . . . . . .42 E8
Lichfield WS14. . . . . .9 D7
Maryvale RC Prim Sch
B44. . . . . .44 E1
Mary Vale Rd B30 . . . . . .103 F6
Marywell Cl B32 . . . . . . .102 B7
Masefield Ave
Dudley DY1 . . . . .51 C7
Warwick CV34 . . . . .160 C4
Masefield Cl
Bilston WV14 . . . . .40 F2
Lichfield WS14. . . . . .9 B6
Masefield Dr B79 . . . . . . .21 A6
Masefield Gdns [1] DY10. .117 B6
Masefield Gr WS11. . . . . . .1 E4
Masefield Mews WV10 . . .12 A1
Masefield Rd
Dudley DY3 . . . . .50 A4
Walsall WS3 . . . . .28 E7
Wolverhampton WV10. . . .11 E2
Masefield Rise B62 . . . . . .83 D3
Masefield Sq B31. . . . . . .103 C4
Masham Cl B33. . . . . .68 E3
Mashie Gdns B38 . . . . . . .103 D1
Maslen Pl B63. . . . . .83 B3
Maslin Dr WV14 . . . . .40 A1
Mason Ave CV32. . . . . . . .157 C3
Mason Ct B97 . . . . .158 D7
Mason Cotts B24 . . . . .57 B5
Mason Cres WV4 . . . . .38 E5
Mason Ct LE10. . . . . .75 B8
Mason Gr CV8 . . . . .148 B5
Mason La B94. . . . . .125 F1

Masonleys Rd B31 . . . . . .102 D3
Mason Rd
Birmingham B24 . . . . .57 A4
Coventry CV6. . . . . .95 F1
Kidderminster DY11 . . . . .116 C6
Redditch B97 . . . . .158 D8
Walsall WS2 . . . . .28 B5
Masons Cl B63 . . . . .82 C6
Mason St
Dudley WV14. . . . . .51 B7
West Bromwich B70 . . . . .53 B4
Wolverhampton WV2. . . . .39 C7
Masons View B24 . . . . . . .57 A2
Mason's Way B92. . . . . . . .88 E2
Masons Yd DY11. . . . . . . .116 D6
Massbrook Gr WV10 . . . . .25 F6
Massbrook Rd WV10 . . . . .25 F6
Masser Rd CV6 . . . . .95 D4
Masshouse La
Birmingham,Digbeth B5. . .164 D3
Birmingham,King's Norton
B38. . . . . .103 F1
Masters La B62. . . . . .63 E1
Masters Rd CV31 . . . . . . .162 A4
Matchborough Ctr B98. . . .154 E1
Matchborough Fst Sch
B98. . . . . .154 E1
Matchborough Way B98. . .154 E1
Matchlock Cl B74. . . . . . . .44 E7
Matfen Ave B13. . . . . .45 F2
Mathe Croft CV31. . . . . . .162 C5
Math Mdw B32 . . . . .84 F5
Matlock Cl
Dudley DY2 . . . . .62 D3
Walsall WS3 . . . . .14 C3
Matlock Dr WS11. . . . . . . .2 A4
Matlock Rd
Birmingham B11. . . . . .87 F3
Coventry CV1 . . . . .113 D6
Walsall WS3 . . . . .14 C3
Matlock Villas [2] B12. . . .87 B5
Matterson Rd CV6 . . . . . .113 A5
Matthew Boulton Coll
Matthew Boulton Coll Prim
Sch B21. . . . . .65 C7
Matthew La (Road 3)
DY10. . . . . .116 F1
Matthews Cl B65. . . . . . . .63 B1
Matthews Wlk WS13 . . . . .3 A2
Mattox Rd WV11. . . . . . . .26 D6
Matty Rd B68. . . . . .64 C4
Maud Rd
Water Orton B46. . . . . . . .59 D3
West Bromwich B70 . . . . .53 C1
Maudslay Rd CV5 . . . . . . .112 E2
Maughan St
Brierley Hill DY5 . . . . .82 A8
Dudley DY1 . . . . .51 B1
Maund Cl B60. . . . . .150 E7
Maureen Cl CV4 . . . . .111 C1
Maurice Gr WV10 . . . . . . .26 A6
Maurice Mead Ct [12]
CV31. . . . . .162 A6
Maurice Rd
Birmingham B14 . . . . .104 E5
Smethwick B67 . . . . .64 E2
Mavis Gdns B68 . . . . .84 B8
Mavis Rd
Birmingham B31 . . . . . . .102 E1
Cannock WS12. . . . . .2 B7
Mavor Dr CV12 . . . . .77 D1
Mawgan Dr WS14. . . . . . . .9 D6
Mawnan Cl CV7. . . . . .96 B8
Maw St WS1. . . . . .42 F6
Maxholm Rd B74 . . . . .44 E8
Max Rd
Birmingham B32 . . . . .84 D5
Coventry CV6. . . . . .112 F5
Maxstoke Cl
Birmingham B32 . . . . .102 A7
Meriden CV7 . . . . .92 B1
Redditch B98. . . . . .154 D1
Sutton Coldfield B73 . . . . .45 E2
Tamworth B77 . . . . .35 C4
Walsall WS3 . . . . .14 A3
Maxstoke Croft B90. . . . . .126 C8
Maxstoke Gdns CV31. . . . .161 F6
Maxstoke La
Meriden CV7 . . . . .92 B2
White Stitch CV7 . . . . .92 B3
Maxstoke Rd B73 . . . . .45 E1
Maxstoke St B9. . . . . .67 B2
Maxted Rd B23 . . . . .56 C7
Maxtock Ave WS13. . . . . . .9 A6
Maxwell Ave B20 . . . . .54 F1
Maxwell Cl WS14 . . . . .9 C7
Maxwell Ct B33. . . . . .68 F3
Maxwell Rd WV2. . . . . . . .163 C1
Mayall Dr B75. . . . . .32 D4
Mayama Rd B78 . . . . .34 F8
May Ave [3] B12. . . . . . . .87 A5
Maybank B9. . . . . .67 F3
Maybank Cl WS14. . . . . . . .9 E8
Maybank Pl B44 . . . . .55 E6
Maybank Rd DY2 . . . . . . .62 C3
Mayberry Cl B14. . . . . . . .105 B2
Maybridge Dr B91. . . . . . .127 B8
Maybrook Ind Est WS8. . . .15 F5
Maybrook Rd
Brownhills WS8 . . . . .15 F5
Sutton Coldfield B76 . . . . .58 A5
Maybush Gdns WV10. . . . .11 C1
Maycock Rd CV6. . . . . . . .113 D7
Maycroft Cl WS12 . . . . .1 F7
Maydene Croft B12. . . . . . .86 F6
Mayfair B37 . . . . .69 F5

Mayfair Cl
Birmingham B44. . . . . .56 B7
Dudley DY1 . . . . .51 A2
Mayfair Dr
Fazeley B78. . . . . .35 A7
Kingswinford DY6 . . . . . . .60 C7
Mayfair Gdns
Tipton DY4. . . . . .52 A4
Wolverhampton WV3. . . . .24 D2
Mayfair DY9 . . . . .81 D2
May Farm Cl B47 . . . . . . .125 A6
Mayfield Ave B29 . . . . . . .86 B2
Mayfield Cl
[9] Royal Leamington Spa
CV31. . . . . .162 C6
Bedworth CV12 . . . . .78 B3
Fairfield B61 . . . . .120 F1
Kidderminster DY11 . . . . .116 A8
Solihull B91 . . . . .107 C1
Mayfield Cres B65. . . . . . .63 A3
Mayfield Ct
Birmingham B13. . . . . .87 A2
Kidderminster DY11 . . . . .116 C7
Mayfield Dr CV8 . . . . .148 C4
Mayfield Prep Sch WS1. . . .43 A8
Mayfield Rd
Birmingham,Acock's Green
B11. . . . . .88 A3
Birmingham,Lozells B19 . . .66 C8
Birmingham,Moseley B13 . .87 A3
Birmingham,Stirchley B30. .104 A6
Coventry CV5 . . . . .113 A1
Dudley DY1 . . . . .51 C4
Halesowen B62 . . . . .63 F1
Halesowen,Hasbury B63 . . .82 E2
Nuneaton CV11 . . . . .73 E2
Sutton Coldfield,Boldmere
B73. . . . . .46 A2
Sutton Coldfield,Streetly
B74. . . . . .44 F8
Wolverhampton WV1. . . . .26 B8
Mayfield Sch B19. . . . . . . .66 C8
Mayfields Dr WS8. . . . . . . .6 B2
Mayfields B98 . . . . .153 E2
Mayfield B77 . . . . .36 C8
Mayfield The WV1. . . . . . . .26 B1
Mayflower Cl B19. . . . . . . .66 D6
Mayflower Dr
Brierley Hill DY5 . . . . .61 A7
Coventry CV2 . . . . .114 E2
Mayford Gr B13. . . . . . . .105 B6
Maygrove Rd DY6 . . . . . . .60 C7
Mayhurst Cl
Hollywood B47. . . . . .125 C6
Tipton DY4. . . . . .52 A8
Mayhurst Rd B47 . . . . . . .125 B6
May La
Birmingham B14 . . . . .104 F5
Hollywood B47. . . . . .125 A7
Mayland Dr B74. . . . . .45 A5
Mayland Rd B16. . . . . .65 C2
Maynard Ave
Bedworth CV12 . . . . .95 D8
Stourbridge DY8 . . . . .80 D3
Warwick CV34 . . . . .161 A7
Mayo Dr CV8 . . . . .148 A4
Mayor's Croft CV4 . . . . . .132 B7
Mayou Cl WS3. . . . . .15 A4
Maypole Cl B64. . . . . .82 B8
Maypole Ct WV5 . . . . .49 A6
Maypole Dr B9. . . . . .80 E5
Maypole Fields B63. . . . . .82 A7
Maypole Gr B14 . . . . .105 B2
Maypole Hill B63 . . . . .82 A7
Maypole La B14 . . . . .105 B2
Maypole Rd B68 . . . . .64 B1
Maypole St WV5 . . . . .49 A6
May St
Coventry CV6. . . . . .113 E8
Walsall WS3 . . . . .28 D6
Mayswood Dr WV6. . . . . . .23 F1
Mayswood Rd B92. . . . . . .89 C2
Maythorn Ave B76. . . . . . .58 A6
Maythorn Gdns
Codsall WV8 . . . . .10 A4
Wolverhampton WV6. . . . .24 C3
Maytree Cl B37 . . . . .70 A2
May Tree Gr B20 . . . . .54 F3
May Trees B47 . . . . .124 F6
Maywell Dr B92 . . . . .107 F8
Maywood Cl DY6 . . . . .60 B6
Meaburn Cl B29 . . . . .103 A7
Mead Cl WS9 . . . . .30 B6
Mead Cres B9 . . . . .68 B3
Meadfoot Ave B14 . . . . . .104 F3
Meadfoot Dr DY6. . . . . . . .60 B7
Meadfoot Rd CV3 . . . . . . .134 E6
Meadow Ave B71. . . . . . . .53 E8
Meadowbank Dr B46. . . . . .59 D1
Meadowbank Grange WS6 . .4 E4
Meadow Bank B78. . . . . . .21 B1
Meadowbrook Gdns WV6. .10 B4
Meadow Brook Rd B31. . . .102 F5
Meadowbrook Rd
Halesowen B63 . . . . .82 E3
Lichfield WS13 . . . . .3 B3
Meadow Cl
Ansty CV7 . . . . .97 D3
Birmingham B17 . . . . .85 D6
Hockley Heath B94 . . . . . .143 C6
Royal Leamington Spa
CV31. . . . . .162 D8
Solihull B90 . . . . .126 D8
Sutton Coldfield B74 . . . . .30 F2
Sutton Coldfield B76 . . . . .46 F4
Walsall WS4 . . . . .29 C8

Meadow Croft WS12 . . . . . . .1 C4
Meadowcroft Cl CV4 . . . . .131 F8
Meadow Croft
Perton WV6 . . . . .23 D3
West Hagley DY9 . . . . .98 F4
Wythall B47 . . . . .125 A3
Meadow Ct
Birmingham B17 . . . . .65 B1
Nuneaton CV11 . . . . .73 B4
Meadow Dr
Hampton-in-A B92 . . . . . .109 B7
Hinckley LE10 . . . . .76 A7
Meadowfield Rd B45. . . . .122 A6
Meadowfields Cl DY8 . . . . .60 E2
Meadow Grange Dr WV12 . .27 B7
Meadow Green Prim Sch
B47. . . . . .125 A3
Meadow Gr
Great Wyrley WS6 . . . . .5 A2
Solihull B92 . . . . .88 D1
Meadow Hill Cl DY11 . . . . .116 A8
Meadowhill Cres B98. . . . .153 F5
Meadow Hill Dr [6] WS11. . .2 A3
Meadowhill Dr DY8 . . . . . .60 E2
Meadow Hill Rd B38 . . . . .103 C2
Meadowhill Rd B98. . . . . .153 F5
Meadow Ho [5] CV1. . . . . .113 B3
Meadow La
Alvechurch B48 . . . . .139 B6
Coven Heath WV10 . . . . . .11 C6
Kingswood B94 . . . . .144 D3
Meadowlands Dr WS4. . . . .15 D1
Meadow Lark Cl WS12 . . . .2 B4
Meadow La
Wednesfield WV12 . . . . . . .27 A5
Wolverhampton WV4. . . . .40 B2
Wombourne WV5. . . . . . . .49 B8
Meadow Mills Ind Est
DY10. . . . . .116 E5
Meadowpark Rd DY8. . . . . .80 D8
Meadow Pk B79 . . . . .20 F5
Meadow Pleck La B90 . . . .126 A6
Meadow Rd
Aldridge WS9 . . . . .30 A4
Birmingham B17 . . . . .65 B1
Birmingham,Harborne B17 . .65 B1
Catshill B61. . . . . .136 F8
Coventry CV6. . . . . .95 B4
Dudley DY1 . . . . .51 B3
Halesowen B62 . . . . .83 C8
Hartshill CV10 . . . . .72 A8
Oldbury B68. . . . . .64 A4
Smethwick B67 . . . . .65 A4
Tamworth B78 . . . . .20 D3
Warwick CV34 . . . . .161 A7
Wolverhampton WV3. . . . .38 D8
Wythall B47 . . . . .125 A3
Meadow Rise
Balsall Common CV7 . . . . .130 C7
Birmingham B30 . . . . .103 E7
Meadows Fst Sch B61 . . . .137 A3
Meadows Gr WV8 . . . . .10 A4
Meadows Rd B43. . . . . . . .43 E1
Meadowside CV11 . . . . . . .73 B2
Meadowside Rd B74. . . . . .31 F3
Meadows Prim Sch The
B31. . . . . .102 E1
Meadows The
Coventry CV4. . . . . .111 E3
Oldbury B69. . . . . .2 F2
Smethwick B67 . . . . .99 B7
Meadow St
Nuneaton CV11 . . . . .73 B5
Tamworth B77 . . . . .21 C3
Walsall WS1 . . . . .42 D8
Meadowsweet Ave B38. . .123 F8
Meadowsweet Pl DY10. . . .116 D8
Meadowsweet Way
Cannock WS12. . . . . .1 C6
Kingswinford DY6 . . . . . . .61 A6
Meadow Vale WV8 . . . . . . .10 B2
Meadowvale Rd B60 . . . . .137 C6
Meadow View
Birmingham B13 . . . . .105 C8
Burntwood WS7 . . . . .7 D6
Meadow View Cvn Pk
WV10. . . . . .11 C6
Meadow View JMI Sch
B43. . . . . .54 C8
Meadow View B10 . . . . . . .39 C1
Meadow View Terr WV6 . . .24 E4
Meadow Way
Cannock WS12. . . . . .2 C1
Stourbridge DY8 . . . . .60 C2
Meadow Wlk
Birmingham B14 . . . . .104 E1
Cradley Heath B64 . . . . . . .82 D8
Mead Rise B15 . . . . .85 F6
Mead The DY3 . . . . .50 B8
Meadthorpe Rd B44 . . . . . .55 D8
Meadvale Rd B45 . . . . . . .122 B6
Meadway B33 . . . . .69 B2
Meadway Cl WS12 . . . . .2 C3
Meadway N CV2 . . . . .114 B6
Meadway St WS7 . . . . .7 A8
Meadway The
Hinckley LE10 . . . . .75 F7
Redditch B97 . . . . .153 C1

Meadway The continued
Wolverhampton WV6. . . . .24 A5
Meadwood Ind Est WV14 . .40 E5
Meakins Cl CV34 . . . . .160 B4
Mears Cl B23. . . . . .56 D8
Mears Coppice DY5. . . . . . .81 E6
Mears Dr B33 . . . . .68 D4
Mearse Cl B18. . . . . .66 A5
Mearse La
Barnt Green B45 . . . . .122 A1
Madeley Heath DY9. . . . . .120 B6
Mease Ave WS7. . . . . .7 D6
Mease Croft [2] B9 . . . . . .67 B2
Measham Gr B26 . . . . .88 E5
Measham Way WV11. . . . . .26 E7
Meaton Gr B32 . . . . .102 B8
Medcroft Ave B20 . . . . . . .54 E4
Medici Rd B60. . . . . .137 C2
Medina Cl WV10 . . . . .11 F4
Medina Rd
Birmingham B11 . . . . .87 E4
Coventry CV6. . . . . .95 E1
Medina B77 . . . . .21 E1
Medina Way DY6. . . . . .60 C6
Medland Ave CV3. . . . . . . .132 F5
Medley Gdns DY4 . . . . .52 E4
Medley Gr CV31 . . . . .161 F3
Medley Rd B11 . . . . .87 D5
Medlicott Rd B11. . . . . . . .87 C6
Medway Cl DY5. . . . . .61 A6
Medway Croft B36 . . . . . . .69 F7
Medway Ct B73. . . . . .46 B5
Medway Gr B38 . . . . .123 E8
Medway Rd WS8. . . . . .6 C2
Medway B77 . . . . .21 E1
Medway Twr B7. . . . . .67 B5
Medway Wlk WS8. . . . . . . .6 C2
Medwin Gr B23. . . . . .56 D7
Meerash La WS7 . . . . .7 C3
Meer End B38 . . . . .123 D7
Meer End Rd CV8. . . . . . .130 D1
Meerhill Ave B90 . . . . . . .127 A6
Meeting Ho The [3] WS10. .41 E3
Meeting House La
Balsall Common CV7 . . . . .130 C6
Birmingham B13 . . . . .103 A4
Meeting Lane Ind Est DY5 .61 B1
Meeting St
Dudley DY2 . . . . .62 C5
Tipton DY4. . . . . .52 D5
Wednesbury WS10 . . . . . .41 E3
Meg La WS7. . . . . .7 C8
Meir Rd B98 . . . . .159 C8
Melbourne Ave
Birmingham,Newtown
B19. . . . . .66 D5
Birmingham,Selly Oak B66 . .65 B7
Bromsgrove B61. . . . . . . .136 E4
Melbourne Cl
Bromsgrove B61. . . . . . . .136 E3
Kingswinford DY6 . . . . . . .60 E4
Nuneaton CV11 . . . . .78 E8
West Bromwich B70 . . . . .53 A7
Melbourne Cres WS12 . . . . .2 B7
Melbourne Ct [3] CV12 . . . .77 F2
Melbourne Gdns WS5. . . . .43 B6
Melbourne Rd
Bromsgrove B61. . . . . . . .136 E3
Cannock WS12. . . . . .2 F2
Coventry CV5. . . . . .113 A2
Halesowen B63 . . . . .82 E5
Smethwick B66 . . . . .65 B7
Melbourne St WV2 . . . . . .163 C2
Melbury Cl WV3 . . . . .25 A1
Melbury Gr B14. . . . . .104 E5
Melbury Way [1] WS11. . . .1 F2
Melchester Wlk [2] WS11. .1 F2
Melchett Rd B30. . . . . . . .104 A4
Melcote Gr B44. . . . . .55 E8
Meldon Dr WV14 . . . . .41 A2
Meldrum Rd CV10 . . . . . . .72 D4
Melen St B97. . . . . .153 D4
Melford Cl DY3 . . . . .39 C2
Melford Hall Rd B91 . . . . .106 F7
Melford B79 . . . . .20 E6
Melfort Cl
Coventry CV3. . . . . .114 F2
Nuneaton CV10 . . . . .72 C5
Melfort Gr B14. . . . . .105 A3
Meksham Sq B35. . . . . . . .58 A3
Mellis Gr B23 . . . . .56 A5
Mellish Dr WS4 . . . . .29 A3
Mellish Rd WS4 . . . . .29 B3
Mellor Dr B74. . . . . .31 E3
Mellors Cl B17 . . . . .85 B3
Mellowdew Rd
Coventry CV2 . . . . .114 C2
Stourbridge DY8 . . . . .60 C3
Mellowship Rd CV5 . . . . . .111 D5
Mell Sq B91 . . . . .107 C4
Mellwaters B77. . . . . .36 C8
Melmerby B77. . . . . .36 C8
Melplash Ave B91. . . . . . .107 A4
Melrose Ave
Bedworth CV12 . . . . .95 D8
Birmingham,Sparkbrook
B12. . . . . .87 A6
Birmingham,Sparkhill B11. . .87 C6
Stourbridge DY8 . . . . .81 A2
Sutton Coldfield B73 . . . . .45 E2
West Bromwich B71 . . . . .42 D1
Melrose Cl
Birmingham B38 . . . . .103 F1
Hinckley LE10 . . . . .75 B8
Melrose Ct WS4 . . . . .29 A3

Melrose Dr
  Cannock WS12 . . . . . . 1 F7
  Perton WV6 . . . . 23 E4
Melrose Gr B19 . . . . . . 66 B7
Melrose Pl B66 . . . . . . 64 D8
Melstock Cl DY4 . . . . . 51 D5
Melstock Rd B14 . . . . . 104 D7
Melton Ave B92 . . . . . . 89 B4
Melton Dr B15 . . . . 86 B7
Melton Rd
  Birmingham B14 . . . . . 104 F8
  Royal Leamington Spa
    CV32 . . . . 157 B4
Melverley Gr B44 . . . . . 55 F7
Melverton Ave WV10 . . . . 25 E8
Melville Cl CV7 . . . . . . 96 A8
Melville Hall 1 B16 . . . 65 D1
Melville Rd
  Birmingham B16 . . . . . 65 D1
  Coventry CV1 . . . . . . 113 A3
Melvina Rd B7 . . . . 67 B5
Melzer Ho DY10 . . . . . . 116 E7
Membury Rd B8 . . . . 67 D6
Memorial Cl WV13 . . . . . 27 A2
Memory La
  Darlaston WS10 . . . . . 41 D8
  Wolverhampton WV11 . . . 26 B5
Menai Cl WV12 . . . . 27 C6
Menai Wlk B37 . . . . 70 B4
Mendip Ave B8 . . . . 67 E5
Mendip Cl
  Bromsgrove B61 . . . . . 137 A5
  Dudley DY3 . . . . 50 D3
  Wolverhampton WV2 . . . . 39 F7
Mendip Dr CV10 . . . . . . 72 B3
Mendip Ho B98 . . . . . . 154 D6
Mendip Rd
  Birmingham B8 . . . . . . 67 E5
  Halesowen B63 . . . . . . 82 D1
  Stourbridge DY8 . . . . . 81 B6
Mendip Way B77 . . . . . . 22 C1
Menin Cres B13 . . . . . . 105 B7
Menin Rd
  Birmingham B13 . . . . . 105 B8
  Tipton DY4 . . . . 51 D5
Mentone Ct B20 . . . . . . 54 E3
Menzies High Sch B71 . . 53 C8
Meon Gr
  Birmingham B33 . . . . . 89 B8
  Perton WV6 . . . . 23 F4
Meon Rise DY9 . . . . 81 C3
Meon Way WV11 . . . . . . 26 F7
Meranti Cl WV12 . . . . . 27 C8
Mercer Ave
  Coventry CV2 . . . . . . 114 A5
  Water Orton B46 . . . . . 59 A3
Mercer Gr WV11 . . . . . . 26 D7
Mercers Mdw CV7 . . . . . 95 A6
Merchants Ct 5 CV32 . . 157 A1
Merchants Pk WS9 . . . . . 30 A7
Merchants Way WS9 . . . . 30 A7
Mercia Ave CV8 . . . . . . 147 F4
Mercia Bsns Village CV4 131 F6
Mercia Cl
  Bromsgrove B60 . . . . . 150 F7
  Tamworth B79 . . . . . . 20 E7
Mercia Dr
  Birmingham B14 . . . . . 104 D6
  Perton WV6 . . . . 23 E5
Mercia Ho CV1 . . . . . . 165 B3
Mercian Cl WS14 . . . . . . 9 C7
Mercian Pk B77 . . . . . . 22 A3
Mercian Way B77 . . . . . 22 B3
Mercia Way CV34 . . . . . 161 B7
Mercot Cl B98 . . . . . . 159 A6
Mercury Pk B77 . . . . . . 22 B3
Mercury Rd WS11 . . . . . . 2 A5
Mere Ave B35 . . . . 58 B3
Mere Cl WV12 . . . . 27 A5
Merecote Rd B92 . . . . . 106 D7
Mere Croft WS11 . . . . . . 5 F4
Meredith Gn DY11 . . . . . 116 A1
Meredith Pool Cl B18 . . . 65 F6
Meredith Rd
  Coventry CV2 . . . . . . 114 D2
  Dudley DY3 . . . . 50 A5
  Wolverhampton WV11 . . . 26 C8
Meredith St B64 . . . . . . 62 D1
Mere Dr B75 . . . . 32 B2
Mere Green Ct B75 . . . . . 32 C2
Mere Green Comb Sch
  B75 . . . . 32 B2
Mere Green Rd B75 . . . . . 32 C2
Mere Oak Rd WV6 . . . . . 23 E5
Mere Pool Rd B75 . . . . . 32 E2
Mere Rd
  Birmingham B23 . . . . . 56 D3
  Stourbridge DY8 . . . . . 80 D3
Mereside Way B92 . . . . . 106 E8
Meres Rd B63 . . . . 82 C5
Mere St B23 . . . . 56 B4
Merevale Ave
  Hinckley LE10 . . . . . . 75 C7
  Nuneaton CV11 . . . . . . 73 A4
Merevale Cl
  Hinckley LE10 . . . . . . 75 C7
  Redditch B98 . . . . . . 159 D8
Merevale Ct CV11 . . . . . 73 A4
Merevale Rd B92 . . . . . . 89 B2
Mere View WS4 . . . . 29 C8
Mereways B90 . . . . 126 A5
Merganser B77 . . . . 36 A4
Meriden Ave DY8 . . . . . . 80 D6
Meriden Bsns Pk CV5 . . . 111 B8
Meriden CE Prim Sch
  CV7 . . . . 92 C1

Meriden Cl
  Birmingham B25 . . . . . 88 B7
  Cannock WS11 . . . . 4 B8
  Stourbridge DY8 . . . . . 80 D6
Meriden Cross* CV7 . . . . 92 B1
Meriden Ct 3 WV4 . . . . . 39 F4
Meriden Dr B37 . . . . . . 70 A6
Meriden Hill CV7 . . . . . 110 E8
Meriden Park Homes
  CV7 . . . . 110 C8
Meriden Rd
  Berkswell CV7 . . . . . . 110 C4
  Chapel Green CV7 . . . . 93 B7
  Hampton-in-A B92 . . . . 109 C7
  Wolverhampton WV10 . . . 25 A8
Meriden Rise B92 . . . . . 89 D3
Meriden St
  Birmingham B5 . . . . . . 164 D2
  Coventry CV1 . . . . . . 113 B3
Meridian Pl B60 . . . . . 137 A1
Merino Ave B31 . . . . . . 123 A8
Merlin Ave CV10 . . . . . . 72 B6
Merlin Cl
  Birmingham B35 . . . . . 58 A3
  Cannock WS11 . . . . 1 C2
  Dudley DY1 . . . . 61 F8
  Tamworth B77 . . . . . . 36 A6
Merlin Dr DY10 . . . . . . 117 B3
Merlin Gr B26 . . . . 89 B5
Merrick Cl B63 . . . . . . 82 D2
Merrick Ct 1 LE10 . . . . 75 F5
Merrick Rd WV11 . . . . . . 27 A6
Merridale Ave WV3 . . . . . 24 F2
Merridale Cres WV3 . . . . 25 A2
Merridale Ct WV3 . . . . . 24 F1
Merridale Gdns WV3 . . . . 25 A1
Merridale Gr WV3 . . . . . 24 E1
Merridale Jun & Inf Sch
  WV3 . . . . 25 A1
Merridale La WV3 . . . . . 25 A1
Merridale Rd WV3 . . . . . 25 A1
Merridale St WV3 . . . . . 39 A8
Merridale St W WV3 . . . 163 A2
Merridale Terr WV3 . . . . 25 A1
Merrifield Gdns LE10 . . . 75 E5
Merrill Cl WS6 . . . . 4 E2
Merrill Gdns B60 . . . . . 121 D2
Merrills Hall Island WV11 26 D4
Merrills Hall La WV11 . . . 26 D4
Merrington Cl 5 B91 . . . 127 C8
Merrion's Cl B43 . . . . . 43 E4
Merrishaw Rd B31 . . . . . 122 E8
Merritts Brook Cl B29 . . 103 A5
Merritt's Brook La B31 . . 102 E5
Merritts Hill B31 . . . . . 102 E6
Merrivale Rd
  Coventry CV5 . . . . . . 112 E3
  Halesowen B62 . . . . . . 83 F8
  Smethwick B66 . . . . . . 65 A2
Merryfield Cl B92 . . . . . 107 D7
Merryfield Gr B17 . . . . . 85 C4
Merryfield Rd DY1 . . . . . 50 E1
Merryfields Way CV2 . . . 96 F1
Merry Hill DY5 . . . . 61 F2
Merry Hill Ctr DY5 . . . . 61 F3
Merryhill Dr B18 . . . . . 65 F6
Merrylees Ent Pk WV10 . . 25 F5
Merry Hurst Pl LE10 . . . . 74 E7
Merse Rd B98 . . . . 154 E6
Mersey Gr B38 . . . . 123 E8
Mersey Rd
  Bulkington CV12 . . . . . 79 A3
  Walsall WS3 . . . . 14 E1
Merstal Dr B92 . . . . . . 107 F7
Merstone Cl WV14 . . . . . 40 C6
Merstone Sch B37 . . . . . 70 A1
Merstowe Cl B27 . . . . . . 88 B3
Merton Cl
  Kidderminster DY10 . . . 117 B7
  Oldbury B68 . . . . 64 B2
Merton Ct WS7 . . . . 7 D8
Merton Ho B37 . . . . 69 F2
Merton Rd B13 . . . . 87 B3
Mervyn Pl WV14 . . . . . . 41 A3
Mervyn Rd
  Bilston WV14 . . . . . . 41 A3
  Birmingham B21 . . . . . 54 E1
Meryhurst Rd WS10 . . . . 42 B5
Merynton Ave CV4 . . . . . 132 E5
Meschines St CV3 . . . . . 133 D6
Mesnes Ave WS14 . . . . . . 9 C7
Messenger La B70,B71 . . 53 D3
Messenger Rd B66 . . . . . 65 B6
Mesty Croft Prim Sch
  WS10 . . . . 42 B3
Metalloys Ind Est B76 . . 58 B5
Metcalf Cl WS12 . . . . . . 7 C8
Metcalfe Cl WS12 . . . . . 7 C8
Metchley Abbey 11 B17 . . 85 D5
Metchley Cl B17 . . . . . . 85 D4
Metchley Dr B17 . . . . . . 85 D5
Metchley Ho 8 B17 . . . . 85 D5
Metchley La B17 . . . . . . 85 D5
Metchley Park Rd B15 . . . 85 E4
Metfield Cl B79 . . . . . . 21 C8
Metfield Croft
  Birmingham B17 . . . . . 85 D4
  Kingswinford DY6 . . . . . 60 F6
Metlin Gr B33 . . . . 69 E3
Metric Wlk 2 B67 . . . . . 65 A5
Metro Way B66 . . . . 65 E7
Mews Rd CV32 . . . . 161 D8
Mews The
  Bedworth CV12 . . . . . . 78 B2
  Birmingham B27 . . . . . 88 B3
  Cannock WS11 . . . . 1 D1

Mews The continued
  Kenilworth CV8 . . . . . 147 E3
  Rowley Regis B65 . . . . . 63 B2
Mey Coppice B36 . . . . . 69 F7
Meynell Ho 5 B20 . . . . . 54 F3
Meyrick Rd B70 . . . . . . 53 A6
Meyrick Wlk B16 . . . . . . 65 F1
Miall Park Rd B91 . . . . . 106 E5
Miall Rd B28 . . . . 106 A8
Mica Cl B77 . . . . 22 B2
Michael Banning Pl CV7 . 130 B7
Michael Blanning Gdns
  B93 . . . . 127 C3
Michael Blanning Ho 10
  B13 . . . . 87 B2
Michael Ct B15 . . . . . . 86 C6
Michael Drayton Jun Sch
  CV10 . . . . 72 B8
Michael Dr B15 . . . . . . 86 C6
Michaelmas Rd CV3 . . . . 165 B1
Michael Rd
  Darlaston WS10 . . . . . 41 B7
  Smethwick B67 . . . . . . 64 E6
Michaelwood Cl B97 . . . 152 F2
Michel Ho CV1 . . . . . . 165 C4
Michell Cl CV3 . . . . . . 134 B8
Michelle Cl B13 . . . . . 105 A5
Michigan Cl WS11 . . . . . 2 B2
Micklehill Dr B90 . . . . 126 B8
Mickle Mdw B46 . . . . . . 59 B3
Mickleover Rd B8 . . . . . 68 C5
Mickleton Ave B33 . . . . 89 C8
Mickleton Cl B98 . . . . . 158 E7
Mickleton Rd
  Coventry CV5 . . . . . . 133 A8
  Solihull B92 . . . . . . 106 D8
Mickley Ave WV10 . . . . . 25 E5
Midacre WV13 . . . . 27 A1
Middelburg Cl CV11 . . . . 74 A1
Middle Acre Rd B32 . . . . 84 E2
Middle Ave WV13 . . . . . . 40 E8
Middle Bickenhill La B92 91 A4
Middleborough Rd CV1 . . 165 A4
Middlecotes CV4 . . . . . . 112 B1
Middle Cres WS3 . . . . . . 29 A7
Middle Cross WV1 . . . . . 163 D3
Middle Dr B45 . . . . 122 D4
Middle Entry B79 . . . . . 21 B4
Middlefield Ave
  Dorridge B93 . . . . . . 128 B4
  Halesowen B62 . . . . . . 63 F1
Middlefield Cl
  Halesowen B62 . . . . . . 63 F1
  Hinckley LE10 . . . . . . 71 D2
Middlefield Ct LE10 . . . . 71 D2
Middlefield Dr CV3 . . . . 115 B1
Middlefield Gdns B62 . . . 83 F8
Middlefield Ho B14 . . . . 104 F3
Middlefield La
  Hinckley LE10 . . . . . . 71 D3
  West Hagley DY9 . . . . . 99 B6
Middlefield Pl LE10 . . . . 71 D3
Middle Field Rd B31 . . . 103 D2
Middlefield Rd
  Bromsgrove B60 . . . . . 151 B7
  Oldbury B69 . . . . 63 A8
Middle Gdns WV13 . . . . . 27 B2
Middle House Dr B60 . . . 121 D1
Middlehouse La B97 . . . . 153 E6
Middle La
  Wolverhampton WV9 . . . 11 A5
  Wythall B38 . . . . 124 D5
Middle Leaford B34 . . . . 69 A5
Middle Leasowe B32 . . . . 84 D4
Middlemarch Bsns Pk
  CV3 . . . . 134 C2
Middlemarch Rd
  Coventry CV6 . . . . . . 113 C7
  Nuneaton CV10 . . . . . . 73 C1
Middlemarch Sch CV10 . . 73 B1
Middlepark Dr B31 . . . . 103 B6
Middlepark Rd DY1 . . . . . 61 F8
Middle Park Rd B29 . . . . 103 C8
Middle Piece Dr B97 . . . 153 B1
Middle Rd
  Fairfield B61 . . . . . . 120 F4
  Upper Bentley B60 . . . . 152 A2
Middle Ride CV3 . . . . . . 134 E5
Middlesmoor B77 . . . . . . 36 C8
Middleton Cl
  Hammerwich WS7 . . . . . 7 D4
  Walsall WS5 . . . . 43 C4
Middleton Gdns B30 . . . 103 D4
Middleton Grange B31 . . 103 C4
Middleton Hall
  Birmingham B30 . . . . . 103 E4
  Middleton B78 . . . . . . 34 E1
Middleton Hall Rd B30 . . 103 E4
Middleton La B78 . . . . . 47 F6
Middleton Mews B98 . . . 154 F2

Middleton Rd
  Birmingham B14 . . . . . 104 F7
  Bromsgrove B61 . . . . . 136 F4
  Brownhills WS8 . . . . . . 7 A1
  Solihull B90 . . . . . . 106 A2
  Sutton Coldfield B74 . . . 31 A1
Middleton Trad Est WV13 26 E4
Middletown La B96,B80 . 159 D1
Middletree Rd B63 . . . . . 82 C7
Middle Vauxhall 4 WV1 . 25 A2
Middleway Ave DY8 . . . . 60 C3
Middleway Gn WV14 . . . . 40 C8
Middleway Rd WV14 . . . . 40 C7
Middleway View B18 . . . . 66 A3
Midford Gr B15 . . . . . . 86 C8
Midgley Dr B74 . . . . . . 32 A2
Midhill Dr B65 . . . . . . 63 C6
Midhurst Dr WS12 . . . . . 2 C7
Midhurst Gr WV6 . . . . . . 24 C5
Midhurst Rd B30 . . . . . . 104 B3
Midland Air Mus* CV8 . . 134 B3
Midland Ct B21 . . . . . . 66 A7
Midland Croft B33 . . . . . 69 D3
Midland Dr B72 . . . . . . 46 C5
Midland Oak Trad Est
  CV6 . . . . 95 E2
Midland Rd
  Birmingham B30 . . . . . 103 F5
  Coventry CV6 . . . . . . 113 E5
  Darlaston WS10 . . . . . 41 C8
  Huntington WS12 . . . . . 1 C5
  Nuneaton CV11 . . . . . . 73 A5
  Sutton Coldfield B74 . . . 46 A6
  Walsall WS1 . . . . 28 E1
Midland St B9 . . . . 67 C3
Midpoint Ctr WV6 . . . . . 24 F5
Midpoint Park Ind Est
  B76 . . . . 58 C5
Midvale Dr B14 . . . . . . 104 D2
Mikado Rd B60 . . . . . . 137 D1
Milburn Hill Rd CV4 . . . 132 B6
Milburn Rd B44 . . . . . . 45 A3
Milby B77 . . . . 36 C8
Milby Ct CV11 . . . . 73 C2
Milby Dr CV11 . . . . 73 A7
Milby Prim Sch CV11 . . . 73 F8
Milcote Dr
  Sutton Coldfield B73 . . . 45 C3
  Willenhall WV13 . . . . . 26 C1
Milcote Rd
  Birmingham B29 . . . . . 103 A8
  Smethwick B67 . . . . . . 64 F1
  Solihull B91 . . . . . . 107 B4
Milcote Way DY6 . . . . . . 60 B7
Mildenhall Rd B42 . . . . . 44 A1
Mildenhall B79 . . . . . . 21 C8
Mildred Rd B64 . . . . . . 62 E2
Mildred Way B65 . . . . . . 63 C6
Milebrook Gr B32 . . . . . 102 B8
Mile End B94 . . . . 142 A2
Mile Flat DY6 . . . . 60 A7
Mile La CV1 . . . . 165 C3
Mile Oak Cross Rds B78 . 20 C2
Milesbush Ave B36 . . . . . 58 D1
Miles Gr DY2 . . . . 62 F7
Miles Mdw CV6 . . . . 96 A3
Miles Meadow Cl WV12 . . 27 C8
Milestone Ct WV6 . . . . . 24 A3
Milestone Dr DY9 . . . . . 98 F4
Milestone Ho 2 CV1 . . . 113 B2
Milestone La B21 . . . . . 65 D8
Milestone Way WV12 . . . . 27 C8
Milford Ave
  Birmingham B12 . . . . . 87 A6
  Willenhall WV12 . . . . . 27 A5
Milford Cl
  Allesley CV5 . . . . . . 112 B6
  Redditch B97 . . . . . . 158 C6
  Stourbridge DY8 . . . . . 60 E3
Milford Copse B17 . . . . . 85 B5
Milford Croft B65 . . . . . 62 F6
Milford Ct
  Birmingham B19 . . . . . 164 B5
  Royal Leamington Spa
    CV31 . . . . 162 A8
Milford Gr B90 . . . . . . 126 F3
Milford Pl B14 . . . . . . 104 E8
Milford Rd
  Birmingham B17 . . . . . 85 B5
  Wolverhampton WV2 . . . . 39 C7
Milford St CV10 . . . . . . 73 B2
Milhill Rd B98 . . . . . . 154 E1
Milholme Gn B92 . . . . . 107 D8
Milking Bank DY1 . . . . . 50 E2
Milking Bank Prim Sch
  DY1 . . . . 50 E2
Milk St B5 . . . . 66 F1
Millais Cl CV12 . . . . . . 77 A4
Millard Cl LE10 . . . . . . 71 A3
Millard Ind Est B70 . . . . 53 A1
Millard Rd WV14 . . . . . . 40 B1
Mill Bank Cotts DY11 . . 116 D6
Mill Bank Mews CV8 . . . 148 B6
Mill Bank WV11 . . . . . . 12 F1
Millbank CV34 . . . . 156 B6
Millbrook Cl 4 WS11 . . . 1 F2
Millbrook Ct B62 . . . . . 83 A7
Mill Brook Dr B31 . . . . . 122 E8
Millbrook Rd B14 . . . . . 104 C6
Millbrook Way DY5 . . . . . 81 B8

Mill Burn Way 3 B9 . . . . 67 B2
Mill Cl
  Blakedown DY10 . . . . . 98 B2
  Bromsgrove B60 . . . . . 150 F6
  Coventry CV2 . . . . . . 96 B3
  Dudley DY3 . . . . 50 D6
  Hollywood B47 . . . . . . 125 A7
  Nuneaton CV11 . . . . . . 73 F1
  Wolston CV8 . . . . 135 F3
Mill Cres WS11 . . . . 2 B2
Mill Croft WV14 . . . . . . 40 E6
Millcroft Cl B32 . . . . . 84 E2
Millcroft Rd B74 . . . . . 45 A8
Mill Ct WS14 . . . . 18 A6
Milldale Cl DY10 . . . . . 116 E8
Milldale Cres WV10 . . . . 11 D3
Milldale Rd WV10 . . . . . 11 D4
Mill Dr B66 . . . . 65 B5
Mill End CV8 . . . . 148 A6
Millennium Pk B70 . . . . . 53 A5
Millennium Cl WS3 . . . . . 15 A4
Millennium Forge DY4 . . . 51 D5
Millennium Gdns B64 . . . 62 F2
Millennium Way
  Codsall WV8 . . . . 10 B4
  Wolston CV8 . . . . 135 F3
Miller Cl
  Bromsgrove B60 . . . . . 150 E6
  Lichfield WS13 . . . . . . 3 B2
Miller Cres WV14 . . . . . 40 A1
Millers Cl WS2 . . . . . . 27 B3
Millers Ct
  1 Kidderminster DY11 . . 116 D6
  Solihull B90 . . . . . . 105 F2
Millersdale Dr B71 . . . . 42 F2
Millers Gn LE10 . . . . . . 75 F6
Millers Green Dr DY6 . . . 60 A8
Miller St B6 . . . . 66 E8
Millers Rd CV34 . . . . . . 160 E8
Millers Vale WS12 . . . . . 2 D1
Millers Wharf B78 . . . . . 22 F1
Millers Wlk WS3 . . . . . . 14 E3
Mill Farm Cl CV22 . . . . . 79 B6
Mill Farm Rd B17 . . . . . 85 C3
Millfield Ave
  Walsall,Little Bloxwich
    WS3 . . . . 14 D3
  Walsall WS4 . . . . 15 B1
Millfield B31 . . . . 103 A4
Millfield Gdns 2 DY11 . . 116 D6
Millfield Prim Sch
  Brownhills WS8 . . . . . . 16 A7
  Fazeley B78 . . . . 35 A8
Millfield Rd
  Birmingham B20 . . . . . 54 F5
  Bromsgrove B61 . . . . . 136 E1
  Smethwick B67 . . . . . . 16 A7
Millfields CV31 . . . . . . 162 A8
Millfields B33 . . . . . . 69 E3
Millfields Cl B71 . . . . . 42 B1
Millfields Fst Sch B61 . . 136 E1
Millfields Rd
  Bilston WV14 . . . . . . 40 B5
  West Bromwich B71 . . . . 42 B1
Millfield View B63 . . . . 82 C4
Mill Gdns
  Birmingham B14 . . . . . 105 D5
  Smethwick B67 . . . . . . 64 F3
Mill Gr WV8 . . . . 10 C3
Mill Green Nature Pk*
  WS11 . . . . 1 F1
Millhaven Ave B30 . . . . . 103 D6
Mill Hill CV8 . . . . 133 D3
Mill Hill B63 . . . . 82 C4
Mill Hill Rd LE10 . . . . . 71 C1
Mill Ho B67 . . . . 68 C8
Mill House Cl CV32 . . . . 161 C8
Mill House Ct CV6 . . . . . 113 F7
Mill House Dr CV32 . . . . 161 C8
Millhouse Rd B25 . . . . . 88 C8
Millicent Cl WS12 . . . . . 2 B6
Millicent Pl 1 B12 . . . . 87 A6
Millichip Rd WV13 . . . . . 26 E1
Millington Rd
  Birmingham B36 . . . . . 68 E7
  Tipton DY4 . . . . 40 F1
  Wolverhampton WV10 . . . 25 E6
Millison Gr B90 . . . . . . 127 A7
Mill La
  Bentley Heath B93 . . . . 127 F4
  Birmingham B32 . . . . . 84 E2
  Birmingham,Digbeth B5 . 164 D1
  Birmingham,Northfield
    B31 . . . . 103 A2
Mill La Arc B91 . . . . . . 107 C3
Mill La
  Blakedown DY10 . . . . . 98 B2
  Bramcote CV11 . . . . . . 79 F8
  Bromsgrove B60 . . . . . 136 E4
  Bulkington CV12 . . . . . 79 A3
  Coventry CV3 . . . . . . 134 C4
  Cubbington CV32 . . . . . 157 F5
  Earlswood B94 . . . . . . 141 B8
  Fairfield B61 . . . . . . 120 F3
  Fazeley B78 . . . . 83 C4
  Halesowen B63 . . . . . . 83 C4
  Hammerwich WS7 . . . . . 7 D4
  Kidderminster,Blakebrook
    DY11 . . . . 116 C6
  Kidderminster,Hoobrook
    DY10 . . . . 116 F2
  Kingswood B94 . . . . . . 144 C4

Mill La continued
Oldbury B69 . . . .**64** A5
Shenstone WS14 . . . .**18** A6
Solihull B91 . . . .**107** C4
Stonnall WS9,WS14 . . . .**17** A4
Tamworth B79 . . . .**21** C5
Walsall WS3,WS4 . . . .**28** F4
Willenhall WV12 . . . .**27** C5
Wolverhampton,Scotlands
  WV11 . . . .**26** B7
Wolverhampton,Tettenhall Wood
  WV6 . . . .**24** A3
Wombourne WV5 . . . .**49** B6
Wythall B47,B94 . . . .**125** B1
Mill Lodge Prim Sch
  B90 . . . .**105** C2
Millmead Lodge B13 . . . . . .**105** D8
Millmead Rd B32 . . . .**84** E1
Mill Park Ind Est WS11 . . . . .**2** A1
Mill Pk WS11 . . . .**2** A2
Mill Pleck B80 . . . .**159** E3
Mill Pl WS3 . . . .**28** E4
Mill Pond The WS13 . . . .**3** C2
Millpool Cl DY9 . . . .**99** A4
Millpool Gdns B14 . . . .**104** F3
Millpool Hill B14 . . . .**104** F4
Mill Pool La B93 . . . .**144** A8
Mill Pool Rd WS12 . . . .**2** B6
Millpool Way B66 . . . .**65** A4
Mill Race La
  Coventry CV6 . . . .**96** B3
  Stourbridge DY8 . . . .**81** A6
Millrace Rd B98 . . . .**153** E5
Mill Rd
  Brownhills WS8 . . . .**16** A7
  Cradley Heath B64 . . . .**82** E7
  Royal Leamington Spa
    CV31 . . . .**162** A8
  Walsall WS4 . . . .**15** C1
Mills Ave B76 . . . .**46** E4
Millsborough Rd B98 . . . . .**153** F3
Mills Cl WV11 . . . .**26** B8
Mills Cres WV2 . . . .**163** D1
Millside B28 . . . .**105** E3
Mills Rd WV2 . . . .**163** D1
Mill St
  Barwell LE9 . . . .**71** F5
  Bedworth CV12 . . . .**78** B3
  Bilston WV14 . . . .**40** D6
  Birmingham B6 . . . .**164** D5
  Brierley Hill DY5 . . . .**61** E2
  Cannock WS11 . . . .**1** E1
  Coventry CV1 . . . .**165** A3
  Darlaston WS10 . . . .**41** C6
  Halesowen B63 . . . .**82** C7
  Kidderminster DY11 . . . .**116** D6
  Nuneaton CV11 . . . .**73** C4
Millstone Cl B76 . . . .**46** F1
Mill Stream Cl WV8 . . . .**10** B4
Mill St
  Redditch B97 . . . .**153** D4
  Royal Leamington Spa
    CV31 . . . .**162** A7
  Stourbridge DY8 . . . .**60** F2
  Sutton Coldfield B72 . . . .**46** C5
  Tipton DY4 . . . .**52** D5
  Walsall WS2 . . . .**28** E3
  Warwick CV34 . . . .**52** E5
  West Bromwich B70 . . . .**53** C4
  Willenhall WV12 . . . .**27** C2
Millsum Ho 6 WS1 . . . .**28** F1
Mills Wlk DY4 . . . .**51** F7
Mill Terr CV12 . . . .**78** B5
Mill The WV1 . . . .**163** D3
Millthorpe Cl B8 . . . .**67** F5
Mill View
  Birmingham B33 . . . .**69** C4
  Hinckley LE10 . . . .**71** E1
Millwalk Dr WV9 . . . .**11** A3
Millward St
  Birmingham B9 . . . .**67** C1
  West Bromwich B70 . . . .**53** A3
Mill Wlk WS11 . . . .**73** C4
Mill Wlk The B31 . . . .**102** F1
Millwright Cl 1 DY4 . . . .**52** B5
Milner Cl CV12 . . . .**79** D2
Milner Cres CV2 . . . .**96** E1
Milner Dr B79 . . . .**22** E7
Milner Rd B29 . . . .**86** A1
Milner Way B13 . . . .**105** D8
Milnes Walker Ct B44 . . . . . .**44** E1
Milo Cres B78 . . . .**21** A2
Milrose Way CV4 . . . .**131** F8
Milsom Gr B34 . . . .**69** C6
Milstead Rd B26 . . . .**69** A1
Milston Cl B14 . . . .**104** E1
Milton Ave
  2 Birmingham B12 . . . .**87** A6
  Tamworth B79 . . . .**21** A7
  Warwick CV34 . . . .**160** C5
Milton Cl
  Bedworth CV12 . . . .**78** D1
  Bentley Heath B93 . . . .**127** F4
  Hinckley LE10 . . . .**71** C1
  Kidderminster DY11 . . . .**116** A6
  Redditch B97 . . . .**158** C8
  Stourbridge DY8 . . . .**81** A7
  Walsall WS1 . . . .**42** D6
  Willenhall WV12 . . . .**27** E7
Milton Cres
  Birmingham B25 . . . .**88** D7
  Dudley DY3 . . . .**50** A5
Milton Ct WV6 . . . .**23** E4
Milton Dr WV9 . . . .**99** D7

Milton Gr
  Birmingham,Edgbaston
    B29 . . . .**85** F3
  Birmingham,Handsworth
    B21 . . . .**65** C8
Milton Ho B63 . . . .**82** B5
Milton Pl WS1 . . . .**42** D6
Milton Rd
  Bentley Heath B93 . . . .**127** F4
  Cannock WS11 . . . .**1** E4
  Catshill B61 . . . .**137** A8
  Dudley WV14 . . . .**51** D8
  Smethwick B67 . . . .**64** E5
  Wolverhampton WV10 . . . .**26** A5
Milton St
  Birmingham B19 . . . .**66** E6
  Brierley Hill DY5 . . . .**61** D7
  Coventry CV2 . . . .**114** A4
  Walsall WS1 . . . .**42** D7
  West Bromwich B71 . . . .**53** B5
Milverton Cl
  Halesowen B63 . . . .**83** A6
  Sutton Coldfield B76 . . . .**57** F7
Milverton Cres 1 CV32 .**156** E1
Milverton Cres W 3
  CV32 . . . .**156** E1
Milverton Ct
  3 Birmingham B62 . . . .**84** A7
  Royal Leamington Spa
    CV32 . . . .**161** E8
Milverton Hill CV32 . . . . . .**161** E8
Milverton House Prep Sch
  CV11 . . . .**73** D3
Milverton Lodge 2
  CV32 . . . .**156** E1
Milverton Prim Sch
  CV32 . . . .**156** E1
Milverton Rd
  Birmingham B23 . . . .**56** E4
  Coventry CV2 . . . .**96** D2
  Knowle B93 . . . .**128** C5
Milverton Terr CV32 . . . . .**161** E8
Milward Sq 7 B97 . . . .**153** E3
Mimosa Cl B29 . . . .**103** B7
Mimosa Wlk DY6 . . . .**60** E8
Mincing La B65 . . . .**63** D3
Mindelsohn Way B15 . . . . . .**85** D4
Minden Gr B29 . . . .**85** B1
Minehead Rd
  Dudley DY1 . . . .**61** D8
  Wolverhampton WV10 . . . .**11** B2
Miner St WS2 . . . .**28** C3
Miners Way WS7 . . . .**6** C7
Miners Wlk B78 . . . .**22** F1
Minerva Cl
  Tamworth B77 . . . .**21** D5
  Willenhall WV12 . . . .**27** E4
Minerva La WV1 . . . .**25** E1
Minewood Cl WS3 . . . .**13** F3
Minith Rd WV14 . . . .**51** D8
Miniva Dr B76 . . . .**47** A2
Minivet Dr B12 . . . .**86** E6
Miniey Ave B17 . . . .**84** F7
Minories B4 . . . .**164** C3
Minories The 1 DY2 . . . .**51** D1
Minors Hill WS14 . . . .**9** C6
Minstead Rd B24 . . . .**56** D1
Minster Cl
  Knowle B93 . . . .**128** B8
  Rowley Regis B65 . . . .**63** E3
Minster Dr B10 . . . .**87** D7
Minsterley Cl WV3 . . . .**38** E8
Minsterpool Wlk WS13 . . . . .**9** B8
Minster Rd CV1 . . . .**113** B3
Minster The WV3 . . . .**39** A7
Minster Wlk B61 . . . .**136** F8
Mintern Rd B25 . . . .**88** C8
Minton Cl WV1 . . . .**26** A1
Minton Ho 8 B12 . . . .**86** F5
Minton Mews B60 . . . .**151** B8
Minton Rd
  Birmingham B32 . . . .**84** F4
  Coventry CV2 . . . .**96** E1
Minworth B97 . . . .**153** B2
Minworth Ind Pk B76 . . . . . .**58** B5
Minworth Jun & Inf Sch
  B76 . . . .**58** D5
Minworth Rd B46 . . . .**59** A3
Miranda Cl
  Birmingham B45 . . . .**102** A2
  Coventry CV3 . . . .**134** D7
Miranda Dr CV34 . . . .**161** E2
Miras Bsns Est WS12 . . . .**2** D3
Mirfield Cl WV9 . . . .**11** A3
Mirfield Rd
  Birmingham B33 . . . .**69** B2
  Solihull B91 . . . .**107** A6
Mission Cl B64 . . . .**63** A1
Mission Dr DY4 . . . .**52** A3
Mistletoe Dr WS5 . . . .**43** B3
Mistral Cl LE10 . . . .**75** F8
Mitcham Cl WS12 . . . .**1** F7
Mitcham Gr B44 . . . .**45** B1
Mitcheldean Cl B98 . . . . . .**158** E7
Mitcheldean Covert B14 .**104** D2
Mitchell Ave
  Coventry CV4 . . . .**132** A7
  Dudley WV14 . . . .**40** B1
Mitchell Ho
  Coventry CV4 . . . .**132** A7
  Warwick CV34 . . . .**160** D6
Mitchell Rd CV12 . . . .**78** C2
Mitchel's Ct B79 . . . .**21** B5
Mitchel Rd DY6 . . . .**60** F4
Mitford Dr B92 . . . .**107** D7
Mitre Cl
  Essington WV11 . . . .**13** A3
  Willenhall WV12 . . . .**27** D7

Mitre Ct
  Bromsgrove B61 . . . .**137** A3
  Sutton Coldfield B74 . . . .**46** C6
Mitre Fold WV1 . . . .**163** B3
Mitre Rd
  Cheslyn Hay WS6 . . . .**4** D2
  Stourbridge DY9 . . . .**81** E5
Mitten Ave B45 . . . .**102** A1
Mitton Rd B20 . . . .**54** E2
Moat Ave CV3 . . . .**132** F5
Moat Coppice B62 . . . .**84** A1
Moat Croft
  Birmingham B37 . . . .**70** A2
  Sutton Coldfield B76 . . . .**58** B7
Moat Dr
  Drayton Bassett B78 . . . .**34** E5
  Halesowen B62 . . . .**63** F1
Moat Farm Dr
  Bedworth CV12 . . . .**95** C8
  Birmingham B32 . . . .**84** A1
Moat Farm Inf Sch B68 . . . .**64** C3
Moat Farm Jun Sch B68 . . . .**64** C3
Moat Farm Way WS3 . . . .**15** A5
Moatfield Terr 2 WS10 . . . . .**42** A3
Moat Gn CV35 . . . .**160** E1
Moat Green Ave WV11 . . . . . .**26** E7
Moat Hall Prim Sch WS6 . . . .**4** F3
Moat House La CV4 . . . .**132** C7
Moathouse La E WV11 . . . . . .**26** E7
Moathouse La W WV11 . . . . . .**26** D7
Moat House Prim Sch
  Coventry CV2 . . . .**96** D1
  Wednesfield WV11 . . . .**26** E7
Moat House Rd B8 . . . .**68** A4
Moat La
  Birmingham,Digbeth B5 . . .**164** C1
  Birmingham,South Yardley
    B26 . . . .**88** E7
  Great Wyrley WS6 . . . .**5** A2
  Solihull B91 . . . .**107** C6
Moat Mdws B32 . . . .**84** E4
Moatmead Wlk B36 . . . .**68** E8
Moat Rd
  Oldbury B68 . . . .**64** B3
  Tipton DY4 . . . .**52** A7
  Walsall WS2 . . . .**28** D3
Moatside Cl WS3 . . . .**15** A5
Moat St WV13 . . . .**27** A2
Moat Way LE9 . . . .**71** F6
Moatway The B38 . . . .**123** E7
Mobberley Rd WV14 . . . .**40** A1
Mob La WS4 . . . .**15** C3
Mockley Wood Rd B93 . . . .**128** B7
Modbury Ave B32 . . . .**84** D1
Modbury Cl CV3 . . . .**133** D5
Moden Cl DY3 . . . .**50** D6
Moden Hill DY3 . . . .**50** C7
Mogul La B63 . . . .**82** A7
Moillett St B18 . . . .**65** E4
Moilliett Ct B66 . . . .**65** C6
Moira Cres B14 . . . .**105** C4
Moises Hall Rd WV5 . . . .**49** B7
Moland St B4 . . . .**164** C4
Mole St B11 . . . .**87** B6
Molesworth Ave CV3 . . . . . .**114** A4
Molineux Grounds
  (Wolverhampton
    Wanderers FC) WV1 . . . . .**163** B4
Molineux St WV1 . . . .**163** B4
Mollington Cres B90 . . . . . .**106** C3
Mollington Rd CV31 . . . . . .**162** A3
Molyneux Rd DY2 . . . .**62** E2
Momus Bvd CV2 . . . .**114** C2
Monarch Dr DY4 . . . .**52** C6
Monarch Ho B68 . . . .**64** C6
Monarch Ind Est B11 . . . .**88** A5
Monarch Way DY2 . . . .**62** C4
Monarch Works 7 DY9 . . . . .**81** F5
Monastery Dr B91 . . . .**106** E6
Monckton Rd B68 . . . .**84** A7
Moncrieff Dr CV31 . . . .**162** C5
Moncrieffe Cl DY2 . . . .**62** E8
Moncrieffe St WS1 . . . .**29** A1
Mondrian Rd B60 . . . .**137** C1
Money La B61 . . . .**121** A7
Monica Rd B10 . . . .**87** F8
Monins Ave DY4 . . . .**52** A2
Monk Cl DY4 . . . .**52** B3
Monkgate Dr B71 . . . .**53** C6
Monk Rd B8 . . . .**68** A5
Monk's Croft The CV3 . . . . .**133** C7
Monks Dr B80 . . . .**159** D4
Monkseaton Rd B72 . . . .**46** B2
Monksfield Ave B43 . . . .**43** D1
Monks Field Cl CV4 . . . .**112** A1
Monkshood Mews B23 . . . . . .**56** B7
Monkshood Retreat B38 . .**123** F8
Monks Kirby Rd B76 . . . .**46** F3
Monkspath Bsns Pk B90 .**126** F8
Monkspath Cl B90 . . . .**126** D7
Monkspath Hall Rd B90,
  B91 . . . .**127** B7
Monkspath Jun & Inf Sch
  B90 . . . .**127** B6
Monks Path B97 . . . .**152** F4
Monkspath
  Solihull B90 . . . .**127** A6
  Sutton Coldfield B76 . . . .**46** F1
Monks Rd
  Binley Woods CV3 . . . .**135** C7
  Coventry CV1 . . . .**113** F2
Monksway B38 . . . .**104** B1
Monks Way
  Tamworth B77 . . . .**21** F5
  Warwick CV34 . . . .**160** D6
Monkswell Cl
  Birmingham B10 . . . .**87** D7

Monkswell Cl continued
  Brierley Hill DY5 . . . .**61** D1
Monkswood Cres CV2 . . . . .**114** D8
Monkswood Rd B31 . . . .**103** C2
Monkton Rd B29 . . . .**85** A2
Monmer Close Ind Est
  WV13 . . . .**27** B3
Monmer Cl WV13 . . . .**27** B3
Monmer Ct WV12 . . . .**27** B5
Monmer La WV12,WV13 . . . . .**27** B5
Monmore Bsns Pk WV2 . . . . .**39** F7
Monmore Park Ind Est
  WV2 . . . .**40** A6
Monmore Rd WV1 . . . .**40** A7
Monmouth Cl
  Coventry CV5 . . . .**112** B3
  Kenilworth CV8 . . . .**147** F6
Monmouth Dr
  Sutton Coldfield B73 . . . .**45** D3
  West Bromwich B71 . . . .**53** B7
Monmouth Gdns CV10 . . . . . .**72** E3
Monmouth Ho B33 . . . .**69** E2
Monmouth Rd
  Birmingham,Bartley Green
    B32 . . . .**102** D8
  Birmingham,Warley Woods
    B67 . . . .**84** E8
  Walsall WS2 . . . .**27** E3
Monnington Ho CV8 . . . . . .**148** B7
Monsal Ave WV10 . . . .**25** E4
Monsaldale Cl WS8 . . . .**15** D7
Monsal Rd B42 . . . .**55** D7
Monsieurs Hall La B61 . . . .**136** B3
Mons Rd DY2 . . . .**51** F1
Montague Ho
  Birmingham B16 . . . .**65** D1
  Warwick CV34 . . . .**161** A8
Montague Rd
  Birmingham,Birches Green
    B24 . . . .**57** A1
  Birmingham,Edgbaston B16 .**65** E1
  Birmingham,Handsworth
    B21 . . . .**65** F8
  Smethwick B66 . . . .**65** C3
  Warwick CV34 . . . .**161** A8
Montague St
  Birmingham,Aston B6 . . . .**67** B8
  Birmingham,Bordesley B9 . . .**67** A2
Montalt Rd CV3 . . . .**133** E7
Montana Ave B42 . . . .**55** A5
Montana Wlk CV10 . . . .**72** E3
Monteagle Dr DY6 . . . .**49** D1
Montford Gr DY3 . . . .**50** D7
Montfort Rd
  Coleshill B46 . . . .**70** F5
  Walsall WS2 . . . .**42** B6
Montfort Wlk B32 . . . .**84** A2
Montgomery Cl
  Coventry CV3 . . . .**134** C4
  Upper Catshill B61 . . . .**121** A1
Montgomery Cres DY5 . . . . . .**81** F7
Montgomery Croft B11 . . . . . .**87** C7
Montgomery Prim Sch
  B11 . . . .**87** C7
Montgomery Rd
  Walsall WS2 . . . .**27** E2
  Whitnash CV31 . . . .**161** F4
Montgomery St Bsns Ctr
  B11 . . . .**87** D7
Montgomery St B11 . . . .**87** D7
Montgomery Way B8 . . . .**68** A4
Montgomery Wlk 1 B71 . . .**53** D4
Montjoy Cl CV3 . . . .**134** F7
Montley B77 . . . .**36** C8
Montpelier Ho CV8 . . . .**147** F5
Montpelier Rd B24 . . . .**57** A1
Montpellier Cl CV3 . . . .**133** C6
Montpellier Gdns DY3 . . . . . .**50** E2
Montpellier St B12 . . . .**87** A6
Montreal Ho B5 . . . .**86** D7
Montrose Ave CV32 . . . .**157** B5
Montrose Cl CV11 . . . .**1** F5
Montrose Dr
  Birmingham B35 . . . .**58** A4
  Dudley DY1 . . . .**62** A8
  Nuneaton CV10 . . . .**72** F3
Montsford Cl B93 . . . .**127** F6
Monument Ave DY9 . . . .**81** E4
Monument Dr WV10 . . . .**12** C8
Monument Ho 6 B16 . . . .**65** F1
Monument La
  Birmingham B45 . . . .**121** F4
  Hagley DY9 . . . .**99** D7
  Sedgley DY3 . . . .**39** E1
Monument Rd B16 . . . .**65** F2
Monway Bldgs 1 WS10 . . . .**41** E3
Monway Ind Est WS10 . . . . . .**41** E3
Monway Terr WS10 . . . .**41** E3
Monwood Gr B91 . . . .**106** F2
Monyhull Hall Rd B30 . . . . .**104** C3
Moodyscroft Rd B33 . . . .**69** C3
Moon's La WS6 . . . .**4** D1
Moons Moat Dr B98 . . . .**154** E5
Moons Moat Fst Sch
  B98 . . . .**154** D5
Moons Pk B98 . . . .**154** E6
Moorborooke CV10 . . . .**72** A7
Moor Cl WS7 . . . .**7** B7
Moorcroft Cl
  Nuneaton CV11 . . . .**74** B1
  Redditch B97 . . . .**158** B6
Moorcroft Dr WS10 . . . .**41** C2
Moorcroft Gdns B97 . . . . . .**158** B6
Moorcroft Pl 5 B7 . . . .**67** A4
Moorcroft Rd B13 . . . .**86** E3
Moorcroft Wood Prim Sch
  WV14 . . . .**40** E5
Moor Ct B24 . . . .**56** F3

Moor Ctr The DY5 . . . .**61** D3
Moordown Ave B92 . . . .**89** A2
Moore Cl
  Coventry CV6 . . . .**96** A5
  Perton WV6 . . . .**23** F4
  Sutton Coldfield B74 . . . .**31** F6
  Warwick CV34 . . . .**155** E2
Moore Cres B68 . . . .**64** C3
Moorend Ave B37 . . . .**70** B2
Moor End Ct B24 . . . .**57** B4
Moor End La B24 . . . .**57** B4
Moor Rd WV12 . . . .**27** D8
Moore's Row B5 . . . .**66** F1
Moore St
  Cannock WS12 . . . .**2** C1
  Wolverhampton WV1 . . . .**25** F1
Moore Wlk CV34 . . . .**161** C7
Moorfield Ave B93 . . . .**127** F6
Moorfield Dr
  Bromsgrove B61 . . . .**136** F3
  Halesowen B63 . . . .**83** A5
  Sutton Coldfield B73 . . . .**57** A8
Moorfield Rd
  Birmingham B34 . . . .**69** B6
  Wolverhampton WV2 . . . .**39** C7
Moorfields Cl WS9 . . . .**30** A7
Moorfield The CV3 . . . .**134** B8
Moorfoot Ave B63 . . . .**82** C1
Moorgate B79 . . . .**21** A5
Moorgate Cl B98 . . . .**154** E6
Moorgate Com Prim Sch
  B79 . . . .**21** A5
Moorgate Rd B60 . . . .**151** A2
Moorgate B79 . . . .**21** A5
Moor Green Inf Sch B13 .**86** C1
Moor Green Jun Sch B13 .**86** C1
Moor Green La B13 . . . .**86** D2
Moor Hall Dr
  Clent DY9 . . . .**100** A1
  Sutton Coldfield B75 . . . .**32** D1
Moor Hall Prim Sch B75 . . . .**32** D2
Moorhen Cl WS8 . . . .**15** E7
Moorhill Prim Sch
  Cannock WS11 . . . .**1** E4
  Cannock WS11 . . . .**1** E5
Moorhill Rd CV31 . . . .**162** A3
Moorhills Croft B90 . . . .**126** B8
Moor Ho B14 . . . .**104** C2
Moorings Bsns Pk The
  CV6 . . . .**96** A6
Moorings The
  Birmingham B18 . . . .**65** F5
  Brierley Hill DY5 . . . .**62** A4
  Oldbury B69 . . . .**63** E8
  Royal Leamington Spa
    CV31 . . . .**161** D7
  Wolverhampton WV9 . . . .**10** F2
Moor La B6 . . . .**56** A4
Moorland Ave WV10 . . . .**25** C6
Moorland Ct B16 . . . .**65** D1
Moorland Rd
  Birmingham B16 . . . .**65** D1
  Cannock WS11 . . . .**1** E5
  Walsall WS3 . . . .**28** A8
Moorlands Ave CV8 . . . .**147** F3
Moorlands Cl 1 B75 . . . . . .**46** F6
Moorlands Dr B90 . . . .**106** C2
Moorlands Lodge CV8 . . . . .**147** F3
Moorlands Prim Sch B71 . . .**53** B8
Moorlands Rd B71 . . . .**42** C1
Moorlands The B74 . . . .**45** F8
Moor Lane Ind Est B6 . . . .**55** F5
Moor La
  Rowley Regis B65 . . . .**63** B3
  Shenstone WS14 . . . .**17** E2
  Tamworth B77 . . . .**22** A6
  Tamworth,Bolehall B77 . . . . . .**21** D5
Moor Leasow B31 . . . .**103** C2
Moor Meadow Rd B75 . . . .**46** D7
Moorpark Cl CV11 . . . .**79** C8
Moorpark Rd B31 . . . .**103** A1
Moor Pk
  Perton WV6 . . . .**23** D5
  Walsall WS3 . . . .**14** B3
Moor Pool Ave B17 . . . .**85** C6
Moor Rd CV10 . . . .**72** A8
Moor St S WV2 . . . .**39** C7
Moors Croft B32 . . . .**84** B1
Moorside Gdns WS2 . . . .**28** B3
Moorside Rd B14 . . . .**105** D3
Moors La B31 . . . .**102** E7
Moors Mill La DY4 . . . .**52** D7
Moorsom St B6 . . . .**66** E5
Moorsom Way B60 . . . .**151** B7
Moor St
  Brierley Hill DY5 . . . .**61** C3
  Coventry CV5 . . . .**112** F1
Moors The B36 . . . .**68** F8
Moor Street Ind Est DY5 . . . .**61** C3
Moor Street Queensway
  B5 . . . .**164** C2
Moor Street Sta B5 . . . .**164** C2
Moor St
  Tamworth B79 . . . .**21** A5
  Wednesbury WS10 . . . .**42** B2
  West Bromwich B70 . . . .**53** C2
Moor The B76 . . . .**58** A8
Moorville Wlk B11 . . . .**87** A7
Moorwood Cres CV10 . . . .**72** A8
Moorwood La
  Hartshill CV10 . . . .**72** A7
  Hartshill CV10 . . . .**72** A8
Moray Cl
  Halesowen B62 . . . .**83** E8
  Hinckley LE10 . . . .**75** A8
Morcom Rd B11 . . . .**87** D6
Morcroft WV14 . . . .**41** A3

Mordaunt Dr B75 . . . . .32 E2
Morden Rd B33. . . . . .68 D3
Mordern Mobile Home Pk WV10. . . . . .11 C6
Mordiford Cl B98 . . . . 154 E4
Moreall Mdws WV4. . . . . . 132 D3
Morecroft Dr CV34. . . . . . 160 B4
Moreland Croft B76. . . . . . .58 B6
Moreland Pl B31. . . . . 102 F1
Morelands The B31. . . . . . 103 B1
Morestead Ave B26 . . . . . . .89 C5
Moreton Ave
  Birmingham B43 . . . . .44 C3
  Wolverhampton WV4. . . . . .39 E4
Moreton Cl
  Birmingham,Queen's Park B32. . . . . .84 F5
  Birmingham,Yardley B25 . . .88 B7
  Wednesbury DY4 . . . . .41 B2
Moreton Com Sch WV10 . .11 F1
Moreton Rd
  Solihull B90 . . . . 106 C2
  Wolverhampton WV10. . . . . .11 D1
Moreton St
  Birmingham B1 . . . . .66 B4
  Cannock WS11. . . . . .1 F4
Morfa Gdns CV6 . . . . 112 D5
Morgan Ave WS2. . . . . . . .30 A7
Morgan Cl
  ▪ Cradley Heath B64. . . . . .82 E8
  Oldbury B69. . . . . .63 D8
  Studley B80 . . . . 159 F2
  Willenhall WV12 . . . . .27 B4
Morgan Ct B24 . . . . .57 C6
Morgan Gr B36 . . . . .58 F1
Morgan Rd B8 . . . . .21 A2
Morgans Rd CV5. . . . . . . 111 C4
Morgrove Ave B93 . . . . . . 127 F6
Morillon Ct DY10 . . . . 117 A1
Morjon Dr B43 . . . . .43 F2
Morland Cl CV12. . . . . .79 D2
Morland Dr LE10. . . . . .71 B3
Morland Rd
  Birmingham B43 . . . . .44 C4
  Coventry CV6. . . . . .95 C2
Morley Gr WV6 . . . . .25 C4
Morley Rd
  Birmingham B8 . . . . .68 B6
  Burntwood WS7 . . . . .7 B7
Morley Road Sh Ctr WS7. .7 B7
Morlings Dr WS7 . . . . .7 B8
Morning Pines DY8 . . . . . . .80 E4
Morningside
  Coventry CV5. . . . . 133 B8
  Sutton Coldfield B73 . . . . . .46 B6
Mornington Rd B66. . . . . . .65 B7
Morpeth B77 . . . . .35 C7
Morrell St CV32. . . . . 156 F1
Morris Ave
  Coventry CV2. . . . . 114 D4
  Walsall WS2 . . . . .27 E2
Morris Croft B35. . . . . .88 D4
Morris Ct B36. . . . . .58 F1
Morris Ct
  ▪ Wolverhampton WV4 . . . . .39 F4
  Brierley Hill DY5 . . . . .61 B1
Morris Dr
  Nuneaton CV11 . . . . .73 D1
  Whitnash CV31 . . . . 162 B2
Morris Field Croft B28 . . . 105 E4
Morris Hill B78. . . . . .36 F7
Morrison Ave WV10 . . . . . .25 D8
Morrison Rd DY4 . . . . .52 C4
Morris Rd B8. . . . . .68 C6
Morris St B70 . . . . .53 C1
Morris Wlk B66 . . . . 150 E8
Morsefield La B98 . . . . . . 154 D1
Morse Rd CV31. . . . . 162 B3
Morsom B77 . . . . .35 D4
Mortimer Rd CV8 . . . . 147 F2
Mortimers Cl B14. . . . . . . 105 B1
Morton Cl CV6. . . . . .95 A1
Morton Ho B97 . . . . 153 A3
Morton La B97 . . . . 158 B7
Morton Rd
  Brierley Hill DY5 . . . . .81 D7
  Harvington DY10 . . . . 118 B2
Morton St CV32. . . . . 156 F1
Morvale Ct DY9 . . . . .81 E5
Morvale Gdns DY9 . . . . . . .81 E5
Morvale St DY9. . . . . .81 E5
Morven Rd B73. . . . . .46 A3
Morville Croft WV14 . . . . . .40 B5
Morville Rd DY2 . . . . .62 E4
Morville St B16. . . . . .66 B2
Mosborough Cres B19 . . . . .66 C5
Mosedale Dr WV11. . . . . . .26 F5
Moseley Ave CV6 . . . . 113 A4
Moseley CE Prim Sch B13 .86 F2
Moseley Cl
  ▪ Birmingham B13. . . . . . . .87 B2
  Essington WV11. . . . . .12 F3
  Willenhall WV13 . . . . .26 D1
Moseley Ct B37 . . . . .89 F8
Moseley Gate B13. . . . . . . .86 F3
Moseley Hall Hospl B13. . . .86 E3
Moseley Old Hall* WV10 . .12 A5
Moseley Old Hall La WV10. . . . . .12 A5
Moseley Park Sch WV14 . . .40 E8
Moseley Prim Sch CV6 . . . 113 A4
Moseley Rd
  Bilston WV14 . . . . .40 E8
  Birmingham B12 . . . . .86 F6
  Kenilworth CV8 . . . . 148 B3
  Willenhall WV14,WV13 . . . .26 D1

Moseley Rd continued
  Wolverhampton WV10 . . . . .12 A4
Moseley Sch B13 . . . . .87 C2
Moseley St
  Birmingham B12 . . . . .86 F8
  Tipton DY4. . . . . .52 C7
  Wolverhampton WV6. . . . . .25 C4
Mossbank Ave WS7 . . . . . . .7 A6
Moss Cl
  Aldridge WS9. . . . . .30 A5
  Walsall WS4 . . . . .29 A3
Moss Cres WS12 . . . . .1 C5
Mossdale Cl CV6. . . . . 113 B6
Mossdale Cres CV10 . . . . . .72 F2
Mossdale B77 . . . . .36 C8
Mossdale Way DY3. . . . . . .50 E7
Moss Dr B72 . . . . .46 C3
Mossfield Rd B14. . . . . 104 F7
Moss Gdns WV14 . . . . .40 B3
Moss Gr
  Birmingham B14 . . . . 104 D6
  Kenilworth CV8 . . . . 148 B7
  Kingswinford DY6 . . . . .60 D7
Moss House Cl B15. . . . . . .66 B1
Moss La B98 . . . . 154 F8
Moss Lane Cl B98 . . . . 154 F8
Mossley Cl WS3. . . . . .13 F1
Mossley La WS3 . . . . .13 F1
Mossley Prim Sch WS3. . . .13 F2
Mosspaul Cl CV32. . . . . . . 156 D2
Moss Rd WS11. . . . . .2 A3
Mossvale Cl
  ▪ Royal Leamington Spa CV31. . . . . 162 A7
  Cannock WS11. . . . . .2 A4
Mossvale Cl B64. . . . . .62 F1
Mossvale Gr B8 . . . . .67 F5
Moss Way B74. . . . . .44 F7
Mosswood La WS11 . . . . . . .4 D7
Mostyn Cres B71 . . . . .53 A7
Mostyn Rd
  Birmingham,Edgbaston B16. . . . . .65 F2
  Birmingham,Handsworth B21. . . . . .65 F8
Mostyn St WV1 . . . . .25 A4
Mother Teresa Ho B70 . . . .53 B3
Mott Cl DY4 . . . . .52 C8
Mottistone Cl CV3 . . . . . . 133 D6
Mottram Cl B70 . . . . .53 B2
Mottrams Cl B72 . . . . .46 C2
Mott St B19 . . . . 164 B4
Moule Cl DY11. . . . . 116 C6
Moundsley Gr B14. . . . . . . 105 A3
Moundsley Ho B14. . . . . . . 104 F2
Mounds The B38. . . . . 123 E8
Mountain Ash Dr DY9. . . . . .81 C2
Mountain Ash Rd WS8 . . . . .15 F5
Mountain Pine Cl WS12 . . . .2 A8
Mount Ave
  Brierley Hill DY5 . . . . .61 C4
  Cannock WS12. . . . . .2 B7
Mountbatten Ave CV8. . . . 148 C3
Mountbatten Cl B70 . . . . . .53 F2
Mountbatten Rd WS2 . . . . .27 F2
Mount Cl
  Birmingham B13 . . . . .86 F4
  Cheslyn Hay WS6. . . . . .4 E2
  Dudley DY3 . . . . .50 C2
  Wombourne WV5. . . . . . . .24 B2
Mount Ct WV6 . . . . .24 B2
Mount Dr
  Bedworth CV12 . . . . .78 A3
  Wombourne WV5. . . . . . . .49 A7
Mountfield Cl B14 . . . . 105 A2
Mount Field Ct CV1. . . . . . 165 D4
Mountford Cl ▪ B65. . . . . . .63 C3
Mountford Dr WS9. . . . . . . .30 C8
Mountford Dr B75 . . . . .46 B8
Mountford Ho B70 . . . . .53 E1
Mountford La WV14. . . . . . .40 D6
Mountford Rd B90. . . . . . . 105 D1
Mountford St B11. . . . . .87 D5
Mount Gdns CV5 . . . . 133 B2
Mount Grace High Sch LE10. . . . . .71 E1
Mountjoy Cres B92 . . . . . . .89 C3
Mount La
  Clent DY9. . . . . .99 E4
  Dudley DY3 . . . . .50 C2
Mount Nod Prim Sch CV5 . . . . 112 A3
Mount Nod Way CV5 . . . . . 112 B3
Mount Pleasant Ave B21 . . .54 E1
Mount Pleasant
  Bilston WV14 . . . . .40 E6
  Birmingham,King's Heath B14. . . . . .86 F1
  Birmingham,Small Heath B10. . . . . .87 A7
  Brierley Hill DY5 . . . . .61 E1
  Cheslyn Hay WS6. . . . . .4 F2
Mount Pleasant Cotts CV2 . . . . 115 A7
Mount Pleasant Ct ▪ B10 .67 B1
Mount Pleasant Rd CV6. . . .60 C4
Mount Pleasant Mobile Home Pk B77 . . . . .21 C1
Mount Pleasant Prim Sch DY5 . . . . .61 E1
Mount Pleasant Rd CV12 . .78 A3
Mount Pleasant B97 . . . . . 153 D2
Mount Pleasant Terr CV10 . . . . .72 F3

Mountrath St WS1 . . . . .28 E1
Mount Rd
  Birmingham B21 . . . . .65 D7
  Burntwood WS7 . . . . .7 B6
  Fairfield B61 . . . . 120 E2
  Hinckley LE10 . . . . .75 D8
  Oldbury B69. . . . . .63 C8
  Rowley Regis B65 . . . . .63 E3
  Stourbridge,Stambermill DY8. . . . . .81 B5
  Stourbridge,Wollescote DY8 .60 E2
  Wolverhampton WV4 . . . . . .39 A4
  Willenhall WV13 . . . . .40 E8
  Birmingham,Goldthorn Hill WV4 . . . . .39 A4
  Wolverhampton,Tettenhall Wood WV6 . . . . .24 A3
  Wolverhampton,Woodcross WV14 . . . . .39 F2
  Wombourne WV5. . . . . . . .49 A7
Mount Road Ind Est WS7 . . .7 B6
Mountserrat Rd B60 . . . . . 137 B1
Mount Side St WS12 . . . . . . .2 C7
Mounts Rd WS10 . . . . .41 F2
Mount St
  Birmingham B7 . . . . .67 C7
  Cannock WS12. . . . . .2 B7
  Coventry CV5. . . . . 112 F2
  Halesowen B63 . . . . .83 A3
  Nuneaton CV11 . . . . .73 B4
  Redditch B98 . . . . 153 E3
  Walsall WS1 . . . . .42 E8
Mount Street Bsns Ctr B7 .67 C6
Mount Street Ind Est B7 . . .67 D7
Mount Street Pas CV1 . . . . .73 B4
Mount The
  Stourbridge DY8 . . . . .81 B5
  Tipton DY4. . . . . .52 C6
  Walsall WS1 . . . . .42 E8
Mounts Way B7 . . . . .67 C7
Mount Vernon Dr B61. . . . 137 A5
Mount View B75 . . . . .46 E4
Mountwood Covert WV6 . . .24 B3
Mousehall Farm Rd DY5 . . .81 D7
Mouse Hill WS3 . . . . .14 F3
Mouse La DY11. . . . . 116 B8
Mousesweet Cl DY2 . . . . . .62 E4
Mousesweet La DY2. . . . . . .62 E3
Mousesweet Wlk B64. . . . . .82 B8
Mowbray Cl B45. . . . . 102 A2
Mowbray St
  Birmingham B5 . . . . .86 E8
  Coventry CV5. . . . . 113 F3
Mowe Croft B37 . . . . .90 B7
Mows Hill Rd B94. . . . . . . 143 A1
Moxhall Cl WV12 . . . . .13 C1
Moxhall Dr B76. . . . . .57 F7
Moxhall Gdns WV12. . . . . . .13 C1
Moxhull Rd B37 . . . . .70 A5
Moxley Ind Ctr WS10. . . . . .41 C4
Moxley Jct WS10 . . . . .41 B4
Moxley Rd WS10 . . . . .41 C5
Moyle Cres CV5. . . . . 111 D4
Moyle Dr B63. . . . . .82 B7
Moyses Croft B66. . . . . .48 B7
Mozart Ct WS11 . . . . .2 A2
Muchall Rd WV4 . . . . .39 A5
Much Park St CV1 . . . . 165 C2
Mucklow Hill B62. . . . . .83 D5
Mucklow Hill Trad Est B62. . . . . .83 C5
Muirfield Cl WS3 . . . . .14 A3
Muirfield Cres B69. . . . . . . .63 B7
Muirfield Gdns B38. . . . . . 103 D1
Muirfields Cl CV11 . . . . .79 C8
Muirfield Rd B77. . . . . .22 C5
Muirville Cl ▪ DY8 . . . . . . .60 D3
Mulberry Cl CV32 . . . . 157 A2
Mulberry Cl CV8. . . . . 147 F4
Mulberry Dr
  ▪ Lichfield WS13. . . . . .9 E8
  ▪ Warwick CV34. . . . . 160 F8
  Birmingham B13. . . . . .87 B1
Mulberry Dr WS3 . . . . .50 F5
Mulberry Pl WS3 . . . . .13 F1
Mulberry Rd
  Birmingham B30 . . . . 103 C5
  Cannock WS11. . . . . .1 E3
  Coventry CV6 . . . . 114 A7
  Walsall WS3 . . . . .14 A1
Mulberry Way CV10 . . . . . . .72 A8
Mulberry Wlk B74 . . . . .44 E8
Muldoon Cl WS12 . . . . .1 B4
Mullard Dr CV31. . . . . 162 B3
Mull Croft B36 . . . . 101 E1
Mull Croft B36. . . . . .70 B7
Mullein B77 . . . . .31 F5
Mullensgrove Rd B37. . . . . .70 A5
Mullett Rd WV11. . . . . .26 B7
Mullett St DY5. . . . . .61 B5
Mulliners Cl ▪ B37. . . . . . . .70 D2
Mulliner St CV1. . . . . 113 F5
Mullion Croft B38. . . . . . . 103 E1
Mulroy Rd B74 . . . . .46 B6
Mulwych Rd B33 . . . . .69 E3
Munches La B62. . . . . 120 C8
Munnings Dr CV10. . . . . . . .72 A8
Muntz Ho B16. . . . . .66 A1
Muntz St B10 . . . . .87 D8
Murcott Ct CV31 . . . . 162 A3

Murcott Rd E CV31. . . . . . 162 A3
Murcott Rd W CV31. . . . . . 162 A3
Murcroft Rd DY9 . . . . .81 E1
Murdoch Dr DY6. . . . . .60 C7
Murdoch Rd WV14 . . . . .41 A6
Murdock Ct WV12. . . . . .27 C7
Murdock Gr B21. . . . . .65 C4
Murdock Rd
  Birmingham B21 . . . . .65 E8
  Smethwick B66 . . . . .65 D6
Murdock Way ▪ WS2 . . . . .28 A5
Murray Ct
  Birmingham B20 . . . . .55 A2
  Sutton Coldfield B73 . . . . . .46 A3
Murrayfield Way CV3 . . . . . .115 B8
Murray Ho WV14. . . . . .40 D5
Murray Rd CV6 . . . . 113 A7
Murrell Cl B5. . . . . .86 D7
Murton B77 . . . . .36 C8
Musborough Cl B36. . . . . . .58 C1
Muscott Gr B17. . . . . .85 B5
Muscovy Rd B23. . . . . .56 C3
Musgrave Cl B76. . . . . .46 E3
Musgrave Rd B18. . . . . .65 F6
Mushroom Hall Rd B68. . . . .64 B5
Musketts Ct B97 . . . . 153 B2
Musk La DY3 . . . . .50 B3
Musk La W DY3 . . . . .50 B3
Mus of British Road Transport* CV6 . . . . .11 D4
Mus of Cannock Chase* WS12. . . . . .2 D6
Mus of the Jewellery Quarter* B19. . . . . .66 C5
Muswell Cl B91. . . . . 107 D5
Muxloe Cl WS3 . . . . .14 A3
Myatt Ave
  Aldridge WS9. . . . . .29 F5
  Burntwood WS7 . . . . .7 B7
  Wolverhampton WV2. . . . . .39 E6
Myatt Cl WV2 . . . . .39 E6
Myatt Way WV9 . . . . .29 F5
Myddleton St B18. . . . . .66 A4
Myles Ct DY5 . . . . .61 D4
Mylgrove CV3 . . . . 133 D3
Mynors Cres B47 . . . . 125 A6
Myring Dr B75. . . . . .46 F5
Myrtle Ave
  ▪ Birmingham,Balsall Heath B12. . . . . .87 A5
  Birmingham,Higher's Heath B14. . . . . 104 F2
  Redditch B98 . . . . 153 E2
  Myrtle Cl WV12 . . . . .27 E7
Myrtle Gr
  ▪ Birmingham B19. . . . . . . .66 C8
  Coventry CV5. . . . . 112 F1
  Wolverhampton WV3. . . . . .38 B2
Myrtle Pl B29. . . . . .86 B3
Myrtle Rd DY1 . . . . .51 B3
Myrtle St WV2 . . . . .39 F6
Myrtle Terr DY4 . . . . .52 B6
Myton Cres CV34 . . . . 161 C6
Myton Crofts CV31 . . . . . . 161 D7
Myton Dr B90 . . . . 105 D1
Myton Gdns CV34 . . . . 161 A6
Myton La CV34 . . . . 161 C6
Myton Rd CV31,CV34. . . . . 161 B6
Mytton Cl DY2 . . . . .51 E1
Mytton Gr DY4. . . . . .51 E5
Mytton Rd
  Birmingham B30 . . . . 103 C5
  Water Orton B46 . . . . .58 F3
Myvod Rd WS10 . . . . .42 A5

N

Naden Ho WS12 . . . . .1 C5
Naden Rd B19. . . . . .66 B6
Nadin Rd B73. . . . . .57 A8
Naesby Rd WV6. . . . . .23 F3
Nafford Gr B14. . . . . 104 F2
Nagersfield Rd DY5. . . . . . .61 A4
Nailcote Ave CV4. . . . . 131 C8
Nailcote La CV7 . . . . 131 A7
Nailers Cl
  Birmingham B32 . . . . .83 F2
  Stoke Heath B60 . . . . 150 E6
Nailers Ct ▪ B60. . . . . 136 F2
Nailers Dr WS7 . . . . .7 D6
Nailers Fold WV14 . . . . .40 D2
Nailstone Cres B27 . . . . . . 106 C8
Nailsworth Rd
  Dorridge B93 . . . . 127 D2
  Redditch B98 . . . . 153 F2
Nairn Cl
  Birmingham B28 . . . . 105 F5
  Nuneaton CV10 . . . . .73 A2
  Redditch B98 . . . . 154 A4
Nairn Rd WS3 . . . . .14 A4
Nally Dr WV14 . . . . .40 A2
Nanaimo Way DY6. . . . . . . .61 A4
Nansen Prim Sch B8. . . . . .67 F5
Nansen Rd
  Birmingham,Sparkhill B11. . .87 C3
  Birmingham B8 . . . . .67 F5
Nantmel Gr B32 . . . . 102 C8
Naomi Way WS9 . . . . .16 B4
Napier Dr DY4 . . . . .52 C6
Napier Rd
  Walsall WS2 . . . . .28 A5
  Wolverhampton WV2. . . . . .39 D7
Napier St CV1 . . . . 113 E3
Napley Ho B77 . . . . .21 D2
Napton Cl B98 . . . . 154 D1
Napton Dr CV32 . . . . 157 A2

Napton Gn CV5 . . . . 112 A3
Napton Gr B29. . . . . .84 F2
Narberth Way CV2 . . . . 114 F8
Narraway Gr DY4 . . . . .52 D8
Narrowboat Cl CV6 . . . . . . .96 B6
Narrowboat Way DY5,DY2. .62 A5
Narrow Hall Mdw CV34 . . . 160 B4
Narrow La
  Brownhills WS8 . . . . .15 F8
  Halesowen B62 . . . . .83 E8
  Walsall WS2 . . . . .42 B7
Narrows The ▪ LE10 . . . . . .75 C8
Naseby Cl
  Coventry CV3 . . . . 134 F8
  Redditch B98 . . . . 154 D6
Naseby Dr B63 . . . . .82 D2
Naseby Rd
  Birmingham B8 . . . . .67 F5
  Solihull B91 . . . . 107 B6
Nash Ave WV6 . . . . .23 C3
Nash Cl B65 . . . . .63 C1
Nash Croft B37 . . . . .90 B8
Nashe Cl DY10 . . . . 117 C5
Nash Ho B15. . . . . .86 D8
Nash La
  Belbroughton DY9 . . . . . . 119 D7
  Lichfield WS13. . . . . .3 A5
Nash Rd B98 . . . . 154 B1
Nash Sq B42 . . . . .55 B7
Nash Wlk ▪ B66 . . . . .65 C5
Nately Gr B29 . . . . .85 C3
Nathan Cl B75 . . . . .46 C8
Nathaniel Newton Inf Sch CV10 . . . . .72 B8
National Ex Ctr B40. . . . . . .90 E4
National Indoor Arena* B1. . . . . .66 B2
National Motorcycle Mus The* B92. . . . . .91 A2
National Sea Life Ctr* B1 .164 B2
Naul's Mill Ho CV1. . . . . . . 165 B4
Naunton Cl B29. . . . . 103 A7
Naunton Rd WS2 . . . . .28 A3
Navenby Cl B90. . . . . 105 C3
Navigation Dr DY5. . . . . . . .62 A4
Navigation La B71 . . . . .42 F2
Navigation Rdbt DY4. . . . . .52 E6
Navigation St
  Birmingham B2 . . . . 164 B2
  Walsall WS2 . . . . .28 D1
  Wolverhampton WV1. . . . . .25 E1
Navigation Way
  Birmingham B18 . . . . .65 F5
  Cannock WS11. . . . . .1 A2
  Coventry CV6. . . . . 114 A8
  West Bromwich B70 . . . . . . .52 F2
Nayland Croft B28 . . . . 106 A5
Naylor Cl DY11 . . . . 116 B3
Naylors Gr DY3 . . . . .50 E4
Neachells Ct WV13 . . . . . . .26 E1
Neachells Lane Ind Est WV11. . . . . .26 D4
Neachells Lane Island WV11. . . . . .26 D4
Neachells La
  Wednesfield WV11 . . . . . . .26 D5
  Willenhall WV13 . . . . .26 D5
Neachless Ave WS5 . . . . . . .49 A5
Neachley Gr B33. . . . . .68 F4
Neal Ct CV2 . . . . 115 A8
Neale Ave CV5 . . . . 112 A6
Neale Cl CV12 . . . . .79 C1
Neale Ho
  ▪ West Bromwich B70. . . . . .53 D1
  Wolverhampton WV2. . . . . .39 C7
Neale St WS2 . . . . .28 C2
Neander B79 . . . . .20 F6
Near High Dr ▪ DY4. . . . . . .52 B5
Nearhill Rd B38 . . . . 123 C8
Near Lands Cl B32. . . . . . . .84 B4
Near Oak Ho B32 . . . . .69 D6
Near Oak Ho B32 . . . . 102 D8
Neasden Gr B44 . . . . .56 B8
Neath Rd WS3 . . . . .13 F2
Neath Way
  Dudley DY3 . . . . .51 A6
  Walsall WS3 . . . . .13 F2
Nebsworth Cl CV5 . . . . 106 D5
Nechells Jun & Inf Sch B7. . . . . .67 C8
Nechells Park Rd B7 . . . . . .67 C7
Nechells Parkway B7 . . . . . .67 A5
Nechells Pl B7 . . . . .67 C7
Needham St B7 . . . . .67 C8
Needhill Cl B93. . . . . 127 F6
Needle Mill La B98 . . . . . . 153 E4
Needle Mill La B98 . . . . . . 153 E6
Needlers End La CV7 . . . . . 130 A7
Needless Alley B2. . . . . . . 164 B2
Needwood Cl WV2 . . . . .39 B6
Needwood Dr WV4. . . . . . . .39 F4
Needwood Gr B71 . . . . .42 E1
Needwood Hill WS13. . . . . . .3 A2
Needwood Ho B27 . . . . .88 D3
Neighbrook Cl B97 . . . . . . 152 F2
Nelson Ave
  Bilston WV14 . . . . .40 C7
  Warwick CV34 . . . . 161 A8
Nelson Ct ▪ B13 . . . . .86 F4
Nelson Dr
  Cannock WS12. . . . . .2 F4
  Hinckley LE10 . . . . .71 D4
Nelson Ho DY4 . . . . .52 A7
Nelson La CV34 . . . . 161 A8

Nelson Mandela Sch B12..**87** B5
Nelson Prim Sch B1 ......**66** B3
Nelson Rd
Birmingham B6 ....**55** F1
Dudley DY1 ....**51** B1
Nelson St
7 Coventry CV1.........**113** E4
Birmingham B1 ....**66** B3
Oldbury B69...........**64** B6
West Bromwich B71 ......**53** C5
Willenhall WV13 ....**27** B3
Nemesia B77.........**22** B4
Nene Cl
Coventry CV3..........**134** D7
Stourbridge DY8 ....**81** A5
Nene Way B36.........**69** F8
Neptune Ind Est WV13 ...**41** B8
Neptune St DY4 ....**51** E5
Nesbit Gr B9 ....**68** B3
Nesfield Cl B38.......**103** C1
Nesfield Gr B92......**109** B7
Nesscliffe Gr B23....**56** D7
Nest Comm WS3 ....**14** D1
Neston Gr B33........**68** C2
Nestor Ho B13.......**105** D7
Netheravon Cl B14...**104** D1
Nether Beacon WS13 ....**3** A1
Netherbridge Ave WS14 ..**9** E7
Netherbrook Prim Sch
DY2 ....**62** D2
Netherby Rd DY3 ......**50** C8
Nethercote Gdns B90..**105** E3
Netherdale Cl B72 ....**57** C7
Netherdale Rd B14 ...**105** A1
Netherend Cl B63......**82** A7
Netherend La B63 .....**82** B7
Netherend Sq B63 .....**82** A7
Netherfield Gdns B27...**88** B3
Netherfield B98 ......**159** A8
Nethergate DY3 ....**50** F5
Nether La WS7 ....**7** D8
Netherley Ct LE10......**71** D3
Netherley Rd LE10....**71** D3
Nethermill Rd 1 CV6 ..**113** A5
Netherstone Gr B74....**31** F5
Nether Stowe High Sch
WS3 ....**3** B1
Netherstowe La WS13 ...**3** D2
Netherstowe WS13......**3** C2
Netherton Bsns Pk DY2 .**62** E3
Netherton CE Prim Sch
DY2 ....**62** B4
Netherton Gr B33......**69** C3
Netherwood Cl B91...**106** E6
Netherwood La B93....**145** A7
Nether Dr WV6 ....**24** B5
Netley Gr B11 ....**87** C4
Netley Ho B32 ....**84** F5
Netley Rd WS3........**13** E2
Netley Way WS3 ....**13** E2
Network Pk B7 ....**67** C4
Nevada Way B37.......**70** C1
Neve Ave WV10 ....**25** F8
Nevill Cl CV31......**161** F6
Neville Ave
Kidderminster DY11 ....**116** D3
Wolverhampton WV4 .....**39** D5
Neville Cl B98 ....**154** A5
Neville Ct
5 Warwick CV34 ......**160** E6
Birmingham B13 ....**104** F6
Kidderminster DY11 ....**116** D3
Neville Gr CV34......**155** F1
Neville Ho DY3 ....**50** D7
Neville Rd
Birmingham,Castle Bromwich
B36 ....**58** E1
Birmingham,Stockland Green
B23 ....**56** C3
Solihull B90 ....**105** F1
Neville St B77 ....**21** E3
Neville Wlk B35 ......**58** A2
Nevill St B79 ....**21** A5
Nevin Gr B42 ....**55** C5
Nevis Ct WV6 ....**24** E2
Nevis Gr WV12........**13** B1
Nevison Gr B43.......**44** B4
Newall Ho B97 ....**153** D2
Newark Croft B26.....**89** B6
Newark Rd
Dudley DY2 ....**62** D2
Willenhall WV12 ....**27** C7
New Art Gall The WS8 ..**28** E2
New Ash Dr CV5......**111** F5
Newbank Gr B9 ....**68** A3
New Barns La WS14.....**17** B3
New Bartholomew St
B5.....................**164** D2
New Birmingham Rd B69,
DY2 ....**52** B1
New Bldgs
Coventry CV1..........**165** C3
Darlaston WS10.........**41** E6
Hinckley LE10 ....**71** D1
Newbold Cl
Bentley Heath B93....**127** F5
Coventry CV3..........**114** F1
Lichfield WS13 ....**9** A5
Newbold Comyn Pk* ....
CV32 ....**162** D8
Newbold Croft B7 .....**67** B5
Newbold Ct B63 ......**83** B3
Newbold Lawn CV32 ...**162** A8
Newbold Pl CV32 .....**162** A8
Newbolds Rd WV10 .....**26** A6
Newbold St CV32 .....**162** A8
Newbold Terr E CV32...**162** B8
Newbold Terr CV32....**162** A8
Newbolt Rd WV14......**40** E6
Newbolt St WS5 ....**42** E5
New Bond St
2 Dudley DY2.........**62** A8
Birmingham B9 ....**67** B1
Newborough Gr B28,B90..**105** F3
Newborough Rd
Birmingham B28 ....**105** F4
Solihull B90 ....**106** A3
Newbourne Hill B48...**139** E4
Newbridge Ave WV6 ....**24** E3
Newbridge Cres WV6 ...**24** E4
Newbridge Dr WV6 .....**24** E4
Newbridge Gdns WV6....**24** E4
Newbridge Mews 3 WV6 .**24** E4
Newbridge Prep Sch WV6 .**24** E4
Newbridge Rd
Birmingham B9 ....**68** B1
Kingswinford DY6 ......**60** C8
Newbridge St WV6......**24** E4
New Brook St 3 CV32...**161** E8
Newburgh Cres CV34...**160** E8
Newburgh Prim Sch
CV34 ....**160** C4
Newburn Croft B32....**84** B5
Newbury Cl
4 Royal Leamington Spa
CV31 ....**162** C6
Great Wyrley WS6 ....**4** F2
Halesowen B62 ....**83** F7
Lower Marlbrook B61...**121** B1
Newbury Ho 8 B69.....**63** D5
Newbury La B69 ....**63** D6
Newbury Rd
Birmingham B19 ....**66** E7
Norton Canes WS11 ......**6** A5
Stourbridge DY8 ....**60** D1
Wolverhampton WV10....**11** C2
Newbury Wlk B65......**63** C6
Newby Cl CV3........**133** E6
Newby Gr B37 ....**70** B5
New Canal St B5.....**164** D2
Newcastle Croft B35..**58** C3
New Century Pk CV3...**114** C2
New Century Way CV11...**73** B4
Newchurch Gdns 8 B24 .**56** E2
New Church Rd B73.....**57** A8
New Cole Hall La B33,B34 .**69** B5
New College Cl WS1...**43** A7
Newcombe Rd
Birmingham B21 ....**54** D2
Coventry CV5..........**113** A1
Newcome Ct B24......**57** D4
Newcomen Cl
Bedworth CV12 ....**95** D8
Burntwood WS7..........**7** C8
Newcomen Ct WS4 ......**29** B7
Newcomen Dr DY4......**51** F3
Newcomen Rd CV12 .....**77** D1
New Coppice Ct B97...**158** E6
New Coventry Rd B26...**89** A5
New Croft B19........**66** E7
New Cross Ave WV10 ....**26** B4
New Cross Hospl WV11...**26** B5
New Cross Ind Est WV1...**26** A3
New Cross Junc WV10 ...**26** B4
New Cross St
Darlaston WS10.........**41** D5
Tipton DY4 ....**51** E5
New Ct 7 DY5.........**61** D2
Newdegate Cl CV11.....**73** C4
Newdegate Pl CV11....**73** C4
Newdegate Rd CV12 ....**78** A3
Newdegate St CV11....**73** C4
Newdigate Prim Sch
CV12 ....**77** C1
Newdigate Rd
Coventry CV6..........**113** F6
Sutton Coldfield B75...**47** A5
New Dudley Rd DY6.....**60** C8
Newells Dr DY4.......**52** D7
Newells Rd B26.......**89** B8
New England Cl B69....**52** E1
New England B62......**83** D7
Newent Cl WV12.......**27** D3
Newent Rd B31.......**103** C4
New Ent Workshops B18..**66** A5
Newey Ave CV12 ....**95** D8
Newey Cl B45 ....**122** A6
Newey Dr CV8 ....**148** A3
Newey Rd
Birmingham B28 ....**105** F6
Coventry CV2..........**114** D4
Wednesfield WV11 ......**27** A8
Newey St DY1.........**51** A2
New Farm Rd DY9......**81** C4
Newfield Ave CV8....**148** B3
Newfield Cl
Solihull B91 ....**107** D6
Walsall WS3 ....**28** C5
Newfield Cres B63....**83** A5
Newfield Dr DY6......**60** E4
Newfield Gdns DY9....**99** A4
Newfield La B63......**83** A5
Newfield Park Prim Sch
B63 ....**83** A5
Newfield Pl DY9......**99** A4
Newfield Rd
Coventry CV1..........**113** C5
Oldbury B69............**63** F8
West Hagley DY9........**99** A4
New Forest Rd WS3......**28** F6
Newgale Wlk CV31....**162** C7
New Gas St B70........**53** A5
New Gate Ct CV1......**165** C2
Newgate St WS7 ....**7** A5
New Gdns WS7..........**6** F5
New Green Pk CV2 ....**114** D7
Newhall Cres WS11.....**2** B3
Newhall Ct 9 B3......**66** C3
New Hall Dr
Sutton Coldfield,Maney
B75....................**46** D4
Sutton Coldfield,Wylde Green
B76....................**46** E2
Newhall Farm Cl B76...**46** D4
Newhall Gdns WS11.....**1** F2
Newhall Hill B1......**66** C3
New Hall Ho 6 WS1.....**42** E8
New Hall Ind Est B75...**47** B5
New Hall Jun Sch B75...**47** B5
Newhall Pl B1........**66** C3
New Hall Pl WS10.....**42** A3
Newhall Rd
Coventry CV2..........**114** D7
Rowley Regis B65.......**63** C3
Newhall St
Birmingham B3 ....**164** B3
Cannock WS11 ....**1** D1
Tipton DY4 ....**51** E8
Walsall WS1............**42** E8
West Bromwich B70 .....**53** C2
New Hall St WV13......**27** B2
Newhall Wlk B72......**46** C4
Newham Gn CV10.......**72** D3
Newhampton Rd E WV1..**163** A4
New Hampton Rd W WV6..**24** F4
Newhaven Cl
Birmingham B7 ....**67** A5
Coventry CV6..........**112** E6
Newhay Croft B19......**66** C7
New Heath Cl WV11.....**26** B5
New Henry St B68......**64** B4
Newhope Cl 2 B15......**86** D8
New Hope Rd B66.......**65** C4
New Horse Rd WS6......**4** E3
Newhouse Croft CV7....**130** A6
Newhouse Farm Cl B76..**46** F3
New House Farm Dr
B31....................**103** C6
Newick Ave B74.......**31** B3
Newick Gr B14.......**104** C4
Newick St DY2.......**62** C4
Newington Cl CV6....**112** D6
Newington Rd B37.....**90** B8
New Inn Rd 2 B19.....**66** D8
New Inns Cl B21.....**65** D8
New Inns La B45.....**101** E1
New John St W B19.....**66** D5
New John St
Birmingham B6 ....**66** E5
Halesowen B62 ....**83** C8
New King St 7 B1.....**51** C1
Newland Cl
Redditch B98 ....**159** B7
Walsall WS4 ....**15** C2
Newland Ct B23......**56** C3
Newland Gdns B64.....**82** E7
Newland Gr DY2......**62** A4
Newland La CV7.......**61** F7
Newland La CV7.......**95** B7
Newland Rd
Birmingham B9 ....**67** F1
Coventry CV1..........**113** D5
Royal Leamington Spa
CV32 ....**157** C3
Newlands Cl
Kidderminster DY11 ....**116** C7
Willenhall WV13 ....**27** A1
Newlands Ct
Cannock WS12 ....**5** E8
Coventry CV3..........**113** F2
Newlands Dr B62.......**83** E7
Newlands Gn B66......**65** A4
Newlands La
Birmingham B37 ....**90** A6
Norton Canes WS12 ......**5** D8
Newlands Rd
Bentley Heath B93....**127** F4
Birmingham B30 ....**104** C7
Newlands The
Birmingham B34 ....**69** C7
Studley B80 ....**159** D3
New Landywood La WS6..**13** E7
New Leasow B76.......**58** A7
Newlyn Cl
Lichfield WS14 ....**9** D7
Nuneaton CV11 ....**73** F4
Newlyn Rd
Birmingham B31 ....**102** F3
Cradley Heath B64.....**82** D8
Newman Ave WV4 ....**39** F4
Newman College B32...**102** C8
Newman Coll of Higher Ed
B32....................**102** D8
Newman Pl WV14.......**40** F7
Newman Rd
Birmingham B24 ....**56** F4
Wednesbury DY4........**41** C1
Wolverhampton WV10....**12** A1
Newmans Cl B66.......**65** C4
Newman Way B45......**122** A6
Newmarket Cl
Coventry CV6..........**96** A4
Wolverhampton WV6.....**25** A5
Newmarket Rd WS11.....**6** B1
New Market St B3.....**164** B3
Newmarket Way B36....**68** B7
Newmarsh Rd B76......**58** A6
New Meadow Cl B31...**103** B2
New Meadow Rd B45...**122** A6
New Meeting St B69....**64** A8
New Mill La B78.......**35** A7
New Mills St WS1......**42** D7
New Mill St DY2......**51** C1
Newmore Gdns WS5.....**43** C5
New Moseley Rd B12....**87** A8
Newnham Gr B23......**56** E6
Newnham Ho B36.......**70** B5
Newnham Rd
Birmingham B16 ....**65** C2
Coventry CV1..........**113** F5
Royal Leamington Spa
CV32 ....**157** B3
Newnham Rise B90....**106** D3
New Oscott Prim Sch B73..**45** C3
New Park Sch W6......**24** F5
New Penkridge Rd WS11..**1** C1
New Plant La WS7......**6** C8
New Pool Rd B64.......**82** B8
Newport Cl B97......**158** B6
Newport Rd
Birmingham,Balsall Heath
B12...................**87** A4
Birmingham,Buckland End
B36...................**68** F8
Coventry CV6..........**95** D1
Newport St
4 Walsall WS1........**28** E1
Wolverhampton WV10....**25** E4
Newport B77 ....**21** F5
Newquay Cl
Hinckley LE10 ....**71** E4
Nuneaton CV11 ....**73** F5
Walsall WS5............**43** E7
Newquay Rd WS5.......**43** D7
New Railway St WV13...**27** B2
New Rd
Aldridge WS9...........**30** A5
Ash Green CV7..........**95** B6
Astwood Bank B96.....**158** C1
Birmingham B45 ....**121** F7
Bromsgrove B60 ....**151** A7
Bromsgrove,Sidemoor B61 .**136** E3
Brownhills WS8 ....**15** F7
Burntwood WS7..........**7** B6
Coventry CV6..........**94** F1
Dudley DY2 ....**62** C7
Fairfield B61 ....**120** E2
Halesowen B63 ....**83** B4
Hinckley LE10 ....**71** C4
Hollywood B47.........**125** A8
Kidderminster DY10 ...**116** E5
Shenstone WS14 ....**17** F6
Shuttington B79........**22** E8
Solihull B91 ....**107** D3
Stourbridge DY8 ....**81** A5
Studley B80 ....**159** E3
Tamworth B77..........**35** F7
Tipton DY4 ....**52** D6
Water Orton B46........**59** B3
Willenhall WV13 ....**27** A2
Wolverhampton,Newbridge
WV6 ....**24** A4
Wolverhampton,Scotlands
WV10 ....**26** B8
New Row WS6.........**34** E5
New Rowley Rd DY2....**62** E7
New Shipton Cl B76....**46** F1
Newshire Ind Est B11...**87** D6
Newsholme Cl 1 B34...**155** E1
New Spring St N B18...**66** A4
New Spring St B18....**66** A4
New St 6 Cannock,Mill Green
WS11 ....**4** E8
Bedworth CV12 ....**78** C2
Birchmoor B78.........**36** E7
Birmingham B23 ....**57** A4
Birmingham,Castle Bromwich
B36 ....**69** B8
Birmingham,Digbeth B2...**164** C2
Birmingham,Erdington B23 .**56** E5
Birmingham,Frankley B45 .**102** A1
Brierley Hill DY5 .....**82** A8
Bulkington CV12 ....**79** D2
Burntwood,Chase Terrace
B77 ....**60** C8
Burntwood,Chasetown WS7 ..**6** E5
Cannock,Bridgtown WS11....**4** D6
Cannock WS12 ....**2** C4
Cubbington CV32......**157** E5
Darlaston WS10.........**41** D6
Dudley,Eve Hill DY1....**51** D1
Dudley,Gornalwood DY3 ..**50** D4
Kingswinford,Wall Heath
DY6 ....**60** C8
Oldbury B69...........**64** A8
New Street Sta B2......**164** B2
New St
Royal Leamington Spa
CV31 ....**162** A7

New St continued
Smethwick B66 ....**65** B6
Stourbridge DY8 ....**80** F5
Stourbridge,Wordsley DY8 ..**60** D2
Tamworth,Bolehall B77...**21** E4
Tamworth,Mount Pleasant
B77 ....**21** C1
Tipton DY4 ....**51** F5
Walsall,Rushall WS4 ...**29** B7
Walsall,The Chuckery WS1 .**28** F1
Walsall,Wallington Heath
WS3 ....**14** B1
Walsall WS4 ....**15** C1
Warwick CV34..........**160** E6
Wednesbury WS10 ....**41** F1
West Bromwich,Hill Top
B70 ....**53** A7
West Bromwich,Mayer's Green
B70 ....**53** D3
Willenhall WV13 ....**26** E1
Wolverhampton,Merry Hill
WV3 ....**38** D7
Wolverhampton,Parkfield
WV4 ....**39** E6
New Summer St B19....**164** B4
New Swan La B70......**53** A5
New Swinford Hall DY9..**81** C4
Newton Chambers 1
B2....................**164** B2
Newton Cl
Birmingham B43 ....**43** C1
Coventry CV2..........**114** F7
Redditch B98 ....**159** A6
Newton Gdns B43......**54** B8
Newton Gr 5 B29......**85** F2
Newton Ind Est B9......**67** D2
Newton Manor Cl B43...**54** D8
Newton Pl
Birmingham B18 ....**66** A7
Walsall WS2............**28** B6
Newton Rd
Birmingham,Balsall Heath
B11...................**87** B5
Birmingham,Newton B43...**54** B8
Bromsgrove B60 ....**151** A7
Hinckley LE10 ....**74** E7
Knowle B93 ....**128** B7
Walsall WS2............**28** B5
West Bromwich B71.....**53** F6
Newton's Coll WS13 ....**9** B8
Newton Sq
Birmingham B43 ....**43** C1
Bromsgrove B60 ....**151** A7
Newton St
Birmingham B4 ....**164** C3
West Bromwich B71.....**53** C7
Newton Works B60......**151** A6
Newtown Bldgs CV12....**78** B3
New Town Dr B19......**61** C4
New Town DY2.........**62** C2
Newtown La
Cradley Heath B64......**62** D1
Madeley Heath B62....**120** D8
Romsley B62 ....**101** D2
Newtown Middleway B6..**66** E5
Newtown Prim Sch B70...**52** D3
Newtown Rd
Bedworth CV12 ....**78** A2
Nuneaton CV11 ....**73** C5
New Town Row B6.....**66** E5
Newtown St Cnr Ctr B19...**66** E5
Newtown St B64.......**62** D1
New Union St CV1....**165** B2
New Village DY2......**62** C2
New Wharf Cotts B60..**152** B7
New Wlk 3 B97.......**153** E4
New Wood Cl DY7......**80** C8
New Wood Dr B31.....**102** D1
New Wood Gr WS9......**16** A3
New Wood La DY10....**113** B8
Ney Ct DY4...........**51** F2
Niall Cl B15.........**85** E8
Nibletts Hill B61...**136** F4
Nicholas Chamberlaine Tec
Coll CV12 ....**78** D3
Nicholas Cl CV12.....**78** C3
Nicholas Rd B74......**44** E8
Nicholls Cl WV14.....**40** B1
Nicholls Fold WV11 ..**26** D5
Nicholls Rd DY4......**40** E1
Nicholls St
Coventry CV2..........**113** F4
West Bromwich B70.....**53** E2
Nicholls Way WS12.....**2** F1
Nichols Cl B92......**107** F7
Nicholson Cl CV34...**155** F1
Nickson Rd CV4......**111** E1
Nigel Ave B31.......**103** A5
Nigel Ct B16.........**65** E1
Nigel Rd
Birmingham B8 ....**67** E6
Dudley DY1 ....**51** A2
Nightingale Ave B36...**70** A8
Nightingale Cl
Birmingham B23 ....**56** C7
Hartlebury WS11.........**1** C7
Nightingale Cres
Brierley Hill DY5 .....**81** D7
Willenhall WV12 ....**27** C8
Nightingale Ct
Burntwood WS7..........**7** F8
Royal Leamington Spa
CV31 ....**162** B8
Solihull B91 ....**107** C4
Nightingale Dr
Kidderminster DY10 ...**117** B2
Tipton DY4 ....**52** C5

Nightingale La CV5 . . . . . .132 E7
Nightingale Pl WV14 . . . . . .40 D7
Nightingale B77 . . . . .36 A6
Nightingale Wlk
1 Birmingham B15 . . . . .86 C7
Burntwood WS7 . . . . .7 F8
Nightjar Gr B23 . . . . .56 C6
Nighwood Dr B74 . . . . .44 F7
Nijon Cl B21 . . . . .54 D1
Nimbus B77 . . . . .35 D4
Nimmings Cl B31 . . . . .122 F6
Nimmings Rd B62 . . . . .63 D1
Nimmings Visitor Ctr*
B62 . . . . .100 B6
Nineacres Dr B37 . . . . .70 A3
Nine Days La B98 . . . . .159 B6
Nine Elms La WV10 . . . . . . .25 E4
Ninefoot La
Tamworth,Belgrave B77 . . . .35 E8
Tamworth,Wilnecote B77 . . .35 F7
Nine Leasowes B66 . . . . .64 E7
Nine Locks Ridge DY5 . . . .61 D2
Nine Pails Wlk 2 B70 . . . .53 D1
Ninestiles Sch (Tech Coll)
B27 .88 B1
Nineveh Ave B21 . . . . .65 F7
Nineveh Rd B21 . . . . .65 F7
Ninfield Rd B27 . . . . .88 A4
Ninian Pk B77 . . . . .35 D6
Ninian Way B77 . . . . .35 E6
Nirvana Cl WS11 . . . . .1 C2
Nith Pl DY1 . . . . .51 B3
Niton Rd CV10 . . . . .73 D6
Niven Cl CV5 . . . . 112 A6
Noakes Ct WS10 . . . . .41 F7
Noble Cl CV34 . . . . 160 D5
Nocke Rd WV11 . . . . .12 F1
Nock St DY4 . . . . .52 C7
Noddy Park Rd WS9 . . . . . .30 B7
Noddy Pk WS9 . . . . .30 B7
Node Hill Cl B80 . . . . 159 D3
Node Hill B80 . . . . 159 D3
Nod Rise CV5 . . . . .112 B3
Noel Ave B12 . . . . .87 A6
Noel Ct B97 . . . . 158 C8
Noele Gordon Gdns 10
WS1 .42 E8
Noel Rd B16 . . . . .65 F1
Nolan Cl CV6 . . . . .95 D4
Nolton Cl B43 . . . . .54 D8
No Name Rd WS7 . . . . .6 E7
Nonsuch Prim Sch B32 . . .84 D2
Nooklands Croft B33 . . . . . .69 A2
Nook The
Brierley Hill DY5 . . . . .61 B5
Cheslyn Hay WS6 . . . . .4 C1
Nuneaton CV11 . . . . .73 E2
Noonan Cl B97 . . . . .153 B2
Noose Cres WV13 . . . . .26 E2
Noose La WV13 . . . . .26 E3
Nora Rd B11 . . . . .87 C3
Norbiton Rd B44 . . . . .56 A8
Norbreck Cl B43 . . . . .43 D1
Norbury Ave WS3 . . . . .15 A3
Norbury Cl B98 . . . . .154 B7
Norbury Cres WV4 . . . . .40 A4
Norbury Dr DY5 . . . . .61 D1
Norbury Gr B92 . . . . .89 A3
Norbury Rd
Bilston WV14 . . . . .40 F6
Birmingham B44 . . . . .44 F3
West Bromwich B70 . . . . . . .53 A7
Wolverhampton WV10 . . . . . .25 F6
Norcombe Gr B90 . . . . . . 127 A5
Nordic Drift CV2 . . . . 115 A6
Nordley Rd WV11 . . . . .26 C5
Norfolk Ave B71 . . . . .53 D7
Norfolk Cl
Birmingham B30 . . . . .104 B6
Hinckley LE10 . . . . .75 D4
Norfolk Cres
Aldridge WS9 . . . . .30 B8
Nuneaton CV10 . . . . .72 E4
Norfolk Ct
6 Birmingham,Selly Oak
B29 . . . . 103 C7
Birmingham B16 . . . . .65 D1
Norfolk Dr
Tamworth B78 . . . . .21 A1
Wednesbury WS10 . . . . .42 D4
Norfolk Gdns B75 . . . . .46 B7
Norfolk Gr WS6 . . . . .4 F1
Norfolk Ho
Birmingham,Short Heath
B23 .56 F5
Birmingham,Walker's Heath
B30 . . . . 104 A3
Norfolk House Sch B15 . . .85 D8
Norfolk New Rd WS2 . . . . . .28 A4
Norfolk Pl WS2 . . . . .28 D5
Norfolk Rd
Birmingham,Brandhall
B68 .84 B7
Birmingham,Chad Valley
B15 .85 D8
Birmingham,Erdington B23 . .56 F5
Birmingham,Frankley B45 . .101 F2
Dudley DY2 . . . . .62 A7
Stourbridge DY8 . . . . .80 D8
Sutton Coldfield B75 . . . . . . .46 C7
Wolverhampton WV3 . . . . . . .39 A8
Norfolk St
Coventry CV1 . . . . .113 B3
Royal Leamington Spa
CV32 . . . . 157 A1
Norfolk Twr B18 . . . . .66 B5
Norgrave Rd B92 . . . . .89 C2
Norlan Dr B14 . . . . .104 F3
Norland Rd B27 . . . . .88 C1
Norley Gr B13 . . . . 105 C7
Norman Ashman Coppice
CV3 . . . . 135 C7
Norman Ave
Birmingham B32 . . . . .84 E7
Coventry CV2 . . . . .96 F1
Nuneaton CV11 . . . . .73 B4
Normanby Mdws CV31 . . 162 A2
Norman Cl B79 . . . . .20 E7
Normandy Cl CV35 . . . . . . 160 A7
Normandy Rd B20 . . . . .55 E1
Normandy Way LE10 . . . . . .71 C3
Norman Place Rd CV6 . . . .112 F7
Norman Rd
Birmingham B31 . . . . .103 B3
Smethwick B67 . . . . .64 E2
Walsall WS5 . . . . .43 D7
Normansell Twr B6 . . . . . . .67 B8
Norman St
Birmingham B18 . . . . .65 E5
Dudley DY2 . . . . .62 E7
Norman Terr B65 . . . . .63 C4
Normanton Ave B26 . . . . . .89 D5
Normanton Twr B23 . . . . . . .57 A6
Normid Ct B13 . . . . .87 A4
Norrington Gr B31 . . . . . . 102 C3
Norrington Rd B31 . . . . . . 102 D3
Norris Dr B33 . . . . .68 E3
Norris Rd B6 . . . . .55 F1
Norris Way B75 . . . . .46 D5
Northampton St B18 . . . . . .66 C4
Northam Wlk WV6 . . . . .25 B4
Northanger Rd B27 . . . . . . .88 B2
North Ave
Bedworth CV12 . . . . .78 D2
Birmingham B40 . . . . .90 F5
Coventry CV2 . . . . 114 A3
Wolverhampton WV11 . . . . . .26 C6
Northbourne Dr CV11 . . . . .78 F7
North Bromsgrove High Sch
B60 . . . . .137 B3
Northbrook Ct B90 . . . . . . 106 C5
North Brook Rd CV6 . . . . . 112 D8
Northbrook Rd B90 . . . . . 106 D5
Northbrook St B16 . . . . .65 F4
North Cl
Cubbington CV32 . . . . .157 E5
Hinckley LE10 . . . . .75 E6
Northcliffe Hts DY11 . . . . 116 C7
Northcote Rd B33 . . . . .68 D4
Northcote St
7 Royal Leamington Spa
CV31 . . . . .162 B7
Walsall WS2 . . . . .28 D4
Northcott Rd
Bilston WV14 . . . . .40 F4
Dudley DY2 . . . . .62 D4
North Cres WV10 . . . . .12 C7
Northdale WV6 . . . . .24 B4
Northdown Rd B91 . . . . . .106 F1
North Dr
Birmingham,Balsall Heath
B5 . . . . .86 C5
Birmingham,Lozells B20 . . . .66 B8
Sutton Coldfield B75 . . . . . . .46 C6
North East Worcestershire
Coll (Bromsgrove Campus)
B60 . . . . .137 B3
North East Worcestershire
Coll (Redditch Campus)
B98 . . . . .153 E4
Northey Rd CV6 . . . . 113 D8
Northfield Children's Farm*
B31 . . . . 102 C4
Northfield Cl B98 . . . . 154 D6
Northfield Gr WV3 . . . . .38 C7
Northfield Manor Prim Sch
B29 . . . . .103 B7
Northfield Rd
Birmingham B17,B32 . . . . . . .85 A3
Birmingham,King's Norton
B30 . . . . .103 E4
Coventry CV1 . . . . .113 F2
Dudley DY2 . . . . .62 D4
Hinckley LE10 . . . . .75 C7
Northfield Road Prim Sch
DY2 .62 D5
Northfield Sta B31 . . . . . . 103 A2
Northfields Way WS8 . . . . .15 D7
Northfolk Terr CV4 . . . . . . .132 B7
Northgate WS9 . . . . .30 A7
North Gate B17 . . . . .85 C7
Northgate Cl
2 Dudley DY1 . . . . .51 B2
Kidderminster DY11 . . . . . 116 A4
Northgate B64 . . . . .82 D8
Northgate St CV34 . . . . . . .160 E7
Northgate CV34 . . . . .160 E7
Northgate Way WS9 . . . . . .30 A8
North Gn WV4 . . . . .38 D6
North Holme B9 . . . . .67 C2
Northicote Recn Ctr
WV10 . . . . .11 E3
Northicote Sch The WV10 .11 E3
Northland Rd B90 . . . . .106 E1
Northlands Rd B13 . . . . .87 A1
Northleach Ave B14 . . . . . . 104 D2
Northleach Cl B98 . . . . . . .154 B5
North Leamington Com Sch
& Arts Coll CV32 . . . . . . .156 F4
North Leamington Com Sch
& Arts Coll (Sixth Form)
CV32 . . . . .156 F2
Northleigh Rd B8 . . . . .68 A6
Northmead B33 . . . . .69 A2
Northolt Dr B35 . . . . .58 A4
Northolt Gr B42 . . . . .43 F1
North Oval DY3 . . . . .50 E5
Northover Cl WV9 . . . . .11 A2
North Park Rd B23 . . . . .56 B3
North Pathway B17 . . . . . . .85 B7
North Rd
Birmingham,Edgbaston
B29 .85 F3
Birmingham,Handsworth
B20 .55 E2
Birmingham,Harborne B17 . .85 D6
Bromsgrove B60 . . . . 137 A2
Tipton DY4 . . . . .52 B8
Wolverhampton,Dunstall Hill
WV1 . . . . .25 C4
Wolverhampton,Parkfield
WV4 . . . . .39 F5
North Roundhay B33 . . . . . .69 A4
Northside Cl B98 . . . . .158 E7
Northside Dr B74 . . . . .44 F8
North Springfield DY3 . . . .39 E1
North St
Brierley Hill DY5 . . . . .61 C2
Cannock WS11 . . . . .4 E6
Coventry CV2 . . . . .114 B5
Dudley DY2 . . . . .51 D1
Nuneaton CV10 . . . . .72 F3
North Street Ind Est DY5 . .61 C2
North St
Smethwick B67 . . . . .64 F5
Walsall WS2,WS4 . . . . .28 E3
Wednesbury WS10 . . . . .41 F3
Wolverhampton WV1 . . . . . .163 B3
Northumberland Ave
Kidderminster DY11 . . . . . 116 D3
Nuneaton CV10 . . . . .72 F3
Northumberland Cl B78 . . .21 A1
Northumberland Lodge
CV32 . . . . .156 F3
Northumberland Mews
CV32 . . . . .156 F3
Northumberland Pk
CV32 . . . . .156 F3
Northumberland Rd
Coventry CV1 . . . . 113 A3
Royal Leamington Spa
CV32 . . . . .156 E2
Northumberland St B7 . . . .67 A3
Northvale Cl CV8 . . . . .148 B6
North View CV2 . . . . .97 A1
North View Dr DY5 . . . . .61 E5
North Villiers St CV32 . . . 157 A1
North Walsall Prim Sch
WS2 .28 E4
North Warwickshire &
Hinckley Coll LE10 . . . . . .71 E1
North Warwickshire &
Hinkley Coll
Hinckley LE10 . . . . .75 F8
Nuneaton CV11 . . . . .73 E6
North Warwick St 1 B9 . .67 D1
Northway
Birmingham B40 . . . . .90 F5
Sedgley DY3 . . . . .39 C2
Whitnash CV31 . . . . 162 A5
North Western Arc B2 . . 164 C3
North Western Rd B66 . . . .65 A6
North Western Terr B18 . . .65 F7
Northwick Cres B91 . . . . . .107 B1
North Wlk B31 . . . . 103 C1
Northwood Ct 9 DY5 . . . . .61 D2
Northwood Park Cl WV10 .11 E3
Northwood Park Prim Sch
WV10 . . . . .11 E1
Northwood Park Rd WV10 11 E3
Northwood St B3 . . . . 164 A4
Northwood Way DY5 . . . . . .81 B8
Northycote Farm & Ctry Pk*
WV10 . . . . .11 F3
Northycote La WV10 . . . . . .11 F4
Norton Canes High Sch
WS11 . . . . .6 A7
Norton Canes Prim Sch
WS11 . . . . .6 A6
Norton Cl
Birmingham B31 . . . . 103 A3
Redditch B98 . . . . .154 F2
Smethwick B66 . . . . .65 C5
Tamworth B79 . . . . .21 C7
Wolverhampton WV4 . . . . . . .38 C3
Norton Cres
Bilston WV14 . . . . .40 D1
Birmingham B9 . . . . .68 B3
Dudley DY2 . . . . .62 E3
Norton Dr
Warwick CV34 . . . . .155 E2
Wythall B47 . . . . 125 C4
Norton East Rd WS11 . . . . . .6 B6
Norton Gate B38 . . . . .103 F1
Norton Grange CV5 . . . . . . 112 C6
Norton Grange Cres WS11 . .5 F4
Norton Grange WS11 . . . . . . .5 F4
Norton Green La
Dorridge B93 . . . . 128 C2
Norton Canes WS11 . . . . .5 F4
Norton Hall La WS11 . . . . . . .5 D4
Norton Hill Dr CV2 . . . . . . .114 E6
Norton La
Burntwood WS7 . . . . .7 C6
Great Wyrley WS6 . . . . .5 A4
Norton Lakeside Sta*
WS11 . . . . .6 C6
Norton La
Norton Canes WS12 . . . . .5 B7
Tidbury Green B47,B90,
B94 . . . . .125 E3
Norton Mews B61 . . . . 137 A4
Norton Rd
Coleshill B46 . . . . .70 F8
Norton Rd *continued*
Kidderminster DY10 . . . . . .117 B6
Norton Canes WS11,WS12 . . .5 F8
Stourbridge DY8 . . . . .80 E2
Walsall WS3 . . . . .15 A5
Norton Springs WS11 . . . . . .5 F5
Norton St
Birmingham B18 . . . . .66 A6
Coventry CV1 . . . . 165 C3
Norton Terr
Birmingham B30 . . . . .104 B6
Norton Canes WS11 . . . . .5 F6
Norton Twr B1 . . . . .66 C2
Norton View B14 . . . . 104 D7
Norton Wlk B23 . . . . .56 C3
Nortune Cl B38 . . . . 103 D2
Norwich Cl
Lichfield WS13 . . . . .3 C3
Nuneaton CV11 . . . . .74 A8
Norwich Croft B37 . . . . .69 F1
Norwich Dr
Birmingham B17 . . . . .84 F8
Coventry CV3 . . . . .133 B5
Norwich Rd
Dudley DY2 . . . . .62 D2
Walsall WS2 . . . . .28 B1
Norwood Ave B64 . . . . .82 E7
Norwood Cl LE10 . . . . .71 E3
Norwood Gr
Birmingham B19 . . . . .66 B7
Coventry CV2 . . . . .96 E2
Norwood Ho 13 CV32 . . . .156 F2
Norwood Rd
Birmingham B9 . . . . .67 E2
Brierley Hill DY5 . . . . .61 C3
Norwood Villas B16 . . . . . . .65 F1
Nottingham Dr WV12 . . . . .27 C7
Nottingham New Rd WS2 .28 A5
Nottingham Way DY5 . . . . .61 F2
Nova Croft CV5 . . . . 111 C4
Nova Ct B43 . . . . .44 B1
Nova Lodge CV32 . . . . .156 E3
Nova Scotia St B4 . . . . . . 164 D3
Nowell St WS10 . . . . .41 E5
Nuffield Ho B36 . . . . .70 A8
Nuffield Hospl WV6 . . . . . . .24 C4
Nuffield Rd
Coventry CV6 . . . . 114 A7
Hinckley LE10 . . . . .74 E7
Nugent Cl B6 . . . . .66 E7
Nugent Gr B90 . . . . 126 D3
Nuneaton Borough Football
Club CV11 . . . . .73 A4
Nuneaton Mus & Art Gal*
CV11 . . . . .73 C3
Nuneaton Rd
Bedworth CV12 . . . . .78 B4
Bulkington CV12 . . . . .79 B4
Nuneaton CV10 . . . . .72 D8
Nuneaton Trent Valley Sta
CV11 . . . . .73 C5
Nunts La CV6 . . . . .95 B3
Nunts Park Ave CV6 . . . . . .95 B4
Nursery Ave
Aldridge WS9 . . . . .30 B5
Birmingham B12 . . . . .86 F5
Nursery Cl
Birmingham B30 . . . . .103 F5
Kidderminster DY11 . . . . . .116 B8
West Hagley DY9 . . . . .99 A4
Nursery Dr B30 . . . . .103 F5
Nursery Gdns
Solihull B90 . . . . .125 E8
Stourbridge DY8 . . . . .60 F1
Nursery Gr DY11 . . . . .116 B8
Nursery La
Hopwas B78 . . . . .20 B6
Sutton Coldfield B74 . . . . . . .32 A2
Whitnash CV31 . . . . 162 A5
Nursery Rd
Birmingham,Cotteridge
B30 . . . . .103 E5
Birmingham,Harborne B15 . .85 D7
Birmingham,Lozells B19 . . . .66 C6
Walsall WS3 . . . . .28 B7
Nursery St WV1 . . . . .163 B4
Nursery View Cl WS9 . . . . . .30 E2
Nursery Wlk WV6 . . . . .24 D4
Nurton Bank WV6 . . . . .23 A3
Nutbrook Ave CV4 . . . . . . .111 E2
Nutbush Dr B31 . . . . 102 D6
Nutfield Wlk B32 . . . . .84 F5
Nutgrove Cl B14 . . . . .104 F7
Nuthatch Dr DY5 . . . . .81 C7
Nuthurst Dr WS11 . . . . .4 F4
Nuthurst Grange Rd B94 143 C4
Nuthurst Gr
Birmingham B14 . . . . .104 F2
Dorridge B93 . . . . 128 A4
Nuthurst Rd
Birmingham B31 . . . . .122 F6
Kemps Green B94 . . . . 143 A2
Nuthurst B75 . . . . .47 B4
Nutley Dr DY4 . . . . .52 D8
Nutmeg Gr WS1 . . . . .29 A2
Nuttall Gr B21 . . . . .65 C7
Nutt's La LE10 . . . . .75 A7
Nymet B77 . . . . .35 E8

O

Oakalls Ave B60 . . . . .137 B2
Oak Apple Rd B61 . . . . .137 B8
Oak Ave
Birmingham B12 . . . . .87 A5
Great Wyrley WS6 . . . . .5 A1
Huntington WS12 . . . . .1 D8
Oak Ave *continued*
Walsall WS2 . . . . .27 E3
West Bromwich B70 . . . . .53 B3
Oak Bank B18 . . . . .66 A6
Oak Barn Rd B62 . . . . .83 E8
Oak Cl
Baginton CV8 . . . . .133 F2
Bedworth CV12 . . . . .78 C4
Birmingham B17 . . . . .85 A6
Hinckley LE10 . . . . .75 E5
Wednesbury DY4 . . . . .41 A1
Oak Cottage Prim Sch
B91 .106 F6
Oak Cotts B14 . . . . 105 C2
Oak Cres
Oldbury B69 . . . . .52 B1
Walsall WS3 . . . . .28 D6
Oak Croft B37 . . . . .69 E3
Oakcroft Rd B13 . . . . 105 C7
Oak Ct
Coventry CV3 . . . . .133 F7
Halesowen B63 . . . . .82 F2
Oldbury B66 . . . . .64 C8
Royal Leamington Spa
CV34 . . . . .161 E2
Stourbridge DY8 . . . . .81 A4
Sutton Coldfield B74 . . . . . . .31 E5
Walsall WS5 . . . . .43 A4
Oakdale Cl
Brierley Hill DY5 . . . . .61 A7
Oldbury B68 . . . . .64 A2
Oakdale Rd
Binley Woods CV3 . . . . 135 C7
Birmingham B36 . . . . .68 E7
Oldbury B68 . . . . .64 A2
Oakdale B74 . . . . .31 A1
Oakdale Trad Est DY6 . . . . .49 E1
Oakdene Cl WS6 . . . . .4 D2
Oakdene Cres CV10 . . . . . . .73 D7
Oakdene Dr B45 . . . . 138 C8
Oakdene Rd WS7 . . . . .7 A6
Oakden Pl DY11 . . . . 116 C7
Oak Dr
Birmingham B23 . . . . .56 C7
Hartshill CV10 . . . . .72 A8
Mile Oak B78 . . . . .20 C1
Oaken Dr
Solihull B91 . . . . .106 F5
Willenhall WV12 . . . . .27 E7
Oakenfield WS13 . . . . .3 A2
Oaken Gdns WS7 . . . . .7 A8
Oaken Grange WS6 . . . . .4 F1
Oakenhayes Cres
Brownhills WS8 . . . . .6 F1
Minworth B76 . . . . .58 C5
Oakenhayes Dr WS8 . . . . . . .6 F1
Oaken Pk WV8 . . . . .10 A2
Oakenshaw Rd
Redditch B98 . . . . 154 A1
Solihull B90 . . . . 106 D1
Oakeswell St WS10 . . . . . . .42 A3
Oakey Cl CV6 . . . . .95 F4
Oakeywell St DY2 . . . . .51 D1
Oak Farm Cl B76 . . . . .58 A7
Oak Farm Craft Ctr* B78 .34 B5
Oak Farm Rd B30 . . . . .103 E5
Oakfield Ave
9 Birmingham,Balsall Heath
B12 .87 A6
Birmingham,Sparkbrook
B11 .87 C6
Dudley DY1 . . . . .51 B6
Kingswinford DY6 . . . . .60 E5
Oakfield Cl
Smethwick B66 . . . . .65 C6
Stourbridge DY8 . . . . .60 F1
Oakfield Ct 6 DY5 . . . . .61 D2
Oakfield Dr
Birmingham B45 . . . . 122 D4
Walsall WS3 . . . . .15 B5
Oakfield Ho
12 Royal Leamington Spa
CV32 . . . . .156 F2
Coventry CV3 . . . . 115 A1
Oakfield Rd
Birmingham,Balsall Heath
B12 .86 E5
Birmingham,Erdington B24 . .56 F3
Birmingham,Selly Oak B29 . .86 B3
Codsall WV8 . . . . .10 C2
Coventry CV6 . . . . .112 F5
Kidderminster DY11 . . . . . .116 B5
Smethwick B66 . . . . .65 C6
Stourbridge DY8 . . . . .61 A1
Stourbridge,Wollescote DY9 .81 F2
Oakfields Way B91 . . . . . . .108 B5
Oakford Dr CV5 . . . . .111 F6
Oak Gn
Dudley DY1 . . . . .51 A5
Wolverhampton WV6 . . . . . . .24 B3
Oak Gr B31 . . . . .102 E1
Oak Green Way B68 . . . . . . .64 A4
Oak Gr
Kidderminster DY10 . . . . . 117 A5
Wolverhampton WV11 . . . . . .26 B7
Oakhall Dr B93 . . . . .127 F4
Oakham Ave DY2 . . . . .62 E7
Oakham Cl B98 . . . . 159 A5
Oakham Cres
Bulkington CV12 . . . . .79 D2
Dudley DY2 . . . . .62 E7
Oakham Ct 9 DY2 . . . . .62 E8
Oakham Dr DY2 . . . . .62 F8
Oakham Prim Sch B69 . . . .63 B7

Oakham Rd
Birmingham B17 . . . 85 B7
Dudley DY2 . . . 62 F7
Oldbury B69 . . . 63 A7
Oakham Way B92 . . . 89 A1
Oakhill Ave DY10 . . . 116 E4
Oakhill Cl B17 . . . 85 B8
Oakhill Cres B27 . . . 106 B8
Oak Hill Dr B15 . . . 85 E7
Oakhill Dr DY5 . . . 81 B7
Oak Hill Fst Sch B98 . . . 154 A2
Oakhill Prim Sch B77 . . . 21 F2
Oakhill Rd WS11 . . . 1 F2
Oak Hill WV3 . . . 24 C1
Oak Ho
7 Warwick CV34 . . . 161 D8
Great Wyrley WS6 . . . 5 A1
Sutton Coldfield B74 . . . 31 B5
Oak House Mus* B70 . . . 53 B2
Oakhurst Ct B72 . . . 57 C8
Oakhurst Dr B60 . . . 137 A3
Oakhurst WS14 . . . 9 C7
Oakhurst Rd
Birmingham B27 . . . 106 B8
Sutton Coldfield B72 . . . 57 C8
Oak Ind Pk The DY6 . . . 49 E1
Oakington Dr B35 . . . 58 A3
Oak La
Barston B92 . . . 109 B2
Harvest Hill CV5 . . . 93 E1
Kingswinford DY6 . . . 50 A1
Oakland Cl B91 . . . 107 E4
Oakland Ct B79 . . . 21 A5
Oakland Dr DY3 . . . 50 B2
Oakland Gr B61 . . . 137 B4
Oakland Ho B74 . . . 32 A4
Oakland Rd
Birmingham,Handsworth B21 . . . 65 E8
Birmingham,Moseley B13 . . . 87 A3
Walsall WS3 . . . 28 E7
Oaklands Ave B17 . . . 85 B5
Oaklands
Birmingham B62 . . . 84 A4
Birmingham,Moseley B13 . . . 87 A3
Birmingham,Northfield B31 . . . 102 F4
Oaklands Cl WS12 . . . 1 C6
Oaklands Croft B76 . . . 58 B7
Oaklands Ct
Bromsgrove B61 . . . 150 D6
Kenilworth CV8 . . . 148 A2
Oaklands B76 . . . 59 B6
Oaklands Dr B20 . . . 54 F2
Oaklands Gn WV14 . . . 40 D8
Oaklands Ind Est WS12 . . . 2 B3
Oaklands Prim Sch The B27 . . . 88 C2
Oaklands Rd
Sutton Coldfield B74 . . . 46 B8
Wolverhampton WV3 . . . 39 B8
Oaklands The
Birmingham B37 . . . 90 A7
Coventry CV4 . . . 112 A2
Halesowen B62 . . . 83 F6
Kidderminster DY10 . . . 117 A7
Oaklands Way
Birmingham B31 . . . 102 C1
Walsall WS3 . . . 15 B3
Oaklands WV3 . . . 39 B8
Oak La B70 . . . 53 B3
Oaklea Dr B64 . . . 62 F2
Oakleaf Cl B32 . . . 84 C2
Oak Leaf Dr B13 . . . 87 A3
Oak Leasow B32 . . . 84 B4
Oakleigh B31 . . . 103 C2
Oakleigh Ct 3 WV3 . . . 25 B2
Oakleigh Dr
Codsall WV8 . . . 10 A3
Sedgley DY3 . . . 50 C7
Oakleigh Rd DY8 . . . 81 B2
Oakleighs DY8 . . . 60 C1
Oakleigh Trad Est WV14 . . . 40 B2
Oakleigh Wlk DY6 . . . 60 E8
Oakley Ave
Aldridge WS9 . . . 30 A5
Tipton DY4 . . . 52 A6
Oakley CV8 . . . 129 F1
Oakley Cl WS13 . . . 3 B2
Oakley Ct
Bedworth CV12 . . . 77 D1
Birmingham B15 . . . 85 E5
Oakley Gr WV4 . . . 38 D5
Oakley Ho
Bromsgrove B60 . . . 137 A1
Smethwick B66 . . . 65 C6
Oakley Rd
Birmingham,Sparkbrook B10 . . . 87 C7
Birmingham,Stirchley B30 . . . 104 B5
Wolverhampton WV4 . . . 38 D5
Oak Leys WV3 . . . 24 C1
Oakley Wood Dr B91 . . . 107 E4
Oakley Wood Rd CV33 . . . 161 F1
Oakly Rd B97 . . . 153 D3
Oakmeadow Ave B24 . . . 57 D3
Oakmeadow Cl
Birmingham,Acock's Green B26, B27 . . . 88 D4
Birmingham,Tile Cross B33 . . . 69 D3
Oak Meadow Jun & Inf Sch WV11 . . . 27 A7
Oakmeadow Way B24 . . . 57 D3
Oakmoor Pl WS9 . . . 30 F2
Oakmoor Rd CV6 . . . 96 A4
Oakmount Cl WS3 . . . 14 F3
Oakmount Rd B74 . . . 45 A7
Oak Park Ct
5 Sutton Coldfield B74 . . . 31 E3
Stourbridge DY8 . . . 60 F1
Oak Park Rd DY8 . . . 60 F1
Oak Rd
Birmingham B68 . . . 84 C7
Brownhills WS9 . . . 16 A3
Catshill B61 . . . 137 B8
Dudley DY1 . . . 51 C3
Tipton DY4 . . . 51 E6
Walsall,Pelsall Wood WS3 . . . 14 F5
Walsall WS4 . . . 15 C1
West Bromwich B70 . . . 53 B2
Willenhall WV13 . . . 26 E2
Oakridge Cl
Redditch B98 . . . 154 C7
Willenhall WV12 . . . 27 C4
Oakridge Dr
Cheslyn Hay WS6 . . . 4 E2
Willenhall WV12 . . . 27 C4
Oakridge Rd
Birmingham B31 . . . 103 D2
Royal Leamington Spa CV32 . . . 157 C4
Oak Rise B46 . . . 70 F5
Oakroyd Cres CV10 . . . 72 D7
Oaks Cres WV3 . . . 25 A1
Oaks Dr
Cannock WS11 . . . 1 C1
Featherstone WV10 . . . 11 F8
Wolverhampton WV3 . . . 25 B2
Wombourne WV5 . . . 49 A5
Oakslade Dr B92 . . . 107 E8
Oaks Pl CV6 . . . 96 A3
Oaks Prec CV8 . . . 147 E3
Oaks Prim Sch The B14 . . . 104 D2
Oaks Rd CV8 . . . 147 E2
Oak St
Brierley Hill DY5 . . . 61 F1
Cradley Heath B64 . . . 62 D1
Dudley,Darby End DY2 . . . 62 E4
Dudley,West Coseley DY1, WV14 . . . 51 B7
Oaks The
Bedworth CV12 . . . 77 F2
Birmingham B34 . . . 69 B7
Birmingham,Hawkesley B38 . . . 123 F7
Portway B47 . . . 140 F8
Redditch B98 . . . 158 F7
Royal Leamington Spa CV32 . . . 161 D8
Smethwick B67 . . . 64 F5
Sutton Coldfield B76 . . . 47 A3
Walsall WS3 . . . 14 A1
Wolverhampton,Merridale WV3 . . . 25 A2
Wolverhampton WV11 . . . 26 B5
Oak St DY6 . . . 60 D6
Oakstreet Ent Ctr B64 . . . 62 D1
Oak Street Trad Est DY5 . . . 61 F1
Oak St WV3 . . . 25 A1
Oakthorpe Dr B37 . . . 69 F5
Oakthorpe Gdns B69 . . . 52 A2
Oak Tree Ave
Coventry CV3 . . . 133 A6
Redditch B97 . . . 153 B4
Oaktree Cl B48 . . . 139 A7
Oak Tree Cl
Bentley Heath B93 . . . 127 E4
Royal Leamington Spa CV32 . . . 157 A2
Oak Tree Cres B62 . . . 83 F6
Oak Tree Ct
Birmingham B28 . . . 106 A5
Royal Leamington Spa CV32 . . . 157 A2
Oaktree Farm Mobile Homes Pk B94 . . . 141 B7
Oak Tree Gdns
2 Stourbridge DY8 . . . 61 A1
Birmingham B28 . . . 105 E3
Oak Tree Ho B30 . . . 103 E7
Oak Tree La
Birmingham B29 . . . 85 E1
Hollywood B47 . . . 125 B6
Sambourne B96 . . . 159 B2
Oak Tree Pk B98 . . . 154 F6
Oak Tree Rd
Birmingham B8 . . . 67 D6
Coventry CV3 . . . 135 A7
Oaktree Rd WS10 . . . 42 B3
Oak Trees B47 . . . 125 A7
Oak Tree Wlk B79 . . . 20 F7
Oak View WS2 . . . 27 E3
Oak Way
Coventry CV4 . . . 111 D2
Sutton Coldfield B76 . . . 46 F2
Oak Wlk The B31 . . . 103 A1
Oakwood Cl
Brownhills WS9 . . . 15 E4
Essington WV11 . . . 13 B3
Shenstone WS14 . . . 18 A6
Oakwood Cres DY2 . . . 61 F6
Oakwood Croft B91 . . . 107 C1
Oakwood Ct B63 . . . 83 A4
Oakwood Dr
Birmingham B14 . . . 104 D4
Sutton Coldfield B74 . . . 44 E8
Oakwood Gr CV34 . . . 156 A1
Oakwood Rd
Birmingham B11 . . . 87 C3
Hollywood B47 . . . 125 A6
Smethwick B67 . . . 64 F4
Sutton Coldfield B73 . . . 45 E1
Walsall WS3 . . . 28 E7
Oakwoods WS11 . . . 4 D8
Oakwood Specl Sch WS9 . . . 16 A3
Oakwood St B70 . . . 53 B5
Oakworth Cl CV2 . . . 114 F8
Oasis The DY9 . . . 98 F5
Oast Ho B8 . . . 68 D4
Oasthouse Cl
Kingswinford DY6 . . . 60 A7
Stoke Heath B60 . . . 150 D6
Oaston Rd
Birmingham B36 . . . 69 D8
Nuneaton CV11 . . . 73 D4
Oatfield Cl WS7 . . . 7 A4
Oatlands Cl CV6 . . . 95 C4
Oatlands Way WV6 . . . 23 D3
Oatlands Wlk 3 B14 . . . 104 C2
Oatmill Cl WS10 . . . 41 E5
Oban Dr CV10 . . . 73 A2
Oban Rd
Coventry CV6 . . . 95 F5
Hinckley LE10 . . . 75 A7
Solihull B92 . . . 88 F1
Oberon Cl
Birmingham B45 . . . 102 A2
Nuneaton CV11 . . . 74 A1
Royal Leamington Spa CV34 . . . 161 E4
Oberon Dr B90 . . . 106 B1
Occupation Rd
Brownhills WS8 . . . 16 A4
Coventry CV2 . . . 114 C3
Occupation St DY1 . . . 51 A2
Ocean Dr WS10 . . . 41 E1
Ockam Croft B31 . . . 103 C2
Ocker Hill Inf Sch DY4 . . . 52 C8
Ocker Hill Jun Sch DY4 . . . 41 C1
Ocker Hill Rd DY4 . . . 52 C8
O'Connor Dr DY4 . . . 41 C1
Oddicombe Croft CV3 . . . 133 D5
Oddingley Ct B23 . . . 56 C3
Oddingley Rd B31 . . . 103 C2
Odell Cres WS3 . . . 28 C7
Odell Pl B5 . . . 86 C5
Odell Rd WS3 . . . 28 B7
Odell Way WS3 . . . 28 B7
Odensil Gn B92 . . . 89 B2
Odiham Cl B79 . . . 21 C7
Odin Cl WS11 . . . 2 A5
Odnall La DY9 . . . 99 F3
Odstone Dr LE10 . . . 74 F8
Offadrive B79 . . . 21 B5
Offa Dr CV8 . . . 148 A4
Offa Rd CV31 . . . 162 B5
Offa's Dr WV6 . . . 23 E5
Offa St B79 . . . 21 B5
Offchurch La CV31 . . . 162 F6
Offchurch Rd CV32 . . . 157 E4
Offenham Cl B98 . . . 154 B6
Offenham Covert B38 . . . 123 E8
Offini Cl B70 . . . 53 F2
Offmoor Rd B32 . . . 102 B8
Offmore Ct DY10 . . . 117 C6
Offmore Farm Cl DY10 . . . 117 C6
Offmore Fst Sch The DY10 . . . 117 B6
Offmore La DY10 . . . 117 A6
Offmore Rd DY10 . . . 116 F6
Offwell Rd B98 . . . 154 D1
Ogbury Cl B14 . . . 104 C2
Ogley Cres WS8 . . . 16 A7
Ogley Dr B75 . . . 47 A5
Ogley Hay Rd
Burntwood,Gorstey Ley WS7 . . . 7 B8
Burntwood,Triangle WS7, WS8 . . . 7 A3
Ogley Rd WS8 . . . 16 A7
Ogley Vale WS7 . . . 7 B8
O'Hare Ho WS4 . . . 28 F3
O'keeffe Cl B11 . . . 87 B6
Okeford Way CV10 . . . 73 A1
Okehampton Dr B71 . . . 53 C6
Okehampton Rd CV3 . . . 133 E5
Okement Dr WV11 . . . 26 C5
Oken Ct CV34 . . . 160 D7
Oken Rd CV34 . . . 160 D8
Olaf Pl CV2 . . . 115 A7
Old Abbey Gdns B17 . . . 85 D4
Oldacre Cl B76 . . . 57 D6
Old Acre Dr B21 . . . 65 E7
Oldacre Rd B68 . . . 84 A7
Oldany Way CV10 . . . 72 F2
Old Bakery Ct DY9 . . . 99 A5
Old Bank Pl B72 . . . 46 C5
Old Bank Top B31 . . . 103 B2
Old Barn Rd
Birmingham B30 . . . 103 D6
Stourbridge DY8 . . . 61 A1
Old Beeches B23 . . . 56 C8
Old Bell Rd B23 . . . 57 B6
Oldberrow Cl 4 B90 . . . 127 A6
Old Birchills WS2 . . . 28 C3
Old Birmingham Rd
Alvechurch B48 . . . 139 B8
Catshill B60 . . . 137 C8
Lower Marlbrook B60,B45 . . . 121 E1
Old Bridge St B19 . . . 66 C6
Old Bridge Wlk B65 . . . 62 F5
Old Bromford La B8 . . . 68 C6
Old Brookside B33 . . . 68 E2
Old Budbrooke Rd CV35 . . . 160 A8
Oldbury Bsns Ctr B68 . . . 64 A2
Oldbury Cl B98 . . . 154 B6
Oldbury Ct B79 . . . 21 B5
Oldbury Green Ret Pk B69 . . . 63 F8
Oldbury Rd
Hartshill CV10 . . . 72 A8
Oldbury Rd *continued*
Rowley Regis B65 . . . 63 D2
Smethwick B66 . . . 64 D7
West Bromwich B70 . . . 52 F2
Oldbury Ringway B69 . . . 63 F8
Oldbury Road Ind Est
Smethwick B66 . . . 64 D7
West Bromwich B70 . . . 52 F2
Oldbury St WS10 . . . 42 B3
Old Bush St DY5 . . . 61 E3
Old Bush Trad Est DY5 . . . 61 E3
Old Camp Hill B12 . . . 87 A8
Old Canal Wlk 1 DY4 . . . 52 B5
Old Castle Gr WS8 . . . 6 F2
Old Chapel Rd B67 . . . 64 F3
Old Chapel Wlk B68 . . . 64 A4
Old Chester Rd S DY10 . . . 116 E2
Old Church CE Prim Sch WS10 . . . 41 C6
Old Church Ct 4 B17 . . . 85 B5
Old Church Gn B33 . . . 68 E2
Old Church Rd
Birmingham B17 . . . 85 B4
Coventry CV6 . . . 96 A1
Water Orton B46 . . . 59 B3
Old Crescent Ct 8 B68 . . . 84 B8
Old Crest Ave B98 . . . 153 E2
Old Croft La
Birmingham B34 . . . 69 C7
Birmingham,Castle Bromwich B36 . . . 69 B7
Old Cross St DY4 . . . 51 E5
Old Crown Cl B32 . . . 84 B1
Old Crown Mews CV2 . . . 96 D5
Old Damson La B92 . . . 90 A2
Old Dickens Heath Rd B90 . . . 126 A5
Old Dominion Wks WV1 . . . 40 A7
Olde Hall La WS6 . . . 4 F3
Olde Hall Rd WV10 . . . 12 C7
Old End La WV14 . . . 51 C7
Old Fallings Cres WV10 . . . 25 F6
Old Fallings La WV10 . . . 25 F8
Old Fallow Ave WS11 . . . 1 E3
Old Fallow Rd WS11 . . . 1 E3
Old Falls Cl WS6 . . . 4 D3
Old Farm Dr WV8 . . . 10 A4
Old Farm Gr B14 . . . 105 D5
Old Farm Mdw WV3 . . . 38 C8
Old Farm Rd B33 . . . 68 E4
Oldfield Dr DY8 . . . 81 A3
Oldfield Rd
Birmingham B12 . . . 87 A6
Coventry CV5 . . . 112 E3
Dudley WV14 . . . 51 A8
Oldfields
Cradley Heath B64 . . . 82 D8
West Hagley DY9 . . . 99 B6
Oldfield Trad Est B64 . . . 82 D8
Old Fire Sta The B17 . . . 85 D6
Old Flour Mills 6 B70 . . . 53 C2
Old Fordrove B76 . . . 46 D3
Old Forest Way B34 . . . 69 B6
Old Forge Bsns Ctr B98 . . . 159 C8
Old Forge Cl WS1 . . . 42 F8
Old Forge Dr B98 . . . 159 C8
Old Forge Trad Est DY9 . . . 81 E6
Old Grange Rd B11 . . . 87 C4
Old Green La CV8 . . . 129 C1
Old Grove Gdns DY9 . . . 81 D3
Old Hall Cl DY8 . . . 81 A8
Old Hall Ct WS9 . . . 44 A5
Old Hall Ind Est WS3 . . . 28 C8
Old Hall La
Norton Canes WS11,WS12 . . . 5 B7
Walsall WS9 . . . 44 B5
Old Hall Sch WS2 . . . 27 E5
Old Hall St WV1 . . . 163 C2
Oldham Ave CV2 . . . 114 E4
Old Ham La DY9 . . . 81 D2
Old Hampton La WV11 . . . 12 C2
Old Hawne La B63 . . . 83 A5
Old Heath Cres WV1 . . . 26 A1
Old Heath Rd WV1 . . . 26 A2
Old Hedging La B77 . . . 35 D5
Old Hednesford Rd WS11 . . . 2 A3
Old High St DY5 . . . 61 F1
Old Hill Prim Sch B64 . . . 62 F1
Old Hill Sta B64 . . . 83 A8
Old Hill WV6 . . . 24 D5
Old Hinckley Rd CV10 . . . 73 D5
Old Hobicus La B68 . . . 64 B5
Old Horns Cres B43,B44 . . . 44 C2
Oldhouse Farm Cl B28 . . . 105 F6
Old House La
Hawkes End CV7 . . . 94 A7
Romsley B62 . . . 101 B1
Oldington Gr B91 . . . 127 B8
Oldington Trad Est DY11 . . . 116 B1
Old Kingsbury Rd B76 . . . 58 C5
Old Know Ct B10 . . . 87 E7
Oldknow Jun Sch B10 . . . 87 E7
Oldknow Rd B10 . . . 87 E7
Old La WV10 . . . 12 C7
Old Landywood La WS6 . . . 13 D7
Old Langley Hall B75 . . . 47 C4
Old La
Rowney Green B48 . . . 140 D4
Walsall WS3 . . . 28 C8
Wolverhampton WV6 . . . 23 F2
Old Level Way DY2 . . . 62 D4
Old Lime Gdns B38 . . . 123 E8
Old Lindens Cl B74 . . . 44 E7
Old Lode La B92 . . . 89 C3
Old London Rd WS14 . . . 9 D1
Old Manor Cl B78 . . . 34 E5
Old Manor Flats WV6 . . . 24 D5
Old Masters Cl WS1 . . . 29 A1
Old Meadow Rd B31 . . . 123 C7
Old Meeting Rd WV14 . . . 51 C8
Old Meeting St B70 . . . 53 B5
Old Meeting Yd 1 CV12 . . . 78 B3
Old Mill Ave CV4 . . . 132 D5
Old Mill Cl B90 . . . 105 D2
Old Mill Gdns
Birmingham B33 . . . 68 E2
Walsall WS4 . . . 15 C2
Old Mill Gr B20 . . . 55 C2
Old Mill House Cl WS4 . . . 15 B1
Old Mill Rd B46 . . . 70 F7
Old Milverton La CV32 . . . 156 E5
Old Milverton CV32 . . . 156 C3
Old Milverton Rd CV32 . . . 156 C2
Old Moat Dr B31 . . . 103 B3
Old Moat Way B8 . . . 68 B6
Oldnall Cl DY9 . . . 81 F4
Oldnall Rd
Kidderminster DY10 . . . 117 A4
Stourbridge B63,DY9 . . . 82 A4
Old Oak Cl WS9 . . . 30 B8
Old Oak Rd B38 . . . 104 A2
Old Oscott Hill B44 . . . 44 F2
Old Oscott La B44 . . . 55 E8
Old Park Cl B6 . . . 66 E7
Old Park La B69 . . . 64 A5
Old Park Prim Sch WS10 . . . 41 E5
Old Park Rd
Darlaston WS10 . . . 41 E5
Dudley DY1 . . . 51 A5
Old Park Special Sch DY1 . . . 61 F8
Old Park Trad Est WS10 . . . 41 E4
Old Park Wlk B6 . . . 66 E7
Old Penkridge Mews WS11 . . . 1 D1
Old Penkridge Rd WS11 . . . 1 C2
Old Penns La B46 . . . 70 F7
Old Penn's Yd 4 CV12 . . . 78 A2
Old Pk B29 . . . 103 A5
Old Pleck Rd WS2 . . . 42 C7
Old Pl WS3 . . . 28 C8
Old Port Cl DY4 . . . 52 B2
Old Portway B38 . . . 123 E7
Old Postway B19 . . . 66 D7
Old Quarry Cl B45 . . . 121 F8
Old Quarry Dr DY3 . . . 50 D5
Old Rd CV7 . . . 92 E1
Old Rectory Gdns WS9 . . . 30 C6
Old Rectory La B48 . . . 139 B7
Old School Cl WV13 . . . 27 A2
Old School Dr 2 B65 . . . 63 C3
Old School Mews CV32 . . . 157 B3
Old School Wlk B79 . . . 21 B6
Old School Yd The B77 . . . 22 A5
Old Scott Cl B33 . . . 69 C2
Old Smithy Pl B18 . . . 66 A5
Old Snow Hill B3 . . . 164 B4
Old Sq B4 . . . 164 C3
Old Sq The 1 WS1 . . . 28 E1
Old Sq CV34 . . . 160 E6
Old Stables Wlk 2 B7 . . . 67 C7
Old Stafford Rd WV10 . . . 11 C8
Old Station Rd
Birmingham B33 . . . 68 D4
Bromsgrove B60 . . . 137 A1
Hampton-in-A B92 . . . 109 A8
Old Stone Cl B45 . . . 101 F1
Old Stone Yd CV32 . . . 156 E1
Old Stowheath La WV1 . . . 26 C1
Old Stratford Rd B60 . . . 137 C2
Oldswinford CE Prim Sch DY8 . . . 81 A3
Old Swinford Hospl DY8 . . . 81 A4
Old Tokengate 2 B17 . . . 85 D6
Old Town Cl B38 . . . 103 F2
Old Town La WS3 . . . 14 F3
Old Union Mill B16 . . . 66 B2
Old Vicarage Cl
Walsall WS3 . . . 15 A2
Wombourne WV5 . . . 49 B7
Old Vicarage Gdns B80 . . . 159 E4
Old Walsall Rd B42 . . . 54 F7
Old Warstone La WV11 . . . 13 B8
Old Warwick Ct 1 B92 . . . 88 E1
Old Warwick Rd
Kingswood B94,CV35 . . . 144 D3
Royal Leamington Spa CV31 . . . 161 E7
Solihull B92 . . . 88 E1
Old Waste La CV7 . . . 130 E6
Oldway Dr B91 . . . 107 E2
Old Well Cl WS4 . . . 29 B7
Old Wharf Rd DY8 . . . 80 F6
Oldwich La E
Balsall Common CV8 . . . 129 D1
Honiley CV8 . . . 145 E8
Oldwich La W B93 . . . 145 C8
Old Winnings Rd CV7 . . . 94 F6
Old Woodyard The DY9 . . . 99 D6
Old Yd The CV2 . . . 114 F7
Olga Dr DY4 . . . 41 B1
Olinthus Ave WV11 . . . 26 E7
Olive Ave
Coventry CV2 . . . 114 D5
Wolverhampton WV4 . . . 39 E5
Olive Dr B62 . . . 83 C8
Olive Hill Prim Sch B62 . . . 83 D7
Olive Hill Rd B62 . . . 83 D8
Olive La B62 . . . 83 D8
Olive Mount B69 . . . 63 D8
Olive Pl B14 . . . 104 E7
Oliver Cl 1 DY2 . . . 62 E8
Oliver Cres WV14 . . . 40 F2
Oliver Ct B65 . . . 63 B2
Oliver Rd
Birmingham,Erdington B23 . . . 56 F6
Birmingham,Ladywood B16 . . . 65 F2

Oliver Rd *continued*
Smethwick B66 . . . . .65 C3
Oliver St
Birmingham B7 . . . . .67 B5
Coventry CV6 . . . . .113 F6
Olivier Way CV2 . . . . .115 B8
Ollerton Rd B26 . . . . .88 F7
Ollison Dr B74 . . . . .30 F2
Olliver Cl B62 . . . . .84 A3
Olorenshaw Rd B26 . . . . . .89 D5
Olton Ave CV5 . . . . .111 E4
Olton Bridge B92 . . . . . . .106 F8
Olton Bvd E B27 . . . . .88 C2
Olton Bvd W B11 . . . . .87 F3
Olton Croft B27 . . . . .88 D2
Olton Mere B92 . . . . .88 E1
Olton Rd B90 . . . . .106 B5
Olton Sta B92 . . . . .88 E1
Olton Wharf B92 . . . . .88 E2
Olympus Ave CV34 . . . . . .161 D5
Olympus Cl CV5 . . . . .111 B8
Olympus Dr DY4 . . . . .52 D6
Omar Rd CV2 . . . . .114 D2
Ombersley Cl
Oldbury B69 . . . . .63 D5
Redditch B98 . . . . .159 C7
Ombersley Rd
Birmingham B12 . . . . .87 A6
Halesowen B63 . . . . .82 D7
Ombersley Way 4 B31 . .103 D2
One Stop Sh Ctr B42 . . . . .55 D3
Onibury Rd B21 . . . . .54 D1
Onley Terr CV4 . . . . .132 C7
Onslow Cres B92 . . . . .89 A1
Onslow Croft CV32 . . . . . .156 F2
Onslow Rd B11 . . . . .88 A4
Ontario Cl B38 . . . . .124 A8
Oozells St N B1 . . . . .66 B2
Oozells Sq B1 . . . . .66 B2
Oozells St B1 . . . . .66 C2
Open Field Cl B31 . . . . . .103 C2
Openfield Croft B46 . . . . . .59 C2
Ophelia Dr CV4 . . . . .161 E3
Orangery The DY9 . . . . . . .99 D7
Oratory Dr CV3 . . . . .134 C6
Oratory RC Prim Sch The
B16 . . . . .65 F2
Orbital Way WS11 . . . . .4 F6
Orchard Ave
Cannock WS11 . . . . .1 C2
Solihull B91 . . . . .107 D5
Orchard Cl
Cheslyn Hay WS6 . . . . .4 E3
Coleshill B46 . . . . .70 F7
Curdworth B76 . . . . .59 B7
Halesowen B63 . . . . .82 C6
Hartshill CV10 . . . . .72 B7
Hinckley LE10 . . . . .76 A5
Rowley Regis B65 . . . . . . .63 A3
Sutton Coldfield B73 . . . . .57 A8
Tamworth B77 . . . . .35 C5
Walsall WS4 . . . . .29 C5
West Hagley DY9 . . . . .99 B4
Willenhall WV13 . . . . .27 B2
Orchard Cres
Coventry CV3 . . . . .133 C8
Stoke Prior B60 . . . . .150 C3
Orchard Croft B45 . . . . . .138 D8
Orchard Ct
Birmingham,Erdington
B23 . . . . .57 A5
Birmingham,Stockland Green
B23 . . . . .56 B4
Coventry CV3 . . . . .115 A1
Kingswinford DY6 . . . . .60 D6
Rowley Regis B65 . . . . . . .63 B3
Orchard Ctr PRU WV3 . . . .25 B1
Orchard Dr
Solihull B91 . . . . .107 E6
Wolverhampton WV3 . . . . . .38 B7
Orchard Dr
Birmingham B31 . . . . . . .122 F7
Coventry CV5 . . . . .111 C4
Orchard Gdns WS12 . . . . . . .1 F6
Orchard Gr
Aldridge WS9 . . . . .30 B4
Dudley DY3 . . . . .50 B3
Sutton Coldfield B74 . . . . .31 F3
Wolverhampton WV4 . . . . .39 A4
Orchard Ho CV6 . . . . .96 A4
Orchard La
Codsall WV8 . . . . .10 B3
Kenilworth CV8 . . . . .148 C3
Orchard Leigh B13 . . . . . . .87 A3
Orchard Meadow Wlk
B35 . . . . .58 B3
Orchard Pl B80 . . . . .159 F8
Orchard Rd
Birmingham B24 . . . . .57 B5
Bromsgrove B61 . . . . .136 F4
Dudley DY2 . . . . .62 C2
Hockley Heath B94 . . . . . .143 C6
Walsall WS5 . . . . .43 B3
Willenhall WV13 . . . . .27 B1
Wolverhampton WV11 . . . . .26 C7
Orchard Ret Pk CV3 . . . . .134 D4
Orchard Rise B26 . . . . .88 F7
Orchard Sch The B67 . . . . .65 A5
Orchard St
Bedworth CV12 . . . . .78 B4
Brierley Hill DY5 . . . . .61 D4
Orchards The
Astwood Bank B96 . . . . . .158 D1
Cheswick Green B90 . . . . .126 D4
Hollywood B47 . . . . .125 A7

Orchards The *continued*
Sutton Coldfield B74 . . . . .46 A8
Orchard St
Hinckley LE10 . . . . .75 E8
Kidderminster DY10 . . . . .116 E6
Nuneaton CV11 . . . . .73 D4
Redditch B98 . . . . .153 E3
Tamworth,Kettlebrook B77 . .21 C3
Tamworth,The Leys B77 . . .21 B5
Tipton DY4 . . . . .51 F2
Orchard The
Bilston WV14 . . . . .40 E5
Birmingham B37 . . . . .89 F8
Bromsgrove B61 . . . . .136 E4
Burntwood WS7 . . . . .7 B7
Oldbury B68 . . . . .64 C4
Walsall WS3 . . . . .14 D2
Wolverhampton WV6 . . . . . .24 E6
Orchard Villas
Fairfield B61 . . . . .120 D2
Wythall B47 . . . . .124 F1
Orchard Way
Birmingham,Acock's Green
B27 . . . . .88 B4
Birmingham,Balsall B12 . . .86 E6
Birmingham,Great Barr B43 . .43 F1
Hollywood B47 . . . . .125 A8
Nuneaton CV10 . . . . .72 C6
Studley B80 . . . . .159 E2
Orcheston Wlk B14 . . . . . .104 D2

Orchid Cl
Bedworth CV12 . . . . .77 E2
Smethwick B66 . . . . .64 D7
Orchid Dr B19 . . . . .66 D6
Ordnance Rd CV6 . . . . . . .113 E5
Oregon Cl DY6 . . . . .60 F6
Oregon Dr WV12 . . . . .27 E7
Orford Gdns WS7 . . . . .6 F8
Orford Gr B21 . . . . .65 C8
Oriel Cl
Cannock WS11 . . . . .4 E8
Dudley DY1 . . . . .50 E2
Oriel Dr WV10 . . . . .11 D3
Oriel Ho B37 . . . . .70 A3
Oriel Villas 4 B11 . . . . . . .87 C5
Oriole Gr DY10 . . . . .117 B2

Orion Cl
Birmingham B8 . . . . .68 B4
Great Wyrley WS6 . . . . .4 F1
Orion Cres CV2 . . . . .96 E2
Orion Way WS11 . . . . .1 F5
Orkney Ave B34 . . . . .68 F7
Orkney Cl
Hinckley LE10 . . . . .71 C1
Nuneaton CV10 . . . . .73 A2
Orkney Croft B36 . . . . .70 B7
Orkney Dr B71 . . . . .35 F7
Orlando Cl WS1 . . . . .42 E8
Orlando Ho 4 WS1 . . . . . .42 E8
Orlescote Rd CV4 . . . . . . .132 E6
Ormande Cl B63 . . . . .82 B7
Orme Cl DY5 . . . . .81 B8
Ormes La WV6 . . . . .24 C3
Ormond Pl WV14 . . . . .40 F6
Ormond Rd B45 . . . . .101 F1
Ormonds Cl WS13 . . . . .3 B1
Ormsby Gr B27 . . . . .106 B7
Ormscliffe Rd B45 . . . . . . .122 B6
Orphanage Rd B24 . . . . . . .57 B6
Orpington Dr CV6 . . . . .95 D4
Orpington Rd B44 . . . . .44 E3
Orpwood Rd B33 . . . . .69 B2
Orsino Cl CV34 . . . . .161 E2
Orslow Wlk WV10 . . . . .26 A5
Orton Ave B76 . . . . .58 A6
Orton Cl B46 . . . . .59 A3
Orton Gr WV4 . . . . .38 D4
Orton La WV4,WV5 . . . . . . .38 D2
Orton Rd CV6 . . . . .95 D4
Orton Way B35 . . . . .58 A1

Orwell Cl
Nuneaton CV10 . . . . .72 A5
Stourbridge DY8 . . . . .80 D4
Wednesfield WV11 . . . . . . .26 F5
Orwell Ct CV1 . . . . .165 C4
Orwell Dr
Birmingham B38 . . . . .123 C8
West Bromwich B71 . . . . . .53 D6
Orwell Pas B5 . . . . .164 C2
Osbaston Cl
Coventry CV5 . . . . .111 E4
Hinckley LE10 . . . . .71 F3
Osberton Dr DY1 . . . . .50 F2
Osborn Ct B73 . . . . .46 B1
Osborne Cl
Birmingham B6 . . . . .67 A7
Brierley Hill DY5 . . . . .81 F8
Kidderminster DY10 . . . . .117 B6
Osborne Ct CV31 . . . . . . .162 A4
Osborne Dr WS10 . . . . .41 D8
Osborne Gr B19 . . . . .66 C7
Osborne Prim Sch B23 . . . .57 A5
Osborne Rd
Birmingham,Erdington
B23 . . . . .56 F5
Birmingham,Handsworth
B21 . . . . .65 F8
Bromsgrove B61 . . . . .137 C1
Coventry CV5 . . . . .133 A8
Osborne Rd S 1 B23 . . . . .56 F4
Osborne Rd
West Bromwich B70 . . . . . .53 C3
Wolverhampton WV4 . . . . . .38 D5
Osborne B79 . . . . .20 D7
Osborne Twr B6 . . . . .67 A8

Osborn Rd B11 . . . . .87 C6
Osbourne Croft B90 . . . . . .126 D5
Osbourne Ho CV1 . . . . . . .165 A2
Oscott Cir WS5 . . . . .55 F3
Oscott Coll B73 . . . . .45 D1
Oscott Gdns B42 . . . . .55 E3
Oscott Rd B6,B42 . . . . .55 E3
Oscott School La B44 . . . . .44 E2
Osier Gr B23 . . . . .56 B6
Osier Pl WV1 . . . . .25 F2
Osier St WV1 . . . . .25 F2
Osler St B16 . . . . .65 F3
Oslo Gdns CV2 . . . . .115 A7
Osmaston Rd
Birmingham B17 . . . . .85 B3
Stourbridge DY8 . . . . .80 F2
Osmington Gr B63 . . . . .82 D6
Osnor Ct B60 . . . . .151 B7
Osprey Cl
Coventry CV2 . . . . .115 B6
Nuneaton CV11 . . . . .79 B8
Osprey Ct WS7 . . . . .7 F8
Osprey Dr DY1 . . . . .50 F1
Osprey Gr B23 . . . . .2 C1
Osprey Ho B80 . . . . .159 D4
Osprey Park Dr DY10 . . . . .117 B3
Osprey Rd
Birmingham,Acock's Green
B27 . . . . .88 D2
Birmingham,Perry Common
B23 . . . . .56 C6
Osprey B77 . . . . .36 A6
Ostler Cl DY6 . . . . .60 B7
Oswald Rd CV32 . . . . .161 D8
Oswald St B69 . . . . .153 E3
Oswestry Cl B97 . . . . .158 C7
Oswestry Ct B11 . . . . .87 B6
Oswin Gr CV2 . . . . .114 C4
Oswin Pl WV3 . . . . .28 F5
Oswin Rd WS3 . . . . .28 F5
Othello Ave CV34 . . . . . . .161 F3
Other Rd B98 . . . . .153 E4
Otley Gr B9 . . . . .68 C3
Ottawa Twr 2 B5 . . . . .86 D7
Otterburn Cl WS12 . . . . .2 E2
Otter Croft B34 . . . . .69 E5
Otters Rest CV31 . . . . .162 C5
Otterstone Cl DY3 . . . . .39 C2
Ottery B77 . . . . .36 B5
Ottile Hild Sch B60 . . . . . .150 E5
Oughton Rd B12 . . . . .87 A7
Oulsnam Ct 15 B13 . . . . . . .87 B2
Oulton Cl DY11 . . . . .116 D8
Oundle Ct 7 B74 . . . . .31 F2
Oundle Rd B44 . . . . .55 F7
Ounsdale Cres WV5 . . . . . . .49 A6
Ounsdale Rd WV5 . . . . .49 A6
Ounty John La B48 . . . . . . .81 A1
Our Lady & Kenelm RC Sch
B63 . . . . .83 A4
Our Lady of Compassion RC
Prim Sch B92 . . . . .106 D7
Our Lady of Fatima RC Prim
Sch B17 . . . . .84 F7
Our Lady of Lourdes RC Prim
Sch B13 . . . . .105 D5
Our Lady of Mount Carmel
RC Fst Sch B97 . . . . . . .153 A2
Our Lady of the Angels RC
Inf Sch CV11 . . . . .73 C3
Our Lady of the Assumption
RC Prim Sch CV4 . . . . . .111 E1
Our Lady Of the Wayside RC
Prim Sch B90 . . . . .126 D8
Our Lady & St Chad's RC Sch
WV10 . . . . .25 F7
Our Lady & St Rose of Lima
RC Prim Sch B29 . . . . . . .85 B1
Our Lady & St Teresa's RC
Prim Sch CV32 . . . . .157 D5
Our Lady's RC Prim Sch
B35 . . . . .69 D2
Outermarch Rd CV6 . . . . . .113 C7
Outfields B13 . . . . .104 E6
Outlands Dr LE10 . . . . .71 B2
Outmore Rd B33 . . . . .69 B1
Outwood Cl B98 . . . . .158 E7
Out Wood Dr B31 . . . . .102 D1
Outwoods The LE10 . . . . . .75 F8
Oval Prim Sch The B33 . . . .68 F2
Oval Rd
Birmingham B24 . . . . .56 E1
Tipton DY4 . . . . .51 F6
Oval The
Dudley DY1 . . . . .61 E8
Smethwick B67 . . . . .64 D2
Wednesbury WS10 . . . . . . .41 F4
Overbare Cl B94 . . . . .142 A1
Overberry Cl CV2 . . . . .96 D2
Overbrook DY3 . . . . .50 C2
Over Brunton Cl B31 . . . . .103 B2
Overbury Cl
Birmingham B31 . . . . . . .103 C3
Halesowen B63 . . . . .83 B2
Overbury Rd B31 . . . . .103 C3
Overdale B96 . . . . .158 E1
Overdale Ave B76 . . . . .57 C3
Overdale Cl B13 . . . . .36 F4
Overdale Dr WS2 . . . . .27 D3
Overdale Rd
Birmingham B32 . . . . .84 E5
Coventry CV5 . . . . .112 C3
Overell Gr CV32 . . . . .156 D2
Overend Rd B63,B64 . . . . . .82 D7
Overend St B70 . . . . .53 D3
Overfield Dr WV14 . . . . . . .40 A3

Overfield Rd
Birmingham B32 . . . . .84 F1
Dudley DY1 . . . . .61 E8
Over Green Dr B37 . . . . . . .69 F5
Overhill Rd WS7 . . . . .7 B5
Overlea Ave B27 . . . . .88 B3
Over Mill Dr B29 . . . . .86 B2
Overmoor Cl B19 . . . . .66 C7
Over Pool Rd B8 . . . . .68 A6
Overseal Rd WV11 . . . . . . .26 E8
Overslade Cres CV6 . . . . . .112 E8
Overslade Rd B91 . . . . . . .106 F2
Oversley Cl B98 . . . . .154 A4
Oversley Rd B76 . . . . .58 A6
Over St CV6 . . . . .114 A8
Overstrand WV9 . . . . .10 F3
Overton Cl B28 . . . . .106 A6
Overton Dr B46 . . . . .59 C3
Overton Gr B27 . . . . .106 C8
Overton La WS7 . . . . .7 C4
Overton Pl
Birmingham B7 . . . . .67 A3
West Bromwich B71 . . . . . .53 D6
Overton Rd B27 . . . . .106 C8
Overtons Cl CV31 . . . . . . .162 F5
Overton Wlk WV4 . . . . .38 C6
Overwood Croft B8 . . . . . . .67 E3
Overwoods Rd B77 . . . . . . .36 A4
Owenford Rd CV6 . . . . . . .113 C7
Owen Pl WV14 . . . . .40 D6
Owen St
Bilston WV14 . . . . .40 D6
Darlaston WV13 . . . . .41 C8
Wolverhampton WV3 . . . . . .39 A8
Owen Road Ind Est WV13 . .27 C1
Owens Croft B38 . . . . .104 A1
Owen St
Darlaston WS10 . . . . .41 D7
Dudley DY2 . . . . .62 E8
Tipton DY4 . . . . .51 E5
Owens Way B64 . . . . .63 A1
Ownall Rd B34 . . . . .69 E6
Oxbarn Ave WV3 . . . . .38 E7
Ox Bow Way DY10 . . . . . . .116 E8
Oxbridge Way B79 . . . . . . .20 E6
Ox Cl CV2 . . . . .114 A6
Oxendon Way CV3 . . . . . . .134 E8
Oxenton Croft B63 . . . . . . .82 D2
Oxford Cl
Birmingham B8 . . . . .68 B5
Great Wyrley WS6 . . . . .4 F3
Nuneaton CV11 . . . . .73 F8
Oxford Ct 8 B29 . . . . . . .103 C7
Oxford Dr
Birmingham B27 . . . . .88 D4
Stourbridge DY8 . . . . .80 F4
Oxford Gn WS11 . . . . .4 F8
Oxford Pl 14 CV32 . . . . . .156 F1
Oxford Rd
Birmingham,Acock's Green
B27 . . . . .88 C3
Birmingham,Moseley B13 . .87 A2
Cannock WS11 . . . . .4 F8
Ryton-on-D CV8 . . . . .134 F1
Smethwick B66 . . . . .65 A7
West Bromwich B70 . . . . . .53 B3
Oxford Row 10 CV32 . . . . .156 F1
Oxford St
Bilston WV14 . . . . .40 E5
Birmingham,Digbeth B5 . . .164 D2
Birmingham,Stirchley B30 . .104 A7
Coventry CV1 . . . . .113 E3
Dudley DY1 . . . . .51 B1
Kidderminster DY10 . . . . .116 E5
Oxford Street Ind Pk
WV14 . . . . .40 F5
Oxford Street Island
WV14 . . . . .40 E5
Oxford St
Royal Leamington Spa
CV32 . . . . .156 F1
Walsall WS2 . . . . .42 C7
Wednesbury WS10 . . . . . . .42 B3
Wolverhampton WV1 . . . . .163 D2
Oxford Terr WS10 . . . . .42 B2
Oxford Trad Est B5 . . . . . .164 D1
Oxford Way DY4 . . . . .51 D5
Oxhayes Cl CV7 . . . . .130 C6
Oxhill Cl B98 . . . . .154 E1
Oxhill Rd
Birmingham B21 . . . . .54 E2
Solihull B90 . . . . .105 C2
Ox Leasow Rd B32 . . . . . . .84 C2
Oxleasow Rd B98 . . . . .154 E4
Oxley Ave WV10 . . . . .25 C6
Oxley Cl
Dudley DY2 . . . . .62 B2
Great Wyrley WS6 . . . . .4 F3
Oxley Dr CV3 . . . . .133 C3
Oxley La B29 . . . . .103 A8
Oxley La WV1 . . . . .163 B4
Oxley Links Rd WV10 . . . . . .25 B8
Oxley Moor Rd WV9,WV10 . .25 C7
Oxley Prim Sch WV10 . . . . .25 C7
Oxleys Rd B75,B76 . . . . . . .47 D3
Oxley St WV1 . . . . .25 C4
Oxlip Cl WS5 . . . . .43 A3
Oxpiece Dr B36 . . . . .68 D8
Oxstall Cl B76 . . . . .58 D5
Ox St DY3 . . . . .50 D5
Oxted Cl WV11 . . . . .26 F5
Oxted Croft B23 . . . . .56 F4
Oxwood La B32 . . . . .101 D4

Pace Cres WV14 . . . . .41 A2
Pacific Ave WS10 . . . . .41 D1
Packenham Dr B76 . . . . . . .57 F8
Packhorse La B38,B47 . . . .124 E6
Packington Ave
Allesley CV5 . . . . .112 B6
Birmingham B34 . . . . .69 D5
Packington Ct B74 . . . . . . .31 E4
Packington La
Little Packington CV7 . . . . .91 C6
Coleshill B46,CV7 . . . . . . .92 B8
Weeford B78 . . . . .19 F5
Packington Pl 6 CV31 . . . .162 A7
Packmores B90 . . . . .126 A5
Packmore St CV34 . . . . . . .160 F8
Packwood Cl
Bentley Heath B93 . . . . . .127 E4
Birmingham B20 . . . . .55 A2
Nuneaton CV11 . . . . .78 F8
Redditch B97 . . . . .152 F1
Royal Leamington Spa
CV31 . . . . .162 C5
Willenhall WV13 . . . . .40 F8
Packwood Cotts B93 . . . . .127 F1
Packwood Ct
1 Birmingham B29 . . . . . . .84 F1
Solihull B91 . . . . .107 C5
Packwood Dr B43 . . . . .43 D1
Packwood Gn CV5 . . . . . . .112 A3
Packwood Ho
Birmingham B15 . . . . .86 C8
Lapworth B94 . . . . .144 A5
Sutton Coldfield B73 . . . . .46 A3
Packwood La B94 . . . . .144 A4
Packwood Mews 5
CV34 . . . . .161 B8
Packwood Rd
Birmingham B26 . . . . .89 B8
Lapworth B94 . . . . .144 A7
Oldbury B69 . . . . .52 A1
Padarn Cl DY3 . . . . .39 C1
Padbury Ho B31 . . . . .102 D5
Padbury WV9 . . . . .11 B3
Paddiford Pl CV10 . . . . .72 C3
Paddington Rd B21 . . . . . . .54 C1
Paddington Wlk WS2 . . . . . .27 F4
Paddock Dr
Birmingham B26 . . . . .89 A7
Dorridge B93 . . . . .128 A2
Paddock La
Aldridge WS9 . . . . .30 A5
Great Wyrley WS6 . . . . .5 A3
Redditch B98 . . . . .158 E7
Walsall WS1 . . . . .28 F1
Paddocks Cl B78 . . . . .22 F1
Paddocks Gn B18 . . . . .66 A4
Paddocks The B47 . . . . . . .124 F6
Paddocks The
Bulkington CV12 . . . . .79 B3
Kenilworth CV8 . . . . .148 B5
Warwick CV34 . . . . .160 F7
Paddock The
Birmingham B31 . . . . .103 C4
Dudley DY3 . . . . .50 E5
Lichfield WS14 . . . . .9 C5
Perton WV6 . . . . .23 D4
Stoke Heath B60 . . . . . . .150 D6
Stourbridge DY9 . . . . .99 C8
Sutton Coldfield B76 . . . . .47 A4
Paddock View WV6 . . . . . . .25 B5
Paddock Way LE10 . . . . . . .74 E6
Paddys Wide Water Est
DY5 . . . . .61 C5
Padgate Cl B35 . . . . .58 B3
Padgets La B98 . . . . .154 D4
Padmore Ct CV31 . . . . . . .162 B6
Padstow Cl CV11 . . . . .73 F5
Padstow Rd
Birmingham B24 . . . . .57 D4
Coventry CV4 . . . . .131 E8
Padstow B77 . . . . .21 F5
Padua Rd B60 . . . . .137 C1
Paganal Dr B70 . . . . .53 E1
Paganel Dr DY1 . . . . .51 A3
Paganel Prim Sch B29 . . . . .85 A2
Paganel Rd B29 . . . . .85 A2
Pageant Ct B12 . . . . .86 E5
Pageant La CV4 . . . . .131 E7
Pages Cl B75 . . . . .46 C5
Pages Ct B43 . . . . .43 E1
Pages La B43 . . . . .43 E1
Paget Cl
Bromsgrove B61 . . . . .136 E2
Dudley DY3 . . . . .51 B8
Lichfield WS13 . . . . .3 B2
Paget Ct CV2 . . . . .96 B3
Paget Ho DY4 . . . . .52 B3
Paget Mews B76 . . . . .46 F2
Paget Prim Sch B24 . . . . . .57 C4
Paget Rd
Birmingham B24 . . . . .57 D4
Wolverhampton WV3,WV6 . .24 F3
Paget St WV1 . . . . .163 A4
Pagham Cl WV9 . . . . .10 F2
Pagnell Gr B13 . . . . .105 C6
Paignton Rd B16 . . . . .65 D3
Pailton Cl CV2 . . . . .96 C2
Pailton Gr B29 . . . . .85 B1
Pailton Rd B90 . . . . .106 B5

Painswick Cl
　Redditch B98.........158 E6
　Walsall WS5.........43 B3
Painswick Rd B28.........105 F7
Paint Cup Row DY2.........62 C2
Painters Cnr [7] B66.........65 C5
Painters Croft WV14.........40 E1
Pakefield Rd B30.........104 C3
Pakenham Cl B76.........57 F8
Pakenham Ho B76.........57 F8
Pakenham Rd B15.........86 C7
Pakenham Village B15.........86 C7
Pake's Croft [3] CV6.........113 A5
Pakfield Wlk B6.........66 F8
Palace Cl B65.........63 D4
Palace Dr B66.........64 D8
Palace Rd B9.........67 E1
Palefield Rd B90.........126 F6
Pale La B17.........84 F8
Palermo Ave CV3.........133 E6
Pale St DY3.........50 E5
Palethorpe Rd DY4.........52 A8
Palfrey Inf Sch WS1.........42 D7
Palfrey Rd DY8.........80 D5
Pallasades Sh Ctr The
　B2.........164 B2
Pallett Dr CV11.........73 F7
Palmcourt Ave B28.........105 E7
Palm Croft DY5.........81 C8
Palmer Cl WV11.........12 F1
Palmer La CV1.........165 B3
Palmer Rd
　Hinckley LE10.........71 B2
　Whitnash CV31.........162 B4
Palmers Cl
　Codsall WV8.........10 C1
　Solihull B90.........106 B5
Palmers Cross Prim Sch
　WV6.........24 D8
Palmers Gr B36.........68 E8
Palmers Rd B8.........154 F5
Palmer St B9.........67 A2
Palmerston Ave B7.........35 E6
Palmerston Ct B77.........35 F6
Palmerston Dr B69.........52 D2
Palmerston Rd
　Birmingham B11.........87 B6
　Coventry CV5.........132 F8
Palmers Way WV8.........10 C1
Palm Tree Ave CV2.........96 C2
Palmvale Croft B26.........89 A6
Palmyra Rd B60.........137 C2
Palomino Pl B16.........65 F2
Pamela Rd B31.........103 A3
Pancras Cl CV2.........96 E1
Pan Croft B36.........68 C7
Pandora Rd CV2.........114 E7
Pangbourne Cl CV11.........73 F8
Pangbourne Rd CV2.........114 C8
Pangfield Pk CV5.........112 C4
Panjab Gdns B67.........64 F6
Pannel Croft B19.........66 D6
Panther Croft B34.........69 D5
Papenham Gn CV4.........132 A8
Paper Mill Cotts B97.........152 E5
Paper Mill End B98.........154 B5
Paper Mill End Ind Est
　B42.........55 D6
Papworth Dr B61.........136 F5
Papyrus Way B36.........57 F1
Parade
　Birmingham B1.........164 A3
　Royal Leamington Spa
　CV32.........161 F8
Parade The
　[6] Hinckley LE10.........75 D8
　Birmingham B37.........70 A5
　Brownhills WS8.........6 E1
　Cradley Heath B64.........82 E8
　Dudley DY1.........51 B2
　Kingswinford DY6.........60 B7
　Nuneaton CV11.........73 C3
　Sutton Coldfield B72.........46 C5
Parade View WS8.........15 E8
Paradise Circus Queensway
　B1,B3.........164 A2
Paradise Ct DY2.........62 D8
Paradise Dr DY2.........62 D8
Paradise Gr WS3.........14 F3
Paradise Ho [4] CV6.........113 F7
Paradise La
　Birmingham B28.........105 E6
　Walsall WS3.........14 F3
　Wolverhampton WV10.........11 E8
Paradise Row B60.........136 F2
Paradise St
　Birmingham B3.........164 B2
　Coventry CV1.........165 C1
　Warwick CV34.........160 F8
Paradise Way CV2.........97 B1
Paradise Works CV6.........113 F7
Paragon Pk CV1.........113 F7
Paragon Way CV6.........96 B8
Parbrook Cl CV4.........131 E8
Parbury B77.........35 D5
Parchments The WS13.........3 B1
Pardington Cl B92.........107 E8
Pargeter Ct [1].........28 C2
Pargeter Rd B67.........64 C6
Pargeter St
　Stourbridge DY8.........80 F4
　Walsall WS2.........28 C3
Par Gn B38.........103 D1

Parish End CV31.........162 C4
Parish Gdns DY9.........81 C1
Parish Hill B61.........120 D1
Parisienne Ho CV5.........112 E2
Park App B23.........56 C2
Park Ave
　[1] Birmingham,Balsall Heath
　B12.........86 F5
　Birmingham,Hockley B18...66 A6
　Birmingham,King's Norton
　B30.........104 A5
　Burntwood WS7.........7 B5
　Coleshill B46.........70 F6
　Coventry CV6.........95 C3
　Norton Canes WS11.........6 A5
　Nuneaton CV11.........73 E3
　Oldbury B68.........64 B3
　Rowley Regis B65.........63 C3
　Smethwick B67.........64 F6
　Solihull B91.........107 D3
　Studley B80.........159 E3
　Tipton DY4.........51 E5
　Willenhall WV13.........26 F2
　Wolverhampton,Goldthorn Park
　WV4.........39 C5
　Wolverhampton WV1.........163 A4
　Wombourne WV5.........49 A5
Park Bldgs DY3.........50 C4
Parkbrook Ind Est [5] DY9.81 F5
Park Butts Ringway
　DY11.........116 D6
Park Cir B6.........66 F7
Park Cl
　Brownhills WS8.........15 F8
　Cheslyn Hay WS6.........4 E3
　Dudley DY1.........51 B7
　Kenilworth CV8.........148 B5
　Oldbury B69.........63 C7
　Solihull B92.........89 D2
　Sutton Coldfield B24.........57 D5
Park Cres
　West Bromwich B71.........53 D4
　Wolverhampton WV1.........163 A3
Park Croft
　Burntwood WS7.........6 C8
　Hollywood B47.........125 A5
Park Ct
　Allesley CV5.........112 B6
　Kidderminster DY11.........116 D5
　Redditch B98.........154 A3
　Rowley Regis B65.........63 C3
　Sutton Coldfield B73.........45 F1
Parkdale Ave WS10.........42 A4
Parkdale Cl B24.........56 F2
Parkdale Dr WS10.........42 A4
Park Dale Ct WV1.........25 A3
Parkdale Dr B31.........123 A7
Park Dale E WV1.........25 A3
Parkdale Rd B26.........89 D6
Parkdale DY3.........50 A3
Park Dale W WV1.........25 A3
Park Dr
　[17] Sutton Coldfield,Four Oaks
　B74.........31 F2
　Royal Leamington Spa
　CV31.........161 E7
　Sutton Coldfield,Streetly
　B74.........31 C4
　Wolverhampton WV4.........39 C5
Park Edge B17.........85 C7
Park End Dr B32.........84 D1
Park End WS14.........9 E7
Parker Ho B14.........104 F3
Parker Paul Ind Est WV2..39 C7
Parker Rd WV11.........12 F1
Parker St
　Birmingham B16.........65 F1
　Walsall WS3.........14 A1
Parkes Ave WV8.........10 B2
Parkes Ct WV4.........160 D7
Parkes Fold WV4.........51 F8
Parkes Hall Rd DY1.........51 A6
Parkes Ho [8] B69.........64 A7
Parkes La
　Dudley DY3.........51 A7
　Tipton DY4.........51 F8
Parkes St
　Brierley Hill DY5.........61 D3
　Smethwick B67.........64 F4
　Warwick CV34.........160 D7
　Willenhall WV13.........27 B1
Parkeston Cres B44.........45 C1
Park Farm Ind Est B98..159 C7
Park Farm Rd
　Birmingham B43.........44 B3
　Tamworth B77.........21 C1
Parkfield Ave B77.........21 C1
Park Meadow Ave WV14..40 C8
Parkfield Chalet Pk WV2..39 D6
Parkfield Cl
　Birmingham,Lee Bank B15..86 C7
　Birmingham,Quinton B62...84 A5
　Redditch B98.........154 B6
　Tamworth B77.........35 C8
Parkfield Colliery WV4...39 F5
Parkfield Cres
　Tamworth B77.........35 C8
　Wolverhampton WV2.........39 E6
Parkfield Ct [1] B46.........70 F7
Parkfield Dr
　Birmingham B36.........58 C1
　Kenilworth CV8.........148 B5
Parkfield Gr WV2.........39 E6
Parkfield High Sch WV4..39 E5
Parkfield Jun & Inf Sch
　B8.........67 D2
Parkfield Prim Sch WV4...39 E6

Parkfield Rd
　Birmingham B8.........67 E4
　Coleshill B46.........70 F6
　Dudley DY2.........62 E6
　Keresley CV7.........95 A6
　Oldbury B68.........64 A3
　Stourbridge DY8.........81 B5
　Wolverhampton WV2,WV4...39 E6
Parkgate Prim Sch CV6...95 B3
Parkgate Rd CV6.........95 C3
Park Gr
　Birmingham B10.........87 D8
　Water Orton B46.........59 C2
Park Hall Cres B36.........69 C8
Parkhall Croft B34.........69 C7
Park Hall Inf Sch WS5....43 C7
Park Hall Jun Sch WS5....43 C7
Park Hall Rd
　Walsall WS5.........43 D6
　Wolverhampton WV4.........39 D5
Park Hall Sch B36.........58 E1
Park Head Cres DY2.........62 B8
Park Head Rd DY2.........62 B8
Park Hill B13.........86 E4
Parkhill Dr CV5.........112 A5
Park Hill Jun Sch CV8...148 B5
Park Hill La
　Allesley CV5.........112 A6
　Coventry CV5.........112 A5
Park Hill Prim Sch
　Birmingham B13.........86 F4
　Coventry CV5.........112 A4
　Wednesbury WS10.........42 C4
Park Hill Rd B17.........85 B6
Parkhill Rd WS7.........7 A8
Park Hill Rd B65.........63 A5
Parkhill Rd B76.........57 F6
Park Hill St DY2.........62 E8
Park Ho
　[1] Smethwick B66.........65 C5
　Essington WV11.........13 A3
　Kidderminster DY11.........116 C3
Parkhouse Ave WV11.........26 B6
Parkhouse Dr B23.........56 B5
Parkhouse Gdns DY3.........50 C4
Park Inn DY4.........52 A4
Park La
　Berkswell CV7.........110 B2
　Birmingham,Aston B6.........66 F7
　Birmingham,Castle Vale
　B35.........58 C4
　Birmingham,Handsworth
　B21.........54 B3
　Fazeley B78.........20 E2
　Great Wyrley WS6.........5 A3
　Halesowen B63.........82 B6
　Harvington DY10.........118 A2
　Kingswinford DY6.........60 E7
　Nuneaton CV11.........73 D3
　Oldbury B69.........63 F6
Parkland Ave DY11.........116 B5
Parkland Cl CV6.........157 C4
Parklands Ave B97.........153 A5
Parklands Cl B97.........153 A5
Parklands Ct B74.........45 F8
Parklands Gdns WS1......43 A8
Parklands Rd
　Bilston WV14.........40 D3
　Darlaston WS10.........41 E5
　Wolverhampton WV1.........26 A1
Parklands The
　Birmingham B23.........56 D6
　Kingswinford DY6.........60 D6
　Stourbridge DY9.........81 D3
　Wolverhampton WV3.........24 D1
Park Lane E WV4.........52 B4
Park Lane Ind Est
　West Bromwich B21.........54 B1
　Wolverhampton WV10.........11 E4
Park Lane Trad Est B69..64 A6
Park La
　Nuneaton CV10.........72 A3
　Oldbury B69.........64 A6
　Shenstone WS14.........18 B4
　Wolverhampton WV10.........25 C6
Park La W DY4.........51 F4
Park Lime Dr WV1.........26 A4
Park Lime Pits Ctry Pk*
　WS4.........29 C4
Park Mall WS1.........28 E2
Park Meadow Ave WV14..40 C8
Park Mews B29.........85 B1
Park Paling The CV3.........133 E7
Park Pl B7.........67 C7
Park Rd
　Bedworth CV12.........78 B2
　Bilston WV14.........40 C5
　Birmingham,Aston B6.........66 F7
　Birmingham,Hockley B18...66 A6
　Birmingham,Moseley B13..86 E4
　Birmingham,Sparkhill B11..87 C3
　Birmingham,Stockland Green
　B23.........56 C2
　Brierley Hill DY5.........81 F8
　Burntwood,Chase Terrace
　WS7.........6 F8
　Cannock WS11.........1 D1
　Coleshill B46.........70 F6
　Coventry CV1.........165 B1
　Darlaston WS10.........41 C6

Park Rd continued
　Dudley,Lower Gornal DY3..50 C4
　Dudley,Netherton DY2.....62 C6
　Dudley,West Coseley DY1..51 B7
Park Rd E WV1.........163 A4
Park Rd
　Featherstone WV10.........12 D8
　Halesowen B63.........82 B5
　Hinckley LE10.........75 E8
　Kenilworth CV8.........148 A6
Park Rd N B6.........67 A7
Park Rd
　Norton Canes WS11.........6 A5
　Oldbury B69.........63 C8
　Royal Leamington Spa
　CV32.........157 A4
Park Rd S B18.........66 B5
Park Rd
　Smethwick B67.........64 F1
　Stourbridge DY8.........80 D5
　Sutton Coldfield B73.........46 B5
　Tamworth B77.........35 C5
　Walsall,Daw End WS4.........29 C5
　Walsall,The Chuckery WS5..43 D8
　Walsall,Wallington Heath
　WS3.........14 B1
　West Hagley DY9.........99 B6
　Willenhall WV13.........26 F3
Park Rd W
　Stourbridge DY8.........80 D5
　Wolverhampton WV1.........25 A3
Park Retreat B66.........65 B5
Park Ridge DY3.........82 B6
Park Ridge Dr B74.........46 A7
Park Rise
　Kidderminster DY11.........116 D5
　Wolverhampton WV3.........24 E2
Parkrose Ind Est B66.........65 B7
Park St Arc [4] WS1.........28 E2
Park St S WV2.........39 C6
Park St B79.........21 A7
Parks Cres WV11.........26 B6
Parkside Ave WV13.........26 E2
Parkside B32.........84 C2
Parkside Cl WS10.........42 B3
Parkside Cl CV1.........165 C2
Parkside Ct LE10.........75 E8
Parkside Ind Est WV1.........25 F1
Parkside La WS11.........1 A2
Parkside Mid Sch B61...137 A3
Parkside Rd
　Birmingham B20.........54 E6
　Halesowen B63.........82 D5
　Redditch B77.........21 E1
Parkside Way
　Birmingham B31.........102 C1
　Sutton Coldfield B74.........31 A1
Park Sq B37.........90 D8
Park St
　Birmingham,Aston B6.........67 A7
　Birmingham,Digbeth B5...164 D2
　Cannock WS11.........4 E6
　Cheslyn Hay WS6.........4 E3
　Coventry CV6.........113 E7
　Cradley Heath B64.........62 E2
　Darlaston WS10.........41 C5
　Kidderminster DY11.........116 D5
　Kingswinford DY6.........60 E8
　Nuneaton CV11.........73 D3
　Oldbury B69.........63 F6
Parkstone Ave B61.........150 D8
Parkstone Cl WS4.........15 C1
Parkstone Rd CV6.........95 F2
Park Street Gdns DY11..116 D6
Park St
　Rowley Regis B65.........63 D1
　Royal Leamington Spa
　CV32.........156 F1
　Stourbridge DY8.........80 F8
　Stourbridge,Lye DY9.........81 F5
　Stourbridge,Stambermill
　DY8.........81 A5
　Tamworth B79.........21 A5
　Tipton DY4.........52 A5
　Walsall WS1.........28 E2
　Wednesbury WS10.........41 F3
　West Bromwich B70.........53 D3
Park Terr
　Birmingham B21.........65 E8
　Darlaston WS10.........41 B6
Park The B97.........152 C7
Park Trad Est B18.........66 A6
Parktree Wlk B24.........57 D4
Park Venture Ctr WS11....4 E6
Park View
　Birmingham,Rotton Park
　B18.........65 C4
　Birmingham,Small Heath
　B10.........87 D7
　Burntwood WS7.........6 E8
Park View CV7.........96 A8
Park View CV3.........114 A2
Parkview CV5.........165 A1
Parkview Cres WS2.........28 A4
Park View Ct WS10.........41 D1
Parkview Ct WV10.........60 B8
Park View Rd WS10.........41 C6
Parkview Dr
　Birmingham B8.........68 A6
　Burntwood WS7.........6 E8
Park View B94.........143 C6
Park View Rd WV14.........40 C8
Park View Rd
　Birmingham B31.........102 F3
　Stourbridge DY9.........81 F8
　Sutton Coldfield B74.........31 D3
Park View Sch B8.........67 F5

Park View B73.........46 A5
Parkview Trad Est B38..103 F3
Park Villas [18] B9.........67 B2
Parkville Ave B17.........85 B3
Parkville Cl CV6.........95 C3
Parkville Highway CV6...95 B3
Park Way B45.........122 B8
Parkway
　Birmingham B8.........68 A5
　Coventry CV2.........115 B8
Parkway Ind Ctr B7.........67 A4
Parkway Rdbt WS10.........41 E1
Parkway Rd B69.........52 A2
Parkway The
　Perton WV6.........23 F4
　Walsall WS4.........29 C8
Park Wlk WS11.........13 A1
Park Wlk
　[4] Redditch B97.........153 E3
　Brierley Hill DY5.........81 F8
Parkwood Cl WS8.........16 A5
Parkwood Croft B43.........44 B1
Parkwood Ct CV8.........148 B5
Parkwood Dr B73.........45 C2
Park Wood La CV4.........131 D7
Parkwood Rd B61.........136 E3
Parkyn St WV2.........163 D1
Parliament St
　Birmingham,Aston B6.........66 F6
　Birmingham,Small Heath
　B10.........87 C8
　West Bromwich B70.........53 D1
Parlows End B38.........123 D7
Parmington Cl B97.........158 B6
Parmiter Ho CV32.........156 F2
Parnell Ave WS13.........9 A6
Parolles Cl CV34.........161 E3
Parr Cl CV34.........161 D6
Parrotts Gr CV2.........96 D5
Parry Rd
　Coventry CV2.........114 C7
　Kidderminster DY11.........116 B3
　Wednesfield WV11.........27 A8
Parsonage Dr
　Birmingham B45.........122 D4
　Halesowen B63.........82 A7
Parsonage St
　Oldbury B69.........64 B7
　West Bromwich B71.........53 D6
Parsons Hill B30.........104 B2
Parsons Ho B38.........64 B2
Parsons Hollow B77.........35 B7
Parson's La LE10.........75 F8
Parson's Nook CV2.........114 A5
Parsons Rd B61.........101 A2
Parsons St DY4.........51 C1
Parson St B77.........35 E7
Parsons Way WS2.........27 F6
Parson's Way B14.........104 D6
Partridge Ave WS10.........41 B6
Partridge Cl
　Birmingham B37.........70 D3
　Cannock WS11.........2 A1
　Huntington WS12.........1 D7
Partridge Croft
　Coventry CV6.........96 A1
　Lichfield WS13.........9 C8
Partridge Ct
　[4] Wednesbury WS10.........41 F3
　Birmingham B4.........164 C4
Partridge Gr DY10.........117 A2
Partridge Ho B97.........153 D2
Partridge La B77.........35 A7
Partridge Mill WS3.........14 E3
Partridge Rd
　Birmingham B26.........69 A1
　Stourbridge DY8.........80 C4
Passey Rd B13.........87 D2
Passfield Ave WS12.........2 C7
Passfield Rd B33.........69 A3
Pastorale Rd B60.........137 C1
Pasture Gate WS11.........1 C2
Pastures The WV6.........23 D4
Pastures Wlk B38.........123 D7
Pasture Way CV34.........160 B4
Patch La B98.........158 F6
Pat Davis Ct DY10.........116 E7
Patent Dr WS10.........41 D3
Patent Shaft Rdbt WS10..41 D3
Paternoster Row
　[4] Kidderminster DY11....116 D6
　Wolverhampton WV1.........163 B3
Paterson Ct B93.........128 C6
Paterson Pl WS8.........16 B3
Pathlow Cres B90.........106 A1
Pathway The B14.........104 C5
Patience Gr CV34.........161 F3
Patios The DY11.........116 F7
Patman Gdns B15.........65 C1
Paton Gr B13.........86 F2
Patricia Ave
　Birmingham B14.........105 C4
　Wolverhampton WV4.........39 D5
Patricia Cl CV4.........111 C1
Patricia Cres DY1.........51 B7
Patricia Dr DY4.........52 A7
Patrick Gregory Rd WV11..26 A7
Patrick Ho [2] WS11.........2 A2
Patrick Rd B26.........88 E7
Patriot Cl WS1.........42 D5
Patshull Ave WV10.........11 B3
Patshull Cl B43.........43 D1
Patshull Gr WV10.........11 B3
Patshull Ho WV6.........24 E5

Patshull Pl **7** B19 . . . . .66 C7
Pattens Rd CV34 . . . . .156 B1
Patterdale Rd
Birmingham B23 . . . . .56 D4
Cannock WS11 . . . . .2 A4
Patterdale Way DY5 . . . . . .81 B8
Patterton Dr B76 . . . . .58 A7
Pattingham Rd WV6 . . . . . . .23 C2
Pattison Coll CV3 . . . . .114 A2
Pattison Gdns B23 . . . . .56 D2
Pattison St WS5 . . . . .42 E5
Paul Byrne Ct B20 . . . . .55 B1
Pauline Ave CV6 . . . . .96 B2
Paul Pursehouse Rd
WV14 . . . . .40 D3
Pauls Coppice WS8 . . . . . . .16 A5
Paul Stacy Ho CV1 . . . . . . .165 D4
Paul St
Dudley WV14 . . . . .40 A1
Wednesbury WS10 . . . . .42 B2
Wolverhampton WV2 . . . . . .163 B2
Pauls Wlk WS13 . . . . .3 A3
Paul Vale DY4 . . . . .52 B5
Pavenham Dr B5 . . . . .86 C4
Pavilion Ave B66 . . . . .64 D3
Pavilion Dr B6 . . . . .55 F3
Pavilion Gdns
Bromsgrove B61 . . . . .136 F5
Dudley DY2 . . . . .62 C2
Pavilions Sh Ctr B4 . . . . . .164 C2
Pavilions The B37 . . . . .90 E8
Pavilion The B77 . . . . .22 B3
Pavilion Way CV5 . . . . .112 F3
Pavillion Cl WV9 . . . . .30 C7
Pavior's Rd WS7 . . . . .6 E4
Paxford Cl B98 . . . . .154 B6
Paxford Way B31 . . . . .102 F6
Paxmead Cl CV6 . . . . .95 A2
Paxton Ave WV6 . . . . .23 E3
Paxton Cl B60 . . . . .137 B1
Paxton Rd
Birmingham B18 . . . . .66 A5
Coventry CV6 . . . . .113 A4
Stourbridge DY9 . . . . .82 A4
Payne Cl CV32 . . . . .157 A2
Paynell Cl CV6 . . . . .95 B2
Payne's La CV1 . . . . .113 F3
Payne St B65 . . . . .63 C1
Payton Cl B69 . . . . .52 E1
Payton Rd B21 . . . . .65 C8
PDH Ind Est
Wednesbury WS10 . . . . .41 C3
Willenhall WV13 . . . . .26 D3
Peace Cl WS6 . . . . .4 E3
Peace Wlk B37 . . . . .70 B1
Peach Ave WS10 . . . . .41 C6
Peachley Cl **8** B63 . . . . . . .83 B3
Peach Ley Rd B29 . . . . .102 F7
Peach Rd WV12 . . . . .27 A6
Peacock Ave
Coventry CV2 . . . . .96 F1
Wednesfield WV11 . . . . .27 A7
Peacock Cl DY4 . . . . .52 B4
Peacock Mews DY10 . . . . . .116 E8
Peacock Rd
Birmingham B13 . . . . .104 F6
Darlaston WS10 . . . . .41 B7
Peacocks Est B64 . . . . .62 C1
Peacocks The CV34 . . . . . .160 B2
Peak Croft B36 . . . . .68 D8
Peak Dr DY3 . . . . .50 E3
Peake Ave CV11 . . . . .73 E7
Peake Cres WS8 . . . . .15 F5
Peake Dr DY4 . . . . .52 B4
Peake Rd WS8 . . . . .16 A5
Peak House Rd B43 . . . . . . .43 E4
Peakman Cl B45 . . . . .122 A6
Peakman St B98 . . . . .153 E4
Peaks La DY9 . . . . .81 B6
Peaks L Ctr B79 . . . . .21 B3
Peal St WS1 . . . . .28 F1
Pearce Cl DY1 . . . . .61 D8
Pearl Gr
3 Birmingham,Rotton Park
B18 . . . . .65 E4
Birmingham,Acock's Green
B27 . . . . .88 B3
Pearl Hyde Com Prim Sch
CV2 . . . . .115 A5
Pearl Hyde Ho **4** CV1 . . .165 C4
Pearman Rd
Birmingham B45 . . . . .101 D1
Smethwick B66 . . . . .65 A3
Pearmans Croft B47 . . . . . .125 A6
Pearsall Dr B69 . . . . .63 E8
Pears Cl CV8 . . . . .147 F5
Pearson Ave CV6 . . . . .96 B2
Pearson Ct WV12 . . . . .27 D4
Pearson St
Brierley Hill DY5 . . . . .61 D3
Cradley Heath B64 . . . . .62 E1
Stourbridge DY9 . . . . .81 F4
West Bromwich B70 . . . . . . .53 B4
Wolverhampton WV2 . . . . . .163 B1
Peart Dr B80 . . . . .159 C4
Pear Tree Ave
Nuneaton CV10 . . . . .72 E6
Tipton DY4 . . . . .51 F5
Peartree Ave WV13 . . . . . . .27 B1
Pear Tree Cl
4 Coventry CV2 . . . . .96 B2
Birmingham,Grove Vale B43 .43 B1
Birmingham,Stechford B33 . .68 D2
Huntington WS12 . . . . .1 C7
Kidderminster DY11 . . . . . .117 B7
Shuttington B79 . . . . .22 E7
Solihull B90 . . . . .105 D2
Pear Tree Cres B90 . . . . . .105 C2

Pear Tree Ct
Birmingham B43 . . . . .54 C8
Rowley Regis B65 . . . . .63 D3
Pear Tree Dr
Birmingham B43 . . . . .43 C1
Rowley Regis B65 . . . . .63 D3
Peartree Dr B91 . . . . .81 A2
Pear Tree Dr B90 . . . . .105 D2
Peartree Ind Est DY7 . . . . . .62 A6
Pear Tree La **1** B4 . . . . .6 C2
Peartree La
Cradley Heath B64 . . . . .62 E1
Dudley DY2 . . . . .62 A6
Pear Tree La
Dudley WV14 . . . . .51 D8
Wolverhampton WV11 . . . . . .26 B8
Pear Tree Rd
Birmingham B34 . . . . .69 C6
Birmingham,Grove Vale B43 .43 B1
Smethwick B67 . . . . .64 E4
Peascroft La WV14 . . . . .40 E6
Peasefield Cl B21 . . . . .65 C8
Pebblebrook Way CV12 . . . .78 C1
Pebble Cl
Stourbridge DY8 . . . . .81 B5
Tamworth B77 . . . . .22 B3
Pebble Island Way CV31 . .162 C5
Pebble Mill Cl WS11 . . . . . . .1 F2
Pebble Mill Dr WS11 . . . . . . .2 A2
Pebble Mill Rd B5 . . . . .86 C4
Pebworth Ave B90 . . . . . . .127 B6
Pebworth Cl
Birmingham B29 . . . . .86 B2
Coventry CV5 . . . . .112 B3
Redditch B98 . . . . .154 C7
Pebworth Gr
Birmingham B33 . . . . .89 C8
Dudley DY1 . . . . .51 B3
Peckham Rd B44 . . . . .45 A2
Peckingham St **2** B63 . . .83 B3
Peckover Cl B65 . . . . .63 C1
Peckstone Cl CV1 . . . . .165 C1
Pedimore La B76 . . . . .58 C7
Pedmore CE Prim Sch
DY9 . . . . .81 C1
Pedmore Cl B98 . . . . .159 B7
Pedmore Court Rd DY8 . . . .81 A3
Pedmore Gr B44 . . . . .44 F2
Pedmore Hall La WV9 . . . . .99 C8
Pedmore La
Hagley DY9 . . . . .99 F8
Stourbridge DY9 . . . . .81 E1
Pedmore Rd
Brierley Hill DY5,DY2 . . . . . .61 F4
Stourbridge DY9 . . . . .81 E3
Pedmore Road Ind Est
DY5 . . . . .61 F4
Pedmore Tech Coll & Com
Sch DY9 . . . . .81 D1
Pedmore Wlk B69 . . . . .63 D5
Peel Cl
Coventry CV6 . . . . .113 E6
Darlaston WS10 . . . . .41 D8
Drayton Bassett B78 . . . . . . .34 E5
Hampton-in-A B92 . . . . .109 B6
Willenhall WV13 . . . . .27 A1
Peel Ct
Cannock WS12 . . . . .1 B8
Tamworth B77 . . . . .35 F6
Peel Dr
Cannock WS12 . . . . .1 B8
Tamworth B77 . . . . .35 F6
Peelers Way B77 . . . . .21 C1
Peel Ho B79 . . . . .21 A4
Peel La CV6 . . . . .113 F5
Peel Rd CV34 . . . . .160 E8
Peel St
Birmingham B18 . . . . .65 E5
Coventry CV6 . . . . .113 E6
Dudley DY2 . . . . .62 E8
Kidderminster DY11 . . . . . .116 D5
Tipton DY4 . . . . .52 A4
West Bromwich B71 . . . . . . .53 C5
Willenhall WV13 . . . . .27 A1
Wolverhampton WV3 . . . . . .163 B2
Peel Way B69 . . . . .52 C1
Peel Wlk **3** B17 . . . . .84 F7
Pegasus Ct
Halesowen B62 . . . . .83 F5
Sutton Coldfield B74 . . . . . . .32 A3
Pegasus Wlk
Birmingham B29 . . . . .85 D1
Tamworth B79 . . . . .20 F7
Pegleg Wlk **2** B14 . . . . . .104 C2
Pegmill Cl CV3 . . . . .133 F8
Pelham Dr DY1 . . . . .51 A2
Pelham Lodge DY10 . . . . . .117 A5
Pelham Rd B8 . . . . .68 B4
Pelham St WV3 . . . . .25 B1
Pelsall La
Walsall,Little Bloxwich
WS3 . . . . .14 D3
Walsall,Shelfield WS4 . . . . . .29 D8
Pelsall Rd WS8 . . . . .15 D7
Pelsall Village Sch WS3 . . . .14 F4
Peltland Trad Ctr B98 . . . . .154 D4
Pemberley Rd B27 . . . . .88 A2
Pemberton Cl B66 . . . . .65 B3
Pemberton Cres WS10 . . . . .42 D5
Pemberton Rd
Dudley WV14 . . . . .40 D1
West Bromwich B70 . . . . . . .53 A6
Pemberton St B18 . . . . .66 B4
Pembridge Cl
Birmingham B32 . . . . .102 A7
Brierley Hill DY5 . . . . .61 F1

Pembridge Cl continued
Redditch B98 . . . . .154 D2
Pembridge Rd B93 . . . . . . .127 E3
Pembroke Ave WV2 . . . . . . .40 A7
Pembroke Cl
1 Warwick CV34 . . . . . . .160 F8
Bedworth CV12 . . . . .77 C1
Tamworth B79 . . . . .20 D6
West Bromwich B71 . . . . . . .42 B1
Willenhall WV12 . . . . .27 B6
Pembroke Croft B28 . . . . . .106 A5
Pembroke Ct **8** CV32 . . . .156 F2
Pembroke Gdns DY8 . . . . . . .60 C2
Pembroke Ho **4** WS3 . . . .28 E5
Pembroke Rd
Birmingham B12 . . . . .87 A4
West Bromwich B71 . . . . . . .42 B1
Pembroke Way
Birmingham,Vauxhall B8 . . . .67 C5
Birmingham,Yardley Wood
B28 . . . . .106 A5
Nuneaton CV11 . . . . .73 D3
West Bromwich B71 . . . . . . .53 B7
Pembrook Rd CV6 . . . . .95 C2
Pembury Ave CV6 . . . . .96 A3
Pembury Cl B74 . . . . .44 F6
Pembury Croft B44 . . . . .45 A1
Penarth Gr CV3 . . . . .134 F7
Pencombe Dr WV4 . . . . .39 D5
Pencraig Cl CV8 . . . . .148 C5
Pencroft Rd B34 . . . . .69 C6
Penda Ct B20 . . . . .66 A8
Penda Gr WV6 . . . . .23 F5
Pendeen Rd B14 . . . . .105 C4
Pendeford Ave WV6 . . . . . . .24 E8
Pendeford Bsns Pk WV9 . . .10 F3
Pendeford Cl WV6 . . . . .24 E8
Pendeford Hall La WV9 . . . .10 D5
Pendeford High Sch
WV10 . . . . .11 B2
Pendeford La WV9 . . . . .11 A3
Pendeford Mill La WV8 . . . . .10 C2
Pendeford Mill Nature
Reserve* WV9 . . . . .10 E4
Pendene Ct WV4 . . . . .39 A5
Pendenis Cl CV6 . . . . .114 A8
Pendennis Cl B30 . . . . .103 D5
Pendennis Dr B69 . . . . .63 A8
Penderel Ct CV6 . . . . .95 C3
Penderell Cl WV10 . . . . .12 A6
Penderel St WS3 . . . . .14 C1
Pendigo Way
Birmingham B40 . . . . .90 E3
Birmingham B40 . . . . .90 F4
Pendinas Dr WV8 . . . . .10 B3
Pendine Ct **4** CV32 . . . . .161 D8
Pendle Hill WS12 . . . . .2 C4
Pendleton Gr B27 . . . . .106 B8
Pendock Ct B23 . . . . .56 C3
Pendragon Rd B42 . . . . .55 C4
Pendrel Cl WS6 . . . . .13 F8
Pendrell Cl
Birmingham B37 . . . . .70 A3
Codsall WV8 . . . . .10 A3
Pendrill Rd WV10 . . . . .11 B6
Penfields Rd DY8 . . . . .81 B8
Penge Gr B44 . . . . .44 E3
Penhallow Dr WV4 . . . . .39 E5
Penhurst Ave B20 . . . . .55 D1
Penk Dr WS7 . . . . .7 D4
Penkridge Cl WS2 . . . . .28 D3
Penkridge Ct WS11 . . . . .1 D1
Penkridge Gr B33 . . . . .68 E4
Penkridge St WS2 . . . . .28 D3
Penk Rise WV6 . . . . .24 B4
Penley Gr B8 . . . . .68 B6
Penmakers Ct B67 . . . . .65 B4
Penmanor B60 . . . . .151 D8
Pennine Dr
Cannock WS11 . . . . .1 E2
Dudley DY3 . . . . .50 D3
Pennine Rd B61 . . . . .137 A5
Pennine Way
Birmingham B8 . . . . .67 D6
Nuneaton CV10 . . . . .72 B3
Stourbridge DY9 . . . . .81 A6
Willenhall WV12 . . . . .27 D4
Pennington Cl B70 . . . . .53 A3
Pennington Way CV6 . . . . .113 E8
Penn La B94 . . . . .141 C4
Penn Rd
Gospel End Village DY3 . . . . .49 F8
Rowley Regis B65 . . . . .63 E3

Penn Rd continued
Wolverhampton WV2,WV3,
WV4 . . . . .39 A6
Penn Road Island WV3 . . . .163 B2
Penns Cl CV32 . . . . .157 E5
Penns Ct B76 . . . . .57 F7
Penns Lake Rd B76 . . . . .57 E7
Penns La B72,B73 . . . . .57 C7
Penns Prim Sch B72 . . . . . . .57 D6
Penn St
6 Cradley Heath B64 . . . . .82 F8
Birmingham B4 . . . . .67 A3
Wolverhampton WV3 . . . . . .163 A1
Penns Wood Cl DY3 . . . . . . .39 C2
Penns Wood Dr B76 . . . . . . .57 F7
Pennwood Ct WV4 . . . . .38 D6
Pennwood La WV4 . . . . .38 F3
Pennyacre Rd B14 . . . . .104 C2
Pennycress Gdns WS11 . . . . .2 C7
Penny Cress Gn WS11 . . . . . .5 F4
Pennycroft Ho B33 . . . . .68 E3
Penny Ct
Great Wyrley WS6 . . . . .13 F8
Tamworth B79 . . . . .21 B5
Penny Farthing Arc DY3 . . .50 D8
Pennyfield Croft B33 . . . . . . .68 E3
Pennyford Cl B97 . . . . .153 A5
Pennyhill La B71 . . . . .53 F7
Pennymoor Rd B77 . . . . .36 B7
Penny Park La CV6 . . . . .95 A3
Penny Royal Cl DY3 . . . . . . .50 D1
Pennyroyal Cl WS5 . . . . .43 B3
Pennys Croft WS13 . . . . .3 E1
Pennystone Cl CV31 . . . . . .162 D6
Penrice Dr B69 . . . . .52 A1
Penrith Cl
Brierley Hill DY5 . . . . .81 B8
Coventry CV6 . . . . .95 C2
Royal Leamington Spa
CV32 . . . . .156 C2
Penrith Croft B32 . . . . .102 D8
Penrith Gr B37 . . . . .70 C2
Penrose Cl CV4 . . . . .132 A7
Penryhn Cl CV8 . . . . .148 C5
Penryn Cl
Nuneaton CV11 . . . . .74 A4
Walsall WS5 . . . . .43 D7
Penryn Rd WS5 . . . . .43 D7
Pensby Cl B13 . . . . .105 B6
Pensford Rd B31 . . . . .103 C3
Pensham Croft B90 . . . . . . .127 A6
Penshaw Cl WV9 . . . . .11 A2
Penshaw Gr B13 . . . . .87 D1
Penshurst Rd B60 . . . . .137 C1
Pensilva Way **7** CV1 . . . .113 E4
Pens Meadow Sch DY8 . . . . .60 E3
Pensnett Rd
Brierley Hill DY5 . . . . .61 C4
Dudley DY1 . . . . .61 F7
Pensnett Sch of Tech
DY5 . . . . .61 B6
Pensnett Trad Est The
DY6 . . . . .60 F8
Penstock Ct DY10 . . . . .117 C8
Penstock Dr B69 . . . . .64 A4
Penstone La WV4 . . . . .37 E4
Pentire Cl CV11 . . . . .73 F5
Pentire Rd WS14 . . . . .9 D6
Pentland Cl LE10 . . . . .71 B1
Pentland Croft B12 . . . . .86 F7
Pentland Gdns WV6 . . . . . . .24 E2
Pentos Dr B11 . . . . .87 D3
Pentridge Cl B76 . . . . .57 F5
Penwood Gdns WV14 . . . . . .51 C8
Penzance Cl LE10 . . . . .71 E4
Penzance Way CV11 . . . . . . .74 A5
Penzer Dr B45 . . . . .138 D8
Penzer St DY6 . . . . .60 D7
Peolsford Rd WS3 . . . . .15 A4
Peony Wlk B23 . . . . .56 B3
Peplins Way B30 . . . . .104 B3
Peplow Rd B33 . . . . .69 A4
Pepper La CV1 . . . . .165 B2
Pepperbox Dr DY4 . . . . .52 A5
Peppercorn Pl B70 . . . . .53 C4
Pepper Hill DY8 . . . . .81 A4
Pepper La CV1 . . . . .165 B2
Pepperwood Cl B61 . . . . . . .136 F6
Pepper Wood Dr B31 . . . . .102 C1
Pepys Cnr CV4 . . . . .111 E3
Pepys Ct B43 . . . . .54 E2
Perch Ave B37 . . . . .70 A3
Perch Cl WV10 . . . . .26 B4
Perchfoot Cl CV1 . . . . .165 C1
Perch Rd WS2 . . . . .28 A4
Percival Rd B16 . . . . .65 C1
Percy Bsns Pk B69 . . . . .63 F7
Percy Cres CV8 . . . . .147 E2
Percy Rd
Birmingham B11 . . . . .87 D4
Kenilworth CV8 . . . . .147 E2
Warwick CV34 . . . . .160 E8
Percy Shurmer Prim Sch
B12 . . . . .86 E7
Percy St CV1 . . . . .165 A3
Percy Terr **5** CV32 . . . . .156 D1
Peregrine Cl DY1 . . . . .50 F1
Peregrine Dr CV5 . . . . .112 A5
Peregrine Gr DY10 . . . . . . .117 A2
Pereira Rd B17 . . . . .85 C7
Pericles Cl CV34 . . . . .161 E3
Perimeter Rd
Birmingham B40 . . . . .90 E4
Birmingham B40 . . . . .90 E4
Perivale Gr
Bilston WV14 . . . . .40 D1
Dudley WV14 . . . . .51 D8

Perivale Way B18 . . . . .81 A8
Periwinkle Cl WS8 . . . . .15 D6
Perkins Cl DY1 . . . . .51 C6
Perks Rd WV11 . . . . .13 A1
Perott Dr B75 . . . . .32 D2
Perrett Wlk **5** DY11 . . . . .116 D6
Perrin Ave DY11 . . . . .116 B4
Perrins Gr B8 . . . . .68 A6
Perrins La DY9 . . . . .81 F4
Perrins Rise DY9 . . . . .81 F4
Perrott Gdns DY5 . . . . .61 B1
Perrott St B18 . . . . .65 E6
Perry Ave
Birmingham B42 . . . . .55 C5
Wolverhampton WV10 . . . . . .25 F1
Perry Barr Stad (Greyhound)
B42 . . . . .55 D3
Perry Beeches Inf Sch
B42 . . . . .55 C5
Perry Beeches Jun Sch
B42 . . . . .55 C5
Perry Beeches Sch B42 . . . .55 C8
Perry Cl
Dudley DY2 . . . . .62 D8
Tamworth B79 . . . . .21 B6
Perry Common Jun & Inf Sch
B23 . . . . .56 C6
Perry Common Rd B23 . . . . .56 C5
Perrycrofts Cres B79 . . . . . .21 C7
Perry Ct B68 . . . . .84 B7
Perryfields Cl B98 . . . . .158 F6
Perryfields Cres B61 . . . . . .136 F5
Perryfields High Sch B68 . . .84 A8
Perryfields Prim Sch B68 . . .84 A7
Perryfields Rd B61 . . . . .136 A3
Perryford Dr B91 . . . . .127 C8
Perry Green B42 . . . . .55 D5
Perry Hall Dr WV12 . . . . .27 B5
Perry Hall Prim Sch WV11 . .26 F6
Perry Hill Ho B68 . . . . .84 C4
Perry Hill La B68 . . . . .84 B7
Perry Hill Rd B68 . . . . .84 B7
Perry La B61 . . . . .136 F2
Perrymill La B96 . . . . .159 E1
Perry Park Cres B42 . . . . . . .55 C6
Perry Park Rd B64 . . . . .63 B1
Perry St
Bilston WV14 . . . . .40 E3
Darlaston WS10 . . . . .41 D8
Smethwick B66 . . . . .65 A7
Tipton DY4 . . . . .52 A4
Wednesbury WS10 . . . . .41 F2
Perry Trad Est WV14 . . . . . . .40 E3
Perry Villa Dr B42 . . . . .55 D5
Perrywell Rd A4 . . . . .56 A4
Perry Wood Rd B42 . . . . .55 A8
Persehouse St WS1 . . . . . . .28 F2
Pershore Ave B29 . . . . .86 B2
Pershore Cl WS3 . . . . .13 F2
Pershore Ct DY11 . . . . .116 D5
Pershore PL CV4 . . . . .132 E6
Pershore Rd
Birmingham,Balsall Heath
B5 .86 C4
Birmingham,Breedon Cross
B30 . . . . .104 A5
Birmingham,Ten Acres
B30 . . . . .104 B8
Halesowen B63 . . . . .83 A3
Kidderminster DY11 . . . . . .116 A6
Pershore Rd S B30 . . . . . . .103 F3
Pershore Rd WS3 . . . . .13 F2
Pershore St B5 . . . . .164 C1
Pershore Way WS3 . . . . .13 F2
Perth Rd WV12 . . . . .27 B6
Perth Rise CV5 . . . . .112 A4
Perton Brook Vale WV6 . . . .23 F2
Perton Fst Sch WV6 . . . . . . .23 E5
Perton Gr
Birmingham B29 . . . . .103 A8
Wolverhampton WV6 . . . . . . .24 A5
Perton Mid Sch WV6 . . . . . .24 A5
Perton Rd WV6 . . . . .23 F2
Perton Sandown Fst Sch
WV6 . . . . .23 F4
Pestilence La
Alvechurch,Arrowfield Top
B48 . . . . .139 C8
Alvechurch B48 . . . . .139 D8
Petard Cl B77 . . . . .35 C8
Petchells Cl DY5 . . . . .61 B5
Peter Ave WV14 . . . . .40 F2
Peterborough Dr WS12 . . . . .2 C1
Peterbrook Cl B98 . . . . .158 F7
Peterbrook Prim Sch
B90 . . . . .105 D2
Peterbrook Rd B90 . . . . . . .105 D1
Peterbrook Rise B90 . . . . . .105 D1
Peterdale Dr WV4 . . . . .38 F3
Peter Hall La CV7 . . . . .115 F6
Peterhead B77 . . . . .21 F5
Peterhouse Mews **1** B13 .87 A2
Peterlee Wlk **6** CV2 . . . . .115 A7
Peters Ave B31 . . . . .102 F2
Petersbourne Ct B28 . . . . . .105 F8
Petersfield WS11 . . . . .1 F4
Petersfield Ct B28 . . . . .105 F8
Petersfield Dr B65 . . . . .63 E3
Petersfield Rd B28 . . . . .105 E7
Peter's Finger B60 . . . . .136 F1
Petersham Pl B15 . . . . .85 E6
Petersham Rd B44 . . . . .45 C1

Peter's Hill Prim Sch DY5 81 C7
Peter's Hill Rd DY5 ....81 C6
Petershouse Dr B74 ..31 F5
Peter's La WS7 ....8 A5
Peters St B70 ....53 A7
Peters Wlk
  Coventry CV6 ....96 A4
  Lichfield WS13 ....3 A2
Petford St B64 ....62 E1
Petitor Cres CV2 ....96 C1
Peto Gr CV4 ....161 F2
Pettitt Cl B14 ....104 E2
Petton Cl B98 ....99 C3
Pettyfield Cl B26 ......89 A6
Pettyfields Cl B93 ....128 A5
Petunia Cl CV10 ......78 A8
Petworth Cl 3 WV13...40 F8
Petworth Gr B26 ....88 E6
Pevensey Cl B69 ....62 F8
Pevensey Rd B60 .....137 C1
Peveril Dr B28 ....105 F7
Peveril Dr CV3 ....133 B5
Peveril Gr B76 ....46 E4
Peverill Rd
  Perton WV4 ....23 F4
  Wolverhampton WV4...39 E3
Pevril Way B43 ....43 F2
Peyto Cl CV6 ....95 C2
Pheasant Cl
  Bedworth CV12 ......77 D1
  Kidderminster DY10 .117 A2
Pheasant Croft B36....70 A8
Pheasant La B98.......158 F7
Pheasant Oak CV4 ....111 C2
Pheasant Rd B67 ......64 D1
Pheasant St DY5 ......61 C3
Pheasant Way WS11 ...2 A1
Pheasey Park Farm Prim Sch
  B43..................44 C4
Philip Cl
  1 Royal Leamington Spa
  CV31.................161 F6
  Sutton Coldfield B76 ..46 F3
Philip Gr WS11 ....1 E6
Philip Rd
  Halesowen B63 ......82 F3
  Tipton DY4 ....52 D5
Philip Sidney Rd B11 ..87 C3
Philip St WV14 ....40 D1
Philip Victor Rd B20 ..54 F1
Phillimore Rd B8 ......67 D5
Phillip Docker Ct CV12..79 B2
Phillippes Rd 6 CV34...155 F1
Philips Ave WV11......12 F1
Phillips St B6 ....66 E6
Phillips Street Ind Est B6..66 F6
Phillips Terr B98......153 F4
Phipson Rd B11 ....87 B3
Phoebe Cl CV34 ......161 E3
Phoenix Bsns Pk
  Birmingham B7 ......67 A6
  Hinckley LE10 ....74 E8
Phoenix Cl
  Birmingham,Castle Vale
  B35..................58 A3
  Birmingham,Edgbaston B5 ..86 C5
Phoenix Ctr WS11......4 E6
Phoenix Gn B15 ....85 E7
Phoenix Ind Est
  Bilston WV14 ....40 F4
  Willenhall WV11 .....26 D3
Phoenix International Ind Est
  B70..................52 F5
Phoenix Pk Ind Est CV7..96 B7
Phoenix Pk B62 ....63 E2
Phoenix Rd
  Cannock WS11........2 A2
  Tipton DY4 ....51 F6
  Willenhall WV11 .....26 D3
Phoenix Rise
  Birmingham B23 .....56 B7
  Wednesbury WS10 ...41 E4
  Wolverhampton WV2..39 C6
Phoenix St
  West Bromwich B70 ..52 F4
  Wolverhampton WV3..39 D6
Phoenix Way CV6 .....95 E3
Picasso Cl WS11.......2 C3
Piccadilly Arc 8 B2 ...164 B2
Piccadilly Cl B37 .....70 C1
Piccadilly Cres B78 ...35 F1
Piccadilly B78 ....35 F1
Pickard St CV34 ......161 A7
Pickenham Rd B14....105 A1
Pickering Croft B32 ...84 D1
Pickering Rd WV11 ...26 D5
Pickersleigh Cl 6 B63..63 A3
Pickford Cl CV11......74 A1
Pickford Grange La CV5..111 C7
Pickford Green La CV5..111 C7
Pickford St B5.........66 F2
Pickford Way CV5.....112 B6
Pickrell Rd WV14 .....40 B1
Pickwick Cl B13 ....87 B2
Pickwick Gr B13 ......87 C2
Pickwick Pl WV14 .....40 E4
Picton Croft 3 B37 ...70 D2
Picton Gr B13 ....105 B6
Picturedrome Way 4
  WS10.................41 C6
Piddock Rd B66 ....65 A5
Pierce Ave WV92 ......88 E3
Piercy St B70 ....53 A3
Piers Cl CV34 ....160 F8

Piers Rd B21 ....66 A7
Pier St WS8 ....15 F7
Piggots Croft B37.....69 F3
Pike Cl
  Birmingham B20 .....54 F1
  Hinckley LE10 ....75 D5
Pike Dr B37 ....70 C3
Pikehelve St B70 ......52 E7
Pike Hill B60 ....138 A7
Pikehorne Croft B36...58 D2
Pike Rd WS2 ....28 A4
Pikers La CV7 ....94 A3
Pikes Pool La B60 ....137 E2
Pikes The B45 ....121 F8
Pikewater Rd B9 ......67 D2
Pilgrims Gate LE10 ...76 A6
Pilgrims Wlk CV6,CV7 ..95 B6
Pilkington Ave B72 ...46 C2
Pilkington Rd CV5 ....132 D8
Pillaton Dr WS12 ......1 C6
Pilling Cl CV2 ....114 F8
Pilson Cl B36 ....68 F8
Pimbury Rd WV12.....27 D7
Pimlico Ct DY3 ....50 D3
Pimpernel Dr WS5 ....95 B6
Pinbury Croft B37 ....70 B1
Pinchers Cl DY9 .....119 E7
Pineapple Cl B14 ....104 C6
Pineapple Gr B30 ....104 C8
Pineapple Pl B14 ....104 D6
Pineapple Rd B30 ....104 C7
Pine Ave
  Smethwick B66 ......64 E7
  Wednesbury WS10 ...41 F4
Pine Cl
  Great Wyrley WS6 ....4 F4
  Kingswinford DY6 ....60 D5
  Solihull B91 ....106 F2
  Tamworth B79 ....21 B8
  Wolverhampton WV3..25 A1
Pine Ct
  Coventry CV5 ....111 C4
  Royal Leamington Spa
  CV32.................157 B3
  Stourbridge DY9 .....81 B1
  Wolverhampton WV11..26 C6
Pine Gn DY1...........51 A5
Pine Gr
  Birmingham B14 .....105 A5
  Burntwood WS7 ......6 F5
  Lower Marlbrook B45..121 F2
Pine Ho B36 ....68 F8
Pinehurst CV32 ......157 E6
Pinehurst Dr B38 ....103 F3
Pine Leigh Rd B74 ...32 B1
Pineneedle Croft WV12 ..27 E4
Pine Rd
  Dudley DY1 ....51 C4
  Oldbury B69 ....63 A8
Pineridge Dr WV11 ..116 B5
Pines Park Home Est The
  WS12.................1 D5
Pine Sq B37 ....70 B2
Pines Specl Sch The B36..68 F8
Pines The
  Bedworth CV12 ......77 E2
  Birmingham B45 .....102 A1
  Cheswick Green B90..106 D6
  Coventry CV4 ....131 D7
  Lichfield WS14.......9 F7
  Walsall WS1 ....42 D1
  Wolverhampton WV3..24 D1
Pine St WS3 ....14 D2
Pine Tree Ave CV4 ...112 A2
Pine Tree Cl B97......152 F3
Pine Tree Ct CV12 ....78 C4
Pinetree Dr B74 ......30 D1
Pine Tree Rd CV12 ...78 C4
Pineview B31 ....102 F2
Pinewall Ave B38 ....104 A1
Pineways Dr WV6.....24 E4
Pineways
  Stourbridge DY8 .....60 C2
  Sutton Coldfield B74 ..31 C3
Pineways The B69 ....63 C5
Pine Wlk
  Birmingham B31 ....103 B3
  Stourbridge DY9 .....81 D3
Pinewood Ave
  Cannock WS11........1 D4
  Wood End CV9 ....36 C1
Pinewood Bsns Pk B37 ..90 B8
Pinewood Cl
  Birmingham B44 ....121 D8
  Birmingham,Great Barr B44 ..55 E7
  Brownhills WS8 ......6 E2
  Walsall WS5 ....83 B4
  Willenhall WV12 .....27 E7
  Wolverhampton WV3..38 A8
  Wombourne WV5.....49 A6
Pinewood Dr
  Binley Woods CV3 ...135 C7
  Birmingham B32 .....84 A1
Pinewood Gr CV5 ....133 B8
Pinewoods Ave DY9...98 F4
Pine Woods B32......84 A4
Pinewoods
  Birmingham,Hurst Green
  B62..................84 A2
  Birmingham,Woodcock Hill
  B31..................102 F8
Pinewoods Cl DY9 ....98 F4
Pinewoods Ct DY9 ...98 F4
Pinewood Wlk DY6 ...60 E8
Pinfield Dr B45 ......122 B1
Pinfold Cl LE10 ......74 F7
Pinfold Cres WV4 ....38 D6
Pinfold Ct WS10 .....41 C6

Pinfold Gdns WV11 ...26 D5
Pinfold Gr WV4 ....38 D6
Pinfold Hill WS14 ....17 F6
Pinfold Ind Est WS3...28 C8
Pinfold La
  Cheslyn Hay WS6.....4 C2
  Norton Canes WS11 ...5 E4
  Walsall WS9 ....44 B6
  Wolverhampton WV4..38 E5
Pinfold Rd B91 ....107 E5
Pinfold St
  Bilston WV14 ....40 D5
  Birmingham B2 ......164 B2
  Darlaston WS10......41 A5
  Oldbury B69 ....64 A8
Pinfold Street Extension
  WS10.................41 C5
Pinfold Street JMI Sch
  WS10.................41 A5
Pinfold WS3 ....28 C8
Pingle Cl B71 ....42 F1
Pingle Ct CV11 ....73 D2
Pingle La WS7 ....7 D5
Pink Green La B97 ...153 C5
Pinkney Pl B68 ....64 C3
Pinley Fields CV3 ....134 B8
Pinley Gr B43 ....43 C3
Pinley Way 2 B91 ....107 A1
Pinnacle Ho B97 .....158 E5
Pinner Ct B17 ....85 C6
Pinner Gr B32 ....84 E4
Pinner's Croft CV2 ...114 A5
Pinnock Pl CV4 ....111 F1
Pinson Gdns WV13 ...26 F1
Pinson Rd WV13 .....26 F2
Pintail Dr B23 ....56 C2
Pintail Gr DY10 ......117 B3
Pinto Cl B16 ....65 F7
Pinvin Ho B97 ....153 A3
Pinza Croft B36.......68 D8
Pioli Pl WS2 ....28 D5
Pioneer Cl B97 ......153 D4
Pioneer Ho CV1 .....165 D4
Pioneer Way B35 ....58 B2
Pipe Hall Farm Nature
  Reserve* WS13 ....8 A8
Piper Cl WV6 ....23 F4
Piper Pl DY8 ....80 E7
Piper Rd WV3 ....38 C8
Pipers Cl B61 ....150 D7
Pipers Croft WS13 ...3 A2
Pipers Ct CV3 ....132 F4
Pipers Gn B28 ....105 F5
Piper's La CV9 ....148 A5
Pipers Rd B98 ....159 D7
Piper's Row CV1 .....163 C3
Pipes Mdw WV14 ....40 E5
Pipit Ct DY10 ....117 A2
Pipkin Ct CV1 ....165 D1
Pippin Ave B63 ......82 B7
Pirbright Cl WV14....40 E3
Pirrey Cl WV14 ....40 E1
Pitcairn Cl B30 ......104 B6
Pitcairn Dr B62 ......83 B5
Pitcairn Ho B67 ......64 E2
Pitcairn Rd B67 ......64 E2
Pitchcombe Cl B98 ..154 A2
Pitcheroak Cotts B97..153 A3
Pitcheroak Sch B97..153 A4
Pitclose Rd B31 ......103 B1
Pitfield Rd B33 ......69 E1
Pitfield Row 17 DY1 ..51 B1
Pitfields Cl B68 ......84 A8
Pitfields Rd B68 .....84 A8
Pitfield St 5 DY1.....51 C1
Pithall Rd B34 ....69 D5
Pit Leasow Cl B30 ...104 B8
Pitman Rd B32 ....84 B3
Pitmaston Ct B13 ....86 D3
Pitmaston Rd B28 ...106 B6
Pitmeadow Ho B14 ..104 E2
Pitsford St B18 ......66 B4
Pitt La B92 ....90 D2
Pitts Farm Rd B24 ...57 C6
Pitt St
  Birmingham B4 ......67 A3
  Wolverhampton WV3..163 B2
Pixall Dr B15 ....86 B6
Pixhall Wlk B35 ......58 B3
Plainview Cl WS9 ....30 E2
Plaistow Ave B36 ....68 C7
Plane Cl CV10 ....72 E7
Plane Gr B37 ....70 B1
Planetary Ind Est WV13 ..26 C4
Planetary Rd WV13...26 C3
Planet Rd DY5 ....61 D4
Planetree Cl B60 ....137 B2
Plane Tree Cl DY10 ..116 F7
Plane Tree Rd B74 ...44 D8
Plane Tree Rd WS5...43 C4
Plank La B46 ....59 A2
Planks La WV5 ....49 A7
Plantagenet Pk CV34..161 E3
Plantation La DY3 ...46 F6
Plantation La
  Himley DY3 ....49 B3
  Hopwas B78 ....20 B4
Plantation Rd WS5...43 A4
Plantation The DY5 ..61 B7
Plant Ct 10 DY5......61 D2
Plant La WS7 ....6 E7
Plants Brook Rd B76..57 F6
Plantsbrook Sch B72..46 C4
Plants Cl
  Great Wyrley WS6 ...14 A8
  Sutton Coldfield B73..45 D1
Plants Gr B24 ....57 D5
Plants Hill Cres CV4..111 E1

Plants Hollow DY5....61 D1
Plant St
  Cradley Heath B64 ...62 D1
  Stourbridge DY8 .....60 E2
Plant Way WS3 ....14 F4
Plascom Rd WV1 .....26 A1
Plato Cl CV34 ....161 E5
Platts Cres DY8 ......80 E8
Platts Dr DY8 ....80 F8
Platts Rd DY8 ....80 E8
Platt St
  Cannock WS11........2 A5
  Darlaston WS10......41 D5
Playdon Gr B14 .....105 A3
Pleasant Cl DY6 .....60 C4
Pleasant St
  Kidderminster DY10 ..116 F7
  West Bromwich,Hill Top
  B70..................53 A8
  West Bromwich,Lambert's End
  B70..................53 C2
Pleasant View DY3 ...50 D2
Pleasant Way CV32 ..157 A2
Pleck Bsns Pk WS2 ..28 C1
Pleck Ho B14 ....104 C1
Pleck Ind Est WS2 ...42 C8
Pleck Rd WS2 ....42 C6
Pleck Wlk B38 ....104 A1
Plestowes Cl B90 ...106 B5
Pleydell Cl CV3 .....134 C5
Plimsoll Gr B32 ......84 C5
Plimsoll St DY11 ....116 D5
Plough Ave B32 .....84 C2
Plough & Harrow Rd B16 ..65 F1
Plough Hill Rd CV10..72 A6
Ploughmans Wlk B75 ..32 D4
Ploughmans Wlk
  Kingswinford DY6 ....60 A7
  Lichfield WS13.......3 C3
  Stoke Heath B60 ....150 D6
  Wolverhampton WV8..10 F1
Plover Cl WV10 ....12 B7
Ploverdale Cres DY6..61 A6
Plover Gr DY10 ......117 B1
Plowden Rd B33 .....68 F4
Plume St B6 ....68 C6
Plumstead Cl B97....153 C6
Plumstead Rd B44 ...56 B8
Plym Cl WV11 ....26 C5
Plymouth Cl
  Birmingham B31 ....123 A7
  Coventry CV2 ....114 C7
Plymouth Ct B97 ....153 C1
Plymouth Dr B45 ....138 A8
Plymouth Ho B60 ...152 B7
Plymouth Pl CV31....162 A7
Plymouth Rd
  Barnt Green B45 ....138 A8
  Birmingham B30 ....104 B7
  Redditch B97 ....153 D2
Plympton Mews B71..53 C6
Pochard Cl DY10 ....116 F1
Poets Cnr B10 ....87 D7
Poins Cl CV34 ....161 F3
Pointon Cl WV14 ....40 A2
Poitiers Rd CV3 .....133 D6
Polden Cl B63 ....82 C1
Polesworth Cl B98 ..154 D1
Polesworth Gr B34 ..69 B6
Polesworth High Sch B78..36 F7
Pollard Rd B27 ......88 E2
Pollards The B23 ....56 E8
Polly Brooks Yd DY9..81 E5
Polo Fields DY9 .....81 B1
Polperro Dr CV5 ....112 A5
Pomeroy Cl CV4 .....131 D7
Pomeroy Rd
  Birmingham B32 .....84 C1
  Birmingham,Pheasey B43 ..44 D4
Pommel Cl WS5 ......42 F4
Pond Cres WV2 ......39 E2
Pond Farm Mews CV5..111 E5
Pond Gr WV2 ....39 E2
Pond La WV2 ....39 D7
Pondthorpe CV3 .....134 C6
Ponesfield Rd WS13..3 B2
Ponesgreen WS13 ...3 B2
Pontypool Ave CV3..134 F6
Pool Ave WS11 ......6 B5
Pool Bank B45 ......153 E2
Pool Bank St CV11...73 B4
Poole Cres
  Birmingham B17 ....85 C3
  Bilston WV14 ....40 D2
Poolehouse Rd B43..43 E3
Pool End Cl B93 ....127 F6
Poole Rd CV6 ....113 A6
Pooles La WV12 .....27 D8
Poole St
  Stourbridge DY8 .....80 E4
Poole's Way WV10 ...25 E4
Pooley La B78 ....22 F2
Pool Farm Rd B27 ...88 C1
Pool Field Ave B31 ..102 E2
Poolfield Dr B91 ....106 F3
Poolfield Rd WS13...8 E6
Pool Furlong DY9 ...99 E1
Pool Gn WS9 ....30 A5
Pool Green Terr WS9..30 A5
Pool Hall Cres WV3..38 A8
Pool Hall Rd WV3 ...38 A8
Pool Hayes Com Sch
  WV12.................27 B5
Pool Hayes La WV12..27 B5

Pool Hayes Prim Sch
  WV12.................27 B6
Poolhead La
  Earlswood B94.......141 C7
  Tanworth-In-A B94 ..141 E5
Pool La B69 ....63 F3
Pool Mdw
  Cheslyn Hay WS6.....4 D1
  Sutton Coldfield B76 ..58 A8
Pool Meadow Cl
  Birmingham B13 .....87 C1
  Solihull B91 ....107 F2
Pool Rd
  Brownhills WS7 ......6 E3
  Burntwood WS7 ......6 E4
  Halesowen B63 ......83 B3
  Nuneaton CV10 ......72 F5
  Smethwick B66 ......65 B5
  Studley B80 ....159 E4
  Wednesfield WV11 ...26 A3
Pool Road Bsns Ctr CV10..72 F5
Poolside Gdns CV3 ..133 A5
Pool St
  Birmingham B6 ......66 F6
  Dudley DY1 ....51 A6
  Walsall WS1 ....28 F1
  Wolverhampton WV2..163 B1
Pooltail Wlk B31 ....102 D1
Pool View
  Great Wyrley WS6 ....5 A4
  Walsall WS4 ....29 D7
Pool Way B33 ....69 A1
Pope Gr WS12 ....1 F6
Pope Rd WV10 ....12 B1
Popes La
  Astwood Bank B96 ..158 E2
  Birmingham B30,B31,B38 ..103 D3
Pope's La B69 ....64 B7
Popes La WV6 ....24 A6
Pope St
  Birmingham B1 ......66 B3
  Smethwick B66 ......65 B7
Poplar Arc B91 ......107 C4
Poplar Ave
  2 Birmingham,Erdington
  B23..................56 F4
  Birmingham,Lozells B19..66 C8
  Bedworth CV12 ......78 D2
  Birmingham,Balsall Heath
  B12..................87 A5
  Birmingham,Coleshill Heath
  B37..................90 C8
  Birmingham,Edgbaston B17..65 B2
  Birmingham,King's Heath
  B14..................104 F8
  Brownhills WS8 ......16 A8
  Burntwood WS7 ......6 F6
  Cannock WS11 ......1 F4
  Oldbury,Grace Mary Estate
  B69..................63 C8
  Oldbury,Langley B69..64 A4
  Sutton Coldfield B75 ..46 F7
  Tipton DY4 ....51 D5
  Walsall,Yew Tree WS5..43 A4
  West Bromwich B70 ..53 E2
  Willenhall WS2 ......27 E4
  Wolverhampton WV3..26 B7
Poplar Cl
  Catshill B61 ....136 F8
  Oldbury B69 ....52 C1
  Willenhall WS2 ......27 E4
  Wombourne WV5.....49 A6
Poplar Cres
  Dudley DY1 ....51 B3
  Stourbridge DY8 .....80 D3
Poplar Dr
  Barnt Green B45 ....138 D8
  Birmingham,Washwood Heath
  B8...................67 D6
  Birmingham,Witton B6 ..55 F5
Poplar Gn DY1........51 B3
Poplar Gr
  7 Birmingham B19...66 C8
  Ryton-on-D CV8 .....135 B1
  Smethwick B66 ......65 B3
  West Bromwich B70 ..53 E1
Poplar Ho CV12......78 D2
Poplar La
  Cannock WS11........1 B1
  Romsley B62 ....101 A4
Poplar Rd
  Bilston WV14 ....40 F7
  Birmingham,Moseley B14..86 E1
  Birmingham,Sparkhill B11..87 C5
  Brownhills WS8 ......16 A8
  Coventry CV5 ....112 F1
  Dorridge B93 ....127 F3
  Great Wyrley WS6 ....5 A1
  Kidderminster DY11 ..116 C4
  Kingswinford DY6 ....60 E5
  Oldbury B69 ....64 A8
  Redditch B97 ....153 A3
  Smethwick B66 ......65 A1
  Solihull B91 ....107 C4
  Stourbridge DY8 .....80 E3
  Wednesbury WS10 ...42 A4
  Wolverhampton WV3..39 A6
Poplar Rise
  Birmingham B42 .....55 B7
  Oldbury B69 ....63 C8
  Sutton Coldfield B74 ..31 D6
Poplar Row DY11 ....116 C4
Poplars Dr B35 ......58 A1
Poplars La B96 ......158 A1
Poplars The
  Birmingham,Rotton Park
  B16..................65 F3
  Birmingham,Sparkhill B11..87 C6

Poplars The continued
Brierley Hill DY5 . . . . .61 B7
Cannock WS11. . . . . 1 E4
Nuneaton CV10 . . . . .72 D3
Smethwick B66 . . . . .65 C4
Stourbridge DY8 . . . . .60 F2
Poplar St WS11 . . . . .1 A6
Poplars Trad Est B80. . . . .159 D6
Poplar St
Smethwick B66 . . . . .65 C5
Wolverhampton WV2 . . . . .39 D6
Poplar Trad Est B6. . . . . . .55 F5
Poplar Trees B47 . . . . . . .125 A6
Poplar Way B91 . . . . .107 C4
Poplarwoods B32. . . . . . . .84 B2
Poppy Cl CV10. . . . . .78 A8
Poppy Ct CV3. . . . . .134 D6
Poppy Gr B8 . . . . .57 C5
Poppy La B24 . . . . .57 C5
Poppymead B23 . . . . .56 B8
Porchester Cl
Brownhills WS9 . . . . .16 A2
Coventry CV3. . . . . .115 A2
Porchester Dr B19. . . . . . .66 D6
Porchester St B19 . . . . . . .66 D6
Porlock Cl CV3 . . . . .133 E5
Porlock Cres B31. . . . . . . .102 D3
Porlock Rd DY8 . . . . .81 A6
Portal Rd WS2. . . . . .27 F2
Portchester Dr WV11 . . . . .26 D5
Porter Cl
Coventry CV4. . . . . .131 E8
Sutton Coldfield B72 . . . . . .57 B7
Porters Croft B17. . . . . . . .85 A8
Porters Field 8 DY2 . . . . . .51 D1
Portersfield Ind Est B64. . . .82 D8
Portersfield Rd B64. . . . . . .82 C8
Portershill Dr B90 . . . . . . .106 C1
Porter St DY2 . . . . .51 D1
Porter Street S 9 DY2. . . . .51 D1
Porters Way B9. . . . . .67 E2
Portfield Dr DY4. . . . . .52 A3
Portfield Gr B23. . . . . .57 A6
Porthkerry Gr DY3 . . . . . . .50 C5
Port Hope Rd B11 . . . . . . .87 A7
Porthouse Gr WV14. . . . . .40 B3
Portia Ave B90 . . . . .106 B1
Portia Cl CV11. . . . . .74 A1
Portia Way CV34. . . . . . . .161 E3
Portland Ave
Aldridge WS9. . . . . .30 B5
Tamworth B79 . . . . .20 F8
Portland Cres DY9 . . . . . . .81 B1
Portland Ct
9 Royal Leamington Spa
CV32. . . . . .161 F8
Aldridge WS9. . . . . .30 B6
Portland Dr
Hinckley LE10 . . . . .71 E4
Nuneaton CV10 . . . . .72 C4
Oldbury B69. . . . . .52 D3
Stourbridge DY9 . . . . .81 B1
Portland Mews 10 CV32. .161 F8
Portland Pl
Cannock WS11. . . . . .4 C7
Dudley WV14. . . . . .51 B7
Portland Pl E CV32. . . . . .161 F8
Portland Pl W 5 CV32. . . .161 F8
Portland Rd
Aldridge WS9. . . . . .30 B6
Birmingham B16 . . . . .65 D1
Portland St
Birmingham B6 . . . . .67 A7
Royal Leamington Spa
CV32. . . . . .161 F8
Walsall WS2 . . . . .28 E3
Portland Terr 6 B18. . . . . .66 A5
Portleys La B78. . . . . .34 D4
Portman Rd B13. . . . . . . .104 F7
Portmanteau Mews B94. .143 C6
Portobello Cl WV13. . . . . .26 D1
Portobello Rd B70. . . . . . .53 A8
Portreath Dr CV11 . . . . . . .74 A5
Portree Ave CV34 . . . . . . .114 F2
Portrush Rd WV6. . . . . . . .23 D4
Portsdown Cl WV10. . . . . .25 F7
Portsdown Rd B63. . . . . . .82 D7
Portsea Cl CV3 . . . . .133 D6
Portsea St WS3. . . . . .28 C6
Portswood Cl WV9. . . . . . .10 F1
Portway Cl
Coventry CV4. . . . . .131 E8
Kingswinford DY6 . . . . .60 E5
Royal Leamington Spa
CV31. . . . . .162 D6
Solihull B91. . . . . .106 E1
Portway Hill B65 . . . . .63 C6
Portway Rd
Bilston WV14. . . . . .40 E7
Oldbury B69. . . . . .63 F7
Rowley Regis B65 . . . . . . .63 C6
Wednesbury WS10 . . . . . .41 E2
Portway The DY6. . . . . . . .60 E5
Portway Wlk B65 . . . . .63 C6
Portwrinkle Ave CV6. . . . .114 A6
Poseidon Way CV34. . . . .161 F4
Posey Cl B21. . . . . .54 C3
Post Box B1. . . . . .164 B1
Postbridge Rd CV3. . . . . .133 D5
Post Office Wlk B96 . . . . .158 E1
Poston Croft B14. . . . . . . .104 D3
Potter Cl B23. . . . . .56 D8
Potter Ct 8 DY5. . . . . .61 D2
Potters Brook 8 DY4. . . . .52 B5

Potters Green Prim Sch
CV2 . . . . .96 E2
Potters Green Rd CV2. . . . .96 E1
Potters La
Birmingham B6 . . . . .66 F7
Wednesbury WS10 . . . . . .41 F2
Potters Rd CV12 . . . . .77 E1
Potterton Way B66. . . . . . .64 F8
Pottery Rd B68. . . . . .64 D1
Potton Cl CV3 . . . . .134 E6
Potts Cl CV8. . . . . .148 C4
Pouk Hill Cl WS2. . . . . . . .28 A3
Pouk La WS14 . . . . .16 F7
Poultney Rd CV6. . . . . . . .113 A6
Poultney St B70 . . . . .52 F7
Poulton Cl B13. . . . . .87 A2
Pound Cl
Berkswell CV7 . . . . .110 D3
Lapworth B94. . . . . .144 B3
Oldbury B68. . . . . .63 F3
Pound Gn B8. . . . . .67 F6
Pound House La
Nuthurst B94. . . . . .143 A4
Tanworth-in-A B94. . . . . .142 F4
Pound La
Birmingham B32. . . . . . . .101 F3
Royal Leamington Spa
CV32. . . . . .157 A3
Poundley Cl B36. . . . . .69 C8
Pound Rd
Birmingham B14 . . . . .104 E2
Oldbury B68. . . . . .64 A2
Wednesbury WS10 . . . . . .42 A3
Pountney St WV2 . . . . . . .163 B1
Pourbaix Ho WS13. . . . . . . .9 B6
Poverty B96 . . . . .158 E2
Powell Ave B32. . . . . .84 A6
Powell Pl
Bilston WV14. . . . . .40 E3
Tipton DY4 . . . . .52 C5
Powell Rd CV2 . . . . .114 A4
Powells Cl B72 . . . . .46 C2
Powells Ho B73. . . . . .45 C2
Powell St
7 Halesowen B63. . . . . . . .83 B3
Birmingham B1 . . . . .66 B3
Wolverhampton WV10. . . . .25 F4
Powell Way CV11 . . . . .73 C4
Power Cres B16. . . . . .66 A2
Powers Ct 4 CV32. . . . . . .156 F1
Powers Rd LE9 . . . . .71 F5
Power Way DY4. . . . . .52 D8
Powick Rd B23 . . . . .56 E6
Powis Ave DY4. . . . . .52 B7
Powis Gr CV8. . . . . .148 C5
Powke La B65 . . . . .63 A2
Powke Lane Ind Est B65 . .63 A2
Powlers Cl DY9. . . . . .81 E2
Powlett St WV2 . . . . .163 C2
Poxon Rd WS9. . . . . .16 A3
Poynings The WV6 . . . . . . .24 C5
Poyser Rd CV10. . . . . .78 C8
Praetor Ho 8 LE10 . . . . . . .71 D1
Pratts La B95 . . . . .159 F7
Precinct The
Tamworth B79 . . . . .21 B5
Willenhall WV12 . . . . .27 B5
Premier Bsns Ctr 8 DY9. .81 F5
Premier Bsns Pk WS2. . . . .28 D1
Premier Ct B30. . . . . .104 C3
Premier Partnership Ind Est
DY5 . . . . .61 A3
Premier St B7. . . . . .67 D8
Premier Trad Est B7. . . . . .66 F5
Prescelly Cl CV10 . . . . .72 B3
Prescelly Ct B45. . . . . . . .147 F5
Prescot Rd DY9. . . . . .81 C3
President Kennedy Sch &
Com Coll CV6 . . . . .95 B4
Prestbury Rd B6. . . . . .66 E8
Presthope Rd B29 . . . . . . .103 B7
Prestley Smith Sch B42 . . .55 C8
Preston Ave B76. . . . . .46 E3
Preston Cl
Coventry CV4. . . . . .131 F7
Redditch B98. . . . . .154 B6
Preston Ho 4 WS1 . . . . . . .28 F1
Preston Rd
Birmingham,Hockley B18. .65 E6
Birmingham,South Yardley
B26 . . . . .88 D7
Hinckley LE10 . . . . .71 B2
Prestons Row WV14. . . . . .40 A3
Prestwick Cl B75. . . . . . . .46 C7
Prestwick Rd
Birmingham B35. . . . . . . .58 B4
Kingswinford DY6 . . . . . . .60 C6
Prestwood Ave WV11 . . . . .26 D7
Prestwood Dr DY7 . . . . . . .80 B7
Prestwood Rd
Birmingham B29 . . . . .103 B8
Wolverhampton WV11. . . . .26 A5
Prestwood Rd W WV11 . . .26 B7
Pretoria Rd B9 . . . . .67 E3
Priam Cir CV34 . . . . .161 F3
Priam Gr WS3. . . . . .14 B3
Price Cl E CV34. . . . . .160 B4
Price Cl W CV34. . . . . . . .160 B4
Price Cres WV14. . . . . .40 D7
Price Rd
Cubbington CV32. . . . . . .157 E5
Stourbridge DY9 . . . . .82 A6
Wednesbury WS10 . . . . . .42 C3
Price St
Bilston WV14. . . . . .40 F5
Birmingham B4 . . . . .164 C4

Price St continued
Cannock WS11. . . . . .1 E1
Dudley DY2 . . . . .51 E1
Smethwick B66 . . . . .65 B5
West Bromwich B70 . . . . . .53 C3
Pridmore Rd CV6 . . . . . . .113 D7
Priestfield Cl B44. . . . . . . .44 D2
Priestfield Rd B97. . . . . . .158 E5
Priestfield Sta WV2. . . . . . .40 A7
Priestfield St WV14 . . . . . .40 B6
Priesthills Rd LE10. . . . . . .75 D8
Priestland Rd B34 . . . . . . .69 B7
Priestley Cl
Birmingham B20 . . . . .55 A2
Halesowen B63 . . . . .82 B6
Priestley Rd
Birmingham B11 . . . . .87 A7
Walsall WS2 . . . . .28 A5
Priest Meadow Cl B96. . . .158 D1
Priest St B64. . . . . .62 F1
Primley Ave
Birmingham B36. . . . . .68 D7
Tamworth B77 . . . . .35 F5
Walsall WS2 . . . . .28 B2
Primley Cl WS2 . . . . .28 B2
Primrose Ave
Birmingham B11 . . . . .87 C5
Tipton DY4 . . . . .52 C8
Wolverhampton WV10. . . . .11 D3
Primrose Bank B68. . . . . . .64 B4
Primrose Cl
Cradley Heath B64 . . . . . . .82 B8
Lickey End B60 . . . . .137 C6
Walsall WS3 . . . . .15 A5
Primrose Cres DY1. . . . . . .51 C4
Primrose Croft
Birmingham,Perry Common
B23 . . . . .56 C7
Birmingham,Yardley Wood
B28 . . . . .105 F5
Primrose Dr
Bedworth CV12 . . . . .77 E1
Hinckley LE10 . . . . .75 E5
Primrose Gdns
Birmingham B38 . . . . .123 F8
Codsall WV8 . . . . .10 A3
Featherstone WV10. . . . . .12 B7
Primrose Hill B38. . . . . . .124 A8
Primrose Hill Com Sch
B38. . . . . .123 F8
Primrose Hill B67. . . . . . . .64 D4
Primrose Hill St CV1 . . . . .165 C4
Primrose Hill DY8. . . . . . . .60 E1
Primrose Hill Trad Est
DY2 . . . . .51 D1
Primrose Hill CV34. . . . . .155 E2
Primrose La
Birmingham B28 . . . . .105 F5
Solihull B90 . . . . .126 A5
Wolverhampton WV10. . . . .26 A8
Primrose Mdw 9 WS11. . . . .2 C2
Primrose Pk DY5. . . . . .61 C7
Primrose Rd DY2 . . . . .62 C4
Primroses The WS5 . . . . . .43 B4
Primrose Way DY10. . . . . .116 F4
Primrose Woods B32 . . . . .84 B2
Primsland Cl B90. . . . . . . .127 C7
Prince Albert Inf & Jun Sch
B6. . . . . .65 C5
Prince Albert St B9. . . . . . .67 D1
Prince Andrew Cres B45 . .101 E2
Prince Charles Cl B45 . . . .101 E2
Prince Charles Rd WV14 . .40 F3
Prince Edward Dr B45. . . .101 E2
Prince George Rd WS10 . . .42 A5
Prince Of Wales La B14. . .105 C3
Prince Of Wales Rd CV5. .112 E3
Prince of Wales Wlk 3
B65 . . . . .65 C5
Princep Cl B43 . . . . .44 D4
Prince Philip Cl B45. . . . . .101 E2
Prince Rd B30. . . . . .104 A3
Prince Regent Ct 3
CV31 . . . . .161 F6
Prince Rupert Mews WS13 . .9 A8
Prince's Rupert's Way WS13 . .9 A8
Prince's Ave
Nuneaton CV11 . . . . .73 B3
Walsall WS1. . . . . .29 B1
Princes Cl CV3 . . . . .134 B8
Princes Dr
Codsall WV8 . . . . .10 A2
Coventry CV6. . . . . .96 B1
Kenilworth CV8 . . . . .148 A7
Princes End Ind Pk DY4 . . .40 E1
Princes Gate
Solihull B91. . . . . .107 B4
West Bromwich B70 . . . . . .53 E2
Princes Gdns WV8 . . . . . . .10 A2
Princes Rd DY8. . . . . .80 D3
Prince's Rd B69. . . . . .52 B2
Princess Alice Dr B73. . . . .45 D2
Princess Alley WV1. . . . . .163 C3
Princess Anne Dr B45 . . . .101 E2
Princess Anne Rd
Bilston WV14. . . . . .40 F3
Willenhall WV13. . . . . .27 F3
Princess Cl WS7. . . . . .6 E7
Princess Cres B63. . . . . . . .82 E6
Princess Ct WV10. . . . . . . .26 A6
Princess Gr B71. . . . . .53 D6
Princess of Wales Com Hospl
The B41. . . . . .137 A4
Princess Rd
Birmingham B5 . . . . .86 E7

Princess Rd continued
Hinckley LE10 . . . . .75 E8
Oldbury B68. . . . . .64 D2
Princess Sq WV14 . . . . . . .40 F3
Princess St
Burntwood WS7. . . . . .6 E8
Cannock WS11. . . . . .1 F5
Coventry CV6. . . . . .113 F7
Wolverhampton WV1. . . . .163 C3
Princess Way WS10 . . . . . .41 C8
Prince St
Brownhills WS9 . . . . .15 F2
Cannock WS12. . . . . .1 E6
Cradley Heath B64 . . . . . . .82 D8
Dudley DY2 . . . . .62 C6
Walsall WS2 . . . . .42 C8
Prince's Way B91. . . . . . .107 B3
Princethorpe Cl
Birmingham B34 . . . . .69 D7
Solihull B90 . . . . .106 A2
Princethorpe Inf Sch B29 .85 A1
Princethorpe Jun Sch
B29. . . . . .85 A1
Princethorpe Rd B29. . . . . .85 A1
Princethorpe Way CV3 . . .134 D8
Princeton Gdns WV9 . . . . .10 F2
Prince William Cl
Birmingham B23. . . . . .69 D7
Coventry CV6. . . . . .112 E6
Princip St B4. . . . . .164 C4
Principal Ct 867. . . . . .65 A5
Printing House St B4 . . . . .164 C3
Prior Ave B60 . . . . .150 C3
Prior Cl DY10 . . . . .117 C5
Prior Deram Wlk CV4 . . . .132 C7
Priors Cl CV7 . . . . .130 B6
Priors Field Prim Sch
CV8 . . . . .147 D7
Priorsfield Rd
4 Coventry CV6. . . . . . . .113 A4
Kenilworth CV8 . . . . .147 D6
Priorsfield Rd N 3 CV6. . .113 A4
Priorsfield Rd S CV6. . . . .113 A4
Priors Harnall CV1. . . . . . .165 D4
Priors Mill DY3 . . . . .50 E5
Priors Oak B97 . . . . .153 B4
Priors The CV12 . . . . .78 C2
Priors Way B23 . . . . .56 C8
Prior Ave B29 . . . . .86 B2
Priory Cl
Dudley DY1 . . . . .51 B2
Kingswood B94 . . . . .144 D5
Smethwick B66 . . . . .65 C4
Stourbridge DY8 . . . . .81 B3
Tamworth B79 . . . . .20 F7
Priory Croft CV8. . . . . . . .148 A4
Priory Ct
3 Dudley DY1 . . . . .51 C1
Brownhills WS9 . . . . .16 A4
Coventry CV5. . . . . .113 A1
Nuneaton CV11 . . . . .73 A4
Solihull B90 . . . . .127 B7
Priory Cts The B2. . . . . . .164 C3
Priory Ct
Stourbridge DY8 . . . . .81 B3
Studley B80 . . . . .159 E5
Wolverhampton WV1. . . . .163 B4
Priory Dr B68. . . . . .64 C5
Priory Field Cl WV14 . . . . .39 F1
Priorygate Way B7. . . . . . .67 E3
Priory Gdns B16. . . . . .65 F1
Priory Green Prim Sch
WV9 . . . . .11 A2
Priory Ho
Halesowen B63 . . . . .82 F5
Kenilworth CV8 . . . . .147 F4
Priory Hospl The B5. . . . . .86 C5
Priory La DY3 . . . . .50 D7
Priory Mews CV34 . . . . . .160 E2
Priory New Way Ind Est
B6. . . . . .165 C4
Priory Pl CV1. . . . . .165 C3
Priory Prim Sch DY1. . . . . .51 B3
Priory Prim Sch The
WS10. . . . . .42 D2
Priory Queensway The
B4. . . . . .164 C3
Priory Rd
Birmingham,Aston B6 . . . . .67 B8
Birmingham,Edgbaston B5,
B15. . . . . .86 B5
Birmingham,Warstock B28 .105 D3
Cannock WS12. . . . . .2 C7
Dodford B61. . . . . .136 A6
Dudley DY1 . . . . .51 C3
Halesowen B62 . . . . .83 F5
Warwick CV34 . . . . .160 E7
Priory Row CV1. . . . . .165 B3
Priory Sch B15 . . . . .86 B6
Priory Sq
Birmingham B4 . . . . .164 C3
Studley B80 . . . . .159 E5
Priory St
Coventry CV1. . . . . .165 C3
Dudley DY1 . . . . .51 C1
Nuneaton CV10 . . . . .72 D4
Royal Leamington Spa
CV31. . . . . .161 F6
Priory Terr CV31. . . . . . . .162 A7

Priory The DY3 . . . . .50 D8
Priory Visitors Ctr* CV1. .165 C3
Priory Wlk
10 Warwick CV34 . . . . . .160 F7
Birmingham B4 . . . . .164 C3
Hinckley LE10 . . . . .71 E1
Sutton Coldfield B72. . . . . .57 C7
Pritchard Ave WV11. . . . . .26 E6
Pritchard Cl B66. . . . . .65 B5
Pritchard St
Brierley Hill DY5 . . . . .61 B7
Wednesbury WS10 . . . . . .42 A3
Pritchatts Rd B15. . . . . . . .85 F5
Pritchett Ave WV4 . . . . . . .39 F3
Pritchett Rd B31. . . . . . . .123 B7
Pritchett St B6. . . . . .66 E5
Pritchett Twr 4 B10 . . . . . .67 B1
Private Way B45 . . . . .122 C4
Privet Cl B44. . . . . .44 E3
Privet Rd CV2 . . . . .96 B2
Proctors Barn La B98. . . . .154 B4
Proctor St B7 . . . . .67 A4
Proffitt Ave CV6. . . . . .96 A1
Proffitt Cl
Brownhills WS8 . . . . .16 A5
Walsall WS3 . . . . .28 E4
Proffitt St WS2 . . . . .28 E4
Progress Cl CV3 . . . . .135 A7
Progress Dr WS11 . . . . .4 F6
Progress Ind Ctr WS11 . . . .4 F7
Progress Way CV3 . . . . . .135 A8
Prole St WV10 . . . . .25 E4
Prologis Pk CV6 . . . . .95 B5
Promenade The DY5 . . . . . .61 D2
Prophets Cl B97 . . . . .153 D3
Prospect Gdns DY8 . . . . . .81 A4
Prospect Hill
Kidderminster DY10 . . . . . .116 E6
Redditch B97. . . . . .153 E4
Stourbridge DY8 . . . . .81 A4
Prospect La
Kidderminster DY10 . . . . . .116 E6
Solihull B91. . . . . .106 D4
Prospect Manor Ct WS12. . .2 C3
Prospect Pl 812. . . . . .86 F5
Prospect Rd
Birmingham B13 . . . . .86 F1
Burntwood WS7. . . . . .7 B6
Dudley DY2 . . . . .50 C2
Halesowen B62 . . . . .83 C5
Prospect Rd N B98. . . . . .154 A4
Prospect Rd S B98. . . . . .154 A4
Prospect Rd CV31. . . . . . .162 B5
Prospect Row
Dudley DY2 . . . . .62 D8
Stourbridge DY8 . . . . .81 A3
Prospect St
Bilston WV14. . . . . .40 E6
Tamworth B79 . . . . .21 A5
Wednesbury DY4 . . . . .41 C1
Prosper Mdw DY6. . . . . . . .60 F7
Prospero Cl B45. . . . . . . .102 A2
Prospero Dr CV34. . . . . . .161 E3
Prosser St
Bilston WV14. . . . . .40 D5
Wolverhampton WV10. . . . .25 V9
Prossers Wlk B46. . . . . . . .70 F7
Proud Cross Ringway
DY11. . . . . .116 C6
Proud's La WV14 . . . . .40 D6
Providence Cl WV10. . . . . .25 F4
Providence Ct B64. . . . . . .82 C8
Providence Dr DY9 . . . . . . .81 E6
Providence Ind Est DY9 . . .81 E6
Providence La WS3. . . . . . .28 C6
Providence Rd B61. . . . . .136 F3
Providence Row B61. . . . . .51 B8
Providence St
Coventry CV5. . . . . .132 F8
Cradley Heath B64 . . . . . . .62 D1
Stourbridge DY9 . . . . .81 F5
Tipton DY4 . . . . .52 C5
Providence Terr WS10. . . . .41 E6
Provost Williams CE Prim
Sch CV8 . . . . .135 A1
Pruden Ave WV4. . . . . .39 F3
Pryor Rd B68. . . . . .64 C4
Ptarmigan Pl CV11. . . . . . .73 F3
Puckering's La 11 CV34 . .160 E6
Pudsey Dr B75. . . . . .32 C3
Pugh Cres WS2. . . . . .27 E2
Pugh's Cl LE10 . . . . .76 A6
Pugh Rd
Bilston WV14. . . . . .40 E3
Birmingham B6 . . . . .67 A8
Wolverhampton WV4,WV14. .39 F2
Pugin Cl WV6. . . . . .23 D3
Pugin Gdns B23. . . . . .56 D8
Pullman Cl B77. . . . . .22 A2
Puma Way CV1. . . . . .165 C1
Pump House La
Blackwell B45,B60. . . . . . .137 F7
Pumphouse La 2 B69 . . . . .52 D1
Pumphouse Way 3 B69 . . .52 D1
Pump St
Kidderminster DY10 . . . . . .116 C6
Wolverhampton WV2. . . . . .40 A7
Puppy Gn DY4 . . . . .52 B5
Purbeck Cl B63. . . . . .82 D1

Purbeck Croft B32 . . . . .84 F4
Purbrook Rd WV1. . . . . . . .40 A8
Purbrook B77 . . . . .35 E8
Purcell Ave
 Lichfield WS13. . . . . .3 C2
 Nuneaton CV11 . . . . .79 A7
Purcell Cl CV32. . . . . . . .162 A8
Purcell Rd
 Coventry CV6. . . . . .114 B8
 Wolverhampton WV10. . . . .25 D8
Purdy Rd WV14 . . . . .40 E2
Purefoy Rd
 Birmingham B13 . . . . . . .105 C5
 Coventry CV3. . . . . .133 D8
Purley Gr B23 . . . . .56 A5
Purlieu La CV8 . . . . .147 D5
Purnells Way B93. . . . . . .128 A5
Purser Dr CV34. . . . . .160 B4
Purshall Cl B97. . . . . . . .153 C3
Purslet Rd WV1. . . . . .26 A2
Purslow Gr B31. . . . . .103 A1
Purton Mews CV31. . . . . .162 C6
Putney La B62. . . . . .55 C1
Putney La B62. . . . . .101 B1
Putney Rd B20. . . . . .55 C1
Putney Wlk B37 . . . . .70 B3
Puxton Dr DY11. . . . . . . .116 D8
Puxton La DY11. . . . . . . .116 C7
Pye Green Rd WS11. . . . . . .1 D4
Pye Green Valley Prim Sch
 WS12. . . . . .2 A7
Pyeharps Rd LE10. . . . . . .75 E5
Pype Hayes Cl B24. . . . . . .57 D4
Pype Hayes Rd B24. . . . . . .57 D4
Pyree Sq CV34. . . . . .160 B4
Pytchley Ho 6 B20. . . . . . .54 F3
Pytman Dr B76. . . . . .58 A7
Pyt Pk CV5 . . . . .112 D4

Q

Quadrangle The B90. . . . .126 E8
Quadrant Ho B32. . . . . . . .84 E7
Quadrant The
 Coventry CV1. . . . . .165 B2
 Nuneaton CV11. . . . . .73 E3
 Sedgley DY3. . . . . .39 D1
Quadrille Lawns WV9 . . . .10 F2
Quail Gn WV6 . . . . .23 F2
Quail Park Dr DY10 . . . . .117 A2
Qualcast Rd WV1,WV10. . . .25 F2
Quantock Cl
 Birmingham B45 . . . . . . .102 B2
 Brownhills WS8 . . . . .16 A4
 Halesowen B63 . . . . .82 D2
Quantock Dr
 Kidderminster DY10 . . . . .117 A6
 Nuneaton CV10 . . . . .72 B3
Quantock Rd DY8. . . . . . . .81 B6
Quantry La DY9. . . . . . . .120 F8
Quarrington Gr B14. . . . . .105 A3
Quarry Bank Prim Sch
 DY5. . . . . .62 A1
Quarry Brow DY3 . . . . . . .50 E6
Quarry Cl
 Cheslyn Hay WS6. . . . . . . .4 E3
 Leek Wootton CV35. . . . . .155 F7
Quarryfield La CV1. . . . . .165 D1
Quarry Fields CV35. . . . . .155 F7
Quarry Hill B63. . . . . .82 F2
Quarry Hills La WS14 . . . . .9 D8
Quarry House Cl B45. . . . .101 F1
Quarry La
 Birmingham B31 . . . . . . .103 A2
 Bromsgrove B61 . . . . . . .150 D8
 Halesowen B63 . . . . .83 A2
 Nuneaton CV11 . . . . .73 F1
 Rowington Green CV35. . . .145 C1
Quarry Lodge WS14. . . . . . .9 D5
Quarry Park Rd DY8 . . . . .99 A8
Quarry Rd
 Birmingham B29 . . . . . . .103 A8
 Dudley DY2. . . . . .62 B4
 Kenilworth CV8 . . . . .147 E6
Quarry Rise B69 . . . . .63 B8
Quarry St CV32 . . . . .161 C8
Quarry The DY10. . . . . . . .116 F8
Quarry Wlk B45 . . . . .122 A4
Quarrywood Gr CV2. . . . . .114 A4
Quarry Yd CV10. . . . . .72 C4
Quasar Cir 3 WV1. . . . . . .28 E2
Quatford Gdns WV10. . . . . .25 E5
Quayle Gr 3 DY8. . . . . . . .60 C3
Quayside B18. . . . . .66 A5
Quayside Cl B69. . . . . .63 E8
Quayside WS2 . . . . .42 C8
Queen Alexandra Coll
 B17. . . . . .85 E4
Queen Eleanors Dr B93 . . .128 B8
Queen Elizabeth Ave WS2 . .27 F2
Queen Elizabeth Ct B19. . . .66 B6
Queen Elizabeth Hospl
 B15. . . . . .85 E4
Queen Elizabeth Psychiatric
 Hospl B15 . . . . .85 E4
Queen Elizabeth Rd
 Birmingham B45 . . . . . . .101 E2
 Kidderminster DY10 . . . . .117 B5
 Sutton Coldfield B72. . . . . .46 C4
Queen Elizabeth's Mercian
 Sch B79 . . . . .21 C6
Queen Isabel's Ave CV3 . . .133 D8
Queen Margaret's Rd
 CV4 . . . . .132 C8
Queen Mary's Gram Sch
 WS1. . . . . .43 A8
Queen Mary's High Sch
 WS4 . . . . .28 F3
Queen Mary's Rd
 Bedworth CV12 . . . . .78 C5
 Coventry CV6. . . . . .113 E8
Queen Mary St WS1. . . . . .42 D6
Queen Philippa St CV3. . . .133 D6
Queens Arc CV11 . . . . .73 C4
Queen's Arc WV1. . . . . . . .163 B3
Queens Ave B14. . . . . . . .104 E8
Queen's Ave B69. . . . . . . .52 A1
Queens Ave B90. . . . . . . .106 B1
Queensbridge Rd B13. . . . .86 E2
Queensbridge Sch B13. . . . .86 E2
Queensbury Sch B24. . . . . .56 F2
Queens CE Jun Sch CV11. . .73 A4
Queen's Cl B24. . . . . .56 F2
Queen's Cl CV8. . . . . .147 F3
Queen's Cl B67. . . . . .65 A5
Queen's Coll The B15. . . . . .85 F5
Queen's Cotts B97. . . . . . .153 B4
Queens Court Trad Est
 B70. . . . . .52 F3
Queens Cres WV14. . . . . . .40 A1
Queen's Cres DY8. . . . . . .81 A7
Queen's Croft Com Sch
 WS13. . . . . .9 B7
Queen's Cross DY1. . . . . . .62 B8
Queens Ct
 Birmingham B3 . . . . .164 B4
 Brierley Hill DY5 . . . . .61 C6
 Nuneaton CV11. . . . . .73 A4
Queen's Ct WV10 . . . . .26 A6
Queens Dr
 Birmingham B5 . . . . .164 C2
 Birmingham,Lifford B30. . . .104 A4
 Burntwood WS7. . . . . .6 F5
Queen's Dr CV35. . . . . . . .145 A1
Queens Dr B65. . . . . .63 D4
Queen's Dr The B62. . . . . .83 C5
Queens Gdns
 4 Birmingham B23. . . . . . .56 B7
 Bilston WV14. . . . . .40 D7
 Dudley DY2 . . . . .62 C4
Queens Head Rd B21. . . . . .65 E7
Queens Hill DY9 . . . . .119 D7
Queens Hospital Cl B15. . . .66 C1
Queensland Ave CV5. . . . .112 F2
Queensland Gdns 4 CV12. . .77 F2
Queen's Lea WV12 . . . . . . .27 C5
Queen's Park CB 3 LE10. . . .75 E8
Queen's Park Flats 2
 LE10. . . . . .75 E8
Queen's Park Rd B32. . . . . .84 F6
Queen's Park Terr 4
 LE10. . . . . .75 E8
Queens Par WS3. . . . . .14 B1
Queen Sq WV1. . . . . .163 B3
Queens Rd B6. . . . . .67 A8
Queen's Rd B23 . . . . .56 C3
Queens Rd B26. . . . . .68 F5
Queen's Rd
 Coventry CV1. . . . . .165 A2
 Hinckley LE10 . . . . .75 E8
 Kenilworth CV8 . . . . .147 F3
 Nuneaton CV11. . . . . .73 B4
 Oldbury B68. . . . . .64 D5
Queens Rd DY3 . . . . .50 E8
Queen's Rd
 Smethwick B67. . . . . .64 D4
 Stourbridge DY8 . . . . .80 F6
 Tipton DY4. . . . . .51 F5
Queens Rd WS4 . . . . .29 C7
Queen's Ride B12. . . . . . . .86 D4
Queens Sq WS11. . . . . .1 E1
Queen's Sq CV34 . . . . . . .160 D5
Queen St
 Astwood Bank B96. . . . . .158 E1
 Bedworth CV12 . . . . .78 C3
 Bilston,Bunker's Hill WV14 . .40 E5
 Birmingham B12 . . . . .87 B5
 Brierley Hill,Pensnett DY5. . .61 C6
 Brierley Hill,Quarry Bank
  DY5. . . . . .82 A8
 Brownhills WS9 . . . . .15 F2
 Burntwood WS7. . . . . .6 F5
 Cannock,Blackfords WS11. . .1 D1
 Cannock WS11. . . . . .2 A5
 Cheslyn Hay WS6. . . . . . . .4 D3
 Coventry CV1. . . . . .165 C4
 Cradley Heath B64 . . . . . . .62 D1
 Cubbington CV32. . . . . . .157 E5
 Darlaston,Darlaston Green
  WS10 . . . . .41 D8
 Darlaston,Moxley WS10 . . . .41 B4
 Halesowen B63 . . . . .83 A4
 Kidderminster DY10 . . . . .116 E7
 Kingswinford DY6 . . . . . . .60 D7
 Lichfield WS13. . . . . .9 A7
 Oldbury B69. . . . . .64 A8
 Redditch B98 . . . . .153 E4
Queen Street Pas 1 DY5. . .82 A8
Queen St
 Royal Leamington Spa
  CV32. . . . . .157 A1
 Stourbridge DY8 . . . . .80 F6
 Stourbridge,Wordsley DY8 . .60 E3
 Sutton Coldfield B72. . . . . .46 C4
 Tipton DY4. . . . . .51 E4
 Walsall WS2 . . . . .28 D1
 Wednesbury WS10 . . . . . . .41 E3
 West Bromwich B70. . . . . .53 D3
 Wolverhampton WV1. . . . .163 C3
Queensway B6 . . . . .55 F2
Queensway Cl B68. . . . . . . .64 B1
Queens Way B78. . . . . .36 F6
Queensway
 Halesowen B63 . . . . .83 B3
 Nuneaton CV10 . . . . .73 E6
 Oldbury B68. . . . . .64 B1
 Royal Leamington Spa
  CV31. . . . . .161 E6
 Stourbridge DY9 . . . . .81 E2
 Sutton Coldfield B74. . . . . .45 A8
 Tamworth B79. . . . . .21 A8
Queensway Trad Est
 Birmingham B5 . . . . .164 D3
 Royal Leamington Spa
  CV31. . . . . .161 E6
Queensway (Tunnel) B1. . .164 B3
Queenswood Ct CV7. . . . . .94 D4
Queens Wood Ho B14. . . . .104 D4
Queenswood Rd
 Birmingham B13 . . . . .87 A4
 Sutton Coldfield B75. . . . . .32 B1
Queen Victoria Ct 4
 LE10. . . . . .71 D1
Queen Victoria Prim Sch
 DY3. . . . . .50 E8
Queen Victoria Rd
 Coventry CV1. . . . . .165 B2
 Coventry CV1. . . . . .165 B3
Quenby Dr DY1. . . . . .51 A3
Quentin Dr DY1. . . . . .61 F8
Queslade Cl B43. . . . . .44 A1
Queslett Rd B43. . . . . .44 C2
Queslett Rd E B74,B43. . . . .44 F5
Quibery Cl B98 . . . . .154 F3
Quicksand La WS9. . . . . . . .29 F4
Quigley Ave B9. . . . . .67 B2
Quillets Rd DY8. . . . . .60 C3
Quilletts Cl CV6. . . . . .96 A1
Quilter Cl
 Dudley WV14 . . . . .51 A8
 Willenhall WS2 . . . . .27 F3
Quilter Rd B24 . . . . .57 B2
Quince B77 . . . . .22 B3
Quince Tree Sch B77. . . . . .22 A3
Quincey Dr B24. . . . . .57 C3
Quincy Rise DY5. . . . . .81 C7
Quinn Cl CV3 . . . . .134 B7
Quinneys La B98. . . . . . . .159 B6
Quinton Ave WS6. . . . . .4 F3
Quinton Bsns Pk B32. . . . . .84 A4
Quinton Church Prim Sch
 B32. . . . . .84 A6
Quinton Cl
 Redditch B98 . . . . .154 D1
 Solihull B92 . . . . .89 D3
Quintondale 5 B90. . . . . .126 C8
Quinton Expressway B32. . .84 B4
Quinton Flats CV3 . . . . . . .133 D7
Quinton La B32. . . . . .84 D6
Quinton Par CV3. . . . . . . .133 D7
Quinton Pl CV3 . . . . .133 D7
Quinton Pl WS11. . . . . .4 A6
Quinton Rd
 Birmingham B17 . . . . .85 C3
 Coventry CV1. . . . . .165 C1
Quinton Rd W B32. . . . . . .84 D4
Quonians La WS13. . . . . . . .9 B8
Quorn Cres DY8 . . . . .60 C3
Quorn Gr B24 . . . . .57 B2
Quorn Ho 3 B20. . . . . .54 F3
Quorn Way CV3. . . . . .134 E7

R

Rabbit La WV11. . . . . .12 A8
Rabone La B66. . . . . .65 C6
Raby Cl B69 . . . . .62 F8
Raby St WV2 . . . . .163 C2
Racecourse La DY8. . . . . . .80 F1
Racecourse Rd WV6. . . . . . .25 A5
Race Leys Inf Sch CV12 . . . .78 B3
Race Leys Jun Sch CV12 . . .78 B4
Racemeadow Cres B64. . . . .62 C1
Rachael Gdns WS10. . . . . . .42 C4
Rachel Cl DY4. . . . . .41 C1
Rachel Gdns B29. . . . . .85 D2
Radbourn Dr B74. . . . . .46 A6
Radbourne Dr B63. . . . . . . .82 A7
Radbourne Rd B90. . . . . . .106 C3
Radbrook Way CV31. . . . . .162 D6
Radcliffe Dr B62. . . . . .83 E6
Radcliffe Gdns 6 CV31. . . .162 A6
Radcliffe Rd CV5. . . . . . . .132 F8
Radcliffe Twr 3 B12. . . . . .86 F8
Radclyffe Ho B16. . . . . . . .86 A8
Raddens Rd B62. . . . . .83 F3
Raddington Dr B92. . . . . . .106 E8
Raddlebarn Dr B29 . . . . . . .86 A1
Raddlebarn Farm Dr
 B29. . . . . .103 F8
Raddlebarn Prim Sch B29. .85 F1
Raddlebarn Rd B29. . . . . . .103 F8
Radford Ave DY10. . . . . . .116 E7
Radford Cl WS5. . . . . .43 A3
Radford Ct WS5. . . . . .43 A3
Radford Ct DY10. . . . . . . .116 E7
Radford Dr B14. . . . . .15 C0
Radford Hall CV31. . . . . . .162 E6
Radford Ho
 2 Redditch B97 . . . . . . .153 A4
 Coventry CV1. . . . . .113 A7
Radford La WV3,WV4. . . . . .37 F7
Radford Prim Sch CV6. . . .113 B5
Radford Rd
 Alvechurch B48. . . . . . . .139 D7
 Birmingham B29 . . . . . . .103 A6
Radford Rd continued
 Coventry CV1,CV6 . . . . . .113 B5
 Royal Leamington Spa
  CV31. . . . . .162 C7
Radford Rise WS1. . . . . . .107 E5
Radford Semele CE Prim Sch
 CV31. . . . . .162 E5
Radley Ct B26. . . . . .89 C7
Radley Dr CV10 . . . . .73 A1
Radley Gr B29 . . . . .85 A2
Radley Rd
 Stourbridge DY9 . . . . .81 F4
 Walsall WS4 . . . . .29 C7
Radleys Prim Sch The
 WS4 . . . . .29 D7
Radleys The B33 . . . . .89 D8
Radleys Wlk B33. . . . . .89 D8
Radlow Cres B37 . . . . .90 B8
Radmore Cl WS7. . . . . .6 D8
Radmore Rd LE10. . . . . . . .71 D3
Radnor Cl B45. . . . . .102 B2
Radnor Croft WS5 . . . . .43 C3
Radnor Ct WS9 . . . . .15 F4
Radnor Dr CV10. . . . . .72 E2
Radnor Gn B71. . . . . .53 C7
Radnor Rd
 Birmingham,Brandhall
  B68. . . . . .84 B7
 Birmingham,Lozells B20 . . . .66 B8
 Sedgley DY3. . . . . .50 C8
Radnor Rise WS12 . . . . .2 B4
Radnor St B18. . . . . .66 A6
Radnor Wlk CV2. . . . . .114 F8
Radstock Ave B36 . . . . .68 C7
Radstock Rd WV12. . . . . . .13 C1
Radway Cl B98. . . . . .154 B6
Radway Ind Est B90. . . . . .126 E7
Radway Rd B90. . . . . .126 E8
Raeburn Rd B43 . . . . .44 C4
RAF Cotts B35. . . . . .57 F2
Raford Rd B23. . . . . .56 D6
Ragees Rd DY6 . . . . .60 F4
Raglan Ave
 Perton WV6. . . . . .23 D7
 Smethwick B66. . . . . .65 C4
Raglan Cl
 Nuneaton CV11 . . . . .73 D4
 Sedgley DY3. . . . . .39 C1
 Sutton Coldfield WS9. . . . . .30 F3
Raglan Ct
 7 Coventry CV1. . . . . . . .113 E3
 Bromsgrove B60 . . . . . . .137 A1
Raglan Gr CV8. . . . . .148 B5
Raglan Ho B33. . . . . .69 A2
Raglan Rd
 Birmingham,Balsall Heath
  B5. . . . . .86 D5
 Birmingham,Handsworth
  B21. . . . . .65 C8
 Smethwick B66. . . . . .65 C4
Raglan St
 Brierley Hill DY5 . . . . .61 C4
 Coventry CV1. . . . . .165 D3
 Wolverhampton WV3 . . . . .163 A2
Raglan Way B37. . . . . .70 D1
Ragley Cl
 Knowle B93 . . . . .128 B7
 Walsall WS3 . . . . .14 A1
Ragley Cres B60. . . . . . . .151 A8
Ragley Dr
 2 Willenhall WV13. . . . . . .40 F8
 Birmingham,Grove Vale B43 .43 D2
 Birmingham,Sheldon B26 . . .89 C6
Ragley Ho 8 B97. . . . . . . .153 A4
Ragley Way CV11 . . . . .73 F2
Ragley Wlk 3 B65. . . . . . . .63 C3
Raglis Cl B97 . . . . .153 A1
Ragnall Ave B33. . . . . .89 D7
Raikes La WS14 . . . . .17 C7
Rail Bridge Est B70. . . . . . .53 A1
Railswood Dr WS3 . . . . . . .15 B3
Railway Cl B80. . . . . .159 D4
Railway Dr
 Bilston WV14. . . . . .40 E5
 Wolverhampton WV1. . . . .163 C3
Railway La WV13 . . . . .27 A1
Railway Rd
 Birmingham B20 . . . . .55 C2
 Sutton Coldfield B73. . . . . .46 B5
 Sutton Coldfield 8 B66 . . . .64 E7
Railway St
 Bilston WV14. . . . . .40 E5
 Cannock WS11. . . . . .4 E8
 Norton Canes WS11 . . . . . .6 A5
 Tipton DY4. . . . . .52 C5
 West Bromwich B70. . . . . .53 B4
 Wolverhampton WV1. . . . .163 C3
Railway Terr
 4 Wednesbury WS10. . . . .41 F2
 Bedworth CV12 . . . . .78 C2
 Birmingham,Aston B7 . . . . .67 B6
 Birmingham,Hamstead B42. .54 F6
Railway View B10. . . . . . . .87 C7
Railway Wlk B60. . . . . . . .151 A6
Railwharf Sidings DY2 . . . .62 F4
Rainbow St
 Dudley WV14 . . . . .40 D2
 Wolverhampton WV2. . . . .163 D1
Rainford Way B38 . . . . . . .123 C8
Rainham Cl DY4. . . . . .51 D5
Rainsbrook Dr
 Nuneaton CV11. . . . . .74 A1
 Solihull B90. . . . . .126 F6
Rainscar B77. . . . . .36 B7
Rainsford Cl CV35. . . . . . .146 B1
Raison Ave CV11. . . . . .73 F3
Rakegate Prim Sch WV10 . .11 B1
Rake Hill WS7 . . . . .7 B8
Rake Way B15. . . . . .66 B1
Raleigh Cl
 Birmingham B21 . . . . .54 B8
 Hinckley LE10 . . . . .71 D7
Raleigh Croft B43. . . . . . . .43 E1
Raleigh Ind Est B21. . . . . . .54 B8
Raleigh Rd
 Bilston WV14. . . . . .41 A4
 Birmingham B9 . . . . .67 D1
 Coventry CV2. . . . . .114 B3
Raleigh St
 Walsall WS2 . . . . .28 C2
 West Bromwich B71. . . . . .53 C4
Ralph Barlow Gdns B44. . . .56 B8
Ralph Rd
 Birmingham B8 . . . . .67 D5
 Coventry CV6. . . . . .112 F6
 Solihull B90. . . . . .106 C4
Ralphs Mdw B32. . . . . .84 D2
Ralston Cl WS3 . . . . .14 A4
Rambures Cl CV34. . . . . . .161 F1
Ramillies Cres WS6 . . . . . . .4 F3
Ramp Rd B26. . . . . .90 C4
Ramsay Cl B71. . . . . .53 F8
Ramsay Cres CV5. . . . . . . .112 B2
Ramsay Rd
 Oldbury B68. . . . . .64 C3
 Tipton DY4. . . . . .51 F2
 Walsall WS2 . . . . .28 A5
Ramsden Ave CV10 . . . . . . .72 D6
Ramsden Cl B29. . . . . .103 B2
Ramsden Ct CV10 . . . . .72 C7
Ramsey Cl
 Birmingham B45 . . . . . . .101 F1
 Hinckley LE10 . . . . .71 B1
Ramsey Rd
 1 Royal Leamington Spa
  CV31. . . . . .162 B2
 Tipton DY4. . . . . .51 F5
 Walsall WS2 . . . . .28 A5
Ramsey Ho 5 WV3. . . . . . . .67 C7
Randall Ave B48. . . . . . . .139 A6
Randall Cl DY6 . . . . .60 F4
Randall Rd CV8. . . . . .147 F3
Randle Dr B75 . . . . .32 C3
Randle Rd
 Nuneaton CV10 . . . . .72 C4
 Stourbridge DY9 . . . . .81 C4
Randolph Cl 11 CV31. . . . .162 C6
Randwick Gr B44 . . . . .44 E1
Ranelagh Ho WV2 . . . . .39 D7
Ranelagh Rd WV2. . . . . . . .39 D7
Ranelagh St CV31. . . . . . .162 A6
Ranelagh Terr CV31. . . . . .161 F6
Range Meadow Cl CV32 . . .156 C3
Rangemoor CV3 . . . . .134 D6
Rangeway Rd CV8. . . . . . . .44 F6
Rangeways Rd
 Kidderminster DY11 . . . . .116 A8
 Kingswinford DY6 . . . . . . .60 F4
Rangeworthy Cl B97. . . . . .158 C7
Rangifer Rd B78 . . . . .20 F1
Rangoon Rd B92. . . . . .89 E4
Ranleigh Ave DY6. . . . . . . .60 F4
Rankine Cl B16. . . . . .66 A1
Rannoch Cl
 Brierley Hill DY5 . . . . .81 B8
 Hinckley LE10 . . . . .75 B8
Rannoch Dr CV10 . . . . .72 C5
Rannoch Cl CV3 . . . . .114 F2
Ranscombe Dr DY3 . . . . . . .50 D2
Ransom Rd
 Birmingham B23 . . . . .56 C4
 Coventry CV6. . . . . .113 E8
Ran-tan The B97 . . . . .158 E5
Ranton Park Area 3 WS11 . .2 A2
Ranulf Croft CV3. . . . . . . .133 C7
Ranulf St CV3 . . . . .133 C7
Ranworth Rise WV4. . . . . . .39 D4
Raphael Cl CV5. . . . . .112 C3
Rashwood Cl B94. . . . . . . .143 B6
Ratcliffe Ave B30 . . . . .104 D3
Ratcliffe Cl DY3. . . . . .50 F6
Ratcliffe Ct CV10. . . . . .72 C4
Ratcliffe Dr WV13. . . . . . . .41 B8
Ratcliffe Rd
 Hinckley LE10 . . . . .75 F6
 Solihull B91. . . . . .107 C4
 Wednesfield WV11. . . . . . .27 A6
Ratcliffe Way DY4. . . . . . . .52 D6
Ratcliff Wlk 3 B69 . . . . . . .64 A7
Rathbone Cl
 Bilston WV14. . . . . .40 D5
 Birmingham B5 . . . . .86 E7
 Keresley CV7. . . . . .94 F6
 Keresley CV7. . . . . .95 A6
Rathbone Rd B67. . . . . .64 F2
Rathlin Cl WV9 . . . . .11 A3
Rathlin Croft B36. . . . . .70 B6
Rathmell Cl WV9. . . . . .11 A3
Rathvale Dr B27. . . . . .103 B3
Rathwell Cl WV9 . . . . .11 A1
Rattle Croft B33 . . . . .68 E3
Raveloe Dr CV11. . . . . .73 D1
Ravenall Cl B34. . . . . .69 B7
Raven Cl
 Cannock WS12. . . . . .2 E4
 Cheslyn Hay WS6. . . . . . . .4 D2
Raven Cragg Rd CV5. . . . . .132 E8
Raven Cres WV11. . . . . . . .26 F8
Raven Ct
 21 Brierley Hill DY5. . . . . . .61 D2
 Wolverhampton WV10. . . . .11 B3
Ravenfield Cl B8. . . . . .68 A5
Ravenhayes La B32. . . . . .102 A6
Raven Hays Rd B31. . . . . . .102 C2
Ravenhill Dr WV8. . . . . . . .10 A4
Ravenhurst Dr B43. . . . . . . .43 E3

Ravenhurst Mews B23 . . . .56 E3
Ravenhurst Rd B17 . . . . . . .85 C6
Ravenscroft St B12 . . . . . . .87 A8
Raven Rd WS5 . . . . .43 B6
Ravens Bank Dr B98 . . . .154 E7
Ravens Bank Fst Sch
B98 . . . . .154 D6
Ravensbourne Gr WV13 . .27 C2
Ravenscroft Rd
 Solihull B92 . . . . .107 A8
 Willenhall WV12 . . . . .27 B5
Ravenscroft DY8 . . . . .80 C6
Ravens Ct WS8 . . . . .15 F7
Ravensdale Ave CV32 . . .156 C2
Ravensdale Cl WS5 . . . . . .43 B7
Ravensdale Gdns WS5 . . .43 B7
Ravensdale Prim Sch
CV2 . . . . .114 D4
Ravensdale Rd
 Birmingham B10 . . . . .87 F7
 Coventry CV2 . . . . .114 D3
Ravenshaw La B91 . . . . .108 A4
Ravenshaw Rd B16 . . . . . .65 C2
Ravenshaw Way B91 . . .108 A3
Ravenshill Rd B14 . . . . . .105 D4
Ravensholme WV6 . . . . . . .23 F2
Ravensholt CV4 . . . . .132 D6
Ravensitch Wlk DY5 . . . . .61 E1
Ravensmere Rd B98 . . . .154 E1
Ravensthorpe Cl CV3 . . .134 E8
Ravenstone B77 . . . . .36 B8
Ravenswood B15 . . . . .85 E8
Ravenswood Cl B74 . . . . . .46 B8
Ravenswood Dr B91 . . . .106 F1
Ravenswood Dr S B91 . .106 E1
Ravenswood Hill B46 . . . .70 F7
Raven Way CV11 . . . . .73 F2
Raven Wlk B15 . . . . .86 C7
Rawdon Gr B44 . . . . .56 B8
Rawlett Sch B79 . . . . .21 A8
Rawlings Rd B67 . . . . .65 A2
Rawlins Croft B35 . . . . . . .58 C3
Rawlinson Rd CV32 . . . . .157 B2
Rawlins St B16 . . . . .66 A1
Rawnsley Dr CV8 . . . . . . .148 C6
Rawnsley Rd WS12 . . . . . . .2 E6
Raybolds Bridge Rd WS2 .28 C4
Raybon Croft B45 . . . . . .122 A6
Raybould's Fold DY2 . . . . .62 C5
Rayford Dr B71 . . . . .43 A2
Raygill B77 . . . . .36 B8
Ray Hall La
 Birmingham B43 . . . . .54 B8
 West Bromwich B43,B71 . .43 A1
Rayleigh Rd B27 . . . . .88 D3
Rayleigh Rd WV3 . . . . .39 A8
Ray Mercer Way DY10. .116 F5
Raymond Ave B42 . . . . . . .55 B6
Raymond Cl
 Coventry CV6 . . . . .95 F5
 Walsall WS2 . . . . .28 D5
Raymond Gdns WV11 . . .26 E6
Raymond Rd B8 . . . . .67 E4
Raymont Gr B43 . . . . .44 B4
Rayners Croft B26 . . . . . . .68 F2
Raynor Cres CV12 . . . . . . .77 D1
Raynor Rd WV10. . . . . .25 F6
Raynsford Wlk CV34 . . .155 D1
Raywoods The CV10. . . . . .72 F3
Rea Ave B45. . . . . .121 E8
Reacroft Rd B31. . . . . . . .122 F8
Rea Cl B31. . . . . .123 A7
Rea St S B5 . . . . .86 F8
Reaside Cres B14. . . . . . .104 B5
Reaside Croft B12. . . . . . .86 E6
Reaside Dr B45. . . . . .102 B1
Reaside Jun Sch B45. . . .101 E1
Rea St B5 . . . . .164 D1
Rea Terr B5 . . . . .86 F8
Rea Twr B19. . . . . .66 C5
Rea Valley Dr B31. . . . . . .103 B2
Reaview Dr B29 . . . . .86 B2
Reaymer Cl WS2. . . . . .28 B6
Reay Nadin Dr B73 . . . . . .45 B4
Rebecca Dr B29 . . . . .85 E2
Rebecca Gdns WV4 . . . . .38 F4
Recreation Rd
 Bromsgrove B61 . . . . .136 F3
 Coventry CV6. . . . . .96 A3
Recreation St DY2 . . . . . . .62 D5
Rectory Ave WS10 . . . . . . .41 D6
Rectory Cl
 Allesley CV5. . . . . .112 C6
 Bedworth CV7 . . . . .78 A1
 Drayton Bassett B78. . . . .34 E5
 Stourbridge DY8 . . . . .81 B3
 Whitnash CV31 . . . . .162 B4
Rectory Ct B97 . . . . .153 D1
Rectory Dr CV7 . . . . .78 A1
Rectory Fields DY8 . . . . . .60 E2
Rectory Gdns
 Birmingham B36 . . . . .69 A8
 Oldbury B68. . . . . .64 C5
 Solihull B91 . . . . .107 D5
 Stourbridge DY8 . . . . .81 B3
Rectory Gr B18 . . . . .65 E6

Rectory La
 Allesley CV5. . . . . .112 C6
 Birmingham B36 . . . . .69 A8
 Upton Warren B61. . . . . . .150 A4
Rectory Park Ave B75 . . . .46 E4
Rectory Park Cl B75 . . . . .46 E4
Rectory Park Ct B75 . . . .46 F6
Rectory Park Rd B26. . . . .89 C5
Rectory Rd
 Birmingham B31 . . . . .103 B3
 Redditch B97 . . . . .153 D1
 Solihull B91 . . . . .107 C3
 Stourbridge DY8 . . . . .81 B3
 Sutton Coldfield B75 . . . . .46 E6
Rectory St DY8 . . . . .60 E3
Redacre Rd B73 . . . . .45 F2
Redacres WV6 . . . . .24 E8
Redbank Ave B23 . . . . .56 C3
Redbourn Rd WS3 . . . . . .14 A4
Red Brick Cl B64 . . . . .82 D7
Redbrook Cl WS12. . . . . . . .2 D2
Redbrook Covert B38 .123 E8
Red Brook Rd WS2. . . . . .28 A5
Redbrooks Cl B91 . . . . . .107 A1
Redburn Dr B14 . . . . .104 D2
Redcap Croft CV6. . . . . . . .95 D4
Redcar Cl
 Lower Marlbrook B60 . . . .121 B1
 Royal Leamington Spa
 CV32 . . . . .157 C4
Redcar Croft B36 . . . . .68 C8
Redcar Rd
 Coventry CV1 . . . . .113 E5
 Wolverhampton WV10 . . .11 D4
Redcliffe Dr WV5 . . . . .49 B6
Redcliff B77 . . . . .21 F5
Redcotts Cl WV10. . . . . . . .26 A8
Redcroft Dr B24 . . . . .57 C5
Redcroft Rd DY2 . . . . .62 E3
Reddal Hill Prim Sch B64 .62 E1
Reddal Hill Rd B64 . . . . . .62 E2
Red Deeps CV11. . . . . .78 D8
Reddicap Heath Rd B75. .46 F4
Reddicap Hill B75 . . . . . . .46 E4
Reddicap Trad Est B64 . .46 D4
Reddicroft B73 . . . . .46 C5
Reddings B13. . . . . .86 D3
Reddings La B11,B28 . . . .87 E3
Reddings Rd B13 . . . . .86 E2
Reddings The B47 . . . . . .125 A5
Redditch Ho B69. . . . . .69 E2
Redditch Rd
 Alvechurch,Arrowfield Top
 B48. . . . . .139 B8
 Alvechurch,Rowney Green
 B48. . . . . .139 C3
 Birmingham B31,B38. . . .123 C8
 Hopwood B48 . . . . .123 B1
 Stoke Heath B60 . . . . . . .150 D5
 Studley B80 . . . . .159 D5
Redditch Ringway B97,
 B98. . . . . .153 D4
Redditch Sta B97 . . . . . .153 D4
Redditch Wlk CV2. . . . . . .115 A7
Redesdale Ave CV6. . . . . .112 F5
Redfern Ave CV8. . . . . . . .148 A6
Redfern Cl B92 . . . . .89 B1
Redfern Dr WS7 . . . . .7 B5
Redfern Park Way B11. . . .88 A5
Redfern Rd B11. . . . . .88 A6
Redfly La DY5 . . . . .61 C6
Redford Cl B13 . . . . .87 B2
Redgate Cl B38 . . . . .103 D2
Redgrave Cl CV2. . . . . . . .115 B8
Red Hall Prim Sch DY3. . .50 C3
Redhall Rd
 Birmingham B32 . . . . .84 E7
 Dudley DY3 . . . . .50 C2
Redhill Ave WV5. . . . . .49 A6
Redhill Cl DY8 . . . . .81 B4
Red Hill Cl B80 . . . . .159 E6
Redhill Ct DY8 . . . . .81 B4
Redhill Furrows CV31. . .162 C5
Red Hill Gr B38 . . . . .123 F7
Redhill Jun & Inf Sch B25 .88 A6
Redhill La B45,B61. . . . . .121 C5
Red Hill Pl B62 . . . . .1 F4
Redhill Prim Sch WS11. . .1 F4
Redhill Rd
 Birmingham,King's Norton
 B38. . . . . .123 D7
 Birmingham,Tyseley B25 . . .88 A6
 Cannock WS11 . . . . .1 F4
Red Hill St WV1 . . . . .153 F2
Redhill Sch DY8 . . . . .81 B4
Red Hill St WV1. . . . . .25 B4
Red House Ave WS10 . . . .42 B3
Red House Park Rd B43 . .43 C2
Red House Rd B33. . . . . . .68 E2
Redhouse Rd WV6 . . . . . . .24 B5
Redhouse St WS1. . . . . . . .42 E7
Redhurst Dr WV10. . . . . . .11 B3
Red La
 Burton Green CV8 . . . . . .131 C2
 Coventry CV6 . . . . .113 F5
 Essington WV11. . . . . .13 C3
 Gospel End Village DY3 . . .50 B8
Redlake Dr WV9. . . . . .99 B8
Red La CV8. . . . . .147 D8

Redlake Rd DY9 . . . . .81 B1
Redlake B77. . . . . .35 E8
Redland Cl
 Coventry CV2. . . . . .96 E2
 Lower Marlbrook B60 . . . .121 C1
Redland La CV8. . . . . .135 A2
Redland Rd CV31. . . . . . .162 B5
Redlands CI B91 . . . . .107 D5
Redlands Rd B91 . . . . . . .107 D5
Redlands Way B74 . . . . . . .31 A1
Red Leasowes Rd B63. . . .83 A3
Redliff Ave B36 . . . . .58 D1
Red Lion Ave WS11 . . . . . . .6 A4
Red Lion Cl B69 . . . . .52 A1
Red Lion Cres WS11 . . . . . .6 A4
Red Lion La WS11 . . . . .6 B4
Red Lion St
 Alvechurch B48 . . . . .139 B6
 Redditch B98 . . . . .153 E4
 Wolverhampton WV1 . . . .163 B3
Redlock Field WS14. . . . . . .9 A5
Redmead Cl B30. . . . . . . .103 C4
Redmoor Gdns WV4 . . . . .39 A5
Redmoor High Sch LE10 .71 B3
Redmoor Way B76. . . . . . .58 D6
Rednal Hill Jun & Inf Sch
 B45. . . . . .122 C7
Rednal Hill La B45. . . . . .122 A6
Rednal Mill Dr B45 . . . . .122 C3
Rednal Park Dr B38. . . . .103 F2
Rednal Rd B38 . . . . .103 E1
Rednell Ho B69. . . . . .63 D6
Redpine Crest WV12 . . . . .27 D5
Red River Rd WS2 . . . . . . .28 A5
Redruth Cl
 Coventry CV6 . . . . .114 A8
 Kingswinford DY6 . . . . .60 D8
 Nuneaton CV11 . . . . .74 A4
 Walsall WS5 . . . . .43 D7
Redruth Rd WS5 . . . . .43 D7
Red Sands Rd B64 . . . . . .116 C6
Redstart Ave DY10 . . . . . .117 B2
Redstone Cl B98. . . . . . . .154 E8
Redstone Dr WV11. . . . . . .26 F5
Redstone Farm Rd B28 .106 B6
Redstone Way DY3. . . . . . .50 D4
Redthorne Gr CV8 . . . . . .148 B8
Redthorn Gr B33 . . . . .68 D3
Redvers Rd B9 . . . . .67 F1
Redway Ct B75 . . . . .46 E4
Redwell Cl B77 . . . . .21 D5
Redwing Cl WS7 . . . . .7 D5
Redwing Dr DY10 . . . . . . .117 A1
Redwing Gr B23 . . . . .56 B7
Redwing Rd B36 . . . . .70 A6
Red Wing Wlk B36 . . . . . . .70 A8
Redwood Ave DY1 . . . . . . .50 F5
Redwood Bsns Pk B66 . . .64 C7
Redwood Cl
 Birmingham B30 . . . . .103 E4
 Sutton Coldfield B74 . . . . .30 F2
Redwood Croft
 Birmingham B14 . . . . .104 C7
 Nuneaton CV10 . . . . .73 A1
Redwood Dr
 Burntwood WS7 . . . . .6 F8
 Cannock WS11 . . . . .2 A3
 Tipton B69. . . . . .52 B2
Redwood Gdns B27 . . . . .88 B5
Redwood Ho B37 . . . . .69 F5
Redwood Rd
 Birmingham B30 . . . . .103 E4
 Dudley DY1 . . . . .40 D2
 Walsall WS5 . . . . .43 B4
Redwood Way WV12 . . . . .27 B8
Reedham Gdns WV4. . . . .38 D5
Reedly Rd WV12 . . . . .13 C1
Reedmace Cl B38. . . . . . .123 F8
Reedmace Dr B61. . . . . . .137 A5
Reedmace B77 . . . . .21 C2
Reedswood Cl WS2 . . . . . .28 C3
Reedswood Gdns WS2 . . .28 C3
Reedswood La WS2 . . . . . .28 B3
Reedswood Way WS2 . . . .28 B4
Rees Dr
 Coventry CV3 . . . . .133 D4
 Wombourne WV5. . . . . .49 B7
Reeve Ct DY10. . . . . .117 A1
Reeve Dr CV8. . . . . .148 A4
Reeves La WS3 . . . . .9 B8
Reeves Cl DY4 . . . . .52 B2
Reeves Gdns WV8. . . . . . .10 A4
Reeves Rd
 Birmingham B14 . . . . .104 C6
 Hinckley LE10 . . . . .75 F6
Reeves St WS3 . . . . .28 B8
Reflex Ind Pk WV13. . . . . .27 A3
Reform St B70 . . . . .53 D3
Regal Cl B77 . . . . .35 C8
Regal Croft B36 . . . . .68 F8
Regal Dr WS2 . . . . .42 C8
Regal Ho DY11 . . . . .73 D3
Regan Ave B90 . . . . .106 A1
Regan Cres B23 . . . . .56 E6
Regan Dr B69 . . . . .63 D8
Regan Ho B13 . . . . .105 D7
Regency Arc CV32. . . . . .161 F8
Regency Cl
 Birmingham B9. . . . . .67 D1
 Nuneaton CV10 . . . . .73 D6
Regency Ct
 Coventry CV5 . . . . .132 F8
 Hinckley LE10 . . . . .76 A7
 Walsall WS1 . . . . .43 A7

Regency Ct continued
 Wolverhampton WV1 . . . .163 B4
Regency Dr
 Birmingham B38 . . . . .103 F2
 Coventry CV3 . . . . .132 F5
 Kenilworth CV8 . . . . .147 F3
Regency Gdns B14 . . . . .105 C3
Regency Ho
 Birmingham B16 . . . . .66 A1
 Royal Leamington Spa
 CV32 . . . . .162 A8
Regency Mews CV32 . . . .162 A8
Regency Wlk B74 . . . . .31 D5
Regent Ave B69 . . . . .52 A1
Regent Cl
 Birmingham B5 . . . . .86 D6
 Halesowen B63 . . . . .83 A4
 Kingswinford DY6 . . . . .60 C6
 Oldbury B69. . . . . .63 A8
Regent Ct
 Smethwick B66. . . . . .65 A5
 Birmingham B62. . . . . .84 A7
 Hinckley LE10 . . . . .75 D8
 Darlaston WS10 . . . . .41 D6
Regent Gr CV21 . . . . .52 A1
Regent Gr CV32. . . . . . . .161 F8
Regent Ho
 Walsall WS2 . . . . .28 D3
 Oldbury B69. . . . . .64 B2
Regent Mews B61 . . . . . .150 E8
Regent Par B61. . . . . .66 C4
Regent Park Rd B10 . . . . .67 C1
Regent Pl
 Royal Leamington Spa
 CV31. . . . . .162 A7
 Birmingham B1 . . . . .66 C4
 Tipton B69. . . . . .52 B2
Regent Rd
 Birmingham B17 . . . . .85 D8
 Birmingham,Handsworth
 B21. . . . . .65 D8
 Oldbury B69. . . . . .63 A8
 Wolverhampton WV4 . . . . .38 E5
Regents Park Com Prim Sch
 B10. . . . . .87 B8
Regents Park Rd B60 . . .137 C2
Regent St
 Bedworth CV12 . . . . .78 C4
 Bilston WV14 . . . . .40 D6
 Birmingham,Hockley B1. . .66 C4
 Birmingham,Stirchley B30 .104 A7
 Coventry CV1 . . . . .165 A2
 Cradley Heath B64 . . . . . . .82 F8
 Dudley DY1 . . . . .51 C6
 Hinckley LE10 . . . . .75 D8
 Nuneaton CV11 . . . . .73 D5
 Royal Leamington Spa
 CV32 . . . . .161 F8
 Smethwick B66. . . . . .65 A6
 Tipton DY4 . . . . .51 F4
 Willenhall WV13 . . . . .27 A3
Regents Wlk B75 . . . . .46 F6
Reg Hadden Ct CV10. . . . .73 D6
Regiment Ct CV6 . . . . .95 E1
Regina Ave B44. . . . . .101 E2
Regina Cres
 Coventry CV2 . . . . .115 A7
 Wolverhampton WV6 . . . . .24 B4
Regina Dr
 Birmingham B42 . . . . .55 D3
 Walsall WS4 . . . . .29 B4
Reginald Rd
 Birmingham B8 . . . . .67 D4
 Smethwick B67 . . . . .64 F2
Regis Beeches WV6. . . . . .24 C5
Regis Gdns B65. . . . . .63 C2
Regis Heath Rd B65 . . . . .63 E2
Regis Rd
 Rowley Regis B65 . . . . .63 C2
 Wolverhampton WV6 . . . . .24 B4
Regis Wlk CV2 . . . . .115 A7
Reid Ave WV12 . . . . .27 D6
Reid Cl WS7 . . . . .7 A4
Reid Rd B68. . . . . .64 D1
Reigate Ave B8 . . . . .68 B4
Reignier Pl CV34. . . . . . . .161 F2
Reindeer Rd B78 . . . . .20 E1
Relay Dr B77 . . . . .36 C7
Reliance Trad Est WV14 . .40 B5
Relko Dr B36 . . . . .68 C7
Relton Mews CV6. . . . . . .113 F6
Rembrandt Cl
 Cannock WS11. . . . . .2 D2
 Coventry CV5 . . . . .112 B4
Remburn Gdns CV34 . . .160 F8
Remembrance Rd
 Coventry CV3 . . . . .134 D6
 Wednesbury WS10 . . . . . .42 C3
Remington Dr WS11 . . . . . .4 F8
Remington Pl WS2. . . . . . .28 C5
Remington Rd WS2 . . . . . .28 B5
Renaissance Ct B12. . . . . .87 A1
Rene Rd B77 . . . . .21 E5
Renfrew Cl DY8 . . . . .60 C7
Renfrew Gdns DY11. . . . .116 C5
Renfrew Sq B35 . . . . .58 B4
Renison Rd CV12 . . . . .77 E1
Rennie Gr B32. . . . . .84 D5
Rennison Dr WV5. . . . . . . .49 A6
Renolds Cl CV4 . . . . .112 C2
Renown Ave CV5. . . . . . . .132 E8
Renown Cl DY5 . . . . .61 B7
Renshaw B91 . . . . .108 A3

Renshaw Ind Est B80 . . .159 B4
Renton Gr WV10. . . . . .11 A1
Renton Rd WV10. . . . . .11 A1
Repington Rd B77 . . . . . . .22 A5
Repington S B77 . . . . .22 A5
Repington Way B75. . . . . .47 B5
Repton Ave WV6 . . . . .23 E3
Repton Cl WS11 . . . . .4 B8
Repton Dr CV6 . . . . .96 B2
Repton Gr B9. . . . . .68 B3
Repton Ho B23 . . . . .56 F6
Repton Rd B9 . . . . .68 B3
Reservoir Cl WS2 . . . . .28 B8
Reservoir Pas WS10. . . . . .41 F3
Reservoir Pl WS2 . . . . .42 B8
Reservoir Rd
 Birmingham B29 . . . . .85 C3
 Birmingham,Edgbaston B16 .65 F2
 Birmingham,Rednal B45 .122 C3
 Birmingham,Stockland Green
 B23 . . . . .56 E4
 Cannock WS12. . . . . .2 D4
 Kidderminster DY11 . . . . .116 C3
 Oldbury B68. . . . . .64 C4
 Rowley Regis B65 . . . . .63 D3
 Solihull B92 . . . . .106 F8
Reservoir Retreat B16 . . .65 F1
Reservoir St WS2 . . . . .42 B8
Reswood Ct B24 . . . . .56 F3
Retallack Cl B66 . . . . .64 C3
Retford Dr B76 . . . . .46 E4
Retford Gr B25 . . . . .88 C6
Retreat Gdns DY3. . . . . . . .50 E7
Retreat St
 Astwood Bank B96 . . . . . .158 E1
 Wolverhampton WV3 . . . .163 A1
Retreat The B64 . . . . .82 E7
Reuben Ave CV10 . . . . .72 B6
Revesby Wlk B7 . . . . .67 A4
Revival St WS3 . . . . .14 B1
Rex Cl CV4 . . . . .131 D8
Reyde Cl B97 . . . . .153 A2
Reynalds Cross Sch B92 .106 D7
Reynard Cl B97 . . . . .152 F3
Reynards Cl DY3. . . . . .51 A7
Reynolds Cl
 Hinckley LE10 . . . . .71 A3
 Lichfield WS13. . . . . .3 B2
Reynolds Gr WV6 . . . . .23 F5
Reynolds Ho B19 . . . . .66 E7
Reynolds Rd
 Bedworth CV12 . . . . .78 A4
 Birmingham B21 . . . . .65 F2
Reynoldstown Rd B36. . . .68 E8
Reynolds Wlk WV11. . . . . .27 B8
Rhayader Rd B31. . . . . . . .102 E5
Rhodes Alms Houses The
 B21. . . . . .65 F5
Rhodes Cl DY3 . . . . .50 A4
Rhone Cl B11. . . . . .87 C3
Rhoose Croft B35. . . . . . . .58 B3
Rhuddlan Way DY10. . . . .116 E1
Rhyl Rd CV11. . . . . .79 F6
Rhys Thomas Cl WV12. . .27 D4
Rian Ct B44 . . . . .32 D8
Ribbesford Ave WV10 . . . .25 B8
Ribbesford Cl B63 . . . . . . .82 D6
Ribbesford Cres WV14 . . .40 D1
Ribble Cl CV12. . . . . .79 B2
Ribble Ct B73 . . . . .46 B5
Ribble Rd CV3 . . . . .113 F2
Ribblesdale Ave LE10 . . . .71 E3
Ribblesdale Rd B29,B30 .104 E2
Ribblesdale B77 . . . . .36 B7
Ribble Wlk B36. . . . . .69 F8
Ribbonbrook CV11. . . . . . .73 D3
Ribbonfields CV11 . . . . . . .73 D3
Richard Cooper Rd WS14. .17 F1
Richard Joy Cl CV6 . . . . . .95 C2
Richard Lee Prim Sch
 CV2 . . . . .114 E3
Richard Lighton Ho B1. .66 C3
Richard Pl WS5 . . . . .43 C8
Richard Rd WS5 . . . . .43 C8
Richard St S B70 . . . . .53 C2
Richards Cl
 Birmingham B31 . . . . .122 F6
 Kenilworth CV8 . . . . .147 F5
 Rowley Regis B65 . . . . .63 E4
Richards Gr CV31 . . . . . . .162 A5
Richards Ho
 Walsall WS2 . . . . .28 D3
 Oldbury B69. . . . . .63 E4
Richardson Cl CV34 . . . .155 F1
Richardson Dr WS7 . . . . . .6 E8
Richardson Dr B79 . . . . . . .20 E8
Richardson Way CV2 . . . .115 B8
Richards Rd DY4 . . . . .40 F1
Richards St WS10 . . . . .41 D7
Richard St B7 . . . . .66 F4
Richard St S B70 . . . . .53 C2
Richard Williams Rd
 WS10. . . . . .42 B2
Richborough Dr DY1. . . . . .50 F4
Rich Cl CV34 . . . . .161 B7
Riches St WV6. . . . . .24 F3
Richford Gr B33 . . . . .69 D2
Richmere Ct WV6 . . . . .23 F3
Richmond Aston Dr DY4 . .52 A5
Richmond Ave
 Birmingham B12 . . . . .86 F5
 Wolverhampton WV3 . . . . .24 F1

Richmond Cl
Birmingham B20 . . . .**55** A3
Cannock WS11. . . . .**2** A5
Hollywood B47. . . . .**125** C7
Tamworth B79. . . . .**21** A5
Richmond Croft B42 . . . . . .**54** F6
Richmond Ct
2 Sutton Coldfield B72 . . .**57** B7
4 Birmingham,Weoley Castle
B29. . . . .**103** C7
6 Royal Leamington Spa
CV31. . . . .**162** B7
Birmingham,Calthorpe Fields
B15. . . . .**86** B8
Halesowen B63 . . . .**82** E3
Oldbury B68. . . . .**64** C5
Stourbridge DY9 . . . .**81** B1
Richmond Dr
Lichfield WS14. . . . .**9** D7
Perton WV6 . . . .**23** F3
Sutton Coldfield B75 . . . . . .**46** F6
Wolverhampton WV3. . . . . .**24** E1
Richmond Gdns
Stourbridge DY8 . . . .**80** F7
Wombourne WV5. . . . .**49** A5
Richmond Gr DY8. . . . .**80** E8
Richmond Hill Gdns B15 . .**85** E7
Richmond Hill B68. . . . . . .**64** C5
Richmond Hill Rd B15 . . .**85** F6
Richmond Ho 2 B37 . . . . .**70** C1
Richmond Mews WV3. . . .**25** A1
Richmond Pk DY6 . . . .**60** C8
Richmond Pl B14 . . . .**104** F8
Richmond Prim Sch LE10 .**71** C3
Richmond Rd
Birmingham B45 . . . .**121** E7
Birmingham,Hockley B18...**54** A6
Birmingham,Yardley B33 . . .**68** D2
Dudley DY2 . . . .**62** C8
Hinckley LE10 . . . .**71** C3
Nuneaton CV11. . . . .**73** A4
Sedgley DY3 . . . .**50** E7
Smethwick B66 . . . .**65** A2
Solihull B92 . . . .**88** F2
Sutton Coldfield B73 . . . . . .**46** B6
Wolverhampton WV3. . . . . .**24** E1
Richmond St S B70 . . . . . .**52** E5
Richmond St
Coventry CV2 . . . .**114** A3
Halesowen B63 . . . .**83** A4
Walsall WS1 . . . .**29** A1
West Bromwich B70 . . . .**52** F6
Richmond Way 2 B37 . . . .**70** C3
Rickard Cl B93 . . . .**127** E6
Rickman Dr B15. . . . .**86** D8
Rickyard Cl
Birmingham,Northfield
B29. . . . .**103** A6
Birmingham,Yardley B25. . . .**68** D1
Rickyard La B98 . . . .**154** D5
Rickyard Piece B32 . . . . . .**84** E4
Ricoh Arena (Coventry City
FC) CV6. . . . .**95** E3
Riddfield Rd B36 . . . .**68** E8
Ridding La WS10. . . . .**41** F2
Riddings Cres WS3 . . . .**14** F4
Riddings Hill CV7 . . . .**130** C8
Riddings The
Birmingham B33 . . . .**68** F4
Coventry CV5. . . . .**132** E7
Stourbridge DY9 . . . .**81** D2
Sutton Coldfield B76 . . . . . .**58** B8
Tamworth B77. . . . .**21** E5
Wolverhampton WV10. . . . . .**26** A7
Riddon Dr LE10. . . . .**75** B8
Ridesvell Gr CV31. . . . . . .**162** A1
Ridgacre Ent Pk B71. . . . . .**53** B6
Ridgacre La B32. . . . .**84** C6
Ridgacre Rd B32. . . . .**84** C6
Ridgacre Rd W B32. . . . .**84** A6
Ridgacre Rd B71. . . . .**53** B6
Ridge Cl
Birmingham B13 . . . .**105** C6
Willenhall WS2 . . . .**27** D3
Ridge Ct CV5 . . . .**112** A6
Ridgefield Rd B62 . . . .**83** C7
Ridge La WV11 . . . .**26** D7
Ridgeley Cl CV34 . . . .**155** E2
Ridgemount Dr B38. . . . .**123** D8
Ridge Prim Sch The DY8 . . .**80** C5
Ridge Gr B25 . . . .**60** C5
Ridge St DY8 . . . .**80** C6
Ridgethorpe CV3 . . . .**134** E6
Ridgewater Cl B45. . . . .**122** B6
Ridge Way WS9. . . . .**30** B4
Ridgeway Ave
Birmingham B62 . . . .**84** A6
Coventry CV3. . . . .**133** C6
Ridgeway B17 . . . .**65** B2
Ridgeway Rd B80 . . . .**159** E2
Ridgeway Cl WS2 . . . .**27** E2
Ridgeway Dr WV4. . . . .**38** F3
Ridgeway Prim Sch WS7...**7** A5
Ridgeway The
1 Tipton DY4 . . . .**52** A8
Stourbridge DY8 . . . .**60** F2
Ridgeway Sch The CV34.**156** A1
Ridgeway DY3. . . . .**50** D7
Ridgeway The
Birmingham,Quinton B32...**84** A4
Birmingham,Upper Witton
B23. . . . .**56** A5
Burntwood WS7. . . . .**7** A4
Hinckley LE10 . . . .**75** D6

Ridgeway The continued
Warwick CV34 . . . .**156** A1
Ridgeway Trad Est B98 . . .**158** E1
Ridgewood Ave DY8 . . . . . .**80** C7
Ridgewood B34. . . . .**69** B6
Ridgewood Cl
7 Walsall WS1. . . . .**42** F8
Royal Leamington Spa
CV32. . . . .**156** C1
Ridgewood Dr B75. . . . . . .**32** B1
Ridgewood Gdns B44. . . . . .**55** F7
Ridgewood High Sch DY8 .**80** C5
Ridgewood Rise B77. . . . . . .**22** A5
Ridgley Rd CV4 . . . .**131** E8
Ridgmont Croft B32 . . . . . .**84** E5
Riding B71. . . . .**53** F7
Ridings Brook Dr 3 WS11..**2** A2
Ridings La B98 . . . .**154** B6
Ridings Park Trad Est
WS11. . . . .**2** A3
Ridings The WS11. . . . .**4** F8
Riding Way WV12. . . . .**27** D6
Ridley St B1. . . . .**164** A1
Ridpool Prim Sch B33 . . . . .**69** B3
Ridpool Rd B33. . . . .**69** B3
Ridware Ho WS13. . . . .**3** E1
Rifle Range Rd DY11 . . . .**116** B3
Rifle St WV14 . . . .**51** A8
Rigby Cl CV34 . . . .**161** D4
Rigby Dr WS11. . . . .**1** F4
Rigby Hall B60 . . . .**151** C8
Rigby Hall Day Specl Sch
B60. . . . .**151** C8
Rigby La B60 . . . .**151** C8
Rigby St WS10. . . . .**42** A1
Rigdale Cl CV2 . . . .**114** E2
Righton Ho B77 . . . .**21** D1
Riland Ave B75 . . . .**46** D5
Riland Ct B72 . . . .**57** C7
Riland Gr B75 . . . .**46** C5
Riland Ind Est B75. . . . .**46** D5
Riland Rd B75 . . . .**46** D5
Riley Cl CV4 . . . .**148** D4
Riley Cres WV4 . . . .**39** A6
Riley Dr B36. . . . .**58** E1
Riley Ho CV1 . . . .**165** B2
Riley Rd B14 . . . .**105** D3
Riley Sq CV2 . . . .**96** B1
Riley St WV13 . . . .**27** B2
Riley B77. . . . .**21** E3
Rills The LE10 . . . .**71** E2
Rilstone Rd B32 . . . .**84** F5
Rindleford Ave WV4. . . . . .**38** C6
Ringhills Rd WV8 . . . .**10** B2
Ringinglow Rd B44 . . . .**44** D2
Ringmere Ave B36. . . . .**69** B7
Ring Rd WS7 . . . .**6** E7
Ring Rd N B15. . . . .**85** F4
Ring Road St B15 . . . .**85** F3
Ring Road St Andrews
WV1. . . . .**163** A3
Ring Road St Davids
WV2. . . . .**163** B2
Ring Road St Georges
WV2. . . . .**163** C2
Ring Road St Johns
WV2. . . . .**163** B2
Ring Road St Marks
WV3. . . . .**163** B2
Ring Road St Patricks
WV1. . . . .**163** C4
Ring Road St Peters
WV1. . . . .**163** B3
Ringswood Rd B92. . . . .**88** E4
Ring The B25 . . . .**88** C8
Ringway WS11. . . . .**1** E1
Ringway Hill Cross CV1 .**165** A3
Ringway Ind Est WS13 . . . . .**3** C3
Ringway Queens CV1 . . . . .**165** A2
Ringway Rudge CV1 . . . . . .**165** A2
Ringway St Johns CV1. . . .**165** A2
Ringway St Nicholas
CV1. . . . .**165** B3
Ringway St Patricks CV1 .**165** B1
Ringway Swanswell CV1 .**165** C3
Ringway The DY10 . . . .**116** F0
Ringway Whitefriars
CV1. . . . .**165** C3
Ringwood Ave WV9 . . . .**30** B5
Ringwood Dr B45. . . . .**102** A1
Ringwood Highway CV6 . . .**96** E2
Ringwood Rd WV10 . . . .**11** D1
Rinhill Gr CV31. . . . .**162** D6
Ripley Cl B69. . . . .**62** F8
Ripley Gr B23. . . . .**56** B5
Riplingham 3 CV32 . . . . .**156** F2
Ripon Cl CV5. . . . .**112** B8
Ripon Dr B71. . . . .**42** D1
Ripon Rd
Birmingham B14 . . . .**105** C4
Walsall WS2 . . . .**28** B2
Wolverhampton WV10. . . . . .**25** C7
Rippingille Rd B43. . . . . . .**44** C4
Ripple Rd B30 . . . .**103** E5
Risborough Cl CV5. . . . . . .**112** C3
Rischale Way WS4 . . . .**29** D8
Risdale Cl CV32 . . . .**156** D2
Rise Ave B45 . . . .**122** A7
Riseley Cres B5. . . . .**86** D7
Rise The
Birmingham,Great Barr
B42. . . . .**55** A8
Birmingham,Marston Green
B37. . . . .**90** A7
Hopwood B48 . . . .**123** B4
Kingswinford DY6 . . . .**60** E5
Lichfield WS13. . . . .**8** F7
Rising Brook WV6. . . . .**24** B4

Rising La
Chadwick End B93. . . . .**145** B5
Kingswood B94,B93. . . . . . .**144** F5
Rising Rd B94. . . . .**144** C5
Rissington Ave B29 . . . . .**104** A8
Ritchie Cl B13. . . . .**87** A1
Rivendell Ct B28. . . . .**87** E1
Rivendell Gdns WV6 . . . . . .**24** B5
Riverbank Rd WV13 . . . .**27** D2
River Brook Dr B30 . . . . .**104** B8
River Cl
Bedworth CV12 . . . .**77** F1
Royal Leamington Spa
CV32. . . . .**161** D8
River Ct 3 CV1. . . . .**113** B3
Riverdrive B78,B79. . . . .**21** B3
Riverfield Gr B77 . . . .**21** D5
Riverford Croft CV4 . . . . .**132** D4
River Lee Rd B11. . . . .**87** B5
Rivermead CV11 . . . .**73** A4
Rivermead Rd B34. . . . .**69** A6
Riversdale 6 CV32 . . . . . .**161** E8
Riversdale Rd B14 . . . .**105** D3
Riverside Cl
Coventry CV3. . . . .**134** A7
Lickey End B60 . . . .**137** C6
Riverside Cres B28 . . . . . .**105** D4
Riverside Ct
1 Coleshill B46. . . . .**70** F7
Birmingham B38 . . . .**103** D3
Riverside Dr
Birmingham,Cannon Hill
B29. . . . .**86** C3
Birmingham,Stechford B33 . .**68** D4
Solihull B91 . . . .**107** E2
Riverside Gdns WV8 . . . . . .**10** B5
Riverside Ind Est B21 . . . . .**21** B1
Riverside
Royal Leamington Spa
CV32. . . . .**161** E8
Studley B80 . . . .**159** F5
Riverslea Rd CV3 . . . .**114** C1
Riversleigh Dr DY8. . . . . . .**80** E8
Riversleigh Rd CV32 . . . .**156** C1
Riversley Rd CV11 . . . .**73** B4
River St B5. . . . .**67** A2
Riverway WS10 . . . .**42** B2
River Wlk CV2 . . . .**96** C2
Rivington Cl DY8 . . . .**80** E4
Rivington Cres B44 . . . .**45** C1
Roach Cl
Birmingham B37 . . . .**70** C3
Brierley Hill DY5 . . . .**61** D5
Roach Cres WV11 . . . .**26** F8
Roach Pool Croft B16. . . . .**65** C2
Roach B77 . . . .**35** D6
Road No 1 DY10 . . . .**116** E2
Road No 2 DY10 . . . .**116** E2
Road No 3 DY10 . . . .**116** E2
Roadway CV12 . . . .**78** B2
Roanne Ringway CV11 . . . .**73** B4
Robert Ave B23. . . . .**56** E6
Robert Cl
Coventry CV3. . . . .**134** C4
Tamworth B79. . . . .**20** F7
Robert Cramb Ave CV4..**131** F8
Robert Ct
5 Birmingham,Wake Green
B13. . . . .**87** B2
Birmingham,Pheasey B44...**44** D4
Robert Rd
Bedworth CV7 . . . .**95** F8
Birmingham B20 . . . .**55** B1
Tipton DY4. . . . .**51** F6
Roberts Cl
Brownhills WS9 . . . .**15** F2
Darlaston WS10. . . . .**41** B4
Roberts Ct B24 . . . .**57** C6
Roberts Green Rd DY3 . . . .**50** E4
Roberts La DY9 . . . .**99** B8
Robertson Knoll B36 . . . . .**68** F7
Robertsons Gdns 5 B7 . . . .**67** C7
Roberts Prim Sch DY3 . . . .**50** D4
Roberts Rd
Birmingham B27 . . . .**88** D3
Walsall WS3 . . . .**28** F5
Wednesbury WS10 . . . .**42** E2
Robert Wynd WV14 . . . .**40** A1
Robeson Cl DY4 . . . .**51** D5
Robey's La B78 . . . .**22** D3
Robin Cl
Birmingham B36 . . . .**70** A8
Huntington WS12. . . . .**1** C7
Kingswinford DY6 . . . .**61** A6
Tamworth B77 . . . .**35** C8
Robin Gr WV11 . . . .**26** A7
Robin Hood Cres B28 . . .**105** F7
Robin Hood Croft B28 . . .**105** F6
Robin Hood La B28 . . . . .**105** F7
Robin Hood Rd
Brierley Hill DY5 . . . .**61** F2
Coventry CV3. . . . .**133** E4
Robin Hood Sch B28. . . . .**106** B6
Robinia Cl CV32 . . . .**157** B2
Robinia B77 . . . .**22** A4
Robin Rd B23. . . . .**56** E5
Robins Bsns Pk B70 . . . . . .**52** E7
Robins Cl WS6 . . . .**4** D1
Robin's Cl DY8 . . . .**81** A3
Robins Croft WS11. . . . .**2** A1
Robins Ct B46 . . . .**86** F1
Robinsfield Dr B31 . . . . . .**123** A7
Robins Gr CV34. . . . .**160** C4
Robins Hill Dr B48. . . . . . .**139** A5
Robins La B47. . . . .**153** C6
Robinson Cl B79. . . . .**20** E7

Robinson Rd
Bedworth CV12 . . . .**95** D8
Burntwood WS7. . . . .**7** A5
Robinson's Way B76 . . . . . .**58** D5
Robinson Way LE10 . . . . . .**75** F4
Robins Rd WS7 . . . .**6** E7
Robins Way CV10 . . . .**72** A3
Robin Wlk WS2 . . . .**27** F3
Robottom Cl WS2. . . . .**28** B6
Robson Cl WS8 . . . .**15** F5
Rocester Ave WV11 . . . .**26** E7
Rochdale Wlk B10 . . . .**87** C7
Roche Rd WS3 . . . .**13** F1
Rochester Ave WS7 . . . .**7** A7
Rochester Cl
Nuneaton CV11 . . . .**73** B3
Redditch B97 . . . .**158** C3
Rochester Croft WS2. . . . . .**28** A4
Rochester Rd
Birmingham B31 . . . .**103** A4
Coventry CV5. . . . .**132** E8
Rochester Way CV3 . . . .**2** C1
Rochester Wlk DY10 . . . . .**117** C5
Roche The WS13 . . . .**8** A8
Roche Way WS3 . . . .**13** F1
Rochford Cl
Birmingham B45 . . . .**121** E7
Halesowen B63 . . . .**82** F2
Sutton Coldfield B76 . . . . . .**58** A8
Rochford Ct
Royal Leamington Spa
CV31. . . . .**161** E7
Solihull B90 . . . .**127** A6
Rochford Gr WV4. . . . .**38** D5
Rochford Rd B42 . . . .**55** A7
Rock Gr B92. . . . .**88** E3
Rock Hill
Bromsgrove B61 . . . .**150** D7
Redditch B78,WS14. . . . .**19** C4
Rockingham Cl
Dorridge B93 . . . .**127** D2
Dudley DY3 . . . .**50** B3
Walsall WS3 . . . .**4** F5
Rockingham Dr
Nuneaton CV11 . . . .**78** F7
Perton WV6 . . . .**23** F3
Rockingham Gdns B74 . . . .**44** F8
Rockingham Hall Gdns
DY9. . . . .**99** D7
Rockingham Rd B25 . . . . . .**88** D8
Rock La CV7. . . . .**94** C7
Rockland Dr B33 . . . .**68** E4
Rockland Gdns WV13 . . . . .**40** F8
Rocklands Cres WS13 . . . . .**3** D1
Rocklands Dr B75 . . . .**46** B8
Rockley Gr B45 . . . .**122** A7
Rockley Rd B65. . . . .**63** A6
Rockmead Ave B44 . . . .**44** F2
Rock Mill La CV32 . . . . . .**161** D8
Rock Rd CV32 . . . .**156** C1
Rockmoor Cl B37. . . . .**69** E3
Rock Rd
Sedgley DY3 . . . .**50** F8
Solihull B92 . . . .**88** E3
Rockrose Gdns WV10 . . . . .**12** A7
Rock St DY3 . . . .**50** E5
Rock The WV6 . . . .**24** D5
Rockville Rd B8 . . . .**68** A4
Rockwell La B48. . . . .**139** E4
Rockwood Rd B27 . . . .**88** B4
Rocky La
Birmingham,Aston B6 . . . . . .**67** A6
Birmingham,Great Barr B42 . .**55** B5
Birmingham,Nechells Green
B7. . . . .**67** B6
Catshill B61 . . . .**136** E7
Kenilworth CV8 . . . .**148** D2
Rodborough Rd
Birmingham B26 . . . .**89** B7
Dorridge B93 . . . .**127** E3
Roddis Cl B23 . . . .**56** D8
Roddis Cl B23 . . . .**56** D8
Roden Ave DY10 . . . .**117** A7
Roderick Dr WV11 . . . .**26** D7
Roderick Rd B11. . . . .**87** C5
Rodhouse Cl CV4 . . . .**111** D1
Rodlington Ave B44. . . . . . .**44** F1
Rodman Cl B15. . . . .**85** D8
Rodney Cl
Birmingham B16 . . . .**66** A2
Hinckley LE10 . . . .**71** D4
Solihull B92 . . . .**89** B1
Rodney Rd B92 . . . .**89** B1
Rodway Cl
Birmingham B19 . . . .**66** E7
Brierley Hill DY5 . . . .**81** D7
Wolverhampton WV4. . . . . . .**39** D3
Rodwell Gr B44. . . . .**44** E2
Rodyard Way CV1 . . . .**165** C1
Roebuck Glade WV12 . . . . .**27** E4
Roebuck La
Smethwick B66 . . . .**64** F8
West Bromwich B70 . . . .**53** E1
Roebuck Pl WS3 . . . .**28** E6
Roebuck Rd WS3 . . . .**28** E6
Roe Cl CV34. . . . .**160** F8
Roedean Cl B44 . . . .**56** B7

Roford Ct DY3 . . . .**50** E5
Rogerfield Rd B23 . . . .**57** AC
Rogers Cl WV11 . . . .**13** A2
Rogers Rd B8 . . . .**55** B5
Rogers Way CV34 . . . .**160** B4
Rogue's La LE9,LE10. . . . . .**71** C4
Rokeby Cl B76. . . . .**46** E4
Rokeby Rd B43 . . . .**43** F2
Rokeby Wlk B34 . . . .**69** A6
Rokewood Cl DY6. . . . .**49** D3
Rokholt Cres WS11 . . . .**1** C1
Roland Ave CV6 . . . .**95** C3
Roland Gdns 3 B19 . . . .**66** C8
Roland Gr 4 B19. . . . .**66** C8
Roland Mount CV6 . . . .**95** C3
Roland Rd B19 . . . .**66** C8
Rolan Dr B90. . . . .**125** C8
Roland Terr 3 B19 . . . .**66** C8
Roland Vernon Way DY4..**52** C7
Rolfe St B66. . . . .**65** A6
Rollason Cl CV6 . . . .**113** C8
Rollason Rd
5 Dudley DY2. . . . .**62** D8
Birmingham B24 . . . .**57** A3
Coventry CV6. . . . .**113** B8
Rollason's Yd CV6 . . . .**96** A3
Rollesby Dr WV13. . . . .**40** F8
Rolling Mill Cl B5. . . . .**86** E7
Rolling Mill Rd WS11 . . . . . .**1** E4
Rollingmill St WS2 . . . .**28** C1
Rollswood Dr B91 . . . .**107** A4
Rolvenden Ct WV13 . . . . . .**27** C2
Roman Cl WS8. . . . .**6** E2
Roman Ct
Birmingham B38 . . . .**124** B8
Cannock WS11. . . . .**4** E5
Tamworth B77. . . . .**35** E7
Romani Cl CV34 . . . .**160** D7
Roman La B74. . . . .**31** B4
Roman Pk
Coleshill B46. . . . .**59** F1
Sutton Coldfield B74 . . . . . .**31** B4
Roman Pl B74 . . . .**31** B2
Roman Rd CV2 . . . .**114** B3
Roman Rd (Sandy La)
CV3. . . . .**114** B3
Roman Rd B74 . . . .**31** C4
Romans Grange B74 . . . . . .**31** C5
Roman View WS11 . . . .**4** F5
Roman Way
Birmingham B15 . . . .**85** D3
Bromsgrove B61 . . . .**137** B4
Coleshill B46. . . . .**59** F2
Coventry CV3. . . . .**133** C6
Roman Way Fst Sch B98 .**154** E3
Roman Way
Lichfield WS14. . . . .**9** D7
Rowley Regis B65 . . . .**63** C3
Tamworth B79. . . . .**20** E7
Roman Wlk WS13 . . . .**8** D2
Romany Rd B45 . . . .**101** D1
Romany Way DY8. . . . .**80** C3
Roma Rd B11. . . . .**87** E5
Romeo Arbour CV34 . . . .**161** E3
Romford Cl B26 . . . .**89** B6
Romford Rd CV6 . . . .**95** B2
Romilly Ave B20 . . . .**55** B3
Romilly Cl
Lichfield WS14. . . . .**9** E7
Stourbridge DY8 . . . .**80** E6
Sutton Coldfield B76 . . . . . .**47** A4
Romney Cl
Birmingham B28 . . . .**105** F7
Hinckley LE10 . . . .**71** A3
Romney House Ind Est
WS10. . . . .**41** B7
Romney B77 . . . .**35** F8
Romney Rd B43 . . . .**44** D4
Romney Way B43 . . . .**44** D4
Romsey Ave CV10 . . . .**73** D8
Romsey Rd WV10 . . . .**11** C3
Romsey Way WV11 . . . .**42** C7
Romsey Way WV10 . . . .**11** C3
Romsey Way WS3 . . . .**13** F1
Romsley Cl
Birmingham B45 . . . .**121** E8
Halesowen B63 . . . .**83** B2
Redditch B98. . . . .**154** F3
Walsall WS4 . . . .**15** C2
Romsley Hill Grange
B62. . . . .**100** F1
Romsley Rd
Birmingham B32 . . . .**102** B3
Coventry CV6. . . . .**113** C6
Oldbury B68. . . . .**64** B2
Stourbridge DY9 . . . .**81** C5
Romsley,St Kenelm's CE Fst
Sch B62 . . . .**101** A4
Romulus Cl B20 . . . .**55** B3
Ronald Pl B9 . . . .**67** E2
Ronald Rd B9 . . . .**67** D2
Ron Davis Cl B66 . . . .**65** B5
Ro-Oak Rd CV6 . . . .**112** F5
Rood End Prim Sch B68 . . .**64** C6
Rood End Rd B68 . . . .**64** C7
Rooker Ave WV2 . . . .**39** F6
Rooker Cres WV2 . . . .**39** F6
Rookery Ave
Brierley Hill DY5 . . . .**61** A2
Wolverhampton WV4. . . . . . .**40** A3
Rookery Cl B97. . . . .**153** D1
Rookery Ct WS13 . . . .**8** E7
Rookery La
Aldridge WS9. . . . .**30** B6
Coventry CV6. . . . .**95** C4
Weeford B75,B78 . . . .**19** E2
Wolverhampton WV4. . . . . . .**39** B6
Rookery Par WS9 . . . .**30** B6

Rookery Pk DY5 61 B5
Rookery Rd
Birmingham B29 85 F2
Birmingham,Handsworth B21 54 E1
Wolverhampton WV14,WV4 40 A3
Wombourne WV5 49 B6
Rookery Rise WV5 49 B6
Rookery Sch B21 54 E1
Rookery St WV11 26 C5
Rookery The B62 84 A2
Rooks Mdw DY9 99 B6
Rookwood Dr WV6 23 F2
Roosevelt Dr CV4 111 E2
Rooth St WS10 42 B4
Roper Way DY3 50 F6
Roper Wlk DY3 50 F6
Rosafield Ave B62 83 F6
Rosalind Ave DY1 51 B6
Rosalind Gr WV11 27 A5
Rosamond St WS1 42 D7
Rosary RC Prim Sch B8 67 E3
Rosary Rd B23 56 D3
Rosary Villas 1 B11 87 C5
Rosaville Cres CV5 112 A6
Rose Ave
Alvechurch B48 139 A5
Birmingham B68 84 C7
Coventry CV6 112 F5
Kingswinford DY6 60 F5
Rosebank Dr WS3 28 E4
Rosebay Ave B38 123 F8
Rose Bay Mdw 2 WS11 2 C2
Roseberry Ave CV2 96 C1
Rosebery Rd
Smethwick B66 65 C4
Tamworth B77 35 D4
Rosebery St
Birmingham B18 66 A4
Wolverhampton WV3 25 B1
Rosebriars B90 125 E7
Rose Cl B66 65 C5
Rose Cottage Dr 3 DY8 60 D3
Rose Cottage Flats CV5 111 D5
Rose Cotts
6 Birmingham B29 85 F2
Birmingham,Stirchley B30 104 A6
Rose Croft CV8 147 E6
Rosecroft Rd B26 89 C6
Rose Ct
Balsall Common CV7 130 B8
Dudley DY2 51 F1
Rosedale Ave
Birmingham B23 56 E3
Smethwick B66 65 C5
Rosedale CE Inf Sch WV12 27 D5
Rosedale Cl B97 153 A4
Rosedale Gr B25 88 C8
Rosedale Pl WV13 41 A8
Rosedale Rd B25 88 C8
Rosedale Wlk DY6 60 E8
Rosedene Dr B20 54 F2
Rose Dr WS8 15 E5
Rosefield Croft B6 66 F7
Rosefield Ct B67 65 A4
Rosefield Pl 4 CV32 161 F8
Rosefield Rd B67 65 A4
Rosefield St CV32 162 A8
Rosefield Wlk 3 CV32 161 F8
Rosegardens The B63 82 E2
Rosegreen Cl CV3 133 E6
Rosehall Cl
Redditch B98 158 E6
Solihull B91 106 F1
Rose Hill
Barnt Green B45 122 B4
Brierley Hill DY5 62 A1
Rosehill WS12 1 F8
Rose Hill Cl B36 69 B8
Rose Hill WV13 41 A8
Rose Hill Gdns WV13 27 B1
Rose Hill Rd B21 66 A7
Rosehip Cl WS5 43 A3
Rosehip Dr CV2 114 B6
Rose La
Burntwood WS7 7 C7
Dodford B61 136 A6
Roseland Ave DY2 51 F1
Roseland Rd CV8 147 F3
Roselands Ave CV2 114 D8
Roseland Way 7 B15 66 B1
Rose La
Nuneaton CV11 73 C3
Oldbury B69 52 C2
Roseleigh Rd B45 122 B6
Rosemary Ave
Bilston WV14 40 F6
Cheslyn Hay WS6 4 D3
Wolverhampton WV4 39 C6
Rosemary Cl
Brownhills WS8 15 D6
Coventry CV4 111 E3
Rosemary Cres
Dudley DY1 51 A6
Wolverhampton WV4 39 C5
Rosemary Cres W WV4 39 B5
Rosemary Ct B74 31 D4
Rosemary Dr
Huntington WS12 1 D5
Stoke Prior B60 150 C1
Sutton Coldfield B74 31 C3
Rosemary Hill CV8 147 F5
Rosemary Hill Rd B74 31 D4
Rosemary La DY8 80 D3
Rosemary Mews CV8 147 F5
Rosemary Nook B74 31 D5
Rosemary Rd
Birmingham B33 68 F2
Cheslyn Hay WS6 4 D3
Halesowen B63 82 E2
Kidderminster DY10 117 B7
Tamworth B77 21 F4
Tipton DY4 52 A6
Rosemary Way LE10 75 B7
Rosemont Ho B93 127 F3
Rosemoor Dr DY5 81 B7
Rosemount B32 84 E5
Rosemount Cl CV2 114 E7
Rosemount WV6 24 D5
Rosemullion Cl CV7 96 B8
Rose Rd
Birmingham B17 85 D6
Coleshill B46 70 F8
Rose St WV14 40 F2
Rose Terr B45 138 D8
Rosetti Cl DY10 117 C6
Roseville Ct 4 WV14 51 C8
Roseville Gdns WV8 10 A4
Roseville Prec 5 WV14 51 C8
Rosewood Cl
Hinckley LE10 75 F6
Tamworth B77 21 D4
Rosewood Cres CV32 157 B2
Rosewood Ct B77 21 D4
Rosewood Dr
Barnt Green B45 138 C7
Birmingham B23 56 D2
Willenhall WV12 27 B8
Rosewood Gdns WV11 13 B3
Rosewood CV11 73 F1
Rosewood Pk WS6 4 D2
Rosewood Rd DY1 51 B5
Rosewood Sch DY1 50 E1
Roshven Rd B12 87 A4
Roslin Cl B60 137 B1
Roslin Gr B19 66 C6
Roslyn Cl B66 65 A6
Ross Cl
Coventry CV5 112 A5
Wolverhampton WV6 24 E2
Ross Dr DY6 60 C7
Rosse Ct B92 107 F8
Rossendale Cl B63 82 D6
Rossendale Way CV10 72 E2
Ross Hts B65 63 B3
Rosslyn Ave CV6 112 E6
Rosslyn Rd B76 57 F6
Ross Rd WS3 28 F6
Ross B65 63 B2
Ross Way CV11 79 B7
Roston Dr LE10 71 A1
Rostrevor Rd B10 67 F1
Rosy Cross B79 21 B5
Rotary Ct 2 WV3 25 B2
Rotary Ho DY1 50 F1
Rothay B77 35 F8
Rothbury Gn WS12 2 E2
Rotherby Gr B37 90 B7
Rotherfield Cl CV31 162 B7
Rotherfield Rd B26 89 B8
Rotherham Rd CV6 95 C2
Rotherhams Oak La B94 142 F7
Rothesay Ave CV4 112 B2
Rothesay Cl CV10 73 A2
Rothesay Croft B32 102 B7
Rothesay Dr DY8 60 C3
Rothesay Way WV12 27 B6
Rothley Wlk B38 123 C8
Rothwell Dr B91 106 D4
Rothwell Rd CV34 155 C1
Rotten Row Barns B93 128 C4
Rotten Row WS14 9 C7
Rotton Park Rd B16 65 D2
Rotton Park St B16 65 F3
Rough Coppice Wlk B35 58 A2
Rough Hay Pl WS10 41 C7
Rough Hay Prim Sch WS10 41 C7
Rough Hay Rd WS10 41 C7
Rough Hill Dr
Redditch B98 158 F6
Rowley Regis B65 62 F6
Rough Hills Cl WV2 39 F6
Rough Hills Rd WV2 39 F6
Roughknowles Rd CV4 131 D6
Roughlea Ave B36 68 F7
Roughley Dr B75 32 C2
Roughley Farm Rd B75 32 E3
Rough Rd B44 45 A3
Rough The B97 158 D8
Rough Wood Ctry Pk WV12 27 E6
Rouncil Cl B92 107 D7
Rouncil La CV8 155 C8
Roundabout The B31 102 D1
Round Cl B90 126 A6
Round Croft WV13 27 A2
Round Hill Ave DY9 81 C1
Roundhill Cl B76 46 E4
Round Hill DY3 39 D2
Roundhills Rd B62 83 F8
Roundhill Terr B62 63 E1
Roundhill Way WS8 7 A2
Round Hill Wharf DY11 116 D5
Round House Rd
Coventry CV3 134 B8
Dudley DY3 50 E4
Roundlea Cl WV12 27 B7
Roundlea Rd B31 102 E7
Round Moor Wlk B35 58 A3
Round Oak Sch The CV32 157 A3
Round Rd B24 57 B2
Round Saw Croft B45 121 F8
Rounds Green Prim Sch B69 63 E7
Rounds Green Rd B69 63 F7
Rounds Hill CV8 147 E2
Rounds Hill Rd WV14 51 D8
Rounds Rd WV14 40 D3
Round St DY2 62 C6
Roundway Down WV6 23 F3
Rounton Cl B74 31 D4
Rousay Cl B45 101 F1
Rousdon Gr B43 54 D8
Rover Dr
Birmingham,Acock's Green B27 88 D4
Birmingham,Castle Bromwich B36 58 F1
Rover Rd CV1 165 B2
Rovex Bsns Pk B11 87 F5
Rowallan Rd B75 32 D2
Rowan Cl
Binley Woods CV3 135 D7
Bromsgrove B61 136 E2
Hollywood B47 125 B5
Lichfield WS14 9 D8
Sutton Coldfield B76 46 F2
Rowan Cres
Dudley WV14 40 B1
Redditch B97 153 A4
Wolverhampton WV3 38 E7
Rowan Ct
Birmingham B30 104 A2
Oldbury B66 64 D8
Rowan Dr
6 Warwick CV34 160 F8
Birmingham B28 106 A5
Essington WV11 13 B3
Rowan Gr
Burntwood WS7 6 F7
Coventry CV2 96 E2
Rowan Rd
Cannock WS11 1 C2
Nuneaton CV10 72 C6
Redditch B97 153 A4
Sedgley DY3 39 F1
Sutton Coldfield B72 46 C3
Walsall WS5 42 F4
Rowan Rise DY6 60 E6
Rowans The CV12 77 E2
Rowantrees B45 122 B5
Rowan Way
Birmingham,Chelmsley Wood B37 70 C1
Birmingham,Longbridge B31 122 F8
Hartshill CV10 72 A8
Roway La B69 52 F1
Rowborough Cl B96 158 E2
Rowbrook Cl B90 125 E8
Rowcroft Covert B14 104 C2
Rowcroft Rd CV2 115 A6
Rowdale Rd B42 55 C6
Rowden Dr
Birmingham B23 57 A6
Solihull B91 106 E2
Rowena Gdns DY3 39 C2
Rowheath Ho B30 103 E5
Rowheath Rd B30 103 F4
Rowington Ave B65 63 D3
Rowington Cl CV6 112 D5
Rowington Gn CV35 144 F1
Rowington Rd B34 69 E6
Rowington Terr B25 88 B7
Rowland Ave B80 159 E3
Rowland Gdns WS2 28 C3
Rowland Hill Ave DY11 116 B5
Rowland Hill Ctr 9 DY10 116 E6
Rowland Hill Dr DY4 52 C5
Rowlands Ave
Walsall WS2 27 E3
Wolverhampton WV1 26 B2
Rowlands Cl WS2 27 E4
Rowlands Cres B91 107 B8
Rowlands Rd B26 88 E7
Rowland St WS2 28 C3
Rowland Way (Road 1a) DY11 116 E1
Rowley Cl WS12 2 B8
Rowley Dr CV3 134 B4
Rowley Gr B33 69 D3
Rowley Hall Ave B65 63 C4
Rowley Hall Prim Sch B65 63 C4
Rowley Hill View B64 82 F8
Rowley La CV3 134 D3
Rowley Pl WS4 29 B7
Rowley Rd
Coventry CV3,CV8 134 B3
Whitnash CV31 162 A2
Rowley Regis Com Hospl B65 63 B2
Rowley Regis Sta B65 63 E2
Rowley's Green La CV6 95 E4
Rowleys Green Lane Ind Est CV6 95 E4
Rowley St WS1 29 A2
Rowley View
Bilston WV14 41 A3
Darlaston WS10 41 C4
West Bromwich B70 53 B3
Rowley Village B65 63 C3
Rowney Croft B28 105 E4
Rowney Green La B48 139 F5
Rowood Dr B91,B92 107 D7
Row The CV7 97 D3
Rowthorn Cl B74 45 A7
Rowthorn Dr B90 127 A6
Rowton Ave WV6 23 E3
Rowton Dr B74 44 F5
Roxall Cl DY10 98 C2
Roxboro Ho B97 153 D2
Roxburgh Croft CV32 157 C6
Roxburgh Gr B43 44 C4
Roxburgh Rd
Nuneaton CV11 73 E1
Sutton Coldfield B73 46 A3
Roxby Gdns WV6 25 A5
Royal Brierley Glassworks* DY5 61 C2
Royal Cl
Brierley Hill DY5 81 C8
Rowley Regis B65 63 C5
Royal Cres CV3 134 C5
Royal Ct
Hinckley LE10 75 D7
Sutton Coldfield B73 46 B2
Royal Gr 3 B23 56 B7
Royal Leamington Spa Rehabilitation Hospl CV34 161 E4
Royal London Bldgs WV1 163 C3
Royal Mail St B1 164 B2
Royal Oak La CV7,CV12 95 C7
Royal Oak Rd
Halesowen B62 83 F5
Rowley Regis B65 62 F5
Royal Oak Yd CV12 78 B4
Royal Orthopaedic Hospl The B31 103 B5
Royal Priors 18 CV32 156 F1
Royal Rd B72 46 C4
Royal Scot Gr WS1 42 D5
Royal Star Cl B33 69 C2
Royal Sta The WV1 163 D2
Royal Way DY4 52 A2
Royal Wolverhampton Sch The WV3 39 B7
Royal Worcester Cres B60 137 C1
Roy Carver Ctr The (St John Ambulance HQ) WV1 163 D2
Roydon Rd B27 106 C8
Roylesden Cres B73 45 C2
Royston Chase B74 31 A3
Royston Cl CV3 115 A3
Royston Croft B12 86 F6
Royston Ct 7 B13 87 B2
Royston Way DY3 50 C8
Rubens Cl
Coventry CV5 112 C3
Dudley DY3 50 D5
Rubery Ct WS10 41 C7
Rubery Farm Gr B45 121 F7
Rubery Field Cl B45 102 B1
Rubery La B45 102 A1
Rubery La S B45 121 F8
Rubery St WS10 41 D8
Ruckleigh Sch B91 107 C4
Ruckley Ave 4 B19 66 C7
Ruckley Rd B29 103 B8
Rudd Gdns WV10 26 B4
Rudgard Rd CV6 96 A4
Rudge Ave WV1 26 B3
Rudge Cl WV12 27 C4
Rudge Croft B33 69 A4
Rudgewick Croft 1 B6 66 F6
Rudge Wlk B18 66 A3
Rudyard Cl WV10 11 E4
Rudyard Gr B33 69 B3
Rudyngfield Dr B33 68 F4
Rufford Cl
Birmingham B23 56 D8
Hinckley LE10 75 D3
Rufford Prim Sch DY9 81 C5
Rufford Rd DY9 81 C4
Rufford St DY9 81 D5
Rufford B79 20 E6
Rufford Way WS9 29 E7
Rugby Rd
Binley Woods CV3 135 D8
Bulkington CV12 79 D2
Cubbington CV32 157 E6
Hinckley LE10 75 D5
Royal Leamington Spa CV32 156 D1
Stourbridge DY8 80 D7
Rugby St WV1 25 B4
Rugeley Ave WV12 27 D8
Rugeley Cl DY4 51 E5
Rugeley Rd
Burntwood,Gorstey Ley WS7 7 C7
Cannock,Hednesford WS12 2 F6
Cannock,West Hill WS12 2 D7
Ruislip Cl B35 58 A4
Ruiton St DY3 50 D4
Rumbow B63 83 B4
Rumbow La B62 100 D3
Rumbush La
Earlswood B90,B94 125 F3
Solihull B90 126 A5
Rumer Hill Bsns Est WS11 4 E7
Rumer Hill Rd WS11 4 F8
Runcorn Cl
Birmingham B37 70 C4
Redditch B98 158 F8
Runcorn Rd B12 87 A5
Runcorn Wlk 10 CV2 115 A7
Runneymede Gdns CV10 72 F3
Runnymede Dr CV7 130 C5
Runnymede Rd B11 87 E3
Rupert Rd CV6 113 B8
Rupert St
Birmingham B7 67 A4
Wolverhampton WV3 25 A2
Rushall Cl
Stourbridge DY8 80 E8
Walsall WS4 29 B4
Rushall Com Coll WS4 29 B6
Rushall Ct B43 54 E7
Rushall JMI Sch WS4 15 B1
Rushall Manor Cl WS4 29 B4
Rushall Manor Rd WS4 29 B4
Rushall Rd WV10 11 E2
Rushbrook Cl
Brownhills WS8 15 D6
Solihull B92 88 E2
Rushbrooke Cl B13 86 F4
Rushbrooke Dr B73 45 C3
Rushbrook Gr B14 104 C4
Rushbrook La B94 141 D3
Rushbury Cl
Bilston WV14 40 B5
Solihull B90 106 D4
Rushden Croft B44 44 F1
Rushes Mill WS3 14 E3
Rushey La B11 88 A4
Rushford Ave WV5 49 A6
Rushford Cl B90 127 A7
Rush Gn B32 84 E2
Rushlake Gn B34 69 B5
Rush La
Redditch B98 154 B6
Tamworth B77,B78 35 D4
Rushleigh Rd B90 125 E8
Rushmead Gr B45 122 A7
Rushmere Rd DY4 52 A8
Rushmoor Cl B74 46 B6
Rushmoor Dr CV5 112 F3
Rushmore St CV31 162 B7
Rushmore Terr 9 CV31 162 B7
Rushock Cl B98 159 C7
Rushton Cl CV7 130 C7
Rushton Hall Sch CV7 95 D5
Rushwick Croft B34 69 D6
Rushwick Ct B23 56 B3
Rushwick Gr B90 127 A6
Rushwood Cl WS4 29 A3
Rushy Piece B32 84 D3
Rusina Ct CV31 161 F6
Ruskin Ave
Dudley DY3 50 A5
Kidderminster DY10 117 C6
Rowley Regis B65 63 D2
Wolverhampton WV4 39 F2
Ruskin Cl
Birmingham B6 66 F7
Coventry CV6 112 D6
Nuneaton CV10 72 A5
Ruskin Ct 5 B68 84 B8
Ruskin Glass Ctr* DY8 80 F7
Ruskin Gr B27 88 B2
Ruskin Hall Gr B6 66 F7
Ruskin Rd WV10 12 A1
Ruskin St B71 53 C5
Russel Croft B60 151 A7
Russell Bank Rd B74 31 E4
Russell Cl
Oldbury B69 52 D2
Tamworth B77 35 E6
Wednesbury DY4 41 C1
Wolverhampton WV11 12 F1
Russell Ct
7 Royal Leamington Spa CV31 162 A7
Sutton Coldfield B74 31 D3
Wolverhampton WV3 163 A2
Russell Ho
Tamworth B77 21 F2
Wednesbury WS10 41 F2
Russell Rd
Bilston WV14 40 F7
Birmingham,Hall Green B28 87 E1
Birmingham,Moseley B13 86 D3
Kidderminster DY10 116 F4
Russell St N 2 CV1 165 C4
Russells Hall Hospl DY5 61 E7
Russells Hall Prim Sch DY1 50 E1
Russell's Hall Rd DY1 50 F1
Russell St
Coventry CV1 165 C4
Dudley DY1 51 B1
Russells The B13 86 D3
Russell St
Royal Leamington Spa CV32 156 F1
Wednesbury WS10 41 F2
Willenhall WV13 27 B2
Wolverhampton WV3 163 A2
Russell Terr CV31 162 A7
Russet Gr CV4 132 D3
Russett Cl
Burntwood WS7 7 A6
Walsall WS5 43 D8
Russett Way DY5 61 B7
Russet Way B31 102 E6
Russet Wlk WV8 10 E1
Ruston St B16 66 B1
Ruthall Cl B29 103 C7
Ruth Chamberlain Ct 3 DY11 116 D6
Ruth Cl DY4 41 C2
Rutherford Glen CV11 73 F1
Rutherford Rd
Birmingham B23 56 E7
Bromsgrove B60 151 B7
Walsall WS2 28 A5
Rutherglen Ave CV3 134 A6

Rutland Ave
Hinckley LE10 . . . . .75 C7
Nuneaton CV10 . . . . .72 F4
Wolverhampton WV4 . . . . . . .38 D4
Rutland B17 . . . . .85 A6
Rutland Cres
Aldridge WS9 . . . . .16 B1
Bilston WV14 . . . . .40 E7
Rutland Croft **3** CV3 . . . . . .134 F8
Rutland Ct **2** B29 . . . . .103 C7
Rutland Dr
Birmingham B26 . . . . .88 E7
Bromsgrove B60 . . . . .151 A8
Tamworth B78 . . . . .21 A1
Rutland Pas **3** DY1 . . . . . . .51 C1
Rutland Pl DY8 . . . . .80 D8
Rutland Rd
Cannock WS12 . . . . .2 E1
Smethwick B66 . . . . .65 A1
Wednesbury WS10 . . . . .42 D4
West Bromwich B71 . . . . . . .53 C7
Rutland St WS3 . . . . .28 E5
Rutland Terr **5** B18 . . . . . . .66 A5
Rutley Gr B32 . . . . .84 F4
Rutters Mdw B32 . . . . .84 B4
Rutter St WS1 . . . . .42 E8
Ryan Ave WV11 . . . . .27 A7
Ryan Pl DY2 . . . . .62 C6
Rycroft Gr B33 . . . . .69 C2
Rydal Ave CV11 . . . . .74 A6
Rydal Cl
Allesley CV5 . . . . .112 B8
Cannock WS12 . . . . .2 A8
Hinckley LE10 . . . . .74 F7
Sutton Coldfield B74 . . . . . . .30 F2
Wolverhampton WV11 . . . . . .26 C7
Rydal Dr WV6 . . . . .23 F4
Rydal Ho **6** B69 . . . . .63 D5
Rydal B77 . . . . .36 A7
Rydal Way B28 . . . . .105 F7
Rydding La B71 . . . . .53 B8
Rydding Sq B71 . . . . .53 B8
Ryde Ave CV10 . . . . .73 D7
Ryde Gr B27 . . . . .88 A1
Ryde Park Rd B45 . . . . .122 C7
Ryders Green Prim Sch
B70 . . . . .53 A4
Ryders Green Rd B70 . . . . . .52 F4
Ryders Hayes Com Sch
WS3 .15 A5
Ryders Hayes La WS3 . . . . . .15 B4
Ryders Hill Cres CV10 . . . . . .72 C7
Ryder St
Birmingham B4 . . . . .164 C3
Stourbridge DY8 . . . . .60 D2
West Bromwich B70 . . . . . . .52 F5
Ryebank Cl B30 . . . . .103 C5
Ryeclose Croft B37 . . . . .70 D3
Rye Croft **2** B27 . . . . .88 C5
Ryecroft Ave WV4 . . . . .39 B5
Ryecroft Cl DY3 . . . . .50 C8
Ryecroft Dr **3** WS7 . . . . .7 A8
Rye Croft B47 . . . . .125 A5
Ryecroft Pk **1** WS2 . . . . . . .28 E3
Ryecroft Pl WS3 . . . . .28 F6
Ryecroft Sh Ctr WS7 . . . . .7 A8
Ryecroft St **2** WS2 . . . . . . .28 E3
Rye Croft DY9 . . . . .81 E2
Ryefield Cl
Solihull B91 . . . . .106 E5
West Hagley DY9 . . . . .99 A4
Ryefield La B76 . . . . .48 B2
Ryefields Rd B60 . . . . .150 C3
Ryefield WV8 . . . . .10 E1
Ryegrass La B97 . . . . .158 C6
Rye Grass Wlk B35 . . . . .58 B3
Rye Gr B11 . . . . .87 F4
Rye Hill CV5 . . . . .112 A6
Rye Hill Office Pk CV5 . . . . .112 A7
Ryemarket Sh Ctr **7** DY8 . .81 A5
Rye Piece Ringway CV12 . . .78 C3
Ryhope Cl CV12 . . . . .77 C1
Ryhope Wlk WV9 . . . . .11 A3
Ryknild Cl B74 . . . . .31 F6
Ryknild Dr B74 . . . . .45 A7
Ryknild St WS14 . . . . .9 B6
Ryland Cl
3 Tipton DY4 . . . . .52 B5
Halesowen B63 . . . . .82 E2
Royal Leamington Spa
CV31 . . . . .162 C6
Ryland Ho B19 . . . . .66 D5
Ryland Rd
Birmingham,Edgbaston
B15 .86 C8
Birmingham,Gravelly Hill
B24 .56 F1
Rylands Dr WV4 . . . . .39 A4
Ryland St B16 . . . . .66 B1
Rylcroft **7** WV4 . . . . .39 F4
Ryle St WS3 . . . . .14 D1
Ryley St CV1 . . . . .165 A3
Rylston Ave CV6 . . . . .95 A1
Rylstone Way **4** CV34 . . . .155 E1
Rymond Rd B34 . . . . .68 C6
Ryton Cl
Coventry CV4 . . . . .132 B8
Redditch B98 . . . . .154 D1
Sutton Coldfield B73 . . . . . . .46 B5
Wolverhampton WV10 . . . . . .26 A5
Ryton Gr B34 . . . . .69 D7
Ryton Organic Gdns*
CV8 . . . . .135 E1
Ryton B77 . . . . .35 F8

S

Sabell Rd B67 . . . . .64 F6
Sabrina Rd WV6 . . . . .23 E1
Sackville Ho **1** CV1 . . . . . .165 D4
Sacred Heart Prim Sch
DY4 .52 A4
Sacred Heart RC Prim Sch
CV2 . . . . .114 A3
Sacred Heart Sch B20 . . . . . .55 D1
Saddington Rd CV3 . . . . . . .134 E8
Saddlers Cl
Halesowen B63 . . . . .82 B5
Hinckley LE10 . . . . .75 F6
Lichfield WS14 . . . . .9 E8
Saddlers Ctr WS1 . . . . .28 A7
Saddlers Court Ind Est
WS2 .28 A7
Saddlers Ctr WS1 . . . . .28 A7
Saddlers Mews B91 . . . . . . .107 C1
Saddlestones The WV6 . . . . .23 D4
Saddleworth Rd WS3 . . . . . . .14 A4
Sadler Cres B11 . . . . .87 D2
Sadler Ctr WS8 . . . . .16 A8
Sadler Gdns CV12 . . . . .78 C2
Sadler Ho B19 . . . . .66 C6
Sadler Rd
Brownhills WS8 . . . . .16 A8
Coventry CV6 . . . . .113 A8
Sutton Coldfield B75 . . . . . . .47 A6
Sadlers Cl WS2 . . . . .42 B7
Sadlers Mill WS8 . . . . .16 A7
Sadlerswell La B94 . . . . .143 B6
Sadlers Wlk B16 . . . . .66 A1
Saffron Gdns WV4 . . . . .39 A4
Saffron Ho **8** B38 . . . . .123 E8
Saffron B77 . . . . .22 B4
Sagebury Dr B60 . . . . .150 C1
Sage Croft B31 . . . . .102 F5
St Agatha's Rd
Birmingham B8 . . . . .68 B5
Coventry CV2 . . . . .114 A3
St Agnes Cl
Birmingham B13 . . . . .87 B2
Studley B80 . . . . .159 C4
St Agnes Rd B13 . . . . .87 B1
St Agnes Way CV11 . . . . .73 F4
St Aidan's Ct WV4 . . . . .39 A5
St Aidan's Rd WS11 . . . . .1 E5
St Aidans Wlk **3** B10 . . . . . .87 C8
St Alban's Ave CV11 . . . . .116 A7
St Alban's CE Prim Sch
WV11 . . . . .27 B8
St Alban's CE Sch B12 . . . . .86 F7
St Albans Cl
Royal Leamington Spa
CV32 . . . . .156 C2
Smethwick B67 . . . . .64 E6
Wednesfield WV11 . . . . .27 A8
St Albans Ho B32 . . . . .84 F5
St Alban's RC Prim Sch
B14 .104 F4
St Albans Rd
Birmingham B13 . . . . .87 B2
Smethwick B67 . . . . .64 E6
St Alphege CE Inf Sch
B91 .107 C3
St Alphege CE Jun Sch
B91 .107 C2
St Alphege Cl B91 . . . . .107 C3
St Ambrose Barlow RC Prim
Sch B28 . . . . .106 A6
St Ambrose RC Prim Sch
DY10 . . . . .116 F8
St Andrews Ave WS3 . . . . . . .15 B4
St Andrew's CE Fst Sch
B45 .138 D8
St Andrew's CE Inf Sch
CV5 .111 C5
St Andrews CE Prim Sch
WV6 .24 F4
St Andrews Cl B32 . . . . .85 A3
St Andrew's Cl DY3 . . . . .50 A3
St Andrews Dr
Nuneaton CV11 . . . . .74 B1
Oldbury B69 . . . . .63 D6
Perton WV6 . . . . .23 D5
St Andrew's Gd (Birmingham
City FC) B9 . . . . .67 C1
St Andrews Gn DY10 . . . . . .116 E4
St Andrews Ho WV6 . . . . .25 B4
St Andrews Ind Est B9 . . . . . .67 C1
St Andrew's Jun & Inf Sch
B9 . . . . .67 B2
St Andrew's RC Prim Sch
B92 .89 A2
St Andrew's Rd
Birmingham B9 . . . . .67 B2
Dudley DY2 . . . . .62 C5
St Andrews B77 . . . . .22 B4
St Andrews Way B61 . . . . . .150 D8
St Annes Cl B20 . . . . .55 D4
St Anne's Cl WV13 . . . . .6 E4
St Anne's Ct B13 . . . . .86 E4
St Annes Ct B44 . . . . .56 A7

St Anne's Ct WV13 . . . . .27 B1
St Annes Gr B93 . . . . .128 A6
St Annes Ind Est WV13 . . . . .27 B3
St Anne's RC Prim Sch
Birmingham B37 . . . . .70 A2
Birmingham,Deritend B12 . . .87 A8
Coventry CV3 . . . . .134 C6
Nuneaton CV10 . . . . .72 D7
Sutton Coldfield B64 . . . . . . .44 E8
St Anne's Rd B64 . . . . .62 C1
St Ann's Cl CV31 . . . . .162 C7
St Ann's Rd CV2 . . . . .114 A3
St Anthonys Dr WS3 . . . . . . .15 B5
St Anthony's RC Prim Sch
CV31 . . . . .162 C7
Wolverhampton WV10 . . . . . .11 D3
St Antony's RC Prim Sch
B37 . . . . .70 A5
St Asaphs Ave B80 . . . . .159 D4
St Athan Croft B35 . . . . .58 B3
St Audries CV6 . . . . .94 B2
St Augustine's RC High Sch
B97 .158 D5
St Augustine's RC Prim Sch
Birmingham B21 . . . . .54 D2
Coventry CV6 . . . . .113 A7
Kenilworth CV8 . . . . .147 E7
Solihull B91 . . . . .107 A2
St Augustine's Rd B16 . . . .65 D1
St Augustine's Wlk CV6 . . . .113 A7
St Augustus Cl B70 . . . . .53 F2
St Austell Cl
Nuneaton CV11 . . . . .74 A5
Tamworth B79 . . . . .21 A6
St Austell Rd
Coventry CV2 . . . . .114 E3
Walsall WS5 . . . . .43 E7
St Barnabas CE Prim Sch
B57 . . . . .47 A3
St Bartholomews Cl CV3 . .115 A2
**St Bartholomew's CE Prim
Sch**
Coventry CV3 . . . . .134 E7
Wolverhampton WV4 . . . . . . .38 E3
St Bartholomew Terr **3**
WS10 . . . . .41 F2
St Bede's RC Mid Sch
B98 .153 F3
**St Benedict Bishop CE Prim
Sch** WV5 . . . . .49 B7
St Benedict's Cl B70 . . . . . . .53 F2
St Benedict's Inf Sch B10 . . .87 F7
St Benedicts Rd B10 . . . . . . .87 F8
St Benedicts Rd WV5 . . . . . . .49 A6
St Bernadette's RC Prim Sch
Birmingham B25 . . . . .88 B8
Brownhills WS8 . . . . .15 F8
St Bernard's Rd
B13 . . . . .87 C1
St Bernard's Rd B92 . . . . . . .106 E7
St Bernards Rd B72 . . . . .46 C4
St Bernard's Wlk CV3 . . . . . .134 D6
St Blaise Ave B46 . . . . .59 C2
St Blaise Rd B75 . . . . .32 D3
St Brades Cl B69 . . . . .63 C7
St Bride's Cl CV31 . . . . .162 C6
St Brides Cl DY3 . . . . .50 C8
St Brigid's RC Prim Sch
B31 .102 F3
St Buryan Cl CV11 . . . . .74 A5
Saintbury Dr B91 . . . . .127 C8
St Caroline Cl B70 . . . . .53 F2
St Catharines Cl WS1 . . . . . .43 A7
**St Catherine of Siena RC
Prim Sch** B1 . . . . .66 D3
St Catherine's Cl
Coventry CV3 . . . . .134 B8
Hinckley LE10 . . . . .75 F7
St Catherines Cl
Oldbury B72 . . . . .52 A1
Sutton Coldfield B75 . . . . . . .46 F7
St Catherine's Cres
Whitnash CV34 . . . . .161 F3
Wolverhampton WV4 . . . . . . .38 F4
St Catherine's Lodge **7**
CV6 .113 A4
St Catherine's Rd B60 . . . . .138 A5
St Catherine's Rd WS13 . . . . .3 B3
St Cecilia Cl DY10 . . . . .116 E2
St Cecilia's WV11 . . . . .26 C5
St Chad Ct B77 . . . . .21 F2
St Chad's CE Prim Sch
WS13 .9 C8
St Chad's Circus Queensway
B3 . . . . .164 B3
St Chad's Cl
Cannock WS11 . . . . .2 A4
Dudley DY3 . . . . .50 B3
St Chads Cl **3** WS13 . . . . . . .9 B8
St Chads Ind Est B19 . . . . . .66 F5
St Chads Mews B94 . . . . . . .144 D3
St Chads Queensway B4 . . .164 C4
St Chad's RC Prim Sch
DY3 .50 D7

St Chad's Rd
Bilston WV14 . . . . .40 F7
Birmingham B45 . . . . .121 F7
Lichfield WS13 . . . . .3 C1
St Chads Rd B80 . . . . .159 C4
St Chad's Rd
Sutton Coldfield B75 . . . . . . .46 F5
Wolverhampton WV10 . . . . . .25 F8
St Christian's Croft CV3 . . . .133 E8
St Christian's Rd CV3 . . . . . .133 E8
St Christopher Cl B70 . . . . . . .53 E2
St Christopher Dr WS10 . . . . .42 E3
St Christopher Prim Sch
CV5 .112 D4
St Christophers B20 . . . . .54 F4
St Christopher's Cl CV34 . . .160 D8
St Christopher's Dr B77 . . . . .21 C1
St Christophers RC Prim Sch
WV8 .10 A3
St Clare's RC Prim Sch
B20 . . . . .55 B1
St Clement's Ave WS3 . . . . . .28 D7
St Clement's CE Prim Sch
B7 . . . . .67 C7
St Clements Cl CV2 . . . . .114 D8
St Clements Ho **3** B71 . . . . .53 D4
St Clement's La B71 . . . . .53 D4
St Clement's Rd B7 . . . . .67 C6
St Columba's Cl CV1 . . . . .165 B4
St Columbas Dr B45 . . . . . . .122 D7
St Columba's RC Prim Sch
B45 .122 D7
St Cuthbert's Cl B70 . . . . .53 F2
St Cuthberts RC Prim Sch
B8 . . . . .68 C4
St David Dr WS10 . . . . .42 E3
St David's Cl CV31 . . . . .162 C7
St Davids Cl WS3 . . . . .15 B5
St David's Dr B32 . . . . .84 B5
St Davids Orch CV3 . . . . . . .134 F7
St Davids Pl WS3 . . . . .14 D2
St Denis Rd B29 . . . . .103 B7
St Dennis Ho **5** B15 . . . . . . .65 D1
St Dominic's Rd B24 . . . . . . .56 E1
St Dunstan's RC Prim Sch
B14 .104 F8
St Edburghs Rd B25 . . . . .68 E1
St Editha's Cl B79 . . . . .21 B5
St Editha's Ct B79 . . . . .21 B7
St Edith's Gn **3** CV34 . . . . .161 B8
St Edith's Rd CV34 . . . . .161 B8
St Edmund Campion RC
Lower Sch B24 . . . . .57 C6
St Edmund Campion RC Sch
B23 . . . . .57 B5
St Edmund's Cl
West Bromwich B70 . . . . .53 F2
Wolverhampton WV6 . . . . . . .24 F3
St Edmund's RC Sch WV3 . . .24 E3
St Edward's RC Prim Sch
B29 . . . . .86 B1
St Edward's Rd B29 . . . . .85 F2
Sainte Foy Ave WS11 . . . . .9 A6
SS John & Monica RC Prim
Sch B13 . . . . .86 E4
St Eleanor Cl B70 . . . . .53 F3
St Elizabeth's RC Prim Sch
Coventry CV6 . . . . .113 E7
Tamworth B79 . . . . .20 F8
St Elizabeth's Rd CV6 . . . . . .113 E7
St Foy Ave WS13 . . . . .8 F5
St Francis Ave B91 . . . . . . .106 E6
St Francis CE Prim Sch
B30 .103 D6
St Francis Cl
Hinckley LE10 . . . . .71 C3
Walsall WS3 . . . . .15 B5
St Francis Factory Est
B70 . . . . .53 F2
St Francis of Assisi Tech Coll
WS9 .30 C5
St Francis RC Prim Sch
Bedworth CV12 . . . . .78 C3
Birmingham B19 . . . . .66 B6
Walsall WV4 . . . . .15 C1
St Francis Xavier RC Sch
B69 . . . . .64 A8
St Fremund Way CV31 . . . . .162 C5
St Gabriel's RC Prim Sch
B77 . . . . .21 E1
St George Cl WS10 . . . . .42 E3
St George Dr B60 . . . . .151 B8
**St George & St Teresa RC
Prim Sch** B93 . . . . .128 A4
St Georges Ave B23 . . . . .57 A5
St George's Ave LE10 . . . . . . .71 C1
St George's CE Fst Sch
Kidderminster DY10 . . . . . . .116 F7
Redditch B98 . . . . .153 F3
St George's CE Prim Sch
Birmingham B19 . . . . .164 B5
Birmingham,Ladywood B16 . .65 F1
St Georges Cl B15 . . . . .86 A7
St George's Cl
Darlaston B9 . . . . .50 B3
Sutton Coldfield B75 . . . . . . .46 F6
St Georges Ct
10 Kidderminster DY10 . . .116 E6
5 Walsall WS1 . . . . .28 F2
St George's Ct
Birmingham B30 . . . . .103 E2
Wolverhampton WS10 . . . . . .41 D7
St Georges Ct B74 . . . . .31 E5

St George's Gdns **3** B98 . .153 F4
St George's Par WV1 . . . . . .163 C2
St George's Pl
4 Walsall WS1 . . . . .28 F2
Kidderminster DY10 . . . . . . .116 E7
St Georges Pl B70 . . . . .53 C4
St George's Rd CV1 . . . . . . .113 F2
St Georges Rd
Dudley DY2 . . . . .62 E6
Redditch B98 . . . . .153 F4
St George's Rd
Royal Leamington Spa
CV31 . . . . .161 F6
Solihull B90 . . . . .126 D8
Stourbridge DY8 . . . . .80 D2
St George's Sta WV1 . . . . . .163 C2
St George's St
Birmingham B19 . . . . .164 B4
Darlaston WS10 . . . . .41 D7
St George's Terr DY10 . . . . .116 E7
St Georges Way DY10 . . . . . .78 B8
St George's Way B77 . . . . . . .21 F4
St Gerards Ct B91 . . . . .106 E2
St Gerards RC Prim Sch
B35 . . . . .58 B4
St Gerards Rd B91 . . . . .106 E2
St Giles Ave B65 . . . . .63 B4
St Giles' CE Prim Sch
WV13 . . . . .27 B2
St Giles Cl B65 . . . . .63 C4
St Giles Cres WV1 . . . . .26 A2
St Giles Ct B65 . . . . .63 D3
St Gile's Ct WV13 . . . . .27 B1
St Giles Jun Sch CV7 . . . . . . .95 F8
St Giles Rd
Birmingham B33 . . . . .69 D2
Burntwood WS7 . . . . .7 C4
Coventry CV7 . . . . .95 D6
Willenhall WV13 . . . . .27 B1
Wolverhampton WV1 . . . . . . .26 A2
St Giles Row DY8 . . . . .81 A6
St Giles St DY2 . . . . .62 C5
St Godwald's Cres B60 . . . . .151 B8
St Godwald's Rd B60 . . . . . .151 C2
St Govan's Cl **2** CV31 . . . .162 C6
St Gregory's RC Prim Sch
Coventry CV2 . . . . .114 E3
Smethwick B67 . . . . .64 F2
St Helens Ave DY4 . . . . .52 C5
St Helens Pas B1 . . . . .66 C3
St Helens Rd WS13 . . . . .3 B3
St Helen's Rd
Solihull B91 . . . . .107 A6
Whitnash CV31 . . . . .162 A5
St Helen's Way CV5 . . . . . . .112 B8
St Helens Rd B31 . . . . .102 F4
St Hellier Ho **4** B15 . . . . . . .65 D1
St Hubert's RC Prim Sch
B68 . . . . .84 C8
St Ives Cl B79 . . . . .21 B6
St Ives Rd
Coventry CV2 . . . . .114 E3
Walsall WS5 . . . . .43 D7
St Ives Way CV11 . . . . .73 F5
St James Ave B65 . . . . .63 B4
St James CE Jun Sch
Bulkington CV12 . . . . .79 C2
Solihull B90 . . . . .106 B2
St James CE Prim Sch
Birmingham B21 . . . . .54 D1
Oldbury B69 . . . . .63 D5
Stourbridge DY8 . . . . .80 D7
St James Cl
Walsall WS3 . . . . .15 B5
West Bromwich B70 . . . . .53 F2
St James Ct
Bromsgrove B60 . . . . .137 A3
Coventry CV3 . . . . .134 E6
St James Gdns
Brownhills WS8 . . . . .15 F7
Bulkington CV12 . . . . .79 C2
St James' La CV3 . . . . .134 D6
St James Meadow Rd
CV32 . . . . .156 C2
St James' Pl B15 . . . . .86 B8
St James' Pl B7 . . . . .67 A3
St James Pl B90 . . . . .106 B2
St James Prim Sch WS8 . . . .15 F8
St James' RC Jun & Inf Sch
B45 .122 A7
St James Rd B15 . . . . .86 B8
St James' Rd B21 . . . . .65 D8
St James Rd
Cannock WS11 . . . . .1 C1
Norton Canes WS11 . . . . .6 B5
Oldbury B69 . . . . .63 E8
Sutton Coldfield B75 . . . . . . .32 C2
St James's Rd DY1 . . . . .51 B2
St James's Rd DY1 . . . . .51 B2
St James' St DY3 . . . . .50 D3
St James' Terr DY1 . . . . .51 A2
St James St
Wednesbury WS10 . . . . .41 E2
Wolverhampton WV1 . . . . . . .163 D3
St James Wlk WS8 . . . . .15 F7
**St John Bosco RC Jun & Inf
Sch** B71 . . . . .53 D4
St John Cl B75 . . . . .32 D4
St John Fisher RC Prim Sch
Birmingham B31 . . . . .123 B7
Coventry CV2 . . . . .114 D5
St John's Arc WV1 . . . . .163 B2
St John's Ave
Kenilworth CV8 . . . . .148 A3
Kidderminster DY11 . . . . . . .116 A6
St Johns Ave B65 . . . . .63 A4
**St John's CE Foundation Mid
Sch** B61 . . . . .136 F1

St John's CE Fst Sch
DY11. . . . . .116 B6
St John's CE Mid Sch
DY11. . . . . .116 B6
St John's CE Prim Sch
Birmingham B11 . . . . .87 C4
Brownhills WS9 . . . . .16 A3
Coventry CV5 . . . . .112 C4
Essington WV11 . . . . .13 A4
Wednesbury WS10 . . . . . . .41 F2
St John's Cl
6 Kidderminster DY11. . 116 C6
Brownhills WS9 . . . . .15 F3
Cannock WS11. . . . . .4 D8
St Johns Cl B93 . . . . .128 B6
St John's Cl
Lichfield WS13. . . . . .9 B6
West Bromwich B70 . . . . . .53 F3
St Johns Ct
20 Brierley Hill DY5. . . . . .61 D2
2 Birmingham,Harborne
B17 . . . . .85 B6
St John's Ct **4** CV34. . . .160 F7
St Johns Ct
5 Wednesbury WS10. . . . .41 F2
Birmingham,Turves Green
B31. . . . . .103 B1
St John's Ct
Cannock WS12. . . . . .2 E1
Walsall WS3 . . . . .14 B1
St John's Dr WS14. . . . . . . .17 F5
St John's Flats CV8. . . . . .148 A3
St Johns Gr B37 . . . . .69 F3
St John's Hill WS14. . . . . . .17 F5
St Johns Ho LE10 . . . . .71 E1
St Johns Ho **2** B74. . . . . .31 E3
St John's House Mus*
CV34 . . . . .160 F7
St John's Ladywood CE Prim
Sch B16 . . . . .66 A2
St John's Prim Sch CV8. .147 F2
St John's Rd B11. . . . . .87 C5
St John's Rd B17 . . . . .85 D6
St Johns Rd WS8 . . . . .16 A5
St John's Rd
Cannock WS11. . . . . .4 E7
Darlaston WS10. . . . . .41 C5
Dudley DY2 . . . . .51 E1
St Johns Rd WV11. . . . . . . .13 A3
St Johns Rd B63 . . . . .82 E4
St Johns Rd B68. . . . . .64 C5
St John's Rd
Royal Leamington Spa
CV31. . . . . .162 A6
Stourbridge DY8 . . . . .81 A5
Tipton DY4 . . . . .51 F8
St Johns Rd
Walsall,Pleck WS2. . . . . . . .42 B8
Walsall WS3 . . . . .15 B5
St Johns Ret Pk WV2 . . . .163 B1
St John's Sq WV2. . . . . . . .163 B2
St John's St
5 Kidderminster DY11. . 116 C6
Coventry CV1. . . . . .165 C2
Dudley DY2 . . . . .62 C5
Kenilworth CV8 . . . . .148 A3
Tamworth B79 . . . . .21 B5
Wolverhampton WV1. . . . .163 B2
St John St B61. . . . . .136 F2
St John's Terr **13** CV31. .162 A6
St John St WS13. . . . . .9 B7
St John Vianney CE Prim Sch
CV3 . . . . .134 C5
St John Vianney RC Prim Sch
CV5 . . . . .112 B3
St John Wall RC Sch B21. .54 C2
St Joseph & St Theresa RC
Prim Sch WV6 . . . . .6 E6
St Josephs Ave B31. . . . . .103 B5
St Josephs Cl WS3. . . . . . . .15 A4
St Joseph's Convent Sch
WV6. . . . . .24 E6
St Josephs Ct WV4. . . . . . .38 D6
St Joseph's RC Jun Sch
CV11 . . . . .73 C3
St Josephs RC Prim Sch
B30. . . . . .103 F5
St Joseph's RC Prim Sch
Birmingham B7 . . . . .67 B6
Cannock WS12. . . . . .2 C4
Darlaston WS10. . . . . .41 D7
Dudley DY2 . . . . .51 E1
Lichfield WS14. . . . . .9 C7
Sutton Coldfield B75 . . . . .46 C7
Whitnash CV31. . . . . .162 A3
St Josephs Rd B8. . . . . . . .68 C5
St Joseph St **7** DY2 . . . . .51 D1
St Judes Ave B80 . . . . . . .159 D4
St Jude's CE Prim Sch
WV3. . . . . .24 F3
St Judes Cl
4 Sutton Coldfield B75 . . .46 F6
Birmingham B14 . . . . .104 F2
St Jude's Cres CV3 . . . . . .134 D7
St Jude's Ct B14. . . . . . . .104 F7
St Jude's Pas B5 . . . . .164 B1
St Jude's RC Prim Sch
B14. . . . . .104 F2

St Jude's Rd WV6. . . . . . . .24 F3
St Jude's Rd W WV6. . . . . .24 F3
St Katherine's Rd B68 . . . .64 B2
St Kenelms Ave B63 . . . . . .82 E1
St Kenelm's Cl B70. . . . . . .53 F2
St Kenelm's Rd B62. . . . . .100 E5
St Kilda's Rd B8. . . . . .67 E5
St Laurence Ave CV34. . . .160 D5
St Laurence CE Inf Sch
B31. . . . . .103 B4
St Laurence CE Jun Sch
B31. . . . . .103 B4
St Laurence Cl B48. . . . . .139 B6
St Laurence Rd B31. . . . . .103 B5
St Lawrence Cl
1 Birmingham B5. . . . . . .86 D7
Knowle B93 . . . . .128 B5
St Lawrence Dr WS11. . . . . .2 B2
St Lawrence Ho **6** B15 . .65 D1
St Lawrence Mews B31. . .103 A3
St Lawrence's Rd CV6. . . . .95 F1
St Lawrence Way WS10 . . .41 D6
St Leonards Cl B37. . . . . . .90 A7
St Leonards View B78. . . . .36 F8
St Leonard's Wlk CV8. . . .135 A1
St Loye's CE Prim Sch
B97. . . . . .153 D1
St Luke's CE Fst Sch
WV2. . . . . .39 B7
St Luke's Cl WS11 . . . . .4 D8
St Lukes Cl B65. . . . . .63 B4
St Luke's Cotts B97 . . . . .153 D1
St Lukes Prim Sch (Inf Site)
WV2 . . . . .39 C7
St Luke's Rd
Birmingham B5 . . . . .86 E7
Burntwood WS7. . . . . .7 C6
Coventry CV6. . . . . .95 D3
Wednesbury WS10 . . . . . . .42 A3
St Lukes St B64. . . . . .62 D1
St Luke's Terr DY1 . . . . . . .62 A8
St Lukes Way CV10. . . . . . .72 C4
St Margaret Mary RC Jun &
Inf Sch B23. . . . . .56 C6
St Margaret Rd CV1. . . . .113 F2
St Margarets Ave B8 . . . . .68 B6
St Margaret's CE Jun Sch
CV31. . . . . .162 B7
St Margaret's CE Prim Sch
Birmingham B43 . . . . .43 E4
Solihull B92 . . . . .88 F2
St Margaret's Ct **3** B92. . .88 E1
St Margarets Dr B63 . . . . .82 F2
St Margaret's Ho CV31. . .162 B8
St Margaret's Rd
2 Solihull B92 . . . . .88 E1
Birmingham B43 . . . . .43 F2
St Margarets Rd
Birmingham B8 . . . . .68 B6
Lichfield WS13. . . . . .3 B3
St Margaret's Rd B79 . . . . .21 B7
St Margarets Rd WS3 . . . . .15 A4
St Margaret's Rd CV31. . .162 B5
St Margaret's B74 . . . . . . .31 C3
St Mark's Annexe (Coventry
& Warwickshire Hospl)
CV1 . . . . .165 C4
St Mark's CE Prim Sch
DY5 . . . . .61 C7
St Marks Cl
Great Wyrley WS6 . . . . .4 F4
Nuneaton CV10 . . . . .72 C4
St Marks Cres B1. . . . . . . .66 B3
St Mark's Ct DY5 . . . . .61 D7
St Mark's Mews CV32. . . .156 E1
St Mark's RC Prim Sch
B42. . . . . .54 F6
St Marks Rd WS8 . . . . .16 A5
St Mark's Rd
Burntwood WS7. . . . . .7 C6
Dudley DY2 . . . . .51 F1
Royal Leamington Spa
CV32. . . . . .156 D1
Smethwick B67 . . . . .64 D3
Stourbridge DY9 . . . . .81 D5
St Marks Rd WS3 . . . . .15 A4
St Mark's Rd WV3 . . . . .25 B1
St Mark's St B1. . . . . .66 B3
St Mark's St WV3 . . . . . . .163 A2
St Martin De Porres RC Prim
Sch B13 . . . . .87 A3
St Martins Ave B80 . . . . . .159 D4
St Martin's CE Prim Sch
Bilston WV14. . . . . .41 A2
Tipton WV14. . . . . .52 B5
St Martin's Cl
West Bromwich B70 . . . . . .53 F2
Wolverhampton WV3. . . . . .39 E6
St Martin's Dr DY4. . . . . . .52 A5
St Martins Ind Est B69 . . .64 A4
St Martin's Mkt B5. . . . . .164 C1
St Martin's Queensway B2. . .164 C2
St Martin's Rd CV3 . . . . . .133 C2
St Martins Rd B75 . . . . . . .46 F5
St Martin's Sch B91 . . . . .107 D3
St Martin's Terr WV14. . . . .40 E4
St Mary Magdalene CE Jun &
Inf Sch B71. . . . . .53 D4
St Mary of the Angels RC
Prim Sch WV9. . . . . .30 B5
St Mary & St Benedict RC
Prim Sch CV1. . . . . .113 E4

St Mary & St John RC Prim &
Inf Sch WV2. . . . . .163 C1
St Mary & St Jun & Inf Sch
B23. . . . . .56 E3
St Mary & St Margaret's CE
Prim Sch B36 . . . . .69 B8
St Mary's Ave LE9 . . . . .71 F5
St Mary's CE Fst Sch
DY10. . . . . .116 E8
St Mary's CE Jun & Inf Sch
B20. . . . . .55 B1
St Mary's CE Prim Sch
Birmingham B29 . . . . .85 D1
Hinckley LE10 . . . . .75 D8
Kingswinford DY6 . . . . .60 D7
St Marys Cl B27 . . . . .88 B3
St Mary's Cl
Sedgley DY3. . . . . .50 F8
Sutton Coldfield B24 . . . . .57 D4
Warwick CV34 . . . . .160 D8
St Mary's Cres CV31 . . . . .162 B7
St Marys Cl **12** DY5. . . . . .61 D2
St Mary's Ct
3 Willenhall WV13. . . . . .27 A2
Kenilworth CV8 . . . . .147 F2
Nuneaton CV11 . . . . .73 B5
St Mary's Hall WV1 . . . . . .163 C2
St Mary's Ho **4** B15. . . . .86 D8
St Mary's Immaculate RC
Prim Sch CV34 . . . . .160 E8
St Mary's La DY8 . . . . .81 B3
St Marys Park Cvn Pk
B47. . . . . .124 E2
St Mary's RC Prim Sch
Birmingham B17 . . . . .85 C5
Brierley Hill DY5 . . . . .61 E2
Cannock WS11. . . . . .4 E8
Studley B80 . . . . .159 E4
Wednesbury WS10 . . . . . . .41 F4
Wolverhampton WV10. . . . .26 A7
St Marys Rd B17. . . . . .85 C5
St Mary's Rd
Hinckley LE10 . . . . .75 D8
Lichfield WS13. . . . . .3 B3
Nuneaton CV11 . . . . .73 B5
Royal Leamington Spa
CV31. . . . . .162 B7
Smethwick B67 . . . . .64 F1
Wednesbury WS10 . . . . . . .41 F3
St Marys Ringway DY10 . .116 E6
St Mary's Row
Birmingham,Moseley B13 . .86 F3
Birmingham,New Town Row
B4 . . . . .164 C3
St Mary's St WV1 . . . . . . .163 C3
St Mary St CV1. . . . . .165 C2
St Mary's Terr CV31. . . . . .162 B7
St Mary's The Mount RC Prim
Sch WS1. . . . . .42 F8
St Marys View B23. . . . . . .56 D8
St Mary's Way
Aldridge WS9. . . . . .30 B5
Tamworth B77 . . . . .21 E4
St Matthew's Ave WS7 . . . .7 F7
St Matthews CE Prim Sch
B7. .67 A4
St Matthew's CE Prim Sch
B66. . . . . .65 C5
St Matthews Cl CV10. . . . .72 C4
St Matthew's Cl WS1. . . . .28 F1
St Matthews Cl WS3 . . . . .15 B5
St Matthew's Rd WS7 . . . . .7 F7
St Matthews Rd
Oldbury B68. . . . . .64 A2
Smethwick B66 . . . . .65 C5
St Matthew St WV1 . . . . . .25 F1
St Mawes Rd WV6 . . . . . . .24 A3
St Mawgen Cl B35. . . . . . . .58 B4
St Michael Ho **3** B15. . . .65 D1
St Michael Rd WS13 . . . . . . .9 C8
St Michael's CE High Sch
B65. . . . . .63 C5
St Michaels CE Inf & Jun Sch
B21. . . . . .66 A7
St Michael's CE Jun & Inf Sch
WV6 . . . . .24 E5
St Michael's CE Prim Sch
Bedworth CV12. . . . . .78 D3
Birmingham B32 . . . . .102 C8
Lichfield WS14. . . . . .9 C7
Lichfield WS14. . . . . .9 C8
St Michaels CE Prim Sch
Walsall WS3 . . . . .14 F2
Walsall WS3 . . . . .15 A3
St Michael's Cl WS3 . . . . .15 A2
St Michael's Cl CV9 . . . . . .36 D1
St Michael's Cres B69 . . . .64 A4
St Michael's Ct B18 . . . . . .66 B4
St Michael's Ct B68. . . . . .64 A4
St Michaels Dr WS12. . . . . .2 F5
St Michael's Gr DY2 . . . . . .52 A1
St Michael's Hill B18 . . . . .66 A7
St Michael's Hospl
Lichfield WS13. . . . . .9 B8
Warwick CV34 . . . . .161 A3
St Michael's Mews B69. . . .52 A2
St Michael's RC Prim Sch
WV3. . . . . .38 D7
St Michael's Rd
Birmingham B18 . . . . .66 A7
Coventry CV2 . . . . .114 A3
St Michaels Rd DY9 . . . . . .49 F5
St Michael's Rd
Sutton Coldfield B73 . . . . .46 B5
Warwick CV34 . . . . .160 D8

St Michael St
Walsall WS1 . . . . .42 E8
West Bromwich B70 . . . . . .53 C3
St Michael's Way CV10. . . .72 C4
St Michaels Way DY4 . . . . .52 A3
St Nicholas Ave CV8 . . . . .147 F3
St Nicholas CE Com Prim
Sch CV8 . . . . .147 F5
St Nicholas Church St
CV34 . . . . .160 F6
St Nicholas Ct
Coventry CV1. . . . . .113 C5
Walsall WS3 . . . . .15 A4
St Nicholas Ct
3 Coventry,Edgwick
CV6. . . . . .113 F7
Coventry,Radford CV6 . . . .113 B6
St Nicholas Pk CV34. . . . .160 F6
St Nicholas RC Prim Sch
B73. . . . . .45 F2
St Nicholas Rd CV31. . . . .162 F5
St Nicholas St CV1. . . . . .165 B4
St Nicholas Terr CV31. . . .162 E4
St Nicholas Wlk B76 . . . . .59 B6
St Nicolas CE Prim Sch
CV11 . . . . .73 F6
St Nicolas Gdns B38 . . . . .103 F2
St Nicolas Park Dr CV11 . . .73 F7
St Nicolas Rd CV11 . . . . . .73 D5
St Osburg's RC Prim Sch
CV1 . . . . .165 A3
St Osburg's Rd CV2 . . . . .114 A3
St Oswalds Cl DY10. . . . . .116 F8
St Oswald's Ct B10 . . . . . .87 E8
St Oswalds Rd B10 . . . . . .87 E8
St Patrick's CE Jun & Inf Sch
CV1 . . . . .89 B4
St Patricks Cl B14 . . . . . .104 E5
St Patrick's Ct DY11 . . . . .116 B1
St Patricks RC Prim Sch
B18. . . . . .65 F4
St Patrick's RC Prim Sch
Birmingham B37. . . . . .70 C2
Coventry CV2. . . . . .96 D1
St Patricks RC Prim Sch
CV1 . . . . .161 F6
St Patrick's RC Prim Sch
Walsall WS2 . . . . .28 E3
Wolverhampton WV11. . . . .26 C5
St Patrick's Rd CV1 . . . . . .165 B2
St Paul's Ave
Birmingham B12 . . . . .87 A5
Kidderminster DY11 . . . . .116 A6
St Paul's CE Prim Sch
Nuneaton CV10 . . . . .72 C3
Royal Leamington Spa
CV32. . . . . .157 B1
Tipton DY4 . . . . .51 F6
St Pauls CE Prim Sch
WV9 . . . . .11 A2
St Paul's Cl
5 Walsall WS1 . . . . .28 E2
Cannock WS11. . . . . .2 B1
Warwick CV34 . . . . .160 D6
St Paul's Cres **5** B46. . . .70 F7
St Paul's Cres WS3 . . . . . .15 B5
St Paul's Cres B70. . . . . . .52 E7
St Paul's Ct B77 . . . . .35 C4
St Paul's Ct B46. . . . . .59 B3
St Pauls Dr B62. . . . . .63 D1
St Pauls Dr DY4 . . . . .52 B4
St Paul's Gdns LE10 . . . . . .71 E1
St Paul's RC Prim Sch
B38. . . . . .104 A1
St Paul's Rd
Birmingham B12 . . . . .87 A5
Burntwood WS7. . . . . .7 C6
Cannock WS12. . . . . .2 D8
Coventry CV6. . . . . .113 E6
Dudley DY2 . . . . .62 D5
Nuneaton CV10 . . . . .72 D3
Smethwick B66 . . . . .64 E7
Wednesbury WS10 . . . . . . .42 C5
St Paul's Sch for Girls
B16. . . . . .65 E1
St Paul's Sq
4 Royal Leamington Spa
CV32. . . . . .157 A1
Birmingham B3 . . . . .164 A4
St Paul's Sta B19 . . . . . . .164 B4
St Paul's St WS1. . . . . .28 E2
St Paul's Terr CV34 . . . . . .160 D6
St Peter & St Paul RC Prim
Sch
Birmingham B24 . . . . .57 C3
Lichfield WS13. . . . . .3 B1
St Peter's CE Prim Sch
Birmingham B17 . . . . .85 B5
Cannock WS12. . . . . .2 D4
Stonnall WS9 . . . . .16 E4
St Peters Cl
Birmingham B28 . . . . .105 D6
Bromsgrove B61. . . . . .136 E1
St Peter's Cl
Redditch B97 . . . . .158 E5
Stonnall WS9 . . . . .16 E4
St Peters Cl B72. . . . . .46 B3
St Peter's Cl
Tamworth B77 . . . . .21 D1
Water Orton B46. . . . . .59 B2
West Bromwich DY4 . . . . . .52 D8
St Peter's Collegiate CE Sch
WV3. . . . . .24 E3
St Peter's Croft B73. . . . . .46 B3

St Peters Ct **2** LE10 . . . .71 E1
St Peter's Ct CV1 . . . . . . .165 D4
St Peters Ct
Lichfield WS13. . . . . .3 B2
Walsall WS3 . . . . .14 B1
St Peters Dr WS3. . . . . . . .15 A4
St Peters La B92. . . . . .90 D1
St Peter's RC First Sch
B61. . . . . .150 E8
St Peters RC Prim Sch
B32. . . . . .84 C1
St Peter's RC Prim Sch
Royal Leamington Spa
CV32. . . . . .161 F8
Walsall WS3 . . . . .14 B2
St Peter's RC Sch
Hinckley LE10 . . . . .71 E1
Solihull B91. . . . . .107 B2
St Peter's Rd B17 . . . . .85 B5
St Peter's Rd
Birmingham B20 . . . . .66 C8
Burntwood WS7. . . . . .7 C6
Cannock WS12. . . . . .2 D4
Dudley DY2 . . . . .62 D5
Stourbridge DY9 . . . . .81 C1
St Peters Terr WS2. . . . . . .28 E4
St Philip's Cath* B3. . . . .164 B3
St Philip's Pl B2 . . . . .164 C3
St Philip's RC Prim Sch
B66. . . . . .65 B6
St Phillip's Ave WV3 . . . . .38 F7
St Phillips Ave WV3 . . . . . .38 F7
St Phillip's Gr WV3. . . . . . .38 F7
St Quentin St WV3. . . . . . .42 C7
St Saviour's CE Prim Sch
B8. .67 D5
St Saviour's Cl WV2. . . . . .39 D7
St Saviour's Cl WV9 . . . . . .99 A6
St Saviour's Rd B8. . . . . . .67 D4
St Silas' Sq B19 . . . . .66 B7
St Simons Cl **3** B75 . . . . .46 F6
Saint's Peter & Paul RC Prim
Sch CV2 . . . . .114 F7
St Stephan's Ho B97 . . . . .153 E14
St Stephen's CE First Sch
B98. . . . . .153 F5
St Stephen's CE Prim Sch
WV10. . . . . .25 F4
St Stephen's Gdns **1**
WV13. . . . . .27 A1
St Stephens Gdns B98 . . .153 F5
St Stephen's Rd B29. . . . .104 B8
St Stephen's Rd WS7 . . . . . .7 C6
St Stephens Rd B71. . . . . .65 B8
St Stephens St B6. . . . . . .66 E6
Saints Way CV10. . . . . .73 C5
St Teresa's RC Prim Sch
Birmingham B20 . . . . .55 A3
Wolverhampton WV4 . . . . . .39 E5
St Thomas Aquinas RC Sch
B38. . . . . .103 D3
St Thomas' CE Prim Sch
B15. . . . . .86 D8
St Thomas CE Prim Sch
WV1 . . . . .26 D7
St Thomas' Cl WS9. . . . . . .16 B1
St Thomas Cl
Sutton Coldfield B75 . . . . .46 F5
Walsall WS3 . . . . .28 E6
St Thomas More RC Fst Sch
B98. . . . . .159 B7
St Thomas More RC Prim
Sch
Coventry CV3. . . . . .133 D5
Great Wyrley WS6 . . . . .5 A4
St Thomas More RC Sch
Bilston WV14. . . . . .41 A7
Nuneaton CV10 . . . . .73 A3
St Thomas More's RC Prim
Sch B26 . . . . .89 B5
St Thomas of Canterbury RC
Prim Sch WS3. . . . . .28 F6
St Thomas' Rd
Birmingham B23 . . . . .56 D3
Coventry CV6. . . . . .96 A3
St Thomas's Cl CV10 . . . . .72 C3
St Thomas's Ct **13** CV1 . .113 B2
St Thomas's Ho **12** CV1. .113 B2
St Thomas St DY2. . . . . . . .62 C5
St Valentines Cl CV10 . . . .53 F2
St Vincent Cres B70. . . . . .52 F4
St Vincent St W B16 . . . . .66 A2
St Vincent St B16 . . . . . . .66 A2
St Wilfrid's RC Prim Sch
B36. . . . . .68 F8
Saladin Ave B69 . . . . .63 E5
Salcombe Ave B26. . . . . . .89 C5
Salcombe Cl
Cannock WS11. . . . . .4 C7
Coventry CV3. . . . . .134 D6
Nuneaton CV11 . . . . .73 F5
Salcombe Dr DY5. . . . . . . .81 C1
Salcombe Gr WV14. . . . . . .40 D1
Salcombe Rd B66. . . . . . . .65 B5
Saldavian Ct WS2. . . . . . . .42 B6
Salem St WV14. . . . . .40 F5
Salem Sch DY4 . . . . .52 D5
Salford Cl B23. . . . . .56 F5
Salford Cl
Coventry CV2. . . . . .114 A5

Salford Cl continued
Redditch B98 . . . . .159 B6
Salford St B6 . . . . .67 C8
Salford Trad Est B6 . . . . .67 C8
Salisbury Ave CV3 . . . .133 C6
Salisbury Cl
Birmingham B13 . . . . .86 E3
Dudley DY1 . . . . .50 F3
Lichfield WS13 . . . . .3 C3
Wolston CV8 . . . . .135 F3
Salisbury Dr
Cannock WS12 . . . . .2 B1
Kidderminster DY11 . . . . .116 A6
Nuneaton CV10 . . . . .72 B7
Water Orton B46 . . . . .59 C3
Salisbury Gr B72 . . . . .57 C7
Salisbury Ho
3 Birmingham B24 . . . . . .56 F4
Hinckley LE10 . . . . .71 C4
Salisbury Pl WV3 . . . . .25 B1
Salisbury Prim Sch WS10 .41 F7
Salisbury Rd
Birmingham,Lozells B19 . . .66 C3
Birmingham,Moseley B13 . .86 E3
Birmingham,Saltley B8 . . . .67 E5
Hinckley LE10 . . . . .76 B7
Smethwick B66 . . . . .65 B4
West Bromwich B70 . . . . . .53 E1
Salisbury St
Darlaston WS10 . . . . .41 E7
Wolverhampton WV3 . . . . .25 B1
Salisbury Twr B18 . . . . .66 A3
Sallow Gr WS8 . . . . .7 A1
Sally Ward Dr WS9 . . . . . .16 A4
Salop Cl B71 . . . . .53 B6
Salop Dr
Cannock WS11 . . . . .4 F8
Oldbury B68 . . . . .64 C2
Salop Rd
Oldbury B68 . . . . .64 C2
Redditch B97 . . . . .153 D3
Salop St
Bilston WV14 . . . . .40 E4
Birmingham B12 . . . . .86 F8
Dudley DY1 . . . . .51 B2
Oldbury B69 . . . . .52 E1
Wolverhampton WV3 . . . .163 B2
Salstar Cl B6 . . . . .66 E6
Saltash Gr B25 . . . . .68 C1
Saltbrook Rd B63 . . . . .82 A7
Saltbrook Trad Est B63. . .82 A7
Salter Rd DY4 . . . . .51 F7
Salter's La B97 . . . . .153 B5
Salters La B79 . . . . .21 B6
Salter's La B71 . . . . .53 E4
Salter's Rd WS9 . . . . .16 A3
Salter St B94 . . . . .126 C2
Salters Vale B70 . . . . .53 E1
Saltisford Canal Ctr*
CV34 . . . . .160 C8
Saltisford Gdns CV34. . . .160 C8
Saltisford CV34 . . . . .160 D7
Salt La CV1 . . . . .165 B2
Saltley Ind Ctr B8. . . . . . . .67 C3
Saltley Rd B7 . . . . .67 A5
Saltley Sch B9 . . . . .68 A3
Saltley Trad Est B8. . . . . . .67 C6
Saltley Viaduct B8 . . . . . . .67 C5
Saltney Cl B24 . . . . .57 D5
Salts La B78 . . . . .34 E5
Saltwells La DY2 . . . . .62 B2
Saltwells Nature Reserve*
DY5,DY2 . . . . .62 A2
Saltwells Rd DY2 . . . . .62 C2
Salwarpe Gr B29 . . . . .84 F2
Salwarpe Rd B60 . . . . .150 F8
Sam Barber Ct WS12. . . . . .2 E1
Sambar Rd B78. . . . . .20 F1
Sambourn CI B91. . . . . . . .107 E6
Sambourne Dr B34 . . . . . . .69 D7
Sambourne La
Astwood Bank B96 . . . . . .158 F1
Sambourne B96 . . . . .159 A1
Sambourne Park La B96 .159 A1
Sambrook Rd WV10 . . . . . .26 A6
Sam Gault Cl CV3 . . . . . . .134 E7
Sammons Way CV4 . . . . .111 D1
Sampson Cl
Birmingham B21 . . . . .54 C1
Coventry CV6 . . . . .114 C8
Oldbury B69 . . . . .63 C7
Sampson Ho B11 . . . . .87 B8
Sampson Rd B11 . . . . .87 B7
Sampson Rd N B11 . . . . . . .87 B8
Sampson St WS10 . . . . . . .42 B3
Samsara Rd B60 . . . . .137 C1
Sams La B70 . . . . .53 C1
Sam Spencer Ct DY10. . . .118 A2
Samuel Cl WS13 . . . . .3 C2
Samuel Hayward Ho 5
CV2 .96 B1
Samuel Ho WS3 . . . . .14 B1
**Samuel Johnson's Birthplace
Mus*** WS13. . . . . .9 B8
Samuels Rd B32 . . . . .84 A5
Samuel St WS3 . . . . .14 A1
Samuel Vale Ho CV1 . . . .165 B4
Sanby Cl CV12 . . . . .78 A4
Sanda Croft B36 . . . . .70 B6
Sandalls Cl B31. . . . . .102 D1
Sandal Rise B91 . . . . .107 E3
Sandals Rise B62 . . . . .83 D3
Sandalwood Cl WV12 . . . . .27 B8
Sand Bank WS3. . . . . .14 A1
Sandbarn Cl B90. . . . . .126 F6

Sandbeds Rd WV12 . . . . . .27 C4
Sandbourne Rd B8 . . . . . . .68 A4
Sanderling Cl WV10. . . . . .12 B7
Sanderling Ct DY10 . . . . . .117 A1
Sanderling Rise
Burntwood WS7 . . . . .7 B8
Kingswinford DY6 . . . . .61 A6
Sanders Cl
Dudley DY2 . . . . .62 E7
Redditch B97 . . . . .153 B4
Sanders Ct CV34. . . . . .161 C8
Sanders Ind Est 1 B61 . .136 E1
Sanderson Ct DY11 . . . . . .116 C5
Sanders Rd
Bedworth CV6 . . . . .96 B6
Bromsgrove B61 . . . . .136 E1
Sandfield Bridge DY5 . . . .50 B1
Sandfield Cl B90. . . . . .126 B8
Sandfield Gr DY3 . . . . .50 B2
Sandfield Mdw WS13 . . . . . .9 A6
Sandfield Rd
Stourbridge DY8 . . . . .60 F2
West Bromwich B71 . . . . . .42 E2
Sandfields Ave B10 . . . . . . .87 B8
Sandfields Rd B64 . . . . .62 C2
Sandford Ave B65 . . . . .63 C3
Sandford Cl
Coventry CV2 . . . . .96 E3
Hinckley LE10 . . . . .71 F1
Sandford Ho WS13. . . . . . . .9 A7
Sandford Rd
Birmingham B13 . . . . .87 A3
Dudley DY1 . . . . .50 E1
Sandford Rise WV6 . . . . . .24 E6
Sandford St WS13 . . . . .9 B7
Sandgate Cres CV2 . . . . . .114 E2
Sandgate Rd
Birmingham B28 . . . . .106 A4
Tipton DY4. . . . . .52 A8
Sandhill Farm Cl 1 B19 .66 D7
Sandhills Cres B91. . . . . . .127 B8
Sandhills Gn B48 . . . . .138 E7
Sandhills La B45. . . . . .138 D7
Sandhills Rd B45 . . . . .138 D8
Sandhill St WS3 . . . . .14 A1
Sandhurst Ave
Birmingham B36 . . . . .68 D6
Stourbridge DY9 . . . . .81 D2
Sandhurst Cl B98 . . . . .154 C6
Sandhurst Dr WV4 . . . . . . .39 A4
Sandhurst Gr
Coventry CV6 . . . . .113 B5
Stourbridge DY8 . . . . .60 E3
Sandhurst Ho B38 . . . . . . .104 B1
Sandhurst Rd
Birmingham B13 . . . . .86 F2
Kingswinford DY6 . . . . .61 A4
Sutton Coldfield B74 . . . . .31 F5
Sandliffe Cl DY11 . . . . .116 C8
Sandlands Cl CV2 . . . . .114 E4
Sandland Cl WV14 . . . . .40 F6
Sandland Rd WV12. . . . . . .27 D8
Sandmartin Cl DY2 . . . . . . .62 D2
Sandmeadow Pl DY6 . . . . .60 C5
Sandmere Gr B14. . . . . . . .105 D3
Sandmere Rd B14 . . . . . . .105 D3
Sandmere Rise WV10 . . . .11 E1
Sandon Cl B98 . . . . .154 A3
Sandon Gr B24 . . . . .57 B4
Sandon Ho WV6 . . . . .24 E5
Sandon Rd
Birmingham B17 . . . . .65 B1
Nuneaton CV11 . . . . .73 B5
Stourbridge DY9 . . . . .81 F4
Wolverhampton WV10. . . . .11 B2
Sandown Ave
Cheslyn Hay WS6. . . . . .4 E3
Coventry CV6 . . . . .95 F2
Sandown Cl CV32 . . . . .157 B2
Sandown Ct 10 B29 . . . . .103 C7
Sandown Dr
Lower Marlbrook B61 . . . . .121 B1
Perton WV6 . . . . .23 F4
Sandown Rd B36 . . . . .68 D8
Sandown B77 . . . . .21 E5
Sandown Twr 3 B31. . . . .103 A1
Sandpiper Cl
Cannock WS12 . . . . .2 C7
Kidderminster DY10 . . . . .117 B2
Stourbridge DY9 . . . . .81 F5
Sandpiper Gdns B38 . . . . .123 F7
Sandpiper Rd CV2 . . . . .96 B3
Sandpiper B77 . . . . .36 A5
Sandpiper Way B23 . . . . . . .56 C6
Sandpit Cl WS10 . . . . .42 E2
Sand Pits B1 . . . . .66 B3
Sandpits Cl B76 . . . . .59 C6
Sandpits Ind Est 4 B1. . . .66 B3
Sandpits La CV5 . . . . .94 F2
Sandpits The
Birmingham B30 . . . . .103 E8
Bulkington CV12 . . . . .79 C2
Sandra Cl WS9 . . . . .30 B5
Sandringham Ave WV12 . .27 B6
Sandringham Cl CV4. . . . .131 F5
Sandringham Dr
Aldridge WS9. . . . . .16 B1
Rowley Regis B65 . . . . .63 C4
Sandringham Ho WV3. . . .163 A1
Sandringham Pl DY8 . . . . .60 D1
Sandringham Rd
Birmingham B42. . . . . .55 D6
Halesowen B62. . . . . .83 B7
Stourbridge DY8 . . . . .60 D1

Sandringham Rd continued
Wolverhampton WV4. . . . . .39 A4
Sandringham Way DY5. . . .81 C8
Sandstone Ave B45 . . . . . .122 A8
Sandstone Cl DY3. . . . . . . .50 D4
Sandstone Ct B77. . . . . . . .36 A7
Sandstone B77. . . . . .36 A7
Sandway Gdns B8 . . . . .67 D6
Sandway Gr B13 . . . . .105 C7
Sandwell Ave WS10 . . . . . .41 B5
**Sandwell Bsns Development
Ctr** B66 . . . . .64 C7
Sandwell Bsns Pk B66 . . . .64 C8
**Sandwell Coll Oldbury
Campus** B68 . . . . .64 A3
**Sandwell Coll (Smethwick
Campus)** B66 . . . . .65 A5
**Sandwell Coll (West
Bromwich Campus)** B70 .53 C3
Sandwell Ctr B21. . . . . .65 D8
Sandwell Ctr B70. . . . . .53 D3
Sandwell & Dudley Sta
B70. .53 C2
Sandwell General Hospl
B71 .53 F3
Sandwell Pl WV12 . . . . .27 D7
Sandwell Rd B21 . . . . .54 D8
Sandwell Rd N B71 . . . . . . .53 D4
Sandwell Rd
West Bromwich B70 . . . . . .53 C4
Wolverhampton WV10. . . . .11 B1
Sandwell Road Pas B70. . .53 C4
Sandwell St WS1 . . . . .42 F8
Sandwell Valley Country Pk*
B70,B71. . . . . .53 F5
Sandwell Valley Ctry Pk
B71. .54 A5
Sandwell Valley Nature Ctr*
B43 .54 C6
Sandwell Wlk 8 WS1. . . . .42 F8
Sandwick Cl CV3 . . . . .134 F8
Sandwood Dr B44 . . . . .55 F8
Sandyacre Way DY8. . . . . .81 B5
Sandy Cres
Hinckley LE10 . . . . .71 C1
Wednesfield WV11 . . . . . . .27 A8
Wolverhampton WV11. . . . .13 A1
Sandy Croft
Birmingham B13 . . . . .105 C2
Sutton Coldfield B72 . . . . .46 C3
Sandyfields Rd DY3 . . . . . .50 B6
Sandygate Cl B97. . . . . . . .152 F2
Sandy Gr WS8 . . . . .6 F1
Sandy Hill Rd B90 . . . . . . .106 A4
Sandy Hill Rise B90. . . . . .106 A4
Sandy Hollow WV6. . . . . . .24 C2
Sandy La
Birmingham,Aston B6 . . . . .67 B7
Birmingham,Great Barr B42 .55 D8
Blackdown CV32 . . . . .156 F6
Blakedown DY10 . . . . .118 F2
Cannock WS11. . . . . .1 B1
Codsall WS8 . . . . .10 A4
Coventry CV1. . . . . .113 C5
Madeley Heath B61,B62 . .120 E5
Sandy Lane Bsns Pk CV1 .113 C5
Sandy La
Royal Leamington Spa
CV32 . . . . .156 D4
Wednesbury WS10 . . . . . . .42 F3
Wolverhampton,Bushbury
WV10 . . . . .11 E1
Wolverhampton WV6. . . . . .24 E6
Sandymount Rd WS1. . . . . .42 F8
Sandy Mount WV5 . . . . . . .49 B7
Sandy Rd DY8 . . . . .80 D1
Sandys Gr DY4 . . . . .51 E5
Sandythorpe CV3 . . . . . . .134 E6
Sandy Way
Birmingham B15 . . . . .66 B1
Tamworth B77 . . . . .22 B3
Sandy Wlk LE10 . . . . .71 B2
Sangwin Rd WV14 . . . . .51 C7
Sankey Rd WS11 . . . . .1 F3
Sankey's Cnr WS7 . . . . .6 F7
Sanders Cres DY4. . . . . . . .52 B5
Sansome Rd B90 . . . . .105 F2
Sansome Rise B90 . . . . . . .105 F2
Sanstone Cl WS3 . . . . .14 C3
Sanstone Rd WS3 . . . . .14 C3
Santolina Dr WS5 . . . . .43 A3
Santos Cl CV3 . . . . .134 F8
Sant Rd B31 . . . . .123 B7
Santridge Ct B61 . . . . .137 A4
Santridge La B61. . . . . . . .137 A4
Sapcote Gr CV2 . . . . .96 B4
Sapcote Ind Est B64 . . . . . .62 F3
Sapcote Rd LE10. . . . . .76 B7
Sappings The B76 . . . . .58 A8
Sapphire Cl
3 Solihull B92 . . . . .88 F1
Birmingham B3 . . . . .164 A4
Sapphire Ct
Cannock WS11. . . . . .2 C3
Royal Leamington Spa
CV31. . . . . .161 F5
Sapphire Gate CV2 . . . . . .114 C2
Sapphire Hts B1 . . . . .66 B4
Sapphire Twr 2 B6. . . . . . .66 B4
Saracen Dr
Balsall Common CV7 . . . . .129 C6
Sutton Coldfield B75 . . . . .47 A6
Sara Cl B74 . . . . .32 A3
Sarah Cl WV14. . . . . .40 E1

Sarah Ct B73 . . . . .45 D1
Sarah Gdns WS5 . . . . .42 F4
Sarah Siddons Ho 2 WS13 .9 B7
Sarah St B9 . . . . .67 B2
Saredon Cl WS3 . . . . .15 A1
Saredon Rd WS6,WS11,
WV10. . . . . .4 B3
Saredon Mill Mus* B13 .105 D8
Sarehole Rd B28 . . . . .87 E1
Sargeaunt St CV31 . . . . . .161 F7
Sargent Cl B43 . . . . .44 D4
Sargent Turner Trad Est
DY9 .81 E6
Sark Dr B36 . . . . .70 B6
Satchwell Ct 15 CV32 . . . .161 F8
Satchwell Wlk 16 CV32. . .161 F8
Satellite Ind Pk WV11 . . . .26 D4
Saturday Bridge 7 B1. . . .66 C1
Saturn Rd WS11 . . . . .2 A5
Saumur Way CV34 . . . . . .161 C6
Saunders Ave CV12 . . . . . .78 B2
Saunders Cl DY10 . . . . . . .117 B8
Saunton Cl CV5 . . . . .112 B8
Saunton Way B29 . . . . .85 C2
Saveker Dr B76 . . . . .46 E4
Savernake Cl B45 . . . . .102 A2
Saville Cl
Birmingham B45 . . . . .122 B7
Hinckley LE10 . . . . .71 E2
Saville Gr CV8 . . . . .148 C5
Savoy Cl B32 . . . . .85 A5
Saw Mill Cl WS4 . . . . .28 E3
Saxelby Cl B14 . . . . .104 E2
Saxelby Ho B14 . . . . .104 E2
Saxifrage Pl DY10 . . . . . . .116 F4
Saxon Bsns Pk B60 . . . . . .150 E2
Saxon Cl
Binley Woods CV3 . . . . . . .135 D7
Great Wyrley WS6 . . . . .5 A2
Polesworth B78. . . . . .22 F1
Studley B80 . . . . .159 E5
Tamworth B77 . . . . .35 F6
Saxoncourt WS15 . . . . .6 A6
Saxon Ct WS13 . . . . .8 E7
Saxondale Ave B26 . . . . . . .88 F6
Saxondrive B79. . . . . .21 C5
Saxon Dr B65 . . . . .63 C4
Saxonfields WV6 . . . . .24 C5
Saxon Hill Sch WS14 . . . . . .9 C6
Saxon Mill La B79 . . . . .21 C4
Saxon Rd CV2 . . . . .114 B4
Saxons Way B14 . . . . .105 A2
Saxon Way B37 . . . . .69 F3
Saxon Wlk WS13 . . . . .8 E7
Saxon Wood Cl 2 B31. . .103 A4
Saxon Wood Rd B90 . . . . .126 D5
Saxton Dr B74 . . . . .31 F6
Scafell Cl CV5 . . . . .112 A4
Scafell Dr
Bilston WV14 . . . . .40 F7
Birmingham B23 . . . . .56 D5
Scafell Rd DY8. . . . . .81 B6
Scaife Rd B60 . . . . .151 B7
Scammerton B77. . . . . .36 B7
Scampton Cl WV6. . . . . . . .23 E5
Scampton Way B79 . . . . . . .21 C8
Scar Bank CV34 . . . . .155 D1
Scarborough Cl 2 WS2. . .42 B8
Scarborough Rd WS2 . . . . .42 B8
Scarborough Way CV4 . . .131 F7
Scarecrow La B75 . . . . .32 E4
Scarfield Hill B48 . . . . .138 E5
Scarman Rd CV4. . . . . .132 B5
Scarsdale Rd B42. . . . . .55 D8
Schofield Ave B71 . . . . .53 B8
Schofield Bsns Pk B60 . .151 A7
Schofield Rd B37 . . . . .70 A5
Scholars Cl B21 . . . . .66 A6
Scholars Ct DY10 . . . . .116 E4
Scholars Gate
Birmingham B33 . . . . .69 B2
Burntwood WS7. . . . . .7 D7
Scholars Wlk WS14. . . . . . .29 B7
Scholefield Twr B19. . . . . . .66 D5
Scholfield Rd CV7 . . . . .96 C7
Scholocare Rd B34 . . . . . . .69 B6
Scholocare Rise B74. . . . . .30 E1
School Ave WS8 . . . . .15 F8
School Bell Mews B64 . . .149 B6
School Cl
Birmingham,Castle Vale
B35. .58 B3
Birmingham,Kingshurst B37 .70 A6
Burntwood WS7. . . . . .7 D7
Codsall WV8 . . . . .10 A4
Coventry CV3. . . . . .113 F2
Hinckley LE10 . . . . .76 A6
Norton Canes WS11. . . . . . . .6 B6
Oldbury B69. . . . . .63 C7
Wolverhampton WV3. . . . . .38 B7
School Cotts CV35 . . . . . . .145 F3
School Cres WS11 . . . . .6 A6
School Croft CV35 . . . . . . .146 C2
School Ct WS12. . . . . .2 C6
School Dr
Bilston WV14 . . . . .41 A2
Bromsgrove B60 . . . . .137 A3
Stourbridge DY8 . . . . .80 F8
School Dr The DY2. . . . . . .62 D7
School Dr B47. . . . . .125 A3
Schoolfields Rd WS14 . . . .18 A5
Schoolgate Cl
Birmingham B8. . . . . .68 A6
Walsall WS4 . . . . .15 D1
School Gn WV14 . . . . .40 C8
School Hill CV10 . . . . .72 A8
School Ho The WS7 . . . . . . .7 D7

Schoolhouse Cl B38 . . . . .104 B2
School House La CV2 . . . .115 A6
School La
Alvechurch B48 . . . . .139 B5
Bedworth CV7 . . . . .95 F7
Birmingham,Buckland End
B34. .69 B7
Birmingham,Kitt's Green
B33 .68 F1
Brierley Hill DY5 . . . . .61 B4
Burntwood WS7. . . . . .6 D8
Hagley DY9 . . . . .99 D6
Halesowen B63. . . . . .82 F2
Hopwas B78 . . . . .20 B7
Kenilworth CV8 . . . . .147 F5
Lickey End B60 . . . . .137 B6
Little Packington CV7 . . . . .91 D7
Norton Canes WS3 . . . . .5 E2
Radford Semele CV31 . . . .162 E5
Shuttington B79 . . . . .22 F7
Solihull B91. . . . . .107 D4
Tamworth B77 . . . . .35 D5
Walsall WS3 . . . . .14 F4
Weeford B78 . . . . .19 D2
Wolverhampton WV10. . . . .11 E2
Wroxall CV35 . . . . .145 E4
School Rd
Birmingham B45 . . . . .121 E6
Birmingham,Hall Green
B28. . . . . .106 A8
Birmingham,Moseley B13 . .86 F1
Birmingham,Yardley Wood
B14. . . . . .105 C4
Brierley Hill DY5 . . . . .62 A2
Bulkington CV12 . . . . .79 C2
Himley DY3. . . . . .49 B3
Hockley Heath B94 . . . . . .143 B7
Norton Canes WS11 . . . . . . .6 A6
Solihull B90 . . . . .106 B2
Trysull WV5 . . . . .37 C1
Wednesbury WS10 . . . . . . .42 D2
Wolverhampton,Nordley Hill
WV11 . . . . .26 C6
Wolverhampton,Tettenhall Wood
WV6 .24 B3
Wombourne WV5 . . . . .49 B7
School St W 2 WV14 . . . . .51 C8
School St
Brierley Hill DY5 . . . . .61 D7
Cradley Heath B64 . . . . . . .62 D1
Darlaston WS10 . . . . .41 E5
Dudley,Eve Hill DY1 . . . . . .51 B1
Sedgley DY3. . . . . .50 E8
Stourbridge DY8 . . . . .80 F6
Tamworth B77 . . . . .21 E4
Tipton WV14 . . . . .51 C8
Walsall WS4 . . . . .15 D1
Willenhall WV13 . . . . .26 F1
Wolverhampton WV3. . . . .163 B2
School Terr 1 B29 . . . . . . .85 F2
School Wlk
Bilston WV14 . . . . .40 C8
Burntwood WS7. . . . . .6 D8
Nuneaton CV11 . . . . .73 E2
Tamworth B79 . . . . .21 B6
Scimitar Cl B79 . . . . .21 B6
Scorers Cl B90 . . . . .106 B6
Scotchill The CV6. . . . . . . .95 A1
Scotchings The B36. . . . . .68 E8
Scotch Orchard Prim Sch
WS13. . . . . .3 D1
Scotch Orch WS13 . . . . .3 D1
Scotia Rd WS11. . . . . .1 D3
Scotland La B32 . . . . .102 C7
Scotland St B1 . . . . .66 C3
Scots Cnr B14 . . . . .104 E8
Scots La CV6 . . . . .112 F6
Scott Arms Sh Ctr B43 . . .43 F1
Scott Ave
Nuneaton CV10 . . . . .73 D8
Wednesbury WS10 . . . . . . .42 B2
Wolverhampton WV4. . . . . .38 E4
Scott Cl
Lichfield WS14. . . . . .9 B6
West Bromwich B71 . . . . . .53 D5
Scott Gr B92 . . . . .88 E3
Scott Ho B43. . . . . .54 F7
Scott Rd
Birmingham B43 . . . . .43 F2
Kenilworth CV8 . . . . .147 E2
Redditch B97 . . . . .158 C8
Royal Leamington Spa
CV31. . . . . .162 B6
Solihull B92 . . . . .88 E2
Tamworth B77 . . . . .21 E4
Walsall WS5 . . . . .43 D6
Scott's Green Cl DY1. . . . .62 A8
Scotts Green Island DY1 .61 F7
Scott's Rd DY8 . . . . .80 F6
Scott St WS12. . . . . .2 A2
Scotwell Cl B65 . . . . .63 B3
Scout Cl B33 . . . . .69 C2
Scribban Cl B66 . . . . .65 B4
Scriber Cl B28 . . . . .105 E4
Scribers Mdw B28. . . . . . .105 E4
Scrimshaw Ho 1 WS2. . . . .42 C7
Sculthorpe Rd DY10. . . . . .99 B2
Seacole Ho B97 . . . . .153 B2
Seacroft Ave B25 . . . . .68 E1
Seafield Cl DY6 . . . . .60 E4
Seafield La
Beoley B48,B98. . . . . .141 A2
Portway B48,B98. . . . . . . .140 E4
Seafield B77. . . . . .21 F5
Seaford Cl CV6 . . . . .96 B4
Seaforth Dr LE10 . . . . .71 A1
Seaforth Gr WV11. . . . . . . .13 B1
Seagar St B71 . . . . .53 E4

Seager's La DY5 . . . . .61 D2
Seagrave Rd CV1 . . . . 165 D1
Seagull Bay Dr WV14 . . . .40 D1
Sealand Dr CV12. . . . . .78 A3
Seal Cl B76 . . . . .46 E3
Seals Gn B38 . . . . .123 D7
Seamless Dr WV11 . . . . . .26 D4
Sear Hills Cl CV7 . . . . . .130 B6
Seaton Cl
  Hinckley LE10 . . . . .76 B7
  Nuneaton CV11 . . . . .73 F5
  Wednesfield WV11 . . . . . .26 F5
Seaton Gr B13. . . . . .86 D1
Seaton Pl D9 . . . . .60 C2
Seaton Rd B66 . . . . .65 B5
Seaton B77. . . . . .35 F8
Sebastian Cl DY3 . . . . . .42 E8
Seckham Rd **3** WS13 . . . . .9 A8
Second Ave
  Birmingham B29 . . . . .86 B3
  Birmingham,Bordesley Green
    B9. . . . . .67 D3
  Birmingham,Witton B6 . . .55 F3
  Brownhills WS8 . . . . .4 E1
  Coventry CV3. . . . . .114 C1
  Kingswinford,Barrow Hill
    DY6. . . . . .61 D7
  Kingswinford,Wall Heath
    DY6. . . . . .60 F8
  Wolverhampton WV10. . . .25 E7
Second Exhibition Ave
  B40. . . . . .90 D4
Securehold Bsns Ctr
  B98. . . . . .154 B2
Sedge Ave B38 . . . . .103 F3
Sedgeberrow Covert **4**
  B38. . . . . .123 D8
Sedgeberrow Rd B63 . . . .83 A2
Sedgebourne Way B31. . .102 C1
Sedge Gr B61 . . . . .137 A6
Sedgefield Cl DY1 . . . . . . .50 E3
Sedgefield Gr WV6. . . . . .23 F4
Sedgefield Wlk B61. . . . .121 B1
Sedgeford Cl DY5. . . . . . .81 D8
Sedgehill Ave B17 . . . . . .85 B4
Sedgemere Gr
  Balsall Common CV7 . . . .130 C5
  Walsall WS4 . . . . .29 C8
Sedgemere Rd B26 . . . . . .68 F1
Sedgemoor Ave WV7 . . . . .7 B5
Sedgemoor Rd CV3 . . . .134 B5
Sedgefield Way WS11 . . . .6 A8
Sedgley Cl B98 . . . . .153 F4
Sedgley Gr B20. . . . . .54 E4
Sedgley Hall Ave DY3 . . . .50 C8
Sedgley Rd
  Dudley DY1 . . . . .51 B6
  Gospel End Village WV4 . .38 F2
Sedgley Rd W DY4 . . . . . .51 D5
Sedgley Road E DY4 . . . . .52 A3
Sedgley St WV2. . . . . .39 C7
Seed Field Croft CV3. . . .133 E7
Seedhouse Ct B64 . . . . . .83 B8
Seeds La WS8 . . . . .15 F8
Seekings Dr CV8. . . . . . .148 B4
Seekings The CV31. . . . . .162 B3
Seeleys Rd B11. . . . . .87 E5
Seeswood Cl CV10. . . . . .72 C2
Sefton Dr B65 . . . . .62 F6
Sefton Gr DY4 . . . . .41 C2
Sefton Rd
  Birmingham B16 . . . . .65 F2
  Coventry CV4. . . . . .132 E6
  Tamworth B77. . . . . .35 E5
Segbourne Rd B45. . . . . .121 F8
Segundo Cl WS5 . . . . .42 F4
Segundo Rd WS5 . . . . . . .42 F4
Seisdon Rd WV5 . . . . .37 A1
Selba Dr DY11 . . . . .116 A6
Selborne Cl WS1. . . . . . . .29 A1
Selborne Gr B13. . . . . . .105 C5
Selborne Rd
  Birmingham B20 . . . . .55 A2
  Dudley DY2 . . . . .62 D7
Selborne St WS1. . . . . . . .29 A1
Selbourne Cres WV1 . . . .26 B1
Selby Cl B26 . . . . .68 F1
Selby Gr B13 . . . . .105 C6
Selby Ho B69. . . . . .63 D6
Selby Way
  Nuneaton CV10 . . . . .72 B5
  Walsall WS3 . . . . .13 E2
Selcombe Way B38. . . . .123 F7
Selco Way B76 . . . . .58 A5
Selcroft Ave CV3 . . . . . . .84 F5
Selecta Ave B44 . . . . .44 D2
Selina Dix Ho CV1 . . . . .165 C4
Selker Dr B77 . . . . .36 A7
Selkirk Cl B71. . . . . .53 C6
Selly Ave B29. . . . . .86 A2
Selly Gr B29. . . . . .86 B2
Selly Hall Croft B30. . . . .104 A6
Selly Hill Rd B29 . . . . . . .85 F2
Selly Manor Mus* B30. . .103 F7
Selly Oak Colls B29 . . . .103 D8
Selly Oak Hospl B29 . . . .85 F1
Selly Oak Ind Est B29 . . . .85 E1
Selly Oak Rd B30 . . . . . .103 E5
Selly Oak Specl Sch B29.103 E8
Selly Oak Sta B29. . . . . . .85 E2
Selly Park Rd B29 . . . . . . .86 A2
Selly Park Tech Coll For Girls
  B29. . . . . .86 B1
Selly Wharf B29 . . . . .85 E2
Selly Wick Dr B29 . . . . . .86 B2
Selly Wick Rd B29 . . . . . .86 B2
Sellywood Rd B29,B30. . .103 E8
Selma Gr B14 . . . . .105 D5

Selmans Hill WS3. . . . . . .14 C2
Selman's Par WS3 . . . . . .14 C2
Selsdon Cl
  Kidderminster DY11 . . . .116 B5
  Wythall B47. . . . . .125 C5
Selsdon Rd WS3 . . . . .13 F3
Selsey Ave B66 . . . . .65 B3
Selsey Cl CV3. . . . . .134 C4
Selsey Rd B17. . . . . .65 B3
Selston Rd B6 . . . . .66 E7
Selvey Ave B43 . . . . .44 C3
Selworthy Rd
  Birmingham B36 . . . . .69 F8
  Coventry CV6. . . . . .95 E3
Selwyn Cl WV2 . . . . .39 C7
Selwyn Ho B37 . . . . .70 D3
Selwyn Rd
  Bilston WV14. . . . . .40 F7
  Birmingham B16 . . . . .65 D2
  Burntwood WS7. . . . . .7 F8
Selwyn Wlk B74 . . . . .31 C4
Semele Cl CV31 . . . . . . .162 E5
Seneschal Rd CV3 . . . . .133 E7
Senior Cl WV11. . . . . .13 A3
Senneleys Park Rd B31. . .84 E1
Sennen Cl
  Nuneaton CV11 . . . . .74 A5
  Willenhall WV13 . . . . .26 F1
Sensall Rd DY9 . . . . .81 F3
Sentry Way B75 . . . . .46 F6
Sephton Dr CV6 . . . . .96 C6
Serin Cl DY10 . . . . .117 A1
Serpentine Rd
  Birmingham,Aston B6 . . . .56 A1
  Birmingham B17 . . . . .85 B5
  Birmingham,Selly Oak B29 .86 A2
Serpentine The DY11. . . .116 C4
Servite Ct B14. . . . . .105 A2
Servite Ho
  2 Coleshill B46 . . . . .70 F7
  Kenilworth CV8 . . . . .147 F3
Seton Ho B74 . . . . .31 E2
Settle Ave B34. . . . . .68 F6
Settle Croft B37 . . . . .69 F1
Setton Dr DY3 . . . . .50 E7
Seven Acres WS9 . . . . . . .30 B5
Seven Acres La B98. . . . .154 C5
Seven Acres Rd
  Birmingham,Quinton B62. . .84 A5
  Birmingham,Turves Green
    B31. . . . . .103 C1
Sevendwellings View WS5.61 C1
Seven Star Rd B91. . . . . .107 B5
Seven Stars Ind Est CV3 .134 A2
Seven Stars Rd B69. . . . . .64 A7
Severn Cl
  Birmingham B36 . . . . .69 F7
  Catshill B61 . . . . .137 A8
  Royal Leamington Spa
    CV32. . . . . .157 C3
  Tipton DY4 . . . . .51 F5
  Wednesfield WV12 . . . . . .27 A7
Severn Ct
  Birmingham B23 . . . . .56 B3
  Sutton Coldfield B73 . . . . .46 B5
Severn Dr
  Brierley Hill DY5. . . . . .61 B7
  Burntwood WS7. . . . . .7 D6
  Perton WV6 . . . . .23 E4
Severne Gr B27. . . . . .88 C1
Severne Jun & Inf Sch
  B27. . . . . .106 C8
Severne Rd B27 . . . . . . .106 C8
Severn Gr
  5 Birmingham B19. . . . . . .66 C7
  3 Birmingham B19. . . . . . .66 C7
  Kidderminster DY11 . . . .116 B3
Severn Ho
  4 Birmingham B68. . . . . . .84 B8
  Dudley DY3 . . . . .50 D3
Severn Rd
  Brownhills WS8 . . . . .6 C2
  Bulkington CV12 . . . . .79 A3
  Coventry CV1. . . . . .113 F1
  Halesowen B63 . . . . .82 B5
  Stourbridge DY8 . . . . .80 F3
  Walsall WS3 . . . . .14 E1
Severn St B1. . . . . .164 B1
Severn Twr B7. . . . . .67 B5
Severn Valley Rly* DY10,
  DY11 . . . . .116 D2
Severn Way B47. . . . . . .124 E2
Sevilla Cl CV3 . . . . .115 A2
Sevington Cl B91 . . . . . .127 C8
Sewall Ct CV6 . . . . .114 A8
Sewall Highway CV2 . . . .114 B6
Seward Cl WS14 . . . . .9 D6
Seymour Cl
  Birmingham B29 . . . . .86 A2
  Cheslyn Hay WS6. . . . . . . .4 D1
  Coventry CV3. . . . . .134 C5
Seymour Dr B98 . . . . . . .154 A5
Seymour Gdns B74 . . . . . .31 E3
Seymour Gr CV34 . . . . . .161 D6
Seymour Ho CV1 . . . . . .133 C8
Seymour Rd
  Kidderminster DY11 . . . .116 B8
  Nuneaton CV11 . . . . .73 D3
  Oldbury B69. . . . . .64 C7
  Stourbridge DY9 . . . . .82 A4
  Wednesbury DY4 . . . . .41 C1
Shackleton Dr
  Hinckley LE10 . . . . .75 E4
  Perton WV6 . . . . .23 E5
Shackleton Rd WS3 . . . . .14 C1
Shadowbrook La B92 . . .108 E2
Shadowbrook Rd CV6 . . .113 A5

Shadwell Dr DY3. . . . . . . .50 D3
Shadwell St B4. . . . . . . .164 C4
Shady La B44. . . . . .44 E2
Shadymoor Dr DY5 . . . . . .81 C8
Shaftesbury Ave
  Keresley CV7 . . . . .95 A7
  Stourbridge DY9 . . . . .81 C2
Shaftesbury Cl B60 . . . . .137 B2
Shaftesbury Dr WS12 . . . .2 C7
Shaftesbury Rd
  Coventry CV5. . . . . .132 F8
  Wednesbury WS10 . . . . . .42 B2
Shaftesbury Sq B1. . . . . . .53 C5
Shaftesbury St B70,B71. .53 C4
Shaft La CV7. . . . . .93 A4
Shaftmoor Ind Est B28. . .87 F2
Shaftmoor La B27,B28. . . .87 F2
Shaftsbury Ave B63. . . . . .82 B7
Shaftsbury Cl WV14. . . . . .40 F7
Shaftsbury Dr WS7. . . . . . .7 F7
Shaftsbury Rd B26. . . . . . .89 C5
Shahjalal Rd B8 . . . . .67 D5
Shakels Cl B97 . . . . .158 E4
Shakespeare Ave
  Bedworth CV12 . . . . .78 D2
  Lichfield WS14 . . . . .9 B6
  Redditch B98 . . . . .154 A2
  Warwick CV34 . . . . .160 C4
Shakespeare Cl
  Hinckley LE10 . . . . .71 C1
  Kidderminster DY10 . . . .117 B6
  Nuneaton CV11 . . . . .74 A1
  Solihull B90 . . . . .106 B1
Shakespeare Ho WS11. . .123 A8
Shakespeare Ho B31 . . .123 A8
Shakespeare Pl WS3 . . . . .28 F7
Shakespeare Rd
  Birmingham B23 . . . . .56 B3
  Burntwood WS7. . . . . .6 F8
  Dudley DY3 . . . . .50 A4
  Smethwick B67 . . . . .64 E4
  Solihull B90 . . . . .106 B1
  Tipton DY4 . . . . .52 A8
Shakespeare St
  Birmingham B11 . . . . .87 C5
  Coventry CV2. . . . . .114 B4
  Wolverhampton WV1 . . . .163 D2
Shakleton Rd CV5 . . . . . .113 A2
Shaldon Wlk **4** B66 . . . . . .65 B5
Shale St WV14. . . . . .40 C5
Shalford Rd B92 . . . . .88 E4
Shallcross La DY3 . . . . . . .50 D3
Shalnecote Gr B14. . . . . .104 C5
Shambles **2** WS10. . . . . . . .41 F2
Shandon Cl B32. . . . . .84 F3
Shanklin Cl CV10 . . . . . . .73 D6
Shanklin Dr CV10. . . . . . .134 B4
Shanklin Rd CV3 . . . . .6 C2
Shannon Dr WS8 . . . . .6 C2
Shannon Rd B38. . . . . . .123 E7
Shannon's Mill B79 . . . . . .21 A5
Shannon B77 . . . . .35 F8
Shannon Wlk WS8 . . . . . . .6 C2
Shanti Niketan WV2 . . . . .39 D7
Shapinsay Dr B45. . . . . . .101 F1
Shard End Cres B34 . . . . .69 C6
Shardlow Rd WV11. . . . . .26 E8
Shardway The B34 . . . . . .69 C5
Sharesacre St WV13 . . . . .27 B3
Sharington Cl **3** DY2 . . . . .62 E8
Sharman Rd WV10 . . . . . .25 E6
Sharmans Cross Jun Sch
  B91. . . . . .106 A4
Sharmans Cross Rd B91. .106 A4
Sharnford Rd LE10. . . . . . .76 F6
Sharon Cl WV4 . . . . .39 E5
Sharon Ct B27. . . . . .88 C5
Sharon Way WS12 . . . . . . .2 D3
Sharp Cl CV6 . . . . .95 C2
Sharpe Cl CV34 . . . . . . .160 E8
Sharpe St B77 . . . . .22 A5
Sharpless Rd LE10 . . . . . .75 F7
Sharpley Ct CV2 . . . . . . .115 A8
Sharps Cl B45 . . . . .122 A7
Sharrat Field B75. . . . . . . .32 D2
Sharratt Rd CV12 . . . . .78 A8
Sharrocks St WV1 . . . . . .163 D2
Shaw Ave DY10 . . . . .117 B6
Shawbank Rd B98 . . . . . .154 B3
Shawberry Ave B35. . . . . .58 A4
Shawberry Rd B37. . . . . . .69 F5
Shawbrook Gr **4** B14. . . .105 A3
Shawbury Cl B98 . . . . . . .154 E3
Shawbury Gr
  Birmingham B12 . . . . .86 F8
  Perton WV6 . . . . .23 E5
Shawhurst Rd WV10 . . . . .25 F5
Shaw Cl WS11. . . . . .6 A5
Shaw Dr B33 . . . . .68 E2
Shawe Ave CV10 . . . . .73 C7
Shawfield B47 . . . . .125 A5
Shaw Hall La WV9 . . . . . .11 C7
Shaw Hellier Ave DY5. . . .61 C6
Shaw Hill Gr B8 . . . . .68 A4
Shaw Hill Prim Sch B8. . . .67 F4
Shaw Hill Rd B8 . . . . .68 A4
Shawhurst Croft B47. . . .125 A7
Shawhurst La B47 . . . . . .125 A6
Shaw La WS13 . . . . .9 A8
Shaw Lane Ind Est B60. . .150 C2
Shaw La
  Stoke Prior B60. . . . . . . .150 C3
  Wolverhampton WV6. . . . .24 B3

Shawley Croft B27 . . . . . .88 E4
Shaw Park Bsns Village
  WV10. . . . . .25 D6
Shaw Rd
  Dudley,Netherton DY2 . . . .62 C7
  Hurst Hill WV14. . . . . .40 B1
  Tipton DY4. . . . . .52 C4
  Wolverhampton WV4 . . . . .39 C6
Shaws Cl B97. . . . . .152 F2
Shawsdale Rd B36 . . . . . .68 F7
Shaw's Pas B5. . . . . .164 D2
Shaw's Pas B5 . . . . .164 D2
Shaw St B70. . . . . .52 E7
Shayler Gr WV2. . . . . .39 D7
Sheaf La B26. . . . . .89 B4
Sheapecoate Ho **1** B71. . .42 F1
Shearers Pl B75 . . . . .32 E3
Shearwater Cl
  Birmingham B45 . . . . . . .121 F6
  Kidderminster DY10 . . . .117 B2
Shearwater Ct WV10 . . . .11 B3
Shearwater Wlk B23. . . . .56 B7
Sheaves Cl WV14 . . . . . . .40 B3
Shedden St **3** DY2 . . . . . .62 D8
Sheddington Rd B23. . . . .56 D7
Sheen Ho CV2 . . . . .114 D8
Sheen Rd B44 . . . . .44 E4
Sheepclose Dr B37 . . . . . .70 A3
Sheepcote Cl CV32. . . . .157 A1
Sheepcote Grange B61 . .136 F5
Sheepcote La DY4 . . . . . . .21 F4
Sheepcote St B16. . . . . . .66 B2
Sheepcroft Cl B97 . . . . . .152 F2
Sheepfold Cl B65 . . . . . . .63 A4
Sheepmoor Cl B17 . . . . . .84 F8
Sheepwash La DY4 . . . . . .52 D5
Sheepy Cl LE10 . . . . .71 F1
Sheerwater Dr DY5. . . . . .81 D7
Sheffield Rd B73 . . . . .57 A7
Sheffield St DY5 . . . . .62 A1
Shefford Rd B6 . . . . .66 F5
Sheila Ave WV11 . . . . .26 E7
Shelah Rd B63. . . . . .83 A6
Shelbourne Cl B69 . . . . . .52 D2
Sheldon Ave WS10 . . . . . .42 A4
Sheldon Cl WV14 . . . . . . .40 D4
Sheldon Ctry Pk* B26 . . . .89 E5
Sheldon Dr B31 . . . . .102 D2
Sheldonfield Rd B26. . . . .89 D5
Sheldon Gr
  Birmingham B26 . . . . .89 B5
  Warwick CV34 . . . . .155 F2
Sheldon Hall Ave B33 . . . .69 E6
Sheldon Heath Com Arts Coll
  B26. . . . . .89 B8
Sheldon Heath Rd B26. . . .89 B8
Sheldon Rd
  Redditch B98 . . . . .159 A8
  West Bromwich B71 . . . . . .53 E8
  Wolverhampton WV10. . . .11 A1
Sheldon Wlk B33 . . . . . . .69 C1
Sheldrake Cl CV3 . . . . . .115 A1
Shelduck Cl DY10 . . . . . .117 B3
Shelfield Cl
  Coventry CV5. . . . . .112 B3
  Hockley Heath B94 . . . . .143 C6
Shelfield Rd B14. . . . . . . .104 C3
Shelfield Sports & Com Coll
  WS4 . . . . .15 C2
Shell Corner Trad Est
  B62. . . . . .83 D8
Shelley Ave
  Kidderminster DY10 . . . .116 E7
  Tipton DY4 . . . . .52 B8
  Warwick CV34 . . . . .160 C4
Shelley Cl
  Bedworth CV12 . . . . .78 D1
  Catshill B61 . . . . .137 A8
  Dudley DY3 . . . . .50 A5
  Redditch B97 . . . . .158 C8
  Stourbridge DY8 . . . . .81 A8
Shelley Dr
  Birmingham B23 . . . . .56 B5
  Sutton Coldfield B74 . . . . .31 F6
Shelley Gdns LE10 . . . . . .71 E3
Shelley Ho
  1 Oldbury B68. . . . . .64 C4
  Halesowen B63 . . . . .82 B5
Shelley Rd
  2 Burntwood WS7 . . . . . . .7 A8
  Cannock WS11 . . . . .1 E5
  Coventry CV2. . . . . .114 C3
  Tamworth B79 . . . . .21 A7
  Willenhall WV12 . . . . .27 E7
  Wolverhampton WV10. . . .11 D2
Shellon Cl CV3 . . . . .134 F8
Shelly Cl B37 . . . . .70 B2
Shelly Cres B90. . . . . . . .127 B6
Shelly Croft B33 . . . . .69 A3
Shelly La B90 . . . . .127 B6
Shelly Twr B31. . . . . .103 C3
Shelsley Ave B69 . . . . . . .63 D5
Shelsley Dr B13 . . . . .87 C2
Shelsley Way B91. . . . . . .107 B1
Shelton Cl WS10 . . . . .42 E5
Shelton La B63. . . . . .82 E5
Shelton Sq CV1. . . . . . . .165 B2
Shelton St B77 . . . . .35 F7
Sheltwood Cl B97. . . . . . .153 A2
Sheltwood La B60,B97. . .152 A3
Shelwick Gr B93 . . . . . . .127 F6
Shenley Ave DY1 . . . . .51 C6
Shenley Court Sch B29 . .102 F7
Shenley Fields Dr B31 . . .102 E8
Shenley Fields Rd B29 . . .103 B8
Shenley Gdns B29 . . . . . .102 F6
Shenley Green B29 . . . . .102 E6
Shenley Hill B31. . . . . . . .102 F6
Shenley La B29 . . . . .102 F6

Shenstone Ave
  Halesowen B62 . . . . .83 E5
  Stourbridge DY8 . . . . .80 D3
Shenstone Cl
  Bromsgrove B60 . . . . . . .137 B3
  Sutton Coldfield B74 . . . . .31 E6
Shenstone Ct
  Bromsgrove B60 . . . . . . .137 B3
  Solihull B90 . . . . .105 D2
  Wolverhampton WV3. . . . .39 A6
Shenstone Dr
  Aldridge WS9. . . . . .30 A8
  Balsall Common CV7 . . . .130 A6
Shenstone Flats B62 . . . . .83 F5
Shenstone Ho WS13 . . . . . .3 E1
Shenstone Lodge Sch
  WS14. . . . . .18 A3
Shenstone Rd
  Birmingham,Edgbaston
    B16. . . . . .65 C3
  Birmingham,Great Barr B43 .54 E8
  Birmingham,Highter's Heath
    B14. . . . . .105 A1
Shenstone Sta WS14. . . . .17 F6
Shenstone Trad Est B63 . .83 C4
Shenstone Valley Rd B62 . .83 F4
Shenton Wlk B37. . . . . . . .69 F5
Shepeard Rd B26. . . . . . . .89 D5
Shepheards La CV7 . . . . . .92 A3
Shepherd Cl
  Coventry CV4. . . . . .111 F3
  Lichfield WS13. . . . . .3 E3
Shepherd Dr WV12. . . . . .27 C5
Shepherds Brook Rd DY9 .81 D5
Shepherds Fold B65 . . . . .63 B2
Shepherds Gdns **8** B15. . .66 B1
Shepherds Green Rd B24 . .56 F1
Shepherds Pool Rd B75. . .32 E2
Shepherds Standing B34. . .69 B6
Shepherds Way B23 . . . . .56 C8
Shepherds Wlk
  Bromsgrove B60 . . . . . . .150 E7
  Wolverhampton WV8. . . . .10 F2
Shepley Mdw B45 . . . . . .138 B8
Shepley Rd
  Barnt Green B45 . . . . . . .138 A7
  Birmingham B45 . . . . . . .122 B6
Shepperton Bsns Pk CV11 .73 C1
Shepperton Ct CV11 . . . . .73 C1
Shepperton St CV11. . . . . .73 C2
Sheppey Dr B36 . . . . .70 B5
Shepwell Gdns WV10 . . . .12 C7
Shepwell Gn WV13. . . . . .27 C1
Sherard Croft B36 . . . . . . .70 B6
Sheraton Cl
  Aldridge WS9. . . . . .30 B6
  Cannock WS12. . . . . .2 A7
Sheraton Dr DY10. . . . . . .117 B6
Sheraton Grange DY8 . . . .80 F2
Sheraton Rd B60 . . . . . . .137 C1
Sherborne Cl WS3. . . . . . .28 C7
Sherborne Ct WV10 . . . . .11 E1
Sherborne Gdns WV8 . . . .10 A3
Sherborne Gr B1 . . . . .66 A3
Sherborne Rd
  Hinckley LE10 . . . . .76 B7
  Wolverhampton WV10. . . .11 D1
Sherborne St B16. . . . . . . .66 B2
Sherbourne Arc CV1 . . . .165 B2
Sherbourne Ave
  Cannock WS12. . . . . .2 E4
  Nuneaton CV10 . . . . .72 B4
Sherbourne Cl B97 . . . . .154 D2
Sherbourne Cres CV5 . . .112 E4
Sherbourne Ct CV1 . . . . .165 B1
Sherbourne Dr B27 . . . . . .88 C4
Sherbourne Fields Sch
  CV6 . . . . .112 D5
Sherbourne Rd
  Birmingham,Acock's Green
    B27. . . . . .88 C3
  Birmingham,Balsall Heath
    B12. . . . . .86 F7
  Cradley Heath B64 . . . . . . .83 B8
  Stourbridge DY8 . . . . .81 B4
Sherbourne St CV1 . . . . .113 A2
Sherbrook Rd WS11. . . . . . .1 C1
Sherdmore Croft B90 . . . .126 F6
Sheridan Cl **3** WS2. . . . . .42 B7
Sheridan Gdns DY3 . . . . . .49 F5
Sheridan St
  Walsall WS2 . . . . .42 B7
  West Bromwich B71 . . . . . .53 D4
Sheridan Wlk B35 . . . . . . .58 A3
Sheriff Ave CV4 . . . . .132 B7
Sheriff Dr DY5. . . . . .61 F2
Sheriffs Cl WS14 . . . . .9 E6
Sheriffs Orch CV1 . . . . . .165 B2
Sherifoot La B75. . . . . . . .32 B4
Sheringham B15. . . . . .85 E8
Sheringham Cl CV11. . . . . .73 F2
Sheringham Rd B30 . . . . .104 B3
Sherington Ave CV5. . . . .112 C4
Sherington Dr WV4 . . . . . .39 D5
Sherlock Cl WV12. . . . . . . .27 D5
Sherlock Rd CV5. . . . . . . .112 D3
Sherlock St B5. . . . . .86 E8
Sherrans Dell WV4. . . . . . .39 D4
Sherratt Cl B76. . . . . .57 F8
Sherringham Dr WV11 . . . .13 C1
Sherron Gdns B12 . . . . . . .86 F5
Sherston Covert **11** B30. .104 C2
Shervale Cl WV4 . . . . .39 A6
Sherwin Ave DY4 . . . . .40 A2

Sherwood Ave DY4. . . . . . . .51 F4
Sherwood Cl
  Birmingham B28 . . . . .105 F5
  Solihull B92 . . . . .106 F7
  Wood End CV9. . . . . .36 C1
Sherwood Dr
  Brierley Hill DY5 . . . . .61 F2
  Cannock WS11. . . . . .2 A3
Sherwood Ho **1** B64 . . . . . .82 F8
Sherwood Jones Cl CV6. .13 B6
Sherwood Mews B28 . . . .105 E6
Sherwood Rd
  Birmingham B28 . . . . .105 E7
  Bromsgrove B60 . . . . .151 A6
  Smethwick B67 . . . . .65 A1
  Stourbridge DY8 . . . . .80 E7
  Sherwood St WV1. . . . . . .163 B4
Sherwood Wlk
  Birmingham B45 . . . . .102 B2
  Royal Leamington Spa
    CV32. . . . . .157 C4
  Walsall WS9 . . . . .29 F7
Shetland Ave B37. . . . . . . .35 F7
Shetland Cl
  Birmingham B16 . . . . .65 F2
  Coventry CV5. . . . . .112 A4
  Wolverhampton WV6. . . . . .25 B5
Shetland Dr
  Nuneaton CV10 . . . . .73 A2
  Smethwick B66 . . . . .64 D8
Shetland Wlk B36 . . . . . . .70 B6
Shevlock Way CV6 . . . . . .114 A6
Shidas La B69 . . . . .63 E7
Shifnal Wlk B31 . . . . .122 F8
Shifnall Way B75 . . . . .46 F7
Shillcock Gr B19. . . . . .66 E5
Shillingstone Cl CV2 . . . .115 A4
Shillingstone Dr CV10. . . .73 A1
Shilton & Ansty CE Fst Sch
  CV7 .97 E5
Shilton Cl B90. . . . . .126 F6
Shilton Gr B29. . . . . .102 F8
Shilton Ind Est CV7 . . . . . .97 E7
Shilton La
  Barnacle CV2,CV7. . . . . . . .97 B4
  Bulkington CV12 . . . . .79 D1
  Coventry CV2. . . . . .96 F3
  Shilton CV7,CV12. . . . . . . .97 D8
Shinwell Cres B69 . . . . . . .52 D2
Shipbourne Cl B32. . . . . . .84 F5
Shipley Fields B24. . . . . . .57 A3
Shipston Rd
  Birmingham B31 . . . . .103 B1
  Coventry CV2. . . . . .114 C6
Shipton Cl
  Dudley DY1 . . . . .50 F3
  Redditch B97 . . . . .153 A5
Shipton Rd B72. . . . . .46 C3
Shiral Way WS3. . . . . .88 A7
Shirebrook Cl CV2 . . . . . . .96 D2
Shire Brook Ct **2** B19 . . .66 D7
Shire Cl
  Birmingham B16 . . . . .65 F2
  Coventry CV6. . . . . .96 B1
  Oldbury B68. . . . . .64 B2
Shirehall Pl WS11. . . . . .2 B2
Shirehampton Cl B97 . . . .152 F2
Shireland Brook Gdns **1**
  B18. .65 E3
Shireland Cl B20. . . . . .54 F3
Shireland Hall Jun & Inf Sch
  B66. .65 C3
Shireland Language Coll
  B66. .65 B3
Shireland La B97 . . . . .153 A4
Shireland Rd B66. . . . . .65 B3
Shire Lea WS8. . . . . .16 B6
Shirelea Cl WS7 . . . . .7 B8
Shire Oak Sch WS9 . . . . . . .16 A5
Shire Ridge WS9. . . . . .16 A4
Shirland Rd B37. . . . . .70 A1
Shirlett Cl CV2. . . . . .96 B4
Shirledale **2** B90. . . . . . .126 C8
Shirley Dr B72. . . . . .46 C4
Shirley Heath Jun Sch
  B90. . . . . .106 C1
Shirley La CV7. . . . . .111 A5
Shirley Park Rd B90 . . . . .106 B2
Shirley Rd
  Birmingham,Hall Green B27,
  B28 . . . . .106 A4
  Birmingham,King's Norton
    B30. . . . . .104 A5
  Coventry CV2. . . . . .115 A4
  Dudley DY2 . . . . .62 E8
  Oldbury B68. . . . . .64 C6
Shirley Sta B90. . . . . .105 F1
Shirley Wlk B79 . . . . .20 F7
Shirral Gr B37. . . . . .69 F5
Shirrall Dr B78 . . . . .33 E4
Shoal Hill Cl WS11. . . . . . . .1 B2
Sholing Cl WV8. . . . . .10 F1

Shooters Cl B5. . . . . .86 D6
Shooters Hill B72. . . . . .46 D2
Shop La WV6 . . . . .37 B7
Shopping Ctr The CV31. . .162 B5
Shopping Prec The
  CV34. . . . . .156 A1
Shops The DY6 . . . . .60 D4
Shopton Rd B34 . . . . .69 A7
Shoreham CV WV13 . . . . . . .26 D1
Shorncliffe Rd CV6 . . . . . .112 E6
Short Acre St WS2. . . . . . . .28 D3
Shortbutts La WV14. . . . . . .40 E5
Shortcroft B14 . . . . .105 B4
Shortfield Cl CV7. . . . . . . .130 B7
Short Heath B23 . . . . .56 F5
Short Heath Jun Sch
  WV12. . . . . .27 D5
Short Heath Prim Sch
  B23. .56 D6
Short Heath Rd B23 . . . . . .56 E6
Short La WS6. . . . . .4 E3
Shortland Cl B93 . . . . .128 A7
Shortlands Cl B30 . . . . . . .104 A2
Shortlands CV7. . . . . .95 D6
Shortlands La WS3. . . . . . . .14 F3
Shortley Rd CV3 . . . . .133 F8
Short Rd
  Smethwick B67 . . . . .64 D3
  Wolverhampton WV10. . . . .11 E1
Short St
  Bilston WV14. . . . . .40 D6
  Brownhills WS8 . . . . .15 F7
  Cannock WS11. . . . . .1 F3
  Coventry CV1. . . . . .165 C2
  Darlaston WS10. . . . . .41 F7
  Dudley DY1 . . . . .51 A2
  Halesowen B63 . . . . .82 F5
  Nuneaton CV10 . . . . .72 D4
  Rowley Regis B65 . . . . .63 C2
  Solihull B90. . . . . .126 A5
  Stourbridge DY8 . . . . .80 F5
  Tipton DY4 . . . . .51 E8
  Walsall WS2 . . . . .28 D1
  Wednesbury WS10 . . . . . . .41 E3
  Willenhall WV12 . . . . .27 C5
  Wolverhampton WV1. . . . .163 C3
Shortwell Pl DY5 . . . . .61 B1
Shottery Cl
  Coventry CV5. . . . . .112 B3
  Sutton Coldfield B76 . . . . . .46 F1
Shottery Gr B76 . . . . .46 F1
Shottery Rd B90 . . . . .106 B1
Shotteswell Rd B90. . . . . .126 B8
Showell Cir WV10. . . . . .25 E2
Showell Green La B11. . . . .87 C3
Showell La
  Eaves Green CV7. . . . . .93 A1
  Wombourne WV4. . . . . .38 B3
Showell Rd WV10 . . . . .25 D6
Showell Road Ind Est
  WV10. . . . . .25 D6
Showells Gdns B7. . . . . . . .67 C7
Showmans Cvn Site WS3. .14 E2
Shrawley Ave DY11 . . . . . .116 B3
Shrawley Cl
  Birmingham B45 . . . . .121 F7
  Halesowen B63 . . . . .83 A2
Shrawley Rd B31 . . . . .103 C2
Shreres Dyche CV34 . . . . .160 C4
Shrewley Cres B33. . . . . . . .69 E1
Shrewsbury Cl WS3 . . . . . .13 F1
Shrewsbury Rd DY11. . . . .116 A6
Shrewton Ave B14 . . . . . . .104 D2
Shrubberies The CV4. . . . .132 E4
Shrubbery Ave DY4 . . . . . . .51 D5
Shrubbery Cl
  Sutton Coldfield B76 . . . . . .57 D6
  Walsall WS1 . . . . .29 B1
Shrubbery Ct B10. . . . . . . .116 F7
Shrubbery Rd B61. . . . . . . .136 E1
Shrubbery Sch The B76 . . .57 F7
Shrubbery St DY10. . . . . . .116 F7
Shrubbery The
  4 Dudley DY1. . . . . .51 B2
  Birmingham B16 . . . . .65 F3
Shrub La B24. . . . . .57 B4
Shrublands Ave B68 . . . . . .84 B7
Shrubland Street Com Prim
  Sch CV31. . . . . .162 A6
Shrubland St CV31 . . . . . .162 A6
Shuckburgh Gr **3** CV32. .157 A2
Shugborough Cl WS3 . . . . .14 B1
Shugborough Dr DY1 . . . . .50 E2
Shugborough Way WS11. . . .2 C1
Shulman's Wlk CV2 . . . . . .114 D7
Shultern La CV4 . . . . .132 C6
Shuna Croft CV2. . . . . .115 B7
Shustoke La WS5 . . . . .43 B4
Shustoke Rd
  Birmingham B34 . . . . .69 C6
  Solihull B91 . . . . .107 D5
Shutlock La B13. . . . . .86 D1
Shut Mill La B62. . . . . .100 D3
Shuttington Rd B77,B79 . . .22 B6
Shutt La B94. . . . . .126 B1
Shuttle St CV6. . . . . .114 B8
Shylock Gr CV34. . . . . .161 E2
Shyltons Croft B16. . . . . . . .66 A2
Sibdon Gr B31. . . . . .123 A8
Sibree Rd CV3 . . . . .134 B4
Sibton Cl CV2 . . . . .96 C1
Sidaway Cl B65. . . . . .63 C6
Sidaway St B64. . . . . .62 E1
Sidbury Gr B93 . . . . .127 E3
Sidbury Rd CV6 . . . . .113 C6
Sidcup Cl WV14. . . . . .40 B3
Sidcup Rd B44. . . . . .45 A1

Siddeley Ave
  Coventry CV3. . . . . .114 B1
  Kenilworth CV8. . . . . .147 E3
Siddons Factory Est B70. .52 F8
Siddons Rd WV14. . . . . .40 A7
Siddons Way B70 . . . . .53 A7
Sidemoor Fst Sch B61. . . .136 E3
Sidenhill Cl B90 . . . . .126 B8
Sidestrand WV9 . . . . .10 F3
Sidford Gdns B24. . . . . .57 C3
Sidford Gr B23 . . . . .56 E7
Sidings The
  5 West Bromwich B70. . .53 C2
  B23. .56 E3
  Birmingham,Lozells B20 . . .66 C8
  Cannock WS12. . . . . .2 C7
Sidlaw Cl
  Halesowen B63 . . . . .82 D2
  Wolverhampton WV10. . . . .25 C6
Sidmouth Cl
  Coventry CV2. . . . . .114 C7
  Nuneaton CV10 . . . . .73 F5
Sidney Stringer Com Tech
  Coll CV1. . . . . .165 C3
Sidney St WV2 . . . . .163 B1
Sidon Hill Way WS11. . . . . .2 C2
Sidwick Cres WV2 . . . . .40 B6
Sigmund Cl WV1. . . . . .26 B3
Signal Gr WS3. . . . . .14 A1
Signal Hayes Rd B76. . . . . .47 A2
Signal Wlk B77 . . . . .22 A2
Silesbourne Cl B36 . . . . . . .69 C8
Silhill Hall Rd B91 . . . . . . .107 A5
Silica Rd B77 . . . . .22 B2
Silken Ct CV11. . . . . .73 B4
Silksby St CV3 . . . . .133 D8
Sillins Ave B98 . . . . .154 A3
Silva Ave DY6. . . . . .60 F4
Silver Birch Ave CV12. . . . .77 E2
Silver Birch Cl
  Binley Woods CV3 . . . . . . .135 D7
  Birmingham B8 . . . . .67 D6
Silverbirch Cl CV10 . . . . . . .72 A7
Silver Birch Coppice B74. .31 D5
Silverbirch Ct B24. . . . . . . .57 B6
Silver Birch Dr
  Hollywood B47 . . . . .125 B6
  Kidderminster DY10 . . . . .117 C5
Silver Birches Bsns Pk **3**
  B60. . . . . .150 F6
Silver Birch Gr **5** CV31 . .161 F5
Silver Birch Rd
  Birmingham,Erdington
    B24. . . . . .57 B6
  Birmingham,Kingshurst B37 .69 F6
  Huntington WS12. . . . . .1 D8
  Norton Canes WS11. . . . . . .6 B5
Silverbirch Rd B91. . . . . . .107 E3
Silver Birch Rd
  Sutton Coldfield B74 . . . . . .30 F1
  Wolverhampton WV2. . . . . .39 E7
Silver Court Gdns WS8. . . .15 F7
Silvercroft Rd B21. . . . . . . .54 D3
Silver Ct WS8. . . . . .15 F7
Silverdale B61. . . . . .136 F4
Silverdale Cl CV2 . . . . .96 B4
Silverdale Dr
  Burntwood WS7. . . . . .6 D7
  Wolverhampton WV10. . . . .25 E5
Silverdale Gdns DY8 . . . . . .60 C3
Silverdale Rd B24. . . . . .57 D5
Silver End Ind Est & Bsns Pk
  DY5. .61 C1
Silverfield Cl B14. . . . . . . .104 E8
Silver Fir Cl WS12 . . . . .2 A8
Silver Innage B63 . . . . .82 C7
Silverlands Ave B68. . . . . . .64 B3
Silverlands Cl B28 . . . . .87 F1
Silver Link Rd B77. . . . . . . .21 F1
Silvermead Rd B47 . . . . . .124 F5
Silvermead Rd B73. . . . . . . .46 A1
Silvermere Rd B26. . . . . . . .89 D6
Silver's Cl WS3. . . . . .14 F4
Silver St
  Birmingham B14 . . . . .104 E8
  Brierley Hill DY5 . . . . .61 C1
  Brownhills WS8 . . . . .15 F7
  Coventry CV1. . . . . .165 B3
  Hollywood B47 . . . . .124 E5
  Kidderminster DY10 . . . . .116 E6
Silverstone Ave DY11. . . . .116 D8
Silverstone Cl WS2 . . . . . . .27 D3
Silverstone Ct B30. . . . . . .104 B8
Silverstone Dr
  Coventry CV6. . . . . .95 E5
  Sutton Coldfield B74 . . . . . .44 F6
Silver St
  Redditch B97,B98. . . . . . . .153 E4
  Tamworth B79 . . . . .21 A3
Silverthorne Ave DY4 . . . . .51 D5
Silverthorne La B64. . . . . . .82 D8
Silverton Cres B13. . . . . . . .87 D1
Silverton Hts B67. . . . . .64 F6
Silverton Rd
  Coventry CV6. . . . . .113 F7
  Smethwick B67. . . . . .64 E6
Silverton Way WV11. . . . . . .26 F5
Silver Trees Dr CV12. . . . . .79 A4
Silvertrees Rd DY4. . . . . . . .51 E5
Silver Wlk CV10 . . . . .72 F3
Silvester Rd WV14 . . . . .40 F7
Silvester Way DY5 . . . . .81 B8
Silvington Cl B29 . . . . .103 C2
Simcox Gdns B32. . . . . .84 D2
Simcox Rd WS10. . . . . .41 F5

Simcox St WS12 . . . . .2 D4
Simeon Bissell Cl DY4. . . .52 A5
Simeon's Wlk DY5 . . . . .81 F7
Simmonds Cl WS3 . . . . .14 D3
Simmonds Pl WS10 . . . . . . .41 F7
Simmonds Rd WS3 . . . . . . .14 D3
Simmonds Way B8. . . . . . . .16 A6
Simmons Cl B78. . . . . .34 B1
Simmons Dr B32. . . . . .84 D4
Simmons Leasow B32. . . . .84 E2
Simmons Rd WV11. . . . . . . .13 B1
Simms La
  Dudley DY2 . . . . .62 C5
  Hollywood B47. . . . . .125 A5
Simon Cl
  Nuneaton CV11 . . . . .73 D2
  West Bromwich B71 . . . . . .42 E1
Simon Ct CV7. . . . . .96 A8
Simon Rd B47. . . . . .125 A7
Simon Stone St CV6 . . . . .113 F8
Simpkins Cl WS9 . . . . .16 A3
Simpson Gr
  Coventry CV3. . . . . .134 C6
  Wolverhampton WV10. . . . .25 E6
Simpson Rd
  Lichfield WS13. . . . . .3 B2
  Sutton Coldfield B72 . . . . . .46 C1
  Walsall WS2 . . . . .28 B5
  Wolverhampton WV10. . . . .25 E6
Simpson St B69 . . . . .64 A8
Sinclair Ct B13 . . . . .86 E4
Sinclair Dr CV6 . . . . .96 C6
Singer Cl CV6 . . . . .114 B8
Singer Croft B36. . . . . .58 F1
Singh Cl B21 . . . . .54 E1
Sion Cl DY5 . . . . .61 D3
Sir Alfreds Way B76 . . . . . .46 E3
Sir Frank Whittle Prim Sch
  CV2 . . . . .114 F8
St George's Mall **6**
  DY10. . . . . .116 E6
Sir Harrys Rd B5 . . . . .86 C6
Sir Henry Parkes Rd
  CV5 . . . . .132 D7
Sir Hilton's Rd B31 . . . . . .123 C7
Sir John's Rd B29 . . . . .86 C3
Sir Richards Dr B17. . . . . . .84 F7
Sir Robert Peel Hospl
  B78. .20 D2
Sir Thomas White's Rd
  CV5 . . . . .112 F2
Sir Toby Belch Dr CV34. . .161 F3
Sir Walter's Mall **8**
  DY10. . . . . .116 E6
Sir William Lyons Rd
  CV4 . . . . .132 C6
Sir Winston Churchill Pl
  CV3 . . . . .134 E8
Sisefield Rd B38. . . . . .104 A1
Siskin Cl
  Hammerwich WS7 . . . . .7 D5
  Oldbury B68. . . . . .64 C2
Siskin Dr
  Birmingham B12 . . . . .86 E6
  Coventry CV3. . . . . .134 C4
Siskin Parkway E CV3. . . .134 C2
Siskin Parkway W CV3 . . .134 C2
Siskin Rd DY9 . . . . .81 C3
Sisley Way DY10. . . . . .117 B1
Sister Dora Ave WS3. . . . . .28 E1
Sister Dora Bldgs **2** WS1.28 E1
Sister Dora Gdns **1** WS1. .42 E8
Siviter's Cl B65. . . . . .63 B3
Siviter's La B65. . . . . .63 B3
Six Acres B32 . . . . .84 C4
Sixth Form Coll Solihull The
  B91. . . . . .107 D2
Six Towers Rd WS2. . . . . . .28 C4
Six Ways B23 . . . . .56 F4
Six Ways Ho B23. . . . . .56 F4
Skelcher Rd B90 . . . . .106 A3
Skelwith Rise CV11 . . . . . . .74 A6
Skemp Cl WV14. . . . . .40 D6
Sketchley Cl B66. . . . . .65 A6
Sketchley Hall Gdns LE10 .75 C5
Sketchley Hill Prim Sch
  LE10. . . . . .75 E5
Sketchley La Ind Est LE10 .75 C5
Sketchley Manor La LE10. .75 D5
Sketchley Mdws LE10 . . . . .75 C5
Sketchley Meadows Bsns Pk
  LE10. . . . . .75 C5
Sketchley Old Village
  LE10. . . . . .75 C5
Sketchley Rd LE10 . . . . .75 E6
Skey Dr CV10. . . . . .72 B6
Skidmore Ave
  Tamworth B77 . . . . .35 C5
  Wolverhampton WV3. . . . . .38 F8
Skidmore Dr B70. . . . . .53 A3
Skidmore Rd WV14 . . . . . . .40 D2
Skilts Ave B98 . . . . .153 F1
Skinner La B5. . . . . .66 E1
Skinner St WV1. . . . . .163 B3
Skip La WS5. . . . . .43 E6
Skipton Gdns CV2 . . . . . . .114 B6
Skipton Gn WV6 . . . . .25 A5
Skipton Lodge CV2 . . . . . .114 B6
Skipton Pl WS11. . . . . .4 B7
Skipton Rd B16. . . . . .66 A8
Skipworth Rd CV3 . . . . . . .115 A1
Skomer Cl B45 . . . . .101 E1
Sky Blue Way CV1 . . . . . . .113 E3
Skydome The CV1. . . . . . . .165 A2

Skye Cl
  Birmingham B36 . . . . .70 B6
  Nuneaton CV10 . . . . .72 F2
  Tamworth B77 . . . . .35 F7
Skye Wlk **5** B64. . . . . .62 E1
Skylark Cl
  Birmingham B23 . . . . .56 C7
  Dudley DY5 . . . . .50 C1
  Huntington WS12. . . . . .1 C7
Skylark Way DY10. . . . . . . .117 A2
Slack La B20 . . . . .54 E2
Slacky La WS3. . . . . .14 F1
Slade Ave WS7 . . . . .7 A8
Slade Cl
  Nuneaton CV11 . . . . .79 C8
  West Bromwich B71 . . . . . .42 F2
Sladefield Inf Sch B8. . . . .68 A5
Sladefield Rd B8 . . . . .68 A5
Slade Gdns WV8 . . . . .10 A4
Slade Gr B93 . . . . .127 F6
Slade Hill **1** WV6. . . . . . . .24 F3
Slade Jun & Inf Sch B23. . .56 C2
Slade La B28 . . . . .105 E3
Slade Lanker B34. . . . . .69 A5
Slade La
  Sutton Coldfield B75. . . . . .33 A3
  Tamworth B77 . . . . .35 C4
Slade Mdw CV31. . . . . .162 E5
Slade Rd
  Birmingham B23 . . . . .56 D3
  Halesowen B63 . . . . .82 C6
  Sutton Coldfield B75 . . . . . .32 E3
  Wolverhampton WV10. . . . .11 C3
Slaithwaite Rd B71. . . . . . . .53 E4
Slaney Ct WS2. . . . . .42 C7
Slaney Rd WS2 . . . . .42 B6
Slatch House Rd B67 . . . . . .64 E2
Slateley Cres B90. . . . . . . .126 F6
Slater Cl B64. . . . . .62 F1
Slater Rd B93 . . . . .127 F4
Slaters La WS2 . . . . .42 B7
Slaters Pl WS2 . . . . .42 B7
Slater St
  Bilston WV14. . . . . .40 E3
  Darlaston WS10. . . . . .41 D6
  Tipton,Dudley Port DY4. . . .52 A4
  Tipton,Great Bridge DY4 . . .52 C7
  Willenhall WV13 . . . . .27 C3
Sleaford Gr B28 . . . . .106 A7
Sleaford Rd B28 . . . . .106 B7
Sleath's Yd CV12. . . . . .78 B3
Sledmere Cl CV2 . . . . .96 A3
Sledmere Prim Sch DY2. . .62 D6
Sledmore Rd DY2. . . . . .62 E7
Sleets Yd CV12 . . . . .78 A2
Slideslow Ave B60 . . . . . . .137 B2
Slideslow Dr B60. . . . . .137 B3
Slieve The B20. . . . . .55 A3
Slim Ave WV14 . . . . .40 E3
Slimbridge Cl
  2 Solihull B90 . . . . .127 A6
  Redditch B97 . . . . .158 E5
Slim Rd WS2 . . . . .27 E2
Slims Gate B63 . . . . .83 A3
Slingfield Rd B31. . . . . . . .103 C1
Slingsby Cl CV11. . . . . .73 F2
Slingsby B77 . . . . .35 C7
Sling The
  Dudley DY2 . . . . .62 C6
  Kidderminster DY10 . . . . .116 E6
Slitting Mill Cl B21. . . . . . . .65 C8
Sloane Ho **6** B1. . . . . .66 C3
Sloane St B1. . . . . .66 C3
Slough The B97,B80. . . . . .159 B4
Smallbrook La WS5. . . . . . .49 B7
Smallbrook Queensway
  B5. .164 C1
Small Cl B67. . . . . .64 D5
Smalldale Rd B42. . . . . .55 D7
Smalley Cl WS11. . . . . .2 A5
Small Heath Bridge B10,
  B11. .87 B8
Small Heath Bsns Pk B10 .87 F7
Small Heath Highway B10,
  B11. .87 D6
Small Heath Sch
  Birmingham B10 . . . . .87 D7
  Birmingham B10 . . . . .87 D8
Small Heath Sta B10 . . . . . .87 C7
Small Heath Trad Est B10 .87 D6
Small La B94 . . . . .141 E6
Smallman Rd CV21 . . . . . . .72 A7
Smallshire Cl WV11 . . . . . . .26 F5
Smallshire Way DY8 . . . . . .80 E8
Small St
  Walsall WS1 . . . . .42 E8
  West Bromwich B71 . . . . . .53 B5
Smallwood Almshouses
  B98. . . . . .153 E4
Smallwood Arch **6** B98. .153 E4
Smallwood Cl
  Birmingham B24 . . . . .57 D3
  Sutton Coldfield B76 . . . . . .46 E3
Smallwood Rd WV8. . . . . . .10 E2
Smallwood St B98. . . . . . . .153 E3
Smarts Ave WS14 . . . . .33 E2
Smarts Rd CV12. . . . . .77 F1
Smeaton Gdns B18. . . . . . . .65 F4
Smedley Crooke Pl B48. . .123 C2
Smeed Gr B24. . . . . .57 B3
Smercote Cl CV12 . . . . .77 D1
Smestow Ho B68 . . . . .64 B1
Smestow Sch WV3 . . . . .24 B1
Smestow St WV10 . . . . .25 C4

Smethwick Galton Bridge Sta
 B66 . . . . 64 E7
Smethwick Rolfe Street Sta
 B66 . . . . 65 A6
Smillie PI WS11 . . . . 1 F3
Smirrells Rd B28 . . . . 105 E5
Smith Ave WS10 . . . . 41 D4
Smith CI
 Smethwick B67 . . . . 64 D3
 Wolverhampton WV14 . . . . . 40 A1
Smithfield Rd WS3 . . . . 14 D1
Smithfield Rise WS3 . . . . . . 14 D1
Smithfields ◀ DY8 . . . . 81 A5
Smithford Way CV1 . . . . . . 165 B3
Smith Ho WS3 . . . . 14 C3
Smithmoor Cres B71 . . . . . . 53 F8
Smith PI DY4 . . . . 52 B4
Smith Rd
 Walsall WS2 . . . . 42 C6
 Wednesbury WS10 . . . . 41 F1
Smiths CI B32 . . . . 84 B1
Smith's CI WS7 . . . . 6 D6
Smiths La B93 . . . . 127 E7
Smith St
 ❷ Royal Leamington Spa
 CV31 . . . . 161 F7
 Bedworth CV12 . . . . 77 E1
 Bilston WV14 . . . . 40 D5
 Birmingham B19 . . . . 66 C5
 Coventry CV6 . . . . 113 F5
 Dudley DY2 . . . . 62 D7
 Warwick CV34 . . . . 160 F7
 Wood End CV9 . . . . 36 C1
Smiths Way B46 . . . . 59 A3
Smiths Wood Sch B36 . . . . . 70 A6
Smithy Dr WS3 . . . . 15 A4
Smith La
 Aston Flamville LE9 . . . . 76 C8
 Aston Flamville LE9 . . . . 76 D8
 Dudley DY5 . . . . 50 B1
 Lichfield WS13 . . . . 3 A1
 Tamworth B77 . . . . 35 F7
Smithy The B26 . . . . 89 C6
Smorrall La CV12 . . . . 77 C2
Smout Cres WV14 . . . . 39 F2
Smythe Gr CV34 . . . . 155 E1
Snake La B48 . . . . 139 A6
Snakes Lake La B61 . . . . . . 136 D6
Snake Terr B48 . . . . 139 A6
Snapdragon Dr WS5 . . . . . . 43 A3
Snape Rd
 Coventry CV2 . . . . 114 F5
 Wolverhampton WV11 . . . . . 13 B1
Sneyd Com Sch WS3 . . . . . 13 E2
Sneyd Hall CI WS3 . . . . 28 A8
Sneyd Hall Rd WS3 . . . . 14 A1
Sneyd Ho WS3 . . . . 13 F1
Sneyd La
 Walsall WS3 . . . . 13 F1
 Willenhall WV11 . . . . 13 C1
Snipe CI WV10 . . . . 12 B7
Snowberry Dr DY5 . . . . 50 C1
Snowberry Gdns ❻ B27 . . . 88 C5
Snowdon CI CV11 . . . . 72 B3
Snowdon Gr B63 . . . . 82 D1
Snowdon Rd
 Cannock WS11 . . . . 1 E6
 Stourbridge DY8 . . . . 81 B6
Snowdon Rise DY3 . . . . 50 D6
Snowdon Way
 Willenhall WV12 . . . . 13 B1
 Wolverhampton WV10 . . . . . 25 B6
Snowdrop CI
 Bedworth CV12 . . . . 77 E1
 Brownhills WS8 . . . . 15 D6
Snowford CI B90 . . . . 105 F1
Snow Hill Queensway
 B4 . . . . 164 C3
Snow Hill Sta B3 . . . . 164 B3
Snows Drive Hill B90 . . . . . 126 D5
Snowshill CI
 Nuneaton CV11 . . . . 78 F8
 Redditch B98 . . . . 154 B6
Snowshill Gdns DY1 . . . . . . 50 F4
Soar Way LE10 . . . . 75 A8
Soberton CI WV11 . . . . 26 F7
Soden CI CV3 . . . . 134 D6
Soden's Ave CV8 . . . . 135 A1
Soho Ave B18 . . . . 66 A7
Soho, Benson Road Sta
 B18 . . . . 65 F6
Soho CI B66 . . . . 65 C6
Soho Hill B19 . . . . 66 B7
Soho House Mus* B18 . . . . . 66 A7
Soho Pool Way B18 . . . . 66 A6
Soho Rd B21 . . . . 65 E8
Soho St B66 . . . . 65 C6
Soho Way B66 . . . . 65 B6
Solari CI DY4 . . . . 52 C8
Solent CI WV9 . . . . 10 F2
Solent Ct B73 . . . . 46 B5
Solent Dr CV2 . . . . 96 F1
Solihull By-Pass B91 . . . . . 107 E4
Solihull Coll (Chelmsley
 Campus) B37 . . . . 70 C4
Solihull Coll B91 . . . . 107 A3
Solihull Hospl B91 . . . . 107 C4
Solihull Ln B28 . . . . 106 A6
Solihull Parkway B37 . . . . . 90 E8
Solihull Parkway Hospl
 B91 . . . . 107 E5
Solihull Rd
 Birmingham B11 . . . . 87 D3
 Hampton-in-A B92 . . . . 108 E6
 Solihull B90 . . . . 106 D3
Solihull Ret Pk B90 . . . . . . 126 C8

Solihull Sch B91 . . . . 107 D4
Solihull Sta B91 . . . . 107 A4
Solly Gr DY4 . . . . 52 D7
Solva CI WV1 . . . . 26 B1
Solway CI
 Royal Leamington Spa
 CV31 . . . . 162 C6
 Tamworth B79 . . . . 21 A7
 Wednesbury WS10 . . . . 42 C4
Somerby Dr B91 . . . . 127 A8
Somercotes Rd B42 . . . . 55 D8
Somerdale Rd B31 . . . . 103 C4
Somerfield CI WS4 . . . . 15 C1
Somerfield Rd WS3 . . . . 28 C7
Somerfield CI WS6 . . . . 4 E1
Somerford Gdns WV10 . . . . 11 E2
Somerford PI WV13 . . . . 26 F1
Somerford Rd B29 . . . . 102 F8
Somerford Way WV14 . . . . . 51 B8
Somerland Rd B26 . . . . 69 A1
Somerleyton Ave DY10 . . . 117 A5
Somerleyton Ct ❸ DY10 . . 117 A5
Somerly CI CV3 . . . . 134 F8
Somerset CI WS10 . . . . 42 D4
Somerset Dr
 Birmingham B31 . . . . 122 F7
 Nuneaton CV10 . . . . 72 E4
 Stourbridge DY8 . . . . 80 D7
Somerset Ho B33 . . . . 69 A2
Somerset PI WS11 . . . . 1 F3
Somerset Rd
 Birmingham B15 . . . . 85 F5
 Birmingham,Erdington B23 . . 56 F6
 Birmingham,Handsworth
 B20 . . . . 54 F2
 Coventry CV1 . . . . 113 C5
 Walsall WS4 . . . . 29 A4
 West Bromwich B71 . . . . . . 53 D6
 Willenhall WV13 . . . . 27 D2
Somers PI ❹ CV32 . . . . . . 161 E8
Somers Rd
 Halesowen B62 . . . . 83 C5
 Keresley CV7 . . . . 95 A6
 Meriden CV7 . . . . 91 F1
 Walsall WS2 . . . . 42 A7
 Somers Sq ❺ B63 . . . . 83 B3
Somerton Dr
 Birmingham,Erdington
 B23 . . . . 57 A6
 Birmingham,Marston Green
 B37 . . . . 90 B7
Somerville Ct
 ❷ Sutton Coldfield B73 . . . 46 A2
 Tamworth B79 . . . . 20 D6
Somerville Ho B37 . . . . 70 D3
Somerville Prim Sch B10 . . . 87 D8
Somerville Rd
 Birmingham B10 . . . . 87 E8
 Sutton Coldfield B73 . . . . . . 46 A3
Somery Rd
 Birmingham B29 . . . . 85 A2
 Dudley DY1 . . . . 51 C3
Sommerfield Rd B32 . . . . . . 84 D3
Sommerville Dr B73 . . . . . . 46 A4
Sommerville Rd CV2 . . . . . 114 C4
Sonata Rd B60 . . . . 137 C1
Sonning Dr WV9 . . . . 10 F2
Sopwith Croft B35 . . . . 58 A2
Sorbus B37 . . . . 22 B4
Soredale Croft CV3 . . . . . . 115 A1
Sorrel CI
 Coventry CV4 . . . . 131 E8
 Featherstone WV10 . . . . . . 12 B7
 Lichfield WS13 . . . . 8 E6
 Tipton B69 . . . . 52 B2
Sorrel Dr
 Birmingham B27 . . . . 88 B2
 Walsall WS5 . . . . 43 A3
Sorrel Gr B24 . . . . 57 D3
Sorrel Ho B24 . . . . 57 D3
Sorrel PI CV10 . . . . 78 D8
Sorrell Rd CV10 . . . . 78 D8
Sorrell Wlk DY5 . . . . 81 B6
Sorrel B77 . . . . 22 B5
Sorrento Ct B13 . . . . 87 A3
Soudan B97 . . . . 153 D2
Souters Ho B32 . . . . 102 D8
Southacre Ave B5 . . . . 86 F8
Southall Cres WV14 . . . . . . 40 C1
Southall Rd WV11 . . . . 27 A8
Southall's La DY1 . . . . 51 B1
Southam CI
 Birmingham B28 . . . . 105 E8
 Coventry CV4 . . . . 131 E7
Southam Dr B73 . . . . 46 B1
Southampton St WV1 . . . . . 163 C4
Southam Rd
 Birmingham B28 . . . . 105 E8
 Radford Semele CV31 . . . . 162 E6
South Ave
 Coventry CV2 . . . . 114 A2
 Stourbridge DY8 . . . . 80 F4
 Wolverhampton WV11 . . . . . 26 C5
Southbank Ct CV8 . . . . 147 F4
Southbank Ho ❹ CV34 . . . 161 D8
Southbank Rd CV6 . . . . 112 E5
Southbank Rd B64 . . . . 82 E8
Southbank View DY6 . . . . . 60 E4
South Birmingham Coll
 (Digbeth Ctr for Arts
 & Digital Media) B5 . . . . . . 66 F1
South Birmingham Coll (Hall
 Green Campus) B28 . . . . . 105 E8

Southborough Terr ❶
 CV31 . . . . 162 A6
Southbourne Ave
 Birmingham B34 . . . . 68 D6
 Walsall WS2 . . . . 28 A2
Southbourne CI B29 . . . . . . 86 A2
Southbourne PI WS11 . . . . . 1 D2
Southbourne Rd WV10 . . . . 11 C3
South Bromsgrove Com High
 Sch (Tech Coll) B60 . . . . 150 F1
South Car Park Rd B40 . . . . 90 E3
South CI WS11 . . . . 4 C8
Southcote Gr B38 . . . . 103 D1
Southcott Ave DY5 . . . . 81 D8
Southcott Way CV2 . . . . 96 F1
South Cres
 Bromsgrove B60 . . . . 137 A1
 Featherstone WV10 . . . . . . 12 C6
Southcrest Gdns B97 . . . . . 153 D1
Southcrest Rd B98 . . . . 154 A2
Southcroft Rd B23 . . . . 56 E3
South Dene B67 . . . . 64 F5
Southdown Ave B18 . . . . . . 66 A6
Southdown Ct DY6 . . . . 60 D6
South Dr
 Birmingham B5 . . . . 86 C4
 Coleshill B46 . . . . 70 F6
 Sutton Coldfield B75 . . . . . . 46 C6
South East Quadrant ❽
 B98 . . . . 153 E4
Southern CI DY6 . . . . 60 F3
Southern Cross WS14 . . . . . 9 C7
Southerndown Rd DY3 . . . . 50 B7
Southern Dr B30 . . . . 104 D3
Southern Ho B13 . . . . 105 A7
Southern Rd B8 . . . . 68 A6
Southern Way WS10 . . . . . . 41 C3
Southey CI
 Solihull B90 . . . . 127 B8
 Willenhall WV12 . . . . 27 E8
Southfield Ave
 Birmingham,Castle Bromwich
 B36 . . . . 69 B8
 Birmingham,Edgbaston B16 . 65 D3
Southfield CI
 Aldridge WS9 . . . . 30 A4
 Nuneaton CV10 . . . . 73 D5
Southfield Dr
 Birmingham B28 . . . . 106 A5
 Kenilworth CV8 . . . . 148 A6
Southfield Gr WV3 . . . . 38 C7
Southfield Rd
 Birmingham B16 . . . . 65 D3
 Hinckley LE10 . . . . 75 E7
 Wednesfield WV11 . . . . 26 F5
Southfields Prim Sch
 CV1 . . . . 113 E3
Southfields Rd B91 . . . . . . 106 F1
Southfields CV32 . . . . 157 A3
Southfield Way WS6 . . . . 4 F2
Southgate WS11 . . . . 4 F8
Southgate CI DY11 . . . . . . 116 A4
Southgate End WS11 . . . . . . 4 B7
Southgate Rd B44 . . . . 44 E2
Southgate Way ❸ DY1 . . . 51 B2
Southgate WS11 . . . . 163 A3
South Gdns DY9 . . . . 99 A4
South Gn WV4 . . . . 38 D5
South Gr
 Birmingham,Aston B6 . . . . . 66 D8
 Birmingham,Erdington B23 . . 56 F5
 Birmingham,Lozells B19 . . . 66 B8
South Holme B9 . . . . 67 C2
South Oval DY3 . . . . 50 E5
South Park Mews DY5 . . . . . 61 C2
South Par B72 . . . . 46 C4
Southport CI CV3 . . . . 134 B5
South Range ❹ B11 . . . . . . 87 B6
South Rd
 Birmingham,Erdington
 B23 . . . . 56 F4
 Birmingham,Hockley B18 . . . 66 A6
 Birmingham,King's Heath
 B14 . . . . 104 E8
 Birmingham,Northfield
 B31 . . . . 102 F2
 Birmingham,Sparkbrook
 B11 . . . . 87 B7
 Bromsgrove B60 . . . . 151 B7
 Smethwick B67 . . . . 64 F5
 Stourbridge DY8 . . . . 80 F8
 Tipton DY4 . . . . 52 B8
 West Bromwich B71 . . . . . . 53 D4
 Wolverhampton WV4 . . . . . 39 F4
South Ridge CV5 . . . . 112 B4
South Road Ave B18 . . . . . . 66 A6
South Roundhay B33 . . . . . . 69 A3
Southside Bsns Ctr B12 . . . 87 A5
South St ❸ DY10 . . . . 116 F6
South Staffordshire Bsns Pk
 WS11 . . . . 4 C4
South St
 Birmingham B17 . . . . 85 D5
 Brierley Hill DY5 . . . . 61 C2
 Coventry CV1 . . . . 113 E3

South St continued
 Redditch B98 . . . . 153 E3
South Street Gdns WS1 . . . 42 D8
South St
 Walsall WS1 . . . . 42 D8
 Willenhall WV13 . . . . 26 F1
 Wolverhampton WV10 . . . . . 25 C6
South Terr CV31 . . . . 162 B3
South View B43 . . . . 54 E7
South View CI
 Coaluvll WV8 . . . . 10 B2
 Featherstone WV10 . . . . . . 12 B6
South View CV35 . . . . 160 A6
South View Rd
 Royal Leamington Spa
 CV32 . . . . 157 C5
 Sedgley DY3 . . . . 50 C8
Southview Ridge DY5 . . . . . 81 D7
Southville Bglws For Old
 People B14 . . . . 105 B4
Southwark CI WS13 . . . . 3 C3
South Way B40 . . . . 90 F3
Southway CV31 . . . . 162 A5
Southwick PI WV14 . . . . 40 D7
Southwick Rd B62 . . . . 83 D8
Southwold Ave B30 . . . . . . 104 C3
Southwood Ave B34 . . . . . . 69 B7
Southwood CI DY6 . . . . 60 E5
Southwood Covert B14 . . . 104 C2
Sovereign CI CV8 . . . . 147 F1
Sovereign Ct ⑦ B1 . . . . 66 C3
Sovereign Dr DY1 . . . . 50 E2
Sovereign Hts B31 . . . . . . 102 C1
Sovereign Rd
 Birmingham B30 . . . . 104 A4
 Coventry CV5 . . . . 113 A2
Sovereign Row CV5 . . . . . . 113 A2
Sovereign Way B13 . . . . 86 F4
Sovereign Wlk ⑦ WS1 . . . . 28 F2
Sovereign Works DY1 . . . . . 50 E4
Sowerby March B24 . . . . . . 57 D4
Sowers CI WV12 . . . . 27 D5
Sowers CI B75 . . . . 32 D4
Sowers Gdns WV12 . . . . 27 D5
Sowe Valley Prim Sch
 CV3 . . . . 134 D7
Spa CI LE10 . . . . 71 E1
Spadesbourne Rd B60 . . . . 137 C6
Spa Gr B30 . . . . 104 C8
Spa La LE10 . . . . 71 E1
Sparkbrook St CV1 . . . . . . 113 F3
Sparkbrook Workshops
 CV1 . . . . 113 F3
Spark St B11 . . . . 87 A7
Sparrey Dr B30 . . . . 104 A8
Sparrow CI WS10 . . . . 42 B5
Sparrow Cock La B93 . . . . 129 C1
Spartan CI CV34 . . . . 161 E4
Spartan Ind Ctr B70 . . . . . . 52 E6
Spa View CV31 . . . . 162 B4
Speakers CI B69 . . . . 63 B7
Spearhill WS14 . . . . 9 E8
Speed Rd DY4 . . . . 51 E7
Speedway La CV8 . . . . 135 F7
Speedwell CI
 ❻ Bedworth CV12 . . . . 77 D2
 Aldridge WS9 . . . . 30 A5
 Birmingham B25 . . . . 88 A6
 Wednesfield WV11 . . . . 26 E5
Speedwell Dr CV7 . . . . 130 A6
Speedwell Gdns
 Brierley Hill DY5 . . . . 81 B6
 Featherstone WV10 . . . . . . 12 B8
Speedwell Ho B38 . . . . 104 A1
Speedwell Rd
 Birmingham,Balsall Heath
 B5 . . . . 86 D6
 Birmingham,Tyseley B25 . . . 88 A6
Speedwell Trad Est B11 . . . . 88 A6
Speedy CI WS11 . . . . 1 E5
Spencer Ave
 Coventry CV5 . . . . 113 A1
 Tipton WV14 . . . . 51 C8
Spencer CI
 ❺ West Bromwich B71 . . . . 53 F8
 Birmingham B24 . . . . 57 D2
 Dudley DY3 . . . . 50 A4
 Oldbury B69 . . . . 52 E8
Spencer Dr WS7 . . . . 6 E8
Spencer Rd
 Coventry CV5 . . . . 165 A1
 Lichfield WS14 . . . . 9 E7
Spencer's La CV7 . . . . 110 E1
Spencer St
 Birmingham B18 . . . . 66 C4
 Hinckley LE10 . . . . 71 D1
 Kidderminster DY11 . . . . . 116 C4
 Royal Leamington Spa
 CV31 . . . . 161 F7
Spencer Yd CV31 . . . . 161 F7
Spennells Fst Sch B60 . . . . 137 A2
Spennells Valley Nature
 Reserve* DY10 . . . . 117 A3
Spennells Valley Rd
 DY10 . . . . 117 A3
Spenser Ave WV6 . . . . 23 F4
Spenser St CV31 . . . . 21 A6
Spenser Wlk B61 . . . . 137 A8
Spernal Ash B80 . . . . 159 F1
Spernal La B80 . . . . 159 F1
Spernall Gr B29 . . . . 85 A1
Spetchley CI B97 . . . . 158 C6
Spey CI B5 . . . . 86 D6
Sphinx Dr CV3 . . . . 114 B1
Spiceland Rd B31 . . . . 102 F6

Spiers CI B93 . . . . 128 A6
Spies CI B62 . . . . 83 F6
Spies La B62 . . . . 83 F5
Spills Mdw DY3 . . . . 50 E5
Spilsbury CI CV32 . . . . 156 E2
Spilsbury Croft B91 . . . . . . 127 A8
Spindle La B90 . . . . 126 A6
Spindle St CV1 . . . . 113 D6
Spindles The LE10 . . . . 75 F5
Spindlewood CI ❶ WS12 . . . 2 D1
Spinners End Dr B64 . . . . . . 62 D1
Spinners End Ind Est B64 . . 82 D8
Spinney CI
 Binley Woods CV3 . . . . 135 E7
 Birmingham B31 . . . . 103 B3
 Kidderminster DY11 . . . . . 116 A7
 Norton Canes WS11 . . . . 5 F5
 Polesworth B78 . . . . 36 F8
 Stourbridge DY8 . . . . 60 C3
 Walsall WS3 . . . . 15 A2
Spinney Dr B90 . . . . 126 D6
Spinney Farm Rd WS11 . . . . 4 B7
Spinney Hill CV34 . . . . 156 A1
Spinney La CV10 . . . . 72 C4
Spinney Mews B97 . . . . . . 153 C1
Spinney The
 Birmingham B15 . . . . 85 E5
 Birmingham,Brown's Green
 B20 . . . . 54 E4
 Coventry CV4 . . . . 132 D3
 Dudley DY3 . . . . 50 C2
 Royal Leamington Spa
 CV32 . . . . 156 D1
 Solihull B91 . . . . 127 C8
 Sutton Coldfield B74 . . . . . . 31 B6
 Wolverhampton WV3 . . . . . 24 D1
 Wythall B47 . . . . 125 B4
Spinning School La B79 . . . 21 B5
Spiral CI B62 . . . . 83 E8
Spiral Ct
 Birmingham B24 . . . . 56 E2
 Dudley DY3 . . . . 50 D3
 Stourbridge DY8 . . . . 81 A4
 Sutton Coldfield B76 . . . . . . 46 F3
 Wednesfield WV11 . . . . 26 C1
Spiral Gn B24 . . . . 57 C4
Spirehouse La B60 . . . . . . 137 C5
Spires The
 Lichfield WS14 . . . . 9 E6
 Nuneaton CV10 . . . . 72 C4
Spires View B61 . . . . 136 F3
Spitfire Pk B24 . . . . 57 C2
Spitfire Rd B24 . . . . 57 D2
Spitfire Way B35 . . . . 58 A2
Splash La WS12 . . . . 2 C1
Spode PI WS11 . . . . 2 B2
Spondon Gr B34 . . . . 69 C5
Spondon Rd WV11 . . . . 26 E8
Spon End CV1,CV5 . . . . . . 113 A3
Spon Gate Ho CV1 . . . . . . 113 A2
Spon Gate Prim Sch
 CV1 . . . . 113 A3
Spon La S B70 . . . . 53 D1
Spon Lane Trad Est B70 . . . 53 D2
Spon La S B66 . . . . 64 D8
Spon La B70 . . . . 53 D3
Spon St CV1 . . . . 165 A3
Spoon Dr B38 . . . . 103 D2
Spooner Croft B5 . . . . 86 E8
Spooners CI B92 . . . . 107 F8
Spouthouse La B43 . . . . 54 F7
Spout La
 Walsall WS1 . . . . 42 E7
 Walsall WS1 . . . . 42 E8
Spreadbury CI B17 . . . . 84 F8
Sprig Croft B36 . . . . 68 C8
Spring Ave B65 . . . . 63 D2
Springacorn Croft B17 . . . . 85 B6
Springbank B9 . . . . 68 A3
Springbank Rd B15 . . . . 86 D7
Springbrook CI B36 . . . . 58 D1
Springbrook La B47 . . . . . . 142 A7
Spring CI
 ❹ Coventry CV1 . . . . 113 E2
 Solihull B91 . . . . 106 F3
 Walsall WS4 . . . . 15 C2
 West Hagley B90 . . . . 99 F4
Spring Coppice Dr B93 . . . 128 A3
Spring Cres B64 . . . . 82 F7
Springcroft Rd B11 . . . . 87 F2
Spring Ct
 Walsall WS1 . . . . 43 A8
 West Bromwich B70 . . . . . . 53 D2
Springdale Ct CV11 . . . . 73 D2
Springdale Jun & Inf Schs
 WV4 . . . . 38 D5
Springfield Ave
 ❻ Birmingham B12 . . . . . . 87 A6
 Bromsgrove B60 . . . . 151 A8
 Oldbury B68 . . . . 64 C5
 Sedgley DY3 . . . . 39 E1
 Stourbridge DY9 . . . . 81 E4
Springfield CI B23 . . . . 56 E3
Springfield CI B65 . . . . 63 A5
Springfield Cres
 Bedworth CV12 . . . . 78 B2
 Dudley DY2 . . . . 62 F8
 Solihull B92 . . . . 89 C3
 Sutton Coldfield B76 . . . . . . 47 A4
 West Bromwich B70 . . . . . . 53 E1
Springfield Ct
 Birmingham B28 . . . . 105 E4
 Sutton Coldfield B75 . . . . . . 47 C5

Springfield Ct continued
Wolverhampton WV10 . . . . . .11 D4
Springfield Dr
Birmingham B14 . . . . .86 E1
Halesowen B62 . . . . .83 D7
Springfield Gn DY3 . . . . .39 E1
Springfield Gr DY3 . . . . .20 D1
Springfield Ho DY10 . . . . .116 F8
**Springfield House Com Specl
Sch** B93 . . . . .129 A5
Springfield Ind Est B69 . . . .64 B7
Springfield La
Kidderminster DY10 . . . . . .116 F8
Rowley Regis B65,DY2. . . . . .62 F5
Wolverhampton WV10 . . . . . .11 D4
Springfield Mill Ct WS10 . .41 E6
Springfield Pk LE10 . . . . . . .71 A3
Springfield Pl CV1 . . . . . . .165 C4
Springfield Prim Sch
Birmingham B13 . . . . .87 D2
Rowley Regis B65 . . . . .63 A4
Springfield Rd
Bilston WV14 . . . . .40 E7
Birmingham,Castle Bromwich
B36. . . . . .69 D8
Birmingham,King's Heath
B14 . . . . .104 F8
Coventry CV1 . . . . .165 C4
Halesowen B62 . . . . .83 D7
Hinckley LE10 . . . . .75 D7
Nuneaton CV11 . . . . .73 E2
Oldbury B68 . . . . .64 C4
Sutton Coldfield B75,B76. . . .47 A4
Tamworth B77 . . . . .35 D8
Wolverhampton WV10 . . . . . .25 E3
Springfield Rise WS12 . . . .2 C2
Springfields B46 . . . . .70 F5
Springfields Rd DY5 . . . . . .61 B2
Springfield St B18 . . . . .66 A3
Springfields WS4 . . . . .29 C6
Springfield Terr B65 . . . . . .62 F5
Spring Gdns
🖪 Dudley DY2 . . . . .62 D8
Birmingham B21 . . . . .65 F7
Smethwick B66 . . . . .65 B3
Spring Gr B19 . . . . .66 B6
Spring Grove Cres DY11. .116 B3
Spring Groves Gdns B18 . . .65 F6
Spring Grove Rd DY11 . . .116 B3
Spring Head WS10 . . . . .41 F2
Springhill Ave WV4 . . . . . . .38 C4
Spring Hill
Birmingham,Erdington
B24 . . . . .56 F3
Birmingham,Hockley B18. . . .66 A4
Springhill Cl
Walsall WS4 . . . . .15 D1
Willenhall WV12 . . . . .27 D7
Springhill Ct 🖪 WS1. . . . . .42 F8
Springhill Gdns B97 . . . . .152 F2
Springhill Gr WV4 . . . . .38 C4
Springhill CV10 . . . . .72 A8
Spring Hill Ind Est B18. . . .66 A4
Springhill La WV4 . . . . .38 B4
Spring Hill Pas B18. . . . . . . .66 A3
Spring Hill Prim Sch WS7 . .7 B6
Springhill Rd
Brownhills WS8 . . . . .16 A7
Burntwood WS7 . . . . .7 A6
Spring Hill Rd CV10 . . . . . . .72 C6
Springhill Rd
Walsall WS4 . . . . .28 F1
Wednesfield WV11 . . . . .26 E7
Spring La
Birmingham B24 . . . . .57 A3
Hockley Heath B94 . . . . . . .143 B5
Kenilworth CV8 . . . . .148 A5
Lapworth B94 . . . . .143 D3
Radford Semele CV31 . . . . .162 E5
Romsley B62 . . . . .100 D4
Walsall WS4 . . . . .15 C2
Willenhall WV12 . . . . .27 C4
Spring Mdw
🖪 Cradley Heath B64 . . . . . .62 F1
Cheslyn Hay WS6. . . . . .4 D1
Halesowen B63 . . . . .82 F2
Tipton DY4. . . . . .52 C6
Springmeadow Gr B19 . . . .66 D6
Springmeadow Rd B15. . . . .86 D7
Spring Meadow Rd DY2 . . . .62 C2
Spring Meadows Cl WV8 . .10 B4
Spring Parklands DY1. . . . .62 A8
Spring Pool CV34 . . . . .160 E7
Spring Rd
Barnacle CV7 . . . . .97 E4
Birmingham,Balsall Heath
B15 . . . . .86 D7
Birmingham,Tyseley B11. . . .87 F3
Coventry CV6 . . . . .95 F1
Dudley DY2 . . . . .62 D6
Lichfield WS13 . . . . .3 E2
Smethwick B66 . . . . .64 D8
Walsall WS4 . . . . .15 D1
Wolverhampton WV4 . . . . . . .39 A6
Spring Road Ind Est WV4 .40 A4
Spring Road Sta B28. . . . . .88 A2
Springs Ave B61. . . . . .121 A1
Springside B98 . . . . .159 C8
Springslade B32. . . . . .84 F5
Springslade Dr B24. . . . . . .57 D3
Spring St
Birmingham B15 . . . . .86 D8
Cannock WS11. . . . . .4 E8

Spring St continued
Halesowen B63 . . . . .82 D6
Springs The B64 . . . . .63 A1
Spring St
Stourbridge DY9 . . . . .81 E4
Tipton DY4. . . . . .52 C8
Spring Terr WS7 . . . . .6 E5
Springthorpe Gn B24 . . . . .57 C4
Springthorpe Rd
Birmingham,Pype Hayes
B24 . . . . .57 D5
Birmingham,Tyburn B24 . . . .57 D3
Springvale Ave
Bilston WV14 . . . . .40 B4
Walsall WS5 . . . . .43 C7
Springvale Bsns Pk WV14 .40 B4
Spring Vale Cl WV14 . . . . . .40 A1
Spring Vale Ind Est WV4 . . .40 C5
Spring Vale Island WS11 . .4 E8
Spring Vale Prim Sch
WV4 . . . . .39 E4
Springvale Rd B97 . . . . . . .152 F2
Spring Vale Rd B65 . . . . . . .63 A5
Springvale St WV13 . . . . . . .27 B3
Springvale Way WV14 . . . . .40 C4
Spring Vale Way CV31. . . .162 D6
Spring Wlk
Halesowen B63 . . . . .82 D1
Oldbury B69 . . . . .64 A5
Walsall WS2 . . . . .28 B3
Sproat Ave WS10 . . . . .41 C5
Spruce Gr
🖪 Royal Leamington Spa
CV31 . . . . .161 F5
Birmingham B24 . . . . .57 B2
Spruce Rd
🖪 Coventry CV2 . . . . .96 B2
Nuneaton CV10 . . . . .72 E7
Walsall WS3 . . . . .43 B3
Spruces The DY9 . . . . .98 F4
Spruce B77. . . . . .22 B4
Spruce Way WV3 . . . . .24 D1
Spur Tree Ave WV3 . . . . . . .24 A1
Squadron Ct B35 . . . . .58 C4
Square Cl B32. . . . . .84 C3
Square The
🖪 Birmingham,Ladywood
B15. . . . . .66 B1
🖪 Birmingham B17. . . . . .85 C5
Aldridge WS9. . . . . .30 B6
Alvechurch B48 . . . . .139 B6
Birmingham B17 . . . . .85 B7
Brierley Hill DY2 . . . . .61 F6
Coventry CV2 . . . . .115 A7
Fazeley B78 . . . . .35 A8
Kenilworth CV8 . . . . .147 F4
Nuneaton CV11 . . . . .73 E2
Solihull B91 . . . . .107 C3
Tipton DY4. . . . . .52 D7
Willenhall WV12 . . . . .27 D8
Wolverhampton WV4 . . . . . .163 C1
Squires Croft
Coventry CV2 . . . . .96 F1
Sutton Coldfield B76 . . . . . . .47 A2
Squires Ct DY5 . . . . .81 C8
Squires Gate WS7 . . . . .7 C8
Squires Gate Rd 🖪 WV13 .22 B7
Squires Gate Wlk B35. . . . .58 A3
Squires La B18 . . . . .75 F6
Squires Way CV4 . . . . .132 D6
Squire's Wlk WS10 . . . . . . .41 F3
Squirhill Pl 🖪 CV31. . . . . .162 B7
Squirrel Cl
Cannock WS12. . . . . .2 D2
Huntington WS12. . . . . .1 C6
Squirrel Hollow B76 . . . . . .47 A2
Squirrels Hollow B68 . . . . .84 D7
Squirrels The WS14 . . . . .9 C7
Squirrel Wlk
Sutton Coldfield B74 . . . . . . .31 C5
Wolverhampton WV4 . . . . . . .39 A5
Stable Croft B71. . . . . .53 F7
Stable Ct DY3 . . . . .50 E6
Stableford Cl
Birmingham B32 . . . . .84 F3
Redditch B97 . . . . .158 D7
Stables The
Berkswell CV7 . . . . .110 C4
Birmingham B29 . . . . .86 A2
Hinckley LE10 . . . . .75 D5
Royal Leamington Spa
CV32 . . . . .156 C1
Stable Way B60 . . . . .150 E6
Stable Wlk CV11. . . . . .73 F2
Stacey Cl B64 . . . . .62 E1
Stacey Dr B13 . . . . .105 A5
Stacey Grange Gdns
B45. . . . . .122 A6
Stackhouse Cl WS9 . . . . . . .16 A4
Stackhouse Dr WS3. . . . . . .15 A4
Stadium Cl
Coventry CV6. . . . . .95 D2
Kidderminster DY10 . . . . . .116 F4
Willenhall WV13 . . . . .27 B3
Stadium Dr B64 . . . . .62 C1
Stafford Cl
Bulkington CV12 . . . . .79 C2
Walsall WS3 . . . . .14 B2
Stafford Ct
Birmingham B43 . . . . .54 E7
Wolverhampton WV10 . . . . .11 B8
Stafford Dr B71. . . . . .53 B6
Stafford Ho B33 . . . . .69 E2
Stafford La WS12 . . . . .2 B5
Stafford Rd
Birmingham B21 . . . . .65 F8

Stafford Rd continued
Cannock WS11. . . . . .1 D1
Coven Heath WV10 . . . . .11 D4
Darlaston WS10. . . . . .41 C6
Huntington WS11,WS12 . . . .1 D1
Walsall WS3 . . . . .14 B4
Staffordshire Pool Cl 🖪
B6. .55 F1
Staffordshire Univ WS13 . . .9 B7
Stafford St
Bilston WV14 . . . . .40 D5
Birmingham B5 . . . . .164 D3
Cannock WS12. . . . . .2 E1
Dudley DY1 . . . . .51 B1
Walsall WS3 . . . . .28 E3
Wednesbury WS10 . . . . .41 F2
Willenhall WV13 . . . . .27 A2
Wolverhampton WV1 . . . . . .163 C4
Stafford Way B43 . . . . .54 E7
Staff Way B23 . . . . .56 E4
Stagborough Way WS12. . . .2 B4
Stag Cres
Norton Canes WS11 . . . . .6 A6
Walsall WS3 . . . . .28 E6
Stag Dr WS12 . . . . .1 C6
Stag Hill Rd WS3 . . . . .28 E7
Stag Ind Est WV14 . . . . . . .40 F4
Stag Wlk B76 . . . . .57 D7
Staines CT CV11. . . . . .73 F7
Stainforth Cl CV11 . . . . .74 A2
Stainsby Ave B19 . . . . .66 C5
Stainsby Croft B90. . . . . . .127 B5
Staircase La CV5. . . . . .112 C7
Stakenbridge La DY10. . . . .98 D4
Staley Croft WS12. . . . . .1 C4
Stalling's La DY6 . . . . .60 E6
Stambermill Cl DY9 . . . . . . .81 D5
Stambermill Ho DY9 . . . . . . .81 E5
Stambermill Ind Est DY9 .81 D6
Stamford Ave CV3 . . . . . . .133 C6
Stamford Cres WS7 . . . . .7 A8
Stamford Croft B91 . . . . . .107 B2
Stamford Gdns CV32 . . . . .156 E1
Stamford Gr B20. . . . . .55 C1
Stamford Rd
Birmingham B20 . . . . .55 C1
Brierley Hill DY5 . . . . .81 C6
Dudley DY8 . . . . .80 F7
Stamford Way WS9 . . . . . . .16 A4
Stanbrook Rd B90 . . . . . . .127 A5
Stanbury Ave WS10 . . . . . . .41 B6
Stanbury Rd B14. . . . . .105 B4
Stancroft Gr B26 . . . . .89 A8
Standard Ave CV4 . . . . . . .132 B1
Standard Way B24 . . . . .67 F8
Standbridge Way DY4. . . . .52 A5
Standedge B77 . . . . .22 A4
Standhills Rd DY6 . . . . .60 E6
Standish Cl CV2 . . . . .114 E2
Standlake Ave B36. . . . . . . .68 D7
Standlake Mews 🖪
CV31. . . . . .162 C6
Standsbury Terr B23 . . . . . .57 A6
Stand St CV34 . . . . .160 D5
Stanfield Rd
Birmingham B32 . . . . .84 E6
Birmingham,Pheasey B43 . . .44 D3
Stanford Ave B42 . . . . .55 A7
Stanford Cl B97 . . . . .158 B6
Stanford Dr B65. . . . . .63 B4
Stanford Rd B23 . . . . .82 C1
Stanford Way B46 . . . . .163 B1
Stanford Way 🖪 B69. . . . . .63 E4
Stanhoe Cl DY5 . . . . .81 D8
Stanhope Ho B79 . . . . .21 A4
Stanhope Rd B67. . . . . .64 F3
Stanhope St
Birmingham B12 . . . . .86 F7
Dudley DY2 . . . . .62 E4
Wolverhampton WV3 . . . . . .163 A2
Stanhope Way B43. . . . . . . .44 E4
Stanhurst Way B71 . . . . . . .43 A2
Stanier Ave CV1 . . . . .113 B4
Stanier Cl WS4 . . . . .29 B7
Stanier Gr B20 . . . . .55 B2
Staniforth St B4 . . . . .164 C4
Stanklyn La DY10 . . . . .117 C1
Stanley Ave
Birmingham B32 . . . . .84 E7
Solihull B90 . . . . .106 B4
Sutton Coldfield B75 . . . . . . .46 F4
Stanley Cl
Birmingham B28 . . . . .106 A5
Redditch B98 . . . . .154 A5
Wednesfield WV11 . . . . .26 F8
Stanley Ct
🖪 Birmingham B13. . . . . .87 B2
Perton WV6 . . . . .23 E4
Royal Leamington Spa
CV31 . . . . .162 C7
Stanley Gr 🖪 B11. . . . . . . .87 B6
Stanley Pl
Bilston WV14 . . . . .40 B5
Birmingham B13 . . . . .87 B2
Walsall WS4 . . . . .29 B6
Stanley Rd
Birmingham B6 . . . . .84 C7
Birmingham,King's Heath
B14 . . . . .104 D7
Birmingham,Nechells B7. . . .67 C7
Cannock WS12. . . . . .2 A6
Coventry CV5 . . . . .132 F8
Darlaston WS10. . . . . .41 D5
Hinckley LE10 . . . . .71 C2
Nuneaton CV10 . . . . .72 F3
Stourbridge DY8 . . . . .80 F3
Walsall WS4 . . . . .29 B6
West Bromwich B71. . . . . . . .53 E7

Stanley Rd continued
Wolverhampton WV10. . . . . .11 D1
Stanley St WS3 . . . . .14 D1
Stanmore Gr B62 . . . . .84 A3
Stanmore Rd B16. . . . . .65 C1
Stansbury Ho 🖪 WS2 . . . . .42 C8
Stansfield Gr CV8. . . . . . . .148 D4
Stanton Ave DY1. . . . . .51 A6
Stanton Bridge Prim Sch
CV6 . . . . .113 F6
Stanton Gr
Birmingham B26 . . . . .88 F8
Solihull B90 . . . . .106 A4
Tipton DY4. . . . . .52 A5
Stanton Ho 🖪 B71. . . . . . . .42 F1
Stanton Rd
Birmingham B43 . . . . .54 D8
Royal Leamington Spa
CV31. . . . . .162 C6
Solihull B90 . . . . .106 A4
Wolverhampton WV1. . . . . . .25 F2
Stanton Wlk CV34 . . . . . . .155 D1
Stanville Rd B26. . . . . .89 C6
Stanville Jun & Inf Sch
B26. . . . . .89 C6
Stanway Gdns B71. . . . . . . .53 D6
Stanway Gr B44 . . . . .44 F3
Stanway Rd
Coventry CV5. . . . . .133 A8
Solihull B90 . . . . .106 C4
West Bromwich B71 . . . . . . .53 D6
Stanwell Gr B23 . . . . .56 E6
Stanwick Ave B33. . . . . .69 E3
Stan Williams Ct CV11 . . . .73 D4
Stapenhall Rd B90 . . . . . . .127 A5
Staple Flat B60 . . . . .137 C8
Stapleford Croft B14 . . . . .104 C2
Stapleford Gdns WS7 . . . . . .7 D6
Stapleford Gr DY8 . . . . .60 E2
Staple Hall Rd B31. . . . . . . .103 B2
Staplehurst Rd B28 . . . . . .105 F8
Staple Lodge Rd B31 . . . .103 C2
Staples Cl CV12. . . . . .79 C3
Stapleton Cl
Birmingham B80 . . . . .154 D3
Studley B80 . . . . .159 D3
Sutton Coldfield B76 . . . . . . .58 B6
Stapleton Dr B37. . . . . .70 A4
Stapleton La
Barwell LE9 . . . . .71 F8
Hinckley CV13 . . . . .71 A8
Stapleton Rd
Aldridge WS9. . . . . .29 F5
Studley B80 . . . . .159 D4
Stapylton Ave B17 . . . . .85 B5
Stapylton Cl 🖪 B17. . . . . . .85 B5
Starbank Prim Sch (Annexe)
B10. . . . . .68 B1
Starbank Prim Sch B10 . . .88 A8
Starbank Rd B10 . . . . .88 A8
Starbold Cres B93 . . . . . . .128 B5
Starbold Ct B93 . . . . .128 A6
Star City B7 . . . . .67 D8
Star Cl
Tipton DY4. . . . . .52 C5
Willenhall WS2 . . . . .28 A4
Starcrest Ind Est DY5 . . . . .61 E1
Starcross Cl CV2. . . . . .114 C7
Starcross Rd B27 . . . . .88 C2
Star Ct B91. . . . . .107 D6
Starley Ct CV1 . . . . .165 B2
Starley Rd CV1 . . . . .165 A2
Star Ind Pk CV2 . . . . .114 F5
Starkey Croft B37. . . . . .70 D2
Starkie Dr B68. . . . . .64 C4
Starley Ct CV3 . . . . .135 A7
Starley Pk CV7 . . . . .96 B8
Starley Rd CV1 . . . . .165 A2
Starley Way B37. . . . . .90 C6
Star St
Stourbridge DY9 . . . . .81 F5
Wolverhampton WV3. . . . . . .38 E8
Startin Cl CV7. . . . . .95 F7
Startpoint Trad Est B11 . . .87 D4
Statham Dr B16 . . . . .65 C2
Station App
Barnt Green B45 . . . . .138 D8
Birmingham B73 . . . . .127 F2
Kidderminster DY10 . . . . . .116 F5
Lichfield WS13. . . . . .9 F8
Royal Leamington Spa
CV31 . . . . .161 F7
Solihull B91 . . . . .107 A4
Sutton Coldfield B74 . . . . . . .31 F6
Sutton Coldfield,Maney B73 .46 B6
Station Ave
Birmingham B16 . . . . .65 C1
Coventry CV4 . . . . .131 D8
Warwick CV34 . . . . .160 F8
Station Bldgs B46 . . . . .59 B3
Station Cl WS3 . . . . .28 B8
Station Cotts
Blackwell B60 . . . . .138 A4
Stourbridge DY8 . . . . .60 C7
Sutton Coldfield B73 . . . . . . .45 D6
Station Dr
Blakedown DY10 . . . . .98 C2
Brierley Hill,Quarry Bank
DY5. . . . . .61 E1
Brierley Hill,Silver End DY5. .61 B1
Earlswood B94. . . . . .125 D1
Solihull B92 . . . . .88 E1
Sutton Coldfield B74 . . . . . . .46 B8
Tipton DY4. . . . . .52 B4
West Hagley DY9 . . . . .99 A6

Stationfields Park Homes
B79 . . . . .21 C5
Station La B94 . . . . .144 D3
Station Link Rd B26 . . . . . . .90 D4
Station Pl WS3 . . . . .28 B8
Station Rd
Aldridge WS9. . . . . .30 A5
Alvechurch B48 . . . . .139 A5
Balsall Common CV7 . . . . . .130 B7
Bilston WV14 . . . . .40 E5
Birmingham,Acock's Green
B27 . . . . .88 C3
Birmingham,Aston B6 . . . . . .55 F1
Birmingham B17 . . . . .85 C6
Birmingham,Erdington B23 . .56 F5
Birmingham,Handsworth
B21. . . . . .65 C8
Birmingham,King's Heath
B14. . . . . .86 E1
Birmingham,King's Norton
B30. . . . . .103 D4
Birmingham,Marston Green
B37. . . . . .90 A8
Birmingham,Northfield
B31. . . . . .103 A2
Birmingham,Stechford B33 . .68 C3
Blackwell B60 . . . . .138 A5
Brierley Hill DY5 . . . . .61 C3
Cannock WS12. . . . . .2 E1
Coleshill B46 . . . . .59 F1
Cradley Heath,Haden Cross
B64 . . . . .83 A8
Dorridge B93. . . . . .128 B4
Great Wyrley WS6 . . . . .4 F4
Hammerwich WS7 . . . . .7 E3
Hampton-in-A B92 . . . . .109 B7
Hinckley LE10 . . . . .75 D6
Kenilworth CV8 . . . . .147 F4
Kingswood B94 . . . . .144 D4
Lichfield WS13. . . . . .9 C7
Oldbury B69 . . . . .64 A5
Rowley Regis B65 . . . . .63 D2
Shenstone WS14 . . . . .17 F6
Solihull B91 . . . . .107 B4
Studley B90 . . . . .81 E6
Studley B80 . . . . .159 D4
Sutton Coldfield B73 . . . . . . .46 A1
Walsall,Rushall WS4 . . . . . . .29 A7
Walsall WS3 . . . . .15 A3
Warwick CV34 . . . . .160 F7
West Hagley DY9 . . . . .99 A6
Wombourne WV5. . . . . .49 A8
Wythall B47 . . . . .125 B3
Station Road Ind Est B65 .63 D2
Station St E CV6 . . . . .113 E7
Station St W CV6 . . . . .113 E7
Station Sq CV1 . . . . .165 B1
Station St
Birmingham B5 . . . . .164 B2
Bromsgrove B60 . . . . .136 F1
Cheslyn Hay WS6. . . . . .4 E3
Cradley Hay WS6. . . . . .82 C8
Cannock WS12. . . . . .2 E1
Tipton DY4. . . . . .52 B5
Walsall,Blakenall Heath
WS3 . . . . .28 B8
Walsall WS1 . . . . .28 E1
Station Villas WS10 . . . . . . .41 A6
Station Way DY1 . . . . .153 D3
Staulton Gn 🖪 B69 . . . . . . .63 E4
Staunton Rd
Walsall WS3 . . . . .14 A3
Whitnash CV31 . . . . .162 A5
Staveley Rd
Birmingham B14 . . . . .104 D6
Wolverhampton WV1. . . . . . .25 C4
Staverton Cl CV5 . . . . .112 A3
Stead Cl
Walsall WS2 . . . . .28 C5
Wednesbury DY4 . . . . .41 B1
Steadman Croft DY4 . . . . . .52 D8
Stechford La B8. . . . . .68 D2
Stechford Prim Sch B33 . . .68 D2
Stechford Rd B34. . . . . .68 E5
Stechford Ret Pk B33. . . . . .68 E4
Stechford Trad Est B33 . . . .68 E3
Steel Bright Rd B66. . . . . . .65 C6
Steel Dr WV10 . . . . .25 D8
Steel Gr B25 . . . . .88 C7
Steelhouse La
Birmingham B4 . . . . .164 C3
Wolverhampton WV2. . . . . . .39 E8
Steelmans Rd WS10 . . . . . . .41 F7
Steelpark Rd B62 . . . . .83 C7
Steelpark Way WV11 . . . . . .26 E4
Steel Rdbt B31. . . . . .102 F2
Steene Gr B31. . . . . .102 D3
Steeplefield Rd CV6 . . . . . .113 A5
Steeples The DY8 . . . . .81 B3
Steepwood Croft B30. . . . .103 D4
Steere Ave B79 . . . . .21 C7
Steetley Ind Est B77 . . . . . .21 C3
Stella Croft B37 . . . . .70 C2
Stella Gr B43 . . . . .54 C8
Stella Rd DY4 . . . . .51 F6
Stenbury Cl WV10. . . . . .11 F4
Stencills Dr WS4 . . . . .29 B3
Stencills Rd WS4 . . . . .29 B4
Stennels Ave B62 . . . . .83 E4
Stennels Cl CV6 . . . . .112 F8
Stennels Cres B62. . . . . .83 E4
Stephanie Gr B77 . . . . .22 A4

Stephens Cl WV11 . . . . .26 F8
Stephens Ct DY4 . . . . .52 A6
Stephens Ind Est B11 . . . . . .87 F4
Stephenson Ave WS2 . . . . .28 B5
Stephenson Cl
 Royal Leamington Spa
  CV32 . . . . .156 C1
 Tamworth B77 . . . . .22 A2
Stephenson Dr
 Birmingham B37 . . . . .70 B2
 Perton WV6 . . . . .23 E5
Stephenson Pl B2 . . . . . . .164 C2
Stephenson Rd
 Bedworth CV7 . . . . .96 C7
 Hinckley LE10 . . . . .74 E7
Stephenson Sq WS2 . . . . .28 B5
Stephenson St
 Birmingham B2 . . . . .164 B2
 Wolverhampton WV1 . . . .163 A2
Stephenson Way WS12 . . . .2 B5
Stephens Rd B76 . . . . .47 A4
Stepping Stone Cl WS2 . . .27 F4
Stepping Stones Rd CV5 .112 F4
Stepping Stones DY8 . . . .81 B5
Steppingstone St DY1 . . . .51 B1
Sterling Pk
 Brierley Hill DY5 . . . . .61 F4
 Hinckley LE10 . . . . .74 D8
 Tamworth B77 . . . . .35 E7
Sterling Way CV11 . . . . . . .78 E8
Sterndale Rd B42 . . . . .55 C6
Stevenage Wlk 2 CV2 . . .115 A7
Steven Dr WV14 . . . . .40 E1
Stevens Ave B32 . . . . .84 D2
Stevens Dr WS12 . . . . .2 D6
Stevens Gate WV2 . . . . . .163 B1
Stevens Ho CV1 . . . . .165 C4
Stevenson Ave B98 . . . . . .153 F3
Stevenson Rd
 Coventry CV6 . . . . .113 A8
 Tamworth B79 . . . . .21 A6
Stevenson Wlk WS14 . . . . . .9 B6
Stevens Rd DY9 . . . . .81 D2
Steve Roberts Ct DY11 . .116 A6
Steward St B18 . . . . .66 A3
Stewart Cl CV4 . . . . .112 D2
Stewart Ct DY10 . . . . .116 F5
Stewart Rd
 Brownhills WS9 . . . . .16 A3
 Kingswinford DY6 . . . . . . .60 D4
Stewarts Rd B62 . . . . .83 D7
Stewart St
 Nuneaton CV11 . . . . .73 C3
 Wolverhampton WV2 . . . .163 B1
Stewkins Ct 4 DY8 . . . . . . .80 E8
Steyning Rd B14 . . . . .104 E3
Stickley La DY3 . . . . .50 C4
Stidfall Gr CV31 . . . . .162 D6
Stilehouse Cres B65 . . . . . .63 C2
Stilthouse Gr B45 . . . . . . .122 A7
Stirchley Com Sch B30 . .104 A6
Stirchley Trad Est B30 . . .104 B6
Stirling Ave
 Hinckley LE10 . . . . .71 A1
 Royal Leamington Spa
  CV32 . . . . .157 B6
Stirling Cl CV3 . . . . .134 F8
Stirling Cres WV12 . . . . . . .27 B6
Stirling Ct B16 . . . . .65 F1
Stirling Ho DY5 . . . . .46 C5
Stirling Pk B90 . . . . .126 E8
Stirling Pl WS11 . . . . .4 B8
Stirling Rd
 Bilston WV14 . . . . .40 F2
 Birmingham B16 . . . . .65 F1
 Dudley DY2 . . . . .62 E6
 Solihull B90 . . . . .126 E8
 Sutton Coldfield B73 . . . . .45 E2
Stirrup Cl WS5 . . . . .42 F4
Stivichall Croft CV3 . . . . .133 B6
Stivichall Prim Sch CV3 . .133 A6
Stivichall Cl WV6 . . . . .23 F2
Stockdale Pl B15 . . . . .85 D8
Stockfield Rd B25,B27 . . . . .88 B5
Stockhay La WS7 . . . . .7 D5
Stockhill Dr B45 . . . . .121 F6
Stockingford Inf & Jun Schs
 CV10 . . . . .72 D3
Stocking Leys LE10 . . . . . . .76 A7
Stocking Sq DY9 . . . . .81 F5
Stockland Ct B74 . . . . .44 F8
Stockland Green Sch B23 .56 C4
Stockland Rd B23 . . . . .56 D4
Stockley Cres B90 . . . . . . .106 D3
Stockley Rd CV6 . . . . .96 C6
Stockmans Cl B38 . . . . . . .123 E8
Stocks Wood B30 . . . . .103 F8
Stockton Cl
 Dorridge B93 . . . . .128 B4
 Sutton Coldfield B76 . . . . .58 C5
 Walsall WS2 . . . . .28 D4
Stockton Ct WV14 . . . . .51 B8
Stockton Gr
 2 Royal Leamington Spa
  CV32 . . . . .157 A2
 Birmingham B33 . . . . .69 D1
Stockton Rd CV1 . . . . .165 D4
Stockwell Ave DY5 . . . . .81 D8
Stockwell End WV6 . . . . . . .24 D6
Stockwell Head LE10 . . . . . .71 D1
Stockwell Rd
 Birmingham B21 . . . . .54 E2
 Wolverhampton WV6 . . . . .24 D6
Stockwell Rise B92 . . . . . . .107 D7
Stoke Cross B60 . . . . .151 E7

Stoke Gn CV3 . . . . .114 A2
Stoke Green Cres CV3 . . .114 B1
Stoke Heath Prim Sch
 CV2 . . . . .114 A6
Stoke La B98 . . . . .154 B7
Stoke Park Mews CV2 . . .114 A3
Stoke Park Sch & Com Tech
 Coll CV2 . . . . .114 A4
Stoke Pound La
 Stoke Pound B60 . . . . . . .151 A4
 Stoke Prior B60 . . . . .150 F3
Stoke Prim Sch CV2 . . . . .114 A4
Stoke Prior Fst Sch B60. .150 C3
Stoke Rd
 Bromsgrove,Aston Fields
  B60 . . . . .151 A7
 Bromsgrove,Charford B60. .150 F7
 Hinckley LE10 . . . . .71 B4
Stoke Row CV2 . . . . .114 A4
Stokes Ave
 7 Tipton DY4 . . . . .52 A8
 Willenhall WV13 . . . . .40 F8
Stokesay Ave WV6 . . . . . . .23 F3
Stokesay Cl
 Kidderminster DY10 . . . . .116 E2
 Nuneaton CV11 . . . . .73 A3
 Oldbury B69 . . . . .63 A8
Stokesay Gr B31 . . . . .122 F8
Stokesay Ho B23 . . . . .56 F6
Stokesay Rise DY1 . . . . . . .50 E3
Stoke's La WS11 . . . . .5 F7
Stoke Turn Ct B61 . . . . . . .150 D6
Stoke Way B15 . . . . .66 C1
Stom Rd WV14 . . . . .40 B5
Stoneacre Cl WV3 . . . . .24 A1
Stone Ave B75 . . . . .47 A5
Stonebow Ave B91 . . . . . .127 B8
Stonebridge Cres B37 . . . . .69 F4
Stonebridge Highway
 CV3 . . . . .133 C4
Stonebridge Rd
 Birmingham B46 . . . . .91 A7
 Coleshill B46 . . . . .70 F5
Stonebridge Trad Est
 CV3 . . . . .134 B4
Stonebrook Way
 Birmingham B29 . . . . .84 F2
 Coventry CV5 . . . . .95 F3
Stonebury Ave CV5 . . . . . .111 E4
Stonebury B15 . . . . .85 D8
Stone CE Fst Sch DY10. . .117 E2
Stonechat Cl DY10 . . . . . .117 B2
Stonechat Dr B23 . . . . .56 C2
Stone Cl B38 . . . . .103 F2
Stone Cotts B31 . . . . .103 A3
Stonecroft Ave B45 . . . . . .122 A7
Stonecrop Cl
 Birmingham B38 . . . . . . .123 F8
 Brownhills WS8 . . . . .15 D6
Stonedown Cl WV14 . . . . . .40 A3
Stonefield Dr DY5 . . . . .61 A7
Stonefield Rd WV14 . . . . . .40 D5
Stoneford Rd B90 . . . . . . .106 A4
Stonehaven Dr CV3 . . . . . .133 B6
Stonehaven Gr B28 . . . . . .106 B8
Stonehaven B77 . . . . .21 F5
Stonehenge Croft B14 . . .104 D1
Stonehill Croft B90 . . . . . .126 F6
Stone Hill WV10 . . . . .117 E2
Stonehill Wlk 5 B77 . . . . . .35 F4
Stonehouse Ave WV13 . . . .26 F4
Stonehouse Cl
 Cubbington CV32 . . . . . . .157 D5
 Redditch B97 . . . . .153 D1
Stonehouse Cres WS10. . . .42 B3
Stonehouse Dr B74 . . . . . . .31 C4
Stonehouse Gr B32 . . . . . . .84 D2
Stonehouse Hill B29 . . . . . .85 A3
Stonehouse La
 Birmingham B32 . . . . .84 E2
 Birmingham B32 . . . . .84 F3
Stone House La CV7 . . . . . .93 F6
Stonehouse La
 Coventry CV3 . . . . .134 C4
 Hopwood B48 . . . . .123 E2
Stonehouse Rd
 Bromsgrove B60 . . . . . . .137 A1
 Sutton Coldfield B73 . . . . .45 F3
Stonehurst Rd B43. . . . . . . .44 E3
Stoneleigh WS9 . . . . .30 B5
Stonelea Cl B71 . . . . .53 E8
Stoneleigh Abbey* CV8..148 F3
Stoneleigh Ave
 Coventry CV5 . . . . .132 F7
 Kenilworth CV8 . . . . .148 A6
Stoneleigh Cl
 Redditch B98 . . . . .158 F6
 Stoneleigh CV8 . . . . .149 D6
 Sutton Coldfield B74 . . . . .45 F8
Stoneleigh Ct CV11 . . . . . . .73 C3
Stoneleigh Deer Park Bsns
 Village CV8 . . . . .149 A8
Stoneleigh Gdns CV11 . . . .73 C3
Stoneleigh Ho B32 . . . . . . .84 F5
Stoneleigh Park National Ag
 Ctr* CV8 . . . . .149 A4
Stoneleigh Rd
 Baginton CV8 . . . . .133 F1
 Birmingham B20 . . . . .55 B2
 Blackdown CV32 . . . . . . .157 A7
 Coventry CV4 . . . . .132 D6
 Kenilworth CV8 . . . . .148 A6
 Solihull B91 . . . . .106 E6
 Stoneleigh CV8 . . . . .149 B3
Stoneleigh Way DY3 . . . . . .50 D6

Stone Mdw CV7 . . . . .95 A6
Stone Pine Cl WS12. . . . . . . .1 F8
Stonepine Pl DY3 . . . . .50 E6
Stonepits La B97 . . . . .158 D4
Stonepit B77 . . . . .21 C1
Stone Rd B15. . . . . .86 D7
Stonerwood Ave B28 . . . . .105 E8
Stones Gn B23. . . . . .56 F6
Stone St
 Dudley DY1 . . . . .51 C1
 Oldbury B69. . . . . .64 A7
Stoneton Cres CV7. . . . . . . .130 A6
Stoneton Gr B29 . . . . .103 A8
Stoneway Gr CV31 . . . . . . .162 D6
Stonewell Cres CV11 . . . . . .79 B8
Stoney Cl B92 . . . . .107 E7
Stoney Ct CV3 . . . . .135 A7
Stone Yd
 Birmingham B12 . . . . .66 F1
 Cradley Heath B64 . . . . . .82 C8
Stoneydelph Prim Sch
 B77 . . . . .22 A1
Stoneyfield Cl 3 WS11. . . .1 F2
Stoneyford Gr B14 . . . . . . .105 B4
Stoneygate Dr LE10 . . . . . .71 F3
Stoney Hill Cl B60 . . . . . . .137 A1
Stoneyhurst Rd B24. . . . . . .56 F1
Stoney La
 Birmingham B32 . . . . .84 B6
 Birmingham,Balsall Heath
  B12 . . . . .87 B6
 Birmingham,Stechford B25 .68 E1
 Blackwell B60 . . . . .138 C2
 Dudley DY2 . . . . .62 C3
 Kidderminster DY10 . . . . .116 E8
Stoney Lane Ind Est
 DY10. . . . . .116 E8
Stoney La
 Stakenbridge DY10 . . . . . . .98 E3
 Walsall WS3 . . . . .14 D3
 West Bromwich B71 . . . . . .53 D4
 Wolverhampton WV4 . . . . .39 B5
Stoney Lea Rd WS11 . . . . . .1 F1
Stoneymoor Dr B36. . . . . . .58 D1
Stoney Rd
 Coventry CV1,CV3 . . . . . .165 B1
 Nuneaton CV10,CV11,. . . .73 B6
Stoney Stanton Rd CV1,
 CV6. . . . . .113 E5
Stoneythorpe Cl B91. . . . . .107 B1
Stoneywood Rd CV2 . . . . .114 F8
Stonnal Gr B23 . . . . .57 A6
Stonnall Gate WS9 . . . . . . .30 C8
Stonnall Rd WS9. . . . . .30 C8
Stonor Park Rd B91 . . . . . .106 F5
Stonor Rd B28 . . . . .106 A5
Stonydelph La B37. . . . . . . .36 A7
Stony La B67 . . . . .64 F5
Stony St B67 . . . . .64 F6
Stoop The CV3 . . . . .115 B1
Stornoway Rd B35 . . . . .58 B4
Storrage La B48 . . . . .139 E3
Storrs Cl B9 . . . . .67 D1
Storrs Way The B32. . . . . . .102 B7
Stotfold Rd B14 . . . . .104 F2
Stourbridge Coll (Longlands
 Ctr) DY8 . . . . .80 E5
Stourbridge Coll DY8 . . . . .81 A4
Stourbridge Juntion Sta
 DY8 . . . . .81 B3
Stourbridge Rd
 Brierley Hill DY1,DY2,DY5 . .61 E6
 Catshill B61 . . . . .136 F7
 Churchill DY10 . . . . .98 A6
 Clent DY9 . . . . .99 E3
 Dudley DY1 . . . . .62 A8
 Fairfield B61 . . . . .120 D2
 Hackman's Gate DY9 . . . . .98 F1
 Hagley DY9 . . . . .99 C7
 Halesowen B63 . . . . .82 F3
 Kidderminster DY10 . . . . .116 F8
 Madeley Heath DY9 . . . . .120 B7
 Stourbridge DY9 . . . . .81 D5
 Wombourne WV5,DY3 . . . .49 B5
Stourbridge Town Sta
 DY8 . . . . .81 A4
Stourbridge Trad Est DY8 .81 A6
Stour Cl
 Burntwood WS7 . . . . .7 D6
 Halesowen B63 . . . . .82 E6
Stourdale Rd B64 . . . . .82 E6
Stourdell Rd B63 . . . . .82 E6
Stour Hill DY5 . . . . .82 A8
Stour Ho 2 B68. . . . . .84 B8
Stourminster Specl Sch
 DY10. . . . . .117 B4
Stourmore Cl WV12 . . . . . . .27 D6
Stourport Rd DY11. . . . . . .116 C2
Stour St
 Birmingham B18 . . . . .66 A3
 West Bromwich B70 . . . . . .52 E3
Stour B77 . . . . .36 A5
Stourton Cl
 Knowle B93 . . . . .128 B7
 Sutton Coldfield B76 . . . . .46 F4
Stourton Dr WV4 . . . . .38 C4
Stourton Rd B32 . . . . .84 B5
Stourvale Ind Est DY9 . . . . .81 F6
Stourvale Rd B63 . . . . .82 F5
Stourvale Trad Est B63. . . . .82 D6
Stour Valley Cl DY5 . . . . . . .81 B6
Stow Dr DY5. . . . . .81 B6
Stowecroft WS13 . . . . .3 C1
Stowe Hill Gdns WS13 . . . . .3 C1
Stowell Rd B44 . . . . .55 F8

Stowe Pl CV4. . . . . .111 C1
Stowe Rd WS13. . . . . .9 C8
Stowe St
 Lichfield WS13. . . . . .9 C8
 Walsall WS3 . . . . .28 C7
Stow Gr B36. . . . . .68 C8
Stowhealth Ind Est & New Ent
 Ctr WV1. . . . . .40 A8
Stow Heath Jun & Inf Schs
 WV13. . . . . .26 D1
Stow Heath La
 Bilston WV1. . . . . .40 B8
 Wolverhampton WV1 . . . . .26 C1
Stow Heath Pl WV1 . . . . . . .40 C8
Stowlawn Jun & Inf Sch
 WV14. . . . . .40 C8
Stowmans Cl WV14 . . . . . . .40 B3
Strachey Ave CV32. . . . . . .156 E2
Stradey Cl CV3 . . . . .115 B1
Straight Rd WV12. . . . . .27 D6
Straits Gn DY3 . . . . .50 B5
Straits Prim Sch DY3 . . . . .50 B5
Straits Rd DY3 . . . . .50 B3
Straits The DY3 . . . . .50 B3
Strand The B61 . . . . .137 A3
Stratford Cl DY1 . . . . .50 E2
Stratford Ct B72 . . . . .46 B3
Stratford Dr WS9 . . . . .30 C8
Stratford Gdns B60 . . . . . .137 A2
Stratford Pl B12 . . . . .87 A8
Stratford Rd
 Birmingham,Sparkbrook B11,
  B28 . . . . .87 B6
 Birmingham,Sparkhill B11. .87 D3
 Bromsgrove B60 . . . . . . .137 A2
 Dorridge B94 . . . . .127 B3
 Longbridge CV34 . . . . . . .160 C3
 Nuthurst B94 . . . . .143 C5
 Solihull B90 . . . . .126 D7
 Stratford St N B11. . . . . . .87 A8
Stratford St
 Birmingham B11 . . . . .87 C5
 Coventry CV2 . . . . .114 A4
 Nuneaton CV11 . . . . .73 C4
Stratford Way WS11 . . . . . .1 F5
Stratford Wlk B36 . . . . .68 C8
Strathdene Gdns B29 . . . . .85 C1
Strathdene Rd B29 . . . . . . .85 C2
Stratheam Rd CV32. . . . . . .156 E1
Strathern Dr WV14. . . . . . . .40 A1
Strathfield Wlk WV3,WV4 . .38 C6
Strathmore Ave CV1 . . . . .113 E1
Strathmore Cres WV5. . . . .38 A1
Strathmore Pl 6 WS11 . . . .1 F2
Strathmore Rd
 Hinckley LE10 . . . . .75 A7
 Tipton DY4 . . . . .52 A8
Stratton St WV10 . . . . .25 E4
Strawberry Cl B69 . . . . .63 C7
Strawberry Fields CV7 . . . .92 B1
Strawberry La WS6 . . . . . . .13 E8
Strawberry Lane Ind Est
 WV13. . . . . .26 C2
Strawberry La WV13 . . . . . .26 D3
Strawberry Wlk CV2 . . . . . .96 D2
Stream Mdw WS4. . . . . .15 D1
Stream Pk DY6 . . . . .60 C6
Stream Rd DY6,DY8 . . . . . .60 C6
Streamside Cl CV5. . . . . . . .112 A8
Streamside Way
 Solihull B92 . . . . .89 D4
 Walsall WS4. . . . . .29 B3
Streatham Gr B44 . . . . .45 A2
Streather Rd B75. . . . . .32 C2
Streetly Cres B74 . . . . .31 D3
Streetly La B74 . . . . .31 D3
Streetly Rd B23. . . . . .56 D5
Streetly Sch The B74. . . . . .45 A6
Streetly Wood B74. . . . . . . .31 A2
Streetsbrook Inf Sch
 B90. . . . . .106 C4
Streetsbrook Rd B90,B91 .106 D5
Streets Corner Gdns WS9 .16 A4
Streets La WS6 . . . . .4 F1
Streetway Rd WS14 . . . . . . .18 B7
Strensham Ct B13 . . . . .86 E4
Strensham Hill B13 . . . . . . .86 E4
Strensham Rd B12 . . . . .86 E5
Stretton Ave CV3 . . . . .134 D6
Stretton Cl LE10 . . . . .75 D6
Stretton Cres CV31. . . . . . .162 B5
Stretton Ct
 Birmingham B23 . . . . .56 E2
 Hinckley LE10 . . . . .75 D3
Stretton Dr B45. . . . . .122 A2
Stretton Gr
 2 Birmingham,Lozells
  B19. . . . . .66 C7
 Birmingham,Sparkbrook
  B11. . . . . .87 C6
Stretton Ho B97 . . . . .153 A4
Stretton Pl
 Dudley DY2 . . . . .62 D5
 Wolverhampton WV14 . . . .40 A1
Stretton Rd
 Kidderminster DY11 . . . . .116 B4
 Nuneaton CV10 . . . . .73 A3
 Solihull B90 . . . . .126 B8
 Willenhall WV12 . . . . .13 D1
Stretton St B77 . . . . .21 E3
Stringer Cl B75. . . . . .32 A4
Stringes Cl WV13 . . . . .27 C3
Stringes Hill WS12 . . . . .2 D7
Stringes La WV13 . . . . .27 B3

Strode Ho B79. . . . . .21 A4
Strode Rd WV2 . . . . .39 C6
Stroma Way CV10. . . . . .72 F2
Stronsay Cl B45 . . . . .101 F1
Stroud Ave WV12 . . . . .27 D5
Stroud Cl WV13 . . . . .27 C4
Stroud Rd B90. . . . . .105 F2
Strutt Cl B15 . . . . .85 D8
Strutt Rd LE10. . . . . .76 A5
Stuart Bathurst RC High Sch
 WS10. . . . . .42 B5
Stuart Cl CV34. . . . . .160 D5
Stuart Cres DY2 . . . . .51 E1
Stuart Ct
 7 Royal Leamington Spa
  CV32. . . . . .156 E1
 Coventry CV6. . . . . .114 A8
Stuart Rd
 Halesowen B62 . . . . .83 F5
 Rowley Regis B65 . . . . . . .63 C4
Stuarts Cl DY9. . . . . .99 A5
Stuart's Dr B33 . . . . .68 C1
Stuarts Gr DY9 . . . . .99 B8
Stuarts Rd B33 . . . . .68 C1
Stuart St
 Birmingham B7 . . . . .67 C7
 Walsall WS3 . . . . .28 B8
Stubbers Green Rd
 Aldridge WS9. . . . . .30 A7
 Walsall WS9 . . . . .29 F6
Stubbington Cl WV13 . . . . .26 D1
Stubbs Cl CV12 . . . . .78 A4
Stubbs Gr CV2 . . . . .114 B5
Stubbs Rd WV3 . . . . .39 A6
Stubby La WV11 . . . . .27 F6
Stubley Dr WV10 . . . . .25 E6
Stud Farm Cotts B78. . . . . .20 E2
Studland Gn CV2 . . . . .115 A4
Studland Rd B28. . . . . .106 A8
Studley Croft B92 . . . . .89 D3
Studley Dr DY5. . . . . .81 C8
Studley Gate WS9 . . . . .16 B2
Studley High Sch B80. . . . .159 E3
Studley Inf Sch B80. . . . . .159 E4
Studley Rd
 Redditch B98 . . . . .154 A2
 Wolverhampton WV3 . . . . .38 C6
Studley St Mary's CE Jun Sch
 B80. . . . . .159 E3
Studley St B12. . . . . .87 B5
Studley Twr B12 . . . . .86 F7
Sturgeon's Hill WS14 . . . . . .9 C7
Sturley Cl CV8 . . . . .148 B6
Sturman Dr B65. . . . . .63 C1
Sturminster Cl CV2 . . . . . .115 A4
Stychbrook Gdns WS13 . . . .3 B2
Styles Cl CV31 . . . . .162 A4
Styvechale Ave CV5. . . . . . .133 A8
Suckling Green La WV8 . . . .10 A2
Sudbury Cl
 Royal Leamington Spa
  CV32. . . . . .157 C3
 Wednesfield WV11 . . . . . . .26 E7
Sudbury Gr B44. . . . . .45 B2
Sudeley Cl B36 . . . . .58 B1
Sudeley Gdns DY1 . . . . .50 D2
Sudeley Rd CV10 . . . . .78 C8
Sudeley B77. . . . . .35 C8
Suffield Gr B23 . . . . .56 B5
Suffolk Cl
 Bedworth CV12 . . . . .78 A3
 Coventry CV5. . . . . .112 B3
 Nuneaton CV10 . . . . .72 E3
 Oldbury B68. . . . . .64 A2
 Wolverhampton WV11. . . . .26 C6
Suffolk Dr DY5 . . . . .81 C7
Suffolk Gr WS9 . . . . .30 B8
Suffolk Ho B23 . . . . .56 F5
Suffolk Pl
 Birmingham B5 . . . . .164 B3
 Walsall WS2 . . . . .28 D5
Suffolk Rd
 Dudley DY2 . . . . .62 A2
 Wednesbury WS10. . . . . . .42 C3
Suffolk Street Queensway
 B1. . . . . .164 B2
Suffolk St CV32. . . . . .157 A1
Suffolk Way B78 . . . . .21 A1
Suffrage St B66 . . . . .65 B4
Sugarbrook Ct 1 B60. . . . .150 F6
Sugarbrook Rd B60 . . . . . .151 A5
Sugar Loaf La DY10. . . . . . .98 B7
Sugden Gr B5 . . . . .86 E8
Sulgrave Cl
 Coventry CV2. . . . . .114 E7
 Dudley DY1. . . . . .51 A3
Sullivan Ct CV6 . . . . .114 B7
Sullivan Rd CV6. . . . . .114 B7
Sullivan Way WS13 . . . . . . .3 C2
Sullivan Wlk WS13 . . . . . . .3 C2
Sumburgh Croft B35. . . . . . .58 A3
Summercourt Dr DY6 . . . . . .60 C6
Summercourt Sq DY6 . . . . .60 C5
Summer Croft B19. . . . . . . .66 C6
Summer Dr DY3 . . . . .50 C3
Summerfield Ave
 Kingswinford DY6 . . . . . . .60 C7
 West Bromwich B70 . . . . . .53 C4
Summerfield Cl B78 . . . . . . .65 E3
Summerfield Cres B16. . . . .65 E3
Summerfield Dr 2 B29 . .103 A7
Summerfield Gr 5 B18 . . . .65 E4

Summerfield Jun & Inf Sch
B18. . . . . .65 E4
Summerfield Rd
Birmingham B16 . . . . .65 E3
Burntwood WS7. . . . . .7 A5
Dudley DY2 . . . . .62 D7
Holy Cross DY9 . . . . .99 E2
Solihull B92 . . . . .89 A1
Tamworth B77 . . . . .21 D4
Wolverhampton WV1 . . . . .25 B2
Summerfields Ave B62. . . .83 F7
Summergate DY3 . . . . .50 C4
Summer Gr WS13 . . . . .3 D2
Summer Hill **6** B63 . . . . . .83 B3
Summerhill Ave DY11 . . . 116 A5
Summer Hill Ind Pk **2** B1 **66** B3
Summer Hill DY6 . . . . .60 C6
Summerhill Prim Sch
DY4 . . . . .52 A6
Summer Hill Rd B1 . . . . . . .66 B3
Summerhill Rd
Dudley WV14 . . . . .40 D1
Tipton DY4. . . . . .51 F7
Summerhill Sch The DY6. . .60 B6
Summer Hill St B1. . . . . . . .66 B3
Summerhill WS14. . . . . . . .16 E8
Summer Hill Terr B1 . . . . .66 A3
Summerhouse Cl B97. . . . 158 A6
Summerhouse Rd WV14. . .40 A1
Summer La
Birmingham B19 . . . . .66 D5
Dudley DY3 . . . . .50 C3
Minworth B76 . . . . .58 D6
Walsall WS4 . . . . .15 C2
Summerlee Rd B24 . . . . . . .57 B2
Summer Pl DY11. . . . . . . .116 C5
Summer Rd
Birmingham,Acock's Green
B27. . . . . .88 A2
Birmingham,Edgbaston B15 .86 C7
Birmingham,Erdington B23 . .56 F5
Dudley DY1 . . . . .51 A4
Kidderminster DY11 . . . . 116 C3
Rowley Regis B65 . . . . . . .63 D3
Summer Row
Birmingham B3 . . . . 164 A3
Wolverhampton WV2. . . .163 B2
Summer St
Kingswinford DY6 . . . . . . .60 D6
Redditch B98 . . . . .153 E3
Stourbridge DY8 . . . . .80 F5
Stourbridge,Lye DY9 . . . . .81 E5
West Bromwich B71 . . . . .53 D4
Willenhall WV13 . . . . .26 F2
Summerton Rd
Oldbury B69. . . . . .52 D1
Whitnash CV31 . . . . .162 A3
Summervale Cl DY9. . . . . .99 A5
Summervale Rd DY9 . . . . .99 A5
Summerville Terr **4** B17 .85 C5
Summit Cres B66 . . . . .64 E8
Summit Gdns B63 . . . . . . .82 F3
Summit Pl DY3 . . . . .50 B2
Summit The DY9 . . . . .81 F4
Summer Rd B46. . . . . .70 F6
Sunart Way CV10 . . . . .72 C5
Sunbeam Cl B36. . . . . .58 F1
Sunbeam Dr WS6. . . . . .4 F3
Sunbeam St WV2 . . . . .39 C7
Sunbeam B77 . . . . .21 E3
Sunbeam Way B33. . . . . . .69 C2
Sunbury Ave WS14 . . . . .9 E7
Sunbury Cl WV14 . . . . .40 E1
Sunbury Cotts B31. . . . . . 103 A4
Sunbury Rd
Birmingham B31 . . . . . . .122 E7
Coventry CV3. . . . . .134 C5
Halesowen B63 . . . . .82 F4
Suncliffe Dr CV8. . . . . . . .148 A2
Suncroft B32 . . . . .84 C5
Sundbury Rise B31 . . . . .103 B5
Sunderland Dr DY8 . . . . . .81 A8
Sunderton Rd B14 . . . . . .104 E4
Sundew Croft B36 . . . . . . .68 D8
Sundew St CV2 . . . . .96 D2
Sundial La B43 . . . . .43 F1
Sundorne Cl CV5 . . . . . . .112 A4
Sundour Cres WV11. . . . . .12 B1
Sundridge Prim Sch B44. .44 E4
Sundridge Rd B44 . . . . . . .44 E4
Sundridge Wlk WV4 . . . . .38 C6
Sunfield Rd WS11. . . . . .1 B1
Sunleigh Gr B27 . . . . .88 E4
Sunley Dr WS12 . . . . .2 D7
Sunningdale Ave
Coventry CV6. . . . . .95 D2
Kenilworth CV8 . . . . .148 B4
Perton WV6. . . . . .23 D5
Sunningdale B60 . . . . . . .137 A1
Sunningdale Cl
Birmingham B20 . . . . .54 E4
Nuneaton CV11 . . . . .74 A1
Redditch B98 . . . . .153 F4
Stourbridge DY8 . . . . .80 F2
Sutton Coldfield B73 . . . . .46 A2
Sunningdale Dr B69 . . . . .63 A7
Sunningdale B62 . . . . .83 E4
Sunningdale Rd
Birmingham B11 . . . . .88 A3
Bromsgrove B61 . . . . 150 D8
Sedgley DY3 . . . . .39 B1
Sunningdale
Sutton Coldfield B73 . . . . .46 B1
Tamworth B77 . . . . .22 C5
Sunningdale Way WS3 . . .14 A3

Sunny Ave B12 . . . . .87 A5
Sunnybank Ave
Birmingham B44 . . . . .56 B7
Coventry CV3. . . . . .134 B5
Sunnybank Cl WS9. . . . . . .30 E2
Sunny Bank CV1 . . . . 165 A3
Sunny Bank Rd B68. . . . . .84 C7
Sunnybank Rd
Dudley DY3 . . . . .50 F5
Sutton Coldfield B73 . . . . .57 A8
Sunnydale Cres LE10. . . . .75 A7
Sunnydale Rd LE10 . . . . . .74 F7
Sunnydale Wlk B71. . . . . .53 C4
Sunnydene B8. . . . . .68 A5
Sunny Hill Cl WV5 . . . . . . .49 B6
Sunnyhill LE10. . . . . .75 F7
Sunnyhill S LE10. . . . . . . .75 F6
Sunnymead B60 . . . . 137 A1
Sunnymead Rd
1 Burntwood WS7 . . . . .7 A8
Birmingham B26 . . . . .88 F6
Sunnymead Way B74 . . . . .44 F7
Sunnymede Rd B64 . . . . . .61 A4
Sunnyside Ave B23 . . . . . .56 E3
Sunnyside WS9 . . . . .16 A2
Sunnyside Cl
Balsall Common CV7 . . . . 130 C7
Coventry CV5 . . . . .112 F3
Sunnyside Ct CV10. . . . . . .72 F3
Sunnyside LE10. . . . . .71 D3
Sunnyside Hospl LE10. . . .71 D5
Sunnyside Ind Est LE10 . .71 D4
Sunnyside La CV7. . . . . . .130 C7
Sunnyside B69 . . . . .63 B7
Sunridge Ave
Birmingham B19 . . . . .66 D6
Wombourne WV5. . . . . . . .49 A7
Sunrise Ct B15 . . . . .86 D7
Sunrise Hill WS12. . . . . . . .2 B6
Sunrise Wlk B68. . . . . .64 C3
Sunset Cl
Great Wyrley WS6. . . . . . . .4 F3
Tamworth B79 . . . . .21 A5
Sunset Pl WV4. . . . . .39 F3
Sunshine Cl CV8 . . . . . . .148 A2
Sunshine Inf Sch The
WS3 . . . . .28 C8
Sun St
Brierley Hill DY5 . . . . .61 F1
Walsall WS1 . . . . .42 E7
Wolverhampton WV10. . .163 D3
Sunway Gr CV3 . . . . .133 B6
Surfeit Hill Rd B64. . . . . . .82 D8
Surrey Cl
Cannock WS11. . . . . .4 F8
Hinckley LE10 . . . . .75 E4
Nuneaton CV10 . . . . .72 E3
Surrey Cres B71 . . . . .53 A8
Surrey Ct CV34 . . . . .160 E8
Surrey Dr
Kingswinford DY6 . . . . . . .60 F3
Tamworth B78 . . . . .21 A1
Wolverhampton WV3. . . . .24 E1
Surrey Ho **2** DY8 . . . . .80 F8
Surrey Rd
Birmingham B44 . . . . .44 F4
Dudley DY2 . . . . .62 A7
Surrey Wlk WS9 . . . . .16 A1
Sussex Ave
Aldridge WS9. . . . . .30 A8
Wednesbury WS10 . . . . . .42 D4
West Bromwich B71 . . . . .53 C6
Sussex Cl CV10 . . . . .72 E3
Sussex Ct
7 Birmingham B29. . . . .103 C7
Warwick CV34 . . . . .160 E8
Sussex Dr
Cannock WS12. . . . . .2 B5
Wolverhampton WV3 . . . . .24 E1
Sussex Rd CV5. . . . . .112 F4
Sutherland Ave
Coventry CV5. . . . . .112 A4
Solihull B90 . . . . .106 C3
Wolverhampton WV2. . . . .40 A8
Sutherland Cl
Birmingham B43 . . . . .44 D4
Warwick CV34 . . . . .155 E1
Sutherland Dr
Bedworth CV12 . . . . .78 A4
Birmingham B13. . . . . . . .86 F4
Wombourne WV5. . . . . . . .38 A1
Sutherland Gr WV6 . . . . . .23 F4
Sutherland Ho WV2. . . . .163 C2
Sutherland Rd
Cheslyn Hay WS6. . . . . . . .4 E2
Cradley Heath B64. . . . . . .82 E8
Wolverhampton WV4. . . . .39 B5
Sutherland St B6 . . . . .67 B8
Sutton App B8. . . . . .68 A4
Sutton Ave
Coventry CV5. . . . . .111 D4
Tamworth B78 . . . . .21 A2
Sutton Cl
Hinckley LE10 . . . . .71 F3
Redditch B98 . . . . .154 D2
Sutton Coldfield Coll Design
Ctr B72. . . . . .46 C4
Sutton Coldfield Coll
(Erdington Ctr B24 . . . . . .57 A4
Sutton Coldfield Coll (Great
Barr Campus) B44. . . . . . .55 E7
Sutton Coldfield Cottage
Hospl B72 . . . . .46 B4
Sutton Coldfield Gram Sch
For Girls B73. . . . . .46 B3
Sutton Coldfield Sta B73. .46 B5

Sutton Cres B70 . . . . .53 A3
Sutton Ct
3 Birmingham,Erdington
B24. . . . . .57 B6
Bedworth CV6 . . . . .96 C6
Birmingham,Hamstead B43. .54 E7
Sutton Coldfield B75 . . . . .46 B7
Wolverhampton WV4. . . . .39 E2
Sutton Lodge B91 . . . . . .107 A3
Sutton New Rd B23. . . . . .56 F4
Sutton Oak Cnr B73. . . . . .45 A5
Sutton Oak Rd B73. . . . . . .45 A5
Sutton Park Ct B73 . . . . . .46 B2
Sutton Park Fst Sch
DY11. . . . . .116 B4
Sutton Park Gr DY11. . . .116 C3
Sutton Park Rd DY11. . . .116 B3
Sutton Park Rise DY11 . .116 B3
Sutton Park Visitor Ctr*
B74 . . . . .46 A5
Sutton Pk
Nuneaton CV10 . . . . .72 B7
Sutton Coldfield B74 . . . . .45 D6
Sutton St
Aldridge WS9. . . . . .30 A1
Birmingham B23 . . . . .57 B6
Darlaston WS10. . . . . .41 A4
Kidderminster DY11 . . . . 116 C3
Mile Oak B78. . . . . .34 A8
Tamworth B78 . . . . .20 C1
Walsall WS5 . . . . .43 C8
Sutton's Dr
Birmingham B43 . . . . .44 A4
Walsall B43 . . . . .43 F4
Sutton Specl Sch The
DY1 . . . . .61 F8
Sutton Sq B70 . . . . .58 E6
Sutton St
Birmingham,Aston B6 . . . . .66 F4
Birmingham B1 . . . . .66 D1
Stourbridge CV6. . . . . .96 B5
Sutton St DY6 . . . . .60 F1
Swadling St CV31 . . . . . .161 F6
Swaffield Pk WS11. . . . . . .2 B2
Swain Crofts CV31 . . . . . .162 B6
Swains Gn LE10. . . . . .75 F6
Swains Gr B44. . . . . .44 F4
Swaledale Cl B60. . . . . . .150 E6
Swaledale CV4 . . . . .132 D6
Swale Gr
Birmingham B38 . . . . . . .103 F1
Willenhall WV13 . . . . .27 D2
Swale Rd B76. . . . . .47 A1
Swallow Ave B36 . . . . .70 A8
Swallow Cl
Birmingham B12 . . . . .87 B5
Dudley DY2 . . . . .62 D2
Huntington WS12. . . . . .1 C7
Wednesbury WS10. . . . . . .42 B4
Swallow Croft WS13 . . . . . .3 A1
Swallow Ct
Bedworth CV12 . . . . .95 C8
Hinckley LE10 . . . . .74 F6
Wolverhampton,Fordhouses
WV10 . . . . .11 B3
Wolverhampton,Low Hill
WV10 . . . . .25 D7
Swallowdale
Brownhills WS9 . . . . .16 B4
Wolverhampton WV6. . . . .23 F2
Swallowdean Rd CV6 . . . .112 E8
Swallow Dr DY10 . . . . . . .117 A2
Swallowfall Ave DY8 . . . . .80 C4
Swallowfields Dr WS12. . . .2 B3
Swallowfields Rd DY3. . . .39 C2
Swallowfield B79 . . . . .20 E6
Swallowgate Bsns Pk
CV6 . . . . .95 C1
Swallow Rd CV6. . . . . .95 C1
Swallows WS13 . . . . .15 A5
Swallows Ind Est The
B90. . . . . .126 D8
Swallows' Mdw B90. . . . .126 D8
Swallows Rise Bsns Pk
. . . . .61 E3
Swallow St
Birmingham B2 . . . . .164 B2
West Bromwich B70 . . . . .53 A4
Swanage Gn CV2 . . . . . . .115 A4
Swanage Rd B10 . . . . .87 D8
Swan Ave B66 . . . . .64 E7
Swan Bank WV4 . . . . .38 F4
Swan Cl
Blakedown DY10 . . . . .98 B1
Cheslyn Hay WS6. . . . . . . .4 D2
Swan Copse B25. . . . . .88 C5
Swan Corner Sh Ctr WS7. .7 C6
Swancote Dr WV4 . . . . . . .38 C6
Swancote Rd
Birmingham B33 . . . . .68 F5
Dudley DY1 . . . . .62 A8
Swancote B69 . . . . .63 A5
Swancroft Ho **11** DY4 . . . .52 A8
Swancroft Rd
Coventry CV2. . . . . .114 A5
Tipton DY4. . . . . .51 F8
Swan Ctyd B25 . . . . .88 D6
Swan Dr WS8. . . . . .15 F8
Swanfield Rd DY8. . . . . . . .61 A2
Swanfields B78. . . . . .34 F8
Swan Gdns B23 . . . . .56 F4
Swan La
Coventry CV2. . . . . .113 F4
Fairfield B61 . . . . .120 E3
Swan Lane Ind Est B70. . .53 A5
Swan La
Stourbridge DY5,DY8. . . . .61 A2

Swan La continued
Upton Warren B61. . . . . . 150 A3
West Bromwich B70 . . . . .53 A5
Swanley Cl B62. . . . . .84 A3
Swan Mews WS13 . . . . .9 A8
Swanmore Cl WV3 . . . . . . .38 E8
Swannote B79 . . . . .20 F5
Swann Rd WV14 . . . . .40 A2
Swan Wlk **10** DY4. . . . . . . .52 A8
Swan Pk B77 . . . . .21 C3
Swan Pool Gr WS4. . . . . . .15 D1
Swan Rdbt B70 . . . . .52 F5
Swan Rd WS13 . . . . .9 A7
Swansbrook Gdns **4**
B38. . . . . .104 C2
Swanshurst La B13 . . . . .105 C8
Swanshurst Sch B13. . . .105 B7
Swans Length B48. . . . . .139 A7
Swan St
Alvechurch B48 . . . . .139 B5
Brierley Hill DY5 . . . . .61 C6
Dudley DY2 . . . . .62 C6
Royal Leamington Spa
CV32. . . . . .157 A1
Stourbridge DY8 . . . . .80 F5
Warwick CV34 . . . . .160 E6
Wolverhampton WV1 . . . . .25 F2
Swanswell Rd B92 . . . . . .106 D7
Swanswell St CV1 . . . . . .165 C4
Swans Wlk B48 . . . . .139 A6
Swanswood Gr **3** B37 . . . .70 C3
Swan Village Ind Est B70. .53 A5
Swarthmore Rd B29 . . . . .103 B7
Sweetbriar La WV12 . . . . .27 D5
Sweetbriar Rd WV2. . . . . .40 A7
Sweetbriar Way WS12. . . . .2 D2
Sweetbrier Dr **4** DY8. . . . .60 E1
Sweetman Pl WV6 . . . . . . .25 A3
Sweetman St
Wolverhampton WV6. . . . .24 F4
Wolverhampton WV6. . . . .25 A3
Sweetmoor Cl B36. . . . . . .69 C8
Sweetpool La DY9 . . . . . . .98 F5
Swift Cl
Birmingham B36 . . . . .70 A8
Bromsgrove B61 . . . . 150 E8
Kenilworth CV8 . . . . .148 A2
Swift Park Gr DY10 . . . . .117 B2
Swift's Cnr CV3 . . . . .133 E8
Swift B77 . . . . .21 E3
Swift Ho B77 . . . . .21 C3
Swinbrook Gr B44 . . . . . . .44 E1
Swinbrook Way B90 . . . . 106 D4
Swinburne Ave CV2 . . . . .114 D2
Swinburne Cl CV10 . . . . . .72 A5
Swinburne Rd
Hinckley LE10 . . . . .71 C1
Redditch B97 . . . . .158 C7
Swincross Rd DY8 . . . . . . .81 B3
Swindale CV4 . . . . .132 B7
Swindale Croft CV3 . . . . .134 F8
Swindell B77 . . . . .36 B7
Swindell Rd DY9. . . . . .81 C1
Swindon Rd
Birmingham B17 . . . . .65 B2
Kingswinford DY6 . . . . . . .60 B6
Swinfen Broun Rd WS13 . . .9 A8
Swinford Gr B93. . . . . . . .127 E3
Swinford Old Hall DY8 . . .81 B3
Swinford Rd
Birmingham B29 . . . . .85 B3
Stourbridge DY8 . . . . .81 A3
Wolverhampton WV10. . . .25 E5
Swiss Dr DY9. . . . . .60 F2
Swiss Lodge Dr B78 . . . . .34 F8
Sword Dr LE10. . . . . .71 B3
Swynnerton Dr WV11 . . . .12 F4
Sycamore Ave
Birmingham B12 . . . . .87 A5
Redditch B98 . . . . .153 E2
Sycamore Cl
Birmingham B24 . . . . .56 F3
Hinckley LE10 . . . . .75 E5
Kidderminster DY10 . . . .116 F7
Stourbridge DY8 . . . . .80 D2
Sutton Coldfield B76 . . . . .46 F2
Walsall WS4 . . . . .29 B8
Sycamore Cres
Birmingham,Erdington
B24. . . . . .56 F3
Birmingham,Marston Green
B37. . . . . .90 A8
Sycamore Ct
Allesley CV5. . . . . .111 F7
Birmingham,Cotteridge
B30. . . . . .103 C6
Birmingham,Perry Common
B23. . . . . .56 C7
Sycamore Dr
Hollywood B47. . . . . .125 B6
Wolverhampton WV3 . . . . .24 D1
Sycamore Gn
Cannock WS11. . . . . .1 E6
Dudley DY1 . . . . .50 F5
Sycamore Green Prim Sch
DY1 . . . . .50 F5
Sycamore Gr CV34 . . . . . 156 A1
Sycamore Ho
Birmingham B13 . . . . .87 A3
Redditch B98 . . . . .158 F8
Sycamore Ind & Trad Est
DY8 . . . . .61 A1
Sycamore Paddock **1**
. . . . .61 A1
Sycamore Pl
Bilston WV14 . . . . .41 A3
Burntwood WS7. . . . . .7 A6
Smethwick B66 . . . . .64 F4

Sycamore Rd
Birmingham,Aston B6 . . . . .67 A8
Birmingham,Bournville
B30. . . . . .103 F7
Birmingham,Erdington B23 . .56 F7
Birmingham,Great Barr B43 .43 E4
Birmingham,Handsworth
B21. . . . . .65 D7
Burntwood WS7. . . . . .6 F7
Cannock WS12. . . . . .2 F4
Coventry CV2. . . . . .96 B2
Kingswinford DY6 . . . . . . .60 E6
Nuneaton CV10 . . . . .72 D6
Oldbury B69. . . . . .64 A4
Smethwick B66 . . . . .65 B3
Tipton DY4. . . . . .51 F7
Walsall,Shelfield WS4 . . . .29 B8
Walsall,The Delves WS5 . . .42 F5
Wednesbury WS10 . . . . . .42 A2
Sycamores The
2 Sutton Coldfield B74 . .31 F2
Bedworth CV12 . . . . .77 E2
Lichfield WS14. . . . . .9 B5
West Hagley DY9. . . . . . . .98 F5
Wolverhampton,Elston Hall
WV11. . . . . .26 B5
Wolverhampton WV11. . . .26 B5
Sycamore B77 . . . . .35 E7
Sycamore Terr B14. . . . . .104 C7
Sycamore Way
1 Birmingham B27. . . . . .88 C5
Huntington WS12. . . . . .1 D8
Sydenham Dr CV31 . . . . .162 B6
Sydenham Ind Est B37. . .162 B6
Sydenham Prim Sch
CV31 . . . . .162 C6
Sydenham Rd
Birmingham B11 . . . . .87 C6
Smethwick B66 . . . . .65 A7
Wolverhampton WV1. . . . .26 B2
Sydnall Cl B97 . . . . .152 F2
Sydnall Fields CV6. . . . . . .95 F4
Sydnall Rd CV6 . . . . .95 F4
Sydney Cl B70. . . . . .53 A7
Sydney Ct **1** CV12. . . . . . .77 F2
Sydney Ho B34 . . . . .69 E6
Sydney Rd
Birmingham B9 . . . . .67 C2
Bromsgrove B61 . . . . 136 E3
Cradley Heath B64 . . . . . .82 C8
Smethwick B67. . . . . .64 F2
Sykesmoor B77 . . . . .36 B7
Sylvan Ave B31. . . . . .102 F3
Sylvan Dr CV3 . . . . .132 F6
Sylvan Gn B62 . . . . .83 D5
Sylvan Gr B90 . . . . .106 B5
Sylvia Ave B31. . . . . .123 B8
Symphony Ct B16. . . . . . . .66 B2
Synkere Cl CV7 . . . . .95 A6
Sytch La WV5. . . . . .49 A5

T

Tabbs Gdns DY10 . . . . . . .117 A6
Table Oak La CV8. . . . . . .130 B1
Tachbrook Cl CV2 . . . . .96 C2
Tachbrook Link CV34. . . .161 E4
Tachbrook Park Dr CV34 .161 E5
Tachbrook Rd CV31. . . . . .161 F4
Tachbrook St CV31. . . . . .162 A6
Tack Farm Rd DY8 . . . . . . .60 D1
Tackford Cl B36 . . . . .58 D1
Tackford Rd CV6. . . . . . . .114 A8
Tackley Cl B90. . . . . .126 B8
Tadmore Cl WV14 . . . . . . .40 D5
Tadworth Cl WV1 . . . . .26 A2
Tainters Hill CV8. . . . . . . .148 A6
Tait Croft B92 . . . . .107 F8
Talaton Cl WV9 . . . . .11 A2
Talbot Ave B74 . . . . .31 B3
Talbot Cl
Birmingham B23 . . . . .56 D8
Walsall WS2 . . . . .28 C6
Talbot Ct CV32. . . . . .157 A1
Talbot Ho
Birmingham B24. . . . . . . .56 F4
6 Wednesbury WS10. . . .41 F2
Talbot Pass **6** DY8 . . . . .81 A5
Talbot Pl WV14 . . . . .40 C6
Talbot Rd
Bromsgrove B60 . . . . 150 E7
Dudley DY2 . . . . .62 B4
Smethwick B66 . . . . .65 A3
Wolverhampton WV2. . . . .39 C6
Talbots La DY5 . . . . .61 F1
Talbot St
Birmingham B18 . . . . .65 F6
Brierley Hill DY5 . . . . .61 D3
Halesowen B63 . . . . .82 C6
Kidderminster DY11 . . . . 116 C4
Stourbridge,Lye DY9 . . . . .81 F5
Stourbridge,Stambermill
DY8. . . . . .81 A5
Talbot B77 . . . . .21 E3
Talbot Way B10. . . . . .87 F7
Talfourd St B9. . . . . .67 D1
Talgarth Covert B38 . . . . .123 E7
Talisman Cl CV8 . . . . .147 F3
Talisman Sq CV8. . . . . . . .147 F4
Talke Rd WS5. . . . . .43 A4
Talladale B32. . . . . .102 B7
Talland Ave
Coventry CV6. . . . . .114 A6
Tamworth B77 . . . . .21 E5
Tallants Cl CV6. . . . . .114 A8
Tallants Rd CV6. . . . . .114 A8
Tallington Rd B33. . . . . . . .89 D7

Tall Trees Cl
Catshill B61 . . . . **136** F8
Sutton Coldfield B74 . . . . . **31** D4
Willenhall WV12 . . . . **27** D6
Tall Trees Dr DY9 . . . . **81** D2
Talton Cl B90 . . . . **127** A5
Tamar Cl WS8 . . . . **6** C2
Tamar Dr
Birmingham B36 . . . . **69** F8
Dudley DY3 . . . . **50** F6
Sutton Coldfield B76 . . . . . **58** B7
Tamar Rd
Perton WV6 . . . . **23** E4
Willenhall WV13 . . . . **27** C2
Tamarisk Cl B29 . . . . **103** B8
Tamar Rd
Bulkington CV12 . . . . **79** B2
Tamworth B77 . . . . **36** A5
Tamar Rise DY8 . . . . **81** A8
Tame Ave
Burntwood WS7 . . . . **7** D6
Wednesbury WS10 . . . . **42** C4
Tamebridge Ind Est B42 . . **55** E4
Tame Bridge Sta B71 . . . . . **42** F2
Tame Cl WS1 . . . . **42** E4
Tame Cres B71 . . . . **53** C6
Tame Ct
Fazeley B78 . . . . **35** B8
Tamworth B79 . . . . **21** A5
Tamedrive B78,B79 . . . . **21** A4
Tame Dr WS3 . . . . **15** A1
Tame Gr WS11 . . . . **4** D8
Tame Rd
Birmingham,Brandhall
B68 . . . . **84** B8
Birmingham,Witton B6 . . . . **56** A1
Tipton DY4 . . . . **52** C5
Tame Rise B68 . . . . **84** B8
Tame Road Ind Est B6 . . . . **56** B1
Tamerton Rd B32 . . . . **84** D1
Tame St WS1 . . . . **42** F6
Tameside Dr
Birmingham,Castle Bromwich
B35 . . . . **58** A1
Birmingham,Erdington B6 . . **56** A3
Tameside Prim Sch WS10 **.42** C2
Tame St
Bilston WV14 . . . . **40** F5
Tamworth B77 . . . . **21** C3
Walsall WS1 . . . . **42** E6
West Bromwich B70 . . . . . . **52** F8
Tame Valley Bsns Pk B77 **.35** E6
Tame Valley Com Sch
B36 . . . . **69** E8
Tame Valley Ind Est B77 **.35** E6
Tame Way LE10 . . . . **75** A8
Tamora Cl CV34 . . . . **161** D3
Tamworth Bsns Ctr B77 **.22** B3
Tamworth Bsns Pk B70 **. . .52** E8
Tamworth Castle Mus★
B79 . . . . **21** B4
Tamworth Castle★ B78 **. . .21** B4
Tamworth Cl WS8 . . . . **6** F2
Tamworth & Lichfield Coll
(Tamworth Campus)
B79 . . . . **21** B6
Tamworth Rd (Amington)
B77 . . . . **21** F5
Tamworth Rd B78 . . . . **35** C2
Tamworth Rd (Dosthill)
B77 . . . . **35** C6
Tamworth Rd
Keresley CV6,CV7 . . . . **94** D5
Lichfield WS14 . . . . **9** E5
Polesworth B78 . . . . **22** E1
Sutton Coldfield B75 . . . . . **33** A2
Tamworth,Mount Pleasant
B77 . . . . **21** C1
Tamworth,Two Gates B77 **.35** D8
Wood End CV9 . . . . **36** C1
Tamworth Sta B79 . . . . **21** C5
Tamworth St WS13 . . . . **9** B8
Tanacetum Dr WS5 . . . . **43** B3
Tancred Cl CV31 . . . . **161** F5
Tandy Ct B14 . . . . **104** F3
Tandy Dr B14 . . . . **104** F3
Tandy's La DY10 . . . . **118** E4
Tanfield Cl WV6 . . . . **24** B3
Tanfield Rd
Birmingham B33 . . . . **68** F3
Dudley DY2 . . . . **62** B7
Tanford Rd B92 . . . . **89** C3
Tanglewood Cl
Birmingham,Castle Bromwich
B34 . . . . **69** C5
Blackwell B60 . . . . **138** A5
Tanglewood Gr DY3 . . . . **39** C2
Tangmere CV6 . . . . **23** E5
Tangmere Dr B35 . . . . **58** A3
Tanhill B77 . . . . **36** B7
Tanhouse Ave B43 . . . . **54** C7
Tanhouse Farm Rd B92 **. . .89** C2
Tanhouse La
Halesowen B63 . . . . **82** C5
Redditch B98 . . . . **154** C6
Tanners Cl B75 . . . . **46** F7
Tanners Ct WS1 . . . . **42** E8
Tanners Ctyd CV34 . . . . **160** D5
Tanners Gr CV6 . . . . **95** D4
Tanners Green La B47,
B94 . . . . **125** B2
Tanners' La CV4,CV7 . . . . . **111** B1
Tanners Cl WS2 . . . . **28** D3
Tannery Cl CV8 . . . . **147** F4
Tannery Ct CV8 . . . . **61** B7
Tansey Green Rd
Brierley Hill DY5,DY6 . . . . . **61** B8

Tansey Green Rd *continued*
Kingswinford DY6 . . . . **50** A1
Tansley Cl B93 . . . . **127** F4
Tansley Gr B44 . . . . **44** F1
Tansley Hill Ave DY2 . . . . . **62** F8
Tansley Hill Rd DY2 . . . . . . **62** E8
Tansley Rd B44 . . . . **55** F8
Tansley View WV2 . . . . **39** D7
Tansy
Sutton Coldfield B74 . . . . . **31** F4
Tamworth B77 . . . . **21** C3
Tantallon Dr B32 . . . . **84** D1
Tantany La B71 . . . . **53** C4
Tantarra St
Walsall,The Chuckery
WS1 . . . . **29** A1
Walsall WS1 . . . . **28** F1
Tanwood Barns DY10 . . . . . **119** B2
Tanwood Cl
Redditch B97 . . . . **158** A6
Solihull B91 . . . . **127** B8
Tanwood Cross DY10 . . . . . **119** B2
Tanwood La DY10 . . . . **119** B2
Tanworth Gr B12 . . . . **86** F6
Tanworth-in-Arden CE Prim
Sch B94 . . . . **142** A2
Tanworth La B90 . . . . **126** C5
Tanyard Cl
Alvechurch B48 . . . . **139** B6
Coventry CV4 . . . . **111** D1
Tanyard La B48 . . . . **139** B6
Tanyard WS13 . . . . **9** C8
Tanyards B27 . . . . **88** D3
Tapcon Way CV2 . . . . **114** F5
Tapestries Ave B70 . . . . **53** A4
Taplow Pl WS11 . . . . **1** F4
Tappinger Gr CV8 . . . . **148** C5
Tapster La B94 . . . . **143** F2
Tapton Cl WS3 . . . . **14** C3
Tara Ct CV2 . . . . **114** B4
Tardebigge CE First Sch
B60 . . . . **152** B7
Tardebigge Ct B97 . . . . **152** C6
Tardebigge Ho B60 . . . . **137** B3
Tarlington Rd CV6 . . . . **112** E6
Tarmac Rd WV14 . . . . **40** B5
Tarn Cl CV12 . . . . **78** A2
Tarquin Cl CV3 . . . . **134** D7
Tarragon Cl CV2 . . . . **96** D1
Tarragon Gdns B31 . . . . . . **102** C2
Tarrant Gr B32 . . . . **84** F5
Tarrant B77 . . . . **35** F8
Tarrant Wlk CV2 . . . . **115** A5
Tarrington Covert 6
B38 . . . . **123** E8
Tarry Hollow Rd DY5 . . . . . **61** A7
Tarry Rd B8 . . . . **67** E5
Tarvin Mews DY5 . . . . **61** D1
Tasker St
Walsall WS1 . . . . **42** D8
West Bromwich B70 . . . . . . **52** E4
Tasman Gr WV6 . . . . **23** E5
Tat Bank Rd B69 . . . . **64** B6
Tatchbrook Ct 5 CV31 . . . **161** F6
Tatnall Gr CV34 . . . . **160** E8
Taunton Ave WV10 . . . . **11** D4
Taunton Cl B31 . . . . **103** C1
Taunton Rd B12 . . . . **87** B4
Taunton Way CV6 . . . . **95** A2
Taverners Cl WV12 . . . . **13** C1
Taverner's Gn B20 . . . . **54** F7
Tavistock Dr WV10 . . . . **21** C7
Tavistock Rd B27 . . . . **106** C8
Tavistock St CV32 . . . . **156** F1
Tavistock Way CV11 . . . . **73** E5
Tavistock Wlk CV2 . . . . **114** C7
Taw Cl B36 . . . . **69** F7
Tay Croft B37 . . . . **70** C4
Tay Gr
Birmingham B38 . . . . **123** F8
Halesowen B62 . . . . **83** E8
Taylor Ave
Royal Leamington Spa
CV32 . . . . **157** B2
Walsall WS3 . . . . **28** D8
Taylor Cl CV8 . . . . **148** B6
Taylor Ct CV34 . . . . **160** D7
Taylor Ho 4 WS2 . . . . **42** C7
Taylor Rd
Birmingham B13 . . . . **104** F5
Dudley DY2 . . . . **62** E2
Wolverhampton WV4 . . . . . **39** F5
Taylors La B69 . . . . **63** E7
Taylor's La
Smethwick B67 . . . . **64** F5
West Bromwich B71 . . . . . . **53** D4
Taylors Orch B43 . . . . **54** D1
Taylor St WV11 . . . . **26** D5
Taylor Way B69 . . . . **63** D6
Taynton Covert 4 B30 **. . 104** C3

Tean Cl
Birmingham B11 . . . . **88** A3
Burntwood WS7 . . . . **7** D6
Teasdale Way DY9 . . . . **81** D4
Teasel Gr WV10 . . . . **12** B7
Teasel Rd WV11 . . . . **26** F5
Teazel Ave B30 . . . . **103** D6
Tebworth Cl WV9 . . . . **10** F2
Tedbury Cres B23 . . . . **56** E6
Tedder Rd WS2 . . . . **27** F2
Teddesley Ct WS11 . . . . **1** E3
Teddesley Gr B33 . . . . **69** C4
Teddesley St WS4 . . . . **28** F3
Teddesley Way WS12 . . . . **1** D6
Teddington Cl 4 B73 . . . . . . **46** A2
Teddington Gr B42 . . . . **55** D3
Ted Pitts La CV5 . . . . **94** B2
Tedstone Rd B32 . . . . **84** E5
Teesdale Ave B34 . . . . **68** F6
Teesdale Cl WV1 . . . . **26** A2
Tees Gr B38 . . . . **123** F8
Teeswater Cl B60 . . . . **150** E6
Teign Bank Cl LE10 . . . . **71** D2
Teign Bank Rd LE10 . . . . **71** D2
Teignmouth Rd B29 . . . . **86** A1
Teign B77 . . . . **36** A5
Telephone Rd CV3 . . . . **114** C2
Telfer Rd CV6 . . . . **113** B7
Telford Ave
Great Wyrley WS6 . . . . **4** F3
Royal Leamington Spa
CV32 . . . . **157** B5
Telford Cl
Burntwood WS7 . . . . **7** C8
Smethwick B67 . . . . **64** D1
Walsall WS2 . . . . **28** A5
West Bromwich B71 . . . . . . **53** A8
Telford Gdns WV3 . . . . **38** D7
Telford Gr WS12 . . . . **2** B8
Telford Inf & Jun Schs
CV32 . . . . **157** C5
Telford Rd
Bedworth CV7 . . . . **96** C8
Tamworth B79 . . . . **20** F8
Walsall WS2 . . . . **28** A5
Telford Way B66 . . . . **64** F8
Teme Ave DY11 . . . . **116** B3
Teme Ct B23 . . . . **56** B3
Teme Gr WV13 . . . . **27** D2
Teme Rd
Halesowen B63 . . . . **82** B5
Stourbridge DY8 . . . . **80** F3
Tempest St
Tamworth B79 . . . . **21** A5
Wolverhampton WV2 . . . . . **163** C2
Templar Ave CV4 . . . . **112** A1
Templar Ct CV11 . . . . **73** C3
Templars' Fields CV4 . . . . . **132** B7
Templars Prim Sch CV4 **.132** A1
Templars The
Oldbury B69 . . . . **63** E5
Warwick CV34 . . . . **160** F5
Temple Ave
Balsall Common CV7 . . . . . **129** F6
Birmingham B28 . . . . **106** A6
Temple Bar WV13 . . . . **27** A2
Temple Ct B98 . . . . **153** F4
Temple Ct B46 . . . . **59** F1
Templefield Gdns 2 B9 **. . .67** C1
Templefield Sq B15 . . . . **86** B7
Templefield St B9 . . . . **67** C1
Temple Gr CV34 . . . . **160** D5
Temple La B93 . . . . **129** A4
Temple Meadow Prim Sch
B64 . . . . **63** A1
Temple Meadows Rd B71 **.53** E6
Templemore Dr B43 . . . . **54** E7
Temple Pas B2 . . . . **164** B2
Temple Rd
Dorridge B93 . . . . **128** A3
Willenhall WV13 . . . . **27** B3
Temple Row B2 . . . . **164** C3
Temple Row W B2 . . . . **164** B3
Temple Sq WV13 . . . . **27** A3
Temple St
Bilston WV14 . . . . **40** E5
Birmingham B2 . . . . **164** B2
Dudley DY3 . . . . **50** D3
West Bromwich B70 . . . . . . **53** C4
Wolverhampton WV2 . . . . . **163** B2
Templeton Cl B93 . . . . **128** A3
Templeton Rd B44 . . . . **44** F2
Temple Way
Coleshill B46 . . . . **59** F1
Oldbury B69 . . . . **52** D2
Temple Wlk WV13 . . . . **27** A2
Tenacre La DY3 . . . . **50** E6
Ten Acres End B30 . . . . **104** B8
Tenacres Est Sch B98 **. . .154** F3
Tenacres La B98 . . . . **154** F3
Ten Ashes La B45 . . . . **122** C4
Tenbury Cl
Aldridge WS9 . . . . **30** C8
Redditch B98 . . . . **154** C6
Willenhall WS2 . . . . **27** D3
Tenbury Ct WV4 . . . . **38** D5
Tenbury Gdns WV4 . . . . **38** E5
Tenbury Ho 2 B63 . . . . **83** A3
Tenbury Rd B14 . . . . **104** E6
Tenbury Cl CV12 . . . . **78** A3
Tenby Ct CV32 . . . . **161** E8
Tenby Rd B13 . . . . **105** C6
Tenby St N B1 . . . . **66** B4
Tenby St B1 . . . . **66** B4
Tenby Twr 2 B31 . . . . **103** A1
Teneriffe Rd CV6 . . . . **95** F1
Tenlands Rd B63 . . . . **82** F3
Tenlons Rd CV10 . . . . **72** F2

Tennal Dr B32 . . . . **84** F6
Tennal Gr B32 . . . . **84** F6
Tennal La B32 . . . . **84** F6
Tennal Rd B32 . . . . **84** F6
Tennant St
Birmingham B15 . . . . **66** B1
Nuneaton CV11 . . . . **73** E3
Tennessee B13 . . . . **86** E2
Tennis Ct B30 . . . . **103** D4
Tennis Ct The B15 . . . . **86** A5
Tennscore Ave WS6 . . . . **4** E3
Tennyson Ave
Sutton Coldfield B74 . . . . . **31** F6
Tamworth B79 . . . . **21** A6
Warwick CV34 . . . . **160** C4
Tennyson Cl CV8 . . . . **148** C4
Tennyson Ho
3 Oldbury B69 . . . . **64** C4
Birmingham B31 . . . . **123** A8
Tennyson Rd
Birmingham B10 . . . . **87** E7
Coventry CV2 . . . . **114** C3
Dudley DY3 . . . . **50** A4
Hinckley LE10 . . . . **71** C1
Redditch B97 . . . . **158** C8
Walsall WS3 . . . . **28** E8
Willenhall WV12 . . . . **27** E8
Wolverhampton WV10 . . . . **12** A1
Tennyson St DY5 . . . . **61** D7
Tennyson Way DY10 . . . . . . **117** C6
Ten Shilling Dr CV4 . . . . . . **131** E6
Tenter Ct B63 . . . . **83** B3
Tenter Dr B63 . . . . **83** C4
Tenterfields B63 . . . . **83** B4
Tenterfields Prim Sch
B63 . . . . **83** C4
Terminal Rd B26 . . . . **89** F3
Tern Cl WV4 . . . . **39** D3
Tern Gr B38 . . . . **103** E1
Terrace Rd
Birmingham B15 . . . . **85** F3
Birmingham,Lozells B19 . . **66** B7
Terrace St
Brierley Hill DY5 . . . . **61** E5
Rowley Regis B65 . . . . **63** B1
Wednesbury WS10 . . . . **42** A3
Terrace The
Cradley Heath B64 . . . . **82** E8
Wolverhampton WV3 . . . . . **24** C1
Terret Cl WS1 . . . . **28** F2
Terry Ave CV32 . . . . **156** C1
Terry Dr B76 . . . . **46** F2
Terry Rd CV1 . . . . **113** F1
Terrys Cl B98 . . . . **153** F5
Terrys La B24 . . . . **57** C3
Terry St DY2 . . . . **51** E1
Tessall La B31 . . . . **102** D8
Tetbury Gr B31 . . . . **102** D3
Tetley Ave WS4 . . . . **29** B4
Tetley Rd B11 . . . . **87** E3
Tetnall St DY2 . . . . **62** D8
Tettenhall Arc WV6 . . . . **24** D5
Tettenhall Coll WV6 . . . . **24** D4
Tettenhall Gate 9 WV3 **. . .25** A2
Tettenhall Rd WV1,WV3,
WV6 . . . . **24** F4
Tettenhall Wood Sch
WV6 . . . . **24** B3
Teviot Gdns
Brierley Hill DY5 . . . . **61** B6
Wolverhampton WV8 . . . . . **10** A5
Teviot Gr B38 . . . . **123** F8
Teviot Twr B19 . . . . **66** C5
Tewe Pl WS13 . . . . **9** A6
Tewkesbury Dr
Bedworth CV12 . . . . **78** C3
Dudley DY2 . . . . **62** D3
Tewkesbury Rd
Birmingham B20 . . . . **55** E2
Walsall WS3 . . . . **13** E2
Tew Park Rd B21 . . . . **65** E7
Thackeray Cl CV10 . . . . **72** A4
Thackeray Dr B79 . . . . **21** B7
Thackeray Rd B30 . . . . **103** D5
Thackhall St CV2 . . . . **113** F4
Thame Ct B47 . . . . **124** E2
Thames Cl
Brierley Hill DY5 . . . . **61** B7
Bulkington CV12 . . . . **79** A3
Thames Ct B73 . . . . **46** B5
Thames Ho DY3 . . . . **50** D3
Thames Rd WS3 . . . . **14** E1
Thames Twr B7 . . . . **67** B5
Thamley Rd CV6 . . . . **113** A4
Thane Cl B80 . . . . **159** F4
Thanet Cl CV34 . . . . **160** C7
Thanet Gr B42 . . . . **55** C4
Thatchers Ct WV5 . . . . **37** C1
Thatchers The B62 . . . . **83** E8
Thatcher Way CV34 . . . . . . **160** B7
Thaxted Rd B33 . . . . **69** E3
Theatre App B5 . . . . **164** C1
Theatre Ct CV34 . . . . **160** D6
Theatre St CV34 . . . . **160** D7
Thebes Cl CV5 . . . . **111** B8
Theddingworth Cl CV3 **. .134** E8
Thelbridge Rd B31 . . . . **122** E6
Thelma Rd DY4 . . . . **51** E5
Thelma St WS1 . . . . **42** D7
Thelsford Way B92 . . . . **107** D8
Theodore Cl
4 Birmingham B17 . . . . **85** D4
Oldbury B69 . . . . **52** E1
Theresa Rd B11 . . . . **87** A7
Thetford Cl DY4 . . . . **51** D5
Thetford Gdns WV11 . . . . **26** E5
Thetford Rd B42 . . . . **55** B7
Thetford Way WS5 . . . . **43** C3

Thicket Cl WS2 . . . . **42** B8
Thicknall Dr DY9 . . . . **81** C2
Thicknall La DY9 . . . . **99** B3
Thicknall Rise DY9 . . . . **99** B4
Thickthorn Cl CV8 . . . . **148** B2
Thickthorn Mews CV8 **. . .148** B2
Thickthorn Orchs CV8 **. . .148** B2
Thimble Dr B76 . . . . **46** F1
Thimble End Rd B76 . . . . **47** A2
Thimble Mill La B6,B7 . . . . . **67** B7
Thimblemill Rd B67 . . . . **64** E3
Thimbler Rd CV4 . . . . **132** C7
Thinktank Mus & IMAX
Theatre★ B4 . . . . **66** F3
Third Ave
Birmingham,Bordesley Green
B9 . . . . **67** F2
Birmingham,Selly Oak B29 **.86** C3
Birmingham,Witton B6 . . . . **55** F3
Brownhills WS8 . . . . **7** A1
Kingswinford DY6 . . . . **60** F8
Wolverhampton WV10 . . . . **25** F7
Third Exhibition Ave B40 **.90** D4
Third Rd B61 . . . . **120** F4
Thirlestane Cl CV8 . . . . **148** C6
Thirlmere Ave CV11 . . . . **73** F6
Thirlmere Cl
Cannock WS11 . . . . **1** E1
Coventry CV4 . . . . **111** E3
Wolverhampton WV6 . . . . . **24** D8
Thirlmere Dr
Birmingham B13 . . . . **105** D8
Essington WV11 . . . . **13** A2
Thirlmere Gr WV6 . . . . **23** F4
Thirlmere Ho 3 B15 . . . . . . **85** D3
Thirlmere Rd
Bedworth CV12 . . . . **78** A2
Hinckley LE10 . . . . **75** A7
Wolverhampton WV6 . . . . . **24** D8
Thirlmere Wlk DY5 . . . . **81** B7
Thirsk Croft B36 . . . . **68** C8
Thirsk Rd CV3 . . . . **133** C5
Thirsk Way B61 . . . . **121** B1
Thirston Cl WV11 . . . . **27** A5
Thistle Cl DY3 . . . . **50** F6
Thistle Croft WV11 . . . . **26** D5
Thistledown Ave WS7 . . . . . . **7** A6
Thistledown Dr
3 Cannock WS12 . . . . **2** D1
Featherstone WV10 . . . . . . **12** A7
Thistledown Rd B34 . . . . **69** C7
Thistledown Wlk DY3 . . . . . . **39** C1
Thistle Gn B38 . . . . **123** E7
Thistlegreen Rd B65 . . . . **62** F5
Thistlegreen Rd DY2 . . . . . . **62** E4
Thistle Ho B36 . . . . **68** D8
Thistle La B32 . . . . **102** B7
Thistlewood Gr B93 . . . . . . **145** B6
Thistley Field E CV6 . . . . . **113** A7
Thistley Field N CV6 . . . . . **113** A7
Thistley Field S CV6 . . . . . **112** F6
Thistley Field W CV6 . . . . **112** F7
Thistley Nook WS13 . . . . **3** A1
Thomas Barnes Prim Sch
B78 . . . . **34** E6
Thomas Benson Pl 8 B12 **.86** F7
Thomas Cres 2 B66 . . . . . . **65** C5
Thomas Greenway WS13 . . . **3** A2
Thomas Guy Rd B70 . . . . **52** F6
Thomas Hardy Ct B79 . . . . . **21** A7
Thomas Ho WS3 . . . . **14** D3
Thomas King Ho 6 CV1 **.113** E4
Thomas Landsdail St
CV3 . . . . **133** D8
Thomas Lane St CV6 . . . . **96** A1
Thomas Mason Cl WV11 **. . .26** D7
Thomas Naul Croft CV4 **.111** F3
Thomas Sharp St CV4 **. . .132** A7
Thomas St
Bedworth CV12 . . . . **78** A2
Birmingham B6 . . . . **66** F6
Royal Leamington Spa
CV32 . . . . **157** A1
Smethwick B66 . . . . **65** B5
Tamworth B77 . . . . **21** D4
Walsall WS2 . . . . **28** D3
West Bromwich B70 . . . . . . **53** D2
Wolverhampton WV2 . . . . . **163** B1
Thomas Wlk B35 . . . . **58** B3
Thompson Ave
Tamworth B77 . . . . **21** C3
Wolverhampton WV2 . . . . . **39** E6
Thompson Cl
Dudley DY2 . . . . **62** B2
Willenhall WV13 . . . . **27** A3
Thompson Dr B24 . . . . **67** F8
Thompson Gdns B67 . . . . . . **64** F4
Thompson Ho WV10 . . . . **52** C8
Thompson Rd
Oldbury B68 . . . . **64** B5
Smethwick B67 . . . . **64** F4
Thompson's La CV7 . . . . **94** E6
Thompson's Rd CV7 . . . . **94** F6
Thompson St
Bilston WV14 . . . . **40** D5
Willenhall WV13 . . . . **27** A3
Thomson Ave B38 . . . . **103** D1
Thor Cl WS11 . . . . **2** A5
Thoresby Croft DY1 . . . . **50** F3
Thornberry Dr DY1 . . . . **61** E8
Thornberry Wlk B7 . . . . **67** C6
Thornbridge Ave B42 . . . . . . **55** D7
Thornbridge Gr WS9 . . . . **15** F3

Thornbrook Ct [1] WS4 ....28 F3
Thornbury Ct WV6 ....24 A3
Thornbury Ho CV8 ....148 A3
Thornbury La B98 ....154 C7
Thornbury Rd B20 ....55 D2
Thornby Ave
 Kenilworth CV8 ....148 B3
 Solihull B91 ....107 B5
 Tamworth B77 ....35 E8
Thornby Rd B23 ....56 C8
Thorncliffe Cl B97 ....158 A6
Thorncliffe Rd B44 ....44 E2
Thorn Cl WS10 ....41 F4
Thorncroft Way WS5 ....43 B4
Thorne Ave WV10 ....25 E7
Thorne Pl B65 ....63 C2
Thorne Rd WV13 ....27 A4
Thornes Croft WS9 ....16 E4
Thorne St WV2 ....40 A7
Thorneycroft La WV10 ....26 A6
Thorneycroft Pl WV14 ....41 B3
Thorneycroft Rd WV14 ....41 B4
Thorney Rd
 Coventry CV2 ....114 B6
 Sutton Coldfield B74 ....30 F1
Thornfield Cres WS7 ....7 A8
Thornfield Croft DY3 ....50 E7
Thornfield Rd B27 ....88 D2
Thornfield Way WV10 ....75 E8
Thorngrove Ave B91 ....127 C8
Thornham Way B14 ....104 D1
Thornhill Dr CV11 ....79 C8
Thornhill Gr B21 ....65 F8
Thornhill Pk B74 ....45 A8
Thornhill Rd
 Birmingham,Handsworth
 B21 ....65 F8
 Birmingham,Sparkhill B11 ....87 D3
 Brierley Hill DY5 ....81 E8
 Cannock WS12 ....1 F7
 Coventry CV1 ....113 D5
 Dudley DY1 ....51 C4
 Halesowen B63 ....82 E3
 Redditch B98 ....154 E6
 Solihull B91 ....107 C7
 Sutton Coldfield B74 ....31 B1
Thornhurst Ave B32 ....84 E7
Thornleigh DY3 ....50 D5
Thornleigh Trad Est DY2 ....62 A7
Thornley Cl
 Birmingham B13 ....87 A1
 Radford Semele CV31 ....162 F5
 Wolverhampton WV11 ....12 F1
Thornley Croft WS6 ....4 D1
Thornley Gr B76 ....58 C6
Thornley Rd WV11 ....12 F1
Thornley St WV1 ....163 C3
Thorn Rd B30 ....103 E7
Thorns Ave DY5 ....61 E1
Thorns Com Coll DY5 ....81 E8
Thorns Com Inf Sch CV8 ....148 B4
Thornsett Gr B90 ....106 B6
Thorns Prim Sch DY5 ....81 E7
Thorns Rd DY5 ....81 E7
Thorn Stile Cl CV32 ....157 E6
Thornthwaite Cl B45 ....102 B2
Thornton Cl
 Coventry CV5 ....111 C4
 Oldbury B69 ....52 C2
 Warwick CV34 ....155 F1
Thornton Dr DY5 ....61 E1
Thornton Ho B19 ....66 E5
Thornton Jun Sch B8 ....68 B5
Thornton Rd
 Birmingham B8 ....68 B5
 Solihull B90 ....126 F6
 Wolverhampton WV1 ....25 F4
Thorntons Way CV10 ....72 A3
Thornton Way B77 ....35 C8
Thornwood Cl B68 ....64 C5
Thornycroft Rd LE10 ....75 E8
Thornyfield Cl B90 ....106 D3
Thornyfield Rd B90 ....106 C3
Thornyhurst La WS14 ....17 A6
Thorpe Ave WS7 ....6 D8
Thorpe Cl
 Burntwood WS7 ....6 D8
 Sutton Coldfield B75 ....46 C7
Thorpe Ct B91 ....106 F6
Thorpe Rd B12 ....87 A5
Thorpe St WS7 ....6 D8
Thorp St B5 ....164 B1
Threadneedle St CV1 ....113 D6
Three Acres La B90 ....125 F6
Three Corner Cl B45 ....125 F6
Three Cornered Cl CV32 ....157 E6
Three Crowns Specl Sch
 WS5 ....43 F8
Three Oaks Rd B47 ....125 B4
Three Pots Rd LE10 ....75 E4
Three Shires Oak Rd B67 ....64 F2
Three Spires Ave CV6 ....113 A6
Three Spires Ind Est CV6 ....96 A5
Three Spires Jct CV6 ....95 E1
Three Spires Sch CV6 ....112 D6
Three Spires Sh Ctr WS13 ....9 B7
Three Tuns La WV10 ....11 C2
Three Tuns Par WV10 ....11 C2
Threshers Dr WV12 ....27 D6
Threshers Way WV12 ....27 D6
Throckmorton Rd B98 ....159 A8
Throne Cl B65 ....63 D5
Throne Cres B65 ....63 D4
Throne Rd B65 ....63 D5
Throstles Cl B43 ....54 E7

Thruppence Cl CV4 ....131 E6
Thrushel Wlk WV11 ....26 C5
Thrush Rd B68 ....63 F2
Thruxton Cl
 Birmingham B14 ....104 F3
 Redditch B98 ....154 E3
Thunderbolt Way DY4 ....51 D6
Thurcroft Cl B8 ....67 F4
Thuree Rd B67 ....64 E2
Thurlby Ct WV1 ....25 A3
Thurleigh Cl DY9 ....81 C2
Thurlestone Rd
 Birmingham B31 ....122 E7
 Coventry CV6 ....112 F8
Thurloe Cres B45 ....101 E1
Thurlston Ave B92 ....88 F4
Thurlstone Dr WV4 ....38 F4
Thurlstone Rd WS3 ....14 B3
Thurne B77 ....37 F8
Thursfield Rd
 Royal Leamington Spa
 CV32 ....157 B3
 Tipton DY4 ....52 A6
 West Bromwich B71 ....53 E7
Thurso B77 ....21 E5
Thurston Ave B69 ....63 F6
Thynne St B70 ....53 E2
Tibbats Cl B32 ....84 A1
Tibberton Cl
 Halesowen B63 ....83 C4
 Solihull B91 ....127 A8
 Wolverhampton WV3 ....38 D7
Tibberton Ct B60 ....150 E7
Tibbets La B17 ....85 B4
Tibbington Rd DY4 ....51 E7
Tibbington Terr DY4 ....51 F7
Tibbits Ct [8] CV34 ....160 E6
Tibbits Ho [1] WS2 ....28 D3
Tibbletone B90 ....126 A5
Tiber Cl CV5 ....111 F4
Tiberius Cl B46 ....59 F1
Tibland Rd B27 ....88 D2
Ticknall Cl B97 ....153 A4
Tidbury Cl B97 ....153 B2
Tidbury Green Sch B90 ....125 E4
Tiddington Cl B36 ....58 B1
Tideswell Cl CV3 ....115 A1
Tideswell Rd B42 ....55 C7
Tidmarsh Cl CV7 ....130 A6
Tidmarsh Rd CV35 ....156 A7
Tidworth Croft B14 ....105 A3
Tierney Dr DY4 ....52 C6
Tiffany La WV9 ....10 F2
Tiffield Rd B25 ....88 C5
Tigley Ave B32 ....84 D1
Tilbury Cl WV3 ....38 A8
Tilbury Gr B31 ....86 D1
Tildasley St B70 ....53 B4
Tildesley Dr WV12 ....27 B5
Tile Cross Rd B33 ....69 E2
Tile Cross Trad Est B33 ....69 E1
Tiled House La DY5 ....61 B6
Tile Gr B37 ....70 A5
Tile Hill La
 Coventry,Allesley CV4,
 CV5 ....112 D2
 Coventry,Tile Hill CV4 ....112 B1
Tile Hill Sta CV4 ....131 C8
Tile Hill Wood Sch &
 Language Coll CV4 ....111 D2
Tilehouse Green La B93 ....127 F6
Tilehouse La B90 ....125 C6
Tilehouse B97 ....153 D2
Tilehurst Dr CV4 ....111 D1
Tilesford Cl B90 ....127 A6
Tilewood Ave CV5 ....111 F4
Tilia Rd B77 ....22 B5
Tiller Gr B75 ....32 D4
Tilley St WS10 ....41 E6
Tillington Cl B98 ....154 E3
Tillyard Croft B29 ....85 C1
Tilshead Cl B14 ....104 E3
Tilsley Gr B23 ....56 B5
Tilston Dr DY5 ....61 D1
Tilton Rd
 Birmingham B9 ....67 C1
 Hinckley LE10 ....75 E6
Timberdine Cl B63 ....82 D6
Timberhonger La B61 ....136 B2
Timberlake La B90 ....127 B6
Timberley Croft B34 ....69 C6
Timberley La B34 ....69 C6
Timberley Prim Sch B34 ....69 B6
Timber Mill Ct [4] B17 ....85 B6
Timbers Way
 Birmingham B11 ....87 A6
 Sutton Coldfield B24 ....57 F4
Timbertree Cres B64 ....82 E7
Timbertree Prim Sch B64 ....82 E7
Timbertree Rd B64 ....82 F7
Times Square Ave DY5 ....61 F7
Timmins Cl B91 ....107 E6
Timmis Cl WV14 ....40 B3
Timmis Rd DY9 ....81 C6
Timon View CV34 ....161 E3
Timothy Gr CV4 ....112 B1
Timothy Rd B69 ....63 D7
Tinacre Hill WV6 ....23 E2
Tinchbourne St [1] DY1 ....51 C1
Tindal St B12 ....86 F5
Tink-A-Tank CV34 ....160 E6
Tinkers Farm Gr B31 ....102 E3
Tinkers Farm Rd B31 ....102 E3
Tinkers Green Rd B77 ....35 F6
Tinkers La
 Earlswood B94 ....142 E4
 Lapworth B94 ....143 E1

Tinmeadow Cres B45 ....122 C7
Tinsley St DY4 ....52 E5
Tintagel Cl
 Coventry CV3 ....134 D5
 Perton WV6 ....23 F3
Tintagel Dr DY1 ....50 E2
Tintagel Gr CV8 ....148 B4
Tintagel Way
 Nuneaton CV11 ....74 A5
 Walsall WS9 ....29 E7
Tintern Cl
 Bromsgrove B61 ....136 E1
 Sutton Coldfield B74 ....45 A7
Tintern Cres WS3 ....13 F2
Tintern Ct WV6 ....23 E4
Tintern Ho B32 ....84 E5
Tintern Rd B20 ....55 E3
Tintern Villas [4] B12 ....87 B5
Tintern Way
 Bedworth CV12 ....78 C3
 Walsall WS3 ....13 F2
Tipperary Cl B36 ....68 E8
Tipperary Wlk [2] B69 ....63 F7
Tipper Trad Est DY9 ....82 A5
Tippett Cl CV11 ....79 A7
Tipping's Hill B97 ....158 C5
Tippity Gn B65 ....63 B4
Tipps Stone Cl DY4 ....52 A4
Tipton Green Jun Sch
 DY4 ....51 F4
Tipton Rd
 Dudley,Tipton Green DY1 ....51 E3
 Dudley,Woodsetton DY3 ....50 E7
 Oldbury B69 ....52 C2
 Tipton Sta DY4 ....51 E6
 Tipton DY3 ....50 E7
Tirley Rd B33 ....69 A4
Tisdale Rise CV8 ....148 B6
Titan Bsns Ctr CV34 ....161 E4
Titania Cl B45 ....102 A3
Titan Way WS13 ....9 F8
Titchfield Cl WV10 ....11 E4
Titford Cl B69 ....63 A4
Titford La B69 ....63 E4
Titford Rd B69 ....63 F4
Tithe Barn La B94 ....142 C6
Tithe Croft WV10 ....25 F3
Tithe Rd WV11 ....26 D6
Titterstone Rd B31 ....123 A8
Tiverton Cl DY6 ....61 A3
Tiverton Dr
 Nuneaton CV11 ....73 F5
 West Bromwich B71 ....53 C6
Tiverton Gr
 Coventry CV2 ....114 D5
 Smethwick B67 ....64 F6
Tiverton Jun & Inf Sch
 B29 ....85 F2
Tiverton Rd
 Birmingham B29 ....85 F2
 Coventry CV2 ....114 D5
 Smethwick B67 ....65 B5
Tiverton Sch CV6 ....112 D5
Tiveycourt Rd CV6 ....96 A3
Tividale Com Arts Coll
 B69 ....52 B2
Tividale Com Prim Sch
 B69 ....52 B2
Tividale Rd B69 ....52 A2
Tividale St DY4 ....52 A2
Tivoli The B26 ....88 D6
Tixall Rd B28 ....105 E5
Tobruk Wlk
 Brierley Hill CV7 ....61 D3
 Willenhall WV13 ....40 E8
Tocil Croft CV4 ....132 D4
Toledo Cl CV5 ....112 C1
Toler Rd CV11 ....73 B5
Tollard Cl CV2 ....114 F5
Toll End Rd DY4 ....52 C7
Tolley Rd DY11 ....116 B1
Tollgate Cl B31 ....122 F8
Tollgate Dr B20 ....66 B7
Tollgate Prec B67 ....64 F6
Toll House Rd B45 ....122 E7
Tollhouse Rd B60 ....150 E6
Tollhouse Way B66 ....64 F6
Tolman Dr B77 ....21 D3
Tolson Ave B78 ....35 B8
Tolson Cl B77 ....35 D5
Tolworth Gdns WV2 ....39 E7
Tolworth Hall Rd B24 ....57 B3
Tom Ellis Ct CV7 ....96 A8
Tomey Rd B11 ....87 D5
Tom Henderson Cl CV3 ....134 F7
Tom Hill B94 ....142 B3
Tomkinson Dr DY11 ....116 B4
Tomkinson Rd CV10 ....72 F4
Tomlan Rd B31 ....123 C7
Tomlinson Rd B36 ....58 D1
Tompstone Rd B71 ....53 F8
Tomson Ave CV6 ....113 A4
Toms Town La B80 ....159 E3
Tom Ward Cl CV3 ....134 E7
Tom Williams Way B77 ....35 C8
Tonadine Cl WV11 ....13 A1
Tonbridge Rd
 Birmingham B24 ....57 A1
 Coventry CV3 ....134 A6
Tong Ct [9] WV3 ....25 C4
Tong St WS1 ....29 C3
Tongue Ave B78 ....35 A8
Topcliffe Prim Sch B35 ....58 A3
Top Croft Rd B23 ....56 F7
Topfield Ho B14 ....104 E1
Top Field Wlk B14 ....104 D2
Topland Gr B31 ....102 C2
Topp's Dr CV12 ....77 E1

Topp's Heath CV12 ....77 E1
Top Rd
 Barnacle CV7,CV12 ....97 B7
 Upper Catshill B61 ....121 A4
Topsham Croft B14 ....104 D5
Topsham Rd B67 ....64 E6
Torbay Rd CV5 ....112 C4
Torbay B77 ....21 E6
Torcastle Cl CV6 ....113 F7
Torc Ave B77 ....21 E4
Torc High Sch B77 ....21 F1
Torcross Ave CV2 ....114 C6
Torfield WV8 ....10 E2
Toronto Gdns B32 ....84 E6
Torpoint Cl CV2 ....114 C7
Torre Ave B31 ....102 E2
Torres Cl CV34 ....160 B4
Torrey Gr B8 ....68 C4
Torridge Dr WV11 ....26 C5
Torridge B77 ....36 A5
Torridon Croft B13 ....86 D3
Torridon Rd WV11 ....13 B1
Torridon Way CV8 ....71 B1
Torrington Ave CV4 ....131 E8
Torside B77 ....37 E7
Tor St DY9 ....153 D2
Torside B77 ....36 B7
Torvale Rd WV6 ....24 A2
Tor Way WS3 ....14 F3
Torwood Cl CV4 ....131 F6
Totnes Cl CV2 ....114 C7
Totnes Gr [2] B29 ....85 F2
Totnes Rd B67 ....64 F6
Tottenham Cres B44 ....45 B2
Touchstone Rd CV34 ....161 F2
Touchwood Hall Cl B91 ....107 C4
Touchwood Sh Ctr [1]
 B91 ....107 C3
Towbury Cl B98 ....158 F5
Towcester Croft B36 ....68 D8
Tower Cl B67 ....70 B4
Tower Dr B61 ....137 A6
Tower Hill B42 ....55 A6
Tower Rd
 Bedworth CV12 ....78 B2
 Birmingham,Aston B6 ....67 A7
 Birmingham,Aston New Town
 B6 ....66 F7
 Birmingham B23 ....56 E4
 Oldbury B69 ....63 C7
 Sutton Coldfield B75 ....32 B3
Towers Cl
 Kenilworth CV8 ....147 F2
 Kidderminster DY10 ....117 B5
Tower St
 Royal Leamington Spa
 CV31 ....162 A7
 Birmingham B19 ....164 B5
 Coventry CV1 ....165 B3
 Dudley DY1 ....51 C1
 Sedgley DY3 ....39 D1
 Walsall WS1 ....28 E2
 Wolverhampton WV1 ....163 C3
Tower View Cres CV10 ....72 B3
Tower View Rd WS6 ....13 F8
Townend St WS2 ....28 E2
Townesend Cl CV34 ....155 F1
Town Feilds Cl CV5 ....112 B7
Townfields WS13 ....9 A7
Townfold WS3 ....15 A4
Townley Gdns B6 ....55 E1
Townsend Ave
 Bromsgrove B61 ....137 B4
 Sedgley DY3 ....50 D8
Townsend Croft CV3 ....133 C7
Townsend Dr
 Nuneaton CV11 ....73 F3
 Sutton Coldfield B76 ....57 F7
Townsend Ho B79 ....21 A4
Townsend Pl DY6 ....60 D6
Townsend Rd CV3 ....133 C8
Townsends Cl CV11 ....75 A1
Townsend Way [5] B1 ....66 B3
Townshend Gr B37 ....69 F4
Townson Rd WV11 ....27 A8
Townwell Fold WV1 ....163 B3
Town Wharf Bsns Pk
 WS2 ....28 D2
Towpath Cl
 Bedworth CV6 ....96 B6
 Birmingham B9 ....67 B2
Towyn Rd B13 ....87 D2
Toys La B63 ....82 C5
Tozer St DY4 ....51 F7
Traceys Mdw B45 ....122 A7
Tractor Spares Ind Est
 WV13 ....26 D2
Trafalgar Ct WS12 ....2 E4
Trafalgar Ct B69 ....52 B1
Trafalgar Gr B25 ....88 A6
Trafalgar Ho
 Coventry CV1 ....113 B2
 Birmingham B11 ....87 B8
 Cannock WS12 ....2 E4
Trafalgar Rd
 Birmingham,Erdington
 B24 ....56 F3
 Birmingham,Handsworth
 B21 ....65 E8
 Birmingham,Moseley B13 ....86 F4
 Oldbury B69 ....52 B1
 Smethwick B66 ....65 A5
Trafford Dr CV10 ....72 C6
Trafford Lodge [4] CV31 ....162 B7
Trafford Pk The B98 ....153 F3
Trafford Rd LE10 ....71 F2

Trajan Hill B46 ....59 F1
Tram St DY10 ....116 E5
Tramway Cl
 [1] Bilston WV14 ....41 A7
 Darlaston WS10 ....41 A7
Tram Way B66 ....64 C7
Tranter Ave B48 ....139 A5
Tranter Cres WS11 ....2 B3
Tranter Rd B8 ....68 A5
Tranwell Cl WV9 ....10 F2
Traquain Dr DY1 ....51 A3
Travellers Cl WS7 ....4 A3
Travellers Way B37 ....70 D3
Treaford La B8 ....68 C4
Treasure Cl B77 ....21 E4
Treddles La B70 ....53 D3
Tredington Cl
 [1] Birmingham B29 ....103 A3
 Redditch B98 ....159 B7
Tredington Rd CV5 ....111 F4
Tree Acre Gr B63 ....82 C2
Treedale Cl CV4 ....131 D8
Treeford Cl B91 ....106 E5
Trees Rd WS1 ....42 F6
Tree Tops Ct B33 ....69 A2
Treetops Dr WV12 ....27 E4
Trefoil Cl B29 ....103 A4
Trefoil B77 ....22 B5
Treford St B8 ....67 A5
Treforest Rd CV3 ....134 C8
Tregarron Rd B63 ....82 C5
Tregea Rise B43 ....54 C7
Tregony Rise WS14 ....9 D6
Tregorrick Rd CV7 ....96 A8
Tregullan Rd CV7 ....96 A8
Trehern Cl B93 ....128 A5
Treherne Rd CV6 ....113 B8
Trehernes Dr DY9 ....81 B1
Trehurst Ave B42 ....55 C7
Trejon Rd B64 ....82 F7
Trelawney Rd CV7 ....96 A7
Tremaine Gdns WV10 ....25 E4
Tremont Ho WV10 ....25 E3
Tremont St WV10 ....25 E3
Trenance Cl WS14 ....9 D7
Trenance Rd CV7 ....96 A8
Trenchard Cl B75 ....46 F5
Treneere Rd CV7 ....96 A8
Trensale Ave CV6 ....112 F4
Trent Cl
 Burntwood WS7 ....7 D6
 Perton WV6 ....23 E4
 Stourbridge DY8 ....81 A4
Trent Cres B47 ....124 E2
Trent Ct B73 ....46 B5
Trent Dr B36 ....69 F8
Trentham Ave WV12 ....27 B5
Trentham Cl
 Cannock WS11 ....2 B1
 Nuneaton CV11 ....78 F8
Trentham Gdns CV8 ....148 C5
Trentham Gr B26 ....88 E5
Trentham Rd CV1 ....113 F4
Trentham Rise WV2 ....39 F7
Trent Ho
 Cannock WS12 ....2 E4
 Dudley DY3 ....50 E3
Trent Pl WS3 ....28 D8
Trent Rd
 Bulkington CV12 ....79 A2
 Cannock WS11 ....1 E5
 Hinckley LE10 ....75 A8
 Nuneaton CV11 ....73 D5
 Walsall WS3 ....15 A1
Trent St B5 ....164 D3
Trent Twr [3] B7 ....67 A4
Trent Valley Rd WS13,WS14 ....9 D8
Trenville Ave B11 ....87 B5
Tresco Cl B45 ....101 E1
Trescott Jun & Inf Sch
 B31 ....102 D3
Trescott Rd
 Birmingham B31 ....102 D4
 Redditch B98 ....153 F3
Tresham Rd
 [2] Kingswinford DY6 ....60 D8
 Birmingham B44 ....44 F1
Tresillian Rd CV7 ....96 B8
Tressel Croft CV34 ....161 E2
Trevanie Ave B32 ....84 C6
Trevelyan Cres B75 ....33 C1
Trevelyan Ho [1] B37 ....70 C1
Treville Cl B98 ....154 E3
Treviscoe Cl CV7 ....96 A7
Trevithick Cl WS7 ....7 C8
Trevor Ave WS6 ....5 A3
Trevor Cl CV4 ....131 D8
Trevorne Cl B12 ....86 F6
Trevor Rd
 Hinckley LE10 ....71 F1
 Walsall WS3 ....14 F5
Trevor St W B7 ....67 C6
Trevor St B7 ....67 C6
Trevose Ave B77 ....96 B8
Trevose Cl WS3 ....13 F3
Trevose Retreat B12 ....86 F5
Trewint Cl CV7 ....96 A8
Trewman Cl B76 ....57 F8
Treyamon Rd WS5 ....43 D7
Treynham Cl WV1 ....26 C1
Triangle The
 Birmingham B18 ....65 F5
 Coventry CV5 ....112 B4
Trianon Rd B60 ....137 C1
Tribune Ho [7] LE10 ....71 D1
Trickley Dr [2] B75 ....47 A6
Trident Bsns Pk CV11 ....73 D3
Trident Bvd B35 ....58 B2

Trident Cl
Sutton Coldfield,Walmley
B76......................57 F7
Sutton Coldfield,Wylde Green
B23......................57 A7
Trident Ct
Birmingham,Coleshill Heath
B37......................90 E8
Birmingham,Handsworth Wood
B20......................55 A3
Trident Ctr The DY1.....51 C1
Trident Dr
Oldbury B68.............64 B5
Wednesbury WS10 ......41 D3
Trident Ho 🔼 B15......66 C1
Trident Rd B26..........90 C4
Trident Ret Pk B9.......67 A2
Trigo Croft B36..........68 E8
Trimpley Cl B93.........127 E3
Trimpley Dr
Coventry CV6............113 C6
Kidderminster DY11 ....116 A7
Trimpley Gdns WV4 ....38 E3
Trimpley Rd B32.........84 B1
Trinculo Gr CV34.........161 F2
Trinder Rd B67...........64 D2
Trindle Rd DY2 ....51 D1
Tring Ct WV6.............24 F4
Trinity CE Prim Sch WV10 25 F4
Trinity Churchyard CV1 .165 B3
Trinity Cl
🔳 Birmingham B19.......66 D8
Cannock WS11...........4 E8
Shenstone WS14 ....17 F6
Solihull B92.............89 B1
Stourbridge DY8 ....60 D2
Trinity Ct
Kidderminster DY10.....116 F6
🔼 Cradley Heath B64....62 E1
Birmingham B6...........55 D1
Bromsgrove B60.........151 B7
Hinckley LE10...........75 C8
Trinity Ctr 🔳 B64.......62 E1
Trinity Ct WV3...........25 A2
Trinity Dr B79...........20 D6
Trinity Fields DY10......116 F6
Trinity Grange DY10.....116 F7
Trinity Gr WS10..........42 A3
Trinity High Sch & Sixth
Form Ctr B98 ....153 F4
Trinity Hill B72..........46 C5
Trinity Ho B70...........53 E1
Trinity La
Coventry CV1............165 B3
Hinckley LE10...........71 C1
Trinity Pk B40 ....90 D3
Trinity RC Sch CV32....156 D2
Trinity RC Sch The CV34. 161 C6
Trinity Rd
Bilston WV14............40 F5
Birmingham B6 ....55 E1
Dudley DY1..............51 C1
Freasley B78,CV9.......36 B3
Stourbridge DY8 ....81 B8
Sutton Coldfield B75....32 C1
Willenhall WV12.........27 D7
Trinity Road N B70......53 D2
Trinity Road S B70......53 D1
Trinity St
Brierley Hill DY5........61 D7
Coventry CV1............165 B3
Cradley Heath B64......62 E1
Oldbury B69.............64 A6
Royal Leamington Spa
CV32...................156 F1
Smethwick B67..........65 A6
West Bromwich B70.....53 D2
Trinity Terr 🔳 B11.......87 A8
Trinity Vicarage Rd LE10 .75 C8
Trinity Way Sta B70.....53 D1
Trinity Way B70.........53 D2
Trinity Wlk CV11........73 E3
Trippleton Ave B32.....102 B8
Tristram Ave B31.......103 B1
Triton Cl WS6............4 F1
Trittiford Rd B13........105 C6
Triumph Cl CV2..........114 E3
Triumph Ho CV1.........165 B2
Triumph B77.............21 E3
Triumph Wlk B36........59 A1
Troilus Ct CV34..........161 F3
Trojan B77...............21 E3
Tromans Cl B64..........82 E7
Tromans Ind Est DY2....62 D3
Troon Cl
Sutton Coldfield B75....46 D8
Walsall WS3.............14 A3
Troon Ct WV6............23 D5
Troon Pl DY8............70 A7
Troon B77...............22 C4
Troon Way LE10.........75 D4
Trossachs Rd CV5.......111 F3
Trotter's La B71.........53 A7
Troughton Cres CV6.....113 A5
Trouse La WS10.........41 F3
Troutbeck Ave CV32....156 C2
Troutbeck Dr DY5.......81 B8
Troutbeck Rd CV5.......111 F4
Troyes Cl CV3............133 E7
Troy Gr B14.............104 D4
Troy Ind Est B96........159 E3
Truck Stop Bsns Pk B11..88 B5
Truda St 🔳 WS1.........42 D7
Trueman Cl CV34.........160 E8
Truemans Heath La B47,
B90....................125 C7
Truggist La CV7.........130 E8
Trundalls La B90........126 A5

Truro Cl
Hinckley LE10...........71 E4
Lichfield WS13...........3 B3
Nuneaton CV11..........73 F5
Rowley Regis B65.......63 E4
Truro Dr DY11...........116 A5
Truro Pl WS12...........5 C8
Truro Rd WS5............43 D7
Truro Twr 🔳 B16........66 A2
Truro Wlk B37...........70 B2
Trustin Cres B92........107 E8
Tryan Rd CV10...........72 E4
Tryon Pl WV14..........40 E6
Tryst The B61............137 B5
Trysull Ave B26.........89 C4
Trysull Gdns WV3.......38 D7
Trysull Holloway WV5...37 C3
Trysull Rd
Orton WV5...............37 E1
Wolverhampton WV3....38 D7
Trysull Way DY2........62 C4
Tudbury Rd B31.........102 E4
Tudman Cl B36..........58 A7
Tudor Ave CV5...........111 F4
Tudor Bsns Ctr 🔳 B98 ..153 E3
Tudor Cl
Balsall Common CV7....130 A6
Birmingham,Highter's Heath
B14....................105 A1
Birmingham,King's Heath
B13....................104 F6
Burntwood WS7..........7 C6
Cheslyn Hay WS6........4 E3
Lichfield WS14...........9 F6
Sutton Coldfield B73....45 D2
Tudor Cres
Tamworth B77...........21 F4
Wolverhampton WV2....39 B6
Tudor Croft B37.........69 F1
Tudor Ct
Bedworth CV7...........95 E7
Coventry CV3............133 C8
Essington WV11.........12 F4
Sutton Coldfield B74....32 A2
Tipton DY4..............52 A4
Sutton Coldfield WS14...30 C5
Tudor Eaves 🔳 B17.....85 C5
Tudor Gdns
Birmingham B23.........56 E3
Stourbridge DY8 ....80 E5
Tudor Grange Sch B91...107 A2
Tudor Gr B74............45 A8
Tudor Hill B73...........46 B6
Tudor Ho
Dudley DY2..............61 F6
Walsall WS1.............28 E2
Tudor Ind Est B11.......88 B5
Tudor Park Ct 🔳 B74....31 F3
Tudor Park Gdns WS7....7 C6
Tudor Pl DY3............50 E6
Tudor Rd
Birmingham B13.........86 F3
Burntwood WS7..........7 C6
Cannock WS12...........1 F8
Darlaston WV14..........41 B4
Dudley DY3..............50 E6
Hinckley LE10...........71 C3
Nuneaton CV10..........72 C6
Oldbury B68.............64 C4
Rowley Regis B65.......63 C5
Sutton Coldfield B73....46 A4
Tudor Row 🔳 WS13......9 B7
Tudors Cl 🔼 B10........87 C8
Tudor St
Birmingham B18.........65 E4
Tipton DY4..............52 A4
Tudor Terr
Birmingham B17.........85 C6
Dudley DY2..............51 E1
Tudor Vale DY3..........50 E6
Tudor Way
Cheslyn Hay WS6........4 D1
Sutton Coldfield B72....46 B2
Tufnell Gr B8............68 B7
Tugford Rd B29..........103 C7
Tuisi Ctr B19............164 A4
Tulip Gdns B29..........102 F7
Tulip Tree Ave CV8......148 B5
Tulip Tree Ct CV8.......148 B4
Tulip Wlk B37...........90 C8
Tulliver Cl CV12.........78 B3
Tulliver Rd CV10........73 C1
Tulliver St CV6...........113 B5
Tulyar Cl B36............68 C8
Tunnel Dr B98...........153 E2
Tunnel La
Birmingham,Brandwood End
B14....................104 C4
Birmingham,Lifford B30...104 B4
Tunnel Rd B70...........53 A7
Tunnel St WV14..........51 C4
Tunstall Rd DY6.........61 A5
Turchill Dr B76..........58 B8
Turf Cl WS11.............6 A4
Turf Cotts WV4..........38 E2
Turfpits La B23..........56 D6
Turf Pitts La B75........32 F4
Turks Head Way B70....53 C2
Turlands Cl CV2.........115 A7
Turley St DY1...........51 A6
Turls Hill Rd
Sedgley DY3............50 E8
Sedgley WV14...........50 E8
Turls St DY3..........50 E8
Turnberry Dr CV11......79 C8
Turnberry Gr WV6 ......23 D5

Turnberry Rd
Birmingham B42.........55 B8
Walsall WS3.............14 A4
Turnberry B77...........22 C5
Turner Ave WV4,WV14 ..39 F2
Turner Cl
Bedworth CV12..........78 A4
Cannock WS11...........2 D2
Warwick CV34...........160 B4
Turner Dr
Brierley Hill DY5........81 D7
Hinckley LE10...........71 A3
Turner Gr WV6...........24 A4
Turner Rd CV5...........112 D3
Turners Croft B71.......54 A8
Turner's Gr DY3.........50 C4
Turner's Hill Rd DY3....50 C4
Turner's Hill B65........63 B6
Turner's La DY5.........61 D1
Turner St
🔼 Dudley,Old Dock DY1...62 B8
Birmingham B11.........87 A6
Dudley,Gornalwood DY3..50 D3
Tipton DY4..............51 F7
West Bromwich B70.....53 A4
Turney Rd DY8..........80 F6
Turnham Gn WV6.........23 E3
Turnhouse Rd B35.......58 B4
Turnley Rd B34..........69 C6
Turnpike Cl
Balsall Common CV7....130 B7
Birmingham B11.........87 A6
Turnpike Dr B46.........59 C2
Turnpike La B97.........153 A4
Turnstone Dr WV10.....12 B7
Turnstone Rd DY10 .....117 A1
Turpin Ct CV31..........161 F6
Turquoise Gr WS11.....2 C3
Turton Cl WS3............14 A4
Turton Rd
Tipton DY4..............40 F1
West Bromwich B70.....53 B2
Turtons Croft WV14.....40 B3
Turton St DY10 ....117 A8
Turton Way CV8.........148 C4
Turves Gn
Birmingham,Turves Green
B31....................103 A1
Birmingham,West Heath
B31....................122 F8
Turves Green Boys' Tech Coll
B31....................103 A1
Turves Green Girls Sch &
Tech Coll B31...........103 A1
Turves Green Prim Sch
B31....................103 A1
Turville Cl LE10.........75 F5
Turville Rd B20..........55 C1
Tustin Gr B27...........106 C8
Tutbury Ave
Coventry CV4............132 E6
Perton WV6.............24 A3
Tutbury Cl WS11.........2 C3
Tutbury B77.............35 C7
Tutehill Rd B97.........36 B7
Tutnall Cl B60...........137 F1
Tutnall Dr B98...........143 B6
Tutnall Grange B60.....138 A1
Tutnall La
Blackwell B60...........138 A1
Finstall B60.............137 F1
Tutors Way DY10........116 E4
Tuttle Hill CV10.........72 F6
Tuxford Cl WV10........25 E4
Twatling Rd B45.........122 A2
Tweedside Cl LE10......71 F3
Tweeds Well B32........102 B7
Tweed Twr B20..........55 D2
Twickenham Ct DY8.....80 C7
Twickenham Dr B13 ....86 E2
Twickenham Prim Sch
B44....................45 C1
Twickenham Rd B44....45 C1
Twickenham Way CV3..115 B1
Twiners Rd B98.........153 F1
Two Gates Com Prim Sch
Tamworth B77...........35 C8
Tamworth,Mount Pleasant
B77....................21 C1
Two Gates La B63.....82 C5
Two Gates Ind Est B77...35 D7
Two Gates La B63.......82 C5
Two Locks DY5...........62 A4
Two Oaks Ave WS7......6 D8
Two Trees Cl B78.......20 B6
Two Woods La DY5......61 F1
Two Woods Trad Est DY5..61 F1
Twycross Gr B36........68 D8
Twycross Rd LE10.......75 F6
Twycross Wlk CV34.....155 D1
Twydale Ave B69.........52 C2
Twyford Cl WS9.........30 B5
Twyford Gr WV11........26 F7
Twyford Rd B8..........68 C5
Twyning Rd
Birmingham,Edgbaston
B16....................65 D3
Birmingham,Stirchley B30..104 B7
Tybalt Cl
Coventry CV3............134 C5
Royal Leamington Spa
CV34...................161 D2
Tyber Dr B20............55 A3
Tyburn Gr B24..........57 D3
Tyburn Gr B24..........57 C2
Tyburn Rd
Birmingham B24.........57 C2
Wolverhampton WV1....26 C2

Tyburn Sq B24........57 D3
Tyburn Trad Est B24....57 D2
Tyebeams B34..........69 C5
Tye Gdns DY9...........81 B1
Tyler Ct B24............56 F3
Tyler Gdns WV13........27 B1
Tyler Gr B43............44 A1
Tyler Rd WV13...........27 B1
Tylers Gn B38...........104 B1
Tylers Gr B90...........126 F6
Tylney Cl
Birmingham B5..........86 D7
Coventry CV3............115 B2
Tyndale Cres B43.......44 C3
Tyndall Wlk B32.........84 A2
Tyne Cl
Birmingham B37.........70 C4
Brownhills WS8..........6 C2
Tyne Ct B73.............46 B5
Tynedale Cres WV4.....39 E3
Tynedale Rd B11........87 F3
Tyne Gr B25.............88 D8
Tynemouth Cl CV2......96 D5
Tyne Pl DY5.............61 F2
Tynes The B60..........150 E7
Tyning Cl WV9...........11 A2
Tyninghame Ave WV6...20 D7
Tynings La WS9.........30 A5
Tynsall Ave B97.........152 F2
Tynward Cl CV3.........133 B5
Tyrley Cl WV6...........24 B2
Tyrol Cl DY8.............80 D6
Tyseley Hill Rd B11.....88 A4
Tyseley Ind Est B11.....87 E5
Tyseley La B11..........88 A4
Tyseley Locomotive Wks
Visitor Ctr* B11.........87 E5
Tyseley Sta B11.........88 A5
Tysoe Cl
Hockley Heath B94.....143 C6
Redditch B98...........154 D2
Tysoe Croft CV3........134 F8
Tysoe Dr B76...........46 F4
Tysoe Rd B44...........55 F7
Tythe Barn Cl B60......150 D6
Tythebarn Dr DY6.......60 A7
Tythe Barn La B90......126 A6
Tyzack Cl DY5...........61 C2

U

Udall Rd WV14..........40 D3
Uffculme Rd B30........104 D8
Uffculme Specl Sch B13 .86 E1
Uffmoor Est B63.........82 E2
Uffmoor La B62..........100 D7
Ufton Cl B90............106 E3
Ufton Cres B90.........106 D3
Ufton Croft CV5.........112 A3
Ullapool Cl B97.........158 D5
Ullenhall Rd
Dorridge B93............128 A6
Sutton Coldfield B76....57 F8
Ullenwood B21..........65 D7
Ulleries Rd B92.........89 A2
Ullrik Gn B24...........56 F2
Ullswater Ave
Nuneaton CV11.........73 F6
Royal Leamington Spa
CV32...................156 C2
Ullswater Cl B32........84 F2
Ullswater Gdns DY6.....60 D6
Ullswater Ho 🔼 B69....63 D5
Ullswater Pl WS11......1 E1
Ullswater Rd
Bedworth CV12.........78 A2
Coventry CV11..........114 F1
Wolverhampton WV11...13 B1
Ullswater Rise DY5......61 E5
Ullswater B77...........36 B7
Ulster Cl WS11..........2 A3
Ulster Dr DY6...........60 E4
Ulverley Cres B92.......106 F8
Ulverley Green Rd B92..88 F1
Ulverley Sch B92........89 B1
Ulverscroft Rd CV3......133 D7
Ulwine Dr B31...........103 A4
Umberslade Children's
Farm* B94..............142 C2
Umberslade Rd
Birmingham B29.........100 A8
Earlswood B94..........142 C7
Tanworth-In-A B94.....142 E3
Uncle Ben's Cl 🔳 B69 ..63 F4
Underhill Cl
Coventry CV3............133 D3
Redditch B98...........158 F6
Underhill La WV10.......12 A2
Underhill Prim Sch WV10 .12 B1
Underhill Rd
Birmingham B8..........67 F3
Tipton DY4..............52 C6
Underhill St B69.........64 A5
Underhill Wlk B69.......64 A5
Underley Cl DY6.........60 B7
Underpass The B40.....90 E4
Underwood Cl
Birmingham B15.........85 D4
Birmingham,Stockland Green
B23....................56 C4
Redditch B97...........158 A7
Underwood Rd B20.....54 E6
Unett Ct 🔳 B66.........65 C5
Unett St
Birmingham B19.........66 C5
Smethwick B66.........65 C5
Unett Wlk B19..........66 C5

Unicorn Ave CV5......111 E4
Unicorn Hill B97........153 D4
Unicorn La CV5..........111 F4
Union Bldgs CV1.......165 B2
Union Dr B73..........45 F2
Union Ho B73............45 F2
Union La WV5...........37 D2
Union Mill St WV1......163 D3
Union Pas B2...........164 C2
Union Pl
Birmingham B29.........86 B2
Coventry CV6............95 F4
Union Rd
Birmingham B6..........67 B8
Oldbury B69.............52 F2
Royal Leamington Spa
CV32...................156 E1
Solihull,Lode Heath B91 ..107 C4
Solihull,Shirley B90.....106 C2
West Bromwich B70.....52 F2
Union Row B21.........65 F7
Union St
🔼 Dudley DY1..........51 D2
Bilston WV14............40 C5
Birmingham B2..........164 C2
Burntwood WS7.........6 E5
Cannock WS11...........4 E6
Kidderminster DY10.....116 E7
Redditch B98...........153 F3
Rowley Regis B65.......63 C1
Stourbridge,Lye DY9....81 E5
Stourbridge,Stambermill
DY8....................81 A4
Tipton,Princes End DY1 ..51 F8
Tipton,Tipton Green DY4..51 F5
Walsall WS1.............28 F1
Wednesbury WS10 .....41 F2
West Bromwich B70.....64 D8
Willenhall WV13.........27 A2
Wolverhampton WV1....163 C3
Unisant Trad Est B64....62 F2
United Coll of the Ascension
B29....................85 C1
Unitt Dr B64............82 E8
Unity Cl WS10...........41 C4
Unity Ho CV1............165 C4
Unity Pl
🔳 Birmingham B29.....85 F2
Oldbury B69.............64 A8
Unity Wlk DY4..........51 F5
University Rd CV4.......132 C5
University Road W B15...85 F4
University Sta B15.......85 E4
Univ of Birmingham B15..85 F4
Univ of Birmingham The
(Halls of Residence)
B15....................66 C1
Univ of Central England
B4.....................164 D4
Univ of Central England
Edgbaston Ctr B15......86 A8
Univ of Central England in
Birmingham B42.........55 D2
Univ of Warwick CV4...132 C4
Univ of Warwick (Gibbet Hill)
CV4....................132 D3
Univ of Warwick Science Pk
CV4....................132 C5
Univ of Warwick (Westwood)
CV4....................132 B6
Univ of Wolverhampton
(Annexe) WV1..........163 C3
Univ of Wolverhampton (City
Campus North) WV1....163 B4
Univ of Wolverhampton (City
Campus South) WV1....163 B3
Univ of Wolverhampton
Compton Park Campus
WV6...................24 C2
Univ of Wolverhampton
(Walsall Campus) WS1 ..43 A7
Unketts Rd B67.........64 E3
Unwin Cres DY8.........80 E5
Upfield Cl B35...........58 A4
Upfield Cotts WS7.......7 A6
Upland Gr B61...........137 A4
Upland Rd
Birmingham B29.........86 B3
Bromsgrove B61.........137 B4
Uplands Ave
Rowley Regis B65.......63 D3
Wolverhampton WV3....38 D8
Uplands Cl DY2.........62 E7
Uplands CV2.............114 A5
Uplands Dr
Sedgley DY3............50 D8
Wolverhampton WV3....38 E8
Wombourne WV5........49 A6
Uplands Gr WV13........26 C1
Uplands Jun Sch WV3....38 D8
Uplands Jun Sch WS3....38 D8
Uplands Manor Prim Sch
B67....................64 F3
Uplands Rd
Birmingham B21.........54 D2
Dudley DY2.............62 F7
Wolverhampton WV13..26 C1
Uplands The B67.......64 E3
Upleadon Cl B97........158 A6
Upper Abbey St CV11...73 B5
Upper Ashley St B62....63 C1
Upper Balsall Heath Rd
B12....................86 F6
Upper Bond St LE10....71 D1

Upper Brook St WS2 . . . . .28 D1
Upper Cape CV34 . . . . .160 D8
Upper Chapel St B69 . . . . .52 B2
Upper Church La DY4 . . . .52 A6
Upper Cl B32 . . . . .84 D3
Upper Clifton Rd B73 . . . .46 B6
Upper Conybere St [6]
  B12 . . . . .86 F7
Upper Crossgate Rd B98 159 C8
Upper Dean St B5 . . . . . . .164 C1
Upper Eastern Green La
  CV5 .111 E5
Upper Ettingshall Rd
  WV14 .51 B8
Upper Field Cl B98 . . . . .154 C6
Upperfield Way CV3 . . . . .115 A1
Upper Forster St WS4 . . . . . . .28 F3
Upper Gambolds La B60 151 C5
Upper Gn WV6 . . . . .24 D5
Upper Gough St B1 . . . . .164 B1
Upper Green La WS2 . . . . . .28 C4
Upper Grosvenor Rd B20 . .55 B2
Upper Grove St [8] CV32 .156 E1
Upper Gungate B79 . . . . . .21 B6
Upper Hall La B45 . . . . . .154 D2
Upper Hall La [4] WS1 . . . .28 E1
Upper Hattons Cotts WV9 .10 D5
Upper Highgate St B12 . . .86 F7
Upper High St
  Cradley Heath B64 . . . . . . .62 D1
  Wednesbury WS10 . . . . . . .41 F3
Upper Hill St
  Coventry CV1 . . . . .165 A3
  Royal Leamington Spa
  CV32 . . . . .157 A1
Upper Holland Rd B72 . . .46 C4
Upper Holly Wlk CV32 . . .157 A1
Upper Keys Bsns Pk WS12 . .2 E3
Upper Ladyes Hills CV8 . 148 A6
Upper Landywood La
  Cheslyn Hay WS6 . . . . .4 D1
  Great Wyrley WS6 . . . . .13 D8
Upper Lichfield St WV13 .27 A2
Upper Marshall St B1 . . .164 B1
Upper Meadow Rd B32 . . .84 C5
Upper Mill La B5 . . . . . . .164 C1
Upper Navigation St WS2 .28 D2
Upper Norgrove Ho B97 .152 F1
Upper Pk CV3 . . . . .134 D6
Upper Portland St B6 . . . .67 A7
Upper Perc CV1 . . . . .165 B3
Upper Ride CV3 . . . . .134 D5
Upper Rosemary Hill
  CV8 .147 F5
Upper Rushall St WS1 . . . .28 F1
Upper Russell St [1] WS10 41 F2
Upper St John St WS1 . . . . .9 B6
Upper Short St WS2 . . . . . .28 D1
Upper Sneyd Rd WV11 . . . .13 B2
Upon Spon St CV1 . . . . . .113 A3
Upper Spring La CV47 . . .147 F7
Upper Stone Cl B76 . . . . . .46 E4
Upper Sutton St B6 . . . . . . .67 F7
Upper Thomas St B6 . . . . . .66 F7
Upper Trinity St B9 . . . . . . .67 A1
Upper Vauxhall WV1 . . . . .25 A2
Upper Villiers St WV2 . . . .39 C6
Upper Well St CV1 . . . . . .165 B3
Upper William St B1 . . . . . .66 C1
Upper York St CV1 . . . . . .113 B2
Upper Zoar St WV3 . . . . . .163 A1
Upton Cl B98 . . . . .154 F3
Upton Ct B23 . . . . .56 B3
Upton Dr CV11 . . . . .78 F8
Upton Gdns WV14 . . . . .40 C5
Upton Gr B33 . . . . .68 C1
Upton Rd B33 . . . . .68 C1
Upton St DY2 . . . . .62 C5
Upwey Ave B91 . . . . .107 A4
Usam Trad Est WV10 . . . . . .11 D2
Usk Cl WS3 . . . . .28 D8
Usk Way B36 . . . . .69 F8
Usmere Rd DY10 . . . . .116 F8
Utrillo Cl CV5 . . . . .112 C3
Uttoxeter Cl WV6 . . . . .25 B5
Uxbridge Ave CV3 . . . . . . .114 C2
Uxbridge Cl DY3 . . . . .50 D2
Uxbridge Ct
  Burntwood WS7 . . . . .6 F5
  Cannock WS12 . . . . .2 C4
  Kidderminster DY11 . . . . .116 D5
Uxbridge St
  Birmingham B19 . . . . .66 D5
  Cannock WS12 . . . . .2 C4

V

Valbourne Rd B14 . . . . . .104 C4
Vale Ave
  Aldridge WS9 . . . . .30 D3
  Dudley DY3 . . . . .50 D6
Vale Cl
  Birmingham B32 . . . . .84 F3
  Lichfield WS13 . . . . .3 B1
Vale Ct B64 . . . . .82 D7
Vale Gr B60 . . . . .151 A7
Vale Head Dr WV6 . . . . . . .24 A2
Vale Ind Est DY11 . . . . . . .116 C1
Valencia Croft B35 . . . . . . .58 B4
Valencia Rd
  Bromsgrove B60 . . . . .137 D1
  Coventry CV3 . . . . .115 A2

Valentine Cl B74 . . . . .44 F7
Valentine Ct B14 . . . . .86 E1
Valentine Rd
  Birmingham B14 . . . . .86 F1
  Oldbury B68 . . . . .64 C2
Valepits Rd B33 . . . . .69 C1
Vale Rd DY2 . . . . .62 E4
Valerian
  Kidderminster DY10 . . . . .116 E2
  Sutton Coldfield B74 . . . . . .31 F4
Valerie Gr B43 . . . . .54 C8
Vale Row DY3 . . . . .50 D5
Vales Cl B76 . . . . .57 E7
Vale St
  Dudley DY3 . . . . .50 D5
  Stourbridge DY8 . . . . .81 A8
  West Bromwich B71 . . . . . . .53 C6
  Wolverhampton WV2 . . . . . .40 A6
Vale The
  Birmingham,Edgbaston
  B15 . . . . .86 A6
  Birmingham,Moseley B11 . .87 B2
  Coventry CV3 . . . . .134 C8
Vale View
  Aldridge WS9 . . . . .30 B4
  Nuneaton CV10 . . . . .72 E4
Valiant Cl LE10 . . . . .75 E4
Valley Cl B97 . . . . .158 A6
Valley Farm Rd B45 . . . . .122 A6
Valley Gn WS6 . . . . .4 E2
Valley Heritage Ctr* WS12 .2 D6
Valley Int Sch B92 . . . . .89 D3
Valley La
  Kingswood B94 . . . . .144 E7
  Lichfield WS13 . . . . .9 D8
  Tamworth B77 . . . . .35 E7
Valley Park Nature Reserve*
  WV6 .24 D3
Valley Rd
  Birmingham B43 . . . . .54 C7
  Bournheath B61 . . . . .136 E2
  Cannock,Hednesford WS12 . .2 D6
  Coventry CV2 . . . . .114 A6
  Cradley Heath B64 . . . . . . .82 E7
  Dudley DY3 . . . . .50 E6
  Earlswood B94 . . . . .126 A1
  Halesowen B62 . . . . .83 F8
  Radford Semele CV31 . . . .162 E4
  Royal Leamington Spa
  CV32 . . . . .157 C3
  Smethwick B67 . . . . .64 F3
  Solihull B92 . . . . .89 D4
  Stourbridge DY9 . . . . .81 F6
  Sutton Coldfield B74 . . . . . .44 F7
  Walsall WS3 . . . . .14 D1
  Wolverhampton WV10 . . . . .25 F5
Valley Side WS3 . . . . .14 F2
Valley Stad (Redditch FC)
  B97 .153 C4
Valley The
  Burntwood WS7 . . . . .6 F6
  Radford Semele CV31 . . . .162 E4
Valley View WS9 . . . . .16 A7
Vallian Croft B36 . . . . .68 E7
Vanborough Wlk DY1 . . . . .51 A2
Vanbrugh Ct WV6 . . . . .23 E3
Van Dyke Cl CV5 . . . . .112 C3
Van Gogh Cl WS11 . . . . .2 D2
Vanguard Ave CV5 . . . . . .112 C1
Vanguard Cl [1] B36 . . . . . .68 E8
Vanguard Ctr CV4 . . . . . . .132 C6
Vanguard Rd B26 . . . . .90 C4
Vanguard B77 . . . . .35 D6
Vann Cl [2] B10 . . . . .87 C8
Vantage Point [4] B70 . . . .53 C2
Varden Croft B5 . . . . .86 D7
Vardon Dr CV3 . . . . .133 D4
Vardon Way B38 . . . . .103 D1
Varley Rd B24 . . . . .57 D4
Varley Vale B24 . . . . .57 D4
Varlins Way B38 . . . . .123 D6
Varney Ave B70 . . . . .53 D2
Vaughan Cl B74 . . . . .31 F6
Vaughan Rd WV13 . . . . .26 E5
Vaughan Trad Est DY4 . . . .52 B3
Vaughton Dr B75 . . . . .46 E6
Vaughton Ho B15 . . . . .86 C7
Vaughton St S B12 . . . . .86 E8
Vaughton St B12 . . . . .86 F8
Vauxhall Ave [4] WV1 . . . .25 A2
Vauxhall Cl CV1 . . . . .113 E3
Vauxhall Cres B36 . . . . .58 F1
Vauxhall Gdns DY2 . . . . . . .62 E7
Vauxhall Gr [7] B7 . . . . .67 B3
Vauxhall Ho [2] WV1 . . . . . .25 A2
Vauxhall Pl B7 . . . . .67 A3
Vauxhall Rd
  Birmingham B7 . . . . .67 A3
  Stourbridge DY8 . . . . .81 A5
Vauxhall St
  Coventry CV1 . . . . .113 E3
  Dudley DY1 . . . . .62 B8
Vauxhall Trad Est B7 . . . . . .67 B4
Vaynor Dr B97 . . . . .158 D8
Vaynor Frst Sch The B97 . 158 C7
Veasey Cl CV11 . . . . .73 E3
Vecqueray St CV1 . . . . .113 E2
Vector Ind Pk B71 . . . . .53 C6
Velsheda Rd B90 . . . . .106 A2
Venetia Rd B9 . . . . .67 C2
Venice Ct [2] B13 . . . . .87 B2
Venning Gr B43 . . . . .54 D7
Ventnor Ave
  Birmingham,Lozells B19 . . .66 D7
  Birmingham,Ward End B36 . .68 D7
Ventnor Cl
  Birmingham B66 . . . . .84 C7
  Coventry CV2 . . . . .114 E3

Ventnor Rd B92 . . . . .89 C3
Ventnor St CV10 . . . . .73 D6
Ventura Park Rd B78 . . . . . .20 F3
Ventura Pk Rd B78 . . . . .21 A3
Venture Pl B8 . . . . .21 A3
Venture Ct LE10 . . . . .74 E8
Venture Way B7 . . . . .66 F4
Vera Rd B26 . . . . .88 E7
Vera Roberts Way DY11 . 116 B3
Verbena Cl
  Coventry CV2 . . . . .96 B1
  Stoke Prior B60 . . . . .150 C1
Verbena Gdns B7 . . . . .67 A5
Verbena Rd B31 . . . . .102 F6
Vercourt B74 . . . . .31 B3
Verden Ave CV34 . . . . .160 B4
Verdi Cl WS13 . . . . .3 C2
Verdun Cl CV31 . . . . .162 B2
Verdun Cres DY2 . . . . .51 F2
Vere St B5 . . . . .86 D8
Verity Wlk DY8 . . . . .60 E1
Vermont Gn [4] WS11 . . . . . .2 A3
Vermont Gr CV31 . . . . .162 D6
Verney Ave B33 . . . . .89 D7
Vernier Ave DY6 . . . . .61 A5
Vernolds Croft B5 . . . . .86 E8
Vernon Ave
  Birmingham B20 . . . . .54 F4
  Brownhills WS8 . . . . .16 A8
  Tipton DY4 . . . . .51 E4
Vernon Cl
  [9] Coventry CV1 . . . . .113 C3
  Essington WV11 . . . . .12 F4
  Halesowen B62 . . . . .83 D8
  Redditch B98 . . . . .154 A5
  Royal Leamington Spa
  CV32 . . . . .156 E3
  Sutton Coldfield B74 . . . . . .31 E5
  Willenhall WV13 . . . . .26 E1
Vernon Ct
  [9] Coventry CV1 . . . . .113 C4
  Birmingham B16 . . . . .65 E1
Vernon Rd
  Bilston WV14 . . . . .40 F6
  Birmingham B16 . . . . .65 E1
  Halesowen B62 . . . . .83 C8
  Oldbury B68 . . . . .64 C6
Vernons Ct CV10 . . . . .72 F4
Vernons La CV10,CV11 . . . .72 F4
Vernons Mews CV10 . . . . . .72 F4
Vernon St B70 . . . . .52 E3
Vernon Trad Est B62 . . . . . .83 C8
Vernon Way WS3 . . . . .13 E1
Verona Cl CV11 . . . . .74 A1
Verona Rd B60 . . . . .137 A2
Veronica Ave WV4 . . . . .39 E5
Veronica Cl B29 . . . . .103 A6
Veronica Rd CV2 . . . . .61 A6
Verstone Croft B31 . . . . . .103 A3
Verstone Rd B90 . . . . .106 C4
Verwood Cl WV13 . . . . .26 D1
Vesey Cl
  Sutton Coldfield B74 . . . . . .31 F2
  Water Orton B46 . . . . .59 B2
Vesey Rd B73 . . . . .46 B1
Vesey St B4 . . . . .164 C4
Vestry Cl B64 . . . . .62 F1
Vestry Ct DY8 . . . . .80 E6
Viaduct Dr WV6 . . . . .25 B6
Viaduct St B7 . . . . .67 A3
Vibart Rd B26 . . . . .88 F8
Vicarage Cl
  Birmingham,Great Barr
  B42 . . . . .55 D7
  Birmingham,Strichley B30 .104 C7
  Brierley Hill DY5 . . . . .81 C8
  Bromsgrove B60 . . . . .151 B8
  Brownhills WS8 . . . . .16 A7
  Dordon B78 . . . . .36 F5
  Tipton DY4 . . . . .51 E5
Vicarage Cres
  Kidderminster DY10 . . . . .116 F5
  Redditch B97 . . . . .153 C3
Vicarage Ct WS7 . . . . .6 F6
Vicarage Field CV34 . . . . .161 B8
Vicarage Gdns
  Halesowen B62 . . . . .63 D1
  Sutton Coldfield B76 . . . . . .57 F7
Vicarage La
  Brierley Hill DY5 . . . . .61 D7
  Coventry CV7 . . . . .95 D7
  Longbridge CV35 . . . . .160 A1
  Water Orton B46 . . . . .59 B2
Vicarage Prospect DY1 . . . .51 B1
Vicarage Rd
  Birmingham,Aston B6 . . . . .67 A7
  Birmingham,Chad Valley
  B15 . . . . .85 F8
  Birmingham,Handsworth
  B18 . . . . .66 A7
  Birmingham,Harts Green
  B17 . . . . .85 B5
  Birmingham,King's Heath
  B14 .104 E8
  Birmingham,Stechford B33 . .68 E1
  Birmingham,Stirchley B30 . .104 D6
  Brownhills WS8 . . . . .16 A7
  Cheswick Green B90,B94 . 126 C3
  Dudley,West Coseley WV14 . .51 C7
  Dudley,Woodsetton DY3 . . .50 F5
  Halesowen B62 . . . . .63 C1
  Hockley Heath B94 . . . . . .143 F7
  Oldbury B68 . . . . .64 C5

Vicarage Rd continued
  Royal Leamington Spa
  CV32 . . . . .157 B3
  Smethwick B67 . . . . .64 F5
Vicarage Rd S DY9 . . . . .81 E5
Vicarage Rd
  Stone DY10 . . . . .117 E2
  Stoneleigh CV8 . . . . .149 B6
  Stourbridge DY9 . . . . .80 D7
  Stourbridge,Lye DY9 . . . . . .81 F5
  Walsall WS3 . . . . .15 B2
Vicarage Rd W DY1 . . . . . . .51 C6
Vicarage St
  Nuneaton CV11 . . . . .73 C4
  Oldbury B68 . . . . .64 B5
Vicarage Terr [1] WS2 . . . .42 C8
Vicarage View B97 . . . . . . .153 D3
Vicarage Wlk [9] WS1 . . . . .28 E1
Vicar's Cl WS13 . . . . .9 A8
Vicar St
  Dudley DY2 . . . . .62 C8
  Kidderminster DY10 . . . . .116 E6
  Sedgley DY3 . . . . .50 D8
  Wednesbury WS10 . . . . . . .42 A3
Vicars Wlk DY9 . . . . .81 E2
Viceroy Cl
  Birmingham B5 . . . . .86 C6
  Kingswinford DY6 . . . . .61 A5
Victor Bsns Ctr B98 . . . . .154 B3
Victoria Arc WV1 . . . . .163 B3
Victoria Ave
  Birmingham B21 . . . . .65 F8
  Birmingham,Small Heath
  B10 . . . . .87 D8
  Halesowen B62 . . . . .83 F6
  Smethwick B66 . . . . .65 A5
  Walsall,Blakenall Heath
  WS3 .28 D8
  Walsall,Wallington Heath
  WS3 .14 C1
Victoria Bldgs B16 . . . . . . .65 E3
Victoria Bsns Ctr [11]
  CV31 . . . . .162 A7
Victoria Colonnade [5]
  CV31 . . . . .161 F7
Victoria Com Specl Sch
  B31 .103 A5
Victoria Ct
  [2] Birmingham,Showell Green
  B13 . . . . .86 F4
  [2] Kidderminster DY10 . . .116 F6
  [9] Birmingham,Hurst Green
  B62 . . . . .84 A7
  Brierley Hill DY5 . . . . .61 D3
  Coventry CV5 . . . . .112 D4
  Halesowen B62 . . . . .83 F6
  Norton Canes WS11 . . . . . . .6 B5
Victoria Dr B78 . . . . .35 A8
Victoria Fold WV1 . . . . . . .163 B2
Victoria Gdns
  Cradley Heath B64 . . . . . . .62 F2
  Lichfield WS13 . . . . .8 F6
Victoria Gr
  [1] Birmingham B18 . . . . . .65 E4
  Wombourne WV5 . . . . .49 A8
Victoria Ho
  [2] Birmingham B2 . . . . . .164 C2
  [2] Darlaston WS10 . . . . . . .41 C6
  [4] Birmingham,Ladywood
  B16 . . . . .66 B2
  Birmingham,Small Heath
  B10 . . . . .87 D8
Victoria Hospl WS13 . . . . . . .9 A6
Victoria Inf Sch DY4 . . . . . .51 F5
Victoria Law Cts B2 . . . . .164 C3
Victoria Mews
  Barnt Green B45 . . . . .138 C8
  Coventry CV3 . . . . .114 C2
  Oldbury B69 . . . . .63 F3
  Walsall WS4 . . . . .29 A3
  Warwick CV34 . . . . .160 D7
Victoria Park Prim Sch
  B66 . . . . .65 B5
Victoria Park Rd B66 . . . . . .65 B5
Victoria Pass [5] DY8 . . . . .81 A5
Victoria Pas WV1 . . . . .163 B3
Victoria Pl DY11 . . . . .116 B2
Victoria Rd
  Birmingham,Acock's Green
  B27 . . . . .88 C2
  Birmingham,Aston B6 . . . . .66 F7
  Birmingham B17 . . . . .85 B5
  Birmingham,Handsworth
  B21 . . . . .65 D7
  Birmingham,Stechford B33 . .68 D3
  Birmingham,Stirchley B30 .104 A4
  Birmingham,Stockland Green
  B23 . . . . .56 D5
  Brierley Hill DY5 . . . . .62 A1
  Bromsgrove B61 . . . . .137 A3
  Cradley Heath B64 . . . . . . .62 F2
  Darlaston WS10 . . . . .41 D6
  Dodford B61 . . . . .136 A7
  Halesowen B62 . . . . .83 D8
  Hartshill CV10 . . . . .72 B8
  Hinckley LE10 . . . . .75 F5
  Oldbury B68 . . . . .64 D6
  Royal Leamington Spa
  CV31 . . . . .161 E8
  Sedgley DY3 . . . . .50 E8

Victoria Rd continued
  Sutton Coldfield B72 . . . . . .46 C5
  Tamworth B79 . . . . .21 C5
  Tipton DY4 . . . . .52 A4
  Walsall WS3 . . . . .15 A3
  Wolverhampton,Newbolds
  WV10 . . . . .25 F5
  Wolverhampton,New Cross
  WV11 . . . . .26 B6
  Wolverhampton,Oxbarn
  WV3 .38 E7
  Wolverhampton,Tettenhall
  WV6 .24 E4
Victoria Sq
  Birmingham B3 . . . . .164 B2
  Wolverhampton WV1 . . . .163 C3
Victoria St
  [7] Redditch B98 . . . . .153 E4
  Birmingham B9 . . . . .67 D1
  Brierley Hill,Barrow Hill
  DY5 . . . . .61 C7
  Brierley Hill,Merry Hill DY5 .61 D3
  Cannock,Bridgtown WS11 . . .2 D8
  Cannock,Broomhill WS11 . . .1 E4
  Cannock WS12 . . . . .2 C6
  Coventry CV1 . . . . .165 C4
  Halesowen B63 . . . . .83 A4
  Hinckley LE10 . . . . .71 D1
  Kingswinford DY6 . . . . .49 B1
  Nuneaton CV11 . . . . .73 C4
  Royal Leamington Spa
  CV31 . . . . .161 E8
  Stourbridge DY8 . . . . .81 A5
  Warwick CV34 . . . . .160 D7
  Wednesbury WS10 . . . . . . .41 E2
  West Bromwich,Lambert's End
  B70 . . . . .53 C3
  West Bromwich,Swan Village
  B70 . . . . .52 F5
  Willenhall WV13 . . . . .27 B3
  Wolverhampton WV1 . . . .163 B3
Victoria Terr
  [4] Walsall WS4 . . . . .28 E1
  Royal Leamington Spa
  CV31 . . . . .161 F7
Victor Rd
  Birmingham B18 . . . . .65 E6
  Solihull B92 . . . . .89 D3
Victor St
  Walsall,Caldmore WS1 . . . .42 E8
  Walsall WS3 . . . . .15 A1
Victor Twr B7 . . . . .67 B6
Victory Ho
  Burntwood WS7 . . . . .6 F7
  Darlaston WS10 . . . . .41 C5
Victory La [2] 41 C5
Victory Ho B [2] B13 . . . . . .86 F4
Victory La WS2 . . . . .28 A4
Victory Rd CV6 . . . . .95 E1
Victory Rise B71 . . . . .53 D5
Victory Terr B78 . . . . .35 B8
Vienna Ho CV5 . . . . .112 E2
View Dr DY2 . . . . .62 E8
Viewfield Ave WS12 . . . . .1 F7
Viewfield Cres DY3 . . . . . . .50 D6
Viewlands Dr WV6 . . . . .24 A2
View Point B69 . . . . .63 A3
View St WS12 . . . . .1 F6
Vigo Cl WS9 . . . . .15 F2
Vigo Pl WS9 . . . . .30 A8
Vigo Rd WS9 . . . . .15 F2
Vigo Terr WS9 . . . . .15 F2
Viking Rise B65 . . . . .63 C4
Viking B77 . . . . .35 D7
Villa Cl LE10 . . . . .75 F4
Villa Cl CV12 . . . . .79 C2
Villa Cotts B19 . . . . .66 E6
Villa Cres CV12 . . . . .79 C1
Villa Cross B19 . . . . .66 D6
Village Mews The WV6 . . . .24 C5
Village Rd B6 . . . . .56 A1
Village The DY6 . . . . .60 E7
Village Wlk WS10 . . . . .42 B3
Villa Park (Aston Villa FC)
  B6 . . . . .55 F1
Villa Rd
  Birmingham B19 . . . . .66 B7
  Coventry CV6 . . . . .113 B6
Villa St
  Birmingham B19 . . . . .66 C6
  Stourbridge DY8 . . . . .81 A8
Villa Wlk B19 . . . . .66 C6
Villebon Way CV31 . . . . . .162 A2
Villette Gr B14 . . . . .105 C4
Villiers Ave WV14 . . . . .40 D7
Villiers Ho [1] WV14 . . . . . .39 B7
Villiers Jun & Inf Sch
  WV14 . . . . .40 D7
Villiers Rd
  Bromsgrove B60 . . . . .150 E7
  Kenilworth CV8 . . . . .148 B5
Villiers Sq WV14 . . . . .40 D7
Villiers St
  Birmingham B18 . . . . .65 E5
  Coventry CV2 . . . . .114 A3
  Kidderminster DY10 . . . . .117 A5
  Nuneaton CV11 . . . . .73 B3
  Royal Leamington Spa
  CV32 . . . . .157 A1
  Walsall WS1 . . . . .42 E7
  Willenhall WV13 . . . . .27 B2
Vimy Rd
  Birmingham B13 . . . . .105 B8
  Wednesbury WS10 . . . . . . .42 A4
Vimy Terr WS10 . . . . .42 A4
Vincent Cl B12 . . . . .86 F6
Vincent Dr B15 . . . . .85 E4

Vincent Par B12 . . . . .86 F6
Vincent Rd B75 . . . . .46 E7
Vincent St
  Birmingham B12 . . . . .86 F5
  Coventry CV1 . . . . .113 B2
  Royal Leamington Spa
    CV32 . . . . .157 A1
  Walsall WS1 . . . . .42 F7
Vincent Wyles Ho CV2 . .114 E3
Vince St B66 . . . . .65 A3
Vinculum Way WV13 . . . . . .41 B8
Vine Av B12 . . . . .87 A5
Vine CI WV10 . . . . .11 D3
Vinecote Rd CV6 . . . . .95 F4
Vine Cres B71 . . . . .53 D6
Vine Ct
  Cradley Heath B64 . . . . . . .82 D8
  Warwick CV34 . . . . .160 F8
Vine Gdns B64 . . . . .62 F2
Vine La
  Cannock WS11 . . . . .4 D5
  Clent DY9 . . . . .99 F3
  Halesowen B63 . . . . .83 B3
  Warwick CV34 . . . . .160 F8
Vineries The B27 . . . . .88 E4
Vine St
  Birmingham B6 . . . . .67 B7
  Brierley Hill DY2,DY5 . . . . . .61 D5
  Kidderminster DY10 . . . . . .117 A8
  Redditch B97 . . . . .153 D4
  Stourbridge DY8 . . . . .60 E1
Vineyard Rd B31 . . . . .102 F5
Vinnall Gr B32 . . . . .102 B8
Vintage CI B34 . . . . .69 A5
Vinyard CI B18 . . . . .65 F7
Violet CI
  Bedworth CV12 . . . . .77 E2
  Coventry CV2 . . . . .96 C3
Violet Croft CV4 . . . . .41 B1
Violet La DY9 . . . . .99 E4
Virginia Dr WV4 . . . . .38 F4
Virginia PI CV10 . . . . .72 E3
Virginia Rd CV1 . . . . .113 E3
Viscount CI
  Birmingham B35 . . . . .58 A2
  Royal Leamington Spa
    CV31 . . . . .161 F6
Viscount Dr B35 . . . . .58 B2
Vista Gn B38 . . . . .104 B1
Vista The DY3 . . . . .39 D2
Vittle Dr CV34 . . . . .160 D7
Vittoria St
  Birmingham B1 . . . . .66 C4
  Smethwick B66 . . . . .65 D6
Vittoria Works B1 . . . . .66 C4
Vivian CI B17 . . . . .85 C5
Vivian Rd B17 . . . . .85 C5
Vixen CI B76 . . . . .57 D7
Vodena Ct **5** CV32 . . . .156 F1
Vogue CI CV1 . . . . .165 D3
Vowchurch CI B97 . . . . . . .153 A5
Voyager Dr WS11 . . . . .4 F6
Vulcan Ho B91 . . . . .107 C6
Vulcan House Ind Est
  B91 . . . . .107 C6
Vulcan Ind Est WS2 . . . . . . .28 C6
Vulcan Rd
  Bilston WV14 . . . . .40 F5
  Lichfield WS13 . . . . .3 E1
  Solihull B91 . . . . .107 C7
Vulcan Road Ind Est WV14 .40 F5
Vyrnwy Gr B38 . . . . .123 E8
Vyse St
  Birmingham,Aston B6 . . . . . .67 B8
  Birmingham,Hockley B18. . . .66 C4

W

Wackrill Dr CV32 . . . . .157 C3
Wadbarn B90. . . . . .126 A5
Waddam's Pool DY2 . . . . . . .51 D1
Waddell CI WV14 . . . . .39 F2
Waddens Brook La WV11. . .26 E5
Waddington Ave B43. . . . . . .43 E1
Wade Ave CV3 . . . . .133 B5
Wadebridge Dr CV11. . . . . . .73 F5
Wade La CV3 . . . . .62 E3
Wades CI **8** DY4. . . . . . . .51 E5
Wadesmill Lawns WV10 . . . .11 E4
Wade St WV13 . . . . .9 B7
Wadham CI B65 . . . . .63 C6
Wadham Ho B37. . . . . .70 D3
Wadham's Fold WV1 . . . . . .163 B3
Wadhurst Rd B17 . . . . .65 B2
Wadleys Rd B91 . . . . .106 F6
Waen CI DY4 . . . . .52 B8
Waggestaff Dr CV10 . . . . . . .72 A7
Waggoners CI **1** B60 . .150 E6
Waggoner's La B78. . . . . . . .33 E8
Waggon La DY10. . . . . .98 A3
Waggon St B64 . . . . .62 F2
Waggon Wlk B38 . . . . .123 C8
Wagoners CI B8 . . . . .67 F6
Wagon La B26,B92 . . . . .88 F4
Wagstaff CI WV14 . . . . .51 D8
Wagstaff Way B37 . . . . .90 A8
Wainbody Ave N CV3 . . . . .133 A6
Wainbody Ave S CV3 . . . . .132 F5
Wainbody Wood Sch
  CV4 . . . . .132 D2
Wainrigg B77 . . . . .36 B7
Wainwright CI DY6. . . . . .60 A8
Wainwright St B6. . . . . .67 A7
Waite Rd WV13 . . . . .40 E8
Wakefield CI
  Coventry CV3. . . . . .134 F7

Wakefield CI continued
  Sutton Coldfield B73 . . . . . . .46 A2
Wakefield Ct B13 . . . . .87 B2
Wakefield Gr B46 . . . . .59 B3
Wakeford Rd B31 . . . . .103 C1
Wake Green Pk B13. . . . . . . .87 B2
Wake Green Rd
  Birmingham B13 . . . . .87 A2
  Wednesbury B71 . . . . .41 A1
Wake Gr CV34 . . . . .160 B5
Wakehurst Cl CV11 . . . . .78 F8
Wakelam Gdns B43 . . . . . . .43 D1
Wakelams Fold DY3 . . . . . . .50 C3
Wakeley Hill WV4 . . . . .38 F4
Wakelin Rd B90. . . . . .126 B7
Wakeman Ct WV11. . . . . .12 F3
Wakeman Dr B69. . . . . .63 B8
Wakeman Gr B33 . . . . .89 D7
Wakes CI WV13 . . . . .27 B1
Wakes Rd WS10. . . . . .42 A2
Walcot CI B75. . . . . .32 B3
Walcot Dr B43. . . . . .54 F6
Walcot CI LE10 . . . . .74 F8
Walcot Gdns WV14. . . . . . . .40 B4
Walcot Gn CV34 . . . . .128 A2
Waldale CI WV11 . . . . .13 C1
Walden Gdns WV4 . . . . .38 E6
Walden Rd B11. . . . . .88 A3
Waldeve Gr B92 . . . . .107 F8
Waldley Gr B24 . . . . .57 D3
Waldon Wlk B36. . . . . .69 F8
Waldron Ave DY5 . . . . .61 B2
Waldron CI WS10 . . . . .41 F6
Waldrons Moor B14. . . . . . .104 C5
Walford Ave WV3 . . . . .38 B8
Walford Dr B92. . . . . .89 D3
Walford Gn B32. . . . . .102 B7
Walford Gr CV34 . . . . .155 F1
Walford Rd B11. . . . . .87 C6
Walford St B69 . . . . .52 A2
Walford Wlk **6** B97 . . . .153 E3
Walhouse CE Jun Sch
  WS11 . . . . .1 C1
Walhouse CI **6** WS11 . . .28 F2
Walhouse Rd WS1 . . . . .29 A2
Walhouse St WS11 . . . . .4 E8
Walker Ave
  Brierley Hill DY5 . . . . .81 D7
  Oldbury B69. . . . . .63 C7
  Stourbridge DY9 . . . . .81 E3
  Wolverhampton WV10. . . . . .25 E8
Walker Dr B24. . . . . .67 E8
Walker Grange DY4 . . . . .51 F6
Walker PI WS3. . . . . .28 E8
Walker Rd WS3 . . . . .28 E8
Walkers Croft WS13 . . . . .3 C2
Walkers Fold WV12 . . . . .27 E6
Walkers Heath Rd B38 . . . .104 B1
Walkers Orch CV8 . . . . .149 B6
Walkers Rd B98. . . . . .154 E6
Walkers Rise WS12 . . . . .2 D8
Walker St
  Bedworth CV12 . . . . .77 F1
  Kenilworth CV8 . . . . .147 F2
Walk La WV5 . . . . .49 A6
Walkmill Bsns Pk WS11 . . . . .4 D5
Walkmill La WS11. . . . . .4 D5
Walkmill Way WS11 . . . . .4 D5
Walk The DY3. . . . . .39 F8
Walkwood CE Mid Sch
  B97. . . . . .158 C8
Walkwood Cres B97 . . . . . .158 C6
Walkwood Rd B97 . . . . .158 D6
Wallace CI
  Norton Canes WS11 . . . . .5 F5
  Oldbury B69. . . . . .63 D6
  Walsall CV56. . . . . .4 D1
Wallace Ho
  8 Oldbury B69. . . . . . . .63 D5
  Warwick CV34. . . . . .160 D7
Wallace Rd
  Bilston WV14. . . . . .41 A2
  Birmingham B29 . . . . .86 B2
  Brownhills WS8 . . . . .15 E8
  Coventry CV6. . . . . .113 A8
  Oldbury B69. . . . . .63 D6
Wallace Rise B64 . . . . .82 E7
Wall Ave B46. . . . . .70 F5
Wallbank Rd B8 . . . . .68 A6
Wallbrook Prim Sch
  WV14. . . . . .51 E8
Wallbrook St WV14*. 51 D8
Wall Croft WS9 . . . . .30 B7
Wall End CI WS5 . . . . .31 F4
Wall End Ct WS5 . . . . .28 A7
Waller CI CV35. . . . . .155 F7
Waller St CV32 . . . . .157 A2
Wallface B71. . . . . .53 B7
Wallheath Cres WS14 . . . . . .16 F5
Wallheath La WS14 . . . . .16 F5
Wall Hill Rd CV5,CV7 . . . . . . .94 B3
Walling Croft WV14 . . . . .40 B3
Wallington CI WS3 . . . . .14 B2
Wallington Heath WS3 . . . . . .14 B2
Wallis Ct **1** B13 . . . . .87 B2
Wall La WS13,WS14. . . . . .8 D3
Wall (Letocetvm) Roman Site
  (Town)* B13. . . . . .8 E2
Wallnut Wlk WS11 . . . . .5 B5
Wallows Ind Est The DY5. . .61 D5
Wallows La WS1,WS2. . . . . . .42 C6
Wallows Rd DY5. . . . . .61 D5
Wallows Rd DY5. . . . . .61 D5
Wallows Wood DY3. . . . . . . .50 A4

Wall Roman Site (Letocetvm)
  Mus* WS14. . . . . .8 D2
Wallsgrove CI CV32 . . . . . .157 B3
Wall's Rd B60 . . . . .150 C3
Wall St WV1 . . . . .26 B2
Wall Well B63 . . . . .82 F3
Wall Well La B63 . . . . .82 F3
Wallwin Ct CV34 . . . . .160 D6
Walmead Croft **1** B17 . . .84 F7
Walmer Ct B16 . . . . .65 D2
Walmer Gr B23 . . . . .56 B5
Walmer Mdw WS9 . . . . .30 B7
Walmers The WS9 . . . . .30 B7
Walmers Wlk The B31. . . . .102 D1
Walmer Way B37 . . . . .70 C3
Walmesley Way B31 . . . . . .102 E3
Walmley Ash Ct B76 . . . . . . .57 F8
Walmley Ash La B76. . . . . . .58 C6
Walmley Ash Rd B76. . . . . . .58 A7
Walmley CI
  Halesowen B63 . . . . .82 B7
  Sutton Coldfield B76 . . . . . . .57 F8
Walmley Jun & Inf Schs
  B76. . . . . .58 A7
Walmley Park Ct B76 . . . . . .57 F8
Walmley Rd B76. . . . . .46 F2
Walney CI LE10 . . . . .71 B1
Walnut Ave WV8 . . . . .10 B3
Walnut CI
  Birmingham B37 . . . . .70 B1
  Cannock WS11. . . . . .1 F3
  Hartshill CV10 . . . . .72 A8
  Nuneaton,Camp Hill CV10 . . .72 E6
  Stourbridge DY9 . . . . .81 B1
Walnut Dr
  5 Smethwick B66 . . . . . . .65 B5
  Cannock WS11. . . . . .1 F3
  Royal Leamington Spa
    CV32. . . . . .157 B3
  Wolverhampton WV3 . . . . . . .24 D1
Walnut Gr WV14 . . . . .9 F7
Walnut La
  Finstall B60 . . . . .151 D8
  Wednesbury WS10 . . . . .42 A2
Walnut Rd WS5. . . . . .43 A4
Walnut St CV2 . . . . .96 B2
Walnut Tree CI CV8 . . . . . . .148 A3
Walnut Way B31 . . . . .122 F8
Walpole St WV6 . . . . .25 A3
Walpole Wlk **3** B70 . . . . .53 D1
Walsal End La B92. . . . . . . .108 F3
Walsall Acad WS3 . . . . .14 C2
Walsall Arboretum* WS3. . . .29 A2
Walsall Coll of Arts & Tech
  (Shelley Campus) WS2 . . . . .28 C1
Walsall Coll of Arts & Tech
  Walsall WS1 . . . . .28 E2
  Walsall WS2 . . . . .28 D3
Walsall Ent Pk WS2. . . . . . . .42 C8
Walsall New Firms Ctr
  WS1. . . . . .42 D8
Walsall Rd
  Aldridge WS9. . . . . .30 A5
  Birmingham B42 . . . . .55 B6
  Brownhills WS9 . . . . .15 E2
  Cannock WS11. . . . . .4 E7
  Darlaston WS10. . . . . .41 E6
  Great Wyrley WS6 . . . . .5 A2
  Leamonsley WS13 . . . . .3 D4
  Lichfield,Christ Church WS13 . .9 A7
  Lichfield,Pipehill WS13,WS14 . .8 C5
  Norton Canes WS11 . . . . .5 F4
  Stonnall WS14 . . . . .16 E8
  Sutton Coldfield B74 . . . . . . .31 D4
  Walsall,The Delves WS5 . . . . .42 F4
  Walsall WS3 . . . . .15 A1
  Wednesbury WS10,B71,
    WS5. . . . . .42 F2
  West Bromwich B71 . . . . . . .53 E8
  Willenhall WV13 . . . . .27 C2
Walsall Sta WS1 . . . . .28 E2
Walsall St
  Bilston WV14. . . . . .40 D8
  Coventry CV4. . . . . .132 B7
  Darlaston WS10. . . . . .41 D7
  Dudley WV14. . . . . .51 B8
  Walsall WS1 . . . . .28 F2
  Willenhall WV13 . . . . .27 B3
  Wolverhampton WV1 . . . . . .163 D3
Walsall Wood Jun Mix & Inf
  Sch WS8. . . . . .16 A4
Walsall Wood Rd WS9. . . . . .30 B7
Walsgrave CE Prim Sch
  CV2 . . . . .115 A6
Walsgrave CI B92. . . . . .107 D6
Walsgrave Dr B92. . . . . .107 D6
Walsgrave Gdns **5** CV2 .115 A7
Walsgrave Hospl CV2 . . . . .115 A5
Walsgrave Rd CV2 . . . . .114 B3
Walsgrave Ret Pk CV2 . . . .115 B7
Walsham Croft B34 . . . . .69 C5
Walsh Dr B76 . . . . .46 F4
Walsh Gr B23. . . . . .56 D8
Walsh La CV7 . . . . .92 E2
Walsingham St WS1 . . . . . . .29 A1
Walstead CI WS5 . . . . .43 C5
Walstead Rd WS5. . . . . .43 B5
Walstead Rd W WS5 . . . . . . .42 F5
Waltdene CI B43 . . . . .43 E3
Walter Burden Ho B66 . . . . .65 C3
Walter Cobb Dr B73 . . . . . . .46 A1
Walter Ct B20 . . . . .55 C2
Walter Nash Rd E DY11. 116 A1
Walter Nash Rd W DY11. 116 A1
Walter Rd
  Bilston WV14. . . . . .40 F3
  Smethwick B67. . . . . .64 E6
Walters CI B31. . . . . .122 F6

Walter Scott Rd CV12 . . . . . .78 C1
Walters Rd B68. . . . . .84 B6
Walters Row DY1 . . . . .51 A1
Walter St
  Birmingham B7 . . . . .67 B6
  Walsall WS3 . . . . .15 A1
  West Bromwich B70 . . . . . . .53 E2
Waltham CI B61 . . . . .136 E1
Waltham Cres CV10 . . . . . . .72 B5
Waltham Gr B44. . . . . .45 B2
Waltham Ho
  Birmingham B38 . . . . .104 B1
  West Bromwich B70 . . . . . . .53 D3
Walthamstow Ct DY5. . . . . . .61 D1
Walton Ave B65. . . . . .83 B8
Walton CI
  Coventry CV34. . . . . .134 E7
  Halesowen B63 . . . . .82 F2
  Kidderminster DY11 . . . . . .116 B2
  Nuneaton CV11 . . . . .79 A7
  Redditch B98 . . . . .154 E3
  Rowley Regis B65 . . . . .63 A4
Walton Cres WV4 . . . . .39 E5
Walton Croft B91 . . . . .107 B1
Walton Ct B63 . . . . .82 F3
Walton Dr DY9. . . . . .81 C5
Walton Gr B30. . . . . .104 B2
Walton Heath WS3 . . . . .13 F3
Walton Pool La DY9. . . . . . . .99 F2
Walton Rd
  Aldridge WS9. . . . . .16 A1
  Bromsgrove B61 . . . . .137 B4
  Oldbury B68. . . . . .64 C2
  Stourbridge DY9 . . . . .81 A6
  Wednesbury WS10 . . . . .42 C2
  Wolverhampton WV4 . . . . . .39 F5
Walton Rise DY9 . . . . .100 A3
Walton St DY4 . . . . .51 F5
Wanderers Ave WV2 . . . . . . .39 C6
Wanderer Wlk B36. . . . . .57 E1
Wandle Gr B11 . . . . .88 A4
Wandsbeck B77 . . . . .35 E8
Wandsworth Rd B44 . . . . . . .44 F3
Wanley Rd CV3 . . . . .133 D6
Wannerton Rd DY10. . . . . . . .98 B1
Wansbeck Gr B38. . . . . .123 E8
Wansbeck Wlk DY3 . . . . .50 F6
Wansfell CI CV4 . . . . .132 A7
Wanstead Gr B44. . . . . .45 A1
Wantage Rd B46. . . . . .59 E1
Wappenbury CI CV2. . . . . . . .96 C2
Wappenbury Rd CV2 . . . . . . .96 D2
Warbage La
  Belbroughton DY9 . . . . . . .119 F1
  Dodford B61 . . . . .136 A7
Warbank CI B48 . . . . .139 A6
Warbler PI DY10 . . . . .117 A2
Ward CI B8. . . . . .68 A5
Warden Ave B73 . . . . .56 F8
Ward End CI B8 . . . . .67 F6
Ward End Hall Gr B8. . . . . . . .68 A6
Ward End Park Rd B8 . . . . . .67 F5
Ward End Prim Sch B8 . . . . .68 B6
Wardend Rd B8. . . . . .68 A6
Warden Rd
  Coventry CV6. . . . . .113 B6
  Sutton Coldfield B73 . . . . . . .56 F8
Wardens Ave The CV5 . . . . .112 B6
Wardens The CV8 . . . . .148 C5
Ward Gr
  Warwick CV34 . . . . .161 C7
  Wolverhampton WV4 . . . . . .39 F3
Wardle CI B75 . . . . .32 A4
Wardle PI WS11 . . . . .1 E5
Wardles La WS6. . . . . .4 F2
Wardle St B79 . . . . .21 A5
Wardlow CI WV4 . . . . .39 B6
Wardlow Rd B7 . . . . .67 B4
Wardour Dr B37 . . . . .70 C2
Wardour Gr B44. . . . . .45 B1
Ward Rd WV4 . . . . .39 D5
Ward St
  Bilston WV2. . . . . .40 B6
  Birmingham B19 . . . . .164 C5
  Cannock WS12. . . . . .1 F6
  Dudley WV14. . . . . .51 B8
  Walsall WS1 . . . . .28 F2
  Willenhall WV13 . . . . .27 B3
  Wolverhampton WV1 . . . . . .163 D3
Wareham CI WS3 . . . . .28 F5
Wareham Gn CV2 . . . . .115 A5
Wareham Ho B28 . . . . .105 E3
Wareham Rd B45 . . . . .102 B2
Wareing Dr B23 . . . . .56 D8
Warewell CI **5** WS1 . . . . .28 F2
Warewell St **8** WS1. . . . . .28 F2
Waring CI DY4. . . . . .51 E8
Waring Rd DY4. . . . . .52 A8
Warings Green Rd B94. . . .126 D1
War La B17. . . . . .85 B5
Warley Croft B68. . . . . .84 E8
Warley Hall Rd B68. . . . . . . .64 B2
Warley High Coll of Sport
  B68. . . . . .64 C2
Warley Ho B67 . . . . .64 F2
Warley Inf Sch B68. . . . . . . .64 C1
Warley Rd B68. . . . . .64 C1
Warmington Dr B73 . . . . . . .46 A4
Warmington Gr CV34 . . . . .160 B8
Warmington Rd
  Birmingham B26 . . . . .89 C5
  Hollywood B47. . . . . .125 A6
Warmley CI
  Solihull B90 . . . . .107 D5
  Wolverhampton WV6. . . . . . .25 B5
Warmstry Rd B60 . . . . .137 C1

Warmwell CI CV2 . . . . .114 F4
Warneford Mews **9**
  CV31 . . . . .162 A7
Warner CI CV34. . . . . .155 D1
Warner Dr DY5 . . . . .61 D1
Warner PI **1** WS3 . . . . . . .28 F6
Warner Rd
  Walsall WS3 . . . . .29 A6
  Wednesbury WS10 . . . . .42 C2
Warner Row **2** CV6. . . . .113 F7
Warner St **1** B12. . . . . . . .87 A8
Warners Wlk **1** B10. . . . . .87 C8
Warnford Wlk WV4 . . . . .38 C6
Warnford Wlk WV4 . . . . .38 C6
Warple Rd B32 . . . . .84 C5
Warren Ave
  Birmingham B13 . . . . .86 F2
  Wolverhampton WV10. . . . . .25 F5
Warren CI
  Earlswood B94. . . . . .142 A8
  Lichfield WS14. . . . . .9 E7
  Royal Leamington Spa
    CV32. . . . . .157 A3
  Ryton-on-D CV8. . . . . .135 A1
  Tipton DY4 . . . . .52 A7
Warren Dr
  Dorridge B93. . . . . .128 A3
  Rowley Regis B65 . . . . .62 F5
  Sedgley DY3. . . . . .39 C1
Warren Farm Prim Sch
  B44. . . . . .56 A8
Warren Farm Rd B44 . . . . . .56 A8
Warren Field CV8 . . . . .135 A1
Warren Gdns DY6 . . . . .60 C6
Warren Gn CV4 . . . . .131 F7
Warren Hill Rd B44 . . . . .56 A7
Warren House Ct B76 . . . . . .46 F1
Warren House Wlk B76 . . . . .46 F1
Warren La B45 . . . . .122 B3
Warren PI WS8 . . . . .16 A7
Warren Rd
  Birmingham,Perry B44 . . . . .56 A7
  Birmingham,Stirchley B30. . .104 A6
  Birmingham,Washwood Heath
    B8. . . . . .67 E6
  Burntwood WS7. . . . . .7 A5
Warrens Croft WS5 . . . . .43 D5
Warrens End **1** B38 . . . .103 F1
Warrens Hall Rd DY2 . . . . . .62 E7
Warrington CI B76 . . . . .47 A1
Warrington Dr B23 . . . . .56 D7
Warsash CI WV1 . . . . .40 B8
Warstock La B14 . . . . .105 A4
Warstock Rd B14. . . . . .105 A3
Warston Ave B32. . . . . .84 C2
Warstone Dr B71 . . . . .53 E4
Warstone La B18 . . . . .66 C4
Warstone Mews **2** B18 . .66 C4
Warstone Par E B18 . . . . . . .66 B4
Warstone Rd WS6 . . . . .13 C7
Warstones Cres WV4 . . . . . .38 C5
Warstones Dr WV4 . . . . .38 C6
Warstones Gdns WV4 . . . . . .38 C6
Warstones Jun & Inf Schs
  WV4 . . . . .38 E6
Warstones Rd WV4 . . . . .38 C6
Warstone Terr B21. . . . . .65 E8
Warstone Twr B36 . . . . .68 D8
Wartell Bank Ind Est DY6 . .60 D7
Wartell Bank DY6. . . . . .60 D7
Warton CI CV8 . . . . .148 C4
Warwards La B29. . . . . .86 B8
Warwell La B26. . . . . .88 D6
Warwick Ave
  Bromsgrove B60 . . . . .151 A8
  Coventry CV5. . . . . .133 A8
  Perton WV6 . . . . .23 F3
  Wednesbury WS10 . . . . .42 C4
  Willenhall WV13 . . . . .27 D2
Warwick By-Pass
  Hampton Magna CV34,
    CV35. . . . . .160 A5
  Warwick CV34 . . . . .161 A1
Warwick Castle* CV34 . .160 E6
Warwick CI
  Cannock WS12. . . . . .4 F8
  Oldbury B68. . . . . .64 B2
  Studley B80. . . . . .159 D3
  West Bromwich B70 . . . . . . .52 E7
Warwick Crest B15 . . . . .86 B7
Warwick Ct
  1 Birmingham,Acock's Green
    B27. . . . . .88 C2
  1 Birmingham,Weoley Castle
    B29. . . . . .103 C7
  5 Birmingham,Chelmsley Wood
    B37. . . . . .70 D2
  5 Solihull B91 . . . . .106 F3
  9 Wolverhampton WV4 . . .39 F4
  Birmingham,Moseley B13 . . .87 A2
  Coventry CV3. . . . . .165 B1
  Dudley DY3. . . . . .50 D3
  Solihull,Lode Heath B91 . . .107 B4
Warwick Gdns
  Hinckley LE10 . . . . .71 E3
  Nuneaton CV10 . . . . .72 E4
  Oldbury B69. . . . . .52 C2
  Willenhall WV13 . . . . .27 D2
Warwick Gn CV12. . . . . .78 C2
Warwick Grange B91 . . . . .106 F7
Warwick Gr B92 . . . . .88 E1
Warwick Hall Gdns B60 . . .151 A8
Warwick Highway B98 . . . .154 C2
Warwick Ho B73. . . . . .46 A3

Warwick La CV1 . . . . .165 B2
Warwick New Rd CV32 . .161 C8
Warwick Park Ct B92 . . . .106 F8
Warwick Parkway CV35 . .160 A7
Warwick Pas **3** B2 . . . . .164 C2
Warwick Pl CV32 . . . . . . .156 E1
Warwick Race Course
CV34 . . . . .160 C6
Warwick Rd
Birmingham,Birchfield
B42 . . . . .55 E2
Birmingham,Sparkhill B11 . .87 D4
Birmingham,Warley Woods
B68 . . . . .84 D7
Chadwick End B93 . . . . . .145 A7
Coventry CV3 . . . . .165 B1
Dudley DY2 . . . . .62 E3
Kenilworth CV8 . . . . .148 A1
Knowle B93 . . . . .128 D3
Leek Wootton CV35 . . . . .155 F7
Solihull B27,B91,B92 . . . .106 F7
Stourbridge DY8 . . . . .60 D1
Sutton Coldfield B73 . . . . .45 C2
Tamworth B77 . . . . .21 E4
Wolston CV8 . . . . .135 F3
Warwick Road Trad Est
B11 . . . . .87 D4
Warwick Row CV1 . . . . . .165 B2
Warwick Sch CV34 . . . . . .161 A6
Warwickshire Coll CV32 . .161 D8
Warwickshire Mus*
CV34 . . . . .160 E6
Warwickshire Nuffield Hospl
The CV32 . . . . .156 E5
Warwick Sta CV34 . . . . . .160 F7
Warwick St
Bilston WV14 . . . . .40 E5
Birmingham B12 . . . . .67 A1
Coventry CV5 . . . . .112 F1
Royal Leamington Spa
CV32 . . . . .156 F1
Walsall WS4 . . . . .28 F3
Wolverhampton WV1 . . . .163 D2
Warwick Tech Pk CV34 . .161 B5
Warwick Terr CV32 . . . . . .156 E1
Warwick Way WS9 . . . . . .16 A1
Wasdale Cl CV32 . . . . . . .156 C2
Wasdale Dr DY6 . . . . .60 E6
Wasdale Rd
Birmingham B31 . . . . .102 F4
Brownhills WS8 . . . . .15 D6
Waseley Hills Country Pk*
B45 . . . . .121 C8
Waseley Hills High Sch &
Sixth Form Ctr B45 . . . .121 D7
Waseley Hills Visitor Ctr*
B45 . . . . .101 C1
Waseley Rd B45 . . . . .121 E8
Washbourne Rd CV31 . . .162 A2
Washbrook La
Hawkes End CV5 . . . . .94 A1
Norton Canes WS11 . . . . . .5 D5
Washbrook Rd B8 . . . . . . .68 A6
Washford Dr B98 . . . . . . .159 D7
Washford Gr B25 . . . . .88 B8
Washford Ind Est B98 . . .159 E8
Washford La B98 . . . . . . .159 D8
Washington Ct B1 . . . . . . .164 A1
Washington Ctr DY2 . . . . .62 D4
Washington Ct WV3 . . . . . .24 D1
Washington Dr B20 . . . . . .55 B3
Washington St
Birmingham B1 . . . . .164 A1
Dudley DY2 . . . . .62 D3
Kidderminster DY11 . . . . .116 C5
Washington Wharf B1 . . .164 A1
Wash La B25 . . . . .88 C8
Washwood Heath Rd B8 . .67 E6
Washwood Heath Tech Coll
B8 . . . . .68 C5
Wasperton Cl
6 Coventry CV3 . . . . . .134 F8
Wasperton La B58 . . . . . . .69 B8
Wassall Ct B63 . . . . .82 E2
Wassell Grove Bsns Ctr
DY9 . . . . .82 A2
Wassell Grove Rd
Hagley DY9 . . . . .99 F8
Halesowen B63 . . . . .82 A2
Wassell Rd
Bilston WV14 . . . . .40 D7
Halesowen B63 . . . . .82 E2
Stourbridge DY9 . . . . .81 E2
Waste La
Balsall Common CV7 . . . .130 F5
Coventry CV6 . . . . .94 F1
Wast Hill Gr B38 . . . . .123 F7
Wasthill La B38,B48 . . . . .123 D5
Wastwater Ct WV6 . . . . . .23 F4
Watchbury Cl B36 . . . . . . .58 C1
Watch Cl CV1 . . . . .165 A3
Watchmaker Ct CV1 . . . . .165 A2
Watchman Ave DY5 . . . . . .81 F7
Watcombe Rd CV2 . . . . . .114 E8
Waterbrook Way WS11 . . . .4 E6
Watercall Ave CV3 . . . . . .133 C6
Waterdale B90 . . . . .126 D5
Water Dale WV3 . . . . .24 E1
Waterfall Cl
Meriden CV7 . . . . .92 C1
Smethwick B66 . . . . .64 E7
Waterfall La B64 . . . . .63 A1
Waterfall Lane Ind Est
B64 . . . . .63 A1
Waterfall Rd DY5 . . . . .81 D7

Waterfall Way LE9 . . . . . . .71 F5
Waterfield Cl DY4 . . . . .51 D5
Waterfield Gdns CV31 . . .162 C7
Waterfield Way
Birmingham B26 . . . . .89 C7
Hinckley LE10 . . . . .75 C5
Watford Cl B23 . . . . .56 B4
Waterford Pl B33 . . . . .69 D3
Waterford Rd DY6 . . . . . . .60 D7
Waterford Way CV3 . . . . .114 C1
Waterfront Bsns Pk B69,Y1 . .51 F4
Waterfront E DY5 . . . . .61 E4
Waterfront Way
2 Walsall WS2 . . . . .28 D2
Brierley Hill DY2,DY5 . . . . .61 F4
Waterfront W DY5 . . . . . . .61 E4
Waterglade La WV13 . . . . .27 A1
Waterhaynes Cl B45 . . . . .122 A6
Waterhead Cl WV10 . . . . . .12 A2
Waterhead Dr WV10 . . . . . .12 B2
Water La B71 . . . . .53 F7
Waterlily Cl WS12 . . . . .2 E3
Water Lily Gr WS8 . . . . . . .15 E7
Water Lily Way CV10 . . . . .78 A8
Waterlinks Blvd B6 . . . . . . .67 A7
Waterloo Ave B37 . . . . . . .70 B4
Waterloo Bvd WS12 . . . . . .2 E4
Waterloo Ct CV34 . . . . . . .161 A8
Waterloo Ind Est B37 . . . . .70 B5
Waterloo Pl **5** CV32 . . . .156 F1
Waterloo Rd
Birmingham,King's Heath
B14 . . . . .104 E8
Birmingham,South Yardley
B25 . . . . .88 C6
Hinckley LE10 . . . . .75 D8
Smethwick B66 . . . . .65 A5
Wolverhampton WV1 . . . .163 B4
Waterloo St E DY4 . . . . . . .51 F5
Waterloo St
8 Coventry CV1 . . . . . .113 E4
Birmingham B2 . . . . .164 B2
Dudley DY1 . . . . .62 B8
Kidderminster DY10 . . . . .116 E6
Royal Leamington Spa
CV31 . . . . .162 B7
Tipton DY4 . . . . .51 F5
Waterloo Terr WV1 . . . . . .163 A4
Waterman Rd CV6 . . . . . .113 F6
Watermarque **2** B16 . . . . .66 B2
Watermead Grange WS8 . .15 E7
Watermeadow Dr WS4 . . .15 D1
Watermere WS4 . . . . .29 D8
Water Mill Cl B29 . . . . .85 D3
Water Mill Cres B76 . . . . . .46 F1
Water Mill Prim Sch B29 . .85 D3
Watermint Cl WS12 . . . . . . .2 E4
Water Orton La B46,B76 . . .58 E4
Water Orton Prim Sch
B46 . . . . .59 B2
Water Orton Rd B36 . . . . . .58 E1
Water Orton Sta B46 . . . . .59 A3
Water Rd DY3 . . . . .50 C2
Watersbridge Gdns CV10 . .73 C1
Waters Dr B74 . . . . .31 D3
Waters Edge The B1 . . . . . .66 C2
Waterside
1 Birmingham B15 . . . . .66 C1
Bedworth CV6 . . . . .96 C6
Birmingham,Egbaston B15 . .86 C8
Birmingham,Hamstead B43 . .54 E7
Waterside Cl
Birmingham,Bordesley B9 . .67 B2
Birmingham,Pype Hayes
B24 . . . . .58 A5
Wolverhampton WV2 . . . .39 D7
Waterside Ct
1 Birmingham B16 . . . . . .66 B2
Hinckley LE10 . . . . .74 F7
Royal Leamington Spa
CV31 . . . . .162 B6
Tamworth B77 . . . . .21 F5
Waterside Dr B18 . . . . .65 F5
Waterside Est DY2 . . . . . . .62 C3
Waterside Grange DY10 . .116 E8
Waterside Ind Est
Rowley Regis B65 . . . . . . .62 F4
Wolverhampton WV2 . . . .40 A6
Waterside Orch B48 . . . . .123 B2
Waterside CV31 . . . . .161 D7
Waterside View
Birmingham B18 . . . . .66 A5
Brierley Hill DY5 . . . . .81 B8
Waterside Way
Brownhills WS8 . . . . .6 D2
Wolverhampton WV9 . . . . .11 A3
Watersmead Cl WS12 . . . . .2 F4
Watersmeet Gr CV2 . . . . .114 B6
Watersmeet Ho CV2 . . . . .114 B6
Watersmeet Rd CV2 . . . . .114 B6
Waterson Croft B37 . . . . . .70 D3
Water St
Birmingham B3 . . . . .164 B3
Burntwood WS7 . . . . .6 E8
Kingswinford DY6 . . . . .60 D7
West Bromwich B70 . . . . . .53 D2
Wolverhampton WV10 . . .163 D4
Waters View WS3 . . . . .15 B5
Waterward Cl B17 . . . . .85 C5
Waterway Ct B14 . . . . .105 C3
Waterways Dr B69 . . . . .63 E8
Waterways Gdns DY8 . . . . .60 E1
Waterworks Dr B31 . . . . . .102 D4
Waterworks Rd B16 . . . . . .65 F1
Waterworks St B6 . . . . .67 B8
Watery La
Alvechurch B48 . . . . .124 C1

Watery La continued
Birmingham B62 . . . . .84 A3
Blakedown DY10 . . . . .118 F2
Cheswick Green B90 . . . . .126 D4
Codsall WV8 . . . . .10 A5
Corley Moor CV7 . . . . .93 D5
Coventry CV6 . . . . .95 A4
Hopwood B48 . . . . .123 F2
Keresley CV7 . . . . .94 F4
Knowle B93 . . . . .128 E4
Lichfield WS13 . . . . .3 E2
Longbridge CV35 . . . . . . .160 A1
Watery Lane Ind Est
WV13 . . . . .26 E3
Watery Lane Middleway
B9 .67 B2
Watery La
Portway B47,B48 . . . . . . .140 D7
Redditch B98 . . . . .154 B2
Smethwick B67 . . . . .65 A5
Stourbridge DY8 . . . . .60 E2
Tipton DY4 . . . . .51 F5
Walsall WS1 . . . . .42 E8
Willenhall WV13 . . . . .26 E3
Watford Gap Rd WS14 . . . .32 A7
Watford Gap SW14 . . . . . . .32 A7
Watford Rd B30 . . . . .103 F5
Wathan Ave WV14 . . . . . . .39 F1
Wathen Rd
Royal Leamington Spa
CV32 . . . . .157 A2
Warwick CV34 . . . . .160 E8
Watkins Gdns B31 . . . . . . .103 C4
Watkins Rd WV12 . . . . .27 C5
Watland Gn B34 . . . . .69 B5
Watling Cl LE10 . . . . .75 C4
Watling Ct CV11 . . . . .73 F3
Watling Dr LE10 . . . . .75 C4
Watling Rd CV8 . . . . .148 B6
Watling St
Brownhills WS8 . . . . .6 D1
Cannock WS11 . . . . .4 D6
Dordon B77,B78 . . . . .36 D6
Hinckley CV11,LE10 . . . . . .74 C8
Hints B78 . . . . .19 D3
Norton Canes WS11 . . . . . . .5 D3
Watling Street Bsns Pk
WS11 . . . . .6 A2
Watling Street Prim Sch
WS8 . . . . .6 C1
Watling St
Tamworth,Bonehill B78 . . . .20 E1
Tamworth,Wilnecote B77 . . .35 E7
Watney Gr B44 . . . . .56 C8
Watson Cl
3 Warwick CV34 . . . . . .155 E1
Sutton Coldfield B72 . . . . . .46 C2
Watson Rd
Birmingham B7 . . . . .67 D7
Birmingham,Nechells B24 . .67 D8
Birmingham,Saltley B8 . . . .67 F5
Coventry CV5 . . . . .112 D2
Darlaston WS10 . . . . .41 A5
Watson Rd E B7 . . . . .67 D7
Watson Rd
Wolverhampton,Pendeford
WV10 . . . . .11 B2
Wolverhampton WV14 . . . .39 F2
Watsons Cl DY2 . . . . .62 E8
Watson's Green Fields
DY2 . . . . .62 F8
Watson's Green Rd DY2 . . .51 E1
Watson Way CV7 . . . . .130 C8
Watt Cl B60 . . . . .136 F1
Watt Ho DY6 . . . . .60 F7
Wattisham Sq B35 . . . . . . .58 A4
Wattis Rd B67 . . . . .65 A2
Wattle Gn B70 . . . . .53 A3
Wattle Rd B70 . . . . .53 A3
Watton Cl WV14 . . . . .40 A1
Watton Ct B6 . . . . .66 E8
Watton Gn B35 . . . . .58 A2
Watton La B46 . . . . .59 D2
Watton St B70 . . . . .53 D2
Watt Rd
Birmingham B23 . . . . .56 E4
Tipton DY4 . . . . .52 B8
Watts Cl DY4 . . . . .51 D5
Watt's Rd B10 . . . . .87 D8
Watts Rd B80 . . . . .159 E2
Watt St
Birmingham B21 . . . . .65 D7
Smethwick B66 . . . . .65 B6
Wattville Ave B21 . . . . .65 C8
Wattville Prim Sch B21 . . .65 B8
Wattville Rd B21 . . . . .65 C8
Watt Wood Rd B28,B90 . . .105 F3
Waugh Cl B37 . . . . .70 B2
Waugh Dr B63 . . . . .100 D8
Waveley Rd CV1 . . . . .113 A3
Wavell Rd
Birmingham B8 . . . . .67 E5
Brierley Hill DY5 . . . . .81 F7
Walsall WS2 . . . . .27 F2
Wavendon Cl CV2 . . . . .96 F1
Waveney Ave WV6 . . . . . . .23 F4
Waveney Cl LE10 . . . . .75 A8
Waveney Croft B36 . . . . . . .69 F8
Waveney B77 . . . . .35 E8
Wavenham Cl B74 . . . . . . .31 E5
Waverhill Rd B21 . . . . .65 F7
Waverley Ave
Birmingham B43 . . . . .44 B4
Nuneaton CV11 . . . . .73 F1
Waverley Cl DY10 . . . . . . .117 A8
Waverley Cres
Romsley B62 . . . . .100 F4

Waverley Cres continued
Wolverhampton,Goldthorn Hill
WV4 . . . . .39 B6
Wolverhampton,Lanesfield
WV4 . . . . .39 F3
Waverley Gdns WV5 . . . . . .49 B7
Waverley Gr B91 . . . . .106 F3
Waverley Rd
Birmingham B10 . . . . .87 D7
Darlaston WS10 . . . . .41 D6
Kenilworth CV8 . . . . .148 A4
Royal Leamington Spa
CV31 . . . . .162 B6
Walsall WS3 . . . . .13 F2
Waverley Sch B10 . . . . .88 A8
Waverley Sq CV11 . . . . . . .73 F1
Waverley St DY2 . . . . .62 A8
Wavers Marston B37 . . . . . .90 A8
Waverton Mews **2** CV31 .162 C6
Waxland Rd B63 . . . . .83 B2
Wayfield Cl B90 . . . . .106 C3
Wayfield Rd B90 . . . . .106 C3
Wayford Dr B72 . . . . .57 D7
Wayford Glade WV13 . . . . .40 F8
Wayford Gr B8 . . . . .68 B4
Waynecroft Rd B43 . . . . . . .43 E2
Wayside B37 . . . . .90 A8
Wayside Dr B74 . . . . .31 C3
Wayside Gdns WV12 . . . . . .27 E5
Wayside Wlk WS2 . . . . .28 A3
Wayside WV8 . . . . .10 F2
Waystone La DY9 . . . . . . .119 D4
Wealden Hatch WV10 . . . . .11 E4
Wealdstone Dr DY3 . . . . . .50 D2
Weale Gr CV34 . . . . .155 E1
Weaman St B4 . . . . .164 C3
Weates Yd B27 . . . . .88 C4
Weatheroak Cl B97 . . . . . .153 A1
Weatheroak Hill B48 . . . . .124 B1
Weatheroak Rd B11 . . . . . .87 C5
Weather Oaks B17 . . . . . . .85 B6
Weatheroaks
Birmingham B62 . . . . .84 A7
Brownhills WS9 . . . . .16 B4
Weaver Ave
Birmingham B26 . . . . .89 B6
Sutton Coldfield B76 . . . . . .47 A1
Weaver Cl DY5 . . . . .61 B6
Weaver Gr WV13 . . . . .27 D2
Weavers Cl B97 . . . . .158 D4
Weavers Rise DY2 . . . . .62 D3
Weavers Wharf DY10 . . . .116 D6
Weavers Wlk CV6 . . . . .96 A4
Weaving Gdns **1** WS11 . . . .1 E1
Webb Ave WV6 . . . . .23 E5
Webbcroft Rd B33 . . . . . . .68 F4
Webb La B28 . . . . .105 E6
Webb Rd DY4 . . . . .52 C7
Webb St
Dudley WV14 . . . . .40 C1
Nuneaton CV10 . . . . .72 D3
Webheath Fst Sch B97 . . .153 A2
Webley Rise WV10 . . . . . . .11 F4
Webner Ind Est WV2 . . . . . .40 A6
Webster Ave CV8 . . . . .148 B5
Webster Cl
Birmingham B11 . . . . .87 B6
Sutton Coldfield B72 . . . . . .57 B7
Webster Rd
Walsall WS2 . . . . .28 E5
Willenhall WV13 . . . . .27 A3
Webster Way CV6 . . . . .58 B8
Webster Wills WS11 . . . . . . .2 A4
Weddell Wynd WV14 . . . . . .40 F1
Weddington Cty Wlk*
CV10 . . . . .73 B8
Weddington Prim Sch
CV10 . . . . .73 D7
Weddington Rd CV10 . . . . .73 C7
Weddington Terr CV10 . . . .73 D5
Wedgbury Cl WS10 . . . . . . .42 A1
Wedgbury Way DY5 . . . . . .61 B1
Wedge St **10** WS1 . . . . . . .28 F2
Wedgewood Ave B70 . . . . .52 F7
Wedgewood Cl
Burntwood WS7 . . . . .7 C7
Coventry CV2 . . . . .114 E8
Wedgewood Ct WS4 . . . . . .15 C1
Wedgewood Dr B20 . . . . . .55 B2
Wedgewood Ho B37 . . . . . .70 B4
Wedgewood Pl B70 . . . . . . .52 F7
Wedgewood Rd B32 . . . . . .84 D5
Wedge-Woods CV5 . . . . . .132 F8
Wedgnock Gn CV34 . . . . . .160 D8
Wedgnock Ind Est CV34 . .160 C8
Wedgnock La CV34 . . . . . .155 C1
Wedmore Rd B73 . . . . .45 F1
Wednesbury, Great Western
Street Sta WS10 . . . . . . .41 E2
Wednesbury Mus & Art Gall*
WS10 . . . . .41 E4
Wednesbury Oak Prim Sch
DY4 . . . . .41 A1
Wednesbury Oak Rd DY4 . .41 A1
Wednesbury Parkway Sta
WS10 . . . . .41 D2
Wednesbury Rd WS1 . . . . .42 D7
Wednesbury Trad Est
WS10 . . . . .41 E4

Wednesfield High Sch
Specialist Engineering Sch
WV11 . . . . .26 E5
Wednesfield Rd
Willenhall WV13 . . . . .27 A3
Wolverhampton WV1,
WV10 . . . . .163 D6
Wednesfield Village Prim
Sch WV11 . . . . .26 D5
Wednesfield Way Ind Est
WV11 . . . . .26 D4
Wedon Cl CV4 . . . . .131 E7
Weeford Dell **2** B75 . . . . . .32 E3
Weeford Rd B20 . . . . .54 F4
Weeford Rd B75 . . . . .32 F3
Weethley Ho **6** B97 . . . . .153 A4
Weights Farm B97 . . . . . . .153 C7
Weights La B97 . . . . .153 C7
Weirbrook Cl B29 . . . . .103 C2
Weland Cl B46 . . . . .59 B2
Weland Ct B46 . . . . .59 B2
Welbeck Ave
Hinckley LE10 . . . . .75 D4
Wolverhampton WV10 . . . .25 D7
Welbeck Cl B62 . . . . .83 G6
Welbeck Dr
Kidderminster DY11 . . . . .116 B5
Walsall WS4 . . . . .29 D7
Welbeck Gr B23 . . . . .56 B5
Welbury Gdns WV6 . . . . . . .24 F5
Welby Gate CV7 . . . . .130 B5
Welby Rd B28 . . . . .87 F1
Welch Cl DY4 . . . . .52 B7
Welches Cl B31 . . . . .103 B5
Welcombe Dr B76 . . . . .57 F7
Welcombe Gr B91 . . . . . . .106 F4
Welcome Dr B61 . . . . .121 A1
Welford Ave B26 . . . . .88 F8
Welford Cl B98 . . . . .158 F5
Welford Gr B74 . . . . .31 F3
Welford Pl CV6 . . . . .113 D7
Welford Prim Sch B20 . . . .66 A8
Welford Rd
Birmingham B20 . . . . .66 A8
Solihull B90 . . . . .106 C4
Sutton Coldfield B73 . . . . . .45 E1
Tamworth B77 . . . . .35 C5
Welgarth Ave CV6 . . . . . . .112 F6
Welham Croft B90 . . . . . . .127 A6
Welland Dr DY8 . . . . .81 A8
Welland Gr
Birmingham B24 . . . . .57 D3
Willenhall WV13 . . . . .27 C2
Welland Rd
Coventry CV1 . . . . .113 F1
Halesowen B63 . . . . .83 A2
Welland Way B76 . . . . .58 A7
Well Cl
Birmingham B36 . . . . .68 E8
Redditch B97 . . . . .158 E5
Wellcroft Rd B34 . . . . .69 A7
Wellcroft St WS10 . . . . .41 F3
Weller Cl WV3 . . . . .24 D1
Wellesbourne Cl
Redditch B98 . . . . .153 E4
Wolverhampton WV3 . . . . .38 B8
Wellesbourne Dr WV14 . . . .51 B7
Wellesbourne Rd
Birmingham B20 . . . . .55 B1
Coventry CV5 . . . . .112 A3
Wellesbourne Twr **3** B5 . .86 E8
Wellesley Dr DY4 . . . . .51 F5
Wellesley Gdns B13 . . . . . .87 D1
Wellesley Rd B68 . . . . .64 B6
Wellfield Cl
Balsall Common CV7 . . . .130 C5
Cannock WS11 . . . . .4 B7
Wellfield Gdns DY2 . . . . . . .62 E6
Wellfield Rd
Aldridge WS9 . . . . .30 B8
Birmingham B28 . . . . .106 B6
Wellhead La B42 . . . . .55 E3
Wellhead Way B42 . . . . . . .55 F2
Wellington Ave WV3 . . . . . .38 F7
Wellington Cl
Hinckley LE10 . . . . .75 E4
Kingswinford DY6 . . . . .60 E4
Wellington Cres B20 . . . . . .55 B2
Wellington Ct
Birmingham B32 . . . . .84 F5
Birmingham,Handsworth Wood
B20 . . . . .55 C2
Cradley Heath B64 . . . . . . .62 F2
Kidderminster DY11 . . . . .116 C5
Willenhall WV13 . . . . .27 B1
Wellington Dr WS11 . . . . . . .4 B8
Wellington Gdns **1** CV1 . .113 B2
Wellington Gr B91 . . . . . . .106 F6
Wellington Ho B32 . . . . . . .84 F7
Wellington Ind Est WV14 . .51 C7
Wellington Pl WV13 . . . . . .26 F1
Wellington Rd
Bilston WV14 . . . . .40 D6
Birmingham B20 . . . . .55 C2
Birmingham,Edgbaston B15 . .86 C7
Bromsgrove B60 . . . . .151 A8
Dudley DY1 . . . . .51 B1
Royal Leamington Spa
CV32 . . . . .157 C2
Smethwick B67 . . . . .65 A3
Tipton DY4 . . . . .52 A4
Walsall WS5 . . . . .43 C3
Wellington St S B70 . . . . . .53 C4
Wellington St
6 Redditch B98 . . . . . .153 E4

Wellington St *continued*
Birmingham B18 . . . . .65 D5
Coventry CV1 . . . . .165 D4
Cradley Heath B64 . . . . .62 F2
Oldbury B69 . . . . .42 A1
Walsall WS2 . . . . .42 B7
West Bromwich B71 . . . . . . .53 C4
Wellington Terr 3 B19. . .66 B7
Wellington Way B35 . . . . .58 B2

Well La
Birmingham B5 . . . . .164 D2
Great Wyrley WS6 . . . . .5 A1
Hinckley LE10 . . . . .71 D1
Tanworth-In-A B94 . . . . . . .142 A1
Walsall,Harden WS3 . . . . . . .28 D7
Walsall WS3 . . . . .28 E8
Wolverhampton WV11 . . . . .26 C4
Wellman Croft B29 . . . . . .85 D1
Wellman's Rd WV13 . . . . .27 C1
Well Mdw B45 . . . . .122 A6
Wellmeadow Gr B27 . . . .109 A7
Wellmead Wlk B45 . . . . .121 F8
Well Pl WV13 . . . . .28 E8
Wells Ave WS10 . . . . .41 B6

Wells Cl
Cannock WS11 . . . . .1 E6
Kidderminster DY11 . . . . . .116 A6
Perton WV6 . . . . .23 D4
Wolverhampton DY4 . . . . . . .41 A1
West Bromwich B71 . . . . . . .53 D8

Wells Ct
Coventry CV3 . . . . .133 F7
Dudley DY2 . . . . .62 C5
Wellsford Ave B92 . . . . . .89 B4
Wells Green Rd B92 . . . . .89 A4

Wells Rd
Bilston WV14 . . . . .40 E3
Brierley Hill DY5 . . . . .61 B3
Rowley Regis B65 . . . . .63 E4
Solihull B92 . . . . .89 C4
Wolverhampton WV4 . . . . . .38 F5

Well St
Birmingham B19 . . . . .66 C5
Coventry CV1 . . . . .165 B3
Darlaston WS10 . . . . .41 E6
Wells Ter B16 . . . . .66 A2
Wells Wlk B37 . . . . .70 A1
Welney Gdns WV9 . . . . . . .11 A3
Welsby Ave B43 . . . . .54 E7
Welsh Cl CV34 . . . . .155 E2
Welsh House Farm Com Sch
B32 .84 F4
Welsh House Farm Rd
B32 .84 F4
Welshmans Hill B73 . . . . .45 C3

Welsh Rd
Coventry CV2 . . . . .114 B4
Cubbington CV32,CV33 . . .157 F7
Welton Cl B76 . . . . .47 A2
Welton Rd CV34 . . . . .155 D1
Welwyndale Rd B72 . . . . .57 C6
Welwyn Rd LE10 . . . . .71 F1
Wembley Gr B25 . . . . .88 C8
Wembley La WS7 . . . . .6 D8
Wembrook Cl CV11 . . . . . .73 D2
Wembrook Ho CV11 . . . . .73 E2
Wembrook Prim Sch
CV11 . . . . .73 C2
Wembury B77 . . . . .21 E5
Wem Gdns WV11 . . . . .26 D6
Wendell Crest WV10 . . . . .11 F4
Wendiburgh St CV4 . . . . .132 B7
Wendover Dr LE10 . . . . . . .71 E4

Wendover Rd
Birmingham B23 . . . . .56 C7
Rowley Regis B65 . . . . .63 A5
Wolverhampton WV4 . . . . . .39 F2
Wendover Rise CV5 . . . . .112 C4
Wendron Cl B60 . . . . .137 B2
Wendron Gr B14 . . . . . . .104 D4
Wenlock Ave WV3 . . . . . . .38 E8

Wenlock Cl
Halesowen B63 . . . . .82 D2
Sedgley DY3 . . . . .50 C7
Wenlock Dr B61 . . . . .137 A5
Wenlock Gdns WS3 . . . . . .28 E5

Wenlock Rd
Birmingham B20 . . . . .55 F1
Stourbridge DY8 . . . . .81 B6
Wenlock B71 . . . . .21 D3
Wenlock Way CV10 . . . . . .72 B3
Wenman St B12 . . . . .86 F6
Wensley Croft B90 . . . . . .106 B6
Wensleydale Rd B42 . . . . .55 B6
Wensley Rd B26 . . . . .88 F6
Wensum Cl LE10 . . . . .75 B8
Wentbridge Rd WV1 . . . . .26 C1
Wentworth Ave B36 . . . . . .69 B8

Wentworth Cl
Burntwood WS7 . . . . .7 C7
Hinckley LE10 . . . . .71 E3

Wentworth Ct
Birmingham B24 . . . . .56 F2
Sutton Coldfield B75 . . . . . .32 B1

Wentworth Dr
Blackwell B60 . . . . .138 A5
Coventry CV6 . . . . .95 B4
Lichfield WS14 . . . . .9 D5
Nuneaton CV11 . . . . .74 A1
Oldbury B69 . . . . .63 A7
Wentworth Gate B17 . . . . .85 B6
Wentworth Gr WV6 . . . . . .23 E5
Wentworth Park Ave B17. .85 B6

Wentworth Rd
Birmingham B17 . . . . .85 B6
Royal Leamington Spa
CV31 . . . . .162 D6

Wentworth Rd *continued*
Solihull B92 . . . . .88 F2
Stourbridge DY8 . . . . .80 E7
Sutton Coldfield B74 . . . . . .46 A8
Walsall WS3 . . . . .13 F3
Wolverhampton WV10 . . . . .11 F3
Wentworth Rise B62 . . . . .83 D3
Wentworth Way B32 . . . . .84 F3
Wenyon Cl DY4 . . . . .52 B4
Weoley Ave B29 . . . . .85 C2
Weoley Castle Rd B29 . . . .84 F1
Weoley Hill B29 . . . . .103 C8
Weoley Park Rd B29 . . . . .85 C1
Wergs Dr WV6 . . . . .24 A7
Wergs Hall WV8 . . . . .23 F7
Wergs Hall Rd WV6,WV8 . .24 A7

Wergs Rd
Codsall WV6 . . . . .23 F7
Wolverhampton WV6 . . . . . .24 B6
Werneth Gr WS3 . . . . .14 A4
Wesleyan Ct WS4 . . . . .29 A4

Wesley Ave
Cheslyn Hay WS6 . . . . .4 D3
Codsall WV8 . . . . .10 B2
Halesowen B63 . . . . .82 B8
Wesley Cl B64 . . . . .62 F1

Wesley Ct
4 Cradley Heath B64 . . . . . .82 F8
5 Wolverhampton WV4 . . . .39 F4
Birmingham B16 . . . . .65 C2
Cannock WS11 . . . . .1 E1
Wesley Gr WS10 . . . . .41 E3
Wesley Ho 3 WS2 . . . . . . .42 C7

Wesley Pl
Cannock WS12 . . . . .2 C7
Tipton DY4 . . . . .52 C7

Wesley Rd
Birmingham B23 . . . . .56 F5
Brierley Hill DY5 . . . . .61 B5
Codsall WV8 . . . . .10 B2
Willenhall WV12 . . . . .27 C6
Wesley's Fold WS10 . . . . .41 D6

Wesley St
Bilston WV14 . . . . .40 E2
Oldbury B69 . . . . .64 A8
West Bromwich B70 . . . . . . .53 B3
Wolverhampton WV2 . . . . . .40 A6
Wesley Wlk B60 . . . . .150 E7
Wessenden B77 . . . . .36 B7

Wessex Cl
Bedworth CV12 . . . . .78 A4
Brownhills WS8 . . . . .15 F7
Wessex Ct B79 . . . . .22 F7
Wessex Dr WS11 . . . . .1 E2
Wessex Rd WV2 . . . . .39 F6
Wesson Gdns B63 . . . . . . .83 A3
Wesson Rd WS10 . . . . .41 C8
Westacre Cres WV3 . . . . . .24 C1
Westacre Dr DY5 . . . . .81 F8
Westacre Gdns B33 . . . . . .68 F3
Westacre Inf Sch WV3 . . . .24 C1
West Acre WV13 . . . . .26 F1

West Ave
Bedworth CV12 . . . . .78 D2
Birmingham,Castle Bromwich
B36 .69 D8
Birmingham,Handsworth
B20 .55 A4
Coventry CV6,CV7 . . . . .95 A5
Coventry,Middle Stoke
CV2 . . . . .114 A2
Oldbury B69 . . . . .63 B7
Redditch B98 . . . . .153 E3
Wolverhampton WV11 . . . . .26 C6
Westbourne Ave
Birmingham B34 . . . . .68 E6
Cannock WS11 . . . . .1 D3
Cheslyn Hay WS6 . . . . .4 E3
Westbourne Cl 3 B61 . . .136 E1
Westbourne Cres
Birmingham B15 . . . . .86 A8
Burntwood WS7 . . . . .7 B7

Westbourne Ct
Darlaston WS10 . . . . .41 F7
Walsall WS4 . . . . .29 A3
Westbourne Gdns B15 . . . .86 A7
Westbourne Gr B21 . . . . . .65 F7

Westbourne Rd
Birmingham,Edgbaston
B15 .86 A8
Birmingham,Handsworth
B21 .54 D1
Darlaston WS10 . . . . .41 F7
Halesowen B62 . . . . .83 E7
Solihull B92 . . . . .106 F8
Walsall,Ryecroft WS4 . . . . . .28 F4
Walsall WS4 . . . . .29 A4
Wolverhampton WV3 . . . . . .39 A5
Westbourne St WS4 . . . . . .28 F3
Westbourne Terr 2 B61. .136 E1
West Bromwich Central Sta
B70 .53 D2
West Bromwich Rd WS5 . .42 F5
West Bromwich Ringway
B70 .53 D2

West Bromwich St
Oldbury B69 . . . . .52 F1
Walsall WS1 . . . . .42 E7
Westbrook Ave B77 . . . . . .85 A8
Aldridge WS9 . . . . .29 F5
Aldridge WS9 . . . . .30 A5
Westbrook Ct CV5 . . . . . .112 A4
Westbury Ave WS10 . . . . .41 C7

Westbury Ct
22 Brierley Hill DY5 . . . . . . .61 D2
Coventry CV2 . . . . .114 A3

Westbury Ct *continued*
Warwick CV34 . . . . .161 A7
Westbury Ho B97 . . . . . . .153 B2

Westbury Rd
Coventry CV5 . . . . .112 D5
Nuneaton CV10 . . . . .72 D3
Smethwick B17 . . . . .65 B3
Wednesbury WS10 . . . . .41 F6
Westbury St WV1 . . . . .163 C3
West Bvd B32 . . . . .84 F4
West Cl LE10 . . . . .75 D7
West Dr CV34 . . . . .155 E2
Westcliff Dr CV3 . . . . .133 B5
Westcliff Pl B31 . . . . .102 F4
Westcombe Gr B32 . . . . . .84 A1
West Coppice Rd WS8 . . .15 C8
Westcote Ave B31 . . . . . .102 C2
Westcote Cl B92 . . . . .89 A2
Westcott Cl DY6 . . . . .60 F3
Westcott Rd B26 . . . . .89 A8
Westcroft Ave WV10 . . . . .12 A1
Westcroft Gr B38 . . . . . . .103 D3

Westcroft Rd
Sedgley DY3 . . . . .39 B2
Wolverhampton WV6 . . . . . .23 F6
Westcroft Sch & Sports Coll
WV10 . . . . .12 B2
Westcroft Way B14 . . . . . .105 B1
West Cross Sh Ctr B66 . . .64 D7
West Ct B60 . . . . .150 F6
Westdean Cl B62 . . . . .83 C4

West Dr
Birmingham,Edgbaston B5 . .86 C5
Birmingham,Handsworth
B20 .66 B8
Fazeley B78 . . . . .20 E2
West End Ave B66 . . . . . . .64 D7
West End Ct CV34 . . . . . .160 D6
West End Villas B38 . . . . .103 F2
Westerdale Cl DY3 . . . . . . .51 A4
Westerham Cl B93 . . . . . .127 F6
Westerhope Gr B19 . . . . . .66 C5
Westeria Cl B36 . . . . .69 C8
Westeria Ho B36 . . . . .69 C8
Westering Parkway WV10 . .11 F4
Westerings B20 . . . . .55 C2

Western Ave
Brierley Hill DY5 . . . . .61 B2
Halesowen B62 . . . . .83 E4
Sedgley DY3 . . . . .50 B8
Willenhall WS2 . . . . .27 D3
Western Bsns Pk
Birmingham B18 . . . . .65 E6
Halesowen B62 . . . . .83 B7
Western By-Pass WS13 . . . .8 F8
Western Cl WS2 . . . . .27 D3
Western Hill Cl B96 . . . . .158 E1

Western Rd
Birmingham,Edgbaston
B18 .65 F4
Birmingham,Erdington B24 . .57 A3
Cannock WS12 . . . . .2 A5
Cradley Heath B64 . . . . .82 E8
Oldbury B69 . . . . .64 B5
Stourbridge DY8 . . . . .80 F4
Sutton Coldfield B73 . . . . . .46 A1
West Hagley DY9 . . . . .99 B4
Western Way
Darlaston WS10 . . . . .41 C3
Kidderminster DY11 . . . . . .116 A5
Westfield Ave B14 . . . . . .105 B1

Westfield Cl
Dorridge B93 . . . . .127 F2
Nuneaton CV10 . . . . .73 D5
Westfield Ct LE10 . . . . .75 C7
Westfield Dr WS9 . . . . .30 A6
Westfield Grange B14 . . . . .86 E1
Westfield Hall 2 B16 . . . . .65 D1
Westfield Ho B36 . . . . .70 A7
Westfield Inf Sch LE10 . . . .75 B7
Westfield Jun Sch LE10 . . .75 B7
Westfield Manor B75 . . . . .32 A4
Westfield Prim Sch WV5 . .49 A7

Westfield Rd
Bilston WV14 . . . . .40 B7
Birmingham,Acock's Green
B27 .88 B3
Birmingham,Edgbaston
B15 .85 D7
Birmingham,Moseley B14 . . .86 E1
Brierley Hill DY5 . . . . .81 F8
Dudley DY2 . . . . .62 D7
Halesowen B62 . . . . .63 E1
Hinckley LE10 . . . . .75 B7
Sedgley DY3 . . . . .39 E1
Smethwick B67 . . . . .64 F5
Willenhall WV13 . . . . .40 E8
Westfields
Birchmoor B78 . . . . .36 D8
Catshill B61 . . . . .136 F8
Westford Gr B28 . . . . .105 E3

Westgate
Aldridge WS9 . . . . .29 E6
Birmingham B15 . . . . .85 E4
West Gate Gdns B16 . . . . .65 E3
Westgate WS12 . . . . .2 F6

Westgate Cl
Sedgley DY3 . . . . .39 E1
Warwick CV34 . . . . .160 F7
Westgate Ho 10 CV34 . . .160 E6
Westgate B65 . . . . .63 E4
Westgate Prim Sch
CV34 . . . . .160 D6
Westgate Trad Est WS9 . . .29 E6
West Gn WV4 . . . . .38 C5
West Green Cl B15 . . . . . . .86 B8
Westgrove Ave 6 B90 . . .127 A6

Westgrove Terr 1 CV32 . .161 D8
Westhall Gate WS3 . . . . . .14 B2
Westham Ho B37 . . . . .70 B4
Westhaven Dr B31 . . . . . .102 E7
Westhaven Rd B72 . . . . . . .46 C5
Westhay Rd B28 . . . . .106 B7
West Heath Hospl B38 . . .123 C8
West Heath Prim Sch
B38 . . . . .123 C8

West Heath Rd
2 Birmingham,Edgbaston
B18 .65 D4
Birmingham,Northfield
B31 . . . . .103 B1
West Hill Ave WS12 . . . . . . .2 B6
Westhill Cl B29 . . . . .106 E8
Westhill CV6 . . . . .95 B3
West Hill Prim Sch WS12. . .2 B6

Westhill Rd
Birmingham B38 . . . . .103 F3
Blackdown CV32 . . . . .157 A6
Coventry CV6 . . . . .112 F6
Westhill WV3 . . . . .24 C2
West Holme B9 . . . . .67 C2
Westholme Croft B30 . . . .103 E8
Westhouse Gr B14 . . . . . .104 D6
Westhouse Gr B14 . . . . . .104 D6
West House Sch B15 . . . . .86 C8
West Hyde LE10 . . . . .74 F7
Westland Ave WV3 . . . . . . .24 F2
Westland Cl B23 . . . . .56 F5

Westland Gdns
6 Wolverhampton WV3 . . . .25 A2
Stourbridge DY8 . . . . .80 F7
Westland Rd WV3 . . . . .24 F2

Westlands Rd
Birmingham B13 . . . . .87 A1
Sutton Coldfield B76 . . . . . .57 F6
Westlands Wlk B35 . . . . . . .57 F2
Westlea Rd CV31 . . . . .161 E6
Westleigh Ave CV5 . . . . . .132 F7
Westley Brook Cl B26 . . . .89 B5
Westley Gdns B28 . . . . . . .106 B6
Westley Rd B27 . . . . .88 B3

Westley St
6 Dudley DY1 . . . . .62 B8
Birmingham B9 . . . . .67 A2
West Lodge WV1 . . . . .25 A3
Westmead Ave B80 . . . . . .159 E4
Westmead Cres B24 . . . . . .57 C4
West Mead Dr B14 . . . . . .104 E6
Westmede Ctr CV5 . . . . . .112 C4
West Mews B44 . . . . .44 D3
West Midlands Hospl B63 .82 D5
West Mill Croft B38 . . . . .123 E7
Westminster Ave WV4 . . . .39 B5
Westminster B37 . . . . .69 F5

Westminster Cl
Bromley DY1 . . . . .136 D1
Dudley DY1 . . . . .51 A2
Westminster Ct
3 Bromsgrove B60 . . . . . . .137 A2
Birmingham B20 . . . . .55 C2
Westminster Dr
Birmingham B14 . . . . .104 E6
Hinckley LE10 . . . . .75 F4
Nuneaton CV10 . . . . .72 B7
Westminster Ind Est DY2 . .62 D2
Westminster Prim Sch
B20 .55 C1

Westminster Rd
Birmingham,Handsworth
B20 .55 C1
Birmingham,Stirchley B29 . .104 A8
Cannock WS11 . . . . .1 E6
Coventry CV1 . . . . .116 A6
Stourbridge DY8 . . . . .60 D2
Walsall WS4 . . . . .29 B7
West Bromwich B71 . . . . . . .53 D8
Westminster Sch The
Smethwick B67 . . . . .65 A5
West Bromwich B71 . . . . . . .53 D8
Westmoreland Ave CV10 . .72 E4
Westmore Way WS10 . . . . .42 E5
Westmorland Ct B71 . . . . .21 A1
Westmorland Ct B71 . . . . .53 D7

Westmorland Rd
Coventry CV2 . . . . .114 F4
West Bromwich B71 . . . . . . .53 D7
Weston Ave
6 Birmingham,Lozells
B19 .66 C7
Birmingham,Sparkbrook
B11 .87 C6
Oldbury B69 . . . . .52 B1
Westonbirt Cl CV8 . . . . . .148 C6
Weston Cl
5 Royal Leamington Spa
CV31 . . . . .162 C6
Cannock WS11 . . . . .2 C1
Dorridge B93 . . . . .128 A2
Hinckley LE10 . . . . .75 F4
Walsall WS1 . . . . .42 E6
Warwick CV34 . . . . .160 F7
Weston Cres WS9 . . . . .30 B4
Weston Ct 10 WV3 . . . . . . .25 B4
Weston Dr
Bilston WV14 . . . . .40 B5
Great Wyrley WS6 . . . . .4 F1
Wednesbury DY4 . . . . .41 C2
Westonhall Rd B60 . . . . . .150 D1
Weston Hall Stables CV12 .79 A3

Weston Ho
Birmingham B19 . . . . .66 E6
Wolverhampton WV6 . . . . . .24 E5
Weston Ind Est B11 . . . . . .87 E4

Weston La
Birmingham B11 . . . . .87 E4
Bulkington CV12 . . . . .79 B3

Weston Rd
Birmingham B19 . . . . .66 B7
Lichfield WS13 . . . . .3 A2
Smethwick B67 . . . . .64 F2

Weston St
Coventry CV1 . . . . .165 C4
Walsall WS1 . . . . .42 E7
Weston Terr 3 B19 . . . . . .66 D8
West Orchards Sh Ctr
CV1 . . . . .165 B3
Westover Rd B20 . . . . .54 E4
West Park Ave B31 . . . . . .102 E2
West Park Cl WS9 . . . . .29 E5
West Park Ct WV1 . . . . .25 A4
West Park Prim Sch
WV1 . . . . .163 A4
West Park Rd B67 . . . . .64 D6
West Pathway B17 . . . . . . .85 C6
West Point B17 . . . . .85 C8
Westport Cres WV11 . . . . . .26 F5
Westray Cl B45 . . . . .101 F1
Westray Dr LE10 . . . . .71 C1

West Rd
Birmingham,Hamstead
B43 .54 E7
Birmingham,Handsworth B6 .55 E2
Bromsgrove B60 . . . . .137 A2
Halesowen B60 . . . . .82 B6
West Rd S B63 . . . . .82 B6

West Rd
Tipton DY4 . . . . .52 B8
Wolverhampton WV4 . . . . . .39 F5
West Ridge CV5 . . . . .112 A5
Westridge Rd B13 . . . . . . .105 C6
Westridge DY3 . . . . .50 C8
West Rise B75 . . . . .46 C6
West Rock CV34 . . . . .160 D7
West Side Bsns Ctr CV4 . .131 E8
Westside Dr B32 . . . . .84 D1

West St
17 Royal Leamington Spa
CV31 . . . . .162 A7
Brierley Hill DY5 . . . . .81 F8
Cannock WS11 . . . . .4 E6
Coventry CV1 . . . . .113 E3
Redditch B98 . . . . .153 E3
Rowley Regis B65 . . . . .63 C1
Stourbridge DY8 . . . . .80 F5
Tamworth B79 . . . . .21 C5
Tamworth,Kettlebrook B77 . .21 C3
Walsall WS3 . . . . .28 C7
Wolverhampton WV6 . . . . . .25 C5

West View
Birmingham B8 . . . . .68 C4
West View B75 . . . . .46 E6
West View Dr DY6 . . . . .60 D7

West View Rd
Royal Leamington Spa
CV32 . . . . .157 C5
Sutton Coldfield B75 . . . . . .46 E6
Westville Ave DY11 . . . . . .116 A5
Westville Rd WS2 . . . . .28 A3
Westward Cl B44 . . . . .55 F8
West Way B31 . . . . .123 B7
Westway Ho WS4 . . . . .15 B1
Westway WS4 . . . . .15 B2
Westwick Cl WS9 . . . . .16 E4
West Winds WV10 . . . . .12 C7

Westwood Ave
Birmingham B11 . . . . .87 D4
Stourbridge DY8 . . . . .80 D3
Westwood Bsns Pk
Birmingham B6 . . . . .56 B1
Coventry CV4 . . . . .131 F6
Westwood Cl CV10 . . . . . . .72 E3
Sutton Coldfield B73 . . . . . .45 B4
Westwood Dr B45 . . . . . . .102 B1
Westwood Heath Rd
CV4 . . . . .131 E6
Westwood Holdings WS12. .1 B6
Westwood Rd
Birmingham,Aston B6 . . . . . .56 A2
Coventry CV5 . . . . .113 A1
Sutton Coldfield B73 . . . . . .45 A4
Westwoods Hollow WS7 . . .7 B8
Westwood St DY5 . . . . .61 A1
Westwood View B24 . . . . . .57 C3
Westwood Way CV4 . . . . .132 A6

Wetherby Cl
Birmingham B36 . . . . .68 D8
Wolverhampton WV10 . . . . .11 D5

Wetherby Rd
Birmingham B27 . . . . .88 C2
Walsall WS3 . . . . .14 A4
Wetherfield Rd B11 . . . . . . .88 A3
Wexford Cl DY1 . . . . .50 F2
Wexford Rd CV2 . . . . .96 D1
Weybourne Rd B44 . . . . . . .44 E2
Weycroft Rd B23 . . . . .56 B7
Weyhill Cl WV9 . . . . .10 F2
Weymoor Rd B17 . . . . .85 B3
Weymouth Cl CV3 . . . . . . .134 D5
Weymouth Dr B74 . . . . .31 E4
Weymouth Ho WV9 . . . . . . .21 B5
Whaley's Croft CV6 . . . . . .113 B8
Wharf App WS9 . . . . .29 F7

Wharf Cl WS14 . . . . 9 C7
Wharfdale Rd B11 . . . . 88 A5
Wharfedale Cl DY6 . . . . 60 B7
Wharfedale St WS10 . . . . . 42 A2
Wharf La
　Birmingham B18 . . . . 66 A6
　Burntwood WS8 . . . . 6 F3
　Nuthurst B94 . . . . 143 D4
　Solihull B91 . . . . 107 D6
　Tardebigge B60 . . . . 138 B1
Wharf Lodge CV31 . . . . . 161 D7
Wharf Rd
　Birmingham,King's Norton
　　B30 . . . . 104 A2
　Birmingham,Tyseley B11 . . 88 B5
　Coventry CV6 . . . . 113 F5
　Wharfdale B69 . . . . 63 F7
Wharf St
　Birmingham,Aston B6 . . . . 67 A7
　Birmingham,Hockley B18 . . 66 A6
　Walsall WS2 . . . . 28 C1
　Warwick CV34 . . . . 161 A8
　Wolverhampton WV1 . . . . 163 D2
Wharf The B1 . . . . 164 A2
Wharf Yd LE10 . . . . 75 A7
Whar Hall Rd B92 . . . . 107 E8
Warrington Cl B98 . . . . . . 159 A8
Warrington Hill B98 . . . . . 159 A8
Wharton Ave B92 . . . . 107 E7
Wharton St Ind Est B7 . . . . 67 D8
Wharton St B7 . . . . 67 D8
Wharwell La WS6 . . . . 5 A1
Whatcote Gn B92 . . . . 107 E8
Whatecroft The B17 . . . . . . 85 B6
Whateley Ave B45 . . . . 26 F6
Whateley Cres B36 . . . . . . 69 D8
Whateley Ct CV11 . . . . 73 B4
Whateley Gn B74 . . . . 44 A4
Whateley Hall Cl B93 . . . . 128 C7
Whateley Hall Rd B93 . . . 128 B7
Whateley La B77,B78 . . . . . 35 F4
Whateley Lodge Dr B36 . . . 69 C8
Whateley Pl WS3 . . . . 28 F6
Whateley Rd
　Birmingham B21 . . . . 65 E8
　Walsall WS3 . . . . 28 F6
Whateley's Dr CV8 . . . . . . 148 A5
Whateley Villas CV9 . . . . . 36 A2
Wheatcroft Cl
　Burntwood WS7 . . . . 7 A5
　Halesowen B62 . . . . 83 F8
　Redditch B97 . . . . 153 A5
Wheatcroft Dr B37 . . . . . . 70 C1
Wheatcroft Gr DY2 . . . . . . 51 F1
Wheatcroft Rd B33 . . . . . . 68 F2
Wheate Croft CV4 . . . . . . 111 F2
Wheaten Cl B37 . . . . 70 D3
Wheatfield Cl B36 . . . . 70 A7
Wheatfield View B31 . . . . 102 D6
Wheatfield Way LE10 . . . . . 71 C4
Wheathill Cl
　Royal Leamington Spa
　　CV32 . . . . 156 C2
　Wolverhampton WV4 . . . . . 38 E3
Wheat Hill WS5 . . . . 43 E8
Wheatland Gr WS9 . . . . . . 30 B4
Wheatlands Cl [1] WS12 . . . 2 C1
Wheatlands Croft B33 . . . . 69 E3
Wheatlands The WV6 . . . . . 23 D3
Wheatley Cl
　Birmingham B68 . . . . 84 C8
　Solihull B92 . . . . 107 E8
　Sutton Coldfield B75 . . . . . 32 C3
Wheatley Grange B46 . . . . 70 F6
Wheatley Gr WS6 . . . . 5 A2
Wheatley Rd B68 . . . . 84 D8
Wheatley St
　West Bromwich B70 . . . . . . 53 A3
　Wolverhampton WV2 . . . . . 39 F6
Wheatmill Cl DY10 . . . . 98 B2
Wheatmoor Rd B75 . . . . . . 47 A6
Wheatmoor Rise B75 . . . . . 46 E6
Wheaton Cl WV10 . . . . 25 C7
Wheaton Vale B20 . . . . 54 E3
Wheatridge Cl DY6 . . . . . . 60 A8
Wheatridge Rd B60 . . . . . 150 E6
Wheats Ave B17 . . . . 85 B3
Wheatsheaf Cl B75 . . . . . . 32 E4
Wheatsheaf Rd
　Birmingham B16 . . . . 65 D2
　Oldbury B69 . . . . 63 A8
　Wolverhampton WV8 . . . . . 10 E1
Wheat St CV11 . . . . 73 D4
Wheatstone Cl DY3 . . . . . . 50 E6
Wheatstone Gr B33 . . . . . . 68 F5
Wheeldon Ho B26 . . . . 88 E4
Wheeler Cl B93 . . . . 145 B7
Wheeler Ho [12] B69 . . . . . . 64 A7
Wheeler Rd WV11 . . . . 26 C8
Wheeler's Fold WV1 . . . . . 163 C3
Wheelers La B13 . . . . 104 F7
Wheelers La B13 . . . . 105 A7
Wheelers Lane Prim Sch
　B13 . . . . 104 F7
Wheelers Lane Prim Sch
　(Annexe) B13 . . . . 105 A6
Wheelers Lane Tech Coll
　B13 . . . . 104 F7
Wheeler St La B97 . . . . . . 153 C6
Wheeler St B19 . . . . 66 D7
Wheeler Street Sh Ctr
　B19 . . . . 66 D6
Wheeler St B19 . . . . 80 F5
Wheeley Moor Rd B37 . . . . 70 A5

Wheeley Rd
　Alvechurch B48 . . . . 138 D5
　Solihull B92 . . . . 107 D7
Wheeley's La B15 . . . . 66 C1
Wheeleys Rd B15 . . . . 86 B8
Wheelock Cl B74 . . . . 44 F7
Wheelwright Cl
[4] Darlaston WS10 . . . . . . 41 C6
　Bromsgrove B60 . . . . 150 E6
Wheelwright Ct [5] B24 . . . 56 E2
Wheelwright La CV6,CV7 . . 95 C4
Wheelwright Lane Prim Sch
　CV7 . . . . 95 D5
Wheelwright Rd B24 . . . . . 56 F1
Wheldrake Ave B34 . . . . . . 69 C6
Wheler Rd CV3 . . . . 134 A7
Whernside Dr WV6 . . . . 25 A5
Wherretts Well La B91 . . . 107 E6
Whetstone Cl B15 . . . . 85 F5
Whetstone Field Prim Sch
　WS9 . . . . 30 B4
Whetstone Gn WV10 . . . . . 11 D1
Whetstone Gr WV10 . . . . . 25 D8
Whetstone La WS9 . . . . . . 30 B4
Whetstone Rd WV10 . . . . . 25 D8
Whettybridge Rd B45 . . . 121 E6
Whetty La B45 . . . . 121 F7
Whichcote Ave CV7 . . . . . . 92 C1
Whichford Cl B76 . . . . 57 A6
Whichford Gr B9 . . . . 68 C2
While Rd B72 . . . . 46 B4
Whilmot Cl WV10 . . . . 12 B6
Whimbrel Gr DY10 . . . . . . 117 A1
Whinberry Rise DY5 . . . . . 50 C1
Whinchat Gr DY10 . . . . . . 117 A2
Whinfield Rd B61 . . . . 136 B6
Whinyates Rise WS11 . . . . . 4 F8
Whisley Brook La B28 . . . . 87 F2
Whistler Gr WV10 . . . . 26 A8
Whiston Ave WV11 . . . . 27 A7
Whiston Gr B29 . . . . 103 B8
Whiston Ho [9] WS11 . . . . . 28 F1
Whitacre La WS14 . . . . 16 E7
Whitacre Rd
[3] Royal Leamington Spa
　CV32 . . . . 157 A2
　Birmingham B9 . . . . 67 F3
Whitacre Rd Ind Est CV11 . 73 E4
Whitacre Rd CV5 . . . . 112 C3
Whitaker Rd CV5 . . . . 112 C3
Whitburn Ave B42 . . . . 55 A5
Whitburn Cl
　Kidderminster DY11 . . . . 116 B5
　Wolverhampton WV9 . . . . . 11 A2
Whitburn Rd CV12 . . . . 77 C1
Whitby Cl WS3 . . . . 13 F3
Whitby Rd B12 . . . . 87 A4
Whitby Way WS11 . . . . 4 C8
Whitchurch Cl B98 . . . . . . 158 F6
Whitchurch Way CV4 . . . . 131 F8
Whitcot Gr B31 . . . . 122 F8
White Bark Cl WS12 . . . . . . 2 A8
Whitebeam Cl
　Brownhills WS8 . . . . 15 E6
　Coventry CV4 . . . . 111 D1
　Dudley DY3 . . . . 50 C4
Whitebeam Croft [3] B38 . 103 E1
White Beam Rd B37 . . . . . 90 D8
Whitebeam Way CV10 . . . . 72 D7
White City Rd DY5 . . . . 62 A1
White Cl DY9 . . . . 81 C2
Whitecrest B43 . . . . 44 A2
Whitecrest Jun & Inf Sch
　B43 . . . . 44 A2
Whitecroft Rd B26 . . . . . . 89 D5
White Falcon Ct CV8 . . . . 148 C6
White Farm Rd B74 . . . . . . 31 E4
White Field Ave B17 . . . . . 85 A6
Whitefield Cl
　Codsall WV8 . . . . 10 B2
　Coventry CV4 . . . . 131 D6
Whitefields Cres B91 . . . . 107 B2
Whitefields Gate B91 . . . . 107 A1
Whitefields Rd B91 . . . . . 107 A2
Whitefriars Dr B63 . . . . 83 A4
White Friars La CV1 . . . . . 165 C2
White Friars St CV1 . . . . . 165 C2
Whitefriars Dr WS13 . . . . . 3 A1
Whitegates Rd WV14 . . . . . 40 D2
Whitehall Dr WV3 . . . . 38 F6

Whiteheath Ct [6] B65 . . . . 63 E4
Whiteheath PRU B65 . . . . 63 D4
White Hill B31 . . . . 103 B6
Whitehill La B29,B31 . . . . 103 A5
Whitehill Rd DY11 . . . . . . 116 A4
White Hollies WS3 . . . . 14 F4
Whitehorse Cl CV6 . . . . . . 96 B6
White Horse Rd WS8 . . . . . 6 E2
Whitehouse Ave
　Darlaston WS10 . . . . 41 B7
　Wednesbury WS10 . . . . . . 41 F3
White House Ave WV3 . . . . 38 D8
Whitehouse Ave WV3 . . . . 38 D8
White House Cl B91 . . . . . 106 F3
Whitehouse Common Prim
　Sch B75 . . . . 46 D7
Whitehouse Common Rd
　B75 . . . . 46 E7
Whitehouse Cres
　Burntwood WS7 . . . . 7 B7
　Nuneaton CV10 . . . . 72 D3
　Sutton Coldfield B75 . . . . . 46 E7
　Wolverhampton WV11 . . . . 12 F1
Whitehouse Ct [8] B75 . . . . 46 F6
White House Dr B45 . . . . . 122 A2
Whitehouse Dr
　Lichfield WS13 . . . . 8 F6
　Smethwick B66 . . . . 65 A7
　White House Gn B91 . . . . 106 F3
Whitehouse La
　Codsall WV8 . . . . 10 A6
　Redditch B98 . . . . 154 E4
Whitehouse Pl B45 . . . . . 121 F6
Whitehouse Rd
　Kidderminster DY10 . . . . 116 D4
　Polesworth B78 . . . . 36 F7
White Houses La WV10 . . . 12 B5
Whitehouse St
　Birmingham B6 . . . . 66 F6
　Tipton,Burnt Tree DY4 . . . 52 A2
　Tipton,Wallbrook WV14 . . 51 C8
　Walsall WS2 . . . . 28 D3
Whitehouse Way WS9 . . . . 30 A5
White House Way B91 . . . 107 A3
Whitelaw Cres CV5 . . . . . . 112 C6
Whitemoor Dr B90 . . . . . . 127 A7
Whitemoor Rd CV8 . . . . . . 148 B5
White Oak Dr
　Kingswinford DY6 . . . . 60 C6
　Wolverhampton WV3 . . . . . 24 C1
Whitepits La B48 . . . . 140 F4
Whitepoplars Cl DY5 . . . . . 61 C4
White Rd
　Birmingham B32 . . . . 84 D6
　Birmingham,Sparkbrook
　　B11 . . . . 87 C7
White Rose Ho [4] CV32 . . 156 F2
White Row WV5 . . . . 37 C1
Whitesands Cl B77 . . . . . . 21 E5
White's Dr DY3 . . . . 50 E8
Whiteside Cl CV3 . . . . 134 F8
Whiteslade Cl B93 . . . . . . 128 A8
Whitesmith Croft B14 . . . 104 E8
Whitesmiths Cl DY5 . . . . . . 50 D8
Whitesmore Sch B37 . . . . . 69 F1
White's Rd B71 . . . . 53 C6
Whites Row CV8 . . . . 148 A3
White St
　Birmingham B12 . . . . 87 A5
　Coventry CV1 . . . . 165 C3
Whitestitch La CV7 . . . . . . 92 C3
Whitestone Inf Sch CV11 . . 79 A8
Whitestone Rd
　Halesowen B63 . . . . 83 A6
　Nuneaton CV11 . . . . 79 B7
White St WS1 . . . . 42 E8
Whites Wood WV5 . . . . 49 A5
Whitethorn Cl WS12 . . . . . . 2 A8
Whitethorn Cres B74 . . . . . 30 D1
Whitethorn Dr CV32 . . . . . 157 B2
Whitethorn Rd DY8 . . . . . . 61 A1
Whitewood Glade WV12 . . 27 E4
Whitfield Gr B15 . . . . 86 D8
Whitfield Rd WS12 . . . . 2 C7
Whitford Bridge Rd B60 . 151 A2
Whitford Cl B61 . . . . 150 D6
Whitford Dr B90 . . . . 127 C7
Whitford Gates B61 . . . . . 136 D2
Whitford Rd B61 . . . . 136 D2
Whitgreave Ave
　Featherstone WV10 . . . . . 12 B7
　Wolverhampton WV10 . . . . 25 F8
Whitgreave Ct WV10 . . . . . 12 B7
Whitgreave Inf Sch WV10 . 25 E8
Whitgreave Jun Sch
　WV10 . . . . 25 E8
Whitgreave Prim Sch
　WV10 . . . . 12 B7
Whitgreave St B70 . . . . . . 52 E3
Whiting B77 . . . . 35 D7
Whitland Cl B45 . . . . 122 B6
Whitland Dr B14 . . . . 104 F3
Whitley Abbey Com Sch
　CV3 . . . . 133 F6
Whitley Abbey Prim Sch
　CV3 . . . . 133 F6
Whitley Ave B77 . . . . 54 E3
Whitley Cl WV6 . . . . 24 B2
Whitley Court Rd B32 . . . . 84 D5
Whitley Ct
　Birmingham B20 . . . . 54 E3
　Coventry CV3 . . . . 133 F7
Whitley Dr B74 . . . . 45 A8
Whitley St WS10 . . . . 41 E3
Whitley Village CV3 . . . . . 133 F7
Whitlock Gr B14 . . . . 105 A3
Whitlocks End Halt B90 . . 125 E7

Whitminster Ave B24 . . . . 57 B3
Whitminster Cl WV12 . . . . 27 C4
Whitmore Hill WV1 . . . . . 163 B3
Whitmore Ho WV6 . . . . 25 A4
Whitmore Park Prim Sch
　CV6 . . . . 95 A1
Whitmore Park Rd CV6 . . . 95 D3
Whitmore Rd
　Birmingham B10 . . . . 87 C8
　Stourbridge DY8 . . . . 80 D5
　Whitnash CV31 . . . . 162 A3
Whitmore St
　Birmingham B18 . . . . 66 B6
　Walsall WS1 . . . . 42 D7
　Wolverhampton WV1 . . . . 163 C3
Whitnash Cl CV7 . . . . 130 A6
Whitnash Gr CV2 . . . . 114 D5
Whitnash Prim Sch
　CV31 . . . . 162 A4
Whitnash Rd CV31 . . . . . . 162 B4
Whitney Ave DY8 . . . . 80 D6
Whittaker St WV2 . . . . 39 E6
Whittall Dr E DY11 . . . . . . 116 B1
Whittall Dr W DY11 . . . . . 116 A1
Whittall St B4 . . . . 164 C3
Whittimere St WS1 . . . . . . 28 F2
Whittingham Gr WV11 . . . . 26 F7
Whittingham Rd B63 . . . . . 83 A5
Whittington Cl
[4] Warwick CV34 . . . . . . 161 B8
　Birmingham B14 . . . . 104 E5
　West Bromwich B71 . . . . . 53 F8
Whittington Gr B33 . . . . . . 68 F2
Whittington Hall La DY7 . . 80 B3
Whittington Ho WS13 . . . . . 3 E1
Whittington Oval B33 . . . . 69 A2
Whittington Rd DY8 . . . . . . 80 C3
Whittle Cl CV3 . . . . 134 F8
Whittle Croft B35 . . . . 57 F3
Whittle Ct CV32 . . . . 157 A1
Whittleford Rd B36 . . . . . . 58 C1
Whittleford Rd CV10 . . . . . 72 C4
Whittle Rd LE10 . . . . 74 E7
Whittles Ct DY11 . . . . 116 B8
Whitton St WS10 . . . . 41 E6
Whitville Cl DY11 . . . . 116 C7
Whitwell Cl B90 . . . . 127 A6
Whitworth Ave
　Coventry CV3 . . . . 114 B1
　Hinckley LE10 . . . . 74 F7
Whitworth Dr B71 . . . . 42 E1
Whitworth Ind Pk B9 . . . . . 67 C2
Whoberley Ave CV5 . . . . . 112 D2
Whoberley Hall Prim Sch
　CV5 . . . . 112 C3
Whyley St B70 . . . . 53 A4
Whyley Wlk B69 . . . . 64 A5
Whynot Cl B60 . . . . 150 C2
Whynot St B63 . . . . 82 B5
Whytes The WS13 . . . . 8 F5
Wibert Cl B29 . . . . 86 A1
Wichnor Rd B92 . . . . 88 F5
Wickets Twr B35 . . . . 86 C5
Wickham Cl CV6 . . . . 94 F2
Wickham Ct CV32 . . . . . . 157 B3
Wickham Gdns WV11 . . . . 26 A6
Wickham Rd B80 . . . . 159 F4
Wickham Sq B70 . . . . 53 B2
Wicklow Cl B63 . . . . 82 D1
Wickmans Dr CV4 . . . . . . 111 C2
Wiclif Way WV10 . . . . 72 B3
Widdecombe Cl CV2 . . . . 114 D7
Widdrington Rd CV1 . . . . . 113 C5
Wideacre Dr B44 . . . . 55 E7
Wide Acres B45 . . . . 101 F1
Widgeon Gr WV10 . . . . 12 A3
Widney Ave
　Aldridge WS9 . . . . 16 B1
　Birmingham B29 . . . . 85 C1
Widney Cl B93 . . . . 127 F5
Widney Ho B97 . . . . 153 C4
Widney Jun Sch B91 . . . . 106 F1
Widney La B91 . . . . 127 B8
Widney Manor Rd B91,
　B93 . . . . 127 D7
Widney Manor Sta B91 . . 127 C6
Widney Rd B93 . . . . 127 F5
Wigford Rd DY4 . . . . 35 C5
Wiggin Cotts B17 . . . . 85 C5
Wiggin Ho WS3 . . . . 14 A3
Wiggins Croft B76 . . . . 46 F3
Wiggins Hill Rd B76 . . . . . 58 F7
Wigginsmill Rd WS10 . . . . 41 D1
Wiggin St B16 . . . . 65 F3
Wigginton Rd B79 . . . . 21 B7
Wight Croft B36 . . . . 70 B6
Wightman Cl WS14 . . . . 9 E6
Wightwick Bank WV6 . . . . 24 A2
Wightwick Cl WS3 . . . . 14 B1
Wightwick Ct WV6 . . . . 24 A3
Wightwick Gr WV6 . . . . 24 A2
Wightwick Hall Rd WV6 . . 23 C1
Wightwick Manor* WV6 . . 23 F1
Wigland Way B38 . . . . 104 A1
Wigmore Gr B44 . . . . 56 B8
Wigmore La B71 . . . . 54 A8
Wigorn Ho B67 . . . . 84 F8
Wigorn La DY9 . . . . 99 B8
Wigorn Rd B67 . . . . 64 F1
Wigston Rd CV2 . . . . 96 F1
Wilberforce Way B92 . . . . 107 F7
Wilbraham Rd WS2 . . . . . . 28 C1
Wilcote Gr B27 . . . . 106 C8
Wilcox Ave WS12 . . . . 2 D2
Wildacres DY8 . . . . 80 C6
Wilday Cl DY4 . . . . 52 A5

Wildcroft Rd CV5 . . . . 112 C3
Wilde Cl B14 . . . . 104 D4
Wilden Cl B31 . . . . 102 C3
Wilden La DY10,DY11 . . . 116 E1
Wilderness La B43 . . . . . . 43 D3
Wildey Rd [1] CV12 . . . . . . 77 D2
Wildfell Rd B27 . . . . 88 D2
Wild Goose La B98 . . . . . 159 D8
Wildmoor Cl CV2 . . . . 96 B4
Wildmoor La B61 . . . . 121 A3
Wildmoor Rd B90 . . . . 106 B5
Wildtree Ave WV10 . . . . . . 12 A2
Wiley Ave WS10 . . . . 41 C5
Wiley Ave S WS10 . . . . 41 C5
Wilford Gr
　Solihull B91 . . . . 107 B2
　Sutton Coldfield B76 . . . . . 58 B6
Wilford Rd B71 . . . . 53 D6
Wilhelmina Cl CV32 . . . . . 161 E8
Wilkes Ave WS2 . . . . 27 F2
Wilkes Cl WS3 . . . . 14 E3
Wilkes Croft DY3 . . . . 50 A3
Wilkes Green Jun & Inf Sch
　B21 . . . . 54 E1
Wilkes St
　West Bromwich B71 . . . . . 53 E7
　Willenhall WV13 . . . . 27 A1
Wilkin Rd WS8 . . . . 6 C2
Wilkins Ho WS3 . . . . 14 A1
Wilkinson Ave WV14 . . . . . 40 E3
Wilkinson Cl
　Burntwood WS7 . . . . 7 B8
　Sutton Coldfield B73 . . . . . 46 A2
Wilkins Croft B8 . . . . 68 A6
Wilkinson Jun & Inf Sch
　WV14 . . . . 40 F3
Wilkinson Rd WS10 . . . . . . 41 A4
Wilkinson Way B46 . . . . . . 70 D7
Wilks Gn B21 . . . . 54 D1
Willard Rd B25 . . . . 88 C6
Willaston Rd B33 . . . . 89 D7
Willclare Rd B26 . . . . 89 A6
Willcock Rd WV2 . . . . 39 E7
Willenhall Ind Est WV13 . . 27 C3
Willenhall La CV3 . . . . 134 F7
Willenhall Lane Cvn Site
　WS2 . . . . 28 A3
Willenhall Lane Ind Est
　WS3 . . . . 28 A8
Willenhall Mus* WV13 . . . 27 B1
Willenhall Rd
　Bilston WV14 . . . . 40 F7
　Darlaston WS10 . . . . 41 D8
　Wolverhampton WV1,WV13 . 26 C1
Willenhall Sch Sports Coll
　WV12 . . . . 27 E5
Willenhall St WS10 . . . . . . 41 C7
Willenhall Trad Est WV13 . 27 A1
Willenhall Wood Prim Sch
　CV3 . . . . 134 D6
Willerby Fold WV10 . . . . . . 11 F4
Willersey Rd B13 . . . . 105 D8
Willes Ct
[2] Birmingham B62 . . . . . 84 A7
[3] Royal Leamington Spa
　CV31 . . . . 162 B7
Willes Rd
　Birmingham B18 . . . . 65 E6
　Royal Leamington Spa CV31,
　　CV32 . . . . 162 A8
Willes Terr CV31 . . . . 162 B8
Willett Ave WS7 . . . . 7 A5
Willett Rd B71 . . . . 53 E8
Willetts Dr B63 . . . . 82 B4
Willetts Rd B31 . . . . 103 A1
Willetts Way B64 . . . . 62 F2
Willey Gr B24 . . . . 57 B2
William Arnold Cl CV2 . . . 114 A4
William Batchelor Ho
　CV1 . . . . 165 B4
William Baxter Sch WS12 . 2 A6
William Beesley Cres
　CV11 . . . . 79 E6
William Bentley Ct WV11 . 13 A1
William Booth La B4 . . . . 164 B4
William Bree Rd CV5 . . . . 111 C5
William Bristow Rd CV3 . . 133 E7
William Cook Rd B8 . . . . . 68 B5
William Cowper Prim Sch
　B19 . . . . 66 E6
William Cree Cl CV8 . . . . . 135 F3
William Ct
[7] Birmingham,Showell Green
　B13 . . . . 86 F4
　Birmingham,Rotton Park
　　B16 . . . . 65 E1
William Edward St [1] B12 86 F7
William Green Rd WS10 . . 42 C3
William Groubb Cl CV3 . . 134 D7
William Hanke Ind Est
　DY5 . . . . 61 E1
William Harper Rd WV13 . 27 B2
William Henry St B7 . . . . . 67 A6
William Iliffe St LE10 . . . . 75 B7
William Ker Rd DY4 . . . . . . 52 C5
William Kirby Cl CV4 . . . . 112 A1
William Lunn's Homes [2]
　WS14 . . . . 9 D8
William McCool Cl CV3 . . 134 F7
William MacGregor Prim Sch
　B77 . . . . 21 D4
William McKee Cl CV3 . . . 134 E7
William Malcolm Ho
　CV2 . . . . 114 E3
William Morris Gr WS11 . . . 1 E4
William Rd
　Birmingham B31 . . . . 102 F1

William Rd *continued*
Smethwick B67 64 D3
William St N B19 164 B4
William St W B66 65 B7
Williams Cl WV12 27 C5
William Sheriden Ho
CV2 114 E3
Williamson St WV3 163 A2
Williams Rd CV31 162 E4
William St
Bedworth CV12 78 D2
Birmingham B15 66 C1
Brierley Hill DY5 61 C3
Nuneaton CV11 73 E3
Redditch B97 153 E4
Royal Leamington Spa
CV32 162 A8
Walsall WS4 28 F3
West Bromwich B70 52 E5
William Tarver Cl CV34 161 A7
William Thomas Ho 7
CV32 157 A1
William Thomson Ho 2
CV1 165 D4
William Tolson's Ind Est
B78 35 A8
William Wiggin Ave WS3 14 B2
Willingsworth High Sch
DY4 41 B2
Willingsworth Rd WS10 41 D1
Willington Rd B79 21 B7
Willington St CV11 73 B5
Willingworth Cl WV14 40 A3
Willis Gr CV12 78 C3
Willis Ho CV11 73 E1
Willis Pearson Ave WV14 41 A3
Willis St DY11 116 C5
Willmore Gr 4 B38 123 F8
Willmore Rd B20 55 D2
Willmott Cl B75 32 D3
Willmott Rd B75 32 D3
Willoughby Ave CV8 147 E3
Willoughby Cl CV3 134 E8
Willoughby Ct B76 46 F2
Willoughby Dr B91 107 B1
Willoughby Gr B29 85 A1
Willoughby Rd B79 20 E7
Willow Ave
Birmingham B17 65 A2
Burntwood WS7 7 C6
Wednesbury WS10 41 F4
Wolverhampton WV11 26 B8
Willowbank Rd LE10 75 C7
Willow Bank Rd B93 127 F6
Willowbank B78 21 B1
Willow Bank WV3 24 C1
Willow Brook Rd B48 139 A7
Willowbud Ho B98 158 F8
Willow Cl
Bedworth CV12 78 A5
Bromsgrove B61 136 E2
Cradley Heath B64 62 E1
Hinckley LE10 75 E5
Nuneaton CV10 72 A7
West Hagley DY9 98 F5
Whitnash CV31 162 B2
Willow Coppice B32 84 C1
Willow Ct
Birmingham B13 87 A3
Bromsgrove B61 136 E3
Lichfield WS14 9 C5
Oldbury B66 64 D8
Smethwick B17 65 A2
Willow Ctyd CV2 114 D7
Willowdale Grange WV6 24 E5
Willowdale LE10 75 A7
Willow Dr
Birmingham B21 54 C1
Cheswick Green B90 126 D4
Codsall WV8 10 B3
Oldbury B69 63 C7
Willow End DY9 81 D3
Willowfield Dr DY11 116 C8
Willowfields Rd CV11 74 A1
Willow Gdns
Birmingham B16 65 F4
Bromsgrove B61 136 E3
Willow Gr
Coventry CV4 112 B2
Essington WV11 13 B3
Willenhall WV13 27 B1
Willowherb Cl
4 Walsall WS5 43 A3
5 Coventry CV3 134 F8
Cannock WS11 2 C2
Willowherb Way B90 126 A5
Willow Ho
11 Warwick CV34 161 D8
Birmingham B7 67 B4
Walsall WS4 15 D1
Willow Hts B64 83 A8
Willow Meer CV8 148 B5
Willow Mews B29 85 B1
Willow Park Dr DY8 81 B2
Willow Rd
Birmingham,Bournville B29,
B30 103 F8
Birmingham,Great Barr B43 44 A2
Bromsgrove B61 136 E3
Dudley DY1 51 A4
Nuneaton CV10 72 F5
Solihull B91 106 E2
Wolverhampton WV3 38 D8
Willow Rise DY5 61 C1
Willowsbrook Rd B62 83 F8
Willows Cres B12 86 E5
Willow Sheets Mdw
CV32 157 E6
Willowside WS4 29 C8
Willowsmere Dr WS14 9 F7
Willows Prim Sch WS13 3 B2
Willows Rd
Birmingham B12 86 E5
Walsall,Shelfield WS4 29 C8
Walsall,The Chuckery WS1 29 A1
Willows The
10 Sutton Coldfield B74 31 F2
Bedworth CV12 77 E2
Birmingham B27 88 B2
Cannock WS11 1 C1
Dudley DY2 62 E5
Hollywood B47 125 A6
Portway B47 140 F7
Sutton Coldfield,Walmley
B76 46 F2
Wolverhampton WV11 26 B5
Willowtree Cl WS13 3 B2
Willow Tree Dr B45 138 D8
Willow Way
Birmingham B37 70 B1
Redditch B97 153 B4
Studley B80 159 E2
Willow Wlk WS12 1 D8
Wills Ave B71 53 B7
Willsbridge Covert 8
B14 104 C2
Wills Ho B70 53 C2
Willson Croft B28 105 D3
Wills St B19 66 C7
Wills Way B66 65 C4
Wilmcote Cl B12 86 E6
Wilmcote Ct B61 150 D8
Wilmcote Dr B75 32 B3
Wilmcote Gn CV5 112 A3
Wilmcote Ho B97 153 B4
Wilmcote Rd B91 106 F6
Wilmcote Twr 5 B12 86 F7
Wilmhurst Rd CV34 160 C8
Wilmington Rd B32 84 B6
Wilmore Ho B20 55 D1
Wilmore La B47 124 F4
Wilmot Ave B46 70 F6
Wilmot Cl CV7 130 B8
Wilmot Dr
Birmingham B23 57 A6
Tipton DY4 51 E6
Wilmot Gdns DY1 51 A2
Wilmott Cl WS13 9 A7
Wilnecote Gr
Birmingham B42 55 D4
Whitnash CV31 162 B5
Wilnecote High Sch B77 35 F6
Wilnecote Jun Sch B77 35 F7
Wilnecote La B77 21 D2
Wilnecote Sta B77 35 D7
Wilner's View WS3 14 F5
Wilsford Cl
Birmingham B14 104 D1
Walsall WS4 29 C8
Wilsford Gn B15 85 E7
Wilson Dr B75 47 A5
Wilson Gn CV3 114 F1
Wilson Gr
Cannock WS11 2 C2
Kenilworth CV8 148 C4
Wilson Rd
Birmingham B19 66 D8
Brierley Hill DY5 61 C4
Dudley WV14 51 C7
Oldbury B68 64 D1
Smethwick B66 65 B3
Wilsons La CV7 96 A6
Wilson's La CV6 95 F6
Wilsons Rd B93 128 C6
Wilson St DY4 52 A5
Wilson Stuart Sch B23 56 C6
Wilson St WV1 163 C4
Wiltell Rd Ind Est WS14 9 B7
Wiltell Rd WS14 9 B6
Wilton Ave DY11 116 B8
Wilton Cl DY3 50 E7
Wilton Rd
Balsall Common CV7 130 B5
Birmingham,Balsall Heath
B11 87 B5
Birmingham,Erdington B23 57 A5
Birmingham,Handsworth
B20 55 B1
Wilton St B19 66 D8
Wiltshire Cl
Bedworth CV12 78 A3
Coventry CV5 112 B3
Walsall WS2 28 D4
Wiltshire Ct 10 B29 103 C7
Wiltshire Dr B63 82 B7
Wiltshire Ho 3 DY8 80 F8
Wiltshire Way B71 53 C7
Wimberger Ho 2 B71 53 D4
Wimblebury Rd WS12 2 F2
Wimbledon Dr DY8 81 B2
Wimborne Dr CV2 115 A4
Wimborne Rd WV10 26 A6
Wimbourne Cl CV10 72 B5
Wimbourne Rd
Birmingham B16 65 D3
Sutton Coldfield B76 47 A4
Wimperis Way B43 44 C4
Wimpole Gr B44 56 B7
Wimshurst Mdw WV10 11 F4
Wincanton Croft B36 68 C8
Winceby Pl CV4 111 D1
Winceby Rd WV6 23 F3
Winchat Cl CV3 114 F1
Winchcombe Cl
Dudley DY1 50 E3
Solihull B92 89 B2
Winchcombe Rd B92 89 B2
Winchester Ave
Kidderminster DY11 116 A6
Nuneaton CV10 73 C7
Winchester Cl
8 Rowley Regis B65 63 E4
Lichfield WS13 3 C3
West Hagley DY9 99 A6
Winchester Ct 4 B74 31 F2
Winchester Dr
Birmingham B37 70 A2
Hinckley LE10 76 B7
Stourbridge DY8 81 A3
Winchester Gdns B31 103 A3
Winchester Gr B21 65 C8
Winchester Mews WS9 30 B4
Winchester Rd
Birmingham B20 55 D1
Cannock WS11 2 A3
Tamworth B78 20 F3
West Bromwich B71 53 B8
Wolverhampton WV10 11 C3
Winchester Rise DY1 51 A2
Winchester St CV1 113 E3
Winchfield Dr B17 84 F7
Wincote Dr WV6 24 C4
Wincrest Way B34 69 C5
Windermere Ave
Coventry,Binley CV3 114 E1
Coventry,Upper Eastern Green
CV5 111 E4
Nuneaton CV11 73 F6
Windermere Dr
Kingswinford DY6 60 D6
Royal Leamington Spa
CV32 156 D2
Sutton Coldfield B74 30 F3
Windermere Ho
11 Oldbury B69 63 D5
Kidderminster DY10 116 E7
Windermere Pl WS11 1 E1
Windermere Rd
Birmingham,Handsworth
B21 54 E2
Birmingham,Moseley B13 87 B1
Wolverhampton WV6 24 D8
Windermere B77 36 A7
Windermre Ho 2 B15 85 D3
Windfall Ct B24 57 D4
Winding House La CV6,
CV7 95 C4
Winding Mill N DY5 81 E7
Winding Mill S DY5 81 E7
Windings The WS13 3 A1
Windleaves Rd B36 69 E8
Windley Ho B73 45 C2
Windmill Ave
4 Coleshill B46 70 F7
Birmingham B45 121 E8
Windmill Bank WV5 49 A7
Windmill Cl
Birmingham B31 103 C5
Kenilworth CV8 148 A6
Lichfield WS13 3 A2
Tamworth B79 21 A8
Windmill Cres
Smethwick B66 65 C5
Wolverhampton WV3 24 A1
Windmill Croft CV32 157 D5
Windmill Ct CV6 96 A3
Windmill Dr B97 158 C6
Windmill End DY2 62 E5
Windmill Gdns B97 158 B6
Windmill Gr DY6 60 B8
Windmill Hill
Birmingham B31 103 B5
Cubbington CV32 157 D5
Halesowen B63 82 D5
Windmill Hill The CV5 112 A7
Windmill Ind Est CV5 111 F7
Windmill La
Balsall Common CV7 130 D4
Corley Moor CV7 93 D6
Dorridge B93 127 F1
Lichfield WS13 3 A2
Smethwick B66 65 B5
Tanworth-in-A B94 144 A8
Wolverhampton WV3 24 A1
Windmill Prec B66 65 C5
Windmill Rd
Bedworth CV7 96 A8
Coventry CV6 96 A3
Nuneaton CV10 72 D7
Solihull B90 105 E2
Whitnash CV31 161 F5
Windmill St
Birmingham B1 164 B1
Dudley DY1 51 A2
Dudley,Gornalwood DY3 50 D5
Walsall WS1 42 F8
Wednesbury WS10 42 A3
Windmill Terr WS10 42 A3
Windmill View DY1 51 B7
Windmill Works Ind Pk
DY2 62 B6
Windridge Cl CV3 134 C6
Windridge Cres B92 107 F8
Windrow The WV6 23 D4
Windrush Cl
Redditch B97 158 D6
Solihull B92 89 A2
Walsall WS3 15 A1
Windrush Dr LE10 75 A8
Windrush Gr B29 104 A8
Windrush Rd
Cannock WS11 1 E6
Hollywood B47 125 B7
Windsor Arc B2 164 C3
Windsor Ave
Cannock WS12 2 B6
Oldbury B68 64 A3
Wolverhampton WV4 38 E6
Windsor Cl
Birmingham,Coft Common
B31 123 A6
Birmingham,Frankley B45 102 A2
Dudley DY3 50 B2
Halesowen B63 82 F3
Rowley Regis B65 63 C4
Tamworth B79 21 C7
Windsor Cres DY2 62 D6
Windsor Ct
12 Royal Leamington Spa
CV32 161 F8
Birmingham B38 103 F1
Cannock WS12 2 B6
Coventry CV4 112 B2
Hinckley LE10 76 A5
Lichfield WS14 9 B6
Nuneaton CV10 72 E6
Windsor Dr
Birmingham B24 57 C5
Kidderminster DY10 116 E7
Solihull B92 89 B2
Windsor Gate WV12 27 C4
Windsor Gdns
Bromsgrove B60 137 A2
Nuneaton CV10 72 E4
Wolverhampton WV3 38 A8
Windsor Gr
Stourbridge DY8 60 E1
Walsall WS4 15 C2
Windsor High Sch B63 82 F4
Windsor Ho
Birmingham B23 56 F6
Dudley DY2 61 F7
Wolverhampton WV3 163 A1
Windsor Ind Est B7 67 A5
Windsor Lodge B92 106 D8
Windsor Pl
10 Royal Leamington Spa
CV32 156 F1
Birmingham B7 67 A3
Birmingham,Erdington B23 56 E3
Windsor Rd
Birmingham,Castle Bromwich
B36 69 F7
Birmingham,New Oscott
B73 45 D1
Birmingham,Stirchley B30 104 B5
Cheslyn Hay WS6 4 E4
Halesowen B63 82 F4
Oldbury B68 64 A3
Redditch B97 153 D5
Rowley Regis B65 63 C5
Stourbridge DY8 80 E3
Tipton DY4 52 A8
West Bromwich B71 42 B1
Wolverhampton WV4 39 F5
Windsor St S B7 67 A4
Windsor St
Bilston WV14 40 C6
Birmingham B7 67 A4
Bromsgrove B60 137 A2
Coventry CV1 113 B2
Hinckley LE10 76 A5
Nuneaton CV11 73 B4
Royal Leamington Spa
CV32 161 F8
Walsall WS1 42 E7
Windsor Terr 5 B16 65 F1
Windsor View B32 102 B7
Windsor Way WS4 29 D7
Windsor Wlk WS10 41 D8
Winds Point DY9 99 A6
Windward Way B36 70 B6
Windward Way Ind Est
B36 69 F8
Windy Arbor Prim Sch
B37 70 D2
Windy Arbour CV8 148 B4
Windyridge Rd B76 58 A6
Winfield Rd CV11 73 B5
Winford Ave DY6 60 E4
Winforton Cl B98 154 E3
Wingate Cl B30 103 F4
Wingate Ct B74 31 E4
Wingate Rd WS2 27 E2
Wing Cl WS2 27 F4
Wingfield Cl B37 69 F3
Wingfield Ho B37 69 F5
Wingfield Rd
Birmingham B42 55 C7
Coleshill B46 70 F5
Wingfield Way CV6 95 A2
Wingfoot Ave WV10 25 E8
Wingrave Cl CV5 112 A6
Winifred Ave CV5 113 A1
Winifride Ct B17 85 B5
Winkle St B70 53 B4
Winleigh Rd B20 54 F2
Winnall Cl WV14 40 D2
Winnallthorpe CV3 134 E6
Winn Ho 3 WS2 28 D3
Winnie Rd B29 85 E1
Winnington Rd B8 68 A7
Winnipeg Rd B38 124 A8
Winrush Cl DY3 50 D3
Winscar Croft DY3 50 D3
Winsford Ave CV5 112 B4
Winsford Cl
Balsall Common CV7 130 A6
Halesowen B63 83 A6
Sutton Coldfield B76 46 E3
Winsford Ct CV5 112 C4
Winsham Gr B21 65 E8
Winsham Wlk CV3 133 C3
Winslow Ave B8 68 B4
Winslow Cl
Coventry CV5 112 B3
Redditch B98 154 F3
Royal Leamington Spa
CV32 156 C1
Winslow Dr WV6 24 E4
Winslow Ho 11 CV1 113 B2
Winson Green, Outer Circle
Sta B21 65 E7
Winson Green Rd B18 65 E5
Winson St B18 65 D4
Winsor Ave WS12 2 B6
Winspear Cl CV7 92 B1
Winstanley Rd B33 68 D2
Winster Ave B93 127 E4
Winster Cl CV7 95 A7
Winster Gr B44 44 D2
Winster Grove Ind Ctr
B44 44 D2
Winster Rd
Birmingham B43 54 D8
Wolverhampton WV1 26 B1
Winston Ave CV2 114 D8
Winston Churchill Ct
WV14 40 C8
Winston Cl CV2 114 D8
Winston Dr
Birmingham B20 55 B1
Romsley B62 101 A4
Winstone Cl B98 154 A4
Winterborne Gdns CV10 73 A2
Winterbourne Botanic Gdn*
B15 86 A5
Winterbourne Croft B14 104 C1
Winterbourne Rd B91 106 F4
Winter Cl WS13 3 D2
Winterdene CV7 130 B7
Winterfold Cl DY10 117 B6
Winterley Gdns DY3 50 E6
Winterley La WS4 29 C6
Winterton Rd
Birmingham B44 45 A3
Bulkington CV12 79 C2
Winthorpe Dr B91 127 C8
Wintney Cl B17 85 A7
Winton Gr B76 58 A6
Wintour Wlk B60 150 E7
Winward Rd B98 154 F1
Winwood Ct DY8 80 F4
Winwood Heath Rd B62 100 E2
Winwood Rd B65 63 E3
Winwoods Gr B32 102 A8
Winyate Hill B98 154 A2
Winyates Crafts Ctr B98 154 E3
Winyates Ctr B98 154 E3
Winyates Way B98 154 E4
Wirehill Dr B98 153 F1
Wiremill Cl B44 55 E6
Wirral Rd B31 102 F6
Wiseacre Croft B90 105 E2
Wise Gr CV34 155 E2
Wiseman Gr B23 45 D1
Wisemore WS2 28 E2
Wise St CV31 161 F7
Wise Terr CV31 161 F7
Wishaw Cl
Redditch B98 159 A8
Solihull B90 105 E2
Wishaw Gr B37 69 F5
Wishaw La
Curdworth B76 59 A7
Middleton B76,B78 48 C6
Minworth B76 58 E7
Wisley Gr CV8 148 C5
Wisley Way B32 84 F5
Wissage Ct WS13 9 D8
Wissage La WS13 3 D1
Wissage Rd WS13 9 D8
Wistaria Cl
2 Coventry CV2 96 B2
Birmingham B31 103 A6
Wisteria Dr
2 Walsall WS5 42 F4
Brownhills WS8 6 C2
Wisteria Gr B44 44 E2
Wistmans Cl DY1 50 E2
Wistwood Hayes WV10 11 F4
Witham Cl B76 47 A1
Witham Croft B91 107 C1
Withdean Cl B11 87 D6
Witherford Cl B29 103 C8
Witherford Croft B91 106 E2
Witherford Way B29 103 C8
Withern Way DY3 50 D3
Withers Rd WV8 10 B3
Withers Way B71 53 D4
Withington Covert B14 104 D2
Withington Gr B93 127 E4
Withybed Cl B48 139 A6
Withybed La B48 139 A6
Withybrook Cl CV2 96 D2
Withybrook La CV7 97 F5
Withybrook Rd
Bulkington CV12 79 D2
Solihull B90 126 B8
Withy Gr B37 69 F5
Withy Hill Rd B75 47 B8
Withymere La WV5 49 C8
Withymoor Prim Sch DY5 61 D1
Withymoor Rd
Dudley DY2 62 E4
Stourbridge DY8 81 A7
Withymore Ct WV3 25 A1

Withy Rd WV14 . . . . .40 C3
Withy Road Ind Est WV14 .40 C3
Withywood Cl WV12 . . . . .13 C1
Witley Ave
  Halesowen B63 . . . . .82 E4
  Solihull B91 . . . . .107 C2
Witley Cl DY11 . . . . .116 B2
Witley Cres B69 . . . . .63 E5
Witley Dr 🔢 WV13 . . . . . . .9 E8
Witley Farm Cl B91 . . . . . .107 C2
Witley Rd 🔢 B31 . . . . . . .103 D2
Witnell Rd CV6 . . . . .113 C6
Witney Cl B79 . . . . .20 F7
Witney Dr B37. . . . . .69 F2
Witney Gr WV10 . . . . .11 B3
Wittersham Ct 🔢 WV13 . .27 B2
Witton Bank B62 . . . . .83 F7
Witton La
  Birmingham B6 . . . . .55 F1
  West Bromwich B71 . . . . . .53 B8
Witton Lodge Rd B23 . . . .56 D7
Witton Rd
  Birmingham B6 . . . . .66 E8
  Wolverhampton WV4. . . . . .39 A6
Witton Sta B6 . . . . .55 F1
Witton St
  Birmingham B9 . . . . .67 B2
  Stourbridge DY8 . . . . .80 F4
Wixford Gr WV0 . . . . .106 D2
Wobaston Ct WV10. . . . . . .11 B3
Wobaston Rd
  Codsall WV9 . . . . .10 E4
  Wolverhampton WV9,WV10. .11 B4
Woburn Ave WV12 . . . . . . .27 B6
Woburn Cl
  Bromsgrove B61 . . . . . . .136 D1
  Hinckley LE10 . . . . .71 E3
  Royal Leamington Spa
    CV31. . . . . .162 C6
Woburn Cres B43. . . . . . .43 D1
Woburn Dr
  Brierley Hill DY5 . . . . . . .81 B8
  Cradley Heath B62 . . . . . .83 B7
  Nuneaton CV10 . . . . .73 A2
Woburn Gr B27. . . . . .88 C1
Woburn Ho B15 . . . . .86 C7
Woburn B77. . . . . .21 D3
Wodehouse Cotts WV5...49 D8
Wodehouse La WV5,DY3 ..49 E8
Woden Ave WV11 . . . . .26 C6
Woden Cres WV10. . . . . . .26 C6
Woden Cres Park WV10...25 E4
Woden Rd E WS10 . . . . . . .42 B4
Woden Rd N WS10 . . . . . . .41 F5
Woden Rd S WS10 . . . . . . .42 A1
Woden Rd W WS10 . . . . . . .41 D4
Woden Rd WV10 . . . . .25 F4
Wodensborough Com Tech
  Coll WS10. . . . . .42 B2
Wodensfield Prim Sch
  WV11. . . . . .26 B6
Wodensfield Twr WV11...26 C5
Woden Way WV11. . . . . . . .26 C6
Wold Wlk
  Birmingham B13 . . . . . . .105 C6
  Birmingham B13 . . . . . . .105 C6
Wolfe Rd CV4. . . . . .131 F8
Wolfsbane Dr WS5. . . . . . .43 A3
Wolfson Dr B11. . . . . .85 E4
Wollaston Cres WV11 . . . .26 D6
Wollaston Ct
  🔢 Walsall WS1. . . . . .28 F2
  Stourbridge DY8 . . . . .80 C6
Wollaston Rd
  Stourbridge DY7 . . . . .80 C7
  Stourbridge DY8 . . . . .80 F5
Wollerton Gr 🔢 B75. . . . . .46 F6
Wollescote Bsns Pk 🔢 B
  DY9 . . . . .81 F5
Wollescote Dr B91. . . . . . .107 B2
Wollescote Prim Sch DY9..81 F4
Wollescote Rd DY9 . . . . . .81 D3
Wolmer Rd WV11. . . . . . . .13 A2
Wolseley Ave B27. . . . . . . .88 D4
Wolseley Bank WV10. . . . .25 F7
Wolseley Cl
  Birmingham B36 . . . . .59 A1
  Wolverhampton WV10. . . .25 F7
Wolseley Dr B8. . . . . .68 A7
Wolseley Gate WV10 . . . . .25 F7
Wolseley Rd
  Bilston WV14 . . . . .40 C7
  West Bromwich B70 . . . . . .52 F6
Wolseley St B9 . . . . .67 B2
Wolseley B77. . . . . .21 F3
Wolston Cl B90. . . . . .106 B5
Wolston La CV8. . . . . .135 E2
Wolston Way CV3 . . . . . . .134 C6
Wolverhampton Coll Wulfrun
  Campus WV6. . . . . .24 E3
Wolverhampton (Dunstall
  Park) Race Course WV6.25 A6
Wolverhampton Girls' High
  Sch WV6. . . . . .24 F3
Wolverhampton Gram Sch
  WV3 . . . . .24 F2
Wolverhampton & Midland
  Cties Eye Infmy WV3 . . . .35 A2
Wolverhampton Mus & Art
  Gall* WV1. . . . . .163 B3
Wolverhampton Rd
  Cannock WS11. . . . . .4 D8
  Cheslyn Hay WV10,WS6. . . . .8 B2
  Codsall WV8 . . . . .10 A3
  Essington WV11. . . . . .13 A3

Wolverhampton Rd E
  WV4 . . . . .39 D5
Wolverhampton Rd
  Kingswinford DY6 . . . . . . .49 C1
  Nurton WV6. . . . . .23 A3
  Oldbury B69. . . . . .63 F4
Wolverhampton Rd S B32 84 E7
Wolverhampton Rd
  Sedgley DY3. . . . . .39 D2
  Walsall,Birchills WS2. . . . .28 B2
  Walsall,Pelsall WS3. . . . . .14 B1
  Walsall,Wallington Heath
    WS3 . . . . .14 B1
  Wedges Mills WS11. . . . . . .4 B6
  Wolverhampton WV10,
    WV11. . . . . .26 B4
Wolverhampton Rd W WV13,
  WS2 . . . . .27 D2
Wolverhampton Sta
  WV1 . . . . .163 C3
Wolverhampton St
  Bilston WV14 . . . . .40 C6
  Darlaston WS10. . . . . .41 C6
  Dudley DY1 . . . . .51 B1
  Walsall WS2 . . . . .28 D2
  Willenhall WV13 . . . . .27 A1
Wolverley Ave
  Stourbridge DY8 . . . . .80 C6
  Wolverhampton WV4. . . . . .38 D5
Wolverley Cres B69 . . . . . .63 E5
Wolverley Rd
  Birmingham B32 . . . . . . .102 B8
  Halesowen B63 . . . . .82 F2
  Solihull B92 . . . . .89 D2
Wolverson Cl WV12 . . . . . .27 C4
Wolverson Rd WV9. . . . . . .16 A4
Wolverton Cl B98. . . . . . .154 E2
Wolverton Rd
  Birmingham,Marston Green
    B37. . . . . .90 B7
  Birmingham,Rednal B45 . .122 C6
  Coventry CV5. . . . . .112 A3
  Dudley DY2 . . . . .51 E1
Wolvey Rd
  Bulkington CV12 . . . . .79 E2
  Hinckley LE10 . . . . .75 E4
Wombourne Cl DY3 . . . . . .50 C8
Woodacre Rd B24 . . . . . . .57 C4
Woodall Ho WS3. . . . . .28 C8
Woodall Rd B6 . . . . .55 F1
Woodall St
  Cradley Heath B64 . . . . . .62 C1
  Walsall WS3 . . . . .28 C8
Woodard Rd DY4 . . . . .52 C7
Wood Ave
  Dudley DY3 . . . . .50 C4
  Wednesfield WV11. . . . . . .26 D6
Woodbank Dr B61 . . . . . . .136 F8
Woodbank LE10 . . . . .76 A7
Woodbank Rd DY3. . . . . . . .50 C7
Wood Bank Rd WV3. . . . . .38 A8
Woodberrow La B97 . . . . .158 D6
Woodberry Dr B76. . . . . . .47 A2
Woodberry Wlk B27 . . . . .88 D3
Woodbine Ave B10. . . . . . .87 D8
Woodbine Cotts
  🔢 Royal Leamington Spa
    CV32. . . . . .161 E8
  Kingswood CV35 . . . . . . .144 D3
Woodbine Croft B26 . . . . .89 A6
Woodbine St 🔢 CV32 . . .161 E8
Woodbine Wlk B37 . . . . . .70 D2
Woodbourne B15. . . . . . . .85 D8
Woodbourne Cl
  Birmingham B15,B16. . . . .85 C8
  Smethwick B67 . . . . .64 E2
Woodbridge Cl
  Walsall,Wallington Heath
    WS3 . . . . .14 A3
  Walsall WS4 . . . . .15 D1
Woodbridge Rd B13 . . . . .86 F3
Woodbrooke Gr B31. . . . .103 C6
Woodbrooke Rd B30. . . .103 E7
Woodbrook Ho 🔢 B37. . . .70 D2
Woodburn Cl CV5. . . . . . . .112 B4
Woodburn Rd B66. . . . . . .65 D7
Woodbury Cl
  Brierley Hill DY5 . . . . . . .61 E2
  Halesowen B62 . . . . .83 F8
  Redditch B97 . . . . .158 A6
Woodbury Gr B91. . . . . . .107 B1
Woodbury Rd
  Birmingham B62 . . . . .84 A8
  Kidderminster DY11 . . . .116 B2
Woodchester Rd B93 . . . .127 E2
Woodchester DY9. . . . . . . .99 B4
Woodchurch Grange B73..56 F8
Woodclose Cl B46 . . . . . . .70 F7
Woodclose Ave DY4. . . . .112 F6
Woodclose Rd B37. . . . . . .69 F3
Woodcock Cl
  Birmingham B31 . . . . . . .102 C1
  Tanworth-In-A B94 . . . . .141 E3
Woodcock Gdns WV10 . .12 B7
Woodcock Hill Jun & Inf Sch
  B31. . . . . .102 C7
Woodcock La
  Birmingham,Acock's Green
    B27. . . . . .88 D3
  Birmingham,Northfield
    B31. . . . . .102 E8
Woodcock La N B27 . . . . .88 D4
Woodcock St B7. . . . . . . .66 F4
Woodcombe Cl DY5. . . . . .81 B7
Wood Common Grange
  WS14. . . . . .14 F4
Woodcote Ave
  Kenilworth CV8 . . . . .147 D6

Woodcote Ave continued
  Nuneaton CV11 . . . . .73 F8
Woodcote Cl B98. . . . . . . .154 E3
Woodcote Dr
  Birmingham B8 . . . . .67 F5
  Dorridge B93. . . . . .128 B2
  Leek Wootton CV35. . . . .155 F7
Woodcote La
  Belbroughton DY9 . . . . . .119 E1
  Leek Wootton CV8,CV35 . .155 F7
Woodcote Rd
  Birmingham B24 . . . . .57 D5
  Royal Leamington Spa
    CV32. . . . . .156 F3
  Warwick CV34. . . . . .160 F8
  Wolverhampton WV6. . . . .24 C4
Woodcote Way
  Birmingham B18 . . . . .66 A4
  Sutton Coldfield B74 . . . .44 F6
Woodcraft Cl CV4. . . . . . . .112 A2
Woodcroft Ave
  Birmingham B20 . . . . .54 E3
  Dudley DY4 . . . . .51 C4
  Tamworth B79 . . . . .21 B6
Woodcroft Cl
  Blackwell B60 . . . . .137 F5
  Cradley Heath B64 . . . . . .82 F8
Wood Croft B47 . . . . .125 B6
Woodcross La WV14 . . . . .40 A2
Woodcross St WV14 . . . . .39 F2
Wood Ct
  Birmingham B20 . . . . .55 A2
  Coventry CV2. . . . . .114 D7
  Redditch B97 . . . . .153 C1
Woodend B20 . . . . .54 E6
Woodend Cl B97. . . . . .153 B2
Woodend Croft CV4. . . . . .131 E8
Wood End Dr B45. . . . . . .138 A8
Wood End La
  Birmingham B24 . . . . .56 F3
  Lichfield WS13. . . . . .3 B7
  Tanworth-In-A B94 . . . . .141 F5
Woodend Pl WV6 . . . . .24 B4
Wood End Prim Sch
  Wolverhampton WV11. . . .26 C7
  Wolverhampton WV6. . . . .36 C1
Wood End Rd
  Birmingham B24 . . . . .56 F3
  Walsall WS5 . . . . .43 D8
  Wednesfield WV11. . . . . . .26 D7
  Wolverhampton WV11. . . .12 C1
Wood End Way WS9 . . . . . .16 B1
Woodfall Ave B30. . . . . . .103 F5
Woodfield Ave
  Brierley Hill DY5 . . . . . . .61 B7
  Cradley Heath B64 . . . . . .82 D8
  Oldbury B69. . . . . .64 A4
  Stourbridge DY9 . . . . .81 F2
  Wolverhampton WV4. . . . .38 F6
Woodfield Dr WV9. . . . . . .119 E2
Woodfield Cl
  Norton Canes WS11 . . . . . .5 F7
  Redditch B98 . . . . .154 A5
  Sutton Coldfield B74 . . . .46 B8
  Walsall WS5 . . . . .43 E5
Woodfield Cres
  Birmingham B12 . . . . .87 A6
  Kidderminster DY11 . . . .116 D5
Woodfield Ct B14. . . . . . .104 F8
Woodfield Dr WS15 . . . . . .5 F7
Woodfield Ho WV10. . . . . .11 C2
Woodfield Hts WV6 . . . . . .24 D4
Woodfield Jun & Inf Schs
  WV4 . . . . .38 F6
Woodfield La B62. . . . . . . .120 D8
Woodfield Mid Sch B98 .154 A2
Woodfield Rd
  Birmingham,Balsall Heath
    B12. . . . . .87 A6
  Birmingham,King's Heath
    B13. . . . . .104 F8
  Coventry CV5. . . . . .132 E8
  Dudley DY3 . . . . .50 C4
  Hinckley LE10 . . . . .75 C6
  Solihull B91 . . . . .107 B6
Woodfields Dr WS14 . . . . .9 E5
Woodfield St 🔢 DY11 . . .116 C6
Woodfold Croft WV9 . . . . .30 B7
Woodford Ave B36. . . . . . .69 B8
Woodford Cl
  Coventry CV7. . . . . .95 D5
  Nuneaton CV10 . . . . .72 D4
  Wolverhampton WV9. . . . .10 F2
Woodford Cres WV12 . . . .7 D6
Woodford End 🔢 WS11 . .1 F4
Woodford Green Rd B28 106 B8
Woodford Way WS12 . . . . .2 D1
Woodfort Rd B43 . . . . .65 D1
Woodgate Bsns Pk B32 . .84 B2
Woodgate Dr B32. . . . . . . .84 A1
Woodgate Gdns B32. . . . . .84 A2
Woodgate Ho 🔢 B97. . . .153 B4
Woodgate La B32. . . . . . . .84 A2
Woodgate Prim Sch B32 .84 B1
Woodgate Rd
  Hinckley LE10 . . . . .76 A8
  Stoke Prior B60. . . . . . . .151 B1
Woodgate Valley Ctry Pk*
  B32. . . . . .84 D3
Woodglade Croft B38 . . .103 E2
Woodgreen WS6. . . . . .4 E5
Woodgreen Cl B97. . . . . . .158 B7
Woodgreen Croft B68 . . . .84 C7
Wood Green High Sch
  WS10. . . . . .42 B5

Wood Green Jun Sch
  WS10. . . . . .42 A4
Wood Green Rd B18 . . . . .65 D4
Woodgreen Rd B68 . . . . . .84 C7
Wood Green Rd WS10. . . .42 B4
Woodhall Cl
  Nuneaton CV11 . . . . .74 A2
  Tipton DY4. . . . . .52 A8
Woodhall Croft B92. . . . . .88 F3
Woodhall Rd WV4 . . . . . . .38 E5
Woodham Cl B45. . . . . . . .101 E1
Woodhams Rd CV3 . . . . . .134 C3
Woodhaven
  Walsall WS4 . . . . .15 D1
  Wedges Mills WS11. . . . . .4 B5
Wood Hayes Croft WV10.12 C2
Wood Hayes Rd WV11. . . .12 C1
Wood Hill Rise CV6. . . . . .95 D2
Wood Ho 🔢 WS1 . . . . .42 E7
Woodhouse Cl CV3 . . . . . .134 E8
Woodhouse Fold WV11...26 D5
Woodhouse High Sch B77 22 E4
Woodhouse La B77 . . . . . . .22 A5
Woodhouse Orch DY9 . . .119 E7
Woodhouse Prim Sch
  B32. . . . . .84 E6
Woodhouse Rd B32. . . . . .84 E5
Woodhouse Rd N WV6 . .24 B4
Woodhouse Rd WV6 . . . . .24 B4
Woodhouses La WV5 . . . . .8 A7
Woodhouses Rd WS7 . . . .8 A2
Woodhouse St CV34 . . . . .160 D6
Woodhouse Way B64 . . . .62 C1
Woodhurst Cl B77 . . . . . . .21 F5
Woodhurst Rd B13. . . . . . .87 A4
Wooding Cres DY4. . . . . . .41 B1
Woodington Rd B75. . . . . .47 B5
Wood La
  Birmingham,Erdington
    B24. . . . . .57 C1
  Birmingham,Handsworth
    B20. . . . . .55 B2
  Birmingham,Marston Green
    B37. . . . . .90 A8
  Birmingham,Queen's Park
    B17. . . . . .85 A6
  Birmingham,Woodgate B32. .84 A1
  Cannock WS12. . . . . .2 C4
  Earlswood B94. . . . . .125 E1
  Eastcote B92. . . . . .108 F2
  Fairfield B61 . . . . .120 C3
  Hartshill CV10 . . . . .72 A8
Woodland Ave
  Brierley Hill DY5 . . . . . . .62 A1
  Coventry CV5. . . . . .132 F7
  Dudley DY1 . . . . .51 C3
  Hinckley LE10 . . . . .76 A7
  West Hagley DY8. . . . . . . .98 F5
  Wolverhampton WV6. . . . .24 B3
Woodland Cl
  Cannock WS12. . . . . .2 B8
  Stourbridge DY9 . . . . .81 D2
  Willenhall WV12 . . . . .27 D6
Woodland Cres WV3 . . . . .38 D7
Woodland Ct
  Cannock WS11. . . . . .1 C4
  Shenstone WS14 . . . . .32 A7
Woodland Dr
  Barnt Green B45 . . . . . . .122 A2
  Cheslyn Hay WS6. . . . . . . .4 E4
  Smethwick B66 . . . . .64 F5
Woodland Gr
  Birmingham B43 . . . . .43 E3
  Dudley DY3 . . . . .50 B3
Woodland Rd
  Birmingham,Handsworth
    B21. . . . . .65 C8
  Birmingham,Northfield
    B31. . . . . .103 B3
  Dodford B61 . . . . .136 A7
  Halesowen B62 . . . . .83 D8
  Hinckley LE10 . . . . .71 F1
  Kenilworth CV8 . . . . .148 B7
  Redditch B97 . . . . .153 B3
  Tamworth B77 . . . . .22 A3
  Wolverhampton WV3. . . . .38 D7
Woodland Rise
  Cradley Heath B64 . . . . . .82 F8
  Sutton Coldfield B73 . . . .46 B4
Woodlands Ave
  Walsall WS5 . . . . .43 E5
  Water Orton B46. . . . . . . .59 B2
Woodlands Com Prim Sch
  The B77. . . . . .21 E4
Woodlands Cotts WV4 . . .38 F4
Woodlands Cres WS3 . . . .14 F5
Woodlands Ct
  Binley Woods CV3 . . . . . .135 D7
  Coventry CV5. . . . . .133 A8
Woodlands Farm Rd B24 .57 F4
Woodlands Inf Sch B90 .126 B8
Woodlands La
  Bedworth CV12 . . . . .77 E4
  Solihull B90 . . . . .126 B8
Woodlands Paddock WV4 38 E4
Woodlands Park Rd B30 103 C5
Woodlands Prim Sch
  WV12. . . . . .27 D6
Woodlands Rd
  Bedworth CV12 . . . . .77 F3
  Binley Woods CV3 . . . . . .135 D7
  Birmingham B45 . . . . . . .121 D7
  Birmingham,Moseley B11. .87 C2
  Birmingham,Saltley B8 . . .67 A5
  Wombourne WV5. . . . . . . .49 A5
Woodlands The CV5 . . . . .111 D3
Woodlands St B66 . . . . . . .65 C5

Woodlands The
  Cradley Heath B64 . . . . . .83 A7
  Hartshill CV10 . . . . .72 A7
  Lichfield WS13. . . . . .3 C2
  Stourbridge DY8 . . . . .81 C7
  Sutton Coldfield B75 . . . .47 A7
  Wood End DY9. . . . . .36 C7
Woodlands Way B37 . . . . .70 C7
Woodland Way
  Burntwood WS7. . . . . .7 A5
  Polesworth B78. . . . . .36 F6
Wood Lane Cl WV12 . . . . .27 E8
Wood La
  Shenstone WS14 . . . . .17 E8
  Shilton CV7 . . . . .97 C1
  Sutton Coldfield B74 . . . .30 E8
  Walsall WS3 . . . . .14 F1
  Wedges Mills WS11. . . . . .4 F4
  West Bromwich B70 . . . . .53 A4
  Willenhall WV12 . . . . .27 E8
Woodlawn Gr DY6 . . . . . . .60 D8
Woodleas B91 . . . . .107 E6
Wood La WV10 . . . . .11 C2
Woodlea Dr
  Birmingham B24 . . . . .56 F4
  Solihull B91 . . . . .106 E5
Wood Leasow B32 . . . . . . .84 D7
Woodleaves B47. . . . . .124 F6
Woodleigh Ave B17 . . . . .85 C5
Wood Leigh Cl B63 . . . . . .83 A7
Woodleigh Cl B38 . . . . . .103 F1
Woodleigh Rd
  Coventry CV4. . . . . .131 F7
  Sutton Coldfield B72 . . . .46 C4
Woodleys The B14 . . . . . . .105 C6
Woodloes Ave N CV34...155 E1
Woodloes Ave S CV34...155 E1
Woodloes Inf Sch CV34 .155 E1
Woodloes Jun Sch CV34 155 E1
Woodloes La CV34,CV35 .155 E3
Woodloes Rd B90. . . . . . .126 B6
Woodman Cl
  Halesowen B63 . . . . .83 C4
  Wednesbury WS10 . . . . . .42 E4
Woodman Gr 🔢 B75. . . . .32 E2
Woodman La
  Cheslyn Hay WS6. . . . . . . .4 E3
  Clent DY9. . . . . .99 E1
Woodman Rd
  Birmingham B14 . . . . . . .105 A2
  Halesowen B63 . . . . .83 C4
Woodman Wlk B23 . . . . . .56 A4
Woodmeadow Rd B30. . .104 B8
Woodmill Mdw CV8. . . . . .148 B8
Woodnorton Dr B13 . . . . .86 E6
Woodnorton Rd B65 . . . . .63 F7
Woodpecker Gr
  Birmingham B36 . . . . .70 A4
  Kidderminster DY10 . . . .117 B8
Woodpecker Way WS11 . .2 C2
Woodperry Ave B91. . . . . .107 C1
Wood Piece La B98 . . . . .154 D7
Wood Rd
  Dudley DY3 . . . . .50 C1
  Wolverhampton WV6. . . . .24 C1
  Wombourne WV5. . . . . . . .49 B8
Woodridge Ave
  Birmingham B32 . . . . .84 B6
  Coventry CV5. . . . . .112 A4
Woodridge B6. . . . . .55 E
Woodridge Rd B63. . . . . . .83 A4
Wood Ridings WS13. . . . . .3 A4
Woodroffe Wlk CV6. . . . . .96 A
Woodrough Dr B13 . . . . . .86 F7
Woodrow Cl B61. . . . . .120 F7
Woodrow Cres B93 . . . . . .128 A3
Woodrow Ctr B98. . . . . . .159 B8
Woodrow Dr B98. . . . . . . .159 B8
Woodrow Fst Sch B98 . . .159 B8
Woodrow La
  Bluntington DY10. . . . . . .118 C5
  Lower Marlbrook B61 . . .121 B2
Woodrow N B98 . . . . .159 B8
Woodrow S B98 . . . . .159 B8
Woodrow Wlk B98. . . . . . .159 A1
Woodruff Way WS5. . . . . .43 E4
Woodrush Com High Sch The
  B47. . . . . .125 A6
Woodrush Dr B47. . . . . . . .125 A5
Woodsbank Ind Est The
Woods Bank Terr WS10...41 C5
Woods Cres DY5 . . . . .62 A1
Woods Croft WS13. . . . . . .3 A1
Woodsetton Cl DY1 . . . . .51 B6
Woodsetton Sch The DY3..50 F4
Woodshill Ave B45. . . . . . .122 A2
Woodshires Rd
  Coventry CV6. . . . . .95 F1
  Solihull B92 . . . . .106 F1
Woodside Ave N CV3 . . .132 F6
Woodside Ave S CV3 . . . .132 F6
Woodside Cl
  Walsall WS5 . . . . .43 D6
  Wood End CV9 . . . . .36 C2
Woodside Cres B93 . . . . .128 A4
Woodside Dr
  Barnt Green B45 . . . . . . .138 A8
  Sutton Coldfield B74 . . . .31 C5
Woodside Gr WV8 . . . . . . .10 B2
Woodside Ind Est DY2 . . .61 F6
Woodside Pk Mobile Homes
  Pk B94. . . . . .141 B2
Woodside Pl WS11. . . . . . .1 E5
Woodside Rd
  Birmingham B29 . . . . .86 A1

Woodside Rd continued
Dudley DY2 . . . . .61 F7
Walsall WS5 . . . . .43 E6
Woodside B74 . . . . .31 E2
Woodside Way
Aldridge WS9 . . . . .30 B5
Birmingham B32 . . . . .102 A8
Solihull B91 . . . . .106 E5
Willenhall WV12 . . . . .27 E1
Wood Side WV11 . . . . .27 A8
Woods La
Brierley Hill DY5 . . . . .81 D7
Cradley Heath B64 . . . . .82 C8
Woodsome Gr B23 . . . . .56 C7
Woodsorrel Rd DY1 . . . . . . .50 F4
Woods Piece CV7 . . . . .94 F6
Wood St
Bedworth CV12 . . . . .78 B5
Bilston WV14 . . . . .40 D5
Birmingham B16 . . . . .66 A2
Darlaston WS10 . . . . .41 F6
Dudley DY2 . . . . .61 F6
The B14 . . . . .86 F1
Wood St LE10 . . . . .71 D1
Woodstile B34 . . . . .69 B6
Woodstock Cl B75 . . . . .32 D3
Woodstock Cross 3
DY10 . . . . .116 E5
Woodstock Ct
2 Walsall WS5 . . . . .43 A3
Dudley DY1 . . . . .62 A8
Hinckley LE10 . . . . .76 A5
Stourbridge DY9 . . . . .60 C1
Woodstock Cres B93 . . . . . .127 F3
Woodstock Ct B13 . . . . .87 B4
Woodstock Dr
Huntington WV12 . . . . .1 C7
Stourbridge DY8 . . . . .60 C2
Sutton Coldfield B74 . . . . . . .31 D4
Woodstock Ho B13 . . . . .87 B2
Woodstock Rd
Birmingham,Handsworth
B21 . . . . .65 F8
Birmingham,Moseley B13 . . .87 B3
Coventry CV3 . . . . .133 D7
Nuneaton CV11 . . . . .73 E1
Wolverhampton WV1 . . . . . . .26 B1
Wooston Gr B91 . . . . .127 C8
Wood St LE10 . . . . .71 E1
Wood St
Royal Leamington Spa
CV32 . . . . .162 A8
Stourbridge DY8 . . . . .80 D6
Stourbridge,Lye DY9 . . . . . . .81 F5
Tipton DY4 . . . . .51 E5
Willenhall WV13 . . . . .27 B2
Wolverhampton,Park Village
WV10 . . . . .25 F5
Woodcross WV4 . . . . .40 A3
Wood End CV9 . . . . .36 C1
Wood Terr B96 . . . . .159 B1
Woodthorne Cl DY1 . . . . . . .50 D2
Woodthorne Prim Sch
WV6 . . . . .24 A4
Woodthorne Rd WV6 . . . . . .24 A5
Woodthorne Rd WV6 . . . . . .24 A5
Woodthorne Wlk DY6 . . . . . .60 E8
Woodthorpe Dr DY9 . . . . . . .81 C3
Woodthorpe Gdns B14 . . . .104 E5
B14 . . . . .104 E5
Woodthorpe Rd B14 . . . . . .104 E5
Woodvale Dr B28 . . . . .105 E4
Woodvale Rd
Birmingham B32 . . . . .84 A1
Birmingham,Yardley Wood
B28 . . . . .105 E4
Woodview Dr B15 . . . . .86 C7
Woodview Primary Sch
B15 . . . . .86 C7
Woodville Ct
3 Birmingham B23 . . . . .56 E2
Warwick CV34 . . . . .160 F7
Woodville Gdns DY8 . . . . . . .39 F1
Woodville Rd
Birmingham B17 . . . . .85 A6
Birmingham,King's Heath
B14 . . . . .104 E8
Warwick CV34 . . . . .160 E8
Woodward Cl CV31 . . . . . . .162 A2
Woodward Pl DY9 . . . . .81 C4
Woodward Rd DY11 . . . . . .116 C4
Woodwards Cl WS2 . . . . . . .42 B8
Woodwards Pl WS2 . . . . . . .42 B8
Woodwards Rd WS2 . . . . . . .42 B8
Woodward St B71 . . . . .53 E4
Woodway B24 . . . . .57 B5
Woodway Cl CV2 . . . . .114 F8
Woodway La CV2 . . . . .96 F1
**Woodway Park Sch & Com
Coll** CV2 . . . . .96 F1
Woodway Wlk CV2 . . . . .114 E8
Woodwells Rd B8 . . . . .68 B5
Woody Bank WS6 . . . . .4 E2
Woolacombe Lodge Rd
B29 . . . . .85 E1
Woolaston Rd B98 . . . . .159 C8
Woolgrove St CV6 . . . . .96 A3
Woolhope Cl B98 . . . . .154 F3
Woolmore Rd B23 . . . . .56 C5
Woolpack Cl B65 . . . . .63 A4
Woolpack St WV1 . . . . .79 F6
Woolpack The 9 CV34 . . . .160 E6
Woolwich Rd CV11 . . . . .79 F6
Wooton Cl B97 . . . . .153 A4
Wooton Gr B44 . . . . .56 C8

Wootton Ave WV11 . . . . .26 D7
Wootton Cl WS11 . . . . .2 B3
Wootton Ct
6 Royal Leamington Spa
CV32 . . . . .156 F2
Coventry CV2 . . . . .114 D7
Wootton Green La CV7 . . . .130 A8
Wootton La CV7 . . . . .109 E1
Wootton Rd
Birmingham B31 . . . . .123 A6
Wolverhampton WV3 . . . . . . .38 D8
Woottons Ct WS11 . . . . .1 F1
Wootton's Sq WV14 . . . . . . .40 E2
Wootton St CV12 . . . . .78 D3
Worcester Cl
Allesley CV5 . . . . .112 B7
Cannock WS11 . . . . .4 F8
Lichfield WS13 . . . . .3 C3
Sutton Coldfield B75 . . . . . . .32 D3
West Hagley DY9 . . . . .99 A5
Worcester Cross 3
DY10 . . . . .116 E5
Worcester Ct
Coventry CV6 . . . . .96 B4
Wolverhampton WV3 . . . . . . .39 A6
Worcester Gr B71 . . . . .53 C7
Worcester Gr WV6 . . . . .23 D4
Worcester Ho
4 Halesowen B63 . . . . .83 A3
Birmingham B36 . . . . .70 A8
Worcester La
Stourbridge DY9 . . . . .99 B7
Sutton Coldfield B75 . . . . . . .32 D4
Worcester Rd
Birmingham,Birchfield B6 . . .55 F2
Birmingham,Brandhall B68 . .84 A8
Bromsgrove B61 . . . . .136 F1
Dudley DY2 . . . . .62 E3
Harvington DY9,DY10 . . . . .118 C4
Kenilworth CV8 . . . . .148 B3
Kidderminster DY10 . . . . . . .116 E2
Mustow Green DY10 . . . . . .117 F1
Stoke Heath B61 . . . . .150 B4
West Hagley DY9 . . . . .99 A5
Willenhall WV13 . . . . .27 D2
Worcester Rise B29 . . . . . . .86 B1
Worcester Sq 1 B97 . . . . . .153 E4
Worcester St
Birmingham B2 . . . . .164 C2
Kidderminster DY10 . . . . . . .116 E6
Stourbridge DY8 . . . . .81 A4
Wolverhampton WV2 . . . . . .163 B2
Worcester Wlk B37 . . . . .70 A1
Word Hill B17 . . . . .84 F7
Wordsley Cl B98 . . . . .154 B7
Wordsley Ct DY8 . . . . .60 E3
Wordsley Green Sch Ctr
DY8 . . . . .60 D2
Wordsley Hospl DY8 . . . . . . .60 E3
Wordsley Sch The DY8 . . . . .60 E3
Wordsworth Ave
Redditch B97 . . . . .158 C8
Tamworth B79 . . . . .21 A6
Warwick CV34 . . . . .160 D5
Wolverhampton WV4 . . . . . . .39 F4
Wordsworth Cl
Cannock WS11 . . . . .1 D4
Lichfield WS14 . . . . .9 B5
Tipton DY4 . . . . .52 A8
Wordsworth Cres DY10 . . . .117 B6
Wordsworth Ct WV1 . . . . . . .23 E4
Wordsworth Dr CV8 . . . . . . .148 C4
Wordsworth Ho
4 Oldbury B68 . . . . .64 C4
Birmingham B31 . . . . .123 A8
Halesowen B63 . . . . .82 B5
Wordsworth Rd
Bedworth CV12 . . . . .78 D1
Birmingham B10 . . . . .87 D7
Burntwood WS7 . . . . .7 D8
Coventry CV2 . . . . .114 C4
Dudley DY3 . . . . .50 B5
Walsall WS3 . . . . .28 E8
Willenhall WV12 . . . . .27 E7
Wolverhampton WV10 . . . . . .26 A8
Wordsworth St B71 . . . . .53 C5
Worfield Gdns WV3 . . . . .38 F6
Workhouse La LE10 . . . . .76 A4
Works Rd B26 . . . . .90 A3
World's End Ave B32 . . . . . . .84 D6
World's End Ho B32 . . . . .84 D6
World's End La B32 . . . . .84 D5
Worlds End Rd B20 . . . . .55 A3
Worleys Wharf Ave WS10 . . .42 E2
Worsdell Cl CV1 . . . . .113 B4
Worsey Dr DY4 . . . . .52 D6
Worsfold Cl CV5 . . . . .112 B6
Worthen Gr B31 . . . . .123 A8
Worthings The B30 . . . . . . .104 B6
Worthy Down WV11 . . . . .26 F5
Worthy Down Wlk B35 . . . . . .58 B3
Wortley Ave WV10 . . . . .25 E6
Worton Rd DY9 . . . . .81 F2
Wragby Cl WV9 . . . . .11 B3

Wrekin Cl
Halesowen B63 . . . . .82 C1
Kidderminster DY11 . . . . . . .116 B2
Wrekin Cl 3 B74 . . . . .31 F2
Wrekin Dr
Bromsgrove B61 . . . . .137 A5
Stourbridge DY9 . . . . .81 D4
Wolverhampton,Bradmore
WV3 . . . . .38 E8
Wolverhampton,Wergs
WV6 . . . . .24 A5
Wrekin Gr WV11 . . . . .13 B1
Wrekin La WV6 . . . . .24 A5

Wrekin Rd
Birmingham B44 . . . . .56 A6
Sutton Coldfield B73 . . . . . . .46 A1
Wrekin View
Brownhills WS8 . . . . .16 A5
Huntington WS12 . . . . .1 C7
Wrekin View Rd DY3 . . . . . . .50 C8
Wrekin View WV1 . . . . .163 B3
Wren Ave WV6 . . . . .23 D3
Wrenbury Dr
Coventry CV6 . . . . .96 A4
Coventry CV6 . . . . .96 A4
Wrens Ave
Kingswinford DY6 . . . . .61 A4
Tipton DY4 . . . . .51 D4
Wrens Croft WS11 . . . . .2 B1
Wrens Hill Rd DY1 . . . . .51 B5
Wren's Nest Cl B90 . . . . . . .126 A5
**Wren's Nest Nature Reserve*
. . . . .51 B4
Wren's Nest Rd DY1 . . . . . . .51 A4
Wren's Nest Prim Sch
DY1 . . . . .51 A4
Wrens Nest Rd DY1 . . . . .51 A5
Wren's Nest Rd DY1 . . . . . . .51 A5
Wrens Park Ave B76 . . . . . . .57 F7
Wren St
Coventry CV2 . . . . .113 F3
Dudley DY1 . . . . .51 C6
Dudley,Netherton DY2 . . . . . .62 B5
Wrentham St B5 . . . . .86 E8
Wretham Ct B19 . . . . .66 E8
Wretham Rd B19 . . . . .66 E8
Wrexham Ave WS2 . . . . .27 F1
Wright Ave WV11 . . . . .26 E7
Wrighton Cl WV12 . . . . .27 C8
Wrighton Dr DY5 . . . . .50 C1
Wrighton Gr B39 . . . . .88 B4
Wright Rd B8 . . . . .67 E5
Wright's Ave WS11 . . . . .1 F5
Wright's La B64 . . . . .63 A1
Wright St
Bilston WV14 . . . . .40 E4
Birmingham B10 . . . . .87 D8
Coventry CV1 . . . . .113 E4
Halesowen B63 . . . . .83 B4
Wolverhampton WV10 . . . . . .25 D8
Wrigsham St CV3 . . . . .133 D8
Wrottesley Rd WV8 . . . . .23 C8
Wrottesley Park Rd WV6,
WV8 . . . . .23 C8
Wrottesley Rd
Birmingham B43 . . . . .43 D1
Wolverhampton WV6 . . . . . . .24 B5
Wrottesley Rd W
Perton WV6 . . . . .23 F6
Wolverhampton WV6 . . . . . . .24 A6
Wrottesley St B5 . . . . .164 C1
Wroxall Cl DY5 . . . . .81 C8
Wroxall Dr CV3 . . . . .134 D5
Wroxall Gr B13 . . . . .105 A6
Wroxall Rd B91 . . . . .106 E6
Wroxham Glen WV13 . . . . . . .40 F8
Wroxton Rd B26 . . . . .89 B8
Wr Twr La CV8 . . . . .147 F6
Wulfruna Ct B13 . . . . .163 A2
Wulfruna Gdns WV3 . . . . . . .24 F1
Wulfruna St WV1 . . . . .163 B3
**Wulfrun Coll Annexe,
Newhampton Ctr** WV1 . . .163 B4
Wulfrun Ctr WV1 . . . . .163 B2
Wulfrun Hall 2 WV1 . . . . . .163 B2
Wulfrun Sq WV1 . . . . .163 C2
Wulfrun Trad Est WV6 . . . . . .25 C5
Wulfrun Way WV1 . . . . .163 B2
Wyatt Cl B5 . . . . .86 C5
Wyatt Ho CV2 . . . . .114 D7
Wyatt Rd B75 . . . . .47 B5
Wyatts Ct CV12 . . . . .78 B3
Wychall Dr WV10 . . . . .11 E4
Wychall La B38 . . . . .103 E2
Wychall Park Gr B38 . . . . . .103 D2
Wychall Prim Sch B31 . . . .103 C3
Wychbold Cl
Redditch B98 . . . . .158 A6
Willenhall WV12 . . . . .13 D1
Wychbold Cres B33 . . . . .69 C3
Wychbold Ct DY9 . . . . .99 C8
Wychbold Way WV12 . . . . . . .13 D1
Wychbury Ct B63 . . . . .83 A3
Wychbury Dr DY9 . . . . .99 C7
Wychbury Grange DY9 . . . . .81 C1
Wychbury Rd
Birmingham B32 . . . . .102 B7
Brierley Hill DY5 . . . . .81 E8
Stourbridge DY9 . . . . .81 E2
Wolverhampton WV3 . . . . . . .38 C7
Wychbury B76 . . . . .47 F1
Wyche Ave B14 . . . . .104 D4
Wyche Cotts B60 . . . . .150 C1
Wych Elm Dr 6 CV31 . . . . .161 F5
Wychelm Farm Rd B14 . . . .105 A1
Wych Elm Rd WS8 . . . . .15 E5
Wycherley Way B64 . . . . .82 F8
Wychnor Gr B71 . . . . .42 E2
Wychwood Ave
Coventry CV3 . . . . .133 C3
Knowle B93 . . . . .128 B8
Wychwood Cres B26 . . . . . . .89 A6
Wychwood Dr B97 . . . . .158 D6
Wyckham Cl B17 . . . . .85 A4
Wyckham Rd B36 . . . . .69 F8
Wycliffe Gr CV2 . . . . .114 B5
Wycliffe Rd W CV2 . . . . .114 C5
Wycome Rd B28 . . . . .106 A7
Wye Cl
Bulkington CV12 . . . . .79 B2

Wye Cl continued
Hinckley LE10 . . . . .75 A8
Wye Cliff Rd B20 . . . . .66 B8
Wye Cl
Perton WV6 . . . . .23 F4
Royal Leamington Spa
CV32 . . . . .157 C3
Sutton Coldfield B76 . . . . . . .58 B7
Wyegate Cl B36 . . . . .69 F8
Wye Rd WS3 . . . . .14 E1
Wyemanton Cl B43 . . . . .43 C1
Wye Rd WS3 . . . . .14 E1
Wykeham Gr WV6 . . . . .23 D3
Wyken Ave CV2 . . . . .114 C4
Wyken Cl B93 . . . . .127 E2
Wyken Croft CV2 . . . . .114 D6
Wyken Croft Nature Pk *
CV2 . . . . .114 D6
Wyken Croft Prim Sch
CV2 . . . . .114 C5
Wyken Grange Rd CV2 . . . .114 C5
Wyken Way CV2 . . . . .114 B5
Wyke Rd CV2 . . . . .114 C4
Wykin Rd LE10 . . . . .71 A3
Wyld Cl B71 . . . . .53 A5
Wyld Ct CV5 . . . . .112 B5
Wylde Cres B65 . . . . .63 C4
Wylde Green Cl B72,B76 . . .46 C1
Wylde Green Prim Sch
B73 . . . . .57 A8
Wylde Green Rd B72,B76 . . .46 D1
Wylde Green Sta B73 . . . . . . .46 B1
Wyley Rd CV6 . . . . .113 A8
Wymering Ave WV11 . . . . . . .26 F7
Wynall La DY9 . . . . .82 A3
Wynall La DY9 . . . . .81 F3
Wynbrook Gr B90 . . . . .126 F6
Wynchcombe Ave WV4 . . . . .38 D4
Wyncote Cl CV8 . . . . .148 A4
Wyndcliffe Prim Sch
Birmingham B9 . . . . .67 C1
Birmingham B9 . . . . .67 D1
Wyndcliff Rd B9 . . . . .67 D1
Wyndham Gdns B30 . . . . . .103 D4
Wyndham Rd B16 . . . . .65 F1
Wyndhurst Rd B33 . . . . .68 E5
Wyndley Cl B74 . . . . .31 F6
Wyndley Dr B73 . . . . .46 B4
Wyndley Gr B72 . . . . .46 C2
Wyndley La B73 . . . . .46 A5
Wyndley L Ctr B73 . . . . .46 A5
Wyndley Manor B74 . . . . .32 A6
Wyndmill Cres B71 . . . . .42 F1
Wynds Covert B14 . . . . .104 C2
Wynds Point B31 . . . . .103 B5
Wynd The DY3 . . . . .39 D1
Wynfield Gdns B14 . . . . . . .104 F5
Wynford Rd B27 . . . . .88 C5
Wynford Road Ind Est
B27 . . . . .88 C5
Wyn-Griffith Dr DY4 . . . . . . .52 A3
Wynne Cres WV4 . . . . .38 C3
Wynn Rd WV4 . . . . .38 F5
Wynn St B15 . . . . .86 C8
Wynstead Covert 6 B14 . . .104 C2
Wyntor La B71 . . . . .53 B8
Wynyates B79 . . . . .20 E6
Wyre Cl
Birmingham B45 . . . . .102 B1
Brownhills WS9 . . . . .15 F4
Wyre Rd DY8 . . . . .80 E7
Wyrley Brook Pk WS11 . . . . .4 D6
Wyrley Brook Ret Pk WS11 . .4 D6
Wyrley Cl
Burntwood WS8 . . . . .6 F3
Lichfield WS14 . . . . .9 A5
Willenhall WV12 . . . . .27 D7
Wyrley Ho
Birmingham B23 . . . . .56 C6
Tipton DY4 . . . . .52 B3
Wyrley La WS3 . . . . .14 E8
Wyrley Rd
Birmingham B6 . . . . .56 A2
Sutton Coldfield B75 . . . . . . .32 D1
Wednesfield WV11 . . . . .27 A7
Wyrley St WV10 . . . . .25 F2
Wyrley Trad Est B6 . . . . .56 B2
Wyrley Way B23 . . . . .56 A6
Wythall Green Way B47 . . . .124 E3
Wythall Rd B63 . . . . .83 A2
Wythall Sta B47 . . . . .125 C4
Wythwood Cl DY9 . . . . .81 D1
Wythwood Gr
Hollywood B47 . . . . .125 C6
Tipton DY4 . . . . .52 A8
Wythwood Rd B47 . . . . .125 C6
Wyton Ave B68 . . . . .64 C2
Wyver Cres CV2 . . . . .114 C3
Wyvern
Birmingham B29 . . . . .85 C2
Cannock WS12 . . . . .2 A5
Wyvern Gr
Birmingham B29 . . . . .85 C2
Cannock WS12 . . . . .2 A5
Wyvern Rd B74 . . . . .46 B2
Wyvern B77 . . . . .21 F3
Wyvis Cl WV6 . . . . .24 E2

Y

Yale Dr WV11 . . . . .26 E5
Yale Rd WV13 . . . . .41 A7
Yardley Cl
Oldbury B68 . . . . .64 B1

Yardley Cl continued
Redditch B98 . . . . .154 E3
Warwick CV34 . . . . .155 F2
Yardley Green Rd B9,B25,
B33 . . . . .68 A2
Yardley Prim Sch B26 . . . . . .88 D7
Yardley Rd B27 . . . . .88 C5
Yardleys Sch B11 . . . . .87 F4
Yardley St
Coventry CV1 . . . . .113 E4
Darlaston WS10 . . . . .41 C7
Stourbridge DY9 . . . . .81 E5
Yardley Wood Com Prim Sch
B14 . . . . .105 D4
Yardley Wood Rd B13,
B14 . . . . .105 D5
Yardley Wood Sta B28 . . . . .105 D5
Yardley Works DY9 . . . . .81 C5
Yare Gr WV13 . . . . .27 D1
Yarmouth Gn CV4 . . . . .131 E8
Yarnborough Hill DY8 . . . . . .81 A2
Yarnbury Cl B14 . . . . .104 E1
Yarn Cl B47 . . . . .125 A5
Yarner Cl DY1 . . . . .50 E2
Yarnfield Prim Sch B11 . . . . .88 A3
Yarnfield Rd B11 . . . . .88 A3
Yarningale Cl B98 . . . . .158 F6
Yarningale Rd
Birmingham B14 . . . . .104 D5
Coventry CV3 . . . . .134 D5
Yarningale 7 B90 . . . . .126 C8
Yarn La B90 . . . . .126 A6
Yarnold La
Bournheath B61 . . . . .136 C8
Fairfield B61 . . . . .120 C1
Yarrow Cl
Walsall WS3 . . . . .15 A5
Wednesfield WV11 . . . . .26 F5
Yarrow Dr B38 . . . . .123 F8
Yarwell Cl WV10 . . . . .163 C4
Yateley Ave B42 . . . . .55 A7
Yateley Cres B42 . . . . .55 A7
Yateley Rd B15 . . . . .85 E7
Yatesbury Ave B35 . . . . .58 A3
Yates Croft B74 . . . . .31 F6
Yates Ind Est WS3 . . . . .5 B5
Yates La B65 . . . . .63 F2
Yeadon Cl B97 . . . . .153 A1
Yeadon Gdns WV3 . . . . .38 D8
Yeames Cl B43 . . . . .44 C4
Yellowhammer Ct DY10 . . . .117 A1
Yelverton Cl WS3 . . . . .14 B4
Yelverton Dr B15 . . . . .85 E8
Yelverton Rd CV6 . . . . .113 D8
Yeman Rd B68 . . . . .64 D3
Yemscroft WS6 . . . . .14 A8
Yems Croft WS4 . . . . .29 A6
Yenton Cl B78 . . . . .21 A1
Yenton Gr B24 . . . . .57 C6
Yenton Prim Sch B24 . . . . . .57 C6
Yeoman Cl DY10 . . . . .116 E3
Yeomanry Cl
12 Warwick CV34 . . . . .160 F7
Sutton Coldfield B75 . . . . . . .47 A6
Yeomans Grange 5 B75 . . .46 F6
Yeomans Way B75 . . . . .46 F6
Yeomans Wlk B60 . . . . .150 E8
Yeovil Ct 15 DY5 . . . . .61 D2
Yeovilton B79 . . . . .21 C8
Yerbury Gr B23 . . . . .56 A6
Yew Cl CV3 . . . . .134 C1
Yew Croft Ave B17 . . . . .85 B6
Yewdale B17 . . . . .85 C4
Yewdale Cres CV2 . . . . .96 F1
Yewdale Ct CV2 . . . . .96 F1
Yewhurst Rd B91 . . . . .106 E4
Yews The CV12 . . . . .77 E2
Yew St WV3 . . . . .25 A1
Yew Tree Ave
Belbroughton DY9 . . . . .119 E8
Birmingham B26 . . . . .88 E7
Lichfield WS14 . . . . .9 E8
Yew Tree Com Jun & Inf Sch
B6 .56 A5
Yew Tree Ct 1 CV31 . . . . . .161 F5
Yewtree Dr B60 . . . . .137 B2
Yew Tree Gdns WV8 . . . . . . .10 A4
Yew Tree Hills DY2 . . . . .62 C4
Yew Tree Inf & Jun Sch
B91 . . . . .107 E6
Yew Tree La
Birmingham,Frankley
B32 . . . . .101 E3
Birmingham,Yardley B26 . . . .88 E7
Dudley WV14 . . . . .40 D1
Fairfield B61 . . . . .120 D2
Lapworth B94 . . . . .144 B1
Solihull B91 . . . . .107 E5
Wednesbury WS10 . . . . .42 A2
Wolverhampton WV6 . . . . . . .24 A5
Yew Tree Pl
Romsley B62 . . . . .101 A5
Walsall WS3 . . . . .14 D3
Yew Tree Prim Sch WS5 . . . .43 D1
Yew Tree Rd
Birmingham,Castle Bromwich
B36 . . . . .69 E8
Birmingham,Edgbaston B15 . .86 C8

Yew Tree Rd *continued*
Birmingham,Handsworth B6 .**56** A1
Birmingham,Moseley B13 . . .**86** D2
Dudley DY2 . . . .**62** C4
Halesowen B63 . . . .**82** F3
Kidderminster DY10 . . . . . .**116** F5
Smethwick B67 . . . .**64** E4
Yewtree Rd
Sutton Coldfield,Boldmere
B73 . . . .**57** A7
Sutton Coldfield,Streetly
B74 . . . .**44** D8
Yew Tree Rd
Walsall,The Delves WS5 . . . .**43** A5
Walsall WS4 . . . .**15** B1
Yew Tree Ret Pk B25 . . . . .**88** D8
Yew Tree Rise B76 . . . .**46** F3
Yew Tree Villas B73 . . . . . .**57** A7
Yew Wlk B37 . . . .**70** B2
Yockleton Rd B33 . . . .**69** C3

York Ave
Bedworth CV12 . . . .**78** D2
Bromsgrove B61 . . . .**136** E4
Walsall WS2 . . . .**28** B2
Willenhall WV13 . . . .**27** D2
Wolverhampton WV3 . . . . . .**24** E1
Yorkbrooke Dr B26 . . . .**89** B5
York Cl
Birmingham B30 . . . .**104** A6
Bromsgrove B61 . . . .**136** E4
Coventry CV3 . . . .**134** C5
Lichfield WS13 . . . .**3** C3
Studley B80 . . . .**159** C4
Tipton DY4 . . . .**51** D4
York Cres
Birmingham B34 . . . .**69** E6
Darlaston WS10 . . . .**41** D6
Stourbridge DY8 . . . .**80** D7
West Bromwich B70 . . . .**53** A6
Wolverhampton WV3 . . . . . .**24** E1
York Ct DY10 . . . .**116** E7
Yorkdale Cl DY3 . . . .**50** D3
York Dr B36 . . . .**68** B8

Yorke Ave DY5 . . . .**61** A1
York Gdns WV3 . . . .**24** E1
Yorklea Croft B37 . . . .**69** F2
Yorkmead Jun & Inf Sch
B28 . . . .**87** F2
Yorkminster Dr B37 . . . .**70** D3
York Rd
Birmingham B23 . . . .**56** F4
Birmingham,Edgbaston B16 .**65** E1
Birmingham,Handsworth
B21 . . . .**65** F8
Birmingham,King's Heath
B14 . . . .**104** E8
Birmingham,Tyseley B28 . . . .**87** F2
Bromsgrove B61 . . . .**136** F4
Cannock WS11 . . . .**4** F7
Dudley DY2 . . . .**62** E3
Hinckley LE10 . . . .**71** D3
Rowley Regis B65 . . . .**63** E3
Royal Leamington Spa
CV31 . . . .**161** F8
Walsall WS4 . . . .**29** D7
Wolverhampton WV3 . . . . . .**38** B8

Yorksand Rd B78 . . . .**34** F8
Yorkshire Way WS7 . . . .**7** F8
York St
Birmingham B17 . . . .**85** D6
Coventry CV1 . . . .**113** B2
Kidderminster DY10 . . . . . .**116** E7
Nuneaton CV11 . . . .**73** A4
Wolverhampton WV1 . . . . . .**163** D2
Yorks Wood Dr B37 . . . . . .**69** E5
Yorkswood Prim Sch B37 .**69** F5
York Terr B18 . . . .**66** C5
Young Cl CV34 . . . .**160** B5
Young St B70 . . . .**53** A3
Yoxall Gr B33 . . . .**69** A3
Yoxall Rd B90 . . . .**106** D2
Yule Rd CV2 . . . .**114** D5
Yvonne Rd B97 . . . .**158** D7

Z

Zealand Cl LE10 . . . .**71** F3
Zion Cl WS6 . . . .**4** D3

Zions Cl B64 . . . .**62** F
Zion St DY4 . . . .**51** F
Zoar St
Dudley DY3 . . . .**50** C
Wolverhampton WV3 . . . . . .**25** B
Zorrina Cl CV10 . . . .**72** B
Zouche Cl DY8 . . . .**80** E

Any feature in this atlas can be given a unique reference to help you find the same feature on other Ordnance Survey maps of the area, or to help someone else locate you if they do not have a Street Atlas.

The grid squares in this atlas match the Ordnance Survey National Grid and are at 500 metre intervals. The small figures at the bottom and sides of every other grid line are the National Grid kilometre values (**00** to **99** km) and are repeated across the country every 100 km (see left).

To give a unique National Grid reference you need to locate where in the country you are. The country is divided into 100 km squares with each square given a unique two-letter reference. Use the administrative map to determine in which 100 km square a particular page of this atlas falls.

The bold letters and numbers between each grid line (**A** to **F**, **1** to **8**) are for use within a specific Street Atlas only, and when used with the page number, are a convenient way of referencing these grid squares.

Example   *The railway bridge over DARLEY GREEN RD in grid square B1*

Step 1: Identify the two-letter reference, in this example the page is in **SP**

Step 2: Identify the 1 km square in which the railway bridge falls. Use the figures in the southwest corner of this square: Eastings **17**, Northings **74**. This gives a unique reference: **SP 17 74**, accurate to 1 km.

Step 3: To give a more precise reference accurate to 100 m you need to estimate how many tenths along and how many tenths up this 1 km square the feature is (to help with this the 1 km square is divided into four 500 m squares). This makes the bridge about **8** tenths along and about **1** tenth up from the southwest corner.

This gives a unique reference: **SP 178 741**, accurate to 100 m.

Eastings (read from left to right along the bottom) come before Northings (read from bottom to top). If you have trouble remembering say to yourself "Along the hall, THEN up the stairs"!

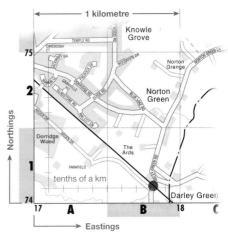

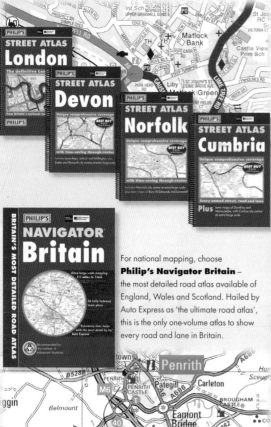